COLLEGES
WORTH
YOUR MONEY

COLLEGES
WORTH
YOUR MONEY

A Guide to What America's Top Schools Can Do for You

Andrew Belasco, Dave Bergman, & Michael Trivette

ROWMAN & LITTLEFIELD

Lanham • Boulder • New York • London

Published by Rowman & Littlefield
An imprint of The Rowman & Littlefield Publishing Group, Inc.
4501 Forbes Boulevard, Suite 200, Lanham, Maryland 20706
www.rowman.com

6 Tinworth Street, London, SE11 5AL, United Kingdom

Distributed by NATIONAL BOOK NETWORK

British Library Cataloguing in Publication Information Available

Library of Congress Control Number: 2020932428

∞™ The paper used in this publication meets the minimum requirements of American National Standard for Information Sciences—Permanence of Paper for Printed Library Materials, ANSI/ NISO Z39.48-1992.

Contents

Before the birth of the modern internet, savvy teens seeking information on prospective colleges cracked open the latest Yellow Pages-thick college guidebook, eager to soak in school-specific admissions data that felt like classified information. Possessors of such guidebooks were the true insiders of the day, privy to admissions statistics that simply could not be found within the glossy brochures delivered to the masses via snail mail. By 2020, those oversized volumes have been rendered far less essential. Basic admissions data such as SAT ranges, grade point averages, tuition costs, and acceptance rates are available via fast and free Google searches. Everyone is now—at least in 1980s or '90s terms—an insider.

The formula for these annual editions is simple. Easy-to-find admissions and tuition data points are complemented by blocks of heavily anecdotal text designed to reveal something about the campus milieu: the quality of food, the architectural style of the buildings, the political leanings of the student body, and the subjective like. While these books all serve as useful starting points for your college search (we read them ourselves each year), they fail to acknowledge the seismic shift taking place in the national conversation about higher education—the idea that students should stop obsessing over gaining admission into the most prestigious schools that will accept them and instead ask, "What can a given college do for me?" If students/parents are going to pony up $200,000 or more in tuition alone, they should first demand to see outcomes data, return on investment (ROI) figures, and a statistically backed account of unique opportunities for undergraduates. That's where the college guide you're holding comes into play.

Why do I need this guide?

There are two main reasons:

(1) Given the absurd cost of a college education, finding a school that will provide an acceptable ROI has never been more challenging.

(2) Your prospective colleges are likely to be more selective than they were only a few years ago; greater information gathering/strategic planning will be required to successfully gain admission.

Let's begin with the issue of price. As we get older, it's easy to fall into a nostalgic trap on the subject of how much things cost. For example, "When I was a boy, you could feed a family of four for a Buffalo nickel." Yet when it comes to lamenting rising college expenses, there is actual data to back up the sticker shock. In 1950, the University of Pennsylvania charged $600 per year to attend—roughly $6,000 in 2020 money. Today, Penn's annual cost of attendance is over $77,000. By 1960, most private institutions charged an annual fee of $1,500–$2,000 that equates to $12,000–$16,000 today. In the current marketplace, a $50,000 annual tuition is considered "reasonable." This is hardly just a private school phenomenon. The University of North Carolina at Chapel Hill's in-state 2019–20 tuition cost of $9,018 is one of the best bargains in all of higher education. Of course, that pales in comparison to the in-state tuition of thirty years ago—only $504 per year. (No, that's *not* a typo).

Turning to the matter of increased selectivity, you don't need to look back to the '50s, '60s, or even '70s to find a college admissions landscape vastly different from today's hyper-competitive environment. In 1980, nearly half of all applicants were accepted into prestigious Swarthmore College while the Class of 2022 had a 9 percent acceptance rate. As recently as the 1990s, the University of Chicago accepted 60–70 percent of those who applied, but for applicants to the Class of 2022, only 7 percent were successful. Less drastic but still significant changes have proliferated as the overwhelming majority of desirable public and private schools have grown more selective in recent years. As of the publication of this book, many of the most prestigious schools in the country boast single-digit acceptance rates, including all the Ivy League schools (except Cornell University, which is a fraction over 10 percent) as well as Stanford University, Johns Hopkins University, Duke University, Northwestern University, Vanderbilt University, and the Massachusetts Institute of Technology. Other elite schools including Pomona College, Bowdoin College, Williams College, Amherst College, Rice University, and the University of Southern California all have inched closer to the single-digit club and will likely join it soon.

The reasons for this increased level of selectivity include an influx of highly-qualified foreign students applying to US colleges, the Common App making it easier for top students to apply to as many elite schools as they wish, and a greater number of applicants paying for services, such as private SAT tutors, that ultimately enhance their academic profiles.

How to use this guide:

We hope the above statistics have convinced you that the college selection and admissions process has never been more of a high-stakes game. Parents/students who are about to essentially take out another mortgage to finance their own or their teens' college education should, at the very least, first perform the equivalent of a home inspection. Just as it is easy to fall in love with a house based on a Zillow photo, many select a college based on surface observations such as the campus is pretty, the school colors would look nice on a bumper sticker, or you've heard good things from other parents in your social circle. Think of this guidebook as an inspection report with no crawlspace left unexplored.

Each profile includes six statistically rich narrative sections and two tables containing in excess of seventy additional data points. The following is a brief overview of the information included for each school and why it is important for prospective college students (and their parents) to know.

Inside the Classroom

We begin each profile by discussing what makes a given institution academically unique. Some schools have a core curriculum that dictates three semesters of study; others have an entirely open curriculum. Some mandate foreign language, physical education, a freshman seminar or two, and a senior thesis; others have no such requirements. Statistics on class size, undergraduate research opportunities, study abroad participation and—when possible—institutional survey data regarding professor availability and the quality of classroom instruction are included. In this section we also highlight particular programs/departments that have standout reputations as well as how seniors fare in landing nationally competitive postgraduate scholarships.

Outside the Classroom

Words such as "vibe," "feel," and "atmosphere" may sound like flaky reasons to pick one college over another, yet when formulating college lists, future applicants absolutely should be mindful of their fit at a given school. The key is to properly size up the vibe/feel/atmosphere through more than merely a brief and heavily sanitized campus tour.

Some traits of a given school are easy to spot, and the contrast between institutions can be stark. For example, attending a small liberal arts school is going to be a wholly different social experience than attending a flagship state university with ten times the enrollment. However, there are many small liberal arts schools with high percentages of student-athletes where Greek life dominates the social scene. While this section is certainly our most anecdotal, we use statistics to dig beyond mere generalizations wherever possible.

For instance, if—like at Wake Forest University—85 percent of the student body participates in National Collegiate Athletic Association (NCAA), club, or intramural sports, and you hate sports, that information may help you cross the school off your list. If you are dead set on joining a fraternity or sorority, Bucknell University's 35-40 percent rate of participation in Greek life will be more attractive than the 4 percent pledge rate at Wesleyan University. If volunteer work is important to you, you may wish to target a school filled with kindred spirits, such as the College of William & Mary, where thousands perform community service every year. If a cappella is an essential creative outlet for you, a school such as Amherst, where one can barely count the number of established singing groups on two hands, may be appealing. Undoubtedly, any personality type can find at least a few like-minded souls at any of the 3,000 four-year colleges in the United States, but it's important that teens find schools where they can develop a true sense of belonging. Research has consistently demonstrated that college students who feel connected to their schools experience far greater academic success than those who do not.

Career Services

In an effort to entice applicants, college brochures are usually filled with group shots of smiling students on picturesque quads, amenities such as Olympic-size pools and rock-climbing walls, and dining halls that look like five-star restaurants. Those images are usually accompanied by some hollow catchphrase such as "Where leaders are born." Yet you likely won't find much (if any) information about the career services offerings—one of the most overlooked but important offices within a university. In reality, the professionals who provide individual career counseling, arrange internships, engage in corporate recruiting, and plan job fairs will do far more for your future than that towering rock climbing wall.

We answer the questions that students should ask when they evaluate their prospective colleges: What is the student-to-counselor ratio? What percent of students engage with career services? Does this happen in freshman year or does counseling only get utilized by seniors? We'll provide information on job fairs, networking events, corporate recruiting on campus, and how helpful staff are with arranging internships. In utilizing this section, you will discover which schools actually give rise to tomorrow's leaders vs. those whose public relations departments merely thought up an empty marketing slogan. And, yes, on occasion we will briefly note rock climbing walls or exceptionally delicious cuisine because, well, those things are nice to know as long as they aren't one of the top reasons you pick School A over School B.

Professional Outcomes

We'll look at how recent graduating classes are faring six months after graduation. In examining the list of companies that hire the most alumni, you'll see which schools serve as a pipeline to many of the nation's premier employers. Geographic information will allow you to see where the largest pockets of alumni settle—a factor that may assist your networking efforts. You'll also be able to identify which undergraduate institutions send large numbers of students to elite graduate and professional schools. Universities that have notable success preparing their students for admission into law and medical schools are highlighted.

Admissions

As wonderful as many high school guidance counselors are, even the best are pulled in a million different directions over the course of the day. To quantify that phenomenon, counselors in public high schools report spending only 22 percent of their time on college-related counseling while their private school counterparts spend a far healthier 55 percent. In either setting, given their breadth of responsibilities, even knowledgeable counselors may not be able to keep track of the latest admissions-related news at every one of the top postsecondary institutions in the country.

Given the aforementioned escalation in selectivity over the last few years, schools that may have been considered *safety schools* when you were a freshman may now be closer to *reach schools*. A multitude of applicants to the University of California's branch campuses discovered that reality the hard way in 2018. It's important to consider the way a given school is trending from a selectivity standpoint, which is why we include our unique "five-year admissions trend" metric that shows the degree to which the school has become more/less competitive in recent years. Further analysis of that number will reveal whether the decreasing acceptance rate is simply the result of an influx of borderline applicants or whether the profile of the average accepted student is actually shifting. We also will identify whether an admissions edge can be gained by applying early, the impact of legacy status, and the factors each admissions office values most.

Worth Your Money?

The worth of a college degree is almost always context-dependent. Plenty of students attend unspectacular universities and go on to incredible levels of success; conversely, plenty of young people have attended prestigious institutions and struggled in their careers. A school that may be an incredible value for an in-state electrical engineering major may be a terrible choice for out-of-state students concentrating in sociology.

The intent of this section is to (a) give you an overview of how generous (or stingy) particular schools are with financial aid; (b) inform you about cost of attendance, in-state vs. out-of-state tuition rates, and the amount of debt students graduate with; and (c) give an assessment of the circumstances in which one might want to be wary of paying the full sticker price for a given school. Think of this as an introductory counseling session that will get you thinking about whether a school's cost makes sense for *you*.

Data Tables

In addition to the data-heavy narrative section, each profile is accompanied by two tables brimming with useful and often underappreciated statistical information. The following data points are included:

Admissions Data

Admission Rate
The overall percentage of the total application pool that is offered admission.

Admission Rate (Men)
The overall percentage of male applicants that are offered admission.

Admission Rate (Women)
The overall percentage of the female applicants that are offered admission.

Early Action Admission Rate
The percentage of applicants admitted during the early action (EA) or single-choice early action (SCEA) rounds.

Early Decsion Admission Rate
The percentage of applicants admitted during the early decision (ED) round.

Admission Rate (five-year trend)
This is the percentage change in the acceptance rate from five years ago. For example, if a school's acceptance rate was 32 percent in 2013 and 27 percent in 2018, the five-year trend would be -5 percent.

Early Decision Admission Rate (five-year trend)
The percentage change in the early decision acceptance rate from five years ago.

Percent of Admits Attending (yield rate)
A school's yield rate is the percentage of accepted students who ultimately elect to enroll in the freshman class divided by the number of accepted applicants. For example, if 5,000 students were accepted and 1,000 chose to enroll, the yield rate would be 20 percent.

Transfer Admission Rate
The overall percentage of the total transfer application pool that is offered admission.

Number Offered Waitlist
The number of students offered a place on a school's waitlist.

Number Accepted Waitlist
The number of students who accepted a place on the waitlist.

Number Admitted Waitlist
The number of students who are admitted to the university from the waitlist.

SAT Math (middle 50 percent)
The 25th-and 75th-percentile SAT math scores for first-year students.

SAT Reading/Writing (middle 50 percent)
The 25th-and 75th-percentile reading/writing SAT scores for first-year students.

ACT Composite (middle 50 percent)
The 25th-and 75th-percentile composite ACT scores for first-year students.

Testing Policy
Whether the school requires the SAT/ACT or has a test-optional or test-flexible policy.

SAT Superscore
Whether the college will combine an applicant's highest scores by section across test administrations.

ACT Superscore
Whether the college will combine an applicant's highest scores by section across test administrations. (Note: More schools superscore the SAT than the ACT, and the policies are not always the same for both tests.)

Percent in Top 10 percent, 25 percent, and 50 percent of High School Class
Among enrolled freshmen who reported their class ranks, the percent that finished in the top tenth, quarter, and half of their graduating classes.

Enrollment Data

Total Undergraduate Enrollment
The number of undergraduate students attending the institution.

Percent Part-Time
The percentage of undergraduates taking fewer than twelve credits per semester.

Percent Male/Female
The percentage of males and percent of females that comprise the undergraduate student body.

Percent Out of State
The percentage of domestic (U.S.) students who are not residents of the state in which the college is located.

Percent Fraternity/Sorority
The percentage of undergraduates who are members of Greek organizations divided by the undergraduate population.

Percent on Campus (Freshmen)
The number of freshmen who live on campus divided by the number of freshmen.

Percent on Campus (All Undergraduates)
The number of undergraduates living on campus divided by the number of undergraduates.

Ethnic/Racial Demographics
The percentage of undergraduate students who identify as African American, Asian, Hispanic, and white.

Percent International
The number of foreign students enrolled at an American university who are studying through a temporary visa divided by the undergraduate population.

Percent Low-Income
The number of students who meet the US Department of Education standard for "low income" (for a family of four, that figure is $37,650 per year) divided by the undergraduate population.

Academics

Student-to-Faculty Ratio
The number of undergraduate students divided by the number of full-time faculty members.

Percent of Classes under Twenty Students
The number of undergraduate course sections with an enrollment under twenty divided by the number of undergraduate course sections.

Percent of Classes under Forty Students
The number of undergraduate course sections with an enrollment under forty divided by the number of undergraduate course sections.

Percent of Full-Time Faculty
The percentage of faculty members who are full-time professors at a given institution.

Percent of Full-Time Faculty with Terminal Degree
The percentage of full-time professors who possess the highest possible degree in their field (typically PhD).

Top Programs
This is not purely a list of the most popular majors by volume. While that is factored into our algorithm, so are other metrics including selectivity, student-to-faculty ratio, class size, peer assessment, graduate earnings (by major), and PhD productivity. (More details are included later in this section.)

Retention Rate
The percentage of freshmen who return to the same institution the following fall to begin their sophomore year.

Four-Year Graduation Rate
The percentage of enrolled undergraduate students who graduate in four years or fewer.

Six-Year Graduation Rate
The percentage of enrolled undergraduate students who graduate in six years or fewer.

Curricular Flexibility
Many colleges have a "core curriculum" and "distributional requirements" that dictate what specific courses and/or general categories of courses all undergraduates must complete in order to graduate. We awarded schools one of three grades: Very Flexible, Somewhat Flexible, or Less Flexible, depending on the extent and specificity of their curricular mandates.

Academic Rating

To construct an academic rating for each college, we rely on ten different indicators of academic quality, namely the average SAT/ACT composite of incoming students, the percentage of incoming students ranked in the top 10 percent of their high school class, student-to-faculty ratio, class size, the percentage of faculty who are full-time employees, the percentage of faculty with terminal degrees, mean faculty salary, freshman retention rate, six year-graduation rate, and graduation performance. This last variable compares an institution's actual graduation rate with its predicted graduation rate, after controlling for the high school class rank and SAT/ACT scores of incoming students as well as the percentage of undergraduates receiving a Pell Grant, a grant primarily given to low-income students.

After collecting data, we normalize and subsequently sum values across all ten indicators, assigning each institution a total score, and by extension, its academic rating. Academic ratings range from one to five stars (institutions receiving a rating of lower than three stars are not featured in this book), with a rating of five stars assigned to colleges and universities receiving the highest total scores. We opted to use a discrete variable (a "star" rating) instead of each college's total numerical score, because incorporating the latter would presume that our assessment is precise. It is not. An institution's academic environment and offerings can never be captured by a single number. That said, we do believe the ratings assigned can prove useful when comparing the academic climates and offerings of the colleges featured in this book.

Financial

Institutional Type
Indicates whether the school is a public or private institution.

In-State Tuition
For public schools, the annual cost of full-time tuition for one academic year charged to state residents. For private schools, we list the general tuition here.

Out-of-State Tuition
For public schools, the annual cost of full-time tuition for one academic year charged to state residents. For private schools, we list the general tuition here.

Room & Board
The annual cost for university-owned housing and meal plans.

Required Fees
Mandatory fees charged by the school for things such as technology, the library, athletics, laboratory experiences, and transportation.

Books and Supplies
The average figure students pay for one academic year's worth of books purchased through the university bookstore.

Average Need-Based Scholarships
Of students who qualified for need-based aid, the average dollar amount the institution awarded.

Average Percent of Need Met
Of students who qualified for need-based aid, the average percentage of the demonstrated need that the institution met.

Average Merit-Based Scholarship
Among those who received a non-need-based financial award, the average annual award that was granted.

Percent Receiving Merit-Based Scholarships
The percentage of undergraduates presently enrolled who received some degree of non-need-based aid.

Average Cumulative Debt
Among students who took out loans to pay for a given college, the average cumulative debt owed upon graduation.

Percentage of Students Borrowing
The percentage of students who are taking out loans in order to fund a portion of their educational expenses.

Career

Who Recruits
A list of high-profile companies that regularly recruit on campus.

Notable Internships
Collected from institutional data sources, this is a list of employers who regularly provide meaningful internships to undergraduate students.

Top Industries
A list of the sectors where the highest number of recent graduates find employment.

Top Employers
According to LinkedIn data, the companies/organizations that employ the largest number of graduates.

Where Alumni Work
According to LinkedIn data, the cities where the largest concentration of alumni currently live.

Earnings
In an effort to give you the most complete picture of alumni earning possible, we include three data points. They are as follows:

College Scorecard: This number is the median earnings of students who received federal financial aid ten years after entering a given college.

The Equality of Opportunity Project: The results of a Harvard economist's look at millions of anonymous tax records. The figures are median salary figures at age thirty-four. This ongoing research endeavor examined more than 30 million tax returns of individuals who were born between 1980 and 1991.

PayScale: The median salary of individuals with 10+ years of work experience based on millions of survey respondents. This figure tends to be higher than the other two because it includes professionals in mid-to-late career, when earnings are typically highest. Additionally, these salaries are self-reported, which makes them the least accurate of the bunch.

Rankings

Forbes Ranking
A college's ranking by *Forbes*, which is determined via the following formula: salary (20 percent), debt (20 percent), student experience (20 percent), American leaders list (15 percent), academic success (12.5 percent), and graduation rate (12.5 percent).

Money Ranking
A college's ranking by *Money*, which is determined via the following formula: six-year graduation rate (30 percent), value-added graduation rate (30 percent), peer quality (10 percent), instructor quality (10 percent), financial troubles (15 percent), and Pell Grant recipient outcomes (5 percent).

US News & World Report Ranking
A college's ranking by *US News & World Report (US News)*, which is determined via the following formula: outcomes (35 percent), faculty resources (20 percent), expert opinion (20 percent), financial resources (10 percent), student excellence (10 percent), and alumni giving (5 percent).

Wall Street Journal/Times Higher Education Ranking
A college's ranking by *The Wall Street Journal/Times Higher Education (THE)*, which is determined via the following formula: resources (30 percent), engagement (20 percent), outcomes (40 percent), and environment (10 percent).

Washington Monthly Ranking
A college's ranking by *Washington Monthly*, which is determined via the following formula: social mobility (33.3 percent), research (33.3 percent), and community and national service (33.3 percent).

Where did this data come from?

Admissions Data

Our primary source for SAT and ACT middle-50 percent ranges is the Common Data Set (CDS), a collaborative effort of data providers in the higher education community in which most institutions participate. We gathered superscoring policies from institutional websites and, in the many cases where nothing was listed publicly, from direct contact with admissions offices. We also gathered regular and early decision (ED) acceptance rates and waitlist statistics from a combination of the CDS and institutional websites.

Enrollment Data

We took enrollment and demographic data directly from each school's CDS. If the school did not publish a CDS, we collected that information from alternative institutional reports.

Academics Data

We pulled class sizes, student-to-faculty ratios, and graduation/retention rates from the CDS or other available institutional publications.

Top Programs Within Colleges

Our methodology for determining each college's top academic programs incorporated the following four factors:

1. Major Emphasis
Indicates the number of students at an institution studying a specific major. If a high percentage of students at a particular college are studying a major, it is likely that the major attracts a relatively large portion of the institution's resources. To measure major emphasis and we relied on data collected by the National Center for Education Statistics as reported by The Integrated Postsecondary Education Data System (IPEDS).

2. Student-to-Faculty Ratio and Class Size
Research consistently shows that class size as well as student–faculty interaction and collaboration leads to better learning and career-related outcomes. We collected data for these indicators from the US Department of Education, institutional websites, and surveys of college administrators.

3. Peer Assessment

To derive a peer assessment score, we relied on questionnaires distributed to both college admission experts (including school counselors, independent education consultants, and college admission officers) and higher education administrators, and then compared responses with "strong programs" data published by U.S. News & World Report, Niche, and other reputable sources that rank colleges within a specific discipline (e.g. *CSRankings.org* for Computer Science, *The Hollywood Reporter* for Film, *Foreign Policy* for International Relations, etc.) Alone, peer assessment surveys are subject to a fair amount of bias. However, when evaluated in sum and considered along with more objective data—such as that examining major emphasis and class size—they can provide more complete and corroborative insight into the strength of a particular program/major.

4. PhD Productivity

While most undergraduates have no intent to pursue a doctoral degree, the rate at which a department/program produces Ph.D. recipients arguably reflects how well the program promotes academic rigor and prepares students to tackle advanced coursework. When available, we used data provided by the National Science Foundation in order to assess which programs graduated the highest percentage of students who later completed a PhD degree.

Top Colleges for America's Top Majors

When choosing which majors to feature in section, we considered both professional prospects (i.e. which majors results in high salaries and ample job opportunities) and popularity of discipline (i.e. how many students pursue the major). In order to identify the top colleges for each major, we relied on the same variables used to select the top programs within each college, as well as three additional variables, namely those for institutional selectivity, major share, and graduate earnings (see descriptions of variables below). It is also important to note that for some areas of study (e.g. Actuarial Science, Information Systems), we list colleges that do not offer a formal major, but that possess offerings (within a minor or informal concentration) so strong that they warrant inclusion.

1. Institutional Selectivity

Though selectivity is not a perfect proxy for college or major/program quality, it is highly correlated with student ability/achievement and institutional expenditures per student, which both contribute significantly to the undergraduate learning experience. We looked to a college's freshman admission rate and average SAT/ACT score (as reported by each institution's CDS) to measure selectivity.

2. Major Share

If a college enrolls a relatively high percentage of all students in the United States studying a particular major, it is likely that the college has been identified by prospective students, employers, and other stakeholders as a leader in that subject area. Though this assumption may result in bias against smaller institutions or programs, it is important to account for the fact that larger programs often have the ability to attract more tuition revenue, meet fixed costs, and reinvest the major's offerings. To measure major share we relied on data collected by the National Center for Education Statistics as reported by IPEDS.

3. Graduate Earnings

To measure graduate earnings, we relied on salary data provided by College Score Card, PayScale, and the Equality of Opportunity Project, all of which indicate both early-career and mid-career wages of students by college. We analyzed both early-career and mid-career wages because the former is typically an indicator of how employers perceive the quality of a particular major/program, while the latter indicates how well a major/program may have prepared students for work.

In addition, when able, we used data indicating graduate earnings by field of study, as doing so provides a more accurate measure of the relationship between a specific academic program and graduate earnings. For example, PayScale provides salary data for a student attending Boston University and majoring in engineering, which is different from salary data for students attending Boston University and majoring in business.

Financial Data

Financial data is taken directly from each school's CDS. If the school did not publish a CDS, we collected this information from alternative institutional reports.

Career/Salary Data

There are two main sources for information related to the most popular industries and the companies at which alumni have the most representation. LinkedIn is an excellent resource for gathering data on how many alumni of all ages are working for a particular employer. Reports the colleges produce for each recent graduating class—often called "First Destination Surveys"—receive high response rates and offer a glimpse into where the Class of 2019 is headed. If your aim is to work at a relatively new mega-company such as SpaceX, Uber, or Airbnb, it may be more helpful to know where recent graduates have landed. Where possible, we included this data in the narrative sections of the profiles.

No one source of salary data is perfect, so we sought to give you as many data points as possible for each college. As previously mentioned, the salary figures provided in each data table come from College Scorecard, PayScale, and the Equality of Opportunity project. We also included First Destination Survey data in instances where reliable institutional data could be reported. This sometimes offers a glimpse at average or median starting salaries for a school's recent graduates; certain universities provide a breakdown of starting salary by major.

Rankings

Taken at face value, a school's rank in a given publication can be unhelpful or even misleading to your unique college search. For instance, the fact that the 2019 *US News & World Report* rankings list Emory University twenty-first and Tufts University is tied for twenty-seventh doesn't mean that one school is superior to the other; Emory and Tufts happen to be two of the finest schools in the country, and assigning any value to a fraction of a point in a ranking algorithm would just be plain silly. However, when considered in proper context and across several different rankings systems utilizing different algorithms, one can get a general idea of a school's reputation in the eyes of graduate schools and top employers. Collectively, we believe that these rankings can provide a degree of insight as you ponder your postsecondary future.

Why some colleges made the cut and others did not.

We wish to be fully transparent about an important issue: There is no definitive algorithm that would determine the dollar-for-dollar "best colleges for your money." Sure, you could base your rankings solely on return on investment figures and just list the top 150 schools in terms of median salaries. However, doing so would pretty much produce a list of the colleges that produce the greatest percentage of business, computer science, and engineering grads because those fields generally pay the best. You could also concoct a pseudoscientific formula with dozens of inputs that would spew out a concrete score that would serve as a defense as to why one school made the 150 and others were left out in the cold.

In truth, selecting these schools was as much art as science. In aiming to create a useful college guide, we drew on our collective experience of having guided thousands of students through the application process over the past decade. In seeking quantifiable evidence of value, we also examined every available report on earnings, social mobility, academic rankings, and school-specific outcomes. In the end, we were genuinely surprised by some of the lesser-known schools that stood out by those metrics and were equally surprised by some big-name schools that fared poorer than expected. Ultimately, we are extremely confident that every institution included in this book does admirable work on behalf of its undergraduates.

On the other hand, there are not only 150 schools that are, in our professional opinion, "Worth Your Money." So before alums or representatives from omitted schools start penning nasty emails to us, this book is not being intentionally exclusionary—150 is an arbitrary cutoff because—well—you have to have an arbitrary cutoff. Depending on one's circumstances, (again, all higher education value is context dependent), there may be 250-300 schools that could serve as fine postsecondary destinations from which to springboard into a successful career/life. Our hope is that this book will help give the tools and mindset to evaluate any prospective institution, whether or not you find that college in the pages that follow.

Final Thoughts

Before you turn to the profiles section of this book, consider the following startling facts:

- Barely half of current college students can provide an accurate estimate of their freshman year cost of attendance.
- Only 55 percent of undergraduates nationwide finish their degree within six years.
- For those who do graduate, the average debt load is roughly $30,000.
- Studies estimate that as many as 43 percent of college grads end up working in jobs that do not require a college degree.
- Fifty-one percent of college grads ultimately wish they had chosen a different school, degree program, or major.

If picking the right college was easy, the numbers above wouldn't be nearly so bleak. Selecting a school that will put you on the right side of those unfortunate statistics takes a great deal of hard work and planning. Applicants are often so swept up in the quest to gain admission into a given school that they fail to stop and consider exactly why their dream school became their dream in the first place.

A dream college—or to be less hyperbolic, a good-fit college—should check boxes in terms of the availability and quality of academic programs of interest, the extracurricular opportunities and aspects of campus life that will promote a sense of connectedness, the level of career services you will need to get on the path to the right career/graduate school, a demonstrated history of positive outcomes for graduates, and a school where you have a genuine chance of being accepted.

Whether you are a parent or high school student, rest assured that by carefully examining the profiles that follow you are about to become a more knowledgeable college consumer than your adult or teenage peers. Ideally, you will enter the pages that follow with an open mind and be willing to consider disconfirming data about a school you previously thought was perfect for you as well as new, unexpected information about a school you would never have considered before. While the college search and admissions process is rife with challenges and stressors, eschewing the cacophony of unhelpful voices in favor of data will result in increased confidence and focus as you make this extremely important life decision.

Enjoy the journey ahead!

America's Top Schools

American University

Washington, District of Columbia | Admissions Phone: 202-885-6000

Inside the Classroom

Located in the heart of our nation's capital, American University's highly desirable location and access to an abundance of government/corporate internships and networking opportunities has contributed to the university becoming far more selective than it was a decade ago. AU presently plays host to 8,100 undergraduate students as well as over 5,700 graduate and law students. Campus is a genuinely diverse place with an undergraduate population comprised 25 percent of underrepresented minorities and another 7 percent of international students. There are sixty-seven undergraduate degrees for students to choose from at AU across six undergraduate colleges: the College of Arts & Sciences, the Kogod School of Business, the School of Communication, the School of Education, the School of International Service, and the School of Public Affairs.

All undergrads are exposed to a recently-adopted core curriculum that focuses on enhancing students' meta-cognitive abilities. Requirements include more than thirty credits of study in courses such as Complex Problems, Quantitative Literacy, Ethical Reasoning, Creative-Aesthetic Inquiry, and Written Communication. As the school itself explains, the "AU Core general education program offers a four-year, inquiry-based liberal arts education, beginning with a Complex Problems seminar (small, nineteen-person seminars that include cocurricular experiences), bridging to essential habits of mind and integrating these skills and habits with the student's major, and culminating in a capstone." The American University Experience Program is designed to provide first-years with the advising and experiences that help students adjust to the academic rigors and social challenges that arise with the transition to college.

A low 12:1 student-to-faculty ratio allows roughly half of offered courses to be capped at nineteen students; the average undergraduate class size is twenty-three. Undergraduate research opportunities are taken advantage of by 50 percent of first-year students and 40 percent of seniors. For the last twelve years AU has hosted an Undergraduate Research Symposium at the end of each year where students can present their research. Students here are not afraid to hop on a plane and pursue a semester's worth of education in a foreign land. A substantial 55 percent of undergrads take a semester abroad with the most popular destination points being the United Kingdom, Italy, Spain, Kenya, and Belgium.

American's School of International Service (SIS) is one of the top-ranked programs in the country—its Public Affairs program also receives universally high marks. In terms of sheer popularity, the most commonly conferred degrees are in the social sciences (36 percent), business (17 percent), communication/journalism (11 percent), and the visual and performing arts (6 percent). Graduates fare quite well in securing service-oriented awards and scholarships. Among medium-sized universities, AU is the number one producer of Peace Corps volunteers in the country. It also boasts the most Boren Scholars, awarded to students who wish to study language for the purpose of national security. AU is also one of only seven schools to produce more than one Truman Scholar in 2017, and it saw thirty-seven undergraduates win Fulbright Scholarships from 2013-18.

Outside the Classroom

This ninety-acre campus receives accolades as one of the most beautiful urban campuses in the country. Off campus, Northwest DC is a happening place, containing a number of other large schools (Georgetown, GW, Howard, and UDC) and Capital One Arena, home to the Wizards, Capitals, and countless concerts. All of the dining, cultural, and museum experiences the District of Columbia offers can be accessed car-free via the Metro. For a flat fee, students receive a University Pass entitling them to unlimited Metro rides. The undergraduate population is 63 percent female, which certainly influences social life on campus. Fraternities attract 9 percent of men and sororities draw 11 percent of women. The Eagles play Division I sports in the Patriot League (except for wrestling) and boast six men's teams and eight women's teams. Another twenty-five club teams provide opportunities for athletic participation. For the less athletically inclined, 250 student organizations are available including student government, political clubs, charitable groups, and those dedicated purely to recreational pursuits. Facilities for student use include three gymnasiums, an aquatic center featuring two eight-lane pools, a two-mile fitness trail, and a beautiful outdoor athletic complex with basketball and tennis courts.

Career Services

The AU Career Center is staffed by thirty full-time professional employees who serve as career counselors, employer relations specialists, merit awards program coordinators, and alumni career coordinators. That works out to a phenomenal student-to-advisor ratio of 240:1, among the best of any midsize institution included in this book. It's no wonder that 99 percent of surveyed undergraduates are happy with the school's career advising services.

AU does an exceptional job hooking up students with internship opportunities; 91 percent of grads had such an experience. Being located in DC is a boon to internship opportunities as the leading host agencies include the Department of Education, State, Homeland Security, DC Public Schools, and the Public Defender Service for the District of Columbia. The Employer-in-Residence program brings organizations including Deloitte, the CIA, CNN, and Google on campus for one-one-one networking opportunities with undergrads. Student-Alumni

Networking Receptions in areas such as human security, public health, education, and energy, the environment, and sustainability allow current students to network with alumni working in their area of interest. In the 2018-19 academic year 504 employers recruited at AU, 238 hiring organizations attended career fairs, and 523 on-campus interviews were conducted. Among the employers that recruited on campus in that same time were the CIA, Politico, Booz Allen Hamilton, the Washington Nationals, the US Department of Defense, EY, Bloomberg, and Yelp.

Professional Outcomes

Within six months of graduation, 92 percent of AU grads have found employment, are enrolled in grad school, or both. There is a 60/40 split on landing jobs in the private sector versus finding employment in nonprofit/government arena. A healthy percentage of grads are attracted to public service in the form of Teach for America and the Peace Corps as both organizations are among the top five employers of recent grads. Ernst & Young, Deloitte, and the US Army round out the list. Across all graduating years, more than one hundred alumni presently work for the US House of Representatives, the US Department of State, Booz Allen Hamilton, Google, EY, IBM, PwC, and Accenture. With a heavy concentration of grads flowing into the public sector, starting salaries are not eye-popping—32 percent start above $50k, and 85 percent start above $40k. Predictably, graduates of the Kogod School of Business fare better than the average AU grad with 58 percent starting at over $50k. Many remain in DC but many others flock to New York City, Boston, San Francisco, Los Angeles, and Philly in substantial numbers.

Many of the most popular grad school destinations are only a Metro stop away. George Washington, Georgetown, Johns Hopkins, and American itself head the list. Seventeen percent of those who graduate from the School of Arts Sciences and the School of Public Affairs go straight into graduate school (including those working and going to grad school). Far lower concentrations of graduates from other schools within the university dive right into continuing their education. Fewer than fifty graduates apply to medical school each year, but some have had success in recent years gaining acceptance into schools including the Georgetown University School of Medicine, the University of Massachusetts Medical School, and Upstate Medical University. Recent grads pursuing a legal education have done so at the University of Pennsylvania, the University of Miami, Villanova University and, of course, American's own Washington College of Law.

Admission

American University had a 46 percent acceptance rate in 2014, hit an all-time low of 26 percent in 2016, and accepted 32 percent of applicants seeking a place in the Class of 2022. While acceptance rates have plummeted at AU in recent years, the profile of the average attending student hasn't changed commensurately. The ACT middle-50 percent range five years ago was 27-31, identical to the range today, and the SAT ranges have remained fairly constant as well. The average GPA for an entering member of the Class of 2022 was 3.6. While 40 percent possessed high school GPAs above a 3.75, 16 percent earned under a 3.25, giving hope to those with more B's than A's on their transcript.

Additionally, it is important to note that American is test-optional, having been one of the earlier competitive institutions to jettison test scores almost a decade ago. The strongest emphasis is placed on the rigor of one's course load, GPA and, most interestingly, applicant's interest. Since AU is a popular backup, the school very much wants to know if it is one of your top choices. This idea is supported by the school's early decision acceptance rate. In 2018, the school accepted 791 of 974 ED applicants, an overwhelming 81 percent. American is a quality institution situated in a city that is a highly desirable destination for young people. While a surface-level glance at its admissions data may suggest an increasingly competitive environment, AU is still accessible to good but not top-of-the-class students who view the school as their number one choice.

Worth Your Money?

Spending big money on tuition to attend American University can be a wise decision, but it really depends on your financial circumstances and academic area of interest. The annual cost of attendance is $64,769, but approximately 50 percent of undergraduates qualify for an average aid award of $29k. Unfortunately, American is not terribly generous with merit aid, awarding scholarships to only one-quarter of students. (The average award is $13k.) Yet, if you want a school that opens doors to jobs in politics, government, and major consulting firms, AU may be worth the expense.

FINANCIAL
Institutional Type: Private
In-State Tuition: $49,070
Out-of-State Tuition: $49,070
Room & Board: $14,880
Required Fees: $819
Books & Supplies: $800

Avg. Need-Based Aid: $29,118
Avg. % of Need Met: 87%

Avg. Merit-Based Aid: $13,347
% Receiving Merit-Based Aid: 25%

Avg. Cumulative Debt: $35,122
% of Students Borrowing: 63%

CAREER
Who Recruits
1. Central Intelligence Agency
2. Politico
3. Yelp
4. Government Accoutability Office
5. AARP

Notable Internships
1. United States Senate
2. Smithsonian
3. American Foreign Service Association

Top Industries
1. Business
2. Education
3. Media
4. Social Services
5. Operations

Top Employers
1. U.S. State Department
2. Deloitte
3. Booz Allen Hamilton
4. U.S. House of Representatives
5. IBM

Where Alumni Work
1. Washington, DC
2. New York City
3. Boston
4. Philadelphia
5. San Francisco

Median Earnings
College Scorecard (Early Career): $61,000
EOP (Early Career): $59,100
PayScale (Mid-Career): $102,900

RANKINGS
Forbes: 126
Money: 456
U.S. News: 77 (T), National Universities
Wall Street Journal/THE: 131
Washington Monthly: 255, National Universities

#CollegesWorthYourMoney

Amherst College

Amherst, Massachusetts | Admissions Phone: 413-542-2328

Inside the Classroom

One of the premier liberal arts colleges in the country—and one the most selective—Amherst College is an Ivy-equivalent institution that offers its brilliant student body a one-of-a-kind academic experience. A mere 1,850 undergraduates grace this picturesque rural campus located seventy-five miles west of Boston. Yet, a small town location is not at all indicative of an isolated existence. If the forty majors and 850 course offerings on campus aren't enough, Amherst belongs to the Five College Consortium that allows students to take any course offered at Mount Holyoke, Smith, Hampshire College, or UMass-Amherst.

Similar to Brown's "New Curriculum," Amherst operates its "Open Curriculum" that requires no specific courses or distribution of credits. Students have the flexibility to pursue their areas of passion and interest from the very start of their collegiate experience. With no burdensome requirements, double majoring is commonplace with over 30 percent of the student body electing to study at least one additional discipline. The college encourages students to "take full responsibility for their intellectual growth, in the same way they will take responsibility for important choices later in life."

If you crave facetime with your professors, Amherst delivers. A 7-to-1 student-to-faculty ratio allows for 71 percent of courses to have fewer than twenty students and 30 percent to have single-digit enrollments. That level of intimacy pays off with the forging of student-faculty relationships. By senior year, 98 percent of seniors report feeling close enough to a faculty member to ask for a letter of recommendation. The eight-to-ten-week Summer Science Undergraduate Research Program is available for students as are plenty of grants aimed at funding original student research projects. A sizable number of students study abroad, 43 percent to be precise, in just about any country you can name from Namibia to Trinidad. The school's student body has become increasingly diverse in recent years, now boasting double-digit percentages of African American, Latino, and first-generation students.

A true liberal arts college, Amherst possesses strong offerings across the board, most notably in economics, English, history, mathematics, and law (through its one-of-a-kind major in Law, Jurisprudence and Social Thought). Amherst also boasts one of the most esteemed (and highest paid) liberal arts faculties in the country. Students are always competitive for postgraduate awards and fellowships. The college has been recognized as one of the top producers of Fulbright Scholars for over a decade; it had eight winners in 2019 and had more Watson Fellows in 2017 than any other institution in the country.

Outside the Classroom

Amherst is the rare school where 98 percent of undergraduates reside in school-owned housing. There are no Greek organizations, but a colossal 37 percent of Amherst students are rostered on one of the college's twenty-seven NCAA Division III sports teams, which means that many are dedicating a good portion of their time to athletics. For everyone else, over 150 student organizations are operating on campus. The schools six a cappella groups and four-ensemble Choral Society play a notable enough role to have earned the school the nickname "The Singing College." Membership in the Five College Consortium opens the door to a variety of other clubs and activities within close proximity. However, it is important to note that the other four campuses are not adjoining—UMass and Hampshire are about a ten-minute drive, and Smith and Mount Holyoke take twenty minutes to reach by car. Guest speakers are regularly on campus. Each year, the Amherst Leads organization brings up to twenty-five well known athletes, business leaders, and writers/journalists to speak on campus. Dorms, food, and other amenities generally receive positive reviews. For students who want to be in touch with nature, a 500-acre wildlife preserve is located on campus, and it can be freely hiked and explored.

Career Services

Unlike at just about every other institution of higher education, the vast majority of the Amherst student body actually takes advantage of the Career Center's offerings. In fact, the Loeb Center for Career Exploration and Planning advises more than 1,400 students and alumni each year for a total of more than 6,000 sessions. That prodigious output comes from the office's thirteen full-time staff members who focus on either career advising or employer relations. Loeb's 142:1 student-to-advisor ratio is among the best of any school featured in this guide.

Amherst does a superb job recruiting companies to campus with more than 175 visiting per year and close to 450 interviews taking place on campus, which is roughly the size of the graduating class. There were fifty-nine days in the 2017-18 school year on which interviews were taking place on campus. Other programs, such as Career Treks, involve organized trips to Boston, New York City, and Los Angeles. Those trips allow students the chance to meet with alumni in the areas of finance, government, entertainment, education, and philanthropy. The Pathways program facilitates hundreds of additional mentoring relationships between alumni and current students each year. Nearly one-quarter of freshmen are enrolled in the Amherst Select Internship Program, which allows first-year students to jump directly into a hands-on learning opportunity.

E-mail: admissions@amherst.edu | Website: www.amherst.edu

Professional Outcomes

Whether you are interested in going directly into the workforce or continuing into graduate school, Amherst's reputation and connected alumni network will open doors. A few months after graduation, 98 percent of the Class of 2018 had already found its way into the world of employment, graduate school, or a volunteer organization. The highest number of recent grads went into finance (37 percent) with education (21 percent) and science/technology (11 percent) next in popularity. Recent graduates found jobs everywhere from Bain Capital to the United Talent Agency to the US Department of State. By sheer volume, the largest employers of Amherst grads is a high-end list including Google, Deloitte, Morgan Stanley, and Goldman Sachs. The average starting salary for Amherst graduates is around $60k, making them among the highest-paid liberal arts grads in the country. That is even more impressive when you consider that Amherst doesn't even have an engineering program, the profession that usually bolsters starting salary figures.

Amherst grads fare well at gaining acceptance to elite schools. It regularly sees 50 percent or more of applicants get into law schools like those at Georgetown, Columbia, Harvard, Berkeley, and Stanford, more than twice those schools' overall acceptance rates. In total, the schools where the highest number of Amherst grads can be found pursuing advanced degrees includes University of Cambridge (UK), MIT, Dartmouth, and the University of Pennsylvania. Fifty to sixty Amherst grads apply to medical school each year, and the acceptance rate hovers around 75-80 percent. As with law schools, students attend many of the finest medical institutions in the world. In order, the greatest number of alumni settle in New York City, Boston, San Francisco, and Washington, DC.

Admission

Amherst accepted under 13 percent of applicants to the Class of 2022. The average test score of admitted students was 33 on the ACT and 1492 on the SAT. That SAT number is twenty points higher than it was one year ago. However, Amherst has long been one of the most selective liberal arts schools in the country, so the landscape hasn't changed all that much. The college has had an acceptance rate of under 16 percent for more than a decade. Unsurprisingly, a high percentage of admitted students finished in the top 10 percent of their high school class—88 percent at last count. An impressive 20 percent of the Class of 2022 were valedictorians. This cohort has mid-50 percent standardized test score ranges of 1390-1540 on the SAT and 31-34 on the ACT.

The admissions office lists a whopping nine categories as having the highest level of influence on admissions decisions. That list includes talent/ability, character/personal qualities, recommendations, and first-generation status. While the process is holistic and genuinely committed to increasing the underrepresented minority and first-generation presence on campus, Amherst remains one of the most selective liberal arts colleges in the United States.

If Amherst is your top choice, applying ED can give you a slight edge; 38 percent of the 2018-19 freshman class were accepted via the ED round, versus 11.5 percent in the regular round; roughly 20 percent of those admitted via the early round were children of alumni. Many of Amherst's varsity athletes are also admitted early; the school claims that fewer than seventy admitted athletes per year are given preferential admissions treatment, a figure that equates to a sizable 15 percent of the class. Successful applicants will be near (or at) the top of their high school class, have earned standardized test scores in the top 1-2 percent, and possess unique gifts/intangibles that help separate them from a mass of similarly qualified peers.

Worth Your Money?

Close to half of Amherst students will pay the full $74,000 cost of attendance, a four-year sum of $296,000. This is because the college does not award merit aid, only need-based. For the 56 percent who qualify for financial aid, Amherst does meet 100 percent of their demonstrated need, which works out to an average of $59k per year, making the school quite affordable. The majority of the students paying full freight come from families in the top income percentiles, rendering the impact of the huge bill minimal. Amherst is an Ivy-level school that is worth attending for most as it will legitimately play a role in opening any and all employment or graduate schools dreams you could conjure up.

FINANCIAL
Institutional Type: Private
In-State Tuition: $55,520
Out-of-State Tuition: $55,520
Room & Board: $14,740
Required Fees: $906
Books & Supplies: $1,000

Avg. Need-Based Aid: $58,880
Avg. % of Need Met: 100%

Avg. Merit-Based Aid: $0
% Receiving Merit-Based Aid: 0%

Avg. Cumulative Debt: $13,710
% of Students Borrowing: 30%

CAREER
Who Recruits
1. Hulu
2. FiscalNote
3. T. Rowe Price
4. RBC Capital
5. Fox Sports

Notable Internships
1. National Center for Health Research
2. U.S. House of Representatives
3. NY State Division of Human Rights

Top Industries
1. Business
2. Education
3. Research
4. Media
5. Legal

Top Employers
1. Google
2. Goldman Sachs
3. JP Morgan
4. Massachusetts General Hospital
5. Citi

Where Alumni Work
1. New York City
2. Boston
3. San Francisco
4. Washington, DC
5. Springfield, MA

Median Earnings
College Scorecard (Early Career): $65,000
EOP (Early Career): $69,300
PayScale (Mid-Career): $116,500

RANKINGS
Forbes: 28
Money: 64
U.S. News: 2, Liberal Arts Colleges
Wall Street Journal/THE: 20
Washington Monthly: 3, Liberal Arts Colleges

#CollegesWorthYourMoney

Tempe, Arizona | Admissions Phone: 480-965-7788

ADMISSION
Admission Rate: 85%
Admission Rate - Men: 83%
Admission Rate - Women: 87%
EA Admission Rate: Not Offered
ED Admission Rate: Not Offered
Admission Rate (5-Year Trend): +5%
ED Admission Rate (5-Year Trend): Not Offered
% of Admits Attending (Yield): 39%
Transfer Admission Rate: 84%

Offered Wait List: Not Offered
Accepted Wait List: Not Offered
Admitted Wait List: Not Offered

SAT Reading/Writing (Middle 50%): 570-670
SAT Math (Middle 50%): 560-690
ACT Composite (Middle 50%): 22-29
Testing Policy: ACT/SAT Required
SAT Superscore: No
ACT Superscore: No

% Graduated in Top 10% of HS Class: 33%
% Graduated in Top 25% of HS Class: 62%
% Graduated in Top 50% of HS Class: 89%

ENROLLMENT
Total Undergraduate Enrollment: 42,844
% Part-Time: 8%
% Male: 56%
% Female: 44%
% Out-of-State: 26%
% Fraternity: 10%
% Sorority: 16%
% On-Campus (Freshman): 76%
% On-Campus (All Undergraduate): 26%

% African-American: 4%
% Asian: 8%
% Hispanic: 21%
% White: 50%
% Other: 4%
% Race or Ethnicity Unknown: 0%
% International: 11%
% Low-Income: 29%

ACADEMICS
Student-to-Faculty Ratio: 20:1
% of Classes Under 20: 38%
% of Classes Under 40: 76%
% Full-Time Faculty: 79%
% Full-Time Faculty w/ Terminal Degree: 89%

Top Programs
Art
Business
Communication
Computer Science
Criminology and Criminal Justice
Earth and Space Exploration
Engineering
Psychology

Retention Rate: 88%
4-Year Graduation Rate: 52%
6-Year Graduation Rate: 69%

Curricular Flexibility: Somewhat Flexible
Academic Rating: ★★★

Inside the Classroom
It may be surprising to see one of the largest universities in the country—one which sports an 85 percent acceptance rate—included in this guidebook. Yet, Arizona State University has flourished across its five desert locations (including the ASU Colleges at Lake Havasu City), enhancing its offerings and academic quality in recent years. Serving over 42,000 students at its Tempe campus alone and close to 60,000 undergraduates overall, ASU offers a staggering 350 academic majors. The renowned Barrett Honors College enrolls an incredible 7,200 students compared to the average honors college size of 1,200. Barrett attracts a talented bunch, enrolling more National Merit Scholars than Duke, Stanford, or MIT.

All students must complete a minimum of twenty-nine credits in General Studies courses. Courses can be used to meet more than one requirement at a time but, ultimately, boxes must be checked in the areas of literacy and critical inquiry; mathematical studies; humanities, arts and design; social-behavioral sciences; and the natural sciences. Three "awareness areas" also must be satisfied: Cultural Diversity in the United States, Global Awareness, and Historical Awareness.

The faculty-to-student ratio is a fairly high 20:1, but not all classes call for stadium seating. In fact, 38 percent of course sections seat fewer than twenty students. You'll find classes of over fifty students 18 percent of the time, not unreasonable for a university of this unmatched size. There are plenty of opportunities for experiential learning as 60 percent of students engage in research, land an internship, or have a practicum experience as part of their academic program. The school also has above-average study abroad rates, ranking in the top ten in the nation by sending approximately 2,500 students to 250 programs in sixty-five countries each year.

Business is the concentration in which over one-quarter (27 percent) of total bachelor's degrees are conferred. Engineering (13 percent), the social sciences (9 percent), and biology (8 percent) are the next three most popular. The WP Carey School of Business offers many highly ranked programs as does the Fulton Schools of Engineering. In the last decade, the number of Sun Devils winning competitive national fellowships has skyrocketed. ASU produced an outstanding twenty-one Fulbright Scholars in 2019. It also is becoming a regular producer of Marshall, Gates-Cambridge, Truman, Goldwater, Udall, and Boren Scholarships. Over the past five years 117 graduates have been awarded National Science Foundation Graduate Research Fellowships.

Outside the Classroom
Young people don't typically come to ASU to live a hermetic existence. While the university has begun to shed its "party school" label in recent years, it remains a vibrant, extremely connected campus. Athletics are popular with ten NCCA Division I men's teams and fourteen women's teams. Sun Devil football stadium plays host to 71,000 raucous fans on game days. In addition, ASU fields forty club teams and at least 6,000 additional students take place in competitive intramural sports leagues. Greek life attracts 10 percent of men and 16 percent of women, giving it substantial influence on the social scene. There are more than 1,000 clubs operating across the five campuses with the ASU Outdoors Club and the school's seven identity-based student coalitions drawing large memberships. Interestingly, only 26 percent of the undergraduate student body lives on campus—however, 76 percent of freshmen do opt for that experience. Due to large numbers of students renting apartments/houses in surrounding neighborhoods, ASU hosts an Off-Campus Housing Fair and provides free advice to undergrads seeking a place to reside. In addition to living in the surrounding communities, Sun Devils like to get involved in volunteer work. Collectively, the student body contributes 1.8 million hours of community service each year. There is plenty to do in the cities of Phoenix, Tempe, Mesa, and Scottsdale, all a short drive from one another.

Career Services
ASU's Career and Professional Development Services (CPDS) has offices on its Tempe, Downtown, Polytechnic, and West locations. When you boast 59,000 undergraduate students across your four metropolitan campuses, things can only be so personalized, but ASU does a solid job making services available on a mass scale. Amazingly, it claims 95,000+ annual interactions with students through job fairs, workshops, and networking events.

Nearly 60,000 jobs are posted each year on Handshake, and the school has been selected as a top choice for recruiting talent by more than one hundred companies including Marriot International, Microsoft, General Mills, Charles Schwab, Geico, Ford, FedEx, and Yelp. For such a behemoth of an institution, ASU has a fairly impressive level of internship participation. Around 50 percent of undergraduates have at least one internship, and 44 percent of those are paid opportunities. In total, more than 13,000 internships are posted each year. Having an alumni base of over half a million Sun Devils is great for networking. It is an active and proud bunch that presently has over 100,000 members who donate annually to the university. Thanks to this strong alumni base, wealth of employer partnerships, and strong internship participation rate, the CPDS succeeds in helping the great majority of its graduates swiftly arrive at their next destination soon after receiving diplomas.

Professional Outcomes

A healthy 92 percent of 2018 ASU graduates were employed or in graduate school within six months of earning their degrees. As you would expect from a large school offering 350 majors, the most prolific employers of Sun Devils represent a broad array of corporations and nonprofit entities. Among the school's top fifty employers are Amazon, Apple, Intel, The Vanguard Group, Walt Disney Company, a number of local school districts, and Arizona-based government organizations. In total, the five industries most frequently entered by alumni are banking and finance, technology and engineering, health care, and public and human services. Arizona also ranks thirteenth in the nation among large universities for graduates entering the Peace Corps. The average salary for a member of the Class of 2018 was $50,529. The majority (55 percent) of newly minted grads were working in Arizona with California (14 percent) next in popularity.

Approximately one-fifth of recent grads enrolled in graduate school. Similar to employment, the size and scope of the university leads to many graduate pathways. Many grads continue at ASU itself, but some continue at various prestigious institutions. For example, Yale Law School typically claims at least one ASU alum in its 1L class. From 2010-14, ASU sent 375 graduates to medical school; today, over 350 apply each year. The school's Mayo Medical Scholars program exclusively offered to Barrett Honors College students can open doors for future doctors. While the majority of ASU grads continuing their education do not enter prestigious graduate or professional programs, getting strong grades at ASU absolutely puts them in a position to be strong applicants at any university in the country, including the elites.

Admission

While ASU's reputation for academics has been climbing in recent years, the school is still only slightly selective, accepting 85 percent of those who apply. Considering that friendly acceptance rate, the academic profile of the typical Sun Devil may surprise you. The average freshman possessed a 1216 SAT score, a 3.54 GPA, and ranked within the top 23 percent of their high school class. One-third of Class of 2022 freshmen ranked in the top 10 percent of their high school class while 62 percent were in the top quartile, and 89 percent were in the top half. Among the students presently enrolled in the superb Barrett Honors College, the average SAT score was 1343 and the average GPA was a touch under 3.8. Only a decade ago, the 75th percentile SAT score was 1210, meaning that despite the high acceptance rate, ASU is attracting a more academically superior crop than in the past.

As you might expect at one of the nation's largest universities, admissions officers will not be agonizing over every detail of your application, carefully weighing the merits of your essay, recommendations, and extracurricular resume. In fact, none of those factors are even considered at ASU. Grades, class rank, and test scores are considered "most important," and the rigor of your secondary school record is "important." Conveniently for those entering the admissions process now, the university began accepting the Common Application in 2018. Getting into Arizona State is a straightforward proposition; those who bring a solid transcript and test scores to the table will be invited to join this thriving institution. Admission into the Honors College requires another level of achievement.

Worth Your Money?

Competitively priced for both in-state and out-of-state students, it's no wonder students from around the globe flock to Arizona State. Those from the Grand Canyon State pay less than $27,000 per year cost of attendance while nonresidents cough up $44,000, not that much more than the in-state rate for many public schools on the East Coast. Further, ASU awards merit aid to 43 percent of undergraduates; the average amount is $9k. Need-based aid is granted to 55 percent of full-time students with an average grant of $14k. Thanks to those extremely reasonable prices (we don't utter that phrase often without major qualifiers), this university produces graduates that carry a below-average debt load relative to their peers. Whether you're a local majoring in American Indian Studies or an out-of-stater learning cybersecurity, your tuition dollar goes far at ASU.

FINANCIAL
Institutional Type: Public
In-State Tuition: $10,104
Out-of-State Tuition: $27,618
Room & Board: $12,648
Required Fees: $718
Books & Supplies: $1,148

Avg. Need-Based Aid: $13,663
Avg. % of Need Met: 71%

Avg. Merit-Based Aid: $9,299
% Receiving Merit-Based Aid: 43%

Avg. Cumulative Debt: $23,731
% of Students Borrowing: 45%

CAREER
Who Recruits
1. Amazon
2. Aetna
3. ExxonMobil
4. Ticketmaster
5. General Motors

Notable Internships
1. Intel
2. Geico
3. Phoenix Suns

Top Industries
1. Business
2. Operations
3. Education
4. Sales
5. Engineering

Top Employers
1. Intel
2. Wells Fargo
3. Amazon
4. American Express
5. Apple

Where Alumni Work
1. Phoenix
2. Los Angeles
3. San Francisco
4. New York City
5. Seattle

Median Earnings
College Scorecard (Early Career): $47,700
EOP (Early Career): $46,300
PayScale (Mid-Career): $100,900

RANKINGS
Forbes: 186
Money: 247
U.S. News: 117, National Universities
Wall Street Journal/THE: 224 (T)
Washington Monthly: 46, National Universities

#CollegesWorthYourMoney

Babson College

ADMISSION
Admission Rate: 24%
Admission Rate - Men: 19%
Admission Rate - Women: 34%
EA Admission Rate: 24%
ED Admission Rate: 39%
Admission Rate (5-Year Trend): -4%
ED Admission Rate (5-Year Trend): -5%
% of Admits Attending (Yield): 35%
Transfer Admission Rate: 36%

Offered Wait List: 1,852
Accepted Wait List: 746
Admitted Wait List: 5

SAT Reading/Writing (Middle 50%): 620-690
SAT Math (Middle 50%): 650-760
ACT Composite (Middle 50%): 28-32
Testing Policy: ACT/SAT Required
SAT Superscore: Yes
ACT Superscore: Yes

% Graduated in Top 10% of HS Class: 53%
% Graduated in Top 25% of HS Class: 84%
% Graduated in Top 50% of HS Class: 98%

ENROLLMENT
Total Undergraduate Enrollment: 2,361
% Part-Time: 0%
% Male: 52%
% Female: 48%
% Out-of-State: 71%
% Fraternity: 13%
% Sorority: 26%
% On-Campus (Freshman): 100%
% On-Campus (All Undergraduate): 82%

% African-American: 4%
% Asian: 12%
% Hispanic: 11%
% White: 36%
% Other: 2%
% Race or Ethnicity Unknown: 5%
% International: 28%
% Low-Income: 18%

ACADEMICS
Student-to-Faculty Ratio: 14:1
% of Classes Under 20: 18%
% of Classes Under 40: 81%
% Full-Time Faculty: 70%
% Full-Time Faculty w/ Terminal Degree: 88%

Top Programs
Accounting
Entrepreneurship
Finance
International Business
Management

Retention Rate: 95%
4-Year Graduation Rate: 89%
6-Year Graduation Rate: 91%

Curricular Flexibility: Somewhat Flexible
Academic Rating:

★★★★

Inside the Classroom
With an unmatched entrepreneurial ethos, tiny but powerful Babson College in Wellesley, Massachusetts, only has one offering on the menu, a BS in business administration, but it is expertly prepared. Instead of offering a smorgasbord of majors, Babson students pick from twenty-seven areas of concentration including business analytics, global business management, and statistical modeling that offer more curricular flexibility than a traditional major. Babson was an all-male college until 1969, but it has completely transformed as women now comprise close to 50 percent of the school's 2,300 undergraduate population. Of equal interest is the college's status as one the best schools for international students; over one-quarter of the population hails from outside the United States.

The Babson experience kicks off with a one-credit first-year seminar designed to help you "better understand your identity, your classmates' identities, and what it takes for all of you to be successful students in the diverse Babson community." While you'll unavoidably spend a good portion of your time swimming in business-related curriculum, roughly half of the courses you will take will be in the liberal arts on engaging subjects such as Art and Ecology; Imagining Nature, Imagining Ourselves; Sports and Literature; Literature and Philosophy of Madness; Constructing and Performing the Self; and Global Pop. One of the many unique experiences at Babson is Foundations of Management and Entrepreneurship, a freshman requirement. Students are given $3,000 in start-up money to launch and run an actual business. They concurrently take part in the Coaching for Teamwork and Leadership Program, working with staff and alumni coaches to enhance personal development, problem-solving skills, and ethical decision-making.

This school's exceptionally interactive and hands-on approach to undergraduate education is evident from the moment students step foot on campus. While a fair number of courses are large—half have more than thirty students—the nature of the instruction is highly interactive with professors and with peers. It is simply not possible to be an anonymous student at Babson. Around one-half of the undergraduate population spends time studying abroad in one of the college's 104 programs spread across forty-one countries. While Babson is more about doing than spending time in the ivory tower, students are encouraged to assist with faculty-led research or propose an independent research study of their own (for credit).

It's little surprise that a business school like Babson has done an excellent job of branding. It is regularly ranked at the top of any list of best colleges for entrepreneurship and business. Babson also ends up toward the top of any list that looks at return on investment as its graduates fare well on the job market. This institution usually produces one or two Fulbright Scholars per year, but the vast majority of graduates are champing at the bit to enter the workforce.

Outside the Classroom
Babson's classrooms are filled with entrepreneurial spirits, and that obsession doesn't disappear when students leave the academic setting. Of the one hundred or so clubs and activities at the college, a large number have the words "investment," "business," or "banking" somewhere in their titles. The school does run twenty-two varsity sports teams, but it does not offer athletic-based scholarships, so while its men's soccer and basketball teams have captured NCAA Division III titles in recent years, sports hardly dominate life at Babson. More than 20 percent of Babson students partake in Greek life, and the number of sorority and fraternity members has grown in recent years. Close to 80 percent of students live in one of the eighteen on-campus residence halls, and some socialize in the surrounding suburb of Wellesley, but with Boston a short T ride away, jaunts into town are commonplace. The campus vibe has a reputation as being somewhat preppy and conservative-leaning. However, the demographic makeup of the student body continues to grow more and more diverse as one-quarter of all students are international, coming from forty-three countries, and 45 percent of US students are nonwhite.

Career Services
The Career Development Services Center at Babson is dedicated solely to the college's undergraduates; a separate career services office exists for MBA students. With twelve full-time, professional staff members, Babson operates with a 190:1 student-to-advisor ratio, far better than the average school featured in this guide. The career center facilitates a number of corporate sponsorships with major companies including PEPSICO, Boston Scientific, EY, and PwC. Events sponsored by the office occur frequently, at least once per week, and are well attended by the student body. Those include regular Industry Spotlights where corporate guests present to and network with students as well as Career Expos.

A global alumni network of more than 40,000 graduates spread across 115 countries and all fifty US states and the Babson Connector, an online resource, help connect current students with alumni. As a result of this type of engagement, a staggering 89 percent of all Babson students embark on at least one internship during their four years of study. Further, thanks to the diligent, hands-on work of this career services office, less than 1 percent of graduates are still looking for employment/grad school within six months of graduating. Considering its well-staffed office and excellent track record for helping graduates find internships and high-paying employment options, Babson's career services is worthy of a great deal of praise.

Professional Outcomes

Babson students are a group of young people with exceptional drive and direction. Within six months of graduation, 99 percent are already employed or in graduate school. The largest numbers flock to finance, technology, and accounting with the highest concentration of recent graduates ending up at EY, PwC, Dell, and Wayfair. Many alumni also work at Fidelity Investment, IBM, Deloitte, Google, Amazon, Siemens, and Accenture. Keeping with the entrepreneurial philosophy of the college, 7 percent of Babson grads start their own businesses soon after graduation. Starting salaries are strong at approximately $58k. The highest average salaries await those entering the oil, financial services, and accounting industries while the lowest average salaries go to those in the sports/entertainment, staffing, and media/publishing fields. Even though only 16 percent of undergrads hail from Massachusetts, many put down roots nearby after graduation, and over 11,000 alumni are clustered in the Boston area.

While many pursue MBAs down the road, only 8 percent enter a program right out of undergrad. Babson students typically enter excellent institutions once they do decide to pursue a graduate or professional track. Recent grads have entered law school at the likes of Harvard, Tulane, Boston University, UVA, and UC-San Diego. Alumni going the MBA route have attended top programs including at the London Business School, Yale, Columbia, Boston College, USC, and Northwestern.

Admission

Babson is a school whose national and international reputation is on the rise, and with that has come shrinking acceptance rates. As recently as five years ago, 40 percent of applicants were accepted. For students entering in the 2018-19 academic year that number fell to an all-time low of 24 percent. Women fared better than men, gaining acceptance 34 percent of the time versus 19 percent for their male counterparts. The caliber of student admitted has risen with the school's selectivity. For those offered a place in the Class of 2022, the mid-50 percent SAT range was 1340-1480 and 29-33 on the ACT. Five years back, a 30 on the ACT would have placed you in the 75th percentile of attending students.

Successful Babson applicants do not have to have perfect grades, but they need to have performed at the B+/A- range within a rigorous high school program. Interviews are not required but are evaluative in nature and would be a good idea for any applicant with borderline statistics. The process is genuinely holistic as admissions staff want to see evidence of leadership and extracurricular involvement during your high school career. Writing ability is also highly valued as evidenced by the requirement of both a personal statement and writing supplement as part of your application. The committee also values recommendations, tests scores, class rank, extracurricular activity, and talent/ability. Those committing to Babson via early decision were admitted 39 percent of the time into the Class of 2022, making ED a wise choice, particularly for those on the admissions bubble. In general, Babson is undoubtedly getting more selective year by year, but students with excellent grades, strong standardized test scores, and a burning passion for business should still fare well in the application process.

Worth Your Money?

With business being the dominant area of focus in the classroom, the $72,000+ annual cost of attendance is not as terrifying as it might otherwise be. The school also offers students the chance to apply for various merit scholarships ranging from the Weissman Scholarship that covers full tuition to a Dean's Scholarship worth $5,000 per year. Babson does award need-based grants of $40k to qualifying students; however, only 40 percent of undergraduates qualify for any financial aid. Nevertheless, if you're committed to a career in business, Babson is worth your money thanks to its distinctive brand of education, industry connections, and solid starting salaries that would allow students to comfortably pay back some level of student loans.

FINANCIAL
Institutional Type: Private
In-State Tuition: $52,608
Out-of-State Tuition: $52,608
Room & Board: $16,776
Required Fees: $0
Books & Supplies: $1,144

Avg. Need-Based Aid: $39,582
Avg. % of Need Met: 100%

Avg. Merit-Based Aid: $21,920
% Receiving Merit-Based Aid: 10%

Avg. Cumulative Debt: $37,866
% of Students Borrowing: 40%

CAREER
Who Recruits
1. Boston Scientific
2. AXA Advisors
3. RxAdvance
4. Applause
5. PepsiCo

Notable Internships
1. Mid-Market Securities
2. CoreAxis Consulting
3. PepsiCo

Top Industries
1. Business
2. Finance
3. Operations
4. Sales
5. Marketing

Top Employers
1. Fidelity Investments
2. PwC
3. EY
4. Dell
5. IBM

Where Alumni Work
1. Boston
2. New York City
3. Sao Paulo, Brazil
4. San Francisco
5. United Kingdom

Median Earnings
College Scorecard (Early Career): $96,100
EOP (Early Career): $95,300
PayScale (Mid-Career): $133,800

RANKINGS
Forbes: 62
Money: 151
U.S. News: N/A
Wall Street Journal/THE: 120
Washington Monthly: N/A

#CollegesWorthYourMoney

Barnard College

New York, New York | Admissions Phone: 212-854-2014

Inside the Classroom

Affiliated with Columbia University, this all-women's college serves 2,500-plus accomplished young women in the heart of Manhattan's Upper West Side. The institution's cosmopolitan locale is appropriately populated by a diverse student body—52 percent of attendees identify as women of color, and 22 percent are first-generation college students. Roughly fifty majors are offered, including crossover programs with Columbia such as the 3:2 engineering program or five-year programs that lead to a BA plus a Master of International Affairs or Master of Public Administration. Barnard also has partnerships with The Jewish Theological Seminary and the Julliard School.

The newly-adopted Foundations curriculum has refined an already rigorous educational tradition at the college. Freshmen must tackle a first-year writing course and a first-year seminar that emphasizes persuasive writing/speaking. In subsequent years, students must fulfill six Modes of Thinking courses that focus on local NYC history, global inquiry, social difference, historical perspective, quantitative and empirical knowledge, and technological thinking. Distributional requirements in a foreign language, arts/humanities, social sciences, and the hard sciences also must be fulfilled. Regardless of major, seniors must complete a semester or year-long thesis/project that is publicly presented or displayed.

All of this unfolds in an academic environment in which students will work closely with professors. Barnard has a 10:1 student-faculty ratio, and a sensational 75 percent of courses are capped at nineteen or fewer students; 26 percent have fewer than ten. Many get the chance to engage in research alongside a professor as 197 undergraduates were granted such an opportunity through the Summer Research Institute in 2018-19. Many students also take advantage of the more than 150 study abroad programs spread over sixty-five countries. Roughly one-third of students elect to take a semester in a foreign country.

Barnard's most popular majors, by number of degrees conferred, are economics, English, political science, history, psychology, biology, neuroscience, computer science, urban studies, and art history. The dance program is notably strong and often places near the top of national rankings. With a strong emphasis on global perspective and public service, it makes sense that the school produces a disproportionately high percentage of Fulbright and Truman Scholars. In 2019, four graduates won Fulbright Scholarships, and three students captured Critical Language Scholarships. Additionally, four Barnard grads were named National Science Foundation fellows in 2018.

Outside the Classroom

Outside the classroom is where Barnard's affiliation with Columbia really comes into play. The school doesn't have its own athletic teams, so Barnard students are recruited to play for Columbia's NCAA Division I teams. Barnard has seventy clubs of its own, mostly of a fairly serious nature (pre-professional and performance-oriented), but the bulk of opportunities for campus engagement come from Columbia's more than 500 student organizations that are open to Barnard students. Parts of dorm life are also a shared experience. For the 91 percent of students who decide to live on campus, two buildings serve as co-ed dorms where Barnard students are mixed with Columbia students, and meal plans for all dorm residents can be utilized at either school's cafeterias. Of course, being located in the heart of New York City, opportunities for fun and excitement are hardly limited to the Barnard and Columbia campuses. Within a single mile of their dorm rooms, students can enjoy multiple parks, theaters, music venues, diners, and countless other attractions.

Career Services

Barnard has ten professionals, a number of peer advisors, and a handful of administrative assistants working in the offices of Beyond Barnard, the recently reorganized/renamed career services center. In past years complaints about the lack of hands-on assistance from the career services office were voiced by the student government and school newspaper. The college responded by beefing up its offerings, and the work being done today is impressive by any quantifiable measure. Beyond Barnard's 256:1 student-to-advisor ratio is superior to many other colleges featured in this guide, and it puts that staffing to good use. In 2018-19, they conducted 4,424 one-on-one appointments, hosted 350+ events, and served 2,500 individuals in some capacity.

The school hosts career and internship fairs in the fall and spring. Fairs are attended by 1,000 students and approximately fifty employers including Brown Brothers Harriman, Uber, and Hearst Magazines. Those sessions also are open to Columbia students, and there is some degree of reciprocity with Barnard students being allowed to attend a good number of Columbia-hosted events. The New York Network mentoring program saw 140 alumni work in person with current students, and an additional seventy individuals participated in a Virtual Mentoring program. Beyond Barnard helps fund internships offering summer stipends of $4,000; it funded 425 internships last year alone. Students interned at exciting locations including the New York Times, the US House of Representatives, Comedy Central, and Christie's.

Barnard College

E-mail: admissions@barnard.edu | Website: www.barnard.edu

Professional Outcomes

Six months after graduation, 93 percent of 2018 Barnard grads had found employment or were enrolled in a graduate program. The school is known for producing women with a wide array of interests, so it makes sense that grads disperse into many different fields. Finance and banking led the way, albeit only representing 10-15 percent of graduates. JP Morgan, Goldman Sachs, Blackrock, Citibank, and Morgan Stanley all appear on the list of the top fifteen employers of Barnard alumni. Education, law, and technology sectors are next in popularity. Across all fields, companies employing twenty-five or more Barnard alums include the NYC Department of Education, Google, IBM, Accenture, and the Metropolitan Museum of Art. The median income for Barnard grads at age thirty-four is $56,000. For comparison, women graduating from Columbia have a median income of $64,000 at the same age. By leaps and bounds, New York City remains home to alumni with small clusters of graduates forming in San Francisco, Boston, Los Angeles, DC, and Philadelphia.

It is rare for a student to call it an academic career after finishing her bachelor's. Within ten years of graduation, over 80 percent of Barnard alums eventually enroll in graduate school. Those entering graduate school flock to a number of other nearby institutions with Columbia, Yeshiva, Rutgers, Fordham, NYU, and Hunter College (CUNY) among the ten most commonly attended schools. Boston University, Georgetown, and Harvard also have a strong representation of Barnard grads in their graduate/professional programs. Medical Schools where 2018 grads enrolled include St. Louis University School of Medicine, Icahn School of Medicine, and Jefferson College of Health. Barnard typically sports a medical school admissions rate of 60-75 percent.

Admission

The last five years have seen the admission rate at Barnard fall from 24 percent (2014) to an all-time low of 14 percent for those entering the Class of 2022. The middle-50 percent SAT range of attending students is 1350-1500; for the ACT it's 30-33. In 2014, the 25th percentile was a far friendlier 1240 SAT/28 ACT. Therefore, it is safe to conclude that Barnard is trending in a more selective direction.

The average weighted high school GPA of a Barnard student was over 4.0, and 84 percent finished in the top 10 percent of their high school class. That aligns with the school's stated beliefs that rigor of secondary record and GPA are among the admissions committees' strongest considerations. Also making this list are more holistic factors including the essay, recommendations, and character/personal qualities. The early decision acceptance rate is 30 percent compared to 12 percent in the regular round, so that may be an avenue worth exploring for those dead-set on attending this fine institution. Additionally, transfer students fare well at Barnard, especially relative to other highly selective liberal arts schools. In 2018, there were 166 applicants accepted as transfers—22 percent of the transfer applicant pool. As at many selective colleges, gaining acceptance into Barnard is more difficult than ever. Sterling grades, solid test scores, and winning personal attributes are the right combination to receive serious consideration at one of, if not the best women's college in existence.

Worth Your Money?

Forty-six percent of Barnard students come from families that fall in the top 5 percent of income-earners in the United States. Those individuals will almost always be asked to pay the full $78,000 cost of attendance as merit aid is nonexistent at this school. Those on the lower end of the income scale see 100 percent of their demonstrated need paid for by the college through an annual grant of $49k. Thanks to this equitable process, the average debt carried by a Barnard graduate is far less than the average college graduate. In addition to its generous financial aid, Barnard is worth the price for the incredible employment and graduate school networks it will open for you postgraduation.

FINANCIAL
Institutional Type: Private
In-State Tuition: $55,781
Out-of-State Tuition: $55,781
Room & Board: $17,856
Required Fees: $1,887
Books & Supplies: $1,150

Avg. Need-Based Aid: $48,845
Avg. % of Need Met: 100%

Avg. Merit-Based Aid: $0
% Receiving Merit-Based Aid: 0%

Avg. Cumulative Debt: $20,829
% of Students Borrowing: 43%

CAREER
Who Recruits
1. Harlem Arts Alliance
2. 826NYC
3. Bank of America
4. Mastercard
5. Hospital for Special Surgery

Notable Internships
1. U.S. Embassy
2. MacMillan Publishers
3. Prudential

Top Industries
1. Business
2. Education
3. Media
4. Social Services
5. Healthcare

Top Employers
1. NYC Department of Education
2. Google
3. JPMorgan Chase
4. Citi
5. IBM

Where Alumni Work
1. New York City
2. San Francisco
3. Boston
4. Los Angeles
5. Washington, DC

Median Earnings
College Scorecard (Early Career): $57,900
EOP (Early Career): $56,300
PayScale (Mid-Career): $109,800

RANKINGS
Forbes: 50
Money: 94
U.S. News: 25, Liberal Arts Colleges
Wall Street Journal/THE: 51
Washington Monthly: 20, Liberal Arts Colleges

#CollegesWorthYourMoney

Baruch College (CUNY)

New York, New York | Admissions Phone: 646-312-1400

Inside the Classroom

Locating a certifiable commuter school with a highly selective admissions process and an outstanding academic reputation sounds about as realistic as stumbling upon a unicorn on your way to the grocery store. Amazingly, there may be only one institution in the country that perfectly fits that description. Baruch College, a gem within the CUNY system, shines bright in the eyes of employers, even those New York City juggernauts with a taste for Ivy League grads. Of course, not every commuter school is situated in Midtown Manhattan, a primo location for high-level internships and flourishing corporate connections. Baruch students take full advantage; of the three undergraduate schools within the college, the Zicklin School of Business attracts a mind-boggling 75 percent of the student population.

All students at Baruch have to complete a forty-five-credit sequence of required courses, but there is some choice within the broad boxes that need to be checked. The nonnegotiable courses are Writing I & Writing II, Speech Communication, Mathematics, and Foreign Language. Students also need to choose classes that fulfill requirements in fine and performing arts, history, literature, philosophy, natural sciences, anthropology/sociology, economics, politics and government, and psychology. Those who are part of the Honors Program complete an honors thesis as a culminating academic experience during their senior year.

With an 18:1 student-to-faculty ratio and more part-time than full-time faculty, one-on-one bonding time with your professors is at a premium. Single-digit classes are a rarity, and only 20 percent of courses have twenty or fewer enrolled students. That being said, Baruch does offer many courses in the twenty- to thirty-student range; 39 percent of sections fall in that span. Tapping into undergraduate research projects is tough at a business-oriented commuter school. Procuring those opportunities requires initiative, but it can be accomplished through connecting with individual faculty members. Those who do make such a connection eventually share their research at the college's Creative Inquiry Day. Studying abroad is an option at any of the CUNY system's 166 programs in fifty-one countries.

Zicklin is not only a great business school for the money, it's a great business school period. Popular majors within this well-respected and well-connected institution include accounting, finance, marketing, and business communication and, as we will cover later, leading companies in those fields have a strong affection for Baruch graduates. With so many entering the job market postgraduation, prestigious scholarships and fellowships are an afterthought, but the school does produce an occasional Fulbright winner.

Outside the Classroom

Only 2 percent of undergraduate students live on campus, and no—that is not a typo—it is simply a reality for this school of 15,000 set on three Manhattan acres. Baruch is not going to provide a typical college campus experience, and for some that's not a bad thing, but it's just important to go in with the right expectations. The surrounding area is not a college town in any way, shape, or form. As a result, the typical student is there for one purpose—to earn a degree. This "nose to the grindstone" ethos shapes campus life. There are no Greek organizations, although there are thirteen NCAA Division III sports teams that play as the Bearcats. While most time spent on campus is time spent in the classrooms themselves, there are ways to get involved through 130+ clubs and activities. The weekly newspaper, The Ticker, and the student-run radio station, WBMB, have lengthy histories. Most clubs meet at specific times during the early afternoon while people are actually on campus, and most of those meetings are held in the Newman Vertical Campus, a seventeen-floor architectural wonder that was erected in 2003 for $327 million dollars. (For a CUNY school, Baruch has some very wealthy donors.)

Career Services

The Starr Career Development Center (SCDC) employs seven full-time professional staff as well as four part-time staff members. Full-timers play roles such as career counselor, internship coordinator, and employer relations director. The part-time staff assists with tasks like pre-law advising and alumni coordination. Baruch's 2,146:1 student-to-advisor ratio (only counting the full-time professionals) may be undesirable but, overall, the data on actual service delivery is far more promising.

More than eighty companies traveled to Baruch's campus for recruiting purposes in 2017-18 including KPMG, Amazon, Moody's, HarperCollins Publishers, and Colgate-Palmolive. In excess of 2,900 students attended those events. Overall, 46 percent of Baruch students land at least one internship; the average student who found employment within six months had 1.5 such experiences. Five or more 2018 graduates interned at each of KPMG, EY, Citi, Deloitte, and JP Morgan. The SCDC provided 3,480 career consultations in 2017-18; for perspective, that is similar to the number of total graduates annually. It also conducted over 2,700 resume reviews, posted 6,600+ jobs online, and facilitated 1,271 on-campus interviews with employers. The online system, cleverly named Starr Search, is utilized by 84 percent of the undergraduate student body, and it offers countless opportunities for those aggressive and motivated enough to follow leads. Additional staffing would likely be needed to ensure a personal connection with all 15,000+ undergrads.

Baruch College (CUNY)

E-mail: admissions@baruch.cuny.edu | Website: www.baruch.cuny.edu

Professional Outcomes

Within six months of graduation, 82 percent of the Class of 2018 were already employed or in full-time graduate programs. Given that over three-quarters of graduates possess business-related degrees, most first jobs are in the realms of accounting, finance, real estate, management, and marketing. Baruch is one of the few accessible public institutions that is a direct feeder to many of Wall Street's top banks. In fact, the top employers of Class of 2018 members were JP Morgan (33 grads), Morgan Stanley (18), EY (14), Citi (14), TD Bank (12), and Bank of America (10). Goldman Sachs, Moody's, Deloitte, and PwC were other companies scooping up eight or more 2018 graduates. The average salary for Arts & Sciences grads was $46,000 while Zicklin School of Business grads earned $53,000. Just about everyone graduating from this college remains in New York City, although some alumni head to Miami, DC, San Francisco, or Los Angeles, but only in dribs and drabs.

Graduate studies are not usually the immediate step after receiving one's diploma from Baruch—only 9 percent of those finishing their bachelor's go right into another degree program. There are few students majoring in the hard sciences at this school, so you don't see a ton on the premed path, but sophomores do have the option of applying for early admission to the Icahn School of Medicine at Mount Sinai through the FlexMed program. Of the alumni who decide to go the law school route, even if they do so years later, many attend local NYC schools like Pace or Brooklyn Law School, but a handful of recent grads have been welcomed to the law schools of the University of Michigan, Tufts, Fordham, and Cornell.

Admission

Baruch admitted 39 percent of the 21,469 students who applied for admission into the Class of 2022; that is significantly higher than the 23 percent acceptance rate the college registered a decade prior. Part of the change is that the school's enrollment has grown during that same period, increasing by a few thousand undergraduates even though admissions standards have become more rigid. Today, 50 percent of entering freshman are top 10 percent finishers at their respective high schools; in 2009, only 32 percent held that distinction. Further, the 75th percentile SAT score from ten years ago is close to the 25th percentile score today. The 2018-19 freshmen had a mid-50 percent range of 1220-1390 on the SAT, the test submitted 83 percent of the time by applicants.

The Baruch College Admissions Office considers GPA, standardized test scores, and rigor of curriculum above all else. Recommendation letters and essays sit alone in the next rung of important categories. This is a school that can be forgiving of a bad grade or two. In fact, the majority of freshmen earned under a 3.5 in high school, and 22 percent had under a 3.0. It's hard to find a school as exceptional as Baruch that is willing to accept late-bloomers and, in some cases, bright AP/honors kids who earned B's and C's throughout high school.

Worth Your Money?

New Yorkers pay under $7,000 in tuition for a school with an alumni network with deep ties to a number of major Wall Street players. This school is unequivocally worth every cent for Big Apple denizens. Outsiders pay a reasonable $18,600 per year in tuition—of course, there is the small matter of finding an affordable place to live. Once again, that's about as likely as spotting that unicorn.

FINANCIAL
Institutional Type: Public
In-State Tuition: $7,921
Out-of-State Tuition: $18,971
Room & Board: $15,499
Required Fees: N/A
Books & Supplies: $1,364

Avg. Need-Based Aid: $9,920
Avg. % of Need Met: 51%

Avg. Merit-Based Aid: $2,452
% Receiving Merit-Based Aid: 7%

Avg. Cumulative Debt: $9,182
% of Students Borrowing: 13%

CAREER
Who Recruits
1. BBC Worldwide Americas
2. FDM Group
3. Home Advisor
4. NYS Department of Civil Service
5. Yelp

Notable Internships
1. PwC
2. RBC Capital Markets
3. Atlantic Records

Top Industries
1. Business
2. Finance
3. Accounting
4. Operations
5. Sales

Top Employers
1. JPMorgan Chase
2. Citi
3. NYC Department of Education
4. Morgan Stanley
5. EY

Where Alumni Work
1. New York City
2. Miami
3. Washington, DC
4. Los Angeles
5. San Francisco

Median Earnings
College Scorecard (Early Career): $57,200
EOP (Early Career): $57,600
PayScale (Mid-Career): $107,100

RANKINGS
Forbes: 174
Money: 2
U.S. News: 16, Regional North
Wall Street Journal/THE: 232 (T)
Washington Monthly: N/A

#CollegesWorthYourMoney

Lewiston, Maine | Admissions Phone: 207-786-6000

ADMISSION
Admission Rate: 18%
Admission Rate - Men: 20%
Admission Rate - Women: 16%
EA Admission Rate: Not Offered
ED Admission Rate: 45%
Admission Rate (5-Year Trend): -6%
ED Admission Rate (5-Year Trend): +2%
% of Admits Attending (Yield): 38%
Transfer Admission Rate: 3%

Offered Wait List: 1,903
Accepted Wait List: 994
Admitted Wait List: 0

SAT Reading/Writing (Middle 50%): 640-720
SAT Math (Middle 50%): 650-740
ACT Composite (Middle 50%): 29-32
Testing Policy: ACT/SAT Required
SAT Superscore: Yes
ACT Superscore: Yes

% Graduated in Top 10% of HS Class: 55%
% Graduated in Top 25% of HS Class: 89%
% Graduated in Top 50% of HS Class: 98%

ENROLLMENT
Total Undergraduate Enrollment: 1,832
% Part-Time: 0%
% Male: 50%
% Female: 50%
% Out-of-State: 83%
% Fraternity: Not Offered
% Sorority: Not Offered
% On-Campus (Freshman): 100%
% On-Campus (All Undergraduate): 95%

% African-American: 5%
% Asian: 4%
% Hispanic: 8%
% White: 71%
% Other: 4%
% Race or Ethnicity Unknown: 0%
% International: 8%
% Low-Income: 11%

ACADEMICS
Student-to-Faculty Ratio: 10:1
% of Classes Under 20: 72%
% of Classes Under 40: 96%
% Full-Time Faculty: 88%
% Full-Time Faculty w/ Terminal Degree: 98%

Top Programs
Art
Biochemistry
Economics
Environmental Studies
Neuroscience
Philosophy
Political Science
Psychology

Retention Rate: 94%
4-Year Graduation Rate: 86%
6-Year Graduation Rate: 89%

Curricular Flexibility: Somewhat Flexible
Academic Rating: ★★★★↲

Inside the Classroom

The nation's second adopter (1984) of a test-optional admissions policy, Bates College has always prided itself on a commitment to egalitarian education—even back to its official founding in the middle of the Civil War when it proudly admitted students regardless of race, religion, or sex. Today, the school is once again on the cutting edge of higher education, advocating a curriculum that honors the liberal arts tradition but also prepares students for "purposeful work" that is both personally meaningful and societally relevant.

Toward those aims Bates students are required to complete (a) three "writing-attentive" courses; (b) three courses focused on scientific reasoning, lab experience, and quantitative literacy; and (c) two four-course concentrations revolving around a particular issue or area of inquiry. General education at Bates is intended to ensure "depth of knowledge" and a "comparative appreciation of how the several disciplines function and what they can teach us." Distinctive features include a mandatory first-year seminar, senior thesis requirement, and a Short Term at the end of the academic year that provides students the opportunity to focus exclusively on one course, field project, internship, or study abroad opportunity. For those wishing to save money and/or fast-track their undergraduate education, the college offers a three-year option that allows students to graduate in three years, provided they register for five courses (as opposed to four) each semester and one course during each Short Term.

Forty-one percent of courses at Bates have a single-digit enrollment, and 72 percent of classrooms contain nineteen or fewer students, allowing for this process to unfold in an intimate academic atmosphere. Additionally, the student-to-faculty ratio is 10:1, and not a single graduate student is present to vacuum up professorial attention. Students interested in research will find opportunities across all disciplines, many of which culminate with a presentation at the Mount David Summit, an annual campus-wide celebration of undergraduate research and creative works. Bates has one of the highest percentages of study abroad participation of any college in the country, typically sending over two-thirds of each class to one of 200+ global destinations.

Twenty-eight percent of all degrees earned at Bates are in the social sciences and biology (15 percent), psychology (8 percent), English (8 percent), and natural resources and conservation (7 percent) are next in popularity. Though strong across many disciplines, Bates boasts exemplary programs in political science, art, philosophy, economics, and psychology. The college has produced more than seventy Fulbright Scholars in the last five years and is recognized as a top recipient of prestigious academic fellowships, even among highly selective institutions. In 2018 alone, Bates produced twenty-three Fulbright Scholars, more than any other undergraduate-only liberal arts college in the United States.

Outside the Classroom

Outside the classroom Bates places a particularly strong emphasis on community and civic engagement, facilitating numerous volunteer and civic leadership opportunities, primarily through the Harward Center. More than half of all Bates students participate in community-engaged learning (for academic credit). Aside from community service, Bates offers more than 110 officially recognized student organizations, including a nationally ranked debate team and an active investment club. Athletic opportunities also abound at the Division III varsity level and within the college's extensive intramural program that encompasses club sports ranging from equestrian to rugby. There are no fraternities or sororities at Bates, and 95 percent of students live in one of the dorms or school-owned Victorian homes that accommodate ten to thirty students each. Lewistown is the state's second most populous city, yet that isn't saying much in Maine because Lewistown is a post-industrial town with only 60,000 residents. Portland, the state's largest city, can be reached in about forty minutes by car.

Career Services

The Bates Career Development Center (BDCD) features nine full-time staff and a student-to-advisor ratio of 204:1, a superior level of support when compared to most other institutions included in this book. Services offered by the center include career/interest assessment, interview preparation, and a guest lecture series. The BDCD hosts an annual graduate and professional school fair (with Bowdoin and Colby), as well as a number of its own networking events throughout the year, one example being a presentation from Google/Pinterest on tech careers for liberal arts majors. Organizations such as The Beacon Group, Analysis Group, Barclays, and the CIA have recruited on campus in recent years. Over 350 interviews are conducted on campus by sixty-five companies in a single academic year.

The Career Discovery Program in Practice, in existence since 1978, affords undergrads the opportunity to job shadow a Bates alum in a field of interest. Roughly 250 Bobcats take advantage of that program each year. The Purposeful Work Internship Program helps fund living expenses of students interning more than 300 summer hours. Despite Bates' location in Maine, internship opportunities are plentiful, particularly in Boston and smaller cities throughout the New England region. This past summer Bates students worked in over 130 companies/organizations throughout the United States and internationally, including at JP Morgan, the Institute of Infectious Diseases, the Conservation Law Foundation, Amazon, and the Sloan Kettering Cancer Center.

Professional Outcomes

Within six months of graduation 98 percent of the Class of 2018 were either employed, enrolled in graduate school, or otherwise meaningfully engaged in a fellowship or internship. The most frequently entered fields were education (21 percent), health care (17 percent), finance/banking (9 percent), and technology (7 percent). Popular employers included Accenture, Fidelity Investments, Google, Wayfair, and Liberty Mutual Insurance whereas common employment destinations of Bates graduates were concentrated primarily in the Northeast, namely Boston, New York, and Portland, Maine. However, sizable numbers of Bates alumni also can be found working in the Washington, DC, and San Francisco areas. Ten years after arriving in Lewiston, alumni are making a median salary of $59,200, a touch more than Colby grads and almost $6k less than Bowdoin alums.

According to the Bates Career Development Center, within ten years of graduation approximately 13 percent of Bates graduates are in, or have competed, law school whereas 7 percent enroll in medical school. In addition, Bates is currently among the top producers of graduates who eventually go on to enroll in PhD programs in the social sciences, especially economics and sociology. In the past three years Bates alumni have enrolled in several selective graduate programs including those at Harvard Law School, Washington University Medical School, and the Stanford Graduate School of Business. By midcareer Bates alumni are most frequently found working in the professional fields of business development, education, and community and social services.

Admission

From 2014 to 2018, Bates experienced a hefty 52 percent increase in applications and, during the same period, the school's acceptance rate fell from 24 percent to 18 percent. SAT scores were submitted by 46 percent of applicants, and 32 percent included ACT results as part of their application. The mid-50 percent ranges were 1290-1460 on the SAT and 29-32 on the ACT. Students typically ranked high in their graduating high school class with 55 percent in the top 10 percent and 89 percent in the top quartile. Those numbers are almost identical to those held by the freshman class of 2013-14, meaning that while the acceptance rate has declined, the profile of the typical accepted applicant has not changed much.

Aside from grades, class rank, and course rigor, Bates places significant emphasis on an applicant's essay, letters of recommendation, extracurricular profile, talent/ability, and character/personal qualities. Demonstrated interest also plays a considerable role. Of course, the ultimate declaration of love is the submission of an early decision application. Those who go the binding ED route enjoy an acceptance rate three times higher than those who apply in the regular cycle (45 percent vs. 15 percent). A massive 64 percent of the 2018-19 freshman class was admitted via early decision, making it a wise strategic maneuver for anyone serious about attending Bates.

Worth Your Money?

A sizable percentage of the undergraduate student body come from fairly wealthy homes—the median family income is $226,500—and over three-quarters come from families with incomes in the top 20 percent nationwide. Many families with hefty salaries will pay the full $73,238 annual cost of attendance. For the 42 percent of students who do qualify for need-based financial aid, Bates delivers in a big way. The college meets 100 percent of the demonstrated need for every qualifying student with grants averaging $44,644 each year. Not only do Bates grads generally find solid-paying jobs after graduation, they also have far less debt, on average, than their peers receiving diplomas from other institutions.

FINANCIAL
Institutional Type: Private
In-State Tuition: $55,683
Out-of-State Tuition: $55,683
Room & Board: $15,705
Required Fees: N/A
Books & Supplies: $900

Avg. Need-Based Aid: $44,644
Avg. % of Need Met: 100%

Avg. Merit-Based Aid: $0
% Receiving Merit-Based Aid: 0%

Avg. Cumulative Debt: $21,525
% of Students Borrowing: 35%

CAREER
Who Recruits
1. Chevron
2. Hulu
3. Oppenheimer & Co.
4. athenaHealth
5. Owl Cybersecurity

Notable Internships
1. CNN
2. United States Senate
3. Morgan Stanley

Top Industries
1. Business
2. Education
3. Operations
4. Social Services
5. Research

Top Employers
1. Fidelity Investments
2. Massachusetts General Hospital
3. Liberty Mutual Insurance
4. Google
5. Amazon

Where Alumni Work
1. Boston
2. New York City
3. Portland, ME
4. Lewiston, ME
5. Washington, DC

Median Earnings
College Scorecard (Early Career): $59,200
EOP (Early Career): $55,900
PayScale (Mid-Career): $111,900

RANKINGS
Forbes: 39
Money: 38
U.S. News: 21, Liberal Arts Colleges
Wall Street Journal/THE: 63 (T)
Washington Monthly: 17, Liberal Arts Colleges

#CollegesWorthYourMoney

Waltham, Massachusetts | Admissions Phone: 781-891-2244

ADMISSION
Admission Rate: 43%
Admission Rate - Men: 40%
Admission Rate - Women: 49%
EA Admission Rate: Not Offered
ED Admission Rate: 69%
Admission Rate (5-Year Trend): -1%
ED Admission Rate (5-Year Trend): Not Offered
% of Admits Attending (Yield): 28%
Transfer Admission Rate: 52%

Offered Wait List: 1,659
Accepted Wait List: 534
Admitted Wait List: 1

SAT Reading/Writing (Middle 50%): 600-680
SAT Math (Middle 50%): 640-730
ACT Composite (Middle 50%): 28-32
Testing Policy: ACT/SAT Required
SAT Superscore: Yes
ACT Superscore: Yes

% Graduated in Top 10% of HS Class: 50%
% Graduated in Top 25% of HS Class: 89%
% Graduated in Top 50% of HS Class: 98%

ENROLLMENT
Total Undergraduate Enrollment: 4,253
% Part-Time: 2%
% Male: 60%
% Female: 40%
% Out-of-State: 50%
% Fraternity: 4%
% Sorority: 7%
% On-Campus (Freshman): 97%
% On-Campus (All Undergraduate): 78%

% African-American: 4%
% Asian: 10%
% Hispanic: 8%
% White: 69%
% Other: 3%
% Race or Ethnicity Unknown: 5%
% International: 16%
% Low-Income: 14%

ACADEMICS
Student-to-Faculty Ratio: 11:1
% of Classes Under 20: 21%
% of Classes Under 40: 93%
% Full-Time Faculty: 63%
% Full-Time Faculty w/ Terminal Degree: 54%

Top Programs
Accounting
Data Analytics
Finance
Management
Managerial Economics
Marketing
Professional Sales

Retention Rate: 93%
4-Year Graduation Rate: 82%
6-Year Graduation Rate: 91%

Curricular Flexibility: Less Flexible
Academic Rating: ★★★✦

Inside the Classroom
Situated just west of Boston, Bentley University is one of the premier business-focused institutions in the country. Rival Babson College is only ten miles away geographically, but the two schools used to be a much greater distance apart in reputation and prestige. That gap has closed quickly in recent years. The school's 4,200 undergraduate students traversing this attractive 163-acre Waltham, Massachusetts, campus are, somewhat surprisingly, exposed to a top-notch liberal arts education while working toward a BA or BS in a business-related field. Of the twenty-five majors and thirty-six minors to choose from, a handful are non-business concentrations such as English, philosophy, and history. These students typically supplement their education with a healthy number of business courses. The majority take the opposite path, majoring in business and supplementing their studies with liberal arts courses. Always innovating, the school recently started three cutting-edge majors in data analytics, professional sales, and creative industries. Regardless of one's major, the core curriculum consisting of sixteen mandatory courses must be tackled. That includes a first-year seminar, information technology and computer system concepts, a sequence of two expository writing classes as well as courses in math, the hard sciences, government, and history.

Earning a Bentley degree is far from a passive experience. The average undergraduate class is comprised of twenty-six students, and academics are intense. Twenty percent of the student body is double majoring, tacking the liberal studies major on to their business concentration. Roughly half of Bentley students elect to study abroad in one of eighty programs spread across twenty-five countries. Just about everyone lands an internship; the majority of students complete two. Undergraduate research participation has increased in recent years as the school has joined The Council on Undergraduate Research. While not a focal point of the school, it is possible to land a position assisting a faculty member with a research project at some point during your four years on campus.

Bentley is a school on the rise. Having just celebrated its one-hundred-year anniversary, it has become a highly-respected name in the corporate world and possesses an international reach. The most popular majors are all within the business domain and include finance, business, management, marketing, accounting, and poetry—just kidding on that last one. Bentley is a one-trick pony, and that's not a bad thing when you examine the outcomes data for recent graduates (more ahead).

Outside the Classroom
A bastion for extraverts, 90 percent of Bentley undergrads belong to at least one student organization; one-third consider themselves "highly involved." Over one hundred clubs and activities are available with a multitude of options in the academic, cultural, religious, arts and media, and recreational realms. Participation in athletics is high. The Falcons compete in eleven men's and ten women's sports in NCAA Division II (men's ice hockey is the lone Division I team). Intramural and club sports are popular, including ultimate Frisbee, sailing, rugby, and equestrian. More than 1,700 students participate in an intramural sport each year. With 78 percent of students living in school-owned housing, most social events are centered on campus. Fraternity and sorority life attract a significant but not dominant 17 percent of undergraduates. Additionally, some students live in defined communities—residential housing for those passionate about areas such as women's leadership, social justice, or service learning. Waltham, also home to Brandeis University, is a historic and pretty New England town with plenty of bars, restaurants, and other attractions. The university is only thirteen miles from downtown Boston, and the school provides free public transportation to-and-from Harvard Square.

Career Services
The Career Services Office at Bentley has thirteen professional staff members who work with the college's undergraduates. That equates to a 323:1 student-to-advisor ratio, placing the university in the average range compared to other schools featured in this guide. Career services may be average in this category, but it is exceptional by just about every other metric. For example, the staff does an incredible job facilitating meaningful internships. Of the 92 percent of Bentley students who had an internship (71 percent complete more than one) as part of their undergraduate education, 37 percent landed their first job directly through this experience. On-campus recruiting events led another 18 percent of employed graduates to their first employment destination, and a sizable number of students also found their way through alumni networking, school-organized career fairs, and referrals from the school. The school has developed close corporate partnerships with companies including Dell, Fidelity Investments, Liberty Mutual, and United Technologies, all of whom hire their fair share of graduates each year.

Offerings include career development seminars that begin freshman year; 97 percent of first-years sign up for the introductory class. Those seminars are part of the school's larger Hire Education Program that helps students formulate career goals, hone job-readiness skills, and build professional networks. The Mentor Marketplace is an online tool that helps connect current students with alumni who work in a relevant field to serve as a career resource. In addition to the full internships taken advantage of by the bulk of the student body, Bentley also offers micro-internships in which alumni can bring in undergraduates to work on short-term, impactful projects within their company. Taking into account the breadth and quality of its services as well as the stellar outcomes achieved by its graduates, Bentley has as high quality of a Career Services Office as you will find anywhere in the country.

Professional Outcomes

A superb 99 percent of 2018 Bentley grads were employed or in graduate school six months after receiving their diplomas. The financial services and technology sectors each account for 22 percent of new hires. Most job functions are in the areas of finance, sales, accounting, analytics, marketing, consulting, and operations/logistics. A hub of entrepreneurship, the school saw 7 percent of its graduating class start their own businesses right out of college. Companies employing the highest number of alumni include Fidelity Investments, PwC, EY, Dell EMC, and Wayfair. The median starting salary for graduates is $59,000, a strong figure compared to other universities of its ilk. By midcareer, Bentley grads have a median income similar to Harvard and Tufts alumni.

Bentley does not see a high number of graduates directly enter graduate school—roughly 10 percent in any given year. While many pursue MBAs or other advanced business degrees later in their careers, those in this field typically gain work experience prior to attending graduate school. Recent graduates have ended up in advanced degree programs at elite business schools like Wharton (Penn), Stern (NYU), Columbia Business School, Yale School of Management, Sloane School of Management (MIT), and the Tuck School of Business (Dartmouth). Whether entering graduate school or chasing their first job, the vast majority of Falcons stay in the Boston area. New York City and San Francisco are the next two most popular US destinations; there is also a large cluster of graduates settled in Brazil, a country from which the university attracts a large number of international students.

Admission

In the 2017-18 admissions cycle Bentley accepted 43 percent of the 9,252 who applied. Members of the Class of 2022 averaged 1321 on the SAT and 29 on the ACT. For perspective, in 2011 the acceptance rate was a nearly identical 46 percent, but the 75th percentile on the SAT was a 1300. The percent of students ranking in the top 10 percent (50 percent) and 25 percent (89 percent) of their high school classes has risen sharply in that same time. Therefore, we can deduce that while acceptance rates have stayed relatively similar at Bentley in recent years, the standardized test scores and grades needed to gain acceptance have risen significantly.

Test scores, grades (including an emphasis on senior year grades), two letters of recommendation, and an on-campus interview are all important components of the admissions process. While the interviews are not mandatory, they can be an excellent opportunity to highlight interpersonal skills and intangible attributes that a top business school like Bentley is seeking. With a relatively low yield of 28 percent, Bentley is competing with many other rival institutions for the same pool of students. Thus, it makes sense that the school accepts 69 percent of applicants through its binding early decision program. It locks down just short of one-quarter of its incoming freshman class via ED. Bentley is a competitive business school and is a notch easier to gain admission into than comparable Babson. Demonstrating interest and/or applying early is a strong strategic move for serious applicants.

Worth Your Money?

Forty-two percent of Bentley's 4,171 undergraduates qualify for financial aid, and 39 percent of that group sees 100 percent of their demonstrated need met by the university. The average annual grant is for just over $38k, helping to alleviate the pain of the $71,320 per year cost of attendance. To help lessen the cost, even for families who can pay, 20 percent of undergrads receive a merit-based award of roughly $9,000. Even at that high cost, Bentley is worth the money for most applicants. The school rates very well in terms of pure salary—both starting and midcareer—and it rates well for social mobility, allowing those from poor-to-modest backgrounds to climb the economic ladder.

FINANCIAL
Institutional Type: Private
In-State Tuition: $51,830
Out-of-State Tuition: $51,830
Room & Board: $16,960
Required Fees: N/A
Books & Supplies: $1,300

Avg. Need-Based Aid: $37,997
Avg. % of Need Met: 95%

Avg. Merit-Based Aid: 10,128
% Receiving Merit-Based Aid: 22%

Avg. Cumulative Debt: $30,997
% of Students Borrowing: 57%

CAREER
Who Recruits
1. Cognex Corporation
2. Boston Scientific
3. Grant Thornton LLP
4. P&G Gillette
5. Lincoln Financial Group

Notable Internships
1. Liberty Mutual Investments
2. KPMG
3. L'Oreal

Top Industries
1. Business
2. Finance
3. Accounting
4. Sales
5. Operations

Top Employers
1. Fidelity Investments
2. PwC
3. Liberty Mutual Insurance
4. EY
5. State Street

Where Alumni Work
1. Boston
2. New York City
3. Hartford
4. San Francisco
5. Providence

Median Earnings
College Scorecard (Early Career): $86,900
EOP (Early Career): $79,800
PayScale (Mid-Career): $116,600

RANKINGS
Forbes: 107
Money: 88
U.S. News: 2, Regional North
Wall Street Journal/THE: 134 (T)
Washington Monthly: N/A

#CollegesWorthYourMoney

Binghamton University (SUNY)

Binghamton, New York | Admissions Phone: 607-777-2171

ADMISSION
Admission Rate: 40%
Admission Rate - Men: 40%
Admission Rate - Women: 40%
EA Admission Rate: 55%
ED Admission Rate: Not Offered
Admission Rate (5-Year Trend): -2%
ED Admission Rate (5-Year Trend): Not Offered
% of Admits Attending (Yield): 19%
Transfer Admission Rate: 43%

Offered Wait List: 5,560
Accepted Wait List: 2,320
Admitted Wait List: 189

SAT Reading/Writing (Middle 50%): 650-710
SAT Math (Middle 50%): 660-730
ACT Composite (Middle 50%): 28-32
Testing Policy: ACT/SAT Required
SAT Superscore: Yes
ACT Superscore: Yes

% Graduated in Top 10% of HS Class: 54%
% Graduated in Top 25% of HS Class: 86%
% Graduated in Top 50% of HS Class: 98%

ENROLLMENT
Total Undergraduate Enrollment: 14,021
% Part-Time: 3%
% Male: 50%
% Female: 50%
% Out-of-State: 5%
% Fraternity: 14%
% Sorority: 11%
% On-Campus (Freshman): 98%
% On-Campus (All Undergraduate): 50%

% African-American: 5%
% Asian: 14%
% Hispanic: 11%
% White: 57%
% Other: 2%
% Race or Ethnicity Unknown: 2%
% International: 8%
% Low-Income: 24%

ACADEMICS
Student-to-Faculty Ratio: 19:1
% of Classes Under 20: 46%
% of Classes Under 40: 81%
% Full-Time Faculty: 73%
% Full-Time Faculty w/ Terminal Degree: 92%

Top Programs
Accounting
Chemistry
Industrial and Systems Engineering
Integrative Neuroscience
Nursing
Political Science
Psychology

Retention Rate: 92%
4-Year Graduation Rate: 72%
6-Year Graduation Rate: 82%

Curricular Flexibility: Very Flexible
Academic Rating: ★★★

Inside the Classroom

Created in the GI Bill era to accommodate the influx of returning soldiers entering college, SUNY Binghamton (a.k.a., Binghamton University) is the shining star of the State University System of New York. Considered a "Public Ivy," the nearly 14,000 undergraduates are an accomplished bunch (average SAT is 1350), and the excellence of the academic offerings is commensurate with the student body. It's no wonder that 92 percent of freshmen return to campus the next fall, a retention rate that is unparalleled among non-flagship public institutions.

The university offers over 130 areas of concentration across its five undergraduate schools: the Harpur College of Arts and Sciences, the College of Community and Public Affairs, the Decker School of Nursing, the School of Management, and the Thomas J. Watson School of Engineering and Applied Science. General education requirements include foreign language (except for engineering majors), creating a global vision, the liberal arts (aesthetics, humanities, laboratory sciences, social sciences, and mathematics), and a series of physical activity and wellness classes. Unlike many state universities there is no long list of required courses awaiting you. Rather, the mandated categories of coursework are broad enough that you'll have plenty of room for exploration.

The student-to-faculty ratio is on the high side at 19:1, but class sizes are reasonably small with 48 percent of sections containing fewer than twenty students. Only 13 percent of courses are held in large lecture halls with fifty+ students. Research opportunities are available with the Freshman Research Immersion program being one shining example. This program welcomes students to college with a year-long authentic research experience in the sciences and engineering. The Office of Undergraduate Research is adept at connecting students in all fields, not just STEM, to research opportunities alongside faculty members. The school's own undergraduate research journal, Alpenglow, gives students the chance to publish scholarly, as well as original creative works. Study abroad opportunities are available at over fifty worldwide locations, and roughly one-fifth of undergraduates spend a semester in a foreign country.

In the spring of 2018 Binghamton awarded the greatest number of degrees in the social sciences (17 percent), biology (16 percent), business (14 percent), engineering (9 percent), and psychology (8 percent). The School of Management is renowned for its accounting program and is well known by NYC-based companies. Programs in chemistry, psychology, and nursing are also well respected. The university's graduates are somewhat competitive in procuring prestigious postgraduate fellowships, and between 2017 and 2019 the school produced seventeen Fulbright Scholars.

Outside the Classroom

Just over half of undergrads reside on campus in dorms or in residential college communities designed for 200 to 1,000 students each, and all have their own distinct personalities. Most off-campus apartment dwellers reside in the city's West Side neighborhood, but some end up in small towns a ten- to twenty-minute drive away. With fifty-six fraternities and sororities and thousands of participants, you might think that Greek life would be a dominant presence, yet only 14 percent of men and 11 percent of women pledge, leaving the majority to carve out their own social scene. The Binghamton Bearcats field twenty-one varsity sports teams in NCCA Division I. However, with no football team, the university is not a sports-centered campus. There is much to do within the university's 930 acres of grounds that includes a 190-acre nature preserve, a 156,000-square-foot multipurpose center, two fully equipped gyms, two pools, twenty-six tennis courts, and a 1,200-seat theater for art/speaking/musical events. Over 2,000 students participate in forty-two recreational and club athletic teams, and another 3,000 play intramural sports. There are 300 other clubs and activities. From their high-achieving speech and debate squad to a plethora of political, cultural, academic, and religious clubs, all 14,000 undergrads can find some way to connect. There are also eighty-five organizations focused on community service and volunteer work. Green initiatives are popular on campus, including energy efficiency, local food sources, recycling, and the bike-share program.

Career Services

The Fleishman Center for Career and Professional Development is not your average state school career services office. Consisting of twenty-one professional employees and fifty peer assistants and interns, the 666:1 student-to-advisor ratio (only counting the professionals) is more supportive than it appears. In a single year Fleischman staff conducted 7,246 1:1 counseling sessions. The 740 career programs hosted by career services personnel drew 27,500 attendees. About 10,000 unique students connected directly with career services, a sizable portion of the undergraduate population.

Binghamton University (SUNY)

E-mail: admit@binghamton.edu | Website: www.binghamton.edu

Recruiting on campus is a regular occurrence with over 2,700 on-site interviews conducted each year. The hireBing platform (run by Handshake) sees 7,000 job and internship postings annually. SUNY Binghamton's Fall Job Fair attracts more than 120 corporate, government, and nonprofit employers including Teach for America, Geico, Wayfair, and Raytheon Company. The school's recently launched Washington, DC, Employer Site Visit Program complements its successful New York City Site Visits Program. Having increased its staffing, outreach, and technological capabilities in recent years, Binghamton's career services is on the rise.

Professional Outcomes

The Class of 2018 saw 77 percent of job-seeking graduates land their first professional job within six months of commencement. Those entering the technology/computing fields found homes at companies like Facebook, IBM, Apple, and Microsoft in large numbers. Graduates entering finance careers were successful in finding employment at firms like Morgan Stanley, JPMorgan, Goldman Sachs, and CitiGroup. In the accounting/consulting realm the most popular employers of Binghamton grads were EY, PwC, Deloitte, and KPMG. The average starting salary procured was nearly $57,425, well above the national average for college grads. Of course, it is important to note that figure does not include the 23 percent of job-seeking graduates who were still looking for jobs at the time of the survey. New York City is, by far, the most common landing spot for Binghamton graduates, but many also remain in Upstate New York or travel to Washington, DC; Boston; San Francisco; Philadelphia; and Los Angeles.

Of the Binghamton grads seeking to transition directly into graduate studies, 90 percent were already enrolled in a program six months after graduation. Many SUNY branch campuses were among the most popular graduate school destinations, but many prestigious universities also graced this list including Harvard, Dartmouth, Georgetown, Columbia, Stanford, Penn, and the University of Michigan. SUNY Binghamton's reputation also helped open the doors to law school as it enjoyed an 84 percent acceptance rate. The school's early admission med school program (during sophomore year) creates a pipeline into SUNY Upstate Medical University. In the 2018-19 academic year, 196 seniors applied to medical school and were accepted at a rate 14 percent higher than the national average.

Admission

SUNY Binghamton received 33,467 applications in 2018 and accepted 40 percent. That acceptance rate was similar to acceptance rates at this selective state university over the past decade, but the profile of the average enrolling freshman indicates that the school is becoming significantly more competitive. Entering freshmen in 2019-20 had solid grades with a mid-50 percent high school GPA of 3.7-3.9. The mid-50 percent range on the SAT for the previous year's freshmen was 1310-1440 and 28-32 for the ACT. Ten years ago, the SAT range was 1190-1350. Even with SAT score inflation, it is safe to say that the average student at this school today is a higher achiever than the average student of a decade ago.

The factors that are considered above all others in admissions decisions are grades, test scores, and rigor of secondary curriculum. Class rank, the essay, recommendations, and extracurricular activities make up the second tier of important considerations. With such a massive applicant pool, interviews are not offered. SUNY Binghamton is a special value, especially by the standards of today's higher education marketplace. With an annual in-state tuition of just over $7,000, this excellent public research university continues to draw more and more qualified applicants each year. The admission formula falls far short of rocket science. Strong test scores and solid grades in AP/honors classes rule the day.

Worth Your Money?

You simply won't find a better combination of quality and price anywhere on the East Coast than Binghamton University. With a total annual cost of attendance of $26,612 (much lower for those who commute) for an in-state student, this SUNY school is worth anyone's money, no matter your major or career path. More than half of students qualify for financial aid and receive an average grant package of almost $10k, making an already affordable school nothing less than a ridiculous bargain.

FINANCIAL
Institutional Type: Public
In-State Tuition: $6,870
Out-of-State Tuition: $23,710
Room & Board: $15,058
Required Fees: $2,934
Books & Supplies: $1,000

Avg. Need-Based Aid: $9,908
Avg. % of Need Met: 70%

Avg. Merit-Based Aid: $6,629
% Receiving Merit-Based Aid: 12%

Avg. Cumulative Debt: $27,470
% of Students Borrowing: 50%

CAREER
Who Recruits
1. AMETEK Aerospace and Defense
2. NYS Department of Transportation
3. Dick's Sporting Goods
4. AXA Advisors
5. Mirabito Energy Products

Notable Internships
1. United Health Services
2. Cushman & Wakefield
3. Deloitte

Top Industries
1. Business
2. Education
3. Engineering
4. Operations
5. Information Technology

Top Employers
1. IBM
2. EY
3. JPMorgan Chase
4. PwC
5. Morgan Stanley

Where Alumni Work
1. New York City
2. Ithaca, NY
3. Washington, DC
4. Boston
5. San Francisco

Median Earnings
College Scorecard (Early Career): $61,600
EOP (Early Career): $65,700
PayScale (Mid-Career): $109,600

RANKINGS
Forbes: 145
Money: 33
U.S. News: 79, National Universities
Wall Street Journal/THE: 153 (T)
Washington Monthly: 90, National Universities

#CollegesWorthYourMoney

Boston College

Chestnut Hill, Massachusetts | Admissions Phone: 617-552-3100

Inside the Classroom

Along with Notre Dame, Georgetown, and Villanova, Boston College, home to 9,300 undergrads and an additional 4,700 graduate students, is among the most academically renowned Catholic universities in the world. The college offers fifty-eight majors across four schools that award undergraduate degrees: the School of Management, the School of Education, the School of Nursing, and the Morrissey College of Arts & Sciences. Certain majors that one takes for granted as being offered at a large research institution, such as engineering, do not yet exist at BC. However, the school is breaking ground on a new $150 million science facility that will offer a full spectrum of engineering degrees in the not-too-distant future.

The core curriculum lays out an extensive series of academic requirements that includes two courses in the natural sciences, social sciences, history, philosophy, and theology as well as one course in the arts, cultural diversity, math, and writing. All told, the core curriculum accounts for three full semesters of coursework. The breadth of the requirements is far from accidental—BC's program is designed to expand students' intellectual horizons and build character at the same time.

This odyssey unfolds in a caring and personal atmosphere. Approximately half of the college's sections contain nineteen or fewer students; there are some larger lecture hall classes, but those are fairly rare. Working closely with their professors pays off for students. In their own self-assessment, 95 percent of graduates reported learning how to think critically at BC, and 93 percent said they learned how to write clearly and effectively. Fifty percent of BC grads pursued a semester abroad in one of 200+ locations around the globe, and 90 percent cited the experience as a source of personal growth.

BC offers highly respected programs in communications, psychology, and business through the renowned Carroll School of Management. Other popular and well-regarded majors include economics, biology, and chemistry. Graduates fare decently in procuring prestigious awards, especially in the realm of fellowships to study abroad. Sixteen members of the Class of 2018 won Fulbright Scholarships, and BC holds the distinction as one of the top twenty Fulbright-producing research universities over the past decade.

Outside the Classroom

Unlike at Boston University, BC is not located in the heart of its namesake city. Fortunately, downtown Boston is only six miles away and easily accessible from the Chestnut Hill section of Newton where BC's main campus is located. With 70 percent of students identifying as Catholic, it is little surprise that religion and spirituality are a big part of campus life. Clubs in this arena are well represented among the 273 student organizations on campus, but there are a multitude of pre-professional, special interest, performing arts, and political offerings as well. There are no Greek houses at BC, a void that is filled by tightly knit groups with common interests. One such galvanizing force is the school's athletic teams. The Eagles compete in thirty-one NCAA Division I and forty-four intramural sports. The men's ice hockey team is always in the national spotlight, regularly appearing in the Frozen Four. For those seeking charitable opportunity, the Volunteer & Service Learning Center connects students with a plethora of organizations all over the country. One of the most popular of those experiences is the Appalachia Volunteers Program that sends around 500 students each year on spring break to forty impoverished cities and towns in the United States.

Career Services

The Career Center is manned by sixteen professionals whose specialty areas include career counseling, exploration, and employer engagement. Not counting the five graduate assistants and nine peer coaches who also are available to work with undergraduate students, this calculates to a student-to-advisor ratio of 581:1, below average compared to the pool of institutions included in this book.

The better news is that the office is effective at what is most important—helping students achieve positive career and graduate school outcomes. In fact, five of the top six resources cited by job-holding recent grads as being most helpful in landing employment had to do with the Career Center—EagleLink interviews, BC career fairs, networking through BC, EagleLink listings, and internships. Over 200 companies recruit on campus each year with most offering in-person interviews. Career fairs occur throughout the year; some events are general while others cater to specific areas of interest including public accounting, government, and sports and entertainment. The Career Center regularly offers job shadowing opportunities, networking nights, Career Treks, workshops covering a host of topics, and the Eagle Intern Fellowship that provides a $3,500 stipend to selected students pursuing unpaid internships. The alumni network is 180,000 strong and is generally very active and willing to help current students.

E-mail: admission@bc.edu | Website: www.bc.edu

Professional Outcomes

Within six months of graduation 96 percent of the Class of 2018 had landed at their next destination, whether that was employment, graduate school, a fellowship, or a volunteer position. The most favored industries were finance/accounting/real estate (23 percent), health care/science (15 percent), business/consulting (14 percent), and technology/engineering (11 percent). More than forty newly minted alumni found employment at both Ernst & Young and PricewaterhouseCoopers. Notable numbers also flocked to Oracle, Citi, Mass General, and KPMG. Across all graduating years, more than 150 alumni also work at Deloitte, Google, Morgan Stanley, and Goldman Sachs.

The median starting salary for a BC grad is $58,500. Those in the School of Education and A&S had a median salary of below $51k while those exiting the management and nursing schools enjoyed median starting incomes of $60k. By a wide margin, the locale where the must alumni settle is the university's home state of Massachusetts; New York City also draws a sizable number of BC grads.

Examining the last five years of graduate data, enrollment in graduate, medical, or law school is a choice made by 18-23 percent of graduates. Of that higher-education-minded cohort, the greatest number are pursuing master's degrees in education or business. Law school was next in popularity at 12 percent followed by a PhD or applied doctorate at 10 percent and medical school at 8 percent. Of the law school attendees, a dozen continued in BC's own program. BC was also, by far, the most common graduate choice for those pursuing advanced degrees in education and business. Tufts was the No. 1 target for medical school and the natural sciences. Graduates also enjoyed acceptances into other elite medical schools including Georgetown, Duke, and Boston University.

Admission

Boston College received more than 31,000 applications for the Class of 2022, a 9 percent increase from the previous year, but fewer than it received in 2012. The acceptance rate fell to 28 percent in 2018; it was 32 percent in 2017. However, this level of selectivity is nothing new for BC. A decade ago, acceptance rates were in the 26-27 percent range.

What is changing is the academic profile of the average student being offered a spot at this high-end Catholic university. The mid-50 percent SAT score for the Class of 2022 was 1320-1460; fifteen years ago that 1320 would have had you close to the 75th percentile. Almost four-fifths of freshmen in the 2018-19 academic year placed in the top decile of their high school graduating class, and 94 percent hailed from the top quartile. The early admission window plays a large role in shaping the freshman class at BC, but there hasn't been much of an admissions edge. BC accepted 33 percent of EA applicants compared to 26 percent during the regular round. Disparities between early and regular admission rates are expected to grow, however, as the school introduced an Early Decision admission plan this past fall.

No matter when you apply, BC places a high value on writing ability and requires completion of the Boston College Writing Supplement. There are no interviews as part of the admissions process. BC attracts some of the most gifted Catholic students in the country as well as a fair number of non-Catholics. SAT scores in the 1400s and A/A- grades in a rigorous curriculum will put applicants on solid footing.

Worth Your Money?

In 1990, Boston College had an annual cost of attendance of around $15,000. Today, you will owe $75,586 per year for the privilege of attending this fine institution. While this jump in price far outpaces the rate of inflation, so goes the entire higher education marketplace. The good news is that BC awards healthy amounts of financial aid to those unable to pay full freight, so 43 percent of undergraduates receive upwards of $45,000 per year, making the cost far more palatable. Many others do pay full price as recent tax return data estimates that approximately one-half of all BC students come from families who are in the top 5-to-10 percent of income earners. If you were in a situation where you had to take on massive loans to study at BC, it would likely be a good investment if you planned on going the finance or consulting route but less so if you planned to study education.

FINANCIAL
Institutional Type: Private
In-State Tuition: $53,346
Out-of-State Tuition: $53,346
Room & Board: $14,142
Required Fees: N/A
Books & Supplies: $1,250

Avg. Need-Based Aid: $45,393
Avg. % of Need Met: 100%

Avg. Merit-Based Aid: $53,346
% Receiving Merit-Based Aid: 1%

Avg. Cumulative Debt: $20,915
% of Students Borrowing: 47%

CAREER
Who Recruits
1. MullenLowe Mediahub
2. Oracle
3. Epsilon
4. Liberty Mutual
5. Accenture

Notable Internships
1. NBC Sports Boston
2. Pfizer
3. IBM

Top Industries
1. Business
2. Education
3. Finance
4. Operations
5. Sales

Top Employers
1. PwC
2. EY
3. Deloitte
4. Morgan Stanley
5. Citi

Where Alumni Work
1. Boston
2. New York City
3. Washington, DC
4. San Francisco
5. Los Angeles

Median Earnings
College Scorecard (Early Career): $72,500
EOP (Early Career): $71,800
PayScale (Mid-Career): $115,400

RANKINGS
Forbes: 41
Money: 151
U.S. News: 37, National Universities
Wall Street Journal/THE: 59 (T)
Washington Monthly: 67, National Universities

#CollegesWorthYourMoney

Boston University

Boston, Massachusetts | Admissions Phone: 617-353-2300

ADMISSION
Admission Rate: 22%
Admission Rate - Men: 23%
Admission Rate - Women: 22%
EA Admission Rate: Not Offered
ED Admission Rate: 28%
Admission Rate (5-Year Trend): -15%
ED Admission Rate (5-Year Trend): -12%
% of Admits Attending (Yield): 25%
Transfer Admission Rate: 43%

Offered Wait List: 5,441
Accepted Wait List: 3,446
Admitted Wait List: 1

SAT Reading/Writing (Middle 50%): 650-720
SAT Math (Middle 50%): 680-780
ACT Composite (Middle 50%): 30-33
Testing Policy: ACT/SAT Required
SAT Superscore: Yes
ACT Superscore: Yes

% Graduated in Top 10% of HS Class: 65%
% Graduated in Top 25% of HS Class: 93%
% Graduated in Top 50% of HS Class: 100%

ENROLLMENT
Total Undergraduate Enrollment: 18,515
% Part-Time: 6%
% Male: 40%
% Female: 60%
% Out-of-State: 72%
% Fraternity: 5%
% Sorority: 2%
% On-Campus (Freshman): 99%
% On-Campus (All Undergraduate): 75%

% African-American: 4%
% Asian: 15%
% Hispanic: 11%
% White: 37%
% Other: 4%
% Race or Ethnicity Unknown: 8%
% International: 21%
% Low-Income: 15%

ACADEMICS
Student-to-Faculty Ratio: 10:1
% of Classes Under 20: 62%
% of Classes Under 40: 83%
% Full-Time Faculty: 70%
% Full-Time Faculty w/ Terminal Degree: 90%

Top Programs
Biomedical Engineering
Business Administration and Management
Communication
Computer Science
Economics
Health Science
International Relations
Psychology

Retention Rate: 94%
4-Year Graduation Rate: 84%
6-Year Graduation Rate: 88%

Curricular Flexibility: Somewhat Flexible
Academic Rating: ★★★★

Inside the Classroom

Growing more selective each year, Boston University is a private research institution playing host to more than 18,000 undergrads as well as an additional 15,000 graduate students. It's hard to imagine a more dynamic locale than BU's sprawling campus that shares a neighborhood with Fenway Park, the Museum of Fine Arts, MIT, and countless culinary and cultural enticements. In total, the university offers more than 250 programs of study, about half of which are distinct undergraduate degrees spread across ten schools/colleges.

Unique programs include the Kilachand Honors College that welcomes 150 new students each year and offers a unique, original, integrated four-year curriculum thematically centered on global challenges and practical solutions. Not shockingly, it's tough to pin down course requirements with so many colleges within the larger university. College of Arts & Sciences students must satisfy basic requirements in foreign language, mathematics, and writing as part of their 128 credits. Engineering students, on the other hand, must complete sixteen credits in mathematics and twelve in the natural sciences. First-year experience courses are available but not required.

Many classes at BU are reasonably small—62 percent contain fewer than twenty students; only 12 percent contain more than fifty. The student–to-faculty ratio is 10:1, quite an achievement for a school of its size. BU's Undergraduate Research Opportunities Program (UROP) funded 650 students in 2018-19, and many additional students participate in BU's research for credit, volunteer, work study, and other independent opportunities. More than ninety study abroad sites in twenty-five countries are available for those seeking a global experience. Participation is relatively high—40 percent of arts and sciences students complete a semester on a foreign campus.

The greatest number of degrees are conferred in business/marketing (21 percent) communications and journalism (14 percent), social sciences (14 percent), biology (10 percent), engineering (9 percent), and health professions/related sciences (7 percent). The Questrom School of Business and the College of Engineering are highly regarded as well as the university's College of Communication and College of Health & Rehabilitation Services. Over the last five years, BU has produced at least five Fulbright Scholars annually. In 2019, grads took home ten Fulbright Scholarships, four Goldwater Scholarships, two Critical Language Scholarships, a Boren Scholarship, and a Truman Scholarship.

Outside the Classroom

Three-quarters of the undergraduate student body reside on campus. Greek life has a modest presence at BU—13 percent elect to pledge one of the school's eight frats and twelve sororities. Nicknamed the Terriers, BU is represented by twenty-three teams (13 women's, 10 men's) in NCAA Division I, highlighted by its perennially stellar men's ice hockey team. In an odd move for a school of its size, BU dissolved its football program in 1997. The basketball team makes an occasional appearance in March Madness. For those a bit less serious about/ skilled at sports, 7,000 students participate in intramural athletics. With close to 500 student organizations and offerings from improv to synchronized swimming, just about everyone can find their niche. The student-run Daily Free Press is recognized as one of the tops in the country and claims the fourth highest circulation of any paper in Boston. Volunteer spirit runs rampant at BU—the Community Service Center has a volunteer base of over 1,500 students and contributes 75,000 hours of service to the Boston-area community each year. Being located in the heart of Boston, students have limitless choices for nightlife and culture and can conveniently hop aboard the Green Line to explore the farthest reaches of the city.

Career Services

Twenty counselors, recruiters, and outreach coordinators comprise the BU Center for Career Development (CCD). That equates to a student-to-advisor ratio of 925:1, well below average compared to the pool of institutions included in this book. Despite limited personnel for a school so large, the office is successful at working with those who engage with them. In fact, students who regularly utilized the career center reported 22 percent higher earnings than their peers. Last year, staff conducted 2,437 one-on-one advising sessions. Remarkably for a school of BU's size, the CCD helps 89 percent of students complete at least one internship over their four years of study.

Every spring and fall the CCD organizes an All-Majors Career Fair with over one-hundred guest employers; individual colleges within BU also host discipline-specific career fairs in business, engineering, nonprofit leadership, and public health. In total, 725 employers attended BU fairs, and 770 recruited on campus in 2018-19. That led to 600+ on-campus interviews being facilitated by the CCD. Freshmen are encouraged to attend a seminar called Career Directions: Starting Your Journey that gives tips on how to maximize one's educational experience with an eye on life beyond college. Through the Career Advisory Network, the CCD also works to connect students with over 6,000 participating alumni who are employed in a wide spectrum of fields. Even with a less-than-ideal number of counselors, BU's career services staff works hard to reach students through seminars, job fairs, and online resources.

Professional Outcomes

Six months after graduation, 96 percent of BU grads have found their way into the world of employment or full-time graduate study. A recent survey of corporate recruiters with international companies revealed that Boston University alums have the sixth highest employability ranking, directly behind the likes of MIT, Caltech, Harvard, and Stanford. Recent graduating classes have seen more than ten graduates join employers like EY, PwC, Deloitte, and TJX Companies. Healthy numbers of engineering grads found their way to Amazon, IBM, Lockheed Martin, and Pfizer. Across all graduating years, companies employing more than 250 BU alums include Google, Oracle, Accenture, and Wayfair. Starting salary data is highly dependent on which school within BU one attended. For the Class of 2018, grads of the Questrom School of Business earned a starting salary of roughly $63k, College of Engineering grads averaged $70k, and Arts & Sciences students came in just shy of $50k.

Respect for the BU degree comes from more than just the corporate world. Of the 19 percent of 2018 grads who moved directly into graduate school, many were welcomed onto the campuses of elite graduate programs. For example, engineering students found new academic homes at MIT, Stanford, Carnegie Mellon, and Columbia. Most top law schools have some level of representation from BU alumni including BU Law itself, a top twenty-five institution that accepts a significant number of its own undergraduates. Those aiming to become medical doctors can apply for the Seven-Year Liberal Arts/Medical Education Program that leads directly to study at the BU School of Medicine. Overall, the university saw almost 300 undergraduates apply to med school in 2018 alone, the eighth highest total in the nation. Whether attending grad school or starting their careers, the greatest number of BU grads remain in Boston with New York City, San Francisco, Los Angeles, DC, and Philadelphia next in popularity.

Admission

Over 64,000 applications rolled into BU for spots in the Class of 2022, and 22 percent gained acceptance. For historical context, 46 percent of applicants were accepted in 2012 and close to three quarters in 2005. The average member of the Class of 2022 finished with a 3.71 GPA and earned a 1421 SAT score. Back in 2012, the 75th percentile on the SAT was 1390, an indicator that gaining acceptance into BU is considerably more difficult than in the not-too-distant past. Most BU students finished in the upper echelon of their high school classes—65 percent were in the top 10 percent, and 93 percent were in the top 25 percent. On a 4.0 scale, 83 percent had GPAs of 3.5 or higher.

The only two admissions criteria rated as "very important" for all applicants are the rigor of one's high school course load and talent/ability. Factors in the second run of importance are class rank, GPA, standardized test scores, recommendations, essays, extracurricular activities, alumni relation (legacy), and the level of an applicant's interest. Those who demonstrate the most fervent interest and commitment by applying early decision receive a slight boost, gaining acceptance at a 28 percent clip. It is critical to remember that this isn't your mother's or father's BU—it's not even your older sibling's BU. Far more highly selective than even a few years ago, Boston University hopefuls need to bring top-tier credentials in order to be offered admission at this fine private research institution.

Worth Your Money?

At $72,000, Boston University has a hefty list price cost of attendance, a sum made slightly more manageable for the 16 percent of undergraduates who receive an annual merit-based award of $24k or some level of need-based financial aid. BU does award need-based aid to 41 percent of its undergraduates, but it fails to meet 100 percent of all demonstrated need for all students. Still, the average annual award to qualifying students is $45k, which cuts the overall costs considerably. Boston University graduates end up with an average debt load of $43,000, a figure that is higher than the national average. If you were in the position that attending BU would necessitate taking out large loans, your decision should come down to whether you intend to major in a field with a high enough starting salary so you could comfortably make monthly payments.

FINANCIAL
Institutional Type: Private
In-State Tuition: $52,816
Out-of-State Tuition: $52,816
Room & Board: $15,720
Required Fees: $1,132
Books & Supplies: $1,000

Avg. Need-Based Aid: $44,891
Avg. % of Need Met: 91%

Avg. Merit-Based Aid: $23,779
% Receiving Merit-Based Aid: 16%

Avg. Cumulative Debt: $42,976
% of Students Borrowing: 46%

CAREER
Who Recruits
1. Marriott
2. Turner Broadcasting System
3. TJX
4. General Electric
5. Bloomberg LP

Notable Internships
1. Amazon
2. Boston Scientific
3. BuzzFeed

Top Industries
1. Business
2. Education
3. Operations
4. Media
5. Information Technology

Top Employers
1. IBM
2. Google
3. Amazon
4. Microsoft
5. Oracle

Where Alumni Work
1. Boston
2. New York City
3. San Francisco
4. Los Angeles
5. Washington, DC

Median Earnings
College Scorecard (Early Career): $65,300
EOP (Early Career): $62,000
PayScale (Mid-Career): $113,600

RANKINGS
Forbes: 74
Money: 209
U.S. News: 40 (T), National Universities
Wall Street Journal/THE: 44 (T)
Washington Monthly: 126, National Universities

#CollegesWorthYourMoney

Bowdoin College

Brunswick, Maine | Admissions Phone: 207-725-3100

Inside the Classroom

Set on 215 lush acres in the quaint town of New Brunswick, Maine, Bowdoin College serves just over 1,800 undergraduate students. This quintessential, elite New England liberal arts college is steeped in history and tradition; its oldest buildings date to the late eighteenth century, and the curriculum is guided by a poem, "The Offer of College," penned by the school's president in 1906. Does it get any more New England liberal-artsy than that?

Among its core beliefs, Bowdoin offers a flexible and broad liberal arts education. Polar Bears can choose from one of thirty-three academic programs or get more creative through an interdisciplinary or student-designed major. One-size-fits-all requirements are minimal. All must take a freshman seminar in an area of interest such as Women of Color in Politics, Intro to Documentary Film Studies, or Food and Foodways in China: A Cultural History. Bowdoin students are required to take one course from each of five distribution areas: (1) mathematical, computational, or statistical reasoning; (2) inquiry in the natural sciences; (3) exploring social difference; (4) international perspectives; and (5) visual and performing arts.

Class sizes are small—70 percent contain fewer than twenty students—and more than one-quarter have fewer than ten students. The student-faculty ratio is 9:1, which leads to ample and meaningful interaction and guidance in and out of the classroom. More than half of Bowdoin undergrads report interacting with a professor outside of regular class time at least once per week. Professors have a reputation for being extremely dedicated to their teaching. Students also enjoy a plethora of study abroad opportunities with over 50 percent electing to spend a semester learning in a foreign locale.

The greatest percentage of degrees are conferred in the social sciences (30 percent), biology (13 percent), area/ethnic/gender studies (9 percent), and mathematics (7 percent). Economics and government and legal studies are two of the more popular majors within the social sciences. Bowdoin is one of the strongest in the country for those on a pre-med track. The school is also a prolific producer of fellowship/scholarship winners. In 2018 alone, twenty graduates were named Fulbright Scholars—the second highest total from any one school. Graduates also routinely win other prestigious awards including National Science Foundation Graduate Research Fellowships, Boren Scholarships, Watson Fellowships, and Critical Language Scholarships awarded by the US State Department.

Outside the Classroom

By sheer numbers, athletics are a driving force of life outside the classroom. An insanely high 43 percent of undergrads are varsity athletes who compete on one of thirty NCAA Division III teams. And that doesn't include those who play on one of the six club teams or participate in one of ten intramural sports, each of which has an A, B, and C level. Over one hundred non-sports clubs are also active, including the Outing Club, which boasts over 400 members and takes over 150 nature-themed excursions per year. Greek life was disbanded around the turn of the new millennium and replaced with a system of eight college houses that serve as the backbone of the campus residential experience. Each house has its own student government and hosts special events throughout the year. The dining halls are known to prepare extravagant meals that receive rave reviews across the board. Over 90 percent of students live on campus, and certain annual events like the Gala and Ivies concert bring together the whole student body. Among the most favored off-campus destinations is Portland, Maine's largest city, which is less than half an hour away.

Career Services

Bowdoin Career Planning is staffed by six full-time career counselors and one employer relations professional. That works out to a student-to-advisor ratio of 304:1, lower than the average institution included in this book. Students are always welcome to schedule a one-on-one counseling session or mock interview or drop by between noon and 2 p.m. each weekday, unannounced, with a quick question. In 2017-18, the office planned 204 programs with over 5,200 attendees, more than two-and-half times the size of the student body. Incredibly, the staff managed to work, in some capacity, with 80 percent of students and 99 percent of the senior class.

The school combines some events with Colby and Bates; the Graduate & Professional School Fair that is held every October, and the annual Maine Employers Career Fair are two examples. The school's outreach efforts pay off with additional companies recruiting on campus each year. In 2017, it added HSBC, Jefferies Group, Wayfair, and LogMeIn to an already long list. Bowdoin also distributes close to a quarter of a million dollars in grants to support unpaid internships each year. Two-thirds of graduates complete some type of internship. To provide further assistance in carving out career pathways, 200 alumni and parents of current students come to campus to help students with career exploration and networking.

Professional Outcomes

An examination of five years' worth of outcomes data (2012-2016) reveals that by the fall after graduation between 70 and 78 percent of recent grads have found full-time employment, and between 15 and 20 percent have gone directly into graduate school. Only 2-4 percent are still seeking employment. Prominent corporations across all sectors love Bowdoin grads. Recent alumni have found positions at Apple, IBM, Goldman Sachs, Google, HBO, and Microsoft. Other companies that employ more than a dozen alumni are Fidelity Investments, Morgan Stanley, Amazon, UBS, Facebook, and Barclays. At age thirty-four, Bowdoin grads have a median salary of $61k per year, placing them in the 73rd income percentile nationwide, slightly higher than nearby Bates or Colby. The cities attracting the greatest numbers of graduates are (in order) Boston; New York City; Portland, Maine; San Francisco; DC; and Los Angeles.

Of those entering graduate school, 20 percent were enrolled in PhD programs, 15 percent were in med school, 8 percent in law school, and 41 percent were in master's programs. The top twenty graduate schools attended, by volume, in the last five years make an exclusive list including six Ivies along with Duke, MIT, Johns Hopkins, Northwestern, and Stanford. Boston University is also one the largest recipients of Bowdoin grads. Those aiming for medical school fare exceptionally well with 90 percent typically earning acceptance into at least one institution. Recent grads are presently studying medicine at Tufts, Harvard, Boston University, NYU, and the University of Michigan.

Admission

Already a highly selective school, Bowdoin has become even more difficult to get into in recent years. The acceptance rate for applicants to the Class of 2022 was a paltry 10.3 percent compared to 13.6 percent the previous year and 20 percent back in 2012. The number of applicants increased by one-quarter since last year. An examination of the middle-50 percent ranges on standardized tests for attending students suggests there is little evidence that the school is accepting a higher caliber of student than it was five years ago. In 2013-14, Bowdoin freshmen scored 1360-1510 on the SAT and 30-33 on the ACT. In 2018-19, those SAT figures were slightly lower at 1300-1510 while the upper-end of the ACT range was slightly higher at 30-34. Bowdoin is famous for becoming the first test-optional school in the country (1969). Nevertheless, 60 percent of the Class of 2022 submitted SAT scores, and 46 percent shared ACT scores. Those numbers add up to more than 100 percent because a decent number of students submitted results from both tests, so it is fair to conclude that the vast majority of successful applicants elected to submit standardized test scores.

Being in the top 10 percent of your high school class is almost required—80 percent of freshmen held that distinction, and 96 percent were in the top 25 percent. The school also ranks essays, recommendations, talent/ability, personal qualities, and extracurricular activities as "very important" in the admissions process. Although Bowdoin is, technically, a test-optional school, it pays to have high SAT/ACTs. The acceptance rate may be shrinking, but the average student profile has held relatively steady. Those with the best chance of acceptance will be near the top of their high school class and possess standardized test scores above the 95th percentile. Applying early decision also will provide a great boost for your prospects; 23 percent of ED applicants are accepted compared to only 8.5 percent in the regular round.

Worth Your Money?

Bowdoin's annual cost of attendance is $73,800, and merit aid awards are not typically large enough to make any kind of a difference. Fortunately, the school is generous with need-based aid, meeting 100 percent of the demonstrated need for qualifying students. At present, 885 of the 1,824 undergraduates receive an average annual grant of $48,856. If you come from a family making an income in the top 5 percent nationwide—it is estimated that nearly half of all Bowdoin students do--you can expect to pay full price. In the end, the average graduate is in roughly $5,000 less debt than the average college student in the United States.

FINANCIAL
Institutional Type: Private
In-State Tuition: $55,822
Out-of-State Tuition: $55,822
Room & Board: $15,360
Required Fees: $528
Books & Supplies: $840

Avg. Need-Based Aid: $48,856
Avg. % of Need Met: 100%

Avg. Merit-Based Aid: $1,000
% Receiving Merit-Based Aid: 1%

Avg. Cumulative Debt: $25,482
% of Students Borrowing: 27%

CAREER
Who Recruits
1. Barclay's
2. Deutsche Bank
3. Prudential
4. Cornerstone Research
5. Teach for America

Notable Internships
1. Athena Global Advisors
2. eBay
3. CBS News

Top Industries
1. Business
2. Education
3. Research
4. Operations
5. Social Services

Top Employers
1. Unum
2. Fidelity Investments
3. Massachusetts General Hospital
4. Google
5. Morgan Stanley

Where Alumni Work
1. Boston
2. New York City
3. Portland, ME
4. San Francisco
5. Washington, DC

Median Earnings
College Scorecard (Early Career): $65,500
EOP (Early Career): $61,000
PayScale (Mid-Career): $112,000

RANKINGS
Forbes: 26
Money: 82
U.S. News: 6, Liberal Arts Colleges
Wall Street Journal/THE: 44 (T)
Washington Monthly: 5, Liberal Arts Colleges

Brandeis University

Waltham, Massachusetts | Admissions Phone: 781-736-3500

ADMISSION
Admission Rate: 31%
Admission Rate - Men: 29%
Admission Rate - Women: 32%
EA Admission Rate: Not Offered
ED Admission Rate: 39%
Admission Rate (5-Year Trend): -6%
ED Admission Rate (5-Year Trend): -6%
% of Admits Attending (Yield): 24%
Transfer Admission Rate: 25%

Offered Wait List: 1,844
Accepted Wait List: 721
Admitted Wait List: 1

SAT Reading/Writing (Middle 50%): 630-720
SAT Math (Middle 50%): 650-780
ACT Composite (Middle 50%): 29-33
Testing Policy: Test Optional
SAT Superscore: Yes
ACT Superscore: No

% Graduated in Top 10% of HS Class: 56%
% Graduated in Top 25% of HS Class: 91%
% Graduated in Top 50% of HS Class: 99%

ENROLLMENT
Total Undergraduate Enrollment: 3,639
% Part-Time: 1%
% Male: 39%
% Female: 61%
% Out-of-State: 70%
% Fraternity: Not Offered
% Sorority: Not Offered
% On-Campus (Freshman): 100%
% On-Campus (All Undergraduate): 76%

% African-American: 5%
% Asian: 14%
% Hispanic: 8%
% White: 46%
% Other: 3%
% Race or Ethnicity Unknown: 3%
% International: 20%
% Low-Income: 18%

ACADEMICS
Student-to-Faculty Ratio: 10:1
% of Classes Under 20: 57%
% of Classes Under 40: 85%
% Full-Time Faculty: 68%
% Full-Time Faculty w/ Terminal Degree: 94%

Top Programs
Biology
Chemistry
Economics
Health: Science, Society, and Policy
History
International Studies
Neuroscience
Sociology

Retention Rate: 92%
4-Year Graduation Rate: 80%
6-Year Graduation Rate: 88%

Curricular Flexibility: Somewhat Flexible
Academic Rating: ★★★★

Inside the Classroom

Unlike many other elite Boston-area universities, this institution does not have 300-400 years of history and tradition. Founded in 1948 by a group of Jewish donors only a few weeks before the modern State of Israel was established, Brandeis has been a nonsectarian university open to talented students of all backgrounds and faiths. Home to 3,600 undergraduates with a male-heavy split (60/40), Brandeis offers forty-four majors, the most popular of which are the social sciences (21 percent), biology (15 percent), business (9 percent), psychology (7 percent), and computer science (7 percent).

An ethos of high academic standards and intellectual curiosity permeates this Waltham, Massachusetts, campus. An awe-inspiring 54 percent of Brandeis undergraduates double major, and 40 percent elect to study abroad in one of over 350 approved programs across the globe. Core requirements for all students include a university writing seminar; one qualitative reasoning course; one diversity, equity, and inclusion course; one difference and justice in the world course; three semesters of a foreign language; and at least one class within each of the schools of humanities, science, social science, and creative arts.

Professors at Brandeis are committed to undergraduate education and will interact with you in close enough quarters that you can rest assured they will learn your name. The student-faculty ratio is 10:1, and 57 percent of courses contain fewer than nineteen students. Invitations to assist faculty members with academic research is common, even for undergraduates. In the Chemistry Department alone, 260 undergrads have coauthored and published papers with their professors in the last fifteen years. International experiences also abound, whether you are interacting with the 20 percent of the student body who are citizens of another country or decide to travel abroad for a semester, which 40 percent of undergraduates do.

Departments with a particularly strong national reputation include economics, international studies, and sociology as well as all of the traditional premed pathways including biology, chemistry, and the health: science, society, and policy program. More than 200 students work each year with the school's Office of Academic Fellowships to pursue sponsored opportunities to pursue their intellectual passions after graduation. Many have successfully landed Fulbright, Boren, and Critical Language Scholarships, among others.

Outside the Classroom

With over 260 student organizations, the club scene plays a prominent role at Brandeis. A cappella, Jewish groups, intramural sports, and theater are among the most popular. Opportunities to volunteer in the local community abound, and many take advantage; forty-four members of the Class of 2017 accrued more than 300 service hours over their four years. Fraternities and sororities do operate on campus and have a genuine presence, although they are unrecognized by the university. The Brandeis Judges (the school is named for famed Supreme Court Justice Louis Brandeis) compete in NCAA Division III and field nineteen teams (10 for women, 9 for men). The school also has nineteen club teams that include Brazilian Jiu-Jitsu, archery, and sailing. With a plethora of activities in which to participate and a generally active social scene, you don't need to venture off campus in order to fill your days with excitement. Of course, with Boston less than ten miles away, many do stray away from Waltham on the weekends. For the 76 percent of undergrads (and 100 percent of freshmen) who choose to live on campus, Brandeis' nineteen dorms are often ranked highly on lists of best collegiate housing.

Career Services

The Hiatt Career Center is staffed by fifteen professionals with expertise in career counseling, giving it a 240:1 student-to-advisor ratio, which is better than average compared to other schools featured in this guide. It deploys its resources effectively, connecting annually with over 50 percent of each class through counseling appointments, workshops, or job fairs. One-on-one counseling is available to all students as often as once per week, and the center encourages developing a relationship with one particular counselor over your four years of study. Specialized counseling is available for those considering pursuing an MD or other health-care-related position after undergrad. Walk-in hours are more generous than most universities and can be utilized for quick questions that require fifteen minutes or less of interaction. Career Services connects students with internship/employment opportunities by a variety of means. Industry Meetups bring Brandeis alumni to campus from a host of fields. Brandeis Networking Nights are held over winter break each year in Washington, DC, and New York City. It also hosts area-specific fairs for students concentrating in computer science, careers with a social impact, or volunteer and internship opportunities. On-site interviews are conducted at fall and spring career fairs. As an additional aid, 19,000 jobs and internships are posted each year on Handshake. This adds up to almost all graduates finding their next destination within months of leaving the university.

Professional Outcomes

Within six months of graduation, 98 percent of the Class of 2018 had found their way to employment (59 percent), graduate school (33 percent), or another full-time activity like travel or volunteer work (6 percent). The most common industries entered by Brandeis grads are (in order) health care, scientific research, computer science, finance/banking, education, and consulting. Three of the four largest employers of recent grads are in the health-care sector: Boston Children's Hospital, Massachusetts General Hospital, and the Dana Farber Cancer Institute. Nonprofits such as Teach for America, City Year, and the Peace Corps are also well represented. The corporations employing the greatest number of recent graduates (classes of 2014-17) are Amazon, Goldman Sachs, and Walt Disney Parks & Resorts. By age thirty-four Brandeis graduates have a median income of $61k, putting them in the 72nd percentile for income nationally. The greatest number of graduates remains in Boston but many flock to New York City, DC, San Francisco, Los Angeles, and Philadelphia.

A large contingent of grads elect to continue at Brandeis for graduate school. The next most commonly attended graduate/professional schools from 2014-2017 were (in order) BU, Columbia, NYU, Harvard, and Tufts. That list is a good indication that Brandeis' reputation for academic excellence leads to positive outcomes for those applying to elite graduate schools. Those applying to medical school are remarkably successful, gaining acceptance between 65 and 75 percent annually, 20-30 points higher than the national average.

Admission

Brandeis is one of the rare, elite New England liberal arts schools that has not experienced an admissions rate freefall over the past decade. Typically, 33-35 percent of applicants find success, the same range as five years ago, although the Class of 2022 faced a slightly harsher 31 percent. The average SAT and ACT scores of accepted students has increased, but that is likely more a result of the school going test-optional in 2013 (lower scores no longer drag down the average) than an indicator that the applicant pool has become more competitive. We should note that Brandeis is test-optional, but with an asterisk. Students must submit one of the following: SAT/ACT scores; 3 AP/SAT Subject Tests, including a math/science and an English/social science discipline; or one graded analytical writing sample as well as an additional recommendation from an eleventh or twelfth grade course. Those who submitted traditional standardized test scores generally earned high scores. The middle 50 percent of Brandeis students earned a 1280-1500 on the SAT and a 29-33 on the ACT.

Excellent performance in the classroom is valued most strongly by the admissions committee with 90 percent of Brandeis undergrads in the top 25 percent of their high school class and 56 percent in the top 10 percent. The other categories that qualify as "very important" to the committee are class rank, character, personal qualities, and the rigor of one's high school curriculum. The rate of acceptance for early decision is only nine points higher than during the regular cycle (39 percent vs. 30 percent), which means that ED may only offer a slight admissions edge. The small gap between ED and RD acceptance rates could also mean that the ED applicant pool is not as strong, on average, as the RD applicant pool—a reasonable hypothesis given the large number of high-achieving applicants who apply to Brandeis but who do not have Brandeis at the top of their college list. Naturally, as a consequence, demonstrated interest is considered as important in the admission process.

Overall, Brandeis remains an accessible destination for students who are extremely strong in the classroom but who may not have aced the SAT. Those with straight A's in a rigorous high school curriculum and winning personal attributes will succeed as part of this holistic process.

Worth Your Money?

Given the annual cost of attendance of $76k you may be surprised to learn that, according to tax return data, Brandeis students come from homes with a significantly more modest median income, on average, than students at other comparable private schools. It is estimated that only about 55 percent come from families in the top 20 percent of income earners nationwide, a much lower percentage than many other prestigious institutions. What does that mean? Even though it does not meet 100 percent of demonstrated need for all undergraduates, Brandeis does prioritize enrolling an economically diverse student body, awarding need-based grants of close to $39,000 to 47 percent of its student population. Due to that generosity, many lower-to-middle income students have the opportunity to attend this school, and graduates hold less debt than the average college graduate in the United States. With solid financial aid offerings (as well as bit of merit aid) and positive graduate outcomes, Brandeis University is worth its net price.

FINANCIAL
Institutional Type: Private
In-State Tuition: $55,340
Out-of-State Tuition: $55,340
Room & Board: $16,080
Required Fees: $2,221
Books & Supplies: $1,000

Avg. Need-Based Aid: $38,944
Avg. % of Need Met: 94%

Avg. Merit-Based Aid: $12,912
% Receiving Merit-Based Aid: 21%

Avg. Cumulative Debt: $29,785
% of Students Borrowing: 46%

CAREER
Who Recruits
1. TIBCO
2. Analysis Group
3. John Hancock
4. Sun Life Financial
5. Kayak

Notable Internships
1. Uber
2. Symantec
3. Goldman Sachs

Top Industries
1. Business
2. Education
3. Research
4. Healthcare
5. Social Services

Top Employers
1. Dell
2. Google
3. IBM
4. Morgan Stanley
5. Amazon

Where Alumni Work
1. Boston
2. New York City
3. Washington, DC
4. San Francisco
5. Los Angeles

Median Earnings
College Scorecard (Early Career): $57,900
EOP (Early Career): $63,100
PayScale (Mid-Career): $113,200

RANKINGS
Forbes: 96
Money: 153
U.S. News: 40 (T), National Universities
Wall Street Journal/THE: 109
Washington Monthly: 106, National Universities

#CollegesWorthYourMoney

Brigham Young University

Provo, Utah | Admissions Phone: 801-422-2507

Inside the Classroom

An almost exclusively Mormon student body of more than 31,000 undergraduates occupy Brigham Young's high-altitude campus in the mountainous and breathtaking area of Provo, Utah. In addition to living by a strict honor code guided by the LDS Church (more on this later), students come to BYU for its more than 200 programs and reputation for academic excellence.

Required coursework for BYU undergraduates includes a number of courses in the Mormon faith including Teachings & Doctrine of the Book of Mormon, Christ and the Everlasting Gospel, Foundations of the Restoration, and The Eternal Family. Mandatory courses in American heritage, global and cultural awareness, first-year writing, advanced oral and written communication, foreign language, and the social, biological, and physical sciences are all part of the core curriculum that supports BYU's larger mission "to provide an education that is (1) spiritually strengthening, (2) intellectually enlarging, and (3) character building, leading to (4) lifelong learning and service."

A 20:1 student-to-faculty ratio translates to some undergraduate sections being a bit large. Roughly 12 percent of sections contain more than fifty students. However, those lecture hall courses are balanced with classes of more modest size; 45 percent of courses have nineteen or fewer students. Despite the size of the university and some classes, the school does an excellent job getting undergraduate students involved in hands-on research. In the Department of Chemistry and Biochemistry, 88 percent of students worked with a faculty mentor on a research project. Additionally, the school offers 206 approved study abroad programs in seventy-five countries, and 17 percent of undergrads participate.

The ten most popular majors at BYU are exercise science, elementary education, psychology, management, English, public health, computer science, family life (a major unique to BYU), chemical engineering, and communications. The programs with the strongest national reputations are those within the Marriott School of Business and, to a slightly lesser extent, the Ira A. Fulton College of Engineering. Brigham Young alumni do occasionally win highly competitive postgraduation recognition, but in 2017 the National Scholarships, Fellowships, and Programs office was shut down, and those duties now fall under the purview of the Honors College. Students can still apply, but this is certainly a program in transition.

Outside the Classroom

While not a requirement, most freshmen (73 percent) live in on-campus dorms. In total, only 15 percent live on campus, but over 23,000 students live in BYU-contracted housing in the immediate area. There is no Greek life; rather, the LDS Church is at the center of much of student life outside the classroom. The school is governed by an Honor Code that includes clauses about facial hair, foul language, chastity, and abstaining from the consumption of caffeinated beverages. A good number of recognized student organizations are related to religion, volunteer work, or professional associations. One of the more recognizable and typical elements of BYU college life is the passion displayed for the school's sports teams. The Cougars send twenty-one athletic squads into high-level competition in NCAA Division I and have seen ten NCAA titles, a Heisman Trophy winner, and over 1,000 All-Americans. Football games draw 56,000 fans to LaVell Edwards Stadium. Over 12,000 students participate in intramural sports each year on this extremely athletically-inclined campus. Outdoor activities are also emphasized and are aided by the overwhelming natural beauty surrounding the school's 550+ acre campus situated at the edge of the Rocky Mountains.

Career Services

Brigham Young's University Career Services Office employs seventeen professionals (not including office managers) who are responsible for career development and counseling. That works out to a counselor-to-student ratio of 1,837:1, one of the poorest figures of any college featured in this guide. BYU's Career Services staff believes that a career is more than just a job; it is a calling to which one is deeply dedicated. To help students find their path, the office offers free assessments such as the Myers-Briggs, the Strong Interest Inventory, and TypeFocus. The university even offers a credited course called Career Exploration intended to help undergrads learn their strengths, define their interests, and begin seriously thinking about a vocation.

The fall 2018 Career Fair was attended by 126 companies and 1,919 students. Fifteen of those employers conducted 189 interviews. A larger operation, the STEM Career Fair, also held in fall 2018, drew 246 companies to campus and was visited by 5,346 students. All students are able to utilize Handshake accounts that allow them to connect with potential employers for jobs and internships. One of the school's greatest career services strengths is the tightknit network of alumni who are always willing to help a fellow Cougar. While this office is understaffed, it does excel in the areas of graduate school placement and career development that is uniquely tailored to this mostly LDS-affiliated population.

Brigham Young University

E-mail: admissions@byu.edu | Website: www.byu.edu

Professional Outcomes

In 2018, the average age of a BYU graduate was nearly twenty-five, a result of the eighteen months to two years of missionary work members of the LDS Church are required to complete. The most popular fields entered are business management, education, operations, engineering, sales, and information technology. By a wide margin, the two largest employers of BYU alums are the university itself and the LDS Church. However, there are hundreds of Cougars working at major corporations including Adobe, Google, Microsoft, and Goldman Sachs. Average salaries for BYU grads are on the low end compared to alumni of other selective universities. Ten years after entering the school, alumni are earning a median salary of $59,700. Unsurprisingly, Provo and the Greater Salt Lake area see the highest concentrations of BYU alumni. Major cities outside of Utah with significant numbers of graduates include San Francisco, Phoenix, LA, and Seattle.

Brigham Young is in the same league with Berkeley, Cornell, the University of Michigan, and the University of Wisconsin in terms of producing future PhDs. Over the past decade, more than 3,000 alumni have gone on to earn doctoral degrees. Many grads pursuing advanced degrees do so at BYU, yet plenty of others relocate to pursue educational opportunities at institutions such as MIT, Harvard, and the University of North Carolina. (In 2005, two-thirds of the UNC PhD in accounting candidates were BYU alums.) Each year, approximately 500 BYU students apply to medical school; 67 percent are accepted, a far better mark than the national average. Those who attend law school flock to BYU's own well-regarded Rueben Clark Law School, but many attend other elite law schools. Harvard Law and Yale Law have BYU representation in just about every one of their entering 1L classes.

Admission

Despite a 64 percent acceptance rate, gaining admission to BYU requires a strong academic profile. The high rate of acceptance is attributable to the school's uniquely self-selecting applicant pool. Unless you are a member of the Church of Jesus Christ of Latter-day Saints, you likely aren't placing the university on your college wish list. Most students who apply favor the ACT over the SAT, and among 2018-19 freshmen, the middle-50 percent ACT range was 26-31. A narrow majority, 54 percent, also finished in the top 10 percent of their high school class; 85 percent placed in the top 25 percent. On a 4.0 scale, 81 percent had a GPA of 3.75 or higher.

Even with roughly 13,000 applicants per year, BYU employs a holistic review of each one. It values eleven factors as being "very important" in influencing admissions decisions. In addition to the usual factors of rigor of curriculum, grades, recommendations, essays, and test scores, the university also places great importance on religious affiliation, volunteer work, work experience, character/personal qualities, talent/ability, and extracurricular involvement. High-achieving LDS teenagers frequently see BYU as their top or, perhaps, even their only choice for postsecondary education. Those who fit the mold will gain acceptance. Only rarely do non-Mormon individuals attend BYU; they comprise less than 2 percent of the student body.

Worth Your Money?

Similar to an in-state and out-of-state rate, BYU charges different tuition to Latter-day Saints than it does to non-Latter-day Saints. Members of the LDS Church pay an annual tuition of only $5,790, an unheard amount in the third decade of the twenty-first century. The total annual cost of attendance is under $20k, and the majority also receive some type of merit aid with the average award being over $4,000. Close to half also receive need-based aid that averages out to the full price of tuition. For members of the LDS Church, BYU is an amazing fit and worth every penny. For the limited numbers of non-LDS members who apply, Brigham Young University is still an exceptional value, even at a higher cost.

FINANCIAL
Institutional Type: Private
In-State Tuition: $5,790 (LDS)
Out-of-State Tuition: $11,580 (non-LDS)
Room & Board: $7,766
Required Fees: $0
Books & Supplies: $872

Avg. Need-Based Aid: $5,378
Avg. % of Need Met: 30%

Avg. Merit-Based Aid: $4,341
% Receiving Merit-Based Aid: 57%

Avg. Cumulative Debt: $15,701
% of Students Borrowing: 24%

CAREER
Who Recruits
1. Podium
2. Qualtrics
3. Domo, Inc.
4. Pluralsight
5. Lucid

Notable Internships
1. Adobe
2. Bain Capital
3. Utah Jazz

Top Industries
1. Business
2. Education
3. Operations
4. Engineering
5. Sales

Top Employers
1. LDS Church
2. Intermountain Healthcare
3. Qualtrics
4. Adobe
5. Vivint Smart Home

Where Alumni Work
1. Provo, UT
2. Salt Lake City, UT
3. Phoenix
4. San Francisco
5. Los Angeles

Median Earnings
College Scorecard (Early Career): $59,700
EOP (Early Career): $32,600
PayScale (Mid-Career): $108,000

RANKINGS
Forbes: 95
Money: 147
U.S. News: 77 (T), National Universities
Wall Street Journal/THE: 143 (T)
Washington Monthly: 15, National Universities

#CollegesWorthYourMoney

Brown University

Providence, Rhode Island | Admissions Phone: 401-863-2378

ADMISSION
Admission Rate: 8%
Admission Rate - Men: 9%
Admission Rate - Women: 7%
EA Admission Rate: Not Offered
ED Admission Rate: 21%
Admission Rate (5-Year Trend): -2%
ED Admission Rate (5-Year Trend): +2%
% of Admits Attending (Yield): 61%
Transfer Admission Rate: 8%

Offered Wait List: N/A
Accepted Wait List: N/A
Admitted Wait List: 100

SAT Reading/Writing (Middle 50%): 700-760
SAT Math (Middle 50%): 720-790
ACT Composite (Middle 50%): 32-35
Testing Policy: ACT/SAT Required
SAT Superscore: Yes
ACT Superscore: Yes

% Graduated in Top 10% of HS Class: 96%
% Graduated in Top 25% of HS Class: 98%
% Graduated in Top 50% of HS Class: 100%

ENROLLMENT
Total Undergraduate Enrollment: 7,043
% Part-Time: 4%
% Male: 46%
% Female: 54%
% Out-of-State: 95%
% Fraternity: 14%
% Sorority: 10%
% On-Campus (Freshman): 100%
% On-Campus (All Undergraduate): 72%

% African-American: 6%
% Asian: 15%
% Hispanic: 11%
% White: 42%
% Other: 6%
% Race or Ethnicity Unknown: 7%
% International: 12%
% Low-Income: 17%

ACADEMICS
Student-to-Faculty Ratio: 6:1
% of Classes Under 20: 70%
% of Classes Under 40: 86%
% Full-Time Faculty: 84%
% Full-Time Faculty w/ Terminal Degree: 95%

Top Programs
Applied Mathematics
Computer Science
Economics
Engineering
English
Geology
History
Neuroscience

Retention Rate: 98%
4-Year Graduation Rate: 85%
6-Year Graduation Rate: 95%

Curricular Flexibility: Very Flexible
Academic Rating: ★★★★★

Inside the Classroom

Founded in 1764, Brown University holds the distinction as one of the oldest colleges in the United States and, of course, as a member of the vaunted Ivy League. Yet, much like its Rhode Island home, Brown possesses an uncommon blend of tradition and extraordinary commitment to the celebration of individuality. Toward that aim, Brown's Open Curriculum has long been the guiding academic force at the university, perfectly capturing its spirit and core values. The 7,000+ undergraduates who choose (and were chosen by) Brown fit the school's ethos and relish the chance to be the architects of their own educational journey.

Students must choose one "concentration program," but there are no required courses. In essence, the guiding philosophy is that students should take control of their learning, pursue knowledge in areas that they are truly passionate about, and learn to integrate and synthesize information across disciplines. Specialized programs include the Brown/RISD five-year Dual Degree program that leads to a bachelor's from Brown as well as a BFA from the famed Rhode Island School of Design. Teens committed to the medical field even before exiting high school can apply for entry into the program in Liberal Medical Education that allows students to graduate in eight years with an MD from Brown's Warren Alpert Medical School.

This one-of-a-kind experience transpires with a student-faculty ratio of only 7:1, and 100 percent of faculty members spend time teaching the undergraduate population of just under 7,000. Class sizes tend to be small—70 percent have fewer than twenty students—and 34 percent are comprised of nine or fewer students. Student surveys reveal an unsurpassed level of satisfaction with the quality of instruction and professor availability. Undergraduates give favorable reviews in those areas at an overwhelming 92-97 percent clip. Undergraduate research is a big part of the Brown experience for many students; 54 percent conduct research alongside a faculty member or work on an independent project with supervision. As is typical in the Ivy League, the majority of students stay grounded on (or near) campus for all four years. The number of students choosing to study abroad has declined in recent years and presently sits at approximately 500 per year.

Biology, economics, computer science, mathematics, and engineering are among the most popular areas of concentration at Brown; however, it is hard to distinguish any one program, because Brown possesses outstanding offerings across so many disciplines. Computer science is a growing department, conferring 10 percent of the school's degrees in 2018; applied math and English are notably strong. Graduates are a scholarly lot and experience high levels of success at procuring prestigious academic fellowships. In 2019 alone, the school produced thirty-eight Fulbright Scholars and, in 2018, graduates and alumni earned thirty National Science Foundation Graduate Research Fellowships. Brown has produced the seventh most Rhodes Scholars of any institution in history.

Outside the Classroom

The Main Green, surrounded by iconic buildings and located at the heart of campus, is almost always a lively hub of activity. There are more than 300 clubs and activities available to what tends to be a highly involved student body. Performance-based groups such as a cappella, improv, music, and theater draw large numbers of participants. A thriving student-run media scene includes the Brown Daily Herald, the nation's second oldest collegiate daily, and two award-winning campus radio stations. Brown fields an unusually large number of varsity athletic teams, thirty-eight, which compete in NCAA Division I. The Brown Bears claim twenty-one women's teams, the largest number of any school in the country. Greek life plays a moderate role on campus with about a 10 percent participation rate for women and a 14 percent rate for men. Seventy-two percent of students (100 percent of freshmen) live on campus in one of forty-nine residence halls as old as 1822 and as new as 2012. Off-campus housing and a multitude of cultural and entertainment options exist in Providence, including the bustling Thayer Street that runs through campus.

Career Services

The CareerLAB ("LAB" stands for Life After Brown) has twelve full-time staff members who focus on career advising, pre-professional advising, employer relations, marketing, and BrownConnect, which connects current students with alumni. The 587:1 student-to-advisor ratio is slightly higher than the ratio for other schools featured in this guide. However, the LAB is extremely effective at outreach and has a measurable impact on student success.

In the 2018-19 academic year career services staff counseled 3,237 students and brought 251 employers to campus, leading to 950 job interviews. Freshmen engaged at an extremely high rate, 68 percent, which has been an institutional goal. Keeping busy, Brown manages to put on more than one hundred career programs and one hundred employer information sessions per year. Its career fairs, alumni events, and workshops drew almost 13,000. If you can name a corporation, chances are it will be visiting Providence at some point this upcoming year. Help finding internships is always available as the school provides 600+ funded opportunities per year. The CareerLAB deploys its resources well in order to meet the needs of its talented population, and it receives high praise from our staff.

Professional Outcomes

Soon after receiving their Brown diplomas, 70 percent of graduates enter the world of employment. The university has placed significant numbers of recent graduates in the top companies within the following fields: the arts (CAA, Lincoln Center), consulting (every major firm), finance (every major investment house), government (United Nations, Federal Reserve Board), technology (Amazon, all major tech companies), and the list goes on and on. Companies employing the most Brown alums all time are Google, Microsoft, Facebook, Goldman Sachs, Amazon, Morgan Stanley, Apple, McKinsey & Company, and Bain & Company. New York, Boston, Providence, San Francisco, and DC are the five cities attracting the greatest number of Brown alumni. That makes sense given that the two most popular areas of employment are in technology and finance, and many such firms are based in those urban areas. At age thirty-four Brown graduates have a median income well above that of the average college grad, but it is the lowest among Ivy League schools.

The Class of 2017 saw one-fifth of graduates go directly into graduate/professional school. Right out of undergrad Brown boasted an exceptional 92 percent admission rate to med school (the national average was 43 percent) and a 91 percent admission rate to law school (national average was 75 percent). A decade after graduating, 80 percent of Brown alumni have earned an advanced degree. Frequently attended institutions include all of the Ivies plus Stanford, Duke, Carnegie Mellon, the London School of Economics, Oxford, Johns Hopkins, Berkeley, UCLA, and UVA. In sum, you can rest assured that if you do well at Brown, there are few graduate or professional schools on the planet that will not welcome you with open arms.

Admission

In 2018, Brown accepted only 7 percent of applicants, and 96 percent of those who went on to enroll were in the top 10 percent of their high school class. A decade earlier, the admit rate was just shy of 16 percent, but it has been in the single digits since 2014. Back in 2014, the middle 25th-75th percentile range for Brown freshmen was 1330-1550 compared to the current range of 1420-1570. Even with a degree of SAT score inflation, those numbers indicate that the university has become even more competitive in recent years. Over three-quarters of freshmen in the Class of 2022 scored better than 700 on their SAT reading section and over 80 percent scored better than 700 on the math section.

The admissions office lists eight areas that are considered most important in determining admission: rigor of courses, grades, class rank, recommendations, essays, test scores, talent/ability, and character/personal qualities. In a typical year, close to half of admitted students were either the valedictorian or salutatorian of their high school class. Those applying early are accepted at a much higher rate than in the regular round. The Class of 2022 saw 732 seats filled through ED with an acceptance rate of 21 percent compared to a 6 percent acceptance rate in the regular cycle. The 737 admits account for roughly 45 percent of the total class. In short, those looking to come to Providence should be individuals at the top of their class who are intellectually curious, open-minded, and who possess intangible qualities that would allow them to flourish in Brown's unique academic program.

Worth Your Money?

With a $77,490 annual cost of attendance, Brown University will cost a great deal for anyone who does not qualify for financial aid. For the 41 percent of current students who receive need-based grants, 100 percent of their demonstrated need will be covered. That equates to an average grant of almost $50,000 per year. Despite the cost, Brown is the type of school worth its hefty price tag. Not only will the Ivy League credentials benefit you in graduate/professional school admissions and the world of employment, but the quality of the educational experience, the flexibility of your coursework, and the chance to take many small, seminar-style classes with distinguished faculty are of incredible value.

FINANCIAL
Institutional Type: Private
In-State Tuition: $57,112
Out-of-State Tuition: $57,112
Room & Board: $15,332
Required Fees: $1,292
Books & Supplies: $1,632

Avg. Need-Based Aid: $49,256
Avg. % of Need Met: 100%

Avg. Merit-Based Aid: $10,000
% Receiving Merit-Based Aid: 0%

Avg. Cumulative Debt: $29,620
% of Students Borrowing: 35%

CAREER
Who Recruits
1. Boston Consulting Group
2. Oracle
3. Millenium Management
4. BlackRock
5. Teach for America

Notable Internships
1. Google
2. Etsy
3. Apple

Top Industries
1. Business
2. Education
3. Research
4. Media
5. Engineering

Top Employers
1. Google
2. Microsoft
3. Facebook
4. Goldman Sachs
5. Amazon

Where Alumni Work
1. New York City
2. Providence
3. Boston
4. San Francisco
5. Washington, DC

Median Earnings
College Scorecard (Early Career): $67,500
EOP (Early Career): $66,900
PayScale (Mid-Career): $127,600

RANKINGS
Forbes: 7
Money: 72
U.S. News: 14, National Universities
Wall Street Journal/THE: 7 (T)
Washington Monthly: 28, National Universities

#CollegesWorthYourMoney

Bryn Mawr College

Bryn Mawr, Pennsylvania | Admissions Phone: 610-526-5152

ADMISSION

Admission Rate: 34%
Admission Rate - Men: Not Offered
Admission Rate - Women: 34%
EA Admission Rate: Not Offered
ED Admission Rate: 53%
Admission Rate (5-Year Trend): -6%
ED Admission Rate (5-Year Trend): 0%
% of Admits Attending (Yield): 36%
Transfer Admission Rate: 15%

Offered Wait List: 450
Accepted Wait List: 244
Admitted Wait List: 0

SAT Reading/Writing (Middle 50%): 660-730
SAT Math (Middle 50%): 640-770
ACT Composite (Middle 50%): 28-33
Testing Policy: Test Optional
SAT Superscore: Yes
ACT Superscore: Yes

% Graduated in Top 10% of HS Class: 59%
% Graduated in Top 25% of HS Class: 91%
% Graduated in Top 50% of HS Class: 99%

ENROLLMENT

Total Undergraduate Enrollment: 1,360
% Part-Time: 1%
% Male: 0%
% Female: 100%
% Out-of-State: 85%
% Fraternity: Not Offered
% Sorority: Not Offered
% On-Campus (Freshman): 100%
% On-Campus (All Undergraduate): 91%

% African-American: 6%
% Asian: 13%
% Hispanic: 10%
% White: 39%
% Other: 6%
% Race or Ethnicity Unknown: 6%
% International: 22%
% Low-Income: 16%

ACADEMICS

Student-to-Faculty Ratio: 9:1
% of Classes Under 20: 71%
% of Classes Under 40: 95%
% Full-Time Faculty: 81%
% Full-Time Faculty w/ Terminal Degree: 97%

Top Programs
Biology
English
Growth and Structure of Cities
History of Art
Mathematics
Physics
Psychology

Retention Rate: 92%
4-Year Graduation Rate: 79%
6-Year Graduation Rate: 87%

Curricular Flexibility: Somewhat Flexible
Academic Rating: ★★★★

Inside the Classroom

Eleven miles west of Philadelphia and situated on the swanky Main Line rests an immaculate, 135-acre campus that serves as the educational home to more than 1,300 brilliant, politically active, and fiercely independent young women. Bryn Mawr College, still an all-female institution, used to serve as the sister school to Haverford College, which was all male until the late 1970s. The two schools still retain a degree of partnership. In fact, Bryn Mawr, Haverford, and Swarthmore (collectively known as the Tri-Co) all run on the same academic calendar so students can take courses at all three schools. Additionally, Bryn Mawr undergraduates can opt to take up to two courses at Penn each semester. There are more than 3,000 cross-registrations exercised each year.

On the home campus, undergraduates can choose from thirty-six majors and forty-six minors. A phenomenal 31 percent of the student body earns degrees in the natural sciences or mathematics, a figure four times the national average for women. However, as a true liberal arts school, all students must take courses in each of Bryn Mawr's four "approaches": critical interpretation, cross-cultural analysis, inquiry into the past, and scientific investigation. Additional courses in quantitative reasoning and a full year studying one of ten foreign languages round out the mandated coursework. The college does point out that "within this structure, variety abounds," noting that students averse to the hard sciences can fulfill their scientific investigation requirement through the likes of anthropology or psychology.

A 9:1 student-to-faculty ratio leads to small class sizes with 71 percent of sections having fewer than twenty students, and 23 percent of sections enrolling nine students or fewer. This type of academic setting leads to close mentoring from professors. Over 500 undergraduates collaborate on research and independent projects with faculty each year. Those electing to study abroad have more than seventy programs to choose from and, in recent years, students have spent a semester in thirty countries across six continents.

This elite liberal arts school offers a number of excellent academic programs that receive national recognition from employers and graduate schools. By volume, the most popular majors are mathematics, psychology, sociology, English, and biology. Nationally competitive fellowship/scholarship programs also look favorably upon Bryn Mawr alumni. Recent graduates have been successful in procuring Boren, Fulbright, and Watson Fellowships.

Outside the Classroom

Bryn Mawr's breathtakingly beautiful and historic campus is where 100 percent of freshmen and 91 percent of the overall student body reside. Sororities are not permitted at Bryn Mawr as the college prefers participation in the 150 nonexclusive student organizations presently active. Clubs in music/performing arts and community service are among the most popular. Student government is also strong as elected members are dedicated to carrying out the institution's Honor Code. This is a tradition-rich school with events such as Parade Night, Lantern Night, and May Day all taken seriously by the student population. The Owls participate in twelve NCAA Division III sports, and casual athletic participation is always an option as the school boasts a 50,000-square-foot gymnasium, Olympic-size swimming pool, and outdoor tennis courts. While there is plenty to do on campus, nearby Haverford College, Swarthmore, and Villanova University provide Bryn Mawr undergrads with additional social scenes to explore. The college's proximity to Philadelphia means that restaurants, concerts, sporting events, museums, and theater are only a short drive away.

Career Services

The Career Services Department at Bryn Mawr is housed within the Leadership, Innovation, and Liberal Arts Center (LILAC). The office is staffed by seven professionals who specialize in areas like career counseling, pre-law advising, and employer relations. With a 189:1 student-to-advisor ratio, Bryn Mawr rates well above average compared to other colleges featured in this guide. That provides undergraduates with ample opportunity to work closely with a career counselor on resume development, internship hunting, and networking.

In terms of employer relations, rather than hosting their own events the college tends to rely more on partnerships with other Seven Sisters schools and the Tri-College Consortium (TCC) with Haverford and Swarthmore. The Fall Policy & Government Career Fair is held at the University of Pennsylvania and is open to members of the TCC. Spring events held at Haverford College include the Tri-College STEM Recruiting Day and the Philadelphia Career Connection that attracts forty employers. Students can find internship and job opportunities online through Handshake or via the Selective Liberal Arts Consortium that can facilitate off-campus interviews. Bryn Mawr has a low student-to-counselor ratio and has an excellent track record for helping its students gain acceptance into top graduate schools. However, its alumni salary figures lag behind its peers, and its on-campus recruiting opportunities are somewhat limited.

Professional Outcomes

One year after receiving their diplomas, 57 percent of Bryn Mawr graduates have found employment, a robust 29 percent have already entered graduate school, and 5 percent are still in the job-hunting phase. Among those who are employed, the five most popular fields are business, education, health/medicine, science, and communications/media. With graduating classes of under 400 students there are no massive numbers of alumni clustered in particular companies as is the case at many larger institutions. Most of the organizations employing the greatest number of alumni are universities and hospital systems although Google, Accenture, JPMorgan Chase, and Vanguard do employ a fair number of Bryn Mawr graduates. Median salaries by age thirty-four are on the low side by elite college standards, in part due to the heavy concentration of students pursing lengthy graduate programs. The median salary figure at the start of midcareer is $47k, significantly lower than other highly selective Pennsylvania liberal arts schools like Franklin & Marshall, Haverford, and Swarthmore, which all sport median income figures of $56k and above.

Of those pursuing further education, 63 percent were in master's programs, 10 percent in medical school, 2 percent in law school, and 13 percent were already working on their PhD. Again, due to the minuscule class sizes, it's rare that multiple graduates flock to particular institutions for graduate school. However, to get a sense of the prestigious programs accepting Bryn Mawr alumni one can simply examine the higher education destinations of members of the Class of 2017. Those included a PhD in applied physics at Rice University, a PhD in machine learning at Carnegie Mellon, and a PhD in chemistry at Princeton. Other 2017 graduates were pursuing advanced degrees at Columbia, Tufts, Yale, University of Chicago, the London School of Economics, and UVA School of Medicine.

Admission

Bryn Mawr accepts 34 percent of those who apply, making it more selective than Mount Holyoke, comparable to Smith, and a touch less selective than Barnard and Wellesley. Freshmen at Bryn Mawr possessed middle-50 percent SAT scores of 1300-1500 and 28-33 on the ACT. A healthy 59 percent finished in the top 10 percent of their high school class; 91 percent were in the top quarter. In terms of class rank/GPA, the average accepted applicant looks similar to those from five years ago. Yet, the SAT scores of admitted applicants has risen rather dramatically. In 2013, the middle-SAT range for the freshman class was 1190-1420.

The admissions office places the greatest emphasis on the rigor of an applicant's high school curriculum and recommendation letters. Grades, essays, extracurricular activities, and character/personal qualities are next. While Bryn Mawr is a test-optional school, 61 percent submitted SAT results, and 34 percent submitted ACT scores, so tests do still play a role in shaping the overall admissions picture. Early decision is the right choice for those who have the school atop their college list. Bryn Mawr fills 45 percent of its freshman class in the early round and accepts 53 percent of those who apply.

A highly selective destination point for high-achieving young women, this member of the Seven-Sisters Colleges is tougher to get into than its acceptance rate would imply. Known as a supportive, collaborative, and academically excellent school, Bryn Mawr draws brilliant and accomplished applicants from around the globe. An impressive resume is needed, and applying early can give you an edge.

Worth Your Money?

Despite a list price above $73,000, Bryn Mawr is generous with aid, leading to graduates who possess lower-than-average debt. Unusual for a school of its ilk, 27 percent of current students receive an annual merit award averaging $16k in value. A healthy 53 percent of students are found eligible for need-based aid, and 100 percent of their demonstrated need is met by the college. The average annual value of these grants is close to $44,000, helping to make Bryn Mawr more accessible to those of varying socioeconomic backgrounds.

FINANCIAL
Institutional Type: Private
In-State Tuition: $53,180
Out-of-State Tuition: $53,180
Room & Board: $17,100
Required Fees: $1,260
Books & Supplies: $1,000

Avg. Need-Based Aid: $43,903
Avg. % of Need Met: 100%

Avg. Merit-Based Aid: $15,759
% Receiving Merit-Based Aid: 27%

Avg. Cumulative Debt: $25,682
% of Students Borrowing: 51%

CAREER
Who Recruits
1. FDIC
2. Moody's Corporation
3. Philadelphia Museum of Art
4. Vanguard
5. Northwestern Mutual

Notable Internships
1. Whitney Museum of Art
2. JetBlue
3. Citi

Top Industries
1. Education
2. Business
3. Healthcare
4. Social Services
5. Media

Top Employers
1. Penn Medicine
2. Children's Hospital of Philadelphia
3. Vanguard
4. Accenture
5. Google

Where Alumni Work
1. Philadelphia
2. New York City
3. Washington, DC
4. Boston
5. San Francisco

Median Earnings
College Scorecard (Early Career): $54,600
EOP (Early Career): $47,400
PayScale (Mid-Career): $95,300

RANKINGS
Forbes: 111
Money: 370
U.S. News: 27 (T), Liberal Arts Colleges
Wall Street Journal/THE: 53
Washington Monthly: 14, Liberal Arts Colleges

#CollegesWorthYourMoney

Bucknell University

Lewisburg, Pennsylvania | Admissions Phone: 570-577-3000

Inside the Classroom

Approximately 3,600 undergraduate students grace this gorgeous, 450-acre campus in bucolic Lewisburg, Pennsylvania. While technically a "university," the number of graduate students is nominal and, academically, the school functions more as a liberal arts college with a strong engineering program. Socially, with its focus on athletics and Greek life, the "university" label may start to feel more apt.

Over fifty majors and sixty-five minors are on tap across three undergraduate schools: the College of Arts & Sciences, Freeman College of Management, and the College of Engineering. Required core curriculum coursework for A&S and Freeman is identical and must include multiple classes under the umbrella categories of intellectual skills, disciplinary perspectives, tools for critical engagement, and a culminating experience that involves research and/or independent study. The College of Engineering keeps the vast majority of its requirements concentrated in the areas of math, science, and engineering. Before classes even commence, all first-year students attend a five-day new student orientation centered around scholarship and community. Further, all freshmen take a foundation seminar course, and that instructor serves as the faculty adviser until the student declares a major in the sophomore year. That supportive environment helps the school maintain a superb 93 percent retention rate.

Getting well-acquainted with your professors is easy with a 9:1 student-faculty ratio, and class sizes are reasonably small. Slightly more than half of courses at Bucknell unfold in a classroom of no more than nineteen students, and 85 percent of all sections enroll fewer than twenty-nine students. All of Bucknell's 350 full-time professors spend some of their time teaching undergraduates. Last year, 268 students took advantage of summer research opportunities on campus. An additional 175 typically engage in research for academic credit during the regular school year. Study abroad semesters are available at over 130 sites across six continents, and 45 percent of the student body takes advantage of that.

The greatest number of degrees are conferred in the areas of the social sciences (26 percent), engineering (16 percent), business (14 percent), biology (9 percent), and psychology (6 percent). The Freeman College of Management and College of Engineering have the most prominent national reputations, but Bucknell is a well-regarded institution across the board. With a career-focused student body, this is a not a college that produces a sizable number of postgraduate fellows or scholars, but two class of 2018 Bucknell grads were awarded Fulbright Scholarships, and the school has averaged one Goldwater Scholar per year over the last five years.

Outside the Classroom

The vast majority of the student body, 92 percent, reside in university housing on campus. Many join the school's thriving Greek life with 35 percent of men and 40 percent of women becoming members of one of the school's eight fraternity or ten sorority chapters. For a university of Bucknell's modest size, athletics are massive in scale. The school fields twenty-seven teams that play in the Patriot League of NCAA Division I. The Bison men's basketball squad has appeared in the most recent March Madness tourneys, and the swimming and lacrosse teams are also strong. On top of that, intramural and club sports attract a high level of participation. Over 150 student clubs run on campus and enjoy small but loyal followings, thanks to the energy pouring into fraternities and athletics. The most popular clubs include the Black Student Union, Bucknell Outing Club, Activities & Campus Events, French Club, and Catholic Campus Ministries. Many Bucknell students also make time for volunteer work; three-quarters perform some degree of community service over the course of their four years. With no major city within a quick driving distance, students seeking some semblance of nightlife settle for Main Street in quiet Lewisburg. Central Pennsylvania does offer limitless opportunity for those who love the great outdoors with camping, hiking, kayaking, and similar activities available in abundance.

Career Services

Manned by fifteen full-time professionals with expertise in career counseling, internship coordination, and company recruitment, the Career Development Center (CDC) offers a 225:1 student-to-advisor ratio, which is better than average compared to other schools featured in this guide. Each year the CDC hosts a fall Job Expo attended by up to one hundred employers and 750 students. Attendees include corporations like Deloitte, Coca Cola, and Hershey Entertainment & Resorts. Additionally, it organizes a separate internship/job fair in the spring, the Health & Law School Fair, Engineering Career Network Event, and several off-campus events in New York and DC to afford Bucknell students the chance to meet with additional companies in the finance and government realms. More than 200 employers attend school-sponsored career fairs each year.

Corporations, including the likes of ExxonMobil and Proctor & Gamble, appear regularly on campus to conduct job interviews. In fact, recent alums listed those opportunities as the number one factor in how they secured employment. In the 2017-18 school year 670 on-campus interviews were conducted with Bucknell seniors. Annually, the CDC helps over 500 students secure summer internships, which also was cited by grads as frequently leading to their maiden jobs. All told, 71 percent of Class of 2017 graduates completed at least one internship. With generous staffing and a track record of helping students, Bucknell's career services does a strong job preparing its undergraduates for the real world.

Professional Outcomes

Nine months after graduation, 96 percent of the Class of 2018 had launched their careers or entered graduate school. Business is the most common sector for Bucknell grads to enter, and 58 percent of graduates that head directly into the working world enter corporate life. The largest concentration of recent grads can be found working at Accenture, Sloan Kettering Cancer Center, PwC, Amazon Robotics, Yelp, and Axis Group. Across all graduating years more than fifty Bucknellians are presently working at Goldman Sachs, Google, Merck, JPMorgan Chase & Co., IBM, and Johnson & Johnson. Starting salaries for recent grads are solid but highly dependent on the field of study. The mean salary for a computer science major is $85k, an accounting and financial management major takes home $63k, and those who studied education have a mean starting income of only $39k. Across all disciplines, the mean salary for a Class of 2018 grad was $60k.

The Class of 2018 saw 17 percent of diploma recipients go directly into an advanced degree program. Bison alumni heading to graduate school predominantly pursue degrees in the medical field, social sciences, or engineering. Recent graduates have found their way into top med schools (e.g., Columbia, Duke, and Johns Hopkins) and to top engineering schools (e.g., Carnegie Mellon, Princeton, Stanford). Ten percent of this group decided to pursue a legal education. Law schools attended by members of the Class of 2018 included Boston University, George Washington, and the University of California, San Diego. Geographically, most Bucknell grads remain concentrated in Pennsylvania, New York, New Jersey, and the DC metro area.

Admission

Bucknell admitted 33 percent of more than 10,144 applicants into the Class of 2022. Surprisingly, the university received more applications three years prior and had a significantly lower acceptance rate of 24.8 percent. Admission into the well-regarded engineering programs is far more difficult (24 percent acceptance rate for the Class of 2021) than it is for the College of Arts & Humanities (43 percent acceptance rate for the Class of 2021). The middle 50 percent SAT range for the Class of 2022 was 1250-1420; the ACT range was 28-32. A hefty 58 percent finished in the top 10 percent of their high school class, and 85 percent were in the top quarter. The average GPA was a 3.56, and one-third of attending students earned better than a 3.75.

Rigor of classes, GPA, test scores, and essays headline the most important factors for acceptance into Bucknell. Admissions staff members have stated that they keep a six-minute timer on their desks while they examine each application as a team. Thus, we know that your measurable achievements need to be within range in order for your intangibles/outside-the-classroom activities to become serious factors in admission. Those who apply early decision enjoy a major edge; last year, 56 percent of ED applicants were accepted compared to 31 percent in the regular round. However, it is important to point out that recruited athletes make up a good number of those early-round success stories. Being a legacy also gives you an admissions boost. The school regularly hosts events for children (or grandchildren) of alumni, and legacy students comprise 7 percent of the average freshman cohort.

Worth Your Money?

A $75,400 list price cost of attendance is made slightly less onerous by the $18,000 (on average) annual merit aid package that goes to 19 percent of undergraduates as well as the $32,000 (on average) need-based aid package that is awarded to 38 percent of current students. However, Bucknell's clientele tends to include many—an estimated 60 percent of current undergraduates come from families in the top 20 percent income-wise. Those falling in between—not qualifying for aid but not well-off enough to pay full freight—will need to consider whether their intended major/future career is likely to make loan payments worth the cost. If you were on a budget and studying to be a teacher, Bucknell may not prove a wise choice. If you were in the same financial boat but studying engineering or business, attending this school absolutely could be worth your money.

FINANCIAL
Institutional Type: Private
In-State Tuition: $57,882
Out-of-State Tuition: $57,882
Room & Board: $14,174
Required Fees: $314
Books & Supplies: $900

Avg. Need-Based Aid: $32,000
Avg. % of Need Met: 92%

Avg. Merit-Based Aid: $18,017
% Receiving Merit-Based Aid: 19%

Avg. Cumulative Debt: $31,087
% of Students Borrowing: 46%

CAREER
Who Recruits
1. Exelon
2. Horizon Media
3. Nielsen
4. Ralph Lauren
5. Southwest Airlines

Notable Internships
1. NBCUniversal
2. CBRE
3. Bloomberg LP

Top Industries
1. Business
2. Education
3. Operations
4. Finance
5. Sales

Top Employers
1. PwC
2. Deloitte
3. Morgan Stanley
4. IBM
5. Merck

Where Alumni Work
1. New York City
2. Philadelphia
3. Washington, DC
4. Boston
5. Williamsport, PA

Median Earnings
College Scorecard (Early Career): $70,800
EOP (Early Career): $71,800
PayScale (Mid-Career): $122,900

RANKINGS
Forbes: 73
Money: 185
U.S. News: 35, Liberal Arts Colleges
Wall Street Journal/THE: 74
Washington Monthly: 44, Liberal Arts Colleges

#CollegesWorthYourMoney

California Institute of Technology

Pasadena, California | Admissions Phone: 626-395-6341

ADMISSION

Admission Rate: 7%
Admission Rate - Men: 4%
Admission Rate - Women: 12%
EA Admission Rate: N/A
ED Admission Rate: Not Offered
Admission Rate (5-Year Trend): -4%
ED Admission Rate (5-Year Trend): Not Offered
% of Admits Attending (Yield): 43%
Transfer Admission Rate: 2%

Offered Wait List: 634
Accepted Wait List: 512
Admitted Wait List: 6

SAT Reading/Writing (Middle 50%): 740-780
SAT Math (Middle 50%): 790-800
ACT Composite (Middle 50%): 35-36
Testing Policy: ACT/SAT Required
SAT Superscore: Yes
ACT Superscore: Yes

% Graduated in Top 10% of HS Class: 96%
% Graduated in Top 25% of HS Class: 100%
% Graduated in Top 50% of HS Class: 100%

ENROLLMENT

Total Undergraduate Enrollment: 948
% Part-Time: 0%
% Male: 55%
% Female: 45%
% Out-of-State: 63%
% Fraternity: Not Offered
% Sorority: Not Offered
% On-Campus (Freshman): 100%
% On-Campus (All Undergraduate): 86%

% African-American: 1%
% Asian: 40%
% Hispanic: 14%
% White: 27%
% Other: 8%
% Race or Ethnicity Unknown: 0%
% International: 10%
% Low-Income: 10%

ACADEMICS

Student-to-Faculty Ratio: 3:1
% of Classes Under 20: 68%
% of Classes Under 40: 89%
% Full-Time Faculty: 89%
% Full-Time Faculty w/ Terminal Degree: 98%

Top Programs
Biology
Chemistry
Computer Science
Engineering
Geological and Planetary Sciences
Physics
Mathematics

Retention Rate: 98%
4-Year Graduation Rate: 81%
6-Year Graduation Rate: 92%

Curricular Flexibility: Somewhat Flexible
Academic Rating: ★★★★★

Inside the Classroom

The setting of television's Big Bang Theory, the California Institute of Technology is, as suggested by the show's focus on a group of socially-awkward physicists, a collection of some of the most brilliant science and engineering minds in the world. Situated in gorgeous Pasadena, California, Caltech enrolls a mere 948 undergraduates, affectionately known as "Techers," very few of whom got a single question wrong on the math portion of the SAT. As tough as it is to gain admission, coursework at the school is perhaps an even more rigorous and consuming process.

The university's common core is, not surprisingly, STEM-heavy with requirements that includes Freshman Mathematics, Freshman Physics, Freshman Chemistry, and Freshman Biology. However, students also must conquer 36 units of the humanities and social sciences, nine units of physical education, and one course in scientific communication in which undergrads write a paper for submission to a peer-reviewed academic journal. There are six academic divisions: biology and biological engineering; chemistry and chemical engineering; engineering and applied science; geological and planetary sciences; the humanities and social sciences; and physics, mathematics, and astronomy, each with more options for specialized concentrations. Across all divisions, there are thirty-two distinct majors.

Possessing an absurdly favorable 3:1 student-to-faculty ratio, plenty of individualized attention is up for grabs. Class sizes are not quite as tiny as the student-to-faculty ratio might suggest, but 68 percent of courses enroll fewer than twenty students, and 30 percent enroll fewer than ten. Summer Undergraduate Research Fellowships (SURF) enjoy wide participation with 80 percent of undergraduates partaking, and 20 percent of that group going on to publish their results. Six approved study abroad programs are available at Cambridge University, University College London, University of Edinburgh, Copenhagen University, the University of Melbourne, and Ecole Polytechnique in France.

Engineering is the most popular major, accounting for 36 percent of all degrees conferred. Computer and information science (26 percent), the physical sciences (20 percent), and mathematics (11 percent) also have strong representation. Grads find a high level of success in obtaining prestigious scholarships for graduate study including Watson, Fulbright, and Hertz Fellowships. The school also sees an incredible number of students win National Science Foundation Fellowships (the head of the organization received her PhD from Caltech). An astounding twenty-seven 2018 graduates won NSF Graduate Research Fellowships.

Outside the Classroom

Given its small undergraduate population, campus is a spacious 124 acres, and 85 percent elect to live in one of the university's eleven residences; freshmen are required to do so. Greek life was long ago banished in favor of a coeducational residential house system. Each house has its own vibe and traditions, and students go through a two-week rotation period (in place of a pledging process) to find the best fit. On the athletics front, the Beavers field nine men's and nine women's teams to compete in intercollegiate sports, mostly at the NCAA Division III level, although they are more noted for insanely long losing streaks than anything else (the baseball team once lost 228 straight games). Four-fifths of undergrads participate in some kind of organized athletics, and the high rate of involvement isn't limited to sports. Roughly 65 percent of students also play a musical instrument, and many join one of the more than one hundred student-run organizations on campus. There are plenty of pre-professional and tech-oriented club options as well as groups like Magic: The Gathering Club or the Anime Society. While students generally report that academic pursuits plus a club or two generally take up 100 percent of their waking hours at Caltech, gorgeous Pasadena and nearby downtown Los Angeles provide limitless opportunities for those seeking some degree of socialization.

Career Services

The Caltech Career Development Center has five full-time professional staff members working on career counseling, internship coordination, and employer recruiting. That equates to a 189:1 student-to-advisor ratio, which is among the best of any university featured in this guide. Caltech hosts two large career fairs per year, one in October and one in January. Anywhere from 150-200 companies attend those fairs, which is a massive number when considering the school has fewer than 1,000 undergraduates. Small events take place pretty much weekly, and samples of those regular offerings include visits from the likes of Harvard Business School, Bain & Company, Yahoo, and the Google Women's Focus Group.

California Institute of Technology

E-mail: ugadmissions@caltech.edu | Website: www.caltech.edu

Caltech students have little trouble procuring summer internships in engineering, computer science, or business/finance. Unlike most schools where undergrads compete for internships at top companies, the top companies typically have to compete to attract Caltech students. (Its website offers advice for companies in that regard.) Similarly, on-campus recruiting is strong with companies constantly visiting campus to try to snag young talent. That list includes NASA, Facebook, Goldman Sachs, Oracle, and SpaceX. Based on its low student-to-counselor ratio, prodigious on-campus recruiting efforts, placement of more math/science PhD candidates than any university in the country, and unmatched starting salaries for graduates, Caltech's Career Development Center easily earns the highest praise from the College Transitions staff.

Professional Outcomes

Caltech is a rare school that sees six-figure average starting salaries for its graduates; the class of 2017 figure was $106,000. Over 60 percent of recent grads go directly into the workforce and find homes at tech giants such as Google, Intel, Microsoft, Apple, and Facebook. Engineering students are routinely courted by the likes of Boeing, Lockheed Martin, SpaceX, and Northrup Grumman. The school also has a strong alumni representation at NASA. Those who go the academic/research route ultimately end up on the faculty at schools such as Stanford, MIT, USC, and Caltech itself. Networking as a Caltech alum is a dream. The university has 22,000 alumni, many of whom are leaders in the tech world including seventeen living Nobel Prize winners and countless founders/execs of major corporations.

Not surprisingly, the largest number of alumni remain in California, settling into careers in Silicon Valley. A healthy 35 percent of those receiving their diplomas continue directly on the higher education path, immediately entering graduate school. Caltech is the number one producer of math/science PhDs in the country. Many continue their education at Caltech or other elite STEM graduate programs. After attaining graduate degrees, careers in research and higher education are popular pursuits. While engineering is where the largest number of grads eventually land, higher education is a close second.

Admission

With an acceptance rate of 6.6 percent, Caltech occupies the same uber-selective air as MIT. Sporting a middle 50 percent SAT range of 1530-1580 and near-perfect ACT range of 35-36, it is next to impossible to gain admission without acing your standardized tests. In fact, 95 percent of accepted applicants possess a 700 or higher on the reading section of the SAT; 99.4 percent have a 700 or higher on the math portion of the exam. SAT subject test scores are just as impeccable with mid-50 percent ranges of 770-800 for the physics and biology tests, 780-800 for the chemistry exam, and 800-800 (not a typo) on math. Ninety-six percent of enrolled freshmen placed in the top 10 percent of their high school class, and 100 percent were in the top quartile.

Directly from the admissions office, five factors carry the heaviest weight in the process: rigor of secondary curriculum, standardized test scores, essay, recommendations, and character/personal qualities. Caltech does not offer early decision, but its nonbinding early action round does offer better odds of gaining acceptance. In previous cycles the regular round saw 6 percent admitted, but 12 percent of those who applied by Nov. 1 found success. Caltech is among the most competitive universities in the world and is a top choice for many of the most brilliant young minds seeking to study computer science, the hard sciences, and engineering. Flawless standardized test scores are necessary but not sufficient for admissions consideration; those whose intangibles shine brightest gain an edge in this highly competitive process.

Worth Your Money?

Anything beyond a simple "Yes" here feels superfluous but, nevertheless, we'll offer a few statistics to back up the claim. While the school rarely offers merit aid, the majority of students do not pay anything close to the almost $75,000 annual cost of attendance. Need-based aid is awarded to 53 percent of the undergraduate population and carries a mean value of $46,749. Regardless of what you have to pay to attend this institution, it will be well worth the cost. As we highlighted previously in the profile, students' average starting salaries right out of Caltech are in the six figures.

FINANCIAL
Institutional Type: Private
In-State Tuition: $52,506
Out-of-State Tuition: $52,506
Room & Board: $16,644
Required Fees: $2,594
Books & Supplies: $1,428

Avg. Need-Based Aid: $46,749
Avg. % of Need Met: 100%

Avg. Merit-Based Aid: $0
% Receiving Merit-Based Aid: 0%

Avg. Cumulative Debt: $16,337
% of Students Borrowing: 31%

CAREER
Who Recruits
1. Goldman Sachs
2. Southern California Edison
3. Amazon
4. Facebook
5. Intel

Notable Internships
1. Facebook
2. Adobe
3. Apple

Top Industries
1. Engineering
2. Business
3. Research
4. Education
5. Information Technology

Top Employers
1. Northrop Grumman
2. Google
3. Boeing
4. NASA Jet Propulsion Laboratory
5. Apple

Where Alumni Work
1. Los Angeles
2. San Francisco
3. New York City
4. Boston
5. San Diego

Median Earnings
College Scorecard (Early Career): $85,900
EOP (Early Career): $83,000
PayScale (Mid-Career): $151,600

RANKINGS
Forbes: 8
Money: 16
U.S. News: 12, National Universities
Wall Street Journal/THE: 5 (T)
Washington Monthly: 73, National Universities

#CollegesWorthYourMoney

California Polytechnic State University, San Luis Obispo

San Luis Obispo, California | Admissions Phone: 805-756-2311

ADMISSION
Admission Rate: 30%
Admission Rate - Men: 26%
Admission Rate - Women: 35%
EA Admission Rate: Not Offered
ED Admission Rate: Not Offered
Admission Rate (5-Year Trend): -4%
ED Admission Rate (5-Year Trend): Not Offered
% of Admits Attending (Yield): 27%
Transfer Admission Rate: 16%

Offered Wait List: 6,643
Accepted Wait List: N/A
Admitted Wait List: 2,436

SAT Reading/Writing (Middle 50%): 620-700
SAT Math (Middle 50%): 620-730
ACT Composite (Middle 50%): 26-32
Testing Policy: ACT/SAT Required
SAT Superscore: Yes
ACT Superscore: Yes

% Graduated in Top 10% of HS Class: 59%
% Graduated in Top 25% of HS Class: 89%
% Graduated in Top 50% of HS Class: 99%

ENROLLMENT
Total Undergraduate Enrollment: 21,037
% Part-Time: 4%
% Male: 52%
% Female: 48%
% Out-of-State: 14%
% Fraternity: 7%
% Sorority: 11%
% On-Campus (Freshman): 91%
% On-Campus (All Undergraduate): 32%

% African-American: 1%
% Asian: 13%
% Hispanic: 17%
% White: 54%
% Other: 8%
% Race or Ethnicity Unknown: 4%
% International: 2%
% Low-Income: 19%

ACADEMICS
Student-to-Faculty Ratio: 19:1
% of Classes Under 20: 15%
% of Classes Under 40: 74%
% Full-Time Faculty: 64%
% Full-Time Faculty w/ Terminal Degree: 75%

Top Programs
Agricultural Business
Biological Sciences
Civil Engineering
Computer Science
Electrical Engineering
Industrial Engineering
Mechanical Engineering

Retention Rate: 94%
4-Year Graduation Rate: 48%
6-Year Graduation Rate: 82%

Curricular Flexibility: Less Flexible
Academic Rating: ★★★

Inside the Classroom

Nestled between San Francisco and Los Angeles, California Polytechnic State University-San Luis Obispo is the more competitive of the state's two public polytechnic schools, Pomona being the less selective branch. Home to more than 21,000 undergraduate students, Cal Poly churns out a jaw-dropping number of engineers each year, but it is far from a unidimensional university.

Cal Poly is comprised of six undergraduate schools: the College of Agriculture, Food & Environmental Sciences, College of Architecture & Environmental Design, College of Engineering, College of Liberal Arts, College of Science & Mathematics, and the Orfalea College of Business. Across all divisions there are sixty-three majors and eighty-four minors offered. While academic requirements vary by college and program, there are a number of general graduation must-haves that apply to all Mustangs. They include seventy-two units of general education, demonstration of writing competency, and the completion of a senior project.

You won't find many small, liberal-arts-style learning spaces—only 3 percent of classes have a single-digit enrollment. Yet you also won't find many classes that enroll one hundred or more students; only 4 percent do. The majority of courses, 59 percent, fall between twenty and forty students. Cal Poly's student-to-faculty ratio is a high 19:1, but such is the cost of an uber-affordable STEM degree from an excellent institution. Still, faculty receive extremely favorable reviews for their accessibility, and opportunities to work intimately with professors are built into the curriculum in many programs. For example, all students in the College of Science & Mathematics are required to participate in faculty-directed research and complete a senior project in order to graduate. More than 20 percent of students take advantage of the school's robust study abroad program that offers learning opportunities in over seventy-five countries.

The School of Engineering is the university's crown jewel. Over one-quarter of all degrees conferred (27 percent) are in engineering, and Cal Poly gets recognition in many specialty areas of the field including industrial engineering, mechanical engineering, aerospace engineering, computer engineering, and civil engineering. The Orfalea College of Business also receives strong national recognition and is recognized as one of the better ROI business degrees one can find; 13 percent of undergrads earn a business degree. Other popular majors include agriculture (12 percent), biology (6 percent), architecture (5 percent), and the social sciences (5 percent).

Outside the Classroom

While more students are living on campus than ever—the university has added 5,600 beds since 2003—only 32 percent of undergraduates presently reside on campus. Eleven percent of men and 8 percent of women sign up for Greek life. However, thirty-six of the school's sororities and fraternities were suspended in the spring of 2018 for racial insensitivity, leaving the future of Cal Poly Greek life in question. With twenty-one NCAA Division I sports on tap, there is always an opportunity to cheer on the Mustangs. Across all men's and women's sports, Cal Poly squads have captured fifty Big West Conference championships. Twenty-seven club sports, from rodeo to surfing, are available, and massive intramural program attracts 10,000 participants each year. There are an additional 300 student-run clubs, including a heavy dose of pre-professional organizations. San Luis Obispo is known as "The Happiest City in America" for a reason. Located on the coast, students have access to the beach and the natural beauty of Big Falls Trail. Outdoor concerts, an art museum, and the Thursday night farmer's market offer a taste of the effervescence of the surrounding town known as SLO Cal.

Career Services

The Cal Poly Career Services Office has eighteen full-time professional staff members working on career counseling, employer relations, and employer recruiting. That includes two counselors—the Freshman Focus Team—who are dedicated solely to first-year students. Overall, the school's 1,184:1 student-to-advisor ratio does not fare well against other colleges featured in this guide. In spite of the high student-to-counselor ratio, the office does accomplish impressive things on behalf of students. Each year Cal Poly hosts ten major career fairs, including three large, non-major-specific events in the fall, winter, and spring that draw 150+ employers each. Additional fairs cover fields that include teaching, architecture and environmental design, computing, and construction management.

A survey of recent graduates revealed that among those already employed, 43 percent attributed obtaining employment directly to the Career Services Office. An additional 22 percent cited MustangJOBS, the office's online database of employment opportunities, and 9 percent were offered employment after an internship experience while in undergrad. An impressive 97 percent of graduates ended up in jobs related to their major. Such success is not merely a byproduct of producing highly employable STEM graduates. Amazingly, the Freshman Focus Team engaged 100 percent of the 4,451 first-year students in over 6,000 counseling sessions. Further, the office has forged official employer/university partnerships with 334 companies, creating excellent networks for current undergrads to lean on while pursuing employment.

California Polytechnic State University, San Luis Obispo

E-mail: admissions@calpoly.edu | Website: www.calpoly.edu

Professional Outcomes

Within nine months of graduating, 99 percent of job-seeking Cal Poly grads have secured employment; 72 percent already have a job offer by the time they complete their degrees. Top employers of Cal Poly grads include many of the top tech/consulting/engineering/financial firms in the country such as Google, Deloitte, KPMG, Microsoft, Northrup Grumman, Adobe, EY, and Apple. Overall, grads enjoy an average starting salary of $62,000. Engineering majors lead the way at $72,000 while liberal arts grads bring in a median income of only $44,000. Given that the in-state tuition is under $10K per year, this makes the university one of the best ROI schools in the country. An overwhelming majority, 88 percent, remain in California upon graduation. Washington, Colorado, and Texas are next three most popular destinations.

Of the 15 percent of alumni who directly enter graduate school, the six most commonly attended schools are all in California. By far the greatest number continue their studies at Cal Poly. UC Davis, USC, UC San Diego, San Jose State, and Berkeley also draw more than a handful of graduates each year. Many graduates of the Orfalea College of Business pursue master's degrees in accounting. The highest number of engineering students pursued MBAs or master's degrees in specific branches of engineering. Pursuing a legal education is a frequent choice of liberal arts graduates, and the University of San Diego, USC, and UCLA are the most commonly attended law schools.

Admission

Cal Poly accepted 30 percent of the nearly 55,000 freshmen applicants and 16 percent of the almost 11,000 transfer students who applied in 2018. Like many California public universities, Cal Poly has become more competitive in recent years. While acceptance rates have remained steady, other indicators strongly suggest this trend. A startling 10,000 students with 4.0 GPAs (or higher) were denied entry to the Class of 2022. Mid-50 percent standardized test scores were 1240-1430 on the SAT and 26-32 on the ACT. Fifty-nine percent of freshmen entering in 2018-19 claimed a spot in the top 10 percent of their high school class, and 89 percent were in the top quartile. Five years ago, those numbers were all significantly lower.

Freshman applicants apply to one of six colleges within the university, and some are more competitive than others. For example, the acceptance rate into the College of Engineering is 23 percent, and the average SAT of an admitted student is 1481. Those aiming for the School of Agriculture, Food & Environmental Sciences enjoy a 44 percent acceptance rate and average a significantly lower 1325 on the SAT. No matter the college to which you apply, Cal Poly is mainly interested in three factors when making admissions decisions: the rigor of your secondary curriculum, GPA, and standardized test scores. Things like extracurricular activities, work experience, and first-generation status also carry a small amount of weight. Getting into Cal Poly is a straightforward, albeit increasingly challenging proposition. Candidates with a sparkling transcript and SATs north of 1350 should fare well. Those aiming to study engineering, business, or science and mathematics will need stronger credentials than those applying to other colleges.

Worth Your Money?

Annual in-state tuition and fees to attend Cal Poly remain below five figures, an astounding value in today's higher education marketplace. Including room, board, and all other expenses, the cost of attendance for California residents sits at $28,988. Out-of-staters pay an annual COA of under $43,000, not at all an unreasonable sum for the quality of education one will receive at this university. The school does not award large sums of need-based or merit-based aid; however, the net price most students pay still remains relatively low given the school's modest sticker price.

FINANCIAL
Institutional Type: Public
In-State Tuition: $5,742
Out-of-State Tuition: $17,622
Room & Board: $13,796
Required Fees: $4,074
Books & Supplies: $1,941

Avg. Need-Based Aid: $3,442
Avg. % of Need Met: 56%

Avg. Merit-Based Aid: $1,561
% Receiving Merit-Based Aid: 26%

Avg. Cumulative Debt: $22,298
% of Students Borrowing: 42%

CAREER
Who Recruits
1. Lockheed Martin
2. NBCUniversal
3. Greystar
4. The Raymond Group
5. Cushman & Wakefield

Notable Internships
1. Nike
2. EY
3. Oracle

Top Industries
1. Business
2. Engineering
3. Operations
4. Education
5. Sales

Top Employers
1. Apple
2. Google
3. Cisco
4. Oracle
5. Amazon

Where Alumni Work
1. San Francisco
2. San Luis Obispo, CA
3. Los Angeles
4. San Diego
5. Orange County, CA

Median Earnings
College Scorecard (Early Career): $66,900
EOP (Early Career): $55,100
PayScale (Mid-Career): $119,500

RANKINGS
Forbes: 115
Money: 75
U.S. News: 4, Regional West
Wall Street Journal/THE: 193 (T)
Washington Monthly: N/A

#CollegesWorthYourMoney

Carleton College

Northfield, Massachusetts | Admissions Phone: 507-222-4190

ADMISSION
Admission Rate: 20%
Admission Rate - Men: 19%
Admission Rate - Women: 20%
EA Admission Rate: Not Offered
ED Admission Rate: 26%
Admission Rate (5-Year Trend): -1%
ED Admission Rate (5-Year Trend): -4%
% of Admits Attending (Yield): 38%
Transfer Admission Rate: 10%

Offered Wait List: 1,486
Accepted Wait List: 556
Admitted Wait List: 34

SAT Reading/Writing (Middle 50%): 670-750
SAT Math (Middle 50%): 680-780
ACT Composite (Middle 50%): 31-34
Testing Policy: ACT/SAT Required
SAT Superscore: Yes
ACT Superscore: No

% Graduated in Top 10% of HS Class: 79%
% Graduated in Top 25% of HS Class: 96%
% Graduated in Top 50% of HS Class: 100%

ENROLLMENT
Total Undergraduate Enrollment: 2,097
% Part-Time: 1%
% Male: 50%
% Female: 50%
% Out-of-State: 84%
% Fraternity: Not Offered
% Sorority: Not Offered
% On-Campus (Freshman): 100%
% On-Campus (All Undergraduate): 96%

% African-American: 5%
% Asian: 8%
% Hispanic: 8%
% White: 58%
% Other: 7%
% Race or Ethnicity Unknown: 1%
% International: 11%
% Low-Income: 11%

ACADEMICS
Student-to-Faculty Ratio: 9:1
% of Classes Under 20: 70%
% of Classes Under 40: 99%
% Full-Time Faculty: 80%
% Full-Time Faculty w/ Terminal Degree: 97%

Top Programs
Biology
Chemistry
Computer Science
Economics
Geology
History
Mathematics
Political Science

Retention Rate: 97%
4-Year Graduation Rate: 88%
6-Year Graduation Rate: 93%

Curricular Flexibility: Somewhat Flexible
Academic Rating: ★★★★↙

Inside the Classroom

One of the top liberal arts schools (if not the top) in the Midwest, Carleton has the reputation as a destination point for studious young people who love to learn for learning's sake. Located in fairly remote Northfield, Minnesota, the college still manages to be a magnet for the academically gifted and intellectually curious from coast to coast. Carleton is a small institution of just over 2,100 undergraduate students. It offers thirty-four majors, the most popular of which are within the disciplines of the social sciences (29 percent), biology (15 percent), English (6 percent), and computer science (5 percent).

Mandated coursework is extensive and includes an argument and inquiry seminar for first-year students, a global citizenship requirement, a class in international studies as well as domestic studies, and three writing-intensive courses. Undergrads also must take a stroll through the usual liberal arts categories of humanistic inquiry, literary/artistic analysis, the arts, science, statistics, and social inquiry. All of this is done via three ten-week terms per academic year during which most students take only three courses per term.

Students work closely with their professors, and the college is routinely rated atop lists of best undergraduate teaching institutions. Small classes are the norm with the average being only sixteen students; in almost one-quarter of your classes you will be surrounded by no more than eight of your peers. Faculty-mentored research is embedded into many courses, independent study opportunities abound, and full-time supervised research is available during summer and winter break. Over three-quarters of the student body elect to study abroad in one of 130 programs offered in sixty countries. Furthermore, 100 percent of students in the Class of 2017 majoring in a foreign language, art history, dance, and photography spent a semester studying in another part of the globe.

All academic programs at this elite liberal arts school are well regarded, particularly by other universities where an exceptional percentage of Carleton grads later pursue doctoral degrees (more on this below). Consistently named a top producer of Fulbright Scholars, the college enjoyed ten award recipients in 2019. The Peace Corps also ranked Carleton thirteenth on its list of Top Volunteer-Producing (small) Colleges.

Outside the Classroom

With 92 percent of students living on campus and no Greek life at Carleton, the dorms take on the role as the preferred social setting. Fourteen theme houses also play a big role on campus, allowing people with aligned interests to live communally. Those include the WHOA House for campus activists, the Culinary House for those committed to gastronomic pursuits, and the Q&A House for the LBGTQA community. Over 200 student-run clubs offer a multitude of niche activities to suit this fairly eclectic student body. The Ravens' eighteen varsity athletic teams are split evenly between men and women, and they all compete in NCAA Division III. Club and intramural sports are popular with ultimate Frisbee in the lead by a wide margin. Northfield is a small town, but it has its share of social/cultural offerings as well as neighboring St. Olaf's College, which opens additional social opportunities. Those looking for more action than Northfield can provide will be pleased to find the bustle of Minneapolis and St. Paul, both less than fifty miles away. Students seeking natural beauty do not have to look any further than the on-campus Cowling Arboretum, a 900-acre wooded area perfect for hiking or cross-country skiing.

Career Services

The Career Center is staffed by ten full-time professionals, just about all of whom have director, assistant director, or manager in their title. However, at such a small school most of these individuals do work directly with students in some capacity, and that results in a student-to-advisor ratio of 210:1, significantly better than the average institution included in this book.

The major career/internship/graduate school fairs that are open to Carleton students are joint efforts with other Minnesota-based universities, yet many companies, nonprofits, and government entities do make the trip to Northfield to directly recruit this talented cohort of undergraduates. Those companies include Amazon, Ernst & Young, Facebook, Google, and Microsoft. The 30 Minutes Program brings current students face-to-face with alums who work in a field of interest for quick (hence the name) informational/networking sessions. Externships with alumni allow students to shadow alumni in their place of employment for one to three weeks. Alumni remain extremely engaged with the school as evidenced by an extremely high percentage who donate. The area in which the career services office truly excels is advising students on graduate school pathways, an area we will explore further in a moment.

E-mail: admissions@carleton.edu | Website: www.carleton.edu

Professional Outcomes

Carleton does not track the activities of every graduating class, but when it last administered a senior survey in 2016, nearly three-quarters of soon-to-be grads were headed into the workforce with the most common job functions being business analyst, project manager, research assistant/associate, software engineer, and medical scribe. There are thirty-five companies that employ more than ten Carleton alums. Many are prestigious academic institutions including the University of Chicago, the University of Michigan, Colombia, Stanford, Northwestern, and Penn; the University of Minnesota is the largest employer of Knights with over 160 alumni in its ranks. Target, Epic Systems, UnitedHealth Group, Wells Fargo, Amazon, 3M, and Facebook all employ more than twenty-five alumni. Geographically, the greatest number of students remain in the Minneapolis-St. Paul area, but many also head to New York City, San Francisco, Chicago, DC, Boston, Seattle, and Los Angeles.

Carleton is a breeding ground for future scholars as a ridiculously high number of graduates go on to earn PhDs. In fact, by percentage, Carleton is one of the top ten producers of any college or university in the country of PhDs in economics, math, political science, sociology, chemistry, physics, biology, and history. In recent years 20-25 percent of graduates immediately entered graduate school; within ten years, 75 percent of graduates have enrolled in or completed an advanced degree program. Such a focus on time-consuming scholarly pursuits helps explain why Carleton graduates have a median income of $52,000 at age thirty-four, a fairly low figure when measured against other elite colleges.

Admission

The 7,100 applications submitted for the Class of 2022 doesn't sound like an overwhelming number, but for tiny Carleton, that figure represented a 9 percent increase from the previous year. Only 20 percent of those applicants received an offer of admission. That was only a slight decrease from the admit rates of the previous five years. Those presently enrolled at Carleton almost exclusively finished near the top of their high school classes; 79 percent of those admitted into the 2018-19 freshman class were in the top 10 percent, and the school typically attracts around fifty National Merit Scholars each cycle. The 25th percentile SAT score was 1350, and the 75th percentile marker was 1530. A larger number of applicants submitted ACT scores to Carleton with a middle-50 percent range of 31-34. Many members of the Class of 2022 also were active in their high school communities; 58 percent played varsity sports, 43 percent studied music, and an overwhelming 83 percent participated in some type of volunteer work.

The college lists three factors as the most significant in the admissions process: rigor of secondary curriculum, GPA, and class rank. Yet, excellent standardized test scores seem to be a prerequisite as 83 percent of enrolling students possess an ACT above 30, and 70 percent scored better than a 700 on the math section of the SAT. With such a low number of applications, those from remote areas of the country may particularly benefit from the quest for geographic diversity; thirteen US states sent 0-1 student to Carleton in 2017. Early decision can also provide a major advantage to those targeting the college as their number one choice. With two rounds of early decision offered, in a typical year Carleton fills 43 percent of its incoming class via ED. Yet, the acceptance rate isn't all that encouraging, as they admitted only 27 percent of ED students in 2018. Carleton is among the most highly selective liberal arts colleges not located on the East or West coasts. Its remote location keeps application numbers in check, but the applicant pool tends to be self-selecting.

Worth Your Money?

With little merit aid and a $73,500 estimated annual cost of attendance, there are many Carleton students who will be paying $294,000 for their bachelor's degree. The good news is that current undergraduates with demonstrated financial need see 100 percent of that need met, which averages to a $44,774 grant. Fifty-five percent of the student body comes from families without need, and most of those families will pay the sticker price, as Carleton offers little in the way of merit aid. While Carleton's excellence isn't directly reflected in the early-to-mid career salaries of its graduates, the tiny classes, professor quality, extensive career services, and preparation for those aiming for prestigious graduate schools makes this school very much worth your money.

FINANCIAL
Institutional Type: Private
In-State Tuition: $56,778
Out-of-State Tuition: $56,778
Room & Board: $14,658
Required Fees: $333
Books & Supplies: $866

Avg. Need-Based Aid: $43,187
Avg. % of Need Met: 100%

Avg. Merit-Based Aid: $4,174
% Receiving Merit-Based Aid: 8%

Avg. Cumulative Debt: $21,020
% of Students Borrowing: 42%

CAREER
Who Recruits
1. U.S. Bank
2. Anderson Corporation
3. Lewin Group
4. SPS Commerce
5. UnitedHealth Group

Notable Internships
1. Moody's Analytics
2. Smithsonian
3. Federal Rserve Bank of St. Louis

Top Industries
1. Education
2. Business
3. Research
4. Social Services
5. Media

Top Employers
1. Google
2. Epic
3. UnitedHealth Group
4. Target
5. Wells Fargo

Where Alumni Work
1. Minneapolis
2. New York City
3. San Francisco
4. Chicago
5. Washington, DC

Median Earnings
College Scorecard (Early Career): $54,200
EOP (Early Career): $51,700
PayScale (Mid-Career): $109,900

RANKINGS
Forbes: 52
Money: 267
U.S. News: 7, Liberal Arts Colleges
Wall Street Journal/THE: 40
Washington Monthly: 24, Liberal Arts Colleges

#CollegesWorthYourMoney

Carnegie Mellon University

Pittsburgh, Pennsylvania | Admissions Phone: 412-268-2082

ADMISSION
Admission Rate: 17%
Admission Rate - Men: 13%
Admission Rate - Women: 24%
EA Admission Rate: Not Offered
ED Admission Rate: 21%
Admission Rate (5-Year Trend): -8%
ED Admission Rate (5-Year Trend): -12%
% of Admits Attending (Yield): 38%
Transfer Admission Rate: 7%

Offered Wait List: 3,677
Accepted Wait List: 2,310
Admitted Wait List: 109

SAT Reading/Writing (Middle 50%): 700-750
SAT Math (Middle 50%): 750-800
ACT Composite (Middle 50%): 33-35
Testing Policy: ACT/SAT Required
SAT Superscore: Yes
ACT Superscore: No

% Graduated in Top 10% of HS Class: 87%
% Graduated in Top 25% of HS Class: 97%
% Graduated in Top 50% of HS Class: 100%

ENROLLMENT
Total Undergraduate Enrollment: 6,947
% Part-Time: 4%
% Male: 50%
% Female: 50%
% Out-of-State: 86%
% Fraternity: 16%
% Sorority: 11%
% On-Campus (Freshman): 100%
% On-Campus (All Undergraduate): 58%

% African-American: 4%
% Asian: 30%
% Hispanic: 9%
% White: 26%
% Other: 4%
% Race or Ethnicity Unknown: 6%
% International: 22%
% Low-Income: 13%

ACADEMICS
Student-to-Faculty Ratio: 13:1
% of Classes Under 20: 66%
% of Classes Under 40: 84%
% Full-Time Faculty: 96%
% Full-Time Faculty w/ Terminal Degree: 93%

Top Programs
Artificial Intelligence
Business Administration
Computer Science
Economics
Engineering
Information Systems
Mathematical Sciences
Statistics

Retention Rate: 97%
4-Year Graduation Rate: 75%
6-Year Graduation Rate: 89%

Curricular Flexibility: Somewhat Flexible
Academic Rating: ★★★★✓

Inside the Classroom

Founded by steel baron Andrew Carnegie in 1900 as an eponymous technical school, CMU's rise to its present position as one of the best research universities in the country is as much a Horatio Alger story as that of its original namesake. Despite its humble roots and gradual ascension into a regional powerhouse, Carnegie Mellon today is home to 6,900 brilliant undergrads and an additional 7,600 graduate students who come from all over the world to reap the benefits of a top-notch educational experience.

Carnegie Mellon is unique in a number of ways; it is both highly segmented by area of study and, at the same time, interdisciplinary. Students are admitted to one of six colleges: the College of Engineering, College of Fine Arts, Dietrich College of Humanities and Social Science (which houses the popular information systems program), Mellon College of Science, Tepper School of Business, and the School of Computer Science. There are a combined ninety undergraduate majors available across the six schools, but young people simply do not come to CMU as "undecided." CMU students are expected to be well-rounded, and that philosophy is reflected in departmental requirements. For example, Dietrich students are required to take courses on data and computer science as freshmen, and students in the College of Engineering must take courses in writing and expression and foreign language.

Impressive, particularly for a school with more graduate students than undergrads and a good but less-than-tiny 13:1 student-to-faculty ratio. class sizes are small with 28 percent containing single digits and two-thirds having an enrollment of nineteen or fewer. In the 2018-19 school year 823 undergraduates conducted research through the University Research Office, and many others participated through various outside arrangements. Between 500-600 students study abroad for a semester each year in such countries as Japan, China, and Germany.

The most commonly conferred degrees are in engineering (25 percent), computer science (13 percent), business (10 percent), mathematics (10 percent), and visual and performing arts (10 percent). CMU boasts a number of programs that have a stellar worldwide reputation. In fact, it's hard to think of a university that accrues such high praise across such a broad spectrum of disciplines. The School of Computer Science is one of the best in the country, perennially ranked right next to (or above) the likes of MIT, Caltech, and Stanford. Also of note, it enrolls women at two or three times the national average. Tepper is recognized as one of the top undergraduate business schools by corporations around the globe. The drama program is a constant producer of top talent and, amazingly, in 2016 seven alumni were nominated for Tony Awards. The School of Engineering and the information technology program are also regulars in any top ten list. In the last five years CMU students also have captured thirty Fulbright Scholarships, six Goldwater Scholarships, and two Churchill Scholarships.

Outside the Classroom

CMU undergrads are known for being so consumed with academics that some might ask, "What life outside the classroom?" Yet, there is plenty of activity, both on campus and in the surrounding Oakland section of Pittsburgh. All freshmen, and 58 percent of the entire student body, live on campus. There are over 280 student organizations including the famed Scotch'n'Soda, one of the oldest student theater groups in the country. It regularly puts on professional quality plays and musicals. More than sixty of the clubs on campus are pre-professional in focus, such as the popular Society of Women Engineers, but there are plenty of options in the LGBTQ, spiritual, tech-hobby realms as well. Fraternities and sororities have twenty-three chapters on campus, and a substantial but not overwhelming 16 percent of men and 11 percent of women participate in Greek life. Star speakers from all walks of life can frequently be heard on CMU's campus. Attending sports events is not among the most favored CMU pastimes, but the Tartans do compete in eight men's and nine women's sports in NCAA Division III. Plenty of club sports are available as well including badminton, cricket, and Alpine skiing.

Career Services

The Career and Professional Development Center at Carnegie Mellon produces enviable results for its students. A fantastically high number of graduates find their first jobs through internships (26 percent), career fairs (14 percent), Handshake (12 percent), or directly through their career advisor (11 percent). The university pours ample resources into career services, employing twenty-seven full-time consultants, experiential learning coordinators, and employee relations specialists. That equates to a student-to-advisor ratio of 257:1, which is better than average when compared to the other institutions included in this book.

The office does a strong job of engaging with students, whether in person or virtually. Over three-quarters of undergrads login to Handshake to view the roughly 12,000 job and 5,000 internship postings. Many job search-related events focus on specific sectors such as the Civil & Environmental Engineering Career Fair, Energy Industry Career Fair, or Tepper Meetup (for business students). Those events have corporate partnerships with a number of top companies that recruit on campus including Google, Facebook, Uber, Microsoft, Apple, and Salesforce. Multiple members of each class intern at companies that include Amazon, Deloitte, and JP Morgan Chase. In 2018-19, an impressive 488 companies recruited at the university and conducted 5,900 on-campus interviews. Close to 80 percent of undergraduates complete at least one internship. Possessing a heavy arsenal of industry connections and hands-on offerings, CMU's Career and Professional Development Center provides exemplary service to its undergraduates.

Professional Outcomes

By the end of the calendar year in which they received their diplomas, 64 percent of grads were employed, and 23 percent were continuing to graduate school. The companies that have routinely scooped up CMU grads include Google, Facebook, Microsoft, Uber, Apple, Disney Research, McKinsey, and Deloitte as well as Pittsburgh-based PNC Bank. Starting salaries for CMU grads are exceptionally high, due in part, of course, to the high number of engineering and computer science diplomas it awards, yet all Tartans tend to do well financially. With an average starting salary of almost $85,000, CMU grads outpace the average starting salary for a college grad nationally ($51k) by a wide margin. Some majors offer even better remuneration, such as computer science ($114k), electrical and computer engineering ($107k), information systems ($90k), and business ($77k). While some do remain in Pittsburgh, graduates flock in large numbers to San Francisco, New York, and DC.

Of those pursuing graduate education, 20 percent enrolled immediately in PhD programs. A perusal of the schools where recent grads have decided to continue their education is a who's who of the Ivy League and includes MIT, Caltech, and Stanford as well as Carnegie Mellon itself (a popular choice). In 2018-19, there were fifty-nine CMU applicants to medical school. Recent grads have gone on to medical institutions at Harvard, Rutgers, Temple, UMass, and SUNY Downstate Medical Center. Those entering law school are currently studying at elite schools including UVA, Columbia, Penn, Yale, and Georgetown.

Admission

Carnegie Mellon received more than 24,000 applications in 2018, a 19 percent increase over the previous year and almost double the number that applied a decade ago. The overall acceptance rate for the Class of 2022 was 17 percent, however, since applicants apply to one of the six schools within the university, it's essential to examine a school-specific breakdown. Further, those applying to the College of Fine Arts (CFA) must indicate their intended area of study from six choices. Acceptance rates vary greatly from program to program. For example, in 2018-19 only 5 percent of applicants were accepted into the School of Computer Science (SCS) while 14 percent were accepted into the Dietrich College of Humanities and Social Sciences (DC). Within the DC, School of Architecture applicants enjoyed a robust 27 percent admit rate while among School of Drama applicants the percent admitted was an infinitesimal 4 percent. You can apply to more than one program at CMU, but you must fill out separate applications, pay the fee for each, and meet the unique requirements for every school you apply to.

The 50 percent SAT range for students admitted into the CFA was 1330-1510; for the SCS it as a markedly more competitive 1530-1580. The average GPA across all schools is 3.84 on a 4.0 scale. Successful applicants to CMU have taken the most rigorous high school schedules available to them, and the school also lists work experience, volunteer work, and extracurriculars among the most important factors for admission. Additionally, it is worth highlighting the fact that women fared much better than their male counterparts, being admitted at a 24 percent rate versus less than 13 percent for men. One almost needs a degree in applying to Carnegie Mellon in order to apply to Carnegie Mellon. It is a complicated process, and each program has highly specific requirements and greatly varying standards for admission, but excellent grades in honors and AP courses and excellent-to-near perfect SAT/ACT scores are pretty much prerequisites for consideration.

Worth Your Money?

A Carnegie Mellon education carries an annual cost of attendance of $74,000 that, for most attendees (except fine arts and many humanities students), will be less than their starting salary when they graduate. Rare for a school of its caliber, CMU does offer merit aid to 12 percent of the undergraduate population with the average award being $15k per year. While it does not meet 100 percent of the demonstrated financial aid for all qualifying students, the 39 percent of students who receive financial aid see grants averaging $43k. With few exceptions, a degree from Carnegie Mellon is worth taking on a bit of debt. The average amount owed by graduates is just shy of $28,000, slightly less than the average college debt nationwide.

FINANCIAL
Institutional Type: Private
In-State Tuition: $55,816
Out-of-State Tuition: $55,816
Room & Board: $14,972
Required Fees: $1,303
Books & Supplies: $2,400

Avg. Need-Based Aid: $43,090
Avg. % of Need Met: 97%

Avg. Merit-Based Aid: $15,308
% Receiving Merit-Based Aid: 12%

Avg. Cumulative Debt: $27,818
% of Students Borrowing: 59%

CAREER
Who Recruits
1. PNC
2. Uber
3. Epic
4. Google
5. Goldman Sachs

Notable Internships
1. GoDaddy
2. Microsoft
3. Chicago Trading Company

Top Industries
1. Engineering
2. Business
3. Education
4. Information Technology
5. Research

Top Employers
1. Google
2. Microsoft
3. Facebook
4. Amazon
5. Apple

Where Alumni Work
1. Pittsburgh
2. San Francisco
3. New York City
4. Washington, DC
5. Boston

Median Earnings
College Scorecard (Early Career): $83,600
EOP (Early Career): $78,400
PayScale (Mid-Career): $136,100

RANKINGS
Forbes: 37
Money: 120
U.S. News: 25, National Universities
Wall Street Journal/THE: 25 (T)
Washington Monthly: 89, National Universities

#CollegesWorthYourMoney

Case Western Reserve University

Cleveland, Ohio | Admissions Phone: 216-368-4450

ADMISSION

Admission Rate: 29%
Admission Rate - Men: 29%
Admission Rate - Women: 30%
EA Admission Rate: 36%
ED Admission Rate: 42%
Admission Rate (5-Year Trend): -13%
ED Admission Rate (5-Year Trend): Previously
Not Offered
% of Admits Attending (Yield): 18%
Transfer Admission Rate: 23%

Offered Wait List: 9,908
Accepted Wait List: N/A
Admitted Wait List: 0

SAT Reading/Writing (Middle 50%): 650-730
SAT Math (Middle 50%): 700-790
ACT Composite (Middle 50%): 30-34
Testing Policy: ACT/SAT Required
SAT Superscore: Yes
ACT Superscore: Yes

% Graduated in Top 10% of HS Class: 66%
% Graduated in Top 25% of HS Class: 92%
% Graduated in Top 50% of HS Class: 99%

ENROLLMENT

Total Undergraduate Enrollment: 5,262
% Part-Time: 3%
% Male: 55%
% Female: 45%
% Out-of-State: 72%
% Fraternity: 28%
% Sorority: 36%
% On-Campus (Freshman): 97%
% On-Campus (All Undergraduate): 80%

% African-American: 4%
% Asian: 21%
% Hispanic: 8%
% White: 47%
% Other: 5%
% Race or Ethnicity Unknown: 1%
% International: 14%
% Low-Income: 20%

ACADEMICS

Student-to-Faculty Ratio: 11:1
% of Classes Under 20: 59%
% of Classes Under 40: 83%
% Full-Time Faculty: 78%
% Full-Time Faculty w/ Terminal Degree: 92%

Top Programs
Accounting
Biochemistry
Biology
Biomedical Engineering
Business Management
Electrical Engineering
Nursing

Retention Rate: 94%
4-Year Graduation Rate: 65%
6-Year Graduation Rate: 85%

Curricular Flexibility: Somewhat Flexible
Academic Rating: ★★★★

Inside the Classroom

A private, midsize institution in Cleveland, Ohio, Case Western Reserve University (CWRU) is a school whose reputation and selectivity are among the fastest risers in the nation. Long an engineering powerhouse with a rich history of technical education, there has been a recent, sharp rise in the caliber of students clamoring to join this undergraduate student body of just over 5,100. In fact, the university granted acceptance to close to three-quarters of applicants a mere decade ago; today, that figure is sliding toward one-quarter.

Unlike many schools of its ilk, CWRU has a single-door admission policy. Those accepted into the broader university are free to pursue any of the nearly one hundred areas of concentration. All students must complete four seminars called SAGEs (one first-year seminar, two university seminars, and one in the major), and two semesters of physical education. From there, most requirements are school/major specific. In their final year students must conquer the senior capstone, which can take many forms, but it must be designed in consultation with a faculty member.

Sporting an 11:1 faculty-to-student ratio, the university does a nice job keeping classes on the small side with 59 percent of course sections capped at nineteen and only 15 percent of courses having fifty students or more. An exceptional 83 percent of students have the opportunity to participate in undergraduate research as the school places heavy emphasis on experiential learning. The same goes for international experiences. Case Western has a high rate of undergraduates who elect to study abroad; just under half spend a semester in a foreign land.

The Weatherhead School of Management and the Case School of Engineering have stellar reputations within the worlds of employment and academia. Engineering is the most commonly conferred undergraduate degree at 33 percent followed by biology (11 percent), business (10 percent), the social sciences (8 percent), and computer science (6 percent). In a typical year Case Western produces between two and four Fulbright Scholars as well as Churchill Scholars and NSF Fellowship recipients. The school counts sixteen Nobel Prize winners among its alumni and faculty, past and present.

Outside the Classroom

The main campus covers 155 acres, not including a verdant 389-acre, university-owned farm located only ten miles away. Freshmen and sophomores are required to live on campus and four-fifths of the overall undergraduate student body reside on the university's grounds. First-year students live in one of four residential colleges designed to foster a sense of community and belonging. Greek life is thriving with twenty-seven fraternities and sororities attracting 28 percent of men and 36 percent of women. An academically focused student body does not pay a ton of attention to the school's nineteen NCAA Division III sports teams. There are over 200 student-run groups, including plenty of opportunities for intramural athletics, volunteer work, and faith-based connections. CWRUbotix, the school's robotics team, has placed near the top of various national competitions in recent years. Case Western's proximity to downtown Cleveland makes off-campus excursions popular even though the immediate surroundings of East Cleveland are less than ideal. An endless array of restaurants, museums, concerts, and professional sporting events are easily within reach for those willing to take an occasional break from studying.

Career Services

The Career Center at CWRU includes twelve full-time staff members, equating to a student-to-advisor ratio of 420:1, a bit higher than the average institution included in this book. The office is guided by a Four-Phase Plan designed to cultivate career-oriented thinking from freshman through senior year. CWRU has implemented the Student Success Initiative in which each freshman is assigned to a "navigator," a single staff person who remains the student's contact throughout the student's time at the school. Workshops are regularly offered on basic topics such as resume development, internship search strategies, interviewing, and graduate school preparation. Two major career fairs take place each year: the University Career Fair held in October and the Get Experienced! Internship & Career Fair held in February.

Annually, more than 300 employers, from global corporations to start-ups, conduct on-campus interviews with undergraduates. Case Western has fifteen official career center partners including IBM Watson Health, GE, Progressive Insurance, and Yelp. A healthy 81 percent of those landing jobs did so in an area relevant to their college major. Thanks to a strong emphasis on hands-on education, 98 percent of graduates report having the opportunity to engage in some type of experiential learning. Those opportunities include both traditional internships and more structured 560-hour practicums. Three-fifths of students complete at least one internship during their undergraduate years. In a given year, more than a handful of Case Western students land internships at organizations including NASA, Proctor & Gamble, Amazon, and Deloitte.

Professional Outcomes

Fifty-four percent of 2018 CWRU graduates head into the world of professional employment upon receiving their diplomas; only 6 percent were still looking for work six months after leaving the university. Members of the Class of 2018 enjoyed a median salary range of $55,000-$59,000 with engineering majors leading the way with a $65-$70K range, and arts and sciences grads earning the lowest salaries in the $35-40K range. The employers of the greatest number of graduates the previous year included the Cleveland Clinic (21), University Hospitals (20), Accenture (8), Microsoft (8), Deloitte (6), and Google (6). Many alumni also presently work for IBM, Medtronic, EY, and PwC. Nearly 40 percent work in the engineering field, 11 percent enter nursing, and 10 percent find employment in the research realm. A good number of alumni stay in the Cleveland area, but San Francisco and New York are other common destinations.

Of the 36 percent of graduates who decide to enroll in an advanced degree program after completing their undergraduate work, many are accepted by elite graduate schools. In 2017, an impressive number of grads were accepted to continue their studies at Columbia (12), Johns Hopkins (7), Cornell (6), Carnegie Mellon (5), Northwestern (5), and Penn (5). However, the most popular option is to continue studying at Case Western as 44 percent of those going on to graduate school elect to stay on the CMU campus. Of those going directly into graduate/professional studies, between 13 and 23 percent have gone on to medical school in recent years. Only 3 percent of those going to graduate school chose to pursue a law degree.

Admission

Case Western received a record 26,642 applications for admittance into its Class of 2022 and accepted an all-time low of 29 percent. For comparison, only a decade ago Case Western received a little over 7,300 applications and accepted 73 percent of those students. SAT/ACT scores in the 75th percentile for incoming freshmen back then would barely crack the 25th percentile now. Freshmen in 2018-19 boasted a middle-50 percent SAT of 1350-1520 and a 30-34 on the ACT, and roughly the same number of applicants submitted each standardized test. Nearly two-thirds of successful applicants finished in the top 10 percent of their high school classes and 92 percent placed in the top 25 percent.

This increasingly selective admissions committee ranks five factors as "very important": rigor of secondary school record, class rank, GPA, standardized test scores, and extracurricular activities. Essays, recommendation letters, interviews, volunteer work, ethnic status, talent/ability, and personal qualities comprise the second tier of considerations. Case Western offers an early action as well as ED I & ED II rounds. Those applying early find success at close to twice the rate of regular round applicants—42 percent versus 23 percent in applications for the Class of 2022. We often see schools make massive jumps in selectivity over the course of a generation where a warning of "This isn't your mother's/father's fill-in-the-blank university" would be apt. Yet, with CWSU, "This isn't your older sibling's Case Western" is a far more accurate statement. Exponential leaps in the profile of the average accepted student have created an extremely competitive environment, so applying prior to the regular cycle is a much-needed admissions edge.

Worth Your Money?

A Case Western degree will cost you $69k per year if you do not qualify for any need-based or merit aid. Fortunately, there aren't many students who fail to qualify for some sort of tuition reduction. Merit aid is awarded to 60 percent of current undergraduates, and the average award is a hefty $24,454. Need-based aid is awarded to 48 percent of students, and the average award is over $34k; the majority of those eligible see 100 percent of their demonstrated need met by the university. When all is said and done, graduates possess reasonable levels of postsecondary debt relative to the national average. Higher-than-average starting salaries make repaying those loans a doable task.

FINANCIAL
Institutional Type: Private
In-State Tuition: $50,450
Out-of-State Tuition: $50,450
Room & Board: $15,614
Required Fees: $1,029
Books & Supplies: $1,200

Avg. Need-Based Aid: $34,419
Avg. % of Need Met: 100%

Avg. Merit-Based Aid: $24,454
% Receiving Merit-Based Aid: 60%

Avg. Cumulative Debt: $31,820
% of Students Borrowing: 45%

CAREER
Who Recruits
1. Progressive Insurance
2. Lubrizol Corporation
3. Rockwell Automation
4. Amazon
5. The MetroHealth System

Notable Internships
1. Merck
2. Deloitte
3. MITRE

Top Industries
1. Business
2. Healthcare
3. Education
4. Engineering
5. Research

Top Employers
1. Cleveland Clinic
2. University Hospitals
3. Rockwell Automation
4. IBM
5. Microsoft

Where Alumni Work
1. Cleveland
2. New York City
3. San Francisco
4. Washington, DC
5. Chicago

Median Earnings
College Scorecard (Early Career): $74,600
EOP (Early Career): $73,400
PayScale (Mid-Career): $117,800

RANKINGS
Forbes: 100
Money: 320
U.S. News: 40 (T), National Universities
Wall Street Journal/THE: 52
Washington Monthly: 155, National Universities

#CollegesWorthYourMoney

Claremont McKenna College

Claremont, California | Admissions Phone: 909-621-8088

ADMISSION
Admission Rate: 9%
Admission Rate - Men: 10%
Admission Rate - Women: 9%
EA Admission Rate: Not Offered
ED Admission Rate: 25%
Admission Rate (5-Year Trend): -2%
ED Admission Rate (5-Year Trend): -6%
% of Admits Attending (Yield): 56%
Transfer Admission Rate: 6%

Offered Wait List: 1,037
Accepted Wait List: 651
Admitted Wait List: 25

SAT Reading/Writing (Middle 50%): 670-730
SAT Math (Middle 50%): 680-770
ACT Composite (Middle 50%): 31-34
Testing Policy: ACT/SAT Required
SAT Superscore: Yes
ACT Superscore: Yes

% Graduated in Top 10% of HS Class: 78%
% Graduated in Top 25% of HS Class: 93%
% Graduated in Top 50% of HS Class: 100%

ENROLLMENT
Total Undergraduate Enrollment: 1,324
% Part-Time: 0%
% Male: 52%
% Female: 48%
% Out-of-State: 54%
% Fraternity: Not Offered
% Sorority: Not Offered
% On-Campus (Freshman): 100%
% On-Campus (All Undergraduate): 96%

% African-American: 4%
% Asian: 11%
% Hispanic: 15%
% White: 41%
% Other: 6%
% Race or Ethnicity Unknown: 6%
% International: 16%
% Low-Income: 11%

ACADEMICS
Student-to-Faculty Ratio: 8:1
% of Classes Under 20: 81%
% of Classes Under 40: 97%
% Full-Time Faculty: 88%
% Full-Time Faculty w/ Terminal Degree: 99%

Top Programs
Accounting
Economics
Environment, Economics, and Politics (EEP)
Government
History
International Relations
Philosophy, Politics, and Economics
Psychology

Retention Rate: 96%
4-Year Graduation Rate: 82%
6-Year Graduation Rate: 93%

Curricular Flexibility: Very Flexible
Academic Rating: ★★★★★

Inside the Classroom

Start with your average elite liberal arts college in the Northeast, cut the size of the student body in half, replace stuffy Gothic edifices with a modern California feel, and physically connect the campus to four other elite schools whose premier offerings can all be shared communally. That's the recipe for Claremont McKenna College (CMC), a liberal arts school that is home to 1,324 bright and motivated undergraduates and is a founding member of the Claremont Consortium that is comprised of four additional undergraduate institutions: Pomona, Pitzer, Scripps, and Harvey Mudd.

CMC offers thirty-two majors and eleven "sequences," series of courses that can be completed across the neighboring schools in addition to one's major. Registering for courses in one or more of the other Claremont Colleges is a staple of academic life at CMC; 99 percent of undergrads do so. An academically focused group, 32 percent of the student population ends up completing a double major. No matter your academic pursuit, required courses will include a first-year writing seminar, a humanities seminar, multiple semesters of a foreign language, a laboratory science, a math or computer science course, physical education and—of most significance—a senior thesis.

The college boasts an average class size of eighteen, and 81 percent of course sections have fewer than twenty students. With an 8:1 student-to-faculty ratio and only one graduate program offered (an MA in finance), undergrads benefit from ample professor attention. In the 2018-19 school year an incredible 79 percent of CMC students had the chance to conduct research with a faculty member, and the school has eleven partner research institutes and centers that provide graduate-level research experiences. Studying abroad is another popular pursuit as CMC offers approved programs on each of the world's six populated continents. Forty-percent of undergrads spend time at one of 115 approved programs in forty countries.

Economics, government, international relations, and psychology are the most popular majors, and among the strongest. Interdisciplinary majors such as Environment, Economics, and Politics (EEP) and Philosophy, Politics and Economics (PPE) also carry outstanding reputations. Claremont graduates annually have representation of Fulbright, US Department of State Critical Language, and Luce Scholarships. Per capita, it is often among the top ten in Fulbright production, boasting five winners in 2019.

Outside the Classroom

Academically, students attending any of the Claremont Colleges are used to crossing campuses to take courses at one of the other schools. Those permeable borders apply to life outside the classroom as well. Pomona, Pitzer, Scripps, Harvey Mudd, and CMC are all located on the same 560-acre property, and many activities are joint efforts between members of the consortium. Even Claremont McKenna's twenty-one NCAA athletic teams are combined squads with Harvey Mudd and Scripps student-athletes; it has won over 300 conference championships since its founding in 1958. Not everything is a shared-venture; there are seventy CMC-exclusive student-run organizations of the academic, identity-based, service, sports, or music/arts nature. The Model UN team has won the world championship four of the last five years. An endless flow of public speakers grace the stage at the Marian Miner Cook Athenaeum that presents guest lectures four nights per week. With 96 percent of CMC students electing to live on campus and no fraternities or sororities, campus life is an open and vibrant experience. Most facilities are shared among the members of the consortium, including the eight-lane pool; Roberts Pavilion, which includes a 2,200 seat arena and a state-of-the-art fitness center; and the Collins Dining Hall, which garners solid culinary reviews. Situated thirty-five miles east of Los Angeles, all of the culture and excitement you could want is never more than a relatively quick car ride away. The SoCal beaches are about an hour drive as is Disneyland and Joshua Tree National Park.

Career Services

The Claremont McKenna Career Services Office has eight full-time professional staff members working on grad school/career advising and employer relations and internship procurement. That equates to a 166:1 student-to-advisor ratio, which is superior to just about every college featured in our guidebook. The college aims to provide individualized career coaching to all of its students and begins that process freshman year. It even has a counselor solely dedicated to the school's 350 first-year students, and that counselor met with 93 percent of the class that entered last year. Annual fall career expos attract representatives from more than one hundred top employers. Events like company information sessions, two-to-five-day networking treks, and job shadowing experiences take place frequently throughout the year.

In 2018, employers recruiting at CMC included Google, Deloitte, Bain, the CIA, NASA, Goldman Sachs, and the National Football League. A phenomenal 90 percent of students participate in at least one internship. Many of those are financially supported by the Sponsored Internship Experiences Program that provided between $500 and $8,000 grants for 340 students in 2018. Also in the 2018 school year, staff conducted 3,000 one-on-one

Claremont McKenna College

E-mail: admission@cmc.edu | Website: www.cmc.edu

counseling appointments, enticed forty-four employers into recruiting on campus, and facilitated 581on-campus interviews, more than one per member of the senior class. Thanks to that focus on hands-on experience, strong employer relations, and ample resources (including personnel), Claremont McKenna's career services easily earns the highest praise from the College Transitions' staff.

Professional Outcomes
Eighty percent of graduates have found employment within six months of graduation, and only 4 percent are still looking for work. Financial services/accounting, consulting, and technology are the most frequently entered sectors. Companies employing the highest number of 2016 and 2017 graduates include Accenture, Ernst & Young, Goldman Sachs, Amazon, Deloitte, and JP Morgan. The average starting salary for a Claremont grad is $68,200, a particularly impressive figure for a liberal arts college. The highest average starting salaries are traditionally earned by those majoring in computer science ($94k) and economics ($70k), but those studying the humanities ($65k) or social sciences ($57k) fare well too.

Of the 2016/2017 graduating classes, 12 percent elected to continue their education rather than immediately enter the working world. You name the prestigious graduate/professional program and, chances are, a recent CMC grad (or two or three) is presently studying there. In the last four years students have been accepted to medical schools at Stanford, Emory, Harvard, Johns Hopkins, and Penn. Students also have enjoyed law school acceptances at institutions including Columbia, NYU, Berkeley, the University of Chicago, and Yale. The list of MBA and other graduate programs attended by alumni is similarly eye-popping. Ten years out, 15 percent of the total alumni have earned a law degree, 5 percent a PhD, 4 percent a medical degree, and 10 percent have completed an MBA.

Admission
Applications to CMC were actually down slightly in the race for a spot in the Class of 2022, but so was the acceptance rate, which fell to the lowest point yet—9.3 percent. (It fell even further, to 8.6 percent, for 2019-20 freshmen.) The mid-50 percent test scores of freshmen entering in 2018-19 were a 1350-1500 on the SAT and a 31-34 on the ACT. The vast majority, 78 percent, placed in the top 10 percent of their high school class, and 93 percent landed in the top quartile. Claremont McKenna has trended in the more selective direction in recent years. Five years ago, the acceptance rate was a slightly higher 12 percent, median test scores were 1410/31, and fewer students placed in the top 10 percent of their graduating classes.

The process is a holistic one with seven factors deemed "very important" by the admissions committee: rigor of secondary coursework, class rank, GPA, standardized test scores, recommendations, extracurricular activities, and character/personal qualities. First-generation status is listed as a factor that is merely "considered," yet 19 percent of the Class of 2022 met that criterion. Applying early decision is a worthwhile strategic maneuver as the ED acceptance rate tends to be up to four times that of the regular cycle; in 2018, it was 25 percent versus 7 percent in the regular round. To gain admission into CMC applicants should bring exceptional credentials, as expected at any highly selective liberal arts college. There are sometimes surprise decisions here. For example, in looking at the freshman class of 2017-18, 4 percent of accepted freshmen scored lower than 600 on the reading portion of the SAT, and a different 4 percent (presumably) finished outside the top 25 percent of their high school cohort. However, in general, students should be closer to the mean to have a genuine chance at being granted admission.

Worth Your Money?
Two-fifths of CMC undergrads qualify for need-based financial aid, taking home an annual grant averaging $55,880. Additionally, one-quarter of students receive merit aid awards that average over $13k, helping make the $73,775 sticker price a bit more manageable. Those who can pay full price at Claremont McKenna likely will, and there are plenty of students capable of handling the bill. Tax return data estimates that nearly 50 percent come from families with incomes in the top 5 percent nationally. Whether you're a full-paying student or the recipient of generous aid, CMC's strong academics, sterling reputation and incredible career service offerings will more than justify your investment in this top-notch liberal arts school.

FINANCIAL
Institutional Type: Private
In-State Tuition: $56,190
Out-of-State Tuition: $56,190
Room & Board: $17,300
Required Fees: $285
Books & Supplies: N/A

Avg. Need-Based Aid: $55,880
Avg. % of Need Met: 100%

Avg. Merit-Based Aid: $13,355
% Receiving Merit-Based Aid: 25%

Avg. Cumulative Debt: $19,355
% of Students Borrowing: 34%

CAREER
Who Recruits
1. Cloudfare, Inc.
2. United Talent Agency
3. Whittier Trust Company
4. Boston Pharmaceuticals
5. Morgan Stanley

Notable Internships
1. BlackRock
2. Adidas
3. House of Representatives

Top Industries
1. Business
2. Education
3. Finance
4. Operations
5. Research

Top Employers
1. Deloitte
2. Google
3. Microsoft
4. EY
5. Accenture

Where Alumni Work
1. Los Angeles
2. San Francisco
3. New York City
4. Seattle
5. Orange County, CA

Median Earnings
College Scorecard (Early Career): $72,900
EOP (Early Career): $69,600
PayScale (Mid-Career): $125,400

RANKINGS
Forbes: 29
Money: 101
U.S. News: 7, Liberal Arts Colleges
Wall Street Journal/THE: 38
Washington Monthly: 10, Liberal Arts Colleges

#CollegesWorthYourMoney

Clarkson University

Potsdam, New York | Admissions Phone: 315-268-6480

ADMISSION
Admission Rate: 71%
Admission Rate - Men: 73%
Admission Rate - Women: 69%
EA Admission Rate: Not Offered
ED Admission Rate: 78%
Admission Rate (5-Year Trend): +7%
ED Admission Rate (5-Year Trend): +18%
% of Admits Attending (Yield): 16%
Transfer Admission Rate: 68%

Offered Wait List: 55
Accepted Wait List: 2
Admitted Wait List: 0

SAT Reading/Writing (Middle 50%): 570-660
SAT Math (Middle 50%): 590-690
ACT Composite (Middle 50%): 25-29
Testing Policy: ACT/SAT Required
SAT Superscore: Yes
ACT Superscore: No

% Graduated in Top 10% of HS Class: 35%
% Graduated in Top 25% of HS Class: 69%
% Graduated in Top 50% of HS Class: 95%

ENROLLMENT
Total Undergraduate Enrollment: 3,091
% Part-Time: 2%
% Male: 69%
% Female: 31%
% Out-of-State: 29%
% Fraternity: 15%
% Sorority: 13%
% On-Campus (Freshman): 95%
% On-Campus (All Undergraduate): 80%

% African-American: 2%
% Asian: 4%
% Hispanic: 5%
% White: 80%
% Other: 3%
% Race or Ethnicity Unknown: 2%
% International: 4%
% Low-Income: 29%

ACADEMICS
Student-to-Faculty Ratio: 13:1
% of Classes Under 20: 52%
% of Classes Under 40: 77%
% Full-Time Faculty: 71%
% Full-Time Faculty w/ Terminal Degree: 85%

Top Programs
Biology
Civil Engineering
Environmental Engineering
Environmental Science and Policy
Global Supply Chain Management
Innovation and Entrepreneurship
Mechanical Engineering

Retention Rate: 89%
4-Year Graduation Rate: 60%
6-Year Graduation Rate: 76%

Curricular Flexibility: Somewhat Flexible
Academic Rating: ★★★

Inside the Classroom

Among the lesser-known of the Upstate New York schools, Clarkson University is even further north than Syracuse, Rochester, or Buffalo. For perspective, it would take a six-hour drive to reach Potsdam from New York City. The good news is that Clarkson's remote location makes getting in much easier than at comparable small, engineering-heavy schools like Lehigh University, Lafayette College, or Union College. The student body is comprised of 3,400+ undergraduate students pursuing more than fifty programs in engineering, business, the arts, education, and sciences and health professions.

All Golden Knights are required to complete the Common Experience Curriculum that includes a First-Year Experience course on adjustment to college life, the Clarkson Seminar, which is an introduction to college-level thinking and writing, and five courses that adequately cover the six broad areas of knowledge: cultures and societies; contemporary and global issues; imaginative arts; science, technology, and society; economics and organizations; and individual and group behavior. The four common threads in all of the introductory coursework are communication, diversity, ethics, and recognizing how technology can better serve humanity. Students in the business and engineering schools have a fairly rigid schedule of courses the first two years of study. For instance, all business students take Principles of Microeconomics their first semester and Principles of Macroeconomics second semester.

A student-to-faculty ratio of 11:1 translates to reasonable undergraduate class sizes. Forty percent of sections enroll fewer than twenty students, but there are a mix of fifty or more or even one hundred or more student sections for some introductory courses. Undergraduate research is embedded in the Honors Program that admits forty to fifty students each year. Everyone else can apply to programs like the Research Experience for Undergrads (REU) that offers a ten-week apprenticeship funded by the National Science Foundation. Within the Biology Department, for example, all students are strongly encouraged to engage in research during their four years via the REU program, departmental connection, or by completing a senior thesis and presenting the findings at the Clarkson Symposium for Undergraduate Research. The school also offers thirty-seven study abroad programs in twenty countries but, as at most engineering-focused schools, the participation is low, approaching 10 percent.

An overwhelming 55 percent of undergrads are studying in the Coulter School of Engineering, 20 percent in the business school, and 18 percent in the School of Arts and Sciences. Overshadowed in most ranking systems by large research institutions, the School of Engineering is, nevertheless, a stud whose quality is fully recognized by big-time employers well outside the region. The National Science Foundation awarded two engineering undergrads and one biology student their prestigious Graduate Research Fellowship in 2019.

Outside the Classroom

Clarkson students tend to be proud nerds. As the admissions office states, "If the idea of working all night on an animated video for physics class sounds more like fun than work, you'll fit right in at Clarkson." This school has a 70 percent male, 30 percent female student body, which impacts the make-up of the social scene. The presence of SUNY Potsdam and its 58 percent female student body does help even the town's gender divide a bit. Four in five undergrads live on campus in one of eight dorm buildings or in one of the four apartment complexes. Additional Living-Learning Communities bring together students with common interests in areas like robotics, gaming, or women in engineering/business. There are nine fraternities and four sororities that, together, attract 10-15 percent of students. The school's 225 intramural teams draw an incredible 80 percent of the student body into recreational athletics. NCCA Division I ice hockey is huge as this tiny powerhouse has produced approximately thirty NHL players in its history; the other ten teams participate in Division III. Overall, there are 250 student-run clubs and activities from which to choose. Like the woods? If so, you're in luck. Not only do you get to enjoy the 640 wooded acres on which the campus is set, but the grounds are adjacent to Adirondack Park that adds another six million acres (not a typo). Like to spend time in a major metropolitan area? You're not so lucky on that front—Ottawa and Montreal, Canada, are closer to Clarkson than any major American city.

Career Services

The Clarkson Career Center (CCC) is staffed by six professionals with expertise in career coaching, employer relations, and graduate school advising. That works out to a 515:1 student-to-advisor ratio, which is in the average range compared to other schools in the guidebook. Despite its distance from major American cities, the CCC still manages to entice companies to campus with regularity, and 200 come to the annual career fairs. Even more impressive are the office's efforts in arranging internship and co-op experiences; the rate of participation is near 100 percent, and many undergrads procure two or more placements. It's no wonder 95 percent of Clarkson grads end up finding a job directly related to their area of study.

Clarkson University

E-mail: admissions@clarkson.edu | Website: www.clarkson.edu

A proactive office, the Clarkson Career Center has a reputation for seeking to connect personally with every student. Whether you are a freshman or a senior, staffers are equally happy to have you stop by to take a personality assessment, discuss career options one-on-one, work on your resume, or arrange an employer site visit. Golden Knights have a powerful alumni base to tap when it comes time for the job hunt. According to the university, among its 42,000 alumni, "One in five is already a CEO, senior executive, or owner of a company." Thanks to a thriving internship/co-op network that leads to fantastic employment/salary results for grads, the CCC gets high marks as an efficient and effective career services office.

Professional Outcomes

Within eight months of graduation the Class of 2018 enjoyed a job/grad school placement rate of 96 percent and an average starting salary of just under $60,100. Annually, 170+ employers snatch up Clarkson seniors. Top employers of this graduating class included BAE Systems, Amazon, IBM, General Electric, Lockheed Martin, and Pratt & Whitney. Other companies that historically hire large numbers of Golden Knights include GlobalFoundries, Corning Incorporated, Xerox, Siemens, Accenture, and Intel. While a fair number of graduates stay in Upstate New York—Utica, Syracuse, Albany, and Rochester rank as the third through sixth most popular cities—the Greater New York and Boston areas are the most common alumni destinations.

Only 13 percent of Class of 2018 members were pursuing advanced degrees immediately after completing their undergraduate education. Students from that cohort were admitted into graduate school at institutions including Duke, Georgia Tech, the University of Rochester, and Rochester Polytechnic Institute. Medical school is usually the direction of choice for around ten graduates each year. Medical school-bound students often attend SUNY schools, including SUNY Upstate Medical University, SUNY Stonybrook Medical School, and SUNY Buffalo Medical School. Recent grads also have landed at Dartmouth, Johns Hopkins, and Penn State. Remaining at Clarkson for graduate study is an option many also pursue, and the school offers approximately forty advanced degree programs.

Admission

Clarkson sports acceptance rates that range from the high 60 percents to the low 70 percents, pretty nice considering that your average engineering school of this quality typically possesses an admit rate that is a mere fraction of those generous figures. Still, many top students choose Clarkson as 37 percent of freshmen hailed from the top decile of their high school class, and roughly three-quarters finished in the top 25 percent. The average high school GPA was 3.6, and the average test scores were 1240 on the SAT and 27 on the ACT. The admissions standards have toughened in recent years. Back in 2012, the university admitted 80 percent of those who applied, and the SAT range was 1100-1270, significantly lower than the 2018-19 freshman class, even when accounting for recent SAT inflation.

Two factors reign supreme in the minds of admissions officials—GPA and a rigorous high school curriculum. Factors on the next rung of importance include standardized test scores, class rank, extracurricular activities, recommendations, and volunteer work. The early decision acceptance rate is even friendlier than the regular round as 78 percent of ED applicants were admitted during the last cycle. A personal visit to Potsdam as well as a face-to-face informational interview with an admissions counselor is highly recommended. Clarkson remains a rare, strong engineering school that is open to B students with less-than-perfect test scores.

Worth Your Money?

The focus on engineering unsurprisingly raises starting salaries into a higher stratosphere than most schools of Clarkson's size. The list price of this university is $65,000, including room and board, but merit and need-based aid are distributed generously; nine of ten students receive financial aid. Middle-class families can expect to pay closer to $30-35k per year in total costs which, depending on one's academic track, can lead to a terrific return on investment.

FINANCIAL
Institutional Type: Private
In-State Tuition: $49,858
Out-of-State Tuition: $49,858
Room & Board: $15,340
Required Fees: $1,270
Books & Supplies: $1,446

Avg. Need-Based Aid: $37,012
Avg. % of Need Met: 90%

Avg. Merit-Based Aid: $30,928
% Receiving Merit-Based Aid: 29%

Avg. Cumulative Debt: $31,000
% of Students Borrowing: 81%

CAREER
Who Recruits
1. Procter & Gamble
2. General Dynamics
3. Tecnica Group
4. Whiting-Turner
5. Novelis

Notable Internships
1. Salesforce
2. Siemens
3. Hewlett Packard

Top Industries
1. Engineering
2. Operations
3. Business
4. Information Technology
5. Sales

Top Employers
1. IBM
2. Lockheed Martin
3. GLOBALFOUNDRIES
4. Corning Incorporated
5. GE

Where Alumni Work
1. New York City
2. Boston
3. Utica, NY
4. Albany, NY
5. Syracuse, NY

Median Earnings
College Scorecard (Early Career): $72,000
EOP (Early Career): $73,300
PayScale (Mid-Career): $130,100

RANKINGS
Forbes: 207
Money: 165
U.S. News: 117, National Universities
Wall Street Journal/THE: 205 (T)
Washington Monthly: 97, National Universities

#CollegesWorthYourMoney

Clemson University

Clemson, South Carolina | Admissions Phone: 864-656-2287

Inside the Classroom

Championship-caliber sports teams, thriving Greek life, and a passionate and generally happy undergraduate population of close to 20,000 young people define the Clemson experience—not to leave out the strong academic reputation, which becomes more pronounced with each passing year. A highly selective school for out-of-staters, Clemson caters to those residing within its home state of South Carolina. Nearly two-thirds of the student body are South Carolina born and bred, and locals enjoy more relaxed entry requirements (not to mention one-third the tuition costs) of those from out of state.

There are seven undergraduate colleges within the larger university: the College of Forestry and Life Sciences; the College of Architecture, Arts, and Humanities; the College of Business; the College of Engineering, Computing and Applied Sciences; the College of Education; the College of Science; and the College of Behavioral, Social, and Health Sciences. All Tigers, regardless of their academic program, must tackle thirty-three hours of required coursework that includes six credits in communications, ten in mathematical, scientific, and technical literacy, six in arts and humanities, six in social science, three in cross-cultural awareness, and three in science and technology in society. Most degree programs also require coursework in a foreign language.

Class sizes are mixed, and many sections are smaller than you would expect for such a large university where the student-to-faculty ratio is 16:1. Seventeen percent of classes have single-digit enrollments, and 55 percent contain fewer than twenty students; 14 percent of courses are larger, playing host to fifty or more undergraduates. More than half of Clemson students participate in some type of undergraduate research, a strong percentage given the size of the school. Each year over 1,400 students elect to study abroad in one of Clemson's own programs or one offered by a third party.

Business and engineering are the two programs with the highest profiles, and the university's highly selective Calhoun Honors College regularly draws national attention and praise. Business and engineering also are the most popular majors with a 19 percent and 20 percent market share of diplomas, respectively. The next most frequently conferred degrees are in biology (10 percent), agriculture (7 percent), and psychology (6 percent). With such an emphasis on professional career tracks there is not a strong emphasis on winning prestigious postgraduate fellowships. In 2018, two graduates received Boren Fellowships and one captured a Fulbright; Clemson had four Fulbright Scholars in 2017.

Outside the Classroom

Only 41 percent of undergrads, mostly underclassmen, reside on Clemson's 1,400-acre campus. Yet, that figure is not indicative of a dull social scene. Athletics are a galvanizing force as the Tigers compete in eight men's and nine women's NCCA Division I sports. Over 81,000 pack Memorial Stadium, nicknamed "Death Valley," on Saturdays to watch their highly ranked football squad; Clemson won the national title in 2016 and again in 2019. Other sports draw large audiences as well. Greek life is almost as big a tradition here as 34 percent of women join a sorority and 16 percent of men are fraternity affiliated. As at many Greek-heavy institutions, there has been increased scrutiny of those organizations in the wake of some incidents of sexual assault and hazing. Other opportunities for involvement abound as Clemson has over 500 student-run organizations. The school's thirty-four club sports attract widespread participation as does the intramural program. The town of Clemson offers plenty of enjoyable bars and restaurants within walking distance. Hiking trails and botanical gardens offer nature lovers everything they could ask for. Greenville, only forty minutes away, provides a more exciting downtown feel.

Career Services

Clemson's Center for Career and Professional Development employs twenty-four full-time staff members who function as counselors, recruiters, and internship coordinators. That equates to a student-to-advisor ratio of 833:1, well above average compared to the other institutions included in this book. Despite a less-than-ideal ratio, Clemson's staff garners much-deserved praise for its dedication to student success through the sheer scope of their offerings. Fall and spring career fairs attract more than 600 employers and more than 5,500 students annually. The school's online database features up to 9,000 job and internship postings each year. The center has forged corporate partnerships with twenty-four large corporations including Home Depot, Vanguard, Bosch, and General Electric.

Even more impressively, the CCPD personally reaches a massive number of students, claiming more than 31,000 engagements in the 2017-18 school year. Fifty-five percent of those engagements were made at workshops, job fairs, and information sessions while the other 45 percent were made via one-on-one counseling sessions. An astonishing 99 percent of those attending information sessions or individualized career counseling rated the experience favorably. Staff also does an exceptional job hooking students up with hands-on learning experiences; 78 percent of graduates had one experiential learning opportunity and 64 percent partook in two.

Just under 900 students participated in the University Professional Co-op/Internship Program with the school's 450 employer partners. An additional 1,400 participated in other co-op placements, and 92 percent reported being satisfied with the experience. As a result, 94 percent of those receiving diplomas believe their resumes demonstrate marketable skills.

Professional Outcomes

Within six months of graduation 96 percent of Clemson alumni have entered the working world or are pursuing a graduate degree. The top employers of Class of 2017 graduates included Michelin (8), Amazon (8), Vanguard (5), and Wells Fargo (4). Including all alumni, the most frequent employers include Bank of America, GE Power, Deloitte, IBM, and Microsoft. Graduates of the College of Engineering, Computing and Applied Sciences reported a median starting salary of $63,000. College of Business graduates enjoyed median earnings of $49,000. Graduates of the College of Architecture, Arts, and Humanities averaged $47k while those completing degrees in the College of Education brought in a university-low $37k per year. Forty-five percent of graduates remain in South Carolina, and most stay in the Southern United States with North Carolina, Georgia, Florida, and Virginia being the next most popular destinations.

Of the 21 percent of 2017 graduates directly entering graduate or professional school, the largest number retained their Tiger stripes by continuing their studies at Clemson. The next most frequently attended institutions were the Medical University of South Carolina (47), the University of South Carolina (33), UNC (12), the University of Georgia (11), and Wake Forest University (9). Clemson grads also enjoyed three or more acceptances to prestigious graduate schools including Duke, Penn, Emory, Vanderbilt, and the University of Virginia. Among all alumni pursuing advanced degrees, 15 percent were in PhD programs, and a robust 33 percent were pursuing professional degrees in law or medicine.

Admission

The number of applicants to Clemson has rapidly risen in the past decade as 28,845 students applied in 2018 compared with 15,542 in 2008. In that time the average SAT score of attending students has climbed from 1221 to 1302; the ACT mid-50 percent range was 27-32. Admitted applicants from South Carolina public schools averaged only a 1058 on the SAT in 2017. No matter where they hail from, most successful applicants— 87 percent—finished in the top 25 percent of their high school class, and 56 percent were in the top 10 percent. The average high school GPA for entering students was 4.43, and 90 percent earned a 3.75 or higher. Those applying to the Calhoun Honors College need to be even stronger. The average accepted Calhoun students have a 1480/32 and are ranked in the top 4 percent of their class.

A healthy 60 percent of first-year students accepted are from South Carolina, but including transfers, home-state students comprise an even larger percentage of the student body. Being a South Carolina resident is listed among the five most important criteria for admission along with rigor of secondary coursework, GPA, class rank, and standardized test scores. Soft factors like essays, recommendations, and extracurricular activities comprise a distant second tier. Legacy status is also considered at Clemson. There is no early admission round at Clemson, but those who apply by the priority deadline of December 1 will receive an answer by February 15. This desirable Southern public university is friendlier toward in-state applicants than outsiders. Applicants not from South Carolina will need to bring above average standardized test scores and strong grades in honors and AP courses to gain acceptance.

Worth Your Money?

The cost of attendance for South Carolina residents is under $30,000 per year, making Clemson a fantastic bargain for them. For nonresidents, the price is over $50k, not a fortune relative to the out-of-control higher education marketplace at large, but not the steal that it is for those from the Palmetto State. Almost 45 percent of current students are recipients of need-based aid awards that average $10,967 per year. For a state university, Clemson awards an usually high number of students some degree of merit aid. Currently, 78 percent of undergraduates receive an average annual amount of $6k. In-state, attending Clemson is worth your money no matter what you are studying. If you hail from outside the state, a little bit of financial aid can keep the university affordable and a strong educational investment.

FINANCIAL
Institutional Type: Public
In-State Tuition: $13,702
Out-of-State Tuition: $35,056
Room & Board: $10,832
Required Fees: $1,268
Books & Supplies: $1,392

Avg. Need-Based Aid: $10,967
Avg. % of Need Met: 55%

Avg. Merit-Based Aid: $5,979
% Receiving Merit-Based Aid: 78%

Avg. Cumulative Debt: $32,285
% of Students Borrowing: 47%

CAREER
Who Recruits
1. Bank of America
2. ScribeAmerica
3. Global Lending Services LLC
4. Insight Global
5. TD Bank

Notable Internships
1. BMW
2. Booz Allen Hamilton
3. Capital One

Top Industries
1. Business
2. Operations
3. Engineering
4. Education
5. Sales

Top Employers
1. Michelin
2. Fluor Corporation
3. Bank of America
4. Wells Fargo
5. Amazon

Where Alumni Work
1. Greenville, SC
2. Charlotte
3. Charleston, SC
4. Atlanta
5. Columbia, SC

Median Earnings
College Scorecard (Early Career): $52,400
EOP (Early Career): N/A
PayScale (Mid-Career): $106,700

RANKINGS
Forbes: 134
Money: 78
U.S. News: 70, National Universities
Wall Street Journal/THE: 188
Washington Monthly: 179, National Universities

#CollegesWorthYourMoney

Colby College

Waterville, Maine | Admissions Phone: 207-859-4828

Inside the Classroom

Situated within the natural splendor of Waterville, Maine, Colby College's location may be remote, but the alluring sheen of this liberal arts gem is spotted each year by a growing number of top students from around the globe. Over the past decade, applications to Colby have tripled, and the school has become commensurately more selective. The 1,917 undergraduates presently on campus are, by far, the highest-achieving group the school has seen in its 205 years.

Offering fifty-eight majors and thirty-five minors, Colby provides a classic liberal arts education with a high degree of flexibility and room for independent intellectual pursuits. Dual engineering degrees with Dartmouth and Columbia, independent majors of your own creation, and a strong premed track are among the bevy of options. Academic requirements for all Colby undergraduates include a freshman writing seminar, three semesters of a foreign language, two natural science courses (including one lab science), two courses dealing with diversity, and one course each in historical studies, literature, quantitative reasoning, history, and social sciences.

A 10:1 student-to-faculty ratio is put to good instructional use as 35 percent of courses have a single-digit enrollment, and 74 percent have fewer than nineteen students. The school's "Jan Plan" tacks on a truncated semester during which students can conduct research alongside faculty, pursue internships, or take an accelerated course; 90 percent of undergraduates participate. An exceptionally high 67 percent of students study abroad at some point during their four years at Colby. The college runs three of its own off-campus study programs and allows participation in hundreds of programs around the globe.

Being a true liberal arts school, Colby has strengths across many disciplines, but biology, economics, and global studies draw especially high praise. These programs, along with other strong programs in government and environmental science, attract the highest number of students as well. Unlike many of its elite Northeastern liberal arts counterparts, Colby does not produce a significant number of fellowship/scholarship winners, but in 2018 three graduates were named Fulbright Scholars. Bates and Bowdoin routinely produce in excess of twenty winners per year. In 2019, Colby also had a Davis Projects for Peace and Watson Fellowship winner.

Outside the Classroom

The vast majority of students—95 percent—live on campus with a smattering of undergraduates living off campus in the surrounding town of Waterville. Colby ditched fraternities and sororities in the 1980s, but underground Greek-like organizations still exist. The Colby Mules field thirty-two NCAA Division III athletic teams (16 men's, 15 women's, 1 co-ed) as well as extensive intramural and club sports programs. An incredible one-third of undergraduates are members of a varsity athletic team. Of the one hundred student-run clubs and activities, the Colby Outing Club has the largest membership, catering to an outdoorsy student body. Wildlife trails and a pond perfect for ice skating are only two of the many natural treasures found on the school's 714-acre campus. In fact, the outdoor life is impossible to avoid as all freshmen participate in an outdoor bonding experience prior to the start of the fall semester. Manmade features of note include three libraries, the Colby College Art Museum that features more than 6,000 works, and an Olympic-size pool. Getting to major cities from Colby will require the use of planes, trains, or automobiles. Portland, Maine, is seventy-eight miles from the college, Boston is 180 miles away, and New York City is a lengthy 390-mile trip.

Career Services

DavisConnects, the office that provides Colby students with career counseling, internship procurement, and facilitates employer recruiting features eight full-time professional staff members and a student-to-advisor ratio of 240:1. That figure is significantly better than average compared to the other institutions included in this book. Career services staff members do an excellent job of directly engaging the undergraduate population, reaching roughly 1,200 students per year in more than 3,300 counseling sessions. The office also runs a job shadowing program, hosts an interview boot camp, and the CampusTap program that hooks undergraduate students up with alumni-parent mentors in their fields of interest.

Due to its small size and remote location, Colby hosts an annual joint career fair with fellow elite Maine-based schools Bowdoin and Bates. However, many companies do host information sessions directly with Colby undergrads, and those employers include Google, Prudential, Epic, and Citigroup. DavisConnects has increased its number of credited internship opportunities in recent years, now facilitating close to 300 summer/winter experiences at Lockheed Martin, Goldman Sachs, Citigroup, Time, Massachusetts General Hospital, and others. Organizations that have formal partnerships with DavisConnects include PwC, Goldman Sachs, Accenture, Hearst Magazines, the US Department of State, and IBM. Overall, with strong graduate school advising, employer relations, and job placement rates, Colby's career services receive high marks from our staff.

E-mail: admissions@colby.edu | Website: www.colby.edu

Professional Outcomes

More than 55 percent of graduates have already secured gainful employment by the time they receive their diplomas. Within six months of graduation 95 percent have either obtained jobs or are enrolled full-time in a graduate program. Over one-quarter of graduates enter the financial industry, 19 percent start careers in education, with government/nonprofit, STEM, and health- care work next in popularity. Organizations hiring recent Colby grads were an eclectic bunch that included Teach for America, Barclays, Harvard Medical School, HBO, Deutsch Bank, and the United States Olympic Committee. The median income for a Colby graduate by age thirty-four is $59,000, which places it slightly behind Bowdoin and slightly ahead of Bates in the Maine liberal arts pecking order.

Medical school results have fluctuated over the past five years with acceptance rates between 48 percent and 81 percent. In that time multiple graduates have enrolled at prestigious medical schools including Tufts University School of Medicine, Emory University School of Medicine, Dartmouth Medical School, and University of Michigan Medical School. Overall, the five-year average for the medical school acceptance rate is double the national average. Over 80 percent of law school applicants also find success. Law schools where multiple recent alumni have studied include the University of Pennsylvania, Georgetown University, Boston College, and Cornell University.

Admission

In 2018, the number of applicants to Colby hit 12,313, a 10 percent increase over the previous year, and 2017 applications had seen a 14 percent spike from 2016. Such has been the pattern at Colby in recent years. A decade ago, Colby attracted fewer than 5,000 applicants and had an acceptance rate greater than 30 percent. The Class of 2014 enjoyed a 28 percent acceptance rate. In stark contrast, those seeking a place in the Class of 2022 were accepted at a paltry 13 percent clip. The average standardized test scores of this cohort were a 1490 SAT with a 33 ACT, and 90 percent of students graduated in the top 10 percent of their high school class. Just four years ago, a 1430 SAT/32 ACT would have placed you in the 75th percentile of attending students.

Among the factors rated as most important by the admissions committee are rigor of secondary curriculum, grades, recommendations, and character/personal qualities. In the fall of 2018 Colby announced it would become a test-optional institution. Serious applicants should strongly consider early decision as the ED rounds usually allow more generous acceptance rates, often more than three times as high as the regular round. The Class of 2022 was comprised of 51 percent ED-round applicants, and the acceptance rate was 38 percent versus 11 percent for those in the regular cycle.

Colby has become exponentially more competitive in recent years and shows no sign of slowing down. Applicants that would have been accepted a mere five years ago may quickly end up on the rejection pile. Those dead-set on Colby should apply early to gain a much-needed edge in this now hypercompetitive admissions process.

Worth Your Money?

While priced at the level one would expect for a premier New England liberal arts school—the current cost of attendance is $73,600—Colby College is generous when it comes to need-based financial aid. In fact, all undergraduates with demonstrated financial need—approximately 46 percent of Colby's student body-- have the full amount of their need met, with the annual grant averaging more than $53,000. Those grants are balanced by the many wealthy families who send their children to the college and pay full price for the pleasure. It is estimated that slightly more than half of the student body comes from families placing in the top 5 percent of incomes. That makes possible the school's new policy that says, "Families with a total household income of $60,000 or less and typical assets may expect a parent or guardian contribution of $0." Overall, given its excellent reputation and generous need-based aid, Colby proves a sound investment for most.

FINANCIAL
Institutional Type: Private
In-State Tuition: $54,870
Out-of-State Tuition: $54,870
Room & Board: $14,720
Required Fees: $2,410
Books & Supplies: $800

Avg. Need-Based Aid: $53,497
Avg. % of Need Met: 100%

Avg. Merit-Based Aid: $0
% Receiving Merit-Based Aid: 0%

Avg. Cumulative Debt: $24,437
% of Students Borrowing: 25%

CAREER
Who Recruits
1. CGI
2. Market Axess
3. Analysis Group
4. Ocean Spray
5. Boston Medical

Notable Internships
1. Morgan Stanley
2. Boston Red Sox
3. Vertex Pharaceuticals

Top Industries
1. Business
2. Education
3. Operations
4. Research
5. Social Services

Top Employers
1. Fidelity Investments
2. Morgan Stanley
3. Goldman Sachs
4. Massachusetts General Hospital
5. Google

Where Alumni Work
1. Boston
2. New York City
3. Lewiston, ME
4. Portland, ME
5. Washington, DC

Median Earnings
College Scorecard (Early Career): $58,100
EOP (Early Career): $59,200
PayScale (Mid-Career): $103,300

RANKINGS
Forbes: 75
Money: 124
U.S. News: 11, Liberal Arts Colleges
Wall Street Journal/THE: 71
Washington Monthly: 37, Liberal Arts Colleges

#CollegesWorthYourMoney

Colgate University

Hamilton, New York | Admissions Phone: 315-228-7401

Inside the Classroom

When the sons of toothpaste/soap magnate William Colgate bailed out the penniless, struggling seminary/college known as Madison University in the late 1800s, the school had no idea that, from that point on, it would bear the family's name and rise to become one of the most respected liberal arts colleges in the country. Today, Colgate University is just that—one of the finest schools of its kind and home to approximately 2,900 high achievers in the rustic, hilly town of Hamilton, New York.

Fifty-six majors are on tap at Colgate, including all of the expected liberal arts concentrations. No matter your discipline, students must work through the extensive core curriculum. The requirements start with five classes that everyone must complete by the end of sophomore year: Legacies of the Ancient World, Challenges of Modernity, Communities and Identities, Scientific Perspectives on the World, and Global Engagements. An additional six courses from a range of the usual disciplines round out the mandated components of the curriculum as well as foreign language and physical education requirements.

With a student-faculty ratio of 9:1 and an average class size of seventeen, Colgate undergraduates work intimately with their instructors. Undoubtedly, the resulting connections help to explain the school's sterling 94-95 percent freshman retention rate. It is commonplace for Colgate students to research alongside professors. Each summer the school funds over 200 undergraduates who assist with research projects and, year-round, it maintains a useful database of professors who are seeking research across all disciplines. Raiders study abroad in overwhelming numbers with a 72 percent participation rate in one hundred programs that operate in fifty countries.

The social sciences account for 29 percent of all degrees conferred and, within that umbrella, economics, political science, and English are among the most popular and most well-regarded majors. International relations and neuroscience are also very strong. Other commonly issued degrees include biology (15 percent), psychology (7 percent), foreign languages (5 percent), and computer science (5 percent). Compared to other elite liberal arts schools, Colgate grads do not pursue competitive fellowships at a high rate. The university produces an occasional Fulbright, Gilman, Watson, Goldwater, or Critical Language Scholarship recipient, but not on the scale of many in its peer group.

Outside the Classroom

Rural Hamilton is not exactly a hotbed of activity, leading many to spend a great deal of time within the bubble of the university's grounds. Fortunately, those grounds happen to be a lush, 575-acre paradise that often receives accolades as one of the most beautiful colleges in the country. The university's eight Greek organizations, dating as far back as 1856, attract over 30 percent of the student body and play a leading role in defining the university milieu. Like many other colleges in frigid Central/Upstate New York, Colgate has, not unfairly, earned a "party school" label. The sports tradition at Colgate is rich as the Raiders field twenty-five teams that compete in NCAA Division I. The ice hockey team is particularly exceptional and has produced many NHL players. Also competing are club teams in forty sports including Aikido, juggling, and Nordic skiing. Including those who play in varsity, club, and intramural sports, a majority of undergraduates find themselves involved in some level of athletic competition. For everyone else, there are 190+ student-run organizations with a fair representation of environment-oriented clubs. That aligns with the university's status as one of the more eco-friendly campuses as it runs almost exclusively on hydroelectric power and places a strong emphasis on organic food, sustainable energy, and increasing the use of bicycles on campus.

Career Services

The Center for Career Services (CCS) is comprised of fourteen professionals with expertise in career advising, employer relations, and alumni engagement. That works out to a 206:1 student-to-advisor ratio, which is better than average compared to other schools featured in this guide. Further, this staff deploys its ample resources effectively, engaging with 90 percent of students each academic year, including 93 percent of seniors and 88 percent of freshmen.

In 2016-17, the CCS held over 10,800 individual meetings with more than 3,000 current students and recent alumni. On-campus workshops and programs attracted over 11,000 attendees. The office also excels in employer relations, having forged formal recruiting partnerships with 177 companies/hiring institutions, which leads to roughly 600 on-campus interviews per year (close to one per senior). Premier employers include many of the top banking, accounting, and consulting firms in the country. The university supplies generous funding to students who wish to take low-paying or nonpaying internships, financially supporting close to 200 students per year. Job shadowing opportunities with alumni were arranged for 322 students in 2016-17, and 4,500 jobs and internships were posted exclusively for Colgate students. Displaying proficiency in undergraduate engagement, recruiting, and generating positive graduate outcomes, Colgate's career services rates among the best anywhere in the country.

Colgate University

E-mail: admission@colgate.edu | Website: www.colgate.edu

Professional Outcomes

Nine months after graduation only a few Colgate alumni are still looking for work; in 2017, that group represented less than 1 percent of the graduating class. A substantial 84 percent had already landed full-time jobs. Business, education, sales, and finance are the most commonly entered sectors, in that order. Employers hiring the most Colgate grads included Bank of America Merrill Lynch, IBM, EY, Sloan Kettering Cancer Center, Massachusetts General Hospital, and the NIH. Including alumni of all ages, the strongest concentrations of Raiders can be found roaming the corporate offices of Google, Goldman Sachs, JPMorgan Chase & Co., Deloitte, Citi, UBS, PwC, and Amazon. At age thirty-four the alumni's median earnings were $71,500, comparable to other elite private universities such as Wake Forest, Bucknell, and Boston College. A sizable portion of alumni set up shop in the Greater New York City area. Boston and DC are the next most popular locales.

In 2017, a healthy 85 percent of law school applicants were accepted into one of their target institutions. The medical school numbers were even more impressive with 100 percent of graduating seniors (who were recommended by the school) gaining acceptance into at least one med school. The other most commonly pursued areas of graduate study are biology, business, engineering, public affairs and policy, and the social and behavioral sciences. Over the last four years the most frequently attended graduate schools were primarily elite institutions that included Boston College, Boston University, Columbia, Cornell, Georgetown, NYU, Northeastern, and the University of Pennsylvania.

Admission

Colgate hit an all-time high in the number of applications received in 2018. The 9,705 applicants represented a 13 percent increase over the previous year. The acceptance rate for a spot in the Class of 2022 was 25 percent, down from 28 percent the previous year. The average standardized test scores of enrolled students in the Class of 2022 were 1402 on the SAT and 32 on the ACT; and unusual for an East Coast school, two-thirds of applicants submitted ACT results. The average unweighted GPA was 3.72. Among freshmen in the 2018-19 school year, 77 percent finished in the top 10 percent of their high school class while 94 percent were in the top 25 percent.

The admissions office ranks only three factors as being "very important": rigor of coursework, GPA, and class rank. Standardized test scores are included in the next tier of factors, however students who gain acceptance tend to score well. Though Colgate claims that demonstrated interest is not a factor, 48 percent of the Class of 2022 was admitted through early decision, so the school does "want you to want them." Those who applied early in 2018 got in at a far more generous 41 percent acceptance rate than those who applied in the regular cycle (23 percent). Children of alumni, so-called legacies, obtained an even more favorable 47 percent. Over the past decade Colgate's admit rate has held fairly steady, but on the metrics of class rank and standardized tests scores, the average admitted student possesses superior credentials to Raiders of the recent past.

Worth Your Money?

Tax return data suggests that, along with schools such as Colorado College, Trinity College, and Washington University in St. Louis, Colgate enrolls the highest percentage of students from the "top 1 percent." It's no wonder the average amount of debt accrued by its graduates is lower than the national average. While the majority of students come from upper-income homes, those from less-fortunate backgrounds are showered with need-based aid. The 35 percent of undergraduates who qualify receive $55k per year, meeting 100 percent of their demonstrated need. One way or another, people are pleased with their decision to invest their time and money in Colgate University.

FINANCIAL
Institutional Type: Private
In-State Tuition: $57,695
Out-of-State Tuition: $57,695
Room & Board: $14,540
Required Fees: $350
Books & Supplies: $1,040

Avg. Need-Based Aid: $55,163
Avg. % of Need Met: 100%

Avg. Merit-Based Aid: $0
% Receiving Merit-Based Aid: 0%

Avg. Cumulative Debt: $24,243
% of Students Borrowing: 32%

CAREER
Who Recruits
1. NYU Langhorne Medical Center
2. Revlon
3. Guidepoint Global
4. AlphaSights
5. Zipcar

Notable Internships
1. ESPN
2. Wells Fargo
3. Barclay's

Top Industries
1. Business
2. Education
3. Operations
4. Finance
5. Sales

Top Employers
1. EY
2. Morgan Stanley
3. Google
4. Goldman Sachs
5. JPMorgan Chase

Where Alumni Work
1. New York City
2. Boston
3. Washington, DC
4. San Francisco
5. Syracuse, NY

Median Earnings
College Scorecard (Early Career): $63,600
EOP (Early Career): $71,500
PayScale (Mid-Career): $130,600

RANKINGS
Forbes: 46
Money: 54
U.S. News: 17 (T), Liberal Arts Colleges
Wall Street Journal/THE: 48
Washington Monthly: 18, Liberal Arts Colleges

#CollegesWorthYourMoney

Ewing, New Jersey | Admissions Phone: 609-771-2131

ADMISSION
Admission Rate: 50%
Admission Rate - Men: 48%
Admission Rate - Women: 51%
EA Admission Rate: Not Offered
ED Admission Rate: 60%
Admission Rate (5-Year Trend): +7%
ED Admission Rate (5-Year Trend): -1%
% of Admits Attending (Yield): 23%
Transfer Admission Rate: 45%

Offered Wait List: 2,207
Accepted Wait List: 602
Admitted Wait List: 8

SAT Reading/Writing (Middle 50%): 580-670
SAT Math (Middle 50%): 580-680
ACT Composite (Middle 50%): 25-30
Testing Policy: ACT/SAT Required
SAT Superscore: Yes
ACT Superscore: Yes

% Graduated in Top 10% of HS Class: 37%
% Graduated in Top 25% of HS Class: 75%
% Graduated in Top 50% of HS Class: 97%

ENROLLMENT
Total Undergraduate Enrollment: 7,048
% Part-Time: 3%
% Male: 43%
% Female: 57%
% Out-of-State: 6%
% Fraternity: 15%
% Sorority: 13%
% On-Campus (Freshman): 90%
% On-Campus (All Undergraduate): 54%

% African-American: 6%
% Asian: 12%
% Hispanic: 13%
% White: 64%
% Other: 0%
% Race or Ethnicity Unknown: 4%
% International: 0%
% Low-Income: 19%

ACADEMICS
Student-to-Faculty Ratio: 13:1
% of Classes Under 20: 42%
% of Classes Under 40: 97%
% Full-Time Faculty: 43%
% Full-Time Faculty w/ Terminal Degree: 91%

Top Programs
Accounting
Business Administration
Biology
Criminology
Communication Studies
Elementary Education
Nursing

Retention Rate: 93%
4-Year Graduation Rate: 76%
6-Year Graduation Rate: 86%

Curricular Flexibility: Somewhat Flexible
Academic Rating: ★★★↓

Inside the Classroom
Let's lead off with a telling factoid: The freshman-to-sophomore retention rate at the College of New Jersey is 94 percent, better than at the majority of selective private schools. As one of only six public colleges in the country to maintain a four-year graduation rate above 70 percent, the school is in the esteemed company of such institutions as UVA, Michigan, and UNC-Chapel Hill. Central Jersey may not draw a flood of applicants from the far reaches of the globe (only 6 percent of the student population comes from out of state), but the TCNJ, a midsize state school with 6,700+ undergraduate students, is simply one the best bargains you can find in the Northeastern United States.

There are more than fifty majors, but whether you're studying art history or computer science, there are an identical series of general requirements known as Liberal Learning awaiting you, beginning as a freshman. As part of the Intellectual and Scholarly Growth phase of your education, new arrivals participate in a First-Year Program, a seminar-style course centered on one of seventy engaging topics. Students also complete an online, not-for-credit course on Information Literacy. A second language requirement exists for the School of Humanities and Social Sciences and selected programs with the arts and sciences, business, and science schools. While you can test out of the introductory course, three writing-intensive classes are on the menu, including a senior capstone. Additionally, you must choose a collective eight courses that fulfill your breadth requirements in the areas of the arts and humanities, social sciences and history, and natural science and quantitative reasoning.

TCNJ sports a 13:1 student-to-faculty ratio, an average class size of twenty-one, and 81 percent of sections contain fewer than thirty students. While you won't find many seminar-style courses with single-digit enrollments, there are plenty of ways to personally connect with faculty thanks to the school's serious commitment to facilitating undergraduate research. In fact, the Council on Undergraduate Research awarded TCNJ its signature honor, the Campus-Wide Award for Undergraduate Research Accomplishment. In addition to plenty of research opportunities in the hard sciences, this school has invested in specialized facilities that include twenty psychology research labs, a digital humanities lab, and a fully equipped quantitative studies lab for criminology and sociology students. The College of New Jersey may not attract many from outside its state borders, but it certainly helps its own expand their global horizons as 30 percent of undergrads participate in one of 500 study abroad programs.

Twenty-percent of degrees conferred are in education as many attend TCNJ to become teachers. The School of Education is widely considered the finest in the state. Next in popularity are business/marketing (16 percent), psychology (9 percent), engineering (8 percent), the social sciences (7 percent) and biology (6 percent). Jersey- and New York-based employers think highly of the school that also has strong programs in biology, criminology, accounting, and nursing. Recent TCNJ students have won or placed as finalists for Fulbright, Marshall, Gates, and Truman awards. Two 2019 graduates won Goldwater Scholarships, and five 2018 graduates were awarded National Science Foundation Graduate Research Fellowships.

Outside the Classroom
While only 55 percent of the undergraduate student body reside on the 289-acre, well-maintained grounds of this suburban campus in Ewing, The College of New Jersey's fourteen residence halls do accommodate 95 percent of freshmen; housing is guaranteed for a student's first two years only. Greek life does have a noticeable presence on campus with 14 percent of men pledging fraternities and 11 percent of women entering sororities. Aikido, knitting, and broadcasting on WTSR 91.3 are only three of the diverse 150+ active clubs available. A strong Division III athletics program features nine men's and nine women's teams that, since 1979, have captured forty team and forty-nine individual NCAA championships. The Student Recreation Center features an indoor track, tennis courts, and a dance studio for those wanting to stay in shape, and there are plenty of intramural sports on tap at that same location. TCNJ is only five miles from the state capital of Trenton, ten miles from Princeton, and an hour's drive from Philly or New York City.

Career Services
A small office, the Career Center at the College of New Jersey employs only six full-time professional staff, not counting secretaries, office assistants, interns, or peer career educators who assist with things like resume reviews and career fair organization. The student-to-counselor ratio of 1,100:1 isn't terribly strong, but it's clearly enough staffing to make plenty of positive things happen for the school's undergraduates.

Over 400 employers recruit on campus, a phenomenal number given that there are only 6,600 undergrads. A solid 71.6 percent of surveyed graduates reported having at least one internship with 63.1 percent participating in an internship for two or more semesters, and 36.2 percent securing a paid position following their internship.

The College of New Jersey

E-mail: tcnjinfo@tcnj.edu | Website: www.tcnj.edu

In large part due to the efforts of the Career Center, 30 percent of graduates say the school did an excellent job in preparing them for entering the workforce, 44 percent rate the center's efforts as "above average," and fewer than 5 percent of respondents gave a mark of "below average." The large presence of graduates, recent and otherwise, in the offices of many top companies and banks around the country speaks to the superb employer engagement efforts of this school.

Professional Outcomes

Checking in with TCNJ grads one year after receiving their degrees, a near-perfect 98.4 percent had entered the working world or started an advanced degree. The list of companies employing significant numbers of Class of 2017 alumni includes Johnson and Johnson (14), JP Morgan Chase & Co., (11), Bank of America (11), Bloomberg LP (8), AT&T (7), Emergency Medical Associates/EmCare (7), EY (6), and PricewaterhouseCoopers (6). Factoring in all alumni, the school also has a huge presence within Verizon, Merrill Lynch, Merck, and Bristol-Meyers Squibb. The starting salary after exiting the College of New Jersey was an impressive $56,200, more than 12 percent higher than the national average for college grads. School of Arts & Communication grads earned $47,350 while School of Business degree-holders took home $60,050. The most popular geographic destinations were New Jersey (65.5 percent), New York (18.1 percent), and Pennsylvania (5.7 percent).

The most frequently attended graduate schools by members of the Class of 2017 were TCNJ (59), Rutgers University (35), University of Pennsylvania (7), New York University (7), Columbia University (7), Penn State University (6), Monmouth University (5), and Johns Hopkins University (5). Class of 2017 graduates entered law schools including William & Mary, Hofstra, Penn State, and Rutgers. Members of the same cohort went on to attend an array of excellent medical schools including Johns Hopkins, the Icahn School of Medicine at Mt. Sanai, NYU, Drexel, and Penn State University. Many also attend Rutgers via the 7-Year Combined BS/MD Program with Rutgers New Jersey Medical School. Overall, undergraduates enjoy a 65 percent medical school acceptance rate, more than 20 points higher than the national average.

Admission

The College of New Jersey is a rare school that isn't terribly hard to get into—the acceptance rate for 2018-19 freshman was right at 50 percent—but it provides a superior and supportive academic experience to its undergraduates. Thirty-seven percent of the Class of 2022 placed in the top 10 percent of their high school class, three-quarters were in the top 25 percent, and 97 percent were in the top 50 percent. The mid-50 percent standardized test score ranges were 25-30 on the ACT and 1160-1350 on the SAT. In a higher education world where many schools have experienced massive spikes in selectivity in recent years, TCNJ remains fairly steady; the profile of an accepted student five years ago is similar to today's freshman.

At the top of the list of "very important" admissions factors sits participation in a rigorous course load, class rank, standardized test scores, extracurricular activities and, most interestingly, volunteer work. The essay, teacher recommendations, talent/ability, character/personal qualities, and state residency are all in the next tier of "important" factors. However, given that the overwhelming majority of TCNJ students come from inside New Jersey, out-of-state applicants should enjoy a slight advantage. This is reality is made more evident by the fact that TCNJ offers an application fee waiver to all students applying from out of state. Finally, applying Early Decision may also offer an edge--of the 686 submitting ED applications in 2018, three-fifths were accepted. Those accepted through early decision comprised 27 percent of the entire freshman class.

Worth Your Money?

Garden State residents will pay around $17,000 per year in tuition and fees, and while the school isn't as cheap as it used to be (what is?), TCNJ represents an exceptional bargain for an East Coast public school with a tremendously successful alumni base. Few out-of-state students seek out this college, but the price is not unreasonable, particularly for those wishing to study business or a STEM field.

FINANCIAL
Institutional Type: Public
In-State Tuition: $16,942
Out-of-State Tuition: $28,921
Room & Board: $13,964
Required Fees: N/A
Books & Supplies: N/A

Avg. Need-Based Aid: $11,889
Avg. % of Need Met: 40%

Avg. Merit-Based Aid: $5,648
% Receiving Merit-Based Aid: 38%

Avg. Cumulative Debt: $37,787
% of Students Borrowing: 62%

CAREER
Who Recruits
1. Target
2. withum
3. NJM Insurance Group
4. Cenlar
5. Johnson & Johnson

Notable Internships
1. U.S. Department of Education
2. Prudential Financial
3. Lockheed Martin

Top Industries
1. Education
2. Business
3. Operations
4. Healthcare
5. Sales

Top Employers
1. Johnson & Johnson
2. Merrill Lynch
3. Bristol-Myers Squibb
4. Merck
5. Prudential Financial

Where Alumni Work
1. New York City
2. Philadelphia
3. Washington, DC
4. Boston
5. Los Angeles

Median Earnings
College Scorecard (Early Career): $58,500
EOP (Early Career): $60,100
PayScale (Mid-Career): $101,800

RANKINGS
Forbes: 149
Money: 48
U.S. News: 4, Regional North
Wall Street Journal/THE: 266 (T)
Washington Monthly: N/A

#CollegesWorthYourMoney

College of the Holy Cross

Worcester, Massachusetts | Admissions Phone: 508-793-2443

Inside the Classroom

The oldest Catholic college in all of New England, the College of the Holy Cross in Worcester, Massachusetts, offers an exceptional liberal arts education with a strong Jesuit influence that permeates the service-oriented undergraduate student body of just under 2,900. The college offers thirty traditional majors as well as additional subjects in which one can pursue a student-designed major. Hands-on learning, interdisciplinary connections, a genuine quest for meaning and value, and faculty guidance that extends beyond the classroom are all staples of academic life for all Crusaders.

So-called "common requirements" that must be fulfilled by all undergraduate students is a comprehensive but straightforward list. Mandatory areas of study include one course each in religion, philosophical studies, arts, literature, history, and cross-cultural studies. Two courses are required in language studies, social science, and natural and mathematical sciences. All freshmen complete a year-long seminar called Montserrat that is centered on an interdisciplinary topic and designed to help students "develop broad foundational skills, including critical thinking, strong writing, and effective communication."

The average class size is a manageable nineteen students, and 60 percent of courses have enrollments lower than that. An undergraduate-only institution, Holy Cross offers ample individualized attention and guidance from faculty. Each year one hundred students participate in the intensive Weiss Summer Research Program that offers STEM majors the opportunity for one-on-one mentorship from a professor. Across all disciplines, research apprenticeships are available to undergrads as early as the sophomore year. Study abroad figures are relatively modest as roughly 300 students travel each year to one of fifty approved locales.

There are no majors that undergrads flock to in overwhelming numbers, but the most popular are economics (14 percent), psychology (12 percent), political science (11 percent), history (7 percent), and English (7 percent). All of those popular departments also rank well nationally. Biology and chemistry are also very strong. Highly competitive postgraduate fellowships are frequently pursued by seniors. In fact, Holy Cross is one of the nation's top Fulbright producers with ninety-three such scholars named since 2005, and seven students and alums took home the award in 2019 alone.

Outside the Classroom

Thanks to a campus regularly voted as one of the country's most beautiful, few undergraduates wish to flee the grounds. Guaranteed housing is available for all four years in one of eleven residence halls, and 90 percent of students elect to live in college-owned housing. The nine campus eateries also receive acclaim and leave students with little reason to seek off-campus dining options. Those seeking the typical university experience of Greek parties and big-time athletics will find themselves batting .500. There are no fraternities or sororities on campus, but with twenty-seven Division I squads, twenty-two club teams, and eleven intramural sports on the menu it seems like most of the student body participates in some form of athletic competition. The Hart Center is replete with amenities including a six-lane swimming pool, ice rink, and a 2,800-square-foot facility dedicated to cardiovascular and strength training. There are 103 student organizations, including a healthy dose of clubs in the performing arts, service, and multicultural realms. While Worcester isn't a town that teems with alluring activities, the college is located only forty-four miles west of Boston and sixty-one miles northeast of Hartford.

Career Services

The Center for Career Development (CCD) is staffed by eight professional employees (not counting office assistants), resulting in a 377:1 student-to-advisor ratio that is in the average range when compared with other schools featured in this guide. The CCD believes in a "three-stage model of career development: self-assessment, exploration, and implementation." Individualized attention is available to undergraduates at each stage of their education, whether it involves discussing the results of an interest inventory, preparing a resume, engaging in a mock interview, or applying to graduate/professional school.

Fall and spring career fairs attract approximately sixty employers and 300 students. Well-known employers such as City Year, GE, EY, PepsiCo, and the FBI are regular attendees. The office excels in coordinating student internships as an impressive 73 percent of graduates end up with at least one such experience. In 2017-18, the school ponied up $209,000 to help defray costs of eighty-two undergrads completing unpaid summer internships. Students who completed internships enjoyed better job placement rates and higher starting salaries than those who did not. Through the Career Advisor Network current students can link up to alumni in fields of interest to arrange a job-shadowing experience or to receive career advice. Thanks to a high level of student engagement and strong employment/graduate school results (more on this in a moment), the Center for Career Development is performing admirably on behalf of its undergraduates.

Professional Outcomes

Seven months after moving their tassels to the left, 72 percent of the Class of 2018 were employed, 14 percent were in graduate school, 7 percent were engaged in volunteer work, and only 1 percent were still seeking full-time employment; the overall success rate was 97 percent. The industries drawing the most Holy Cross grads were health care (17 percent), financial services (16 percent), technology (8 percent), government/politics/law (7 percent), and accounting (7 percent). Organizations employing more than one recent graduate include Fidelity Investments, JP Morgan, Goldman Sachs, Massachusetts General Hospital, Deloitte, EY, PwC, Oracle, and Dell. Large numbers of alumni also can be found at State Street, Morgan Stanley, and the Dana Farber Cancer Institute. The median salary for graduates is $51,600 and varies greatly by industry. Those in finance enjoyed median starting salaries of $67,000 while those entering health care, government, or education took home $35-42k. New England is the most popular home, keeping 56 percent of grads in the area with the Mid-Atlantic region soaking up an additional 30 percent. Boston and New York City are the two most common destinations.

Among those enrolled in graduate school, 19 percent were in law school, 13 percent were pursuing degrees in a health profession, and 12 percent were in PhD programs. Boston College and Fordham are among the most frequently attended law schools. Recent graduates have earned spots in medical schools such as Tufts and acceptances into dental school at the University of Pennsylvania and Boston University. Overall, Holy Cross graduates enjoy 90 percent acceptance rates to both law and medical schools. Grads have been accepted into masters and doctoral programs at elite schools including Georgetown, Johns Hopkins, Princeton, Harvard, the University of Chicago, and Columbia.

Admission

A competitive pool of more than 7,000 applicants for a place in the Holy Cross Class of 2022 encountered a 38 percent acceptance rate. This is in the same ballpark as the acceptances rates over the last five years. Holy Cross is test-optional and, unlike many other highly selective test- optional schools, attending freshmen actually submitted test-free applications. Of the Class of 2022, only 46 percent submitted SAT scores, and 27 percent submitted ACT scores. Given that a fair number of applicants are likely to have submitted both, it is reasonable to assume that a healthy percentage of the class were admitted sans standardized tests scores. Among those that did submit scores, the mid-50 percent range on the SAT was 1280-1420 and 28-32 on the ACT. Crusaders finished in the top 10 percent of their high school class at a 58 percent clip, and 88 percent fell within the top quarter.

According to the admissions committee, six factors rise above the rest when evaluating applicants: rigor of secondary school record, GPA, essays, recommendations, the interview, and character/personal qualities. Extracurricular activities and talent/ability are the only other factors labeled as being "important." Those dead-set on attending this school shouldn't think twice about applying early decision as the ED acceptance rate climbed as high as 81 percent last cycle. (The regular round acceptance rate was 35 percent.) Early decision admits comprised 44 percent of the Class of 2022. The two most notable items related to admissions at the College of the Holy Cross are its test-optional admissions and incredibly generous ED acceptance rate. Serious applicants are advised to strongly consider the latter.

Worth Your Money?

Holy Cross helps to mitigate the impact of its $71,710 sticker price by meeting 100 percent of demonstrated need for every single student who qualifies for financial aid. All told, 53 percent of students qualify for an average grant of $36,173, making the overall cost sting a bit less. Merit aid is awarded to only 16 percent of the student body, so if you don't obtain need-based aid, you're likely to be paying a large portion of the 300k four-year bill. Holy Cross is an excellent school, but you won't get a huge income boost from attending (median salaries are right around average), so you may not want to go deep into debt to afford a full-price tab, especially if you're considering a lower-paying field.

FINANCIAL
Institutional Type: Private
In-State Tuition: $54,050
Out-of-State Tuition: $54,050
Room & Board: $15,070
Required Fees: $690
Books & Supplies: $1,000

Avg. Need-Based Aid: $36,173
Avg. % of Need Met: 100%

Avg. Merit-Based Aid: $15,200
% Receiving Merit-Based Aid: 16%

Avg. Cumulative Debt: $25,260
% of Students Borrowing: 60%

CAREER
Who Recruits
1. Dell
2. General Electric
3. Peace Corps
4. Wayfair
5. Deloitte

Notable Internships
1. National Football League
2. McCann
3. MetLife

Top Industries
1. Business
2. Education
3. Finance
4. Operations
5. Sales

Top Employers
1. Fidelity Investments
2. PwC
3. Deloitte
4. EY
5. Morgan Stanley

Where Alumni Work
1. Boston
2. New York City
3. India
4. Washington, DC
5. United Kingdom

Median Earnings
College Scorecard (Early Career): $71,000
EOP (Early Career): $71,900
PayScale (Mid-Career): $114,600

RANKINGS
Forbes: 77
Money: 43
U.S. News: 27 (T), Liberal Arts Colleges
Wall Street Journal/THE: 125
Washington Monthly: 13, Liberal Arts Colleges

#CollegesWorthYourMoney

College of William & Mary

Williamsburg, Virginia | Admissions Phone: 757-221-4223

ADMISSION
Admission Rate: 37%
Admission Rate - Men: 42%
Admission Rate - Women: 34%
EA Admission Rate: Not Offered
ED Admission Rate: 58%
Admission Rate (5-Year Trend): +4%
ED Admission Rate (5-Year Trend): +11%
% of Admits Attending (Yield): 29%
Transfer Admission Rate: 52%

Offered Wait List: 4,133
Accepted Wait List: 2,172
Admitted Wait List: 94

SAT Reading/Writing (Middle 50%): 660-730
SAT Math (Middle 50%): 650-760
ACT Composite (Middle 50%): 30-33
Testing Policy: ACT/SAT Required
SAT Superscore: Yes
ACT Superscore: Yes

% Graduated in Top 10% of HS Class: 77%
% Graduated in Top 25% of HS Class: 95%
% Graduated in Top 50% of HS Class: 99%

ENROLLMENT
Total Undergraduate Enrollment: 6,377
% Part-Time: 1%
% Male: 42%
% Female: 58%
% Out-of-State: 31%
% Fraternity: 28%
% Sorority: 29%
% On-Campus (Freshman): 100%
% On-Campus (All Undergraduate): 71%

% African-American: 7%
% Asian: 8%
% Hispanic: 9%
% White: 59%
% Other: 5%
% Race or Ethnicity Unknown: 6%
% International: 6%
% Low-Income: 11%

ACADEMICS
Student-to-Faculty Ratio: 12:1
% of Classes Under 20: 47%
% of Classes Under 40: 86%
% Full-Time Faculty: 70%
% Full-Time Faculty w/ Terminal Degree: 96%

Top Programs
Accounting
Business
Biology
Chemistry
Government
History
International Relations
Public Policy

Retention Rate: 95%
4-Year Graduation Rate: 85%
6-Year Graduation Rate: 91%

Curricular Flexibility: Somewhat Flexible
Academic Rating: ★★★★

Inside the Classroom
Brimming with tradition, the College of William & Mary is one of the oldest public institutions in the country (some contend the oldest), the alma mater of three US presidents, and a school that has long been a member of the "Public Ivy" club. Roughly two-thirds of the 6,300+ undergraduates on this spectacularly beautiful Williamsburg campus hail from in-state, and members of the student body known as "the Tribe" tend to be an intellectual and passionate lot who adore their school. Of W&M's nearly 100,000 living alumni, you'll rarely meet one who doesn't have a strong affinity for their school.

Forty undergraduate programs are available with the most popular being business, psychology, economics, biology, and government. All undergraduates must work through the College Curriculum, the school's liberal arts core including two first-year seminars, four COLL 200 courses covering a variety of topics, COLL 300 (that often involves studying abroad), and COLL 400 as a senior, which requires the production of original research. Additional requirements include taking courses in three "knowledge domains" and demonstrating proficiency in mathematics and foreign language.

William & Mary has an 11:1 student-to-faculty ratio. Class sizes are rarely tiny seminars, but close to 50 percent do enroll fewer than twenty students, and only 14 percent contain more than fifty. An extremely high percentage of undergrads study abroad for a semester; by graduation, roughly half of the class has done so, traveling to one of more than sixty countries. Undergraduate research opportunities are widely available. In the Chemistry Department, for example, 80-90 percent of students complete independent/professor-assisted research with many becoming coauthors of studies alongside faculty. Across the college an average 85 percent of undergraduates participate in research each year.

Among the college's most notable academic programs are (1) government and (2) international relations, both of which serve as pipelines to Washington, DC, employers. The Mason School of Business is highly regarded in the corporate world. With a notable service-minded ethos, William & Mary is the top producer of Peace Corps volunteers among midsize universities. In 2018, the college had thirteen Fulbright Scholarship winners, most in the state of Virginia. However, the school doesn't take home other prestigious scholarships in large numbers.

Outside the Classroom
The campus is large and lush with over 1,200 acres, including an amphitheater, Lake Matoaka, and College Woods, the latter two of which can be freely enjoyed by nature-loving students. William and Mary's grounds easily make any list of the most beautiful college campuses in the country. A touch under three-quarters of students live on campus, including a sizable number of Greek houses. Greek life first appeared at W&M in 1776, and the tradition is still alive and well today. Presently, 28 percent of undergrads participate with higher numbers in the school's sororities than fraternities. More than 450 student clubs in every area imaginable are available with volunteer organizations drawing large numbers—3,500+ each year. That spirit of involvement carries over into athletics as well with an 85 percent participation rate when including the school's twenty-three NCAA Division I teams and thriving intramural and club sports. Nightlife in the surrounding Williamsburg area is generally pretty tame unless you happen to be a colonial-era history buff. Most students enjoy a social life more centered around campus activities and dorm life.

Career Services
The Cohen Career Center (CCC) employs thirteen full-time staff members, not counting graduate assistants or administrative assistants, giving it a student-to-advisor ratio of 571:1, which is higher than the average school profiled in this guide. The CCC does arrange several well-attended job fairs each year including the Government & Nonprofit Career Expo that features ninety employers as well as large-scale career and internship fairs in the fall and spring that are attended by as many as 1,000 undergrads. All told, 397 employers attended William & Mary career fairs in 2018-19.

In a typical year the office conducts over 900 mock interviews, one hundred workshops, and information sessions with 125 employers. In the 2018-19 academic year 2,344 one-on-one counseling sessions were conducted with undergraduates. For those interested in graduate school, representatives from more than one hundred programs across the academic spectrum attend the annual Graduate & Professional Fair. Partnerships with Deloitte, PwC, KPMG, EY, and Accenture lead to on-campus recruiting and interviewing with those giants of the accounting and consulting fields. Close to 1,000 on-campus interviews are arranged each year with W&M seniors. A respectable 61 percent of grads participated in at least one internship, externship, or research project. The office does a solid job guiding undergraduates toward meaningful work as 88 percent found first jobs that aligned to some degree with their career goals.

College of William & Mary

E-mail: admission@wm.edu | Website: www.wm.edu

Professional Outcomes

The Class of 2017 (the most recent class for which data is available) saw 60 percent of its cohort join the work-force, and 26 percent enter graduate school within six months of graduation. Over 500 employers snatched up at least one member of the Tribe. Companies hiring the highest number of grads were IBM (25), Deloitte (17), EY (12), Accenture (11), and Booz Allen Hamilton (11).

More than fifty alumni across all graduating years can be found in the corporate offices of Capital One, PwC, Microsoft, Google, Amazon, and Deloitte. Starting salaries varied significantly by industry. The average salary for those entering the world of IT/computing was over $78k, financial services was $69k, the sciences were $36k, and museums and libraries were $29k. The vast majority of alumni remain in the Mid-Atlantic region; the Northeast is a distant second.

Those opting for immediate entry into graduate school enrolled at 132 institutions. The greatest number of fresh alums stayed at their alma mater with 102 continuing their studies at William & Mary. The next most frequented universities were Virginia Commonwealth University (14), Georgetown (10), UVA (9), Eastern Virginia Medical School (8), Columbia (7), Emory (4), Virginia Tech (4), and Yale (4). Thirty-eight grads were pursuing PhDs, twenty-seven were studying to be MDs, and sixteen headed to law school. In previous years a greater number of alumni have entered JD or PhD programs. Most impressively, William & Mary graduates gain acceptance into medical school at a rate twice the national average.

Admission

Of the 14,644 applicants vying for a seat in W&M's Class of 2022, just over 5,400 received the proverbial thick envelope. That calculates to an acceptance rate of 37 percent. Like UNC-Chapel Hill, but not to nearly as extreme a degree, in-state applicants have an easier pathway to acceptance at William & Mary. The accep-tance rate for out-of-state students typically runs under 30 percent while in-staters enjoy closer to a 45 percent acceptance rate. Of those who enrolled in the Class of 2022 the SAT middle-50 percent range was 1310-1490, and the ACT range was 30-33. (A far greater number of applicants submit SAT scores.) Over three-quarters of enrolled freshmen hail from the top 10 percent of their high school class, and 95 percent placed in the top quartile.

The admissions office ranks a dozen factors as being most important in the admissions process. In addition to the obvious factors of grades, test scores, and class rank, the college also prioritizes state residency status, volunteer work, work experience, character/personal qualities, and talent/ability. Applying early decision can work to your advantage as over 58 percent of ED applicants get positive results, and ED admits comprised 35 percent of the 2018-19 freshman class. The regular round acceptance rate is only 36 percent. William & Mary is a highly selective school, but even more so for non-Virginia residents. The school maintains a 65/35 split of in-state versus out-of-state students. Still, in 2018 the school accepted students from all fifty states as well as forty-eight foreign countries, so candidates with strong academic profiles can still find a home here.

Worth Your Money?

High-achieving residents of Virginia are lucky to have two Ivy-level public schools at their disposal. Like UVA, William & Mary comes at a bargain price for those living in Virginia. The cost of attendance is roughly $38,000 in state and $62,000 out of state. Almost one-fifth of the student population receives a merit aid award with an annual value of $13k. The 38 percent who receive need-based aid rarely see 100 percent of their need met, but the average grant amount of $19,108 certainly helps, particularly for those paying the in-state rate. The average amount of debt for a W&M graduate is slightly less than the national average. For in-state students attending this school is a no-brainer. Prospective out-of-state students have to factor in the amount of loans you would need and the starting salaries typical of the field you eventually wish to enter.

FINANCIAL
Institutional Type: Public
In-State Tuition: $17,434
Out-of-State Tuition: $40,089
Room & Board: $12,926
Required Fees: $6,194
Books & Supplies: $1,000

Avg. Need-Based Aid: $19,108
Avg. % of Need Met: 82%

Avg. Merit-Based Aid: $13,080
% Receiving Merit-Based Aid: 19%

Avg. Cumulative Debt: $25,409
% of Students Borrowing: 35%

CAREER
Who Recruits
1. Central Intelligence Agency
2. National Institutes of Health
3. The Carlyle Group
4. Aldi
5. Navigant Consulting

Notable Internships
1. Booz Allen Hamilton
2. Vanguard
3. NFL Films

Top Industries
1. Business
2. Education
3. Operations
4. Social Services
5. Research

Top Employers
1. Capital One
2. Booz Allen Hamilton
3. Deloitte
4. EY
5. IBM

Where Alumni Work
1. Washington, DC
2. Norfolk, VA
3. New York City
4. Richmond, VA
5. Boston

Median Earnings
College Scorecard (Early Career): $58,500
EOP (Early Career): $59,800
PayScale (Mid-Career): $108,900

RANKINGS
Forbes: 47
Money: 45
U.S. News: 40, National Universities
Wall Street Journal/THE: 79
Washington Monthly: 109, National Universities

#CollegesWorthYourMoney

Colorado College

Colorado Springs, Colorado | Admissions Phone: 719-389-6344

Inside the Classroom

With the Rocky Mountains visible from Colorado College's ninety-acre campus, the school's 2,100 undergraduates find themselves in rarefied air—in more ways than one. A magnet for high-achieving, civic-minded, and generally liberally inclined young people, CC is ideally located seventy miles south of Denver and within a reasonable car ride of seven national parks and ten ski resorts. The student body is geographically diverse with about one-quarter hailing from the Northeast, one-quarter from the West Coast, and a sizable representation from the Midwest and the South.

Rather than the typical semester schedule, Colorado College operates on the "block plan," a series of eight three-and-half-week periods during which students take only one course. Requirements are broad, affording undergraduates the opportunity to chart their own course. That course, however, must stay within some boundaries that include a first-year seminar, a foreign language, as well as courses fitting under the umbrellas of global cultures, social inequality, quantitative reasoning, and scientific investigation of the natural world.

You won't find a more intimate liberal arts college than CC. Classes have a cap of twenty-five students, and no more than a handful of courses exceed that figure. The average class consists of sixteen students, and one-quarter of offerings have single-digit enrollments. Face time with your professors is a certainty as the school boasts a 10:1 student-faculty ratio. Although it does offer master's programs for teachers, this is a teaching college that focuses on undergraduate education. In faculty-wide surveys, the vast majority of professors report that quality of instruction is properly factored into their evaluations. Research opportunities are built in to the academic program as 20 percent of CC classes involve some degree of undergraduate research. Another 6 percent of students receive stipends to conduct research. Tigers appear unafraid to go into the world and immerse themselves in other cultures as a healthy 81 percent study abroad.

Regularly ranked among the top liberal arts schools in the country, Colorado College has an excellent reputation. Environmental studies, art, and sociology are considered very strong, but CC doesn't necessarily offer programs that clearly stand above the rest. In its own words, "The most popular majors at CC are those that are popular nationally." In terms of sheer volume, most degrees are conferred in the social sciences (30 percent), biology (13 percent), physical sciences (9 percent), natural resources and conservation (7 percent), and the visual and performing arts (7 percent). This institution is a regular producer of Watson and Fulbright Scholarship winners. It also ranks seventh in the nation for the number of Peace Corps volunteers produced, which is especially impressive given the modest size of each graduating class.

Outside the Classroom

Every freshman lives on Colorado College's campus, and 80 percent of the total undergraduate student body remains in school-owned housing. There is a Greek presence, but it in no way dominates the social scene. Only 12 percent of men join fraternities and 8 percent of women enter a sorority. More than 135 student clubs and organizations are available, the most popular being the Outdoor Recreation Committee. That makes sense given the natural splendor surrounding campus that is conducive to hiking, skiing, cycling, and the like. Students have the dual benefit of attending what is, technically, an urban campus situated in Colorado Springs that is, by area, the largest city in the state. Dorms, food, and campus facilities all receive generally favorable reviews from the student body. Community service projects are inclusive with an 80 percent undergraduate participation rate. While no one would mistake CC for a jock school, it does have sixteen total men's and women's sports teams competing in NCAA Division III, except for the highly competitive Division I ice hockey squad.

Career Services

The Career Center has eight full-time staff members who focus on either career advising or employer relations. Titles include career coach, health professions advisor, and pre-law advisor. The 262:1 student-to-advisor ratio is superior to many schools featured in this guide. The center puts its personnel to excellent use, having conducted a remarkable 1,700 one-on-one counseling sessions in the 2018-19 academic year.

Colorado College is a member of the nine-school Selective Liberal Arts Consortium that is comprised mostly of elite schools on the East Coast such as Vassar and Haverford College. This organization hosts off-campus interview days based in New York City and DC as well as video interviewing days with a host of high-caliber employers. The Career Center also arranges so-called "Tiger Treks" in which current students travel to a major city to meet with alumni in a variety of job settings. On-campus recruiting and interviewing is not a regular occurrence; only twenty-two companies recruited on campus last year. Internship opportunities are available, but assistance in landing one is limited. Roughly 57 percent of graduating seniors report having participated in at least one internship.

E-mail: admission@coloradocollege.edu | Website: www.coloradocollege.edu

Professional Outcomes

Being a small school, Colorado College does not send massive numbers of graduates to any one company or organization, but there are employers that have wrangled their fair share of Tigers. That list includes Microsoft, Wells Fargo, Amazon, Google, and Charles Schwab. The largest number of graduates who pursue employment end up in the fields of education, technology, health care, the arts, and government. Ten years after entering college, CC alumni have a median salary of about $45,000, lower than many schools of its ilk. Again, this is attributable to many graduates pursuing careers in nonprofit sectors and the relatively low number of STEM majors. Further, as we will discuss in a minute, seemingly all graduates of this school continue their educational journeys, a choice that typically delays financial rewards. Roughly one-quarter of grads stay in the state of Colorado while the majority migrate to major cities across the United States with San Francisco, New York, Seattle, and Los Angeles among the most popular destinations.

The bachelor's degree earned at Colorado College is unlikely to be the last degree a graduate will earn. Five years after graduation the typical cohort sees 70-90 percent of its members having either completed or finishing an advanced degree. Over half of that group are in PhD or professional programs with an average of 25 percent going to medical school. Recent graduates pursuing legal training have matriculated at a wide range of law schools including UVA, Columbia, NYU, Fordham, the University of Colorado, Temple, and Vermont Law School.

Admission

With an acceptance rate of only 15 percent, Colorado College unquestionably qualifies as a highly selective school. That figure has been sliced in half over the past five years as the number of applicants continues to soar. The good news is that the profile of the average admitted student has remained fairly steady. An SAT score in the mid-1300s (or an ACT around 30-31) will put you on solid ground if accompanied by a strong academic transcript. The mid-50 percent on standardized tests for those entering the Class of 2022 was 1300-1470 on the SAT and 29-33 on the ACT.

Colorado College's testing policy used to be as unique as its academic calendar. However, starting in 2020 the school made the shift from test-flexible to full-blown test-optional. Superb grades in a challenging high school curriculum are a must as "rigor of secondary school record" is the sole category rated by the admissions staff as "very important." The data suggests that the school means what it says: more than one-quarter of those attending finished in the top 1 percent of their graduating class; over three-quarters finished in the top 10 percent. Applying via early action or early decision can have a profound impact on your chances of gaining admission. Last year, those applying nonbinding early action were accepted 18 percent of the time, ED applicants 27 percent of the time, and regular applicants at only an 8.5 percent clip. Early decision applicants alone made up 57 percent of the incoming freshman class. In short, Colorado College is an institution with a low acceptance rate but a clear idea of what type of applicants it is looking for. While highly selective, those who performed at the top of their high school class can expect to be welcomed here, even if they didn't score perfectly on the SAT/ACT.

Worth Your Money?

The affluent make up a sizable portion of the undergraduate population at Colorado College, rendering the $73,600 annual cost of attendance of little concern to many considering the school. Tax return data estimates that almost one-quarter of students come from one-percenter households. For those who are concerned about the price tag, Colorado College awards minimal merit aid to 12 percent of its students, but it comes through strong for qualifying applicants, meeting 100 percent of demonstrated need for every financial aid recipient. The average annual value of those grants is roughly $50,000, helping make the school a worthy investment to students coming from more modest economic backgrounds. Students coming from families who make too much to qualify for significant need-based aid, but who make too little to comfortably cover CC's hefty price tag, are encouraged to consider their career and/or graduate school plans before committing.

FINANCIAL
Institutional Type: Private
In-State Tuition: $57,612
Out-of-State Tuition: $57,612
Room & Board: $12,956
Required Fees: $474
Books & Supplies: $1,240

Avg. Need-Based Aid: $50,108
Avg. % of Need Met: 100%

Avg. Merit-Based Aid: $8,036
% Receiving Merit-Based Aid: 12%

Avg. Cumulative Debt: $23,714
% of Students Borrowing: 42%

CAREER
Who Recruits
1. US Olympic Committee
2. El Pomar Foundation
3. Accenture
4. SunShare Community Solar
5. Amazon

Notable Internships
1. National Science Foundation
2. Late Show with Stephen Colbert
3. Accenture

Top Industries
1. Business
2. Education
3. Operations
4. Social Services
5. Media

Top Employers
1. Denver Public Schools
2. Microsoft
3. Amazon
4. Google
5. Charles Schwab

Where Alumni Work
1. Denver
2. Cororado Springs, CO
3. San Francisco
4. New York City
5. Seattle

Median Earnings
College Scorecard (Early Career): $45,400
EOP (Early Career): $43,600
PayScale (Mid-Career): $97,900

RANKINGS
Forbes: 92
Money: 345
U.S. News: 27 (T), Liberal Arts Colleges
Wall Street Journal/THE: 111 (T)
Washington Monthly: 66, Liberal Arts Colleges

#CollegesWorthYourMoney

Colorado School of Mines

Golden, Colorado | Admissions Phone: 303-273-3200

ADMISSION
Admission Rate: 49%
Admission Rate - Men: 45%
Admission Rate - Women: 59%
EA Admission Rate: Not Offered
ED Admission Rate: Not Offered
Admission Rate (5-Year Trend): +13%
ED Admission Rate (5-Year Trend): Not Offered
% of Admits Attending (Yield): 19%
Transfer Admission Rate: 47%

Offered Wait List: 1,280
Accepted Wait List: 426
Admitted Wait List: 16

SAT Reading/Writing (Middle 50%): 630-710
SAT Math (Middle 50%): 660-740
ACT Composite (Middle 50%): 28-33
Testing Policy: ACT/SAT Required
SAT Superscore: No
ACT Superscore: No

% Graduated in Top 10% of HS Class: 59%
% Graduated in Top 25% of HS Class: 85%
% Graduated in Top 50% of HS Class: 100%

ENROLLMENT
Total Undergraduate Enrollment: 4,954
% Part-Time: 5%
% Male: 70%
% Female: 30%
% Out-of-State: 41%
% Fraternity: 14%
% Sorority: 21%
% On-Campus (Freshman): 100%
% On-Campus (All Undergraduate): 11%

% African-American: 1%
% Asian: 4%
% Hispanic: 9%
% White: 72%
% Other: 6%
% Race or Ethnicity Unknown: 2%
% International: 6%
% Low-Income: 16%

ACADEMICS
Student-to-Faculty Ratio: 15:1
% of Classes Under 20: 29%
% of Classes Under 40: 66%
% Full-Time Faculty: 53%
% Full-Time Faculty w/ Terminal Degree: 92%

Top Programs
Computer Science
Civil Engineering
Engineering Physics
Environmental Engineering
Geological Engineering
Metallurgical and Materials Engineering
Petroleum Engineering

Retention Rate: 92%
4-Year Graduation Rate: 59%
6-Year Graduation Rate: 81%

Curricular Flexibility: Less Flexible
Academic Rating: ★★★

Inside the Classroom

Less than a half hour ride from Denver and a neighbor of the Coors factory, the Colorado School of Mines, commonly referred to as "Mines," is a public technical institute with an ever-increasing undergraduate enrollment of nearly 5,000, roughly 1,000 more students than a decade ago. The majority of students are Coloradans taking advantage of the reasonable $17,000 in-state tuition. However, the school is becoming more of a draw for out-of-staters and international students. Presently, there are representatives from all fifty states and eighty countries on campus.

There are sixteen bachelor of science degree options to choose from as well as additional areas of specialization. Close to 90 percent of undergraduates are pursuing engineering degrees in areas such as petroleum engineering, mining, mining engineering, geological engineering, mechanical engineering, and chemical engineering. In short, you don't come to Mines to read Tolstoy or intensively study Picasso's Blue Period. That being said, the university does demand that all undergrads complete its core curriculum that does include a smidgeon of work in the humanities and social sciences with an emphasis on "fundamental technical, mathematical, and writing skills."

Classes are rarely small as Mines possesses a student to faculty ratio of 16:1. The average class has thirty-four students, and only 29 percent of sections have an enrollment under twenty. Yet, that does not translate into a lack of hands-on opportunities. All Mines students must take a two-semester sequence of courses called EPICS (Engineering Practices Introductory Course Sequence) in which they tackle an open-ended design problem as part of a small team. Freshmen also take Cornerstone Design in which teams of students must solve real-world design problems. In the 2017-18 school year, 127 students were awarded Mines Undergraduate Research Fellowships and worked as research assistants on faculty-led projects.

The largest number of degrees are conferred in mechanical engineering and petroleum engineering. To be precise, 88 percent of all earned degrees are classified under the engineering umbrella. However, any degree from the Colorado School of Mines, thanks to its terrific academic reputation and extensive alumni base, will open doors in the world of industry. Eight percent major in computer science, 4 percent in math, 2 percent in the physical sciences, and 1 percent in the social sciences. Prestigious postgraduate fellowships are within reach even though they are not pursued in large numbers; four Mines graduates in 2018 were awarded National Science Foundation Graduate Research Fellowships.

Outside the Classroom

The 373-acre campus is populated by mostly modern, recently-renovated buildings, but only five residence halls that mostly house freshmen who are required to live on campus. Just about everyone else lives off campus in apartments in Golden, nearby Lakewood, or in Greek houses. Greek life is prevalent, but not overbearing, with seven fraternities and three sororities attracting 14 percent of men and 21 percent of women. The Orediggers compete in eighteen NCAA Division II sports and generally place well within the Rocky Mountain Athletic Conference. Club and intramural programs enjoy widespread participation. There are 220 registered student clubs and endless opportunities for outdoor recreation. The school's official Outdoor Recreation Center lends equipment for hiking, biking, or rock climbing. A practice rock climbing wall prepares students for organized climbing trips to the Rockies. "E-Days" are campus-uniting events held multiple times per year that feature activities like carnivals, boat races, concerts, and fireworks shows. Golden, Colorado, which many know only through beer commercials "brewed in Golden, Colorado"—is a place of natural beauty where the Great Plains meet the Rocky Mountains. In addition to natural splendor and ample outdoor recreational opportunities, Golden has a nice downtown replete with shops, restaurants, and cafes. Denver is only a quick fifteen-mile car ride away, making Mines' location anything but remote.

Career Services

The Colorado School of Mines Career Center has seven full-time professional staff members working on career counseling and employer relations. That equates to a 708:1 student-to-advisor ratio that is higher than many schools featured in this guide. Yet, that statistic is not at all telling of the level of career services the school provides. For a moderately sized institution, Mines' career fairs draw an exceptional number of companies to campus. In 2017, the Fall Career Day event drew 288 employers and the spring 2018 event attracted 249 hiring organizations. Combined, more than 5,300 Mines students attended. The 2017-18 school year saw 120 companies visit the school for information sessions as well as 2,912 job interviews take place with undergraduate students on campus.

One-on-one counseling was also dispensed at an excellent rate with more than 5,800 sessions taking place in the previous year (including graduate students). Over sixty small-group workshops were held on topics related to career skill acquisition and job and internship search strategies. A fantastic 83 percent of 2018 graduates had at least one hands-on internship or co-op experience. The school's online job database, DiggerNet, is well maintained and features postings from 790 employers.

Professional Outcomes

Members of the Class of 2018 landed industry jobs or full-time graduate school positions at a clip of 88 percent. However, it is important to note that the success rate varied greatly by major. Geology and geological engineering students were placed at a 100 percent rate while only 77 percent of chemical engineering grads quickly found their next home. Within two years 97 percent or more alumni have successfully launched their career or graduate school path. The largest number of students entered the oil and natural gas industry; construction, aerospace/defense/transportation, and information technology were next in line. Companies employing massive numbers of Mines' grads include Lockheed Martin, BP, ExxonMobil, Halliburton, Chevron, and Shell. Those finding employment enjoyed an average starting salary of $68,000. Petroleum engineering majors averaged $76k and had offers as high as $120k; computer science majors scored similar compensation. After graduating, 61 percent of Mines alumni remain in Colorado. Texas and California are the next most popular destinations.

One-fifth of freshly printed diploma-holders directly enter graduate school, and the most popular institution is Mines itself, which is the choice of 75 percent of those pursuing advanced degrees. Other universities attended by recent graduates include Baylor College of Medicine, Boston University, Carnegie Mellon, Columbia University, Imperial College London, Kyoto University, Rice University, and Worchester Polytechnic Institute.

Admission

Accepting 49 percent of the 12,661 who applied for a spot in the Class of 2022, Mines may not sound as highly selective as it actually is. Acceptance rates can fluctuate greatly at this school from year to year. Last year, it was friendlier—56 percent of applicants were admitted—but in 2015 only 38 percent were. Freshmen in 2018-19 sported ACT middle-50 percent ranges of 28-33 (72 percent of applicants submit ACT results) and 1290-1450 on the SAT. Sixty percent finished in the top 10 percent of their high school classes and 85 percent were in the top 25 percent. The profile of the average freshman today is similar to previous years, whether 56 percent or 38 percent of applicants were admitted.

There is nothing complicated about the admissions process at Mines. The committee considers four cut-and-dried factors to be "very important" in evaluating applicants: rigor of secondary school record, class rank, GPA, and standardized test scores. There are no factors considered "important." Criteria including recommendations, essays, and extracurricular activities are "considered." With 71 percent of the student body being male, being a qualified female applicant can yield a significant admissions edge. The acceptance rate for women is 59 percent compared to 45 percent for men. Almost three-fifths of the student body hail from the Rocky Mountain State, and being a resident can give you a slight boost. No early round is offered, but students should aim for the priority deadline of November 1 to maximize their chances. Mines uses about as straightforward a formula as you will find to make its admissions decisions. That makes self-assessment of one's chances for admission simple. Strong grades in rigorous courses + standardized test scores in the 90th percentile = probable acceptance.

Worth Your Money?

With the annual cost of attendance under $35,000 for Colorado residents and under $55,000 for out-of-staters, Mines is a good value for everyone, especially given that the average starting salary is close to $70k. The news only gets sunnier when you look at the fact that 80 percent of attendees also receive a merit aid award averaging $8,875. Another 48 percent of undergraduates receive an annual need-based grant with a mean value of $6,211. Whether you live in the Centennial State or not, the Colorado School of Mines is a wonderful place to study engineering or computer science. You will have no trouble finding well-compensated work after you earn your diploma.

FINANCIAL
Institutional Type: Public
In-State Tuition: $16,650
Out-of-State Tuition: $36,270
Room & Board: $13,169
Required Fees: $2,314
Books & Supplies: $1,500

Avg. Need-Based Aid: $6,211
Avg. % of Need Met: 62%

Avg. Merit-Based Aid: $8,875
% Receiving Merit-Based Aid: 80%

Avg. Cumulative Debt: $32,482
% of Students Borrowing: 53%

CAREER
Who Recruits
1. Rio Tinto
2. Chevron
3. Phillips 66
4. Procter & Gamble
5. Occidental Petroleum

Notable Internships
1. ExxonMobil
2. Cigna
3. Chevron

Top Industries
1. Engineering
2. Operations
3. Business
4. Research
5. Education

Top Employers
1. Lockheed Martin
2. Chevron
3. Aramco
4. BP
5. National Renewable Energy Laboratory

Where Alumni Work
1. Denver
2. Houston
3. San Francisco
4. Colorado Springs, CO
5. Dallas

Median Earnings
College Scorecard (Early Career): $84,900
EOP (Early Career): $81,500
PayScale (Mid-Career): $139,600

RANKINGS
Forbes: 94
Money: 121
U.S. News: 84, National Universities
Wall Street Journal/THE: 169
Washington Monthly: 117, National Universities

#CollegesWorthYourMoney

Columbia University

New York, New York | Admissions Phone: 212-854-2522

ADMISSION
Admission Rate: 6%
Admission Rate - Men: 6%
Admission Rate - Women: 6%
EA Admission Rate: Not Offered
ED Admission Rate: 18%
Admission Rate (5-Year Trend): -1%
ED Admission Rate (5-Year Trend): N/A
% of Admits Attending (Yield): 62%
Transfer Admission Rate: 6%

Offered Wait List: N/A
Accepted Wait List: N/A
Admitted Wait List: N/A

SAT Reading/Writing (Middle 50%): 710-760
SAT Math (Middle 50%): 740-800
ACT Composite (Middle 50%): 33-35
Testing Policy: ACT/SAT Required
SAT Superscore: Yes
ACT Superscore: Yes

% Graduated in Top 10% of HS Class: 96%
% Graduated in Top 25% of HS Class: 99%
% Graduated in Top 50% of HS Class: 100%

ENROLLMENT
Total Undergraduate Enrollment: 8,931
% Part-Time: 0%
% Male: 51%
% Female: 49%
% Out-of-State: 78%
% Fraternity: 19%
% Sorority: 16%
% On-Campus (Freshman): 100%
% On-Campus (All Undergraduate): 92%

% African-American: 7%
% Asian: 17%
% Hispanic: 13%
% White: 37%
% Other: 6%
% Race or Ethnicity Unknown: 2%
% International: 18%
% Low-Income: 23%

ACADEMICS
Student-to-Faculty Ratio: 6:1
% of Classes Under 20: 82%
% of Classes Under 40: N/A
% Full-Time Faculty: 88%
% Full-Time Faculty w/ Terminal Degree: 100%

Top Programs
Chemistry
Computer Science
Economics
Engineering
English
History
Mathematics
Political Science

Retention Rate: 99%
4-Year Graduation Rate: 87%
6-Year Graduation Rate: 96%

Curricular Flexibility: Less Flexible
Academic Rating: ★★★★★

Inside the Classroom

Attending an Ivy League school that also happens to be located in Manhattan is, for many, an opportunity to have your cake and eat it too. It's no wonder that this particular "cake," Columbia University, is one of the most selective schools in the country. It's also one of the most rigorous in the classroom. The 6,323 exceptional students who make it through a treacherous admissions gauntlet are spread across two schools: Columbia College and the Fu Foundation School of Engineering & Applied Sciences. Combined, those schools offer ninety-six unique areas of study as well as a number of pre-professional and accelerated graduate programs.

The academic experience at Columbia is driven by the famed core curriculum that lays out an extensive to-do list that includes highly specified courses rather than categorical requirements. Those courses include Introduction to Contemporary Civilization in the West, Masterpieces of Western Art, Masterpieces of Western Literature & Philosophy, Frontiers of Science, University Writing, and Music Humanities. Additional science, global core, foreign language, and physical education mandates add seven courses to the core as well as two activities (for phys ed). School of Engineering & Applied Science students only tackle approximately half of the core curriculum (depending on your major). Columbia College students will spend roughly a year and a half slogging through this considerable scholarly workload.

Class sizes are small with more than 80 percent containing fewer than twenty students. The student-faculty ratio is 6:1, but you are likely to be instructed by a few graduate students as you work through the core. Fortunately, only full-time professors lead classes within each major. More than 500 students per year participate in the Columbia Overseas Program. A little over one-quarter of the students leave Manhattan for a foreign country during their four years of study. Undergraduate research is taken seriously by the university, which offers multiple avenues through which students can work side-by-side with faculty on their projects or pursue funding for their own original research ideas. Recent student projects included the following: "Analyzing Sediment Levels in New York Harbor to Examine Urban Growth" and "Examining Chemical Pathways in Stimulating Ovarian Follicle Stem Cell Renewal." Those who participate in a ten-week Summer Undergraduate Research Fellowship present their findings the following spring at a school-run symposium and can publish their work in a number of undergraduate academic journals affiliated with the university.

The largest number of degrees are conferred in political science, economics, history, computer science, and mechanical engineering. The Engineering School as a whole can be found near the top of most national rankings, along with nearly every other department and program. Fewer students pursue prestigious postgraduate fellowships at Columbia than at its Ivy-League brethren; Dartmouth produces double the number of Fulbright Scholars, Brown closer to triple. Yet, if earning a Clarendon, Gates Cambridge, Schwarzman, US State Department Critical Language, or Truman Scholarship is your aim, it can certainly be done at Columbia.

Outside the Classroom

Morningside Heights is a quiet, relatively safe section of New York City, and while Columbia is not situated in the traditional heart of the city like NYU, there are plenty of restaurants and cultural experiences within the immediate vicinity of campus. Unusual for an NYC university, 93 percent of the student body lives in college-owned housing. (Try to rent a place in Manhattan at your own risk—or your wallet's.) A decade ago, Greek life was flatlining with a minimal number of participants, but in recent years it has undergone a rebirth, and now nearly one in every five undergrads joins a fraternity or sorority. The Lions field thirty-one NCAA Division I teams and an additional forty+ club squads, including a number of recent strong performers. Columbia has won seventeen Ivy League titles in the last five years. A full cornucopia of opportunities await through the school's more than 500 student-run organizations. With thirteen a cappella groups, twenty-three dance troupes, thirty-one student run media outlets/publications, and forty political organizations, everyone can find a place to explore their passions at Columbia. The volunteer spirit is also strong with the Community Impact organization attracting more than 900 members who work in twenty-seven community service programs throughout New York City.

Career Services

The Columbia Center for Career Education (CCE) has twenty-six professional staff members who are dedicated to undergraduate counseling, employer relations, and other functions related to undergraduate career/graduate school exploration. That 243:1 student-to-advisor ratio is better than average compared to other schools featured in this guide. The CCE is a well-oiled machine that provides meaningful guidance and experiential opportunities from freshman year through graduation. In 2017, staff engaged in 8,473 one-on-one counseling sessions (98 percent of students reported those as helpful), facilitated 3,547 on-campus interviews, and posted more than 36,000 jobs and internships on the LionSHARE database. Hosting over 400 events that attracted 10,305 students, the CCE is dedicated to bringing a range of large-scale career fairs as well as industry showcases where students with targeted interests can learn from professionals in fields such as book publishing, fashion, sports marketing, and health-care technology.

Columbia University

E-mail: ugrad-ask@columbia.edu | Website: www.columbia.edu

Columbia does an excellent job with outreach, but its internship numbers are, perhaps, even more impressive. A staggering 85 percent of undergraduates complete at least one internship. In part, that phenomenal participation rate is due to Columbia's relationships with hundreds of major employers. Thanks to its high level of undergraduate engagement and superb employer relations efforts, the Center for Career Education receives high praise overall from our staff.

Professional Outcomes

Examining the most recent graduates from Columbia College and the Fu Foundation School of Engineering & Applied Science, 72 percent had found employment within six months, and 17 percent had entered graduate school. Financial services, engineering, and consulting were the three most favored industries. The companies hiring the largest number of Lions are among the most desirable employers in the world including IBM, Goldman Sachs, Morgan Stanley, Google, Citigroup, and Credit Suisse. The median starting salary for graduates of Columbia College/Columbia Engineering is $70,000. Six-figure salaries were reported by 13 percent of graduates, primarily those with engineering degrees, while 30 percent of grads earned less than $50k in their first year of full-time work.

Those moving on to graduate/professional school were welcomed in large numbers into other universities of Columbia's ilk. In addition to remaining at Columbia (the most popular choice), top ten institutions attended were Stanford, Harvard, NYU, Yale, Carnegie Mellon, Cambridge, Oxford, Icahn School of Medicine, and Cornell. A significant number of students from each graduating class also generally secure spots at elite law and medical schools that include the university's own top five law school and the esteemed Vagelos College of Physicians & Surgeons.

Admission

As with the rest of the Ivy League, Columbia received a record number of applications for entry into the Class of 2022. Of the 40,203 hopefuls, only 2,214 were offered admission, which works out to a 5.5 percent acceptance rate, on par with Princeton. Infinitesimal chances at admission is not a new phenomenon here—the acceptance rate hasn't been in the double-digits since 2011.

The profile of the average accepted student is impressive. Entering 2018-19 freshmen had a midde-50 percent SAT of 1450-1560, and the ACT range was 33-35. Over 90 percent were in the top 10 percent of their high school class. Straight from the admissions office, there are six main factors that are given primary importance as part of the university's holistic process: curriculum and grades, context (family circumstances), extracurricular activities, character, fit, and recommendations. Columbia is definitely a school where it is advantageous to apply early decision as ED admit rates are typically three to four times higher than in the regular round; it was 18 percent for the Class of 2022. The university fills close to 50 percent of its freshman class through the early round. Among the Ivies, only Penn scoops up a higher percentage of its entering class through ED. Even by Ivy League standards, gaining acceptance into Columbia is an intimidating proposition. The aforementioned admitted student bona fides should give you an idea if you have a puncher's chance at success, but no one is a sure thing when only one of every twenty high school superstars is welcomed aboard.

Worth Your Money?

All qualifying students at Columbia receive an aid package that meets 100 percent of their demonstrated need and averages almost $54,000. Columbia does not offer any degree of merit aid, so those without financial need will end up paying the full annual cost of attendance of $80k+ per year. While $320,000 for a bachelor's degree sounds (and probably is) insane, Columbia certainly has a number of degree programs that will lead you into a high-paying job right out of college. It's also hard to undervalue the social capital accrued by spending four years at Columbia, which makes spending a massive amount of money on undergraduate tuition a less onerous proposition.

FINANCIAL
Institutional Type: Private
In-State Tuition: $56,608
Out-of-State Tuition: $56,608
Room & Board: $14,016
Required Fees: $2,822
Books & Supplies: N/A

Avg. Need-Based Aid: $56,829
Avg. % of Need Met: 100%

Avg. Merit-Based Aid: $0
% Receiving Merit-Based Aid: 0%

Avg. Cumulative Debt: $21,406
% of Students Borrowing: N/A

CAREER
Who Recruits
1. eBay
2. Memorial Sloan Kettering
3. Boeing
4. Calgene
5. Arup

Notable Internships
1. Mount Sinai Hospital
2. Google
3. Glassdoor

Top Industries
1. Business
2. Education
3. Research
4. Media
5. Engineering

Top Employers
1. Google
2. Morgan Stanley
3. Citi
4. Goldman Sachs
5. JPMorgan Chase

Where Alumni Work
1. New York City
2. San Francisco
3. Los Angeles
4. Washington, DC
5. Boston

Median Earnings
College Scorecard (Early Career): $83,300
EOP (Early Career): $75,300
PayScale (Mid-Career): $126,800

RANKINGS
Forbes: 14
Money: 81
U.S. News: 3, National Universities
Wall Street Journal/THE: 15
Washington Monthly: 13, National Universities

#CollegesWorthYourMoney

New London, Connecticut | Admissions Phone: 860-439-2200

ADMISSION

Admission Rate: 38%
Admission Rate - Men: 31%
Admission Rate - Women: 42%
EA Admission Rate: Not Offered
ED Admission Rate: 62%
Admission Rate (5-Year Trend): +1%
ED Admission Rate (5-Year Trend): -3%
% of Admits Attending (Yield): 21%
Transfer Admission Rate: 35%

Offered Wait List: 1,385
Accepted Wait List: 574
Admitted Wait List: 22

SAT Reading/Writing (Middle 50%): 650-710
SAT Math (Middle 50%): 640-720
ACT Composite (Middle 50%): 30-32
Testing Policy: Test Optional
SAT Superscore: Yes
ACT Superscore: Yes

% Graduated in Top 10% of HS Class: 49%
% Graduated in Top 25% of HS Class: 80%
% Graduated in Top 50% of HS Class: 98%

ENROLLMENT

Total Undergraduate Enrollment: 1,844
% Part-Time: 2%
% Male: 39%
% Female: 61%
% Out-of-State: 81%
% Fraternity: Not Offered
% Sorority: Not Offered
% On-Campus (Freshman): 100%
% On-Campus (All Undergraduate): 99%

% African-American: 4%
% Asian: 5%
% Hispanic: 8%
% White: 68%
% Other: 4%
% Race or Ethnicity Unknown: 2%
% International: 7%
% Low-Income: 12%

ACADEMICS

Student-to-Faculty Ratio: 9:1
% of Classes Under 20: 75%
% of Classes Under 40: 97%
% Full-Time Faculty: 74%
% Full-Time Faculty w/ Terminal Degree: 94%

Top Programs
Area Studies
Behavioral Neuroscience
Dance
English
History
International Relations
Psychology
Theatre

Retention Rate: 91%
4-Year Graduation Rate: 78%
6-Year Graduation Rate: 81%

Curricular Flexibility: Somewhat Flexible
Academic Rating: ★★★✦

Inside the Classroom

Founded as a school for women in the early twentieth century, Connecticut College, known affectionately as Conn College, went co-ed in 1969 and operates today as a unique liberal arts school in the sleepy seaport town of New London. Conn College Camels can pick from an academic menu consisting of forty-one majors, most of which are available as minors as well. There are 1,844 undergraduates on campus, but there is not a single graduate student to be found, which means that, beginning freshman year, the full resources of this school are already at your disposal.

In typical liberal arts fashion, students are required to complete one course in every major discipline: physical and biological sciences, mathematics, social sciences, literature, creative arts, philosophy/religion, and history. There are also requirements in foreign language, writing, and technology. For a laid-back group there is no shortage of academic ambitions as over one-quarter of the Class of 2018 completed a double major. Many also complete a thematic minor that is offered in distinct areas including Modern Greece and Its Background, Non-Violence, or Psychoanalysis: Theories of the Unconscious. Close to 800 courses run each academic year.

The student-faculty ratio is an inviting 9:1, and 75 percent of classes contain fewer than twenty students; 29 percent contain fewer than ten. Conn College's faculty has a reputation for being wholly committed to teaching and forging meaningful relationships with students. Evidence of a personalized experience can be found in the numbers—84 percent of seniors complete a capstone project, 30 percent engage in an individual study with a professor's guidance, and roughly the same number report giving a pubic presentation or performance during their undergraduate career. Slightly more than half of students elect to study abroad. The Class of 2017 completed semesters in thirty-eight countries with Denmark, Italy, and the United Kingdom being the most common destinations.

Consistently named a "top producer" of Fulbright Scholars, Conn College has seen thirty-three students selected in the last five years. Many of those students majored in the school's strong programs in international relations or region-specific programs (e.g., Hispanic Studies, Slavic Studies). Other well-regarded majors include neuroscience, psychology, English, dance, and theatre. In terms of the most frequently conferred degrees, the social sciences at large lead the way (29 percent), followed by biology (17 percent), visual and performing arts (12 percent), psychology (7 percent), and area/ethnic/gender studies (7 percent).

Outside the Classroom

This gorgeous 750-acre campus is wedged between two large bodies of water and features its own hiking trails and arboretum. The gender breakdown still skews strongly in one direction; men make up only 36 percent of the undergraduate population. Three-quarters of the student body participate in competitive sports. For a tiny school it manages to field twenty-eight intercollegiate sports teams (NCAA Division III) as well as a number of intramural squads. Outside of athletic clubs there are roughly seventy student organizations on campus high-lighted by six popular a cappella groups. There are no fraternities or sororities at Conn College, but 98 percent of the student body lives on campus in one of twenty-three residence houses. A close-knit community, Camels come together for some notable campus-wide events like Floralia, Harvestfest, or the massive Seinfeld-inspired Festivus celebration. Public transportation options are plentiful, and the campus and surrounding area are easily bikeable. Even with the relatively close proximity to bigger cities like Boston, New York, and Providence, the school itself estimates that 80 percent of its students stay put on the weekends, making campus a vibrant place seven days a week.

Career Services

The Office of Career Professional Development has eight full-time staff members who specialize in employer relations, general advising, pre-law advising, and connecting students with internships. With a 233:1 student-to-advisor ratio, Conn College sports a higher level of support than many other schools featured in this guide. Its four-year career program assures that the only interaction with the office isn't a harried and panicked "What do I do now?" conversation right before graduation. Advisors visit the required first-year seminar courses and begin to engage students right away, encouraging them to keep in touch via one-on-one advising sessions as well as by attending sponsored events like Sundays with Alumni, workshops, and joint career fairs such as the Liberal Arts Recruiting Connection in Boston that features on-site interviews with more than thirty companies.

Rising seniors are eligible to spend their summers in a school-funded internship. That's right— all students are guaranteed $3,000 to help fund an internship experience anywhere in the world. Plenty are advertised on CamelLink, but advisers will also work individually with students to unearth additional opportunities. It's a testament to the career services staff that nearly 80 percent of alumni reported that their first job out of school put them on their permanent career path.

Professional Outcomes

One year after graduating, 69 percent of the Class of 2018 were engaged in full-time employment, 13 percent were in graduate school, 5 percent were employed part time, and 4 percent were still searching for jobs. Connecticut College produces an interesting blend of career pathways. A solid 24 percent of the Class of 2018 entered the finance industry, but a large swath also veered toward education (17 percent); science, technology, and engineering (15 percent); and health care (14 percent). Those in banking frequently find homes at Bank of America, JPMorgan Chase & Co., and Morgan Stanley. On the public service/health side, three of the largest employers are AmeriCorps, Fulbright, and Sloan Kettering Cancer Center. Other companies employing twenty or more alumni include Pfizer, Massachusetts General Hospital, Deloitte, and UBS. The median salary for midcareer alumni is $56k, slightly less than the median for graduates of UConn, the state's flagship university. Camels end up working predominately in New York (33 percent) and Massachusetts (22 percent), but London/Norwich, Connecticut; DC, San Francisco, and Hartford claim sizable pockets as well.

Conn College students are known for being grad school ready as a surprising (given the small size of the school) twenty-seven alumni earn their doctoral degrees each year. Examining the graduate school attendees from the classes of 2014-16, it is common for multiple students to land at prestigious schools such as NYU, Columbia, and Yale as well as nearby state schools like UMass and UConn. In recent years graduates have earned spots at just about every top law school in the country including Harvard, Emory, Columbia, Penn, Duke, and Northwestern. Those pursuing medical and dental degrees do so at the likes of Tufts University School of Medicine, NYU School of Medicine, and the University of Texas School of Medicine.

Admission

The school admitted 38 percent of applicants in the 2018 admissions cycle. Over the last five years its acceptance rate has hovered in the 35-40 percent range; its low ebb was 32 percent in 2010. Conn College is test-optional, and unlike most test-optional colleges, the majority of accepted applicants (52 percent) elected not to submit a standardized test score as part of their applications. For those who did, the middle 50 percent range for attending students is 1290-1430 on the SAT and 30-32 on the ACT.

While test scores occupy the "considered" category for the Conn College admissions staff, rigor of coursework, grades, class rank, and character/personal qualities are deemed "most important." Academic performance needs to be strong, but you don't need to be perfect to be considered as 80 percent are in the top 20 percent of their high school class and 49 percent cracked the top 10 percent. Legacy students have an edge and have access to special Admission 101 sessions hosted by the college while they are still in high school. The Class of 2022 has the largest number of legacy students of any class in the school's history. Conn College offers two rounds of early decision, and for those who consider it a top choice, it would be wise to consider partaking. A stunning 62 percent of early applicants were accepted in 2018, accounting for more than 45 percent of the 2018-19 freshman class. In essence, this is not a school with a strict formula for admission. It tends to attract a distinguished applicant pool but does not require Ivy-level qualifications for acceptance. Those who apply early face the best odds.

Worth Your Money?

While 42 percent of undergrads receive merit aid, the average award of $6,494 barely dents the $74k annual cost of attendance. Yet, for a very sizable 58 percent of the student population, 100 percent of financial need is met to the tune of $43,000 per year, making attending Conn College possible for lower- and middle-income students. This is a school that the rich pay close to full price to attend, and the not-rich get generous aid packages. Still, the average debt load carried by alumni is higher than the national average. Therefore, middle-to upper-income students without a solid financial aid offer should carefully consider their future plans before investing in the school.

FINANCIAL
Institutional Type: Private
In-State Tuition: $56,870
Out-of-State Tuition: $56,870
Room & Board: $15,720
Required Fees: N/A
Books & Supplies: $1,000

Avg. Need-Based Aid: $42,713
Avg. % of Need Met: 100%

Avg. Merit-Based Aid: $6,494
% Receiving Merit-Based Aid: 42%

Avg. Cumulative Debt: $33,608
% of Students Borrowing: 45%

CAREER
Who Recruits
1. Amazon
2. JLL
3. Morgan Stanley
4. Deloitte
5. UBS

Notable Internships
1. Sony Music Entertainment
2. Smithsonian
3. J. Crew

Top Industries
1. Business
2. Education
3. Social Services
4. Operations
5. Media

Top Employers
1. Pfizer
2. Google
3. Fidelity Investments
4. JPMorgan Chase
5. Bank of America

Where Alumni Work
1. New York City
2. Boston
3. Norwich, CT
4. Washington, DC
5. San Francisco

Median Earnings
College Scorecard (Early Career): $54,900
EOP (Early Career): $55,500
PayScale (Mid-Career): $100,800

RANKINGS
Forbes: 128
Money: 174
U.S. News: 46, Liberal Arts Colleges
Wall Street Journal/THE: 103
Washington Monthly: 35, Liberal Arts Colleges

#CollegesWorthYourMoney

New York, New York | Admissions Phone: 212-353-4120

ADMISSION
Admission Rate: 16%
Admission Rate - Men: 17%
Admission Rate - Women: 15%
EA Admission Rate: Not Offered
ED Admission Rate: 29%
Admission Rate (5-Year Trend): +9%
ED Admission Rate (5-Year Trend): +17%
% of Admits Attending (Yield): 55%
Transfer Admission Rate: 16%

Offered Wait List: 182
Accepted Wait List: 182
Admitted Wait List: 10

SAT Reading/Writing (Middle 50%): 630-720
SAT Math (Middle 50%): 650-790
ACT Composite (Middle 50%): 31-34
Testing Policy: ACT/SAT Required
SAT Superscore: Yes
ACT Superscore: Yes

% Graduated in Top 10% of HS Class: 51%
% Graduated in Top 25% of HS Class: 85%
% Graduated in Top 50% of HS Class: 99%

ENROLLMENT
Total Undergraduate Enrollment: 858
% Part-Time: 0%
% Male: 61%
% Female: 39%
% Out-of-State: 35%
% Fraternity: 4%
% Sorority: 0%
% On-Campus (Freshman): 56%
% On-Campus (All Undergraduate): 13%

% African-American: 3%
% Asian: 21%
% Hispanic: 10%
% White: 31%
% Other: 5%
% Race or Ethnicity Unknown: 8%
% International: 21%
% Low-Income: 20%

ACADEMICS
Student-to-Faculty Ratio: 7:1
% of Classes Under 20: 72%
% of Classes Under 40: 99%
% Full-Time Faculty: 16%
% Full-Time Faculty w/ Terminal Degree: 82%

Top Programs
Architecture
Art
Civil Engineering
Electrical Engineering
Mechanical Engineering

Retention Rate: 91%
4-Year Graduation Rate: 71%
6-Year Graduation Rate: 88%

Curricular Flexibility: Less Flexible
Academic Rating: ★★★⌿

Inside the Classroom
Tuition-free from its founding in 1859 until 2013, The Cooper Union is home to under 900 talented undergraduate students concentrating in art, architecture, and engineering. While tuition has returned (at least until 2029), CU remains an immensely popular destination for its unique programmatic offerings and world-class faculty; hence, it has an Ivy-level acceptance rate of 13 percent.

The Irwin S. Chanin School of Architecture offers a five-year bachelor's program. The School of Art offers a bachelor of fine arts degree with concentrations in painting, sculpture, drawing, film and video, graphic design, photography, and printmaking. The Albert Nerken School of Engineering offers bachelor of engineering degrees in chemical, civil, electrical, and mechanical engineering. All undergraduates must pursue a core curriculum consistent with founder Peter Cooper's insistence on not ignoring the humanities and social sciences in the pursuit of a practical education. As such, a four-semester sequence is required of all students that includes a freshman seminar that focuses on poetry and drama, and three history/sociology courses that follow a chronological sequence from the 1500s to modern day.

No matter your area of study at CU, students report receiving a high degree of attention and mentorship from faculty. With nearly three-quarters of class sections containing fewer than twenty students, learning is an intimate endeavor. Roughly 20 percent elect to study abroad through one of the school's six- to eight-week summer offerings. Engineering students can travel to Spain, Iceland, or Germany while art students have additional options in The Netherlands, France, England, and Sweden. Undergraduate research opportunities are most common in the School of Engineering where all students must complete a senior project.

Accounting for 50 percent of the student body, engineering is the subject in which the largest number of degrees are conferred followed by visual arts and then architecture. All three schools shine in the eyes of employers as well as other institutions of higher education. Graduates of The Cooper Union obtain prestigious fellowships and scholarships at impressive rates. CU has enjoyed thirty-nine Fulbright scholars since 2001, thirteen National Science Foundation Graduate Research Fellowships since 2004, and typically sweeps all four annual Royal Society of Arts-Architecture Student Design Awards.

Outside the Classroom
Most of campus is located in three large buildings: The Foundation Building, 41 Cooper Square, and one freshman-only residence hall where 20 percent of undergraduates reside. Yet, being located in the heart of the East Village, your "campus" is really all of New York City. When they aren't up all night working on projects, students can enjoy the array of restaurants, shops, theaters, and museums within easy walking distance of the school or hop one of the nearby subway stops for access to Midtown Manhattan as well as the outer boroughs. CU does have five club sports teams—men's and women's basketball, men's and women's volleyball, and a coed soccer squad. Two fraternities and one sorority have local chapters, but they fall well short of being a dominant force in the social sphere. Over eighty student-run organizations are active on campus including music and drama troupes, a student newspaper, cultural clubs, and professional societies that participate in intercollegiate competitions.

Career Services
The Center for Career Development employs three full-time professional staff members, equating to a 284:1 student-to-advisor ratio that allows for plentiful personalized attention. Undergraduates are always free to book forty-five-minute one-on-one sessions focusing on areas including résumé and cover letter writing, portfolio development, job and internship search strategies, interview preparation, grad school applications, and applications to competitive fellowship and scholarship programs. Current students and alumni can utilize Handshake for a wealth of job postings. Employers attend the fall and spring career fairs and stop by campus for recruiting sessions and on-campus interviews.

The office organizes a multitude of targeted information sessions and networking opportunities for CU students. Recent examples include a roundtable discussion with gallerists and curators, a graduate school information session with Carnegie Mellon, and lunch with alumni. Opportunities for experiential learning are facilitated by career services staff. For instance, art students can partake in the Professional Internship Program for Art that provides undergraduates with a stipend to work at one of a dozen partner NYC-based museums and galleries. Thanks to a full calendar of intimate events catering to art, architecture, and engineering, The Cooper Union's Center for Career Development serves its students admirably.

The Cooper Union for the Advancement of Science and Art

E-mail: admissions@cooper.edu | Website: www.cooper.edu

Professional Outcomes

Due to the exceptionally low numbers of graduates from Cooper Union each year, it is hard to say that large numbers of alumni cluster in any particular company. However, it is fair to state that CU graduates regularly find their way into the most desirable firms within their respective disciplines. Recent graduates of the School of Architecture found homes at many of the world's largest architecture firms such as AECOM, Gensler, Perkins Eastman, and HOK as well as any desirable boutique firm one can name. School of Art alumni can be found at every great museum of art in the county, including the MoMA and the Met, and at prestigious media outlets such as The New Yorker and the New York Times. Engineering grads waltz into an endless list of top companies including Deloitte, ExxonMobil, Google, Goldman Sachs, IBM, and SpaceX. By age thirty-four, alumni of The Cooper Union enjoy median earnings of $64,000.

Forty percent of CU graduates continue their education at top-ranked graduate programs. In the last few years Cooper Union diploma-holders have gone on to advanced study in architecture at Columbia, Harvard, MIT, Princeton, the Rhode Island School of Design, MIT, Penn, and Yale. Art students have been accepted to US-based programs at Cornell, Georgetown, NYU, and Pratt and internationally at The Glasgow School of Art; Oslo Academy of Art; and Goldsmiths, University of London. Engineering students pursuing master's and doctorate degrees have landed spots at Carnegie Mellon, Johns Hopkins, Stanford, Berkeley, and Vanderbilt.

Admission

Among those seeking a spot in the Class of 2022, only 336 of the 2,574 applicants to The Cooper Union gained acceptance, a 13 percent acceptance rate. This is a self-selecting group of students, many of whom have slotted CU as their number one choice, a fact affirmed by the school's robust 61 percent yield rate. The profile of the average accepted student varies greatly by program. Freshmen in the School of Engineering possessed middle-50 percent SAT scores between 1460 and 1540 and ACT composite scores between 33 and 34. Architecture students scored a significantly lower 1190-1410 (26-32 on the ACT). Freshmen studying art held the lowest standardized test scores with middle-50 percent SAT scores between 1080 and 1330 and 24-30 on the ACT. Successful applicants to all three programs generally had A/A- averages. The five categories rated as "most important" to one's admissions prospects at CU are test scores, GPA, rigor of courses, talent/ ability, and the level of an applicant's interest.

The admissions office recommends that all applicants "take a well-rounded high school program, preferably in advanced coursework." Program-specific recommendations include that "engineering students should also be well prepared in calculus, chemistry, and physics. Art and architecture applicants should take visual art classes" and that architecture applicants should take pre-calculus in high school. Additional application components are required by the various programs. Engineering applicants are required to submit two SAT subject tests, one in math and one in physics or chemistry as well as a writing supplement. School of Art students must complete a Hometest and submit a portfolio. Those applying to the School of Architecture must complete a studio test. While standardized test scores differ greatly across the three schools, all successful applicants to Cooper Union boast solid academic credentials along with demonstrated gifts in their area of interest. Those seeking to study art or architecture will face a holistic review process; those applying to study engineering will be judged more heavily by their test scores.

Worth Your Money?

After over one hundred years of providing a tuition-free education to undergraduate students, Cooper Union controversially decided, in light of a depleted endowment, to begin charging tuition. While plans exist to progressively reduce tuition over the next decade before returning to a tuition-free policy, those entering the school now encounter an annual cost of attendance of $63,092. However, the school does remain extremely generous with aid, awarding an average annual amount of $24k via merit aid and meeting 100 percent of demonstrated need for most students. Presently, 53 percent of undergraduates receive grants of over $43k per year. While it's not as great as receiving a world-class education gratis, Cooper Union remains worth every dollar and is, undoubtedly, worth your money.

FINANCIAL
Institutional Type: Private
In-State Tuition: $44,550
Out-of-State Tuition: $44,550
Room & Board: $13,017 (room only)
Required Fees: $2,150
Books & Supplies: $1,800

Avg. Need-Based Aid: $43,118
Avg. % of Need Met: 100%

Avg. Merit-Based Aid: $24,241
% Receiving Merit-Based Aid: 86%

Avg. Cumulative Debt: N/A
% of Students Borrowing: N/A

CAREER
Who Recruits
1. AECOM
2. Bloomberg
3. General Motors
4. AT&T
5. Credit Suisse

Notable Internships
1. Con Edison
2. Bloomberg LP
3. PepsiCo

Top Industries
1. Arts & Design
2. Business
3. Engineering
4. Education
5. Operations

Top Employers
1. Con Edison
2. Google
3. Bloomberg LP
4. IBM
5. Amazon

Where Alumni Work
1. New York City
2. San Francisco
3. Los Angeles
4. Boston
5. Philadelphia

Median Earnings
College Scorecard (Early Career): $64,900
EOP (Early Career): $64,300
PayScale (Mid-Career): $126,200

RANKINGS
Forbes: 58
Money: 66
U.S. News: 1, Regional North
Wall Street Journal/THE: N/A
Washington Monthly: N/A

#CollegesWorthYourMoney

Cornell University

Ithaca, New York | Admissions Phone: 607-255-5241

ADMISSION
Admission Rate: 11%
Admission Rate - Men: 9%
Admission Rate - Women: 12%
EA Admission Rate: Not Offered
ED Admission Rate: 24%
Admission Rate (5-Year Trend): -5%
ED Admission Rate (5-Year Trend): -5%
% of Admits Attending (Yield): 60%
Transfer Admission Rate: 17%

Offered Wait List: 6,683
Accepted Wait List: 4,546
Admitted Wait List: 164

SAT Reading/Writing (Middle 50%): 680-750
SAT Math (Middle 50%): 710-790
ACT Composite (Middle 50%): 32-34
Testing Policy: ACT/SAT Required
SAT Superscore: Yes
ACT Superscore: No

% Graduated in Top 10% of HS Class: 83%
% Graduated in Top 25% of HS Class: 97%
% Graduated in Top 50% of HS Class: 100%

ENROLLMENT
Total Undergraduate Enrollment: 15,182
% Part-Time: 0%
% Male: 47%
% Female: 53%
% Out-of-State: 59%
% Fraternity: 26%
% Sorority: 24%
% On-Campus (Freshman): 100%
% On-Campus (All Undergraduate): 52%

% African-American: 7%
% Asian: 19%
% Hispanic: 13%
% White: 36%
% Other: 5%
% Race or Ethnicity Unknown: 8%
% International: 11%
% Low-Income: 15%

ACADEMICS
Student-to-Faculty Ratio: 9:1
% of Classes Under 20: 57%
% of Classes Under 40: 78%
% Full-Time Faculty: 83%
% Full-Time Faculty w/ Terminal Degree: 93%

Top Programs
Applied Economics and Management
Architecture
Chemistry
Computer Science
Engineering
English
Hotel Administration
Industrial and Labor Relations

Retention Rate: 97%
4-Year Graduation Rate: 88%
6-Year Graduation Rate: 95%

Curricular Flexibility: Somewhat Flexible
Academic Rating: ★★★★★

Inside the Classroom

By a wide margin, Cornell boasts the largest undergraduate enrollment of any school in the Ivy League at almost 15,000 students, roughly 5,000 more than the next largest school, the University of Pennsylvania. Located in Ithaca, a certifiable college town in the Finger Lakes region of Upstate New York, Cornell's campus is a seemingly endless 745 acres, and that is not including the adjacent Botanic Gardens owned by the university. A diverse array of academic programs includes ninety majors and 125 minors spread across the university's seven schools/colleges: the College of Agriculture and Life Sciences; College of Architecture, Art and Planning; College of Arts and Sciences; SC Johnson College of Business; College of Engineering; College of Human Ecology; and School of Industrial and Labor Relations.

Most degrees conferred in 2018 were in engineering (17 percent), business (14 percent), agriculture (12 percent), computer science (11 percent), and the social sciences (9 percent). Beginning with the Class of 2023, required courses within the College of Arts & Sciences will include two first-year writing seminars, mastery of a foreign language, and ten distributional requirements. While that sounds like a substantial number of mandated classes, the school does allow certain courses to simultaneously fill more than one distributional requirement.

Classes are a bit larger at Cornell than at many other elite institutions. Still, 57 percent of sections have fewer than twenty students. Introductory courses sometimes take place in larger lecture halls, so 18 percent of courses have an enrollment of more than forty students. Undergraduates do give their professors generally high marks: 93 percent report being satisfied with the instruction they have received, 71 percent report participating in class discussions, 48 percent report completing a thesis/research project, and 62 percent plan on or already have conducted research with a faculty member. Members of Big Red can choose from study abroad opportunities in more than forty countries, and roughly one-third participate.

The SC Johnson College of Business houses two undergraduate schools, both of which have phenomenal reputations. The Cornell School of Hotel Administration is one of the finest such programs in the world, and the Charles H. Dyson School of Applied Economics and Management cracks most lists of the top 10 business programs in the United States. The School of Engineering offers fourteen areas of specialization and is held in high regard by employers and prestigious graduate schools. Highly-desired postgraduate scholarships are procured by Cornell grads at a steady rate. The university has twenty-nine Rhodes Scholars to its credit as well as a regular flow of Fulbright, Schwarzman, Goldwater, and Truman Scholarship award winners.

Outside the Classroom

Ithaca has as much Upstate New York natural splendor as you can handle, from Lake Cayuga to parks to the many breathtaking ravines and gorges. (You've likely seen the "Ithaca is Gorges" T-shirt.) Yet, thanks to frigid weather and the absence of a major metropolis nearby, campus itself and the nearby neighborhoods are where the action is. With a roughly 25 percent participation rate across the fifty-five fraternity and sorority chapters on campus, Greek life dominates much of the social scene. Freshmen are required to live in university housing, although a substantial 48 percent of undergrads live off campus. Student-run organizations can be found for almost anything your mind can fathom. Over 1,000 clubs are active. The Cornell Concert works to bring major acts to campus that suit a variety of tastes from Bob Dylan to Ke$ha. The university also succeeds in luring a fair share of impressive guest speakers to campus each year. The Cornell Daily Sun, founded in 1880, is one of the finest student papers in the country, and the dining hall cuisine and libraries (Hogwarts-esque Uris in particular) receive high marks. Athletics feature eighteen men's and nineteen women's teams competing against NCAA Division I competition as well countless club and intramural opportunities.

Career Services

The Career Services Department has fifty-two full-time staff members, excluding office assistants, who are spread across the various colleges within the university. Those individuals serve as career counselors, internship co-op coordinators, recruiting coordinators, and graduate school advisors in specified disciplines. The 280:1 student-to-advisor ratio is better than average compared to other schools featured in this guide. Among large universities, Cornell's level of support is unparalleled.

Career fairs at Cornell are two-day affairs involving hundreds of Fortune 500, government, and nonprofit employers. In recent years the fall University Career Fair Days have drawn over 6,000 students and 260 employers. Of the Class of 2018, 16 percent found their jobs through on-campus recruiting, 5 percent through career fairs, and 17 percent through an internship or volunteer experience. In an average year, students make over 16,000 advising appointments, and more than 15,000 students attend programs and presentations. Over 500 students take advantage of job-shadowing opportunities offered during winter and spring breaks. Most importantly, 90 percent of students have completed, or plan to complete, an internship/practicum.

Professional Outcomes

Breaking down the graduates of the College of Arts and Sciences, the largest school at Cornell, 63 percent entered the workforce, 27 percent entered graduate school, 6 percent pursued other endeavors such as travel or volunteer work, and the remaining 4 percent were still seeking employment six months after receiving their diplomas. The top sectors attracting campus-wide graduates in 2018 were financial services (21 percent), consulting (15 percent), technology (14 percent), and health care services (5 percent). Starting salary data varies greatly across schools as well as by major. For example, the average Dyson graduate earns $74,000 while the average College of Agriculture and Life Sciences graduate starts at $60k. College of Engineering students enjoy an average starting salary of $82,000 with a heavy representation at Google, Amazon, Microsoft, and Goldman Sachs. Across all schools the median starting salary was a healthy $66,000.

Of the students from A&S going on to graduate school, 22 percent were pursuing advanced engineering degrees, 9 percent JDs, and 9 percent MDs. Popular destinations included staying at Cornell (especially computer science majors), other Ivies, Stanford, MIT, universities in the UC system, or abroad at Oxford, Cambridge, University of Toronto, or University of St. Andrews. Harvard was the No. 1 destination for biology majors, and Stanford attracted the highest number of chemistry graduates. The ten most frequently attended law schools by Big Red alumni include Columbia, UCLA, Penn, Harvard, and Yale. Those entering medical school typically stay nearby as every one of the ten most popular medical schools was located within the states of New York, New Jersey, or Pennsylvania.

Admission

The deluge of over 51,000 applications for the Class of 2022 was a record setter for Cornell. The acceptance rate of 10.3 percent was an all-time low and has been trending down in recent years. For comparison, Class of 2016 applicants gained acceptance at a 16 percent rate. At Cornell, applicants must apply to one of the eight colleges or schools (counting Dyson and the Hotel School separately), and acceptance rates vary among schools. For example, in the 2017-18 admissions cycle only 3 percent of applicants were accepted into the Dyson School of Applied Economics and Management while the College of Human Ecology admitted 19 percent. Most (83 percent) Cornell freshmen in 2018-19 placed in the top 10 percent of their high school class. The Class of 2022 entered with median SAT/ACT scores of 1480/33; the mid-50 percent ranges were 1390-1540 on the SAT and 32-34 on the ACT. Children of alumni comprised 16.5 percent of the class, and legacy students are believed to have a significant edge, although the school has not been willing to release any statistics in that area. The eight criteria deemed most important by the admissions office are rigor of coursework, grades, test scores, recommendations, essays, extracurriculars, talent/ability, and character/personal qualities. While technically the "easiest" Ivy to get into, that qualifier doesn't mean much these days. Only a fraction away from joining the other seven Ivy League institutions with single-digit acceptance rates, becoming part of Big Red is only a possibility for the crème de la crème of college applicants.

Worth Your Money?

Graduates emerge from their four years of study with an average debt load of just under $30,000, right around the national average. Like many other elite universities, Cornell does not award any merit aid, instead focusing its generosity on students who could not otherwise afford the school. As a result, the $75,000+ list price annual cost of attendance is greatly reduced for students who demonstrate financial need. These students have 100 percent of their need met to the tune of a $43,000 grant. Alumni enjoy starting salaries far superior to those from your average college, making Cornell a phenomenal investment, even if you need to take out sizable loans to attend.

FINANCIAL
Institutional Type: Private
In-State Tuition: $56,550
Out-of-State Tuition: $56,550
Room & Board: $15,201
Required Fees: $672
Books & Supplies: $970

Avg. Need-Based Aid: $42,946
Avg. % of Need Met: 100%

Avg. Merit-Based Aid: $0
% Receiving Merit-Based Aid: 0%

Avg. Cumulative Debt: $29,762
% of Students Borrowing: 41%

CAREER
Who Recruits
1. Four Seasons Hotel and Resorts
2. WeWork
3. Uber
4. Accor
5. Hilton

Notable Internships
1. American Express
2. Lyft
3. PayPal

Top Industries
1. Business
2. Education
3. Operations
4. Research
5. Engineering

Top Employers
1. Google
2. Amazon
3. Microsoft
4. IBM
5. Facebook

Where Alumni Work
1. New York City
2. San Francisco
3. Boston
4. Washington, DC
5. Los Angeles

Median Earnings
College Scorecard (Early Career): $77,200
EOP (Early Career): $79,800
PayScale (Mid-Career): $128,200

RANKINGS
Forbes: 11
Money: 91
U.S. News: 17, National Universities
Wall Street Journal/THE: 9
Washington Monthly: 25, National Universities

#CollegesWorthYourMoney

Dartmouth College

Hanover, New Hampshire | Admissions Phone: 603-646-2875

ADMISSION
Admission Rate: 9%
Admission Rate - Men: 9%
Admission Rate - Women: 8%
EA Admission Rate: Not Offered
ED Admission Rate: 25%
Admission Rate (5-Year Trend): -2%
ED Admission Rate (5-Year Trend): -4%
% of Admits Attending (Yield): 61%
Transfer Admission Rate: 1%

Offered Wait List: 1,925
Accepted Wait List: 1,292
Admitted Wait List: 0

SAT Reading/Writing (Middle 50%): 700-770
SAT Math (Middle 50%): 720-790
ACT Composite (Middle 50%): 31-35
Testing Policy: ACT/SAT Required
SAT Superscore: Yes
ACT Superscore: No

% Graduated in Top 10% of HS Class: 95%
% Graduated in Top 25% of HS Class: 99%
% Graduated in Top 50% of HS Class: 99%

ENROLLMENT
Total Undergraduate Enrollment: 4,417
% Part-Time: 1%
% Male: 51%
% Female: 49%
% Out-of-State: 97%
% Fraternity: 35%
% Sorority: 42%
% On-Campus (Freshman): 100%
% On-Campus (All Undergraduate): 87%

% African-American: 6%
% Asian: 15%
% Hispanic: 10%
% White: 50%
% Other: 5%
% Race or Ethnicity Unknown: 2%
% International: 10%
% Low-Income: 12%

ACADEMICS
Student-to-Faculty Ratio: 7:1
% of Classes Under 20: 62%
% of Classes Under 40: 88%
% Full-Time Faculty: 77%
% Full-Time Faculty w/ Terminal Degree: 95%

Top Programs
Biology
Computer Science
Economics
Engineering
Environmental Studies
Government
History
Neuroscience

Retention Rate: 97%
4-Year Graduation Rate: 86%
6-Year Graduation Rate: 95%

Curricular Flexibility: Very Flexible
Academic Rating: ★★★★★

Inside the Classroom

The smallest school in the Ivy League, Dartmouth plays home to just over 4,400 undergraduate students on its remote, 237-acre New Hampshire campus. Dartmouth has long wrestled with its reputation as one of the most conservative of the Ivy League universities as well as one of the top party schools. Regardless, there are few arguments against the academic superiority of the college that sports sixty majors and a stunning breadth of course selections for an institution of its size.

Dartmouth offers a unique year-round academic calendar with four ten-week terms that allow students maximum flexibility as they pursue internships, paid work, research opportunities, or travel abroad. Undergraduates design their own individual "D-Plan." Needing thirty-five credits for graduation, individuals are free to take anywhere from two to four courses per term. (Most students take three.) Typically, students are expected to spend twelve of the fifteen terms during their natural four-year period on campus, including Sophomore Summer, a mandatory term for rising juniors. All freshmen must take a writing requirement and a first-year seminar course, both designed as intensive workshops to elevate student writing to Dartmouth's high standards.

The learning environment at Dartmouth is extraordinarily intimate. Not only do 62 percent of course sections have under twenty students, but 19 percent have single-digit enrollments. The student-to-faculty ratio is an outstanding 7:1. Undergraduate research opportunities abound with 58 percent of students participating at some point. Further, 88 percent of those participants report having a satisfying experience working with a faculty member in that capacity. The rate of satisfaction is hardly surprising as Dartmouth's faculty consistently rates at the top of rankings/surveys regarding quality of instruction. An extensive study abroad program offers dozens of Dartmouth faculty-led academic experiences around the world, and around half of all students partake.

Top programs offered by Big Green include biology, economics, neuroscience, and government. The social sciences are the most popular, accounting for 34 percent of degrees conferred, followed by mathematics (8 percent), engineering (8 percent), computer science (7 percent), visual and performing arts (5 percent), and history (5 percent). In recent years, an average of fifteen Dartmouth grads have been offered Fulbright Scholarships annually. With sixty-two Rhodes Scholars to its credit, Dartmouth is the sixth highest producer in the history of the award. The Truman Foundation lists Dartmouth as one of its Honor Institutions as many grads have been awarded its $30,000 prize to pursue graduate study in a public service field.

Outside the Classroom

The presence of Greek life at Dartmouth is powerful with over half of the student population belonging to fraternities and sororities. In fact, the school sports one of the highest percentages of Greek-affiliated undergraduates in the entire nation; women join sororities at a 58 percent clip and 48 percent of men sign-up for fraternity life. Over thirty intercollegiate Division I sports are on tap along with two dozen intramural sports and over thirty-five club sports. Roughly three-quarters of Dartmouth men and women participate in some form of athletics. Other highlights include The Dartmouth, America's oldest school newspaper, 170 student-run clubs and organizations, and the Dartmouth Outing Club, the largest collegiate outdoor recreation club in the country. The college owns over 30,000 acres of New Hampshire land that can be enjoyed by students for camping, skiing, hiking, and similar activities. Almost 90 percent of the student body and 100 percent of freshmen live on campus. Dorms earn rave reviews from students, and all are supervised by full-time, live-in community directors. Big Green is living up to its nickname as a green campus with a number of sustainability ventures including transportation, eco-friendly energy options, and its own organic farm/student-operated farmer's market. If you come from an urban environment, the remote feel of Hanover may induce some culture shock, yet Boston is only a two-hour drive away.

Career Services

The Center for Career Development has nine full-time staff members who focus on either career advising or employer relations. The 489:1 student-to-advisor ratio is slightly higher than other schools featured in this guide. However, also available to advise students are the thousands of alumni who volunteer their time as members of the Dartmouth Career Network. Employer Connection Fairs draw over 1,000 students and feature a strong corporate presence. The fall 2019 Engineering Career Fair attracted fifty-one companies including Microsoft, Draftkings, Mastercard, and Wayfair. Students are given a DartBoard account that allows them to access event notifications, on-campus recruiting opportunities, and thousands of internships.

In part because of its unique academic calendar, Dartmouth does an exceptional job facilitating undergraduate internships. Eighty-seven percent of the Class of 2018 participated in at least one internship experience. Many major corporations have elected to become employer partners with the college, a designation that includes, among other things, annual recruiting on campus. Many of those are financial institutions that also grace the list of top employers of Dartmouth grads. (Please see "Professional Outcomes" below.) This alignment of on-campus recruiting and offers of employment at Dartmouth is most impressive.

Dartmouth College

E-mail: admissions.office@dartmouth.edu | Website: www.dartmouth.edu

Professional Outcomes

A great reputation along with a passionate alumni network that is 80,000 strong leads Dartmouth grads to successful transitions into career and graduate school. At the time of receiving their diplomas, 2019 grads had already found employment at a 69 percent clip while 14 percent were headed to graduate school and 14 percent were still weighing their options. Finance is a popular arena for graduates with 26 percent of the Class of 2019 going in that direction. Thus, it is little surprise that included in the top ten employers of Dartmouth grads are a number of investment banks including Goldman Sachs, Morgan Stanley, Bain & Company, Citibank, and Deutsche Bank. Another 21 percent enter the world of consulting. While many start in finance and consulting, a large number of grads plan to enter academia or a career in government down the road. Dartmouth grads will not struggle financially. The median income for Dartmouth grads by age thirty-four is $76,000, thirty-third best of any college in the United States. Upon graduation the majority of the student body migrates to major cities with notably high concentrations in Chicago, DC, New York, Seattle, San Francisco, and Mountain View, California.

Those pursuing graduate and professional degrees often trade one Ivy for another. Harvard, Columbia, and Princeton are three of the most frequent landing spots for Dartmouth grads. Many others continue their studies in one of Dartmouth's own graduate programs or head to other top institutions such as the London School of Economics, Northwestern, or Berkeley. Among the Class of 2019, 20 percent of graduates intended to obtain a medical degree, 10 percent were chasing a law degree, and 14 percent enrolled in PhD programs.

Admission

Like many highly selective schools, Dartmouth's popularity is at an all-time high. The college's yield—the percentage of accepted students who choose to attend—was an all-time high of 61 percent in both 2017-18 and 2018-19. Due to that sky-high yield rate, the number of accepted students fell to only 1,925, the lowest total since the early 1990s. In 2018, Dartmouth shed its double-digit acceptance rate for the first time, falling to 8.7 percent. Five years ago, the admit rate was 12 percent; a decade ago, it was over 18 percent.

The mean SAT is up to 1497, thirty points higher than five years ago, and the mean ACT is 33. Finishing at the top of your class is a must; 95 percent hail from the top 10 percent of their high school graduating class. Legacy students have a fairly strong but not overwhelming presence on campus, comprising 8-9 percent of the student body. Fifteen percent of students are the first in their family to attend college. Alumni interviews are offered but not required. Essays and recommendations are rated as "very important" by the admissions staff. Bottom line: many pine to be part of this Ivy League institution, but earning a spot on the bucolic Hanover campus has never been tougher. Those who wish to experience its renowned teaching faculty and intimate learning environment, rich with hands-on opportunities, will need to bring stellar credentials to the table.

Worth Your Money?

An average annual grant of $53k is delivered to the 2,215 qualifying students, a figure that meets 100 percent of every single student's demonstrated financial need. Most other students will pay the full cost of attendance—$76,718—as there is no merit aid offered at Dartmouth. Those not qualifying for aid are typically in the upper-income brackets with an estimated 20 percent of current undergraduates counting themselves among the 1-percent club, and another 25 percent are from families in the top 5 percent of income levels nationwide. Big Green is unlikely to cost you large amounts of green unless you can comfortably afford it. For that reason, coupled with the stellar postgraduate outcomes you would expect from an Ivy, Dartmouth is, without question, worth the price.

FINANCIAL
Institutional Type: Private
In-State Tuition: $55,605
Out-of-State Tuition: $55,605
Room & Board: $16,374
Required Fees: $2,017
Books & Supplies: $1,100

Avg. Need-Based Aid: $52,542
Avg. % of Need Met: 100%

Avg. Merit-Based Aid: $0
% Receiving Merit-Based Aid: 0%

Avg. Cumulative Debt: $18,903
% of Students Borrowing: 49%

CAREER
Who Recruits
1. Partenon
2. Nomura
3. Oliver Wyman
4. Bridgewater
5. Trinity Partners

Notable Internships
1. PNC
2. Bain & Company
3. ICM

Top Industries
1. Business
2. Education
3. Research
4. Finance
5. Operations

Top Employers
1. Google
2. Goldman Sachs
3. Amazon
4. Morgan Stanley
5. Facebook

Where Alumni Work
1. Boston
2. New York City
3. San Francisco
4. Washington, DC
5. Los Angeles

Median Earnings
College Scorecard (Early Career): $75,500
EOP (Early Career): $76,600
PayScale (Mid-Career): $130,900

RANKINGS
Forbes: 10
Money: 95
U.S. News: 12, National Universities
Wall Street Journal/THE: 12 (T)
Washington Monthly: 34, National Universities

#CollegesWorthYourMoney

Davidson College

Davidson, North Carolina | Admissions Phone: 704-894-2230

ADMISSION
Admission Rate: 19%
Admission Rate - Men: 20%
Admission Rate - Women: 19%
EA Admission Rate: Not Offered
ED Admission Rate: 46%
Admission Rate (5-Year Trend): -7%
ED Admission Rate (5-Year Trend): N/A
% of Admits Attending (Yield): 46%
Transfer Admission Rate: 16%

Offered Wait List: N/A
Accepted Wait List: N/A
Admitted Wait List: N/A

SAT Reading/Writing (Middle 50%): 640-720
SAT Math (Middle 50%): 650-730
ACT Composite (Middle 50%): 29-33
Testing Policy: ACT/SAT Required
SAT Superscore: Yes
ACT Superscore: Yes

% Graduated in Top 10% of HS Class: 73%
% Graduated in Top 25% of HS Class: 97%
% Graduated in Top 50% of HS Class: 100%

ENROLLMENT
Total Undergraduate Enrollment: 1,843
% Part-Time: 0%
% Male: 52%
% Female: 48%
% Out-of-State: 78%
% Fraternity: 30%
% Sorority: 49%
% On-Campus (Freshman): 100%
% On-Campus (All Undergraduate): 95%

% African-American: 7%
% Asian: 5%
% Hispanic: 8%
% White: 67%
% Other: 4%
% Race or Ethnicity Unknown: 1%
% International: 7%
% Low-Income: 12%

ACADEMICS
Student-to-Faculty Ratio: 9:1
% of Classes Under 20: 69%
% of Classes Under 40: 99%
% Full-Time Faculty: 95%
% Full-Time Faculty w/ Terminal Degree: 97%

Top Programs
Biology
Chemistry
Economics
English
History
Physics
Political Science
Psychology

Retention Rate: 95%
4-Year Graduation Rate: 90%
6-Year Graduation Rate: 90%

Curricular Flexibility: Somewhat Flexible
Academic Rating: ★★★★✦

Inside the Classroom

Strolling around Davidson's lush campus, taking in the historic buildings and intellectually engaged student body, it's easy to forget that you are situated about twenty miles north of Charlotte, North Carolina, and not in the heart of New England. The 1,800 students who grace this undergrad-only institution are high achievers who take academics and their school's more-than-just-lip-service Honor Code seriously.

With its small size, the impressive part of the college is the exceptional quality of its offerings, not the breadth of them, as only twenty-nine majors are available. Additional interdisciplinary majors also can be accessed for those seeking another pathway. However, the majority of students stick to traditional areas of concentration with economics, biology, political science, and psychology being the most popular. Required courses include eight classes under the umbrella category of Ways of Knowing that feature, among others, history, rhetoric, quantitative thought, and the visual performing arts. Additional mandated coursework in foreign language, writing, diversity, justice/equality, and physical education must be completed by all students, regardless of major.

The student-to-faculty ratio is 9:1, which allows the college to ensure that 69 percent have fewer than twenty students and 28 percent have enrollments you can count on two hands. Overall, the average number of students per class is only fifteen. Study abroad is encouraged, and more than three-quarters of students elect to study in one of 110 programs around the globe. Undergraduates working side-by-side with their professors is commonplace as over 60 percent of faculty have published with student coauthors at some point.

Top programs at Davidson include political science, chemistry, and English. However, any degree from Davidson is a credential from one of the most respected liberal arts colleges in the country. In fact, it regularly cracks top ten lists of best liberal arts schools and best teaching faculty. Students are no strangers to accolades either; of 467 graduates of the Class of 2018, an almost incomprehensible fifteen students were awarded Fulbright Scholarships. In the same year other members of the graduating class won Boren, Truman, Watson, and Princeton in Africa fellowships/scholarships. In addition, twenty-three alumni have won Rhodes Scholarships.

Outside the Classroom

"Typical" is not a word that applies to any facet of campus life at Davidson. For example, team sports participation is required at the varsity, club, or intramural level. The ten men's and nine women's varsity teams compete in NCAA Division I with the successful men's basketball team atop the popularity charts. Davidson's fourteen Greek houses are all under the purview of one entity, Patterson Court, which ensures that fraternities, sororities, and eating houses all have a social/charitable mission and abide by a common set of rules. Participation is extremely high as 63 percent of male students and 45 percent of females join a Patterson Court house. Students also run over 200 clubs, including Davidson Outdoors, which organizes kayaking, hiking, and climbing trips around the globe as well as in the school's own backyard. The Lake Norman campus, a 110-acre waterfront property only seven miles from the main campus, is reserved for exclusive use by Davidson students. The college's Union Board, the largest student organization, puts on well-attended events including concerts, trivia nights, and movie screenings on a regular basis. The surrounding town of Davidson features many attractions such as an array of student-friendly coffee shops and restaurants as well as a local farmer's market. Those seeking off-campus nightlife and cultural experiences can make that easy twenty-minute drive south to Charlotte.

Career Services

The Center for Career Development (CCD) is staffed by nine full-time staff members, seven of whom have "director" or "assistant director" in their job title. That works out to a student-to-advisor ratio of 205:1, much lower (i.e. better) than the average institution included in this book. Despite the administrative titles, all members of the staff get hands-on with career counseling. In the 2016-17 school year 86 percent of undergrads engaged with the CCD, including 94 percent of all seniors. Over 150 employers recruited on campus including Amazon, Google, Bain, IBM, Deloitte, and Cigna.

One nice aspect of the CCD is its systematic four-year development model that outlines recommended activities for students at all phases of their undergraduate education. As freshmen, Davidson students are encouraged to get comfortable with Handshake and get one-on-one assistance with resume writing. From there, students receive career coaching, help locating an internship, and can participate in the Senior Bootcamp. Close to 150 students per year participate in the school's job-shadowing program, and 98 percent reported that the experience was helpful. The newly launched Insider Series brings professionals in a host of fields (e.g., sports marketing, advertising, and writing careers) to campus to impart career advice. Participation in Career Treks and group visits to corporations and nonprofit agencies has increased significantly in recent years.

E-mail: admission@davidson.edu | Website: www.davidson.edu

Professional Outcomes

Looking at the past five years of available outcomes data, 73-79 percent of graduates landed jobs within six months of graduation, 14-20 percent were enrolled in a graduate program, and 3-4 percent were still seeking employment. Remaining in North Carolina after graduation is a popular choice, but many grads migrate to New York and DC as well. The top three industries favored by graduates are (in order) education, health care, and financial services. Employers of the largest number of Davidson grads include Carolina Healthcare System, Teach for America, the NIH, Wells Fargo, and Bank of America. At age thirty-four, graduates are earning a median salary of slightly over $60k, more than $10k less than Duke and Wake Forest grads but higher salaries than North Carolina rivals UNC or Elon alums.

Of those who attended grad school, the highest number were in health-care-related programs (including MDs), law school, and laboratory sciences. Significant numbers of students pursue advanced degrees at other Southern gems including Vanderbilt, Emory, Duke, Wake Forest, and UNC. In fact, over a five-year period the college sent more law school-bound alumni to UNC Law School (22), Duke (10), and Emory (7) than any other institution. There is also a fair showing of Ivy League acceptances in all graduate disciplines among Wildcat alumni.

Admission

In 2018, Davidson received a modest but all-time high of 5,700 applications, but it accepted an all-time low 19.5 percent into the Class of 2022. For perspective, in 2013, the school accepted 26 percent of applicants, so the school has become a bit more selective in recent years. On standardized tests, enrolled students have a middle 50 percent of 1290-1450 on the SAT and 29-33 on the ACT. The two tests are submitted with equal frequency by Davidson applicants. Davidson students being admitted today do possess slightly higher test scores than students did five years ago. The average GPA of an enrolled student is over 3.93, and 73 percent finished in the top 10 percent of their class; 97 percent finished in the top quartile.

The college has a unique set of admissions criteria atop its list. According to the admissions office, it places the most weight on rigor of coursework, recommendations, volunteer work, and character/personal qualities. Test scores are among the criteria viewed as being next in importance followed by the merely "considered" factors of class rank, GPA, and legacy status. Applying via binding early decision greatly improves your odds. Class of 2022 members who applied ED were accepted at a 46 percent rate compared to only 16 percent in the regular round. Almost two-thirds of the incoming class was filled through the early round, one of the highest figures you will find at any school. One of the most selective liberal arts schools in the South, Davidson's high yield rate (how many accepted students enroll) of 46 percent suggests the applicant pool is self-selecting as well as frequently applying through ED. Those offered admission typically sport excellent grades/test scores, although components of the process are genuinely holistic.

Worth Your Money?

Half of Davidson undergraduates qualify for need-based aid, an area in which the university is notably generous. Almost every student who qualifies for financial aid sees 100 percent of demonstrated need met, and the average annual grant is for over $45,000. Davidson is also more generous with merit aid than your typical highly selective institution, giving 23 percent of current students an average annual award of nearly $20k. At $70,177 in annual cost of attendance, Davidson's list price is a touch lower than many other schools of its ilk and, even better, most of those schools do not pay the full amount. An estimated 50 percent of undergrads have parents who are top 5 percent income-earners, and pretty much everyone else gets a steep discount. With a record of solid graduate outcomes to boot, Davidson is absolutely worth your money.

FINANCIAL
Institutional Type: Private
In-State Tuition: $52,524
Out-of-State Tuition: $52,524
Room & Board: $14,803
Required Fees: $525
Books & Supplies: $1,000

Avg. Need-Based Aid: $45,002
Avg. % of Need Met: 100%

Avg. Merit-Based Aid: $19,973
% Receiving Merit-Based Aid: 23%

Avg. Cumulative Debt: $22,599
% of Students Borrowing: 29%

CAREER
Who Recruits
1. ESPN
2. Barings
3. Deloitte
4. EY
5. BlackArch Partners

Notable Internships
1. Cancer Treatment Centers of America
2. U.S. House of Representatives
3. POLITICO

Top Industries
1. Business
2. Education
3. Social Services
4. Healthcare
5. Operations

Top Employers
1. Wells Fargo
2. Bank of America
3. Wells Fargo
4. US Army
5. Deloitte

Where Alumni Work
1. Charlotte
2. New York City
3. Washington, DC
4. Atlanta
5. Raleigh-Durham, NC

Median Earnings
College Scorecard (Early Career): $58,900
EOP (Early Career): $60,300
PayScale (Mid-Career): $106,900

RANKINGS
Forbes: 48
Money: 87
U.S. News: 17 (T), Liberal Arts Colleges
Wall Street Journal/THE: 54
Washington Monthly: 25, Liberal Arts Colleges

#CollegesWorthYourMoney

Dickinson College

Carlisle, Pennsylvania | Admissions Phone: 717-245-1231

Inside the Classroom

Set in the small town of Carlisle, Pennsylvania, Dickinson College is a liberal arts school with a strong academic reputation that dates back to the earliest days of the United States. In fact, it was founded the same week the United States signed the Treaty of Paris that ended the Revolutionary War. Today, the 2,400 undergraduate students who call Dickinson home are an increasingly diverse group, both in terms of academic/career interests and demographically. In recent years the school has doubled its rate of international students to 13 percent and raised the presence of underrepresented minorities from 15 percent in 2013 to 21 percent in 2017. The school does have a notable gender gap to the tune of a 60/40 split in favor of women.

Freshmen are matched with a professor-advisor and engage in a mandatory first-year seminar intended to hone critical thinking, analysis, and research skills. From there, students must embark on an extensive trek through required coursework in quantitative reasoning, the humanities and arts, the social sciences, laboratory science, foreign language, and four physical education blocks. There are additional boxes to check in the areas of US diversity, global diversity, and a sustainability course.

As students immerse themselves in one of forty-four areas of concentration, Dickinson supports them with a 9:1 student-to-faculty ratio and average class size of fifteen with 75 percent of classes being capped at nineteen students. This type of intimacy allows the school to advertise that "Not only will you have the opportunity to conduct advanced research as an undergraduate that most wouldn't experience until graduate school, you'll also have the chance to work alongside faculty in the process." The majority of students also elect to venture to other continents as part of their undergraduate experience. Offering study abroad opportunities in thirty-nine locations in twenty-four countries across six continents, Dickinson enjoys a 62 percent participation rate.

By discipline, the greatest number of degrees are conferred in the social sciences (27 percent); business (10 percent); biology (9 percent); and area, ethnic, and gender studies (8 percent). The college's foreign language program that features thirteen offerings—including Arabic, Hebrew, and Portuguese—is recognized as one of the top programs in the country. International studies, history, and environmental studies also have particularly strong reputations. Dickinson students are known as a globetrotting and service-oriented bunch. Thus, it is fitting that the college is a leading producer of Fulbright scholars and Peace Corps volunteers.

Outside the Classroom

Dickinson is located in central Pennsylvania about twenty miles from the state capital of Harrisburg. Carlisle may be a small town, yet there are a reasonable number of nearby shopping/dining options, including dozens of restaurants within walking distance. The school's small town location means that a good deal of social life takes place on campus where literally 100 percent of students reside in college-owned housing. Greek life has a strong but not dominant presence with only 4 percent of men joining fraternities but 25 percent of women joining sororities. More than one hundred student clubs exist with the highest concentrations in the performing arts and club sports. For those serious about athletics, the Red Devils compete in NCAA Division III in eleven men's and twelve women's sports. Environmental sustainability is important to the administration and students alike, and with its own organic farm and pledge to be climate neutral by 2020, the college is regularly ranked as one of the top eco-friendly colleges in the country.

Career Services

The Career Center has seven professional employees (not counting the two administrative assistants) who play advising, pre-professional counseling, and employer relations roles. That works out to a 343:1 student-to-advisor ratio, which is about average compared to other schools featured in this guide. One counselor is dedicated to pre-health advising and another guides pre-law students.

Dickinson does not host its own career fairs but does endorse two nearby gatherings, the Capital Region Internship Fair at Penn State Harrisburg and the Not-for-Profit Networking Fair in Philadelphia. However, there are other areas where this office excels. For example, a tremendous 94 percent of students completed an internship, service-learning, or research apprenticeship at some point over their four years of study. In the summer of 2019, more than 400 students completed internships and summer research experiences in thirty states and twenty-one countries. In 2016, the college also launched an externship program in which students can spend between two and ten days over winter break shadowing alums in their workplaces. Unfortunately, only a tiny percentage of alumni report finding their job directly because of the Career Center. Less than 1 percent of 2005-2010 graduates, surveyed in 2015, cited a Dickinson Career Center event as a factor in finding employment. Less than 2 percent (per category) were assisted by an on-campus interview, a job fair, or school-provided online resources. To be fair, there is evidence that the office has made great strides since that time.

Dickinson College

E-mail: admissions@dickinson.edu | Website: www.dickinson.edu

Professional Outcomes

One year after graduating, 93 percent of Dickinsonians have found jobs, full-time volunteer work, or have enrolled in graduate school. The most popular industries are, in order, business and industry, education, health and medical services, and nonprofits. Red Devils head to a wide range of organizations/employers with multiple 2018 grads headed to the US Army, the Peace Corps, Teach for America and, on the other end of the spectrum, the Vanguard Group. Many other well-known financial, pharmaceutical, and consulting companies are represented on the list of 2018 graduate destinations as are a host of other nonprofit organizations. Across all graduating years, companies employing more than twenty-five Dickinson alumni include Deloitte, IBM, Morgan Stanley, JPMorgan Chase & Co., Merck, EY, PNC, PwC, Google, and Amazon. The median salary for a Dickinson alum at age thirty-four is $55,000, slightly less than graduates of rival Franklin & Marshall. It's interesting that more alumni can be found in New York City than in Pennsylvania.

Within five years of receiving their diplomas, 55-60 percent of recent grads have entered or finished graduate school. For the Class of 2018, the majority of graduate school-bound new alums found homes in state universities; however, a fair number of prestigious acceptances were sprinkled in including Penn, Tufts, Emory, and Carnegie Mellon (computer science), Johns Hopkins, Columbia, UVA, and NYU. Law school applicants are accepted at a rate of 97 percent with some applicants finding success in Carlisle at Penn State's Dickinson Law School, and two 2018 grads are now attending Notre Dame Law School. Of students recommended for medical school by the college, 75 percent were accepted into at least one institution.

Admission

From 2013-2018 as the highly rated liberal arts admissions world became increasingly more hyper competitive, Dickinson experienced little change. The admit rate in 2018 was 49 percent, slightly friendlier than the 44 percent in 2013. Standardized test scores for admitted students have also remained fairly constant, and the majority do submit them (60 percent submit SATs and 27 percent submit ACTs) even though the school went test-optional a long time ago. The mid-50 percent range on the ACT is 27-31 and 1200-1390 on the SAT. The same goes for class rank, which in 2018-19 saw 41 percent of freshmen hail from the top 10 percent of their high school cohort, and 74 percent finish in the top 25 percent; only 4 percent of this group did not finish in the top half of their class.

Dickinson shows love to students who love them. Sixty-eight percent of early decision applicants were offered admission in 2018, which was a reduction from the previous year. It is unusual for a college to include "demonstrated interest" as one of the most important factors in admissions decisions, but Dickinson does exactly that. With a yield rate of only 21 percent, the vast majority of those accepted into the college elect to attend another institution. A handful of other soft factors also sit atop the list: volunteer work, talent/ability, and character/personal qualities. Despite its status as a highly selective institution, intelligent students with a blemish still have a chance to find a home here. With its test-optional policy, those who exceled in the classroom but struggled on Saturday mornings with a No. 2 pencil in their hand are still in the running as are those with the opposite imperfection—strong SAT-takers who bloomed late as serious-minded students.

Worth Your Money?

An impressively high 61 percent of Dickinson students are awarded some level of need-based aid. While not all see 100 percent of their demonstrated need met, the majority do, and the average annual grant is $42,448. An additional 18 percent of undergraduates receive annual merit aid awards of $12,685, helping to reduce the total cost of attendance that is estimated at over $73k per year. Thanks to that assistance, the amount of debt incurred by the average Dickinson student is less than that of the average college student in the United States. If you were borrowing $100k+ to study the liberal arts, we would caution against selecting this school without first exploring more cost-effective options. However, for those taking on modest amounts of student loans, this is a college worth attending for the intimate class environment and solid graduate outcomes.

FINANCIAL
Institutional Type: Private
In-State Tuition: $55,948
Out-of-State Tuition: $55,948
Room & Board: $14,176
Required Fees: $575
Books & Supplies: $1,250

Avg. Need-Based Aid: $42,448
Avg. % of Need Met: 100%

Avg. Merit-Based Aid: $12,685
% Receiving Merit-Based Aid: 18%

Avg. Cumulative Debt: $26,977
% of Students Borrowing: 56%

CAREER
Who Recruits
1. Gartner
2. Amazon
3. Booz Allen Hamilton
4. PwC
5. PNC

Notable Internships
1. BlackRock
2. IBM
3. Cushman & Wakefield

Top Industries
1. Business
2. Education
3. Operations
4. Social Services
5. Sales

Top Employers
1. US Army
2. Deloitte
3. IBM
4. Morgan Stanley
5. JPMorgan Chase

Where Alumni Work
1. New York City
2. Philadelphia
3. Washington, DC
4. Boston
5. Harrisburg, PA

Median Earnings
College Scorecard (Early Career): $57,400
EOP (Early Career): $55,100
PayScale (Mid-Career): $100,100

RANKINGS
Forbes: 120
Money: 230
U.S. News: 46, Liberal Arts Colleges
Wall Street Journal/THE: 100
Washington Monthly: 49, Liberal Arts Colleges

#CollegesWorthYourMoney

Drexel University

Philadelphia, Pennsylvania | Admissions Phone: 215-895-2400

ADMISSION
Admission Rate: 77%
Admission Rate - Men: 76%
Admission Rate - Women: 78%
EA Admission Rate: 96%
ED Admission Rate: 86%
Admission Rate (5-Year Trend): -5%
ED Admission Rate (5-Year Trend): Previously Not Offered
% of Admits Attending (Yield): 14%
Transfer Admission Rate: 48%

Offered Wait List: 1,215
Accepted Wait List: N/A
Admitted Wait List: 9

SAT Reading/Writing (Middle 50%): 580-670
SAT Math (Middle 50%): 590-710
ACT Composite (Middle 50%): 25-30
Testing Policy: Test Flexible
SAT Superscore: Yes
ACT Superscore: Yes

% Graduated in Top 10% of HS Class: 33%
% Graduated in Top 25% of HS Class: 64%
% Graduated in Top 50% of HS Class: 90%

ENROLLMENT
Total Undergraduate Enrollment: 15,667
% Part-Time: 11%
% Male: 52%
% Female: 48%
% Out-of-State: 49%
% Fraternity: 11%
% Sorority: 10%
% On-Campus (Freshman): 87%
% On-Campus (All Undergraduate): 22%

% African-American: 7%
% Asian: 18%
% Hispanic: 7%
% White: 52%
% Other: 4%
% Race or Ethnicity Unknown: 2%
% International: 11%
% Low-Income: 18%

ACADEMICS
Student-to-Faculty Ratio: 11:1
% of Classes Under 20: 53%
% of Classes Under 40: 85%
% Full-Time Faculty: 54%
% Full-Time Faculty w/ Terminal Degree: 86%

Top Programs
Biomedical Engineering
Civil Engineering
Design
Information Systems
Mechanical Engineering
Nursing
Public Health

Retention Rate: 89%
4-Year Graduation Rate: N/A
6-Year Graduation Rate: 74%

Curricular Flexibility: Less Flexible
Academic Rating: ★★★

Inside the Classroom

Building your campus adjacent to an Ivy League school like the University of Pennsylvania is a solid recipe to end up a higher education afterthought. Yet Drexel, established in 1891, has carved out its own solid reputation as a private research university specializing in engineering, business, and nursing, all bolstered by a groundbreaking and distinctive co-op program that just celebrated its one hundredth anniversary. Drexel Dragons come to the university for its rigorous programs as well as the emphasis placed on experiential learning. They leave, by and large, with well-paying jobs in their area of interest. Practical, career-minded teens find a good partner institution in Drexel University.

There are eighty-plus undergraduate majors to choose from at Drexel, and the academic culture lets you get down to brass tacks quickly. Other than a Composition & Rhetoric course and introductory classes that provide an overview of university life and the co-op experience, most students dive right into their major-specific coursework as freshmen. Business students take courses like Foundations of Economics, Principles of Economics, and Introduction to Analysis. Engineering students are plopped right into Chemistry, Calculus, and Introduction to Engineering Design and Data Analysis. The robust co-op program sees just about every single undergraduate participate. Students can choose between a five-year plan that includes three co-op experiences or a traditional four-year pathway that allows for one co-op placement. The school runs year-round on a quarter calendar to accommodate students on co-ops.

Drexel offers a reasonable 11:1 student-to-faculty ratio with commensurately reasonable class sizes. Fifty-three percent of sections contain nineteen or fewer students, and just a sliver under 10 percent of sections contain fifty or more. Drexel students are encouraged to begin seeking undergraduate research opportunities "as early as the freshman year." An array of research-oriented co-ops exist at local hospitals, museums, and pharmaceutical companies as well. With the emphasis on co-op education, it can be difficult to carve out time to study abroad while at Drexel. Last year, roughly 900 students managed to study internationally at one of sixty locations. Co-ops in foreign countries are another way to access the benefits of this type of experience.

Looking at the number of degrees conferred by discipline, the big three at Drexel are business (25 percent), health professions (21 percent), and engineering (21 percent). Visual and performing arts (9 percent), computer science (4 percent), biology (3 percent), and mathematics (3 percent) round out the list of majors with a sizable representation. The Westphal College of Media Arts & Design has a growing reputation, as do programs in engineering. Also on the rise is Drexel's number of winners of prestigious postgraduate fellowships. In 2019, four undergraduates won Fulbright Scholarships and six former Drexel undergrads took home National Science Foundation Graduate Research Fellowships.

Outside the Classroom

Set on a ninety-six-acre urban campus in University City, the section of Philadelphia that also includes the University of Pennsylvania, Drexel has 87 percent of freshmen residing in university-owned housing, but only 22 percent of the overall student body live on campus. Greek life draws 11 percent of males and 10 percent of female students. There are eighteen NCAA Division I sports teams that compete in the Colonial Athletic Association. Club and intramural sports are huge with over 9,000 participants each year. The Drexel Recreation Center is an 18,000-square-foot facility with all of the fitness amenities one could desire. There are 300 active student organizations on campus and a ton more opportunities for fun in the surrounding area. Drexel students get in free at the Academy of Natural Sciences, the oldest museum of its kind in the country, and can just as easily walk to World Café Live and catch a free concert with a big-name artist every Friday afternoon. Famed art museums, major sporting events, and an excellent food and bar scene are all within a short distance of campus. Student groups like the Campus Activities Board organize group trips to amusement parks, Broadway plays, and host block parties and other special events on campus.

Career Services

The Steinbright Career Development Center is staffed by thirteen full-time staff members who serve as career counselors, pre-law/pre-health advisors, and employer relations specialists. However, there are twenty-four additional professional employees dedicated to the co-op program, bringing the total to thirty-seven staff members who work with undergraduates on career-related matters. That works out to a 419:1 ratio, a respectable figure for a university of Drexel's size and scope. Its three annual career fairs are well attended by employers, but student attendance is lower than one would expect. The Fall Career Fair drew 228 employers and 1,678 students, the Spring Career Fair attracted 109 companies/organizations and 923 students, and the Engineering Career Fair saw 135 employers and 625 students in attendance.

E-mail: enroll@drexel.edu | Website: www.drexel.edu

When it comes to career services at Drexel the co-op experiences are, to quote Philadelphia-area native Reggie Jackson, "The straw that stirs the drink." Among surveyed graduates, 84 percent had a co-op experience that was relevant to their current job, and 89 percent landed jobs related to their college majors. More importantly, 48 percent of students received a job offer from one of their co-op employers. Placements are available in thirty-one states and thirty-eight countries, and partner organizations include major players like Goldman Sachs, Lockheed Martin, and Exelon. The strength of this one-of-a-kind co-op program combined with strong employment statistics earns the Steinbright Career Development Center high marks from our staff.

Professional Outcomes

One year after graduating, 96 percent of the class of 2018 had arrived at their next destination; 84 percent were employed, and 12 percent had matriculated into graduate or professional school. The largest employers of Drexel alumni are Comcast, Merck, Vanguard, and Johnson & Johnson. There are also at least one hundred Dragons within GlaxoSmithKline, JP Morgan Chase, SAP (software), Amazon, Microsoft, IBM, Accenture, Deloitte, Google, and EY. Six times as many graduates remain in Philadelphia as go to the second most popular postgraduation destination of New York City. Pockets of Drexel alumni can also be found in DC, San Francisco, Baltimore, Boston, and Los Angeles. The average starting salary for Drexel grads with a full-time job was $59,500.

The predominately career-driven group that attends the university does not immediately move on to graduate schools in large numbers. However, those who do have produced some solid results, particularly those applying to medical and law school. Drexel's medical school acceptance rate was 69 percent, almost thirty points higher than the national average. It offers an accelerated BS/MD program with its own Drexel University College of Medicine. Other commonly attended medical schools include local options Rowan, Temple, Sidney Kimmel Medical College, and the Philadelphia College of Osteopathic Medicine. Eighty-four percent of law school applicants ultimately found a home for their legal education. Recent grads have landed at prestigious law schools at Harvard, the University of Michigan, Vanderbilt, and the University of Pennsylvania as well as a number of local options including Drexel's own law school that opened in 2006.

Admission

Drexel's 30,242 applicants for a place in the freshman class of 2018-19 overwhelmingly received favorable admissions news—77 percent were accepted. That healthy percentage is the norm at Drexel as acceptance rates have been in the 70-80 percent range for some time. Its yield rate, the number of accepted students who actually enroll, is around 14 percent. This is because, for many, Drexel is not their first choice. Still, those who end up attending have a strong academic profile. Freshmen in 2018-19 possessed a mid-50 percent SAT of 1170-1380 and an ACT of 25-30. One-third placed within the top 10 percent of their high school class, and 64 percent were in the top quartile; 49 percent of students sported a GPA of 3.75 or higher and, on the other end, 6 percent had a GPA under 3.0.

Admissions decisions are made in a manner consistent with Drexel's STEM-focus—the hard numbers are of utmost importance. GPA, standardized test scores, class rank, and the rigor of one's high school coursework are deemed "very important" while soft factors like recommendations, essays, and character/personal qualities comprise the second tier. With such a low yield rate, the university looks favorably upon those who will commit to it through binding early decision. The ED acceptance rate in 2018 was 86 percent. In short, Drexel is a rare school with a pre-professional focus that is not terribly difficult to get into. Those with standardized test scores around the 80th percentile and solid but imperfect grades should find a welcome home here.

Worth Your Money?

Drexel graduates earn 18.5 percent above the national average which, even given the focus on business, engineering, and nursing is still an impressive achievement. That salary boost is needed thanks to the $71,600 annual cost of attendance, although students receiving merit aid do receive an average annual grant of $33k. Fortunately, the co-op experience is top notch and frequently leads to gainful employment in one's area of study. Students do not pay tuition during their co-op year and, in fact, are paid a median six-month salary of $18,357. This college is unique and connected enough to be worth the high price tag, particularly for students pursing more pre-professional majors.

FINANCIAL
Institutional Type: Private
In-State Tuition: $52,146
Out-of-State Tuition: $52,146
Room & Board: $14,241
Required Fees: $2,370
Books & Supplies: $1,200

Avg. Need-Based Aid: $33,305
Avg. % of Need Met: 81%

Avg. Merit-Based Aid: $15,641
% Receiving Merit-Based Aid: 35%

Avg. Cumulative Debt: N/A
% of Students Borrowing: N/A

CAREER
Who Recruits
1. Seer Interactive
2. Bentley Systems
3. Johnson & Johnson
4. Spark Therapeutics
5. Lockheed Martin

Notable Internships
1. KPMG
2. Anthropologie
3. Delancy Street Partners

Top Industries
1. Business
2. Engineering
3. Operations
4. Education
5. Healthcare

Top Employers
1. Lockheed Martin
2. Comcast
3. Merck
4. Vanguard
5. Johnson & Johnson

Where Alumni Work
1. Philadelphia
2. New York City
3. Washington, DC
4. San Francisco
5. Baltimore

Median Earnings
College Scorecard (Early Career): $68,800
EOP (Early Career): N/A
PayScale (Mid-Career): $114,800

RANKINGS
Forbes: 226
Money: 382
U.S. News: 97, National Universities
Wall Street Journal/THE: 96 (T)
Washington Monthly: 156, National Universities

#CollegesWorthYourMoney

Duke University

Durham, North Carolina | Admissions Phone: 919-684-3214

ADMISSION
Admission Rate: 9%
Admission Rate - Men: 9%
Admission Rate - Women: 9%
EA Admission Rate: Not Offered
ED Admission Rate: 22%
Admission Rate (5-Year Trend): -4%
ED Admission Rate (5-Year Trend): -9%
% of Admits Attending (Yield): 55%
Transfer Admission Rate: 7%

Offered Wait List: N/A
Accepted Wait List: N/A
Admitted Wait List: N/A

SAT Reading/Writing (Middle 50%): 710-770
SAT Math (Middle 50%): 740-800
ACT Composite (Middle 50%): 33-35
Testing Policy: ACT/SAT Required
SAT Superscore: Yes
ACT Superscore: Yes

% Graduated in Top 10% of HS Class: 95%
% Graduated in Top 25% of HS Class: 98%
% Graduated in Top 50% of HS Class: 100%

ENROLLMENT
Total Undergraduate Enrollment: 6,682
% Part-Time: 0%
% Male: 50%
% Female: 50%
% Out-of-State: 85%
% Fraternity: 29%
% Sorority: 42%
% On-Campus (Freshman): 100%
% On-Campus (All Undergraduate): 85%

% African-American: 10%
% Asian: 22%
% Hispanic: 9%
% White: 42%
% Other: 2%
% Race or Ethnicity Unknown: 4%
% International: 10%
% Low-Income: 13%

ACADEMICS
Student-to-Faculty Ratio: 6:1
% of Classes Under 20: 71%
% of Classes Under 40: 90%
% Full-Time Faculty: 95%
% Full-Time Faculty w/ Terminal Degree: 96%

Top Programs
Biology
Economics
English
Engineering
Environmental Sciences
Neuroscience
Political Science
Public Policy

Retention Rate: 98%
4-Year Graduation Rate: 87%
6-Year Graduation Rate: 96%

Curricular Flexibility: Somewhat Flexible
Academic Rating: ★★★★★

Inside the Classroom

Duke is a place where students can be, at once, fanatical, face-painted members of the Cameron Crazies as well as studious, career-minded young people in an Ivy League-caliber academic environment. Close to 6,700 undergrads are joined by more than 9,900 graduate students on this picturesque, 8,800-acre campus in Durham, North Carolina. Nineteen percent go on to earn degrees in the social sciences followed by engineering (15 percent), biology (14 percent), public administration and social services (9 percent), and psychology (7 percent).

The academic offerings at Duke include fifty-three majors, fifty-two minors, and twenty-six interdisciplinary certificates. More than 4,000 undergraduate courses run each semester in the College of Arts & Sciences alone. Rarely do students concentrate solely on one major—83 percent either double major, add a minor, or pursue an additional certificate. Undergraduates encounter a good number of unique academic requirements. All freshmen in the Trinity College of Arts & Sciences must take a first-year seminar and first-year writing course. Before graduation, each individual must take two small group learning experiences that can involve an independent study and/or constructing a thesis. Foreign language and multiple courses under the umbrellas of Areas of Knowledge and Modes of Inquiry also must be tackled.

Class sizes are on the small side—71 percent are nineteen or fewer, and 27 percent are less than ten. A stellar 6:1 student-to-faculty ratio helps keep classes so reasonable even while catering to almost five-figures of graduate students. The Undergraduate Research Support Office does great work connecting students with opportunities to conduct research, either over the summer or during the regular school year. All told, more than half of undergraduates conduct research. More than any other top-ten research institution, Duke students pursue a semester abroad—48 percent elect to venture off to one of the school's 300 partner programs scattered around the world.

Duke has a sterling reputation for academics across the board. The Department of Biology is world class and a leading producer of successful medical school applicants. Programs in economics, English, and public policy consistently earn top ranking as well. Blue Devils win prestigious postgraduate fellowships on a regular basis. Named a top producer of Fulbright Scholars for the last thirteen years, Duke churned out twelve winners in 2018. The university has produced an incredible forty-three Rhodes Scholars in its illustrious history, more than Emory and Vanderbilt combined.

Outside the Classroom

When you enter campus through Duke Gardens, it can feel like you're strolling through a perfectly manicured Disney theme park; everything is pristine and aesthetically pleasing. Thus, no one is anxious to live anywhere other than the university's grounds and 100 percent of freshmen and 85 percent of the entire student body live on campus. With thirty-nine recognized Greek chapters, fraternities and sororities play a major role in social life at Duke. Almost 42 percent of women and 29 percent of men become Greek affiliated. Those who occupy dorms are generally pleased, and the food at Duke is universally praised. Big-time sports is a staple of life on campus as the Blue Devils compete in twenty-three sports in NCAA Division I's vaunted Atlantic Coast Conference. Since the beloved Coach K took over in 1980, the men's basketball squad has made the Final Four a dozen times and has won five national championships. One of the most popular non-sports-related, campus-wide events is the annual Last Day of Classes (LDOC) celebration that draws a large percentage of the student body for activities, beverages, and music. More than 400 student organizations run on campus, including a high-performing mock trial team and The Chronicle, an award-winning student newspaper with a seven-figure budget. The culture of volunteering is strong with an 80 percent participation rate as Blue Devils perform community service in the city of Durham in programs like Engineers Without Borders.

Career Services

The Career Center at Duke is staffed by eight undergraduate career advisors and six employer relations specialists. Not counting other full-time employees who do not work directly with students or the career ambassadors, who are current students, Duke's student-to-advisor ratio calculates to 477:1, which is slightly below average compared to other schools in its weight class. Yet, this is not indicative of anything less than outstanding career services offerings. This assessment can be delivered by one quick fact: An astounding 95 percent of graduating seniors who had lined up their first jobs were hired by companies that work in some capacity with the Duke Career Center.

Undergrads each have their own assigned career counselor, and the school recommends establishing a relationship as a freshman. Two-thirds of graduates reported meeting with a career center staff member at least once over their four years of study. Regular events held include Practice Interview Day, Ignite Your Internship Search, and the Fall Career Fair that includes over one hundred top companies, many of which recruit and offer interviews on campus. Despite having a higher student-to-advisor ratio than the average school profiled in this book, the career center at Duke is among the best in the country at preparing students for high-paying employment and admission into prestigious graduate/professional programs.

Professional Outcomes

At graduation, 71 percent of surveyed seniors in 2018 were set to enter the world of work, 20 percent were continuing into graduate schools, and 2 percent were starting their own businesses. The industries that attract the largest percentage of Blue Devils are finance, IT, health care, business and consulting, and science/research. Companies employing a minimum of three Class of 2018 Duke grads include Google, Capital One, Facebook, Amazon, Microsoft, Oracle, Goldman Sachs, Morgan Stanley, Accenture, and a host of other top-shelf corporations in the areas of technology, finance, and consulting. Thirty-four percent of Duke alumni elect to stay in North Carolina. New York, California, DC, and Massachusetts follow in popularity. The top foreign destinations for employment are the United Kingdom and China. Duke students, on average, do exceptionally well financially, bringing home the eleventh highest salary by age thirty-four of any school in the country, ahead of schools like Georgetown, Stanford, and Caltech.

Of the 20 percent headed into graduate school, a hefty 22 percent are attending medical school, 18 percent are in PhD programs, and 12 percent are entering law school. The med school acceptance rate is 85 percent, more than twice the national average. Eventually, 84 percent of Duke undergraduates will go on to earn an advanced degree. The Class of 2017 saw 146 members apply to law school, scoring an average of 165 on the LSAT, among the highest in the country. Those applicants found their way into just about every top-ranked law school in existence. In the last few years, Blue Devils have pursued a JD at Stanford Law School, University of Chicago Law School, and Harvard Law School, among others.

Admission

Getting into Duke is an Ivy League-level, single-digit proposition. The application pool vying for a place in the Class of 2022 saw only 8.9 percent gain acceptance. That isn't a new trend. Rather, Duke has had an admit rate under 10 percent for the last five years. Among freshmen in 2018-19, 72 percent submitted ACT scores and had a 50th percentile range of 33-35; the SAT range was 1450-1570. An intimidating 95 percent of Blue Devils graduated in the top 10 percent of their high school class, and 98 percent were in the top quartile.

Early decision applicants saw a far more favorable acceptance rate, 21.6 percent versus the regular round rate of 7.3 percent; a sizable 50 percent of the freshman class is cemented during this early round. However, it is worth keeping in mind that athletes and legacy students are typically admitted in the early round, which certainly helps prop up the acceptance rate. Additionally, legacy students comprise 10-13 percent of the student body in any given year, and they typically apply ED. The Duke Admissions Committee considers eight factors as "very important" in admissions decisions: rigor of classes, grades, test scores, essays, recommendations, extracurricular activities, talent/ability, and character/personal qualities. Like the Ivies, Duke routinely rejects valedictorians and teens with perfect standardized test scores. Successful applicants will have exceptional academic credentials, attention-grabbing essays, and special talents that set them apart from a crowded field of aspiring Blue Devils.

Worth Your Money?

Duke's annual cost of attendance is a hair below $77,000, and only 11 percent receive any merit-based aid. The good news for those who are awarded merit aid is that the average award is $57k per year. Further, the 3,103 members of the undergraduate student body who qualify for need-based financial aid receive annual grants of $53k per year, meeting 100 percent of their demonstrated need. The university has the fifteenth largest endowment in the United States ($7 billion), and it puts it to good use, making Duke affordable to those from non-wealthy families. Essentially, the approximately 45 percent of students who come from wealthy families (top 5 percent income) pay the bulk of the sticker price while those from lower-to-middle income homes get significant tuition reductions. Even if you had to take on a lot of debt to attend Duke, this is one school that will almost certainly pay you back many times over; alumni salaries and employment prospects are that strong.

FINANCIAL
Institutional Type: Private
In-State Tuition: $55,880
Out-of-State Tuition: $55,880
Room & Board: $15,588
Required Fees: $2,051
Books & Supplies: $1,434

Avg. Need-Based Aid: $53,214
Avg. % of Need Met: 100%

Avg. Merit-Based Aid: $56,954
% Receiving Merit-Based Aid: 11%

Avg. Cumulative Debt: $21,525
% of Students Borrowing: 32%

CAREER
Who Recruits
1. 4170 Trading LLC
2. Cornerstone Advisors LLC
3. National Security Agency
4. Xerox
5. Qualtrics

Notable Internships
1. Carlyle Group
2. CNBC
3. Instagram

Top Industries
1. Business
2. Education
3. Research
4. Operations
5. Engineering

Top Employers
1. Google
2. Amazon
3. Microsoft
4. Facebook
5. Goldman Sachs

Where Alumni Work
1. Raleigh-Durham, NC
2. New York City
3. Washington, DC
4. San Francisco
5. Boston

Median Earnings
College Scorecard (Early Career): $84,400
EOP (Early Career): $87,500
PayScale (Mid-Career): $132,100

RANKINGS
Forbes: 9
Money: 19
U.S. News: 10, National Universities
Wall Street Journal/THE: 10
Washington Monthly: 5, National Universities

#CollegesWorthYourMoney

Elon University

Elon, North Carolina | Admissions Phone: 336-278-3566

Inside the Classroom

Nestled in the centralized Piedmont region of North Carolina, Elon University is home to 6,100 undergraduates and is—most fittingly for a school whose mascot is the Phoenix—a school on the rise. Not yet an uber-selective school (nearly three-quarters of applicants get in), this modestly sized university is known for its quality undergraduate teaching, experiential learning opportunities, and unparalleled study abroad program. Individualized attention is available at every turn, particularly from a well-staffed and highly effective Career Services Department.

Students choose from sixty majors and can add a number of interesting minors like adventure –based learning, coaching, and multimedia authoring. Regardless of one's area of concentration, all Elon undergrads must work through an extensive core curriculum that is made up of six interrelated parts: two first-year foundations courses focused on developing writing and critical thinking skills; an experiential learning component that requires studying abroad, interning, or conducting independent research; foreign language (can be exempted through AP tests); a total of thirty-two credits in the arts and sciences; eight credit hours of advanced coursework outside one's major; and a capstone seminar as a senior. Ninety-eight percent of students elect to take a one-credit freshman course entitled Elon 101 that, among other things, helps new students map out a graduation plan.

Elon's 12:1 student-to-faculty ratio leads to an average class size of twenty students; 52 percent of sections contain fewer than twenty students. A whopping 78 percent elect to study abroad, the highest participation rate in the country among master's-granting institutions. There are limitless options for overseas study including official Elon Centers Abroad in Shanghai, Dunedin, London, and Florence. Chances for working closely with faculty on research projects are also plentiful; 23 percent of students participate in faculty-mentored research.

Though Elon possesses solid offerings in many disciplines, programs in finance, communication, exercise science, and the performing arts receive the most praise. The areas in which the greatest number of degrees are conferred are business (33 percent), journalism/communication (19 percent), parks and recreation (7 percent), social sciences (7 percent), and social services (7 percent). Elon is recognized as a top producer of Fulbright Scholars seeing eight fellowship winners in 2018; it had forty-five winners between 2013 and 2018. Recent graduates also have received a Truman Scholarship, a Goldwater Scholarship, and grants from the National Science Foundation.

Outside the Classroom

Sixty-four percent of undergrads live on the school's 656-acre grounds. Greek life is a dominant force on the Elon social scene with 39 percent of women joining sororities and 20 percent of men signing up for fraternity life. The 60/40 gender breakdown in favor of women is certainly a factor in social life. It also should be noted that Elon has been rated as one of the LGBTQ-friendlier schools in the country. An athletically inclined student body participates in seventeen NCAA Division I sports as well as twenty-one intercollegiate club teams and eighteen intramural sports. Elon students are known for being involved in their college community as nearly 90 percent contribute some level of volunteer service, and 49 percent hold some type of leadership role in a student organization. There are 250 student-run clubs, including a student-run television station and an award-winning weekly newspaper, The Pendulum. The Elon Speakers Series sees an incredible list of notable figures visit campus each year. In the last few years it has welcomed David Cameron, Anita Hill, and Bob Woodward. The town of Elon is not the world's most exciting place, but those with access to a car are no more than an hour from the larger cities of Durham, Raleigh, and Winston-Salem.

Career Services

The Student Professional Development Center (SPDC) at Elon University has twenty-one professional employees (not counting a number of graduate fellows and apprentices) who play advising, pre-professional counseling, and employer relations roles. That works out to a 295:1 student-to-advisor ratio, which is better-than-average when compared to other schools featured in this guide. This office has sufficient resources to offer individualized services and coordinate large events such as fall and spring job fairs that attract over ninety employers and over 1,000 students. The center also regularly offers smaller events, such as the Accounting Meet and Greet, which attract fifteen firms and 120 undergraduate students. Its Graduate & Professional School Fair brings representatives from fifty institutions to campus each October. In total, 259 employers attended career fairs during the 2017-18 school year.

Thanks to efforts of the Student Professional Development Center, 89 percent of Elon students complete an internship during their four undergraduate years. Members of the class of 2017 interned at a range of employers including The Smithsonian, HBO, Coca-Cola Co., Booz Allen Hamilton, KMPG, and Ralph Lauren. Two-thirds of employed graduates attributed their acquisition of a job directly to networking leads via their internship experience. Companies known to recruit at Elon and/or offer on-campus interviews include Walt Disney Co., ESPN, Oracle, Credit Suisse, EY, PwC, Goldman Sachs, and ABC News. The SPDC facilitates more than 5,600 one-on-one advising appointments per year, an absolutely remarkable number given the modest size of the school.

Elon University

E-mail: admissions@elon.edu | Website: www.elon.edu

Professional Outcomes

Results of a survey administered nine months after graduation found that 94 percent of the class of 2018 had found employment, a graduate school, or an internship. That is a significant improvement from five years ago when only 83 percent of graduates had found their next postsecondary or employment home nine months after receiving their diplomas. Of those accepting employment, a magnificent 93 percent reported that their job directly related to their area of study. Top employers of recent Elon graduates include Bloomberg, Deloitte, EY, Google, Goldman Sachs, Red Ventures, and Wells Fargo. Geographically, alumni are dispersed all over the map. A mere quarter of graduates remained in the Tar Heel State while 15 percent migrated to New York and 14 percent to Massachusetts. The average starting salary for an Elon graduate is $43,000. Salaries by the start of midcareer rank seventh among North Carolina colleges and are significantly lower than graduates of Duke, Davidson, or Wake Forest.

Just under one-quarter of 2018 grads gained acceptance into graduate/professional school. Many remain at Elon or continue at other Carolina-based schools such as UNC-Chapel Hill, Duke, Wake Forest, East Carolina University, or North Carolina State. Class of 2018 members gained acceptance into prestigious graduate schools such as Boston University, Columbia, NYU, Penn, and Georgetown. Applicants to medical school typically gain acceptance at the same rate as the national average, around 40 percent. However, in 2017 and 2018, Elon students enjoyed a 52 percent acceptance rate. That group of students earned average MCAT scores that placed them in the 75th percentile. Few graduates in recent years have been accepted into the top medical schools in the country.

Admission

Elon admitted 72 percent of the more than 10,700 applicants for a place in the 2018-19 freshman class. First-year students possessed an average SAT score of 1242 and ACT of 27. Only 25 percent of admitted students finished in the top 10 percent of their high school class, and 57 percent finished in the top quartile. Interestingly, a decade ago, the acceptance rate was a much stingier 42 percent, but the credentials of accepted students were roughly the same. In that time the quality of applicants has remained consistent, but the school's yield rate has declined from 33 percent to 22 percent, leading to more offers of acceptance in order to meet enrollment goals.

The admissions committee rates five factors as of the greatest importance: rigor of secondary curriculum, GPA, standardized test scores, essays, and recommendations. Attributes such as talent/ability as well as work experience, extracurricular activities, and legacy status round out the next tier of considered factors. Applying early decision offers a sizable advantage as 87 percent are accepted in the early round compared to 72 percent in the regular cycle. ED admits account for one-quarter of the freshman class. A school whose reputation is ascending, Elon, for now, remains a welcoming landing spot for teens with solid but unspectacular transcripts. Applying early further increases your odds but may be unnecessary as an admissions strategy unless you are a borderline applicant.

Worth Your Money?

As far as private universities go, a list price of $49,000 (COA) isn't outlandish. A good number of students, 43 percent, receive some type of merit aid, but the awards aren't overly helpful—the average is less than $7,000. Roughly one-third of the undergraduate student body receives need-based aid averaging $16k per recipient. Elon isn't a bargain for most students, but it is a solid deal for a school that provides ample individualized attention and has largely positive student outcomes.

FINANCIAL
Institutional Type: Private
In-State Tuition: $34,850
Out-of-State Tuition: $34,850
Room & Board: $12,230
Required Fees: $469
Books & Supplies: $900

Avg. Need-Based Aid: $15,516
Avg. % of Need Met: 59%

Avg. Merit-Based Aid: $6,895
% Receiving Merit-Based Aid: 43%

Avg. Cumulative Debt: $30,625
% of Students Borrowing: 35%

CAREER
Who Recruits
1. Walt Disney Company
2. SAS
3. Oracle
4. Net Suite
5. Vanguard

Notable Internships
1. ABC's The View
2. Aflac
3. Merrill Lynch

Top Industries
1. Business
2. Education
3. Sales
4. Operations
5. Media

Top Employers
1. Wells Fargo
2. Bank of America
3. EY
4. PwC
5. IBM

Where Alumni Work
1. Winston-Salem, NC
2. New York City
3. Raleigh-Durham, NC
4. Washington, DC
5. Charlotte

Median Earnings
College Scorecard (Early Career): $51,900
EOP (Early Career): $47,300
PayScale (Mid-Career): $93,700

RANKINGS
Forbes: 133
Money: 319
U.S. News: 84, National Universities
Wall Street Journal/THE: 143 (T)
Washington Monthly: 282, National Universities

#CollegesWorthYourMoney

Atlanta, Georgia | Admissions Phone: 404-727-6036

ADMISSION
Admission Rate: 19%
Admission Rate - Men: 20%
Admission Rate - Women: 18%
EA Admission Rate: Not Offered
ED Admission Rate: 26%
Admission Rate (5-Year Trend): -7%
ED Admission Rate (5-Year Trend): N/A
% of Admits Attending (Yield): 28%
Transfer Admission Rate: 25%

\# Offered Wait List: 4,983
\# Accepted Wait List: 2,660
\# Admitted Wait List: 0

SAT Reading/Writing (Middle 50%): 660-730
SAT Math (Middle 50%): 690-790
ACT Composite (Middle 50%): 31-34
Testing Policy: ACT/SAT Required
SAT Superscore: Yes
ACT Superscore: No

% Graduated in Top 10% of HS Class: 84%
% Graduated in Top 25% of HS Class: 98%
% Graduated in Top 50% of HS Class: 100%

ENROLLMENT
Total Undergraduate Enrollment: 7,086
% Part-Time: 1%
% Male: 40%
% Female: 60%
% Out-of-State: 79%
% Fraternity: 28%
% Sorority: 25%
% On-Campus (Freshman): 99%
% On-Campus (All Undergraduate): 63%

% African-American: 8%
% Asian: 21%
% Hispanic: 10%
% White: 39%
% Other: 4%
% Race or Ethnicity Unknown: 1%
% International: 17%
% Low-Income: 19%

ACADEMICS
Student-to-Faculty Ratio: 9:1
% of Classes Under 20: 60%
% of Classes Under 40: 82%
% Full-Time Faculty: 88%
% Full-Time Faculty w/ Terminal Degree: 96%

Top Programs
Biology
Business Administration
Chemistry
English
Film and Media
International Studies
Neuroscience and Behavioral Biology
Philosophy

Retention Rate: 95%
4-Year Graduation Rate: 83%
6-Year Graduation Rate: 90%

Curricular Flexibility: Somewhat Flexible
Academic Rating: ★★★★✦

Inside the Classroom
Widely viewed as a "Southern Ivy," Emory University hosts almost 8,000 elite undergraduates on its Atlanta-based campus. To be more geographically precise, the prestigious school, which boasts the sixteenth largest endowment of any university in the United States, is located in the Druid Hills section of Atlanta, home to the Centers for Disease Control as well as one of the wealthiest neighborhoods in the entire state of Georgia. This midsize university offers a diverse array of majors (70+) and minors (50+), and more than half of Emory students pursue more than one area of study.

All freshmen must complete a first-year seminar in which they are tasked with stretching their critical thinking and research skills as they explore one of a series of fascinating topics in an intimate setting with a faculty member. The immersion and support don't stop there; all freshmen also must take a one-credit advising program called PACE (Pre-Major Advising Connections at Emory) in which they work with a faculty advisor and peer mentor to explore academic pathways. Ultimately, the greatest number of students go on to earn degrees in the social sciences (17 percent), business (16 percent), biology (14 percent), mathematics (7 percent), and psychology (5 percent).

One unique feature of Emory is that one of its undergraduate divisions, Oxford College, about forty-five minutes away, functions as a small liberal arts college for freshmen and sophomores. Oxford students knock out many of their lower-level courses before declaring a major and attending upper-level courses at Emory. No matter which school you attend, hands-on learning opportunities abound. A healthy 56 percent of Emory's student body works directly with a faculty member on academic research. Also noteworthy is the fact that 60 percent of courses have class sizes of under twenty students, a number comparable to many smaller liberal arts colleges.

Emory is notable for its renowned Woodruff School of Nursing and Goizueta School of Business. It also routinely rates well in biology, neuroscience, creative writing, and political science. Undergrads at Emory have a strong history of winning national awards; the school boasted fourteen Fulbright Scholars in 2018-19 alone and has produced twenty Rhodes Scholars in its history. Further, Emory churns out more Teach for America candidates than any other midsize school in the United States, and it is also a leading producer of students who join the Peace Corps upon graduation.

Outside the Classroom
Ninety-nine percent of freshmen and 63 percent of all undergraduates reside in university-owned housing. Many also live in Greek houses as 28 percent of men pledge fraternities and 25 percent of women join sororities. Emory claims over 550 student-run clubs and sports teams, and Oxford College adds another eighty to that diverse list. Volunteer Emory organizes twenty to thirty service trips per week, and over 80 percent of students participate in one or more of the opportunities for community service each year. If you are looking for top-of-the-line collegiate athletics, Emory may not be a great fit. Despite the absence of nationally televised football games, roughly 400 non-scholarship athletes compete in a variety of Division III athletic competitions. Another 600+ students compete in one or more of Emory's club sports, which include everything from flag football to golf to swimming. Impressive amenities, such as two Olympic-size swimming pools and a rock climbing arena, also are available for recreational use. Notable campus-wide events include Wonderful Wednesdays, a weekly open-invite celebration that can include anything from a petting zoo to a volunteer fair and an annual town hall with former President Jimmy Carter. Off campus there is something for everyone with Atlanta's nightlife and natural beauty (a nature trail begins on Oxford's campus) right in your backyard.

Career Services
The Career Center at Emory is staffed by thirteen full-time professional employees as well as four additional full-time staff members who exclusively serve business majors at Goizueta. That equates to a student-to-advisor ratio of 417:1, slightly below average compared to the other institutions included in this book. Spring and fall job fairs are well attended (over 1,000 students each), and approximately 200 companies recruit on campus each year. Each year, more than 12,000 jobs and internships are posted on Handshake, 350+ events are held, and 1,500 one-on-one counseling sessions take place.

Typical career-prep services are available to undergraduate students. Resumes, cover letters, and personal statements can be submitted online for editing by a staff member with fairly quick turnaround times. High Five networking events are held at least once a year for ten career categories including legal, data science, green, STEM, and government and public policy. A full slate of guests, many of whom are Emory alums, discuss their careers with undergraduate attendees. At any time, students can access alumni as well as internship opportunities through their Handshake account. Emory Connects: Career Discovery Days provides students with job-shadowing opportunities in the Atlanta area.

Professional Outcomes

Within three months of graduation 43 percent of Emory grads are already employed, and 92 percent have arrived at their next destination. The top ten employers of Emory's Class of 2018 include Ernst & Young, PricewaterhouseCoopers, Google, Goldman Sachs, BlackRock, and Accenture. Past graduating classes have had a significant numbers of Eagles (the schools lesser-known mascot) land at Deloitte, PwC, the Home Depot, Facebook, and the Coca-Cola Company. Teach for America is the largest employer of the previous three graduating classes. While a healthy number of Emory grads found employment in Georgia, the top destinations for the Class of 2018 included non-Southern locales New York City, DC, LA, Chicago, and Philadelphia. Graduates of the Goizueta Business School found strong starting salaries with the majority going into either finance (median salary: $80k) or consulting (median salary: $69k). Eighty-eight percent of graduates from the Woodruff School of Nursing found employment within three months at an average salary of $53k. The median salary across all schools in 2018 was $60k.

A healthy number of Emory grads pursue further education upon graduation. Last year, more than ten Emory grads/alums received acceptance letters from the following top law schools: Columbia, Berkeley, Michigan, Northwestern, and Georgetown. Every one of the forty-three seniors who applied directly to law school received at least one acceptance. Med school acceptances included Duke, Johns Hopkins, Vanderbilt, and USC. Overall, the most commonly attended graduate schools included Emory itself, Columbia, Duke, University of Chicago, NYU, Penn, Harvard, and Stanford.

Admission

Emory received a record number of applications in 2018—27,559; only 5,104 were accepted, an overall acceptance rate of 18.5 percent, down from a 25 percent acceptance rate only two years ago and a 22 percent clip in 2017. Admitted students out of the 2018 applicant pool had a median SAT score of 1500 or above. That means half of those accepted into Emory's Class of 2022 scored in the 99th percentile nationally on standardized tests. Among those who went on to enroll, the mid-50 percent ranges were 1350-1420 on the SAT and 31-34 on the ACT. The average GPA on a 4.0 scale was 3.78, and few students possessed a GPA under a 3.5.

While high test scores and near-perfect grades (83 percent were in the top 10 percent of their high school classes) are close to prerequisites, Emory does employ a holistic review process that carefully considers letters of recommendations, essays, and how you spent your time outside the classroom. It is a fairly common strategy for students to submit applications to both Emory and Oxford. The latter is slightly less selective with a 19.8 acceptance rate (vs. a 15.6 acceptance rates at Emory College). It is also important to note that 49 percent of first-year students at Emory were admitted through early decision, and the ED acceptance rate was eight points higher than the regular round rate. Thus, if Emory is your first choice, applying early may be a good idea. In sum, Emory is a highly selective, elite school where competition for a spot-on campus is growing more difficult every year. Nothing short of straight A's in a rigorous selection of courses, along with a 1500+ SAT score, puts you in good standing to earn a place in one of the South's most prestigious universities.

Worth Your Money?

Almost all Emory students who qualify for financial aid see 100 percent of their demonstrated need met by the university. That translates to 48 percent of the undergraduate student body receiving an average grant of $44,463 per year. In addition, 22 percent of students are given a merit award of almost $30k, which means few students pay the full $71,588 annual cost of attendance. Emory does a tremendous job of opening its doors to students from every socioeconomic background as the median family income for current students (estimated by tax return data) is much lower than many other private institutions of its ilk. Given that grads enjoy top-shelf employment prospects and generous financial aid, Emory is likely to be worth every dollar it will cost you.

FINANCIAL
Institutional Type: Private
In-State Tuition: $53,070
Out-of-State Tuition: $53,070
Room & Board: $14,972
Required Fees: $734
Books & Supplies: $1,224

Avg. Need-Based Aid: $44,463
Avg. % of Need Met: 100%

Avg. Merit-Based Aid: $29,911
% Receiving Merit-Based Aid: 22%

Avg. Cumulative Debt: $29,658
% of Students Borrowing: 34%

CAREER
Who Recruits
1. American Express
2. SunTrust
3. Turner Construction
4. Macy's
5. BNP Paribas

Notable Internships
1. ExxonMobil
2. Booz Allen Hamilton
3. BlackRock

Top Industries
1. Business
2. Healthcare
3. Education
4. Research
5. Social Services

Top Employers
1. Centers for Disease Control
2. Deloitte
3. EY
4. PwC
5. Google

Where Alumni Work
1. Atlanta
2. New York City
3. Washington, DC
4. San Francisco
5. Boston

Median Earnings
College Scorecard (Early Career): $66,000
EOP (Early Career): $67,800
PayScale (Mid-Career): $110,800

RANKINGS
Forbes: 55
Money: 127
U.S. News: 21, National Universities
Wall Street Journal/THE: 22
Washington Monthly: 83, National Universities

#CollegesWorthYourMoney

Fairfield University

Fairfield, Connecticut | Admissions Phone: 203-254-4100

ADMISSION
Admission Rate: 60%
Admission Rate - Men: 61%
Admission Rate - Women: 60%
EA Admission Rate: 61%
ED Admission Rate: 88%
Admission Rate (5-Year Trend): -10%
ED Admission Rate (5-Year Trend): +26%
% of Admits Attending (Yield): 16%
Transfer Admission Rate: 34%

\# Offered Wait List: 3,287
\# Accepted Wait List: 1,005
\# Admitted Wait List: 11

SAT Reading/Writing (Middle 50%): 600-660
SAT Math (Middle 50%): 590-680
ACT Composite (Middle 50%): 26-30
Testing Policy: Test Optional
SAT Superscore: Yes
ACT Superscore: Yes

% Graduated in Top 10% of HS Class: 37%
% Graduated in Top 25% of HS Class: 77%
% Graduated in Top 50% of HS Class: 96%

ENROLLMENT
Total Undergraduate Enrollment: 4,177
% Part-Time: 5%
% Male: 40%
% Female: 60%
% Out-of-State: 72%
% Fraternity: Not Offered
% Sorority: Not Offered
% On-Campus (Freshman): 95%
% On-Campus (All Undergraduate): 73%

% African-American: 2%
% Asian: 3%
% Hispanic: 7%
% White: 76%
% Other: 2%
% Race or Ethnicity Unknown: 5%
% International: 4%
% Low-Income: 17%

ACADEMICS
Student-to-Faculty Ratio: 12:1
% of Classes Under 20: 41%
% of Classes Under 40: 98%
% Full-Time Faculty: 45%
% Full-Time Faculty w/ Terminal Degree: 93%

Top Programs
Accounting
Communication
English
Finance
Marketing
Nursing
Politics

Retention Rate: 90%
4-Year Graduation Rate: 78%
6-Year Graduation Rate: 81%

Curricular Flexibility: Less Flexible
Academic Rating: ★★★

Inside the Classroom

If you're seeking a high-caliber Catholic/Jesuit institution and don't have the grades and test scores for Georgetown, Holy Cross, Boston College, or Fordham, say hello to a new friend named Fairfield University. This school may not have the national name recognition of its Jesuit brethren but, rest assured, this Connecticut university of 4,100+ undergraduates has its share of stellar students and no shortage of connections to the nearby corporate world of New York City, including many of Wall Street's premier firms.

No matter which of the forty-seven majors you happen to be pursuing, a significant amount of time will be spent fulfilling the required Magis Core Curriculum, beginning with the Class of 2023. Totaling forty-five credits (15 courses), students must complete Introduction to Rhetoric and Composition and Introduction to Philosophy as well as coursework in math, history, religious studies, modern or classical language, and additional forays into the behavioral and social sciences, literature, natural sciences, and visual and performing arts. Business majors, of which there are many (stats to follow), take a whole extra set of mandated coursework including Calculus, Introduction to Microeconomics, and Introduction to Macroeconomics.

A 12:1 student-to-faculty ratio is fully felt in the classroom as courses average only twenty students per section. While 41 percent come in under that marker and only a smattering of sections contain forty+ students, the greatest number of courses have enrollments in the twenty to twenty-nine range. Each year 300+ faculty-directed undergraduate research projects are completed and shown-off at the university's Annual Research and Creative Accomplishments Symposium. Study abroad programs have a 30 percent participation rate, and opportunities are available to travel to sixty sites across forty countries on five continents.

Fairfield is primarily known for its business program, which serves as a pipeline to many of the top financial/accounting/consulting firms in the country. A whopping 43 percent of degrees conferred are from the highly respected Dolan School of Business. Next in popularity are majors within the health professions (12 percent) and communication (9 percent)—both areas also receive high marks at Fairfield. Fulbright winners have trailed off in recent years, but the school has had as many as nine in a single year in the not-too-distant past. However, landing fellowships is rarely the postgraduate goal of this business-minded group.

Outside the Classroom

Housing is guaranteed for all four years, but just below three-quarters of students elect to live on the school's 200-acres campus. Demographically, two things at Fairfield stand out. One, the lack of ethnic diversity is real—77 percent of the class of 2022 identifies as white, and secondly, women make up 60 percent of the undergraduate population. As at many Jesuit institutions, Greek life doesn't exist here, but there are plenty of social opportunities around; for many years Fairfield made appearances on top party school lists, but today it cracks prominent lists measuring schools with the happiest students and best quality of life. With twenty NCAA Division I teams boasting a combined forty-two NCAA tournament appearances in school history, Fairfield certainly has plenty of sports to offer. While the Stags' fan base is quiet compared to a place like fellow Jesuit school Boston College, it is still significant that 10 percent of the student body are Division I athletes. There are over one hundred clubs and activities to enjoy, including twenty intramural sports and twenty-five club teams. Being just sixty miles from NYC is an advantage not only for networking but for weekend trips. Campus itself cannot unreasonably be assigned adjectives like "idyllic" and "stunning." It's location on the Connecticut coast turns the nearby beach into an extension of campus; in fact, 400 seniors each year live in beachfront homes and apartments.

Career Services

The Career, Leadership, and Professional Development (CLPD) staff at Fairfield is comprised of seven full-time employees who work in employer development, recruitment, and experiential learning and internship coordination. The 570:1 student-to-advisor ratio is only average compared to the schools featured in this guidebook, but that does not appear to prevent the CLPD staff from directly touching the lives of almost every student. The office hosts four career fairs per year, including general expos in the fall and spring and smaller affairs specific to nursing and law school. The most recent Fall Career Fair was attended by 123 employers and 745 students. Companies in attendance included EY, KPMG, Morgan Stanley, and Epsilon.

Events including mock interviews, job shadowing, industry nights, resume-writing workshops, and employer presentations occur on a regular basis. The Stags4Hire platform connects students with job opportunities and can help book on-campus interviews. An impressive 47 percent of Class of 2018 members reported that they found their first job through on-campus recruiting/interviewing opportunities during their senior year. Among that same cohort, 602 participated in internships, and 20 percent of 2018 grads cited that experience as directly leading to their first full-time employment opportunity. Taking full advantage of their proximity to NYC, Fairfield's CLPD provides all of the internship and employment opportunities one could hope for.

Fairfield University

E-mail: admis@fairfield.edu | Website: www.fairfield.edu

Professional Outcomes

Fairfield's Class of 2018 found its next destination within six months of graduating at a hard-to-beat 98 percent clip. Financial services was the most commonly entered industry (21.8 percent), followed by healthcare/nursing (18.2 percent), communications/marketing (17.3 percent), and science/biotech/technology (7.8 percent). Many major investment banks, accounting firms, and consulting companies employ large numbers of Fairfield alumni. For example, PwC, Deloitte, Morgan Stanley, JP Morgan & Chase Co., EY, UBS, and Merrill Lynch all employ one hundred or more Stags, and Fairfield grads also have strong representation at IBM, Goldman Sachs, Citi, and Prudential. Thus, it's no wonder that the average starting salary is a healthy $56,000, not including bonuses. Connecticut is not the primary destination for graduates. Rather, New York City attracts the greatest number of alumni with Boston second and Hartford a distant third.

A shade under 30 percent of 2018 grads enrolled directly in graduate or professional school. The breakdown of programs was as follows: business (42.5 percent), education (14.5 percent), arts and sciences (14.5 percent), engineering (10.7 percent), health care (7.5 percent), and law (7 percent). The university has produced roughly thirty graduates per year that go on to earn their degrees in medicine and dentistry. Medical schools where recent grads have been admitted include Johns Hopkins, Georgetown, and the Albert Einstein College of Medicine. Those headed to law school do so at a range of institutions that includes elite schools Fordham, Boston College, and Cornell. Graduate schools pursued and attended by Stag alumni run the gamut of selectivity, but those with high GPAs are in the running for a place in elite graduate institutions.

Admission

Applications to the Class of 2023 set a record for the school as over 12,300 lined up for the chance to become a Stag. The 11,361 applications Fairfield received for a place in the class of 2022 saw 60 percent admitted, still an unintimidating acceptance rate despite the school's rising reputation. Fairfield is a test-optional school, but the vast majority of the 2018-19 freshman class did submit test scores with the SAT being the people's choice. The mid-50 percent SAT range was 1190-1340 and the ACT range was 26-30. Thirty-seven percent finished in the top 10 percent of their high school class, 77 percent were in the top quartile, but almost 5 percent did not land in the top half, giving hope to late bloomers with some blemishes on their transcripts. The average GPA was 3.65, but plenty of students with lower GPAs received acceptance letters; in fact, 16 percent of accepted students had lower than a 3.25.

The four factors the committee lists as being of supreme importance are rigor of curriculum, GPA, recommendations, and the essay. On the next tier of still "important" factors are an interview, extracurricular activities, first-generation status, character/personal qualities, talent/ability, work experience, volunteer work, and demonstrated interest. It's definitely a good idea to visit campus and interview in order to let the university know you are serious about attending. Fairfield only has a 16 percent yield rate, meaning that 84 percent of those accepted into the school do not ultimately enroll. Applying early decision is a good way to punch your ticket to campus as those going the ED route enjoyed an 88 percent acceptance rate.

Worth Your Money?

On the surface, Fairfield, being a not terribly selective, high-priced private school is an unlikely candidate for this guide. Yet, Fairfield succeeds where many others in its class fail. For one, thanks to generous merit and need-based aid, even parents in high-income brackets can expect to pay an average annual COA of $40k, which is $25k less than the sticker price. Parents in lower-income brackets receive commensurate discounts (90 percent of students receive some type of aid) and, with strong graduate outcomes and connections to major corporations, this university could make financial sense for students of all income levels, especially if they have business-related aspirations. However, it is worth noting that the average cumulative debt for Fairfield grads is higher than the national average.

FINANCIAL
Institutional Type: Private
In-State Tuition: $47,650
Out-of-State Tuition: $47,650
Room & Board: $14,710
Required Fees: $700
Books & Supplies: $1,150

Avg. Need-Based Aid: $16,564
Avg. % of Need Met: 84%

Avg. Merit-Based Aid: $17,099
% Receiving Merit-Based Aid: 92%

Avg. Cumulative Debt: $38,596
% of Students Borrowing: 64%

CAREER
Who Recruits
1. FBI
2. Deloitte
3. Ipsos
4. McIntyre Group
5. TEKsystems

Notable Internships
1. Major League Baseball
2. PwC
3. Deutsche Bank

Top Industries
1. Business
2. Education
3. Finance
4. Sales
5. Operations

Top Employers
1. PwC
2. Deloitte
3. Morgan Stanley
4. UBS
5. EY

Where Alumni Work
1. New York City
2. Boston
3. Hartford, CT
4. Philadelphia
5. Washington, DC

Median Earnings
College Scorecard (Early Career): $72,100
EOP (Early Career): $69,900
PayScale (Mid-Career): $116,900

RANKINGS
Forbes: 135
Money: 139
U.S. News: 3, Regional North
Wall Street Journal/THE: 199 (T)
Washington Monthly: N/A

#CollegesWorthYourMoney

Florida State University

Tallahassee, Florida | Admissions Phone: 850-644-6200

Inside the Classroom

Founded in 1851, FSU is one of the state's oldest institutions of higher education as well as one of the nation's finest public research universities. A wide range of baccalaureate degrees—107 to be precise—are available to more than 33,000 undergraduate students, a group possessing increasingly impressive academic credentials with every passing year. Bound by excellent academics and athletics, FSU's student body and alumni are, with good reason, proud to call themselves Seminoles.

The greater university is comprised of sixteen distinct colleges, and all except the College of Law and College of Medicine offer undergraduate degree programs. All students must meet a number of state and university requirements as they progress through their four years of study. Regardless of academic concentration, thirty-six semester hours of coursework are mandated in the areas of quantitative and logical thinking, English composition, natural sciences, social sciences/history, humanities, and cultural practices/ethics, and two semesters of foreign language.

The student-to-faculty is a rather high 22:1, which translates into larger class sizes. Over 16 percent of sections contain more than fifty students, and 7 percent have more than one hundred. However, that is balanced by the 40 percent of sections that contain fewer than twenty students. Out-of-class undergraduate research is taken advantage of by one-quarter of students, and the school plans to greatly expand such offerings. An abundance of study abroad choices include special summer programs in Panama, Florence, London, and Valencia, Spain. FSU has sixty academic programs available in twenty locations throughout the world; one in five students elects to participate.

FSU boasts a number of standout academic programs including those in the College of Motion Picture Arts, the premier film school in the region. The College of Business is extremely well regarded in the corporate world as the real estate, marketing, accounting, management, and insurance programs are all highly ranked. Twenty-two percent of degrees conferred fall under the business umbrella. The social sciences (17 percent), biology (9 percent), psychology (7 percent), and homeland security (6 percent) are next in popularity. More Seminoles have landed prestigious postgraduate fellowships in recent years than ever. Eight graduates took home Fulbright Scholarships in 2018; Gilman Scholarships have gone to twenty-one recent undergrads, and three have become Rhodes scholars in the past twelve years.

Outside the Classroom

Florida State could easily be called Extrovert U—95 percent of undergrads participate in at least one on-campus activity. Just about everyone cheers on the Seminole football team as well as seventeen other NCAA Division I teams competing in the esteemed Atlantic Coast Conference (ACC). Forty sports clubs and a thriving intramural program draw widespread participation. The Bobby E. Leach center offers students recreational amenities including a sixteen-lane pool and indoor track, and all of the exercise equipment one could ever desire. While campus is a sizable 477 acres, only 20 percent of undergrads live on site, almost exclusively freshmen. Greek life is a driving force on campus despite a temporary ban in 2017 after a tragic hazing death. The school has a 22 percent participation rate across its twenty-eight fraternities and twenty-six sororities. Those seeking non-Greek, non-sports activities can pick from one of more than 650 recognized student organizations. Approximately 2,000 students become engaged in community service projects each year. Club Downunder, a student-run venue in town, brings notable comedy and musical acts to Tallahassee on a regular basis. The Student Life Cinema plays free movies for students six night a week. Tallahassee offers plenty of nightlife and cultural opportunities and can be easily accessed via public transit.

Career Services

The Career Center at Florida State University employs forty-one full-time staff members (not including office assistants) who work in career advising, employer relations, and experiential learning. This student-to-advisor ratio of 805:1 is below average compared to the other institutions included in this book. Of course, the size and scope of the operation is massive, and FSU's Career Center does a solid job of reaching a healthy number of the 30,000 undergraduate students through a variety of means.

The university puts on twenty job fairs per year that attract close to 1,450 employers and 11,500 students. Annually, the office puts on 1,200+ programs/workshops drawing a total audience of greater than 40,000. Florida State's internship participation rate was 66 percent for the Class of 2018. An impressive 7,700+ students obtain internship/co-op positions, and close to 8,600 students find other opportunities for experiential learning. Over 40 percent of graduates who found employment credited the Career Center with providing them the lead. Many big-time corporations recruit on campus including PepsiCo, KPMG, and PricewaterhouseCoopers. Close to 5,000 on-campus interviews are conducted each year. Despite a high student-to-counselor ratio, Florida State's Career Center deploys its resources efficiently, reaching an extremely high percentage of the student body.

Florida State University

E-mail: admissions@admin.fsu.edu | Website: www.fsu.edu

Professional Outcomes

Two-thirds of 2018 FSU grads already had a job offer in hand when they threw their caps toward the sky in celebration. Within six months of graduation, 87 percent had achieved positive outcomes; 69 percent were employed full time. The top five sectors employing Seminoles are (in order) education, technology, retail, financial, and health. Employers hiring the greatest number of FSU alumni include Apple, Northrup Grumman, EY, General Motors, and Deloitte. The average starting salary for graduates is a shade over $50k. Among ACC schools, FSU ranks toward the bottom in terms of median salary by midcareer, coming in at thirteenth of fourteen, behind Pitt and slightly ahead of the University of Louisville with alumni, by some measures, making roughly half as much as Duke graduates. Geographically, the greatest number of alumni remain in Florida but large numbers also relocate to Massachusetts, Georgia, Texas, Washington State, and California.

Roughly one-quarter of Florida State grads elect to immediately pursue admission into an advanced degree program; 75 percent of those who apply receive at least one acceptance. A typical graduating class sees over one hundred students accepted into medical schools and over 200 accepted into law schools. Students enjoy graduate school acceptances at a wide range of state and private universities with some recent alumni landing at prestigious institutions including Emory, Johns Hopkins, MIT, Northwestern, Georgetown, Vanderbilt, and the University of Chicago.

Admission

The acceptance rate into Florida State's Class of 2022 dipped below 40 percent for the first time, hitting 37 percent as the university received a record 50,314 applications. Only five years ago, the university received fewer than 30,000 applications and accepted more than half. Enrolled freshmen possessed middle-50 percent SAT scores of 1200-1350 and ACT scores of 26-30. For perspective, a decade ago, the ranges were 1090-1270 and 23-28, indicating a notable increase in the academic caliber of the average first-year student. A solid 39 percent of FSU freshmen finished in the top 10 percent of their high school class; 84 percent were in the top quarter. A GPA of 3.75 or higher was possessed by 85 percent of first-year students in 2018-19.

The admissions committee ranks the rigor of an applicant's secondary school record above all other factors but also strongly weights GPA, standardized test scores (the ACT is the more commonly submitted test), talent/ability, and state residency (out-of-state applicants face tougher prospects and were admitted at a rate of 19.5 percent). Class rank, extracurricular activities, and essays are merely "considered." Due to the immense volume of applicants, the university does not offer admissions interviews. While FSU does not offer a binding early decision option, it does have two deadlines—one in November and one in February. The November deadline is preferable as this early round typically sees acceptance rates close to 60 percent. Over 80 percent of attendees are residents of the Sunshine State, and admissions standards are more lax for residents than outsiders. With draws like elite sports, beautiful weather, and an excellent academic reputation, the number of applicants to FSU is likely to continue to rise. Candidates should be mindful of the increasingly selective admissions process and the need to post strong ACT/SAT scores and grades, above all else.

Worth Your Money?

An in-state cost of attendance of just over $22,000 puts places like FSU in the "absurd bargain" category. Unusual for a state school, over half of students also receive some level of merit aid that averages a not inconsequential $6k per year. While the school rarely meets full demonstrated need, it does give financial grants to 48 percent of the undergraduate student body with an average award of $14,597. Even for the 20 percent of students who do not have residency status, the out-of-state COA is a reasonable $37k. Attending Florida State and paying $37k per year is especially appealing if you are entering a field in which grads enjoy high average starting salaries like computer science ($66k), engineering ($68k), or math and sciences ($64k).

FINANCIAL
Institutional Type: Public
In-State Tuition: $4,640
Out-of-State Tuition: $19,806
Room & Board: $10,780
Required Fees: $1,877
Books & Supplies: $1,000

Avg. Need-Based Aid: $14,597
Avg. % of Need Met: 81%

Avg. Merit-Based Aid: $6,078
% Receiving Merit-Based Aid: 52%

Avg. Cumulative Debt: $22,840
% of Students Borrowing: 49%

CAREER
Who Recruits
1. Grant Thorton LLC
2. Enterprise
3. Aldi
4. Northrop Grumman
5. KPMG

Notable Internships
1. Equifax
2. Walt Disney Company
3. Royal Carribean Cruises

Top Industries
1. Business
2. Education
3. Operations
4. Sales
5. Social Services

Top Employers
1. IBM
2. Raymond James
3. JPMorgan Chase
4. Amazon
5. Microsoft

Where Alumni Work
1. Tallahassee, FL
2. Miami
3. Tampa, FL
4. Orlando, FL
5. Atlanta

Median Earnings
College Scorecard (Early Career): $46,400
EOP (Early Career): $46,400
PayScale (Mid-Career): $92,700

RANKINGS
Forbes: 151
Money: 102
U.S. News: 57, National Universities
Wall Street Journal/THE: 208 (T)
Washington Monthly: 81, National Universities

#CollegesWorthYourMoney

Fordham University

ADMISSION
Admission Rate: 46%
Admission Rate - Men: 45%
Admission Rate - Women: 47%
EA Admission Rate: 54%
ED Admission Rate: 53%
Admission Rate (5-Year Trend): -1%
ED Admission Rate (5-Year Trend): Previously Not Offered
% of Admits Attending (Yield): 11%
Transfer Admission Rate: 44%

Offered Wait List: 9,215
Accepted Wait List: 2,423
Admitted Wait List: 68

SAT Reading/Writing (Middle 50%): 620-700
SAT Math (Middle 50%): 630-730
ACT Composite (Middle 50%): 28-32
Testing Policy: ACT/SAT Required
SAT Superscore: Yes
ACT Superscore: Yes

% Graduated in Top 10% of HS Class: 44%
% Graduated in Top 25% of HS Class: 76%
% Graduated in Top 50% of HS Class: 97%

ENROLLMENT
Total Undergraduate Enrollment: 9,645
% Part-Time: 5%
% Male: 43%
% Female: 57%
% Out-of-State: 58%
% Fraternity: Not Offered
% Sorority: Not Offered
% On-Campus (Freshman): 76%
% On-Campus (All Undergraduate): 50%

% African-American: 4%
% Asian: 11%
% Hispanic: 15%
% White: 56%
% Other: 4%
% Race or Ethnicity Unknown: 2%
% International: 9%
% Low-Income: 20%

ACADEMICS
Student-to-Faculty Ratio: 15:1
% of Classes Under 20: 50%
% of Classes Under 40: 98%
% Full-Time Faculty: 41%
% Full-Time Faculty w/ Terminal Degree: 92%

Top Programs
Communication and Culture
English
Finance
Global Business
International Studies
Performing Arts
Psychology

Retention Rate: 90%
4-Year Graduation Rate: 79%
6-Year Graduation Rate: 83%

Curricular Flexibility: Somewhat Flexible
Academic Rating: ★★★✦

Inside the Classroom

With campuses in both Manhattan and the Bronx, Fordham University, a private Jesuit school with 175 years of tradition, has hit new heights of popularity and prestige in recent years; it shows no signs of slowing down. As one of the top twenty-five most expensive schools in the United States, paying for Fordham may be even more challenging than getting accepted. Yet, for those who can afford it, this is a wonderful place to live and learn for four years. Of course, paying back loans becomes easier when you enter a high-paying field like business, which accounts for 29 percent of all degrees conferred. Next in popularity are social sciences (19 percent), communication and journalism (13 percent), psychology (7 percent), and the visual and performing arts (6 percent).

The university offers more than seventy majors, minors, and pre-professional programs. Regardless of concentration area, on their way to earning 124 credits all Rams (minus many pursuing a bachelor of science) are required to tackle from one to four semesters of foreign language. Freshmen must complete an advanced composition course, Computational Reasoning, Philosophy of Human Nature, Faith and Critical Reason, and one seminar course designated as *Eloqeuntia Perfecta* that focuses on enhancing students' written and oral communication ability. As students progress to sophomore, junior, and senior year they are required to tackle additional courses in philosophy, literature, life science, theology, the performing arts, natural science, and ethics.

Fordham's 15:1 student-to-faculty ratio leads to average class sizes of twenty-two. Some classes will be on the smaller side as 52 percent of sections contain nineteen or fewer students. Rarely will an undergrad end up in a classroom of more than forty students. A substantial 45 percent of the student body spend a semester abroad at one of the school's 110 programs in fifty-two countries. The undergraduate research program has awarded 1.5 million dollars to students over the last decade and saw thirty-eight undergrads obtain coauthor status on professor-published work in 2017 alone.

The university's theater and dance programs are world-renowned for sending countless alumni to Broadway and Hollywood. Gabelli is a top-rated business program with standout programs in international business and finance and serves as a pipeline to many large firms. Another point of pride is the phenomenal number of graduates who earn competitive national scholarships/fellowships. Fordham has produced 132 Fulbright scholarships since 2003. Grads also regularly win Beinecke, Gates-Cambridge Harriman, and Truman Scholarships/Fellowships.

Outside the Classroom

The undergraduate experience will differ depending on whether you attend the Rose Hill Campus in the Bronx or the Lincoln Center campus in Manhattan. At Lincoln Center there are two large high-rises that offer every convenience imaginable. Of course, Manhattan has all of the culture, shopping, dining, and entertainment you could ever dream of. The Bronx campus offers fourteen residential buildings and is near the New York Botanical Garden, the Bronx Zoo, Yankee Stadium, and Little Italy. Between the two sites, roughly half of the student body lives on campus. Greek Life at Fordham is a complete non-factor—the university does not have any fraternities or sororities. Instead, 160 student-run organizations provide opportunities for social bonding. Athletics are popular as the Rams field twenty-three teams in NCCA Division I and also run twenty-four club and intramural sports. Over 4,000 students participate in community service each year, contributing over one million collective hours. The school's newspaper, *The Observer*, enjoys a loyal readership and has garnered widespread praise. Yet, no feature of campus life will play a bigger role in the Fordham experience than its Big Apple location, which opens the doors to limitless possibilities on a daily basis.

Career Services

The Career Services office at Fordham is staffed by thirteen professional employees who specialize in areas that include undergraduate counseling and employer relations. That 723:1 student-to-advisor ratio is significantly higher than many of the other schools featured in this guide. In order to reach the masses, the office puts on four career fairs in the fall and two in the spring. Some are specific to areas like finance, STEM, or government while others are more general. The school attempts to engage with students beginning in their freshman year, encouraging first-years to meet one-on-one with an advisor, attend a resume/cover letter workshop, and take personality assessments. Subsequent activities are designed for sophomore, junior, and senior year as students master the office's three goals: awareness, preparedness, and presentation.

A phenomenal 81 percent of 2018 graduates completed at least one internship during their undergraduate years. An examination of how recent graduates found their jobs reveals the following breakdown: internships (12 percent), on-campus recruiting (2 percent), career fairs (2 percent), and CareerLink (6 percent). The vast majority found employment primarily through non-school resources. Yet plenty of opportunities exist to expand one's contacts by taking advantage of a Ram alumni network of over 175,000 individuals embedded in top companies across the globe. Despite a less-than-ideal student-to-counselor ratio and a low percentage of students attributing their job acquisition to the direct efforts of career services, Fordham grads do enjoy better-than-average employment and graduate school outcomes.

Professional Outcomes

Class of 2018 graduates found employment, graduate school, or other meaningful activities at a 90 percent clip within six months of receiving their degrees. Almost three-fifths of this group landed employment and enjoyed an average salary of $55,280, higher than the national average. Financial services was, by a large margin, the most common industry followed by advertising/PR, media and communications, health care, and accounting. Significant numbers of 2018 grads found homes at major companies including Ernst & Young (27), JP Morgan Chase & Co. (24), PwC (17), KMPG (15), NBC Universal (14), and Deloitte (12). A sizable number of graduates also moved into working for nonprofit organizations such as the Jesuit Volunteer Corps, AmeriCorps, or the Peace Corps.

Those aiming for graduate school found homes at a variety of excellent institutions. The greatest number of 2018 graduates landed at Fordham (139), NYU (22), and Columbia (17). Some also gained acceptance into Penn, Georgetown, Boston University, and George Washington. Law school applicants were successful 95 percent of the time, a rate 17 percent higher than the national average. In recent years, Fordham alumni have gone on to Harvard Law School, University of Pennsylvania Law School, Cornell Law School, and Northwestern University School of Law. Those applying to professional health programs, including medical school, gained acceptance at a 76 percent rate compared to the national average of 45 percent.

Admission

Fordham offered admission to 46 percent of the over 46,000 applicants vying for a place in the class of 2022. Those who ultimately enrolled possessed a mean test score of 1354 and a mean high school GPA of 3.64 on a 4.0 scale. In 2014, a 1350 would have placed in the 75th percentile of all Fordham freshmen. The mid-50 percent standardized test score ranges were 1250-1430 Forty-four percent of freshmen finished in the top 10 percent of their high school cohort, and 76 percent placed in the top quarter; three percent did not place in the top half. While 45 percent of entering freshmen in 2018-19 possessed better than a 3.75 GPA, 12 percent did earn a 3.25 or under in high school.

The admissions committee prioritizes the usual factors of rigor of coursework, GPA, and standardized test scores. Softer factors including recommendations, essays, talent/ability, volunteer work, and extracurricular activities are given secondary consideration.

In part because it serves as a safety school for many elite students aiming for Ivies or Ivy equivalents, Fordham has an exceptionally low yield rate—around 10 percent of admitted students actually enroll. Therefore, demonstrating your genuine interest in attending and applying early decision are strategic moves that serious applicants should consider. ED applications to the university are surprisingly low, but acceptance rates are higher than during the regular cycle (53 percent versus 40 percent). Like many schools in Manhattan, Fordham's rising popularity can be best summed up by the real estate cliché of location, location, location. Always a school that required students to have reasonably strong credentials, Fordham is entering a new strata and is now a viable option for very accomplished students.

Worth Your Money?

An annual total cost of attendance exceeding $75,000 sounds prohibitive, but a good number of students do obtain aid, either need based or merit. Sixty-three percent of current undergraduates receive an annual merit aid award of $20,744, and 59 percent of students qualify for grants that average over $32k. Unfortunately, only a small number see 100 percent of their need covered by the university. The average graduate owes more than $37k in loans, but starting salaries tend to be solid, making it worth incurring a moderate amount of debt, particularly for students pursuing study within Fordham's strongest programs, most notably business.

FINANCIAL
Institutional Type: Private
In-State Tuition: $52,980
Out-of-State Tuition: $52,980
Room & Board: $18,510
Required Fees: $1,413
Books & Supplies: $1,039

Avg. Need-Based Aid: $32,045
Avg. % of Need Met: 80%

Avg. Merit-Based Aid: $20,744
% Receiving Merit-Based Aid: 63%

Avg. Cumulative Debt: $37,429
% of Students Borrowing: 62%

CAREER
Who Recruits
1. EY
2. Teach for America
3. Standard Motor Products
4. Enterprise
5. Northwestern Mutual

Notable Internships
1. The Philadelphia Zoo
2. NBCUniversal
3. Spotify

Top Industries
1. Business
2. Education
3. Social Services
4. Operations
5. Finance

Top Employers
1. NYC Department of Education
2. Teach for America
3. NBCUniversal
4. JPMorgan Chase
5. US Army

Where Alumni Work
1. New York City
2. Washington, DC
3. Boston
4. Los Angeles
5. Philadelphia

Median Earnings
College Scorecard (Early Career): $59,200
EOP (Early Career): $63,300
PayScale (Mid-Career): $112,500

RANKINGS
Forbes: 141
Money: 376
U.S. News: 74, National Universities
Wall Street Journal/THE: 176 (T)
Washington Monthly: 301, National Universities

#CollegesWorthYourMoney

Franklin & Marshall College

Lancaster, Pennsylvania | Admissions Phone: 717-358-3953

ADMISSION
Admission Rate: 35%
Admission Rate - Men: 31%
Admission Rate - Women: 39%
EA Admission Rate: Not Offered
ED Admission Rate: 58%
Admission Rate (5-Year Trend): -1%
ED Admission Rate (5-Year Trend): -11%
% of Admits Attending (Yield): 26%
Transfer Admission Rate: 38%

Offered Wait List: 2,106
Accepted Wait List: N/A
Admitted Wait List: N/A

SAT Reading/Writing (Middle 50%): 620-690
SAT Math (Middle 50%): 640-750
ACT Composite (Middle 50%): 28-32
Testing Policy: Test Optional
SAT Superscore: Yes
ACT Superscore: Yes

% Graduated in Top 10% of HS Class: 59%
% Graduated in Top 25% of HS Class: 84%
% Graduated in Top 50% of HS Class: 97%

ENROLLMENT
Total Undergraduate Enrollment: 2,309
% Part-Time: 1%
% Male: 45%
% Female: 55%
% Out-of-State: 72%
% Fraternity: 20%
% Sorority: 27%
% On-Campus (Freshman): 100%
% On-Campus (All Undergraduate): 99%

% African-American: 6%
% Asian: 5%
% Hispanic: 10%
% White: 55%
% Other: 2%
% Race or Ethnicity Unknown: 3%
% International: 18%
% Low-Income: 17%

ACADEMICS
Student-to-Faculty Ratio: 9:1
% of Classes Under 20: 68%
% of Classes Under 40: 99%
% Full-Time Faculty: 89%
% Full-Time Faculty w/ Terminal Degree: 95%

Top Programs
Biology
Business, Organizations & Society
Economics
Environmental Studies
Political Science
Public Health
Sociology

Retention Rate: 92%
4-Year Graduation Rate: 78%
6-Year Graduation Rate: 83%

Curricular Flexibility: Somewhat Flexible
Academic Rating: ★★★★

Inside the Classroom

Situated on the pastoral hills of Lancaster County, Pennsylvania, most famous for its large Amish community, Franklin & Marshall has carved out its own stellar reputation ever since its two namesake colleges merged in 1853. An undergraduate population of almost 2,300 gets to choose from a generous liberal arts menu that features fifty-nine academic programs. Never content to rest on its laurels, F&M is in the middle of a $200 million fundraising campaign entitled "Now to Next" that is designed to take this already excellent school to even greater heights.

The educational experience at F&M is guided by its "Connections" curriculum, a series of requirements divided into three phases: Introduction, Exploration, and Concentration. Freshmen must take two small, intensive seminar classes that immerse them in the world of intellectual discourse, academic writing, and the art of oral presentation. Next, students tackle courses in the arts, humanities, social and natural sciences, foreign language, and non-Western cultures. As a culminating experience, students complete a capstone project that may involve research alongside a professor.

Franklin & Marshall's student-faculty ratio is 9:1, and 67 percent of classes have fewer than twenty students enrolled; 29 percent are in the twenty to twenty-nine range. The average classroom contains eighteen students. Juniors are encouraged to spend a semester abroad, and 55 percent oblige, jetting off to locations from Argentina to Vietnam. Grants through the Hackman Scholars program allow approximately seventy-five students to conduct research with faculty each summer. Many more Diplomats research with faculty through other means during the academic year and, by graduation, 35 percent of students have engaged in a research experience.

The greatest number of degrees conferred at the college are in the social sciences (23 percent), interdisciplinary studies (14 percent), biology (12 percent), business (10 percent), physical sciences (7 percent), and psychology (5 percent). Programs in public health and environmental science receive high marks. In addition, students in the official pre-med program and related majors have experienced a high degree of success in earning acceptances into medical school. F&M students are no strangers to prestigious fellowships, having produced six Fulbright Scholars in 2018 and seven in 2017. The Class of 2018 also saw graduates awarded fellowships from Public Policy and International Affairs, Princeton in Asia, and Princeton in Africa.

Outside the Classroom

Lancaster, Pennsylvania, may be notable primarily for its Amish population, but there is a surprisingly large downtown area replete with a full array of shopping, eating, and entertainment options. Those seeking the excitement of a bigger city will have a bit of a car ride ahead of them—Philly is eighty miles away. Being in a relatively remote locale, the center of social life at F&M is on campus where 99 percent of the student population resides. Greek life is a big part of the Franklin and Marshall tradition, dating back to the school's founding, and it enjoys a robust participation rate of 20 percent for men and 27 percent for women. Participation in athletics is also central to campus life. Being a small school and fielding twenty-seven sports teams, mostly in NCAA Division III, translates to over 30 percent of the student body being comprised of varsity athletes. Outside of sports and frats/sororities, there are roughly one hundred active, student-run organizations that cover everything from a cappella to seven student-run publications. The vast majority of incoming freshmen performed community service in high school, and that practice continues while at F&M through numerous volunteer groups as well as through Greek organizations.

Career Services

The Office of Student and Post Graduate Development (OSPGD), a mouthful to say, is staffed by eleven full-time professionals. That works out to a 210:1 student-to-advisor ratio, which is better than average compared to other schools featured in this guide. Noteworthy for a small liberal arts school, F&M employs expert advisors who specialize in health care professions and law school advising so that undergrads on those tracks can receive specialized guidance. In the 2018-19 academic year an impressive 2,540 (more than one per student) one-on-one advising sessions were conducted.

Students seeking a personal touch in advising will appreciate the OPSGD's availability to meet one-on-one to discuss internship opportunities, professional pathways, or graduate school planning. A commendable 80 percent of the student body engages with the office each year. The sixth annual Job and Internship Fair, held in 2018, drew roughly eighty employers, and 106 employers recruited at some point on campus during the same year. The office puts on about 150 events each year with a total attendance of over 3,200. Other career-oriented offerings include Life After F&M, a handy feature that allows current Diplomats to view the types of jobs held by graduates of every major offered at the college. With each student's Handshake account, they also can access a database of 800+ alumni and parent mentors more than happy to dispense career advice. With a high level of engagement and positive graduate outcomes, the OSPGD receives a positive rating from our staff.

Franklin & Marshall College

E-mail: admissions@fandm.edu | Website: www.fandm.edu

Professional Outcomes

Shortly after graduation, 97 percent of 2018 F&M grads are either employed or continuing their educational journey. The most frequently pursued industries are education (20 percent), finance and insurance (16 percent), research and development (7 percent), public administration (7 percent), and social/community service (7 percent). Students find work at a cornucopia of interesting companies and organizations from HBO to the Selective Mutism Research Institute to Sotheby's. Across all graduating years the companies with the greatest number of Diplomats on staff are Morgan Stanley, Deloitte, Vanguard, EY, Merrill Lynch, IBM, Wells Fargo, and Citi. Sixty-five percent of graduates stay in the Northeast, and 19 percent head down South. There are more alumni living in New York City than in Philadelphia. Salary data for alumni at age thirty-four reveals a median income of $58k, slightly higher than grads of more prestigious Pennsylvania-based liberal arts schools Swarthmore and Haverford.

F&M boasts excellent results for premed students. Over a three-year period, 89 percent of students with at least a 3.3 GPA and an MCAT score in the 67th percentile or better were accepted into medical school. That includes admissions into schools of medicine at Harvard, Yale, Johns Hopkins, Penn, and Georgetown. Those seeking a legal education head to universities such as Villanova, Harvard, William & Mary, NYU, Yale, Tulane, and UC Berkeley. Of the 18 percent of graduates furthering their education, there is a genuine mix of prestigious and less prestigious graduate programs, but it is fair to say that excelling at F&M at least puts you in the running for a spot at a top graduate school.

Admission

Applications to F&M surged to record levels as 9,502 poured in for a place in the Class of 2023, and 30 percent were accepted. The implementation of a full-blown test-optional strategy could be behind the massive spike. In 2018, Franklin & Marshall admitted 35 percent of more than 6,500 applicants. The Class of 2022 possessed mid-50 percent standardized test scores of 1260-1440 on the SAT and 28 to 32 on the ACT. Those scores were almost identical to the profile of the average member of the graduating Class of 2018 that had a similar admit rate of 36 percent. In other words, not much has changed in recent years. F&M continues to place the highest value on rigor of coursework, GPA, class rank, and character/personal qualities. On that last factor, it particularly values athletic participation/leadership; an insanely high percentage of incoming students played a varsity sport in high school. Fifty-nine percent of freshmen in the 2018-19 academic year finished in the top 10 percent of their high school cohort; 84 percent were in the top 25 percent.

F&M faces stiff competition for students as it must compete with a high number of other excellent liberal arts schools in PA and the surrounding states. Its yield rate (the percentage of accepted students who enroll) is only 26 percent, which means the admissions staff is particularly interested in qualified applicants for whom F&M is a top choice. Thus, it is no surprise that the early decision acceptance rate is 58 percent, far more favorable than that of the regular round; 57 percent of the 2018-19 freshman cohort came through the ED round. Not a school with a formulaic admissions algorithm, F&M students do typically share two common traits—excellent high school grades and strong interest in attending the college.

Worth Your Money?

Attending Franklin & Marshall will cost you $73k per year unless you are among the 54 percent of undergraduates who demonstrate financial need, in which case you see 100 percent of your financial need met. The average grant is for almost $47,000. Merit-based aid is not offered. Overall, F&M does an admirable job of making the school affordable for those from a wide range of socioeconomic backgrounds. However, middle-to-upper income students who cannot comfortably afford F&M's price and who fail to qualify for significant need-based aid should consider their desired path after college before committing. For everyone else, investing in an F&M degree is likely worth the money.

FINANCIAL
Institutional Type: Private
In-State Tuition: $56,450
Out-of-State Tuition: $56,450
Room & Board: $14,050
Required Fees: $300
Books & Supplies: $1,200

Avg. Need-Based Aid: $46,628
Avg. % of Need Met: 100%

Avg. Merit-Based Aid: $5,000
% Receiving Merit-Based Aid: 13%

Avg. Cumulative Debt: $27,149
% of Students Borrowing: 54%

CAREER
Who Recruits
1. W.B. Mason
2. The JDK Group
3. Travelers
4. ScribeAmerica
5. S&T Bank

Notable Internships
1. New Jersey Office of the Governor
2. Acacia Finance
3. Audible

Top Industries
1. Business
2. Education
3. Operations
4. Finance
5. Sales

Top Employers
1. Morgan Stanley
2. Deloitte
3. UBS
4. Vanguard
5. EY

Where Alumni Work
1. New York City
2. Philadelphia
3. Lancaster, PA
4. Washington, DC
5. Boston

Median Earnings
College Scorecard (Early Career): $58,900
EOP (Early Career): $57,800
PayScale (Mid-Career): $109,700

RANKINGS
Forbes: 114
Money: 166
U.S. News: 38, Liberal Arts Colleges
Wall Street Journal/THE: 91 (T)
Washington Monthly: 21, Liberal Arts Colleges

#CollegesWorthYourMoney

Franklin W. Olin College of Engineering

Needham, Massachusetts | Admissions Phone: 781-292-2222

ADMISSION
Admission Rate: 16%
Admission Rate - Men: 10%
Admission Rate - Women: 32%
EA Admission Rate: Not Offered
ED Admission Rate: Not Offered
Admission Rate (5-Year Trend): -1%
ED Admission Rate (5-Year Trend): Not Offered
% of Admits Attending (Yield): 61%
Transfer Admission Rate: 80%

Offered Wait List: 47
Accepted Wait List: 35
Admitted Wait List: 3

SAT Reading/Writing (Middle 50%): 710-760
SAT Math (Middle 50%): 750-790
ACT Composite (Middle 50%): 34-35
Testing Policy: ACT/SAT Required
SAT Superscore: Yes
ACT Superscore: Yes

% Graduated in Top 10% of HS Class: N/A
% Graduated in Top 25% of HS Class: N/A
% Graduated in Top 50% of HS Class: N/A

ENROLLMENT
Total Undergraduate Enrollment: 390
% Part-Time: 11%
% Male: 50%
% Female: 50%
% Out-of-State: 89%
% Fraternity: Not Offered
% Sorority: Not Offered
% On-Campus (Freshman): 100%
% On-Campus (All Undergraduate): 100%

% African-American: 2%
% Asian: 13%
% Hispanic: 9%
% White: 44%
% Other: 7%
% Race or Ethnicity Unknown: 14%
% International: 11%
% Low-Income: 9%

ACADEMICS
Student-to-Faculty Ratio: 8:1
% of Classes Under 20: 52%
% of Classes Under 40: 96%
% Full-Time Faculty: 72%
% Full-Time Faculty w/ Terminal Degree: 98%

Top Programs
Electrical and Computer Engineering
Engineering
Mechanical Engineering

Retention Rate: 100%
4-Year Graduation Rate: 78%
6-Year Graduation Rate: 93%

Curricular Flexibility: Somewhat Flexible
Academic Rating: ★★★★★

Inside the Classroom

Perhaps the most highly-regarded school of its size in the entire United States, The Franklin W. Olin College of Engineering was founded in the early 2000s as an experimental, cutting-edge training ground for budding engineers. Today, this Boston-area institution has an undergraduate enrollment of 390 students who are every bit as brilliant as the talent at Caltech or MIT. Academically, there is only one item on the menu here but, boy, is it delicious. Every single degree conferred at Olin has "engineering" in its name: electrical and computer engineering, mechanical engineering, or general engineering with a concentration area such as bioengineering, computing, or design and robotics.

No matter one's major, all students most take a collection of core courses that the college deems essential to its mission, giving its students the engineering toolkit needed to "have a positive impact in the real world." Those required classes are tied to three interconnected themes: Design and Entrepreneurship, Modeling and Analysis, and Systems and Control. Students also work through a concentration in either the arts and humanities or entrepreneurship that can be completed at partner colleges Brandeis, Wellesley, or Babson. Unlike most engineering schools where students knock out a laundry list of math and science requirements before taking a deep dive into their engineering-specific coursework, Olin students take three such courses in their first semester.

Many classes are taught in a studio environment to encourage collaboration, and a number of courses are co-taught by professors from different disciplines. Classes are generally reasonably small; 54 percent of class sections contain fewer than twenty students. The school's 8:1 student- to-faculty ratio translates into an enormous amount of individualized attention and invitations to participate in research. Students can easily track down current research projects and contact information on the school's website and can obtain funding for their efforts via the Undergraduate Research Fund. Additionally, students can elect to take advantage of study abroad programs in thirty-five foreign locations. Half of students ultimately do spend a semester in a foreign country, a notably high percentage for an engineering school.

As chronicled in more detail in our "Professional Outcomes" section, the Franklin W. Olin College of Engineering may not be a household name for the average American, but employers and elite graduate schools adore its graduates every bit as much as those from Stanford or Carnegie Mellon. For such an incredibly small school, Olin graduates annually take home a number of prestigious awards. Two students/alumni won Fulbright Scholarships in 2018, and one took home a National Science Foundation Graduate Research Fellowship. Eight recent grads were named Grand Challenge Scholars by the National Academy of Engineers.

Outside the Classroom

Not far from Wellesley and Babson, Olin College of Engineering's Needham locale places it only eighteen miles outside of Boston. It features a seventy-acre campus lined with buildings as new as the college itself. Nearly all students reside on campus in one of two residence halls. No frats or sororities operate at this institution. There are no NCCA sports because it would be interesting to field teams from a pool of 345 engineering geniuses. However, thanks to agreements forged with nearby schools, Olin students can participate in intramural leagues at Babson or Wellesley. Additionally, Olin does field its own intercollegiate soccer and ultimate Frisbee teams. Fans of the outdoors can connect with hiking trails on campus and all around Needham and the town of Wellesley. There are plenty of student-run clubs with an engineering/innovation emphasis, including the Olin robotic sailing team that competes in global competitions, Olin Baja—a vehicle design competition, and AERO—a drone and plane designing team. Historic Needham is a safe suburb with plenty of restaurants, shops, museums, and cultural events.

Career Services

The Office of Postgraduate Planning consists of three professional employees, equating to a superior student-to-advisor ratio of 130:1, among the best of any school in the country. The office's mission is aligned to that of the school's—to assist future engineers in finding meaningful opportunities for hands-on training. This mission is accomplished to the tune of 98 percent of those graduating in 2018 having had a technical internship or research experience; 89 percent had more than one such experience. The Fall Career Fair is attended by more than fifty top companies. Given that this works out to about one company for every two seniors, this attendance is extraordinary and speaks to how desirable Olin students are in the eyes of employers.

With only thirteen years' worth of graduates, the total alumni base has yet to reach 1,000—it will cross that mark in 2020—but the industry connections made via the school's Corporate Partners Program open countless doors. In the past year undergrads landed internships at organizations including Tesla, Bose, GE, Microsoft, and Google. Thanks to a focus on experiential learning, ample industry connections, and exceptional starting salaries for grads, Olin's career services is held in high esteem by our staff.

Franklin W. Olin College of Engineering

E-mail: info@olin.edu | Website: www.olin.edu

Professional Outcomes

For a school exclusively graduating engineers, it isn't a surprise that alumni tend to find good-paying jobs. The average starting salary for recent graduates is in excess of $80,000. Electrical and computer engineers have averaged over $90K while mechanical engineers are at the low end with $67k in compensation. Over the past decade, the companies employing the greatest number of alumni are Google (39), Microsoft (26), athenahealth (22), Apple (14), and Amazon (11). In 2018, Shift, Bose, Cognex, MITRE, Nutonomy, and Raytheon all hired more than one Olin graduate. While a majority of graduates find work in Massachusetts, a large number also migrate to California where Silicon Valley welcomes them with open arms.

Olin College of Engineering undergrads have gone on to prestigious graduate engineering programs in impressive numbers. Since 2006 more than twenty graduates have gone to Stanford, MIT, and Harvard. The school also has sent double-digit numbers of alumni to Carnegie Mellon, Cornell, and Berkeley. Perusing the lists of graduate school acceptances, it is rare that anyone attends anything less than one of the world's most prestigious institutions. The majority of those hopping right into advanced studies are pursuing PhDs.

Admission

The 85 freshmen in the Class of 2022 are an impressive group, no matter the metric. With an average unweighted GPA of 3.9 and middle 50 percent standardized test scores of 1470-1540 on the SAT and 34-35 on the ACT, Olin students are nothing shy of Ivy caliber. In 2018, the school's acceptance rate was 16 percent, but it has dipped as low as 13 percent in recent years.

Applicants can rest assured that they will be viewed in three dimensions as a number of factors beyond grades and test scores are considered "very important" to the admissions committee. Those include essays, recommendations, interview, extracurricular activities, talent/ability, character/personal qualities, and level of demonstrated interest in the college. In fact, those considerations all rate ahead of standardized test results. Yet, consideration of those traditional factors is only half of the acceptance process. Each year, roughly 225-250 applicants are selected by Olin College of Engineering to visit during a Candidates' Weekend—a process closer to how most schools hire faculty than select their undergraduates. The prospective students are put through a design challenge, an individual interview, and group exercise to help evaluate which students would bring the most to and benefit the most from the Olin College of Engineering. Getting into Olin is a marathon; it is not a school you even apply to unless you are 100 percent committed to attending. Elite academic prowess is only one of many prerequisites for consideration to join this small but potent engineering juggernaut.

Worth Your Money?

The total annual cost of attendance at Franklin W. Olin is a hair below $76,000. Thankfully, 39 percent of the undergraduate population receives need-based aid averaging $50k per year, and merit awards with an average yearly value of $25k are distributed generously. Even if you didn't receive any aid, you're always safe investing in a college where the average starting salary exceeds the annual cost of attending. Olin is such a school, and with engineering being the only pathway, you are just about guaranteed a solid return on your educational investment.

FINANCIAL
Institutional Type: Private
In-State Tuition: $52,164
Out-of-State Tuition: $52,164
Room & Board: $16,872
Required Fees: $3,336
Books & Supplies: $200

Avg. Need-Based Aid: $50,188
Avg. % of Need Met: 100%

Avg. Merit-Based Aid: $25,295
% Receiving Merit-Based Aid: 100%

Avg. Cumulative Debt: $20,480
% of Students Borrowing: 40%

CAREER
Who Recruits
1. Cognex Corporation
2. Ford Motor Company
3. General Electric
4. Watts
5. Tableau

Notable Internships
1. Ford Motor Company
2. Raytheon
3. Tableau Software

Top Industries
1. Engineering
2. Education
3. Research
4. Information Technology
5. Business

Top Employers
1. Google
2. Microsoft
3. Apple
4. athenahealth
5. Skydio

Where Alumni Work
1. Boston
2. San Francisco
3. Seattle
4. New York City
5. Los Angeles

Median Earnings
College Scorecard (Early Career): N/A
EOP (Early Career): N/A
PayScale (Mid-Career): N/A

RANKINGS
Forbes: N/A
Money: N/A
U.S. News: N/A
Wall Street Journal/THE: N/A
Washington Monthly: N/A

#CollegesWorthYourMoney

Fairfax, Virginia | Admissions Phone: 703-993-2400

ADMISSION
Admission Rate: 81%
Admission Rate - Men: 77%
Admission Rate - Women: 84%
EA Admission Rate: 85%
ED Admission Rate: Not Offered
Admission Rate (5-Year Trend): +19%
ED Admission Rate (5-Year Trend): Not Offered
% of Admits Attending (Yield): 23%
Transfer Admission Rate: 83%

Offered Wait List: 1,889
Accepted Wait List: 1,770
Admitted Wait List: 187

SAT Reading/Writing (Middle 50%): 570-660
SAT Math (Middle 50%): 550-660
ACT Composite (Middle 50%): 24-30
Testing Policy: ACT/SAT Required
SAT Superscore: Yes
ACT Superscore: No

% Graduated in Top 10% of HS Class: 18%
% Graduated in Top 25% of HS Class: 50%
% Graduated in Top 50% of HS Class: 87%

ENROLLMENT
Total Undergraduate Enrollment: 26,192
% Part-Time: 19%
% Male: 50%
% Female: 50%
% Out-of-State: 10%
% Fraternity: 5%
% Sorority: 8%
% On-Campus (Freshman): 64%
% On-Campus (All Undergraduate): 23%

% African-American: 11%
% Asian: 20%
% Hispanic: 15%
% White: 39%
% Other: 5%
% Race or Ethnicity Unknown: 3%
% International: 6%
% Low-Income: 24%

ACADEMICS
Student-to-Faculty Ratio: 17:1
% of Classes Under 20: 30%
% of Classes Under 40: 73%
% Full-Time Faculty: 48%
% Full-Time Faculty w/ Terminal Degree: 90%

Top Programs
Accounting
Criminology, Law and Society
Computer Science
Economics
Government and International Politics
History
Information Technology

Retention Rate: 86%
4-Year Graduation Rate: 47%
6-Year Graduation Rate: 70%

Curricular Flexibility: Less Flexible
Academic Rating: ★★★

Inside the Classroom
If you had to describe George Mason University in five adjectives or less, large, public, affordable, career-focused, and politically conservative (the Koch brothers are/were major donors) would be apt selections. Outsiders sometimes find the number of GMU students surprising; there are 37,000+ of them, more than 25,000 of whom are undergraduates. The high numbers of commuters can hide the actual scope of the university that features ten undergraduate schools and colleges and approximately seventy distinct academic programs. You can get a sense of the pre-professional feel of the student body simply by examining the areas where the greatest number of degrees are conferred. Business (20 percent) is followed by the social sciences (11 percent), health professions (10 percent), computer and information sciences (9 percent), and engineering (6 percent).

Mason aims to make every one of its graduates an "engaged citizen and well-rounded scholar who is prepared to act." Toward that goal it requires a journey through the "Mason Core," a forty-three credit collection of foundation, exploration, and integration requirements. Among the mandatory topics one must tackle are written communication, oral communication, quantitative reasoning and information technology, literature, arts, natural sciences, and other liberal arts staples. That trek will take you the equivalent of three full semesters. The Honors College requires twelve additional credits.

As a result of a 17:1 student-to-faculty ratio and over 11,000 graduate students, class sizes at GMU are rarely small, but it tends to be a mixed bag, and many sections do feature relatively modest numbers. Thirty percent of sections enroll nineteen or fewer students, 27 percent have forty or more students, and the remaining sections lie in between. More intimate educational experiences can be sought in the form of undergraduate research, which roughly half of all students ultimately engage in. There are plenty of summer research opportunities, but you can also take courses designated as Discovery of Scholarship, Scholarly Inquiry, or Research & Scholarship Intensive that offer built-in supervised research. Presently, only ten percent of GMU students study abroad, but the school does sponsor 140+ programs, including travel to the school's own international campus in South Korea.

The Volgenau College of Engineering, which houses a top-tier Information Technology Department, and the School of Business are both extremely reputable in the eyes of prospective employers, and the school's Northern Virginia location allows many to connections with industry to be forged via internships and face-to-face recruiting opportunities. Recent grads have also captured a growing number of prestigious fellowships and scholarships. In 2018, five students won Boren Awards, and in 2019, the school produced a Truman Scholarship winner and has boasted a handful of Fulbright Scholars in recent years.

Outside the Classroom
Only 63 percent of freshmen and 22 percent of the overall undergraduate population reside in on-campus housing. There are many students who commute and/or live in (sometimes) cheaper off-campus housing in Arlington, Falls Church, Annandale, or Manassas. Because 85 percent of GMU students are Virginia residents, they are usually in fairly close proximity to their families. Greek life exists but doesn't dominate; 5 percent of men join frats, and 8 percent of women join sororities. While DC isn't exactly in your backyard at Mason, it is like having a beautiful park right down the street. The heart of the city is only fifteen miles from campus. Meanwhile, the 677 wooded acres that comprise the school's grounds are home to 500+ student-run clubs. There are hundreds of events to attend for free at the Center for the Arts, organic gardens that can be fully utilized by students, two pools, and loads of intramural and club sports. On the more serious athletic front, the Patriots' 462 student-athletes compete in twenty-two NCAA Division I sports with a men's basketball team good enough to have made a Final Four run this millennium. The Hub Student Center is another place where a student body with a large contingent of commuters can coalesce and mingle, but surveys indicate that, at present, the social scene at Mason has room for improvement. Seniors offer much lower ratings of indicators like "sense of belonging" and "involvement in campus activities" than the quality of academic instruction they received.

Career Services
George Mason University Career Services employs twenty-four professionals (not including office assistants, the webmaster, or peer advisors). Roles include employer outreach, industry advisor, career counselor, and career fair manager. That works out to a 1,041:1 student-to-advisor ratio, poorer than the average ratio when compared to other institutions included in this guidebook but not altogether unusual for a school of Mason's size. The career services staff still manages to help more than 20,000 unique students each year, approximately 81 percent of all undergraduate students, which is impressive.

This level of outreach helps to explain why, among employed class of 2018 members, 82 percent were in jobs that aligned with their career goals. Some connections are made through fall and spring career fairs that draw 150 employers and 1,500+ students each semester. The internship outlook is aided by the prime location of the university as well as cultivated relationships with many companies. There are fifteen Fortune 500 Companies and, of course, every government agency within a stone's throw. Within the Civil Engineering Department over 90 percent of undergrads complete at least one internship. Over 100,000 Mason alumni, who are mainly concentrated in the Beltway area, also greatly aid the job and internship hunt.

Professional Outcomes

Six months after receiving their degrees 82 percent of the class of 2018 had accepted a job offer or started work in a graduate program. The most commonly entered industries were education (21 percent), government (15 percent), technology (11 percent), health (9 percent), consulting (6 percent), and finance (6 percent). GMU grads flow into major consulting firms like Booz Allen Hamilton, Deloitte, and Accenture, financial institutions like Capital One and Freddie Mac, and engineering/tech firms like General Dynamics, IBM, and Microsoft. Class of 2018 graduates also secured employment at Lockheed Martin, the Smithsonian, the Department of Homeland Security, the Kennedy Center, and CBS News. The vast majority of recent grads stay in the area as 92 percent work in DC, Virginia, or Maryland. New York City and San Francisco also have sizable numbers of Mason alumni. Including bonuses, the median first year salary for a GMU grad is $61,000.

George Mason is presently conducting a feasibility study for creating its own medical college. In the meantime, it offers two guaranteed admissions, joint-degree programs with Virginia Commonwealth University and George Washington University. George Mason does have its own institution for legal education—the Antonin Scalia Law School—and it offers a 3+3 bachelor's/JD program. Across all disciplines Mason graduates tend to pursue advanced degrees either at Mason itself or at other area schools including George Washington, American University, or the University of Maryland.

Admission

At 81 percent George Mason has one the highest acceptance rates of any school featured in this guide, making it an excellent choice for someone with less-than-stellar credentials but a desire to attend a school with tremendous resources. The school is test-optional for those with a strong GPA (It cites a mid-50 percent mark as 3.3-3.9, a record of honors and AP courses, and an impressive list of extracurricular activities that demonstrate leadership). Most applicants end up submitting standardized test scores—71 percent of the Class of 2022 submitted SAT scores, and 9 percent produced ACT results. The mid-50 percent ranges were 1120-1320 on the SAT and 24-30 on the ACT. Only 18 percent of 2018-19 freshman placed in the top 10 percent of their high school class, half were in the top quartile, and 87 percent were in the top 50 percent. The average GPA was 3.7, but 27 percent were below 3.5, giving hope to those who may have hit some bumps along their academic road.

GMU values the rigor of one's high school courses and the GPA earned above all else. Class rank, standardized test scores, and intangibles like talent/ability and character/personal qualities come next. There are no interviews offered as part of the process, nor is there an option for binding early decision. An early action deadline of November 1 will get students a decision by December 15. Entry to Mason is competitive, but compared to many other schools of its class, the bar is easier to clear.

Worth Your Money?

As a state resident George Mason is an unequivocal steal at under $12,500 in tuition. Out-of-staters will pay almost three times as much, making it a question of (a) will Mason provide me with significantly better academics/job prospects than public universities in my own state, and (b) will my potential area of study warrant the extra cost? For example, an applicant from Pennsylvania intent on majoring in education would be unlikely to get a solid return on investment depending, of course, on the degree of merit and need-based aid.

FINANCIAL
Institutional Type: Public
In-State Tuition: $9,060
Out-of-State Tuition: $32,520
Room & Board: $11,460
Required Fees: $3,402
Books & Supplies: $1,200

Avg. Need-Based Aid: $7,840
Avg. % of Need Met: 63%

Avg. Merit-Based Aid: $6,312
% Receiving Merit-Based Aid: 36%

Avg. Cumulative Debt: $30,790
% of Students Borrowing: 60%

CAREER
Who Recruits
1. CoStar
2. BAE Systems
3. Andersen Tax
4. Boeing
5. Black Horse

Notable Internships
1. Verizon
2. Cisco
3. BAE Systems

Top Industries
1. Business
2. Education
3. Infromation Technology
4. Operations
5. Engineering

Top Employers
1. Booz Allen Hamilton
2. Deloitte
3. Northrop Grumman
4. Capital One
5. Freddie Mac

Where Alumni Work
1. Washington, DC
2. New York City
3. Richmond, VA
4. San Francisco
5. Baltimore

Median Earnings
College Scorecard (Early Career): $59,900
EOP (Early Career): $56,500
PayScale (Mid-Career): $105,700

RANKINGS
Forbes: 177
Money: 64
U.S. News: 153, National Universities
Wall Street Journal/THE: 184
Washington Monthly: 51, National Universities

#CollegesWorthYourMoney

George Washington University

Washington, District of Columbia | Admissions Phone: 202-994-6040

ADMISSION

Admission Rate: 42%
Admission Rate - Men: 42%
Admission Rate - Women: 42%
EA Admission Rate: Not Offered
ED Admission Rate: 70%
Admission Rate (5-Year Trend): +9%
ED Admission Rate (5-Year Trend): N/A
% of Admits Attending (Yield): 26%
Transfer Admission Rate: 40%

\# Offered Wait List: 4,963
\# Accepted Wait List: 2,081
\# Admitted Wait List: 14

SAT Reading/Writing (Middle 50%): 640-720
SAT Math (Middle 50%): 640-740
ACT Composite (Middle 50%): 29-32
Testing Policy: Test Optional
SAT Superscore: Yes
ACT Superscore: Yes

% Graduated in Top 10% of HS Class: 56%
% Graduated in Top 25% of HS Class: 88%
% Graduated in Top 50% of HS Class: 98%

ENROLLMENT

Total Undergraduate Enrollment: 12,546
% Part-Time: 10%
% Male: 39%
% Female: 61%
% Out-of-State: 96%
% Fraternity: 14%
% Sorority: 17%
% On-Campus (Freshman): 98%
% On-Campus (All Undergraduate): 60%

% African-American: 7%
% Asian: 11%
% Hispanic: 10%
% White: 50%
% Other: 4%
% Race or Ethnicity Unknown: 6%
% International: 11%
% Low-Income: 12%

ACADEMICS

Student-to-Faculty Ratio: 13:1
% of Classes Under 20: 53%
% of Classes Under 40: 80%
% Full-Time Faculty: 43%
% Full-Time Faculty w/ Terminal Degree: 95%

Top Programs
Communication
Finance
History
International Affairs
International Business
Political Science
Public Health
Public Policy

Retention Rate: 93%
4-Year Graduation Rate: 74%
6-Year Graduation Rate: 82%

Curricular Flexibility: Somewhat Flexible
Academic Rating: ★★★✦

Inside the Classroom

Appropriately located only four blocks from the White House, the university named after our nation's first president educates over 12,500 undergraduate students and an additional 15,500 graduate students. One of the pricier schools in the United States, George Washington University, nevertheless, has rarely been in higher demand since its founding in 1821. Thanks to the popularity of DC as a college setting and a number of highly regarded academic programs, GW has become increasingly selective, catering to a more talented group of students today than it did at the turn of the millennium.

GW undergraduates choose from seventy majors spread across nine colleges: the Columbian College of Arts & Sciences, Corcoran School of the Arts & Design, School of Business, School of Engineering & Applied Science, Elliot School of International Affairs, School of Media & Public Affairs, School of Medicine & Health Sciences, School of Nursing, and the Milken Institute School of Public Health. All GW students must complete one course in mathematics or statistics, one course in natural and/or physical laboratory sciences, two courses in social sciences, one course in humanities, and two writing-intensive courses. From there, another set of college/major-specific requirements follow, but general education requirements tend not to be overly restrictive.

The school's 13:1 student-to-faculty ratio translates to a mix of small, medium, and large undergraduate sections. Eleven percent of courses have single-digit enrollments, 10 percent have over fifty students, and the majority fall in the ten to thirty range. In recent years the university has invested in increasing the number of undergraduate research experiences available to its students through the GW Center for Undergraduate Research and Fellowships. The efforts are paying off as a record 160 undergrads presented at the 2017 GW Research Days, a two-day event held in April. Close to half of Colonials study abroad for one semester in Europe (65 percent), Asia (10 percent), Latin America (8 percent), Africa (7 percent), or Australia (6 percent).

Standout programs at GW include political science, international affairs, communications, and public health. Any degree earned from the university will serve students well when they vie for positions at top companies and elite graduate schools. The social sciences (34 percent) are the area in which the greatest number of degrees are awarded followed by business (17 percent), health professions (12 percent), engineering (5 percent), and communications/journalism (5 percent). A service-oriented institution, GW is proudly the number one producer of Peace Corps volunteers among midsize universities, and it also churns out Teach for America members at one of the highest rates in the country. Twelve of the forty-nine GW students who applied were named Fulbright Scholars in 2017. That success rate of 24 percent is higher than the rate at Harvard, Princeton, or Columbia.

Outside the Classroom

Freshmen, sophomores, and (as of 2018) juniors are all required to live in one of twenty-six residence halls situated on the university's two campuses. Three-quarters of freshmen reside at the main Foggy Bottom Campus, and the other 25 percent of first-years live at the Mount Vernon Campus that is three miles away in Northwest DC. Over 2,500 students, 14 percent of men and 17 percent of women, are Greek affiliated, making fraternities and sororities powerful social forces at GW. The school's robust sports program includes twenty-seven NCAA Division I teams. An additional 1,000 students participate in club sports, and the intramural programs scoop up the rest of the athletically inclined undergrads. The 475 registered student organizations collectively offer 1,200 leadership positions, and 87 percent of undergraduates are involved with at least one group. Noteworthy guest speakers appear with regularity through the GW Speaker Series. Of course, what's on campus is only the first layer of recreational opportunities at George Washington. The Foggy Bottom campus is only a few miles from the National Mall and many of the best museums in the country. As a bridge between the school and outside city, GW's flexible meal plans allow you to visit ninety partner restaurants, cafes, and grocery stores around DC. At GW, your life outside the classroom can involve every corner of the District of Columbia.

Career Services

The Center for Career Services is staffed by twenty-four full-time employees, including eight individuals with the title of career coach as well as other professionals focusing on employer relations and graduate school advising. That calculates to a student-advisor ratio of 420:1, within the average range of institutions profiled in this guide. Personalized career coaching is readily available. The office received high marks from students who exited in 2017 as 95 percent agreed that career programs had helped enhance their career development. Large-scale events, such as the Fall Career Fair, attracted more than one hundred employers in 2018. Fall and spring career fairs generally attract in the neighborhood of 1,400 GW undergrads and alumni.

Internships are completed by 68 percent of undergraduates and 54 percent are either paid or awarded a stipend for their work. Thanks to the university's far-reaching connections and prime location, internships are procured at thousands of different companies/organizations each year, from the US Congress to the Smithsonian to the NFL Players Association. More than 800 employers engaged with GW students through a combination of on- and off-campus events. The school also enjoys an alumni base of over 250,000 that leads to ample opportunities for networking. In sum, the Center for Career Services does a solid job facilitating internships and utilizing its DC locale and huge, well-connected alumni base to produce decent outcomes for its graduates.

Professional Outcomes

Within six months of leaving GW 87 percent of the Class of 2018 had found their way to gainful employment or graduate school while 13 percent were still job hunting. Of the 61 percent of grads already in the workplace, two-thirds were in a for-profit industry, 25 percent had entered a nonprofit position, and 8 percent were working in government. Among the most popular sectors for GW grads were health care (9 percent), legal and law enforcement (6 percent), management/consulting (6 percent), accounting (5 percent), public relations (5 percent), and defense (5 percent). Close to one-third enjoyed starting salaries above $60,000 while 49 percent earned less than $50,000. The median salary earned by newly minted grads from 2014-2017 was $46k. Close to four-fifths of recent grads remained in the Mid-Atlantic region with the West and Mountain regions a distant second.

A healthy 23 percent of those earning their diplomas in 2018 immediately turned their attention to earning an advanced degree. Among that group were 66 percent seeking master's degrees, 14 percent entering law school, 6 percent entering a doctoral program, and 7 percent pursuing a medical degree. Looking at the last four graduating classes as a whole, 488 students have continued their studies at George Washington. The next most commonly attended institutions were Columbia University (48), Georgetown (42), Johns Hopkins (37), and NYU (31).

Admission

Of 26,590 Class of 2022 hopefuls, GW admitted 11,100 for an acceptance rate of 42 percent. That number has shown volatility over current attendees' lifetimes, hitting as low as 32 percent in 2010 and as high as 80 percent in 1998 when today's seniors were in diapers. Freshmen during the 2018-19 school year earned excellent grades in high school as 56 percent finished in the top 10 percent of their class, and 88 percent landed in the top 25 percent. Of those submitting standardized test results the middle 50 percent of SAT scores were 1280-1460 and 29-32 on the ACT.

The admissions committee rates two factors—rigor of secondary school record and GPA—as carrying the greatest weight in the process. The next tier of factors includes the essay, volunteer work, recommendations, talent/ability, and extracurricular activities. GW has been test-optional since 2015, and a fair number of applicants do forgo submitting standardized test scores. Of the 2,800 freshmen in the Class of 2022, 1,419 submitted SAT scores and 955 submitted ACT scores. Given that a fair number of students likely submitted results from both tests, more than a quarter of those enrolled are likely to have been accepted sans test scores. Over the past two decades GW has grown into a highly selective and sought-after university in one of the country's hottest cities. Still, this institution is in a dogfight for top students and rewards those who apply early, typically accepting 70 percent through ED versus 40 percent in the regular cycle.

Worth Your Money?

Attending a private college in the fifth most expensive US city isn't going to come cheap. GW will set you back $74k per year for total cost of attendance. Three-fifths of students do receive a merit aid award averaging almost $23k, which makes the university slightly more affordable. For the 47 percent of undergrads who qualify for need-based financial aid, an average annual award of $35,000 puts a dent in the total costs, but the school does not meet 100 percent of the demonstrated need for the majority of eligible students. George Washington grads emerge with higher-than-average debt loads, thus prospective students need to carefully determine whether this school is a good financial fit for them, given their individual circumstances. Students pursuing study in the areas of business, communication, politics and policy enjoy better prospects for a strong ROI.

FINANCIAL
Institutional Type: Private
In-State Tuition: $54,459
Out-of-State Tuition: $54,459
Room & Board: $14,300
Required Fees: $90
Books & Supplies: $1,400

Avg. Need-Based Aid: $35,061
Avg. % of Need Met: 88%

Avg. Merit-Based Aid: $22,777
% Receiving Merit-Based Aid: 60%

Avg. Cumulative Debt: $35,454
% of Students Borrowing: 47%

CAREER
Who Recruits
1. Becton, Dickinson and Co.
2. Consumer Financial Protection Bureau
3. Westat
4. Turner Construction
5. Gunnison Consulting

Notable Internships
1. United States Senate
2. NBC News
3. Macy's

Top Industries
1. Business
2. Education
3. Operations
4. Social Services
5. information Technology

Top Employers
1. Booz Allen Hamilton
2. Deloitte
3. IBM
4. U.S. House of Representatives
5. Capital One

Where Alumni Work
1. Washington, DC
2. New Yor City
3. San Francisco
4. Boston
5. Philadelphia

Median Earnings
College Scorecard (Early Career): $69,600
EOP (Early Career): $63,900
PayScale (Mid-Career): $115,300

RANKINGS
Forbes: 78
Money: 235
U.S. News: 70, National Universities
Wall Street Journal/THE: 72
Washington Monthly: 54, National Universities

#CollegesWorthYourMoney

Georgetown University

Washington, District of Columbia | Admissions Phone: 202-687-3600

Inside the Classroom

The nation's oldest Catholic and Jesuit university also happens to be one of the best institutions in the country and one of the premier training grounds for future political bigwigs. Spired campus buildings, cobblestone walkways, and tree-lined streets give Georgetown an elegant aesthetic and an air of sophistication that perfectly matches the rigorous educational experience and conservative/traditional campus vibe.

The university's 7,400 undergraduates and 11,700 graduate students are divided among nine schools/colleges, but only four are open to undergrads. Applicants to Georgetown must select one of these four schools: Georgetown College, McDonough School of Business, the Walsh School of Foreign Service, or the School of Nursing & Health Studies. Core requirements vary by school but are fairly extensive. For example, Georgetown College requires one course in the humanities and writing and two courses per discipline in theology, philosophy, math/science, social science, foreign language, and diversity for a total of fourteen required courses. There are forty-four majors within Georgetown College, seven business-oriented majors within McDonough, four tracks in the nursing school, and eight majors within the Walsh School of Foreign Service.

For a large university with a heavy presence of graduate students, Georgetown maintains a personalized and intimate learning environment. The student-faculty ratio is 11:1, and 60 percent of classes enroll fewer than twenty students. While some classes are a bit larger, only 6 percent cross the fifty-student threshold. There are many ways that students can seek funding for independent research projects or become an assistant to faculty members via the Georgetown Undergraduate Research Opportunities Program. Summer research can lead to the completion of a senior thesis that can be presented at the College Academic Council Research Colloquium every spring. A phenomenal 57 percent of Hoya undergrads participate in one of the schools 200 study abroad programs that are spread across fifty countries.

Those desiring to join the world of politics or diplomacy are in the right place. The Government and International Affairs programs are among the best in the country. For those with their eyes on a finance career, McDonough is one of the most esteemed business schools one can find. The greatest number of degrees are conferred in the social sciences (35 percent) followed by business (26 percent), interdisciplinary studies (6 percent), and foreign language (5 percent). Georgetown is regularly a top producer of distinguished fellowship winners. In 2018, it produced thirty Fulbright Scholars, placing it in the top five in the nation. It typically also sees multiple Truman, Boren, Gilman International, and Marshall Scholars from each graduating class.

Outside the Classroom

The scenic and safe Georgetown area of DC is littered with high-end restaurants and shops. Only a short Metro ride away, the opportunities for museums, live music, fine cuisine, sporting events, and a pulsating nightlife are endless. A touch over three-quarters of undergrads live on campus.

The twenty-three NCAA Division I sports teams are part of the fabric of Hoya life, particularly the men's basketball team. More than 2,500 students participate in intramural sports, utilizing the school's superb facilities that include Yates Field House. Due to the clash of values between the Jesuits and Greek life, fraternities and sororities are not recognized by the school, but they have enjoyed a recent rise in popularity despite their unofficial status. Religion is a guiding force at the university as more than half of the student body identify as Catholic. The campus ministry is popular, and many students are part of faith-based or secular volunteer organizations. In total, there are 250 active student organizations that offer an array of clubs focused on spirituality, culture, academics, and the arts. The Georgetown University Lecture Fund brings an incredible lineup of luminaries from the realms of politics, entertainment, business, media, and social activism to speak on campus.

Career Services

The Cawley Career Education Center is manned by fourteen professionals (not counting office managers and administrative assistants). That gives it a student-to-advisor ratio of 531:1, below average compared to the pool of institutions included in this book. Yet, that does not translate to a poor delivery of services. In fact, the staff boasts over 13,000 interactions with undergraduate students each year, almost twice the population of the student body; by graduation, over 90 percent have engaged with the career center. In a given year, counselors spend approximately 800 collective hours meeting one-on-one with students to discuss professional pathways and dole out career/graduate school advice.

In a single school year Georgetown arranged for 2,460 interviews on campus and attracted more than 1,800 attendees at both its fall and spring career expos. Over 200 corporations, government, and nonprofit employers met with students at those events. Additionally, sixty-five companies visited campus to host information sessions with undergraduates. With a strong and active alumni base, the Hoya Career Connection sees roughly 15,000 internship/employment opportunities posted per year. Despite not having an elite student-advisor ratio, Cawley's extensive counseling offerings/events, proficiency with facilitating on-campus recruiting by top-level employers, and tremendous student outcomes earned it top grades from our staff.

ADMISSION
Admission Rate: 15%
Admission Rate - Men: 16%
Admission Rate - Women: 14%
EA Admission Rate: N/A
ED Admission Rate: Not Offered
Admission Rate (5-Year Trend): -3%
ED Admission Rate (5-Year Trend): Not Offered
% of Admits Attending (Yield): 49%
Transfer Admission Rate: 7%

Offered Wait List: 2,593
Accepted Wait List: 1,754
Admitted Wait List: 16

SAT Reading/Writing (Middle 50%): 680-750
SAT Math (Middle 50%): 690-780
ACT Composite (Middle 50%): 31-34
Testing Policy: ACT/SAT Required
SAT Superscore: Yes
ACT Superscore: No

% Graduated in Top 10% of HS Class: 89%
% Graduated in Top 25% of HS Class: 97%
% Graduated in Top 50% of HS Class: 99%

ENROLLMENT
Total Undergraduate Enrollment: 7,459
% Part-Time: 6%
% Male: 44%
% Female: 56%
% Out-of-State: 98%
% Fraternity: Not Offered
% Sorority: Not Offered
% On-Campus (Freshman): 100%
% On-Campus (All Undergraduate): 77%

% African-American: 6%
% Asian: 9%
% Hispanic: 10%
% White: 50%
% Other: 5%
% Race or Ethnicity Unknown: 5%
% International: 15%
% Low-Income: 13%

ACADEMICS
Student-to-Faculty Ratio: 11:1
% of Classes Under 20: 60%
% of Classes Under 40: 87%
% Full-Time Faculty: 49%
% Full-Time Faculty w/ Terminal Degree: 80%

Top Programs
Economics
Finance
Global Health
Government
History
International Business
International Politics
Psychology

Retention Rate: 96%
4-Year Graduation Rate: 89%
6-Year Graduation Rate: 94%

Curricular Flexibility: Somewhat Flexible
Academic Rating: ★★★★

Georgetown University

E-mail: guadmiss@georgetown.edu | Website: www.georgetown.edu

Professional Outcomes

Within six months of graduating 75 percent of members of the Class of 2018 entered the workforce, 16 percent went directly into a graduate or professional program of study, and 5 percent were still seeking employment. In past years the number of fresh alums entering grad school has been significantly greater—as high as 24 percent. The Class of 2018 sent massive numbers of graduates to a number of major corporations including Deloitte (26), Citi (24), JPMorgan Chase (22), PricewaterhouseCoopers (21), EY (18), Morgan Stanley (17), McKinsey & Company (11) and Goldman Sachs (10), and a number of other multinational financial institutions. As one might ascertain from this list of companies, the most popular industries were consulting (15 percent), investment banking (14 percent), and internet and software (8 percent). By far, New York and remaining in DC are the two most popular postgraduate destinations, although a fair number also migrate to Virginia, California, Massachusetts, and Maryland. The financial picture for Georgetown graduates is rosy. They enjoy an average starting salary of $61,000, well above the national average.

Over the past six years, medicine and law have been the top two graduate fields chosen by Hoya alumni. Each year roughly forty to fifty-five grads entered law school, and another forty to fifty-five entered med school. An incredibly high percentage elect to remain at Georgetown—forty-seven members of the Class of 2018 entered graduate school at their alma mater. The number two choice was Columbia with eighteen students. In fact, since 2007 Georgetown and Columbia have been the two most frequently attended graduate schools. The other schools on that list are almost exclusively elite institutions including Harvard, Yale, Duke, Northwestern, USC, NYU, Tufts, and the University of Chicago.

Admission

Like many other prestigious universities, Georgetown registered its all-time high in applications received and all-time low acceptance rate for the class of 2022. Of the almost 23,000 applications, slightly more than 3,330 were admitted for an acceptance rate of 14.5 percent. The average SAT score of those accepted was the highest ever at 1467. For enrolled freshmen in 2018-19, the mid-50 percent range was 1370-1530 on the SAT and 31-34 on the ACT. Grades must be equally exceptional for serious consideration; 89 percent of enrolled students finished in the top 10 percent of their high school class. The profile of students admitted today has much in common with those admitted five years ago.

Georgetown does not have an early decision option but does offer nonbinding early action. However, applying early yields little advantage as the university's early round acceptance rates tend to be lower than in the regular round. Also noteworthy, the university does not allow Score Choice, the option that permits applicants to select which standardized scores are reported to prospective schools and which are not. The admissions office rates nine factors as being "very important," most notably first-generation status, a consideration weighted this heavily by few other schools. In the 2018-19 academic year 11 percent of admitted students were the first in their family to attend college. The most selective school in the DC Metro area, Georgetown attracts growing lines of extremely well-qualified candidates each year. There are few admissions surprises here. Test scores around the 97th percentile and near-perfect grades in an AP-heavy course load are required.

Worth Your Money?

A year at Georgetown will cost you close to $78,000 if you do not receive any financial aid. Like many similarly elite institutions, it is more focused on providing sizable grants to those with true financial need. For the 38 percent of current students who qualify for financial aid, Georgetown meets 100 percent of their demonstrated need, which works out to an average annual amount of $45,572. Unless you plan to enter a low-paying field and need to take on an excessive amount of debt, this school is well worth paying for as the Georgetown name will open doors for you well into adulthood.

FINANCIAL
Institutional Type: Private
In-State Tuition: $55,440
Out-of-State Tuition: $55,440
Room & Board: $17,638
Required Fees: $618
Books & Supplies: N/A

Avg. Need-Based Aid: $45,572
Avg. % of Need Met: 100%

Avg. Merit-Based Aid: $0
% Receiving Merit-Based Aid: 0%

Avg. Cumulative Debt: $25,726
% of Students Borrowing: 37%

CAREER
Who Recruits
1. BMO Capital Markets
2. AlphaSights
3. RBC Capital Markets
4. Capital One
5. Charles River Associates

Notable Internships
1. U.S. Securities and Exchange Commission
2. Vanguard
3. Goldman Sachs

Top Industries
1. Business
2. Education
3. Social Services
4. Operations
5. Media

Top Employers
1. Deloitte
2. Google
3. PwC
4. Citi
5. Goldman Sachs

Where Alumni Work
1. Washington, DC
2. New York City
3. San Francisco
4. Boston
5. Los Angeles

Median Earnings
College Scorecard (Early Career): $93,500
EOP (Early Career): $84,400
PayScale (Mid-Career): $122,200

RANKINGS
Forbes: 15
Money: 61
U.S. News: 24, National Universities
Wall Street Journal/THE: 29
Washington Monthly: 9, National Universities

#CollegesWorthYourMoney

Georgia Institute of Technology

Atlanta, Georgia | Admissions Phone: 404-894-4154

Inside the Classroom

Downtown Atlanta is home to one of the world's undisputed best public technological institutes. The Georgia Institute of Technology, more commonly referred to as Georgia Tech, educates more than 16,000 undergraduates as well as another 16,000-plus graduate students who are on track to be the next generation of leaders in the engineering, computer science, and related fields. While still catering to locals (68 percent are Georgia residents), Tech has managed to grow its national reputation in recent years and has blossomed from a top public tech university to simply a top tech university.

Georgia Tech is divided into six colleges: the College of Design, the College of Computing, the College of Engineering, the College of Sciences, Ivan Allen College of Liberal Arts, and Scheller College of Business. Altogether, more than 115 majors and minors are available to undergraduates; all students are held to a stringent list of core requirements that is partially governed by the state. Must-take courses include Constitution & History, Communication Outcomes, Quantitative Outcomes, and Introduction to Computing as well as requirements in humanities/fine arts/ethics, social sciences, and wellness (physical education).

Being a large research university, the student-to-faculty ratio is a less-than-ideal 23:1, leading to some larger undergraduate class sections. In fact, 35 percent of courses had enrollments of more than thirty students in 2018-19. On the other end of the spectrum, 29 percent of sections had single-digit enrollments. While not all of your professors will know you by name, there are plenty of ways that motivated students can strike up meaningful faculty-student relationships. For example, 30 percent of aerospace engineering majors collaborate on research with their professors. In the School of Chemical and Biomolecular Engineering that figure rises to 60 percent. Over half of Tech students have gone abroad by the time they graduate, with a growing number electing to complete internships in a foreign land rather than academic coursework. Last year, 135 undergraduate students participated in a global internship.

Georgia Tech's engineering and computer science programs are at the top of any "best programs" list. The Scheller College of Business boasts top programs in management information systems, production/operation management, quantitative analysis, and supply chain management/logistics. The architecture school also receives national recognition. In terms of total number of degrees conferred, the most popular areas of study are engineering (60 percent), computer science (17 percent), and business (10 percent). Those pursuing prestigious fellowships/scholarships have done well in recent years. In 2016, five students won Fulbright Scholarships. Others have succeeded at taking home Astronaut, Udall, Truman, and Marshall Scholarships. Two undergrads from one major—electrical engineering—won National Science Fellowships in 2018.

Outside the Classroom

Georgia Tech's 400-acre, wooded campus contains the vast majority of freshmen (98 percent), but only 45 percent of the overall student body lives in the school's forty residence halls. The rest find apartments or housing in surrounding neighborhoods like Buckhead, Home Park, Westside, or Atlantic Station. The Yellow Jackets field seventeen varsity intercollegiate athletic teams. The school's nine men's and eight women's teams participate in the Atlantic Coast Conference (ACC). Add twenty intramural sports, forty-three sports clubs, and one of the largest outdoor recreation programs around, and the result is an extremely athletically-inclined student body. Those who aren't involved with sports typically find another place to connect, whether it's in one of the more than 400 student organizations or fifty Greek organizations. Tech is a Greek-heavy school with 28 percent of men and 33 percent of women belonging to a fraternity or sorority. Campus provides plenty of chances for social engagement, but those seeking more can enjoy all that Atlanta has to offer.

Career Services

The Georgia Tech Center for Career Discovery and Development, cleverly nicknamed C2D2, employs twenty full-time staff members (not counting IT professionals and office assistants). That collection of career advisors, employee relations specialists, and graduate school counselors works out to a student-to-counselor ratio of 679:1, below average compared to the pool of institutions included in this book. Despite this unremarkable number, C2D2 is able to put on impressive, large-scale events that enhance student outcomes. The Fall Career Fair is the school's largest, featuring over 400 employers including Accenture, Capital One, GM, and Intel, and 5,000 students attend each year. The school also forges formal corporate partnerships with big-time companies including Google, Airbnb, Qualcomm, Northrup Grumman, and ConocoPhillips. Corporations routinely host information sessions on campus.

Internships and co-op programs receive some of the highest marks in the country. Thirty-five percent of undergrads choose to enter the school's three-semester co-op program, which leads to a five-year degree, while many others complete a one- or two-semester internship. In 2017, C2D2 placed 1,068 students in internships and another 1,307 in co-op programs. Individualized appointments are encouraged as early as freshman year to begin planning potential career and graduate school pathways. Overall, Georgia Tech's career services does a fantastic job of funneling undergraduates into the world's premier employers at high starting salaries.

Professional Outcomes

Graduates in the Class of 2018 procured employment at a rate of 78 percent by the time they were handed their diplomas. The median salary reported by that group was $70,500. The highest median salary of $99k went to graduates of the School of Computer Science. By midcareer, Georgia Tech alumni enjoy the second highest salary of the most selective public universities in the country. You will find alumni at every major technology in the world. Just examining those who have LinkedIn profiles, 969 Yellow Jackets work at Google, 853 at Microsoft, 789 at Amazon, 759 at IBM, 586 at Apple, 327 at Facebook, and 170 at Uber. The bulk of graduates remain in the Atlanta metro area. The next three most popular destinations are San Francisco, New York City, and Washington, DC.

At the time of their exit surveys, 21 percent of 2018 grads planned on pursuing an advanced degree within the next year. Many remain on campus to earn advanced engineering degrees through Georgia Tech, but the school's reputation is such that gaining admission into other top programs including MIT, Carnegie Mellon, Berkeley, Stanford, and Caltech is an achievable feat. Those same schools are institutions where Tech alumni have gone on to work as professors and researchers.

Admission

Only 22 percent of applicants to the Class of 2022 were admitted, a slight decrease from the 23 percent who were admitted the prior year. Freshmen during the 2018-19 school year possessed middle-50 percent scores of 1390-1540 on the SAT and 31-34 on the ACT, and 94 percent had a GPA of over 3.75. A staggering 89 percent of first-year students hailed from the top 10 percent of their high school classes; 97 percent were in the top 25 percent. Only a decade ago, the university admitted 63 percent of applicants, and the 75th percentile of test-takers placed close to the Class of 2022's 25th percentile. Clearly, this school is infinitely more difficult to get into than it was only a short time ago.

Three factors can give you an advantage in your quest to gain acceptance at Tech: (1) if you are from Georgia, (2) if you are female, and (3) if you apply early action. In 2017-18, the acceptance rate for Peach State residents was 44 percent, more than double the out-of-state figure. The following cycle the acceptance rate for female applicants was 29 percent versus only 19 percent for male applicants. The early action acceptance rate was 26 percent versus 17 percent for the general pool. For all applicants, the admissions committee places the most emphasis on the rigor of one's high school coursework, GPA, and extracurricular activities. Test scores, essays, talent/ability, character, and personal qualities, volunteer work, and work experience are among the factors in the next tier. Getting into Georgia Tech has become a harrowing enterprise and is a wholly different experience than for previous generations. Applying early will help, but nonresident men, in particular, will still face extremely unfavorable odds.

Worth Your Money?

Georgia residents are looking at an annual cost of attendance of $31k which, when you consider that the median starting salary is well over two times that amount, makes Georgia Tech an exceptional bargain. Even better, merit aid is generously distributed with 63 percent of undergrads landing, on average, a $12,777 award each year. That includes the Stamps President's Scholars Program that gives a free ride to forty highly qualified applicants each year. Need-based aid is granted to 40 percent of students with the average amount in the range of $12,500. Only a small percentage of aid recipients see 100 percent of their demonstrated need met. Even if you received limited aid and/or were paying out-of-state tuition, which brings the COA to $52k, Tech would still prove a worthwhile investment of your time and money.

FINANCIAL
Institutional Type: Public
In-State Tuition: $10,008
Out-of-State Tuition: $30,604
Room & Board: $11,884
Required Fees: $2,416
Books & Supplies: $800

Avg. Need-Based Aid: $14,630
Avg. % of Need Met: 66%

Avg. Merit-Based Aid: $12,777
% Receiving Merit-Based Aid: 63%

Avg. Cumulative Debt: $32,760
% of Students Borrowing: 36%

CAREER
Who Recruits
1. SunTrust Bank
2. Caterpillar
3. The Clorox Company
4. Equifax
5. Rockwell Automation

Notable Internships
1. NASA
2. Procter & Gamble
3. Uber

Top Industries
1. Engineering
2. Business
3. Operations
4. Information Technology
5. Research

Top Employers
1. Google
2. Microsoft
3. Amazon
4. Home Depot
5. Apple

Where Alumni Work
1. Atlanta
2. San Francisco
3. New York City
4. Washington, DC
5. Seattle

Median Earnings
College Scorecard (Early Career): $79,100
EOP (Early Career): $78,900
PayScale (Mid-Career): $133,400

RANKINGS
Forbes: 65
Money: 27
U.S. News: 29, National Universities
Wall Street Journal/THE: 68 (T)
Washington Monthly: 48, National Universities

#CollegesWorthYourMoney

Grinnell College

Grinnell, Iowa | Admissions Phone: 641-269-3600

ADMISSION
Admission Rate: 24%
Admission Rate - Men: 23%
Admission Rate - Women: 26%
EA Admission Rate: Not Offered
ED Admission Rate: 58%
Admission Rate (5-Year Trend): -11%
ED Admission Rate (5-Year Trend): +9%
% of Admits Attending (Yield): 26%
Transfer Admission Rate: 4%

Offered Wait List: 1,447
Accepted Wait List: 274
Admitted Wait List: 33

SAT Reading/Writing (Middle 50%): 670-750
SAT Math (Middle 50%): 700-790
ACT Composite (Middle 50%): 30-34
Testing Policy: ACT/SAT Required
SAT Superscore: Yes
ACT Superscore: Yes

% Graduated in Top 10% of HS Class: 68%
% Graduated in Top 25% of HS Class: 90%
% Graduated in Top 50% of HS Class: 99%

ENROLLMENT
Total Undergraduate Enrollment: 1,716
% Part-Time: 2%
% Male: 46%
% Female: 54%
% Out-of-State: 92%
% Fraternity: Not Offered
% Sorority: Not Offered
% On-Campus (Freshman): 100%
% On-Campus (All Undergraduate): 88%

% African-American: 5%
% Asian: 8%
% Hispanic: 7%
% White: 50%
% Other: 5%
% Race or Ethnicity Unknown: 6%
% International: 19%
% Low-Income: 22%

ACADEMICS
Student-to-Faculty Ratio: 9:1
% of Classes Under 20: 65%
% of Classes Under 40: 100%
% Full-Time Faculty: 82%
% Full-Time Faculty w/ Terminal Degree: 99%

Top Programs
Biology
Biological Chemistry
Chemistry
Economics
History
Physics
Political Science
Sociology

Retention Rate: 92%
4-Year Graduation Rate: 78%
6-Year Graduation Rate: 84%

Curricular Flexibility: Very Flexible
Academic Rating: ★★★★✦

Inside the Classroom

Long a bastion of progressive, free-thinking liberal arts education, Grinnell College, set in remote Iowa, has never been a more popular destination in its more than 170-year history than it is today. Rising numbers of applications and shrinking acceptance rates have raised the caliber of the nearly 1,700 young people who currently occupy campus.

Grinnell offers twenty-seven distinct bachelor's degrees and over 500 courses each semester, and students have an immense deal of autonomy with course selection. In fact, nothing better epitomizes the school's philosophy than its list of graduation requirements that are more a list of the maximum number of courses a student can take in any one area rather than a list of minimal expectations. The only required course is the First-Year Tutorial, a ten- to fourteen-student, writing-intensive seminar with topics ranging from the artist Kendrick Lamar to the comic strip Calvin & Hobbes. Outside of that one course, your education is personally crafted through the college's Individually-Advised Curriculum that sees students working closely with a faculty advisor to make the most of their educational journey.

Thanks to a 9:1 student/faculty ratio and no competition from graduate students, two-thirds of classes have fewer than twenty students, and 24 percent of sections have single-digit student enrollments. Participating in research is a normal part of an undergraduate education at Grinnell. Overall, 43 percent of Grinnell undergrads participate in one on- or off-campus research experience that was not simply built into their coursework. Mentor Advanced Projects, which see faculty closely work with students on scholarly or creative works, were participated in by 71 percent of the subset who had some type of research experience. Thirty percent of that group conducted research at another location such as Duke University, Georgetown University, or Carnegie Mellon University. International study is also a fairly common part of a Grinnell education with 50 percent of students studying abroad. The Grinnell-in-London program is a popular option, offering a semester's worth of courses on English politics, history, and theater.

A top producer of PhDs in both the sciences and the social sciences, Grinnell has strong offerings across the board, with programs in biology, chemistry, economics, and history receiving particularly high praise. The largest number of degrees are conferred in English, foreign languages, biology, and computer science. A fast riser, the computer science program now graduates seventy students per year versus only fifteen four years ago. Grinnell students fare extraordinarily well at obtaining competitive scholarships. Graduates in the Class of 2017 captured Watson, Fulbright, and NIH scholarships/fellowships. Grinnell is one of the top Fulbright-producing institutions in the country with seven recipients in 2018 and ten in 2016.

Outside the Classroom

Over 85 percent of students live on campus in small residence halls that house between fifty and sixty students. Grinnell has a long tradition of being fraternity and sorority free, instead favoring an "inclusive and open-minded" social scene. One-third of students engage in varsity athletics; the school fields twenty NCAA Division III teams that compete in the Midwest Conference. Intramurals draw heavy participation with soccer, volleyball, flag football, and basketball being among the most popular. Two-thirds of students participate in community service projects, and opportunities include teaching at a local prison, a buddies program for nearby children, and Alternative Breaks at impoverished areas around the United States. There are more than one hundred student organizations as silly and relaxed as the Zombie Movie Club or as serious as the local chapter of the Roosevelt Institute Campus Network. With its remote location amidst the cornfields of Iowa, there's not much to explore in the surrounding area. Fortunately, campus itself is a nurturing and lively place.

Career Services

For a school of just over 1,700, the Center for Careers, Life, and Service (CLS) employs an astounding twenty-two full-time staff members that includes those specializing in career advising (14), employer relations, internships, and fellowships and awards. That equates to a student-to-advisor ratio of 77:1, better than every school except Wellesley that is featured in this guide. The personalized attention that staffing level affords enables the CLS to adhere to its core belief that "one's impact, satisfaction, and sense of purpose are maximized when one is able to align their values, strengths, and curiosities." To that aim, students are assigned a CLS exploratory advisor before they even set foot on campus. In the 2018-19 academic year the office had 4,469 one-one-one advising contacts with students, which works out to more than two per student!

While its somewhat remote location and small student body makes it tough to host a large-scale career fair, the school compensates by hosting/facilitating over 180 smaller events each year including career treks, workshops, alumni panels, and networking receptions. Seventy-seven companies recruited on campus in the last academic year. Grinnell does a solid job facilitating internship experiences with a 44 percent participation rate among 2017 graduates. Of that group, 31 percent completed two internships, and 19 percent completed four.

Internships were procured around the globe including stops at BMW China, Amazon Japan, the White House, the United Nations, Facebook, IBM, and Twitter. Thirty-five percent of the employed members of the class of 2017 stated that their first job was exactly what they wanted to be doing, and 46 percent viewed their position as a "good stepping stone." Grinnell's CLS offers unparalleled support and has an excellent track record of helping students secure valuable internships, meaningful first jobs, and graduate school acceptances.

Professional Outcomes

Upon graduation 59 percent of the Class of 2017 headed into the workforce, 22 percent to graduate school, 7 percent to postgraduate service, and 5 percent earned fellowships. Of the 59 percent entering employment, 88 percent had already procured full-time jobs. Multiple members of this cohort accepted positions with Amazon and Google while others were hired by desirable organizations that included the Federal Reserve Board, Deloitte, the Brookings Institute, Goldman Sachs, and the Centers for Disease Control. The most commonly entered fields were IT/computing (15 percent), education (14 percent), business (13 percent), and research/science (11 percent). The mean salary of those employed was roughly $45,500, and the median was a slightly lower $42,500. Illinois attracted the highest number of graduates, slightly more than Iowa itself. California, New York, and Minnesota were the next most popular locations for Grinnell grads.

Forty percent of those entering graduate school in 2018 were pursuing PhDs in the hard sciences, 10 percent were headed to law school, and an equal percentage were bound for medical school. Law school acceptances included top-tier institutions Harvard and the University of Chicago, and one student was granted admission to the Johns Hopkins University School of Medicine. Other members were admitted to various advanced degree programs at Cambridge, Yale, Carnegie Mellon, and Cornell (NY). Overall, 86 percent of law school applicants received at least one acceptance, and 57 percent of medical school applicants were successful, which was twelve points higher than the national average.

Admission

The acceptance rate has jumped around in the last few years between 20 and 29 percent. That is far more selective than Grinnell was only a short time ago. For example, in the 2010-11 cycle Grinnell accepted 43 percent of applicants. That year it received only 2,969 applications, but it received 7,345 for a place in the Class of 2022. Standardized test scores of attending freshmen are higher as well—the mid-50 percent SAT score is 1320-1530 and 30-33 on the ACT. Approximately 80 percent of Grinnell students hail from the top 10 percent of their high school classes.

Admissions factors rated by the committee as being "very important" are rigor of secondary curriculum, GPA, class rank, and recommendations. The four categories that fall under "important" are standardized test scores, extracurricular activities, and talent/ability. Most members of the Class of 2022 were deeply involved during high school with 81 percent participating in community service, 71 percent in the fine arts, 65 percent in athletics, and 43 percent held jobs. Applying through early decision yields a major advantage as 58 percent of applicants receive positive news, more than double the regular rate. Early decision applicants comprise 44 percent of the incoming class, meaning that a large number of spots are already filled by the time the regular cycle rolls around. Even with Grinnell's transformation into a highly sought-after liberal arts college, the process remains holistic. Grades and test scores certainly matter, but unique talents and high school involvement play a major role as well. We can't stress enough how advantageous applying early is for students dead-set on studying at this now-elite Iowa school.

Worth Your Money?

The cost of attendance at Grinnell College is $67,646. One-quarter of undergrads receive a merit aid award averaging $19k. More encouragingly, two-thirds of attendees receive need-based grants with an annual value of roughly $45,000. Further, Grinnell manages to meet the full-demonstrated need of 100 percent of aid-eligible students. Starting salaries are generally on the lower side coming out of this college, which is perhaps attributed to the many Grinnellians in the academic and non-profit sectors; however, that isn't a big deal for most, thanks to the generosity of the aid packages being distributed. The average graduate comes out of Grinnell with less than $19,000 in debt, a very manageable sum.

FINANCIAL
Institutional Type: Private
In-State Tuition: $53,872
Out-of-State Tuition: $5,387
Room & Board: $13,292
Required Fees: $482
Books & Supplies: N/A

Avg. Need-Based Aid: $45,007
Avg. % of Need Met: 100%

Avg. Merit-Based Aid: $18,811
% Receiving Merit-Based Aid: 25%

Avg. Cumulative Debt: $18,694
% of Students Borrowing: 60%

CAREER
Who Recruits
1. Epic Systems
2. Morningstar
3. Nationwide
4. Teach for America
5. Google

Notable Internships
1. U.S. Forest Service
2. MasterCard
3. Resorative Justice Project

Top Industries
1. Education
2. Business
3. Research
4. Social Services
5. Media

Top Employers
1. Google
2. Amazon
3. Epic
4. U.S. State Department
5. Wells Fargo

Where Alumni Work
1. Des Mones, IA
2. Chicago
3. New York City
4. Washington, DC
5. Minneapolis

Median Earnings
College Scorecard (Early Career): $49,100
EOP (Early Career): $47,300
PayScale (Mid-Career): $96,500

RANKINGS
Forbes: 80
Money: 205
U.S. News: 14 (T), Liberal Arts Colleges
Wall Street Journal/THE: 57
Washington Monthly: 21, Liberal Arts Colleges

#CollegesWorthYourMoney

Hamilton College

Clinton, New York | Admissions Phone: 315-859-4421

Inside the Classroom

Recent years have been kind to Alexander Hamilton. His legacy has sparked a mega-hit Broadway musical, a Pulitzer Prize-winning biography, and the liberal arts college in Clinton, New York, that bears his name—Hamilton College—has achieved new heights of prestige, claiming a place among the best liberal arts schools in the United States.

Close to 1,900 undergraduate students can choose from forty-three areas of concentration, but education at Hamilton is about so much more than merely choosing a major. The unique open curriculum is immensely flexible and caters to student passions and curiosity over a rigid list of required courses. While there are no distributional requirements, certain skill areas must be addressed as you work your way through the thirty-two courses needed for graduation. That includes three writing-intensive courses, one quantitative/symbolic reasoning course, one physical education course, and an area of concentration that includes a senior project.

The student-to-faculty ratio is 9:1, and without any pesky graduate students to get in the way, face time with professors is a regular occurrence. In fact, 37 percent of all classes have nine or fewer students; 76 percent have nineteen or fewer. Each summer more than 140 students engage in high-level undergraduate research with a faculty member. Two-thirds of Hamilton students study off campus for a semester, although those locations are not always foreign countries. Many participate in domestic study programs in NYC, DC, or Boston while others take advantage of international opportunities like the school's own renowned Chinese language program in Beijing or one of one hundred other approved programs around the globe.

Economics, government, and biology are among the strongest and most popular majors; Other standout programs include public policy, mathematics, and environmental studies. Hamilton students fare extremely well in competition for prestigious national fellowships, capturing a shocking number when considering the small size of each graduating class. The Class of 2019 won seven Fulbright Scholarships, a Critical Language Scholarship, a National Science Foundation Graduate Research Fellowship, and a Watson Fellowship; six juniors also won Gilman Scholarships last year.

Outside the Classroom

Just about everyone lives in university housing—roughly 98 percent to be precise—leading to a cohesive atmosphere on the college's 1,350-acre campus. Greek life is strange in that it is nonresidential following a series of reforms over the past decade. While roughly one-quarter of Hamilton students belong to a fraternity or sorority, those organizations do not play nearly as prominent a role on campus as they once did. The school's twenty-nine teams (15 women's, 14 men's) compete as the Colonials in the New England Small College Athletic Conference (NESCAC) with other elite liberal arts schools Amherst, Bates, Bowdoin, Middlebury, Tufts, Wesleyan, and Williams. There are 550 student-athletes donning the buff-and-blue colors, accounting for 30 percent of the total student body. Add that total to the seventeen club and twelve intramural teams and it can feel like just about everyone is, technically, an athlete. Yet, with almost 200 active student organizations, there are plenty of ways to get involved outside of competitive team sports. The Hamilton Association for Volunteering, Outreach, and Charity (HAVOC) attracts hundreds of civic-minded students each year. The Hamilton Outing Club is the largest club on campus and organizes weekend camping/hiking/skiing trips to the Adirondacks as well as more exotic locations around the world. Amazing speakers come to town as part of the Sacerdote Great Names Series. In recent years Hamilton has hosted David Cameron, Bill and Hillary Clinton, Desmond Tutu, Jon Stewart, Colin Powell, and Jimmy Carter.

Career Services

The Maurice Horowitch Career Center is staffed by twelve professionals with expertise in career development, employer development, and health professions advising. That works out to a 155:1 student-to-advisor ratio, which is significantly stronger than most schools featured in this guide. Each student is assigned a career advisor who works with that student throughout the four-year journey. On the job-finding front, the center assists "students in developing skills in self-assessment, career exploration, resume preparation, interviewing, and uncovering job leads that will empower them to proactively manage their own careers." Yet, that is all steeped in the belief that career planning is a developmental process that unfolds over a lifetime.

The college does not host any large-scale career expos, but numerous employers do visit campus each year to host informational sessions or to recruit/interview candidates. Hamilton's Career Center does a superb job assisting students with finding opportunities for experiential learning. Nine in ten members of the class of 2019 had at least one internship over the course of the four years, and an incredible 70 percent had two. Alumni are highly supportive of current students and are willing to present on campus or offer job-shadowing experiences; 75 percent of alumni in a recent survey stated they would be happy to supply current students with career advice. Hamilton's 22,500 alumni rank in the top 1 percent when measured by the percentage that donate to their alma mater. Students can join Handshake to find internship and career possibilities and My Hamilton to network with alumni. Despite not hosting a notable career fair, the individualized attention and care that Hamilton shows its undergrads results in tremendously overall positive postgraduate and career outcomes.

Professional Outcomes

Examining the 477 graduates in Hamilton's class of 2018, an enviable 95 percent wasted no time landing jobs, graduate school acceptances, or fellowships. The most commonly entered industries were business (18 percent), education (13 percent), finance (12 percent), and science and technology (9 percent), health care (9 percent), and marketing/sales (7 percent). Among the employers welcoming multiple graduates aboard were Wayfair, Goldman Sachs, Teach for America, Dana Farber Cancer Institute, Kantar Consulting, and Deutsch Bank. New York City, Boston, and DC were the most popular destinations. Median compensation by midcareer (age thirty-four) is roughly $60,000, comparable to other elite Northeastern liberal arts colleges such as Middlebury, Tufts, and Colby.

Only 11 percent of 2018 graduates went directly into an advanced degree program. Of that group, 35 percent were studying a STEM field, 23 percent health care, and 6 percent went to law school. Law school acceptances over the past three years have included Georgetown, the University of Virginia, NYU, Penn, Yeshiva University, Washington University, Boston College, and Boston University. Medical school/veterinary school acceptances in that same period have included Columbia University, Penn, Temple, Tufts, SUNY, the University of Rochester, and Boston University. Other Hamilton graduates have been accepted into master's programs at Stanford, Cornell, USC, the University of Chicago, Vanderbilt, and others. Clearly, a degree from Hamilton opens doors to some of the world's top graduate/professional programs.

Admission

Hamilton saw 6,240 applicants for a coveted spot in the Class of 2022, but only 21 percent of that group made the cut, and only 36 percent of those admitted ultimately enrolled in the college. Most applicants provide SAT or ACT scores, but this institution is test-flexible and allows three AP/IB/SAT subject tests to be submitted in lieu of the SAT/ACT. The mid-50 percent range on the SAT was 1350-1510 and 31-34 on the ACT. The vast majority of students finished near the top of their high school class; 81 percent were in the top decile and 98 percent placed in the top quartile. Hamilton's admissions statistics have remained highly consistent over the past decade, so the level of selectivity should not come as a surprise to anyone.

The admissions committee's top priorities are an applicant's GPA, class rank, and the rigor of their coursework. Standardized test scores, essays, recommendations, character/personal qualities, and an interview comprise the second tier of key factors. Because Hamilton is competing for applicants with a host of other elite liberal arts schools, it favors those willing to commit via binding early decision; the acceptance rate for early applicants is more than double that (42 percent) of those in the regular pool (19 percent). Further, early acceptances make up 51 percent of the freshman class, leaving only a limited number of seats in the spring. To be a competitive applicant you should be in the top 10 percent of your graduating class and have standardized test scores in the 95th percentile or higher. If you're on the cusp and Hamilton is your top choice, definitely apply ED.

Worth Your Money?

If you have a genuine need for financial aid to make your education possible, Hamilton will usually answer the bell. In the 2018-19 academic year the college awarded over half of its undergraduates an average grant of $45,000, taking some of the sting out of the $70,000 sticker price for full cost of attendance. In 2008 Hamilton ceased offering merit aid to admitted applicants, a rare and admirable practice in the world of higher education. With 100 percent of its focus on making college affordable to lower- and middle-class students, higher-earning families can expect to pay full freight. Still, this school, with its minuscule class sizes, truly exceptional academics, and powerful network is, in the end, worth the money for most teens.

FINANCIAL
Institutional Type: Private
In-State Tuition: $54,080
Out-of-State Tuition: $54,080
Room & Board: $13,870
Required Fees: $540
Books & Supplies: $1,000

Avg. Need-Based Aid: $45,196
Avg. % of Need Met: 100%

Avg. Merit-Based Aid: $0
% Receiving Merit-Based Aid: 0%

Avg. Cumulative Debt: $20,582
% of Students Borrowing: 44%

CAREER
Who Recruits
1. Merrill Lynch
2. NERA Economic Consulting
3. Isaacson Miller, Inc.
4. Teach for America
5. Kantar Consulting

Notable Internships
1. Credit Suisse
2. CNBC
3. UBS

Top Industries
1. Business
2. Education
3. Operations
4. Media
5. Finance

Top Employers
1. Morgan Stanley
2. Goldman Sachs
3. Google
4. Wayfair
5. Citi

Where Alumni Work
1. New York City
2. Boston
3. Washington, DC
4. San Francisco
5. United Kingdom

Median Earnings
College Scorecard (Early Career): $60,200
EOP (Early Career): $60,300
PayScale (Mid-Career): $108,100

RANKINGS
Forbes: 59
Money: 177
U.S. News: 14 (T), Liberal Arts Colleges
Wall Street Journal/THE: 59 (T)
Washington Monthly: 19, Liberal Arts Colleges

#CollegesWorthYourMoney

Harvard University

Cambridge, Massachusetts | Admissions Phone: 617-495-1551

ADMISSION
Admission Rate: 5%
Admission Rate - Men: 5%
Admission Rate - Women: 5%
EA Admission Rate: 15%
ED Admission Rate: Not Offered
Admission Rate (5-Year Trend): -1%
ED Admission Rate (5-Year Trend): Not Offered
% of Admits Attending (Yield): 82%
Transfer Admission Rate: 1%

Offered Wait List: N/A
Accepted Wait List: N/A
Admitted Wait List: N/A

SAT Reading/Writing (Middle 50%): 720-780
SAT Math (Middle 50%): 740-800
ACT Composite (Middle 50%): 33-35
Testing Policy: ACT/SAT Required
SAT Superscore: Yes
ACT Superscore: No

% Graduated in Top 10% of HS Class: 94%
% Graduated in Top 25% of HS Class: 99%
% Graduated in Top 50% of HS Class: 100%

ENROLLMENT
Total Undergraduate Enrollment: 6,788
% Part-Time: 0%
% Male: 51%
% Female: 49%
% Out-of-State: 84%
% Fraternity: Not Offered
% Sorority: Not Offered
% On-Campus (Freshman): 99%
% On-Campus (All Undergraduate): 97%

% African-American: 8%
% Asian: 20%
% Hispanic: 11%
% White: 38%
% Other: 7%
% Race or Ethnicity Unknown: 2%
% International: 13%
% Low-Income: 15%

ACADEMICS
Student-to-Faculty Ratio: 7:1
% of Classes Under 20: 72%
% of Classes Under 40: 87%
% Full-Time Faculty: 85%
% Full-Time Faculty w/ Terminal Degree: 94%

Top Programs
Biology
Chemistry
Economics
Mathematics
Political Science
Physics
Psychology
Statistics

Retention Rate: 98%
4-Year Graduation Rate: 87%
6-Year Graduation Rate: 98%

Curricular Flexibility: Somewhat Flexible
Academic Rating: ★★★★★

Inside the Classroom

The oldest university in the United States, founded 140 years before the United States itself was even a concept, it is also the most iconic and, in many ways, revered institution of higher learning. Worldwide, Harvard is the envy of other universities and the dream destination for countless teenage geniuses and overachievers. For 6,800 young people, the Ivy League university in Cambridge, Massachusetts, is their reality, and learning from Nobel Laureates, Pulitzer Prize winners, and global leaders in every field is an everyday occurrence.

There are fifty undergraduate fields of study referred to as concentrations; many are interdisciplinary. Nearly 3,900 courses are on the menu, so learning options are extensive. Core requirements are minimal outside of expository writing, which all freshmen must conquer, proficiency in a foreign language (which must be achieved by the end of sophomore year), and a trek through the program in general education. The latter requirement ensures that undergrads are exposed to four main areas: aesthetics and culture, ethics and civics; histories, societies, and individuals; and science and technology in society. Roughly half of students complete some type of senior thesis, but there are no requirements in that area.

Even with a graduate population of almost 14,000 to cater to, undergraduate class sizes still tend to be on the smaller side with 42 percent of sections having single-digit enrollments and 72 percent being capped at nineteen. Graduates report an 82 percent satisfaction rate with the experience within their academic concentration. Summer research experiences are taken advantage of by 38 percent of the student body. Approximately 60 percent of students study abroad at a number of locations in South America, Africa, Europe, or Asia.

Economics, government, and computer science are the three most popular areas of concentration at Harvard. Those programs, along with ones in biology, chemistry, physics, math, statistics, sociology, history, English, and psychology all sit atop most departmental ranking lists. The university also occupies the top position in the all-time Rhodes Scholar rankings with 347 to its credit, more than the combined total from Stanford, Penn, Dartmouth, Brown, MIT, Cornell, and Columbia. Other prestigious postgraduate fellowships are awarded to Harvard students with regularity including the Fulbright, which was captured by sixteen members of the Class of 2018. The list of all-time alumni accolades could go on forever and includes ninety-six Nobel Laureates and eight US presidents.

Outside the Classroom

Possessing a bottomless endowment, the school never needs to cut corners on any programs, campus infrastructure, or amenities—and it shows. Freshmen live together at a centralized campus location adjacent to the famed Harvard Yard and then, as sophomores, move into one of twelve stately, upper-class houses, each with its own set of traditions and sense of community. Greek life, once thriving, has taken a dip in recent years after university officials enacted new regulations to deter membership in single-sex clubs. Students who participate forfeit eligibility for leadership positions in athletics or student government and will not be recommended for prestigious scholarships. Fortunately, a bevy of other social clubs exist in the form of 450 student-run organizations including the history-rich Hasty Pudding Club and the Phillips Brooks House Association that runs eighty-six volunteer organizations. Of course, studying is also a popular "hobby," and the Harvard Library is the largest academic library in the world and boasts a staff of nearly 800. The Harvard Crimson is a premier college newspaper with a long and storied history—Franklin Roosevelt and John F. Kennedy are among its alums—and The Harvard Lampoon is one of the world's oldest humor magazines, one that has helped launch talents ranging from John Updike to Conan O'Brien. Athletics also play a prominent role in Harvard's culture, both past and present, as the school fields forty NCAA Division I sports teams, evenly split between men's and women's squads. Cambridge itself is a bustling hub of culture, nightlife, and entertainment. Downtown Boston is only a twelve-minute ride away on the city's easily accessible public transit system.

Career Services

The Center for Career Development (CCD) has nineteen professional staff members (excluding students, assistants, and IT staff) who are dedicated to tasks including employer relations, career counseling, and summer funding opportunities. The 352:1 student-to-advisor ratio is about average compared to other schools featured in this guide. Yet, the closer you look into Harvard's career services, locating another "average" feature is a nearly impossible task.

The CCD hosts more than 300 events annually that are attended by 9,600 students. It also organizes twenty independent career fairs, each targeting a particular sector that attracts just under 6,000 net attendees. The OCS logs 6,700 advising appointments per year and manages to engage with 70 percent of the total undergraduate student body. Crimson Careers, the office's online database, posts 8,000+ jobs/internships from thousands of unique employers. On-campus recruiting occurred on a regular basis with 180 employers, including just about any big-name company you can think of, conducting over 5,100 interviews on site in Cambridge. More than three-quarters of students participate in a summer internship during their four years of study. In short, career services are what you would expect from America's preeminent university—exceptional.

Harvard University

E-mail: college@fas.harvard.edu | Website: www.college.harvard.edu

Professional Outcomes

The Crimson class of 2018 saw 15 percent of students head directly into graduate/professional school. Of the 65 percent of graduates entering the world of work, 18 percent were entering the financial services field, another 18 percent were entering the world of consulting, and technology/engineering attracted 14 percent. Over 1,000 Harvard alumni presently work for Google and over 500 for Microsoft, McKinsey & Company, and Goldman Sachs. More than 250 are employed at Amazon, Facebook, and Bain & Company. Postgraduation, Harvard students tend to cluster in three main states—New York, California, and Massachusetts. Those three states collectively reel in 57 percent of newly minted alumni. Remuneration is excellent with 53 percent of graduates reporting starting salaries over $70k and 11 percent taking home $110k+ in base pay. By midcareer, grads have the third highest median salaries in the Ivy League.

Turning our attention to those moving on to graduate school, Harvard grads with at least a 3.5 GPA typically enjoy acceptance rates into medical school of 90 percent or greater, demolishing the national average. Harvard grads tend to trade one high prestige school for another when pursuing an advanced degree. Many also stay close to home—Harvard Medical School (HMS), Harvard Law School, and the Graduate School of Arts & Sciences all accept more Harvard College graduates than those from any other single institution. It is estimated that approximately one-fifth of the HMS student body already spent four years in Cambridge as an undergraduate.

Admission

Harvard's admission rate for the Class of 2022 was 4.6 percent, an all-time low. Applicants fare better in the early action round that sports a 14.5 percent acceptance rate; the regular round rate is an almost comically low 2.9 percent. This was the first year in school history that the overall percentage of admitted students dipped below 5 percent. For historical context, at the turn of the millennium, 12 percent of applicants were welcomed aboard. The mid-50 percent SAT range for enrolled freshmen in 2018-19 was 1460-1590; over 85 percent of students scored above a 700 on each portion of the exam. It's not shocking that 94 percent of students admitted earned a place in their high school class's top decile. An insanely high number—84 percent—of admitted students elect to enroll. In other words, Harvard is second choice for few students.

The admissions staff does not rank any factor as being "very important" or even "important." All of the usual factors—grades, SATs, essays, and so on—are "considered." Demonstrated interest is not considered, which is unsurprising in light of the aforementioned yield rate. Legacy students comprise roughly one-third of the student body and enjoy an acceptance rate five times that of non-legacy applicants. For information about the role of race in admissions at Harvard, simply consult any newspaper. Getting into Harvard is the subject of plenty of (mostly awful) movies for a reason—it is a mammoth task set against harrowing odds. Even valedictorians with perfect test scores are not immune from rejection. However, impeccable credentials of that nature will at least allow you the opportunity to roll the dice with a realistic chance of success.

Worth Your Money?

Asking if Harvard is worth the money is a bit like John C. Reilly's character in Stepbrothers, Dale Doback, asking if bonito fish are big. Yes, Dale, bonito fish are big, and Harvard is worth the $78,300 annual cost of attendance. Merit aid barely exists at the university but, thanks to a $38 billion endowment, the 54 percent of the undergraduate population that is eligible for financial aid sees 100 percent of its need met; the total annual value is an extremely generous $57,000. Harvard is one of the rare schools where the average graduate's salary exceeds the annual cost of attendance, so even if you did have to take out loans to attend, it would be more than worth the expense.

FINANCIAL
Institutional Type: Private
In-State Tuition: $47,730
Out-of-State Tuition: $47,730
Room & Board: $17,682
Required Fees: $4,195
Books & Supplies: $1,000

Avg. Need-Based Aid: $56,771
Avg. % of Need Met: 100%

Avg. Merit-Based Aid: $0
% Receiving Merit-Based Aid: 0%

Avg. Cumulative Debt: $13,372
% of Students Borrowing: 17%

CAREER
Who Recruits
1. Putnam Investments
2. Akuna Capital
3. Atlantic Media
4. Vertica
5. Environmental Defense Fund

Notable Internships
1. McKinsey & Company
2. NASA Jet Propulsion Laboratory
3. Jane Street Capital

Top Industries
1. Business
2. Education
3. Research
4. Operations
5. Media

Top Employers
1. Google
2. Microsoft
3. Goldman Sachs
4. McKinsey & Company
5. IBM

Where Alumni Work
1. Boston
2. New York City
3. San Francisco
4. Washington, DC
5. Los Angeles

Median Earnings
College Scorecard (Early Career): $89,700
EOP (Early Career): $81,500
PayScale (Mid-Career): $146,800

RANKINGS
Forbes: 1
Money: 14
U.S. News: 2, National Universities
Wall Street Journal/THE: 1
Washington Monthly: 2, National Universities

#CollegesWorthYourMoney

Harvey Mudd College

Claremont, California | Admissions Phone: 909-621-8011

ADMISSION
Admission Rate: 14%
Admission Rate - Men: 10%
Admission Rate - Women: 24%
EA Admission Rate: Not Offered
ED Admission Rate: 19%
Admission Rate (5-Year Trend): -5%
ED Admission Rate (5-Year Trend): -3%
% of Admits Attending (Yield): 39%
Transfer Admission Rate: 7%

Offered Wait List: 509
Accepted Wait List: 327
Admitted Wait List: 0

SAT Reading/Writing (Middle 50%): 720-760
SAT Math (Middle 50%): 770-800
ACT Composite (Middle 50%): 34-34
Testing Policy: ACT/SAT Required
SAT Superscore: Yes
ACT Superscore: Yes

% Graduated in Top 10% of HS Class: 87%
% Graduated in Top 25% of HS Class: 98%
% Graduated in Top 50% of HS Class: 100%

ENROLLMENT
Total Undergraduate Enrollment: 889
% Part-Time: 0%
% Male: 51%
% Female: 49%
% Out-of-State: 56%
% Fraternity: Not Offered
% Sorority: Not Offered
% On-Campus (Freshman): 100%
% On-Campus (All Undergraduate): 98%

% African-American: 3%
% Asian: 19%
% Hispanic: 20%
% White: 31%
% Other: 11%
% Race or Ethnicity Unknown: 6%
% International: 10%
% Low-Income: 16%

ACADEMICS
Student-to-Faculty Ratio: 8:1
% of Classes Under 20: 57%
% of Classes Under 40: 93%
% Full-Time Faculty: 88%
% Full-Time Faculty w/ Terminal Degree: 99%

Top Programs
Biology
Chemistry
Computer Science
Engineering
Mathematical and Computational Biology
Mathematics and Statistics
Physics

Retention Rate: 97%
4-Year Graduation Rate: 85%
6-Year Graduation Rate: 92%

Curricular Flexibility: Somewhat Flexible
Academic Rating: ★★★★★

Inside the Classroom

To the average college-bound teen, Harvey Mudd may not have the name recognition that other schools of its caliber enjoy. While it may sound a bit like a Depression-era comic strip, the smallest of the colleges within the illustrious Claremont Consortium (Pomona, Claremont McKenna, Scripps, and Pitzer are the others) is routinely rated one of the best liberal arts colleges in the entire country and one of the top STEM institutions in the world.

A little under 900 undergraduate students occupy this tiny 33-acre campus; however, it is surrounded by the aforementioned affiliated colleges, giving the experience a less claustrophobic feel. Only six majors are offered: biology, chemistry, computer science, engineering, mathematics, and physics. All are incredibly strong. Students also have the option to combine certain disciplines into what amounts to a double major. In preparing a small army of future engineers and scientists, Harvey Mudd has been at the forefront of preaching a balanced education. The school requires a significant amount of coursework in the humanities, backing up its stated belief that "technology divorced from humanity is worse than no technology at all."

Class sizes are not always as small as the school itself. While 57 percent of courses have an enrollment under twenty, another 37 percent enroll between twenty and thirty-nine students. Regardless, Mudd prides itself on offering graduate-level research opportunities and experiential learning to all undergrads. The college backs up its philosophical stance with cold, hard cash, allocating three million dollars annually to facilitate student-faculty research. Students can participate during the school year or during the Summer Undergraduate Research Program that entails ten weeks of full-time laboratory work. The Clinic Program groups juniors and seniors and lets them work on a real-world problem for corporate or agency sponsors for 1,200 to 1,500 hours over the course of one year. It is not uncommon for participants to end up with their name on a patent.

The college routinely produces winners of scholarships from the National Science Foundation, the Astronaut Scholarship Foundation, the Department of Energy, the Department of Defense, the Watson Fellowship, and the Mindlin Prize for Innovative Ideas in Science. The faculty also regularly receive accolades for their teaching. The National Science Foundation recognized the Chemistry Department as the top per capita producer of chemistry PhDs in the country.

Outside the Classroom

Campus life at Mudd is, in part, defined by the fact that you are not confined to one campus. After all, Pomona, Pitzer, Scripps, and CMC all share the same 560 acres of land, not to mention a whole lot else. For athletics, Harvey Mudd, Claremont, and Scripps combine forces to compete in twenty-one NCAA Division III men's and women's sports. Club and intramural sports from ultimate Frisbee, equestrian, and roller hockey to water polo are available as well. Both cross-consortium and Mudd-only clubs and activities are plentiful and diverse, ranging from a poker club to a lettuce-eating competition (seriously). With Los Angeles just a half-hour drive away, Claremont is located in close proximity to all of the restaurants, museums, theaters, and even Disneyland, if you so desire. Mudd's dorms are known for having district personalities, but one common thread is that the college is known, in general, to be a friendly and accepting place.

Career Services

HMC's Career Services Office has four full-time professional staff members working on grad school/career advising and employer recruitment. That equates to a 222:1 student-to-advisor ratio, which is among the best of any college featured in this guide. Career Services is highly accessible to students, and it even offers walk-in hours from 1 to 4 p.m. each week day. Staff members are more than happy to offer one-on-one attention, and students take advantage as the office held 891 sessions, just over one per student, in the 2017-18 school year.

Harvey Mudd hosts a Fall Software Fair, a Fall General STEM Fair, and a Spring Fair that can be attended by all members of the consortium, which can draw as many as 160+ employers per year. The three fairs draw almost 2,000 student participants per year. Companies that recruit on campus comprise a who's who of tech royalty: Google, Microsoft, Facebook, Space X, and Uber. In fact, many of those companies, along with other major corporations, conducted interviews on HMC's campus. Undergrads routinely land summer internships at an equally impressive array of technology companies. In examining the breakdown of where Mudd grads end up receiving job offers, there is a clear correlation with the employer relations efforts of the Career Services Office. Overall, HMC's career services earns top grades from the College Transitions staff.

Harvey Mudd College

E-mail: admission@hmc.edu | Website: www.hmc.edu

Professional Outcomes

The highest number of recent Harvey Mudd graduates is scooped up by the following companies (in order of representation): Google, Facebook, Microsoft, and Northrup Grumman. Across all graduating years, significant numbers of alumni also can be found at Apple, Raytheon, Intel, Boeing, and the NASA Jet Propulsion Laboratory. Software and technology is, by far, the career field of choice with aerospace a distant second. HMC grads end up in high-paying jobs that are directly related to their major as the 95 percent of seniors who report landing a job related to their college major confirms. The most common job titles held immediately out of college are software engineer, industrial engineer, and electrical engineer. Graduates average an impressive $87,500 starting salary, a phenomenal number even when accounting for the preponderance of STEM majors. By some measures, that is the highest graduate starting salary of any institution in the United States.

Many Harvey Mudd grads—close to one-quarter—go directly into graduate school programs. The highest number of 2018 grads pursued advanced degrees at the following institutions: Stanford (6), Cornell (5), USC (4), UC-Santa Barbara (2), Columbia (2), and the University of Washington (2). One student from the same class attended each of Harvard, Carnegie Mellon, Caltech, and Johns Hopkins. The most pursued graduate field of study at those elite schools are computer science, mathematics, physics, and engineering. A healthy 72 percent of those attending grad school are presently working toward a PhD.

Admission

A decade ago, over 30 percent of applicants to Harvey Mudd were accepted; five years ago, that number fell to 20 percent. In recent years HMC's admit rate has hovered in the 13 to 15 percent range; it was 15 percent for applicants aspiring to join the Class of 2022. However, it is important to note that the profile of the average accepted student has not changed significantly and, unlike many other elite colleges across the United States, the number of applicants has not skyrocketed in the past few years. Early decision applicants made up 39 percent of the acceptance pool, which means applying early may be a good idea if Mudd is your top choice. The ED rate was 19 percent, which was a touch better than the 14 percent encountered during the regular application round.

An overwhelming 87 percent of accepted applicants finished in the top 10 percent of their high school class, and just about everyone placed at least in the top 25 percent. Valedictorians and salutatorians make up an impressive 23 percent of the student body. Standardized test scores need to be high to garner serious consideration. The mid-50 percent range on standardized tests for freshmen in 2018-19 was 1490-1560 on the SAT and 34-35 on the ACT. HMC is one of those rare schools that requires two SAT subject tests in addition to the SAT/ACT. One of those two tests must be the Math Level 2 exam on which accepted students typically score a 750 or better. The school lists essays and recommendations as being "very important" factors in admissions decisions. In sum, Harvey Mudd is not a school that you add to your college list on a whim. It is an institution for those with a proven track record within the realm of science and engineering. Excellent grades in AP/IB course work, along with standardized test scores well above the 95th percentile, are just about prerequisites for serious consideration.

Worth Your Money?

At almost $77,000 per year, a degree from Harvey Mudd won't come cheap, but the majority of undergraduates do not pay the full cost. On the merit aid front, the college awards an average of $15k to 44 percent of the student body. Even better, 49 percent of attendees see 100 percent of their financial need met, which averages out to $45k in aid each year, knocking the total cost down closer to state school levels. As a result, HMC helps many students from lower- and middle-income families attend the school. While that does result in a higher-than-average postgraduate debt load, alumni enjoy such strong job prospects that paying back loans will not be overly worrisome. No matter your circumstances, if you have a chance to go to Mudd, start packing your bags.

FINANCIAL
Institutional Type: Private
In-State Tuition: $56,331
Out-of-State Tuition: $56,331
Room & Board: $18,127
Required Fees: $545
Books & Supplies: $800

Avg. Need-Based Aid: $45,244
Avg. % of Need Met: 100%

Avg. Merit-Based Aid: $14,678
% Receiving Merit-Based Aid: 44%

Avg. Cumulative Debt: $31,594
% of Students Borrowing: 46%

CAREER
Who Recruits
1. Palantir
2. The Aerospace Corporation
3. Oracle
4. Boeing
5. Farmers Insurance

Notable Internships
1. Google
2. Salesforce
3. PayPal

Top Industries
1. Engineering
2. Research
3. Business
4. Education
5. information Technology

Top Employers
1. Google
2. Microsoft
3. Apple
4. Northrop Grumman
5. Facebook

Where Alumni Work
1. Los Angeles
2. San Francisco
3. Seattle
4. San Diego
5. New York City

Median Earnings
College Scorecard (Early Career): $88,800
EOP (Early Career): $82,400
PayScale (Mid-Career): $158,200

RANKINGS
Forbes: 23
Money: 136
U.S. News: 23, Liberal Arts Colleges
Wall Street Journal/THE: N/A
Washington Monthly: 48, National Universities

#CollegesWorthYourMoney

Haverford College

Haverford, Pennsylvania | Admissions Phone: 610-896-1350

Inside the Classroom

Serving 1,353 remarkably accomplished undergraduate students, Haverford College, situated on Philly's ritzy Main Line, has 186 years of history and a reputation as one of the best liberal arts colleges in the country. Affectionately known as "The Ford," the college is part of the Tri-College Consortium with nearby Bryn Mawr and Swarthmore, which also happen to be among the crème de la crème of liberal arts schools. Students can take courses at those two schools as well through Penn's Wharton School of Business via an additional alliance known as the Quaker Consortium.

Haverford offers twenty-nine majors, thirty-one minors, thirteen concentrations, and eleven consortium programs—areas of study that can be pursued at partner campuses. All students must fulfill a first-year writing requirement, a two-course language requirement, and a quantitative or symbolic reasoning requirement, and students need to take an uncredited physical education course prior to their junior year. Every student produces a senior thesis, a work of original research/scholarship under the close supervision of a faculty member. Teens seeking a relatively open curriculum that encourages exploration and the pursuit of one's unique passions will adore Haverford.

The school's 9:1 student-to-faculty ratio and exclusive emphasis on undergraduate education leads to exceptionally intimate classes, 39 percent of which have fewer than ten students, and 76 percent have fewer than twenty. Plenty of summer research opportunities exist in which students can work alongside faculty, and some STEM students conduct and present original research through the Undergraduate Science Research Symposium. The study abroad program has a 49 percent participation rate, and students can choose from seventy-six programs in thirty-four countries.

The most popular areas of study at Haverford include the social sciences (26 percent), physical sciences (13 percent), psychology (10 percent), biology (9 percent), mathematics (8 percent), foreign language (7 percent), and computer science (5 percent). All majors are highly respected in the eyes of graduate institutions and potential employers, but programs in English, physics, and political science receive especially high marks. Science majors and those on a premed track gain acceptance to prestigious PhD programs and medical schools at an eye-popping rate. Graduates are also no strangers to competitive national awards/fellowships. In the school's history it claims twenty Rhodes Scholars, 104 Fulbright Scholars, sixty-three Watson Fellows, forty-eight National Science Foundation Fellows, and two Goldwater Scholars.

Outside the Classroom

Ninety-eight percent of students live on this stunningly beautiful 216-acre campus; first-years are assigned to one of four residence halls. There are no fraternities or sororities at Haverford. Even with such a tiny student body, Haverford fields twenty-three varsity sports teams that compete in NCAA Division III. Combined with the seven club sports teams, 53 percent of undergrads participate in athletics. The college's 145 student-run organizations include an array of pre-professional and service-oriented groups as well as plenty of recreational/performance options such as the Martial Arts Alliance, contemporary dance, and a number of a cappella groups. HAVOC is an outdoor adventure group that has a strong membership. The mock trial team placed second in the nation in 2017. Fellow Tri-Co member schools Bryn Mawr and Swarthmore offer plenty of additional chances for social connection, both formal and informal. All that the city of Philadelphia has to offer is only eight miles away. The Main Line area itself offers plenty of dining, cultural, and entertainment choices. The college's Honor Code and governing Honor Council are central to the life at Haverford. Tenets of the code include un-proctored exams, no RAs in dorms, and tolerance of people of all backgrounds and orientations.

Career Services

The Center for Career & Professional Advising (CCPA) employs four individuals who specialize in career counseling, pre-law advising, and health professions advising; another four staff members are part time. With a 338:1 student-to-advisor ratio, Haverford compares favorably against most of the other colleges featured in this guide. The resources are deployed efficiently as in a given year the CCPA engages in 800+ advising sessions, reaches over 80 percent of the student body in some capacity, and makes a great effort to reach first-year students. In fact, 94 percent of freshmen report engaging with the office. The level of personalized advising is also evident by the annual number of resume critiques, 600+.

In hosting 150 information sessions and workshops per year, there are almost daily opportunities for students to sharpen their pre-professional skills and connect with potential employers. Large- scale career fairs are typically a joint effort of the Tri-College Consortium, along with Bryn Mawr and Swarthmore. Haverford alone draws more than one hundred employers to campus for its career fairs. The CCPA funds more than 140 internships per year and helps facilitate 190 on-campus interviews. Additionally, the college has more than 1,000 alumni association volunteers who provide hundreds of job-shadowing and externship experiences to current students. The CCPA delivers ample personalized attention to undergraduates and does an unsurpassed job assisting students with acceptance into top graduate schools.

E-mail: admission@haverford.edu | Website: www.haverford.edu

Professional Outcomes

Six months after leaving Haverford 63 percent of the Class of 2018 had found employment, 18 percent had enrolled in graduate school, and 9 percent were still job hunting. Among the employed, education was the most common industry (22 percent) followed by business (12 percent), the sciences (10 percent), community services (9 percent), and health care (9 percent). Employers hiring multiple recent Haverford grads include Google, The Vanguard Group, IBM, Booz Allen Hamilton, Amazon, the National Institutes of Health, and the Children's Hospital of Philadelphia. Midcareer salaries are comparable to other elite liberal arts schools such as Wesleyan, Colby, Swarthmore, and Bates; the median income at age thirty-four is $57,200. Staying in the Philly metro area is the number one choice of alumni. New York City, various international destinations, Boston, and DC are next in popularity.

Almost a quarter of Haverford grads continue to advanced degree programs right out of undergrad. In 2018, the most commonly entered fields of study were STEM (41 percent), medicine (18 percent), law (16 percent), and arts and humanities (12 percent). Graduate schools accepting the highest number of recent alumni include Yale, Columbia, the University of Chicago, Penn, Harvard, Johns Hopkins, and the University of North Carolina at Chapel Hill. Those applying to medical school have extraordinary success as the college's 90 percent rate of acceptance from 2015-18 more than doubles the national average of 42 percent. Haverford undergrads average MCAT scores in the 85th percentile of all test takers. In the last three years 100 percent of those applying to law school received at least one letter of acceptance. Of that cohort, 32 percent were accepted into a top fifteen law school, and 94 percent had found homes at a top one hundred law school.

Admission

Admissions for a place in the Class of 2022 was the most selective round in the school's history; a record 4,682 applications were received, and only 18.7 percent were accepted. A staggering 95 percent of enrolled freshmen earned a place in the top 10 percent of their high school class and sported a mid-50 percent test score of 1370-1530 on the SAT and 32-34 on the ACT. Five years ago, the acceptance rate was a slightly higher 22 percent, but the academic profile of the average admitted applicant was similar to that of a 2018 enrollee.

According to the admissions committee the most important factors in the decision-making process are rigor of coursework, GPA, essays, recommendations, extracurricular activities, and character/personal qualities. Class rank, standardized test scores, talent/ability, work experience, and volunteer work make up the second rung of considered data points. Items like the interview, first-generation status, or legacy status are given a lesser degree of consideration. Applying early decision can be a significant advantage. In the most recent cycle ED applicants were accepted at a far more generous 44 percent clip and comprised 55 percent of that year's incoming freshmen. Even with a self-selecting applicant pool that results in modest application numbers, Haverford is an exceptionally difficult school to gain acceptance into. A near 19 percent acceptance rate is almost misleadingly encouraging, and applicants sizing up their chances will be better informed by the high level of academic achievement displayed by successful applicants. Applying ED should be given serious consideration if Haverford is among your top choices.

Worth Your Money?

Haverford's annual cost of attendance is among the highest in the country at $76,414 but, on the positive end, it meets 100 percent of demonstrated need for those who qualify. The total average annual grant is over $52,000, helping make the school affordable for those not in the highest income brackets. However, an estimated 40 percent of attending students come from families in the top 5 percent of annual income nationwide and, typically, those individuals will pay full price. If you can afford the upfront costs, or if you receive a sufficiently sized financial aid award, becoming part of this elite institution will likely prove worth the investment in the long run.

FINANCIAL
Institutional Type: Private
In-State Tuition: $56,200
Out-of-State Tuition: $56,200
Room & Board: $16,770
Required Fees: $752
Books & Supplies: $1,194

Avg. Need-Based Aid: $51,777
Avg. % of Need Met: 100%

Avg. Merit-Based Aid: $0
% Receiving Merit-Based Aid: 0%

Avg. Cumulative Debt: $11,000
% of Students Borrowing: 37%

CAREER
Who Recruits
1. Chatham Financial
2. FDIC
3. Janney Montgomery Scott
4. Boston Consulting Group
5. Analysis Group

Notable Internships
1. Boston Consulting Group
2. Spotify
3. U.S. House of Representatives

Top Industries
1. Education
2. Business
3. Research
4. Healthcare
5. Media

Top Employers
1. Google
2. Children's Hospital of Philadelphia
3. Facebook
4. US State Department
5. Deloitte

Where Alumni Work
1. New York City
2. Philadelphia
3. Washington, DC
4. Boston
5. San Francisco

Median Earnings
College Scorecard (Early Career): $60,700
EOP (Early Career): $57,200
PayScale (Mid-Career): $112,300

RANKINGS
Forbes: 49
Money: 126
U.S. News: 11, Liberal Arts Colleges
Wall Street Journal/THE: 39
Washington Monthly: 11, Liberal Arts Colleges

#CollegesWorthYourMoney

Hofstra University

Hempstead, New York | Admissions Phone: 516-463-6700

ADMISSION
Admission Rate: 63%
Admission Rate - Men: 58%
Admission Rate - Women: 67%
EA Admission Rate: 70%
ED Admission Rate: Not Offered
Admission Rate (5-Year Trend): +4%
ED Admission Rate (5-Year Trend): Not Offered
% of Admits Attending (Yield): 9%
Transfer Admission Rate: 63%

Offered Wait List: 143
Accepted Wait List: 45
Admitted Wait List: 24

SAT Reading/Writing (Middle 50%): 580-660
SAT Math (Middle 50%): 570-670
ACT Composite (Middle 50%): 24-30
Testing Policy: Test Optional
SAT Superscore: Yes
ACT Superscore: Yes

% Graduated in Top 10% of HS Class: 28%
% Graduated in Top 25% of HS Class: 49%
% Graduated in Top 50% of HS Class: 59%

ENROLLMENT
Total Undergraduate Enrollment: 6,701
% Part-Time: 6%
% Male: 45%
% Female: 55%
% Out-of-State: 38%
% Fraternity: 8%
% Sorority: 10%
% On-Campus (Freshman): 65%
% On-Campus (All Undergraduate): 43%

% African-American: 9%
% Asian: 11%
% Hispanic: 12%
% White: 55%
% Other: 3%
% Race or Ethnicity Unknown: 3%
% International: 6%
% Low-Income: 23%

ACADEMICS
Student-to-Faculty Ratio: 13:1
% of Classes Under 20: 48%
% of Classes Under 40: 95%
% Full-Time Faculty: 39%
% Full-Time Faculty w/ Terminal Degree: 93%

Top Programs
Accounting
Criminology
Finance
Journalism
Performing Arts
Public Relations
Radio, Television & Film

Retention Rate: 82%
4-Year Graduation Rate: 52%
6-Year Graduation Rate: 63%

Curricular Flexibility: Somewhat Flexible
Academic Rating: ★★★

Inside the Classroom

Looking at Hofstra University today, one sees a private university of 6,700 undergraduate students spread across a gorgeous and imposing Long Island campus. Its roots as a commuter school for Long Island residents have long since faded from view as the student body is now comprised of almost 50 percent out-of-state and international students. While still a common safety school choice for high-achieving Northeasterners aiming for schools like Fordham and Boston University, Hofstra's national reputation is undoubtedly on the rise. It remains an excellent academic institution with tremendous resources to help students find their way to a successful career. Even better, it also is accessible to students with imperfect academic profiles—at least for now.

There are 160 programs for undergraduates spread across the various colleges housing liberal arts, engineering, business, communications, and nursing/health professions. While the core curriculum varies from school to school, most Hofstra students are required to complete coursework in the humanities, natural sciences, history, philosophy, foreign language, quantitative reasoning, two introductory writing courses, and two advanced writing courses. In total there are thirty-three credits worth of distributional requirements for students in the College of Liberal Arts and Sciences. First-year seminars are courses reserved for freshmen that enroll nineteen or fewer students, focus on a specific topic of interest, and help new students acclimate to college-level work.

The average undergraduate class size is twenty, and the student-faculty ratio is a favorable 13-to-1. The great bulk of courses enroll between eleven and twenty-nine students; 11 percent are single-digit enrollment courses, and only 2 percent of sections contain more than fifty students. Opportunities to participate in undergraduate research are managed by each department separately. Students in the Honors College have an easier time procuring opportunities as supervised independent research is built into the program. Full-length study abroad opportunities are offered in locations that include Amsterdam, China, Florence, Rome, and Ireland. Many students prefer short-term international sessions offered in January (three weeks) or summer (five weeks).

The Zarb School of Business draws almost a quarter of the student body for good reason; it is a well-regarded business school with strong connections to many major banks and consulting firms. It also boasts one of the nation's best simulated trading rooms. The Lawrence Herbert School of Communication is widely known in the media industry, and Hofstra students enter in large numbers—15 percent of the total degrees conferred are in communication/journalism. Health professions, social sciences, and psychology are third, fourth, and fifth in popularity, respectively. Winning national postgraduate fellowships is not a major focus of Hofstra seniors. They have won an occasional Fulbright Scholarship, a Critical Language Scholarship in 2018, and Gilman Scholarship in 2019.

Outside the Classroom

Only 65 percent of freshmen and roughly 45 percent of the overall undergraduate student body live on campus in one of thirty-five residence halls. There are traditional dorms as well as high-rise options that, collectively, offer single, double, triple, quad, and suite-style living options. Within the limits of the 240-acre campus are eighteen eateries, six theaters, an arboretum, bird sanctuary, and an art museum that houses 5,000 works and artifacts. Hofstra's gorgeous, tree-lined grounds are deservedly included on many "most beautiful campus" lists. The twenty-nine fraternities and sororities attract 8 percent of men and 10 percent of women, creating an atmosphere with a noticeable Greek presence, but not a suffocating one. The sports teams, for many years known as the Flying Dutchmen, now compete as the Pride at the NCAA Division I level in the Colonial Athletic Association. There are twenty-one varsity sports—ten men's and eleven women's teams. There are 200+ student-run clubs at Hofstra, including plenty of performance, cultural, or pre-professional options and a big-time collegiate radio station, WRHU, which also serves as the radio home of the National Hockey League's New York Islanders. Hempstead is not the safest area or most desirable part of town, but this is made up for by having an amenity-filled campus and being only a twenty-five-minute drive from famed Jones Beach in Long Island and, of course, being only a forty- to fifty-minute trip from all that New York City has to offer.

Career Services

Hofstra's Career Center is manned by eight professionals with expertise in career coaching, corporate outreach, and diversity and inclusion initiatives. That works out to an 838:1 student-to-advisor ratio, which is higher than the average school in this guide but not awful when compared to other midsize universities. The Fall Career and Internship Fair was attended by 130+ employers, and the center routinely offers in-person and online workshops, field trips to companies, networking events, and on-campus interview days with employers.

Drawing employers to campus and placing current students with big-name organizations is aided by the school's location and the tight connections that the Career Center has forged with New York City employers.

Hofstra's internship numbers for undergraduates are particularly strong. With the help of career services staff members, 73 percent of Hofstra students participate in at least one internship, and the average student completes 2.31 such experiences. Class of 2017 grads interned at hundreds of organizations including Berkshire Hathaway, Last Week Tonight with John Oliver, ABC News, and the Securities and Exchange Commission. Current students can also benefit from connecting with the 140,000 living alumni, 1,000 of whom are active volunteers for the school and more than willing to assist with career exploration and the job search.

Professional Outcomes

Within six months of exiting with their diplomas, 92 percent of Class of 2017 grads had found employment or a graduate school destination; within a year that figure rose to 99 percent, with 91 percent employed and 33 percent pursuing an advanced degree, which includes some overlap as many individuals were doing both. Northwell Health, the largest health care provider in New York State, is also the largest employer of Hofstra alumni. Other companies employing more than one hundred Flying Dutchmen/Pride alums include JPMorgan Chase, Citi, PwC, Morgan Stanley, EY, Deloitte, Estee Lauder, and NBC Universal. Among the Class of 2017, grads went on to a number of interesting careers with professional sports teams, major media outlets, and political groups. The median starting salary was $50,000 with 20 percent of the class bringing home less than $40k and 30 percent making over $60k. Just about everyone stays in the Greater New York City area with Boston, Philly, and DC picking up the crumbs.

Grad school is a common next step for those receiving their Hofstra degree as 33 percent enrolled within a year, and 44 percent planned to pursue further study within five years. Class of 2017 members matriculated into a wide array of graduate and professional schools including every SUNY and CUNY institution as well as many elite universities like Harvard, Yale, Carnegie Mellon, Northwestern, Rice, MIT, and Stanford. The school offers its undergraduates a 4+4 BS/MD option in conjunction with its own Zucker School of Medicine. Other medical schools attended by recent grads include the Albert Einstein College of Medicine, Icahn School of Medicine, and SUNY Downstate. There were eleven different law schools attended by Class of 2017 members with William & Mary highlighting an otherwise middling list.

Admission

Sixty-three percent of the 27,620 applicants for a spot in the Class of 2022 were accepted, but a minuscule 9 percent of those accepted actually enrolled in the university. Of those that became 2018-19 freshmen, 90 percent had over a 3.0 GPA, 28 percent were in top 10 percent of their high school class, and 59 percent were in top 25 percent. The average SAT score was 1238, and the average ACT score was 27. The mid-50 percent ranges were 1150 to 1330 on the SAT and 24 to 30 on the ACT. The university's degree of selectivity has remained constant in recent years. Acceptance rates and grades from the early 2010s are comparable to those today. Standardized test scores have risen, but much of that can be attributed to going test-optional (more on that in a moment).

The five factors viewed as the most important by the admissions committee are GPA, class rank, rigor of secondary school record, recommendations, and the essay. Hofstra went test-optional in 2014 but, presently, three-quarters of applicants still submit standardized test scores. Interviews are listed as "important" but are not a required part of the process. Extracurricular activities, talent/ability, and character/personal qualities also play a major factor in the process. For a school that has such a low yield rate (the percent of accepted students that enroll), it is surprising that it does not offer a binding early decision option, but it does offer early action. Hofstra remains a realistic option for B students who take some advanced coursework in high school.

Worth Your Money?

Hofstra is an expensive school, registering a $63,000 annual cost of attendance, but it is generous with both need-based and merit aid as the average grants in both areas are approximately $20k-23k. The Long Island location can make this school worth the money for those with a clear plan of how to take advantage of the school's New York City connections. Students without a preprofessional focus and for whom costs are a concern should also consider more affordable options.

FINANCIAL
Institutional Type: Private
In-State Tuition: $44,640
Out-of-State Tuition: $44,640
Room & Board: $15,708
Required Fees: $1,060
Books & Supplies: $1,000

Avg. Need-Based Aid: $23,169
Avg. % of Need Met: 70%

Avg. Merit-Based Aid: $20,251
% Receiving Merit-Based Aid: 36%

Avg. Cumulative Debt: N/A
% of Students Borrowing: 63%

CAREER
Who Recruits
1. Cox Media Group
2. Stanley Black & Decker
3. Raytheon
4. Partners Healtcare
5. Boston Children's Hospital

Notable Internships
1. The Tonight Show
2. The Carlyle Group
3. CNN NY News Bureau

Top Industries
1. Business
2. Education
3. Operations
4. Sales
5. Finance

Top Employers
1. Northwell Health
2. JPMorgan Chase
3. Citi
4. Morgan Stanley
5. PwC

Where Alumni Work
1. New York City
2. Boston
3. Philadelphia
4. Washington, DC
5. Los Angeles

Median Earnings
College Scorecard (Early Career): $53,100
EOP (Early Career): $55,700
PayScale (Mid-Career): $110,400

RANKINGS
Forbes: 292
Money: 609
U.S. News: 162, National Universities
Wall Street Journal/THE: 228
Washington Monthly: 379, National Universities

#CollegesWorthYourMoney

Chicago, Illinois | Admissions Phone: 312-567-3025

ADMISSION
Admission Rate: 58%
Admission Rate - Men: 57%
Admission Rate - Women: 61%
EA Admission Rate: Not Offered
ED Admission Rate: Not Offered
Admission Rate (5-Year Trend): +1%
ED Admission Rate (5-Year Trend): Not Offered
% of Admits Attending (Yield): 21%
Transfer Admission Rate: 58%

Offered Wait List: Not Offered
Accepted Wait List: Not Offered
Admitted Wait List: Not Offered

SAT Reading/Writing (Middle 50%): 600-680
SAT Math (Middle 50%): 620-720
ACT Composite (Middle 50%): 26-31
Testing Policy: ACT/SAT Required
SAT Superscore: Yes
ACT Superscore: Yes

% Graduated in Top 10% of HS Class: 50%
% Graduated in Top 25% of HS Class: 78%
% Graduated in Top 50% of HS Class: 95%

ENROLLMENT
Total Undergraduate Enrollment: 3,026
% Part-Time: 8%
% Male: 69%
% Female: 31%
% Out-of-State: 25%
% Fraternity: 7%
% Sorority: 6%
% On-Campus (Freshman): 73%
% On-Campus (All Undergraduate): 43%

% African-American: 5%
% Asian: 15%
% Hispanic: 16%
% White: 35%
% Other: 4%
% Race or Ethnicity Unknown: 3%
% International: 17%
% Low-Income: 34%

ACADEMICS
Student-to-Faculty Ratio: 12:1
% of Classes Under 20: 46%
% of Classes Under 40: 84%
% Full-Time Faculty: 56%
% Full-Time Faculty w/ Terminal Degree: 82%

Top Programs
Aerospace Engineering
Architecture
Computer Science
Finance
Mechanical Engineering
Information Technology and Management

Retention Rate: 90%
4-Year Graduation Rate: 37%
6-Year Graduation Rate: 72%

Curricular Flexibility: Somewhat Flexible
Academic Rating: ★★★

Inside the Classroom

A rare school that educates more advanced degree-seekers than undergraduate students, the Illinois Institute of Technology—traditionally referred to as IIT but rebranded in 2001 as Illinois Tech—is a private research university with roughly 3,000 undergrads and 40+ undergraduate majors, mostly in the realms of engineering, business, computer science, and architecture.

Located on Chicago's South Side, this school has a large international presence with forty-eight countries represented as well as a phenomenally high number of Pell Grant recipients as 30 percent of undergraduates present with serious financial need. This is significant because Illinois Tech has a reputation not just for producing grads who earn excellent salaries but for facilitating social and economic mobility as well.

Undergraduates study in one of six undergraduate divisions: the Armour College of Engineering, the College of Architecture, the College of Science, the Lewis College of Human Sciences, the School of Applied Technology, or the Stuart School of Business. The university has four learning goals associated with its core curriculum: (1) commitment to positive change in their communities, nations, and the world; (2) the ability to think critically and viewing problems as opportunities for innovation; (3) the ability to collaborate professionally and ethically; and (4) communicate effectively. Toward those aims, one must take three courses in the humanities, three in the social or behavioral sciences, three in science or engineering, one computer science course, and complete thirty-six hours of coursework with a substantial focus on oral or written communication. A 600 SAT reading score will get you out of introductory writing.

The student-to-faculty ratio is 12:1, but with so many graduate students to serve, undergraduate course sections are not small across the board; rather, they vary from 20 percent of sections that boast a single-digit enrollment to the 16 percent of courses that enroll more than forty students. Yet, an Illinois Tech education provides many opportunities for students to have close contact with faculty. For example, the Interprofessional Projects (IPRO) Program features "teams of students from a variety of majors that develop solutions to real-world problems using design-centered methodology and innovative thinking." Completing two IPROs is a graduation requirement. The Elevate program connects students with undergraduate research and other experiential learning opportunities as early as freshman year. There are 42 study abroad programs in which IIT students can participate, although as with most technical institutions, the bulk of undergrads remain on campus for all four years.

The most popular major is computer science followed by architecture and mechanical engineering. Overall, 51 percent of the degrees conferred are in engineering, 17 percent in computer science, and 14 percent in architecture. The School of Applied Technology offers one of the most respected information technology programs in the country and serves as a pipeline to many top tech companies. The College of Architecture has a similarly sterling national reputation. Programs in engineering and computer science are also strong.

Outside the Classroom

Illinois Tech's 120-acre urban campus is home to only 43 percent of the undergraduate population; the majority of students live in university-owned housing and are graduate students. Freshmen and sophomores are required to live on campus, but commuters who live with their parents and transfers are often granted exemptions. There are two traditional dormitories and two "villages" that are collections of smaller residence halls. S.R. Crown Hall and the McCormick Tribune Campus Center are architecturally unique, and the campus as a whole sometimes cracks "most beautiful" lists. Many students self-identify as "nerds," and the rigorous academics and male-heavy population (only 37 percent of students are female) can limit social life. Greek life has a moderate presence on campus drawing 8 percent of men and 7 percent of women. There are seventeen varsity intercollegiate sports teams—nine men's and eight women's—many of which compete in NCAA Division III. More than 150 student-run organizations are available, and the BOG serves as a popular hub thanks to its free, eight-lane bowling alley and abundance of arcade games. Campus is only three miles south of downtown Chicago and about one mile from Guaranteed Rate Field where the Chicago White Sox play baseball. Plenty of bars, jazz clubs, museums, zoos, and an aquarium are a short distance from campus.

Career Services

The main Career Services Office at IIT consists of five professional employees, but the Stuart School of Business has its own separate office with three full-time employees bringing the school's total to eight career services professionals. That works out to a student-advisor ratio of 378:1, within the average range of schools profiled in the book. Freshmen are encouraged to begin working with a career counselor during their first semester. In addition to the professional staff members, eight peer counselors also are available to those looking to get the jump on vocational exploration.

Staff members are always willing to assist with "résumé and cover letter writing, networking advice, company research assistance, mock interviews, (and) dinner/business etiquette workshops." Two-day career fairs are held on campus each semester, and more than 150 employers attended the September 2018 fair alone, including industry giants Amazon, Goldman Sachs, NBCUniversal, and Grainger. The school claims 78,500 living alumni, many of whom are concentrated in tech companies in Chicago, making networking conditions favorable. That can come in handy when pursuing for-credit internships or co-ops during the school year or during the summer term. However, the school does not release information about what percentage of students complete one or more internships or what percentage of the undergraduate student body is serviced by the office in any capacity in a given year.

Professional Outcomes

Illinois Tech grads can be found in sizable numbers within major corporations including Motorola, Amazon, Microsoft, Google, Apple, Accenture, JPMorgan Chase, IBM, EY, and Cisco. The Greater Chicago area plays home to more than half of IIT alumni with San Francisco, New York City, Seattle, and Los Angeles and international destinations including India, Brazil, and Spain all attracting fairly large numbers of Scarlet Hawks. Starting salaries as well as midcareer compensation figures are the strongest in the state of Illinois and among the highest anywhere when compared to other highly selective private universities. The school also ranks high for social mobility, lifting more students whose families fall in the bottom 20 percent income bracket into the top 20 percent than any other school in the state.

Those continuing to graduate school often stay at Illinois Tech, which offers degrees in engineering, science, architecture, business, design, human sciences, applied technology, and law. For premed students, the medical school acceptance rate is "often above the national average." A dual degree program is offered in partnership with Midwestern University's Chicago College of Osteopathic Medicine. Recent students have earned it a place among top medical schools like the Northwestern University Feinberg School of Medicine, New York University School of Medicine, and the University of Michigan Medical School.

Admission

With an acceptance rate of 58 percent, the Illinois Institute of Technology is not looking to shut the door on those with imperfect credentials, yet some of that hefty number is attribute to self-selection. The mid-50 percent SAT range of 2018-19 freshmen is 1220-1400 and the ACT range is 26-31. Surprisingly, and perhaps encouragingly—depending on your circumstances—16 percent of attending students scored less than a 600 on the math section of the SAT, 24 percent scored under a 600 on the verbal section. Half of freshmen earned a place in the top 10 percent of their respective high school class, 78 percent were in the top quartile, and 95 percent were in the top 50 percent. All of those numbers, including the overall acceptance rate, are similar to those from five years ago, despite a spike in the total number of applications.

Like most engineering-focused schools, the hard numbers are paramount when it comes to making admissions decisions. Standardized test scores, GPA, and the level of rigor of one's coursework are of the utmost importance while factors such as class rank and recommendations are also given weight by the committee. Female applicants enjoy slightly better admissions prospects with an acceptance rate of 61 percent compared to men at just under 57 percent. There is no early decision process at Illinois Tech, rather, applications are accepted on a rolling basis beginning on October 1 with a priority deadline of December 1. Applying on the early side is your best bet regardless of whether IIT is your number one choice or one of many irons in the fire.

Worth Your Money?

On paper, the cost of attendance at IIT is greater than $65,000 per year. However, 97 percent of students receive some type of aid, and even families with an income above $135,000 receive an average scholarship and grant combo adding up to $32,000 annually. As a result, the school is a worthy investment for most as solid-paying tech, finance, and architecture jobs in the Chicago area await your arrival postgraduation

FINANCIAL
Institutional Type: Private
In-State Tuition: $47,480
Out-of-State Tuition: $47,480
Room & Board: $13,582
Required Fees: $1,800
Books & Supplies: $1,250

Avg. Need-Based Aid: $36,584
Avg. % of Need Met: 86%

Avg. Merit-Based Aid: $26,980
% Receiving Merit-Based Aid: 39%

Avg. Cumulative Debt: $32,671
% of Students Borrowing: 54%

CAREER
Who Recruits
1. Webber, LLC
2. Wise Equation Solutions
3. W.W. Grainger
4. AVG Automation
5. CCC Information Services

Notable Internships
1. BMW
2. Salesforce
3. Motorola

Top Industries
1. Engineering
2. Business
3. Infromation Technology
4. Operations
5. Education

Top Employers
1. Amazon
2. Motorola
3. Google
4. Microsoft
5. Apple

Where Alumni Work
1. Chicago
2. San Francisco
3. India
4. New York City
5. Seattle

Median Earnings
College Scorecard (Early Career): $69,100
EOP (Early Career): $72,300
PayScale (Mid-Career): $118,500

RANKINGS
Forbes: 208
Money: 213
U.S. News: 2, National Universities
Wall Street Journal/THE: 137 (T)
Washington Monthly: 60, National Universities

#CollegesWorthYourMoney

Indiana University Bloomington

Bloomington, Indiana | Admissions Phone: 812-855-0661

ADMISSION
Admission Rate: 77%
Admission Rate - Men: 78%
Admission Rate - Women: 76%
EA Admission Rate: N/A
ED Admission Rate: Not Offered
Admission Rate (5-Year Trend): +5%
ED Admission Rate (5-Year Trend): Not Offered
% of Admits Attending (Yield): 24%
Transfer Admission Rate: 65%

Offered Wait List: 2,835
Accepted Wait List: 467
Admitted Wait List: 427

SAT Reading/Writing (Middle 50%): 580-670
SAT Math (Middle 50%): 570-690
ACT Composite (Middle 50%): 24-31
Testing Policy: ACT/SAT Required
SAT Superscore: Yes
ACT Superscore: Yes

% Graduated in Top 10% of HS Class: 35%
% Graduated in Top 25% of HS Class: 69%
% Graduated in Top 50% of HS Class: 95%

ENROLLMENT
Total Undergraduate Enrollment: 33,301
% Part-Time: 4%
% Male: 50%
% Female: 50%
% Out-of-State: 35%
% Fraternity: 23%
% Sorority: 20%
% On-Campus (Freshman): 89%
% On-Campus (All Undergraduate): 37%

% African-American: 5%
% Asian: 6%
% Hispanic: 6%
% White: 69%
% Other: 4%
% Race or Ethnicity Unknown: 0%
% International: 9%
% Low-Income: 19%

ACADEMICS
Student-to-Faculty Ratio: 16:1
% of Classes Under 20: 37%
% of Classes Under 40: 75%
% Full-Time Faculty: 86%
% Full-Time Faculty w/ Terminal Degree: 88%

Top Programs
Accounting
English
Entrepreneurship
History
Finance
Music
Psychology
Public Management

Retention Rate: 91%
4-Year Graduation Rate: 64%
6-Year Graduation Rate: 78%

Curricular Flexibility: Somewhat Flexible
Academic Rating: ★★★

Inside the Classroom

From coast to coast, flagship public universities have seen their admissions standards skyrocket in recent years. Students for whom the University of Maryland, the University of Wisconsin, or any school within the University of California system would have been a safety school a decade ago now find themselves sweating out admissions decisions each spring. Fortunately, this is not so at Indiana's famed Bloomington campus where more than three-quarters of applicants who apply still receive a friendly Midwestern welcome, and both the quality and price of the education that await are exceptionally solid. That combination of accessibility, quality, and variety — IU offers 200+ majors — draws more out-of-state and international students than you might expect. Only 57 percent of IU undergraduates are from in state, and 7 percent of the student body are international students hailing from 120+ countries.

Unlike many large universities made up of numerous schools and colleges, Indiana is not overeager to assign and confine you to a particular program. Upon entering IU, freshmen are housed within the University Division, and they remain there for one or two years in order to figure out their academic direction. This gives all freshmen time to begin wrestling with the Common Ground Curriculum that involves completing courses in six areas: English composition, mathematical modeling, arts and humanities, social and historical studies, natural and mathematical sciences, and world languages and cultures. Of note for any foreign language averse students, there are ways to fill the latter requirement without learning another language. Students who are members of the Hutton Honors College also typically need to complete a senior thesis within their academic departments.

The university's 16:1 student-to-faculty ratio is not bad for a school of Indiana's size, and it does make an effort to keep undergraduate classes on the small side. While there are a number of introductory courses that transpire in giant lecture halls, 63 percent of all sections contain no more than twenty-nine students. Experiential learning opportunities are available to those who seize them; 27 percent of arts and sciences students completed research with a faculty member. On the study abroad front, 26 percent of 2018 A&S graduates spent a semester in a foreign country. In total, the school offers 360 programs in sixty-five countries and twenty languages.

Business/marketing is the most popular major accounting for 25 percent of the total degrees conferred. Kelley is an acclaimed business school that draws immense national respect, ranking up there in prestige with Goizueta (Emory), McDonough (Georgetown), and its neighbor to the north, Mendoza (Notre Dame). Indiana, notably, did not offer an engineering program until recently, making Purdue a much better local public option for anyone entering that field of study. However, the computer and information science degree program has tight ties to top tech companies, and it is the school's second most frequently conferred degree at 9 percent. The other degrees most commonly awarded are in social services (8 percent), parks and recreation (8 percent), journalism (7 percent), and biology (7 percent). Plenty of students from all academic backgrounds capture competitive postgraduate scholarships. In 2019, the school's haul included eleven Critical Language Scholarships, ten Fulbrights, and a Churchill Scholarship. The previous year undergraduates won a hard-to-fathom twenty-one Fulbright Scholarships.

Outside the Classroom

The university houses 89 percent of freshmen but only 37 percent of the overall undergraduate student body on its sprawling 1,936-acre campus. Living options include thirteen residence halls, eleven apartment complexes, and more than twenty residential thematic communities. For everyone else, there are plenty of affordable off-campus apartments within close proximity. Fraternities and sororities play an enormous role in social life as 23 percent of men and 20 percent of women join Greek organizations; there are seventy to choose from. There are twenty-four varsity sports, and many boast Big Ten championships, yet one shines above the rest as Hoosier hoops is nothing short of a religion in Bloomington, and you'll never find one of the 17,222 seats within Assembly Hall unfilled during men's basketball games. For those looking for lower-key athletics, there are more than seventy club and intramural sports at your disposal. Overall, Indiana University is home to more than 750 student organizations featuring clubs ranging from calligraphy to bass fishing. Bloomington gets high marks as a safe and enjoyable college town, and there are always events going on whether it's a free show at the spectacular Musical Arts Center or a community service opportunity — students donated a total of 225,000 hours last year. Indianapolis is a fifty-mile highway drive away, making it an option for a quick weekend getaway.

Career Services

The university has a main Career Development Center for those who enter undecided as well as discipline-specific career services offices housed within each undergraduate college. There are eighty-six full-time staff members dedicated to career advising, experiential education, and employer relations. The university's overall 389:1 student-to-counselor ratio is one of the best for a public institution of Indiana's immense size. This staff's output is astounding whether measured by its 23,428 one-on-one counseling sessions per year or its large-scale efforts that include booking 1,761 companies to attend the school's many career fairs.

Indiana University Bloomington

E-mail: iuadmit@indiana.edu | Website: www.indiana.edu

Last year alone, 9,778 internships were completed by IU students in both for-credit and noncredit placements. Over 2,000 employers recruited at Bloomington, and hiring organizations conducted a collective 11,020 on-campus interviews. Among the major corporations actively recruiting and interviewing on campus are EY, PwC, Deloitte, Oracle, JPMorgan Chase & Co., Microsoft Corporation, Anheuser-Busch, Epic Systems, Procter & Gamble, and Grainger, Inc. Just a quick glance at the university calendar reveals a frenetic pace of career fairs taking place in the fall of 2019, including targeted events for those interested in business, media, social services, finance, public health, internships, the creative arts, and the hard sciences. Any way you measure it, the IU career services staff's output is prodigious and helps set undergraduates up for successful postgraduation transition.

Professional Outcomes

Indiana University tracks the postgraduate outcomes from each undergraduate school. Looking at the College of Arts & Sciences, by far the largest group of students, Class of 2018 grads reached their next employment or graduate school destination at a 93 percent rate within six months of receiving their degrees. Fifty-three percent had procured their first jobs, and one-quarter of students were in grad school; only 7 percent of those looking for jobs were unable to land one in that time. The most frequently entered industries (from A&S) were arts & entertainment, education, retail, and advertising. The median starting salary for A&S grads was $37,500. In the Kelley School of Business, 96 percent were placed successfully within six months, and the median starting salary was $62,000. School of Informatics, Computing & Engineering grads had comparable starting salaries and an identical 96 percent success rate. Among the largest employers of Hoosier alumni are local pharmaceutical giant Eli Lilly, EY, Amazon, PwC, Salesforce, Deloitte, IBM, Oracle, Microsoft, Accenture, and Google. Indianapolis, Chicago, Bloomington, and New York City are the locales where you can find the greatest concentration of Indiana graduates.

Among the most frequently attended graduate schools by members of the Class of 2018 were Indiana Bloomington (including its own law and medical schools), Purdue, Loyola Chicago, Northwestern, and Columbia. Indiana is a premed factory with 275 applicants to med school in 2018-19 alone; that is the thirteenth highest in the nation. Impressively, the well-regarded Indiana University School of Medicine was the second most frequently attended graduate school overall. That was aided by the fact that the in-state acceptance rate at this medical school is 48 percent, six times higher than the out-of-state rate. The university also operates two separate law schools, one in Indianapolis and one in Bloomington, and both draw large numbers of IU undergraduates. A combined BA/JD program can be completed in six years.

Admission

Of all the flagship universities profiled in this book, Indiana has the most relaxed admissions standards as 77 percent of those who applied for a place in the Class of 2022 were welcomed aboard. The mid-50 percent SAT scores for attending freshman were 1150-1360 and the ACT mid-50th was a wide-ranging 24-31. The school became test-optional in 2020. The majority— 58 percent—sported GPAs of 3.75 or better, and 35 percent finished in the top 10 percent of their high school class. More encouragingly for less-than-perfect applicants is the fact that 31 percent of undergrads did not place in the top quartile of their graduating cohort, and 24 percent possessed cumulative GPAs under 3.5.

With roughly 44,000 applications to wade through, the admissions committee must first rely on the easy-to-assess credentials of class rank, GPA, standardized test scores, and level of academic rigor. The application essay is "important," but factors like extracurricular activities, recommendations, and volunteer work are merely "considered." While there is no binding early decision option available, IU does offer an early action round with a deadline of November 1, also the deadline for the most complete scholarship consideration. The acceptance rate at this university has actually gone up in the last five years—it had been in the high 60s. Thanks to declining enrollment numbers the last three years, the admissions standards show no sign of stiffening any time soon.

Worth Your Money?

Indiana residents enjoy not only a reasonable tuition cost that is a touch under $11,000 but a modest room-and-board price as well when compared to other schools of roughly the same quality. For comparison, room and board alone at Notre Dame would cost an extra $20,000 over four years. Nonresidents should consider their aid package and program of study (business-related fields are your best bet) before packing off to Bloomington, as out-of-state rates are approaching that of many private colleges. Hoosiers cannot go wrong heading to Bloomington for their bachelor's degree, no matter what field of interest they plan to study.

FINANCIAL
Institutional Type: Public
In-State Tuition: $9,342
Out-of-State Tuition: $34,117
Room & Board: $10,466
Required Fees: $1,339
Books & Supplies: $930

Avg. Need-Based Aid: $12,806
Avg. % of Need Met: 71%

Avg. Merit-Based Aid: $7,592
% Receiving Merit-Based Aid: 36%

Avg. Cumulative Debt: $28,352
% of Students Borrowing: 44%

CAREER
Who Recruits
1. Macy's
2. Anheuser-Busch
3. Grant Thornton LLC
4. Oracle
5. Insight Global

Notable Internships
1. The Economist
2. Grant Thornton LLP
3. Bain & Company

Top Industries
1. Business
2. Education
3. Operations
4. Sales
5. Social Services

Top Employers
1. Eli Lily and Company
2. EY
3. Amazon
4. PwC
5. Salesforce

Where Alumni Work
1. Indianapolis
2. Chicago
3. Bloomington, IN
4. New York City
5. Washington, DC

Median Earnings
College Scorecard (Early Career): $47,700
EOP (Early Career): $40,100
PayScale (Mid-Career): $97,100

RANKINGS
Forbes: 131
Money: 97
U.S. News: 79 (T), National Universities
Wall Street Journal/THE: 123 (T)
Washington Monthly: 47, National Universities

#CollegesWorthYourMoney

Baltimore, Maryland | Admissions Phone: 410-516-8171

ADMISSION

Admission Rate: 10%
Admission Rate - Men: 11%
Admission Rate - Women: 10%
EA Admission Rate: Not Offered
ED Admission Rate: 30%
Admission Rate (5-Year Trend): -8%
ED Admission Rate (5-Year Trend): N/A
% of Admits Attending (Yield): 44%
Transfer Admission Rate: 9%

Offered Wait List: 3,555
Accepted Wait List: 2,179
Admitted Wait List: 207

SAT Reading/Writing (Middle 50%): 710-760
SAT Math (Middle 50%): 760-800
ACT Composite (Middle 50%): 33-35
Testing Policy: ACT/SAT Required
SAT Superscore: Yes
ACT Superscore: Yes

% Graduated in Top 10% of HS Class: 96%
% Graduated in Top 25% of HS Class: 99%
% Graduated in Top 50% of HS Class: 100%

ENROLLMENT

Total Undergraduate Enrollment: 5,374
% Part-Time: 1%
% Male: 48%
% Female: 52%
% Out-of-State: 79%
% Fraternity: 18%
% Sorority: 27%
% On-Campus (Freshman): 99%
% On-Campus (All Undergraduate): 51%

% African-American: 8%
% Asian: 30%
% Hispanic: 16%
% White: 34%
% Other: 6%
% Race or Ethnicity Unknown: 6%
% International: 10%
% Low-Income: 15%

ACADEMICS

Student-to-Faculty Ratio: 7:1
% of Classes Under 20: 74%
% of Classes Under 40: 87%
% Full-Time Faculty: 96%
% Full-Time Faculty w/ Terminal Degree: 90%

Top Programs
Biology
Biomedical Engineering
Chemistry
English
International Studies
Mathematics
Physics
Public Health Studies

Retention Rate: 98%
4-Year Graduation Rate: 88%
6-Year Graduation Rate: 94%

Curricular Flexibility: Somewhat Flexible
Academic Rating: ★★★★★

Inside the Classroom

High schoolers who dream of entering the medical profession look to North Baltimore as their Mecca—more specifically, to Johns Hopkins University, Charm City's prestigious, midsized research institution. Yet, four years at Johns Hopkins is so much more than merely a prelude to seven years of medical school. With fifty-two majors as well as forty-seven minors, JHU excels in everything from its bread-and-butter medical-related majors to international relations and dance. Of the five undergraduate schools within the university, the vast majority of students reside in either the Krieger School of Arts and Sciences or the Whiting School of Engineering. However, the Carey School of Business, School of Education, and Peabody Institute also award bachelor's degrees.

All Hopkins bachelor's-seekers must meet distributional requirements covering the basics: humanities, natural sciences, social and behavioral sciences, quantitative and mathematical sciences, and engineering. Writing-intensive courses also are mandated regardless of one's major. Students are encouraged to broaden their horizons by double majoring or selecting a minor, and 70 percent do so. First-year experience courses help to transition students to the school and second-year experience courses assist with community-building and career planning.

Boasting an enviable 8:1 student-to-faculty ratio and 75 percent of course sections with an enrollment under twenty, face time with professors is a reality. That presents a phenomenal opportunity to learn directly from a group that includes four Nobel Laureates, four Medal of Science winners, and two recipients of the Presidential Medal of Freedom. Fittingly for America's first research university, 80 percent of JHU undergraduates complete a research experience while working closely with a faculty member. Each year, hundreds of students receive significant funding for independent projects through the Hopkins Office for Undergraduate Research.

Universally respected by employers and graduate schools alike, many departments carry a high level of clout, including biology, chemistry, English, and international studies. Biomedical engineering, public health, and nursing, which happen to be the three most popular majors, can also be found at the top of the national rankings. In 2019, there were twenty-two Fulbright Scholars named from the university. Johns Hopkins grads also are competitive in landing Luce, Truman, Marshall, Goldwater, and National Science Foundation Graduate Research Fellowships.

Outside the Classroom

The 140-acre Homewood campus located in North Baltimore is the site of the School of Engineering and the School of Arts & Sciences. The dorms located at Homewood house most underclassmen and feature dining halls that garner generally high praise. Despite the excellent chow, upperclassmen tend to outgrow university-owned housing; a slight majority of students, 52 percent, live off campus. The twenty-two Greek organizations each have their own charitable focus and attract 27 percent of the undergraduate student body. Nicknamed the Blue Jays, athletes compete in twelve men's and ten women's sports in NCCA Division III. Over 400 student organizations are active at JHU. Groups centered on community service tend to be the most popular. The Center for Social Concern connects students with over seventy-five local organizations. For those interested in a medical career, you'll have the chance to volunteer in one of fifteen local hospitals, including Johns Hopkins' own facilities. Popular traditions include the three-day Spring Fair, the nation's largest student-run fair. Famous guest speakers from all walks of life regularly visit campus and draw engaged audiences. Homewood is a only a few miles from the bustle of Baltimore's Inner Harbor so, even though the area immediately surrounding campus isn't the most inviting, culture and nightlife can easily be found.

Career Services

The Homewood Career Center is staffed by seventeen full-time professional employees that work with and on behalf of undergraduates in the areas of career development, employer engagement, internship coordination, and event planning. This figure does not include administrative assistants, IT, graduate advisors, or marketing professionals. Possessing a student-to-advisor ratio of 311:1, JHU is superior to many of the institutions included in this book.

In 2018-19, the Career Center engaged 1,999 undergraduates in one-to-one career coach appointments. More than ninety employers, including many Fortune 1000 companies, conducted 716 interviews on campus. Over 15,000 jobs and internship opportunities were available on Handshake. Homewood hosts three major career fairs each year: the flagship Fall Career Fair with more than 150 employers, the STEM & Innovation Career Fair with forty targeted companies attending, and the spring Nonprofit Career Fair that also focuses on internship procurement. All told, 170 companies attended career fairs at JHU, and 247 companies recruited on campus. The university also provides a number of internships that are built-in to each academic department. Those include credit-bearing options in orthopedic surgery, film and media studies, business, and computational biology. An exceptional 85 percent of undergraduates complete one internship over their four years of study; it is not unusual to complete two.

Professional Outcomes

The Class of 2018 saw 97 percent of graduates successfully land at their next destination within six months of exiting the university; 54 percent of graduates entered the world of employment and a robust 35 percent went directly to graduate/professional school. Of those entering the workforce, the most popular industries were research, engineering and IT, consulting, finance, and health care. Johns Hopkins University and its affiliated medical institutions were the largest employer of recent graduates, scooping up sixty-four Class of 2017 members. Other prominent companies landing more than a handful of fresh JHU alums were Deloitte, Accenture, Booz Allen Hamilton, Morgan Stanley, and ScribeAmerica. Across all graduating years you'll find hundreds of Hopkins grads working for IBM, Google, Microsoft, Facebook, and Apple. The average starting salary across all majors was $60,768.

Johns Hopkins' sterling reputation also helps land its undergrads at premier graduate schools. Engineering is the most popular graduate field with 27 percent of 2017 graduates going in that direction. Medical school was the second most common endeavor at 17 percent. The overall admit rate to medical schools was a healthy 79 percent. Law school grads also found homes at an above-average 90 percent clip. Johns Hopkins itself is the most frequently attended graduate school, and it's not even close, with 147 Class of 2017 grads continuing their educations in Baltimore. The next five most frequently attended institutions were Harvard, Penn, Columbia, Duke, and Stanford.

Admission

If Johns Hopkins' aim in 2018 was to become one of a dozen or so elite universities with a single-digit admissions rate, it only missed that goal by a matter of percentage points; 10.6 percent of undergraduates were admitted into the Class of 2022. That follows a pattern of declining acceptance rates over the past few years. For historical context, the school admitted one-quarter of applicants only a decade ago. The SAT middle 50 percent range in 2008 was 1320-1480; today it is 1470-1560. Given that the former 75th percentile SAT score is now the 25th percentile score, it's pretty clear that Johns Hopkins has grown increasingly competitive in recent years. For those taking the ACT, the mid-50 percent is a tight range of 33-34.

Current students landed in the top 10 percent of their high school classes at a 96 percent clip, so impeccable grades in the most competitive curriculum available is pretty much a prerequisite for consideration. The average unweighted GPA for 2018-19 freshman was 3.93, meaning that more than one or two imperfections on a transcript can be a disqualifier. Leadership qualities and community service are also highly valued. In the university's own words, it is "looking for students who can think beyond their limits, who don't see 'impossible' as a roadblock, and who will not only elevate themselves but also those around them." Early decision applicants will see improved odds as their acceptance rate is more than three times that of the regular round (30 percent vs. 9 percent). Further, 46 percent of the Class of 2022 was accepted via ED. Always a highly selective school, Johns Hopkins is now in the upper-upper tier of selectivity along with the Ivies, Stanford, and a small cadre of elite liberal arts colleges. Only those with first-rate test scores and transcripts need apply.

Worth Your Money?

If your family is a lower-to-mid tier income bracket, Johns Hopkins will provide you with every dollar of financial aid you need to attend the university. Presently, 47 percent of the undergraduate population benefits from that generosity with an average need-based grant of $47,492. The annual cost of attendance is approaching $75,000, and of those families making incomes in the top 5 percent nationally (an estimated 40 percent of current students' families do), you can expect to pay close to full price. Even for those taking out loans to attend, JHU is the type of school that it is almost always OK to pay up for. With fantastic job and professional school prospects down the road, the $300,000 investment will be well worth it in the long run.

FINANCIAL
Institutional Type: Private
In-State Tuition: $53,740
Out-of-State Tuition: $53,740
Room & Board: $15,836
Required Fees: N/A
Books & Supplies: $1,240

Avg. Need-Based Aid: $47,492
Avg. % of Need Met: 100%

Avg. Merit-Based Aid: $10,602
% Receiving Merit-Based Aid: 1%

Avg. Cumulative Debt: $25,697
% of Students Borrowing: 46%

CAREER
Who Recruits
1. Dean & Company
2. Bloomberg
3. Lockheed Martin
4. Bain & Company
5. McKinsey & Co.

Notable Internships
1. Twitter
2. NASA Jet Propulsion Laboratory
3. National Institutes of Health

Top Industries
1. Business
2. Education
3. Research
4. Engineering
5. Healthcare

Top Employers
1. Booz Allen Hamilton
2. Google
3. Deloitte
4. IBM
5. Microsoft

Where Alumni Work
1. Baltimore
2. Washington, DC
3. New York City
4. San Francisco
5. Boston

Median Earnings
College Scorecard (Early Career): $73,200
EOP (Early Career): $75,000
PayScale (Mid-Career): $117,100

RANKINGS
Forbes: 22
Money: 125
U.S. News: 10, National Universities
Wall Street Journal/THE: 12 (T)
Washington Monthly: 56, National Universities

#CollegesWorthYourMoney

Kenyon College

Gambier, Ohio | Admissions Phone: 740-427-5776

ADMISSION
Admission Rate: 36%
Admission Rate - Men: 33%
Admission Rate - Women: 38%
EA Admission Rate: Not Offered
ED Admission Rate: 70%
Admission Rate (5-Year Trend): -3%
ED Admission Rate (5-Year Trend): +12%
% of Admits Attending (Yield): 24%
Transfer Admission Rate: 30%

Offered Wait List: 1,857
Accepted Wait List: 907
Admitted Wait List: 4

SAT Reading/Writing (Middle 50%): 640-730
SAT Math (Middle 50%): 640-740
ACT Composite (Middle 50%): 29-33
Testing Policy: ACT/SAT Required
SAT Superscore: Yes
ACT Superscore: Yes

% Graduated in Top 10% of HS Class: 55%
% Graduated in Top 25% of HS Class: 79%
% Graduated in Top 50% of HS Class: 96%

ENROLLMENT
Total Undergraduate Enrollment: 1,719
% Part-Time: 0%
% Male: 45%
% Female: 55%
% Out-of-State: 87%
% Fraternity: 27%
% Sorority: 32%
% On-Campus (Freshman): 100%
% On-Campus (All Undergraduate): 99%

% African-American: 4%
% Asian: 4%
% Hispanic: 8%
% White: 70%
% Other: 5%
% Race or Ethnicity Unknown: 3%
% International: 7%
% Low-Income: 10%

ACADEMICS
Student-to-Faculty Ratio: 10:1
% of Classes Under 20: 80%
% of Classes Under 40: 99%
% Full-Time Faculty: 80%
% Full-Time Faculty w/ Terminal Degree: 88%

Top Programs
English
History
International Studies
Neuroscience
Performing Arts
Political Science
Sociology

Retention Rate: 91%
4-Year Graduation Rate: 85%
6-Year Graduation Rate: 89%

Curricular Flexibility: Very Flexible
Academic Rating: ★★★★

Inside the Classroom

When your list of notable alumni includes Paul Newman, National Humanities Medal recipient E.L. Doctorow, and largely forgotten US President Rutherford B. Hayes, it's clear that your college is a unique and special place. Kenyon College in rural Gambier, Ohio, has a history of excellence in drama, English, and across the broader liberal arts that produces passionate and talented alumni who are ready, willing, and able to carve out their legacies within their chosen disciplines.

Kenyon offers thirty-three majors and an additional thirteen concentrations that allow students to complete their education with few nondepartmental core requirements. All undergrads must demonstrate proficiency in a foreign language (AP opt-out is available) and take a quantitative reasoning course, but other than that, a Kenyon education is open and flexible. A senior capstone awaits all would-be graduates and can take many forms, but the project must demonstrate a student's skills in writing, speaking, collaborating and "distinguish the essential from the trivial." This latter requirement epitomizes Kenyon's emphasis on critical thought throughout one's four years of study.

The student-faculty ratio is 10-to-1, and the most common class size is fifteen. Thirty-two percent of classes are even more intimate, offering single-digit enrollments. Close relationships develop with faculty and often lead to opportunities to engage in undergraduate research. Summer research programs available to students include the Kenyon Summer Scholars Program, a joint program with Ohio State, and the Summer Science Program that sees more than thirty student-professor pairs collaborate on research for an eight- to ten-week period. Roughly half of each junior class packs up its bags and heads off to a distant land for a semester abroad. Students choose from more than 190 programs in fifty countries across Africa, Asia, Australia, Europe, and the Americas; the school also sponsors programs in England and in Rome.

English, economics, psychology, and political science are easily the school's four most popular majors. As alluded to earlier, the drama program is one of the country's finest and has a lengthy alumni list of recognizable actors and performers. It's rare to identify an institution's English program as having an elevated reputation in the minds of employers and graduate schools, but Kenyon's would be one of the exceptions. For a relatively small school, Kenyon graduates procure nationally competitive scholarships and fellowships at an exceptional clip. In 2018, the college had a dozen Fulbright winners and two Goldwater recipients. It has been a top Fulbright producer for the last decade.

Outside the Classroom

Kenyon's 1,000-acre campus is located forty-five miles from bustling Columbus and includes a 500-acre nature preserve. All students live on campus, and freshmen are clustered in special residence halls near the Gund Commons. Facilities receive rave reviews from students including the Kenyon Athletic Center that includes tennis courts, a pool, and an indoor track. Approximately 30 percent of Kenyon undergraduates are involved in Greek life but, uniquely, fraternities and sororities are situated within residence halls, leading to a more integrated experience. Close to one-third of students are on the roster of one of the school's twenty NCAA Division III athletic teams (ten men's and ten women's). Plenty of club and intramural sports are available for those seeking a less formal sports pursuit. Intramurals include offbeat games like cornhole and capture the flag. Beyond Greek organizations and sports teams, there are 120 student organizations to consider including five a cappella groups, numerous community service opportunities, and the Kenyon College Dance & Dramatics Club that puts on high-quality student productions. Nature lovers can hike the six miles of trails in the school's own preserve along the Kokosing River or join the Outdoors Club that takes backpacking and whitewater rafting trips to more adventurous locations such as the Monongahela National Forest of West Virginia.

Career Services

The Career Development Office (CDO) employs six professional staff members who work in career development or graduate school advising. With a 280:1 student-to-advisor ratio, Kenyon provides a higher-than-average level of support when compared against the other institutions in this guidebook. While it doesn't host a large-scale career fair, it does offer employer/graduate school information sessions at a rate of fifteen to twenty per month. The CDO's strengths lie in its willingness to give individualized attention to students and its involved alumni network.

The online Kenyon Career Network helps link current students to alumni working in their field of interest; there are 8,000 alumni willing to offer their advice and assistance. Job-shadowing opportunities are plentiful, and experiences have included trips to the New York Times, Random House, and the Federal Reserve Bank of Chicago. The office is adept at helping students find internships, and recent grads have had stints with organizations such as the Museum of Modern Art, the San Diego Padres, and the Library of Congress. In recent years 65-70 percent of employed graduates reported that their jobs were related to their desired career path. Only 66 percent of graduates reported that Kenyon was effective at preparing them for the work of employment. Those indicators suggest that not all graduates are fully satisfied with the career services delivered at this school.

Kenyon College

E-mail: admissions@kenyon.edu | Website: www.kenyon.edu

Professional Outcomes

Popular fields for Kenyon grads include education, health care, marketing, nonprofit management, research, and writing and editing. Due to Kenyon's small size and the diversity of its academic programs, it lacks dense concentrations of alumni at particular companies. Economics majors often land as financial analysts or advisors at firms including BlackRock, Wells Fargo, JP Morgan, or Goldman Sachs. English and journalism majors end up at a diverse array of publishing houses, talent agencies, news organizations, and consulting companies. New York City, DC, Columbus, Chicago, and Boston are the five cities drawing the greatest numbers of Kenyon alumni. Median salary for Kenyon grads by the start of midcareer is a modest $48,000, but that can partially be explained by the fact that many alumni pursue lengthy graduate/professional programs that typically pay financial dividends later in life. Other comparable schools including Vassar, Carleton, and Occidental rank similarly.

The 18 percent of graduates who directly enter an advanced degree program enjoy extraordinary success. Within five years of completing their undergraduate education at Kenyon, 50 percent have already finished an advanced degree program and 70 percent are enrolled in one. Law and business school applicants find success at a 99 percent clip and, among medical school candidates with a minimum GPA of 3.25, the acceptance rate is a phenomenal 90 percent. Recent grads have been welcomed into the top law schools at Yale, NYU, Berkeley, Stanford, UVA, Michigan, and the University of Chicago. Future doctors are currently training at prestigious medical schools including Johns Hopkins, Duke, Harvard, Tufts, Vanderbilt, and Northwestern. A successful undergraduate career at Kenyon will make possible admission into the finest graduate and professional schools in the world. Across all disciplines, 98 percent of those applying to an advanced degree program are accepted by one of their top three choices.

Admission

A rarity among elite liberal arts schools, Kenyon's acceptance rate has risen in recent years. The class of 2019 acceptance rate hit an all-time low of 24 percent, but the Class of 2022 rate was a significantly friendlier 36 percent. The latest incoming freshman class possessed an average GPA of 3.97 and middle-50 percent standardized test scores of 1280-1470 on the SAT and 29-33 on the ACT. Three years ago, when the acceptance rate was a dozen points lower, the SAT range was 1240-1420; the average GPA was the same. Therefore, one can conclude that the profile of the average Kenyon student has not changed much in recent years.

The admissions committee values four factors above all others: rigor of courses, GPA, recommendations, and essays. Test scores, class rank, the interview, talent/ability, extracurricular activities, character/personal qualities, and the level of an applicant's interest make up the next rung of important considerations. Facing stiff competition from other elite liberal arts schools, Kenyon very much wants to know if you truly want to go there. Applying early decision is the ultimate sign of devotion, and that act is rewarded. Almost 70 percent of ED applicants were accepted, and they comprise a good portion of each incoming class; 43 percent of the Class of 2022 was admitted via ED. Kenyon is looking for academically curious and talented students who are actively involved in their schools/communities. Excellent grades are a must, and demonstrating interest is more valuable here than at your average college. If your heart is set on Kenyon, strongly consider demonstrating your loyalty by applying early.

Worth Your Money?

The 43 percent of current Kenyon students who qualify for financial aid receive grants averaging $41,000 per year; the college meets 100 percent of student need. To help lower the $71k cost of attendance, it also offers annual awards of $13k in merit aid to 42 percent of the undergraduate population. This school is definitely worth your money but, as when considering any institution, we would caution against taking on an excessive amount of debt if you are pursuing a major that is unlikely to lead to fiscal stability upon graduation.

FINANCIAL
Institutional Type: Private
In-State Tuition: $56,430
Out-of-State Tuition: $56,430
Room & Board: $12,580
Required Fees: $2,140
Books & Supplies: N/A

Avg. Need-Based Aid: $41,461
Avg. % of Need Met: 100%

Avg. Merit-Based Aid: $13,317
% Receiving Merit-Based Aid: 42%

Avg. Cumulative Debt: $26,271
% of Students Borrowing: 46%

CAREER
Who Recruits
1. GBQ Partners
2. DHL Supply Chain
3. Skylight Financial Group
4. TEKsystems
5. Verizon

Notable Internships
1. Penguin Random House
2. Guggenheim Museum
3. Morgan Stanley

Top Industries
1. Business
2. Education
3. Media
4. Operations
5. Social Services

Top Employers
1. JPMorgan Chase
2. Cleveland Clinic
3. Google
4. Amazon
5. US State Department

Where Alumni Work
1. New York City
2. Washington, DC
3. Columbus, OH
4. Chicago
5. Boston

Median Earnings
College Scorecard (Early Career): $48,700
EOP (Early Career): $48,000
PayScale (Mid-Career): $103,800

RANKINGS
Forbes: 71
Money: 248
U.S. News: 27 (T), Liberal Arts Colleges
Wall Street Journal/THE: 91 (T)
Washington Monthly: 47, Liberal Arts Colleges

#CollegesWorthYourMoney

Colleges Worth Your Money   Kenyon College   137

Easton, Pennsylvania | Admissions Phone: 610-330-5100

ADMISSION
Admission Rate: 29%
Admission Rate - Men: 26%
Admission Rate - Women: 33%
EA Admission Rate: Not Offered
ED Admission Rate: 52%
Admission Rate (5-Year Trend): -5%
ED Admission Rate (5-Year Trend): -1%
% of Admits Attending (Yield): 27%
Transfer Admission Rate: 14%

Offered Wait List: 2,332
Accepted Wait List: 948
Admitted Wait List: 2

SAT Reading/Writing (Middle 50%): 620-700
SAT Math (Middle 50%): 630-740
ACT Composite (Middle 50%): 27-32
Testing Policy: ACT/SAT Required
SAT Superscore: Yes
ACT Superscore: Yes

% Graduated in Top 10% of HS Class: 52%
% Graduated in Top 25% of HS Class: 78%
% Graduated in Top 50% of HS Class: 96%

ENROLLMENT
Total Undergraduate Enrollment: 2,642
% Part-Time: 1%
% Male: 48%
% Female: 52%
% Out-of-State: 81%
% Fraternity: 24%
% Sorority: 34%
% On-Campus (Freshman): 100%
% On-Campus (All Undergraduate): 92%

% African-American: 5%
% Asian: 4%
% Hispanic: 7%
% White: 65%
% Other: 3%
% Race or Ethnicity Unknown: 6%
% International: 9%
% Low-Income: 9%

ACADEMICS
Student-to-Faculty Ratio: 10:1
% of Classes Under 20: 62%
% of Classes Under 40: 98%
% Full-Time Faculty: 80%
% Full-Time Faculty w/ Terminal Degree: 98%

Top Programs
Economics
Engineering
English
Film and Media Studies
Government and Law
International Affairs
Psychology

Retention Rate: 93%
4-Year Graduation Rate: 83%
6-Year Graduation Rate: 87%

Curricular Flexibility: Somewhat Flexible
Academic Rating: ★★★★

Inside the Classroom

Nearing its 200th birthday, this elite liberal arts school named after the Revolutionary War hero the Marquis de Lafayette, offers a rare blend of an intimate academic experience mixed with big- time sports and prominent Greek life. Roughly 2,500 students comprise the student body at this undergraduate-only liberal arts school in quiet Easton, Pennsylvania. Undergrads are a high-caliber lot, possessing academic credentials only a touch below archrival Lehigh University.

Lafayette offers fifty-one areas over four academic divisions: engineering, humanities, natural sciences, and the social sciences. It also allows for self-designed majors such as behavioral economics, environmental issues and policy, or nanoscience. All undergrads delve into a first- year seminar during fall of their freshman year, a course designed to strengthen writing, thinking, and speaking abilities. Other required components of the school's common course of study include a year of foreign language, a quantitative reasoning course, two classes under the umbrella of global and multiculturalism, and at least a singular foray into each of the college's academic divisions.

One-on-one attention from professors is a reality at Lafayette, thanks to a 10:1 student-to-faculty ratio and no graduate students to compete with. A solid 62 percent of sections contain fewer than twenty students; 16 percent enroll nine or fewer. By the time senior year is nearing its completion, 52 percent of students have completed a research experience with a faculty member. The school invests almost half a million dollars annually in funding undergraduate research. A majority of students also have studied for a semester in a foreign country as 60 percent of graduates elect to study abroad in one of fifty locations. In addition to semester-long options, Lafayette offers truncated study abroad opportunities during semester breaks.

Of the 609 degrees conferred in 2018, engineering was the discipline in which the largest number of degrees were earned, accounting for a whopping 22 percent. The engineering program is one of the best in the country among non-doctoral granting institutions. Economics was the next most commonly conferred degree and is also one of Lafayette's strongest. Other popular and well-regarded programs include psychology, international affairs, and film studies. On the whole, Lafayette students well with employers and top graduate schools but also experience success when applying for prestigious fellowships. Named a top Fulbright producer, Lafayette had four winners in 2017-18. In recent years, it has had graduates land Gilman, Goldwater, and Udall Scholarships.

Outside the Classroom

In sleepy Easton, 96 percent of undergrads lay their heads at night inside college-owned housing. Greek life, which was under a microscope after a 2012 hazing death, has survived and thrived, still drawing 39 percent of the student body into fraternities and sororities. Athletics are also a central part of the Lafayette experience as the Leopards compete in twenty-three NCAA Division I sports as well as in more than fifty club and intramural programs. Games against rival Lehigh garner a high level of interest. Over 200 student-run organizations are active. For those interested in the performing arts, twenty-four such clubs are on the menu. There are forty-three cultural and/or service organizations that help contribute a collective 20,000 annual hours of charitable engagement. Nature lovers aren't far from the Pocono Mountains that offer all of the hiking, snowboarding, skiing, tubing, and fishing you can handle. Almost equidistant (in terms of travel time) between New York City and Philadelphia, big-city fun is only a car ride away. Easton is a small town with plenty of history and some nice eateries, but campus is the hub of the social experience.

Career Services

The recently renamed Gateway Career Center is staffed by eleven professional employees (not counting office assistants or database managers) who work in career counseling, employer relations, internship coordination, or graduate school advising. That 236:1 student-to-advisor ratio is better-than-average when compared to other schools featured in this guide. Thanks to such generous staffing, counselors can offer distinct services to students at every phase of their college education, beginning with career exploration activities during freshman year. Mock interviews, resume development, internship/externship discovery, or individualized career/grad school counseling is available at any time.

Large-scale events, such as the Fall Career Fair, attract more than sixty employers including Goldman Sachs, ExxonMobil, and Fidelity Investments. The Gateway Career Center does an excellent job guiding students into internships and other meaningful opportunities for hands-on learning. By senior year 78 percent of Lafayette undergrads have completed an internship, externship, or other field experience. A robust 40 percent of recent grads found their jobs directly through campus recruiting and/or the alumni network. On-campus interviews take place October-November and again from February-April. With a high level of personalized offerings and excellent career and graduate school outcomes, the Gateway Career Center accomplishes its mission on behalf of its undergraduates.

Professional Outcomes

Within six months of graduation, a stellar 97 percent of the Class of 2018 had already landed full-time jobs or were enrolled in graduate/professional school. The most commonly procured jobs are in business development, education, operations, engineering, sales, finance, and research. Companies employing large numbers of Lafayette alumni include Merck, IBM, Morgan Stanley, Citi, Merrill Lynch, JP Morgan Chase Co., Deloitte, and EY. The average early career salary for a Lafayette graduate is over $62,000; by midcareer the average income reaches $121,000. Despite being a Pennsylvania institution, Philadelphia is the second most popular landing spot for alumni; New York City attracts nearly three times as many Leopards. Large pockets of alumni also can be found in DC, Boston, and San Francisco.

Those attending graduate school frequently land at some of the top programs in the country within their respective disciplines. Recent economics majors have entered business/econ programs at Stanford, the University of Chicago, and Yale. Government majors have gone on to study at Penn, Harvard, and GW. Chemistry majors go on to pursue PhDs at institutions such as Tulane, Princeton, and Emory. Medical school applicants with a 3.6 GPA or above enjoy a 75 percent acceptance rate, and dental school candidates find homes at a 94 percent clip. Recent graduates have matriculated into medical schools at Georgetown, UVA, Brown, Dartmouth, and Boston University. Law school applicants found homes at a perfect 100 percent rate, and those acceptances included many top law schools.

Admission

The 9,236 students jostling for a spot in the Lafayette Class of 2022 were granted acceptance at a 29 percent rate. The Class of 2021 was admitted at a slightly more generous 31 percent. The Class of 2022 possessed an average SAT score of 1345, ACT of 30, and average GPA of 3.51. Twenty-three incoming freshmen were the valedictorian or salutatorian of their high school classes; 52 percent hailed from the top 10 percent, and 78 percent from the top quarter. A decade ago, Lafayette was a touch easier to get into. The acceptance rate in 2008-09 was 37 percent, and the 75th percentile SAT score was 1370, a figure closer to the average SAT score held by today's freshmen. However, students' class rank from that year shows that 65 percent placed in the top 10 percent of their high school classes, and 93 percent were in the top quarter. Taken together, those figures paint a muddled picture of whether Lafayette is more or less difficult to gain acceptance into than it was a decade ago.

In the eyes of the admissions committee at Lafayette, two factors receive the highest level of consideration—rigor of coursework and GPA. The next tier of factors includes test scores, class rank, essays, recommendations, extracurricular activities, the interview, character/personal qualities, and talent/ability. Those applying early decision were accepted at a 52 percent clip and accounted for more than half of entering freshmen in the 2018-19 academic year. Lafayette is a competitive institution but not out of reach for students with SAT scores in the 1300s and/or a less-than-pristine transcript. Applying early yields a strong advantage in the admissions process as the acceptance rate is higher, and a large chunk of the spots in the freshman class are already occupied by the time applicants enter the regular round.

Worth Your Money?

The annual bill to attend Lafayette exceeds $73,000. Eleven percent of undergrads do receive merit aid averaging $29k. Only one-third of undergraduates currently attending Lafayette receive any aid at all. The good news is that those who are awarded a grant see 100 percent of their need met, and the average total is over $45,000. The school's excellent offerings in engineering and strong networks in Philly and NYC lead to generally high starting salaries, making it possible for most to pay their student loans without too much economic pain.

FINANCIAL
Institutional Type: Private
In-State Tuition: $54,512
Out-of-State Tuition: $54,512
Room & Board: $16,264
Required Fees: $1,240
Books & Supplies: $1,000

Avg. Need-Based Aid: $44,741
Avg. % of Need Met: 100%

Avg. Merit-Based Aid: $29,253
% Receiving Merit-Based Aid: 11%

Avg. Cumulative Debt: $26,341
% of Students Borrowing: 39%

CAREER
Who Recruits
1. Gilbane Building
2. Crayola
3. SMC Partners
4. MarketAxess
5. Whiting-Turner Contracting

Notable Internships
1. Disney Streaming Services
2. RCA Records
3. Cisco

Top Industries
1. Business
2. Education
3. Operations
4. Engineering
5. Sales

Top Employers
1. Merck
2. IBM
3. Morgan Stanley
4. Citi
5. Deloitte

Where Alumni Work
1. New York City
2. Philadelphia
3. Allentown, PA
4. Boston
5. Washington, DC

Median Earnings
College Scorecard (Early Career): $68,600
EOP (Early Career): $75,300
PayScale (Mid-Career): $122,500

RANKINGS
Forbes: 57
Money: 67
U.S. News: 39, Liberal Arts Colleges
Wall Street Journal/THE: 87 (T)
Washington Monthly: 26, Liberal Arts Colleges

#CollegesWorthYourMoney

Lawrence University

Appleton, Wisconsin | Admissions Phone: 920-832-6500

ADMISSION
Admission Rate: 62%
Admission Rate - Men: 60%
Admission Rate - Women: 65%
EA Admission Rate: 85%
ED Admission Rate: 83%
Admission Rate (5-Year Trend): -10%
ED Admission Rate (5-Year Trend): -4%
% of Admits Attending (Yield): 18%
Transfer Admission Rate: 39%

Offered Wait List: 87
Accepted Wait List: 23
Admitted Wait List: 2

SAT Reading/Writing (Middle 50%): 610-710
SAT Math (Middle 50%): 600-740
ACT Composite (Middle 50%): 27-31
Testing Policy: Test Optional
SAT Superscore: Yes
ACT Superscore: Yes

% Graduated in Top 10% of HS Class: 35%
% Graduated in Top 25% of HS Class: 69%
% Graduated in Top 50% of HS Class: 91%

ENROLLMENT
Total Undergraduate Enrollment: 1,472
% Part-Time: 4%
% Male: 47%
% Female: 53%
% Out-of-State: 73%
% Fraternity: 8%
% Sorority: 10%
% On-Campus (Freshman): 100%
% On-Campus (All Undergraduate): 94%

% African-American: 5%
% Asian: 5%
% Hispanic: 10%
% White: 62%
% Other: 4%
% Race or Ethnicity Unknown: 1%
% International: 13%
% Low-Income: 25%

ACADEMICS
Student-to-Faculty Ratio: 8:1
% of Classes Under 20: 81%
% of Classes Under 40: 96%
% Full-Time Faculty: 85%
% Full-Time Faculty w/ Terminal Degree: 91%

Top Programs
Biology
Economics
English
Environmental Studies
Government
Music
Physics

Retention Rate: 85%
4-Year Graduation Rate: 66%
6-Year Graduation Rate: 80%

Curricular Flexibility: Somewhat Flexible
Academic Rating: ★★★⌡

Inside the Classroom

The history of Lawrence University, a tiny liberal arts school in Appleton, Wisconsin, is as unique as its present-day educational offerings. One of the earliest (ninth, to be precise) coeducational colleges in the United States and one of the top music conservatories anywhere, the nearly 1,500 undergraduates on campus today enjoy an intimate academic environment in which the largest number of degrees conferred are in the performing arts. It is the only school in the nation whose college of arts and sciences and music conservatory are both 100 percent populated by undergraduates. There are thirty-five distinct majors as well as the option to complete a five-year double major from both the conservatory and A&S; like we said, LU is unique.

Operating on a trimester calendar, the academic year is comprised of ten-week fall, winter, and spring sessions. For more than seventy years, part of the LU core curriculum has been a yearlong Freshman Studies program that in a small, seminar-style classroom explores questions like "What is the best sort of life for human beings? Are there limits to human knowledge? How should we respond to injustice and suffering?" From there, Lawrence undergrads encounter a dose of humanities, natural science, social science, and fine arts offerings and must show competency in a foreign language, quantitative reasoning, and a writing/speaking-intensive course. Every graduate completes a Senior Experience that can take the form of a paper, performance, portfolio, or exhibition.

An 8:1 student/faculty ratio allows for extremely small class sizes—the majority of sections contain only ten to nineteen students, and many independent study/1:1 music instruction courses also are available. With Lawrence being a "university" in name only, undergraduate research opportunities are wide open. Professors are expected to allow undergraduates access to their research studies; for example, every member of the Chemistry Department has to run an active research group. The Lawrence University Research Fellows (LURF) program offers a stipend during ten-week, research-focused terms. All told, close to two-thirds of LU students gain hands-on research experience at some point during their four years of study. The college strongly encourages students to study abroad, and roughly 40 percent take the plunge. Sponsored opportunities include the London Lawrence Center or the Francophile Seminar in Dakar, Senegal.

Biology (14), social sciences (19 percent), and performing arts (22 percent) comprise the most popular areas of study at LU. The latter includes Lawrence's world-renowned Conservatory of Music, which enrolls approximately 350 undergraduates. Extremely strong natural science programs allow the university to be a top producer of future STEM PhDs. It is also a top producer of Fulbright Scholars, with five to its credit in the 2018-19 year. Other prestigious fellowships won by Class of 2018 members include a Watson Fellowship and a Goldwater Scholarship.

Outside the Classroom

Lawrence's 88-acre campus houses 100 percent of freshmen and 94 percent of the undergraduate student body in five residence halls. The Greek presence is minimal with 8 percent of men affiliated with frats and 10 percent of women members of sororities. One-quarter of the population are NCAA Division III varsity athletes competing on one of the ten men's or nine women's squads known as the Vikings. Non-sports events that draw many participants include Fall Festival, Winter Carnival, and the Great Midwest Trivia Contest, a fifty-hour marathon that has drawn national media attention. There are over one hundred clubs and activities, and virtually every student on campus is involved in at least one. Volunteer organizations are popular, and students give a collective 10,000 hours per year. Three or four times per year campus will close for an hour while everyone flocks to Memorial Chapel for convocation where a famous speaker like Maya Angelou or David Sedaris will address the student body. If the Appleton campus that overlooks the Fox River doesn't provide enough natural beauty for you, the college also owns 425+ acres on the shores of Lake Michigan that can be utilized for hiking, ice skating, and camping. Appleton is a safe and enjoyable small town with a population around 70,000 that contains ample bars, restaurants, and shops. The town is only about a thirty-minute drive from Green Bay and about ninety minutes from Milwaukee.

Career Services

The Center for Career, Life and Community Engagement employs eight full-time staff members in employer and alumni relations, Career advisor, and pre-professional advising and major fellowships. That student-to-advisor ratio of 184:1 is strong when compared to other colleges featured in this guide, and it allows the career services staff to carve out time even for freshmen. All first-years are encouraged to come in for at least a fifteen- or twenty-minute counseling session. The center's stated mission is "preparing students for lives of achievement, responsible and meaningful citizenship, lifelong learning, and personal fulfillment," and it offers ample one-on-one counseling toward those aims.

Students can locate internship opportunities through Lawrence Link or through face-to-face counseling sessions. Many students pursue internships with nonprofit institutions, charitable organizations, and museums, although several recent undergrads have landed positions at Apple, Google, and JPMorgan Chase. In part due to the school's small size and location, recruiting or on-campus interviewing visits from major employers are not frequent occurrences, and the school does not host a major job fair. Unfortunately, LU does not publicize data such as the percentage of students who land an internship, the number of in-person counseling sessions per year, or information about employers visiting campus. In the absence of such information and given the low starting salaries of recent graduates, it appears that some improvement may be needed in those areas.

Professional Outcomes

Of the 329 graduates in the Class of 2017, an impressive 98 percent had already reached their next employment or postsecondary destination. Among the 57 percent of that group who had landed their first jobs, fifty-eight grads were working in business/finance, forty-one in social services/nonprofit, eighteen in the arts, thirteen in health care/pharmaceutical, and twelve in media/communications. Companies presently employing more than a dozen Lawrence alumni include Deloitte, Epic Systems, Wells Fargo, Northwestern Mutual, US Bank, and UnitedHealth Group. Most students continue to reside in the Midwest after graduating. Greater Chicago; Oshkosh, Wisconsin; Greater Minneapolis-St. Paul; and Greater Milwaukee boast the greatest number of alums. Starting salaries for recent graduating classes average around $42,000, lower than many in its peer group that includes St. Olaf, Grinnell, and Carleton (whose graduates pull in over $10k more).

Over the last few years graduates have gone on to master's and doctoral programs at a wide range of universities on the prestige spectrum. Highlighting that list are elite schools Carnegie Mellon, Duke, Dartmouth, Emory, Georgetown, University of Pennsylvania, and Washington University in St. Louis. Medical school acceptance rates fluctuate between 67 and 75 percent, significantly higher than the national average, even in down years. Recent graduates have matriculated into medical schools at Johns Hopkins, the University of Chicago, Northwestern, Boston University, and the University of Wisconsin. According to the National Science Foundation, Lawrence produces the fourteenth most future science and engineering PhDs among liberal arts colleges.

Admission

It's hard to find a school of better quality that has a greater acceptance rate than Lawrence's 62 percent. The university is trending in a more selective direction as the admit rate was an even more generous 73 percent five years ago, but chances remain strong, even for less-than-perfect high schoolers. While 35 percent did place in the top 10 percent of their graduating class and 31 percent possessed a GPA of greater than 3.75, many others brought more middling credentials to the table. The average GPA for admitted students is 3.46, and 31 percent did not land in the top 25 percent of their high school cohort. This school does not require SATs or ACTs but, among those who elected to submit scores anyway, the mid-50 percent range was 1210-1450 on the SAT and 27-31 on the ACT.

Lawrence was early to the test-optional party, jettisoning mandatory standardized test submission in 2006. As a result, GPA, rigor of coursework, class rank, talent/ability, and character/personal qualities are perched atop the list of most important factors. The admissions essay, recommendations, extracurricular activities, and an interview, which is recommended but not required, make up the second rung of "important factors." Test scores are merely "considered"; 41 percent of enrolled freshmen did submit SAT scores to go along with 31 percent who submitted results from the ACT. Few apply early decision; only twenty-four did so in 2018, and twenty were accepted. A safety school for many applying to even more prestigious Midwestern liberal arts institutions, only about 20 percent of those admitted actually enroll. Thus, it is advantageous to communicate your genuine interest in attending throughout the application process.

Worth Your Money?

The sticker price (including room and board and all fees) at Lawrence is $61,716, but few receive an annual bill for that amount. Over two-thirds of undergraduates receive need-based aid for an average of $39,000, and 43 percent of those awarded aid see 100 percent of their demonstrated need met. A substantial number of students, approximately one-third, receive an average merit aid award of more than $26k. Because the most commonly studied fields at LU are not among the highest paying, students need to adjust the value of loans they are willing to take out accordingly. That said, this school provides an amazing educational experience, particularly for those interested in performance and academia, and it typically provides enough financial aid to make a Lawrence degree affordable.

FINANCIAL
Institutional Type: Private
In-State Tuition: $48,822
Out-of-State Tuition: $48,822
Room & Board: $10,719
Required Fees: $300
Books & Supplies: $900

Avg. Need-Based Aid: $39,106
Avg. % of Need Met: 95%

Avg. Merit-Based Aid: $26,419
% Receiving Merit-Based Aid: 33%

Avg. Cumulative Debt: $31,136
% of Students Borrowing: 67%

CAREER
Who Recruits
1. M3 Insurance
2. Enterprise Holdings
3. Hauser Advertising
4. McAdam Financial
5. Air Wisconsin Airlines, LLC

Notable Internships
1. American Museum of Natural History
2. Uber
3. EY

Top Industries
1. Education
2. Business
3. Operations
4. Arts & Design
5. Social Services

Top Employers
1. US Bank
2. Epic
3. Northwestern Mutual
4. Target
5. Wells Fargo

Where Alumni Work
1. Chicago
2. Oshkosh, WI
3. Minneapolis
4. Milwaukee
5. New York City

Median Earnings
College Scorecard (Early Career): $44,100
EOP (Early Career): $44,500
PayScale (Mid-Career): $98,800

RANKINGS
Forbes: 193
Money: 183
U.S. News: 58, Liberal Arts Colleges
Wall Street Journal/THE: 189 (T)
Washington Monthly: 107, Liberal Arts Colleges

#CollegesWorthYourMoney

Bethlehem, Pennsylvania | Admissions Phone: 610-758-3100

ADMISSION

Admission Rate: 22%
Admission Rate - Men: 20%
Admission Rate - Women: 25%
EA Admission Rate: Not Offered
ED Admission Rate: 60%
Admission Rate (5-Year Trend): -9%
ED Admission Rate (5-Year Trend): 0%
% of Admits Attending (Yield): 37%
Transfer Admission Rate: 24%

Offered Wait List: 7,737
Accepted Wait List: 3,358
Admitted Wait List: 69

SAT Reading/Writing (Middle 50%): 620-690
SAT Math (Middle 50%): 650-760
ACT Composite (Middle 50%): 29-33
Testing Policy: ACT/SAT Required
SAT Superscore: Yes
ACT Superscore: Yes

% Graduated in Top 10% of HS Class: 58%
% Graduated in Top 25% of HS Class: 88%
% Graduated in Top 50% of HS Class: 99%

ENROLLMENT

Total Undergraduate Enrollment: 5,047
% Part-Time: 1%
% Male: 54%
% Female: 46%
% Out-of-State: 73%
% Fraternity: 30%
% Sorority: 39%
% On-Campus (Freshman): 99%
% On-Campus (All Undergraduate): 63%

% African-American: 3%
% Asian: 8%
% Hispanic: 10%
% White: 63%
% Other: 3%
% Race or Ethnicity Unknown: 4%
% International: 9%
% Low-Income: 17%

ACADEMICS

Student-to-Faculty Ratio: 9:1
% of Classes Under 20: 50%
% of Classes Under 40: 82%
% Full-Time Faculty: 76%
% Full-Time Faculty w/ Terminal Degree: 95%

Top Programs
Accounting
Computer Science
Earth and Environmental Sciences
Engineering
Finance
International Relations
Psychology

Retention Rate: 94%
4-Year Graduation Rate: 72%
6-Year Graduation Rate: 87%

Curricular Flexibility: Somewhat Flexible
Academic Rating: ★★★★

Inside the Classroom

Emblematic of the American economy as a whole, the once great industrial town of Bethlehem, Pennsylvania, is now highlighted by a research university known for preparing the next generation of problem-solving engineers. Lehigh University is a research powerhouse that caters to only 5,075 undergraduate students, allowing for lots of individualized attention from expert faculty in world-class facilities. There are three colleges within the larger university: the College of Arts & Sciences, the College of Business & Economics, and the prestigious Rossin College of Engineering and Applied Sciences.

Despite its modest size, Lehigh offers more than one hundred undergraduate degree programs and runs 2,300+ courses each school year. Academic requirements vary by school but, notably, none possess a foreign language mandate. In the College of Arts & Sciences students must complete two semesters of Composition & Literature, First-Year Seminar, one math course, and eight credits in each of the humanities, natural sciences, and social sciences. The core curricula in the College of Business & Economics includes foundational courses in decision-making and business principles as well as introductory coursework in accounting, economics, marketing, management, and finance (no matter which of those concentrations you choose). Lastly, all business students must complete a senior capstone project. Within the Rossin College of Engineering and Applied Science undergrads must knock out ten credits of English and economics and thirteen credits in the humanities. There are also two innovative programs that require a foray into other disciplines—the Integrated Business & Engineering Honors Program (IBE) and the Integrated Degree Engineering, Arts & Sciences Honors Programs (IDEAS).

Lehigh has a 9:1 student-to-faculty ratio, but classes aren't as tiny as one might expect with such favorable staffing numbers. The average class size is twenty-nine but, on the plus side, 45 percent of courses have enrollments of nineteen or fewer. Undergraduate research is commonplace, particularly within the engineering school. Each year, 40 percent of engineering students gain faculty-led research experience. Additionally, 43 percent of graduates engage in some type of international experience, whether it's a semester of academic study abroad or a foreign-based internship. Roughly half of those students took courses in one of 250 study abroad programs approved by the university.

With a highly ranked engineering school, it's easy to view Lehigh as primarily a techie haven. Surprisingly, the majority of students pursue other programs, with Lehigh's well-regarded business school drawing the most majors (34%). Competitive fellowship and scholarship programs look favorably upon the university. Ten undergrads were awarded Gilman Scholarships in 2018, and three students won National Science Foundation Fellowships the year prior.

Outside the Classroom

Lehigh's three contiguous campuses account for 1,600 picturesque acres. Only 65 percent of students live on campus, and most of those are underclassmen who are required to reside in college-owned housing. The school plans to add 1,000 undergraduate students by 2026 and is presently building additional on-campus housing to accommodate the increased student population. Even with 35 percent of students living off campus, this is an incredibly involved student body with 99 percent involved in some type of extracurricular activity. Greek life is a powerful force with 43 percent of women joining sororities and one-third of men pledging a fraternity. On the athletics front, the Mountain Hawks compete in twenty-five intercollegiate sports, mostly in the NCAA Division I Patriot League. An additional forty-three intramural and club teams claim another 2,900 participants annually. On the non-sports front there are 200+ student organizations at Lehigh and over 250 art events on campus annually. Service-oriented clubs are popular and account for 65,000 collective hours of community service per year. Bethlehem is known more for its industrial history as a hub of steel production than for a thrilling nightlife, but students with a car can get to Philly in an hour and a half or New York City in a little over two hours.

Career Services

The Center for Career and Professional Development (CCPD) is staffed by ten professional employees (not counting business managers or interns) who work in career counseling, employer engagement, or graduate school advising. That 507:1 student-to-advisor ratio is within the average range of universities profiled in this guide. Yet, by almost any metric, the level of support offered to the school's undergraduates is of superior quality.

In 2017-18, the CCPD enticed more than 6,900 attendees to its events (more than the entire undergraduate population). The fall and spring career expos draw large student crowds and are attended by as many as 140 employers, including many major corporations. Counselors held an outstanding 2,468 one-on-one advising sessions and achieved 12,000+ total engagements through in-person and online interaction. Perhaps most impressive is the number of on-campus interviews conducted in 2017-18—2,754—more than double the number of graduating seniors that year. Lehigh's career services staff also does a superb job facilitating internships and other valuable immersive experiences. An exceptional 89 percent of Class of 2018 members completed at least one internship or externship. Lehigh's Center for Career and Professional Development provides a top-notch level of service to its undergraduate clientele, and those efforts translate into stellar employment and graduate school outcomes.

Professional Outcomes

The Class of 2018 quickly found its way toward the next productive step in their lives with 95 percent landing jobs or grad school placements within six months of leaving Lehigh. Among graduates of the School of Business and Economics, the top industries entered by graduates were financial services (28 percent), accounting (19 percent), consulting (9 percent), and marketing (6 percent). Top employers of recent business degree earners include Amazon, CitiGroup, Deloitte, EY, KPMG, Morgan Stanley, and PwC. Rossin College of Engineering and Applied Science graduates flocked to companies such as ExxonMobil, GE, Google, IBM, Lockheed Martin, Merck, and Microsoft. Arts & Sciences graduates secured employment at places like CBS, People Magazine, and the National Institutes of Health. Across all three schools, the average starting salary was $65,000 with computer science majors on the high end at $87k and math and natural sciences majors on the low end at $48k.

Of those heading straight to graduate/professional school, 31 percent were studying engineering, 24 percent were pursuing business degrees, 10 percent were training for health professions, and 4 percent had entered law school. In 2018, a phenomenal 91 percent of medical school applicants found at least one acceptance. That cohort possessed an average GPA of 3.7 and MCAT scores in the 85th percentile. Recent med school acceptances included Boston University School of Medicine, Harvard School of Dental Medicine, and Johns Hopkins School of Medicine. Over the past three years law school applicants were successful 93 percent of the time and were welcomed by institutions such as the University of Pennsylvania, Tulane, Temple, and Villanova. Those pursuing a master's or a PhD from the Class of 2018 did so at Columbia, Duke, Stanford, Berkeley, Brown, Johns Hopkins, and a number of other first-class universities.

Admission

Lehigh experienced a 13 percent spike in applications between 2018 and 2017 that led to an all-time low 22 percent acceptance rate for those jockeying for a spot in the Class of 2022. Freshmen entering Lehigh for the 2018-19 school year possessed middle-50 percent scores of 1270-1450 on the SAT and 29-33 on the ACT. A similar number of students submit scores from each exam. Fifty-eight percent of entering freshmen in 2018-19 placed in the top decile of their high school class, and 88 percent were in the top quartile.

Five factors sit perched atop the list of criteria considered by the Lehigh admissions committee: rigor of courses, GPA, recommendations, extracurricular activities, and character/personal qualities. The next rung of factors deemed "important" include standardized test scores, essays, talent/ability, volunteer work, and demonstrated interest. On the subject of demonstrated interest, Lehigh places high value on an applicant's level of commitment to attending the university. To quantify that importance, early decision applicants are admitted at a rate of 60 percent, almost three times the acceptance rate during the regular cycle. Early decision applicants comprised 56 percent of the incoming class. Women face slightly better odds, generally sporting acceptance rates 5-7 percent better than male applicants. Clearly, applying early is a major edge at Lehigh, but you'll need to be toward the top of your class and have taken a healthy dose of AP and honors courses, particularly in STEM areas.

Worth Your Money?

Those who don't qualify for financial aid will not receive much help from Lehigh—fewer than 10 percent of attendees receive merit aid. Fortunately, the $71,465 annual cost of attendance is knocked down significantly for the 43 percent of undergraduates who qualify for need-based aid; many see 100 percent of their demonstrated need met by the university, and the average annual grant is for $45k. With extremely high starting salaries, this school is likely to pay you back, particularly if you major in the business/engineering realm.

FINANCIAL
Institutional Type: Private
In-State Tuition: $54,790
Out-of-State Tuition: $54,790
Room & Board: $14,160
Required Fees: $450
Books & Supplies: $1,000

Avg. Need-Based Aid: $44,745
Avg. % of Need Met: 97%

Avg. Merit-Based Aid: $11,097
% Receiving Merit-Based Aid: 9%

Avg. Cumulative Debt: $35,109
% of Students Borrowing: 50%

CAREER
Who Recruits
1. Knowles Corporation
2. Mineral Technologies Inc.
3. SIG
4. Tge LiRo Group
5. Crayola

Notable Internships
1. Prudenial Financial
2. Barclays
3. Visa

Top Industries
1. Business
2. Engineering
3. Education
4. Operations
5. Research

Top Employers
1. Merck
2. EY
3. PwC
4. IBM
5. Deloitte

Where Alumni Work
1. New York City
2. Allentown, PA
3. Philadelphia
4. Boston
5. Washington, DC

Median Earnings
College Scorecard (Early Career): $81,900
EOP (Early Career): $81,200
PayScale (Mid-Career): $134,100

RANKINGS
Forbes: 67
Money: 111
U.S. News: 50 (T), National Universities
Wall Street Journal/THE: 55
Washington Monthly: 71, National Universities

#CollegesWorthYourMoney

Loyola University Maryland

Baltimore, Maryland | Admissions Phone: 410-617-5012

Inside the Classroom

College consumers can sometimes find the Loyola brand hard to grasp. After all, there is Loyola University Chicago, Loyola University New Orleans, Loyola Marymount University in Los Angeles, and the school we are profiling here—Loyola University Maryland—and *none* of the schools is affiliated in any way with the others. While all honor St. Ignatius, the Jesuit founder, Loyola University Maryland is its own distinct entity and is a rare school where the acceptance rate and four-year graduation rate both hover around 80 percent. Offering thirty-five undergraduate programs through its three schools, Loyola College (arts and sciences), the Sellinger School of Business and Management, and the School of Education, Loyola services an undergraduate population of 3,879, only 20 percent of whom are Maryland residents

Consistent with the Jesuit ideology of *cura personalis*, Loyola has created a liberal arts curriculum designed to help develop the whole person and produce well-rounded citizens. This extensive seventeen-course set of requirements includes writing, history, literature, foreign language, social sciences, fine arts, mathematics, theology, philosophy, ethics, and diversity. Students in the small-but-excellent Honors Program follow an identical path but complete their core curriculum within honors-only sections.

A 12:1 student-to-faculty ratio leads to average class sizes of only twenty students. The vast majority of courses enroll between ten and twenty-nine students, 12 percent have a single-digit enrollment, and of 906 total sections only fourteen contained forty or more undergraduates. Students are encouraged to apply for undergraduate research opportunities such as the Hauber Summer Research Fellowship Program which, in 2019, gave fourteen students in the natural and applied sciences fields a chance to conduct ten weeks of independent research. Biology majors can enroll in two courses that facilitate experiential research opportunities. Those with wanderlust will find plenty of kindred spirits and no shortage of options; there are twenty countries that students can choose from as study abroad options, and the participation rate exceeds 60 percent, one of the highest figures of any master's-granting school in the nation.

Almost two-fifths of the degrees conferred are in the area of business/marketing, making it, by far, the school's most popular area of concentration. Next are communication/journalism (10 percent), the social sciences (8 percent), psychology (7 percent), and biology (6 percent). The Sellinger School of Business and Management has a solid reputation beyond the immediate region, and the Department of Communication has an excellent record of placing students within media organizations. The school's push for international study translated to a record number of Fulbright Scholars in 2019 with eight winners. Additionally, three current students captured Gilman Scholarships.

Outside the Classroom

If you are looking for a school where just about everyone lives in a tightknit community on campus, then the Loyola Maryland experience is for you. Freshmen occupy university-owned dorms at a 97 percent clip, and 82 percent of the total student body resides on this 81-acre wooded campus that isn't what you'd expect to find in the middle of Baltimore. Loyola's seventeen residence halls are some of the best-rated college accommodations in the entire country. As is the case at many Jesuit institutions, there are no sororities or fraternities at this school, but there are 200+ clubs, including seventeen community service organizations, fourteen dance groups, and twelve honors societies. Service is popular as 80 percent of the student body engages in some type of charitable endeavor. Religion plays a major role as students are predominately Catholic—27 percent attended Catholic high schools. The gender split on campus is approaching 60/40 in favor of women. Loyola has a strong athletics program that features eighteen NCAA Division I teams that play in the Patriot League. Johns Hopkins is its biggest rival, and the annual lacrosse showdown is a big deal. There are also twenty-six club teams, and 20 percent of students participate in intramural leagues. Recreational amenities include a ten-lane pool, rock climbing wall, and indoor track. Not known as a big party school, there are plenty of safe commercial pockets in the city of Baltimore worth exploring, and DC is only an hour away for weekend trips.

Career Services

The Career Center at Loyola Maryland is manned by seven professionals with expertise in career counseling and employer outreach. That works out to a 554:1 student-to-advisor ratio, which is within the average range of colleges featured in this guide. This office keeps careful track of its own statistics that paint a picture of a supportive and highly available career services staff offering ample opportunity to connect with relevant employers.

In the 2017-18 school year the office posted 12,805 jobs and 4,661 internships on Handshake, held 2,218 counseling appointments, and attracted 2,307 students to networking events, workshops, career fairs, and information sessions. For a small university, it's highly impressive that 111 companies and organizations interviewed seniors on campus. In total, 194 unique employers visited campus. A helpful alumni base 60,000 strong is also willing to lend a hand to those about to launch their careers. If you're looking to land a position far from Baltimore, Loyola Marymount's Career Center has reciprocity with twenty-eight other Jesuit institution's career centers around the country. The school also has forged many strong internship partners. For example, within the Department of Writing, partners include nine publications and ten nonprofits that regularly take Loyola interns. Career fairs drew eighty-nine employers, and official sponsors of the fairs included Bank of America, Dixon Hughes Goodman (the largest accounting firm in the South), and CareFirst BlueCross BlueShield. In sum, the Loyola Career Center directly connects with more than half of the undergraduate student body each year and facilitates a solid number of industry connections, making it a highly useful resource for all current students.

Professional Outcomes

Members of the Class of 2017 found their way to their next employment, volunteer, or grad school home within six months of receiving their diplomas at a stellar 97 percent clip. Major companies and organizations employing members of this cohort include Accenture, Booz Allen Hamilton, Bloomberg, Goldman Sachs, NASA, the National Institutes of Health, the New York Giants (NFL), Sony/ATV Music Publishing, and Walt Disney Company. Employers of the overall greatest number of alumni include T. Rowe Price, Northrup Grumman, Morgan Stanley, JPMorgan Chase, PwC, EY, Black & Decker, and Deloitte. The average starting salary for a Loyola graduate is $51,000 with social sciences majors bringing home a mean salary of $41k and degree-earners in the natural and applied sciences averaging $58k. Baltimore, New York City, DC, Philly, and Boston woo the most Greyhound alumni.

Twenty-three percent of the members of the Class of 2017 immediately enrolled in graduate or professional school after completing their undergraduate work at Loyola Maryland. Many stayed in the area, either at Loyola itself, the University of Maryland, or in the DC or Philadelphia areas at schools like George Washington, Temple University, or Villanova. Some members earned a spot at elite graduate institutions like Brown, Columbia, Duke, Northwestern, and the University of Pennsylvania. Over the last decade the percentage of successful law school applicants has vacillated between 77 percent and 93 percent, and Loyola grads are currently pursuing their legal education at Villanova, George Washington, UC Berkeley, and the University of Maryland. From 2015-2019 medical school applicants who obtained a committee letter supporting their candidacy enjoyed a 72 percent acceptance rate. Recent acceptances include some of the top medical schools in the country such as Boston University, Tufts, Harvard, and Georgetown.

Admission

Getting into Loyola is not a harrowing process, even if you hit a few bumps along your academic road. The acceptance rate for a place in the Class of 2022 was an unintimidating 79 percent, and that doesn't show any signs of falling as the school has only a 13 percent yield rate; in other terms, 87 percent of those who are accepted ultimately enroll at another institution. Loyola is test-optional, but most 2018-19 freshman submitted scores—63 percent included SATs and 25 percent included ACTs as part of their applications. The mid-50 percent scores were 25-30 on the ACT and 1140-1320 on the SAT. The average high school GPA earned by entering members of this class was 3.5, and while 28 percent ranked in the top decile of their graduating class and 61 percent were in the top quartile, 10 percent did not even rank in the top 50 percent.

This committee means what it says when it declares that it does "not use a formula or have strict cutoffs. Instead, the admission office's goal is to conduct a balanced and individual review, taking a number of factors into account." At the top of that list are GPA, rigor of secondary school record, recommendations, the essay, and character/personal qualities. Extracurricular activities, volunteer work, and talent/ability also receive strong consideration. Loyola is a school where bright but perhaps late-blooming teens can find a welcoming institution that will offer a top-notch Jesuit education.

Worth Your Money?

Living on campus brings the total annual sticker price to a whopping $67,380, a steep price to pay for any school. At that cost, it is hard to justify attending Loyola University Maryland if you are in a situation where you will need to take out large loans; the average Greyhound's debt is over $32,000. However, it is worth applying to see what kind of aid package you receive. Freshmen in 2018-19 who qualified for some type of aid averaged a package just shy of $19,000. If the total cost of attendance is comparable to other institutions to which you are accepted, a degree from this university can certainly make it worth your money.

FINANCIAL
Institutional Type: Private
In-State Tuition: $48,700
Out-of-State Tuition: $48,700
Room & Board: $14,710
Required Fees: $1,565
Books & Supplies: $1,250

Avg. Need-Based Aid: $18,861
Avg. % of Need Met: 88%

Avg. Merit-Based Aid: $18,390
% Receiving Merit-Based Aid: 75%

Avg. Cumulative Debt: N/A
% of Students Borrowing: N/A

CAREER
Who Recruits
1. Legg Mason
2. Baltimore Orioles
3. T. Rowe Price
4. Cisco
5. Stanley Black & Decker

Notable Internships
1. LGT Capital Partners
2. National Bank of Canada
3. Fidelity Investments

Top Industries
1. Business
2. Education
3. Operations
4. Finance
5. Sales

Top Employers
1. T. Rowe Price
2. Northrop Grumman
3. Morgan Stanley
4. JPMorgan Chase
5. PwC

Where Alumni Work
1. Baltimore
2. New York City
3. Washington, DC
4. Philadelphia
5. Boston

Median Earnings
College Scorecard (Early Career): $68,100
EOP (Early Career): $69,800
PayScale (Mid-Career): $111,200

RANKINGS
Forbes: 124
Money: 303
U.S. News: 4, Regional North
Wall Street Journal/THE: 208 (T)
Washington Monthly: N/A

#CollegesWorthYourMoney

Macalester College

St. Paul, Minnesota | Admissions Phone: 651-696-6357

ADMISSION
Admission Rate: 41%
Admission Rate - Men: 40%
Admission Rate - Women: 42%
EA Admission Rate: Not Offered
ED Admission Rate: 52%
Admission Rate (5-Year Trend): +7%
ED Admission Rate (5-Year Trend): -1%
% of Admits Attending (Yield): 25%
Transfer Admission Rate: 13%

Offered Wait List: 426
Accepted Wait List: 238
Admitted Wait List: 0

SAT Reading/Writing (Middle 50%): 650-730
SAT Math (Middle 50%): 660-770
ACT Composite (Middle 50%): 29-33
Testing Policy: ACT/SAT Required
SAT Superscore: Yes
ACT Superscore: Yes

% Graduated in Top 10% of HS Class: 63%
% Graduated in Top 25% of HS Class: 91%
% Graduated in Top 50% of HS Class: 99%

ENROLLMENT
Total Undergraduate Enrollment: 2,174
% Part-Time: 2%
% Male: 40%
% Female: 60%
% Out-of-State: 82%
% Fraternity: Not Offered
% Sorority: Not Offered
% On-Campus (Freshman): 100%
% On-Campus (All Undergraduate): 60%

% African-American: 3%
% Asian: 8%
% Hispanic: 8%
% White: 58%
% Other: 6%
% Race or Ethnicity Unknown: 0%
% International: 16%
% Low-Income: 17%

ACADEMICS
Student-to-Faculty Ratio: 10:1
% of Classes Under 20: 73%
% of Classes Under 40: 98%
% Full-Time Faculty: 71%
% Full-Time Faculty w/ Terminal Degree: 94%

Top Programs
Anthropology
Chemistry
Economics
Environmental Studies
Geography
International Studies
Mathematics
Political Science

Retention Rate: 96%
4-Year Graduation Rate: 85%
6-Year Graduation Rate: 90%

Curricular Flexibility: Somewhat Flexible
Academic Rating: ★★★★⧏

Inside the Classroom

One might expect a small liberal arts school in Minnesota to be set in a remote tundra, its own little universe surrounded by a stark landscape and frigid air. In the case of Macalester College, the frigid air would be accurate, but this collection of 2,133 undergraduate students is a rarity in the liberal arts world—it is situated in the metropolis of St. Paul on the border of Minneapolis. While typically lagging slightly behind rival Carleton College in most rankings, Macalester is every bit in the same league, boasting a strong reputation for rigorous academics that draw 85 percent of the school's student body from outside Minnesota and a stunning 24 percent from ninety-seven foreign countries.

International students aren't flocking to Mac for the weather or Great Plains scenery; they are here for the academic reputation. Students can choose from thirty-nine majors and over 800 courses that are offered each academic year. Requirements for all students are fairly straightforward and include a first-year course that is a small, writing-intensive seminar, courses in each of the schools four divisions—Fine Arts, Humanities, Social Studies, and Natural Science and Mathematics, and courses in multiculturalism and internationalism. Perhaps the most notable mandate is in foreign language where proficiency equivalent to four semesters of study must be demonstrated.

Being an undergraduate-only institution, Macalester students enjoy the full benefits of the school's 10:1 student-to-faculty ratio. The average class size is only seventeen students, and 17 percent of class sections have single-digit enrollments. Fewer than 2 percent of the overall courses contain more than forty students, so the chances are high that you will never be in a course where the professor does not know your name. That level of intimacy leads to plentiful chances for being part of faculty-led research, including through the Collaborative Summer Research Program that provides stipends for student-faculty research ventures. In total, 54 percent of students participate in some form of undergraduate research. Study abroad opportunities, typically twelve weeks in length, are taken advantage of by 60 percent of Macalester undergrads.

As an elite liberal arts institution with no attached graduate schools, Macalester possesses strong offerings across many different disciplines. Programs in economics, international studies, and mathematics are among the best anywhere. In addition, science majors of all varieties benefit from the school's strong reputation for premed and preparing future PhD scientists. Prestigious postgraduate fellowships are routinely awarded to Mac seniors. In the last decade, grads have walked away with fifty-seven Fulbright Scholarships, including eight such awards in 2018 alone. In that same time, students and alumni have procured a Rhodes Scholarship, thirty-nine National Science Foundation Fellowships, nine Watson Fellowships, four Goldwater Scholarships, and three Truman Scholarships.

Outside the Classroom

Due to limited availability of college-owned housing, only 60 percent of Macalester students live on campus. However, 100 percent of freshmen live in one of four residence halls for first-years; sophomores, who are also required to live on campus, have their own dorms as well. There is no Greek life here, so undergrads find other ways to forge deep bonds. With twenty-one sports teams and roughly 400 student-athletes, one-quarter of the student population dons a Scots jersey as they compete in NCAA Division III. Intramurals and club teams also draw heavy participation, leading to a majority of Mac students being involved in some type of formalized athletics. There are also ninety-nine student-run organizations, including eleven musical ensembles, student theater groups with 125 participants, three student publications, including the popular Mac Weekly, and a campus radio station, WMCN. The LGBTQ+ population on campus is notably large—25 percent identify in that category. This cozy 53-acre campus provides ample activity, but access to the city nightlife is quite easy by car. The Mall of America is less than a fifteen-minute drive from the college, and students also enjoy Minnesota's pro sports scene, museums, restaurants, and nightlife.

Career Services

The Career Development Center is staffed by seven professionals (not counting graduate/undergraduate fellows or office assistants), equating to a student-to-advisor ratio of 305:1, better than the average college included in this book. That level of support allows the CDC to implement its four-phase process of "explore/design/connect/launch" that ultimately results in favorable outcomes for graduates. Events such as the fall and spring career fairs are small in scale—the fall 2018 Career Fair was attended by thirty-five employers. In the 2018-19 school year, it held 1,918 one-on-one advising appointments and enticed 103 employers to recruit on campus.

Internships and/or mentored research experiences are enjoyed by 72 percent of Macalester undergraduates. Internships, specifically, are obtained and completed by 60 percent of students. In 2017-18, almost 400 students engaged in credit-bearing internships at organizations as varied as the US Department of State, EY, Minnesota Public Radio, the New York University School of Medicine, and Lockheed Martin. This strong internship program sets up students for a successful transition into a meaningful first job. Among 2018 grads who found employment within six months of leaving, 91 percent said their first job was congruent with their interests. While Macalester grads do not go on to earn high starting salaries, they do find fulfilling jobs aligned with their interests and have success entering and completing top graduate/professional degree programs.

Professional Outcomes

Six months after graduating 94 percent of the Macalester Class of 2018 had found employment, graduate school, or a fellowship; 6 percent were still actively seeking their next destination. Fifty-five percent of those finding employment landed with for-profit corporations, 20 percent with nonprofit organizations, 15 percent with educational institutions, and 9 percent with federal, state, or local government. Employers of recent grads include ABC News, Google, Goldman Sachs, Dow Chemical Company, McKinsey & Company, the ACLU, the National Cancer Institute, and *National Geographic*. Across all sectors, the average starting salary was $47,000. Geographically, 52 percent of grads elected to stay in the North Star State while many others migrated to the West Coast (13 percent), East Coast (11 percent) or overseas (8 percent).

Graduates from 2012-2017 most frequently attended graduate schools such as the University of Washington – Seattle (28), University of Wisconsin – Madison (25), Harvard (21), Georgetown (19), NYU (17), and Johns Hopkins (16). Those from the classes of 2017 and 2018 who enrolled in graduate school entered science and mathematics programs at a 42 percent rate. In those same years, 100 percent of Macalester grads who applied to graduate school received at least one acceptance. From 2007-2016 the college ranked fourteenth among liberal arts schools with the most grads who went on to earn PhDs. Among students with at least a 3.5 GPA and decent MCAT scores, 90 percent were admitted to at least one medical school. Recent medical school acceptances include Tufts University, Northwestern, Brown, and Washington University in St. Louis. The most popular medical school attended by alumni is the University of Minnesota – Twin Cities.

Admission

Macalester received just under 6,000 applications for admission into the Class of 2022, and it admitted 41 percent; of that group, 25 percent went on to enroll in the school. Admitted students averaged a 1430 on the SAT and a 32 on the ACT. An impressive 70 percent hailed from the top decile of their high school's graduating class. The profile of the average freshman who enrolls is a bit more down to earth with 63 percent in the top 10 percent of their high school class and a 33 ACT representing the 75th percentile. Comparing this incoming freshman class to the freshman cohort of a decade earlier, there are few differences to be found. With a comparable acceptance rate and almost identical standardized test scores, this is one liberal arts school that has not changed much in recent years.

The admissions committee ranks the rigor of one's secondary programming and GPA earned as the two most critical factors in the process. The second rung of still "important" factors is comprised of SAT/ACT scores, recommendations, essays, extracurricular activities, and character/personal qualities. Macalester insists that it does not consider demonstrated interest in the admissions process, an unusual move for a school with a relatively low yield rate (the percent of accepted students who go on to enroll). That being said, applying via early decision is a wise choice for those committed to attending the college as the ED acceptance rate is 52 percent. Attracting students from all fifty states and eighty-eight countries, this school's Minnesota locale draws talented applicants from around the world. Lots of AP courses and excellent grades should set up candidates for success.

Worth Your Money?

Sixty-eight percent of the Macalester student population receives need-based aid for an average grant of $42,916 per year. Of those that qualify, 63 percent see 100 percent of their demonstrated need met by Mac, with many others receiving packages that cover nearly all of their college costs. Unfortunately, if you don't qualify for need-based aid, do not expect much in·the way of merit aid—most likely you'll be paying close to the full annual cost of attendance of $73,500. With so many graduates pursuing advanced degrees, average early career earnings aren't spectacular, but Mac is still a school with phenomenal long-term career outcomes, and a very wise investment for students who can afford the price without racking up higher-than-average debt.

FINANCIAL
Institutional Type: Private
In-State Tuition: $56,062
Out-of-State Tuition: $56,062
Room & Board: $12,592
Required Fees: $230
Books & Supplies: $1,191

Avg. Need-Based Aid: $42,916
Avg. % of Need Met: 100%

Avg. Merit-Based Aid: $15,361
% Receiving Merit-Based Aid: 20%

Avg. Cumulative Debt: $24,880
% of Students Borrowing: 66%

CAREER
Who Recruits
1. ScribeAmerica
2. ESRI
3. BMO Capital Markets
4. Twin Cities Public Television
5. Airbnb

Notable Internships
1. Minnesota Wild
2. U.S. Bank
3. U.S. House of Representatives

Top Industries
1. Business
2. Education
3. Social Services
4. Research
5. Operations

Top Employers
1. Wells Fargo
2. UnitedHealth Group
3. Target
4. Epic
5. 3M

Where Alumni Work
1. Minneapolis
2. New York City
3. San Francisco
4. Washington, DC
5. Chicago

Median Earnings
College Scorecard (Early Career): $47,600
EOP (Early Career): $47,000
PayScale (Mid-Career): $100,400

RANKINGS
Forbes: 86
Money: 371
U.S. News: 25, Liberal Arts Colleges
Wall Street Journal/THE: 83
Washington Monthly: 36, Liberal Arts Colleges

#CollegesWorthYourMoney

Marist College

Poughkeepsie, New York | Admissions Phone: 845-575-3226

Inside the Classroom

Competing for attention in the world of New York State institutions of higher education must feel like raising your hand to volunteer while surrounded by equally eager-to-contribute NBA centers. As a school serving 5,700 undergraduates, Marist College is overshadowed by smaller and more selective options that include Hamilton, Colgate, Vassar, and Skidmore as well as the more famous larger universities Cornell, Rochester, and Syracuse—and that's not even considering schools in New York City. Yet, there are many reasons you should get to know Marist, an accessible school for solid-but-imperfect high schoolers that succeeds in providing a world-class education to undergraduates who go on to land enviable internships with regularity, study abroad at exceptional rates and, as a whole, experience tremendous postgraduate success.

Marist offers forty-seven distinct bachelor's programs but is ultimately a true liberal arts institution that requires its undergrads to complete a core curriculum. As freshmen, students engage in a first-year seminar and a course called Writing for College, both of which incorporate themes related to "Cultural Diversity, Nature & the Environment, Civic Engagement, and/or Quantitative Reasoning." There are thirty-six credits worth of distributional courses of study including ethics and justice, fine arts, history, literature, mathematics, natural science, philosophy, and social science. Additionally, although this can overlap with distributional requirements, students must also tackle a four-course "Pathway," choosing from twenty-three courses including African Diaspora Studies, Gender Studies, and Public Health Studies.

Marist has average class sizes in the eighteen to twenty-six range and a 16:1 student-to-faculty ratio—few sections are single-digit seminars or large lectures. On the less-than-ideal side, the majority of Marist's professors are adjuncts, 348 versus 232 full timers. On the plus side, undergrads enjoy the real-world knowledge brought by those nontenure-track professors, and few complain about availability outside the classroom. Marist is supportive of undergraduate research, particularly in the hard sciences where completion of a research project is often a graduation requirement. Marist sees 50 percent of its students study abroad as part of the college's robust international program that is rated among the best in the country.

The School of Management and the School of Communication are quite popular as business and communication are, by far, Marist's two most commonly conferred degrees. They are also among Marist's strongest. It is also noteworthy that the School of Mathematics and Computer Science has had a joint study program with IBM for more than three decades. This intensive collaboration frequently leads to employment at IBM after graduation. With many grads entering corporate America, applications to prestigious national fellowship programs are sparse, but twenty-six grads have won Fulbright Scholarships in the past fifteen years.

Outside the Classroom

Two-thirds of the undergraduate population at Marist live on campus in a combination of corridor, suite, apartment, and townhouse-style residences. The 150+ acre campus is spectacularly set on the shores of the Hudson River. On the border of what arguably qualifies as "Upstate" New York, Poughkeepsie is about an hour and half drive from the heart of New York City. On campus, there are three fraternities and four sororities with around 300 members, giving Greek life a modest presence of roughly 5 percent of the undergraduate population. Playing in NCAA Division I, the Red Foxes field twenty-three varsity sports teams. For less serious athletes there are eleven club teams as well as an extensive intramural program that draws an incredible 65 percent of students. Overall, there are more than eighty student-run clubs and organizations. The Hudson Valley offers plenty worth exploring, from the ample natural beauty ripe for hiking and canoeing to the commerce of the popular Poughkeepsie Galleria Mall. While the school's Catholic origins are no longer officially linked to the school, the largest student group at Marist is the Campus Ministry that has a membership of 1,300 students. At 58 percent female, there is a noticeable gender gap at this school.

Career Services

The Center for Career Services (CCS) at Marist is staffed by five professionals with expertise in career coaching, employer relations, and graduate school advising. That works out to a 1,140:1 student-to-advisor ratio that is much higher than the average school in this guide. We do, however, take it as a positive sign that the Student Services Department (which includes the CCS) received a thumbs-up from 95 percent of grads. As the CCS states, "It's never too early to begin the process of learning how your interests and passions turn into long-term career aspirations." To back up that ideal, the CCS offers daily walk-in hours, scheduled one-on-one career counseling appointments, and weekly workshops on topics like resumes, cover letters, interviewing, and building a personal brand online.

Marist College

E-mail: admission@marist.edu | Website: www.marist.edu

Large events take place regularly, including the two annual Career and Internship Fairs. The fall 2018 fair attracted sixty employers and 700 students. An annual Graduate School Forum brings forty graduate and professional schools to campus to meet with prospective students. The CCS also maintains an active Alumni Career Network of former students in a variety of fields who are willing to volunteer their time to mentor. Efforts such as those lead to an extremely healthy 83 percent internship participation rate for Marist undergrads. In 2017, over 1,100 internships were completed at organizations including the Brooklyn Nets (NBA), CBS, Goldman Sachs, HBO, Morgan Stanley, Seventeen Magazine, and Madison Square Garden. Success in helping its students secure experiential and networking opportunities ends up leading to positive career and graduate school outcomes for the vast majority of students.

Professional Outcomes

Red Foxes strutting across the graduation stage in 2017 went on to find employment or a graduate school home at a terrific 98 percent rate by the time they filled out their first-destination survey. Major employers of Marist alums include IBM, which presently employees over 700 individuals, as well as JP Morgan Chase, EY, Macy's Citi, Morgan Stanley, Deloitte, and NBC Universal Media. Members of the Class of 2017 headed to a number of media powerhouses including iHeartRadio, Fox News, Random House, and the MLB Network as well as other major companies Adidas, Coach, Lockheed Martin, Northrup Grumman, and Moody's. The Greater New York City area draws approximately two-thirds of grads; Boston, Atlanta, Albany, and Hartford attract their own slivers of each graduating class. Midcareer median salaries are in the same range as other excellent schools in this guide such as UC Santa Barbara, Texas A&M, Colby, and American University.

The percent of Class of 2017 members pursuing graduate/professional degrees varied greatly across disciplines. Thirty-six percent of those in the School of Social & Behavioral Sciences enrolled in graduate school followed by the School of Science (28 percent), the School of Computer Science & Mathematics (16 percent), and the School of Liberal Arts (14 percent). In terms of selectivity, a wide range of institutions were attended including elite universities Cornell, Penn, Harvard, Columbia, and Oxford. Over the last decade, 70 percent of medical school applicants were accepted to at least one institution, a figure that is more than twenty-five points higher than the national average. Acceptances have included Georgetown Medical School, Albany Medical College, New York Medical College, SUNY Upstate Medical Center at Syracuse, Medical College of Virginia, and the Albert Einstein School of Medicine. Recent law school acceptances have included William & Mary, the University of Texas, and Northeastern University.

Admission

In 2018, Marist received over 11,000 applications, accepted 46 percent, and saw one-quarter of those accepted ultimately go on to enroll. The Class of 2022 possessed mid-50 percent SAT scores 1210-1340 and 26-30 on the ACT. In the classroom, this cohort earned an average high school GPA of 3.3, and only 22 percent of its members placed in the top decile of their high school class. Not only can students gain acceptance into Marist without a pristine transcript, but the college also became test-optional back in 2011. Thirty-seven percent of the Class of 2022 elected not to submit standardized test scores, and in the years since it went test-optional, the average scores have predictably gone up a bit because those with lower scores simply do not submit. The other qualifications, such as GPA and class rank, have remained fairly constant over the last decade.

According to the admissions office Marist applicants "should rank in the top half of their graduating class and hold a recalculated average of 3.3 or better." The school also likes to see some honors and/or Advanced Placement courses on an applicant's transcript. Evidence of leadership and extracurricular participation are valued by the committee as well. With lots of liberal arts competition both Upstate and around New York City, Marist finds itself fighting for quality freshmen each year. Thus, committing to the school via early decision gives you a massive edge in the admissions game; in 2018, the college accepted an overwhelming 86 percent of ED applicants. It filled 22 percent of the Class of 2022 via binding early-round applicants.

Worth Your Money?

Tuition fees plus room and board bring the total sticker price to over $58,000, making a four-year degree a $200,000+ venture. Fortunately, through a combination of merit and need-based aid, the net price ends up under $40k per year, even for families in the top income brackets. While not cheap by any means, Marist has the type of NYC corporate connections that can eventually open doors to lucrative and interesting careers that will likely return your investment.

FINANCIAL
Institutional Type: Private
In-State Tuition: $41,800
Out-of-State Tuition: $41,800
Room & Board: $15,920
Required Fees: $700
Books & Supplies: $1,125

Avg. Need-Based Aid: $20,548
Avg. % of Need Met: 73%

Avg. Merit-Based Aid: $11,813
% Receiving Merit-Based Aid: 41%

Avg. Cumulative Debt: $39,035
% of Students Borrowing: 64%

CAREER
Who Recruits
1. IBM
2. EY
3. KPMG
4. UBS
5. The Met

Notable Internships
1. ESPN
2. Sony Music Entertainment
3. American Red Cross

Top Industries
1. Business
2. Sales
3. Operations
4. Education
5. information Technology

Top Employers
1. IBM
2. JPMorgan Chase
3. EY
4. Macy's
5. Citi

Where Alumni Work
1. New York City
2. Boston
3. Atlanta
4. New York City
5. Hartford, CT

Median Earnings
College Scorecard (Early Career): $56,900
EOP (Early Career): $59,500
PayScale (Mid-Career): $101,000

RANKINGS
Forbes: 189
Money: 189
U.S. News: 10, Regional North
Wall Street Journal/THE: 398 (T)
Washington Monthly: N/A

#CollegesWorthYourMoney

Colleges Worth Your Money

Massachusetts Institute of Technology

Cambridge, Massachusetts | Admissions Phone: 617-253-3400

ADMISSION
Admission Rate: 7%
Admission Rate - Men: 5%
Admission Rate - Women: 11%
EA Admission Rate: 7%
ED Admission Rate: Not Offered
Admission Rate (5-Year Trend): -1%
ED Admission Rate (5-Year Trend): Not Offered
% of Admits Attending (Yield): 76%
Transfer Admission Rate: 4%

Offered Wait List: 460
Accepted Wait List: 383
Admitted Wait List: 0

SAT Reading/Writing (Middle 50%): 720-770
SAT Math (Middle 50%): 780-800
ACT Composite (Middle 50%): 34-36
Testing Policy: ACT/SAT Required
SAT Superscore: Yes
ACT Superscore: Yes

% Graduated in Top 10% of HS Class: 97%
% Graduated in Top 25% of HS Class: 100%
% Graduated in Top 50% of HS Class: 100%

ENROLLMENT
Total Undergraduate Enrollment: 4,602
% Part-Time: 1%
% Male: 54%
% Female: 46%
% Out-of-State: 91%
% Fraternity: 43%
% Sorority: 28%
% On-Campus (Freshman): 100%
% On-Campus (All Undergraduate): 92%

% African-American: 6%
% Asian: 28%
% Hispanic: 15%
% White: 31%
% Other: 7%
% Race or Ethnicity Unknown: 2%
% International: 11%
% Low-Income: 16%

ACADEMICS
Student-to-Faculty Ratio: 3:1
% of Classes Under 20: 71%
% of Classes Under 40: 84%
% Full-Time Faculty: 81%
% Full-Time Faculty w/ Terminal Degree: 92%

Top Programs
Biology
Chemistry
Computer Science
Economics
Engineering
Finance
Mathematics
Physics

Retention Rate: 99%
4-Year Graduation Rate: 85%
6-Year Graduation Rate: 94%

Curricular Flexibility: Somewhat Flexible
Academic Rating: ★★★★★

Inside the Classroom

A beacon of egalitarianism and meritocracy, the Massachusetts Institute of Technology is less about legacy and more about the future. MIT doesn't care who your grandfather was or how far you can throw a football; it is seeking the world's sharpest and most innovative minds in engineering, the sciences, mathematics, and related fields who, one day, will create the world the rest of us will merely inhabit. Graduate students account for the majority of students enrolled at MIT, but the nearly 4,500 undergraduates pursue one of fifty-three majors and fifty-eight minors in this world-class research institution that continues to be one of the world's most magnetic destinations for science geniuses.

There are five separate schools within MIT: the School of Architecture and Planning; the School of Engineering; the School of Humanities, Arts, and the Social Sciences; the Sloan School of Management; and the School of Science. There are a number of broad academic requirements across all five schools including an eight-subject humanities, arts, and social sciences requirement and a six-subject science requirement that includes two terms of calculus, two terms of physics, one term of chemistry, and one term of biology. Additionally, students must complete two courses under the designation of "restricted electives" in science and technology, a laboratory requirement, and a physical education course.

The student-to-faculty ratio is an astonishing 3-to-1, and even with a substantial focus on graduate programs, the class sizes are intimate. An exceptional 43 percent of class sections have single-digit enrollments, and 70 percent of courses contain fewer than twenty students. MIT is known for having one of the best formalized undergraduate research programs in the country. The Undergraduate Research Opportunities Program (UROP) operates year-round and helps connect 91 percent of undergrads to a research experience with an MIT faculty member. Studying abroad is strongly encouraged, and the school offers some fantastic opportunities through programs such as MIT Madrid, Imperial College Exchanges (London), and departmental exchange programs in South Africa, France, and Japan.

The highest numbers of degrees conferred in 2018 were in the following majors: computer science and engineering (251), electrical engineering and computer science (161), mathematics (76), and physics (55). Just about every program at MIT sits at or near the top of any rankings. The most sought after employers and grad schools aggressively recruit alumni. Graduates win nationally competitive fellowships and scholarships on a routine basis. In 2019, five students were awarded Marshall Scholarships; in 2018, eight of the forty finalists for Hertz Fellowships were MIT grads, and fourteen students in the Department of Chemistry alone were awarded National Science Foundation Graduate Research Fellowships.

Outside the Classroom

The campus' 166 acres include twenty-six acres of playing fields, twenty acres of green spaces and gardens, and eighteen student residences that house the 90 percent of students who live on campus, a requirement for freshmen. It may be a bit of a surprise that the school's thirty-seven fraternities, sororities, and living groups attract 43 percent of male students and 28 percent of females. Around half live in frat/sorority/living group housing, and the other half reside in dorms. Falling victim to stereotypes, one might not immediately assume that MIT would have an athletically-inclined student body. However, the school fields thirty-three varsity sports teams (16 women's, 15 men's, 2 co-ed), most of which compete in NCAA Division III against other New England colleges. The intramural program is bursting at the seams with over 4,000 participants annually. Another 800 students are members of thirty-three club teams. Plenty of culture/creativity can be found on campus in one of MIT's twelve museums and galleries (The MIT Museum draws 150,000 visitors each year). There are also more than sixty arts, dance, music, and writing organizations for students. The school is devoted to environmental sustainability, and the campus and surrounding area are designed for a car-free lifestyle that remains highly convenient. With forty-four bike-sharing stations, six subway stations, and twenty-nine bus routes in the surrounding area, students can navigate Cambridge with ease. Harvard's campus is less than one mile away, and downtown Boston is easy to reach. For reference, Fenway Park is less than two miles from campus.

Career Services

MIT Global Education & Career Development (GECD) has sixteen professional staff members who are directly involved in employer relations, career counseling, and graduate school advising. That 278:1 student-to-advisor ratio is better than average compared to other schools featured in this guide. The office provides top-notch individualized counseling and also puts on phenomenal large-scale events. The MIT Fall Career Fair is an unmatched event that sees around 450 companies and 5,000 students attend. If you can think of a desirable tech/finance company, chances are it has a booth at the event. Even the less-epic Spring Career Fair attracts seventy employers including Northrup Grumman, Wayfair, Bank of America, the Walt Disney Company, Cisco, and Twitter.

With assistance from the GECD, 87 percent of MIT undergraduates complete at least one internship. Almost one-quarter of those participating in internships received a full-time job offer from that same organization. The GECD played a direct role in helping many others land jobs through various means as 20 percent found employment through on-campus recruiting, 19 percent through faculty/GECD connections, and 18 percent through career fairs. In a single year the GECD hosted 130 different employers, which led to a collective 2,609 interviews held on campus. An additional 1,072 employers posted 2,595 unique jobs online in an effort to lure MIT seniors. MIT students sell themselves, so career services staff have a role akin to managing the '27 Yankees. Still, the office does a world-class job of setting up its highly desired undergrads with premium opportunities.

Professional Outcomes

The Class of 2018 saw 54 percent of its members enter the world of employment and 39 percent continue on their educational paths. By industry, the highest percentage of graduates found jobs in engineering (24 percent), computer technologies (23 percent), consulting (14 percent), and finance/banking (14 percent). The top employers included Accenture, Oracle, Facebook, Amazon, Microsoft, Northrop Grumman, Goldman Sachs, Google, General Motors, the US Navy, Apple, Bain & Company, Boeing, and McKinsey. The mean starting salary for an MIT bachelor's degree holder was $88,381, and the median was $85,000.

The most frequently attended graduate schools are a who's who of elite institutions including MIT itself, which accounted for 177 members of the Class of 2017 with Stanford a distant second, attracting twenty-two graduates. Also making the list were Princeton, California Institute of Technology, Columbia, Northwestern, University of Chicago, University of California at Berkeley, and University of Michigan. The most common degree being pursued was a PhD (43 percent), and the second most common was a master's of engineering (41 percent). Only 6 percent were entering medical/dental/veterinary school, and 1.6 percent were headed to law school. Medical school acceptance rates typically land in the 80-95 percent range for grads/alumni, more than double the national average.

Admission

Applicants for a place in the Class of 2022 encountered a murderous 6.7 percent acceptance rate. Freshmen entering MIT in the fall of 2018 possessed SATs with a middle-50 percent range of 1500-1570 and ACTs with middle-50 percent scores of 34-36. Students were almost unanimously from the top 10 percent of their high school classes—97 percent boasted that achievement. MIT offers a nonbinding early action option with a November 1 deadline, but it yields little in the way of an admissions edge. The acceptance rate for the early round is usually almost identical to that of the regular round.

The MIT admissions committee rates character/personal qualities as "very important," and just about everything else—rigor of courses, GPA, test scores, essays, recommendations, interview, extracurricular activities—in the next tier of importance. While a nice nod to the importance of character, every one of the aforementioned factors ranked as merely "important" have to be close to perfect for it to even enter the equation. Legacy status is not considered at MIT, a rarity among elite universities, meaning that the alumni connection of your mother, grandfather, or brother plays zero role in helping you gain admission. Despite a large intercollegiate sports program, athletic prowess plays a minimal role in admissions decisions as well. MIT is as close to a true meritocracy as you can find in the world of higher education. The most brilliant and innovative minds from around the globe are admitted regardless of family name or lacrosse skills. Rather, a sparkling academic record, near-perfect test scores, and impressive STEM-focused experiences/accomplishments outside the classroom will rule the day.

Worth Your Money?

Yes…Need more? Going to MIT is punching your ticket to any number of lucrative careers. If you need financial assistance, this school will meet 100 percent of your demonstrated need; the average grant is for roughly $49,000. The full cost of attendance is $73,160.

FINANCIAL
Institutional Type: Private
In-State Tuition: $53,450
Out-of-State Tuition: $53,450
Room & Board: $16,390
Required Fees: $340
Books & Supplies: $820

Avg. Need-Based Aid: $49,010
Avg. % of Need Met: 100%

Avg. Merit-Based Aid: $0
% Receiving Merit-Based Aid: 0%

Avg. Cumulative Debt: $22,696
% of Students Borrowing: 29%

CAREER
Who Recruits
1. Hudson River Trading
2. Nvidia
3. Five Rings Technology
4. Stripe
5. AB InBev

Notable Internships
1. Jane Street Capital
2. Airbnb
3. Shell

Top Industries
1. Business
2. Engineering
3. Education
4. Research
5. Operations

Top Employers
1. Google
2. Apple
3. Microsoft
4. Amazon
5. IBM

Where Alumni Work
1. Boston
2. San Francisco
3. New York City
4. India
5. Washington, DC

Median Earnings
College Scorecard (Early Career): $104,700
EOP (Early Career): $98,500
PayScale (Mid-Career): $155,200

RANKINGS
Forbes: 4
Money: 7
U.S. News: 3 (T), National Universities
Wall Street Journal/THE: 2
Washington Monthly: 3, National Universities

#CollegesWorthYourMoney

Middlebury College

Middlebury, Vermont | Admissions Phone: 802-443-3000

ADMISSION
Admission Rate: 17%
Admission Rate - Men: 18%
Admission Rate - Women: 16%
EA Admission Rate: Not Offered
ED Admission Rate: 47%
Admission Rate (5-Year Trend): -1%
ED Admission Rate (5-Year Trend): +12%
% of Admits Attending (Yield): 41%
Transfer Admission Rate: 9%

\# Offered Wait List: 1,215
\# Accepted Wait List: 914
\# Admitted Wait List: 24

SAT Reading/Writing (Middle 50%): 660-730
SAT Math (Middle 50%): 670-770
ACT Composite (Middle 50%): 31-34
Testing Policy: Test Flexible
SAT Superscore: Yes
ACT Superscore: Yes

% Graduated in Top 10% of HS Class: 80%
% Graduated in Top 25% of HS Class: 95%
% Graduated in Top 50% of HS Class: 99%

ENROLLMENT
Total Undergraduate Enrollment: 2,579
% Part-Time: 1%
% Male: 47%
% Female: 53%
% Out-of-State: 94%
% Fraternity: Not Offered
% Sorority: Not Offered
% On-Campus (Freshman): 100%
% On-Campus (All Undergraduate): 95%

% African-American: 4%
% Asian: 7%
% Hispanic: 10%
% White: 62%
% Other: 5%
% Race or Ethnicity Unknown: 2%
% International: 11%
% Low-Income: 12%

ACADEMICS
Student-to-Faculty Ratio: 8:1
% of Classes Under 20: 66%
% of Classes Under 40: 95%
% Full-Time Faculty: 84%
% Full-Time Faculty w/ Terminal Degree: 96%

Top Programs
Economics
English
Environmental Studies
History
International & Global Studies
Neuroscience
Performing Arts
Political Science

Retention Rate: 96%
4-Year Graduation Rate: 83%
6-Year Graduation Rate: 91%

Curricular Flexibility: Somewhat Flexible
Academic Rating: ★★★★✔

Inside the Classroom

Located between the Green Mountains and the Adirondacks, Middlebury College is heading toward the summit of Northeastern liberal arts colleges. In the same conversation as (although always ranked just behind) Williams and Amherst, Middlebury's 2,500 undergraduate students are an exceptionally accomplished crew. Even the frigid Vermont winters do little to take away from the beauty of the college's historic 350-acre campus or the natural grandeur of the surrounding area. A quintessential New England liberal arts college aesthetically, "Midd" also plays that role when it comes to the classroom experience.

Offering forty-seven departments and programs in which to major and minor, the college requires all students to complete one course in seven of the following eight categories: literature, the arts, philosophical and religious studies, historical studies, physical and life sciences, deductive reasoning and analytical processes, social analysis, and foreign language. Undergrads also must complete four additional courses that meet the cultures and civilization requirement. Mandatory writing-intensive seminars must be tackled—one as a freshman and the second by the end of the sophomore year.

The school's 8:1 student-faculty ratio allows 100 percent of courses to be taught by professors, not graduate assistants. Most classes are small; the mean class size is nineteen, and 19 percent of sections contain fewer than ten students. The Summer Research at Middlebury program funds 130 students annually to work along-side faculty in a variety of disciplines. Each year, more than 50 percent of juniors take a semester abroad in one of ninety programs in forty countries. The college's robust international program includes Middlebury Schools Abroad in Argentina, Brazil, Cameroon, Chile, China, France, Germany, India, Israel, Italy, Japan, Jordan, Morocco, Russia, Spain, the United Kingdom, and Uruguay.

Middlebury is renowned for its Language Department as well as international studies. Graduate schools know the value of a Middlebury education (see med school acceptance rates below). The college also produces a large number of national fellowship/scholarship winners. In the 2017-18 school year graduates/alumni took home three Watson Fellowships, Four National Science Foundation Graduate Research Fellowships, thirteen Fulbright Scholarships, and five Critical Language Scholarships.

Outside the Classroom

Implementing the Oxford/Cambridge system of residential housing, all Middlebury undergraduates are required to live in one of more than sixty on-campus buildings. First-year students are assigned to one of five larger Commons where they will reside until the end of their sophomore year. More than thirty faculty/staff members regularly eat in the Commons allowing for classroom discussions to continue over a meal. That leaves no room for Greek life, which vanished two decades ago (limited "social houses" do remain). With thirty-one varsity sports teams competing in the NCAA New England Small College Athletic Conference, the Middlebury Panthers put a sizable portion of its undergraduate population in uniform. Less committed athletes can enjoy a full array of club and intramural sports as well as the school's eighteen-hole golf course, 3.5-mile jogging trail, 2,200-seat ice hockey rink, or six-lane indoor track. Midd offers more than 170 student-run organizations with options in all the usual realms—performing arts, spiritual, social, student government, and more. Outdoor activity clubs that engage in climbing, hiking, kayaking, skiing, and camping are among the most popular groups. Student theater productions are also well attended. The town of Middlebury is tiny and quiet, so some students make the just-under-an-hour drive to Burlington. Montreal, Canada, is the closest cosmopolitan destination with Boston and New York more than three hours away.

Career Services

The Center for Careers and Internships is staffed by sixteen full-time staff members who specialize in areas such as employer relations, career advising, heath professions and STEM advising, and internships and early engagement. Its 156:1 student-to-advisor ratio places it among the most supportive career services offices of any college profiled in this guide. Middlebury's career counselors are rarely found not actively engaging under-graduates in career/grad school planning. In 2017, the office coordinated 240 events and workshops, and advisors held 2,700 individual student sessions.

For a school of modest size, Middlebury brought an impressive ninety employers to campus to host information sessions and facilitated 500 on-campus interviews in 2017. Every year it helps 800 undergrads find internships and contribute $800,000 to help fund unpaid summer work experiences. More than 5,500 opportunities for jobs and internships are posted online. Further, a generous alumni base is more than willing to assist current Panthers—more than 7,500 alums in a range of professions wait to connect on MiddNet. While the Center for Careers and Internships three- to six-months out employment rate is not as high as that of some other comparably staffed elite schools, Middlebury grads regularly find their way to careers they find meaningful and fulfilling, including many at some of the country's best companies.

Middlebury College

E-mail: admissions@middlebury.edu | Website: www.middlebury.edu

Professional Outcomes

Three months after graduating, 70 percent of the Class of 2018 had landed jobs, 12 percent were in graduate school, and 13 percent were still searching for employment. That was an improvement over the classes of 2016 and 2017 that saw 21-22 percent of alumni still hunting for jobs in the same time frame. The most commonly held jobs fell under the category of "social impact-related careers" (21 percent), followed by financial services (15 percent), consulting (12 percent), technology (11 percent), and health care and science (10 percent). Interestingly, the number of Middlebury grads entering tech-related fields has grown by 55 percent in the last three years. Google is now one of the leading employers of alumni alongside Morgan Stanley, Goldman Sachs, Deloitte, Amazon, and JP Morgan. With a median mid-career salary in the range of $62,000, Middlebury grads are in a similar income bracket with those from Williams, Brandeis, and Bowdoin.

Middlebury students with solid grades will be viewed favorably by graduate and professional schools should they wish to continue their education. Graduate schools attended by members of the Class of 2017 included Columbia, Georgia Tech, Harvard Law School, Oxford, Stanford, and Yale. Members of the Class of 2018 who applied to medical school sported an average GPA of 3.7, a median MCAT score in the 90th percentile, and were accepted at an 89 percent clip (the 2017 figure was 83 percent). Over the last eight years, the most frequently attended medical schools include Tufts, Boston University, Geisel (Dartmouth), and NYU.

Admission

Middlebury College admitted 17 percent of the 9,227 applicants for a place in the Class of 2022. Of those receiving an acceptance letter, 41 percent went on to enroll at the college. The middle-50 percent standardized tests scores of those who enrolled were 1330-1500 on the SAT and 31-34 on the ACT. There is a relatively even split between those submitting scores from each exam. One of the rare test-flexible institutions, Middlebury requires students to submit (a) SAT results (b) ACT results or (c) three SAT subject scores. For those choosing the latter option, the three tests must be from three distinct disciplines (i.e., Math I and Math II will not count as two tests).

Six factors sit atop the pecking order of most important as applicants are being evaluated by the admissions committee: rigor of secondary coursework, GPA, class rank, extracurricular activities, talent/ability, and character/personal qualities. Test scores, recommendations, essays, and racial/ethnic status comprise the second tier of "important" factors. Those who commit to the college through binding early decision are rewarded with a 47 percent acceptance rate, more than three times that of the regular cycle. Middlebury has remained similarly selective throughout the twenty-first century. One decade ago, the acceptance rate was a touch lower at 16 percent; the average test scores were a touch lower too, but the average enrollee looked similar to a 2018-19 freshman. The college continues to use a genuinely holistic approach in the admissions process, and the test-flexible policy can be useful for a certain type of applicant. Even when considering the "special" students being accepted via the early round, ED still provides borderline applicants with an increased chance at getting in.

Worth Your Money?

Middlebury's list price is about the going rate for elite liberal arts institutions with a total annual cost of attendance of $74k. However, if you qualify for need-based aid, the college will meet your full level of need; the average award is $49k. As with most schools that meet a student's full demonstrated need, there isn't much, if any, merit aid money to go around. A school of superior quality, Middlebury rates as a rare liberal arts school that will pay you back multiple times over the course of your life, even if the upfront costs are steep.

FINANCIAL
Institutional Type: Private
In-State Tuition: $55,790
Out-of-State Tuition: $55,790
Room & Board: $16,040
Required Fees: $426
Books & Supplies: $1,000

Avg. Need-Based Aid: $48,993
Avg. % of Need Met: 100%

Avg. Merit-Based Aid: $0
% Receiving Merit-Based Aid: 0%

Avg. Cumulative Debt: $18,955
% of Students Borrowing: 50%

CAREER
Who Recruits
1. Analysis Group
2. Goldman Sachs
3. Oak Hill Advisors
4. ScribeAmerica
5. CIA

Notable Internships
1. Tesla
2. Bain & Company
3. Merrill Lynch

Top Industries
1. Business
2. Education
3. Media
4. Social Services
5. Operations

Top Employers
1. Google
2. Goldman Sachs
3. Morgan Stanley
4. Amazon
5. Deloitte

Where Alumni Work
1. New York City
2. Boston
3. Washington, DC
4. San Francisco
5. Glen Falls, NY

Median Earnings
College Scorecard (Early Career): $58,200
EOP (Early Career): $61,800
PayScale (Mid-Career): $109,800

RANKINGS
Forbes: 36
Money: 186
U.S. News: 7, Liberal Arts Colleges
Wall Street Journal/THE: 35
Washington Monthly: 6, Liberal Arts Colleges

#CollegesWorthYourMoney

Mount Holyoke College

South Hadley, Massachusetts | Admissions Phone: 413-538-2023

Inside the Classroom

Stately, majestic, and Hogwarts-esque are three of the most common adjectives used to describe the grounds of Mount Holyoke College, an exclusively female liberal arts school located in South Hadley, Massachusetts. Situated ninety miles west of Boston, MHC is home to over 2,200 undergraduates and is part of the Five College Consortium with nearby Amherst, Smith, Hampshire, and UMass-Amherst. With fifty departmental and interdepartmental majors as well as the option to design your own major, MHC students, nicknamed "Lyons" after the college's founder, are free to follow their academic passions, an attribute that helps explain the incredible percentage of alumni that go on to earn PhDs.

By liberal arts college standards Mount Holyoke requires a minimal amount of core coursework. While working toward the completion of the 128 credits needed for graduation, students must complete one class in each of the humanities, sciences, social sciences, and mathematics. A freshman seminar focused on sharpening writing skills is mandatory as is one semester of foreign language study, one course focused on multicultural perspectives, and physical education. Thanks to membership in the Five College Consortium, undergrads can take a good number of courses at one of the other institutions but must complete two of their final three years of study on the MHC campus.

Professors are known for their accessibility and commitment to undergraduate education. Thanks to a 9-to-1 student-to-faculty ratio, roughly three-quarters of sections contain fewer than twenty students; 14 percent are single-digit seminar classes. Opportunities to research and publish alongside faculty are definitely available, and many 200- and 300-level courses have independent research baked-in as a requirement. Across all disciplines, more ambitious students can arrange summer research internships with professors. More than one hundred study abroad options are on the table, but preferred MHC-affiliated programs are definitely worth considering. Those targeted college-run programs include Globalization, Development, and Environment in Costa Rica; Economic Transformation and Business in Shanghai; and the Associated Kyoto Program that allows students to attend a full academic year of classes in Japan.

MHC isn't a school where one or two programs are more popular and/or more respected than the rest. Rather, strong programs are found across a variety of fields—for example, in biology, English, and international relations. Among undergrads, there is a fairly even distribution between the humanities (28 percent), social sciences (35 percent), and science and mathematics (36 percent). Fellowships award season is usually kind to Mount Holyoke grads. In 2018, MHC students took home seven Fulbright Scholarships, two Davis Project for Peace awards, and two Critical Language Scholarships awarded by the US State Department.

Outside the Classroom

Roughly 95 percent of undergraduates live on campus in one of eighteen residential halls. The last time sororities existed on campus was 1910 when they were dissolved for being "undemocratic." The college's thirteen sports teams compete in NCAA Division III, including a stellar equestrian program. Of the over one hundred student organizations, a cappella and glee are among the most popular along with volunteerism in many forms. Each year over half of MHC students volunteer at local schools, hospitals, YMCAs, and other community organizations. Speakers, including many authors, appear frequently on campus to give well-attended talks. Thanks again to membership in the Five College Consortium, social opportunities are expanded to include those offered at Smith, UMass, Amherst, and Hampshire. Campus, which is almost always cited as one the nation's prettiest, is a spacious 800 acres that features notable man-made highlights such as the MHC Art Museum, a fitness center that is less than a decade old, and an eighteen-hole golf course in addition to natural highlights such as two lakes and several hiking trails. South Hadley is a small town exploding with quaint New England charm. Those seeking more adventure can make the two-hour trip to Boston.

Career Services

The Career Development Center (CDC) is staffed by ten professionals (not counting communications staff or admin assistants) who work directly with, or on behalf of, students in the following capacities: career counseling, internships, experiential learning, and external relations. That 221:1 student-to-advisor ratio is superior to the majority of schools featured in this guidebook. Ample individualized attention is at the fingertips of undergraduates—thirty-minute advising sessions are available as often as once per week for current students or three times per year for recent graduates. The CDC does not host many large events itself; rather, it takes advantage of the school's geographic location and takes part in events such as the Smith College Life Sciences & Technology Fair, the UMASS Amherst Computer Science & Engineering Fair, and the MIT Asian Career Fair.

Through an approach dubbed the "Lynk," Mt. Holyoke strives to systematically assist students in connecting their curriculum to their future career. That goal is accomplished through the offering of experiential learning opportunities, internship connections (funding is guaranteed), industry site visits, and networking with past students who have entered fields of interest. In fact, a thriving career directory maintained by the college connects undergrads with 20,000 willing-to-help alumni, and almost 1,400 students connect with a member of that directory each year. Overall, the CDC excels in helping young women find their next destination as evidenced by a low percentage of students still seeking employment six months out and the strength of its graduate school preparation (more in a moment). Even with salaries on the lower end and a dearth of on-campus recruiting, the Mount Holyoke Career Development Center works hard to connect its students to fulfilling and relevant career paths.

Professional Outcomes

Six months after commencement 63 percent of 2018 grads had found employment, 20 percent had entered graduate/professional school, 7 percent had landed fellowships/internships, and only 5 percent were still searching for jobs. Education was the most frequently entered field (26 percent). It was followed by technology, science, and engineering (11 percent); social services, public administration, or advocacy (10 percent); and health care (8 percent). The top Lyon employers of 2018 included Google, Goldman Sachs, Barclay's, and Boston Children's Hospital. Microsoft, IBM, Harvard University, and Amazon also employ a healthy number of Lyons. Given the number of grads entering the public sector or pursuing graduate degrees, it isn't shocking that average salary statistics for alumni tend to be on the low side. The midcareer median salary is $49k, more than $7,000 less than the median salary for a Wellesley graduate. Over one-third of students remain in Massachusetts after obtaining their diplomas. Plenty of alumni also can be found in New York, California, or international locales.

Ten years after graduation close to 80 percent of alumni have enrolled in graduate or professional school. The college produces an exceptional number of future STEM PhDs. Between 2004-2013 it saw 171 of its graduates go on to earn doctorates in hard sciences. In recent years the law school acceptance rate has fluctuated between 75 percent and 100 percent. Recent acceptances include Harvard Law School, Boston College, University of Michigan, and Stanford. Medical school acceptance rates tend to be above average, and recent graduates have attended Johns Hopkins, Tufts, Emory, Columbia, UVA, and Washington University. Across all disciplines the graduate schools accepting the most recent alumni included Yale, Cornell, NYU, and Duke. Massachusetts-based Simmons, UMASS-Amherst, and Mt. Holyoke itself also cracked the list.

Admission

The 3,699 applicants for membership in the Class of 2022 saw a generous—particularly by the standards of this book—51 percent succeed, and one-third of those who were accepted ultimately enrolled in the college. The profile of the typical Mt. Holyoke student is quite different than your average college that has an acceptance rate of more than 50 percent. The middle-50 percent range for SATs was 1290-1500, and 47 percent of those attending placed in the top decile of their high school class; 83 percent were in the top quartile. Just under 60 percent earned GPAs of 3.75 or higher.

Four factors reign supreme in the eyes of the admissions committee: rigor of coursework, GPA, recommendations, and essays. Factors such as class rank, the interview, extracurricular activities, talent/ability, character/personal qualities, volunteer work, and work experience also are deemed "important" in the evaluation process. Missing from this list are standardized test scores because Mount Holyoke is a test-optional school. Among freshmen in the 2018-19 school year, 57 percent submitted SATs and 23 percent submitted ACTs as part of their applications. Given that some applicants likely submitted both SAT and ACT scores, it is fair to infer that more than one-quarter of current students were admitted via test-optional applications. A self-selecting applicant pool leads to a deceptively high acceptance rate. Yet, the women who are offered admission at Mount Holyoke tend to be high achieving with impressive high school transcripts to their names. Those sure that this is the Seven Sisters school for them can gain a slight advantage by applying early—58 percent of 2018 ED applicants were admitted.

Worth Your Money?

Mt. Holyoke has an annual cost of attendance approaching the $70,000 mark, yet thanks to the generosity of its aid offers, many pay far less. In fact, 63 percent of the undergraduates at the college qualify for need-based aid, and the average grant in $37k, a figure that covers 100 percent of demonstrated need for every single recipient. Further, the school is not stingy with merit aid either, dishing out an average package of $20,000 per year to 26 percent of the student population. While many graduates don't immediately land high-paying jobs, the swarms of alumni earning advanced degrees do just fine financially in the long run.

FINANCIAL
Institutional Type: Private
In-State Tuition: $52,040
Out-of-State Tuition: $52,040
Room & Board: $15,320
Required Fees: $218
Books & Supplies: $950

Avg. Need-Based Aid: $36,597
Avg. % of Need Met: 100%

Avg. Merit-Based Aid: $20,388
% Receiving Merit-Based Aid: 26%

Avg. Cumulative Debt: $25,538
% of Students Borrowing: 66%

CAREER
Who Recruits
1. ESPN
2. Life Technologies
3. Forester Capital, LLC
4. NERA Economic Consulting
5. Analysis Group

Notable Internships
1. United States Senate
2. Nike
3. The Coca-Cola Company

Top Industries
1. Education
2. Business
3. Social Services
4. Media
5. Research

Top Employers
1. Google
2. MassMutual
3. Microsoft
4. Amazon
5. Goldman Sachs

Where Alumni Work
1. New York City
2. Boston
3. Springfield, MA
4. Washington, DC
5. San Francisco

Median Earnings
College Scorecard (Early Career): $48,600
EOP (Early Career): $48,900
PayScale (Mid-Career): $92,100

RANKINGS
Forbes: 137
Money: 234
U.S. News: 32, Liberal Arts Colleges
Wall Street Journal/THE: 61 (T)
Washington Monthly: 38, Liberal Arts Colleges

#CollegesWorthYourMoney

New York University

New York, New York | Admissions Phone: 212-998-4500

ADMISSION
Admission Rate: 20%
Admission Rate - Men: 20%
Admission Rate - Women: 20%
EA Admission Rate: Not Offered
ED Admission Rate: 35%
Admission Rate (5-Year Trend): -12%
ED Admission Rate (5-Year Trend): +3%
% of Admits Attending (Yield): 43%
Transfer Admission Rate: 25%

Offered Wait List: N/A
Accepted Wait List: N/A
Admitted Wait List: N/A

SAT Reading/Writing (Middle 50%): 650-720
SAT Math (Middle 50%): 660-790
ACT Composite (Middle 50%): 29-34
Testing Policy: Test Flexible
SAT Superscore: Yes
ACT Superscore: Yes

% Graduated in Top 10% of HS Class: 71%
% Graduated in Top 25% of HS Class: 100%
% Graduated in Top 50% of HS Class: 100%

ENROLLMENT
Total Undergraduate Enrollment: 26,733
% Part-Time: 4%
% Male: 42%
% Female: 58%
% Out-of-State: 67%
% Fraternity: 4%
% Sorority: 7%
% On-Campus (Freshman): 84%
% On-Campus (All Undergraduate): 42%

% African-American: 7%
% Asian: 19%
% Hispanic: 15%
% White: 28%
% Other: 4%
% Race or Ethnicity Unknown: 6%
% International: 21%
% Low-Income: 22%

ACADEMICS
Student-to-Faculty Ratio: 9:1
% of Classes Under 20: 61%
% of Classes Under 40: 87%
% Full-Time Faculty: 45%
% Full-Time Faculty w/ Terminal Degree: 94%

Top Programs
Business and Political Economy
Computer Science
Film and Television
Finance
Global Public Health
Journalism
Mathematics
Performing Arts

Retention Rate: 94%
4-Year Graduation Rate: 77%
6-Year Graduation Rate: 85%

Curricular Flexibility: Somewhat Flexible
Academic Rating: ★★★★

Inside the Classroom

A genuine melting pot, even by the standards of the city in which it is located, New York University's campus is graced by talented young people of every ethnicity, from every socio-economic status, and from every corner of the globe. All told, there are more than 50,000 students presently enrolled at NYU, just less than half of whom are undergraduates. With more than 230 areas of undergraduate study, the talents and passions of this student body are as diverse as its demographic makeup.

NYU is divided into a number of smaller (but still quite large) colleges organized by discipline. Schools with undergraduate programs include the College of Arts & Sciences; Tisch School of the Arts; Tandon School of Engineering, Steinhardt School of Culture, Education, and Human Development; Silver School of Social Work; Rory Meyers College of Nursing; Stern School of Business; College of Global Public Health; and the Gallatin School of Individualized Study where students can create their own liberal arts course of study. There are five parts to NYU's core curriculum that must be tackled by all arts and sciences students. Within other colleges, alterations are made in some areas. The core is comprised of (1) a research- and writing-focused first-year seminar capped at eighteen students, (2) a course in expository writing, (3) two years of language study, (4) Foundations of Contemporary Culture, and (5) Foundations of Scientific Inquiry.

With over 30,000 graduate students and a similar number of undergrads, you might expect undergraduate courses to be held in large lecture halls, even with a 9:1 student-to-faculty ratio. However, NYU manages to run a commendable 59 percent of its classes with an enrollment under twenty students; only 10 percent of courses contain more than fifty students. The school puts a great deal of money into undergraduate research, and it has been running an Undergraduate Research Conference for over forty years. Summer research opportunities are plentiful, including through the School of Engineering's ten-week summer research program for rising juniors and seniors. With more than 4,400 students studying in foreign countries each year, NYU sends more undergrads abroad than any other US university.

While all schools within NYU have solid reputations that will open doors to top corporations and grad schools alike, Stern holds the distinction as one of the top undergraduate business programs in the country. For those entering film, dance, drama, or other performing arts, Tisch is as prestigious a place as you can find to study, and the alumni list is full of Hollywood legends. In recent years NYU has seen an increase in the number of students winning highly competitive postgraduate scholarships. In 2019, Fulbright Scholarships were awarded to fourteen exiting seniors. The school has seen more than one Rhodes Scholar named each of the last three years with the Abu Dhabi campus producing more Rhodes winners than any other school in the country.

Outside the Classroom

Campus life at NYU is best described in one word: diverse. The make-up of the student body is 28 percent international, the highest percentage of any US school, as its students hail from 115 countries. With sizable Asian, Latino, and African American populations, only about one-fifth of the students are classified as white. Life outside the classroom is every bit as diverse as the demographics as NYU truly has something for everyone. The school's twenty-two dorms provide housing for 12,000 students (including some graduate students); overall, 43 percent of undergrads live on campus. With eleven men's and ten women's varsity teams competing in NCAA Division III sports as well as an extensive club and intramural program, NYU has enough opportunity to satisfy the athletically-inclined but is far from a "sports school." Greek life is also available but tempered with single-digit participation rates in sororities and fraternities. There are 300 student organizations open to all students as well as hundreds more school-specific clubs (e.g., Stern-only, Tandon-only). Performance-based groups abound and often sport incredible alumni lists such as those from the Hammerkatz sketch comedy, Tisch New Theater, and WNYU radio. Plenty of quirky, niche options also are available such as the uber-popular Milk and Cookies Club. The university's Greenwich Village location means all that New York City has to offer is at your fingertips. International cuisine, Broadway shows, world-renowned museums, top musical and comedy acts, and shopping can all be part of your daily existence.

Career Services

The Wasserman Center for Career Development has fifty professional staff members who work in areas such as career counseling, recruitment, and student employment. That 580:1 student-to-advisor ratio is a bit higher than the average school featured in this guide. Catering to the career services needs of more than 25,000 full-time undergrads is a massive task. Fortunately, NYU's staff is up to it, hosting large-scale events such as the Fall Job & Internship Fair as well as other industry-specific events throughout the year including real estate, nursing, government, and hospitality and tourism.

Of the employed members of the Class of 2018, 56 percent landed their jobs through an NYU resource. Among the resources rated "most helpful" by job/internship seekers were NYU CareerNet, NYU Connections, and the NYU On-Campus Recruiting Program. Those landing summer jobs and internships along the way also attributed their procurement of positions directly to Wasserman at a similar 54 percent clip. The top summer internship destinations include PwC, EY, Credit Suisse, Accenture, Barclay's, Bank of America, and Wells Fargo. Thirteen percent of employed graduates were the recipients of promotions stemming from summer internships. A solid 42 percent of employed grads received job offers prior to commencement. More than half a million alumni are situated in companies and organizations around the world, leaving no shortage of networking opportunities.

Professional Outcomes

Within six months of graduating, 97 percent of NYU Class of 2018 graduates had successfully landed at their next destination. Of that group, 85 percent were employed and 15 percent were in graduate school. Over half of grads received more than one job offer. The top industries for employment were entertainment/media (20 percent), financial services/banking (17 percent), health care (13 percent), computer science/technology (11 percent), and consulting (10 percent). Large numbers of alumni can be found at major corporations such as Google, Deloitte, Morgan Stanley, Goldman Sachs, IBM, JP Morgan Chase, Citi, and Amazon. The mean starting salary is $65,000 with a mean signing bonus of almost $12k. In 2018, New York was (by more than ten times) the most popular destination over number two choice California. New Jersey, DC, and Massachusetts were next in attracting the highest numbers of recent alumni.

Of the 15 percent of the Class of 2018 attending graduate school, 18 percent were seeking degrees in arts/humanities/social sciences, 13 percent were in medical school, and 10 percent were in law school. Elite graduate and professional schools are well within the grasp of an NYU alum, including the university's own top-ranked Stern School of Business, School of Law at New York University, and the School of Medicine at New York University (Langone). Even though the number of students directly matriculating into graduate school is relatively small, 48 percent stated that they planned to continue their education within the next five years.

Admission

Acceptance rates at NYU have experienced a rapid decline in recent years. In 2013, a solid 35 percent of applicants were accepted; in 2017, that figure dipped to 28 percent before plummeting to 20 percent in 2018. In total, the university received over 71,000 applications for a place in the Class of 2022. This cohort boasted a mid-50 percent SAT score of 1310-1510, an all-time high for an incoming class at NYU; the ACT mid-50 percent range was 29-34. The average GPA was 3.62, and 40 percent of freshmen possessed a 3.75 or higher. Close to three-quarters of entering freshmen placed in the top decile of their high school class, and every single individual was at least in the top quartile.

The overwhelming volume of applicants makes an in-depth, personalized admissions process unfeasible. Rather, the committee relies primarily on hard numbers like GPA, class rank, and standardized test scores. Participation in a highly rigorous course load is also a must, and special talents/abilities are given serious consideration. Essays, recommendations, extracurricular activities, and character/personal qualities also are deemed important in the process. NYU does offer an early decision round that yields more favorable acceptance rates than those in the regular round. ED applicants to the Class of 2022 were successful 35 percent of the time versus 18 percent in the regular cycle. *Warning:* This is a school where high school guidance counselors, thinking of NYU-bound students they worked with a few years ago, may not be aware of the increased selectivity demonstrated by the university in the last few years. Applicants with a genuine shot will be near the top of their graduating class and will have standardized test scores in the 95th percentile.

Worth Your Money?

NYU is not nearly as generous with financial aid as many other elite schools that strive to meet 100 percent of demonstrated student need. In fact, the university is downright stingy--only 12 percent of those who qualify for aid see all of their need met; instead, the average annual grant for those found eligible is $31,839. The overall cost of attendance is $75,502, and merit aid awards are extremely uncommon and typically for very low amounts. The university is an exceptional place to learn, but for $300,000 in total costs you'll need to weigh your expected future salary (based on the field you intend to enter) versus the amount of debt you are willing to take on. Of course, if you are aiming to study at any New York City school, the living costs will be on the high side, but the benefits may be great.

FINANCIAL
Institutional Type: Private
In-State Tuition: $50,684
Out-of-State Tuition: $50,684
Room & Board: $18,684
Required Fees: $2,624
Books & Supplies: $752

Avg. Need-Based Aid: $31,839
Avg. % of Need Met: 65%

Avg. Merit-Based Aid: $5,040
% Receiving Merit-Based Aid: 5%

Avg. Cumulative Debt: $29,923
% of Students Borrowing: 43%

CAREER
Who Recruits
1. Infosys
2. BNP
3. Netflix
4. PayPal
5. Eileen Fisher

Notable Internships
1. United Nations
2. Credit Suisse
3. NYU Langone Health

Top Industries
1. Business
2. Education
3. Media
4. Arts & Design
5. Operations

Top Employers
1. Google
2. JPMorgan Chase
3. Citi
4. Morgan Stanley
5. Amazon

Where Alumni Work
1. New York City
2. Los Angeles
3. San Francisco
4. Washington, DC
5. Boston

Median Earnings
College Scorecard (Early Career): $61,900
EOP (Early Career): $58,100
PayScale (Mid-Career): $117,700

RANKINGS
Forbes: 35
Money: 206
U.S. News: 29, National Universities
Wall Street Journal/THE: 31
Washington Monthly: 107, National Universities

#CollegesWorthYourMoney

North Carolina State University

Raleigh, North Carolina | Admissions Phone: 919-515-2434

ADMISSION
Admission Rate: 47%
Admission Rate - Men: 44%
Admission Rate - Women: 49%
EA Admission Rate: 61%
ED Admission Rate: Not Offered
Admission Rate (5-Year Trend): 0%
ED Admission Rate (5-Year Trend): Not Offered
% of Admits Attending (Yield): 34%
Transfer Admission Rate: 42%

Offered Wait List: 4,133
Accepted Wait List: 4,127
Admitted Wait List: 20

SAT Reading/Writing (Middle 50%): 620-680
SAT Math (Middle 50%): 630-710
ACT Composite (Middle 50%): 27-31
Testing Policy: ACT/SAT Required
SAT Superscore: Yes
ACT Superscore: Yes

% Graduated in Top 10% of HS Class: 48%
% Graduated in Top 25% of HS Class: 85%
% Graduated in Top 50% of HS Class: 99%

ENROLLMENT
Total Undergraduate Enrollment: 25,199
% Part-Time: 11%
% Male: 53%
% Female: 47%
% Out-of-State: 9%
% Fraternity: 13%
% Sorority: 17%
% On-Campus (Freshman): 97%
% On-Campus (All Undergraduate): 38%

% African-American: 6%
% Asian: 7%
% Hispanic: 6%
% White: 67%
% Other: 4%
% Race or Ethnicity Unknown: 7%
% International: 4%
% Low-Income: 21%

ACADEMICS
Student-to-Faculty Ratio: 14:1
% of Classes Under 20: 35%
% of Classes Under 40: 76%
% Full-Time Faculty: 86%
% Full-Time Faculty w/ Terminal Degree: 92%

Top Programs
Architecture
Agricultural Science
Animal Science
Design
Engineering
Sport Management
Textile Design and Management

Retention Rate: 94%
4-Year Graduation Rate: 54%
6-Year Graduation Rate: 81%

Curricular Flexibility: Less Flexible
Academic Rating: ★★★✔

Inside the Classroom

Of the University of North Carolina System's seventeen campuses, UNC-Chapel Hill, the flagship, understandably has the highest national profile by a wide margin. Yet, those in the know are aware that North Carolina State University (NC State) has emerged as a highly competitive and elite academic institution in its own right. Located in the state capital of Raleigh, NC State is at the heart of the Research Triangle—in fact, the school is one its vertices with the aforementioned UNC-Chapel Hill and Duke University accounting for the others. Some would be surprised to learn that among entering freshmen in 2018-19, the average SAT score was 1320 and that the group included 230 valedictorians and salutatorians. The quality of the 25,200 undergraduates is matched by the school's superb academic offerings in engineering, architecture, agriculture, design, business, and so much more.

The general education program requires all students to conquer thirty-nine credits of mandated coursework in the following areas: mathematical science, natural sciences, humanities, social sciences, health and exercise studies, US diversity, interdisciplinary studies, global studies, and technology fluency. Everyone also engages with an Introduction to Writing class and the demonstration of foreign language proficiency, but it's extremely easy to opt out of a foreign language if you choose, as long as you took two years of courses in the same language in high school.

Thanks to a reasonable 14:1 student-to-faculty ratio, you won't exclusively have classes in enormous lecture halls. Rather, NC State offers its undergraduates a mix of experiences with 64 percent of sections enrolling twenty-nine or fewer students and 16 percent enrolling fifty or more. The Office of Undergraduate Research works diligently to connect star students to faculty research projects, which leads to over 600 student presentations at spring/summer poster sessions. The "Speed-Data-ing" program brings together 250 underclassmen to learn about current research being conducted by NC State professors. The university has put a good deal of emphasis on raising its study abroad participation rate in recent years, and those efforts have been fruitful; 22 percent of undergraduates now study abroad, and there has been a 75 percent increase in participation by underrepresented students over the past seven years.

Engineering is the most popular area of concentration as 27 percent of Class of 2019 graduates earned a degree in that field. Business/marketing comes in second at 15 percent followed by biology (8 percent) and agriculture (7 percent). NC State has an exceptional regional reputation and an expanding national one with the College of Engineering now found near the top of many rankings. Programs in design, architecture, and animal science are also very strong. Wolfpack members also are gaining the attention of the most prestigious postgraduate fellowship organizations. In 2019, National Science Foundation Graduate Research Fellowships went to fourteen NC State students. Another four students won Goldwater Scholarships, four captured Fulbright Scholarships, and thirteen were awarded Gilman Scholarships.

Outside the Classroom

Freshmen overwhelmingly reside on campus as they are required to do; 97 percent of all first-year students live in university-run housing. Among all undergraduates, 38 percent live on campus in one of twenty residence halls that are a mix of suite, hotel, and traditional buildings. Greek houses draw their fair share of the population with 17 percent of women joining sororities and 13 percent of men pledging fraternities. More than 550 athletes participate as part of the twenty-three varsity athletic teams that have combined to capture four national championships, including the legendary 1983 NCAA champion men's basketball team. Wolfpack fans are a rabid bunch, and they rank in the top ten for hoops attendance in the United States. The Talley Student Union, built in 2015, is the central hub for 700+ student organizations including a daily newspaper, a popular college radio station, and plenty of cultural, performance-based, political, and pre-professional organizations. The school's 2,110-acre campus is within a few miles of many of Raleigh's finest attractions including North Carolina's state art, natural history, and history museums; multiple parks and arboretums; and the beautiful Lake Johnson Park.

Career Services

The NCSU Career Development Center employs eighteen professionals who function as career identity coaches, career counselors, employer relations specialists, and pre-professional advisors. There are numerous other departments within individual colleges that employ another five career services staff members to bring the total of full-time, professional employees to twenty-three, which works out to a 1008:1 student-to-advisor ratio, higher than the average school featured in this guidebook.

Still, 50 percent of Class of 2019 members had received counseling in the Career Development Center, and the vast majority found the experience to be a positive one. A solid two-thirds of employed Class of 2019 members stated that their job was "directly related" to their major, a sign that career counseling staff are pointing students in the right direction. The greatest number of students reported that their internship/externship had been most helpful in their job search (43 percent) followed by a career fair at NC State (29 percent). In the Poole College of

Management, the co-op/internship completion rate was 85 percent. Co-op participation is encouraged, and students can complete up to three alternating semesters of paid work experience. NC State offers 1,000 different work rotations, making it one of the largest university co-op programs in the country. Major employers are regular visitors to campus, and career expos such as the Engineering Career Fair, Poole College of Management Career & Internship Fair, and the Ag & Sciences Career Expo collectively draw hundreds of top hiring organizations to Raleigh. Being situated in the Triangle means that many big-time companies are nearby and loaded with Wolfpack alumni.

Professional Outcomes

Approximately 75 percent of students graduating in May 2019 reported that they planned to pursue employment after receiving their diplomas, and half had already secured a job offer. Members of that class obtaining a full-time job reported an average starting salary of $54,734 (with a slightly higher median). Of that cohort, 71 percent were remaining in the state of North Carolina for work with a large percentage situated in the Research Triangle area of Raleigh, Durham, and Chapel Hill. San Francisco, DC, New York City, and Atlanta also attracted a fair number of graduates. Including all graduating years, the companies employing the largest number of Wolfpack alumni are Cisco, Red Hat and SAS (major NC-based software companies), IBM, Lenovo, Amazon, Microsoft, Intel, Google, Deloitte, Facebook, and Salesforce. Many recent graduates also work for the university itself and for the Wake County Public School System.

Upon graduation, one-fourth of Class of 2019 members indicated that their plan was to attend graduate/professional school. Forty-six percent of that group planned to continue their educational journey at NC State, and 70 percent planned to attend a school in North Carolina. An encouraging 88 percent stated that they were attending their first-choice institution. The most commonly pursued degree was a master's (67 percent) followed by a professional degree (18 percent) and a doctoral degree (15 percent). Each year roughly 300 NC State students apply to medical school and another 150 to dental school. Recent med school acceptances include prestigious programs at Duke, UNC-Chapel Hill, UVA, Wake Forest, and Emory. Between 75 and 80 percent of those recommended by the Health Professions Advising Center are accepted into at least one medical school. Law candidates find similar positive results, and schools like Yale, Duke, UNC-Chapel Hill, and Washington & Lee regularly visit NC State to recruit.

Admission

The present iteration of NC State is highly selective, which may come as a shock even to an older relative who attended the university. In fact, the 25th percentile SAT score of attending freshmen in 2018-19 is close to the 75th percentile figure from a decade prior. The acceptance rate is now 47 percent, and the applicant pool is more competitive than ever. Those attending possess impressive mid-50 percent standardized test ranges of 27-31 on the ACT and 1250-1390 on the SAT with an even number of students submitting results from both exams. They also earned the grades to match those test scores with an average unweighted GPA of 3.76 (the average weighted GPA is 4.59). A solid 58 percent hailed from the top 10 percent of their high school class, and 85 percent placed in the top quartile.

With more than 30,000 applicants annually, NC State admissions officers rely heavily on factors like SAT scores, GPA, class rank, and the rigor of one's course load. All other factors are mere considerations, unlikely to exert significant influence on the decision. There are no early action or early decision options at NC State, but we recommend that every serious applicant submit by the Nov. 1 priority deadline rather than waiting until mid-January. Thirty-four percent of those accepted ultimately enroll in the school compared with over 50 percent in 2000 when the school drew one-third as many applicants. Despite the lower yield rate, it is fair to say that NC State is a more desirable landing spot than ever for high-achieving North Carolina residents.

Worth Your Money?

When an annual tuition bill is in the four-figures it instantly qualifies as an absurd bargain. NC State's tuition is actually around one-sixth the cost of North Carolina private schools like Duke, Davidson, or Wake Forest. For the 15 percent of Wolfpack members not from in state, thanks to low housing costs, the total cost of attendance is not obscene, coming in at under $45k. Therefore, the value of this degree for a nonresident would be context dependent—engineering, computer science, and design students are more than likely to see favorable returns. For a resident, it's a no-brainer investment.

FINANCIAL
Institutional Type: Public
In-State Tuition: $6,535
Out-of-State Tuition: $25,878
Room & Board: $11,078
Required Fees: $2,566
Books & Supplies: $1,082

Avg. Need-Based Aid: $10,104
Avg. % of Need Met: 73%

Avg. Merit-Based Aid: $5,811
% Receiving Merit-Based Aid: 11%

Avg. Cumulative Debt: $24,002
% of Students Borrowing: 51%

CAREER
Who Recruits
1. John Deere
2. Smithfield
3. GSK
4. Allstate
5. SAS

Notable Internships
1. Barclays
2. Red Hat
3. Cisco

Top Industries
1. Business
2. Engineering
3. Operations
4. Education
5. Research

Top Employers
1. Cisco
2. SAS
3. IBM
4. Lenovo
5. Red Hat

Where Alumni Work
1. Raleigh-Durham, NC
2. Charlotte
3. Winston-Salem, NC
4. Washington, DC
5. San Francisco

Median Earnings
College Scorecard (Early Career): $52,500
EOP (Early Career): $52,300
PayScale (Mid-Career): $106,500

RANKINGS
Forbes: 139
Money: 40
U.S. News: 84, National Universities
Wall Street Journal/THE: 104
Washington Monthly: 74, National Universities

#CollegesWorthYourMoney

Northeastern University

Boston, Massachusetts | Admissions Phone: 617-373-2200

Inside the Classroom

If Northeastern University was a middle-aged person headed to a twentieth high school reunion, it would easily earn the distinction as the least recognized individual in the room. Few institutions have undergone such a substantial metamorphosis in such a short time. Beginning in the 1990s NU decided to reverse-engineer the *US News* rankings and make a grab for increased prestige. At the time, the school was ranked the 162nd best university in the nation. As of 2019 it is close to cracking the top forty. Today, the average undergraduate student possesses a 4.2 GPA and a 1459 on the SAT, literally 400+ higher than two decades ago. You read that correctly—400 points!

On the menu for this suddenly top-flight breed of undergrads are all the trappings of a major research university, including ninety-two majors and 142 combined majors available at Northeastern's seven undergraduate schools. All students are required to walk the NUpath, the school's core curriculum that is "built around essential, broad-based knowledge and skills—such as understanding societies and analyzing data—integrated with specific content areas and disciplines." There are eleven components to the NUpath that involve forays into the natural and designed world, creative expression and innovation, culture, formal and quantitative reasoning, societies and institutions, analyzing data, differences and diversity, ethical reasoning, writing across audiences, integrating knowledge and skills through experience, and a capstone course as you near completion of your chosen major(s).

More than two-thirds of Husky classrooms contain nineteen or fewer students, and 11 percent have single-digit enrollments. Large lecture hall courses crammed with undergrads are rare at this school—only 6 percent of sections sport a student enrollment of fifty or more. A 14:1 student-to-faculty ratio makes these cozy class sizes possible, an impressive feat considering the school has almost 8,700 graduate students to serve as well. Since 2006 Northeastern has added an incredible 650 tenured and tenure-track faculty members. Undergraduate research opportunities exist in all departments, and experiential learning of some type is had by virtually all graduates, thanks to the school's illustrious and robust co-op program. NU students have not only become more accomplished but also more worldly. Last academic year, 3,820 students had a global experience in one of eighty-eight countries, and 538 students participated in a co-op program overseas.

The D'Amore-McKim School of Business is a top-ranked school and offers one of the best international business programs anywhere, and the both the College of Engineering and College of Computer Science are highly respected as well. Criminal justice, architecture, and nursing are three other majors that rate near the top nationally. Business/marketing (25 percent) and engineering (17 percent) account for the largest percentages of degrees conferred. The social sciences (12 percent), health-related professions (10 percent), and biology (8 percent) round out the list of most popular majors. In 2019, Northeastern grads fared better than ever in procuring nationally competitive scholarships. Nine took home Fulbright Scholarships, five were awarded Gilman Scholarships, and two won Truman Scholarships.

Outside the Classroom

Northeastern is split down the middle in terms of those who live in on-campus housing and those who do not. All freshmen and sophomores are required to live in the dorms, and most have at least one or two roommates. Campus offers six large quad areas and twenty eateries. Greek life is fairly strong with 10 percent of men and 17 percent of women joining frats and sororities. The 73-acre urban campus is situated in the true heart of downtown Boston and within one mile of Fenway Park, Newbury Street, and the Museum of Fine Arts. With such a premier location, the beloved city of Boston is truly an extension of your campus, but there are also plenty of university-sponsored activities to keep you busy. Over 400 student clubs and organizations and the Northeastern University Hus-skiers and Outing Club (NUHOC), student government, and forty club sports teams are among the most popular. In total, 3,000 students participate in club and intramural sports. Spectator sports are not a focal point of NU life—the football program was dissolved in 2009— but of the sixteen existing NCAA Division I squads, the Huskies hockey team reigns supreme. The spirit of volunteerism is huge at NU as students have contributed a collective 1.4 million hours since 2006.

Career Services

Thirty-six counselors, employer relations specialists, and experiential learning coordinators comprise the NU Employer Engagement and Career Design Office (EECD), which doesn't count admin assistants or IT professionals. Working out to a student-to-advisor ratio of 512:1, NU offers a high level of support for an institution with more than 18,000 undergraduates. Northeastern University has long held a reputation as one of the premier career services providers in the nation, and it's not hard to see why.

Career counselors received incredibly high reviews from students as 96 percent report progress on their career goals after only one session; 100 percent felt it was worth their time to return for a follow-up. The EECD has forged relationships with over 3,000 employers and, through its employer-in-residence program, representatives from those organizations spend up to one day per week for an entire year interacting with students, making personal connections, and offering career tips. The fall 2018 Career Fair was attended by 260 employers and the spring Engineering and Technology Career Fair usually draws 4,000+ students and 140 companies. Perhaps the most impactful role of this office is to facilitate co-op placements. Ninety-six percent of NU graduates spend at least one semester in a co-op placement, and 50 percent of students receive a job offer from their co-op partner; 2,900+ employers participate each year. By almost any metric, the Employer Engagement and Career Design services stand out from the pack, easily earning its staff near universal praise.

Professional Outcomes

Nine months after leaving Northeastern 92 percent of students have landed at their next employment or graduate school destination. Huskies entering the job market are quickly rounded up by the likes of State Street, Fidelity Investments, IBM, and Amazon, all of whom employ 500+ Northeastern alums. Between 200 and 500 employees at Wayfair, Google, Amazon, Oracle, IBM, and Apple have an NU lineage. Whether or not they originally hailed from New England, the vast majority of graduates remain in the Greater Boston area. Next in popularity are New York City, San Francisco, DC, Los Angeles, Philadelphia, and Seattle. Starting salaries are above average, in part due to the stellar co-op program, and compensation is in the same range as other highly selective schools including Fordham and Boston University.

Strange for a school with such excellent career services, Northeastern does not publicize its law school or med school acceptance rates or release a list of the most frequently attended graduate schools by NU alumni. The highly ranked Northeastern University School of Law does take a large number of its own undergraduates. More than one alum is currently enrolled at such law schools as Suffolk, Harvard, Fordham, and Boston College. While Northeastern does not have its own medical college, many graduates go on to attend top institutions. Multiple recent grads are currently attending such medical schools as UMass, Harvard, UConn, and Tufts. In short, while NU is strangely mysterious about its graduate/professional school outcomes data, it has no reason to be; Huskies routinely continue their educations at some of the best universities in the United States.

Admission

Only 18 percent of the 62,000 applicants for a place in the 2019-20 freshman class received a letter of acceptance. The middle-50 percent stats for admitted (not committed) students included a 4.1-4.5 GPA, a 1450-1540 SAT range, and 33-35 on the ACT. Over three-quarters placed in the top 10 percent of their high school graduating class. A decade ago, the school received only 34,000 applications, and a far less menacing 41 percent were let through the door. Freshmen in 2009-10 possessed middle 50 percent SAT scores of 1200-1370. Any way you measure it, the level of selectivity is far greater than even in the most recent past.

An applicant's GPA, rigor of courses, standardized test scores, essay, and recommendation letters are all categorized as "very important" admissions factors by this committee. Admissions officers at Northeastern place soft factors such as extracurricular activities, talent/ability, character, personal qualities, volunteer work, and work experience on the next rung of "important" categories. Class rank, first-generation status, ethnic status, geographical residence, and the level of demonstrated interest comprise the "considered" factors in the admissions process. As to why geographical residence is a considered factor, the university received only 49 percent of its applications from outside New England in 2006; in 2019, it received 65 percent from outside the region. That is all part of the university's aforementioned quest to enhance its national reputation. Northeastern's desirability and prestige have risen at a lightning pace, making it exactly the type of school that even a well-intentioned school counselor or parent can easily misjudge in terms of the current odds of gaining admission. This is a school that generally only accepts students with standardized test scores in the top 3 percent and who have virtually flawless transcripts. Applying via binding early decision is definitely a serious consideration. Of the 1,107 who did so last year, 41 percent were successful.

Worth Your Money?

Northeastern has a list price cost of attendance in excess of $72,000 per year, and the need-based aid situation is less than ideal. Only two-thirds of those applying for financial aid received an award. Compare that to nearby Boston College and Boston University, each of which awarded need-based grants to 88 percent and 82 percent, respectively, of those who applied. The better news is that over half of Northeastern students receive a merit aid award averaging $19,500, at least bringing the total four-year costs closer to $200,000. In short, this school is worth your money if you are aiming to enter a high-paying field and/or have parents who can afford the hefty tuition payments. Then the connections the school provides are worth a substantial amount. However, middle-class students set on entering public service would likely not see their investment returned and could accumulate a good deal of debt along the way.

FINANCIAL
Institutional Type: Private
In-State Tuition: $52,420
Out-of-State Tuition: $52,420
Room & Board: $16,930
Required Fees: $1,086
Books & Supplies: $1,000

Avg. Need-Based Aid: $35,299
Avg. % of Need Met: 100%

Avg. Merit-Based Aid: $19,488
% Receiving Merit-Based Aid: 51%

Avg. Cumulative Debt: N/A
% of Students Borrowing: N/A

CAREER
Who Recruits
1. IBM
2. Siemens
3. Staples
4. Coleman
5. Northwestern Mutual

Notable Internships
1. Wayfair
2. Vogue
3. Tesla

Top Industries
1. Business
2. Engineering
3. Operations
4. Education
5. Information Technology

Top Employers
1. State Street
2. Fidelity Investments
3. Amazon
4. IBM
5. Wayfair

Where Alumni Work
1. Boston
2. New York City
3. San Francisco
4. Washington, DC
5. Los Angeles

Median Earnings
College Scorecard (Early Career): $67,400
EOP (Early Career): $61,800
PayScale (Mid-Career): $109,700

RANKINGS
Forbes: 182
Money: 135
U.S. News: 40, 74, National Universities
Wall Street Journal/THE: 93 (T)
Washington Monthly: 141, National Universities

#CollegesWorthYourMoney

Evanston, Illinois | Admissions Phone: 847-491-7271

ADMISSION
Admission Rate: 8%
Admission Rate - Men: 8%
Admission Rate - Women: 8%
EA Admission Rate: Not Offered
ED Admission Rate: 27%
Admission Rate (5-Year Trend): -6%
ED Admission Rate (5-Year Trend): -8%
% of Admits Attending (Yield): 56%
Transfer Admission Rate: 15%

Offered Wait List: 2,861
Accepted Wait List: 1,859
Admitted Wait List: 24

SAT Reading/Writing (Middle 50%): 700-760
SAT Math (Middle 50%): 730-790
ACT Composite (Middle 50%): 33-35
Testing Policy: ACT/SAT Required
SAT Superscore: Yes
ACT Superscore: No

% Graduated in Top 10% of HS Class: 92%
% Graduated in Top 25% of HS Class: 100%
% Graduated in Top 50% of HS Class: 100%

ENROLLMENT
Total Undergraduate Enrollment: 8,231
% Part-Time: 2%
% Male: 49%
% Female: 51%
% Out-of-State: 68%
% Fraternity: 34%
% Sorority: 39%
% On-Campus (Freshman): 100%
% On-Campus (All Undergraduate): 60%

% African-American: 6%
% Asian: 18%
% Hispanic: 13%
% White: 45%
% Other: 6%
% Race or Ethnicity Unknown: 4%
% International: 9%
% Low-Income: 14%

ACADEMICS
Student-to-Faculty Ratio: 6:1
% of Classes Under 20: 78%
% of Classes Under 40: 93%
% Full-Time Faculty: 86%
% Full-Time Faculty w/ Terminal Degree: 100%

Top Programs
Biology
Communication Studies
Economics
Engineering
Journalism
Performing Arts
Political Science
Social Policy

Retention Rate: 97%
4-Year Graduation Rate: 84%
6-Year Graduation Rate: 95%

Curricular Flexibility: Somewhat Flexible
Academic Rating: ★★★★★

Inside the Classroom

Like the neighboring University of Chicago, Northwestern University is a highly selective academic institution that operates on a quarter system and is located in Illinois, but the similarities end there. Where the UChicago has a reputation as a breeding ground for future academics/researchers, Northwestern's vibe is more pre-profession-al, athletic, and Greek-inclined, but the 8,200 undergraduates who attend must bring equally flawless academic credentials to the table—otherwise, they will find themselves among the 92 percent of applicants left outside the gates.

Northwestern is home to six undergraduate schools: Weinberg College of Arts and Sciences; McCormick School of Engineering and Applied Science; School of Education and Social Policy; School of Communication; Medill School of Journalism, Media, Integrated Marketing Communications; and Bienen School of Music. Academic requirements vary by school. Weinberg, which enrolls half of all Wildcats, requires two first-year seminars, the demonstration of proficiency in a foreign language and in writing as well as two courses each in six intellectual divisions. Overall, coursework requirements are extensive but not particularly narrow.

The quarter system allows students to take four courses at a time rather than the typical five. Even so, the aca-demic demands are intense, and Northwestern students work hard for their grades. Fortunately, the academic experience is far from an anonymous endeavor. The university has a phenomenal 6:1 student-faculty ratio, and a spectacular 42 percent of class sections have nine or fewer students enrolled; 78 percent have fewer than twenty enrollees. Faculty receive generally favorable reviews from undergraduate students with 93 percent either "very satisfied" or "generally satisfied" with the quality of instruction; 92 percent awarded one of those two pos-itive ratings when asked about the availability of their professors. A solid 58 percent of Northwestern students have the chance to conduct research with a faculty member at some point during their undergraduate years.

The social sciences account for the greatest numbers of degrees conferred (22 percent), followed by communi-cations/journalism (14 percent), engineering (13 percent), biology (8 percent), visual and performing arts (7 percent), and psychology (7 percent). Medill is widely regarded as one of the country's best journalism schools. The McCormick School of Engineering also achieves top rankings, along with programs in economics, social policy, and theatre. Students from all majors bring home prestigious postgraduate fellowships at an enviable rate. In 2018 alone, the school produced twenty-six Gilman Scholars awarded through the US State Depart-ment, twenty-four Fulbright Scholarships, and twenty National Science Foundation Research Fellowships. In total, the Class of 2018 took home a ridiculous 268 competitive national/global scholarships.

Outside the Classroom

Northwestern, like its elite peers Duke, Stanford, and USC, offers top-level academics without sacrificing any of the major college frills like football and frat parties. With forty-six Greek organizations drawing 30 percent of men and 39 percent of women, fraternities and sororities exert a significant degree of influence over the social scene. Athletics are also a strong part of the university's culture with eight men's and eleven women's teams competing in NCAA Division I. The Wildcats are the lone private school competing in the Big Ten Conference, which is otherwise made up of athletic powerhouses like Penn State, Ohio State, and Michigan. NU undergrads report that 91 percent are "deeply involved" with a student organization or athletic team. Nearly half the student population reported that same level of involvement with a community service project. Of the school's 350 student-run clubs, pre-professional organizations, service-oriented groups, and the *Daily Northwestern*—named the nation's top student paper by the Society of Professional Journalists—are among the most popular. Evanston is roughly thirty to forty-five minutes from downtown Chicago (depending on traffic). One of the famous North Shore suburbs of Chicago, Evanston is an affluent city with plenty of high-end restaurants and coffee shops. Natural beauty is easy to find as the school owns a lakefront beach that is on campus. Approximately 60 percent of students (and 99.9 percent of freshmen) elect to live in on-campus housing that is highlighted by thirteen residence halls, each accommodating anywhere from 25-500 students.

Career Services

Northwestern Career Advancement (NCA) employs nineteen full-time professionals who work directly with or on behalf of undergraduate students. That includes career counselors, career advisors, and employer relations staff but does not include graduate advisors, interns, or IT specialists. The student-to-advisor ratio of 443:1 puts NU in the average range compared to other institutions included in this book. Career counselors keep extensive walk-in hours and arrange a number of career-related events, large and small, from the two-day Fall Internship and Job Fair with over 150 employers to more intimate workshops and employer information sessions that are held throughout the year.

Northwestern University

E-mail: ug-admission@northwestern.edu | Website: www.northwestern.edu

A phenomenal 90 percent of graduates reported they engaged in at least one experiential learning opportunity, and 64 percent reported engaging in between two and four such activities. When looking specifically at internships, 76 percent reported landing at least one summer of paid or unpaid experience. The Northwestern Network Mentorship Program now has 5,000 alumni across ninety industries and sixty-six countries ready and willing to help current students with their career planning. The NCA has corporate partnerships with a host of top-notch companies including Accenture, Deloitte, PwC, Capital One, and JP Morgan. The NCA does not publish statistics related to outreach (percentage of students engaging with the office), but thanks to a stellar record of arranging experiential learning opportunities/internships and strong corporate connections, Northwestern's career services still gets a thumbs up from our staff.

Professional Outcomes

Six months after graduating, 72 percent of the Class of 2018 had found employment, 23 percent were in graduate school, and only 3 percent were still looking for work. The four professional fields attracting more than 10 percent of Wildcat alumni were business/finance (20 percent), consulting (15 percent), communications/marketing/media (13 percent), and engineering (12 percent). Employers included an impressive group of media outlets including the BBC, NBC News, the *Washington Post*, and NPR. Across all other industries Wildcats had strong representation at all of the usual corporate giants including Boeing, Google, IBM, Deloitte, PepsiCo, Northrup Grumman, and Goldman Sachs. More than 50 percent of graduates remained in the Midwest, roughly a quarter moved to the East Coast, and 12 percent migrated to California. Across all majors the average starting salary was $59k while engineering and applied sciences students averaged $78k with the lowest income belonging to communications students who earned $43k.

Of the recent alum's headed straight to graduate school, 18 percent were pursuing medical degrees, 13 percent were beginning PhD programs, and 6 percent were entering law school. Engineering, medicine, and business were the three most popular graduate areas of concentration. Members of the Class of 2017 pursued advanced degrees at seven of the eight Ivy League Schools—Stanford, MIT, Carnegie Mellon, UChicago, and Oxford—among a host of other elite institutions. Northwestern is a prolific producer of future MDs; 232 applied in the 2018-19 school year alone.

Admission

The trend toward increasing selectivity continued at Northwestern in 2018 as, for the ninth straight year, the admission rate fell. After hitting single digits for the first time in 2017, only 8.5 percent were admitted into the Class of 2022. The profile of the average freshman in the 2018-19 school year was a mid-50 percent SAT of 1430-1550 and an ACT (by far the more commonly submitted test) was 33-35. A decade ago, when 26 percent of applicants were accepted, the ACT range was a significantly lower 30-32. The percent of freshmen in the top 10 percent of their high school class also has increased during that time, jumping from 85 percent to 92 percent.

According to the admissions office, rigor of courses, GPA, class rank, and standardized test scores are the only four factors that are "very important" in the admissions process. Last year, early decision applicants comprised 56 percent of the incoming classes and enjoyed increased chances of getting in. The regular decision acceptance rate in 2018 was only 6.4 percent compared to 27 percent in the ED round. Northwestern has always been a highly selective school, but the bar has been raised even higher in recent years. Those who wish to find a home on this picturesque North Shore campus next fall must bring excellent credentials to the table and should strongly consider applying early decision.

Worth Your Money?

The average Northwestern graduate who took out loans owes $32,000+, which is a tad more than the national average. This is to be expected at a school that costs over $77,500 per year and does not award much merit aid. Yet, for the 46 percent of undergrads who qualify for need-based aid, the school could not be more generous. It met 100 percent of every student's demonstrated financial need with the average grant approaching $52,000 per year. Those in the toughest spot are children of the middle-class who do not qualify for aid. Still, with very few exceptions, this is a school worth paying for. Even in programs such as journalism that do not generally lead to high-paying first jobs, the networks you will gain at Northwestern are likely to end up paying career dividends many decades down the road.

FINANCIAL
Institutional Type: Private
In-State Tuition: $56,232
Out-of-State Tuition: $56,232
Room & Board: $17,019
Required Fees: $459
Books & Supplies: $1,638

Avg. Need-Based Aid: $51,686
Avg. % of Need Met: 100%

Avg. Merit-Based Aid: $4,964
% Receiving Merit-Based Aid: 4%

Avg. Cumulative Debt: $32,395
% of Students Borrowing: 35%

CAREER
Who Recruits
1. Nielsen
2. Aldi
3. AQR
4. Roland Berger
5. Flow Traders

Notable Internships
1. Brookings Institute
2. HSBC
3. BlackRock

Top Industries
1. Business
2. Education
3. Media
4. Operations
5. Research

Top Employers
1. Google
2. Accenture
3. Amazon
4. Microsoft
5. Deloitte

Where Alumni Work
1. Chicago
2. New York City
3. San Francisco
4. Los Angeles
5. Washington, DC

Median Earnings
College Scorecard (Early Career): $69,000
EOP (Early Career): $72,600
PayScale (Mid-Career): $115,400

RANKINGS
Forbes: 17
Money: 62
U.S. News: 9, National Universities
Wall Street Journal/THE: 11
Washington Monthly: 32, National Universities

#CollegesWorthYourMoney

Oberlin College

Oberlin, Ohio | Admissions Phone: 440-775-8411

Inside the Classroom

A Midwestern version of Oregon's Reed College in terms of the originality and progressive leanings of the student body, Oberlin College in Ohio is an extremely strong provider of a liberal arts education. Known primarily for its top-ranked Conservatory of Music and as a factory for future PhDs, particularly in the hard sciences, Oberlin enrolls more than 2,800 undergraduates. Boasting fifty majors and an additional forty-three minors and concentrations, the college provides an educational setting where professors in just about all of your classes will not only know your name but, amazingly, perhaps even your goals and interests.

As part of the curriculum exploration requirement, two courses each are required in each of the college's three divisions: Arts & Humanities, Mathematics & Natural Sciences, and the Social Sciences. Two of the thirty-two total courses taken must be classified as writing and another two as meeting the Quantitative & Formal Reasoning requirement. Three additional courses must have a Cultural Diversity designation. Students are encouraged— but not required—to become proficient in a foreign language. Overall, Oberlin's mandated coursework is not cumbersome, especially compared to many liberal arts schools of its ilk.

Thanks to its almost entirely undergraduate student population, the effects of Oberlin's 9:1 student-to-faculty ratio are fully felt. Of all the courses at the college, 78 percent had nineteen or fewer students enrolled, and 37 percent contained fewer than ten students. Professors are generous with their time in an academic environment conducive to the formation of mentorships. Undergraduate research opportunities are not hard to locate. In fact, according to the school, "Many students coauthor articles with faculty, which are published in scholarly journals and presented at national meetings." The Office of Study Away helps arrange for roughly 40 percent of graduates to study in a foreign land. School-run opportunities such as Oberlin-in-London are on the table as are ninety affiliated programs.

In terms of sheer volume, the greatest number of degrees conferred in 2019 were in history (55), politics (51), biology (48), English (46), and economics (45). The Conservatory of Music has a worldwide reputation as one or more of its representative alumni are in every major ensemble in the United States. Programs in the natural sciences have sterling reputations, leading to remarkable medical school acceptance rates and the aforementioned number of future PhD scientists and researchers. Highly competitive postgraduate fellowship-granting organizations adore Oberlin grads. In 2017, an astonishing fourteen grads and alumni were named Fulbright Scholars, and the school routinely produces Gilman, Critical Language, Goldwater, and Marshall winners as well.

Outside the Classroom

If you understand Oberlin's vibe it will not surprise you that there are no frats or sororities on campus. Instead, Oberlin requires students to live in either college-owned housing or student-run co-ops all the way through graduation. Some co-ops offer "theme living" centered on commonalities such as an obsession with sci-fi, disability status, sustainability/environmental concerns, or a love of ancient Mediterranean culture. With more than 175 clubs and organizations, twenty-one varsity teams, and thirty-one intramural and club sports, just about every one of Oberlin's undergraduate students is involved in something. The Yeoman and Yeowomen compete within NCAA Division III with 350 athletes competing at that level. If you happen to like live classical music you're in luck—the school's conservatory puts on hundreds of concerts each year. Guest speakers, often intellectuals and authors, regularly attract large crowds at Oberlin. There are a wealth of organizations catering to political/social causes and musical/theatrical performance as well as seven student-run publications. To generalize, most Oberlin students are politically liberal and enjoy challenging social norms. Most students stick around campus, and the small town of Oberlin's quaintness is best exemplified by its claim of having one of the last single-screen movie theaters in the country. For those with access to a car, Cleveland is only a forty-minute drive away.

Career Services

The Career Development Center employs five professional staff members who work in career development or graduate school advising (not counting technical support or administrative assistants). With a 565:1 student-to-advisor ratio, Oberlin provides a lower-than-average level of career services support than many comparable liberal arts schools featured in this guide. While the office does encourage one-on-one appointments and walk-ins, large-scale events like career fairs are lacking, and on-campus recruiting by major employers is not a routine occurrence.

Beginning in 2019, Oberlin began hosting Career Communities covering nine sectors (e.g., entrepreneurship and innovation, professions in music, and science and technology). Up to thirty juniors and seniors can join each community, which includes a guaranteed summer internship and a set of industry-specific mentors. Each community meets as a group six times per semester. Oberlin helps to arrange summer and winter term internships for all interested students, primarily through the use of its online resources. The Oberlin Alumni Database is a platform from which current students can seek job advice from alumni. The office also recommends connecting with 7,000 alumni via LinkedIn. New programs such as the Career Communities show Oberlin's commitment to expanding its career services offerings.

Professional Outcomes

In the years 2015-2017, graduates entering business found homes at companies such as United Shore, Edward Jones, and Liberty Mutual Insurance. Publishing, media, and entertainment companies that scooped up recent grads include MSNBC, New York Magazine, and NBCUniversal, Inc. In part because so many students go on to enter careers in research and academia, even age thirty-four median salaries are quite low— one study ranked Oberlin sixty-third of sixty-four selective liberal arts schools in this department. However, it is important to note that many Oberlin graduates do go on to remunerative careers. New York is home to the highest number of alumni followed by San Francisco, Cleveland, DC, and Boston.

Over the last few years multiple students have gone on to pursue advanced degrees at Harvard, Stanford, MIT, Brown, Columbia, Princeton, and the University of Michigan. Graduates fare well in gaining acceptance into med school, sporting an 80 percent success rate, nearly double the national average. Recent grads have enrolled in medical school at the University of Pennsylvania, Baylor College of Medicine, and SUNY Upstate Medical University. Law school applicants have enjoyed an 83 percent acceptance rate and have found homes at the likes of Yale, Indiana, and Wake Forest. Oberlin also has a reputation for churning out future PhDs and, in fact, is among the top ten schools across all disciplines in producing graduates who go on to earn their doctoral degrees.

Admission

An unintimidating 39 percent of the 6,269 applicants for a place in the Class of 2022 were successful, but that number hardly tells the story of how competitive the Oberlin admissions process really is. Admitted students possessed middle-50 percent test scores of 30-34 on the ACT and 1320-1520 on the SAT. The average weighted GPA was 4.0, and the average unweighted GPA was 3.7. An overwhelming 91 percent of students ranked in the top quarter of their high school classes, 65 percent placed in the top 10 percent, and 21 percent were in the top 1 percent. Twenty-nine percent of those accepted went on to enroll in the college. Of those who joined the college, the mid-50 percent SAT range was 1280-1480, and 54 percent placed in the top decile of their graduating class.

Standardized test scores, GPA, class rank, and the rigor of one's secondary school record are the four factors weighted most heavily in the process. Secondary factors include essays, recommendations, talent/ability, character/personal qualities, and the seemingly polar opposite categories of legacy and first-generation applicants. Those who apply via early decision enjoy a 49 percent acceptance rate and account for roughly one-third of each incoming class. Oberlin is definitely a college where the self-selecting applicant pool results in a deceptively high acceptance rate. Make no mistake—you need to bring extremely strong grades to the table (only 14 percent of enrolled high school freshmen possessed GPAs under 3.25) and strong standardized test scores (only 7 percent had SAT reading scores under 600). Applying early is a worthwhile maneuver for those clamoring to spend the next four years in rural Ohio at this liberal arts gem. The ED acceptance rate is 49 percent compared with 35 percent in the regular round.

Worth Your Money?

Oberlin is one of the exclusive club of colleges that meets 100 percent of all undergraduates' demonstrated need. Half of all students receive an average annual aid package that exceeds $41,000. Equally encouraging is the fact that 81 percent of students net merit aid; the average award is approximately $19,000. With an annual cost of attendance of $72,628, those "discounts" are most appreciated, especially because many graduates pursue careers that are not among the most lucrative and/or require many additional years of education beyond the bachelor's degree. Admitted students should consider their future plans before committing. However, Oberlin's top-notch academics and generous aid make it a worthy investment for most.

FINANCIAL
Institutional Type: Private
In-State Tuition: $54,346
Out-of-State Tuition: $54,346
Room & Board: $16,338
Required Fees: $706
Books & Supplies: $930

Avg. Need-Based Aid: $41,979
Avg. % of Need Met: 100%

Avg. Merit-Based Aid: $18,961
% Receiving Merit-Based Aid: 81%

Avg. Cumulative Debt: $27,523
% of Students Borrowing: 41%

CAREER
Who Recruits
1. Cleveland Clinic
2. Sony Pictures
3. City Year
4. Epic
5. Microsoft

Notable Internships
1. Gotham Group
2. Colgate-Palmolive
3. Fidelity Investments

Top Industries
1. Education
2. Business
3. Media
4. Arts & Design
5. Social Services

Top Employers
1. Google
2. Apple
3. Amazon
4. Microsoft
5. IBM

Where Alumni Work
1. New York City
2. San Francisco
3. Cleveland
4. Boston
5. Washington, DC

Median Earnings
College Scorecard (Early Career): $40,800
EOP (Early Career): $38,900
PayScale (Mid-Career): $96,800

RANKINGS
Forbes: 85
Money: 539
U.S. News: 33, Liberal Arts Colleges
Wall Street Journal/THE: 96 (T)
Washington Monthly: 101, Liberal Arts Colleges

#CollegesWorthYourMoney

Occidental College

Los Angeles, California | Admissions Phone: 323-259-2700

Inside the Classroom

A rare liberal arts dynamo in an urban setting, Occidental College, one of the oldest schools on the West Coast, is home to 2,055 undergraduate students. Situated only eight miles from downtown Los Angeles, Occidental attracts a diverse set of talented and community-oriented young people. Non higher-education aficionados may have first heard of the college when Barack Obama burst onto the political scene; he attended the school through sophomore year before transferring to Columbia University. Along with the Claremont colleges, the school known affectionately as Oxy is among the best liberal arts institutions west of the Mississippi.

Thirty-four majors are on tap, but all students must plow through the Oxy Core Program that is designed to "encourage critical thinking, problem-solving, effective communication and productive engagement with issues of difference, diversity and community." Before students even arrive on campus they must complete a summer reading assignment centered on an annual theme. Once class commences, students engage in the Cultural Studies Program, two small seminar courses intended to introduce students to collegiate-level writing and discourse.

Oxy offers an enviable 9:1 student-to-faculty ratio and an average class size of eighteen students. Not a single class contains over fifty students, and 90 percent enroll fewer than thirty. The Undergraduate Research Center facilitates a plethora of hands-on experiences including a ten-week mentored summer program and limitless chances to pursue independent and course-based academic research during the regular school year. At the end of the summer, 120+ students present their research findings. Over two-thirds of undergraduates become global citizens during their time at Occidental through international internships and fellowships or through participation in the study abroad program. Faculty-led programs are available at a variety of destinations around the globe including Italy, Costa Rica, China, the Czech Republic, and Austria. Its partnership with the United Nations provides a one-of-a-kind opportunity for a cohort of students to live in New York, intern at the UN, and take courses with Occidental professors at the same time.

The most popular degree programs at Oxy, all of which carry strong reputations with employers and top-tier graduate schools, are economics, biology, sociology, psychology, diplomacy and world affairs, mathematics, and urban and environmental policy. Prestigious postgraduate scholarship programs look kindly on those with a degree from Oxy. Ten Rhodes Scholars graduated from the school that has been a top ten producer of Fulbright Fellowships for the last decade; nine seniors took home Fulbrights in 2019 alone.

Outside the Classroom

Hardly your typical urban campus, Occidental's 120 acres are among the most notably beautiful higher education homes in the entire country. Countless Hollywood productions (e.g., *Clueless*, *90210*) have selected Occidental as a filming location. The amenities are more in line with a private resort than a typical college. It features a 25,000-square-foot facility only for tennis, a thirty-four-meter deep pool only for water polo, and dining services that serve restaurant-quality cuisine. Just over four-fifths of the student population reside in one the school's thirteen residence halls, and there are seven Greek organizations that attract a modest membership. Roughly 25 percent of undergrads compete on one of twenty-one NCAA Division III sports teams. Tigers also have the option of joining eight club sports teams or any number of intramural athletic leagues. A full array of student organizations exist as well—115 in total—with everything from Oxy TV to a microfinance club. Wandering off campus and into the Eagle Rock and Highland Park sections of Northeast Los Angeles provides easily accessible entertainment, and downtown LA is only a short drive away, which is relevant because 60 percent of Oxy students bring a car to school. In addition, destinations including Venice Beach and Disneyland are less than an hour away.

Career Services

The Hameetman Career Center (HCC) has six full-time professional staff members working in career advising, pre-health advising, and national/international fellowship application guidance. The CDO's 343:1 student-to-advisor ratio is better than average when compared to other colleges featured in our guidebook. Additionally, the center trains four career peer advisors to assist their fellow undergrads. The six core services provided by the office are "(1) career education and career advice; (2) access to internships; (3) pre-law advice; (4) employer, alumni, and parent engagement; (5) job search; and (6) employer recruiting events." It conducted 1,650 one-on-one advising appointments last year alone.

The most recent Oxy Career Fair was attended by sixty-three employers and 380 students. Hosting more than 200 events each year, the HCC also brings 120 employers to campus each year for recruiting purposes. Including all events and individual counseling appointments, it interacts with 2,500 students annually. Internships hosting Oxy students in recent years include Mercedes Benz Shanghai, the Office of the Mayor of Los Angeles, the *Los Angeles Times*, and the NASA Jet Propulsion Laboratory. This office aims to reach students in their freshman year and first presents their services to incoming students at orientation with an eye toward preparing them for a productive first summer experience. Impressive employment and graduate enrollment statistics indicate that its approach works, earning Occidental's Hameetman Career Center praise from current and former students alike.

Professional Outcomes

One year after graduation, 94 percent of Occidental alumni are employed, pursuing graduate studies, or engaged in both simultaneously. By sector, the largest numbers of grads enter community service/education (25 percent), STEM (23 percent), and management/business/finance (20 percent). Among the largest employers of Oxy alumni are the Los Angeles Unified School District, Kaiser Permanente, Microsoft, NASA Jet Propulsion Laboratory, Google, Morgan Stanley, and Amazon. Also on the list are a number of universities that employ Occidental grads after they earn advanced degrees. Most Tigers remain on the prowl in California—mainly LA or San Fran, although there are large alumni clusters on the East Coast, especially in New York City and DC. Midcareer average salaries are in the six figures and among the highest of any institution in the country. According to PayScale, recent graduates earn an average of $51,000 and, by midcareer, bring home $108,000.

Close to three-quarters of Oxy alumni eventually earn one or more advanced degrees. Recent graduates have gone on to continue their educations at Harvard, Stanford, NYU, University of Chicago, UCLA, USC, and UC Berkeley. Those pursuing law degrees have done so at Stanford, USC, UCLA, University of Pennsylvania, Yale, Columbia, Vanderbilt, and Emory. Each year Occidental sees roughly twenty graduates and alumni accepted into medical school, including many of the finest universities in the country. On a per capita basis, the college is also one of the most prolific producers of future PhDs in the country. According to the National Science Foundation, Oxy ranks nineteenth among liberal arts colleges in this category. In short, graduate and professional schools respect the college's reputation and know that those who post an impressive undergraduate GPA have fully earned it.

Admission

Of the 7,281 applicants vying for a place in Occidental College's 2018-19 freshman class, 37 percent were admitted, and 565 ultimately enrolled. Members of the Class of 2022 held a median unweighted GPA of 3.7, SAT score of 1350, and an ACT score of 30. Students were generally active outside the classroom as 52 percent of freshmen played a sport in high school, 75 percent volunteered in their community, and 28 percent played a musical instrument. Over three-fifths placed within the top decile of their high school graduating class; 86 percent landed in the top quarter.

An admissions review from the Occidental staff is a genuinely holistic process. As the committee states, "Creative, soulful, funny, introspective—all words to describe some of our most memorable applicants, but the common thread is always authenticity." That philosophy is supported by GPA, rigor of secondary school record, and the application essay as the triumvirate of admissions factors designated as "most important." Class rank, standardized test scores, recommendations, extracurricular activities, character/personal qualities, volunteer work, and work experience make up the next rung of "important" factors. Men may receive a slight edge in the admissions process as they make up 43 percent of the student body, but the admit rate for men and women is generally comparable. Those applying early decision received a "yes" 48 percent of the time. Occidental is a rare elite college that is not test-optional, but it does not make supremely high test scores a firm prerequisite for serious consideration. In fact, 45 percent of freshmen who took the ACT possessed a composite score between 24 and 29. The college has an extremely low yield rate of 12 percent, which means that it is always on the lookout for students who demonstrate interest and view the school as their number one choice.

Worth Your Money?

An education at Occidental is a phenomenal and highly personalized experience. Of course, providing such an intimate and supportive learning environment costs money. As a result, the annual cost of attendance is $73,102, and while 46 percent of students are awarded merit aid, the average amount is $12k, which puts only a small dent in the overall price. Fortunately, those with significant financial need will see 100 percent of their need met by the school. That translates to 57 percent of current undergraduates receiving grants of almost $42k, helping to make the Occidental experience far more affordable and a worth investment. Middle-income students without a significant financial aid offer should consider their career plans before agreeing to attend.

FINANCIAL
Institutional Type: Private
In-State Tuition: $54,090
Out-of-State Tuition: $54,090
Room & Board: $15,496
Required Fees: $596
Books & Supplies: $1,220

Avg. Need-Based Aid: $41,521
Avg. % of Need Met: 100%

Avg. Merit-Based Aid: $12,332
% Receiving Merit-Based Aid: 46%

Avg. Cumulative Debt: $32,055
% of Students Borrowing: 55%

CAREER
Who Recruits
1. NASA Jet Propulsion Laboratory
2. Northwestern Mutual
3. Aflac
4. Bank of America
5. Teach for America

Notable Internships
1. Calvin Klein
2. Paramount Pictures
3. Pfizer

Top Industries
1. Business
2. Education
3. Operations
4. Media
5. Social Services

Top Employers
1. Kaiser Permanente
2. Google
3. NASA Jet Propulsion Laboratory
4. Microsoft
5. Amazon

Where Alumni Work
1. Los Angeles
2. San Francisco
3. New York City
4. Seattle
5. Orange County, CA

Median Earnings
College Scorecard (Early Career): $50,600
EOP (Early Career): $49,000
PayScale (Mid-Career): $105,700

RANKINGS
Forbes: 102
Money: 251
U.S. News: 39, Liberal Arts Colleges
Wall Street Journal/THE: 99
Washington Monthly: 62, Liberal Arts Colleges

#CollegesWorthYourMoney

The Ohio State University – Columbus

Columbus, Ohio | Admissions Phone: 614-292-3980

ADMISSION
Admission Rate: 52%
Admission Rate - Men: 48%
Admission Rate - Women: 56%
EA Admission Rate: 65%
ED Admission Rate: Not Offered
Admission Rate (5-Year Trend): -4%
ED Admission Rate (5-Year Trend): Not Offered
% of Admits Attending (Yield): 32%
Transfer Admission Rate: 84%

Offered Wait List: 5,296
Accepted Wait List: 1,221
Admitted Wait List: 117

SAT Reading/Writing (Middle 50%): 590-690
SAT Math (Middle 50%): 650-760
ACT Composite (Middle 50%): 27-32
Testing Policy: ACT/SAT Required
SAT Superscore: No
ACT Superscore: No

% Graduated in Top 10% of HS Class: 63%
% Graduated in Top 25% of HS Class: 94%
% Graduated in Top 50% of HS Class: 99%

ENROLLMENT
Total Undergraduate Enrollment: 46,820
% Part-Time: 9%
% Male: 51%
% Female: 49%
% Out-of-State: 19%
% Fraternity: 8%
% Sorority: 12%
% On-Campus (Freshman): 95%
% On-Campus (All Undergraduate): 32%

% African-American: 6%
% Asian: 7%
% Hispanic: 4%
% White: 67%
% Other: 4%
% Race or Ethnicity Unknown: 3%
% International: 9%
% Low-Income: 19%

ACADEMICS
Student-to-Faculty Ratio: 19:1
% of Classes Under 20: 27%
% of Classes Under 40: 64%
% Full-Time Faculty: 72%
% Full-Time Faculty w/ Terminal Degree: 98%

Top Programs
Agriculture
Business
Computer Science
Criminology and Criminal Justice
Engineering
Nursing
Political Science
Sport Industry

Retention Rate: 95%
4-Year Graduation Rate: 59%
6-Year Graduation Rate: 84%

Curricular Flexibility: Somewhat Flexible
Academic Rating: ★★★✦

Inside the Classroom

Anyone who has ever seen a college football game, even a flicker of one while flipping channels on a Saturday afternoon, will immediately associate the name Ohio State with gray football helmets covered in buckeye leaves. Yet, football is hardly the only draw at the great state of Ohio's flagship university, one of the top public research institutions anywhere. Over 46,000 undergraduate students now grace the Columbus campus, 66 percent of whom are Ohio natives, 21 percent of whom are from out of state, and 13 percent of whom are international students. As you will see in the "Admissions" section below, if you want to gain access to the 2021 version of OSU, you'd better be one of the best students in your high school graduating class.

With 200+ undergraduate majors and eighteen schools and colleges housed within OSU, there are a number of curricular requirements that vary among the many academic programs. However, all Buckeyes must take a liberal arts core that includes writing, quantitative skills, natural science, literature, visual and performing arts, history, social science, and a foreign language. From there it's all about completing your major, but students can find electives in just about anything you can imagine because the university offers 12,000 courses.

A 19-to-1 student-to-faculty ratio leads to fairly large classes as only 27 percent of sections enroll fewer than twenty students, so expect a fair number of courses in a large lecture hall setting. In fact, 36 percent of courses contain forty or more undergraduate students. Still, aggressive students can find opportunities to work closely with faculty. The Office of Undergraduate Research & Inquiry helps 800 students participate in annual Denman Undergraduate Research Forum and fifty+ students receive funding from OSU for summer research. All told, approximately 20 percent of students gain research experience. The same percentage of undergraduates elect to study abroad in one of 200 programs spread across seventy countries, the highest figure of any Big Ten university.

Business saw the greatest percentage of degrees conferred at 18 percent followed by engineering (14 percent), biology (9 percent), health professions (9 percent), and the social sciences (9 percent). It makes sense that so many flock to the business and engineering schools as they are among the highest rated undergraduate programs in their respective disciplines. Top companies adore new Buckeye grads, and hundreds of alums can be found at some of the top tech companies, banks, and accounting firms in the United States. In recent years the university has produced between five and eleven Fulbright Scholars annually and as many as six Boren Scholars, thirteen Gilman Scholars, four Goldwater Scholars, and eleven National Science Foundation Graduate Research Fellowship honorable mentions.

Outside the Classroom

There's a little something for everyone on this anything-but-little 1,665-acre campus that ranks third largest in the United States in sheer size. If you are seeking Greek life, you can find it—12 percent of women join sororities and 8 percent of men enter fraternities. The sports scene is epic in scope whether you are a casual athlete wanting to join one of the sixty+ club teams and numerous intramural leagues or one of the 1,000+ big-time athletes on the Buckeyes' thirty-six varsity teams. Football Saturdays are kind of a big deal as more than 102,000 fans of the Scarlet and Gray pack Ohio Stadium. In total, 1,300 student organizations are awaiting your participation on the Columbus campus alone. Only 32 percent of students live in university-owned housing so, for many, sports and club activities are a way to stay connected. Many aspects of OSU campus life receive rave reviews in surveys—from the food to general happiness to LGBTQ friendliness, the university gets a giant thumbs up from its own students. Ohio's capital city is almost equidistant from Cincinnati and Cleveland, about a two-hour car ride. Skiing, camping, and hiking opportunities can be found much closer to satisfy those with a craving for nature.

Career Services

Buckeye Careers is a university-wide office staffed by four professionals, yet the bulk of the counseling takes place within discipline-specific career services offices housed within individual colleges. Including career coaches and other professional staff from the College of Arts & Sciences (14), College of Engineering (9), Fisher School of Business (6), and smaller undergraduate schools, there are forty-two professional members on the OSU career services team. The university's overall 1,115:1 student-to-counselor ratio is poor compared to many other schools in this guide, but there are myriad facts and figures that suggest the university is preparing students for successful postgraduation outcomes.

The fall 2018 Career and Internship Fair was attended by 218 employers and more than 4,000 students, 93 percent of whom rated the event as helpful. The Fisher School of Business has its own career fair that brings 185 companies to campus in the fall and another 130 in the spring. In a typical year, an eye-popping thirty-six career fairs are held. A solid 71 percent of Ohio State graduates completed at least one internship, and those students have been 2.8 times more likely to receive a job offer prior to graduation than their peers who did not complete an internship. Within the Fisher School of Business, 95 percent of graduates participated in an internship or other intensive work experience; Fisher also conducts over 1,100 mock interviews per year. Three-quarters of grads believe the university prepared them well for the job market. Within the School of Education and Human Ecology alone there are just shy of 600 one-on-one counseling sessions taking place every academic year. Despite less-than-desirable staffing levels, Ohio State University's career services is well-run and manages to have a positive impact on students' lives.

Professional Outcomes

Class of 2019 graduates were primarily entering the world of employment (71 percent) while 26 percent were already accepted into graduate or professional school. Hordes of Buckeyes can be found in the offices of many of the nation's leading companies. More than 2,000 alumni work for JPMorgan Chase, more than 1,000 are employed by Cardinal Health and Nationwide, and at least 300 OSU grads inhabit the halls of Amazon, Oracle, IBM, Microsoft, Google, and Apple. Roughly half of graduates settle in for the long haul in the Columbus area, and many others remain in the state, residing in Cleveland or Cincinnati. New York, Chicago, DC, and San Francisco also attract a fair number of alumni. Overall, the average starting salary for a recent graduate is $54,000, a figure buoyed by the high number of business and engineering grads the school produces.

Of the more than one-quarter of recent grads directly matriculating into graduate or professional school, many continue in one of OSU's own ninety-four doctoral programs, ninety-seven master's programs, or excellent law and medical schools. In the last few years law school-bound graduates have earned admission at universities including UVA, Penn, Fordham, Harvard, George Washington, Georgetown, Case Western, and Cornell. Over 500 graduates apply to medical school each year, and some have gone on to prestigious medical institutions like Harvard Medical School, Duke University School of Medicine, and Johns Hopkins School of Medicine. In sum, Ohio State grads attend a wide variety of graduate schools, and they can absolutely earn their way into some of the best institutions in the world.

Admission

Fifty-two percent of the 48,077 applicants for a place in the Class of 2022 gained acceptance, but that figure hardly tells the whole story of just how selective the flagship Columbus campus has become. The ACT is, by far, the more commonly submitted test, and members of the 2018-19 freshman class possessed a mid-50 percent ACT composite score of 27-32; the SAT range was 1240-1370. Even more shocking is the fact that 63 percent of enrolled students finished in the top 10 percent of their high school classes; 94 percent were in the top quartile. Ohio State has become significantly more competitive in recent years. A decade ago, it received fewer than half as many applications as it does today, admitted 62 percent of the pool, and the ACT range was far lower than today at 25-30; the average ACT score today is 29.3.

The OSU admissions staff promises a holistic review of each application but does rank the concrete factors of class rank, standardized test scores, GPA, a rigor of curriculum as "very important" in the process. Essays, extracurricular activities, talent/ability, first-generation status (few schools give this factor so much weight), volunteer work, and work experience get second billing. In a broad sense, OSU seeks individuals who are "not only smart but willing to lead; who see strength in diversity of people and ideas; who seek collaboration when solving problems; and who make use of all opportunities to figure out what kind of impact they want to have in the world." In 2008 in-staters represented 82 percent of the student body; today, that figure is only 66 percent. The influx of out-of-staters and international students has caused the school to make huge jumps in selectivity. As a result, Buckeye state residents need to be A/A- students with standardized test scores in at least the 90th percentile to be on solid footing.

Worth Your Money?

Ohio residents have a cost of attendance of $27,000 per year, making the cost of a four-year degree from a well-respected university very reasonable. The out-of-state cost of attendance is a shade over $48,000 per year. Approximately 30 percent of undergrads receive a small merit aid award, but as is typical at public institutions, the need-based aid tends to be a bit more substantial. Close to half of current students receive some level of grant with an average award of $11,692. In state, OSU is an easy choice and a spectacular value; out of state it may be worth paying for certain top programs, particularly those that lead to careers with above-average starting salaries.

FINANCIAL
Institutional Type: Public
In-State Tuition: $11,084
Out-of-State Tuition: $32,061
Room & Board: $12,708
Required Fees: N/A
Books & Supplies: $1,168

Avg. Need-Based Aid: $11,692
Avg. % of Need Met: 72%

Avg. Merit-Based Aid: $6,800
% Receiving Merit-Based Aid: 31%

Avg. Cumulative Debt: $27,453
% of Students Borrowing: 52%

CAREER
Who Recruits
1. Abercrombie & Fitch
2. Cargill
3. Nestle
4. Sherwin-Williams
5. Marriott International

Notable Internships
1. Sun National Bank
2. Walt Disney World
3. U.S. Department of State

Top Industries
1. Business
2. Education
3. Operations
4. Healthcare
5. Sales

Top Employers
1. JPMorgan Chase
2. Nationwide
3. Cardinal Health
4. Amazon
5. IBM

Where Alumni Work
1. Columbus, OH
2. Cleveland
3. Cincinnati
4. New York City
5. Chicago

Median Earnings
College Scorecard (Early Career): $46,100
EOP (Early Career): N/A
PayScale (Mid-Career): $98,600

RANKINGS
Forbes: 121
Money: 152
U.S. News: 54 (T), National Universities
Wall Street Journal/THE: 86
Washington Monthly: 95, National Universities

#CollegesWorthYourMoney

Pennsylvania State University – University Park

University Park, Pennsylvania | Admissions Phone: 814-865-5471

Inside the Classroom

"We are Penn State," the signature slogan of Pennsylvania State University, is one of the more recognizable chants echoing across any college campus in the United States. More than 40,000 undergraduates reside in State College, nicknamed Happy Valley, a moniker that has weathered scandal and continues to be a destination point for Pennsylvanians as well as many out-of-staters and international students who make up 42 percent of today's student population. Not only does PSU have one the world's largest and most passionate alumni bases, it also possesses as diverse an academic menu as you will find anywhere with its 275 majors and a number of top-ranked programs in a host of disciplines.

There are forty-five credits worth of general education requirements that you'll need to fulfill whether you are studying turfgrass science, toxicology, or telecommunications—all actual majors at PSU. Fifteen of those credits will come through introductory courses in writing, speaking, and quantification, and thirty will come via explorations of the humanities, natural sciences, social and behavioral sciences, the arts, and health and wellness. First-year engagement courses help students hone study and research skills and introduce freshmen to resources around campus. Students also must take courses that satisfy the categories of writing across the curriculum, United States cultures, and international cultures, but those can overlap with the aforementioned forty-five credits worth of distributional mandates.

Unlike some public research universities that can have student-to-faculty ratios greater than 20:1, PSU boasts a stellar 14:1 ratio. That level of support allows 61 percent of classes to have an enrollment below thirty students. Still, you will take some intro courses in massive lecture halls, and 17 percent of sections enroll more than fifty undergraduates. Even at such a large institution, it is possible to get involved in undergraduate research. Eberly College of Science professors are running upwards of 3,000 research projects per year, and the school has a well-maintained and up-to-date database of undergraduate research positions. All told, 20 percent of graduates report having engaged in undergraduate research. Twenty-three percent of Penn Staters avail themselves of study abroad opportunities in one of 300 programs in fifty countries.

Penn State University's College of Engineering is rated exceptionally well on a national scale, cracking the top twenty-five on just about everyone's list, and even hits the top ten in some sub- disciplines such as industrial and biological engineering. It's no wonder that engineering is the most popular field of study at the university, accounting for 18 percent of the degrees conferred. The Smeal College of Business is equally well regarded, also earning high rankings in everything from supply chain management to accounting to marketing. This school not only ranks among top undergraduate public business colleges in the United States but among all colleges, and it attracts 16 percent of total degree-seekers. In addition to gaining positive attention from the engineering and business communities, PSU is viewed favorably by prestigious national fellowship organizations. In 2019, ten graduates captured Fulbright Scholarships as well as one or more Boren, Critical Language, Astronaut, Marshall, and Goldwater Scholarships in the last two years.

Outside the Classroom

Only 35 percent of Nittany Lions technically live in university-owned housing, but that doesn't quite capture the cohesive spirit of the PSU community. Greek life is a major social force at the school as 17 percent of men join frats and 20 percent of women become members of sororities. A tragic hazing death a few years back led to a shutdown of one fraternity and increased administrative scrutiny of the practices of others. Unfortunately, the school is no stranger to national controversy. Yet, even after the infamous Sandusky scandal, Penn State football is a tradition like no other as 106,000 pack into Beaver Stadium to watch the Lions battle with Big Ten rivals like Ohio State, Michigan, and Nebraska. Thon, an annual charity dance marathon, is one of the grandest and most impressive events on campus, raising over $10 million to fight childhood cancer in 2019. With over 1,000 clubs and activities to choose from, it's hard not to find your niche at Penn State. Campus itself covers almost 8,000 acres and contains its own arboretum, the Palmer Art Museum, and the famous (and delicious) Penn State Creamery. State College may be in the middle of nowhere, but it truly is the ultimate college town, walkable and brimming with terrific restaurants, bars, and shops.

Career Services

Not counting graduate assistants and office managers, there are thirty full-time employees occupying the Bank of America Career Services Center at University Park. However, there are additional offices that serve specialty groups such as the Career Resources & Employer Relations department housed within the College of Engineering that is staffed by seven professionals, the Smeal College of Business that has nine career services employees, and eleven other staff members are spread across campus in other departments. Based on this grand total of fifty-seven career counselors, internship coordinators, employer relations specialists, and related positions, the student-to-counselor ratio is 708:1, higher than most of the schools featured in this guide, but not at all bad for a school of PSU's size.

Pennsylvania State University – University Park

E-mail: admissions@psu.edu | Website: www.psu.edu

Career fairs, such as the major one held each fall, are massive undertakings, some featuring 300+ companies. The Fall Career Fair is four days in length, and that time is divided to cover technical jobs, nontechnical jobs, internships, and interviews. It also offers many smaller (but still large) targeted fairs in areas such as nursing, education, graduate school, small business and startups, and impact (nonprofits). The majority of graduates, 63 percent, report participating in at least one internship while at University Park. More than one 2018 graduate held an internship position at companies like Amazon, Pfizer, and Xerox. Within the first week of students returning to school for the 2019-20 school year, Microsoft and Lockheed Martin were already actively recruiting on campus. PSU does not publish statistics on how many students take advantage of career services offerings, but it is clear that this staff facilitates powerful, door-opening opportunities for those proactive enough to seek them out.

Professional Outcomes

By the day of graduation, 72 percent of Nittany Lions have found their next employment or graduate school home; within some of the universities many colleges, that rate is even higher. Upon receiving their diplomas, 82 percent of Smeal College of Business Class of 2018 grads already had their next step lined up. They flock in large numbers to some of the nation's best finance, accounting, consulting, and technology firms. More than 500 PSU alumni are currently working at each of IBM, Deloitte, PwC, Amazon, EY, JPMorgan Chase, Microsoft, Google, and Oracle. Hundreds more work at Citi, Salesforce, and Facebook. Philadelphia, New York City, Pittsburgh, DC, San Francisco, Boston, and Los Angeles all have a strong PSU alumni presence. The median salary for Penn State grads ten years after arriving at the school averages $50,000. Of course, salaries vary greatly by academic discipline; business graduates' salaries start at $60,000 while engineering students start at over $70,000.

Medical school acceptance rates for PSU graduates hover around 60 percent, well above the national average, an impressive figure when considering that over 300 students applied in 2019. Seventy percent of those accepted into medical school enroll at Pennsylvania-based institutions including the Penn State College of Medicine. Overall, presently PSU alumni are enrolled in sixty medical schools throughout the country. Likewise, many prelaw students go on to pursue legal educations at one of the university's two law schools (Penn State Law and Dickinson Law), other strong local options like Temple or Villanova, or prestigious national universities like the University of North Carolina, Stanford, Cornell, or Wake Forest.

Admission

The nearly 53,000 Nittany Lion hopefuls seeking a place in the Class of 2022 were accepted at a 56 percent rate, a figure that somewhat undersells how competitive gaining admission right out of high school truly is (transferring later is easier). For some, Penn State is a clear number one choice and often a family tradition, for other Pennsylvania students it occupies mere safety status. Overall, the yield rate—the percentage of accepted students who go on to enroll—is 27 percent. Freshmen who entered the university in 2018-19 possessed mid-50 percent standardized test scores of 1160-1330 on the SAT and a composite score of 25-30 on the ACT. One-quarter of applicants scored over a 700 on the math portion of the SAT; only 12 percent achieved the same on the verbal section. With 43 percent of freshmen having earned a place in the top ten percent of their high school class and 76 percent in the top quartile, most Penn State admits sport strong grades, generally a mix of A's and B's in at least some AP and honors courses.

The only two "very important" factors in the admissions process are GPA and standardized test scores. The rigor of one's high school coursework sits alone in the next tier of still "important" factors. Soft factors like essays, extracurricular activities, work experience, talent/ability, character/personal qualities as well as state residency status and ethnicity are "considered" in candidate evaluation. An early option allows students to submit an application by November 1. After that admission is rolling, but you should absolutely meet the priority date of November 30.

Worth Your Money?

PSU's in-state tuition cost of roughly $18,500 and total cost of attendance of $32,000+ isn't as cheap as, for example, schools in New York's SUNY system that have a COA approximately $10k cheaper. A non-Keystone State resident would pay a COA of over $50,000, which would not make sense in most circumstances. Denizens of Pennsylvania will generally reap the benefits of this flagship institution's strong reputation and incomprehensibly vast alumni network.

FINANCIAL
Institutional Type: Public
In-State Tuition: $17,416
Out-of-State Tuition: $34,480
Room & Board: $11,884
Required Fees: $1,034
Books & Supplies: $1,840

Avg. Need-Based Aid: $6,578
Avg. % of Need Met: 64%

Avg. Merit-Based Aid: $5,444
% Receiving Merit-Based Aid: 33%

Avg. Cumulative Debt: $38,695
% of Students Borrowing: 53%

CAREER
Who Recruits
1. Google
2. Grant Thorton LLP
3. Oracle
4. PNC
5. Accenture

Notable Internships
1. Anheuser-Busch
2. Morgan Stanley
3. Aramark

Top Industries
1. Business
2. Operations
3. Education
4. Engineering
5. Sales

Top Employers
1. IBM
2. PwC
3. Amazon
4. Johnson & Johnson
5. EY

Where Alumni Work
1. Philadelphia
2. New York City
3. Pittsburgh
4. State College, PA
5. Washington, DC

Median Earnings
College Scorecard (Early Career): $50,100
EOP (Early Career): $50,900
PayScale (Mid-Career): $105,500

RANKINGS
Forbes: 117
Money: 291
U.S. News: 57 (T), National Universities
Wall Street Journal/THE: 105 (T)
Washington Monthly: 120, National Universities

#CollegesWorthYourMoney

ADMISSION

Admission Rate: 36%
Admission Rate - Men: 41%
Admission Rate - Women: 32%
EA Admission Rate: N/A
ED Admission Rate: Not Offered
Admission Rate (5-Year Trend): -1%
ED Admission Rate (5-Year Trend): Not Offered
% of Admits Attending (Yield): 20%
Transfer Admission Rate: 31%

Offered Wait List: 1,639
Accepted Wait List: 935
Admitted Wait List: 0

SAT Reading/Writing (Middle 50%): 610-690
SAT Math (Middle 50%): 610-730
ACT Composite (Middle 50%): 26-32
Testing Policy: ACT/SAT Required
SAT Superscore: Yes
ACT Superscore: No

% Graduated in Top 10% of HS Class: 57%
% Graduated in Top 25% of HS Class: 85%
% Graduated in Top 50% of HS Class: 96%

ENROLLMENT

Total Undergraduate Enrollment: 3,627
% Part-Time: 8%
% Male: 41%
% Female: 59%
% Out-of-State: 44%
% Fraternity: 17%
% Sorority: 27%
% On-Campus (Freshman): 99%
% On-Campus (All Undergraduate): 57%

% African-American: 5%
% Asian: 10%
% Hispanic: 14%
% White: 49%
% Other: 6%
% Race or Ethnicity Unknown: 2%
% International: 13%
% Low-Income: 23%

ACADEMICS

Student-to-Faculty Ratio: 14:1
% of Classes Under 20: 70%
% of Classes Under 40: 96%
% Full-Time Faculty: 57%
% Full-Time Faculty w/ Terminal Degree: 88%

Top Programs
Advertising
Business Administration
Communication
International Studies
Psychology
Public Relations
Sports Medicine
Theatre

Retention Rate: 91%
4-Year Graduation Rate: 73%
6-Year Graduation Rate: 83%

Curricular Flexibility: Less Flexible
Academic Rating: ★★★✦

Inside the Classroom

The incongruity of a resort-like university located in Malibu that only lifted its ban on dancing in the late 1980s is hard to reconcile. Maybe the most beautiful campus in the world, Pepperdine is also a bastion of evangelical Christianity and largely conservative politically. On the academic menu for the 3,300 undergrads at Seaver College (the school's undergraduate wing) are forty-five majors and forty minors with the most commonly conferred degrees being in business/marketing (26 percent), communication/journalism (19 percent), general social sciences (11 percent), psychology (10 percent), and parks and recreation (8 percent). Only 2 percent pursue degrees in religion, but its influence is interwoven into the fabric of both the academic experience and the social scene.

Among the nineteen courses that constitute Pepperdine's general education requirements for all undergraduates are three classes under the umbrella of Christianity and Culture. Other mandated areas of study include the American experience, Western cultures, human institutions and behavior, world civilizations, fine arts, mathematics, laboratory science, and speech and rhetoric. First-year seminars are intended to sharpen skills in the areas of communication, critical thinking and learning how to "apply the university's Christian mission." Those seminars tackle big-picture topics that include science and religion, the nature of conscience, and the pain of betrayal. Students must continually update a writing portfolio that is formally evaluated as the junior writing portfolio when students reach their third year of study.

A 13:1 student-to-faculty ratio is solid, and faculty are fully deployed with the aim of creating an intimate liberal arts classroom setting. The average class contains nineteen students, and one-quarter of courses will contain fewer than ten students. There are three formal programs for undergraduate research: the Summer Undergraduate Research Program, the Cross-disciplinary/Interdisciplinary Undergraduate Research Program, and Academic Year Undergraduate Research Initiative. Close to two-thirds of Seaver students study abroad and build global experience in locations such as Buenos Aires, Florence, London, and Shanghai.

The Graziadio Business School has a strong reputation that penetrates far beyond the school's home state. The Communication Division also registers on many national ranking lists. Thanks in part to the school's focus on international experience, five 2018 graduates won Fulbright Scholarships, and six took home the award in 2017. Recent grads also have, on occasion, been awarded Gilman, Boren, and National Science Foundation fellowships.

Outside the Classroom

The university's 835-acre grounds can be found in the number one or two position in just about any nationwide ranking of "most beautiful campuses." Given its size and luxurious feel, it's a bit strange that under 60 percent of the undergraduate population lives on campus, however 98 percent of freshmen do reside in university-owned housing. Dorms and on-campus apartments are single-sex, and overnight visitors of the opposite sex are prohibited. The alcohol policies are also enforced more than at your average college. Gender-wise, Seaver has a 60/40 split in favor of women, 32 percent of whom join sororities while 23 percent of men join fraternities. A relatively athletic undergraduate student body participates on seventeen NCAA Division I sports teams (the Waves) that have produced an impressive fifty-two Olympians in the school's history. There are plenty of intramural and club teams as well as four fitness centers and an Olympic-size swimming pool. One hundred and ten student organizations are active, and more than 1,000 on-campus events are hosted each semester. A focus on service leads three-fifths of students to engage in volunteer work with over 80,000 hours contributed each year. Pepperdine is nestled in the Santa Monica Mountains only minutes from some of the world's premier surfing beaches. As another bonus, campus is only thirty miles west of Los Angeles, so Hollywood is only a short car ride away.

Career Services

Pepperdine Career Services employs eight full-time professional staff members (not counting office managers) working as counselors, industry specialists, events managers, and employer relations coordinators. That works out to a 402:1 student-to-counselor ratio, within the average range of institutions profiled in this book. This department offers a solid blend of one-on-one counseling and large-scale events such as industry-specific career fairs in business, health and sciences, nonprofit and government, and arts/entertainment/media. There is also a more generalized Spring Career Expo attended by fifty+ employers and graduate schools.

A phenomenal 96 percent of Class of 2017 grads had at least one internship, work experience, or formal undergraduate research experience. Four-fifths had a minimum of one internship in their four years of undergraduate education. Over 1,000 unique internship sites hosted members of this cohort. Each year, 150+ employers recruit on site at Pepperdine, conducting information sessions as well as on-campus interviews. The alumni network is always happy to be involved in assisting current students. Over 500 alumni volunteer to work with undergraduates directly, and 110,000 living alumni can be found around the globe. A formalized Career Coaching Program has set up 350 students with alumni mentors who have guided them through each stage of the career exploration and development process since its inception in 2001. An above-average level of next-step support and reasonably successful student outcomes makes Pepperdine Career Services a strong performing outfit.

Professional Outcomes
Members of the Seaver Class of 2018 landed at their next destination within six months of graduating at an 89 percent clip with 68 percent employed full time, 18 percent admitted to graduate school, 3 percent volunteering, and 11 percent seeking their first job or a graduate school home. Of those entering the world of work, three-quarters were in the for-profit sector, 18 percent with nonprofit/government entities, and 8 percent pursuing entrepreneurial ventures. Deloitte, Disney, EY, Facebook, PwC, Sony Pictures, and the US Senate and House of Representatives all hired 2017 graduates. Other companies employing fifty or more alumni include Kaiser Permanente, Apple, Google, Wells Fargo, and Amazon. Many graduates remain in California as Los Angeles and Orange County are the two most common landing spots. Other West Coast locales including San Diego, San Francisco, and Seattle also sport sizable numbers of alums. When compared to other elite California-based schools, mid-career median salaries rank lower than Pomona but higher than Occidental.

Class of 2018 graduates were admitted to graduate/professional school at an 83 percent rate. Training in a medical field was the choice of 22 percent of that group, and 12 percent matriculated into law school. In a typical year, twenty to thirty grads apply to medical school, and 70-80 percent are successful. Recent students have gained acceptance to medical schools at Georgetown; Emory; USC; University of California, San Diego; and Washington University in St. Louis. Those going the law school route study at many fine institutions including Pepperdine's own law school. In the last few years, others have been admitted to Harvard Law School, UCLA School of Law, and NYU School of Law. No matter your postgraduate pursuit, a solid transcript and a Pepperdine degree will leave you with many strong graduate/professional school options.

Admission
In the 2018 admission cycle, the university admitted 35 percent of 12,134 applicants. Those who were offered a place in the Class of 2022 had a mid-50 percent range of 28-32 on the ACT, 1270-1420 on the SAT, and 3.62-3.95 as their cumulative GPA. Applicants who accepted positions at the university and comprised the freshman class had a 25-30 ACT range, a 1200-1390 SAT range, and an average GPA of 3.64. "Only" 49 percent of that cohort placed in the top 10 percent of their high school class, a low figure compared to many other elite universities. Further, 20 percent did not place in the top quartile, so there is some leeway here for students with imperfect academic transcripts.

There are seven factors rated as "very important" by the admissions committee, most notably religious affiliation because Pepperdine, as noted earlier, is a Christian school. The other more common critical factors are: rigor of coursework, GPA, application essay, extracurricular activities, talent/ability, and character/personal qualities. Standardized tests, recommendations, and volunteer work make-up the second rung of still "important" factors. The yield rate (percent of those accepted who actually enroll) is only 18 percent, which means that Pepperdine is definitely interested to know if you are a student who truly places the university at the top of your college list. Since it offers only early action and does not have a binding early decision program, demonstrating interest is a good idea if you are serious about this school. Admissions standards at Pepperdine today are almost identical to those of five years ago. It remains a niche institution for devout Christians with strong academic credentials.

Worth Your Money?
Pepperdine's annual cost of attendance exceeds $74,000, making it one of the most expensive colleges in the country. Just about everyone entering the school applies for need-based aid, but only 53 percent of those seeking a grant actually receive one; the average amount is over $37,000, slicing the COA in half. Roughly one-quarter of current students receive an average merit aid grant of $15k. There aren't exactly dozens of academically competitive, conservative Christian universities with a beachfront view; so, if that's the description of your ideal school, Pepperdine will likely be worth your money, especially if you have plans to enter the fields of business or communication.

FINANCIAL
Institutional Type: Private
In-State Tuition: $55,640
Out-of-State Tuition: $55,640
Room & Board: $15,670
Required Fees: $252
Books & Supplies: $1,250

Avg. Need-Based Aid: $37,652
Avg. % of Need Met: 77%

Avg. Merit-Based Aid: $15,207
% Receiving Merit-Based Aid: 25%

Avg. Cumulative Debt: $34,335
% of Students Borrowing: 51%

CAREER
Who Recruits
1. PennyMac
2. Disney
3. Universalizer
4. Sony Pictures Entertainment
5. REX-Real Estate Exchange Inc.

Notable Internships
1. United Nations
2. U.S. Securities and Exchange Commission
3. Farmers Insurance

Top Industries
1. Business
2. Education
3. Operations
4. Sales
5. Healthcare

Top Employers
1. Boeing
2. Kaiser Permanente
3. Wells Fargo
4. Walt Disney
5. Amazon

Where Alumni Work
1. Los Angeles
2. Orange County, CA
3. San Francisco
4. San Diego
5. New York City

Median Earnings
College Scorecard (Early Career): $65,500
EOP (Early Career): $55,800
PayScale (Mid-Career): $103,900

RANKINGS
Forbes: 129
Money: 244
U.S. News: 50 (T), National Universities
Wall Street Journal/THE: 137 (T)
Washington Monthly: 203, National Universities

#CollegesWorthYourMoney

Pitzer College

Claremont, California | Admissions Phone: 909-621-8129

Inside the Classroom

Every member school within the Claremont Consortium has its own distinct personality—Harvey Mudd is for engineering geniuses, Scripps is a highly selective women's college, Pomona and CMC are premier liberal arts colleges that battle East Coast schools Swarthmore, Amherst, and Williams for the top spot in the national rankings. Then there is Pitzer College, a liberal arts powerhouse in its own right with an emphasis on service learning and global engagement that has experienced logarithmic leaps in selectivity itself since the dawn of the new millennium. Cozy in size, hosting a mere 1,100 students, Pitzer still manages to offer forty+ majors and twenty minors and, as a bonus, students are free to take more than 2,000 courses across the consortium.

Graduating from Pitzer involves the completion of thirty-two courses including a minimum of eleven required courses that are part of meeting the college's education objectives. That involves two courses in the humanities and fine arts, two in the behavioral and social sciences, and one each in written expression, quantitative reasoning, and the natural sciences. Sequences covering social justice/social responsibility and intercultural understanding global/local also must be completed. The class on social justice requires active community engagement. First-year experience courses are taught on a variety of topics, are capped at fifteen students, and involve "close textual analysis, broadly conceived, and effective writing strategies for diverse audiences and purposes."

A 10:1 student-to-faculty ratio and no graduate student presence leads to an average class size of fifteen students, and 69 percent of sections enroll nineteen or fewer students. In 2018-19, only one course section was larger than forty students. Finding mentorship is doable in this atmosphere and can lead to undergraduate research opportunities such as those at the Keck Science Department, which also services CMC and Scripps students. Those opportunities can occur in the summer or during senior year while completing a required thesis. With one of the highest study abroad percentages of any school at 75 percent, Pitzer runs eight foreign programs and offers access to thirty-two international exchange programs.

The most popular majors at Pitzer are (1) psychology, (2) environmental analysis, (3) economics, (4) sociology, (5) media studies, and (6) self-designed degrees. Nearly all programs have the full admiration of graduate/professional schools as well as prestigious scholarship programs, but majors within the social and behavioral sciences (e.g. psychology and sociology) typically draw the most praise. In fact, Pitzer has produced the most Fulbright Scholars from an undergraduate-only institution for six straight years. In 2019, ten seniors and recent alumni captured Fulbrights, three were named Napier Fellows, and two students won Gilman Scholarships. Students also captured one Goldwater Scholarship, a National Science Foundation Graduate Research Fellowship, a Princeton in Asia Fellowship, and a Davis Project for Peace Award. Not bad for a school with fewer than 250 graduates per year.

Outside the Classroom

Every single Pitzer freshman and 73 percent of all students live in six dorms on the school's thirty-one-acre campus. Dorms receive glowing reviews as environmentally responsible housing and their farm-to-table program that is ranked as one of the best in the country. From those two facts you're likely picking up on the school's ethos and can guess that it does not have fraternities or sororities. Pitzer does have a joint athletics department with Pomona College that features twenty-one NCAA Division III varsity sports teams known as the Sagehens. There are 250+ clubs students can join, many of which are of the cross-college variety. Every single member of the Pitzer community gives back through service. In total, students, faculty, and staff commit approximately 100,000 hours to community-based projects each year. Activism carries over to student government, which is consistently passionate and vocal whether the issue is undergraduate housing costs or a recent ban on study abroad in Israel. Pitzer Outdoor Adventure (POA) is also immensely popular and regularly leads its large membership on hiking, cycling, climbing, camping, and surfing trips. Those seeking big-city fun will relish in the fact the City of Angels can be reached in less than an hour.

Career Services

Career Services at Pitzer has only three full-time professional staff members, yet being such a small college, that number still works out to a solid 360:1 student-to-advisor ratio, slightly better than the average college featured in our guidebook. Those individuals work directly with students and hold the titles of director, assistant director, and career counselor; they also have a highly-qualified office assistant. For such a tiny operation, the level of outreach is spectacular as 75 percent of freshmen engage with career services. Overall, approximately two-thirds of the student body utilize career services, and 33 percent take advantage of walk-in counseling appointments each year. It hosts roughly ninety events per year that attract almost 800 student participants.

Being part of the Claremont Consortium has as many advantages with regard to career development as it is does with regard to academics. Over 350 companies recruit annually at the 5Cs, and Pitzer students enjoy full access to networking and on-campus interviews. The office also does an excellent job financially supporting students' job-exploration endeavors. Roughly fifty students per year receive financial assistance from the Pitzer Internship Fund, which enables students to complete unpaid or low-paid experiential learning opportunities. Roughly forty students engage in a job-shadowing experience with an alum over winter break. Overall, this is an accessible office that greatly benefits from its affiliation with its neighbor schools.

Professional Outcomes

Upon receiving their degrees, 50 percent of 2018 Pitzer graduates had already found full-time employers, 18 percent were headed to graduate school, and 12 percent were entering fellowship, internship, or service programs. Among those employed, the most popular industries were finance/business (29 percent), tech/engineering (17 percent), health/medicine/research (17 percent), entertainment/arts (13 percent), education (6 percent), and nonprofit (6 percent). Employers presently issuing paychecks to more than ten Pitzer alumni include Google, Kaiser Permanente, the Los Angeles Unified School District, and Accenture. Graduates tend to be a globetrotting bunch, and the 11,000 living alumni can be found all over the map, although roughly half settle in Los Angeles or San Francisco. Median salaries, even ten years after graduation, are on the lower end of selective colleges. While plenty of Pitzer grads go on to pursue high-paying finance and tech jobs, many others choose PhD programs, medical school, or fellowship programs abroad that can delay financial returns.

Members of the Class of 2018 headed to prestigious graduate schools including Vanderbilt, Oxford, USC, Northwestern, Columbia, and Johns Hopkins. In 2017, it also sent graduates to UC Berkeley, the University of Pennsylvania, and Stanford. For premed students, the college offers a Joint Medical Program with the Western University of Health Sciences admitting up to six students each year. The W.M. Keck Science Department services Scripps, Claremont McKenna, and Pitzer, so all students have access to an excellent premed curriculum and facility. Those heading to law school in recent years have matriculated into a wide range of institutions that includes Notre Dame, UC Berkeley, Georgetown, Santa Clara, and Loyola Marymount University.

Admission

Applicants to the Class of 2022 were admitted at only a 13 percent clip, a rate similar to five years ago but far below that of 2005 when the admit rate was 39 percent. Even that 39 percent figure represented a sharp decline from a more forgiving admissions era in the 1990s. An early adopter of test-optional policies, Pitzer stopped requiring SAT or ACT scores in 2003, and more applicants take advantage of that option here than at most other test-optional institutions. Among 2018-19 freshmen, only 30 percent of students submitted an SAT score, and an identical 30 percent submitted an ACT result. Unsurprisingly, the test scores of freshmen who divulged them tended to be strong; the mid-50 percent range was a 1320-1490 on the SAT and a 30-33 on the ACT. It's within the realm of high school performance that successful Pitzer applicants set themselves apart. Sixty-two percent placed within the top 10 percent of their graduating class, and 83 percent were in the top quartile. The average GPA for an entering member of the Class of 2022 was 3.94.

The admissions process at Pitzer is highly personalized, and each application receives a lengthy review. A rigorous high school course load, a high GPA, a strong essay, and the demonstration of solid and unique character/personal qualities are at the forefront of the decision-making process. Recommendations, volunteer work, talent/ability, and extracurricular activities are also important factors. If you are a borderline applicant who is serious about getting in, applying early decision may be the way to go; 30 percent of applicants were accepted—135 students—almost half the freshman class.

Worth Your Money?

Pitzer has notably generous financial aid as roughly 40 percent of undergraduates received an average annual package of $41,042. That assistance helps greatly lessen the blow of a $56k list tuition price and $73k+ cost of attendance. While median salaries are on the low side, being part of the world-renowned Claremont Consortium allows access to premier facilities and professors and opens doors to the most competitive grad schools, fellowships and, should you choose, major corporations. You wouldn't want to pay $300,000 for a humanities degree without a clear plan for how to pay back those loans. Again, thanks to merit aid and need-based awards from the school, you are unlikely to be asked to pay anything approaching the full sticker price.

FINANCIAL
Institutional Type: Private
In-State Tuition: $55,734
Out-of-State Tuition: $55,734
Room & Board: $17,432
Required Fees: $284
Books & Supplies: $1,100

Avg. Need-Based Aid: $41,042
Avg. % of Need Met: 100%

Avg. Merit-Based Aid: $5,749
% Receiving Merit-Based Aid: 4%

Avg. Cumulative Debt: $17,848
% of Students Borrowing: 40%

CAREER
Who Recruits
1. City Year
2. Apple
3. Amazon
4. JumpStart
5. Accenture

Notable Internships
1. FX Networks
2. Collins Aerospace
3. Apple

Top Industries
1. Business
2. Education
3. Operations
4. Social Services
5. Media

Top Employers
1. Kaiser Permanente
2. Los Angeles Unified School District
3. Google
4. Wells Fargo
5. Accenture

Where Alumni Work
1. Los Angeles
2. San Francisco
3. New York City
4. Seattle
5. Portland, OR

Median Earnings
College Scorecard (Early Career): $48,700
EOP (Early Career): $43,500
PayScale (Mid-Career): $96,600

RANKINGS
Forbes: 54
Money: 522
U.S. News: 35, Liberal Arts Colleges
Wall Street Journal/THE: 77
Washington Monthly: 109, Liberal Arts Colleges

#CollegesWorthYourMoney

Pomona College

Claremont, California | Admissions Phone: 909-621-8134

Inside the Classroom

Considered the preeminent institution among the Claremont Consortium, Pomona College in Claremont, California, is much like the elite liberal arts schools of the Northeast—Williams and Amherst—only with perfect weather, gorgeous beaches, and Disneyland in relatively close proximity. Pomona also boasts one of the lowest acceptance rates in the country, one that is on par, from a selectivity standpoint, with Yale, Columbia, Brown, and MIT. That said, if you are one of the rare individuals capable of gaining entrance, you won't find a better or more rigorous liberal arts education anywhere.

There are forty-eight majors and minors to select from with the most popular being social sciences (20 percent), math/statistics (12 percent), computer science (10 percent), and physical sciences (9 percent). More than 600 courses are on the menu at Pomona alone, but students can access any of the Claremont Consortium's 2,700 courses. Everyone begins with a critical inquiry seminar as a freshman and must complete coursework designated as writing intensive, speaking intensive, and analyzing difference. Breadth of study requirements demand that undergrads complete one course in the following six categories: criticism, analysis, and contextual study of works of the human imagination; social institutions and human behavior; history, values, ethics, and cultural studies; physical and biological sciences; mathematical and formal reasoning; and creation and performance of works of art and literature. There are literally eight ways to meet the college's foreign language requirement including AP scores, SAT IIs, and passing three semesters of language, but all eight demand the demonstration of proficiency.

The school's 186 professors are dedicated to the task of undergraduate education. Pomona's 8:1 student-to-teacher ratio leads to an average class size of only fifteen students. There are only six of 412 courses that ran in 2018-19 that contained more than forty students. Small classes also lead to the forging of student-professor bonds that help 53 percent of the undergraduate population conduct research alongside a faculty member. Each summer 200 students remain on campus for such an endeavor. Close to 50 percent of Pomona students travel abroad to one of fifty-nine programs in thirty-four countries.

All of the college's academic offerings are highly respected by employers, graduate/professional schools, and national fellowship/scholarship competitions. Majors in economics, international relations, chemistry, and mathematics receive especially high marks. One-quarter of Pomona students apply for at least one competitive fellowship. Of the students in the Class of 2019 who applied for Fulbright Scholarships, nine were successful; thirteen won the previous year. Three captured Watson Scholarships in 2019, and a remarkable ten grads and alumni were awarded National Science Foundation Graduate Research Fellowships.

Outside the Classroom

Pomona's bustling campus is spread across 140 acres and contains fifteen residence halls and three dining halls; 98 percent of students live in campus housing. There are two co-ed fraternities on campus that student members themselves describe as "just a bunch of dorks that hang out sometimes." Unlike Claremont, Mudd, and Scripps that combine for athletics, Pomona fields its own squads. The twenty-one varsity teams play as the Sagehens in NCAA Division III; 20 percent of the student body are members of a varsity team, and many others participate in club and intramural athletics. Student life at Pomona is, in part, defined by the multitude of opportunities to enjoy the resources of the other Claremont Colleges—Pitzer, Scripps, Harvey Mudd, and CMC. More than 250 clubs can be accessed by students of any of the five schools. On the Loose is a popular outdoors club that organizes 150 excursions into natural settings each year. Students can tend to their own plot at an on-campus organic farm, perform for the Claremont Colleges Ballroom Dance Company, write for the *Student Life* newspaper, or connect with volunteer opportunities through the Draper Center for Community Partnerships. While campus itself receives rave reviews, few complain about the school's enviable location either. Less than an hour from campus, students can access all of the fun Los Angeles has to offer as well as some of the most beautiful beaches in the country.

Career Services

The Career Development Office (CDO) has seven full-time professional staff members working on grad school/career advising, employer relations, and experiential learning coordination. The CDO's 243:1 student-to-advisor ratio is better than the average college featured in our guidebook. Pomona's staff puts its resources to good use, engaging 80 percent of freshmen through lunches where the CDO's offerings are introduced. Each year, the office engages in over 1,800 one-on-one counseling appointments, more than one per enrolled undergraduate student. Two-thirds of seniors directly engage with counselors.

On a more global scale, Pomona students can connect with more than 8,500 employers through the school's membership in three consortia groups: the Claremont Consortium, the Career and Internship Connection, and the Liberal Arts Career Network. More than 500 employers engage in on-campus recruiting at Pomona each year, including many that attend winter break recruiting programs. Unique internship opportunities are available such as the Pomona College Internship Program (PCIP) that funds students to intern domestically in places like DC or New York or abroad in cities like Bangkok or Tokyo. Roughly 130 students were awarded PCIP positions during the 2017-18 school year along with an additional eighty students in the summer. By senior year 89 percent of students have participated in at least one internship, and 70 percent have completed two or more. Thanks to loads of individualized attention and ways to connect directly with top employers and graduate schools, Pomona's career services is highly regarded by our staff.

Professional Outcomes

Whether entering the corporate world or a nonprofit position, employers adore Pomona grads. Overall, the largest number of Pomona alumni can be found in the offices of Google, Kaiser-Permanente, Microsoft, Amazon, and Facebook. Looking at grads from 2014-2018, many computer science majors ended up at the aforementioned tech giants. In that same time, more than one economics major landed a job at Goldman Sachs, Wells Fargo, Morgan Stanley, or Accenture. Majors in the hard sciences frequently landed at top research laboratories and hospitals. The three most popular geographical landing spots were Los Angeles, San Francisco, and New York City. Midcareer salaries are middle-of-the-pack among elite schools and are commensurate with other highly selective liberal arts schools like Williams, Middlebury, and Colby.

Of the 16 percent of Class of 2018 members who were accepted directly into graduate school, the three most frequently attended institutions were a not-too-shabby list of the University of Cambridge, the University of Oxford, Stanford, Harvard, and Cornell. When Pomona students go to law school they attend only the best. Thirty percent of alumni were admitted into top-five law schools; nearly three-quarters were admitted into top-fourteen schools. Med school applicants were admitted at a 70 percent clip, and in recent years more than one Pomona graduate has enrolled in medical school at USC, UCLA, University of Washington, and Emory University. In short, attending Pomona as an undergraduate will put you in a direct pipeline into the world's best graduate/professional schools.

Admission

Pomona now sits among the most ultra-selective schools in the world after admitting only 6.9 percent of the 10,245 students fighting for a spot in the Class of 2022. It accepted only 8.2 percent and 9.1 percent, respectively, in the previous two cycles. Of those offered spots in the 2018-19 freshman class, 95 percent were in the top decile of their high school class, and 91 percent of those actually attending earned that distinction. The median SAT score was 1495, and the median ACT score was 34. The mid-50 percent ranges for those who actually enrolled were 1400-1540 and 31-34. Students submitted SAT and ACT scores at a fairly even rate. International admits hailed from forty-four countries, and 57 percent of admitted domestic applicants were students of color. A high yield rate of 53 percent indicates that teens who apply to Pomona are likely to attend the college if accepted.

Getting in is a genuinely holistic process that strongly weights wide-ranging factors including rigor of curriculum, GPA, class rank, standardized test scores, essays, recommendations, extracurricular activities, talent/ability, and character/personal qualities. The committee does not factor in demonstrated interest, and interviews are merely "considered." Two hundred seven members of the Class of 2022 were admitted via early decision at a rate of 16.5 percent, which suggests that ED does provide an admissions edge. Of note, Pomona did accept twenty-eight transfer applicants in 2018, a higher number than many other elite institutions. In 1914, the school's president declared, "Let only the eager, thoughtful, and reverent enter here." Over a century later those criteria hold true with the addendum of near-perfect test scores and placement atop your high school graduating class. Like other schools with single-digit acceptance rates, there is an element of randomness that can leave valedictorians and possessors of 1600 SAT scores wondering why they were rejected.

Worth Your Money?

Pomona may have a sky-high sticker price, but it does everything in its power to make attending the school a possibility for students who otherwise could not afford it. In meeting 100 percent of the need of every eligible student, it awards an average of $54,000 per year to 57 percent of its undergraduate population. For everyone who can afford the $74k+ annual cost of attendance, that will be the actual cost because Pomona does not award merit aid. If you are offered a rare chance to attend Pomona, you should take advantage. With a superior reputation in academic and corporate circles alike, this college is definitely worth your money.

FINANCIAL
Institutional Type: Private
In-State Tuition: $54,380
Out-of-State Tuition: $54,380
Room & Board: $17,218
Required Fees: $382
Books & Supplies: $1,000

Avg. Need-Based Aid: $54,404
Avg. % of Need Met: 100%

Avg. Merit-Based Aid: $0
% Receiving Merit-Based Aid: 0%

Avg. Cumulative Debt: $17,303
% of Students Borrowing: 30%

CAREER
Who Recruits
1. Kaiser Permanente
2. Saatchi & Saatchi
3. UPS
4. JPMorgan Chase
5. AlphaSights

Notable Internships
1. :Los Angeles Review of Books
2. U.S. Senate
3. Spotify

Top Industries
1. Business
2. Education
3. Research
4. Media
5. Operations

Top Employers
1. Google
2. Microsoft
3. Kaiser Permanente
4. Amazon
5. Facebook

Where Alumni Work
1. Los Angeles
2. San Francisco
3. New York City
4. Seattle
5. Washington, DC

Median Earnings
College Scorecard (Early Career): $58,100
EOP (Early Career): $62,000
PayScale (Mid-Career): $117,200

RANKINGS
Forbes: 12
Money: 60
U.S. News: 5, Liberal Arts Colleges
Wall Street Journal/THE: 23
Washington Monthly: 8, Liberal Arts Colleges

#CollegesWorthYourMoney

Princeton University

Princeton, New Jersey | Admissions Phone: 609-258-3060

Inside the Classroom

The fourth oldest college in the United States is also an institution whose very name rings of wealth, privilege, and power—Princeton University. A charter member of the so-called Big Three alongside Harvard and Yale, Princeton has the smallest undergraduate population of that elite trio, but that doesn't stop it from churning out a disproportionate number of leaders and luminaries. Alumni include three current members of the US Supreme Court, eighteen Nobel Prize winners, business giants like Jeff Bezos and Steve Forbes, and countless other influential politicians, actors, writers, and scientific geniuses. We're hardly breaking new ground here—suffice to say that Princeton is Princeton.

Once noted for its policy of grade deflation, Princeton ended that practice five years ago, and GPAs have been on the rise since, providing a source of relief to current and future undergraduates. The majority of students are required to take a freshman writing seminar, one course in each of epistemology and cognition, ethical thought and moral values, historical analysis, and quantitative reasoning as well as two courses in each of literature and the arts, social analysis, and science and technology. All students must demonstrate proficiency in a foreign language. Central to a Princeton education is the culminating senior thesis project that is developed through one-on-one mentorship with a faculty member.

An absurdly low 5:1 student to faculty ratio does, as you might expect, translate to tiny class sizes for undergraduates. Just a touch over three-quarters of class sections have an enrollment of nineteen or fewer students, and 35 percent have fewer than ten students. Princeton is known for its commitment to undergraduate teaching, and students consistently rate professors as accessible and helpful. The Office of Undergraduate Research, formed in 2014, assists Tigers in locating faculty members with whom they can jointly conduct research in the summer or during a regular term. The university offers more than one hundred study abroad programs in forty-three countries; over half of its students take advantage.

As evidenced by the partial list of Princeton alumni, graduates of the university find themselves well received by the worlds of employment and top graduate schools. That goes for recipients of any degree, but the Engineering Department is widely recognized as one of the country's best as is the Woodrow Wilson School of Public and International Affairs. Prestigious scholarship programs love to go Tiger hunting. Thirty-three students and alumni made off with Fulbright Scholarships in 2018, three were named Rhodes Scholars, four became Schwarzman Scholars, and so many National Science Foundation Graduate Research Fellowships were procured that seven students won them from the Electrical Engineering program alone.

Outside the Classroom

An attractive and historic 500-acre campus plays home to 96 percent of Princeton undergraduates who are guaranteed housing for all four years. Freshmen and sophomores are required to live in one of six Residential College houses, each staffed by a live-in faculty member and full administrative team intent on creating a "strong sense of community, collaboration, and mutual respect, and to support individual initiative and personal growth."

Sports are serious at Princeton as the Tigers field thirty-seven varsity men's and women's squads that compete in NCAA Division I, and the school is the all-time leader in Ivy League titles. A sizable 18 percent of the undergraduate students compete at that level, and many others join one of the thirty-seven club sports teams. There are no officially recognized Greek organizations on campus, but that doesn't mean fraternities and sororities do not exist. In fact, 15-20 percent of the undergraduate population joins a Greek organization, and many more go through the "Bicker" process in an attempt to gain entry into one of the university's storied and exclusive "Eating Clubs" that are located in mansions on what is known as "The Street." The 135-member Ivy Club, immortalized by F. Scott Fitzgerald in *This Side of Paradise*, is Princeton's version of a Skull and Bones secret society. For everyone else, there are 300 student organizations that include popular dance troupes, singing groups, fifteen chaplaincies, the *Daily Princetonian* (one the oldest collegiate papers), and the 500-member American Whig-Cliosophic Society. The oldest debate team in the country, it was actually founded by James Madison. Princeton's location fifty-five miles from both Philadelphia and New York City means that big-city fun is always only a reasonable car or train ride away.

Career Services

Career Services at Princeton University has twenty professional staff members (excluding peer career advisors, assistants, and IT staff) who are dedicated to tasks such as pre-law advising, employer engagement, career advising, and alumni engagement. That 263:1 student-to-advisor ratio is superior to the average college featured in this guide. In addition to loads of individualized attention, Princeton also offers large-scale events such as the Fall HireTigers Career Fair that features one hundred top employers, and the school's online Handshake system sees over 42,000 applications for 6,500 jobs and internships each year.

Princeton University

E-mail: uaoffice@princeton.edu | Website: www.princeton.edu

An endless stream of impressive data supports the excellent work of the Career Services office. In 2016-17, counselors engaged students in 5,651 one-on-one advising sessions and attracted 11,541 attendees at 396 unique career services events. Close to 3,800 students participated in student-alumni engagement programs, and 46 percent of undergraduate participants reported that those sessions helped influence their postgraduate plans. More than 3,100 on-campus employer interviews took place each year. Overall, Princeton has recruiting relationships with an astronomical 13,669 employers. Highly personalized career and graduate school advising, along with ample resources and a supportive alumni base, assure graduating Tigers that a multitude of wonderful pathways await them post-commencement.

Professional Outcomes

Ninety-four percent of the Class of 2017 (the most recent class for which data is available) achieved their postgraduation plans within six months. Full-time employment was the first destination for 72.5 percent of those surveyed with professional, scientific, and technical services being the top industry, attracting 18 percent of graduates. The next most commonly entered industries were finance and insurance (13 percent), information (6 percent), and educational services (5 percent). Companies presently employing hundreds of Tiger alumni include Google, Goldman Sachs, Microsoft, McKinsey & Company, Morgan Stanley, IBM, and Facebook. The average salary reported by the 293 graduates entering the business and financial operations field was $73k while the school's 107 grads holding computer/mathematical positions averaged $107k. Those finding jobs in education, health care, or social services generally made less than $40k. The majority of grads remain in the Northeast and Mid-Atlantic regions, but 8 percent head to international destinations such as China, the United Kingdom, and South Korea.

The Class of 2017 saw 17.5 percent of its members head directly to graduate/professional school. Princeton alumni typically choose equally prestigious graduate schools to attend. Members of the Class of 2017 flocked in the largest numbers to Stanford (21), Penn (11), Princeton (11), Harvard (11), Cambridge (11), Columbia (10), and Oxford (10). The most frequently pursued degree was a master's (40 percent) followed by a PhD (34 percent), medical school (11 percent), and law school (5 percent). In recent years, Princeton undergrads have received acceptances into medical school 82-90 percent of the time, more than double the national average.

Admission

On the surface, Princeton's 5.5 percent acceptance rate for the Class of 2022 is extremely intimidating, as are the middle-50 percent of enrolled freshman test scores of 1430-1560 for the SAT and 32-35 for the ACT. Taking a granular look only makes things worse. Applicants with an unweighted GPA of 4.0 were only successful 8.1 percent of the time, and those with SATs north of 1500 had an 8 percent acceptance rate. Candidates with a 3.75 GPA or a 1350 SAT score were accepted less than 3 percent of the time.

The committee ranks nine factors as being most important in making admissions decisions: rigorous curriculum, GPA, class rank, essays, recommendations, standardized test scores (Princeton recommends two SAT subject tests), extracurricular activities, talent/ability, and character/personal qualities. Sorry, Risky Business fans, but alumni interviews are merely "considered." In 2018, single-choice early action (SCEA) applicants experienced a 14.7 percent acceptance rate, the lowest early-round acceptance rate in the school's history. There are a fair number of legacy admits, particularly in the early round. Overall, 14 percent of incoming freshmen in 2018-19 had Tiger lineage. One hundred seventy freshmen were international students representing sixty-three countries. Any way you slice it, getting into Princeton is a harrowing undertaking that will, more often than not, result in failure, even for some of the most accomplished applicants. Those who are successful typically have near-perfect to perfect test scores and GPAs and a "hook" to seal the deal.

Worth Your Money?

If you qualify for financial aid, your family won't pay a dime more than it can afford. That is the case for the 61 percent of current undergrads who qualify for need-based aid; they receive an annual award of $54,270. The university does not award merit aid. The average student graduates from Princeton with less than $10k in debt, less than one-third the national average. Of course, graduates also regularly walk into financially rewarding positions, so taking on any amount of debt to attend this school would absolutely be worth the sacrifice.

FINANCIAL
Institutional Type: Private
In-State Tuition: $49,450
Out-of-State Tuition: $49,450
Room & Board: $16,360
Required Fees: $890
Books & Supplies: $1,050

Avg. Need-Based Aid: $54,270
Avg. % of Need Met: 100%

Avg. Merit-Based Aid: $0
% Receiving Merit-Based Aid: 0%

Avg. Cumulative Debt: $9,059
% of Students Borrowing: 18%

CAREER
Who Recruits
1. Bain & Company
2. Schlumberger
3. MIT Lincoln Laboratory
4. Blackstone Group
5. Uber

Notable Internships
1. US Department of State
2. Jane Street
3. Bain & Company

Top Industries
1. Business
2. Education
3. Research
4. Engineering
5. Finance

Top Employers
1. Google
2. Goldman Sachs
3. Microsoft
4. McKinsey & Company
5. Facebook

Where Alumni Work
1. New York City
2. San Francisco
3. Washington, DC
4. Boston
5. Philadelphia

Median Earnings
College Scorecard (Early Career): $74,700
EOP (Early Career): $90,700
PayScale (Mid-Career): $139,400

RANKINGS
Forbes: 5
Money: 3
U.S. News: 1, National Universities
Wall Street Journal/THE: 5 (T)
Washington Monthly: 8, National Universities

#CollegesWorthYourMoney

West Lafayette, Indiana | Admissions Phone: 765-494-1776

ADMISSION
Admission Rate: 58%
Admission Rate - Men: 52%
Admission Rate - Women: 67%
EA Admission Rate: N/A
ED Admission Rate: Not Offered
Admission Rate (5-Year Trend): -2%
ED Admission Rate (5-Year Trend): Not Offered
% of Admits Attending (Yield): 27%
Transfer Admission Rate: 41%

Offered Wait List: 5,276
Accepted Wait List: 4,409
Admitted Wait List: 565

SAT Reading/Writing (Middle 50%): 590-680
SAT Math (Middle 50%): 590-730
ACT Composite (Middle 50%): 25-32
Testing Policy: ACT/SAT Required
SAT Superscore: Yes
ACT Superscore: Yes

% Graduated in Top 10% of HS Class: 32%
% Graduated in Top 25% of HS Class: 69%
% Graduated in Top 50% of HS Class: 96%

ENROLLMENT
Total Undergraduate Enrollment: 32,672
% Part-Time: 4%
% Male: 57%
% Female: 43%
% Out-of-State: 39%
% Fraternity: 18%
% Sorority: 20%
% On-Campus (Freshman): 94%
% On-Campus (All Undergraduate): 41%

% African-American: 3%
% Asian: 9%
% Hispanic: 5%
% White: 63%
% Other: 4%
% Race or Ethnicity Unknown: 2%
% International: 14%
% Low-Income: 19%

ACADEMICS
Student-to-Faculty Ratio: 13:1
% of Classes Under 20: 38%
% of Classes Under 40: 73%
% Full-Time Faculty: 87%
% Full-Time Faculty w/ Terminal Degree: 98%

Top Programs
Agriculture
Business
Chemistry
Computer and Information Technology
Computer Science
Engineering
Nursing
Pharmacy

Retention Rate: 92%
4-Year Graduation Rate: 56%
6-Year Graduation Rate: 81%

Curricular Flexibility: Somewhat Flexible
Academic Rating: ★★★⯪

Inside the Classroom

After dominating Wabash College in an 1892 football contest, a newspaper reporter labeled the brutes from Purdue University as "burly boiler makers." It was intended to be derogatory—a dig at an engineering and agricultural education—but it was almost immediately embraced by not only the football team but the entire university. As the twenty-first century has progressed, Purdue University, the public STEM university in Indiana, has grown to where it now educates roughly 33,000 undergraduates and another 10,000 graduate students and draws bright techie teens from well beyond the Hoosier State's ninety-two counties. Indiana residents comprise only 52 percent of the total undergraduate population at Purdue while 34 percent hail from out of state, and 14 percent are international students.

Waves of new students crash onto Purdue's West Lafayette campus each year filling up ten discipline-specific colleges in the pursuit of 200+ undergraduate majors. Yet, whether you are a member of the College of Engineering or the College of Education, you'll have to complete the same core curriculum, a thirty-credit concoction that lists among its ingredients written communication, information literacy, oral communication, science, quantitative reasoning, human behavior, and human cultures. The school's renowned Honors College welcomes 700 freshmen each fall and offers small class sizes, honors housing, and special leadership opportunities.

But class sizes are reasonable for all students, not only those in the Honors College. For a school of immense size, Purdue offers a strong 13:1 student-to-faculty ratio that leads to 38 percent of course sections having an enrollment of nineteen or fewer. You can also expect a balance of larger lectures as well as 20 percent of courses enroll more than fifty students. Undergraduate research opportunities are afforded to around 2,000 students per year. Undergrads can connect with professors on research projects during the academic year or apply to participate in a Summer Research Fellowship. A similar number, 2,400 students per year, elect to study abroad at one of 400 programs in sixty countries.

Engineering and engineering technologies majors earn 33 percent of the degrees conferred by the university. It makes sense that so many take advantage. After all, Purdue's College of Engineering cracks the top ten on almost every list of best engineering schools. The Krannert School of Management is also well regarded by employers around the country; 16 percent of degrees conferred are in business. Other popular majors include computer science (8 percent), agriculture (6 percent)—both are incredibly strong. Nationally Competitive Scholarships have been captured by recent grads of all academic backgrounds, including as many as six Fulbright Scholarships per year and a multitude of National Science Foundation Graduate Research Fellowships.

Outside the Classroom

Male-heavy to the tune of 57 percent (a typical STEM disproportionality), two-fifths of the Purdue undergraduate student body lives on campus. Freshman housing is only guaranteed to those who sign a housing contract by early May; 94 percent of first-year students follow through. There are over ninety fraternity and sorority houses, and 18 percent of men and 20 percent of women partake in Greek life. Nearly 1,000 clubs and activities are available, and among those who participate, 66 percent cited their involvement as one of the major reasons they remain at the university. A hard-to-fathom 18,000 students participate in one of forty intramural sports— there are 300 flag football teams alone. There is also no shortage of big-time sports to consume as a fan. A top-ranked marching band helps cheer on the eighteen NCAA Division I squads that compete in the Big Ten Conference. Purdue has sent thirty players to the NBA, and the football team has appeared in eighteen post-season bowl games. Campus food receives favorable reviews as does the sprawling 2,000-acre campus and its proximity to traditional college town fare and basic entertainment. In addition, Indianapolis can be reached within about an hour by car, and Chicago is a nice weekend destination that is only a two-hour drive away.

Career Services

There are twenty-one professional staff members (not counting administrative assistants) occupying the offices of Purdue University's Center for Career Opportunities & Pre-Professional Advising (CCO). The majority have the title of career services consultant while others specialize in pre-professional advising. The university's overall 1,556:1 student-to-counselor ratio is high compared to most other schools profiled in this guidebook. Fortunately, the center is adept at organizing large-scale events, connecting with industry leaders, and facilitating experiential learning and networking opportunities for its undergraduate students.

The Industry Roundtable, held every September, is the largest student-run career fair in the United States, drawing 400 companies and 12,000+ students. A business-specific career fair attracts another 2,000 students, the Agricultural Career Fair brings one hundred companies to campus, and Purdue also offers fairs for aviation, civil engineering, hospitality/tourism, aerospace, and construction management. This robust operation brings a total of 1,400 employers to campus each year for recruiting and/or on-campus interviews. Internship numbers are equally impressive—81 percent engage in at least one internship experience during their four years of study, 28 percent complete two experiences, and 24 percent engage in three or more. Catering to the career services needs of nearly 33,000 undergraduates with limited staff may be a logistical battle, but it is one that Purdue's CCO is managing to win. What it lacks in the ability to hand-hold, it makes up for in the scope of offerings and the positive career results for graduates.

Professional Outcomes

Shortly after receiving their diplomas, 70 percent of members of the Class of 2018 were headed to the world of employment, 21 percent were continuing their educational journey in graduate/professional school, and a mere 3.5 percent were still seeking employment. The top industries entered by Purdue grads in 2018 were (1) health care, pharmaceuticals, and medical devices; (2) finance, insurance, and consulting; (3) higher education; and (4) airline, aviation, and aerospace. Companies employing the greatest number of 2018 graduates included General Motors (31), Amazon (24), PepsiCo (22), Lockheed Martin (19), and Boeing (19). The average starting salary was an exceptional $59,500 across all degree programs. Liberal arts and education majors earned an average salary in the neighborhood of $40k while engineering students brought home $68k. The majority of alumni remain in Indiana with Chicago, San Francisco, New York, and DC rounding out the five next most common destinations.

Purdue enjoys professional school acceptance rates that are "slightly above" the national averages. In 2018-19, the school saw 163 of its seniors apply to medical school, and many went on to attend the Indiana University School of Medicine and other Midwestern institutions including the University of Minnesota and the University of Illinois. Given the academic concentrations of many undergrads, law school is not an immensely popular choice. Interestingly, Purdue purchased an unaccredited online law school in 2017, and it is still working toward recognition from the American Bar Association. Looking at all grad school applicants, 346 graduates in the Class of 2018 who continued their educations did so in state. Illinois, New York, and California all attracted fifty+ graduate/professional students including top institutions like NYU, UC Berkeley, and the University of Chicago.

Admission

Purdue – West Lafayette received 53,439 applications for a spot in the Class of 2022 and admitted a friendly 58 percent of wanna-be Boilermakers. Of those who were admitted and ultimately enrolled, the mid-50 percent standardized test scores were 1190-1390 on the SAT and 25-32 on the ACT. Math scores are generally stronger than reading scores—38 percent of freshmen scored above a 700 on the SAT while only 19 percent hit that same target on the reading section. Roughly one-third placed in the top 10 percent of their high school class, but only 69 percent were in the top quartile, giving more than a glimmer of hope to applicants with a few blemishes on their transcripts and who aren't looking to pursue either engineering or computer science. Earning entry into these majors can prove considerably more difficult.

The university's admissions staff looks foremost at the hard numbers of GPA and standardized test scores as well as the rigor of your high school curriculum. First-generation status is among the categories occupying the next rung of "important" factors. It is joined by essays, extracurricular activities, recommendations, and character/personal qualities. Women enjoyed a 67 percent acceptance rate compared to 52 percent for male applicants. There is no binding early decision option, but there is an early action round with a November 1 deadline. Acceptance rates at Purdue are definitely on the decline. In 2007 the school received approximately 20,000 applications and accepted 79 percent of the pool. Despite the rise in selectivity, Purdue remains one of the top STEM-focused universities that accepts solid-but-imperfect applicants.

Worth Your Money?

Tuition for Hoosier State residents remains a tremendous bargain at a hair under $10K. Nonresidents and international students will pay upward of $29k in tuition which, given the graduates' employment and salary data, is still not a bad price. Like most STEM-oriented schools, Purdue is highly likely to return your investment many times over. The only person for which this school would not make complete sense is an out-of-state applicant taking loans to pursue a non-STEM/business degree.

FINANCIAL
Institutional Type: Public
In-State Tuition: $9,208
Out-of-State Tuition: $28,010
Room & Board: $10,030
Required Fees: $784
Books & Supplies: $1,160

Avg. Need-Based Aid: $12,787
Avg. % of Need Met: 77%

Avg. Merit-Based Aid: $5,333
% Receiving Merit-Based Aid: 28%

Avg. Cumulative Debt: $28,440
% of Students Borrowing: 38%

CAREER
Who Recruits
1. Cognex Corporation
2. Endress + Hauser
3. Lockheed Martin
4. General Motors
5. General Electric

Notable Internships
1. Caterpillar
2. Qualcomm
3. PepsiCo

Top Industries
1. Business
2. Engineering
3. Operations
4. Education
5. Sales

Top Employers
1. Amazon
2. Microsoft
3. IBM
4. Google
5. Apple

Where Alumni Work
1. Indianapolis
2. Lafayette, IN
3. Chicago
4. San Francisco
5. New York City

Median Earnings
College Scorecard (Early Career): $55,100
EOP (Early Career): $48,800
PayScale (Mid-Career): $110,000

RANKINGS
Forbes: 118
Money: 55
U.S. News: 57, National Universities
Wall Street Journal/THE: 46
Washington Monthly: 41, National Universities

#CollegesWorthYourMoney

Reed College

Portland, Oregon | Admissions Phone: 503-777-7511

ADMISSION
Admission Rate: 35%
Admission Rate - Men: 34%
Admission Rate - Women: 36%
EA Admission Rate: N/A
ED Admission Rate: 17%
Admission Rate (5-Year Trend): -13%
ED Admission Rate (5-Year Trend): -50%
% of Admits Attending (Yield): 17%
Transfer Admission Rate: 23%

Offered Wait List: 1,331
Accepted Wait List: 477
Admitted Wait List: 80

SAT Reading/Writing (Middle 50%): 670-750
SAT Math (Middle 50%): 640-770
ACT Composite (Middle 50%): 30-33
Testing Policy: ACT/SAT Required
SAT Superscore: Yes
ACT Superscore: Yes

% Graduated in Top 10% of HS Class: 55%
% Graduated in Top 25% of HS Class: 78%
% Graduated in Top 50% of HS Class: 97%

ENROLLMENT
Total Undergraduate Enrollment: 1,483
% Part-Time: 2%
% Male: 46%
% Female: 54%
% Out-of-State: 93%
% Fraternity: Not Offered
% Sorority: Not Offered
% On-Campus (Freshman): 99%
% On-Campus (All Undergraduate): 62%

% African-American: 2%
% Asian: 7%
% Hispanic: 10%
% White: 58%
% Other: 9%
% Race or Ethnicity Unknown: 3%
% International: 10%
% Low-Income: 18%

ACADEMICS
Student-to-Faculty Ratio: 10:1
% of Classes Under 20: 71%
% of Classes Under 40: 97%
% Full-Time Faculty: 99%
% Full-Time Faculty w/ Terminal Degree: 95%

Top Programs
Biology
Chemistry
Economics
English
History
Mathematics
Physics
Political Science

Retention Rate: 88%
4-Year Graduation Rate: 68%
6-Year Graduation Rate: 81%

Curricular Flexibility: Somewhat Flexible
Academic Rating: ★★★✦

Inside the Classroom

"A band of fierce intellectuals and the distinctive institution that nurtures them. All in for rigorous scholarship and the joy of intellectual pursuit." Thus reads the twitter profile of an elite liberal arts school of fewer than 1,500 undergraduates located in Portland, Oregon—the one-and-only Reed College. It would be difficult to create a statement that more aptly sums up this unique institution that, for many, serves primarily as a prelude to a PhD program.

Twenty-three academic departments collectively offer forty majors, fourteen of which are interdisciplinary (e.g., history-literature or mathematics-economics). One of the most storied features of a Reed education is the mandatory, year-long freshman Humanities 110 course that comprehensively explores Greco-Roman culture and its many influences. However, in spring 2018, after a series of student-led protests over the course's "Eurocentrism," the school agreed to alter the course to include the study of other cultures. As with the aforementioned twitter statement, that anecdote also helps paint a picture of the Reed experience.

Grades at the college are, paradoxically, both (a) difficult to earn and (b) completely unknown to the students themselves. To ensure that the emphasis on the classroom remains on learning for learning's sake, grades are issued but not shared with students until graduation. The average GPA earned is 3.1, and only eleven students have graduated with a perfect 4.0 in the last three decades. The educational experience is highly personalized, and students work directly with their professors. Class sizes average seventeen students, and the student-to-faculty ratio is 9:1. Study abroad opportunities exist at fifty-two partner university programs in twenty-three countries. The college funds a number of undergraduate research opportunities for students to work alongside faculty, and all students are required to complete their own senior thesis, which is essentially a mini-dissertation under the guidance of a faculty advisor.

The areas in which the highest number of degrees are conferred are the social sciences (17 percent), biology (13 percent), interdisciplinary studies (11 percent), foreign languages (10 percent), psychology (9 percent), and English (7 percent). All majors are viewed favorably by elite graduate programs that are fully aware of the exceptional level of rigor baked into every academic program at the college. English, math, and physics receive particularly strong praise. Competitive fellowship and scholarship programs are also acutely aware of Reed's excellence and pluck up graduates at exceptionally high rates. In 2018, of a graduating class of just over 300 students, six won Fulbright awards and one took home a Truman Scholarship. In its history, Reed grads have won thirty-two Rhodes Scholarships, sixty-seven Watson Fellowships, and 174 National Science Foundation Fellowships.

Outside the Classroom

Downtown Portland is only ten minutes away, making Reed's location in the southeastern corner of the city ideal for finding culture, the arts, and entertainment. Public transportation is easy to navigate, so just about anything the uber-progressive City of Roses has to offer is accessible. While 98 percent of freshmen live on campus, only 67 percent of the total student body resides in university-owned housing. Others live in affordable off-campus housing that is easy to locate in the immediate area. There are no fraternities or sororities at Reed, nor is there any semblance of highly completive athletics. There are, however, five intercollegiate club teams in which athletically-inclined students may wish to participate. While most Reedies would say their primary outside-the-classroom activity is "studying," there are ninety student-run organizations from which to choose, including KRRC, the campus radio station; *Quest*, the student body's independent newspaper; and typically "Reedish" groups like the Sky Appreciation Society. Renn Fayre, an annual campus-wide, weekend-long party for graduating seniors is an out-of-control event that is truly beloved by students. Notable amenities include a recently renovated ski cabin on Mt. Hood that students are free to use, and the Watzik Sports Center that boasts a pool, sauna, and climbing wall.

Career Services

The Center for Life Beyond Reed (CLBR) employs five full-time staff members giving it a 297:1 student-to-advisor ratio that is about average for a college included in this guidebook. The guiding mission of the office since a 2012 rebranding is to help students "try to connect the intellectual passions they cultivate during their time here to successful careers."

On the practical side, the CLBR offers six full-day senior boot camps where students can receive help with resumes, online professional profiles, interview techniques, and helpful contacts in students' areas of interest. In recent years, it has increased engagement with freshmen and sophomores, encouraging earlier 1:1 advising sessions. The Fall Job Fayre features a limited number of employers and drew only eighty students in 2017. Handshake and the Reed Career Network are the places online to find a job, internships, or connect with alumni. Winter Shadow internships allow current students to join alumni in their places of business. With an intense focus on preparing the next generation of academics and researchers, the campus is not swarming with corporate recruiters, yet Reed does maintain some productive relationships with employers—Microsoft, for example, contributed $500,000 toward the development of the college's computer science program. Acknowledging its immense level of success in placing students at elite graduate and professional schools, the CLBR serves its unique student population well in spite of below-average starting salaries (more on that in a moment).

Professional Outcomes

An examination of Reed's alumni database reveals that the three most common occupational pathways are business (28 percent), education (25 percent), and self-employment (19 percent). Included among the most frequent current employers are Microsoft Corporation, Kaiser Permanente, Portland Public Schools, Intel Corporation, the US Department of State, National Institutes of Health, and Apple. Because of the incredible number of students who flock to academia (more on this later), many institutions of higher education are also employers of large numbers of Reed alumni. Salary figures for graduates are low. In fact, at age thirty-four the median Reed graduate makes only $37k, lowest among any of the nation's elite liberal arts colleges. However, it is important to put that number in proper context because that is the age when many Reed alumni may be completing an advanced degree.

Reed is rarely the final stop on a student's academic journey. In College Transitions' analysis of National Science Foundation data, Reed was the No. 1 producer of future PhD holders across all academic disciplines as determined by percentage of graduates attaining that degree. By discipline, Reed was in either first or second place for English, history, biology, and physics. The list of the universities where the highest concentration of grads pursue their doctorates is phenomenal. Included on that list are MIT, Harvard, Stanford, Yale, Berkeley, and Princeton. MBAs were earned at institutions that include Penn, Georgetown, Columbia, and UChicago. Reedies who went the legal route obtained their JDs primarily from top-tier law schools. Recent med school applicants have enjoyed a 70 percent acceptance rate, and many have attended similarly impressive universities as those in other fields already mentioned.

Admission

Reed College's 35 percent acceptance rate does not do its level of selectivity justice, not that the college cares. Admirably, this institution has long been anti-rankings and has no interest in PR efforts to drum up more applicants for the purpose of enhancing its status. It receives fewer than 6,000 applications per year. Its students are a self-selecting crew who choose to apply to this unique liberal arts school in Portland, Oregon. The middle-50 percent range for enrolled students is 1310-1520 on the SATs and 30-33 on the ACTs. Grades/class rank numbers are impressive but do not automatically exclude those with an imperfect transcript; 55 percent finished in the top 10 percent of their high school class, 78 percent were in the top 25 percent, and 70 percent of students typically sport a GPA of 3.75 or above.

The Reed Admissions Office only designates three factors as being "very important" in its evaluation process: rigor of secondary school record, grades, and essays. Factors deemed "important" are standardized test scores, class rank, interview, demonstrated interest, and recommendations. This is a college that, like Wesleyan on the opposite coast, is looking for intellectual risk-takers whose passion comes through in their writing and in conversation. Applying early definitely helps as 52 percent of ED applicants are accepted (a figure that is unaffected by athletes). Teens who are destined to be Reedies are the ones who fall in love with the school in the first place. Brilliant young people with an open mind who eschew convention will be thrilled to find a home here. Of course, strong credentials will help to make that goal a reality.

Worth Your Money?

At a cost of $75,000 and little available in the way of merit aid, many pay a steep price for attending this institution. Over 50 percent of Reed students do qualify for need-based aid and receive average annual grants of $40k. Undoubtedly, the academic experience here is uniquely wonderful and a perfect fit for a certain type of budding intellectual. Yet, if you don't qualify for need-based aid and don't come from a wealthy family, you would have to make sure that the $300,000+ bill for tuition would make sense as part of your life plan. Interestingly, the average student loan debt among Reed graduates is lower than the national average.

FINANCIAL
Institutional Type: Private
In-State Tuition: $58,130
Out-of-State Tuition: $58,130
Room & Board: $14,620
Required Fees: $310
Books & Supplies: $1,050

Avg. Need-Based Aid: $40,278
Avg. % of Need Met: 100%

Avg. Merit-Based Aid: $0
% Receiving Merit-Based Aid: 0%

Avg. Cumulative Debt: $21,697
% of Students Borrowing: 48%

CAREER
Who Recruits
1. TerraCotta Group LLC
2. First Book
3. Cranial Technologies
4. Teach for America
5. Wayfair

Notable Internships
1. Melville House Publishing
2. RTI International
3. Whitney Museum of American Art

Top Industries
1. Business
2. Education
3. Research
4. Media
5. Operations

Top Employers
1. Google
2. Microsoft
3. Apple
4. Intel
5. Amazon

Where Alumni Work
1. Portland, OR
2. San Francisco
3. New York City
4. Seattle
5. Los Angeles

Median Earnings
College Scorecard (Early Career): $42,200
EOP (Early Career): $36,900
PayScale (Mid-Career): $104,900

RANKINGS
Forbes: 105
Money: 665
U.S. News: 68, Liberal Arts Colleges
Wall Street Journal/THE: 75 (T)
Washington Monthly: 40, Liberal Arts Colleges

#CollegesWorthYourMoney

Rensselaer Polytechnic Institute

Troy, New York | Admissions Phone: 518-276-6216

ADMISSION
Admission Rate: 43%
Admission Rate - Men: 41%
Admission Rate - Women: 47%
EA Admission Rate: Not Offered
ED Admission Rate: 47%
Admission Rate (5-Year Trend): +2%
ED Admission Rate (5-Year Trend): -6%
% of Admits Attending (Yield): 20%
Transfer Admission Rate: 57%

Offered Wait List: 5,769
Accepted Wait List: 3,845
Admitted Wait List: 3

SAT Reading/Writing (Middle 50%): 640-720
SAT Math (Middle 50%): 690-780
ACT Composite (Middle 50%): 29-33
Testing Policy: ACT/SAT Required
SAT Superscore: Yes
ACT Superscore: No

% Graduated in Top 10% of HS Class: 64%
% Graduated in Top 25% of HS Class: 92%
% Graduated in Top 50% of HS Class: 98%

ENROLLMENT
Total Undergraduate Enrollment: 6,628
% Part-Time: 0%
% Male: 68%
% Female: 32%
% Out-of-State: 66%
% Fraternity: 30%
% Sorority: 16%
% On-Campus (Freshman): 100%
% On-Campus (All Undergraduate): 57%

% African-American: 4%
% Asian: 14%
% Hispanic: 9%
% White: 50%
% Other: 6%
% Race or Ethnicity Unknown: 1%
% International: 15%
% Low-Income: 15%

ACADEMICS
Student-to-Faculty Ratio: 13:1
% of Classes Under 20: 52%
% of Classes Under 40: 83%
% Full-Time Faculty: 90%
% Full-Time Faculty w/ Terminal Degree: 94%

Top Programs
Architecture
Business
Engineering
Computer Science
Game Design
Information Technology and Web Science
Physics

Retention Rate: 92%
4-Year Graduation Rate: 62%
6-Year Graduation Rate: 86%

Curricular Flexibility: Somewhat Flexible
Academic Rating: ★★★★

Inside the Classroom

Founded almost 200 years ago, Rensselaer Polytechnic Institute is America's first technological research university and still one of its best. Fittingly situated on the eastern bank of the Hudson River in the Industrial Revolution hotspot of Troy, New York, RPI is the proud home of 6,628 of the brightest and most innovative technical undergraduate minds anywhere. This is merely perpetuating a long history of producing high achievers in the tech world. Including both faculty and alumni, Rensselaer claims eighty-five members of the National Academy of Engineering, five members of the National Inventors Hall of Fame, and a Nobel Prize winner in physics.

There are five undergraduate schools within the larger university: The School of Architecture; the Lally School of Management; the School of Science; the School of Engineering; and the School of Humanities, Arts, and Social Sciences. All students take what is known as the HASS Core, a six course, twenty-four-credit foray into the humanities and social sciences. Beyond that, the academic programs are tailored to different schools and degree programs. There is no foreign language requirement, although the school does offer coursework in Mandarin Chinese for interested students.

The student-to-faculty ratio at RPI is 13:1, and with only about 1,300 graduate students to serve, there is plenty of time and attention left for undergraduates. Students will encounter various class sizes over the course of their four years of study. A solid 51 percent of sections contain fewer than twenty students; 13 percent will have fifty or more students. Being a research institution, RPI attracts $103 million in research funding each year, meaning that the school's 500 faculty members are constantly in the middle of projects that require student assistance. Students can participate during the academic year for credit or during the summer when select individuals receive $4,000 to work full time in a lab. International study is also encouraged at one of the school's affiliate universities in thirteen countries including Australia, Finland, and Singapore.

Engineering is the most commonly conferred degree area, accounting for 54 percent of 2018 graduates. Computer and information sciences was second (17 percent), followed by business/marketing (6 percent), engineering technology (5 percent), and biology (4 percent). The School of Engineering has a brilliant reputation with employers worldwide and is always near the top of the rankings for its programs in mechanical, aerospace, computer, electrical, and biomedical engineering. Physics, architecture, and computer science are also strong. Graduates do not apply to prestigious fellowship programs in droves, but the school does capture an occasional Fulbright or Truman Scholarship. RPI does, however, typically produce more than one annual National Science Foundation Graduate Research Fellowship winner.

Outside the Classroom

The school's 296-acre suburban campus only houses 57 percent of the student body as many upperclassmen seek off-campus apartments or join fraternities or sororities. Slightly over one-quarter of men and women elect to join Greek organizations. Those numbers are down after several chapters were suspended or dissolved in recent years. For a technical school, RPI boasts a highly athletic student body. Sixty-three percent of incoming freshmen participated in varsity athletics in high school, and forty-two individuals were the captains of their squads. There are twenty-three varsity men's and women's sports teams, twenty-two of which compete in NCAA Division III. The exception is men's hockey, which is one of the oldest and best teams in the entire country, having produced a long list of NHL stars over the years. Including the university's thriving intramural and club programs, 80 percent of RPI students are involved in athletics. With over 200 student organizations, students have their pick of non-sports/Greek sources of camaraderie. For example, the RPI Players has put on 300 theatrical shows over its ninety-year history, and there are nineteen service-oriented groups that serve the local community. In addition, fitness classes run by professional instructors are available just about every day at the Mueller Center. Troy itself may lack excitement, but the state capital of Albany is only ten miles away, and scenic retreats like the Berkshires or Catskills are under two hours away.

Career Services

The Center for Career and Professional Development consists of eight professional employees, which calculates to a student-to-advisor ratio of 796:1, a bit higher than the average school featured in this guide. However, that less-than-deal statistic is not at all representative of the exceptional work done by RPI's career services staff. Other numbers tell a different story, such as the ninety-five annual events hosted by the school that draw almost 1,900 undergrads, and the 1,912 one-on-one counseling appointments that take place. And that doesn't even include the employer recruiting numbers that are even more eye-popping.

Rensselaer Polytechnic Institute

In the 2017-18 school year career fairs drew 403 employers to campus, and 102 employers conducted 1,923 on-campus interviews. Companies also hosted 132 information sessions for RPI students that same year. Companies that recruit on campus include Cisco, the Blackstone Group, Deloitte, Johnson & Johnson, and Credit Suisse. Rensselaer Alumni Connect is a platform with over 2,500 active users, 79 percent of whom are willing to introduce others to connections while 83 percent are willing to answer industry-specific questions. Internship and co-op opportunities abound, and large numbers of students land co-op positions at Hasbro (27), NASA Jet Propulsion Laboratory (10), and Walt Disney World (7). Thanks to an endless parade of recruiters flowing into campus, high starting salaries, and plenty of individualized attention, the CCPD has earned a reputation for stellar work.

Professional Outcomes

As they receive their diplomas, 55 percent of RPI grads have already landed a job, 24 percent have committed to a graduate school, and 16 percent are still seeking their next destination. The largest numbers of 2017 grads were hired by companies that included UnitedHealth (17), United Technologies (16), General Dynamics (16), Boeing (14), and IBM (12). Massive numbers of alumni hold leadership positions in corporations like Google, Pratt & Whitney, General Motors, GE, and Microsoft. Geographically, 68 percent of graduates remain in the Northeast, 10 percent head to the West—primarily to Silicon Valley—and 8 percent land in the Southeast. The Class of 2017 enjoyed an average starting salary of $69,220. By midcareer RPI alumni have achieved one of the highest median salaries of any elite college, slightly ahead of other tech powerhouses including Caltech, Carnegie Mellon, and Lehigh University.

Of the nearly one-quarter of 2017 grads who were entering an advanced degree program, many were headed to some of the nation's best schools. Recent grads have been accepted by the likes of Carnegie Mellon University, Duke University, Massachusetts Institute of Technology, Northwestern University, Texas A&M, and the University of Chicago. Those intent on medical school have the option to apply to RPIs seven-year BS/MD program with affiliate Albany Medical College. Recent medically-minded grads have enjoyed acceptances at the likes of Harvard Medical School and Cornell University College of Veterinary Medicine. Those intent on law school also have the option of a combined degree, in this case a BS/JD at either Albany or Columbia University.

Admission

RPI was deluged by applications from Class of 2022 hopefuls, receiving an all-time high of 20,403. While the acceptance rate of 43 percent will do little to scare off prospective students, the composition of the 2018-19 freshman class was an impressive one. The average SAT score was 1409, and 161 netted a perfect score on either the critical reading or math section. A solid 64 percent placed in the top 10 percent of their high school class, 92 percent were in the top quarter, and ninety-five students earned either valedictorian or salutatorian status. The average GPA of an entering freshman was 3.91, and 69 percent of this cohort had a cumulative GPA of over 3.75. Comparing this incoming crop of freshmen to those from five years ago reveals that not much has changed admissions-wise in the recent past.

There is nothing opaque about the way in which applicants are evaluated by the Rensselaer Admissions Committee. The most strongly weighted factors are GPA, test scores (72 percent submit SATs), class rank, and the rigor of one's high school coursework. Of secondary importance are application essays, recommendations, extracurricular activities, and character/personal qualities. Unusual for a tech school, males and females have fairly similar acceptance rates. In 2018, men were accepted at a 41 percent clip, and women were welcomed 46.5 percent of the time. The yield rate at RPI is around 20 percent, which means only one of five admitted students goes on to enroll. However, applying early decision provides only a modest advantage; 47 percent of ED applicants were admitted into the Class of 2022. Also of note, transfer students fare well at this institution as 57 percent of the 496 applicants were accepted in 2018. Rensselaer Polytechnic Institute is looking for students with GPAs above a 3.75 in most or all honors and AP courses and who scored in the 95th percentile on standardized tests. The criteria is fairly simple.

Worth Your Money?

Rensselaer's annual cost of attendance is a pretty high $73,816; the good news is that starting salaries for graduates just about matches that sum. Over one-third of entering students do get an offer of merit aid that averages almost $22k, and more than half of attendees qualify for a need-based grant with an average value of $39k. Attending a STEM-heavy school like RPI is almost always a good bet for getting an excellent return on your educational investment, even if the up-front cost is quite high.

FINANCIAL
Institutional Type: Private
In-State Tuition: $54,000
Out-of-State Tuition: $54,000
Room & Board: $15,580
Required Fees: $1,378
Books & Supplies: $2,858

Avg. Need-Based Aid: $38,861
Avg. % of Need Met: 82%

Avg. Merit-Based Aid: $21,836
% Receiving Merit-Based Aid: 36%

Avg. Cumulative Debt: $34,595
% of Students Borrowing: 63%

CAREER
Who Recruits
1. U.S. Nuclear Regulatory Commission
2. Etsy
3. GlobalFoundries
4. Apprenda
5. American Airlines

Notable Internships
1. Regeneron Pharmaceuticals
2. NASA
3. Pfizer

Top Industries
1. Engineering
2. Business
3. Operations
4. Information Technology
5. Education

Top Employers
1. IBM
2. Pratt & Whitney
3. Google
4. Boeing
5. GE

Where Alumni Work
1. New York City
2. Albany, NY
3. Boston
4. San Francisco
5. Washington, DC

Median Earnings
College Scorecard (Early Career): $82,000
EOP (Early Career): $84,100
PayScale (Mid-Career): $134,100

RANKINGS
Forbes: 113
Money: 217
U.S. News: 50 (T), National Universities
Wall Street Journal/THE: 122
Washington Monthly: 78, National Universities

#CollegesWorthYourMoney

Rhodes College

Memphis, Tennessee | Admissions Phone: 901-843-3700

ADMISSION
Admission Rate: 45%
Admission Rate - Men: 40%
Admission Rate - Women: 48%
EA Admission Rate: 56%
ED Admission Rate: 63%
Admission Rate (5-Year Trend): -13%
ED Admission Rate (5-Year Trend): -23%
% of Admits Attending (Yield): 24%
Transfer Admission Rate: 22%

Offered Wait List: 1,253
Accepted Wait List: 306
Admitted Wait List: 42

SAT Reading/Writing (Middle 50%): 630-700
SAT Math (Middle 50%): 610-710
ACT Composite (Middle 50%): 28-31
Testing Policy: ACT/SAT Required
SAT Superscore: Yes
ACT Superscore: Yes

% Graduated in Top 10% of HS Class: 54%
% Graduated in Top 25% of HS Class: 85%
% Graduated in Top 50% of HS Class: 99%

ENROLLMENT
Total Undergraduate Enrollment: 2,008
% Part-Time: 1%
% Male: 44%
% Female: 56%
% Out-of-State: 71%
% Fraternity: 34%
% Sorority: 40%
% On-Campus (Freshman): 97%
% On-Campus (All Undergraduate): 69%

% African-American: 9%
% Asian: 6%
% Hispanic: 6%
% White: 69%
% Other: 5%
% Race or Ethnicity Unknown: 2%
% International: 5%
% Low-Income: 15%

ACADEMICS
Student-to-Faculty Ratio: 10:1
% of Classes Under 20: 71%
% of Classes Under 40: 98%
% Full-Time Faculty: 80%
% Full-Time Faculty w/ Terminal Degree: 98%

Top Programs
Biology
Business
Chemistry
International Studies
Neuroscience
Political Science
Psychology

Retention Rate: 90%
4-Year Graduation Rate: 82%
6-Year Graduation Rate: 85%

Curricular Flexibility: Somewhat Flexible
Academic Rating: ★★★✦

Inside the Classroom

Rhodes College's Memphis location places it among the rare liberal arts schools located in an urban setting. (Occidental in Los Angeles is another such school featured in this guide.) Just four miles from the world famous Beale Street, Rhodes, founded in 1848, is one of the top colleges in the region. A progressive, service-oriented student body of just over 2,000 students flocks to Rhodes for its small classes, awesome location, and nurturing environment that leads many on the path to top graduate and professional programs.

The school offers fifty majors and minors and a great deal of academic autonomy along the way. The foundations requirements can be meet by roughly 400 varied courses that cover target areas such as written communication, becoming an active and engaged citizen, gaining proficiency in a second language, and understanding scientific approaches to the natural world. As part of this experience students choose between two signature courses: The Search for Values in the Light of Western Religion and History and Life: Then and Now, both of which were developed after World War II. Freshmen also must engage in the first-year experience requirement, an integrative, year-long program focused on becoming an active student-citizen as well as a first year writing seminar.

A 10:1 student-to-faculty ratio leads to an amazingly intimate average class size of only fourteen students. Only 3.7 percent of course sections contain more than twenty-nine students. Ninety-eight percent of the 224 faculty members hold the highest degree available in their fields, so you will not be taught by TAs or adjuncts. A great deal of resources are committed to undergraduate education. For example, Rhodes puts an astounding sum of money into its physical science programs, having committed $34 million to a new science center in 2017. As a result, the school produces an incredible number of PhDs (more on this under "Professional Outcomes"). Three-quarters of students at this institution engage in some form of undergraduate research. Opportunities are plentiful in every academic discipline to collaborate with faculty on research projects, and the annual Undergraduate Research and Creativity Symposium is a chance to show off student projects. An affiliation with St. Jude's Children's Research Hospital leads to intensive summer research opportunities for those in the hard sciences. A solid 65 percent of students elect to study abroad, and the school offers many Rhodes faculty-led locations around the world.

While the sciences may be the area for which Rhodes receives the greatest recognition (biology is the most popular major), business, psychology, and international studies are also strong and attract large numbers of undergrads. Since the turn of the millennium, Rhodes graduates have earned thirty-one Fulbright Scholarships, fourteen Goldwater Scholarships, eleven Watson Fellowships, five Truman Scholarships, five National Science Foundation Graduate Fellowships, two Luce Scholarships, and one Rhodes Scholarship.

Outside the Classroom

This 123-acre wooded oasis in midtown Memphis is home to 70 percent of all undergraduates. Students are required to live in residence halls for their first two years. Most residence halls are intimate places of under one hundred students where everyone knows everyone. A 56/44 percent breakdown in favor of women certainly has an impact on student life. Greek life is a defining characteristic of social life at Rhodes with 40 percent of women joining a sorority and 34 percent of men pledging a fraternity. Participation in sports is also common with twenty-one men's and women's varsity teams competing in NCAA Division III athletics. The Bryan Campus Life Center offers ample facilities for recreational sports and fitness. For non-jocks, there are more than one hundred student-run organizations, and over 80 percent of students engage in community service activities. The mock trial team is exceptionally strong in national competitions. With the Lynx Lair serving as a hub for food, social events, and frequent concerts, lectures, and films there is rarely a dull moment around Rhodes. Of course, with Memphis as your backyard there are always exciting excursions for entertainment, culture, or dining. The Memphis Zoo, the Memphis Brooks Museum of Art, and the National Civil Rights Museum are only a few miles away. Campus is walker-friendly, but bikes are popular as well. The city of Memphis has over 200 miles of bike infrastructure to help ensure safety.

Career Services

The Career Services Office at Rhodes has three full-time staff members—the director, a first- and second-year counselor, and a third- and fourth-year counselor. Its 663:1 student-to-advisor ratio does not compare favorably to other liberal arts schools featured in this guide, but the push for personalized service is evident everywhere you look. The school encourages meeting one-on-one with advisors two or three times in the freshman year as well during sophomore year. Few schools promote that level of contact so early in a student's undergraduate career.

Rhodes College

E-mail: adminfo@rhodes.edu | Website: www.rhodes.edu

Every fall, representatives from over one hundred graduate and professional schools travel to Rhodes' campus to attend the Graduate School Exposition. The 2019 Career Fair was attended by over fifty employers, including many national corporations such as AutoZone, Raymond James, and St. Jude's Research Hospital. Over 80 percent of undergraduates complete at least one internship. Those numbers are bolstered by career services partnerships with over one hundred local, national, and global employers. Many of the 13,000 alums are willing to lend a hand to a current student or recent grad seeking to network.

Professional Outcomes

Within one year of receiving their diplomas, 98 percent of Rhodes grads have found their way into the world of employment or are pursuing an advanced degree program. Among the companies employing the largest number of alumni are St. Jude's Children's Hospital, Deloitte, EY, FedEx, Raymond James, and PwC. Midcareer salaries are the second highest among any Tennessee institution, behind only Vanderbilt. Yet, it is worth noting that Vandy grads earn over $20k more by age thirty-four. Greater Memphis is where most graduates remain. Many others situate themselves in Greater Nashville, Atlanta, DC, New York, or Dallas.

A superb 86 percent of those applying to graduate school get into their top-choice institution. Medical and law school applicants are accepted at higher rates than the national average. Those with a 3.4 GPA and above the 57th percentile on the MCAT are accepted into medical school at an identical 86 percent clip and, overall, applicants enjoy a 65 percent acceptance rate. In 2018, an impressive forty-two graduates were accepted into med school. Rhodes is in the top 10 percent of science PhD-producing undergraduate schools in the country, and it is ranked fifteenth overall in the number of physics majors who go on to receive a doctorate in physics or astronomy. Recent graduates have been accepted into programs at elite universities including Brown, Columbia, Georgetown, Harvard Law School, New York University School of Law, and Yale Divinity School. Medical schools attended by recent grads include Tufts, Dartmouth, Boston University, Wake Forest, and UVA.

Admission

With a 45 percent acceptance rate for a place in the Class of 2022, Rhodes College is a rare school that provides an elite education without putting applicants through a harrowing admissions process with dreadfully unfavorable odds. The 5,092 hopefuls who submitted applications were a strong bunch, but those who were successful didn't have to sport a perfect transcript. The SAT mid-50 percent range was 1240-1410, although the ACT was submitted more than twice as often; 28-31 was the mid-50 percent ACT score, and half of ACT takers had a composite score above 30. Three-quarters of admitted freshmen held a weighted GPA of 3.75 or higher, 54 percent finished in the top decile of their high school class, and 85 percent were in the top quartile. The average GPA of incoming 2018-19 freshman was 3.92.

Rigor of secondary school record, GPA, and class rank sit atop the list of most important factors in the eyes of the admissions office. Factors considered as "important" include standardized test scores, essays, recommendations, character/personal qualities, legacy status, and racial/ethnic status. Only 24 percent of those accepted actually enrolled, thus the college values those who demonstrate interest, particularly in the form of committing through early decision. As a result, 63 percent of ED applicants were accepted in 2018. In their own words, Rhodes uses a "holistic approach to evaluate every facet of your application to get a better sense of the whole you." Obviously, the school is looking for students with strong grades in a demanding curriculum, but students do not need to have perfect test scores and grades for consideration at this fine liberal arts institution.

Worth Your Money?

Rhodes sticker-price cost of attendance of almost $62,000 isn't particularly tough to swallow, at least when considered against the cost of many comparable institutions. Yet, Rhodes delivers merit aid packages to two-thirds of its undergrads, lowering the cost by an average of $26k per year. Further, almost half of all students receive need-based aid at an average annual total of $33k. Given the cost that most people actually pay, Rhodes College is a fairly priced option that will afford you a one-of-a-kind educational experience.

FINANCIAL
Institutional Type: Private
In-State Tuition: $47,580
Out-of-State Tuition: $47,580
Room & Board: $11,403
Required Fees: $310
Books & Supplies: $1,125

Avg. Need-Based Aid: $32,532
Avg. % of Need Met: 93%

Avg. Merit-Based Aid: $26,103
% Receiving Merit-Based Aid: 66%

Avg. Cumulative Debt: $24,187
% of Students Borrowing: 48%

CAREER
Who Recruits
1. St. Jude's Children's Research Hospital
2. Raymond James
3. Methodist Healthcare
4. PeaceCorps
5. Teach for America

Notable Internships
1. Graystar Real Estate
2. Christie's
3. FedEx

Top Industries
1. Business
2. Education
3. Operations
4. Social Services
5. Healthcare

Top Employers
1. St. Jude Children's Research Hospital
2. Deloitte
3. EY
4. Raymond James
5. FedEx

Where Alumni Work
1. Memphis
2. Nashville
3. Atlanta
4. Washington, DC
5. New York City

Median Earnings
College Scorecard (Early Career): $53,600
EOP (Early Career): $52,000
PayScale (Mid-Career): $97,800

RANKINGS
Forbes: 150
Money: 282
U.S. News: 53 (T), Liberal Arts Colleges
Wall Street Journal/THE: 134 (T)
Washington Monthly: 171, Liberal Arts Colleges

#CollegesWorthYourMoney

Rice University

Houston, Texas | Admissions Phone: 713-348-7423

Inside the Classroom

With just shy of 4,000 undergraduates, Rice is at once a powerhouse research institution *and* a place where world-class instruction is the norm. The university's illustrious faculty includes multiple Nobel Prize and National Medal of Science winners as well as countless recipients of any prestigious fellowship or award that one can name. And the best news is that undergraduates have the chance to learn from that distinguished lot.

Rice offers more than fifty majors across six broad disciplines: engineering, architecture, music, social science, humanities, and natural science. Double majoring is more common at Rice than your average university; roughly 20 percent of students graduate with a double major. Speaking of majors, there is a greater diversity of majors than one might assume at a STEM-famous school. The most commonly conferred degrees are in engineering (19 percent), the social sciences (15 percent), parks and recreation (9 percent), computer science (7 percent), biology (7 percent), and mathematics (5 percent).

Boasting a student-to-faculty ratio of 5.6:1, Rice offers a spectacularly intimate learning experience. Class sizes are ideally small with 72 percent containing fewer than twenty students and a median class size of only fourteen. Undergraduate research opportunities abound with 62 percent of graduates participating in academic research during their four years. Those experiences are open to freshmen through the Century Scholars Program and to all underclassmen through the Rice Undergraduate Scholars Program. Study abroad options are available in seventy countries, including collaborative programs with some of the top schools in the world including The London School of Economics, Oxford, and Cambridge; approximately 30 percent of Rice students elect to spend a semester in another country.

Programs in biology, biochemistry, cognitive science, and music are incredibly strong, while the School of Architecture and the George R. Brown School of Engineering are among the highest ranking schools in their disciplines. It is also notable that Rice is doing its part to close the STEM gender gap; the school is among the national leaders in producing female engineers, and it also boasts a 32 percent clip of female computer science majors, almost twice the national average. When it comes to procuring scholarships and fellowships upon graduation, Owls fare well, regularly producing Fulbright Scholars, Marshall Scholars, Watson Fellows, Hertz Fellows, and an occasional Rhodes Scholar (a dozen in its history).

Outside the Classroom

Central to student life at Rice is the Oxford/Cambridge-style (or more familiarly, Yale-style) residential college system. Upon matriculation, students are assigned to one of eleven residential colleges that contain their own dorms, dining halls, common areas, and faculty sponsors. Each college has its own student-run government, unique traditions, and social events. Those seeking a strong Greek life will have to look elsewhere as Rice has always operated free of fraternities and sororities. Rice does not have a particularly fervent sports culture either despite seven men's and seven women's varsity teams competing in NCAA Division I competition. The most notable squad is the baseball team that is always competing for national titles. Opportunities for intramural and club team participation are vast and include sports like aikido, badminton, and water polo. Student-run clubs are plentiful as well with over 250 to select from. The *Rice Thresher*, the student newspaper, is widely read and regularly wins national awards. While campus life is abuzz with activity, many venture into the city of Houston to enjoy the nightlife and cultural events in such close proximity.

Career Services

The Rice Center for Career Development (CCD) is staffed by eleven full-time professional employees, which equals a student-to-advisor ratio of 363:1, better-than-average when compared with the other institutions included in this book. Additional peer career advisors, embedded in each residential college, offer services such as resume reviews or assistance with locating internship opportunities. Internships opportunities can also be discovered at the Career and Internship Expo, which is attended by more than one hundred employers, and through RICElink, which posts internships open exclusively to current Owls. The CCD also facilitates Owl Edge Externships, job-shadowing experiences that last from one day to a full week.

The university does a phenomenal job of facilitating on-campus interviews with roughly 150 employers conducting over 1,600 interviews each year. It also hosts one hundred+ events that connect students to potential employers from formal career fairs to casual events like the Chili Cook-Off. The CCD does a superb job with outreach as it attracts more than 3,500 non-grad student visits per year, close to one visit per undergraduate. It's little surprise that 55 percent of graduates found their first job directly through the CCD office. In short, it is hard to imagine a career services office accomplishing more for its undergraduates than the CCD does for its students at Rice.

Rice University

E-mail: admi@rice.edu | Website: www.rice.edu

Professional Outcomes

Six months after graduation only 6 percent of Rice grads are still seeking employment. The overwhelming majority have found careers or a graduate school home. Companies that are known to pluck more than their fair share of employees each year from Rice's senior class include Deloitte, Capital One, JP Morgan Chase, Google, and Microsoft. Over one hundred alumni are also current employees of companies such as Shell, ExxonMobil, Chevron, Amazon, Accenture, and Facebook. Median starting salaries for Rice grads far exceed national averages. Across all majors the average starting salary is $69k. That encompasses engineering majors at the high end ($79k) and humanities majors at the low end ($52k). Texas is among the most common destinations for recent grads, but many also flock to California, New York, Wisconsin, and Washington State.

Over one-third of graduates move directly into graduate or professional school. That group fares well in gaining admission to elite graduate institutions; Harvard, Yale, Stanford, MIT, Columbia, and Berkeley are among the schools that absorb the highest number of Rice applicants. Rice is also known for producing a strong number of successful medical school applicants each year. A robust 38 percent of graduate school attendees are enrolled in medical school. Baylor College of Medicine and the med schools in the UT system are popular destinations for future doctors. Other recent grads are presently attending Harvard Medical School, Duke University School of Medicine, and Stanford Medical School.

Admission

Rice's acceptance rate for the Class of 2022 plummeted to an all-time low of 11 percent. That flirtation with the single-digit club was a steep fall from the 15-17 percent acceptance rates of the last few years. The number of applications received by the university topped 20,000 for the first time, and that figure has more than doubled in the last decade. The ACT mid-50 percent range is 33-35. The 75th percentile score on the math section was a perfect 800, and the reading range was 700-760. More than 88 percent of students earned above a 700 in math, and 77 percent earned the same in reading. In 2014, "only" 64 percent of Rice's freshman class scored above a 700 on the verbal section, and 75 percent reached that mark on the math portion. This is a clear indicator that Rice's diminishing acceptance rate is, in fact, indicative of an increasingly selective student profile.

Early decision applicants, as would be expected, enjoy a better acceptance rate of 22 percent, but an applicant's bona fides still need to meet the university's sky-high standards. Rice lists more factors as being "very important" than most elite schools, granting this designation to rigor of courses, GPA, class rank, test scores, essays, recommendations, talent/ability, and character/personal qualities. An intimidating 89 percent of Rice students placed in the top 10 percent of their high school class, and 96 percent were in the top quartile. In 2018, Rice instituted an expedited system of reviewing applications; it now takes two admissions officers fewer than ten minutes to review each candidate and assign a numerical rating, a 5 being the highest. With that in mind, to have a realistic chance of getting in, the admissions staff shouldn't have to dig very deep to find reasons to say "Yes." A quality essay and glowing recommendations will help, but you'll need a sparkling academic profile and in-range test scores to make it through the first wave.

Worth Your Money?

For the 39 percent of students who qualify for need-based financial aid, Rice delivers by meeting 100 percent of every individual's demonstrated need. That equates to over $44k per year, which certainly helps make the $67,000 annual cost (already a reasonable list price relative to the marketplace) of attendance more affordable. Further, 11 percent of students qualify for merit-based aid that averages $21,740. Graduates not only encounter incredibly high starting salaries, they also have less debt, on average, than the average college graduate in the United States. Needless to say, Rice is worth the cost of admissions no matter who you are or how much you have to pay.

FINANCIAL
Institutional Type: Private
In-State Tuition: $48,330
Out-of-State Tuition: $48,330
Room & Board: $14,140
Required Fees: $782
Books & Supplies: $1,200

Avg. Need-Based Aid: $44,044
Avg. % of Need Met: 100%

Avg. Merit-Based Aid: $21,740
% Receiving Merit-Based Aid: 11%

Avg. Cumulative Debt: $24,635
% of Students Borrowing: 24%

CAREER
Who Recruits
1. DMC, Inc.
2. INT Software
3. Quantlab
4. Oxy
5. Chevron

Notable Internships
1. The Blackstone Group
2. Jane Street
3. Houston Rockets

Top Industries
1. Business
2. Education
3. Engineering
4. Research
5. Operations

Top Employers
1. Google
2. Shell
3. ExxonMobil
4. Chevron
5. Microsoft

Where Alumni Work
1. Houston
2. San Francisco
3. Dallas
4. Austin
5. New York City

Median Earnings
College Scorecard (Early Career): $65,400
EOP (Early Career): $76,700
PayScale (Mid-Career): $129,500

RANKINGS
Forbes: 21
Money: 24
U.S. News: 17, National Universities
Wall Street Journal/THE: 16
Washington Monthly: 101, National Universities

#CollegesWorthYourMoney

Rochester Institute of Technology

Rochester, New York | Admissions Phone: 585-475-6631

ADMISSION
Admission Rate: 70%
Admission Rate - Men: 75%
Admission Rate - Women: 68%
EA Admission Rate: Not Offered
ED Admission Rate: 84%
Admission Rate (5-Year Trend): +10%
ED Admission Rate (5-Year Trend): -1%
% of Admits Attending (Yield): 19%
Transfer Admission Rate: 56%

Offered Wait List: 914
Accepted Wait List: 346
Admitted Wait List: 40

SAT Reading/Writing (Middle 50%): 600-690
SAT Math (Middle 50%): 620-720
ACT Composite (Middle 50%): 27-32
Testing Policy: ACT/SAT Required
SAT Superscore: Yes
ACT Superscore: Yes

% Graduated in Top 10% of HS Class: 39%
% Graduated in Top 25% of HS Class: 73%
% Graduated in Top 50% of HS Class: 94%

ENROLLMENT
Total Undergraduate Enrollment: 13,513
% Part-Time: 8%
% Male: 62%
% Female: 38%
% Out-of-State: 47%
% Fraternity: 4%
% Sorority: 2%
% On-Campus (Freshman): 96%
% On-Campus (All Undergraduate): 51%

% African-American: 4%
% Asian: 9%
% Hispanic: 7%
% White: 63%
% Other: 4%
% Race or Ethnicity Unknown: 6%
% International: 6%
% Low-Income: 30%

ACADEMICS
Student-to-Faculty Ratio: 13:1
% of Classes Under 20: 49%
% of Classes Under 40: 88%
% Full-Time Faculty: 73%
% Full-Time Faculty w/ Terminal Degree: 54%

Top Programs
Computer Science
Engineering
Film and Animation
Game Design and Development
Imaging Science
Management Information Systems
Photographic Arts

Retention Rate: 89%
4-Year Graduation Rate: 28%
6-Year Graduation Rate: 70%

Curricular Flexibility: Less Flexible
Academic Rating: ★★★

Inside the Classroom

Since 1829 the Rochester Institute of Technology has been more than simply a technical school that churns out large quantities of engineers each year. With additional strengths in art and animation and design, this institution genuinely desires to "shape the future and improve the world through creativity and innovation." Even by STEM-focused school standards, the training at RIT is highly focused on career readiness and launches students into hands-on learning opportunities from the start of their freshman year. Large compared to other schools of its ilk like RPI and WPI, Rochester Institute of Technology educates approximately 16,000 undergraduates and another 3,100 graduate students. Half are from New York State, but students from all over the United States as well as one hundred countries brave the frigid Upstate New York weather in order to attend this accessible school that offers many standout programs and some of the best connections to industry of any school in the country.

The co-op program is the fourth oldest in the country, and just about all students complete a one- or two-semester paid learning experience after finishing their first two years of academic study. There are nine undergraduate colleges at RIT, and while all have distinct course requirements the school's signature general education curriculum touches every single student. Students earning a bachelor's of science degree in engineering, for example, need to take sixty credit hours of general education courses—including first-year writing—and a number of perspectives courses that cover categories such as social, ethical, global, artistic, mathematics, scientific principles, and natural science inquiry. One immersion sequence that involves a three-course, deep dive into a particular topic also must be built into every undergrad's program.

RIT's 13:1 student-to-faculty ratio and a genuine commitment to undergraduate teaching leads to a respectable 49 percent of sections enrolling fewer than twenty students, and only 11 percent of courses contain more than forty students. Additionally, RIT provides an array of undergraduate research opportunities including the Biological Sciences Research Scholars Program, the Chemistry Research Scholars Program, Economics Undergraduate Research, and the Undergraduate Research Symposium that saw 212 students give presentations in the 2018-19 academic year. Ample opportunities exist to study abroad, but few undergraduates elect to take advantage.

The most popular majors at this school are engineering, information sciences, visual and performing arts, and business. The Gleason College of Engineering and the Golisano College of Computing and Information Sciences are top-of-the-line. The latter houses RIT's game design program, which is the best on the entire East Coast. Strong film, art, and design programs also churn out successful graduates. Few pursue postgraduate fellowships, but the school does produce roughly one Fulbright Scholar and two Goldwater Scholars each cycle.

Outside the Classroom

RIT guarantees housing to freshmen and can accommodate about half the total undergraduate population in a mix of residence halls, apartments, the RIT Inn and Conference Center, Greek housing, and the global village. Like too many institutes of technology, the male-to-female ratio is heavily skewed at 2-to-1, which certainly has an impact on aspects of campus life. There are thirty fraternities and sororities on campus, but in the scope of such a large school, Greek life only draws single-digit participation. While RIT doesn't award athletic scholarships, it does field twenty-four NCAA varsity sports teams including Division I men's and women's ice hockey as well as many highly-competitive Division III teams. RIT is so competitive, in fact, rumors have swirled about a step-up to Division I. There are 300 clubs and organizations, including an extensive intramural sports program that signs up roughly half of the student body and plenty of opportunities for competitive or friendly gaming; video games are a way of life here. One of the greenest campuses around with a focus on sustainability, the 1,159 acres owned by the school offer federally designated wetlands, ample native plantings and wildlife, and a 200-acre area where most buildings are concentrated. There's enough to do on campus and in the classroom to mitigate the impact of an otherwise unexciting locale.

Career Services

The Office of Career Services and Cooperative Education (OCSCE) is staffed by twenty-seven professional staff members (not counting office assistants) who play roles such as career advisor, employer engagement and partnerships coordinator, and alumni relations coordinator. Rochester Institute of Technology's 593:1 student-to-advisor ratio is slightly higher than the average school featured in this guide, but it unquestionably has sufficient personnel to get the job done. Large-scale, university-wide career fairs are put on twice per year, drawing 726 companies and 3,500 students. Numerous boutique fairs cater to groups such as future accountants, civil engineers, and teachers. On a more personal level, the office also arranges "tailored orientations, workshops, and one-on-one advisement. It also plans and promotes events such as career fairs, workshops, and speakers from industry," and that's only the tip of the iceberg.

The co-op program, more than a century old, sees 2,300+ participants per year in co-op with employers from all fifty states and forty countries. The list of co-op and internship partners is incredible—Boeing, the CIA, EY, Fisher Price, Walt Disney World, SpaceX, NASA, Google, and literally dozens of other equally impressive organizations. RIT has 2,200 employer partners. The off-the-charts employer relations accomplishments do not stop there; the career services staff posts 10,000 jobs per year and facilitates 5,400 on-campus interviews, far more than the number of seniors at RIT, meaning many are interviewing with multiple companies. More than 850 companies recruit on campus every single year. In sum, the Rochester Institute of Technology offers an exceptional level of support to its undergraduates through its robust co-op program as well as all of the one-on-one attention you could desire.

Professional Outcomes

Within six months of graduation 95.4 percent of the 2,495 members of the Class of 2017 had found employment or a full-time graduate program. Major companies presently employing more 500 RIT alums include Xerox and Paychex, both with offices in Rochester. Between 200 and 450 employees of IBM, Microsoft, Apple, Intel, Amazon, Google, and Cisco were educated at RIT. Many graduates remain in the Upstate New York area while large numbers of other RIT alumni flock to New York City, Boston, DC, and San Francisco. Median income levels by midcareer are in the same neighborhood as fellow New York institutions including the University of Rochester, Fordham, and Syracuse. Starting salary figures vary greatly by major with College of Business grads landing median starting salaries between $43,000 (marketing majors) and $53,000 (finance majors), and just about all engineering grads being compensated at more than $60k. Computer science majors had a median compensation package of $83k right out of school.

The Class of 2017 saw an exceptionally low 8.8 percent of graduates electing to pursue an advanced degree; the prior year saw 12.5 percent continuing their educations postgraduation. While only a small number of RIT grads head directly to grad school, those who do typically head to some of the world's best such as Carnegie Mellon, Duke, Harvard, Johns Hopkins, MIT, Rhode Island School of Design, Penn, UVA, and the University of Michigan. The number of seniors applying to medical school has risen in recent years and is now between forty and forty-five applicants annually. Historically, the school has an 80-85 percent acceptance rate, but that number includes non-MD graduate programs in the health professions. Recent graduates have landed at top medical schools including Columbia University Vagelos College of Physicians and Surgeons, Emory University School of Medicine, Geisel School of Medicine at Dartmouth, and Georgetown University School of Medicine.

Admission

Applicants to the Rochester Institute of Technology benefit from a fairly generous acceptance rate that is typically in the mid-to-high 50-percent range. Students apply to individual colleges within the larger university, and standards vary from program to program. For example, 2018-19 freshmen in the Saunders College of Business had mid-50 percent standardized test scores of 1170-1340 on the SAT and 26-31 on the ACT. Successful College of Engineering applicants had similar ranges of 1190-1350 on the SAT and 25-31 on the ACT. The highest achieving group were freshmen in the Golisano College of Computing and Information Sciences who scored 1380-1450 on the SAT and 29-34 on the ACT. Across all schools and majors the average entering GPA was 3.7; two-fifths placed in the top decile of their high school class, nearly three-quarters were in the top quartile, and all but 5 percent ranked in the top half.

This admissions committee looks, first and foremost, for applicants who engaged in a rigorous high school course load and achieved a solid mix of A's and B's. The four factors that make-up the second tier of admissions considerations are standardized test scores, class rank, recommendations, and the essay. It is important to note that the school is now test-optional, but only for applicants to the College of Liberal Arts. Roughly 1,300 apply via early decision, and RIT rewards their pledge of loyalty with a 66 percent ED acceptance rate. For the level of excellence at this institution, the Rochester Institute of Technology continues to have rather unintimidating admissions standards. While average test scores have risen in recent years, some of that can be attributed to SAT score inflation. The acceptance rate and general academic expectations for entry have remained steady over the past decade.

Worth Your Money?

Yes. That's the short answer for anyone coming to RIT to study engineering or computer science. The school keeps the sticker price reasonable, by market standards, at a bit over $45k for tuition and under $60k total cost of attendance. Over three-quarters of attending students receive some level of need-based aid and, even for families in the upper income brackets, the total COA annually comes out in the mid-$30k range. Those coming for liberal arts, business, or an art and design degree would have to weigh RIT's offer against their other options to find the most sensible deal.

FINANCIAL
Institutional Type: Private
In-State Tuition: $45,244
Out-of-State Tuition: $45,244
Room & Board: $13,540
Required Fees: $646
Books & Supplies: $2,082

Avg. Need-Based Aid: $29,475
Avg. % of Need Met: 87%

Avg. Merit-Based Aid: $11,700
% Receiving Merit-Based Aid: 14%

Avg. Cumulative Debt: $41,202
% of Students Borrowing: 75%

CAREER
Who Recruits
1. General Electric
2. Google
3. Microsoft
4. Intel
5. IBM

Notable Internships
1. GE Aviation
2. Electronic Arts
3. L.L. Bean

Top Industries
1. Engineering
2. Business
3. Operations
4. Information Technology
5. Arts & Design

Top Employers
1. Xerox
2. Paychex
3. IBM
4. Microsoft
5. Apple

Where Alumni Work
1. Rochester, NY
2. New York City
3. Boston
4. Washington, DC
5. San Francisco

Median Earnings
College Scorecard (Early Career): $62,400
EOP (Early Career): $62,400
PayScale (Mid-Career): $106,600

RANKINGS
Forbes: 337
Money: 369
U.S. News: 104 (T), National Universities
Wall Street Journal/THE: 153 (T)
Washington Monthly: 219, National Universities

#CollegesWorthYourMoney

Rose-Hulman Institute of Technology

Terre Haute, Indiana | Admissions Phone: 812-877-8213

ADMISSION
Admission Rate: 68%
Admission Rate - Men: 66%
Admission Rate - Women: 76%
EA Admission Rate: 84%
ED Admission Rate: Not Offered
Admission Rate (5-Year Trend): +12%
ED Admission Rate (5-Year Trend): Not Offered
% of Admits Attending (Yield): 16%
Transfer Admission Rate: 54%

Offered Wait List: 357
Accepted Wait List: 137
Admitted Wait List: 50

SAT Reading/Writing (Middle 50%): 610-700
SAT Math (Middle 50%): 660-780
ACT Composite (Middle 50%): 28-33
Testing Policy: ACT/SAT Required
SAT Superscore: Yes
ACT Superscore: Yes

% Graduated in Top 10% of HS Class: 64%
% Graduated in Top 25% of HS Class: 93%
% Graduated in Top 50% of HS Class: 100%

ENROLLMENT
Total Undergraduate Enrollment: 2,085
% Part-Time: 1%
% Male: 75%
% Female: 25%
% Out-of-State: 65%
% Fraternity: 37%
% Sorority: 26%
% On-Campus (Freshman): 98%
% On-Campus (All Undergraduate): 55%

% African-American: 3%
% Asian: 6%
% Hispanic: 5%
% White: 65%
% Other: 5%
% Race or Ethnicity Unknown: 1%
% International: 15%
% Low-Income: 17%

ACADEMICS
Student-to-Faculty Ratio: 11:1
% of Classes Under 20: 54%
% of Classes Under 40: 100%
% Full-Time Faculty: 96%
% Full-Time Faculty w/ Terminal Degree: 98%

Top Programs
Biomedical Engineering
Chemical Engineering
Civil Engineering
Computer Science
Electrical Engineering
Mechanical Engineering

Retention Rate: 92%
4-Year Graduation Rate: 67%
6-Year Graduation Rate: 81%

Curricular Flexibility: Less Flexible
Academic Rating: ★★★★

Inside the Classroom

When searching for the top engineering schools you naturally encounter a number of prestigious, doctoral-granting research universities like Stanford, MIT, UC Berkeley, and Carnegie Mellon. When looking for small engineering schools, Caltech and Harvey Mudd are typically the easiest ones to locate. Likely off your radar is a small private college in Terra Haute, Indiana, that, year after year, tops the charts among engineering schools whose highest degree is a master's. The Rose-Hulman Institute of Technology offers only nineteen undergraduate degree programs to 2,200 students, mostly from the Midwest, but they go on to phenomenal postgraduate successes.

Operating on the quarter system, courses are swift and rigorous, and pretty much everything you learn will be related to your major. Engineering students (the bulk of the student body) dive right in as first-semester freshmen by taking a heavy dose of math, science, and introductory engineering courses. The whole first year of study has room for only two electives in the realm of rhetoric/composition, the humanities, or social sciences. Foreign language is not among the requirements at this institution.

A student-to-faculty ratio of 11:1 and a minimal presence of graduate students bodes well for both class sizes and having introductory classes that are taught by full-time faculty members. The average class size is twenty, and 54 percent of sections are smaller than that. Giant lecture halls simply don't exist at Rose-Hulman as only two sections of 457 contained greater than forty students. Undergraduate research is commonplace at this school and can be arranged through the Independent Project/Research Opportunities Program that connects you to faculty mentors and sets you on the path toward presenting your work at the End-of-Quarter Symposium. Ten-week summer research apprenticeships also are available. International opportunities can be procured through the Global E3, a consortium of sixty engineering schools of which Rose-Hulman is a member, or through participation in Engineers without Borders. This is a rare institute of technology that pushes its students to pursue an international experience; it even hosts an annual Study Abroad Fair as part of those efforts.

The engineering major accounts for 79 percent of all degrees conferred, and there's a good reason for its popularity; this program is viewed among the best by prospective employers and graduate schools, and not just in the Midwest. Rose-Hulman's reputation for excellence in engineering stretches from Silicon Valley to the East Coast. Unique undergraduate engineering programs include optical engineering and international computer science; CS, in general, is the second-most popular degree program (13 percent).

Outside the Classroom

Even more than your average STEM-focused school, the gender disparity is significant to the tune of a 75/25 split favoring males. (The school didn't become coed until 1995.) Greek life at Rose-Hulman is booming with 37 percent of men joining fraternities and 26 percent of women involved with the school's sororities. All but a handful of freshmen live on campus (it is a requirement). And 55 percent of the total undergraduate student body lives in one of ten dormitories or apartment complexes. Despite its small size, the school still fields twenty NCAA Division III sports teams, the Fightin' Engineers, who compete in the Heartland Collegiate Athletic Conference. That translates to a full quarter of the student body participating in varsity athletics. There are also ninety clubs, including a popular student newspaper, radio station, and film club plus plenty of intramural sports such as archery, ballroom dancing, scuba, and yoga. The general social hub on campus is the Mussallem Unio, with well-reviewed cuisine, a giant Connect Four board, and a lakefront view—what more can you ask for? Rose-Hulman is set on a 1,300-acre property, but the majority of campus is confined to a 200-acre tract. Terra Haute isn't exactly Midtown Manhattan, but it's not that far from a number of major Midwestern destinations with trips to Indianapolis, Chicago, Louisville, Cincinnati, or St. Louis doable on a weekend.

Career Services

The Career Services and Employer Relations Office at Rose-Hulman consists of five professional employees, which computes to a student-to-advisor ratio of 440:1, in the average range compared to other schools featured in this guide. However, it is notable that this career services office puts "employer relations" right in its own title, and the statistics in that area prove that this inclusion is more than warranted.

A stunning 894 companies participated in events hosted by career services or had contact with students that was facilitated by career services staff in the last academic year. As a school of 2,200+ undergraduates, that figure is absurdly good. In total, 1,392 interviews were conducted by companies on campus, also a ridiculously strong number when you consider there were fewer than 500 seniors. Historically, 94 percent of seniors have had at least one opportunity for experiential learning via undergraduate research, co-op placement (50+ companies participate in the school's co-op program), or an internship. Three career fairs held annually in the fall, winter, and spring are extremely well attended by students as well as major hiring organizations. The fall 2018 fair drew a school record 251 companies, some of which conducted on-the-spot interviews with students. In short, thanks to the vast network of employers connected to this career services office, Rose-Hulman job-seekers are not the hunters but the hunted.

Rose-Hulman Institute of Technology

E-mail: admissions@rose-hulman.edu | Website: www.rose-hulman.edu

Professional Outcomes

Of the 487 graduates who strutted the stage in 2018, an enviable 98 percent had landed at their next destination, whether employment or graduate school, within six months of exiting. Further, students in ten of the school's programs enjoyed a 100 percent success rate. Top employers of Class of 2018 graduates included Boston Scientific, Cook Group, Texas Instruments, Caterpillar, Honeywell, Raytheon, and Rolls Royce. Raytheon, Microsoft, and Indianapolis-based pharmaceutical giant Eli Lilly also have a strong representation of Rose-Hulman-affiliated employees. The average first-year salary for a Rose-Hulman grad is just shy of $70,000, and some members of the Class of 2018 took home a not-too-shabby $120,000 in first-year wages. The majority of alumni remain in Indiana with Indianapolis and Terra Haute being the two favorite destinations. Smaller pockets of graduates can be found in Chicago, Cincinnati, San Francisco, and Seattle.

Fifteen percent of the Class of 2018 (74 students) enrolled in graduate school directly out of undergrad. They entered thirty-five universities, including many of the world's most distinguished such as Johns Hopkins, Carnegie Mellon, Duke, Northwestern, Washington University in St. Louis, Georgia Tech, Cornell, Notre Dame, and Rice University. Two 2018 graduates matriculated into medical school, and one 2017 graduate was on the path to becoming a medical doctor. No one from the previous two classes decided to attend law school. Clearly, and not surprisingly, the records demonstrate that students come to Rose-Hulman to enter technology/engineering fields.

Admission

Rose-Hulman's acceptance rate for membership in the Class of 2022 was an unimposing 68 percent. Compare that to other premier institutes of technology with phenomenal job placement rates and starting salaries and you might breathe a sigh of relief. Of course, the applicant pool is a self-selecting group with an affinity for STEM learning, and that leads to an impressive freshman class academic profile. The Class of 2022 had a mid-50 percent SAT range of 1270-1480 and ACT range of 28-33. Sixty-four percent of 2018-19 freshmen earned a place in the top 10 percent of their high school class while 93 percent were in the top quartile. Nearly four-fifths of students had a GPA over 3.75, and only 6 percent had under a 3.5. Suddenly, that sigh of relief feels like a distant memory. Interestingly, the school does accept a lower percentage of applicants in some cycles. Only a few years ago, the acceptance rate was under 60 percent as rates can fluctuate quite a bit at a school with a small applicant pool of under 4,500 students.

Rigor of secondary coursework and grades are the two most important factors for admission followed by standardized test scores, class rank, recommendations, and extracurricular activities. The acceptance rate for female applicants is 76 percent compared to the rate for males of 66 percent. This schools offers multiple early action application deadlines but no binding early decision option. In the admissions office's own words, successful applicants are "typically at the top of their high school graduating classes with scores in the 95th percentile on the SAT or ACT – plus they have taken a lot of high school science, math and English."

Worth Your Money?

This is a rare case where an annual cost of attendance of $70,000 does little to derail the financial futures of the student population. Freshmen receiving need-based aid net an average annual award of more than $30,000; average merit aid packages for those eligible neared $12,000. Even without financial aid, Rose-Hulman is definitely worth the private school cost thanks to phenomenal placement rates at top companies and extremely high starting salaries, even by STEM standards.

FINANCIAL
Institutional Type: Private
In-State Tuition: $46,641
Out-of-State Tuition: $46,641
Room & Board: $14,766
Required Fees: $930
Books & Supplies: $1,500

Avg. Need-Based Aid: $30,676
Avg. % of Need Met: 65%

Avg. Merit-Based Aid: $11,737
% Receiving Merit-Based Aid: 81%

Avg. Cumulative Debt: $43,459
% of Students Borrowing: 58%

CAREER
Who Recruits
1. Archer Daniels Midland
2. Whirlpool
3. Allegant Air
4. Kinze Manufacturing
5. Ingredion Incorporated

Notable Internships
1. Rolls-Royce
2. Halliburton
3. Tesla

Top Industries
1. Engineering
2. Operations
3. Business
4. Information Technology
5. Education

Top Employers
1. Eli Lily and Company
2. Cummins Inc.
3. Rolls-Royce
4. Caterpillar Inc.
5. Google

Where Alumni Work
1. Indianapolis
2. Terra Haute, IN
3. Chicago
4. Cincinnati
5. San Francisco

Median Earnings
College Scorecard (Early Career): $80,900
EOP (Early Career): $83,600
PayScale (Mid-Career): $135,800

RANKINGS
Forbes: 110
Money: 336
U.S. News: N/A
Wall Street Journal/THE: 103
Washington Monthly: N/A

#CollegesWorthYourMoney

Piscataway, New Jersey | Admissions Phone: 732-445-4636

ADMISSION
Admission Rate: 60%
Admission Rate - Men: 60%
Admission Rate - Women: 60%
EA Admission Rate: N/A
ED Admission Rate: Not Offered
Admission Rate (5-Year Trend): +1%
ED Admission Rate (5-Year Trend): Not Offered
% of Admits Attending (Yield): 28%
Transfer Admission Rate: 55%

Offered Wait List: N/A
Accepted Wait List: N/A
Admitted Wait List: N/A

SAT Reading/Writing (Middle 50%): 590-680
SAT Math (Middle 50%): 600-730
ACT Composite (Middle 50%): 25-31
Testing Policy: ACT/SAT Required
SAT Superscore: Yes
ACT Superscore: Yes

% Graduated in Top 10% of HS Class: 38%
% Graduated in Top 25% of HS Class: 72%
% Graduated in Top 50% of HS Class: 95%

ENROLLMENT
Total Undergraduate Enrollment: 36,039
% Part-Time: 6%
% Male: 50%
% Female: 50%
% Out-of-State: 6%
% Fraternity: N/A
% Sorority: N/A
% On-Campus (Freshman): 84%
% On-Campus (All Undergraduate): 43%

% African-American: 7%
% Asian: 27%
% Hispanic: 13%
% White: 38%
% Other: 4%
% Race or Ethnicity Unknown: 2%
% International: 9%
% Low-Income: 30%

ACADEMICS
Student-to-Faculty Ratio: 16:1
% of Classes Under 20: 42%
% of Classes Under 40: 73%
% Full-Time Faculty: 50%
% Full-Time Faculty w/ Terminal Degree: 99%

Top Programs
Accounting
Computer Science
Criminal Justice
English
History
Public Health
Supply Chain Management

Retention Rate: 93%
4-Year Graduation Rate: 61%
6-Year Graduation Rate: 80%

Curricular Flexibility: Somewhat Flexible
Academic Rating: ★★★

Inside the Classroom
Rutgers-New Brunswick, the flagship campus of the school's three locations (Camden and Newark being the others), is one of the oldest universities in the country. Founded in 1766 as one of nine colleges in Colonial America, the New Brunswick campus today is a top state research university that is home to more than 36,000 undergraduates. Garden State residents comprise 83 percent of the student body, but there has been a push in recent years to attract more out-of-staters, partially for monetary reasons. Presently, there are representatives of all fifty states and 115 countries on campus as the number of nonresidents increases each year. No matter where you're from, you'll enjoy the benefits of Rutgers massive operation that is divided into seventeen schools and colleges, collectively offering one hundred+ undergraduate majors.

Core requirements are variable across different programs, but members of the School of Arts & Sciences, by far the university's largest college, have a ten- to fourteen-course core. Mandates include fulfilling coursework in areas such as diversities and inequalities, our common future, natural sciences, social and historical analysis, arts and humanities, writing and communication, and quantitative and formal reasoning. In the School of Engineering, first-year coursework will look quite different as students must conquer courses that include General Chemistry for Engineers, Calculus, Analytical Physics, and Introduction to Computers for Engineers; non-STEM coursework is minimal for engineering students. A host of first-year initiatives, including Byrne Seminars and First Year Interest Group Seminars, leads to a freshman retention rate of 93 percent, a tremendous achievement for a public university.

Impressive for a school its size and scope, Rutgers boasts a 13:1 student-to-faculty ratio. As a result, it can offer a reasonable number of smaller, seminar-style courses to undergraduates. Thirty-nine percent of class sections have an enrollment of nineteen or fewer students compared to only 21 percent of sections that contain more than fifty undergrads. Rutgers offers 180 study abroad programs in fifty countries, but few take advantage; the participation rate is a paltry 2 percent. Undergraduate research, on the other hand, attracts more takers. The Aresty Research Center serves as a clearinghouse that matches undergraduates with faculty members conducting research in an area of interest; there are presently 1,500 faculty partners. An annual Undergraduate Research Symposium has showcased thousands of student projects in its fifteen+ years of existence.

The areas of study in which the greatest number of degrees are conferred are business (17 percent), engineering (11 percent), health professions (10 percent), biology (9 percent), social sciences (8 percent), and computer science (8 percent). Rutgers Business School sends many majors to top Wall Street investment banks, and programs in computer science, public health, and criminal justice have a terrific national reputation. Competitive scholarship and fellowship organizations also show lots of love to Scarlet Knights. Students and alumni received twenty-three Fulbright Scholarships in 2019 to go with three Goldwater Scholarships, two Schwarzman Scholarships, a Gates-Cambridge Scholarship, and a Truman Scholarship.

Outside the Classroom
Rutgers-New Brunswick's sprawling 2,685-acre campus is divided into five distinct, interconnected campuses. Despite one of the largest undergraduate housing operations of any school in the United States, only 43 percent of students (roughly 16,000) live on campus in one of 136 residence hall buildings or university-owned apartment complexes. The Greek scene is on the rise at Rutgers as the school now has over 3,800 members of eighty+ fraternities and sororities, all of which are located off campus. The Scarlet Knights compete in NCAA Division I athletics in ten men's and fourteen women's sports. Highpoint.com Stadium is the only Division I football stadium in the NY/NJ region, but it rarely fills its 52,000-seat capacity. Rutgers students would rather play sports than watch them as a member of one of fifty-seven club teams or fifty intramural leagues. The school's five fitness and recreation centers attract more than 5,000 visitors per day; ten outdoor fields and parks also are available for student use. There are also 500+ student-run organizations, including a top-ranked Model UN team and the Rutgers University Dance Marathon that raised over one million dollars for pediatric illnesses in 2019 alone. The Zimmerli Art Museum houses one of the top collegiate collections around, and there are plenty of live musical and theatrical acts that visit campus. Rutgers' excellent location makes weekend trips to Philly, New York, or the Jersey Shore a painless one-hour car ride.

Career Services
Thirty-seven professional employees staff the Rutgers University Career Services (UCS) Office in areas such as career exploration, career development, and employer relations. The university's overall student-to-counselor ratio of 973:1 is higher than the average school featured in this guidebook, but not alarmingly so when compared to other large public universities. Despite the monumental task of connecting with more than 36,000 students, the UCS has made some inroads as it currently interacts, in some form, with 56 percent of the student population each year. In 2017, the office saw a 90 percent increase in first-year student contact as it aims to connect with more freshmen. In 2018-19, the UCS conducted 4,817 one-on-one advising appointments.

There are plenty of large-scale offerings designed to benefit the student population. Career fair attendance is solid with 3,400 students connecting with 300 companies in the fall and 4,700 engaging with 265 employers in the spring. Another 641 unique employers visited career fairs in 2018-19. There were more than 3,400 on-campus interviews conducted with Rutgers seniors that same year. The CareerKnight online database of job and internship opportunities receives hundreds of thousands of annual hits. The Road to Wall Street mentoring program led to over 90 percent of participants landing competitive summer internships; the overall internship completion rate for graduates is an estimated 28 percent. Job search boot camps draw solid reviews as 100 percent of attendees said they have a better awareness of the next steps in the process as a result of attending. With 352,000 living alumni, there is always a Scarlet Knight networking opportunity in your field of interest. Roughly two-fifths of graduates say that the Rutgers UCS contributed to their career success.

Professional Outcomes

Upon graduation, 80 percent of Rutgers students have their next stop, whether it's a first job or graduate school, squared away. Three-fifths of the Class of 2018 were headed directly to the world of employment where the companies hiring the largest number of grads included Amazon, Johnson & Johnson, L'Oréal, and JP Morgan Chase. Investment banks like Goldman Sachs and Citi also employ hundreds of alumni. More than 300 current employees of Verizon, Bristol- Meyers Squibb, Novartis, Amazon, Pfizer, and Google also have Scarlet Knight lineage. The median starting salary across all majors was $52,500. The median starting salary for engineering majors was $65,000 while arts and sciences grads brought home $47,500. The bulk of graduates, approximately 75 percent, end up settling in New Jersey/the Greater New York area. Philadelphia, DC, and San Francisco are next in popularity.

One-fifth of the 2018 graduating class matriculated into full-time graduate or professional school. The most frequently attended universities were Rutgers, NYU, Columbia, and fellow Jersey institution Rowan University. Of the 483 graduates of the Class of 2018 who applied to medical school, 52 percent gained acceptance, a bit above the national average. Those sporting a 3.7 GPA or higher were even more successful, gaining acceptance at a 75 percent clip. Ninety-one of those accepted matriculated into one of Rutgers' two medical colleges. Rowan University's Cooper Medical School and School of Osteopathic Medicine were by far the most commonly attended institutions. Prestigious acceptances included Duke, Georgetown, Cornell, UVA, and Stanford. Future lawyers also end up in droves at Rutgers own highly reputable law school as well as at Villanova, Penn, Fordham, and Notre Dame.

Admission

Unlike at so many other premier flagship universities around the nation, the acceptance rate at Rutgers-New Brunswick has not plummeted in recent years. Those seeking entry into the Class of 2022 were given the thumbs up 59 percent of the time. Still, the quality of the applicant pool has risen dramatically over the 2000s. Freshmen entering Rutgers' School of Arts & Sciences in the 2018-19 school year had mid-50 percent standardized test scores of 1270-1430 on the SAT, 26-33 on the ACT, and a weighted GPA of 3.6-4.1. Right around two-fifths of current students placed in the top 10 percent of their high school class, and three-quarters landed in the top 25 percent. Five years ago, the acceptance rate at the university was a comparable 61 percent, but the SAT range was a far lower 1040-1290.

The factors deemed most important by the admissions committee are GPA, standardized test scores, and rigor of secondary curriculum. Extracurricular involvement is the lone category dubbed "important," and factors like state residency, essays, class rank, first-generation status, and volunteer work are "considered." Rutgers does offer an early action deadline of November 1, but no binding early decision plan is available. An average in the B+/A- range and standardized test scores in the 85th percentile put you firmly in play for an invitation to attend the New Brunswick campus right out of high school. Otherwise, a start at the Camden or Newark campus may be the only option. Out-of-state applicants may find slightly more relaxed admission standards, given the university's push to recruit applicants from outside New Jersey.

Worth Your Money?

Rutgers doesn't have the endowment to meet anything close to your full level of financial need, but it does award grants averaging $13,025 to 54 percent of current undergraduates. The school, however, is more generous with merit aid than your average public university, giving one-fifth of students an annual award close to $12k. The in-state cost of attendance is $32,443, which is not a bad deal for a flagship public school in the Northeastern United States. Out-of-state students would pay close to $49k per year COA, which would be a curious move for students not receiving aid, given the likelihood that better deals would be available.

FINANCIAL
Institutional Type: Public
In-State Tuition: $12,230
Out-of-State Tuition: $29,012
Room & Board: $13,075
Required Fees: $3,177
Books & Supplies: $1,350

Avg. Need-Based Aid: $13,025
Avg. % of Need Met: 55%

Avg. Merit-Based Aid: $11,734
% Receiving Merit-Based Aid: 20%

Avg. Cumulative Debt: $34,113
% of Students Borrowing: 60%

CAREER
Who Recruits
1. Aerotek
2. Automatic Data
3. Enterprise Holdings
4. Insight Global
5. Robert Half

Notable Internships
1. Colgate-Palmolive
2. NBCUniversal
3. New York Giants

Top Industries
1. Business
2. Education
3. Operations
4. Healthcare
5. Sales

Top Employers
1. Johnson & Johnson
2. Verizon
3. Bristol-Myers Squibb
4. JPMorgan Chase
5. Novartis

Where Alumni Work
1. New York City
2. Philadelphia
3. Washington, DC
4. San Francisco
5. Boston

Median Earnings
College Scorecard (Early Career): $57,900
EOP (Early Career): $58,400
PayScale (Mid-Career): $111,000

RANKINGS
Forbes: 123
Money: 50
U.S. News: 62, National Universities
Wall Street Journal/THE: 130
Washington Monthly: 39, National Universities

#CollegesWorthYourMoney

San Diego State University

San Diego, California | Admissions Phone: 619-594-6336

ADMISSION
Admission Rate: 34%
Admission Rate - Men: 33%
Admission Rate - Women: 35%
EA Admission Rate: Not Offered
ED Admission Rate: Not Offered
Admission Rate (5-Year Trend): -3%
ED Admission Rate (5-Year Trend): Not Offered
% of Admits Attending (Yield): 24%
Transfer Admission Rate: 20%

Offered Wait List: 2,853
Accepted Wait List: 1,276
Admitted Wait List: 46

SAT Reading/Writing (Middle 50%): 560-650
SAT Math (Middle 50%): 550-660
ACT Composite (Middle 50%): 22-28
Testing Policy: ACT/SAT Required
SAT Superscore: Yes
ACT Superscore: Yes

% Graduated in Top 10% of HS Class: 29%
% Graduated in Top 25% of HS Class: 68%
% Graduated in Top 50% of HS Class: 93%

ENROLLMENT
Total Undergraduate Enrollment: 30,393
% Part-Time: 10%
% Male: 45%
% Female: 55%
% Out-of-State: 11%
% Fraternity: 11%
% Sorority: 13%
% On-Campus (Freshman): 72%
% On-Campus (All Undergraduate): 19%

% African-American: 4%
% Asian: 13%
% Hispanic: 31%
% White: 33%
% Other: 7%
% Race or Ethnicity Unknown: 4%
% International: 7%
% Low-Income: 35%

ACADEMICS
Student-to-Faculty Ratio: 25:1
% of Classes Under 20: 28%
% of Classes Under 40: 70%
% Full-Time Faculty: 49%
% Full-Time Faculty w/ Terminal Degree: 88%

Top Programs
Art
Communication
Criminal Justice
International Business
Kinesiology
Psychology

Retention Rate: 89%
4-Year Graduation Rate: 37%
6-Year Graduation Rate: 75%

Curricular Flexibility: Less Flexible
Academic Rating: ★★★

Inside the Classroom

They say that a rising tide lifts all boats. As the University of California system has become ultra-competitive over the past decade, the California State University system has seen many of its schools become beneficiaries of an overflow of uber-qualified applicants. San Diego State University, offering a highly affordable education in a gorgeous and temperate setting, is one such institution. A diverse school of over 30,000 undergraduates, one-third of its students are Hispanic, and roughly the same percentage are first-generation students. Most hail from the Golden State, but 7 percent of the population are international students representing one of 114 countries. Don't be scared off by the low acceptance rate (34 percent); you don't need straight A's in high school to gain access to this excellent research university that boasts nearly 160 undergraduate majors, minors, and pre-professional programs.

The general education requirements at SDSU are the breadth portion of one's education experience and will comprise approximately one-third of an undergraduate's time at the university. Forty-nine units are required, including nine units of communications and critical thinking courses; thirty-one units of foundational study in the humanities; social and behavioral sciences; and natural sciences and quantitative reasoning; and nine units in "explorations" that are upper-division courses you cannot begin until junior year. After completing sixty credits, all students must take and pass a writing placement assessment. Some majors require you to learn a language other than English while some, like engineering, do not. Lastly, there is a mandated course called American Institutions in which you must demonstrate your knowledge of California government, the US Constitution, and American history.

Like many other schools in the California State University system, cheap tuition and heavy enrollment leads to a high student-to-faculty ratio. San Diego State sports a 25:1 ratio and, consequently, classes tend to be on the large side. Thirty percent of course sections enroll more than forty students, and only 28 percent of sections contain fewer than twenty students. To help connect students to faculty mentors and undergraduate research opportunities, the school maintains a useful database of current professors seeking assistance. Summer research programs and an annual Undergraduate Research Symposium provide additional experiences in that realm. In 2018, a solid 33 percent of grads reported studying abroad. In total, 3,000 SDSU students take a semester outside of the United States each year.

Business/marketing accounts for 22 percent of the degrees conferred, making it the school's most popular area of study. Next in line are the social sciences (10 percent), engineering (8 percent), health professions (8 percent), psychology (7 percent), and parks and recreation (7 percent). You won't find the engineering or computer science programs at the top of any rankings lists, but that doesn't have much of an impact on employment, thanks to the booming local tech and startup scene. Because of its emphasis on international study, many graduates go on to win fellowships that take them all around the globe. SDSU has had as many as nine Fulbright award winners in recent years, and it often has multiple recipients of Boren, Critical Language, and Gilman Scholarships. SDSU also has had several undergraduates receive National Science Foundation Graduate Research Fellowships over the last few years.

Outside the Classroom

On-campus housing is limited, and preference is given to freshmen who take advantage at a 72 percent clip. Overall, only 19 percent of undergraduates reside in university-owned housing. However, there is plenty to bond the student body and create cohesion on campus. Eleven percent of men and 13 percent of women belong to the university's fifty+ fraternities and sororities. In addition to Greek life, annual campus-wide events like AzFest and Homecoming Weekend unify the 30,000+ undergrads, as do basketball and football games. The Aztecs field nineteen NCAA Division I sports teams, and famous alumni athletes include Marshall Faulk (NFL), Tony Gwynn (MLB), and 2019 NBA Finals MVP Kawhi Leonard. There are 350+ student organizations including KCR College Radio that has a long history and large listenership, intramural sports that draw thousands of participants, and the Aztec Unity Project that is committed to local community service projects. Viejas Arena, where the Aztecs play basketball, doubles as a major concert venue drawing acts like the Chainsmokers, the Foo Fighters, and Drake—basically a major act every week. San Diego weather, sunsets, and seventeen miles of coastline are all free benefits of attending SDSU. Additionally, there are multiple beaches less than ten miles from campus. The Aquaplex is, essentially, a free resort on campus for student use. It features two outdoor pools and a twenty-person spa; such is life at San Diego State.

Career Services

The main San Diego State Career Services Office employs nineteen full-time professional staff members (not counting administrative assistants) working as internship coordinators, career counselors, employer outreach specialists, and experiential learning specialists. There are an additional four staff members working out of the Fowler College of Business, bringing the campus-wide total to twenty-three, which works out to a 1,304:1 student-to-counselor ratio, poorer than the average school profiled in this book.

SDSU offers four large-scale career fairs in the fall semester and another four fairs in the spring semester. One hundred ten employers attend the Fall 2018 Career and Internship Fair, and the Nonprofit and Education Career Fair in the spring draws thirty employers. In addition, the Graduate & Professional School Fair draws representative from ninety+ institutions. A solid 49 percent of Class of 2018 graduates reported completing at least one internship. Workshops are offered on a regular basis on useful topics such as Applying for Federal Jobs, Personal Branding Using Social Media, and Planning for Graduate School. Career counselors specialize in a variety of fields and encourage fifty-minute one-on-one career exploration sessions or fifteen-minute walk-in appointments. The Aztec Mentor Program connects juniors and seniors to alumni in their fields of interest for a minimum of eight hours of mentorship. In sum, programmatic offerings by SDSU's Career Services Office are impressive, but they do not publicize statistics on how many counseling sessions take place or how many on-campus interviews with employers occur each year.

Professional Outcomes

At the time of receiving their degrees, 72 percent of newly-minted 2018 SDSU graduates already had their next phase of life planned. Thirty-four percent of that group had secured full-time employment, 21 percent were engaged in military service/volunteer work/part-time employment, and 17 percent were entering graduate or professional school. The mean reported salary for those offered full-time employment was $53,000. Qualcomm and Apple are the two largest employers of Aztec alumni, and they are followed by LPL Financial, Amazon, Intuit, Google, ServiceNow (cloud computing), Microsoft, Facebook, Salesforce, and Robert Half. All of the most common geographic landing spots for alumni are within California borders; San Diego keeps a large chunk of grads while Los Angeles, San Francisco, and Orange County also have fairly strong representation.

In 2019, there were sixty-four SDSU graduates applying to medical school and, while the university lacks its own affiliated hospital/medical schools, many future physicians do remain in the state of California at universities like UC-San Diego, UC-Davis, UC-Riverside, UCLA, and Western University of Health Sciences; others move out of state to the University of Michigan, Tufts, and the University of South Carolina. Likewise, many law students remain in state at schools such as the University of San Diego School of Law, the Thomas Jefferson School of Law, Loyola Law School, Santa Clara School of Law, and UC-Davis. SDSU offers a pre-law society, mock trial team, and targeted pre-law advising to those considering a legal education.

Admission

Only 34 percent of the 69,043 applicants for a place in the Class of 2022 were accepted into the university; 24 percent of that group went on to enroll at SDSU. Despite the intimidating acceptance rate, there is plenty of room at this school for solid but less-than-perfect applicants as evidenced by the wide range of test scores and GPAs that are accepted. The mid-50 percent standardized test scores for 2018-19 freshmen were 1110-1310 on the SAT and 22-28 on the ACT. Twenty-nine percent of that cohort placed within the top 10 percent of their high school class, 68 percent were in the top quartile, and 93 percent landed in top half. While 54 percent of Class of 2022 members possessed a high school GPA of 3.75 or above, 21 percent earned under a 3.5. A decade ago, almost 30,000 fewer students applied, but the acceptance rate was similar. Yet, SAT scores were substantially lower, and less than half as many students held 3.75+ GPAs. The school's freshman class today is 1,500+ students larger than the freshman group of ten years ago.

The admissions committee needs to work quickly to sift through the deluge of applications it receives each year. As a result, it reviews standardized test scores, GPA, rigor of courses, state residency, and literally nothing else. Soft factors like essays, recommendations, and extracurricular activities play no role in the admissions process at San Diego State. There is no early action or early decision option at SDSU, but the admissions deadline is extremely early—everything must be completed by November 30. In spite of the low acceptance rate, students should be able to accurately gauge their odds given the relatively formulaic evaluation process. Those solidly in the middle of the wide ranges of standardized test scores can feel good about their chances.

Worth Your Money?

The process to qualify for out-of-state students to earn residency status has tightened in recent years, making it almost certain that international and non-California residents will pay roughly $42,000 per year total cost of attendance. In-state COA is estimated at $30,500, with only $7,500 of that figure covering basic tuition. Thus, those living at home or commuting can attend the university at an absurdly low cost. Like the other twenty-two schools in the California State University System, SDSU is affordable and, with its excellent ties to industry, job prospects for most graduates are bright.

FINANCIAL
Institutional Type: Public
In-State Tuition: $5,742
Out-of-State Tuition: $17,622
Room & Board: $17,752
Required Fees: $1,768
Books & Supplies: $1,969

Avg. Need-Based Aid: $10,300
Avg. % of Need Met: 68%

Avg. Merit-Based Aid: $3,500
% Receiving Merit-Based Aid: 25%

Avg. Cumulative Debt: $21,327
% of Students Borrowing: 45%

CAREER
Who Recruits
1. Bainbridge
2. Cox Communications
3. GoSite
4. ASML
5. Marriott International

Notable Internships
1. BAE Systems
2. Cushman & Wakefield
3. U.S. Senate

Top Industries
1. Business
2. Operations
3. Education
4. Sales
5. Engineering

Top Employers
1. Qualcomm
2. Apple
3. EY
4. Amazon
5. Intuit

Where Alumni Work
1. San Diego
2. Los Angeles
3. San Francisco
4. Orange County, CA
5. Germany

Median Earnings
College Scorecard (Early Career): $51,000
EOP (Early Career): $51,000
PayScale (Mid-Career): $102,800

RANKINGS
Forbes: 181
Money: 74
U.S. News: 147 (T), National Universities
Wall Street Journal/THE: 270 (T)
Washington Monthly: 144, National Universities

#CollegesWorthYourMoney

Santa Clara University

Santa Clara, California | Admissions Phone: 408-554-4700

ADMISSION
Admission Rate: 50%
Admission Rate - Men: 47%
Admission Rate - Women: 52%
EA Admission Rate: 63%
ED Admission Rate: 73%
Admission Rate (5-Year Trend): 0%
ED Admission Rate (5-Year Trend): +18%
% of Admits Attending (Yield): 17%
Transfer Admission Rate: 46%

\# Offered Wait List: 2,620
\# Accepted Wait List: 1,776
\# Admitted Wait List: 149

SAT Reading/Writing (Middle 50%): 630-700
SAT Math (Middle 50%): 640-740
ACT Composite (Middle 50%): 28-32
Testing Policy: ACT/SAT Required
SAT Superscore: Yes
ACT Superscore: Yes

% Graduated in Top 10% of HS Class: 49%
% Graduated in Top 25% of HS Class: 82%
% Graduated in Top 50% of HS Class: 97%

ENROLLMENT
Total Undergraduate Enrollment: 5,520
% Part-Time: 1%
% Male: 51%
% Female: 49%
% Out-of-State: 28%
% Fraternity: Not Offered
% Sorority: Not Offered
% On-Campus (Freshman): 96%
% On-Campus (All Undergraduate): 56%

% African-American: 3%
% Asian: 16%
% Hispanic: 18%
% White: 48%
% Other: 7%
% Race or Ethnicity Unknown: 2%
% International: 4%
% Low-Income: 12%

ACADEMICS
Student-to-Faculty Ratio: 10:1
% of Classes Under 20: 46%
% of Classes Under 40: 98%
% Full-Time Faculty: 62%
% Full-Time Faculty w/ Terminal Degree: 94%

Top Programs
Accounting
Bioengineering
Communication
Computer Science and Engineering
Finance
Public Health
Psychology

Retention Rate: 95%
4-Year Graduation Rate: 84%
6-Year Graduation Rate: 91%

Curricular Flexibility: Less Flexible
Academic Rating: ★★★★✓

Inside the Classroom
If you were asked to name a premier university in the heart of California's Silicon Valley, chances are your immediate answer would be Stanford. Yet, those who aren't likely to be among the 4.3 percent of accepted applicants at Stanford might want to turn their attention to the Valley's second most prestigious school, one that has over ten times the acceptance rate. Santa Clara University is a Jesuit school with a growing national reputation; right now, 73 percent of undergraduates still hail from California, and major tech firms love to recruit at this excellent institution located in their own backyard.

Students can pursue fifty degrees offered by three undergraduate colleges: the College of Arts & Sciences, the School of Engineering, and the Leavey School of Business. Santa Clara's core curriculum is designed to provide "a humanistic education that leads toward an informed, ethical engagement with the world." To accomplish that students must take (1) foundations courses in critical thinking and critical writing, cultures and ideas, a second language, mathematics, and religion, theology, and culture; (2) explorations courses in ethics, civic engagement, diversity, additional religion/theology courses, and all of the traditional prerequisites in the natural sciences, social sciences, and the arts; and (3) integrations courses in advanced writing, experiential learning for social justice, and a pathways class that requires students to make connections across disciplines. It's a tall order, involves a certain amount of religious study, and doesn't leave a ton of room for electives.

Santa Clara caters to 5,500 undergraduate students as well as another 3,100 graduate students but, thanks to a 10:1 student-to-faculty ratio, it keeps classes reasonably sized. While you won't find many single-digit enrollment seminars, 46 percent of course sections do contain fewer than twenty students. Undergraduate research opportunities are built into many academic programs, particularly in the sciences, and students can partner with willing professors for credited research study. In addition, study abroad opportunities are available on all six continents fit for human habitation, and more than 500 students take advantage each year.

The most commonly conferred degrees are in business (25 percent), engineering (17 percent) and the social sciences (14 percent). The Leavey School of Business offers highly ranked management information systems, accounting, and entrepreneurship degree programs. The engineering program is respected by employers, and computer science students fare extraordinarily well in the Silicon Valley job market, which happens to be one of the most competitive in the world. Graduates of SCU do not seek prestigious fellowships in droves, but many of those who do are successful. In 2018, seven grads/alumni procured Fulbright Scholarships, and one took home a Udall Scholarship; an alum even won a Rhodes Scholarship in 2017.

Outside the Classroom
The 106-acre campus houses only 56 percent of the undergraduate student body; however, 96 percent of first-years do reside in university-owned dorms. There are ten fraternities and six sororities at Santa Clara, and although none of them are affiliated with the university (they were dropped in 2001), Greek life still plays a significant social role. For a school of its size, athletics are surprisingly serious at SCU as the Broncos compete at the NCAA Division I level and field nineteen intercollegiate teams. Intramural sports draw an astonishing 3,800 participants every year on 500 teams in sports ranging from soccer to ping-pong. Almost every student is involved in at least one (if not two or three) of the 125 organizations presently operating. The Ruff Riders, a booster organization, is one of the largest groups of its kind with over 1,000 members. Into the Wild is another popular club that plans outdoor excursions to locations such as Big Sur, the beaches of Santa Cruz, and Lake Tahoe. World-class recreational facilities exist on campus for fitness enthusiasts such as the 45,000-square-foot Malley Fitness Center and the Sullivan Aquatic Center. The University's Silicon Valley location means that plenty of high-end cultural, dining, and entertainment options are at your fingertips, and San Francisco is only an hour away by car.

Career Services
Santa Clara's Career Center has seven full-time professional staff members working as career development specialists, employer relations specialists, and coordinators of experiential learning. The 786:1 student-to-advisor ratio is below average when compared with the other institutions featured in this guide. However, the center has many strengths, particularly its deep connections to major Silicon Valley companies. Each year, the Fall Career Fair draws many top employers (including tech companies) as well as over 1,000 undergraduates. Another STEM-specific fair in October brings in another 650 students in search of jobs. Across the school's six annual career fairs, 470 employers manned booths and spoke with SCU students.

Santa Clara University

E-mail: admission@scu.edu | Website: www.scu.edu

More than 6,000 employers recruit Santa Clara undergraduates through a mix of Career Center programs and the online job board available through the Handshake platform, and 65 percent of students utilize their account. Over 900 on-campus interviews take place each academic year. Recruiting companies include Disney, Tesla, Apple, Oracle, Cisco, Kaiser Permanente, and NBC Universal. Almost four-fifths of those completing an SCU degree completed at least one internship position during their time at the university. This school boasts an alumni network 100,000 strong, and many are willing to assist current students with finding their first job. Thanks to the strength of its employer recruiting efforts and internship program, SCU's Career Center gets high marks from our staff.

Professional Outcomes

Within six months of receiving their degrees, 83 percent of Santa Clara graduates have landed jobs, started graduate school, or committed to a full-time service program. Of those employed, the five most commonly entered industries are business development, engineering, education, entrepreneurship, and sales. The companies presently employing the greatest number of Bronco alumni are all tech giants including Cisco, Apple, Google, Oracle, Facebook, and Adobe. The median starting salary for all grads is $53,000 with engineering ($70k) and business majors ($60k) enjoying the highest compensation, and math/natural sciences grads on the low end ($38k). Roughly two-thirds of alumni remain in the Bay Area. Other West Coast destinations such as Los Angeles, Seattle, Portland, Sacramento, and San Diego also attract a fairly large number of grads.

Many graduates who continue their education at the master's or doctoral level do so at one of Santa Clara's own excellent grad programs; the same goes for law school. Over the last fifteen years, 90 percent of SCU medical school applicants with a minimum of MCAT score of 505 and a GPA of 3.5 or higher have been accepted by at least one institution. However, many fail to meet those criteria as only 40 percent of overall applicants in that period have been accepted, slightly lower than the national average. The three most frequently attended medical schools are fellow Jesuit institutions Creighton, Georgetown, and Loyola (Chicago). A look at where Class of 2017 and 2018 grads were pursuing additional education includes a wide range of schools that includes UCLA, Berkeley, USC, the University of Washington, and Duke University.

Admission

Growing in popularity, Santa Clara crossed the 16,000 application mark with the Class of 2022; that represented a 47 percent increase since 2009. A seemingly soft 49 percent of applicants were granted admission, but a glance at the profile of the average accepted applicant is more informative as to the school's level of selectivity. Successful applicants averaged an unweighted GPA of 3.8 and scores of 1407 on the SAT and 31 on the ACT. Notably, only 17 percent of admitted students went on to enroll in the freshman Class of 2018-19. Of those who actually enrolled in the university, the middle-50 percent SAT range was still a solid 1270-1440. Just a shade under 50 percent placed in the top decile of their high school class, and 82 percent finished in the top quartile.

The admissions committee ranks three categories as most important: rigor of secondary school record, GPA, and essays. The list of factors ranked as "important" is far longer and includes class rank, recommendations, standardized test scores, volunteer work, racial/ethnic status, first generation status, legacy status, and extracurricular activities. While the process can be viewed as holistic, the university does not offer an evaluative interview. Due to the aforementioned low yield rate of only 17 percent, Santa Clara is always happy to have strong applicants who are willing to commit to the school. As a result, a whopping 73 percent of early decision applicants gain admission. Santa Clara University is a school that is attracting more applicants every year as its national reputation climbs to new heights. A deceptively high acceptance rate does not do full justice to the caliber of undergraduate it currently attracts. Borderline candidates who have a strong desire to attend should definitely consider applying early decision.

Worth Your Money?

At almost $74,000 in total annual cost of attendance, Santa Clara is an expensive proposition any way you slice it. The university does dangle an average merit aid award of almost $16k to two-fifths of students to bring the price down a bit, but only 37 percent of all undergrads qualify for need-based grants that average close to $33,000. A Santa Clara degree won't come cheap, but that's okay for business and engineering students who will be heading to high-paying careers in Silicon Valley. Those intending to pursue majors in less immediately lucrative disciplines need to calculate whether the finances make sense for them to attend this school.

FINANCIAL
Institutional Type: Private
In-State Tuition: $52,998
Out-of-State Tuition: $52,998
Room & Board: $15,507
Required Fees: $636
Books & Supplies: $1,971

Avg. Need-Based Aid: $33,180
Avg. % of Need Met: 79%

Avg. Merit-Based Aid: $15,875
% Receiving Merit-Based Aid: 41%

Avg. Cumulative Debt: $25,640
% of Students Borrowing: 36%

CAREER
Who Recruits
1. Stryker Corporation
2. Gap Inc.
3. Tesla
4. Teach for America
5. Kiva

Notable Internships
1. McAfee
2. Yelp
3. Vera Wang

Top Industries
1. Business
2. Engineering
3. Education
4. Operations
5. Sales

Top Employers
1. Cisco
2. Apple
3. Google
4. Oracle
5. Facebook

Where Alumni Work
1. San Francisco
2. Los Angeles
3. Seattle
4. Sacramento
5. Portland, OR

Median Earnings
College Scorecard (Early Career): $72,600
EOP (Early Career): $72,500
PayScale (Mid-Career): $134,700

RANKINGS
Forbes: 51
Money: 144
U.S. News: 54 (T), National Universities
Wall Street Journal/THE: 87 (T)
Washington Monthly: 137, National Universities

#CollegesWorthYourMoney

Scripts College

Claremont, California | Admissions Phone: 909-621-8149

ADMISSION
Admission Rate: 24%
Admission Rate - Men: Not Offered
Admission Rate - Women: 24%
EA Admission Rate: Not Offered
ED Admission Rate: 32%
Admission Rate (5-Year Trend): -11%
ED Admission Rate (5-Year Trend): -20%
% of Admits Attending (Yield): 33%
Transfer Admission Rate: 16%

Offered Wait List: 780
Accepted Wait List: 388
Admitted Wait List: 4

SAT Reading/Writing (Middle 50%): 660-740
SAT Math (Middle 50%): 640-740
ACT Composite (Middle 50%): 30-33
Testing Policy: ACT/SAT Required
SAT Superscore: Yes
ACT Superscore: Yes

% Graduated in Top 10% of HS Class: 69%
% Graduated in Top 25% of HS Class: 98%
% Graduated in Top 50% of HS Class: 100%

ENROLLMENT
Total Undergraduate Enrollment: 1,048
% Part-Time: 1%
% Male: 0%
% Female: 100%
% Out-of-State: 55%
% Fraternity: Not Offered
% Sorority: Not Offered
% On-Campus (Freshman): 100%
% On-Campus (All Undergraduate): 94%

% African-American: 4%
% Asian: 17%
% Hispanic: 14%
% White: 53%
% Other: 5%
% Race or Ethnicity Unknown: 3%
% International: 5%
% Low-Income: 12%

ACADEMICS
Student-to-Faculty Ratio: 10:1
% of Classes Under 20: 77%
% of Classes Under 40: 100%
% Full-Time Faculty: 77%
% Full-Time Faculty w/ Terminal Degree: 99%

Top Programs
Area Studies
Art
Biology
English
Media Studies
Politics
Psychology

Retention Rate: 92%
4-Year Graduation Rate: 81%
6-Year Graduation Rate: 88%

Curricular Flexibility: Somewhat Flexible
Academic Rating: ★★★★✦

Inside the Classroom

While the East Coast is swarming with high-end women's colleges such as Wellesley, Smith, Bryn Mawr, Barnard, and Mt. Holyoke, there is only one such jewel resting closer to the Pacific Ocean. Scripps College, a member of the five-school Claremont Consortium, is the West Coast's lone elite all-female institution, making it a highly desirable destination for young women seeking a classic liberal arts education in a nurturing and supportive academic environment without the lonely, harsh winters of the Northeast.

There are sixty-five majors available to Scripps undergrads, including some that are accessible through membership in the Consortium. Curricular requirements at Scripps are extensive, requiring a three-semester dive into interdisciplinary humanities coursework that tackles the essential question of "What makes a community?" through a combination of lecture, seminar-style discussions, and a self-designed project. All undergraduates must demonstrate competency in mathematics, foreign language, and writing. Along the way, one course must be taken in each of the four divisions: fine arts, natural sciences, letters, and social sciences. Within one's major, a minimum of eight courses must be tackled, culminating in the completion of a senior thesis, which 100 percent of graduates must complete.

A 10:1 student to faculty ratio at a school with zero grad students breeds an intimate learning atmosphere where professors are genuinely dedicated to undergraduate learning. A lack of competitiveness should not be mistaken for a lack of rigor. Scripps is loaded with driven students, 28 percent of whom elect to double major. As part of the required senior thesis, many undergraduates also have the chance to assist professors with academic/scientific research. Due to the absence of graduate students who would gobble up such positions, research opportunities are readily available for credit during the academic year as well on a full-time basis during the summer; the Scripps Undergraduate Research Fellowship is one such program. Study abroad programs in forty countries are taken advantage of by nearly two-thirds of the student body, giving Scripps one of the highest participation rates of any college in the United States.

The top five majors are (in order) biology/life sciences; social sciences; psychology; area, ethnic, and gender studies; and visual/performing arts. Each possesses a very strong reputation. Regardless of your major, however, graduate/professional schools know that earning a degree from Scripps is no small achievement. Prestigious scholarship committees also look kindly upon the school as Scripps is regularly a top twenty-five producer of Fulbright winners, taking home an incredible (considering the size of the graduating class) nine awards in 2018. Two additional 2018 grads took home Watson Fellowships, and one was awarded a Davis Projects for Peace Fellowship.

Outside the Classroom

At Scripps, 96 percent of students live on the school's modestly sized 30-acre campus in one of eleven immaculately maintained dorms or in thematic housing options catering to those with goals and interests in common such as The Stem, Pre-Health Living Learning Community, and the Substance Free Community. There are no sororities at Scripps. Sports exist but are a combined effort with Harvey Mudd, and Claremont McKenna that, collectively, field eleven NCAA Division III teams. Fitness and recreational facilities are shared with Pitzer, Pomona, Harvey Mudd, and CMC. That means students have access to four swimming pools, four fitness centers, and a dozen playing fields. There are roughly thirty Scripps-only student-run organizations, but there are also more than 250 clubs that can be accessed by students of any of the five schools. One of the more notable social hubs is the Motley Coffeehouse, founded in 1974 and run entirely by Scripps students. In fact, the feminist, environmental, and social justice vibe makes its coffeehouse a perfect embodiment of the college's values and ethos. The college also boasts its own art museum, the Williamson Gallery, which contains works by many notable American artists. Of course, cultural options are hardly confined to the campus limits with Los Angeles only a forty-five minute car ride away.

Career Services

The Career Planning & Resources Office (CP&R) has four full-time professional staff members working as career counselors. Scripps' 267:1 student-to-advisor ratio is better than the average college featured in our guidebook. It may be a small office, but you won't find a more proactive group of counselors at any college in the country as the CP&R meets with 90 percent of freshmen within the students' first three weeks on campus. Larger events are typically joint affairs with the other esteemed members of the Claremont Consortium.

Scripps takes pride in its facilitation of student internships and has the stats to prove it; 86 percent of graduates held at least one internship, and close to one-quarter completed three or more. Internship locations of note include 20th Century Fox, the California Department of Justice, and the Smithsonian. Career Treks whisk Scripps students off to metropolitan areas around the country to meet with alumni who are working in the same field of interest. Former students are always willing to lend a hand to current ones and can connect with soon-to-be grads through the Alumni Book, a compilation of student resumes. A week-long Emerging Professionals Program featuring alumni, recruiters, and CP&R counselors can be accessed for free. The office also offers a Financial Literacy Program to teach undergraduates about everything from budgeting to investing to filing taxes.

Professional Outcomes

Women land jobs at some of the world's leading companies after receiving their diplomas. The top employers of Scripps alumni include Google, Kaiser Permanente, and Amazon. Many go on to work for universities, particularly after earning additional degrees (more on this in a moment). Schools employing significant numbers of Scripps alumni include Pomona, Scripps, Stanford, UCLA, and UC-San Diego. Recent graduates also have landed positions at BlackRock, CBS, Goldman Sachs, Facebook, and Pfizer. Median salaries by midcareer are quite a bit lower than fellow Consortium member schools Pomona and Claremont McKenna, but they are comparable to other elite women's colleges such as Bryn Mawr. Most Scripps alumni remain on the West Coast with the largest percentage in Los Angeles followed by San Francisco, Seattle, Portland, San Diego, and Orange County. The most popular East Coast destinations are New York City, DC, and Boston.

An advanced degree is in the cards for most Scripps grads, and it isn't usually too far in the future—two-thirds complete a graduate/professional program within five years of receiving their bachelor's degrees. Recent grads have pursued further study at institutions such as Caltech, Harvard, MIT, Vanderbilt, Oxford, Brown, Northwestern, and Tufts. Scripps knows what it's doing when it comes to premeds, thanks to its Post-Baccalaureate Premedical Program that boasts a 98 percent+ acceptance rate; traditional undergrads also fare well above the national average. Those eyeing law school also find favorable results; recent grads have been accepted at top-tier law schools such as Emory, Georgetown, the University of Chicago, Berkeley, and the University of Michigan.

Admission

Thirty-one percent of the 3,160 women who applied for a place in the Class of 2022 were accepted. One-third of the overall applicant pool went on to enroll. Freshmen in 2018-19 possessed a middle-50 percent score of 1300-1480 on the SAT and 30-33 on the ACT. An impressive 69 percent came from the top decile of their high school class; 98 percent placed in the top quarter. Over 80 percent sported a GPA of 3.75 or greater; 92 percent earned above a 3.5.

The admissions committee seeks "to build a community of curious and engaged students who are eager to contribute their diverse interests, backgrounds, and experiences to our academic and residential community." As such, they weight nine factors as being "very important" to admissions decisions: rigor of coursework, GPA, test scores, class rank recommendations, essays, extracurricular activities, talent/ability, and character/personal qualities. Applying early decision at Scripps does yield an edge; 32 percent of ED applicants were accepted into the Class of 2022 versus 24 percent of regular round applicants. Those accepted in the early round comprised 36 percent of the incoming freshman class. Scripps has become more competitive as the 2000s have marched on. A decade ago, the acceptance rate was a healthier 43 percent, and average SAT/ACT scores were a bit lower. The West Coast's highest-ranked women's college is looking for students with not only strong academic credentials but a solid extracurricular resume.

Worth Your Money?

At almost $74,000 the sticker price cost of attendance for Scripps College is undoubtedly on the high side. However, the 38 percent of undergraduates who are determined eligible for need-based aid all see 100 percent of their need met; the average grant is for $40k. Additionally, 15 percent of students do receive a merit aid package that averages $22k. Of course, you would never want to go into six figures worth of debt in order to obtain an undergraduate degree, but if attending Scripps is financially feasible for your family, the quality of the educational experience and networks/resources offered by the Consortium make this school worth some level of sacrifice.

FINANCIAL
Institutional Type: Private
In-State Tuition: $54,806
Out-of-State Tuition: $54,806
Room & Board: $16,932
Required Fees: $218
Books & Supplies: $800

Avg. Need-Based Aid: $39,735
Avg. % of Need Met: 100%

Avg. Merit-Based Aid: $22,131
% Receiving Merit-Based Aid: 15%

Avg. Cumulative Debt: $17,756
% of Students Borrowing: 34%

CAREER
Who Recruits
1. DaVita
2. Nielsen
3. Pfizer
4. Nordstrom
5. Brancart & Brancart

Notable Internships
1. ALCU
2. Louis Vuitton
3. KPMG

Top Industries
1. Education
2. Business
3. Social Services
4. Media
5. Research

Top Employers
1. Google
2. Kaiser Permanente
3. Amazon
4. Microsoft
5. Seattle Children's

Where Alumni Work
1. Los Angeles
2. San Francisco
3. Seattle
4. New York City
5. Portland, OR

Median Earnings
College Scorecard (Early Career): $54,100
EOP (Early Career): $46,400
PayScale (Mid-Career): $98,600

RANKINGS
Forbes: 60
Money: 308
U.S. News: 33, Liberal Arts Colleges
Wall Street Journal/THE: 65
Washington Monthly: 97, Liberal Arts Colleges

#CollegesWorthYourMoney

Sewanee – The University of the South

Sewanee, Tennessee | Admissions Phone: 931-598-1238

ADMISSION
Admission Rate: 65%
Admission Rate - Men: 65%
Admission Rate - Women: 66%
EA Admission Rate: 83%
ED Admission Rate: 86%
Admission Rate (5-Year Trend): +5%
ED Admission Rate (5-Year Trend): +12%
% of Admits Attending (Yield): 21%
Transfer Admission Rate: 70%

Offered Wait List: 513
Accepted Wait List: 101
Admitted Wait List: 9

SAT Reading/Writing (Middle 50%): 610-700
SAT Math (Middle 50%): 590-690
ACT Composite (Middle 50%): 25-31
Testing Policy: Test Optional
SAT Superscore: Yes
ACT Superscore: Yes

% Graduated in Top 10% of HS Class: 30%
% Graduated in Top 25% of HS Class: 61%
% Graduated in Top 50% of HS Class: 92%

ENROLLMENT
Total Undergraduate Enrollment: 1,698
% Part-Time: 1%
% Male: 49%
% Female: 51%
% Out-of-State: 78%
% Fraternity: 56%
% Sorority: 64%
% On-Campus (Freshman): 100%
% On-Campus (All Undergraduate): 99%

% African-American: 5%
% Asian: 2%
% Hispanic: 5%
% White: 81%
% Other: 3%
% Race or Ethnicity Unknown: 0%
% International: 4%
% Low-Income: 20%

ACADEMICS
Student-to-Faculty Ratio: 10:1
% of Classes Under 20: 60%
% of Classes Under 40: 99%
% Full-Time Faculty: 71%
% Full-Time Faculty w/ Terminal Degree: 95%

Top Programs
Biology
Economics
English
Environment & Sustainability
History
International & Global Studies
Politics

Retention Rate: 89%
4-Year Graduation Rate: 78%
6-Year Graduation Rate: 84%

Curricular Flexibility: Somewhat Flexible
Academic Rating: ★★★✦

Inside the Classroom

People flying over the historic campus of the University of the South, sometimes referred to as "Sewanee" might, in a moment of panic, fret that they had accidentally hopped aboard an international flight and were passing directly over Oxford or Cambridge. This breathtaking campus that includes 13,000 acres of natural beauty known affectionately as "The Domain" is situated on Tennessee's Cumberland Plateau. The pretty packaging is not misleading; the University of the South delivers a powerful academic punch, and it isn't quite as picky as many other top schools as to who gets to step into the ring. While designated a "university," Sewanee is really more of a liberal arts college of approximately 1,700 undergrads and fewer than one hundred graduate students.

Offering thirty-six majors and forty-three minors, undergrads are exposed to a wide scope of liberal arts study, no matter their area of concentration. All students must complete a designated writing-intensive course by the end of their sophomore year as well as coursework fulfilling six "learning objectives." Literary analysis, understanding the arts, and seeking meaning require one course each while multiple classes are required in exploring past and present, the scientific and quantitative view, and language and global studies. Two physical education and wellness classes also must be tackled prior to graduation.

A 10:1 student-to-faculty ratio and a limited number of grad students means that undergraduate teaching remains the primary focus at Sewanee. The average class size is seventeen students, and 99+ percent of course sections have an enrollment under thirty. Opportunities to conduct research with faculty members are not only plentiful, they are often funded by the university. Recent students have collaborated on fascinating research projects on topics such as Adolescent Substance use Perception in Southern Appalachia; Synthesis of New, More Effective Anti-Cancer Metallopharmaceuticals; and Corporate Political Contributions and Stock Returns. Study abroad options that are a summer, a semester, or a full year in length are embarked upon by roughly half of all Sewanee students. European Studies and British Studies are two of the most popular global programs offered by the college.

The degrees most commonly conferred are in biology, economics, English, history, international and global studies, and environment studies. All are strong, but Sewanee's English Department has a leading national reputation. Thanks to the Tennessee Williams Writers-in-Residence program, accomplished authors from around the globe come to teach at Sewanee, and English majors routinely continue their studies at the likes of Princeton, Yale, Duke, and the University of Chicago. The school has also historically had success in helping its students procure the most distinguished graduate fellowships. Sewanee was named a top producer of Fulbright Scholars with four winners in 2018 alone, and forty-seven students have claimed Watson Scholarships since they were first made available in 1968. Incredibly, the school claims twenty-six Rhodes Scholars in its history, more than Amherst, the University of Pennsylvania, or Georgetown.

Outside the Classroom

Just about the entire student body, 98.5 percent to be precise, live in the dorms or in other on-campus housing. Greek life is extremely popular at Sewanee as the eleven fraternities and ten sororities attract an overwhelming 80 percent of undergraduates in rushing. When it's all said and done, 64 percent of women and 56 percent of men end up Greek affiliated. Involvement in some type of sport is also common. Eleven men's and thirteen women's Division III athletic teams are joined by 30 percent of the student population. Another eight club teams and plenty of intramural sessions draw many more. More than ninety student-run organizations are active with the most popular being the Student Government Association, the Order of Gown (focusing on campus spirit and traditions), and the Student Activity Board. If climbing, caving, hiking, biking, or canoeing is more your style, then the Sewanee Outing Program (SOP) is a must-join organization. In addition to taking outdoorsy road trips, the SOP also takes full advantage of the pristine beauty of the aforementioned Domain. With Chattanooga only an hour away and Nashville an hour-and-a-half car ride from campus, Sewanee students can access big-city fun on the weekends.

Career Services

The Career and Leadership Development Office (CLD) employs five full-time staff members, four of whom are titled director or assistant director, yet all work directly in counseling undergraduates. That equates to a student-to-staff ratio of 351:1, in the average range compared to the other institutions included in this book. The CLD does manage to reach 97 percent of students by the time they graduate, and a hard-to-beat 99 percent report being satisfied by the guidance they receive. Events such as the annual Graduate and Professional School Fair draws reps from more than thirty-five programs including Tulane, Vanderbilt, and UGA's law schools, Wake Forest's MBA program, and Emory's School of Theology. An annual Beyond the Gates event sees close to fifty alumni from all walks of professional life spend a weekend mentoring current juniors and seniors as they ready themselves for the job search.

Sewanee – The University of the South

E-mail: admiss@sewanee.edu | Website: www.sewanee.edu

Via the Sewanee Pledge, the university guarantees funding for one unpaid internship or research experience for every single student. Each year, more than 200 such stipends are granted for unpaid internships alone. Over 150 Sewanee-exclusive internship opportunities are posted each year, creating a favorable environment for students to gain the inside track on desirable opportunities. Recent students have interned at *Style Magazine*, Accenture, the World Wildlife Fund, and US Forest Service. The CLD at the University of the South, thanks to a high level of connection and personalized counseling, succeeds in assisting the bulk of graduates reach their next destination.

Professional Outcomes

Within six months of their commencement ceremony, 98 percent of Sewanee grads have found some form of employment or have begun their graduate studies. Three-quarters have obtained full-time employment with the most popular sectors being business/finance/consulting (37 percent), arts/entertainment/sports/media/publishing (10 percent), government/politics/policy/law (10 percent), health care/medicine/research (10 percent), education (9 percent), and environment/sustainability/natural resources (7 percent). Organizations employing recent graduates include Booz Allen Hamilton, Sony Pictures, Warby Parker, BlackRock, and Massachusetts General Hospital. The largest number of total alumni can be found at Wells Fargo, Deloitte, Regions Bank, and Vanderbilt University Medical Center. Median income by midcareer is an unspectacular $47k, comparable to the figures at Colorado College, Smith, or Grinnell. Many alumni remain in the South after graduation as Nashville, Atlanta, and Chattanooga are the most frequent destinations. However, DC and New York City also contain large pockets of grads.

The majority of those in the Class of 2018 who pursued advanced degrees entered master's programs (36) followed by law school (10), medical school (8), and PhD programs (6). Elite graduate school acceptances included Johns Hopkins, Georgetown, Vanderbilt, Washington University in St. Louis, and the University of Michigan. Law schools attended included the University of North Carolina, University of Arkansas, NYU, and Samford University. Medical school acceptances in the last several years included East Carolina University and the University of Texas.

Admission

Sewanee is a rare top school that, even in 2020, still lacks a menacing acceptance rate—its 53.9 percent is about as friendly as you will find among top colleges. The entering Class of 2022 held strong academic credentials, sporting middle-50 percent standardized test scores of 1250-1390 on the SAT and 27-32 on the ACT, which is submitted by the majority of applicants, and an average high school GPA of 3.74. You don't need to be at the top of your high school class to gain admittance as only 30 percent placed in the top decile and 61 percent in the top quartile. The school's selectivity level is similar to that of a full decade ago.

A test-optional school, the University of the South places a strong emphasis on the rigor of one's secondary school record, GPA, and recommendations. Second billing is granted to the application essay, extracurricular activities, character/personal qualities, volunteer work, and work experience. A relatively low yield rate of 21 percent means that almost four-fifths of those accepted enroll elsewhere. While the university does not rank demonstrated interest as an important factor in admissions decisions, the committee certainly appreciates those who apply via binding early decision. In fact, 86 percent of those applying ED are accepted. A fine and distinctive education can be yours at this exceptionally beautiful Tennessee campus without the typical crucible of admissions-related stress found at many of the schools featured in this book. Students with strong but not outstanding resumes are welcomed through this holistic-minded and test-optional admissions process.

Worth Your Money?

The overall cost of attendance of $62,290 is high, but it is not an exorbitant sticker price in the world of small liberal arts schools. This is particularly true since three-fifths of undergrads qualify for an average merit aid award of almost $20k. Forty-seven percent of undergrads qualify for an average need-based award of $29,262, but only 32 percent of those who qualify for aid see 100 percent of their need met. If your family has limited funds (like most), you'll want to see how much merit and need-based aid you are awarded before making a decision on whether Sewanee is the right choice for your wallet.

FINANCIAL
Institutional Type: Private
In-State Tuition: $46,200
Out-of-State Tuition: $46,200
Room & Board: $13,268
Required Fees: $272
Books & Supplies: $1,200

Avg. Need-Based Aid: $29,262
Avg. % of Need Met: 83%

Avg. Merit-Based Aid: $19,708
% Receiving Merit-Based Aid: 60%

Avg. Cumulative Debt: $28,976
% of Students Borrowing: 43%

CAREER
Who Recruits
1. Springbot
2. JumpCrew
3. Showtime Networks
4. Accenture
5. Harris Williams & Co.

Notable Internships
1. UBS
2. Wells Fargo
3. U.S. Senate

Top Industries
1. Business
2. Education
3. Social Services
4. Operations
5. Sales

Top Employers
1. Wells Fargo
2. Regions Bank
3. CBRE
4. Deloitte
5. Capital One

Where Alumni Work
1. Nashville
2. Atlanta
3. Chattanooga, TN
4. Washington, DC
5. New York City

Median Earnings
College Scorecard (Early Career): $45,500
EOP (Early Career): $46,600
PayScale (Mid-Career): $97,800

RANKINGS
Forbes: 154
Money: 388
U.S. News: 43, Liberal Arts Colleges
Wall Street Journal/THE: 141 (T)
Washington Monthly: 99, Liberal Arts Colleges

#CollegesWorthYourMoney

Skidmore College

Saratoga Springs, New York | Admissions Phone: 518-580-5570

ADMISSION

Admission Rate: 27%
Admission Rate - Men: 27%
Admission Rate - Women: 27%
EA Admission Rate: Not Offered
ED Admission Rate: 51%
Admission Rate (5-Year Trend): -8%
ED Admission Rate (5-Year Trend): -17%
% of Admits Attending (Yield): 23%
Transfer Admission Rate: 42%

Offered Wait List: 2,459
Accepted Wait List: 486
Admitted Wait List: 137

SAT Reading/Writing (Middle 50%): 610-700
SAT Math (Middle 50%): 610-700
ACT Composite (Middle 50%): 27-31
Testing Policy: Test Optional
SAT Superscore: Yes
ACT Superscore: No

% Graduated in Top 10% of HS Class: 38%
% Graduated in Top 25% of HS Class: 78%
% Graduated in Top 50% of HS Class: 96%

ENROLLMENT

Total Undergraduate Enrollment: 2,612
% Part-Time: 1%
% Male: 39%
% Female: 61%
% Out-of-State: 65%
% Fraternity: Not Offered
% Sorority: Not Offered
% On-Campus (Freshman): 100%
% On-Campus (All Undergraduate): 90%

% African-American: 5%
% Asian: 5%
% Hispanic: 9%
% White: 62%
% Other: 5%
% Race or Ethnicity Unknown: 2%
% International: 12%
% Low-Income: 13%

ACADEMICS

Student-to-Faculty Ratio: 8:1
% of Classes Under 20: 75%
% of Classes Under 40: 99%
% Full-Time Faculty: 74%
% Full-Time Faculty w/ Terminal Degree: 88%

Top Programs
Anthropology
Art
Business
English
History
Human Physiological Sciences
Theater

Retention Rate: 91%
4-Year Graduation Rate: 82%
6-Year Graduation Rate: 86%

Curricular Flexibility: Somewhat Flexible
Academic Rating: ★★★✦

Inside the Classroom

Founded as a women's college at the turn of the twentieth century, Skidmore still serves more women than men today, but going co-ed isn't the most notable shift that has occurred at this private liberal arts college in Upstate New York. The school's 2,500 undergrads, affectionately known as "Skiddies," have become an increasingly higher-achieving lot as the school has transformed from selective to highly selective over the past decade. What has remained is its reputation as a free-spirited student body and extremely accessible and student-friendly faculty that have long defined Skidmore.

An undergraduate-only institution, there are forty-three majors to choose from with the most popular being business, English, psychology, political science, economics, studio art, theater, biology, and environmental studies. All students begin by completing a first-year experience that is highlighted by participation in the Scribner Seminars where students begin to grasp the level of rigor that will be expected as they launch their collegiate studies. Foundations courses include Applied Quantitative Reasoning, Global Cultural Perspectives, Language Study, and Writing. Inquiry courses include Artistic Inquiry through Practice, Humanistic Inquiry and Practice, and Scientific Inquiry through Practice. It's hard to earn a diploma without completing some type of a culminating project; 75 percent complete a senior capstone, 53 percent engage in independent study, and 32 percent produce a senior thesis or advanced research project.

With no graduate students around to suck up professorial attention, undergrads reap the full benefits of the school's student-faculty ratio of 8-to-1. Skidmore's average class size is only sixteen students, and 94 percent of sections have fewer than thirty students. Over one-quarter of sections enroll only single digits. Each year roughly 500 students, 20 percent of the student body, engage in research with a faculty mentor, including eighty students who participate in the Summer Student-Faculty Research Program. Internships and service-learning courses are a normal part of the Skidmore experience. Three-fifths of students study abroad at one of 120 programs in forty-five countries, a rate of participation that places it at the very top in the nation.

Known for its superior undergraduate teaching, a Skidmore degree will carry enough prestige to open doors to top employers and graduate schools, particularly in the aforementioned areas that are among the most popular majors. The school produces a surprisingly modest number of competitive postgraduate scholars and fellows. Many years it produces a finalist for a National Science Foundation, Goldwater, or Mitchell Scholarship, but it does not consistently take home the big prizes.

Outside the Classroom

Approximately 90 percent of students reside in one of Skidmore's eight residence halls, which are split evenly on a North and a South campus spread over 1,000 enchanting acres. The only Greek life at Skidmore can be found in courses in the classics; there are no frats or sororities in the "Skidmore bubble." An almost 60/40 split along gender lines in favor of women certainly has an impact on social life. There are 120 active student-run clubs and nineteen Division III varsity sports teams (10 women's and 9 men's) nicknamed the Thoroughbreds. There are plenty of club sports and intramural leagues for less serious competitors. Amenities are first-class, from the apartment-style dorms to the award-winning dining services to the 150-acre North Woods oasis that can be used for anything from meditation to skiing. Saratoga Springs is a small city of 30,000, but its funky downtown is only a ten-minute walk from campus. Skidmore is located thirty minutes from Albany and three full hours from popular road trip destinations like New York City, Boston, and Montreal. Those seeking more nature-oriented recreation can easily travel to the Berkshires, Adirondacks, or Green Mountains.

Career Services

The Career Development Center (CDC) at Skidmore College is staffed by eight professionals with counseling expertise in a variety of fields. That works out to a 333:1 student-to-advisor ratio that is solidly in the average range compared to other institutions in this guidebook. The CDC hosts an annual networking event called Career Jam that was attended by 219 students and seventy-four alumni, parents, and employers in 2017. The annual Graduate and Professional School Expo attracts representatives from roughly forty-five universities to Skidmore. Students also can travel off campus to corporate destinations along the East Coast as part of the Road Trips to the Real World program.

In the 2017-18 academic year the CDC conducted 2,081 one-on-one counseling sessions, brought seventy-four employers to Saratoga Springs for recruiting purposes, and facilitated 323 on-campus interviews. An impressive 274 employers attend the college's job fairs. Nearly 85 percent of students participate in an internship during their time at Skidmore, and many are funded by the school. Students nab intriguing internships at places such as Tesla, *The Daily Show with Trevor Noah*, the NBA, *Esquire Magazine*, and Memorial Sloan Kettering Cancer Center. The career services staff encourages individual meetings as early as freshman year in its effort to support "all students and alumni through the creative process of integrating their liberal arts education and experiences into a satisfying career." Skidmore's CDC boasts strong internship numbers; however, with 10 percent of grads still seeking employment six months after graduation, there is room for improvement.

Professional Outcomes

Three-quarters of 2018 Skidmore grads were employed within six months of completing their degrees, 14 percent were enrolled in graduate school, and 10 percent were still seeking employment. The most frequently entered industries were arts, audio/visual technology, and communications (15 percent); education and training (14 percent); STEM (13 percent); business (11 percent); and marketing, sales, and service (10 percent). The median starting salary range for Class of 2018 grads was $40,000-$49,999. Intriguing employers included the Metropolitan Opera, Penguin Random House, NBC Universal, Estee Lauder, and Vineyard Vines. Fairly large numbers of Skiddies can be found at major corporations including Google, Morgan Stanley, EY, Amazon, JPMorgan Chase, Fidelity Investments, and IBM. The greatest concentration of alumni can be found in Greater New York City with Boston, Albany, San Francisco, and Washington, DC, the next most popular landing spots.

Graduate acceptances procured by the Class of 2018 included Ivies like Harvard, Cornell, Dartmouth, and Columbia as well as other elite institutions like Johns Hopkins, Tufts, and NYU. Skidmore students are accepted to medical school at a rate "far above the national average." Many recent med school-bound grads have attended NY-based schools like SUNY Upstate, SUNY Stony Brook, or the University of Buffalo. Class of 2017 and 2018 members matriculated into law schools at Duke, Penn State, and the University of Miami.

Admission

For 2018-19 freshman hopefuls, only 27 percent were accepted (24.5 percent were accepted the previous year), and the average SAT was 1250-1380; a dozen years ago, 39 percent of applicants got in. It is important to note that Skidmore adopted a test-optional policy in 2016 that has led to a spike in applications. Among enrolled freshman, 48 percent submitted SAT scores, and another 27 percent submitted ACT scores, so the majority of accepted applicants are not going the test-optional route. Many students, but far from all, rank near the top of their graduating high school classes; 38 percent of members of the Class of 2022 placed in the top decile, and 78 percent earned a spot in the top quartile.

In the eyes of the admissions office the rigor of secondary coursework is the only factor that rises to "most important" status. From there, class rank, GPA, essays, recommendations, extracurricular activities, talent/ability, character/personal qualities, work experience, volunteer work, and demonstrated interest are on equal footing as "important" factors. As a test-optional school, SATs and ACTs are relegated to "considered" status. In the most recent admissions cycle the acceptance rate for early decision applicants was 51 percent compared to 25 percent in the regular cycle, and ED students made up 53 percent of the freshman class. A more competitive school than in the recent past, those set on Skidmore definitely should consider applying ED and should at least go out of their way to demonstrate serious interest in the college. While test-optional, strong standardized test scores can still help you win over the admissions committee.

Worth Your Money?

Need-based grants averaging $46,400 are awarded to 42 percent of undergraduates at Skidmore. That helps defray the $71,480 in total costs each year for those with genuine financial need. Unfortunately, merit aid is only made available to 2.8 percent of the undergraduate population; thus, you are unlikely to get a significant tuition discount unless you qualify for a grant. If your parents can afford Skidmore, it is a wonderful place to spend four years learning and growing. On the other hand, we would not recommend taking on large amounts of debt in order to study theater, English, studio art, or any other popular but typically low-paying major without a clear postgraduate career and financial plan.

FINANCIAL
Institutional Type: Private
In-State Tuition: $53,258
Out-of-State Tuition: $53,258
Room & Board: $14,494
Required Fees: $1,162
Books & Supplies: $1,300

Avg. Need-Based Aid: $46,400
Avg. % of Need Met: 100%

Avg. Merit-Based Aid: $15,000
% Receiving Merit-Based Aid: 3%

Avg. Cumulative Debt: $24,987
% of Students Borrowing: 42%

CAREER
Who Recruits
1. New England Center for Children
2. M&T Bank
3. EY
4. NYS Department of Health
5. Carney Sandoe & Associates

Notable Internships
1. Scholastic
2. WHYY
3. Airbnb

Top Industries
1. Business
2. Education
3. Arts and Design
4. Operations
5. Media

Top Employers
1. Morgan Stanley
2. EY
3. JPMorgan Chase
4. Google
5. Fidelity Investments

Where Alumni Work
1. New York City
2. Boston
3. Albany, NY
4. San Francisco
5. Washington, DC

Median Earnings
College Scorecard (Early Career): $49,700
EOP (Early Career): $47,500
PayScale (Mid-Career): $99,700

RANKINGS
Forbes: 101
Money: 167
U.S. News: 39, Liberal Arts Colleges
Wall Street Journal/THE: 93 (T)
Washington Monthly: 83, Liberal Arts Colleges

#CollegesWorthYourMoney

Smith College

Northampton, Massachusetts | Admissions Phone: 413-585-2500

Inside the Classroom

You will not find a more wide-open curriculum or liberal/progressive ethos at any women's school in the country than that of Smith College; only a few coeducational institutions—perhaps Vassar or Wesleyan—can go toe-to-toe with Smith on both fronts. Its list of alumnae supports that claim with Gloria Steinem, Julia Child, and Sylvia Plath all being Smith grads (Nancy Reagan was the ideological oddball). From a Seven Sisters admissions standpoint, Smith is more selective than Mt. Holyoke but less selective than Wellesley, Bryn Mawr, or Barnard. A member of the Five College Consortium, students can cross-enroll at Mt. Holyoke, UMass, Amherst, and Hampshire. In addition to the forty-five academic departments and programs and 1,000 courses offered each academic year at Smith, an additional 4,000 courses can be accessed at partner universities.

Smith's seven major fields of knowledge are literature, historical studies, social science, natural science, mathematics and analytical philosophy, the arts, and foreign language. Forays into each are "recommended," but the only nonnegotiable requirement is one writing-intensive course in the first or second semester of the freshman year. Otherwise, graduation requirements dictate that sixty-four credits must be taken outside of one's major. What that distribution looks like is entirely up to you. Young women seeking the ultimate level of undergraduate academic freedom will adore the Smith experience.

There are 290 professors at Smith, translating to a student-faculty ratio of 9:1. With only a small number of graduate students to worry about, 22 percent of undergraduate sections have single-digit enrollments, and 70 percent of total class sections enroll fewer than twenty students. Each summer, eighty Smithies spend their time working side-by-side with a professor on a research project. Around 40 percent of undergrads spend a semester abroad in one of a hundred programs on six continents, including some programs taught in the native tongue for those proficient in a foreign language.

The social sciences are most popular at Smith, accounting for 22 percent of the degrees conferred, with programs in economics and government carrying very strong reputations. Next in line is biology (11 percent), psychology (8 percent), foreign language (7 percent), and engineering (6 percent). Thanks to a strong decade-long push toward increasing the number of women studying such fields as engineering, mathematics, and the hard sciences, greater than two-fifths of current students are majoring in a STEM field. Smith is also the Fulbright Scholarship capital of the world producing an awe-inspiring 188 winners in the past dozen years. Recent students also have captured Goldwater and Udall Scholarships as well as National Science Foundation Graduate Research Fellowships.

Outside the Classroom

Every freshman, and 95 percent of the total undergraduate population, lives in college-owned housing. There are thirty-seven self-governing houses, each with its own dining hall, that accommodate between ten and one hundred students; most have a mix of freshmen through seniors. No sororities operate at this school. Smith offers eleven varsity sports that compete in NCAA Division III as well as extensive intramural and club sports programs that include oddities like Quidditch and Futsal. The Outing Club is a popular way to enjoy the area's natural beauty through hikes, canoeing trips, and rock-climbing adventures. Approximately 120 student-run organizations are available with a wide selection of cultural groups, political and student government groups, and community service clubs. Each year 200+ volunteers dedicate 10,000+ hours of community service through the Jandon Center for Community Engagement. Smith's membership in the Five College Consortium leads to additional social and extracurricular opportunities on the campuses of Mt. Holyoke, UMass, Amherst, and Hampshire. Culture and relaxation can be found on campus at the Smith College Museum of Art or the school's own botanical garden. The town of Northampton is two hours west of Boston and features plenty of restaurants and an artsy vibe that meshes well with this particular college community.

Career Services

The Lazarus Center for Career Development at Smith is staffed by ten professionals, including six career advisors and internship and employer relations specialists. The 245:1 student-to-advisor ratio is better than the average school featured in this guidebook. For a small school, it puts on a fairly large Fall Career Fair that draws eighty+ companies and graduate schools. It also organizes the Spring Life Sciences, Technology & Engineering Fair that attracts thirty+ employers. In addition, Smith partners with MIT and UMass Amherst to offer access to additional off-site career fairs. Membership in the Selective Liberal Arts Consortium affords the women of Smith chances to participate in interview days with major corporations in Washington, DC, and New York City.

ADMISSION
Admission Rate: 31%
Admission Rate - Men: Not Offered
Admission Rate - Women: 31%
EA Admission Rate: Not Offered
ED Admission Rate: 49%
Admission Rate (5-Year Trend): -12%
ED Admission Rate (5-Year Trend): +2%
% of Admits Attending (Yield): 34%
Transfer Admission Rate: 33%

\# Offered Wait List: 923
\# Accepted Wait List: 458
\# Admitted Wait List: 68

SAT Reading/Writing (Middle 50%): 670-750
SAT Math (Middle 50%): 670-770
ACT Composite (Middle 50%): 31-34
Testing Policy: Test Optional
SAT Superscore: Yes
ACT Superscore: Yes

% Graduated in Top 10% of HS Class: 72%
% Graduated in Top 25% of HS Class: 96%
% Graduated in Top 50% of HS Class: 100%

ENROLLMENT
Total Undergraduate Enrollment: 2,502
% Part-Time: 0%
% Male: 0%
% Female: 100%
% Out-of-State: 81%
% Fraternity: Not Offered
% Sorority: Not Offered
% On-Campus (Freshman): 100%
% On-Campus (All Undergraduate): 95%

% African-American: 7%
% Asian: 9%
% Hispanic: 12%
% White: 48%
% Other: 5%
% Race or Ethnicity Unknown: 6%
% International: 14%
% Low-Income: 21%

ACADEMICS
Student-to-Faculty Ratio: 8:1
% of Classes Under 20: 70%
% of Classes Under 40: 94%
% Full-Time Faculty: 94%
% Full-Time Faculty w/ Terminal Degree: 98%

Top Programs
Area Studies
Biology
Education & Child Study
Economics
Engineering
Government
Psychology
Sociology

Retention Rate: 93%
4-Year Graduation Rate: 83%
6-Year Graduation Rate: 89%

Curricular Flexibility: Very Flexible
Academic Rating: ★★★★✔

Last year, 176 companies recruited on campus, an exceptional figure for a small liberal arts school. More than 6,600 job and internship opportunities are posted each year on Handshake. Praxis grants of up to $3,500 are awarded to roughly 400 undergraduates per year to pursue unpaid internships. Current students also benefit from the network of 48,000 alumnae spread across 120 countries who are known for being generous with their time and offers of mentorship. While the school's starting salary numbers leave something to be desired, the Lazarus Center for Career Development excels in employer relations, procurement of prestigious scholarships, and offers ample individualized attention for those who seek it.

Professional Outcomes

Two years after graduating 91 percent of Smith alumnae have found employment, and 42 percent have begun their graduate studies. More than twenty-five alumnae can be found at the US Department of State, Google, IBM, Johnson & Johnson, Accenture, Fidelity Investments, Deloitte, Microsoft, JPMorgan Chase, and Amazon. Many Smith women rise to high ranks within their respective organizations and corporations. Twenty years after graduation, 10 percent of alumnae report holding a chief executive position, and an additional 8 percent are stationed in other executive-level positions. Median career incomes are on the lower side compared to other elite schools and are comparable to those of Mt. Holyoke. Surprising given its locale, Boston is only the second-most popular destination for grads. New York City is number one with Springfield (Massachusetts), San Francisco, and DC also toward the top of the list.

Within ten years of receiving their bachelor's degrees more than three-quarters of Smith grads have earned or are working toward an advanced degree. The five most frequently attended graduate schools are Columbia, NYU, Harvard, Smith itself, and Boston University. Medical and law school acceptance rates are strong. Smith undergrads with a 3.3 GPA and a minimum of 507 on the MCAT were accepted into medical school at an 87 percent clip. The law school acceptance rate is consistently over 80 percent.

Admission

In seeking a place in the Class of 2022, almost 5,800 hopefuls applied to Smith; 31 percent were accepted, and 34 percent of that group ultimately enrolled. The college went test-optional a full decade ago, but 43 percent of the 2018-19 freshman class submitted SAT scores, and an additional 30 percent included ACT results as part of their applications. The mid-50 percent ranges on those exams were a 1340-1510 on the SAT and 31-34 on the ACT. Seventy-two percent of freshmen earned a spot in the top 10 percent of their high school class, and 96 percent placed in the top 25 percent; the average GPA was 3.98. Five years ago, 43 percent of women who applied were accepted at Smith, and the standardized test score range was a much lower 1220-1450 on the SAT and 28-31 on the ACT.

As stated by the committee, "Most applications are read by two members of the admission staff, and every part of your folder reveals another facet of your life." That holistic review places the greatest emphasis on five factors: rigor of coursework, GPA, recommendations, essays, and character/personal qualities. The second rung of important factors are class rank, an interview, extracurriculars, and talent/ability. Those applying through the early decision round received a boost to their admissions prospects to the tune of a 49 percent acceptance rate. Further, ED applicants accounted for 47 percent of the incoming freshman class. While not at the selectivity level of Wellesley or Barnard, Smith College has become increasingly more difficult to gain acceptance into in recent years. A sparkling high school transcript is nonnegotiable, and showing commitment through submitting an early decision application is recommended for borderline applicants who have Smith as their clear first choice.

Worth Your Money?

With a cost of attendance of $74,618, a Smith degree won't come cheap for those who do not qualify for institutional aid. The good news is that 61 percent of undergraduates do, indeed, qualify for need-based grants that average almost $50,000 annually. Merit aid awards are harder to come by and, when given, are only for a fraction of the need-based grants. Smith students have superb graduate/professional school and employment outcomes, making this school a solid choice for anyone who can afford it.

FINANCIAL
Institutional Type: Private
In-State Tuition: $53,940
Out-of-State Tuition: $53,940
Room & Board: $18,130
Required Fees: $284
Books & Supplies: $800

Avg. Need-Based Aid: $50,491
Avg. % of Need Met: 100%

Avg. Merit-Based Aid: $14,564
% Receiving Merit-Based Aid: 8%

Avg. Cumulative Debt: $22,083
% of Students Borrowing: 58%

CAREER
Who Recruits
1. Amazon Robotics
2. The Beacon Group
3. Woodard & Curran
4. Audible
5. Collins Aerospace

Notable Internships
1. National Institutes of Health
2. Goldman Sachs
3. Roosevelt Park Zoo

Top Industries
1. Business
2. Education
3. Healthcare
4. Social Services
5. Media

Top Employers
1. Google
2. IBM
3. Johnson & Johnson
4. Accenture
5. JPMorgan Chase

Where Alumni Work
1. New York City
2. Boston
3. Springfield, MA
4. San Francisco
5. Washington, DC

Median Earnings
College Scorecard (Early Career): $46,200
EOP (Early Career): $46,200
PayScale (Mid-Career): $98,200

RANKINGS
Forbes: 81
Money: 206
U.S. News: 11, Liberal Arts Colleges
Wall Street Journal/THE: 41
Washington Monthly: 28, Liberal Arts Colleges

#CollegesWorthYourMoney

Southern Methodist University

Dallas, Texas | Admissions Phone: 214-768-2058

ADMISSION
Admission Rate: 51%
Admission Rate - Men: 52%
Admission Rate - Women: 51%
EA Admission Rate: 55%
ED Admission Rate: 61%
Admission Rate (5-Year Trend): +1%
ED Admission Rate (5-Year Trend): N/A
% of Admits Attending (Yield): 24%
Transfer Admission Rate: 74%

Offered Wait List: 1,746
Accepted Wait List: 736
Admitted Wait List: 21

SAT Reading/Writing (Middle 50%): 630-710
SAT Math (Middle 50%): 650-750
ACT Composite (Middle 50%): 29-33
Testing Policy: ACT/SAT Required
SAT Superscore: Yes
ACT Superscore: Yes

% Graduated in Top 10% of HS Class: 49%
% Graduated in Top 25% of HS Class: 80%
% Graduated in Top 50% of HS Class: 95%

ENROLLMENT
Total Undergraduate Enrollment: 6,479
% Part-Time: 3%
% Male: 51%
% Female: 49%
% Out-of-State: 55%
% Fraternity: 24%
% Sorority: 37%
% On-Campus (Freshman): 98%
% On-Campus (All Undergraduate): 54%

% African-American: 5%
% Asian: 7%
% Hispanic: 12%
% White: 64%
% Other: 4%
% Race or Ethnicity Unknown: 0%
% International: 8%
% Low-Income: 13%

ACADEMICS
Student-to-Faculty Ratio: 11:1
% of Classes Under 20: 59%
% of Classes Under 40: 85%
% Full-Time Faculty: 66%
% Full-Time Faculty w/ Terminal Degree: 84%

Top Programs
Accounting
Finance
Mathematics
Mechanical Engineering
Public Policy
Sport Management
Theatre

Retention Rate: 91%
4-Year Graduation Rate: 68%
6-Year Graduation Rate: 78%

Curricular Flexibility: Somewhat Flexible
Academic Rating: ★★★

Inside the Classroom

Wealthy and moderately conservative—such is the reputation of Southern Methodist University in Dallas, Texas, a midsized private institution with a loyal alumni base and plenty of financial backing. Historically, a large percentage of the school's 6,500 undergraduates come from families earning incomes in the top 5 percent of all families in the United States. While "Methodist" is in its name, only 14 percent of students identify as affiliating with that denomination; twice as many are Catholic. Academically, the Cox School of Business has one of the most respected faculties in the world, but that is by no means the only high-profile academic department; the public policy, sports management, performing arts, music, and film programs shine almost as brightly. In total, SMU offers one hundred+ majors and eighty-five minors.

The university's curriculum was revised in 2016 and now involves fulfilling foundation, depth, and breadth requirements. While that may sound extensive, the school offers great flexibility within those categories, and many courses within one's major will naturally fulfill some of the various mandates. Seven "proficiencies and experiences" can be met through a combination of coursework and noncredit activities that address each of human diversity, information literacy, oral communication, writing, community engagement, global engagement, and quantitative reasoning.

Thanks in part to an 11:1 student-to-faculty ratio, 59 percent of classes enroll fewer than twenty students, and fewer than 9 percent of classes enroll fifty+ undergraduates. Opportunities for personal connection and guidance extend beyond the classroom as 1,000 current SMU students have participated in undergraduate research or apprenticeships. Grants for independent research through an Engaged Learning Fellowship or a Summer Research Assistantship that pays students to work alongside faculty members for twenty-nine hours per week also are available. An annual symposium and an undergraduate-only research journal provide outlets through which you can share those valuable experiences. The 150 study abroad programs in fifty countries attract more than one-quarter of Mustangs at some point during their four years of study.

This career-minded student body gravitates toward preprofessional degrees, particularly in business (26 percent) and engineering (9 percent). SMU's Cox School of Business is top-ranked and has especially strong ties to Wall Street. Programs in engineering, sports management, and the performing arts are also very well regarded. Most fresh SMU grads are targeting high-paying jobs or entering the graduate/professional school of their choosing, but a small number each year aim for (and win) prestigious fellowships. Mustangs are awarded between two and five Fulbright Scholarships per year, two to four Gilman Scholarships, and an occasional Goldwater or Truman Scholarship.

Outside the Classroom

Almost every freshman resides in one of the university's eleven Residential Commons (which also houses sophomores), and 54 percent of all undergraduates call the dorms home; upperclassmen occupy six separate communities. Greek life is a huge part of the social fabric at SMU with 24 percent of men joining fraternities and 37 percent of women affiliating with a sorority. Sports are also a major force as the Mustangs field seventeen teams that compete in the American Athletic Conference against Division I competition. Impressively, SMU has won eighteen conference championships in the last five years. The football tradition at SMU is strong despite a series of recruiting scandals in the '80s that led to the team being banned for the 1987 season. Now, money flows into the program legally, including the $27 million that funded a new indoor practice facility that opened in 2019. New buildings are popping up everywhere you look across campus, whether it's the 50,000-square-foot Gerald J. Ford Hall for Research and Innovation or the Crain Family Centennial Promenade running through the heart of campus. The school routinely places near the top of "most beautiful campus" lists. Those not thrilled by Greeks and sports can still choose from over 200 campus organizations or venture into Dallas as the city's downtown area is only a few miles from the school.

Career Services

The Hegi Family Development Center has eight full-time employees as well as two graduate assistants. Professionals fill roles such as career counselor and employer relations specialist, and the overall student-to-counselor ratio is 807:1, poorer than most midsized universities profiled in this guide. Events that take place on campus, including career fairs, draw as many as one hundred employers and 575 students. The All Majors Career Fair held in the fall of 2019 attracted fifty+ employers including heavy hitters like American Airlines, Southwest, Hershey's, Mary Kay, and Home Depot.

Southern Methodist University

E-mail: ugadmission@smu.edu | Website: www.smu.edu

SMU's connected alumni base helps sustain strong school-to-employer bonds that lead to ample internship opportunities, particularly in the Dallas area. Business majors land internships at major investment firms and banks like Goldman Sachs, Citi, and JPMorgan Chase. A tremendous 90 percent of Lyle School of Engineering undergraduates complete at least one internship. Services offered by the Hegi Family Development Center include one-day externships, one-on-one career counseling that staff recommends "early and often," and the facilitation of on-campus interviews with recruiters from 160 companies, including some in the Fortune 500. Becoming a Mustang enables undergraduates of all socioeconomic backgrounds to connect to industry through networking, experiential learning opportunities, and impactful corporate relationships.

Professional Outcomes

At the moment they receive their diplomas, over two-thirds of graduates already have their first jobs or graduate school destinations in hand. Six months after graduation, that figure rises to 93 percent. The major corporations employing the greatest number of Mustangs are Lockheed Martin, AT&T, EY, IBM, JPMorgan Chase, Microsoft, Deloitte, American Airlines, Accenture, Oracle, Amazon, and Goldman Sachs. While close to half of SMU alums stay close to their alma mater in the Dallas-Fort Worth area, many relocate to New York City, Los Angeles, San Francisco, or DC for work. Average salaries for graduates of the Cox School of Business ranged between $50k for management majors to $70k for finance majors. Across all colleges and majors the average starting salary was $55,000.

In a typical year, one-quarter of seniors elect to continue their education in pursuit of a graduate or professional degree. SMU itself is a popular choice, but graduates have no shortage of options, including at the nation's top universities. Of the eighty-three SMU grads applying to begin medical school in 2018, a solid 58 percent gained acceptance, better than the national average that year of 43 percent. Acceptances included the Baylor College of Medicine, Perelman School of Medicine at the University of Pennsylvania, University of Texas at Austin Dell Medical School, and Vanderbilt University School of Medicine. The roughly one hundred pre-law students enjoy an annual acceptance rate hovering between 70 and 85 percent. Each year, forty students enter the Pre-Law Scholars Program, which puts them on track to attend SMU's Dedman School of Law upon graduation. Other grads in recent years have entered prestigious law schools such as those at Columbia, Cornell, Duke, Penn, Stanford, and Yale.

Admission

The 12,603 applicants to the Class of 2022 was a slight dip from the previous two admissions cycles but a still a big jump from the roughly 8,000 applications received in 2009. Fifty-one percent of Class of 2022 applicants were accepted, and 24 percent of those admitted chose to attend SMU. Standardized test scores have demonstrated a strong and consistent upward trend over the past decade; in 2008 the average SAT score was 1228, and the average ACT score was 27. Today, the average SAT score is 1363, and the average ACT score is a 30. Almost half finished in the top decile of their high school class, and 80 percent were at least in the top quartile. The average GPA for incoming freshmen is 3.63, and 45 percent of that group possessed a 3.75 or higher.

There are five "very important" factors given top priority by the SMU Admissions Committee: GPA, standardized test scores, rigor of coursework, recommendations, and application essays. That holistic and deep review also grants "important" status to class rank, extracurricular activities, talent/ability, and character/personal qualities. Demonstrated interest is a minor factor in the process as are first-generation or legacy status. Southern Methodist University offers an early decision option with a November 15 deadline that yields a small admissions edge; ED applicants get in at a 61percent clip. SMU also offers a second ED option with a January 15 deadline.

Worth Your Money?

Along with schools like Columbia, USC, and the University of Chicago, Southern Methodist University is near the top of the list of schools with the highest sticker prices in the country. The estimated total cost of attendance for an SMU student in 2019-20 was $76,786. So is a non-Ivy worth an Ivy price tag? Perhaps, especially after accounting for financial aid. The university is generous with merit scholarships, awarding 73 percent of students an average of $28,000 per year. Need-based aid is also disbursed freely to the point that the average cost of attendance, even for families in the highest income bracket, is $43,000; families making $75k-$110k pay $32,500 per year, less than half the list price. Many majors within the Cox School of Business and Lyle School of Engineering start their careers with salaries that will easily cover a reasonable student loan payment.

FINANCIAL
Institutional Type: Private
In-State Tuition: $50,200
Out-of-State Tuition: $50,200
Room & Board: $16,750
Required Fees: $6,360
Books & Supplies: $800

Avg. Need-Based Aid: $18,691
Avg. % of Need Met: 86%

Avg. Merit-Based Aid: $27,685
% Receiving Merit-Based Aid: 73%

Avg. Cumulative Debt: $38,086
% of Students Borrowing: 28%

CAREER
Who Recruits
1. Vira Insight
2. Epsilon
3. Dell
4. Frost Bank
5. Bank of America

Notable Internships
1. Dallas Mavericks
2. Cushman & Wakefield
3. Dell

Top Industries
1. Business
2. Education
3. Operations
4. Engineering
5. Sales

Top Employers
1. Lockheed Martin
2. AT&T
3. EY
4. IBM
5. Accenture

Where Alumni Work
1. Dallas
2. India
3. Houston
4. New York City
5. Austin

Median Earnings
College Scorecard (Early Career): $60,700
EOP (Early Career): $55,400
PayScale (Mid-Career): $110,400

RANKINGS
Forbes: 91
Money: 357
U.S. News: 64 (T), National Universities
Wall Street Journal/THE: 84 (T)
Washington Monthly: 308, National Universities

#CollegesWorthYourMoney

St. Olaf College

Northfield, Minnesota | Admissions Phone: 507-786-3025

ADMISSION
Admission Rate: 50%
Admission Rate - Men: 49%
Admission Rate - Women: 50%
EA Admission Rate: Not Offered
ED Admission Rate: 76%
Admission Rate (5-Year Trend): -9%
ED Admission Rate (5-Year Trend): +13%
% of Admits Attending (Yield): 29%
Transfer Admission Rate: 37%

Offered Wait List: 911
Accepted Wait List: 448
Admitted Wait List: 51

SAT Reading/Writing (Middle 50%): 600-700
SAT Math (Middle 50%): 590-710
ACT Composite (Middle 50%): 25-32
Testing Policy: ACT/SAT Required
SAT Superscore: Yes
ACT Superscore: Yes

% Graduated in Top 10% of HS Class: 41%
% Graduated in Top 25% of HS Class: 72%
% Graduated in Top 50% of HS Class: 96%

ENROLLMENT
Total Undergraduate Enrollment: 3,048
% Part-Time: 1%
% Male: 43%
% Female: 57%
% Out-of-State: 53%
% Fraternity: Not Offered
% Sorority: Not Offered
% On-Campus (Freshman): 100%
% On-Campus (All Undergraduate): 94%

% African-American: 3%
% Asian: 7%
% Hispanic: 7%
% White: 69%
% Other: 4%
% Race or Ethnicity Unknown: 1%
% International: 10%
% Low-Income: 15%

ACADEMICS
Student-to-Faculty Ratio: 12:1
% of Classes Under 20: 50%
% of Classes Under 40: 95%
% Full-Time Faculty: 64%
% Full-Time Faculty w/ Terminal Degree: 97%

Top Programs
Area Studies
Biology
Chemistry
Economics
Exercise Science
Mathematics
Religion

Retention Rate: 91%
4-Year Graduation Rate: 82%
6-Year Graduation Rate: 86%

Curricular Flexibility: Less Flexible
Academic Rating: ★★★↓

Inside the Classroom

Easier to gain acceptance into than neighbor/rival Carleton, St. Olaf College is a strong liberal arts school in Northfield, Minnesota, that is home to roughly 3,000 undergraduates. Just as in 1889 when the college first opened its frost-covered doors, St. Olaf retains a strong affiliation with the Lutheran Church. Running on a 4-1-4 schedule, students take four courses during fourteen-week semesters and one course during the one month in between. Students are nicknamed Oles (pronounced OH-Leez), and they enjoy a robust academic program of eighty-five+ majors, concentrations, and pre-professional options.

General education requirements are extensive, even by the standards of a traditional liberal arts school. This intensive regiment of coursework includes Foundation Studies, which is comprised of a first-year writing seminar, mastery of a foreign language, courses in oral communication and writing in context as well as abstract and quantitative reasoning and studies in physical movement. Freshman courses in biblical studies and theology are also mandates as well as a litany of courses across the humanities, natural sciences, and social sciences.

With a 12:1 student-to-faculty ratio and no graduate students there is ample room for mentor-mentee relationships to flourish. Exactly half of all course sections contain fewer than twenty students, and another 36 percent contain twenty to twenty-nine students. Graduation surveys reveal students who are immensely satisfied with the St. Olaf academic experience. Ninety-four percent agreed that faculty made them better critical thinkers, 88 percent touted the quality of outside-the-classroom interactions with professors, and 87 percent said coursework improved their written expression. There are multiple avenues in which students can pursue research experiences on or off campus. On-campus options include applying for ten-week summer stints through the Collaborative Undergraduate Research & Inquiry program, a Steen Fellowship to encourage independent research, or an independent study conducted for credit. Studying abroad is a staple of life for Oles; three-quarters spend a semester studying off campus, the vast majority at an international locale.

The most commonly conferred degrees are in economics, biology, psychology, mathematics, and the visual and performing arts. Many departments at St. Olaf have exceptional national reputations including religion and theology, mathematics/statistics, and physical sciences. The most coveted fellowship and scholarship organizations definitely pay special attention to graduates of this institution. In fact, the college has produced an astounding five Rhodes Scholars since 1995. In that same time, 119 graduates have taken home Fulbright Scholarships, including thirteen members of the Class of 2019.

Outside the Classroom

With 95 percent of students living on campus or in college-owned housing nearby, the student body functions as a fairly cohesive unit. Students remain on campus for a variety of sound reasons. For one, dining hall cuisine is regularly rated among the country's best, and for another no Greek life exists at St. Olaf. So-called "Honor Houses" are the closest thing to frats or sororities, but they are residences based on common academic areas of study or special interests. There are twenty-one such houses at the college, including ones focused on common bonds such as Norwegian languages, Muslim identity, or the environment. The Oles field twenty-five athletic teams (13 men's, 12 women's) that compete in NCAA Division III. A hefty portion of the student body— 500 undergraduates—are members of a varsity sports squad. There are more than 200 clubs active at the school. Those who enjoy the outdoor life will adore the 325 adjoining acres of woodlands, wetlands, and prairie that students can freely roam. Environmentally conscious policies include running 100 percent on carbon-free electrical power and a connection to fifteen local food producers to promote sustainability. The school's location near Carleton College opens additional chances for socialization as does the fact that Minneapolis and St. Paul are both less than fifty miles away.

Career Services

The Piper Center for Vocation and Career is staffed by eleven professional employers serving roles such as counselor, alumni engagement, and employer relations. Additionally, the college trains twenty-eight peer advisors to add an extra layer of student support. Counting only professional employees, St. Olaf sports a student-to-advisor ratio of 276:1, lower than the average school included in this book. Thanks to those favorable numbers, 79 percent of undergraduates meet with either a career coach or peer advisor each academic year. Among graduates, just shy of 90 percent reported they were adequately prepared for life beyond college.

On-campus events include an annual Recruiting Showcase featuring some of the top corporate employers of Oles and a Government and Nonprofit Career Fair open to all Minnesota college students. The college also participates in the statewide Private College and Career Fair that features 260+ employers. Opportunities for experiential learning are wide ranging and taken advantage of by most students as 86 percent of undergrads complete at least one internship, job-shadowing, or field experience over the course of their four years on campus. A tightknit and helpful alumni base regularly avail themselves to assist current undergrads. Alumni events like Ole Biz, which brings over a hundred graduates to Minneapolis, invites current students to learn about ten industries while networking their hearts out. The Piper Center excels in setting students up with meaningful experiences and important alumni connections, and it has a direct line to many of the region's largest corporate employers.

Professional Outcomes

Examining the outcomes for the graduating classes of 2017 and 2018, between 73 and 79 percent immediately enter the workforce and between 17 and 23 percent matriculate into graduate/professional school. In 2017, four percent of grads were still seeking their next step six months after graduation; in 2018 not a single student reported failing to find their next destination. The great majority of alumni remain in the Greater Minneapolis-St. Paul area (more than ten times as many as relocate to second-choice destination Chicago), which impacts what companies hire the most Oles. To name names, alumni have the largest representation at Target, UnitedHealth Group, the Mayo Clinic, Wells Fargo, Medtronic, 3M, and US Bank. Midcareer median salaries fall in the same range as other Minnesota academic powerhouses Carleton and Macalester.

While many pursuing higher education choose to stay in the Midwest, every year the college sends at least one graduate to the likes of Columbia, Yale, or Cornell to pursue an advanced degree. St. Olaf students in a premed area of concentration and who have a GPA of 3.59 or better gain acceptance to medical school at a solid 75 percent clip. The most commonly attended medical school is the University of Minnesota-Twin Cities, but recent grads have gone on to study at the University of Michigan Medical School, Washington University in St. Louis School of Medicine, and Wake Forest Medical School. Law school applicants have gone on to elite universities including Harvard, Emory, Georgetown, and UCLA. The school is also a top producer of future PhDs, placing eleventh among baccalaureate colleges in the number of graduates who go on to earn doctoral degrees in their respective fields.

Admission

Exactly half of those who applied for a position in St. Olaf's Class of 2022 were granted acceptance. One decade ago, the acceptance rate was 59 percent of an applicant pool that was only one-third the size of the 2022 class. Attending freshmen in the 2018-19 school year possessed a middle-50 percent SAT range of 1190-1410 and a wide-ranging ACT composite of 25-32. The ACT was, by far, the test of choice; it was submitted by 73 percent of applicants. Just over 50 percent of freshmen boasted GPAs of over 3.75, but one-quarter of attendees had below a 3.5. Forty-one percent fell within the top decile of their graduating class, and 72 percent placed in the top quarter.

Rigorous coursework, GPA, and the application essay are of paramount importance to the admissions committee followed by a second tier of factors including standardized test scores, class rank, recommendations, an interview, extracurricular activities, talent/ability, and character/personal qualities. Showing a commitment to the college is rewarded on the admissions end; early decision applicants were accepted at a friendly rate of 76 percent. Overall, St. Olaf has a yield rate of 29 percent, which means that just under one-in-three accepted students actually go on to enroll. Earning admission into St. Olaf is more than a simple numbers game; a holistic approach by the committee rewards "smart, ambitious, creative people who want to be challenged." Even if you lack perfect grades or ACT scores, a candidate can still make a compelling case for acceptance into this fine Midwestern liberal arts institution.

Worth Your Money?

Total cost of attendance at St. Olaf will run you just short of $63,000 per year, yet few pay that amount. Two-thirds of Oles receive some form of financial aid, and the overall value of each need-based award is $37k, ultimately making this school affordable for those with financial need. Considering the high rate of internship participation, close contact with major companies, and accessible faculty, St. Olaf is likely worth your money.

FINANCIAL
Institutional Type: Private
In-State Tuition: $49,710
Out-of-State Tuition: $49,710
Room & Board: $11,270
Required Fees: $0
Books & Supplies: $1,000

Avg. Need-Based Aid: $36,531
Avg. % of Need Met: 100%

Avg. Merit-Based Aid: $17,556
% Receiving Merit-Based Aid: 46%

Avg. Cumulative Debt: $29,907
% of Students Borrowing: 64%

CAREER
Who Recruits
1. Lewin Group
2. Cerner Corporation
3. Thomson Reuters
4. North Sky Capital
5. MatrixCare

Notable Internships
1. Game Informer Magazine
2. MITRE
3. 9/11 Tribute Museum

Top Industries
1. Education
2. Business
3. Operations
4. Social Services
5. Healthcare

Top Employers
1. UnitedHealth Group
2. Target
3. Mayo Clinic
4. Wells Fargo
5. U.S. Bank

Where Alumni Work
1. Minneapolis
2. Chicago
3. New York City
4. San Francisco
5. Denver

Median Earnings
College Scorecard (Early Career): $50,400
EOP (Early Career): $48,600
PayScale (Mid-Career): $101,900

RANKINGS
Forbes: 116
Money: 133
U.S. News: 62, Liberal Arts Colleges
Wall Street Journal/THE: 156 (T)
Washington Monthly: 60, Liberal Arts Colleges

#CollegesWorthYourMoney

Stanford University

Stanford, California | Admissions Phone: 650-723-2091

ADMISSION

Admission Rate: 4%
Admission Rate - Men: 4%
Admission Rate - Women: 4%
EA Admission Rate: N/A
ED Admission Rate: Not Offered
Admission Rate (5-Year Trend): -1%
ED Admission Rate (5-Year Trend): Not Offered
% of Admits Attending (Yield): 82%
Transfer Admission Rate: 1%

Offered Wait List: 870
Accepted Wait List: 681
Admitted Wait List: 30

SAT Reading/Writing (Middle 50%): 700-770
SAT Math (Middle 50%): 720-800
ACT Composite (Middle 50%): 32-35
Testing Policy: ACT/SAT Required
SAT Superscore: Yes
ACT Superscore: Yes

% Graduated in Top 10% of HS Class: 96%
% Graduated in Top 25% of HS Class: 100%
% Graduated in Top 50% of HS Class: 100%

ENROLLMENT

Total Undergraduate Enrollment: 7,087
% Part-Time: 0%
% Male: 50%
% Female: 50%
% Out-of-State: 59%
% Fraternity: 18%
% Sorority: 24%
% On-Campus (Freshman): 100%
% On-Campus (All Undergraduate): 93%

% African-American: 7%
% Asian: 22%
% Hispanic: 16%
% White: 34%
% Other: 9%
% Race or Ethnicity Unknown: 1%
% International: 10%
% Low-Income: 15%

ACADEMICS

Student-to-Faculty Ratio: 5:1
% of Classes Under 20: 69%
% of Classes Under 40: 85%
% Full-Time Faculty: 67%
% Full-Time Faculty w/ Terminal Degree: 76%

Top Programs
Computer Science
Economics
Engineering
Human Biology
International Relations
Mathematics
Physics
Psychology

Retention Rate: 99%
4-Year Graduation Rate: 75%
6-Year Graduation Rate: 94%

Curricular Flexibility: Somewhat Flexible
Academic Rating: ★★★★★

Inside the Classroom

Fittingly situated in the heart of Silicon Valley sits one of the tech industry's top feeder schools and one of the premier research universities in the world. Among Stanford's many quantifiable boasts and brags are the lowest acceptance rate in the country, the nation's second-largest college endowment, the best all-around athletic department in the country, the second-highest total of affiliate-won Nobel Prizes, and the highest graduate starting salaries for any non-STEM-exclusive institution. At Stanford, the list of accomplishments could go longer than a vintage John Elway (an alum) deep ball.

Over 7,000 undergrads and another 8,000 graduate students occupy this expansive campus that is the sixth largest in the nation. For perspective on its size, 19,000 bicycle parking spots can be found on university grounds. There are three undergraduate schools at Stanford: The School of Humanities & Sciences that houses 61 percent of the student body, the School of Engineering, and the School of Earth, Energy, and Environmental Sciences. All undergraduates must complete three courses in writing and rhetoric, one year of a foreign language, and a freshman course entitled Thinking Matters in which students choose from a full menu of courses covering a host of intellectual topics from Race in American Memory to How Does Your Brain Work? The Ways of Thinking, Ways of Doing requirement comprises eleven additional courses in ethical reasoning, applied quantitative reasoning, and aesthetic and interpretive inquiry. Further requirements are major specific. Some programs require a senior capstone, research component, practicum or, for foreign language, an oral proficiency review.

A virtually unmatched 4:1 student-to-faculty ratio sets the Cardinal students up for a personalized classroom experience and an incredible amount of face time with some of the leaders in their respective fields. Two-thirds of classes have fewer than twenty students, and 35 percent have a single-digit enrollment. Stanford puts unmatched resources behind undergraduate research; more than $5.6 million in grant funding is allocated each year to support roughly 1,000 student research projects. Close to 900 students study abroad annually through the Bing Overseas Studies Program in eleven international cities.

The School of Engineering is one of the best in the world; all of its sub disciplines sit atop any list of best engineering programs. Programs in computer science, physics, mathematics, international relations and economics are arguably the best anywhere. In terms of sheer volume, the greatest number of degrees are conferred each year in engineering (18 percent), computer science (18 percent), interdisciplinary studies (15 percent), and the social sciences (12 percent). With ninety-six Rhodes Scholars to its credit, Stanford ranks fourth on the all-time list. In 2018, the school produced twenty Fulbright winners, five Schwartzman Scholars, a Truman Scholar, and in recent years has produced a multitude of winners of just about any prestigious post-grad scholarship one can name.

Outside the Classroom

Stanford is where you can receive a world-class education and experience the excitement of a typical college experience. The Cardinal have a rich sports tradition with its sixteen men's and twenty women's NCAA Division I teams. The excellence the university expects in the classroom in matched on the field; the Athletic Department has won the Directors' Cup, given to the most successful college athletic program, for twenty-four consecutive years, and at least one team has won an NCAA national championship in each of the last forty-two years. With an additional forty club teams, over 900 undergraduates compete in intercollegiate athletics. Fraternities and sororities are thriving on campus with a 25 percent participation rate across twenty-nine Greek organizations. Over 600 student organizations are active including sixty student-led community service organizations, the widely circulated Stanford Daily, and a vast array of ethnic/cultural groups. Ninety-two percent of undergrads live on Stanford's sprawling 8,180-acre campus in the heart of the San Francisco Peninsula. The surrounding area of Palo Alto, America's wealthiest town, is full of natural and manmade beauty and any cultural, culinary, or entertainment delight one could seek. The university itself puts its bottomless endowment to use with immaculately manicured grounds, well-maintained dorms, state-of-the-art recreational facilities, and restaurant-quality campus dining options. Simply put, the campus aesthetics at Stanford are every bit as breathtaking as the quality of its academics.

Career Services

BEAM (Bridging Education, Ambition, & Meaningful Work) is Stanford's career services office. It employs twenty-five professional staff members who work in the Career Catalysts, Career Communities, and Career Ventures divisions. The 282:1 student-to-advisor ratio is lower than the average school featured in this guide. The three aforementioned divisions speak to the unique and comprehensive career services approach at Stanford. There is a sincere effort to get students to align their career interests with their identities and passions, cultivate a personalized network of mentors/guides, and connect directly with employers. BEAM does a fantastic job with all three phases of that process.

In 2017-18, the career services staff facilitated 19,344 "meaningful connections" between current students and alumni/industry professionals and initiated 37,818 "meaningful opportunities" for undergraduates to carve out a pathway toward their employment or graduate school destination. BEAM sponsors fourteen to sixteen career fairs per year, posts over 10,000 job and internship opportunities on Handshake, and runs the superb Stanford Alumni Mentoring program. Major companies recruit on campus on a constant basis because (a) of the incredible talent pool and (b) the school is located in Silicon Valley, home to most of the world's largest tech companies. Stanford facilitates internships at over 700 unique sites, and close to half of all students complete two internships as part of their undergraduate education; two-thirds complete at least one. With a robust career services department and spectacular graduate outcomes (see below), BEAM earns every ounce of its stellar reputation.

Professional Outcomes

Stanford grads entering the working world flock to three major industries in equal distribution: business/finance/consulting/retail (19 percent); computer, IT (19 percent); and public policy and service, international affairs (19 percent). Among the companies employing the largest number of recent Stanford alums are Accenture, Apple, Bain, Cisco, Facebook, Goldman Sachs, Google, McKinsey, Microsoft, and SpaceX. Other companies that employ hundreds of Cardinal alums include LinkedIn, Uber, Lyft, Salesforce, and Airbnb. California, New York, Massachusetts, Texas, DC, and Washington state were the top six destinations for recent grads. The mean salary for all Stanford graduates is a staggering $85,000; that figure is substantially higher than the national average and is usually approached only by high-end engineering schools.

Those who are graduate school bound often stay at Stanford with professors they already have a close working relationship with. The other dozen most popular universities attended by recent graduates include Oxford, Harvard, MIT, Yale, Columbia, the University of Chicago, and Johns Hopkins. You would be hard-pressed to find a top-ranked law or medical school that did not have Stanford alums among its ranks. Last year, 241 Stanford graduates applied to medical school, and acceptance rates were nearly double the national average. In sum, if you get an undergraduate degree from Stanford, your opportunities for continuing your education will be limitless.

Admission

The toughest school to get into in the United States doesn't appear to be getting less selective anytime soon. In 2018-19, a meager 4.3 percent of the 47,450 accomplished teens vying for a place in the Class of 2022 were offered admission. The profile of the average current student is about what you would expect at the university with the lowest acceptance rate in the country. The middle-50 percent SAT range for the Class of 2022 was 1420-1570 and 32-35 on the ACT. If you want to become a member of the Cardinal club, near-perfect grades are a prerequisite. Three-quarters of incoming freshmen had a GPA of a 4.0 or above in high school, although it is important to highlight that only 6 percent of applicants meeting that criterion were accepted, and only 1 percent of those with a 3.7 or lower made the cut. Almost all freshmen—96 percent—ranked in the top 10 percent of their high school class.

There are nine factors considered "very important" to the admissions office: rigor of courses, GPA, class rank, standardized test scores, essays, recommendations, extracurricular activities, talent/ability, and character/personal qualities. The last three from that list are of particular importance given that the first five will likely be similarly perfect from the bulk of those applying. First-generation status is not listed as a primary factor, but a healthy 18 percent of those admitted in 2018 are looking to become the first in their family to earn a degree. Stanford admissions has become the ultimate valedictorian meat grinder, now possessing a lower admission rate than Harvard. With so many top-shelf applicants for a limited number of spots, it helps to have a hook—an area in which you truly excel. Whether academic, athletic, or extracurricular, such a hook can help differentiate you from the throngs of other super-qualified applicants.

Worth Your Money?

An endowment of over $26 billion helps the school cover most but, surprisingly, not all of the determined need of its undergraduate students. Still, the average need-based grant is for $52k+, which helps knock the $74,570 cost of attendance down to a manageable sum for the approximately 50 percent of students who qualify. Of course, Stanford is one of those rare universities that would be worth just about any cost.

FINANCIAL
Institutional Type: Private
In-State Tuition: $52,857
Out-of-State Tuition: $52,857
Room & Board: $16,433
Required Fees: $672
Books & Supplies: $1,245

Avg. Need-Based Aid: $52,453
Avg. % of Need Met: 100%

Avg. Merit-Based Aid: $0
% Receiving Merit-Based Aid: 0%

Avg. Cumulative Debt: $21,348
% of Students Borrowing: 19%

CAREER
Who Recruits
1. Masimo
2. Wealthfront
3. Calico
4. Asurion
5. Los Angeles Dodgers

Notable Internships
1. Citadel
2. SpaceX
3. United Nations

Top Industries
1. Business
2. Engineering
3. Education
4. Research
5. Operations

Top Employers
1. Google
2. Apple
3. Facebook
4. Microsoft
5. Amazon

Where Alumni Work
1. San Francisco
2. New York City
3. Los Angeles
4. Seattle
5. Boston

Median Earnings
College Scorecard (Early Career): $94,000
EOP (Early Career): $84,800
PayScale (Mid-Career): $145,200

RANKINGS
Forbes: 2
Money: 6
U.S. News: 6 (T) National Universities
Wall Street Journal/THE: 7 (T)
Washington Monthly: 1, National Universities

#CollegesWorthYourMoney

Stevens Institute of Technology

Hoboken, New Jersey | Admissions Phone: 201-216-5194

Inside the Classroom

With the Manhattan skyline visible across the Hudson River, the Stevens Institute of Technology's Hoboken, New Jersey, campus occupies prime real estate—but the school is not merely about its breathtaking panoramic view of the Big Apple. For this small but growing private research institution with a focus on engineering and business, proximity to New York City is an asset that translates into strong corporate connections, endless internship and co-op opportunities and, ultimately, exceptional job placement rates at top companies.

There are thirty-five undergraduate majors at Stevens across four undergraduate schools: the Schaefer School of Engineering & Science, the School of Business, the College of Arts and Letters, and the School of Systems and Enterprises. There is no core curriculum at Stevens as every set of requirements is school and major dependent. The only common academic experiences for all undergrads is a sequence of two College of Arts and Letters courses that every freshman must complete—Writing and Communications and Colloquium: Knowledge, Nature, Culture. Some engineering students complete a capstone senior design project that is often conducted in coordination with an industry sponsor.

Two-thirds of course sections have an enrollment of under thirty students, and 38 percent of sections contain fewer than twenty students. The student-to-faculty ratio is 10:1 but, of course, with over 2,000 graduate students some attention is diverted in their direction. Undergraduate research possibilities are plentiful and varied. Roughly 10 percent of each freshman class are invited to become Stevens Scholars, which guarantees a paid summer research experience with a faculty member. As a research university, the school also has close ties to industry and federally run labs that can lead to many additional research opportunities. Co-op experiences that also can involve research are embarked upon by slightly less than one-third of students. A number of study abroad programs are available with some of the most popular destinations being the United Kingdom, Belgium, Jamaica, China, Spain, Thailand, and Greece.

Engineering is, by far, the most common undergraduate major, and all programs within the Schaefer School of Engineering & Science are strong. Programs in computer science, cybersecurity, and quantitative finance also receive praise. Over 80 percent of the degrees granted at Stevens are in a STEM field, and most of the remaining grads major in business, finance, and accounting. It is uncommon for Stevens grads to pursue national fellowships or scholarships as they are traditionally focused on career or graduate school as their next step after graduation.

Outside the Classroom

A relatively low 64 percent of the undergraduate student body resides on campus in college-owned housing. Greek life is a major player on campus as fraternities and sororities attract 1,100 students—37 percent of the undergrad population. Greek houses are community service oriented and work closely with charitable organizations including Big Brothers Big Sisters, the Hoboken Shelter, and the Food Bank of New Jersey. Student-athletes participate on one of twenty-six NCAA Division III varsity athletic teams known as the Ducks. There are an additional sixteen intercollegiate club sports teams and a robust intramural program featuring flag football, three-on-three basketball, and floor hockey. There are over one hundred clubs and activities to join. For the extremely adventurous, the Outdoor Adventure Program plans trips to locales like Costa Rica, Utah, and the Grand Canyon. The Stevens Honor System is taken seriously and permeates beyond academic life into the social realm. An Honor Board and Student Government Association are in place to enforce shared values and enhance the student experience. Students publish a weekly student newspaper and run campus radio and television stations. Hoboken is only one jam-packed square mile of land, making it immensely walkable. For those of age, the town holds the distinction of most bars per capita. Running alongside the Hudson is an aesthetically pleasing option and, perhaps best of all, New York City is only fifteen minutes away.

Career Services

The Stevens Career Center is made up of six professional employees who work with undergraduate students as advisors, cooperative education coordinators, or in a director/assistant director capacity; two additional members work exclusively with the university's graduate students. The student-to-advisor ratio of 572:1, which ranks in the average range when compared against other schools featured in this guide, yet Stevens' career services offerings are as strong as they come. This is a career services office that works hard to forge corporate connections and, as a result, 80 percent of seniors have secured competitive employment prior to graduation.

ADMISSION
Admission Rate: 41%
Admission Rate - Men: 39%
Admission Rate - Women: 47%
EA Admission Rate: Not Offered
ED Admission Rate: 59%
Admission Rate (5-Year Trend): +3%
ED Admission Rate (5-Year Trend): N/A
% of Admits Attending (Yield): 26%
Transfer Admission Rate: 23%

Offered Wait List: 1,503
Accepted Wait List: 629
Admitted Wait List: 0

SAT Reading/Writing (Middle 50%): 640-710
SAT Math (Middle 50%): 690-770
ACT Composite (Middle 50%): 30-33
Testing Policy: ACT/SAT Required
SAT Superscore: Yes
ACT Superscore: Yes

% Graduated in Top 10% of HS Class: 72%
% Graduated in Top 25% of HS Class: 96%
% Graduated in Top 50% of HS Class: 100%

ENROLLMENT
Total Undergraduate Enrollment: 3,431
% Part-Time: 0%
% Male: 71%
% Female: 29%
% Out-of-State: 36%
% Fraternity: 31%
% Sorority: 49%
% On-Campus (Freshman): 91%
% On-Campus (All Undergraduate): 60%

% African-American: 2%
% Asian: 15%
% Hispanic: 12%
% White: 67%
% Other: 0%
% Race or Ethnicity Unknown: 4%
% International: 4%
% Low-Income: 15%

ACADEMICS
Student-to-Faculty Ratio: 10:1
% of Classes Under 20: 37%
% of Classes Under 40: 83%
% Full-Time Faculty: 67%
% Full-Time Faculty w/ Terminal Degree: 95%

Top Programs
Business & Technology
Chemical Biology
Computer Science
Cybersecurity
Engineering
Quantitative Finance

Retention Rate: 95%
4-Year Graduation Rate: 45%
6-Year Graduation Rate: 87%

Curricular Flexibility: Somewhat Flexible
Academic Rating: ★★★↗

Stevens Institute of Technology

E-mail: admissions@stevens.edu | Website: www.stevens.edu

In the 2017-18 school year more than 300 companies recruited on campus, a phenomenal number for a school of any size, but for a small university like Stevens, that figure is astounding. It is rare for Stevens students to not complete at least one internship over their four years of study. Ninety percent of undergrads in the School of Business land internships. The co-op track is selected by 30 percent of all students, and that entails working a forty-hour paid work week beginning in the sophomore year. Three annual career fairs in September, December, and March each attract about 900 students. The March 2018 Career Fair alone attracted 125 companies, including the likes of IBM, Verizon, and JPMorgan Chase.

Professional Outcomes

The Class of 2018 found employment or graduate school homes at a 96 percent rate within six months of receiving their degree. Engineering students entered the fields of manufacturing (24 percent), engineering services (17 percent), and construction (12 percent). Bachelor of Science students most frequently entered sector was finance (42 percent) followed by technology/telecom (17 percent), and business/consulting (8 percent). Employers that hired three or more Class of 2018 Stevens grads included Google, EY, Merck, Prudential, and PwC. Massive numbers of alumni (from all graduating years) can be found at major corporations including Verizon, Citi, JPMorgan Chase, Pfizer, and Johnson & Johnson. The average starting salary was $71,400. Many alumni stay local; 53 percent of 2018 graduates remained in New Jersey, and 29 percent crossed the border to New York.

Of the 18 percent of Stevens grads who immediately enroll in graduate school, 85 percent were pursuing master's or PhDs, 11 percent entered medical school, 2 percent law school, and 2 percent dental school. Some enrolled in doctoral programs at prestigious institutions such as Carnegie Mellon, Georgia Tech, Penn, and Vanderbilt and master's programs at Imperial College London, Royal College of Art, Johns Hopkins, and Cornell. The school offers a three-three accelerated law option as well as a three-four accelerated med school program. Recent medical school acceptances include Albert Einstein College of Medicine, Mount Sanai Medical School, and New York University School of Medicine.

Admission

There were 9,265 applications submitted for the 2018-19 freshman class, an 11 percent increase from the previous year. Of those hopefuls, 41 percent received an offer of acceptance compared to 44 percent in 2017-18. However, it's important to understand that the applicant pool is relatively self-selecting and primarily comprised of strongly credentialed teens. The mid-50 percent SAT Range was 1330-1480 with an average of 1399, and the average high school GPA was 3.86. Stevens accepted and enrolled 33 percent more students in the Class of 2022 than in the previous year's class. That expansion meant that more than 1,000 freshmen enrolled while under 700 graduated in 2018.

In addition to strong grades and standardized test scores, the admissions committee at Stevens is looking for students with a track record of "ingenuity, inventiveness, and inspiration." The school does offer admissions interviews, including via Skype for those living more than 250 miles away, but although interviews are recommended, they are optional. Applying early is strongly encouraged if Stevens is your top choice; the acceptance rate for ED applicants approaches 70 percent. The acceptance rate for women is typically ten points higher than the acceptance rate for men. Women make up about 30 percent of the student body. Stevens Institute of Technology is gaining in popularity and rapidly expanding its undergraduate enrollment. Its proximity to Manhattan, corporate connections, and stellar graduate outcomes should continue to draw larger numbers of highly qualified applicants.

Worth Your Money?

Is it good news or bad news that the average graduate's starting salary and annual cost of attendance at Stevens are nearly identical? Perhaps the adage, "You have to spend money to make money," helps answer that question. With a COA of $72k and starting salaries around the same, those paying full price will be just fine, even if they have to take out substantial loans to attend. Financial aid is awarded to 65 percent of the undergraduate population, but the school only meets the full financial need of 18 percent of accepted students. The average grant is for only $12,700 per year, which barely puts a dent in the tuition bill. Again, the good news is that strong career outcomes help balance the upfront costs.

FINANCIAL
Institutional Type: Private
In-State Tuition: $54,014
Out-of-State Tuition: $54,014
Room & Board: $15,770
Required Fees: N/A
Books & Supplies: $1,200

Avg. Need-Based Aid: $35,636
Avg. % of Need Met: 73%

Avg. Merit-Based Aid: $19,632
% Receiving Merit-Based Aid: 26%

Avg. Cumulative Debt: $40,588
% of Students Borrowing: 64%

CAREER
Who Recruits
1. MThree
2. Nasdaq
3. Bristol-Meyers Squibb
4. Calgene6
5. Nielsen

Notable Internships
1. iHeartMedia
2. Merck
3. Johnson & Johnson

Top Industries
1. Engineering
2. Information Technology
3. Business
4. Operations
5. Project Management

Top Employers
1. Verizon
2. JPMorgan Chase
3. Citi
4. Johnson & JOhnson
5. Pfizer

Where Alumni Work
1. New York City
2. Philadelphia
3. San Francisco
4. Washington, DC
5. Boston

Median Earnings
College Scorecard (Early Career): $89,200
EOP (Early Career): $92,100
PayScale (Mid-Career): $139,900

RANKINGS
Forbes: 152
Money: 212
U.S. News: 74 (T), National Universities
Wall Street Journal/THE: 160 (T)
Washington Monthly: 201, National Universities

#CollegesWorthYourMoney

Stony Brook University (SUNY)

Stony Brook, New York | Admissions Phone: 631-632-6868

Inside the Classroom

Like many schools within the SUNY system, Stony Brook University has quietly but steadily ascended into a different tier of public universities since the turn of the millennium. In fact, back in 1999 its acceptance rate was 58 percent, and the 25th percentile SAT score for accepted students was 1050; in recent years the acceptance rate has crept as low as the 30 percents, and the 25th percentile SAT score is now 1230. But shedding its "commuter school" status has been difficult, and 80 percent of undergrads still hail from in state, but today Stony Brook also attracts students from 110 countries, which would have been an unthinkable feat when it opened as a teacher's college in 1957. In 2018-19, Stony Brook was the undergraduate home of 17,500 students who could choose from sixty+ majors and eighty+ minors.

There are six undergraduate colleges within the university and some, like the College of Leadership and Service or the College of Global Studies are, perhaps, unexpected menu options. After a two-day compulsory orientation, the journey through the Stony Brook curriculum begins. All told, that will involve checking off double-digits worth of learning objective boxes via courses in the humanities, arts, global affairs, technology, natural science, writing, human behavior, US history, and language. Additional coursework (this can be overlapping) also must fulfill mandates related to interconnectedness, deep understanding, and lifelong learning. In sum, required coursework outside of your major will take a solid three semesters to complete but, on the plus side, there is a great deal of choice within each category for you to pursue elective areas of interest.

An 18:1 student-to-faculty ratio and 8,700 graduate students isn't exactly a recipe for small classes, but undergrads will find themselves in some first-name basis classes with 36 percent of all sections containing nineteen or fewer students. However, there also will be large numbers of face-in-the-crowd experiences because one-quarter of undergraduate sections enroll fifty or more students. That type of environment is not going to spoon feed you with one-on-one faculty mentoring or the chance to participate in undergraduate research, but such experiences are available to those who show determination. In fact, more than 1,500 students have the chance to engage in undergraduate research each year. The rate of study abroad participation is low, but exciting opportunities exist for those who choose to take advantage; the school features a winter program that whisks students to Ecuador and the Galapagos.

A popular and locally well-regarded nursing program leads to the largest number of degrees being conferred in health professions (18 percent). Strong majors in biology (13 percent), engineering (9 percent), and computer sciences (8 percent) also draw a sizable number of Seawolves (the school's mascot). The school's reputation in the hard sciences, particularly math, chemistry, and biomedical engineering, is aided by the affiliated Stony Brook University Hospital. With regard to prestigious postgraduate scholarships, Stony Brook students have really upped their game in recent years. In 2019, a record-tying eleven Stony Brook seniors earned National Science Foundation Graduate Research Fellowships. It also set an institutional record for the most Fulbright applicants (38), and a phenomenal ten seniors captured the coveted award. Between 2013 and 2018, seven students earned Goldwater Scholarships.

Outside the Classroom

No longer the commuter-heavy school it once was, 83 percent of freshmen and 53 percent of the total student population live on campus in one of thirty residence halls or twenty-three apartment-style buildings. Greek life is close-to-invisible but has a faint heartbeat as 2 percent of men and women join fraternities and sororities. There are approximately 550 student-athletes competing as the Seawolves on seven men's and nine women's NCAA Division I teams. The men's basketball team made its first March Madness tournament in 2016. There also are thirty-six club sports teams and intramural options including bowling, beach volleyball, Wiffle ball, and flag football. Over 350 clubs are on tap, including the full array of cultural, dance, charitable, and pre-professional groups. Notably strong organizations include the African Student Union, the College Democrats, and service groups like Camp Kesem and Project Sunshine. For a school without centuries of history under its belt, it does have a number of cool traditions including the annual Roth Pond Regatta where students race themed boats made of cardboard and duct tape across a campus pond. The spacious Long Island campus of 1,039 acres is located midway between Manhattan and Montauk. A train station on campus will take you the sixty miles into New York City. Parks, beaches, and shopping are all within reach, particularly for those with a car (or a friend with a car).

Career Services

The Career Center at Stony Brook University employs thirteen professional staff members who are tasked with career counseling, experiential learning, and employer relations. That translates to a 1,346:1 student-to-counselor ratio, significantly poorer than the average school featured in this guide. Fortunately, that figure does not appear to be preventing the school from reaching the entire undergraduate population. In the 2018-19 school year the center conducted 6,015 one-on-one counseling sessions, and career presentations attracted another 7,000 individuals; additionally, it facilitates 900,000 online transactions each year. It is also one of the only career centers to offer two credited courses on career development, one geared toward freshmen and sophomores and the other toward upperclassmen.

Stony Brook University (SUNY)

E-mail: enroll@stonybrook.edu | Website: www.stonybrook.edu

Stony Brook's staff helps facilitate roughly 1,200 undergraduate internships each year as well as 2,500 practicums and hundreds of clinical placements. Recently, it has adopted the practice of micro-internships, paid five- to forty-hour placements at companies ranging from Fortune 100 mega-corporations to small tech start-ups. Several job fairs take place each semester, including the Information Technology/Computer Science Job & Internship Fair, Engineering Job & Internship Fair, Business Job & Internship Fair, and the Healthcare, Research, & Human Services Job & Internship Fair. By drawing more than 400 regional and national companies to Stony Brook's campus, the Career Services Office provides ample opportunity for assertive students to make connections and land desirable jobs and internships in New York City and beyond. There were 1,224 on-campus interviews conducted at the university last year.

Professional Outcomes

Based on the most recent data available, within two years of graduation, 63 percent of Stony Brook graduates are employed, 31 percent have entered graduate/professional school, and 6 percent are presently looking for their next opportunity. Graduates of the arts and sciences, social welfare, and nursing schools had the lowest reported figures of "still searching" alumni while health tech and management students had the highest. The overall median salary was $48,470 with nursing grads earning the most ($66k), followed by those who studied engineering ($60k) and business ($52k). The organizations and companies employing the greatest number of Seawolves are Northwell Health, JPMorgan Chase, Google, Amazon, Citi, Morgan Stanley, Microsoft, Apple, Bloomberg, and Facebook. Over three-quarters of alumni are settled in the Greater New York City area; sizable pockets also can be found in San Francisco, Boston, DC, and Los Angeles.

Among those pursuing further education, common choices include Stony Brook itself, other SUNY or CUNY institutions, and NYC-based powerhouses like Columbia, Fordham, and NYU. Some recent grads also have left the region to attend some of the finest schools in the world including the London School of Economics, Oxford, Caltech, Stanford, Harvard, Duke, the University of Michigan, and Yale. Traditionally, premed students with a 3.5 GPA and an MCAT in the 67th percentile gain acceptance into medical school at a 59 percent clip. The most commonly attended medical schools include Stony Brook, Downstate, Upstate, NYMC, Albany, Buffalo, Eastern Virginia, GW, Howard, Georgetown, Penn State, and Drexel. Law schools attended by recent grads include Hofstra, Boston University, Villanova, Brooklyn Law School, Wake Forest, and the Cardozo School of Law at Yeshiva University.

Admission

Members of the Class of 2022 were admitted at a 42 percent rate, a touch higher than the 39 percent of five years ago. However, the school's popularity is definitely on the rise; it attracts double the number of applicants it did fifteen years ago. Twenty-one percent of those accepted ultimately enroll, a comparable figure to past years. The caliber of freshmen Stony Brook reels in today is higher than ever. The mid-50 percent standardized test score ranges are 1230-1420 on the SAT and 26-31 on the ACT. SAT math scores were notably strong with 46 percent of this group scoring a 700 or above. Forty-seven percent of entering 2018-19 freshmen earned a spot in the top 10 percent of their high school class; 80 percent placed in the top quartile. The average high school GPA was 3.85, and 64 percent sported at least a 3.75. Under 2 percent of entering students had less than a 3.0 GPA.

There is nothing complicated about how admissions decisions are made at Stony Brook. With such a mass of applicants, the admissions committee primarily relies on the hard facts of standardized test scores and GPA within a rigorous course load with a fair number of honors and AP selections. Recommendations and the application essay also are considered "important" to the evaluation process. The application deadline for everyone is January 15 as there are no early action or early decision options. The school does receive over 7,000 transfer applications each year and admits 45 percent of that group.

Worth Your Money?

At $7,000 in pure tuition, students living with their parents and commuting could conceivably graduate from Stony Brook for less than the cost of one semester at NYU. To top it off, 78 percent of freshmen receive financial aid. On the other hand, out-of-staters pay $25,550 in tuition and, with living and meal costs, a degree would likely cost around $170,000 total. For the 80 percent of current undergraduates hailing from the state of New York, this university is an otherworldly bargain; for international students and Americans outside the state, the value would depend on financial aid and whether the program you would pursue would be likely to yield a solid starting salary.

FINANCIAL
Institutional Type: Public
In-State Tuition: $6,870
Out-of-State Tuition: $24,540
Room & Board: $13,698
Required Fees: $2,755
Books & Supplies: $900

Avg. Need-Based Aid: $10,482
Avg. % of Need Met: 69%

Avg. Merit-Based Aid: $5,726
% Receiving Merit-Based Aid: 22%

Avg. Cumulative Debt: $28,780
% of Students Borrowing: 52%

CAREER
Who Recruits
1. Travelers
2. North Atlantic Industries
3. GEICO
4. Broadbridge
5. Canon

Notable Internships
1. Moody's Analytics
2. Bank of America
3. Northrop Grumman

Top Industries
1. Business
2. Education
3. Healthcare
4. Engineering
5. Operations

Top Employers
1. Northwell Health
2. JPMorgan Chase
3. Google
4. Citi
5. Amazon

Where Alumni Work
1. New York City
2. San Francisco
3. Boston
4. Washington, DC
5. Los Angeles

Median Earnings
College Scorecard (Early Career): $57,600
EOP (Early Career): $60,100
PayScale (Mid-Career): $107,800

RANKINGS
Forbes: 176
Money: 47
U.S. News: 91, National Universities
Wall Street Journal/THE: 105 (T)
Washington Monthly: 100, National Universities

#CollegesWorthYourMoney

Swarthmore College

Swarthmore, Pennsylvania | Admissions Phone: 610-328-8300

ADMISSION
Admission Rate: 9%
Admission Rate - Men: 11%
Admission Rate - Women: 8%
EA Admission Rate: Not Offered
ED Admission Rate: 26%
Admission Rate (5-Year Trend): -5%
ED Admission Rate (5-Year Trend): -7%
% of Admits Attending (Yield): 41%
Transfer Admission Rate: 19%

Offered Wait List: N/A
Accepted Wait List: N/A
Admitted Wait List: 40

SAT Reading/Writing (Middle 50%): 680-760
SAT Math (Middle 50%): 700-790
ACT Composite (Middle 50%): 31-34
Testing Policy: ACT/SAT Required
SAT Superscore: Yes
ACT Superscore: Yes

% Graduated in Top 10% of HS Class: 90%
% Graduated in Top 25% of HS Class: 99%
% Graduated in Top 50% of HS Class: 100%

ENROLLMENT
Total Undergraduate Enrollment: 1,647
% Part-Time: 0%
% Male: 49%
% Female: 51%
% Out-of-State: 88%
% Fraternity: 11%
% Sorority: 3%
% On-Campus (Freshman): 100%
% On-Campus (All Undergraduate): 96%

% African-American: 8%
% Asian: 16%
% Hispanic: 13%
% White: 39%
% Other: 7%
% Race or Ethnicity Unknown: 4%
% International: 13%
% Low-Income: 13%

ACADEMICS
Student-to-Faculty Ratio: 8:1
% of Classes Under 20: 74%
% of Classes Under 40: 95%
% Full-Time Faculty: 88%
% Full-Time Faculty w/ Terminal Degree: 100%

Top Programs
Biology
Computer Science
Economics
Educational Studies
Engineering
Mathematics
Political Science
Sociology

Retention Rate: 97%
4-Year Graduation Rate: 87%
6-Year Graduation Rate: 94%

Curricular Flexibility: Very Flexible
Academic Rating: ★★★★★

Inside the Classroom

The average person in the United States may not be fully aware that Swarthmore College, located on Philadelphia's Main Line, is one of, if not *the* finest liberal arts schools in the entire country. The good news is that top employers and grad schools know Swarthmore's quality well. The 1,647 undergraduate students who attend Swat are an exceptional group, having been among the 8.7 percent to gain acceptance. The college has never been more difficult to get into as applications have tripled since the turn of the millennium. A quick examination of the superb academics offered at this school is all it takes to fully understand the reasons for the long lines outside the gates.

Despite its small size, the college offers forty undergraduate programs and runs 600+ courses each academic year. A member of the Tri-College Consortium with fellow top institutions Haverford and Bryn Mawr, students can cross-register at those institutions as well as at the University of Pennsylvania. Unusual for a school full of perfect-SAT/valedictorian-types, Swat also offers an honors program that involves highly independent, self-directed study that culminates with a series of oral exams. All undergrads must complete at least three courses in all three divisions: Humanities, Natural Science & Engineering, and Social Sciences. Additional requirements include three courses that are designated "writing intensive," physical education, a foreign language, and one laboratory science course.

Small, seminar-style courses are the norm at Swat—an outstanding 34 percent of sections enroll fewer than ten students, and 70 percent contain a maximum of nineteen students. Overall, the average class size is sixteen. Thanks to an 8:1 student-to-faculty ratio and zero grad students, professors are extremely available in and outside the classroom. As a result, two-thirds of graduates complete at least one undergraduate research or independent creative project, and the college sets aside $800,000 in funding for that express purpose. Forty percent of students elect to study abroad for a semester in one of 300 programs in sixty countries.

Social science degrees are the most commonly conferred, accounting for 26 percent of all 2018 graduates. Future academics and researchers would do well to look at Swat—a whopping 22 percent of graduates go on to earn PhDs. Future businessmen/women, engineers, and techies are also well positioned, given Swat's incredibly strong offerings in economics, engineering, and computer science. When it comes to prestigious scholarships, Swarthmore is winning in disproportionately large numbers. In 2018, ten grads/alumni nabbed Fulbright Scholarships, four have been named Rhodes Scholars in the past decade, and undergraduates have won Gaither Fellowships, Watson Fellowships, and Luce Scholarships in recent years.

Outside the Classroom

Swarthmore is a connected and tight-knit campus community where 95 percent of students live in one of eighteen residence halls spread across the college's 425-acre grounds. Greek organizations do exist, but their presence is minor as only 11 percent of men and 3 percent of women are affiliated with a fraternity or sorority. There are twenty-two sports teams competing in the NCAA Division III ranks, and roughly 20 percent of the undergraduate student body are members of one of the varsity teams. There are also plenty of intramural and club sports options, including the uber-popular ultimate Frisbee. More than one hundred campus organizations include a number of volunteer groups that attract 60 percent of the student body. The other Tri-Co member schools, Haverford College and Bryn Mawr, are in close proximity, further expanding the social scene at Swarthmore. The town itself is located on the Main Line, which means there is plenty of dining and culture available, pretty much all of which comes at a high cost. Fortunately, everything the city of Philadelphia has to offer isn't far from campus. There is a regional rail line nearby affording students access to the entire city, and West Philadelphia and University City are only about a forty-minute bike ride.

Career Services

Career Services at Swarthmore College employs eight individuals who specialize in career education, employer relations, and internships and technology. The 204:1 student-to-advisor ratio is better than average when compared to other colleges featured in this guidebook. As a member of the Tri-College Consortium with Haverford and Bryn Mawr as well as the Fall Recruiting Consortium with schools like Brown and William & Mary, Swarthmore students are afforded innumerable opportunities to get face time with the world's leading employers; over eighty companies recruited on campus last year.

One-on-one attention is available for anyone who wishes to take advantage of it. In the 2017-18 school year Swat engaged 62 percent of the total student body, including 70 percent of seniors. The office conducted 817 counseling appointments with 373 unique individuals to address areas such as interview prep (24 percent), job search (22 percent), internship search (18 percent), and general career exploration (16 percent). A solid 70 percent of graduates completed at least one internship as part of the undergraduate experience; 42 percent completed one or more externships. Locations for those experiences included some of the most desirable organizations around including The World Bank, the FDA, and Capital One. Visitors to campus include more than one hundred alumni mentors per year and companies like Google, which spent two full days at Swat in 2018 meeting with computer science students. Offering an enviable level of service to its undergraduates and producing across-the-board positive outcomes, this career services office is held in high esteem by our staff.

Professional Outcomes

Seventy percent of Class of 2018 graduates had already entered the workforce shortly after graduation; 77 percent had secured a job prior to completing their degree. Popular industries included financial services (30 percent), research (23 percent), and technology/engineering (21 percent). Google is one of the leading employers of Swarthmore grads followed by Amazon, Goldman Sachs, IBM, and a number of the leading universities in the nation. In the last five years the cities attracting the highest percentage of Swat alumni were New York City (20 percent), Philadelphia (19 percent), DC (14 percent), Boston (8 percent), and San Francisco (6 percent). The average starting salary for 2018 graduates entering engineering jobs was $94,000. The mean figure for those in finance was $73,000, and grads working in research took home $43,000.

Over four-fifths of the 2018 senior class planned to enroll in graduate school within the next five years, and 21 percent did so directly after graduation. Among those pursuing advanced degrees the most frequently attended institutions were Harvard, Penn, Yale, Princeton, Stanford, MIT, and Cornell—not a shabby top seven. PhDs were pursued by 46 percent of this cohort while 31 percent entered master's programs, 11 percent headed to law school, and 10 percent matriculated into medical school. The medical school acceptance rate for grads and alumni typically hovers close to 85 percent, an astounding number that is roughly double the national average. The school also has an early acceptance program with Thomas Jefferson University's Sidney Kimmel Medical College. Swarthmore also sports a 97 percent acceptance rate into law schools, and the institutions attended are typically of the elite variety.

Admission

There were 11,400 applications submitted for a spot in the Class of 2023, but fewer than 1,000 were accepted for an acceptance rate of only 9 percent. While the school's acceptance rate has decreased in the last decade (it was 16 percent ten years ago), it's unlikely that anyone will mistake Swat for anything less than one of the most selective schools in the country. Ninety percent of 2018-19 freshmen placed in the top decile of their graduating high school class. Mid-50 percent standardized test scores were 1380-1550 on the SAT and 31-34 on the ACT. For perhaps a better perspective, the median SAT score was 1490 and the median ACT score was 33. An exceptional 70 percent of attending Class of 2022 students scored above a 700 on the SAT's reading section and 81 percent scored higher than 700 on the math section.

The admissions committee ranks six factors as being of paramount importance in the admissions process: rigor of secondary coursework, class rank, GPA, application essay, recommendations, and character/personal qualities. Test scores and extracurricular activities land in the second tier, but they are serious about extracurriculars, particularly those involving community service; 36 percent of those accepted into the Class of 2023 were involved with a community, national, or international service organization. In a typical year Swat enjoys a yield rate in excess of 40 percent, meaning that it has no trouble landing a sizable percentage of those offered admission. Legacy candidates make up 10 percent of the admitted Class of 2023 cohort while 27 percent are first generation. If Swarthmore is your top choice, applying early decision is wise; it fills over half of its class through ED, and the acceptance rate is a less cutthroat 26 percent. Swarthmore remains one of, if the not the best liberal arts school in the country and will continue to sport a single-digit acceptance rate well into the future.

Worth Your Money?

Swarthmore has pledged to fully meet 100 percent of student need, which helps explain why the 56 percent of undergrads who are eligible receive a sizable average grant of $53,395. That certainly makes the $73,524 cost of attendance more manageable for lower-income and middle- class families. On the flip side, Swat rarely awards any merit aid whatsoever, so if your parents earn a nice living, you will likely be paying the sticker price. Of course, for a chance to attend one of the best colleges in the world, that is hardly a bad choice.

FINANCIAL
Institutional Type: Private
In-State Tuition: $54,256
Out-of-State Tuition: $54,256
Room & Board: $16,088
Required Fees: $400
Books & Supplies: $1,400

Avg. Need-Based Aid: $53,395
Avg. % of Need Met: 100%

Avg. Merit-Based Aid: $0
% Receiving Merit-Based Aid: 0%

Avg. Cumulative Debt: $22,060
% of Students Borrowing: 24%

CAREER
Who Recruits
1. Foreseter Capital
2. The Brattle Group
3. Apogee Adventures
4. American Enterprise Institute
5. M&T Bank

Notable Internships
1. Salesforce
2. Deutsche Bank
3. Children's Hospital of Philadelphia

Top Industries
1. Education
2. Business
3. Research
4. Media
5. Social Services

Top Employers
1. Google
2. Amazon
3. Goldman Sachs
4. Apple
5. Facebook

Where Alumni Work
1. Philadelphia
2. New York City
3. San Francisco
4. Washington, DC
5. Boston

Median Earnings
College Scorecard (Early Career): $56,700
EOP (Early Career): $56,700
PayScale (Mid-Career): $123,200

RANKINGS
Forbes: 25
Money: 37
U.S. News: 3, Liberal Arts Colleges
Wall Street Journal/THE: 28
Washington Monthly: 15, Liberal Arts Colleges

#CollegesWorthYourMoney

Syracuse University

Syracuse, New York | Admissions Phone: 315-443-3611

Inside the Classroom

A private research university of over 15,000 undergraduates, Syracuse University has a reputation for more than just its instantly recognizable bright orange colors. The 'Cuse plays home to a diverse group of students, nationally-ranked sports teams, a devoted alumni network, and a broad array of academic offerings, including a number of standout programs.

In total, 200+ majors and one hundred+ minors are spread across ten undergraduate schools/colleges: The School of Architecture, the College of Arts & Sciences, the School of Education, the College of Engineering & Computer Science, the Falk College of Sport & Human Dynamics, the School of Information Studies, the Whitman School of Management, the Maxwell School of Citizenship and Public Affairs, the Newhouse School of Public Communication, and the College of Visual and Performing Arts. Required courses vary significantly by school, but some common areas include two writing-intensive courses, two classes in foreign language, and a smattering of social science, math/science, and humanities selections.

Despite a high number of graduate students also studying at SU, class sizes are kept reasonably low; 59 percent contain twenty students or fewer. A student-to-faculty ratio of 15:1 does mean you are likely to receive some instruction from graduate students/adjuncts along the way. The Undergraduate Research Program runs through the College of Arts & Sciences but is open to all SU students. Willing professors extend offers for research apprenticeships to highly motivated students. Recent student-assisted, faculty-led research projects include Community Theater in Kenya, The Internet's Role in the Political Process, and Cloning of Leukemia Cells. Syracuse Abroad, the university's office of study abroad programs, arranges for 45 percent of undergrads to spend a semester in a foreign land. There are more than a hundred programs in sixty+ countries to choose from.

The most popular majors include information technology, psychology, finance, political science, marketing, economics, and radio and television. The School of Architecture, Maxwell School of Citizenship and Public Affairs, and Newhouse are all revered names that carry a good deal of weight in their respective fields. Newhouse, in particular, is dominant in the worlds of broadcasting and television/radio/film. Students of all academic backgrounds are competitive in procuring prestigious postgraduate fellowships, albeit at a modest clip. In 2018, Orange graduates accepted at least one Fulbright, Beinecke, SMART, Luce, Mitchell, and Astronaut Scholarship; eight students took home Fulbrights in 2019.

Outside the Classroom

Frigid temperatures and snowy conditions make for long, boring winters in Upstate New York. Thus, like many other institutions in the region, Syracuse receives the designation as a top (if not *the* top) "party school" on a fair number of lists. The sixty fraternities and sororities are at the heart of the lively social scene. Roughly one-third join a Greek organization. SU offers a big-time sports program with a rabid following. Many join the sea of orange in the Carrier Dome for football and basketball games; in total, there are seven men's and eleven women's NCAA Division I teams. Non-sports activities come in the form of 300+ student-run clubs, including a wide selection of performing arts troupes (there are seven a cappella organizations), pre-professional meet-ups, or the *Daily Orange* newspaper, which is one of the more widely read campus dailies in the country and a frequent award-winner. On campus, Marshall Street is home to a number of beloved eateries and bars and is rarely quiet. Likewise, the Quad is always abuzz with activity, especially when the weather is decent. The city of Syracuse may not be the most cosmopolitan locale, but it does feature Destiny USA, the nation's sixth largest shopping/entertainment complex, and it's only a short ride from campus.

Career Services

For a school of over 15,000 undergraduates, SU's Career Services Office employs a central staff of eight career counseling professionals as well as smaller branch offices housed within the various colleges. Collectively, there are thirty-three full-time staff members working in career services, which equates to a 462:1 student-to-advisor ratio, higher than the average school featured in this guidebook but not all that concerning given the size of the university.

Flagship events include a Local Internship Fair, Fall Career Fair, and Spring Career Fair. Niche events are held year-round by the various colleges to cater to students in particular fields of study. Students can, at any time, utilize OrangeLink to view 6,000+ job and internship postings and keep abreast of on-campus recruiting/interviewing opportunities. Internship procurement varies greatly by school. The Whitman School of Management requires an internship for graduation, and three-quarters of them are paid positions. Many other undergrads must rely on the university's fervent alumni network comprised of about a quarter million people worldwide to land a position. Within Newhouse, companies recruiting on campus include CBS News, Hearst Television, McCann, Instagram, and NBCUniversal. The school does not publish the total number of one-on-one counseling sessions held or the number of on-campus interviews facilitated by career services.

Professional Outcomes

Six months after exiting the Carrier Dome for the final time, 65 percent of Orangemen and women have found employment (90 percent related to their career goals), 15 percent are continuing to graduate school, and 10 percent are either seeking employment or working part time. The companies employing the most 'Cuse grads include major media/entertainment management companies like Conde Nast, Bloomberg, and Creative Artists Agency as well as big-name corporations like GE, KPMG, EY, Lockheed Martin, and Morgan Stanley. The average starting salary for SU undergraduates across all majors is $51k. Interestingly, due to the nature of the business for which it prepares its students, Newhouse grads earn a mean starting salary of only $40k. Those who studied at the Whitman School of Management, College of Engineering & Computer Science, or School of Information Studies averaged between $59k and $66k. Over 70 percent of graduates tend to remain in the Northeast with the West Coast coming in a distant second, attracting 11 percent of grads.

A fair number of those headed to graduate school remain in New York state. NYU, Hofstra, Fordham, and the University of Buffalo are among the most popular destinations to pursue an advanced degree. Elite universities such as Yale, Johns Hopkins, Columbia, and Northwestern also make the list of most popular graduate schools attended. Examining the past several years of law school admissions data, it is fair to say that Syracuse does not send a high number of graduates to elite law schools. The university does not publish medical school acceptance data, but a review of recent acceptances indicates a strong relationship with nearby SUNY Upstate Medical School. In that time the school also has produced some acceptances into the nation's top medical institutions.

Admission

Most colleges with national name recognition on par with the 'Cuse have experienced an uptick in selectivity since the turn of the millennium. The fact that Syracuse's numbers have held steady for a couple of decades makes it a refreshing oddity. A touch over 50 percent of applicants are granted acceptance, and the academic profile of the average attendee is strong but not overly intimidating. Standardized test scores do not have to be exceptional to gain acceptance into SU. The middle-50 percent range for accepted students is 1180-1370. Last year's freshman class was comprised of 39 percent of students who finished in the top 10 percent of their high school class; 71 percent were in the top 25 percent, and 6 percent failed to crack the top 50 percent. The average GPA for all 2018-19 freshman was 3.67; 17 percent possessed less than a 3.25.

The Newhouse School of Public Communication is more selective than the university at large. The typical student admitted to Newhouse scored over 1300 on the SAT and earned a 3.8 GPA in high school. Whichever school you are applying to, early decision can work to your benefit as ED applicants got in 58 percent of the time in the most recent cycle. However, if you plan on applying ED, make sure you can afford it. While ED applicants get full consideration for financial aid, SU is on the expensive side, so having a chance to compare aid offers can be advantageous. Perfection is not expected by the SU Office of Admissions. It is a selective university that has room for those with B averages and/or non-eye-popping standardized test scores.

Worth Your Money?

With a list-price of $72,371 (annual COA), Syracuse University is not accessible to those on a budget without financial help. Forty-six percent do receive need-based with average annual grants of around $31k. The university does offer merit aid, but generally grants it to only 20 percent of the population, and those awards don't tend to be for massive sums that significantly alter the total cost of attendance. Syracuse is worth spending up for if you have the opportunity to enter a top-flight program like Newhouse, and it's a solid choice if your parents are able to pay the full bill. Those on a budget who do not receive a generous aid package may find a better value elsewhere.

FINANCIAL
Institutional Type: Private
In-State Tuition: $53,849
Out-of-State Tuition: $53,849
Room & Board: $15,910
Required Fees: $1,639
Books & Supplies: $1,536

Avg. Need-Based Aid: $42,060
Avg. % of Need Met: 94%

Avg. Merit-Based Aid: $9,830
% Receiving Merit-Based Aid: 27%

Avg. Cumulative Debt: $37,707
% of Students Borrowing: 59%

CAREER
Who Recruits
1. SmartestEnergy
2. M&T Bank
3. Oppenheimer & Co.
4. City Year
5. General Electric

Notable Internships
1. Gensler
2. WeWork
3. Berksire Hathaway

Top Industries
1. Business
2. Education
3. Operations
4. Arts & Design
5. Media

Top Employers
1. IBM
2. EY
3. Microsoft
4. JPMorgan Chase
5. Amazon

Where Alumni Work
1. New York City
2. Syracuse, NY
3. Boston
4. Washington, DC
5. Los Angeles

Median Earnings
College Scorecard (Early Career): $62,100
EOP (Early Career): $61,100
PayScale (Mid-Career): $104,800

RANKINGS
Forbes: 156
Money: 208
U.S. News: 54, National Universities
Wall Street Journal/THE: 123 (T)
Washington Monthly: 33, National Universities

#CollegesWorthYourMoney

College Station, Texas | Admissions Phone: 979-845-1060

ADMISSION
Admission Rate: 67%
Admission Rate - Men: 69%
Admission Rate - Women: 66%
EA Admission Rate: Not Offered
ED Admission Rate: Not Offered
Admission Rate (5-Year Trend): -2%
ED Admission Rate (5-Year Trend): Not Offered
% of Admits Attending (Yield): 45%
Transfer Admission Rate: 54%

Offered Wait List: Not Offered
Accepted Wait List: Not Offered
Admitted Wait List: Not Offered

SAT Reading/Writing (Middle 50%): 580-680
SAT Math (Middle 50%): 590-700
ACT Composite (Middle 50%): 25-31
Testing Policy: ACT/SAT Required
SAT Superscore: No
ACT Superscore: No

% Graduated in Top 10% of HS Class: 63%
% Graduated in Top 25% of HS Class: 92%
% Graduated in Top 50% of HS Class: 99%

ENROLLMENT
Total Undergraduate Enrollment: 53,743
% Part-Time: 12%
% Male: 53%
% Female: 47%
% Out-of-State: 4%
% Fraternity: 8%
% Sorority: 17%
% On-Campus (Freshman): 67%
% On-Campus (All Undergraduate): 22%

% African-American: 3%
% Asian: 8%
% Hispanic: 24%
% White: 60%
% Other: 3%
% Race or Ethnicity Unknown: 0%
% International: 1%
% Low-Income: 31%

ACADEMICS
Student-to-Faculty Ratio: 20:1
% of Classes Under 20: 21%
% of Classes Under 40: 64%
% Full-Time Faculty: 86%
% Full-Time Faculty w/ Terminal Degree: 86%

Top Programs
Agriculture
Architecture
Business
Communication
Engineering
Kinesiology
Political Science

Retention Rate: 92%
4-Year Graduation Rate: 55%
6-Year Graduation Rate: 82%

Curricular Flexibility: Less Flexible
Academic Rating: ★★★

Inside the Classroom
You've heard it a million times: "Everything's bigger in Texas." Perhaps the origin of that saying stems from the fact that the state is three times the size of the United Kingdom, or perhaps it was first uttered by a visitor to Texas A&M College Station's gargantuan 5,200-acre campus that is home to 54,000+ undergraduates and another 15,000 graduate and professional degree- seekers, making it one of the largest higher education operations in the United States. With nineteen schools and colleges, 130+ undergraduate degree programs, and an emphasis on agriculture, engineering, and business, this public land-grant university educates an army of future professionals who carry their Aggie pride with them for life.

The Texas Core Curriculum dictates a good amount of the coursework underclassmen must knock out, amounting to forty-two credit hours. Mandates include three classes in life and physical sciences, two classes in each of communication, mathematics, American history, government and political science, and one class in each of language philosophy and culture, creative arts, and the social and behavioral sciences. Collectively, these courses are meant to promote six key skill areas: critical thinking, communication, empirical and quantitative, teamwork, personal responsibility, and social responsibility. Students in the university Honors College are typically required to complete a senior thesis within their departmental home.

Class sizes definitely trend large, not terribly shocking considering the 20:1 student-to-faculty ratio and a graduate school population larger than many entire universities. Only 21 percent of courses enroll fewer than twenty students at A&M, and 36 percent enroll more than forty students. In order to forge personal connections with professors, the LAUNCH program encourages students to apply to participate in undergraduate research during the school year or the summer under the mentorship of a faculty member. Some majors—chemistry, for one— require all students to complete undergraduate research as part of their bachelor's program. A&M excels in facilitating study abroad experiences, sending 5,330 students to 105 countries last year, the most of any public university in the United States.

As the name of the university implies, agriculture and engineering are at the core of what A&M does. Over 19,000 students are presently enrolled in the College of Engineering and 7,700 in the College of Agriculture and Life Sciences. Yet, the College of Liberal Arts (8,500), College of Education and Human Development (6,800), and the Mays Business School (6,300) are sizable presences on campus as well. The business, agriculture, and engineering programs all place well in national rankings and garner deep respect from major national corporations and graduate/professional schools. Considering its size, A&M does not produce a large number of prestigious postgraduate scholarship winners. In 2019, it produced twelve National Science Foundation Graduate Research Fellows, seven Gilman Scholars, and two Critical Language Scholars.

Outside the Classroom
While two-thirds of freshmen live on campus, just about everyone else moves into off-campus housing by sophomore year. Housing is not guaranteed to freshmen and is awarded on a first-come, first-served basis. Fortunately, nice and affordable housing in the area is ample, and the school's database, AggieSearch, helps you locate available living spaces. There are sixty+ Greek organizations on campus with women joining sororities at a higher rate (17 percent) than men join fraternities (8 percent). Athletics are huge with 650 varsity athletes competing in twenty NCAA Division I sports, and the "Twelfth Man," the fan base, is extraordinarily passionate about its teams. For non-superstar athletes, there are thirty-four club sports squads and over 12,000 students participate in intramural sports each year, making it one of the largest programs in the country. The Student Recreation Center contains 400,000 square feet of space for fun and fitness and boasts everything from an archery room to multiple pools. Texas A&M has 1,100 student organizations, making it impossible not to find your niche. An incredible 2,600 undergrads are involved in ROTC, and the Cadet Corps is the largest such group in the country. As the name implies, College Station is a happening college town, brimming with locally famous bars and eateries, particularly within the historic Northgate District. Situated in the so-called Texas Triangle in the central part of the state, major cities like Houston or Austin can be accessed easily by car for a weekend road trip.

Career Services
The Texas A&M Career Center was established in 1939, long before the term "career services" was even a concept at most schools. Including all college-specific career advisors, employer relations, and professional school advising staff members, there are twenty-seven full-time professional staff members (not including office managers and admin assistants). That works out to a student-to-advisor ratio of 2,213:1, easily the highest in this guidebook. Irrespective of that bloated ratio, the A&M career services staff does remarkable things for the second largest undergraduate student body in the United States, and it publishes the numbers to prove it.

Texas A&M University – College Station

E-mail: admissions@tamu.edu | Website: www.tamu.edu

In the 2017-18 school year, the A&M Career Center made direct contact with 19,000 students, drew 30,000 individuals to 130 outreach events, and 37,000 to 760 workshops and other career services programs. It posted 60,000 jobs and 13,000 internship opportunities on its online database and, more importantly, it enticed a stupefying 4,000 employers to actively recruit Aggie undergrads. In total, 57 percent of students had an internship, co-op, or study abroad experience while at College Station, and interns worked with 1,000 different companies. Operating on an almost unimaginable scope, Texas A&M's Career Center gets the job done.

Professional Outcomes

On graduation day 2018, a solid 55 percent of soon-to-be degree-holders had already received at least one job offer, 24 percent were heading to graduate/professional school, and 23 percent were still searching for their next career step. Texas A&M supplies a number of major oil, tech, and consulting firms with a hard-to-fathom numbers of employees. More than 500 Aggies presently work for companies such as ExxonMobil, Halliburton, Chevron, EY, Amazon, Microsoft, Intel, Accenture, and PWC. More than 300 alumni work for Apple, Oracle, and Google. Fifty-five engineering students from the Class of 2019 alone were hired by Lockheed Martin. Starting salaries were strong with the average College of Engineering graduate making $70,500, and the average College of Liberal Arts and College of Agriculture & Life Sciences graduate netting $49,500. The vast majority of graduates remain in Texas with Houston, Dallas, College Station, Austin, and San Antonio tops in popularity. However, cities like San Fran, DC, New York, and Denver also have a notable Aggies representation.

Medical and dental school acceptance rates are far above the Texas state average. In 2018, Aggies were admitted to medical school at a 52 percent clip (state average was 28 percent) and to dental school 56 percent of the time (state average was 31 percent). Among those applicants with a 3.5 or higher GPA and a 505+ MCAT score, 91 percent were accepted to medical school. Institutions where 2018 graduates gained acceptance included Columbia, Cornell, Wake Forest, Yale, Vanderbilt, and Northwestern. Given the engineering focus at A&M, it may surprise you that the school is the eighth largest producer of law students in the entire country. The Class of 2018 collectively applied to 173 law schools and earned admission at 146 of them.

Admission

Texas A&M admitted a favorable two-thirds of those who applied for the 2018-19 freshman class. That group had a mid-50 percent SAT range of 1170-1380 and a 25-31 on the ACT. Texas A&M offers automatic admission for anyone in the top 10 percent of their high school class (public or private), and a hefty number of Class of 2022 members met that standard—63 percent. Overall, 92 percent finished at least in the top 25 percent. Five years ago, the acceptance rate was a similar 69 percent, but the average applicant had lower standardized test scores and only 78 percent of students placed in the top quartile. Simply put, you'll need better academic credentials to get into A&M today than you would have in the recent past. This is especially so for engineering and business applicants who face the toughest admission odds and who will likely need to possess grades and standardized test scores at or above the 75th percentile.

The admissions office is looking primarily at class rank, standardized test scores, rigor of courses, GPA, extracurricular activities, and talent/ability. It also looks closely at geographical residence, which translates to 94 percent of undergrads presently on the College Station campus hailing from the Lone Star State. With such a large applicant pool, there are no interviews offered. There is no early action or early decision offered either; the deadline is December 1 for every applicant. Applicants who are not admitted automatically through placing in the top 10 percent of their class have a much lower success rate of 35 percent.

Worth Your Money?

Tuition for in-state students is under $11,000, and the total cost of attendance is less than $30k. Combine those extremely fair rates with favorable return on investment figures, and A&M is clearly one of the great values in higher education. A nonresident will pay twice as much, but if you lack better in-state options close to home, a business or engineering degree from this institution will still pay for itself.

FINANCIAL
Institutional Type: Public
In-State Tuition: $7,406
Out-of-State Tuition: $33,074
Room & Board: $10,436
Required Fees: $3,562
Books & Supplies: $1,222

Avg. Need-Based Aid: $12,193
Avg. % of Need Met: 74%

Avg. Merit-Based Aid: $4,667
% Receiving Merit-Based Aid: 18%

Avg. Cumulative Debt: $24,175
% of Students Borrowing: 41%

CAREER
Who Recruits
1. Air Liquide
2. NBCUniversal
3. Ethos Group
4. Manhattan Associates
5. Nvidia

Notable Internships
1. Phillips 66
2. Novartis
3. CBRE

Top Industries
1. Business
2. Operations
3. Engineering
4. Education
5. Sales

Top Employers
1. Haliburton
2. Deloitte
3. EY
4. Amazon
5. Intel

Where Alumni Work
1. Houston
2. Dallas
3. College Station, TX
4. Austin
5. San Antonio

Median Earnings
College Scorecard (Early Career): $58,000
EOP (Early Career): $59,400
PayScale (Mid-Career): $115,700

RANKINGS
Forbes: 103
Money: 18
U.S. News: 70 (T), National Universities
Wall Street Journal/THE: 78
Washington Monthly: 10, National Universities

#CollegesWorthYourMoney

Trinity College (CT)

Hartford, Connecticut | Admissions Phone: 860-297-2180

ADMISSION
Admission Rate: 34%
Admission Rate - Men: 31%
Admission Rate - Women: 36%
EA Admission Rate: Not Offered
ED Admission Rate: 58%
Admission Rate (5-Year Trend): +2%
ED Admission Rate (5-Year Trend): -5%
% of Admits Attending (Yield): 28%
Transfer Admission Rate: 26%

Offered Wait List: 1,827
Accepted Wait List: 1,103
Admitted Wait List: 11

SAT Reading/Writing (Middle 50%): 630-710
SAT Math (Middle 50%): 670-750
ACT Composite (Middle 50%): 29-32
Testing Policy: Test Optional
SAT Superscore: Yes
ACT Superscore: Yes

% Graduated in Top 10% of HS Class: 46%
% Graduated in Top 25% of HS Class: 76%
% Graduated in Top 50% of HS Class: 95%

ENROLLMENT
Total Undergraduate Enrollment: 2,182
% Part-Time: 3%
% Male: 50%
% Female: 50%
% Out-of-State: 82%
% Fraternity: 29%
% Sorority: 17%
% On-Campus (Freshman): 100%
% On-Campus (All Undergraduate): 86%

% African-American: 6%
% Asian: 4%
% Hispanic: 9%
% White: 63%
% Other: 3%
% Race or Ethnicity Unknown: 3%
% International: 13%
% Low-Income: 10%

ACADEMICS
Student-to-Faculty Ratio: 9:1
% of Classes Under 20: 72%
% of Classes Under 40: 97%
% Full-Time Faculty: 74%
% Full-Time Faculty w/ Terminal Degree: 95%

Top Programs
Anthropology
Economics
Engineering
History
International Studies
Public Policy and Law
Urban Studies

Retention Rate: 91%
4-Year Graduation Rate: 78%
6-Year Graduation Rate: 84%

Curricular Flexibility: Very Flexible
Academic Rating: ★★★✓

Inside the Classroom
Established as Washington College in 1823 before being renamed in 1845, Trinity College was founded as an Episcopalian alternative to Congregationalist Yale; it is the second oldest college in the state of Connecticut. What began as a college of nine male students is today a 100-acre campus within the confines of downtown Hartford that features 2,200 full-time undergraduates, forty-one majors, and more than 900 distinct courses. Famous alumni are a disparate lot that includes both conservative voices like George Will and Tucker Carlson as well as the legendary absurdist playwright Edward Albee of *Who's Afraid of Virginia Woolf* fame.

Freshmen learn the ropes of academic reading and writing in either a first-year seminar or via the invitation-only Gateway Program. An additional course bearing the "writing intensive" designation must be completed at some point during one's undergraduate program. All students are required to demonstrate competency as writers, quantitative thinkers, and in one foreign language. Lastly, all students must either complete a course with a global focus or participate in a study abroad program. Passing one course with a C- or better in each of the arts, humanities, natural sciences, numerical and symbolic reasoning, and the social sciences are the only other requirements in what amounts to a very open curriculum.

With a total graduate student population that doesn't even hit triple digits, the bulk of the resources are directed toward Bantam undergraduates. Thus, a student/faculty ratio of 9:1 translates to 72 percent of course sections boasting an enrollment of nineteen or fewer students, and one-quarter of sections having fewer than ten; the mean number of students in a class is seventeen. Working closely with faculty is a real possibility at this school where one hundred students conduct research each year alongside faculty through the Summer Research Program, and roughly two-thirds engage in some type of undergraduate research. Greater than 60 percent of Trinity students study abroad and have access to Trinity-exclusive programs in Shanghai and Cape Town and school-run programs in Paris, Barcelona, Rome, Vienna, and Trinidad.

Trinity College is well regarded across the board with an economics department that feeds many leading investment banks and an engineering program that is among the best you will find at a small liberal arts school. Most degrees are conferred in the social sciences, biology, and psychology. While only a small percentage of graduates pursue prestigious national fellowships, a few do typically take home Fulbrights and an occasional Watson Scholarship each year, but the school has only two Rhodes Scholars in its history.

Outside the Classroom
Over 90 percent of Trinity undergraduates reside on campus, and 100 percent of freshmen are housed in one of seven first-year exclusive dorms. Greek life is more popular among men (29 percent join a fraternity) than women (17 percent join a sorority). Competing in the New England Small College Athletic Conference within NCAA Division III, the Bantams field twenty-eight varsity teams evenly split between men's and women's squads. Including club sports, over 40 percent of the student body participates in intercollegiate athletics. While sports and frats dominate the social scene, the Students Activities, Involvement, and Leadership Office (SAIL) oversees 150+ student-run clubs and organizations. While the school touts the "real-world" aspect of being located in downtown Hartford, the city presently has one of the highest per-capita crime rates in the United States. Affluent students, of whom there are many at Trinity, often prefer roads trips to Montreal, New York City, or Boston over their "home" city. However, the spirit of volunteerism is strong, and the Office of Community Service and Civic Engagement offers endless opportunities to work in areas such as hunger, housing, the homeless, and education.

Career Services
The Center for Student Success and Career Development features six full-time staff members who specialize in areas such as strategic partnerships, pre-law advising, and pre-health career advising. That equates to a student-to-advisor ratio of 370:1, in the average range when compared against other liberal arts colleges featured in this guide. The college is one of a dozen schools in the country that uses Stanford University's Designing Your Life approach that encourages undergraduates to shed rigid views and fears about career and, instead, use their passions, goals, and creative problem-solving skills to move toward a meaningful path. To pursue that aim, Trinity invites students to join one of six Career Communities designed for those who wish to take advantage of industry-specific career advice, internship opportunities, Career Treks, panel discussions, and Career Skills Labs.

Other perks include a Career Studio where students can stop by any time for help with tangible job search products like resumes, cover letters, or creating a LinkedIn profile. In addition, the Bantam Career Network functions like a private LinkedIn where current students can network with alumni in their fields of interest. The college does not host any large-scale career fairs, but the Career Connections Summit on parents' weekend affords undergraduates the chance to network with representatives from top corporations. Trinity has invested heavily in its career development in the last decade, and that financial commitment is starting to bear fruit. This forward-thinking center is innovating every year, and its efforts are reflected in career/graduate school outcomes, earning it top marks from our staff.

Professional Outcomes

Surveyed members of the Class of 2018 had found a positive outcome at a 95.2 percent clip. Those entering the world of employment landed jobs at desirable organizations like the New York City Ballet, NBC Universal, and Morgan Stanley, a company with a hefty share of alumni. A large Bantam presence also can be felt in the corporate offices of Citi, Merrill Lynch, Fidelity Investments, Google, IBM, and Goldman Sachs. Finance (17 percent), communications and media (16 percent), education (12 percent), science and health care (12 percent), and management (11 percent) are the most frequently entered fields. Starting and midcareer salaries tend to be on the higher side, ranking in the top ten among highly selective private colleges alongside many engineering-heavy schools. While a fair number of graduates remain in the Hartford area, New York City and Boston occupy the one and two slots for highest alumni concentrations.

Many Trinity grads go on to prestigious graduate schools; 60 percent of alumni have entered or completed a graduate or professional program within five years. Class of 2018 members matriculated into the likes of Yale Medical School, Cambridge University, and Columbia University. Medical or other health-related program applicants are successful 80 percent of the time and are presently enrolled at institutions such as Georgetown, Tufts, Penn, Cornell, and Boston University. Graduates eying law school earn an average LSAT of 160 (80th percentile) and enroll at a vast array of universities including Top Fourteen law schools like Duke, Cornell, Columbia, Stanford, and Northwestern.

Admission

The Class of 2023 saw 33 percent of applicants admitted, an acceptance rate identical to that of the previous three cycles. In Trinity's fourth year as a test-optional school, 58 percent of those who ultimately enrolled took advantage of the policy, not submitting an SAT or ACT score. Middle-50 percent scores of those who did submit standardized test results were 1300-1460 on the SAT and 29-32 on the ACT. Transcripts have to be strong but not immaculate as 46 percent of attendees placed in the top decile of their high school class while 76 percent were in the top quartile.

Rigor of secondary school record, GPA, and character/personal qualities constitute the triumvirate of most important factors. The committee genuinely values intangible qualities that research has shown leads to post-secondary success such as "grit, optimism, persistence, a willingness to take risks, and an ability to overcome adversity." A supplemental essay explaining why applicants wish to attend college in an urban setting also is recommended. The college fills almost half its freshman class via two early decision rounds. The 2023 cohort was comprised of 285 ED students, which included 152 varsity athletes. ED admit rates reached 58 percent in 2018-19 cycle, and those admitted via that round comprised 52 percent of the incoming class. Trinity is a more desirable destination than ever. In 2015, only 22 percent of accepted students elected to attend, but that figure has jumped to 30 percent in recent years. Applying ED or ED II is undoubtedly a wise strategic move.

Worth Your Money?

At $76,450 in annual costs, Trinity won't come cheap. It does not offer much in the way of merit aid, instead focusing its efforts on meeting all of the demonstrated need of students eligible for financial aid. In fact, the 54 percent of current undergraduates who are need-eligible receive annual grants of over $48k per year, bringing Trinity's tuition much more within reach. As a school that helps you develop professional networks and connects you to big-time employers, Trinity can be worth taking on a reasonable amount of debt in order to attend.

FINANCIAL
Institutional Type: Private
In-State Tuition: $56,380
Out-of-State Tuition: $56,380
Room & Board: $15,300
Required Fees: $2,670
Books & Supplies: $1,000

Avg. Need-Based Aid: $48,334
Avg. % of Need Met: 100%

Avg. Merit-Based Aid: $58,374
% Receiving Merit-Based Aid: 3%

Avg. Cumulative Debt: $30,893
% of Students Borrowing: 44%

CAREER
Who Recruits
1. Salesforce
2. CBRE
3. UBS
4. Accenture
5. Fidelity Investments

Notable Internships
1. WeWork
2. Wayfair
3. Boston Public Health Commission

Top Industries
1. Business
2. Education
3. Operations
4. Finance
5. Sales

Top Employers
1. Morgan Stanley
2. Google
3. Citi
4. IBM
5. Merrill Lynch

Where Alumni Work
1. New York City
2. Boston
3. Hartford
4. Washington, DC
5. San Francisco

Median Earnings
College Scorecard (Early Career): $66,100
EOP (Early Career): $67,300
PayScale (Mid-Career): $110,900

RANKINGS
Forbes: 109
Money: 163
U.S. News: 46, Liberal Arts Colleges
Wall Street Journal/THE: 89 (T)
Washington Monthly: 23, Liberal Arts Colleges

#CollegesWorthYourMoney

Trinity University

San Antonio, Texas | Admissions Phone: 210-999-7207

ADMISSION

Admission Rate: 34%
Admission Rate - Men: 35%
Admission Rate - Women: 33%
EA Admission Rate: 65%
ED Admission Rate: 79%
Admission Rate (5-Year Trend): -30%
ED Admission Rate (5-Year Trend): +22%
% of Admits Attending (Yield): 23%
Transfer Admission Rate: 30%

Offered Wait List: 876
Accepted Wait List: 455
Admitted Wait List: 7

SAT Reading/Writing (Middle 50%): 630-710
SAT Math (Middle 50%): 630-720
ACT Composite (Middle 50%): 28-32
Testing Policy: ACT/SAT Required
SAT Superscore: Yes
ACT Superscore: Yes

% Graduated in Top 10% of HS Class: 42%
% Graduated in Top 25% of HS Class: 76%
% Graduated in Top 50% of HS Class: 96%

ENROLLMENT

Total Undergraduate Enrollment: 2,477
% Part-Time: 2%
% Male: 47%
% Female: 53%
% Out-of-State: 24%
% Fraternity: 8%
% Sorority: 15%
% On-Campus (Freshman): 100%
% On-Campus (All Undergraduate): 82%

% African-American: 4%
% Asian: 7%
% Hispanic: 21%
% White: 57%
% Other: 4%
% Race or Ethnicity Unknown: 2%
% International: 5%
% Low-Income: 18%

ACADEMICS

Student-to-Faculty Ratio: 9:1
% of Classes Under 20: 62%
% of Classes Under 40: 97%
% Full-Time Faculty: 75%
% Full-Time Faculty w/ Terminal Degree: 95%

Top Programs
Accounting
Biology
Engineering Science
English
History
Mathematical Finance
Neuroscience

Retention Rate: 91%
4-Year Graduation Rate: 65%
6-Year Graduation Rate: 76%

Curricular Flexibility: Less Flexible
Academic Rating: ★★★✦

Inside the Classroom

It is rare to see a jump in selectivity on the scale of San Antonio's top school, Trinity University, which has sliced its acceptance rate in half in only a few years. The school's meteoric rise has occurred contemporaneously with its 150th anniversary, and while the school continues to be majority Texan—two-thirds of enrollees are residents—applications from out-of-staters have risen in recent years. An increasingly gifted undergraduate student body approaching 2,500 enjoys the choice of forty-seven majors and a carefully crafted liberal arts core curriculum that is more demanding than the norm.

The distinct Pathways Program guides the educational journey at Trinity and is defined by six curricular requirements that involve an overwhelming number of manufactured terminologies. First-year experience courses, capped at sixteen students, introduce freshmen to the rigors of university-level reading and writing. In order to fulfill the Approaches to Creation and Analysis pathway, students must complete one course in the humanities, the arts and creative disciplines, social and behavioral sciences, natural sciences, and quantitative disciplines. Undergrads must also check off each of the Core Capacities: (1) written, oral, and visual communication; (2) digital literacy; and (3) engaged citizenship. All must also tackle "the Interdisciplinary Clusters," three-course groupings with themes such as ecological civilization in Asia or constructing and deconstructing language. One physical education course and one academic major round out the complex labyrinth of mandated coursework at Trinity U.

Undergraduates are the primary beneficiaries of a 9:1 student-to-faculty ratio as the university only enrolls around 140 graduate students. You won't encounter any adjuncts or teaching assistants at Trinity, and 97 percent of the 250 full-time faculty members hold terminal degrees in their fields. Sixty-three percent of courses enroll fewer than twenty students, one-quarter of sections enroll between twenty and twenty-nine, and few contain more than that. Over the summer, close to 140 students participate in intensive undergraduate research projects with faculty members. Overall, 80 percent of students engage in some type of hands-on learning, whether through research or an internship. Study abroad programs are taken advantage of by 35 percent of graduates, most of whom participate in affiliated but not Trinity-run offerings.

Trinity's well regarded School of Business attracts the greatest percentage of students as finance, accounting, and business administration degrees account for 23 percent of the total degrees conferred. Communication, biology, foreign language, and computer science also have strong representation. The university's reputation within the state of Texas is strong, and many graduates further their education or begin their careers locally, but the national prestige of the school is growing by the year. That can be seen in the procurement of highly competitive national fellowships. There were two Goldwater Scholars selected from the Class of 2018, and there were four Fulbright Scholars in the Class of 2017.

Outside the Classroom

With undergraduates required to live on campus for their first three years and 74 percent of all undergraduates residing on the 117-acre grounds, the formation of a tight-knit college community is almost unavoidable. Greek life is also alive and well with 16 percent of men pledged to fraternities and 18 percent of women members of sororities; there are sixteen total Greek organizations on campus. Nine men's and nine women's athletic teams compete at the Division III level, and they do so with intensity; they've captured four championships in recent years. The intramural programs scoop up pretty much everyone not playing a varsity sport with roughly three-fifths of the student body participating in intramural athletics. There are also ninety-seven student-run organizations, including groups devoted to animal welfare, fantasy sports and analytics, and indigenous peoples. The spirit of service is strong as 1,600 students contribute 120,000+ volunteer hours annually. Trinity's campus is only three miles from downtown San Antonio, opening possibilities for all sorts of big-city fun, but having a car is useful. Austin is a popular weekend getaway that is roughly an hour-and-a-half drive from the university.

Career Services

The newly-created Center for Experiential Learning and Career Success (CELCS) is staffed by nine full-time employees (not including administrative assistants) who specialize in areas such as career counseling, experiential learning coordination, and employer relations. That equates to a student-to-advisor ratio of 270:1, better than average when compared against other schools in this guidebook. Fall and spring career fairs were attended by fifty-one employers in the 2018-19 academic year, including top companies like KPMG, Booz Allen Hamilton, Valero Energy, and EY. It also regularly hosts smaller-scale events such as Lunch 'n Learns, employer information sessions, and workshops on topics such as networking, interviewing, and professional dining etiquette.

Trinity University

The school switched to the Handshake platform in 2018 and presently has opportunities from 3,600 employers posted in its database. As of the 2018-19 school year, 65 percent of Trinity students participated in at least one internship during their undergraduate education. Close to 200 on-campus interviews are conducted by employers each year. There are 29,000 actively engaged Tiger alumni, and they are more than happy to provide career advice, arrange a job-shadowing experience, or offer mentorship to current students. The office also facilitates a solid number of one-on-one counseling sessions; it held 1,058 such appointments last year. The nascent CELCS is on the rise and is quickly becoming the type of career services center that the university leadership outlined in its most recent strategic plan.

Professional Outcomes

Six months after receiving their diplomas, 45 percent of Trinity grads are employed full time, and 26 percent have matriculated into graduate school; a shade under 10 percent are still seeking employment. The companies employing the largest number of alumni include USAA (a San Antonio based financial firm), PwC, EY, Deloitte, Dell, Accenture, Morgan Stanley, and Amazon. Most Trinity grads stay in the Lone Star State with San Antonio, Houston, Dallas, and Austin being the four most common landing spots. Median salaries at midcareer are solid, ranking third in the state behind Rice and Texas A&M and just in front of UT Austin. Starting salaries are estimated at $51k while median midcareer salaries are estimated at $105,000.

Those graduating in spring 2018 were accepted into graduate school at an overall rate of 76 percent. In the last five years, acceptance rates into medical school have consistently been above national averages, hovering between 55 percent and 75 percent. Graduates have gone on to Dell Medical School (University of Texas), Harvard Medical School, and Tufts Medical School, among other less prestigious institutions. Law school rates have been within the 75-90 percent range in recent years. Among the most popular law schools attended by recent graduates are the University of Texas, Texas Tech, St. Mary's School of Law, and SMU.

Admission

Just five years ago, Trinity University received barely north of 4,500 applicants and admitted an unintimidating 64 percent; freshmen entering in 2018-19 faced an applicant pool of double that size and an acceptance rate of only 34 percent. Today, the mid-50 percent SAT score is 1260-1430 and the mid-50 percent ACT score is 28-32. A solid 42 percent of entering freshmen earned a place in the top 10 percent of their graduating classes, and 76 percent were in the top quartile; the average GPA was a 3.6 on a 4.0 scale. The average profile of a student beginning at Trinity only a few years ago was less impressive.

Trinity may be a small school that gives each application a "thorough review," yet the meat-and- potatoes factors of GPA, class rank, test scores, and engagement in a rigorous curriculum rest atop the list of most important considerations. The next tier of factors includes an interview, essays, recommendations, extracurricular activities, talent/ability, and character/personal qualities. There would have been no reason to apply early to this university in years past, but a sharp spike in competitiveness has put this strategic option firmly in play. In 2018-19, Trinity accepted 114 of 144 early applicants for a hyper-friendly 80 percent acceptance rate. Strong test scores and B+/A- average are now prerequisites for admission to Trinity, a statement that would have been hard to believe a decade ago. If you're a borderline applicant, going the ED route makes a ton of sense.

Worth Your Money?

Amazingly, given the current landscape, a list price cost of attendance of $60,780 isn't incredibly high for a private university. Yet, the truly good news is that this sticker price is rarely what undergraduates pay. Trinity awards a merit aid discount to two-thirds of current students with an average annual value of $22,000. Further, 47 percent of students meet the criteria for need-based grant eligibility, and the average annual award is $32k. With most students receiving sizable discounts, Trinity becomes a solid value, especially when you consider that its grads bring home above-average salaries at each stage of their careers.

FINANCIAL
Institutional Type: Private
In-State Tuition: $44,680
Out-of-State Tuition: $44,680
Room & Board: $13,584
Required Fees: $616
Books & Supplies: $1,000

Avg. Need-Based Aid: $32,162
Avg. % of Need Met: 98%

Avg. Merit-Based Aid: $22,102
% Receiving Merit-Based Aid: 67%

Avg. Cumulative Debt: $42,036
% of Students Borrowing: 44%

CAREER
Who Recruits
1. USAA
2. AXA Advisors
3. Dell
4. Capgemini
5. KPMG

Notable Internships
1. San Antonion Spurs
2. US State Department
3. Apple

Top Industries
1. Business
2. Education
3. Operations
4. Social Services
5. Sales

Top Employers
1. USAA
2. Deloitte
3. PwC
4. EY
5. H-E-B

Where Alumni Work
1. San Antonio
2. Houston
3. Dallas
4. Austin
5. Washington, DC

Median Earnings
College Scorecard (Early Career): $54,900
EOP (Early Career): $58,100
PayScale (Mid-Career): $102,900

RANKINGS
Forbes: 143
Money: 154
U.S. News: 1, Regional West
Wall Street Journal/THE: 111 (T)
Washington Monthly: N/A

#CollegesWorthYourMoney

Tufts University

Medford, Massachusetts | Admissions Phone: 617-627-3170

ADMISSION

Admission Rate: 15%
Admission Rate - Men: 15%
Admission Rate - Women: 14%
EA Admission Rate: Not Offered
ED Admission Rate: 42%
Admission Rate (5-Year Trend): -4%
ED Admission Rate (5-Year Trend): +7%
% of Admits Attending (Yield): 47%
Transfer Admission Rate: 14%

\# Offered Wait List: 1,957
\# Accepted Wait List: 723
\# Admitted Wait List: 8

SAT Reading/Writing (Middle 50%): 680-750
SAT Math (Middle 50%): 700-780
ACT Composite (Middle 50%): 31-34
Testing Policy: ACT/SAT Required
SAT Superscore: Yes
ACT Superscore: Yes

% Graduated in Top 10% of HS Class: 78%
% Graduated in Top 25% of HS Class: 93%
% Graduated in Top 50% of HS Class: 100%

ENROLLMENT

Total Undergraduate Enrollment: 5,643
% Part-Time: 2%
% Male: 48%
% Female: 52%
% Out-of-State: 76%
% Fraternity: 12%
% Sorority: 15%
% On-Campus (Freshman): 100%
% On-Campus (All Undergraduate): 65%

% African-American: 4%
% Asian: 13%
% Hispanic: 7%
% White: 55%
% Other: 5%
% Race or Ethnicity Unknown: 5%
% International: 10%
% Low-Income: 10%

ACADEMICS

Student-to-Faculty Ratio: 9:1
% of Classes Under 20: 69%
% of Classes Under 40: 89%
% Full-Time Faculty: 64%
% Full-Time Faculty w/ Terminal Degree: 94%

Top Programs

Biology
Computer Science
Economics
Engineering
English
International Relations
Quantitative Economics
Science, Technology and Society

Retention Rate: 96%
4-Year Graduation Rate: 87%
6-Year Graduation Rate: 93%

Curricular Flexibility: Very Flexible
Academic Rating: ★★★★⭒

Inside the Classroom

Quite small for being one of the nation's top research universities at just over 5,600 undergraduates, Tufts excels in delivering a highly personalized educational experience that is on par with its upper-echelon liberal arts rivals Williams and Amherst. In fact, like Amherst and Brown University, the school is notable for having no core curriculum. Instead, students are "encouraged to immerse themselves in the full expanse of course offerings, deepening existing interests while discovering new areas of study."

Three schools serve Tufts' undergraduate population: The College of Arts & Sciences, the College of Engineering, and the School of the Museum of Fine Arts. The three schools combined offer more than ninety majors and minors; approximately one-third of all students double major, and half declare a minor. The school encourages freshmen and sophomores to "Go broad, then deep." Students who do not want to be tethered to a laundry list of required introductory courses will relish the freedom Tufts affords its undergrads.

The university prides itself on its undergraduate teaching, and it shows; 82 percent of the Class of 2018 reported feeling satisfied with their educational journey. Nearly every professor is willing to take on research assistants, and plenty of funding is available. In the College of Engineering, 60 percent of students have a chance to participate in a research project at some point during their collegiate experience. Classes are small, especially when considering the school's legitimate research university status. Twenty-two percent of all courses see fewer than ten students enrolled, and 69 percent have sub-twenty enrollments. The student-to-faculty ratio is 9:1. A substantial segment of the student body, 40-45 percent, study abroad at one of eighty preapproved programs in locales such as Chile, Ghana, Hong Kong, and Madrid.

Well-regarded by industry and elite graduate/professional schools, a diploma in any discipline from Tufts will get you where you want to go. The most popular majors by volume are international relations, economics, computer science, engineering, and biology—all of which receive very high marks. The university does a fantastic job helping students land nationally competitive scholarships. Tufts is a leading producer of Fulbright Scholars, hitting double digits most years, and it also has seen its fair share of Goldwater, Udall, Truman, and Astronaut Scholarships in recent memory.

Outside the Classroom

Unlike some of Tufts' graduate programs, the undergraduate schools are not located in downtown Boston. However, Medford is part of the Boston metro area and is only five miles from the city limits, which makes its location far less remote than many of its rival New England colleges. Fewer than 70 percent of students live on campus in one of forty residential options ranging from traditional dorms to shared apartments. Many upper-classmen move off campus or live in fraternity or sorority houses. Close to one-quarter of the student population has traditionally gone Greek. Yet, some recent well-publicized hazing incidents led to dissolution or suspension of many chapters that altered, at least for the time being, the influence of Greek-letter organizations on campus. Presently, only 12 percent of men and 15 percent of women are Greek affiliated. Few Tufts students are lone wolves as a staggering 94 percent join at least one of the school's 341 recognized student organizations. Opportunities for community service are plentiful. Many students are involved in athletics, whether a member of one of the twenty-nine varsity sports teams competing in NCAA Division III, twenty-two club teams, or intramural groups. Campus is attractive and full of perks, including the new 42,000-square-foot Tisch Sports & Fitness Center that features tennis courts, pools, squash courts, and dance studios. As a bonus, dining options are given rave reviews as every Tufts student has a favorite dish.

Career Services

With thirteen full-time staff members who focus on undergraduate advising, career relations, and alumni outreach, the Tufts Career Center sports a 426:1 student-to-advisor ratio, which is within the average range of schools featured in this guide. The career services staff has done an incredible job improving its outreach over the past two decades. In 1998, only 32 percent of graduates were satisfied with the university's career services, but by 2015 a healthy 83 percent expressed positive feelings, and annual interactions with students had risen to over 7,600. In 2017, they increased the number of sessions with engineering students by 41 percent from the previous year, another indicator that this is an office on the rise.

Tufts does an exceptional job of assisting undergraduates with internship procurement. A robust 66 percent of Tufts graduates completed two or more internships during their time at the university; 89 percent completed at least one. The Fall Career Fair is attended by 185+ companies, and on-campus recruiting/interviews take place throughout the academic year. Career Treks and networking events in cities like New York and San Francisco are also regular occurrences. A recent switch from the antiquated Jumbo Jobs platform to Handshake was lauded by students. As an added long-term support, alumni have lifetime access to the spectrum of career services, including one-on-one job counseling. With a solid track record in internship participation, job placement, and graduate school outcomes, Tufts career services does an exceptional job setting its undergraduates up for next level of success.

Tufts University

E-mail: undergraduate.admissions@tufts.edu | Website: www.tufts.edu

Professional Outcomes

Six months after earning their diplomas, 96 percent of 2018 Tufts graduates were employed, attending graduate school, or otherwise productively engaged. The most commonly entered fields were health, life sciences, environmental (22 percent); engineering and technology (17 percent); finance, consulting, real estate (16 percent), and advocacy, education, and social services (15 percent). All of the leading finance, consulting, and technology companies sit atop the list of the most prolific employers of Tufts alums including Booz Allen Hamilton, JPMorgan, Facebook, Google, Deloitte, Amazon, Raytheon, Morgan Stanley, and BlackRock. The median salary at the start of what is considered midcareer is $73k, higher than Amherst and Boston College but lower than Bentley and Harvard. Most Tufts alumni remain in the Boston area, but many also head to New York City, San Francisco, Los Angeles, DC, and Chicago. Of the 16 percent of the Class of 2018 who went directly to graduate school, over three-quarters were accepted into their first-choice institution. Included among the ten universities enrolling the highest number of Tufts alumni were MIT, UCLA, Penn, Carnegie Mellon, and Columbia. Law school applicants routinely gain acceptance into top-tier institutions. In 2017, alumni were admitted into Harvard, Northwestern, University of Michigan, Penn, Duke, Brown, and Yale. Medical school applicants gained acceptance at a 75-90 percent rate, depending on the year. Those with at least a 3.5 undergraduate GPA find a med school home over 90 percent of the time.

Admission

The university's acceptance rate seems to have settled in the 14-15 percent range in recent years and held steady for the Class of 2022 despite an all-time record 21,502 applications. The vast majority of those applicants were for admittance into the School of Arts & Sciences followed by the School of Engineering with the smallest number applying to the fine arts programs. Overall, the mean SAT score was 1467 and the mean ACT was 33. The mid-50 percent ranges are 1380-1530 and 31-34. Last year, over 78 percent of the freshman class finished in the top 10 percent of their high school class, and 93 percent were in the top quartile.

There is nothing unexpected on the list of what factors the admissions committee considers "most important." It is looking for students who achieved top grades in AP classes, scored well on standardized tests, finished in the top 10 percent of their class, come highly recommended by their high school teachers, and are capable of composing a killer essay. Like many schools in its weight class, Tufts loves to scoop up a large portion of its freshman class in the early round—its ED acceptance rate is close to four times that of the regular round (42 percent vs. 11 percent)— and those accepted early comprise 65 percent of the incoming cohort. Even though it is no longer relegated to Ivy League safety status, Tufts is still understandably eager to lock down as many top candidates as possible via ED. Like all Ivy and Ivy-equivalent schools, Tufts is looking for the best and the brightest and is competing with even bigger names to haul in the best candidates. Therefore, demonstrating commitment through ED can pay dividends for qualified applicants.

Worth Your Money?

Boston is America's fourth-most expensive city, so perhaps it is no surprise that Tufts is on the pricey side. At $76k per year in cost of attendance, it ranks as the fifteenth most expensive school in the country. Only 37 percent of current undergrads qualify for need-based aid, and the average annual grant is for just under $49k. Of course, many in attendance don't have to worry too much about the cost because, based on historical data, a high percent of undergrads hail from wealthy families. It's no wonder that despite the high costs, graduates carry a mean amount of debt slightly lower than average (compared against all college grads). Even if you have to make an economic sacrifice to attend, Tufts is a school that will expose you to many personal and professional networks that will come in handy as you enter the world of graduate school or employment.

FINANCIAL
Institutional Type: Private
In-State Tuition: $57,324
Out-of-State Tuition: $57,324
Room & Board: $15,086
Required Fees: $1,254
Books & Supplies: $1,000

Avg. Need-Based Aid: $48,886
Avg. % of Need Met: 100%

Avg. Merit-Based Aid: $0
% Receiving Merit-Based Aid: 0%

Avg. Cumulative Debt: $28,014
% of Students Borrowing: 33%

CAREER
Who Recruits
1. Gelber Group
2. Cogo Labs
3. Amazon Robotics
4. Putnam Investments
5. Oppenheimer & Co.

Notable Internships
1. Deutsche Bank
2. UBS
3. Wayfair

Top Industries
1. Business
2. Education
3. Research
4. Engineering
5. Operations

Top Employers
1. Google
2. Amazon
3. Microsoft
4. Deloitte
5. Facebook

Where Alumni Work
1. Boston
2. New York City
3. San Francisco
4. Washington, DC
5. Los Angeles

Median Earnings
College Scorecard (Early Career): $75,800
EOP (Early Career): $73,100
PayScale (Mid-Career): $118,100

RANKINGS
Forbes: 34
Money: 90
U.S. News: 29 (T), National Universities
Wall Street Journal/THE: 30
Washington Monthly: 50, National Universities

#CollegesWorthYourMoney

Tulane University

New Orleans, Louisiana | Admissions Phone: 504-865-5731

Inside the Classroom

In competition with Vanderbilt and Emory for King of the Southern Ivies status, Tulane University takes the bronze; yet, that is hardly a knock on this private, midsized university in the heart of New Orleans. Home to 6,750 undergraduates, Tulane successfully combines the benefits of a renowned research university with the friendly classroom atmosphere of a liberal arts college. In the wake of Hurricane Katrina, the school dedicated itself to community service, an attribute that is now deeply woven into the fabric of the university.

Tulane offers seventy-five majors within five colleges, but all students, regardless of major, call Newcombe-Tulane College their home base. The school's core curriculum, which consists of thirty credits worth of courses, was redesigned in 2017 to "develop information literacy, critical thinking, and personal and social responsibility." As a result, coursework is required in the areas of writing skills, formal reasoning, foreign language, mathematics and natural sciences, social and behavioral sciences, textual and historical perspectives, aesthetics and the creative arts, and a first-year seminar called the Tulane Interdisciplinary Experience Seminar (TIDES). The TIDES courses center around engaging topics, many of which have to do with local New Orleans culture/history and involve one-on-one meetings with professors and a chance to connect with a student mentor.

Despite the presence of a significant number of graduate students, the university's enviable 8:1 student-to-faculty ratio can still be felt in the classroom. The average undergraduate class size is twenty-one students, and 94 percent of sections have an enrollment under fifty students. A solid 20 percent of courses have single-digit enrollments, providing a seminar-style environment. The overwhelming majority of undergraduate courses, even introductory ones, are taught by full-time professors. Exiting student surveys indicate that this focus on undergraduate education is noted as 94 percent rated their educational experience at Tulane as either "excellent" or "good." Those aiming to engage in undergraduate research at Tulane can find it; over 200 students per year land such opportunities in the School of Science and Engineering alone. An expansive study abroad program offers more than one hundred programs in forty countries, which is taken advantage of by 600 students each year.

Business/marketing, social science, biology, and health professions are the disciplines in which most degrees are conferred. The A.B. Freeman School of Business and programs in architecture, biology, and neuroscience enjoy strong national reputations. In its history, Tulane has produced eighteen Rhodes Scholars, one more than Emory. The university was a top producer of Fulbright Scholars in 2018 with fifteen graduates and recent alumni selected. Beinecke, Boren, Truman, and Marshall Scholarships also go to Green Wave alums with regularity.

Outside the Classroom

Fewer than half of the undergraduate population resides on the university's 110-acre uptown campus. Ample housing exists in the nearby community that is either within walking/biking distance of campus or accessible via the university bus system. The Greek scene is active with ten fraternities and eight sororities that collectively draw 35-40 percent of the student body. Tulane offers big-time athletics with sixteen NCAA Division I teams competing in the American Athletic Conference. The Green Wave shines brightest in baseball, men's tennis, and women's golf. An additional twenty-nine club sports teams and thirteen intramural leagues ensure that athletic participation is open to all. Over 200 student-run clubs currently are active with volunteer opportunities being among the most popular. Tulane undergrads contribute over 780,000 hours of volunteer service annually. Campus boasts thirty libraries/research centers, fifteen eateries, and the 156,000-square-foot Reily Student Recreation Center. The urban campus is located within the New Orleans city limits, only four miles from the bustling French Quarter, which provides students with all the culinary and cultural delights one can handle. The fact that classes shut down during Mardi Gras tells you all you need to know about life at Tulane.

Career Services

Tulane's Career Center is staffed by ten professionals who specialize in areas such as career advising, senior year experience coordination, pre-health advising, and pre-law advising. That works out to a 675:1 student-to-advisor ratio that is above average when compared to other schools in this guidebook. The office's strength is in organizing well-attended career and grad school fairs. The Mardi Gras Invitational Job Fair brings 145 employers to campus, the Gumbo Gathering Job Fair attracts another 134, and 118 schools are represented at the Graduate & Professional School Fair. Additionally, 11,000+ job and internship listings are posted through Tulane's Career Services Center.

A one-credit course entitled Majors, Internships, and Jobs teaches resume building, interview prep, and professional social media use. Many land internships through the UCAN Intern Consortium that Tulane belongs to alongside such schools as Harvard, Notre Dame, Swarthmore, and Washington University. A nationwide alumni network that is 140,000 members strong is another great source that current undergrads can utilize to land internships or their first paid gig. Founded in 2006, post-Hurricane Katrina, The Center for Public Service ensures that all Tulane grads engage in structured volunteer work during their four years of study. At the heart of this program is a three-credit Public Internship Program that allows students to complete sixty to seventy hours with a nonprofit organization. Thanks to an emphasis on public service and large-scale networking events, the Tulane Career Center succeeds in preparing its students for the world of work and graduate school.

Professional Outcomes

Among those receiving their diplomas in the spring of 2017, 61 percent were entering the world of gainful employment. The most popular industries were finance (17 percent), legal (17 percent), accounting (10 percent), education (6 percent), and engineering (4 percent). Significant numbers of Tulane alumni can be found working in the Louisiana-based Ochsner Health System or at corporations such as Shell, EY, Google, PwC, IBM, Morgan Stanley, Deloitte, and Accenture. Depending on the school from which one was graduating, Class of 2017 members reported median starting salaries between $37,000 and $60,000. Geographically, the most popular postgraduate move is to remain in the Greater New Orleans area although New York City, DC, Houston, San Francisco, and Los Angeles attract large numbers of Green Wave alumni as well.

Seventeen percent of Tulane grads immediately enroll in graduate or professional school. The four most commonly attended graduate schools by members of the Class of 2017 were Tulane itself, Louisiana State University, Boston University, and Johns Hopkins University. Students applying to law and medical schools, including Tulane's own institutions, fare better than the national average. Tulane undergraduates gain acceptance to medical school 58 percent of the time, and that figure rises to 93 percent for those with at least a 3.6 GPA and a score of 509 or higher on the MCAT. Recent grads have attended Columbia, Duke, and Johns Hopkins as well as the uber-selective Tulane School of Medicine. Law school hopefuls gain acceptance at an impressive 93 percent rate including roughly seventy admits annually into Tulane's own solidly ranked law school.

Admission

Tulane received 38,816 applications for its Class of 2022 but accepted only 17 percent, part of a pattern of declining admissions rates in recent years; the Class of 2021 rate was 21 percent, the Class of 2020 rate was 26 percent, and the Class of 2019 rate was 30 percent. The average accepted applicant averaged a 1456 on the SAT, and the middle 50 percent range for attending freshmen was 1350-1490. The middle 50 percent ACT composite score range is 30-33; roughly three-quarters of applicants elect to submit the ACT over the SAT. Sixty-three percent of 2018-19 freshmen had earned a place in the top decile of their high school class, and 88 percent were in the top quartile. Not everyone attending Tulane had perfect grades as 38 percent of attendees sported a high school GPA below 3.5.

With a heavy volume of applications streaming in, the Tulane Admissions Office is forced to rely on concrete factors to winnow down the pool. As a result, four factors are ranked as being most important: rigor of course-work, class rank, GPA, and standardized test scores. Essays, recommendations, and character/personal qualities receive second billing. With the school's acceptance rate in fast decline, it is not a surprise that early decision applications are increasing; ED applications rose 37.5 percent between 2017 and 2018. ED applicants to the Class of 2022 were accepted at a 32 percent clip. An institution whose heightened selectivity in recent years may go unnoticed by applicants relying on old data or the school's reputation a decade ago, Tulane has claimed its position in the realm of highly selective research universities. Successful applicants need standardized test scores above the 95th percentile to go with A's and B's in AP/honors coursework.

Worth Your Money?

Don't let the official cost of attendance of $75,000 make you think that Tulane is beyond your financial reach because a large percentage of students receive a discount in the form of merit or need-based aid that bring that sum down to a more reasonable level. Fifty-five percent of current undergrads receive an average merit aid award of $24k, and 31 percent of undergraduates are given grants averaging $34k per year. If you don't receive a sizable aid offer, the wisest move would be to evaluate (a) your other financial aid offers and (b) the amount of debt you would be likely to incur at Tulane versus the expected starting salaries for jobs related to your intended major.

FINANCIAL
Institutional Type: Private
In-State Tuition: $52,760
Out-of-State Tuition: $52,760
Room & Board: $15,774
Required Fees: $4,040
Books & Supplies: $1,200

Avg. Need-Based Aid: $34,434
Avg. % of Need Met: 96%

Avg. Merit-Based Aid: $23,983
% Receiving Merit-Based Aid: 55%

Avg. Cumulative Debt: $41,767
% of Students Borrowing: 35%

CAREER
Who Recruits
1. Facebook
2. Medtronic
3. Tesla
4. Starbucks
5. Amazon

Notable Internships
1. AIG
2. U.S. Senate
3. HBO

Top Industries
1. Business
2. Education
3. Operations
4. Healthcare
5. Social Services

Top Employers
1. Ochsner Health System
2. Shell
3. EY
4. PwC
5. Deloitte

Where Alumni Work
1. New Orleans
2. New York City
3. Washington, DC
4. Houston
5. San Francisco

Median Earnings
College Scorecard (Early Career): $61,700
EOP (Early Career): N/A
PayScale (Mid-Career): $105,300

RANKINGS
Forbes: 106
Money: 390
U.S. News: 44, National Universities
Wall Street Journal/THE: 84 (T)
Washington Monthly: 343, National Universities

#CollegesWorthYourMoney

Union College

Schenectady, New York | Admissions Phone: 518-388-6112

ADMISSION
Admission Rate: 39%
Admission Rate - Men: 37%
Admission Rate - Women: 40%
EA Admission Rate: Not Offered
ED Admission Rate: 56%
Admission Rate (5-Year Trend): +1%
ED Admission Rate (5-Year Trend): -11%
% of Admits Attending (Yield): 22%
Transfer Admission Rate: 30%

Offered Wait List: 1,045
Accepted Wait List: 516
Admitted Wait List: 13

SAT Reading/Writing (Middle 50%): 620-700
SAT Math (Middle 50%): 650-730
ACT Composite (Middle 50%): 28-32
Testing Policy: Test Optional
SAT Superscore: Yes
ACT Superscore: Yes

% Graduated in Top 10% of HS Class: 61%
% Graduated in Top 25% of HS Class: 80%
% Graduated in Top 50% of HS Class: 94%

ENROLLMENT
Total Undergraduate Enrollment: 2,206
% Part-Time: 0%
% Male: 54%
% Female: 46%
% Out-of-State: 60%
% Fraternity: 28%
% Sorority: 34%
% On-Campus (Freshman): 98%
% On-Campus (All Undergraduate): 88%

% African-American: 4%
% Asian: 5%
% Hispanic: 8%
% White: 70%
% Other: 3%
% Race or Ethnicity Unknown: 0%
% International: 9%
% Low-Income: 19%

ACADEMICS
Student-to-Faculty Ratio: 10:1
% of Classes Under 20: 58%
% of Classes Under 40: 97%
% Full-Time Faculty: 88%
% Full-Time Faculty w/ Terminal Degree: 97%

Top Programs
Biology
Economics
Engineering
History
Mathematics
Neuroscience
Political Science
Psychology

Retention Rate: 95%
4-Year Graduation Rate: 84%
6-Year Graduation Rate: 87%

Curricular Flexibility: Less Flexible
Academic Rating: ★★★★⅃

Inside the Classroom

Whether intent on studying the humanities or engineering, Union College in Schenectady, New York, can perfectly meet your needs. One of the select number of schools in the country that has been in existence since the 1700s, Union, while tough to get into, has not, like many of its peer institutions, reached absurd selectivity levels in recent years. A test-optional school looking for strong but not perfect students, this rigorous, well regarded, and exclusively undergraduate institution of 2,200 students is a perfect fit for a certain subset of high schoolers. It's not a bad option considering that, in its illustrious history, Union has produced a US president, thirteen governors, 200 judges, seven cabinet secretaries, a National Book Award winner, and an Olympic Gold medalist.

Union operates on a trimester system of ten-week terms with an extended winter break. The common curriculum is both broad and highly demanding. Students begin with a First-Year Preceptorial that seeks to sharpen skills in the areas of critical reading and thinking as well as analytical writing. The Sophomore Research Seminar mandates that students participate in structured academic research early in their collegiate career. Dutchmen also must plow through requirements in literature, natural science, quantitative and mathematical reasoning, arts and humanities, science/engineering/technology, languages and cultures, and writing across the curriculum. Union is in the exclusive club of undergraduate institutions that require all graduates to complete a senior thesis.

Class sizes at Union are favorable for creating an intimate and friendly learning environment. A 10:1 student-to-faculty ratio leads to average introductory class sizes of twenty-one and average upper-level class sizes of only fourteen. Two-thirds of course sections have an enrollment of nineteen or fewer students. Faculty-mentored research is a staple of Union's undergraduate program and is experienced by 100 percent of the student body in one form or another. During the Steinmetz Symposium, hundreds of students have the chance to showcase their research. Each year, over one hundred students conduct research with a faculty member for an entire summer. The school also takes immense pride in its popular study abroad program that sees more than 60 percent of its students from all disciplines spend a semester of study in a foreign land.

Economics, mechanical engineering, political science, and psychology are the most commonly conferred degrees, and are also very stong, with Union's engineering program having perhaps the strongest national reputation. A top producer of Fulbright Scholars, the Class of 2018 produced seven winners as well as two National Science Foundation Graduate Research Fellows. Traditionally, Union is among the largest producers of Watson Fellows, but it did not have any such winners in the Class of 2018.

Outside the Classroom

Close to 90 percent of undergraduates reside in university-run dorms or one of thirteen student-run theme houses on the 120-acre grounds. The Greek influence is massive with the eighteen sororities and fraternities (ten of which are residential) attracting roughly 40 percent of the student population. Regardless of Greek affiliation, every undergrad belongs to one of seven Minerva Houses, social hubs that serve to bring students and faculty together outside the classroom for social and academic activities. On the sports front, men and women's ice hockey take center stage as each battles NCAA Division I competition; the other twenty-four squads are relegated to Division III status. In total, one-third of all Union students are members of an intercollegiate sports team. Opportunities for physical fitness also exist in the form of yoga, Pilates, dance, and aerobics classes. More than 130 student-run campus clubs are on tap, including fourteen community service groups and a number of cultural, academic, political, and performance-oriented groups. Other notables include WRUC, America's first college radio station that was founded in 1920, and the *Concordiensis* student newspaper that launched in 1877. Schenectady's downtown is a short car ride away, and longer road trips include Saratoga Springs, a little more than half an hour away, and New York and Boston that require three-hour trips.

Career Services

The Becker Career Center is staffed by six professionals, three of whom specialize in employer relations. That works out to a 378:1 student-to-advisor ratio that falls in the average range when compared to other institutions included this guidebook. Philosophically, the staff encourages students to follow their passions by pursuing opportunities that "pique their interest and spur their enthusiasm." The staff aims to work with students early in their undergraduate careers, regularly administering tests such as the Meyers-Briggs to freshmen. Union hosts its own career fairs but also encourages participation in larger, joint efforts with other institutions. For example, Union, Swarthmore, Bard, and Connecticut College combine for the Fall Recruiting Consortium that attracts many major companies to Times Square.

Students are encouraged to connect with alumni via the Union Career Advisory Network. Alumni are eager to help current undergrads as evidenced by participation in events such as the Walk Down Wall Street that includes representatives Goldman Sachs, Barclay's Deutsche Bank, Morgan Stanley, and CITI. On-campus recruiting has doubled in the past decade and includes visits and interview opportunities with a host of desirable employers. Roughly 60 percent of Union students complete at least one internship during their four years. Overall, thanks to strong career outcomes and an influential alumni base, Becker does well for its graduates.

Professional Outcomes

Ninety-four percent of the Class of 2018 landed at their next destination within months of completing their degree with 66 percent entering full-time employment and 21 percent matriculating into graduate school. The most popular fields were finance/banking (16 percent), engineering (14 percent), education/academia (10 percent), sales (7 percent), and research (6 percent). Of the pool of all living alumni, Union has the largest representation at IBM, GE, PwC, Morgan Stanley, Fidelity Investments, and Accenture. Location-wise, the strongest presence of Dutchmen/women can be found in New York City; Boston; Albany; Washington, DC; San Francisco; and Phila-delphia. Median income figures by the start of midcareer are strong, ranking eleventh among seventy-one highly selective colleges, which is in the same range as Boston University, Trinity College, and Northeastern.

The nearly one-quarter of students who pursue further education directly out of their undergraduate experience do so at a wide range of institutions that include many elite universities. Recent graduates have gone on to advanced business degrees at Stanford, Cornell, and UVA; advanced engineering degrees at Yale, MIT, and RPI, and science degrees at Brandeis, UCLA, and WPI. Many of those headed to medical school do so through the combined BS/MD program Union offers in conjunction with Albany Medical College, but other recent grads have gone on to study medicine at the likes of Johns Hopkins, Tufts, and Dartmouth. Likewise, many pursuing a legal education do so through the combined BA/JD program with partner Albany Law School while others have entered Harvard, Boston College, and the University of Michigan.

Admission

With an acceptance rate of 39 percent for the Class of 2022, Union College, while highly selective, offers strong students better odds of success than many others of its ilk. Still, those who ultimately enroll are often toward the top of their respective high school classes with 61 percent of 2018-19 freshmen hailing from the top decile and 80 percent from the top quartile. Of those who submit test scores (more on this in a moment), the mid-50 percent standardized test ranges are 1270-1430 on the SAT and 28-32 on the ACT.

Unless you are applying to the 3+3 Accelerated Law Program, Leadership in Medicine Program, or are a homes-chooled student, Union is a test-optional institution. Yet, in the most recent admissions cycle, 50 percent submitted SAT results and 29 percent included ACT scores on their applications. Atop the list of criteria deemed "very important" in evaluating an applicant are the rigor of secondary coursework, GPA, and class rank. Soft factors like talent/ability, personal qualities, volunteer work, and extracurricular activities also play a role in evaluating candidates. If you are a student on the cusp, applying early decision is absolutely the way to go as ED applicants are given a thumbs up at a 56 percent clip. You don't need perfect grades to get into Union College—the average GPA for Class of 2022 enrollees was 3.4, and only 27 percent were over a 3.75—but you do need an area of notable strength and should be engaged in a mostly AP/honors-level high school curriculum.

Worth Your Money?

Union College sports a hefty cost of attendance of $73,410 per year. One-third of undergrads receive merit aid awards that average $14,500 per student, not greatly altering the high cost of the school. Where Union truly shines is with need-based aid; like the Ivies, it meets 100 percent of demonstrated need for every single student. Half of current students meet those criteria and receive an average grant approaching $40k. Even with the high price tag, Union is a school that opens doors and sends many graduates directly into remunerative fields such as engineering and finance.

FINANCIAL
Institutional Type: Private
In-State Tuition: $56,853
Out-of-State Tuition: $56,853
Room & Board: $14,061
Required Fees: $471
Books & Supplies: $1,500

Avg. Need-Based Aid: $39,942
Avg. % of Need Met: 100%

Avg. Merit-Based Aid: $14,500
% Receiving Merit-Based Aid: 32%

Avg. Cumulative Debt: $35,388
% of Students Borrowing: 58%

CAREER
Who Recruits
1. Rapid7
2. BioSig Technologies
3. Brown Brothers Harriman
4. Northwell Health
5. Stanley Black & Decker

Notable Internships
1. Dow Jones
2. NBCUniversal
3. AIG

Top Industries
1. Business
2. Education
3. Operations
4. Engineering
5. Sales

Top Employers
1. IBM
2. GE
3. PwC
4. Morgan Stanley
5. GE Power

Where Alumni Work
1. New York City
2. Boston
3. Albany, NY
4. Washington, DC
5. San Francisco

Median Earnings
College Scorecard (Early Career): $65,400
EOP (Early Career): $66,600
PayScale (Mid-Career): $117,500

RANKINGS
Forbes: 104
Money: 58
U.S. News: 45, Liberal Arts Colleges
Wall Street Journal/THE: 115
Washington Monthly: 41, Liberal Arts Colleges

#CollegesWorthYourMoney

University at Buffalo (SUNY)

Buffalo, New York | Admissions Phone: 716-645-6900

ADMISSION
Admission Rate: 56%
Admission Rate - Men: 57%
Admission Rate - Women: 54%
EA Admission Rate: N/A
ED Admission Rate: Not Offered
Admission Rate (5-Year Trend): -1%
ED Admission Rate (5-Year Trend): Not Offered
% of Admits Attending (Yield): 24%
Transfer Admission Rate: 63%

Offered Wait List: 2,841
Accepted Wait List: 694
Admitted Wait List: 168

SAT Reading/Writing (Middle 50%): 570-650
SAT Math (Middle 50%): 590-680
ACT Composite (Middle 50%): 24-29
Testing Policy: ACT/SAT Required
SAT Superscore: Yes
ACT Superscore: No

% Graduated in Top 10% of HS Class: 35%
% Graduated in Top 25% of HS Class: 70%
% Graduated in Top 50% of HS Class: 97%

ENROLLMENT
Total Undergraduate Enrollment: 21,607
% Part-Time: 8%
% Male: 56%
% Female: 44%
% Out-of-State: 2%
% Fraternity: 2%
% Sorority: 2%
% On-Campus (Freshman): 76%
% On-Campus (All Undergraduate): 35%

% African-American: 8%
% Asian: 15%
% Hispanic: 7%
% White: 47%
% Other: 2%
% Race or Ethnicity Unknown: 5%
% International: 15%
% Low-Income: 30%

ACADEMICS
Student-to-Faculty Ratio: 14:1
% of Classes Under 20: 29%
% of Classes Under 40: 71%
% Full-Time Faculty: 72%
% Full-Time Faculty w/ Terminal Degree: 97%

Top Programs
Business
Computer Science
English
Exercise Science
Mechanical Engineering
Public Health
Speech and Hearing Science

Retention Rate: 87%
4-Year Graduation Rate: 60%
6-Year Graduation Rate: 76%

Curricular Flexibility: Less Flexible
Academic Rating: ★★★

Inside the Classroom

You can make all the jokes you want about the city of Buffalo (cold jokes from relatives never get old), and you can call the university bearing the city's name a "commuter school" if you want, but they don't care. SUNY University at Buffalo is the most popular destination within the colossal State University of New York system, boasting an undergraduate population of 20,000+. Well-regarded and highly affordable business, engineering, and computer science programs lure an increasingly more selective group of freshmen each year. It is primarily New York residents who come to Buffalo for its robust academic offerings that include 125 undergraduate degree programs. However, the university ranks in the top twenty-five for total number of international students; including graduate students, there are 4,600 foreign students from 101 countries.

Totaling forty credits, the UB curriculum will take the equivalent of almost three full semesters to complete. The program begins freshman year with a small seminar that emphasizes critical thinking and discussion. Next, students will knock out foundations courses in communication literacy, quantitative literacy, scientific literacy, and diversity learning followed by nine credits (each) from thematic and global pathways. Lastly, as a senior, students will complete a one-credit capstone course. Those in the university's Honors Program also must complete twenty-four credits in honors-only courses.

Despite a favorable 14:1 student-to-faculty ratio, undergraduate class sizes do tend to be rather large at the University at Buffalo. That is partially due to the school enrolling almost 10,000 graduate students. Only 29 percent of course sections enroll fewer than twenty students, and 23 percent of courses contain fifty or more students. The Center for Undergraduate Research and Creative Activity (CURCA) can help make a huge university feel a bit smaller by connecting students with faculty mentors for research endeavors. The center advertises that "100 percent of students have the opportunity to participate in research," thus, it is fair to say that procuring opportunities is simply a matter of being proactive. Likewise for those interested in spending a semester at a foreign university; UB offers 1,000 study abroad programs across all seven continents (Antarctica, anyone?).

A good number of Buffalo students flock to the school's strongest offerings with 18 percent of the degrees conferred coming from the School of Management and another 16 percent from the School of Engineering and Applied Sciences. Other commonly conferred degrees are in psychology (11 percent), biology (9 percent), health professions (6 percent), and communication/journalism (6 percent). There has been a slight uptick in recent years in undergraduates capturing prestigious postgraduate scholarships and fellowships. Five seniors/alumni won Fulbright Scholarships in 2019 while others netted Gilman and Critical Language Scholarships.

Outside the Classroom

Even though a sizable number of UB students commute from home or nearby rental homes/apartments, the school does bring 76 percent of freshmen to live in university-owned housing that features twelve residence halls and five apartment communities. Factoring in all undergrads, only 35 percent reside on campus. Greek life has only a faint heartbeat, attracting 2 percent of men and women. Want to see a big-name speaker live? The UB Speakers Series has enticed the likes of Hillary Clinton, Malcom Gladwell, and John Oliver to trek to Buffalo in recent years. There are 300+ student organizations to choose from at the university, and there are many campus-wide events that energize the Bulls community such as Fall Fest, Spring Fest, and Oozefest, which is the muddiest game of volleyball you will ever play. The sports scene is on the rise as the school now supports sixteen NCAA Division I athletic teams that compete in the Mid-American Conference. In the school's own words, the City of Good Neighbors is home to "a vibrant arts scene, quaint neighborhoods, remarkable restaurants, and an affordable cost of living." On campus, the Crossroads Culinary Center is rated the best in the entire SUNY system.

Career Services

The central Career Center at UB employs twelve professional staff members who hold titles such as career counselor, employer relations manager, and employer and alumni relationship associate. The Ciminelli Family Career Resource Center within the School of Management is staffed by nine full-time employees who work with or on behalf of undergraduate students. That translates to a 952:1 student-to-counselor ratio, which is significantly higher than the average school featured in this guide, but it is to be expected at a public university of Buffalo's size. The good news is that in the 2017-18 academic year, 10,896 students utilized the Career Center through attending a job fair, a workshop, or making an individual appointment for career coaching; another 15,858 students used Bullseye, the office's online networking app.

Career Center staff could improve outreach efforts as only about 10 percent of the undergraduate student population seek direct career counseling services each year. However, the center did succeed in bringing many top employers to campus for expos such as for the STEAM Job + Internship Fair which draws one hundred+ employers and 2,000+ students each fall. The Spring Job + Internship Fair also brings out one hundred+ employers and around 1,300 students. Unfortunately, those efforts ultimately result in fewer than 500 on-campus interviews each year. Based on the most recent data available, close to 60 percent of students engage in at least one internship, co-op, or other experiential learning placement during their four years at the university. Like much else at the University of Buffalo, the career services spoils go to those who aggressively track down and utilize the available resources.

Professional Outcomes

Within three months of graduating, three-quarters of School of Management degree-holders in the Class of 2018 had found employment. The median base salary for those who found jobs was $48,000 (business grads only). Ten years after enrolling at the university, alumni from all majors earned a median salary of $52,600. UB graduates are well-represented in the corporate offices of many top finance, accounting, consulting, and technology companies. More than one hundred alumni of the school are currently employed at the likes of M&T Bank, Citi, Amazon, Microsoft, Google, JPMorgan Chase, PwC, Apple, Deloitte, and Cisco. The greatest number of alumni remain in the Buffalo area but many relocate to New York City, San Francisco, DC, and Boston.

There were 64 SUNY Buffalo graduates in 2018 who applied to medical school. Including those applying to osteopathic schools, a GPA of 3.5-3.7 and an MCAT score in the 505-510 range typically led to successful results. Recent graduates are currently attending medical schools at Virginia Commonwealth University and Boston University with the greatest percentage heading to the four SUNY medical training grounds at the Stony Brook, Buffalo, Upstate, and Downstate locations. Many law school attendees also stay within the SUNY system, including Buffalo's own home for legal education, but other recent grads have entered such schools as Duke, Wake Forest, and Notre Dame. That pattern is also true for those pursuing master's and doctoral degrees. Graduating with honors from UB absolutely can put elite graduate and professional schools in play, but the bulk of students select local public options.

Admission

SUNY University at Buffalo receives the largest number of applications of any school in the state system, over 31,000; the school accepted 56 percent of those aiming to join the Class of 2022. Perfect grades aren't necessary, but you need a pretty sound transcript. Over one-third of attending students placed in the top 10 percent of their high school class, and 70 percent finished in the top quartile. Forty-two percent boasted a GPA of 3.75 or greater, but giving hope to those with blemishes on their academic records, 19 percent possessed a 3.25 or under. The average SAT score for a freshman in 2018-19 was a 1242, and the average ACT score was just shy of 27. To give you a sense of the ranges of standardized test scores, the middle-50 percent scores were a 24-29 on the ACT and 1160-1330 on the SAT.

So many applicants, so little time—it's a recipe for a formulaic admissions process, and that's exactly what the University at Buffalo utilizes. At the top of the list are standardized test scores, GPA, and the rigor of one's coursework followed by the still-important factors of class rank and recommendations. State residency is not considered in the admissions process, nor is demonstrated interest. In the end, 24 percent of those admitted go on to enroll. Strangely, while a near-identical number of men and women are accepted into Buffalo, the yield rate for men is substantially higher. Roughly 350 students per year are admitted into the Honors College, and preference is given to those who apply earlier in the rolling process. For all applicants, we highly recommend meeting the priority deadline of November 15.

Worth Your Money?

Those who live with a relative can earn a four-year degree for a grand sum of $28,000, the cost of tuition alone for one semester at many private universities. Total cost of attendance for a New York resident comes to about $29,000 per year, which accounts for direct and indirect living expenses—still an excellent deal for the quality of education the school provides. For those from out of state, costs climb to $47,000 per year, making attending UB a curious choice for those with more affordable options. Over 10,000 undergraduates are determined needy each year, and the school awards an average annual need-based grant of $7,915. For New York residents, SUNY Buffalo is, unequivocally and independent of circumstance, worth your money.

FINANCIAL
Institutional Type: Public
In-State Tuition: $6,870
Out-of-State Tuition: $24,540
Room & Board: $14,213
Required Fees: $3,229
Books & Supplies: $1,203

Avg. Need-Based Aid: $7,915
Avg. % of Need Met: 45%

Avg. Merit-Based Aid: $3,869
% Receiving Merit-Based Aid: 28%

Avg. Cumulative Debt: $26,062
% of Students Borrowing: 57%

CAREER
Who Recruits
1. ACV Auctions
2. Salesforce
3. Facebook
4. PwC
5. Apple

Notable Internships
1. Walt Disney World
2. Wegmnan's Food Markets
3. HSBC

Top Industries
1. Business
2. Education
3. Operations
4. Engineering
5. Healthcare

Top Employers
1. M&T Bank
2. Citi
3. Amazon
4. Ingram Micro
5. Microsoft

Where Alumni Work
1. Buffalo, NY
2. New York City
3. Rochester, NY
4. San Francisco
5. Singapore

Median Earnings
College Scorecard (Early Career): $52,600
EOP (Early Career): $52,700
PayScale (Mid-Career): $98,000

RANKINGS
Forbes: 196
Money: 99
U.S. News: 79 (T), National Universities
Wall Street Journal/THE: 110
Washington Monthly: 114, National Universities

#CollegesWorthYourMoney

University of California, Berkeley

Berkeley, California | Admissions Phone: 510-642-6000

ADMISSION
Admission Rate: 15%
Admission Rate - Men: 13%
Admission Rate - Women: 17%
EA Admission Rate: Not Offered
ED Admission Rate: Not Offered
Admission Rate (5-Year Trend): -3%
ED Admission Rate (5-Year Trend): Not Offered
% of Admits Attending (Yield): 47%
Transfer Admission Rate: 21%

Offered Wait List: 7,824
Accepted Wait List: 4,127
Admitted Wait List: 1,536

SAT Reading/Writing (Middle 50%): 640-740
SAT Math (Middle 50%): 660-790
ACT Composite (Middle 50%): 28-34
Testing Policy: ACT/SAT Required
SAT Superscore: No
ACT Superscore: No

% Graduated in Top 10% of HS Class: 98%
% Graduated in Top 25% of HS Class: 100%
% Graduated in Top 50% of HS Class: 100%

ENROLLMENT
Total Undergraduate Enrollment: 30,609
% Part-Time: 4%
% Male: 47%
% Female: 53%
% Out-of-State: 16%
% Fraternity: 10%
% Sorority: 10%
% On-Campus (Freshman): 96%
% On-Campus (All Undergraduate): 27%

% African-American: 2%
% Asian: 35%
% Hispanic: 15%
% White: 25%
% Other: 6%
% Race or Ethnicity Unknown: 4%
% International: 13%
% Low-Income: 27%

ACADEMICS
Student-to-Faculty Ratio: 20:1
% of Classes Under 20: 53%
% of Classes Under 40: 77%
% Full-Time Faculty: 66%
% Full-Time Faculty w/ Terminal Degree: 99%

Top Programs
Biological Sciences
Business
Chemistry
Computer Science
Economics
Engineering
English
Psychology

Retention Rate: 97%
4-Year Graduation Rate: 75%
6-Year Graduation Rate: 91%

Curricular Flexibility: Somewhat Flexible
Academic Rating: ★★★★⬩

Inside the Classroom

The University of California, Berkeley, more commonly referred to as Berkeley or Cal, is the flagship university in the stellar and gargantuan UC system. Founded in 1868 with the motto "Fiat Lux" (Let there be light), the university today offers enlightenment to over 30,000 undergraduate and 11,000 graduate students. The name *Berkeley* likely conjures up two immediate associations—academic prestige and the protests of the 1960s. While no longer a hotbed of youth unrest on the level of the Vietnam era, Berkeley remains a bastion of liberal thought and idealism. It is fitting that the school is the number one all-time producer of Peace Corps volunteers.

More than 150 undergraduate majors and minors are available across five undergraduate schools: The College of Letters and Science, the College of Chemistry, the College of Engineering, the College of Environmental Design, and the College of Natural Resources. A sixth school, the Haas School of Business, must be applied to separately prior to one's junior year. Over two-thirds of undergrads are housed within the College of Letters and Science, which requires coursework including entry-level writing, American history and American institutions, foreign language, quantitative reasoning, and reading & composition.

Constant budget crises in the UC system haven't dented the school's reputation one iota, but the impact can be felt in measures such as student-to-faculty ratio that, at 18:1, is significantly higher than other elite flagships like UVA or Michigan. However, that doesn't translate to across-the-board large class sizes. Rather, under-grads will encounter a mix of large lectures (19 percent of sections contain more than fifty students) and tiny, single-digit enrollments in seminar-style courses (24 percent of sections contain nine or fewer students). Under-graduate research opportunities do exist despite the school's massive size; 56 percent of students assist faculty with a research project or complete a research methods course in their time at Berkeley. Study abroad opportuni-ties are available for those who desire them, and approximately 1,800 undergrads take a semester in a foreign country each year. Locations where Berkeley faculty deliver instruction include Taiwan, Switzerland, Serbia, Peru, and the Philippines.

Thanks to its equally esteemed graduate schools, many departments have top international reputations including computer science, engineering, chemistry, English, psychology, and economics. In 2017 alone, 105 grads were awarded National Science Foundation Graduate Research Fellowships, which was more than Stanford and more than Harvard and Yale combined. In 2018, there were eleven Fulbright winners, three Schwarzman Scholars, and two alumni were awarded MacArthur Fellowships, sometimes referred to as "genius grants."

Outside the Classroom

Almost 95 percent of incoming freshmen live in university-run housing, upperclassmen are generally left to fend for themselves. Housing is a challenging issue, and while the university is building new dormitories, it presently only has the capacity to house roughly one-quarter of the undergraduate population. A prominent but far from dominant Greek life attracts 10 percent of men and women (3,600 individuals) into sixty+ active fraternities and sororities. Cal's sports program is exceptional as the Golden Bears thirty varsity teams have won a collective eighty-seven NCAA championships in the school's history; they mostly compete in the Pac-12 Conference. With 1000+ clubs and activities, there is truly somethings for everyone, including many political and public-service organizations. Roughly 5,300 undergraduate students volunteer their time to community service projects, and the campus has a genuine focus on sustainability; 87 percent of students walk, bike, or take public transit, and the school has a goal of zero non-recycled waste by 2020. Being a few miles north of Oakland and a few miles east of San Francisco, big-city fun is never far away. Berkeley itself is replete with awesome restaurants (including, of course, many vegan options), a botanical garden, a marina, an art museum, and a 2,000-acre park. Berkeley is considered one of the most socially liberal cities in the United States.

Career Services

With twenty-five full-time employees dedicated to undergraduates, the UC Berkeley Career Center has a 1,234:1 student-to-counselor ratio, much higher than most of the schools featured in this guide but comparable to the other University of California institutions. What the center lacks in its ability to connect one-on-one it makes up for by putting together large-scale events that bring 350+ employers to campus every year. There are large career fairs in the fall and spring, and many industry-specific affairs are held as well including the Social Impact Career Fair, Investment Banking Forum, Law & Graduate School Fair, and the Civil & Environmental Engineering Career Fair .

A survey of employed 2018 graduates reveals that the efforts of the career center directly contributed to their job attainment. Specifically, 17 percent found their first job through on-campus recruiting, 15 percent directly from an internship, 14 percent via a career fair or information session, and 13 percent through Cal's Handshake platform. A hard-to-beat alumni network of 493,000 individuals—100,000 are dues-paying members of the alumni association— can assist you throughout your career. More than 4,500 students attend webinars and in-person events hosted by alums. The average student received two job offers. Overall, despite a high counselor-to-student ratio, Cal's career services provides plenty of opportunities for undergrads to connect with top employers, resulting in students landing positions that align with their career goals while also paying the bills.

Professional Outcomes

Upon graduating, 61 percent of Cal's Class of 2018 members had already secured employment, 19 percent were headed to graduate school, and 14 percent were still seeking their first jobs. Just over three-quarters of that cohort were employed by for-profit companies, 11 percent entered the education field, 7 percent took positions at nonprofits, and 6 percent were working for government entities. Thousands of alumni can be found in the offices of Google, Apple, and Facebook, and 500+ Golden Bears are currently employed by Oracle, Amazon, and Microsoft. Most alumni are concentrated in the San Francisco Bay area with Los Angeles, New York, Seattle, DC, Boston, and the United Kingdom next in popularity. Average starting salaries vary widely by major. Computer science grads are compensated to the tune of $107k, business majors averaged $75k, biology majors made $59k, and psychology majors brought home $57k.

Because almost 8,000 students earn bachelor's degrees each year, it's hard to pinpoint the most commonly attended graduate/professional schools with literally hundreds of institutions absorbing Berkeley undergrads. They range from the most selective Ivy League universities to a host of less selective institutions. For example, political science degree-holders from the Class of 2018 attended graduate schools that included Stanford, Georgetown, San Francisco State, and Eastern Michigan University. Suffice it to say that earning strong grades at Berkeley will set you up for a successful graduate application process at the nation's most elite schools. From 2016-2018 the medical school acceptance rate has hovered in the 51-55 percent range, and law school applicants have been successful 81-89 percent of the time. Among the Class of 2018, master's degrees were the most frequently pursued degree (311) followed by PhD (170), JD (47), and MD (40).

Admission

In 2018, Berkeley received 89,615 applications for a place in the Class of 2022, but only 15 percent were offered admission. A decade prior, the university received 48,000+ applications and sported an admit rate of 22 percent. Acceptance rates fluctuate among three separate groups of candidates: California residents (17 percent), out-of-staters (15 percent), and international students (8 percent). The average SAT of an admitted resident was 1390 while the average admitted out-of-state applicant score was 1484; accepted international students had a mean of 1480. Overall, members of the Class of 2022 possessed a mid-50 percent range of 1300-1530 on the SAT and 28-34 on the ACT. An eye-popping 98 percent placed in the top decile of their high school class, and 88 percent earned a GPA of 3.75 or higher on a 4.0 scale. The average weighted GPA was an intimidating 4.45.

The committee claims that the admissions review is so holistic that it "literally hugs your application." Logistically, with nearly 90,000 applications to sift through, each embrace is surely quite short. As a result, GPA, rigor of secondary school record, and standardized test scores are among the "very important" criteria used to winnow down the initial pool; however, the application essay does rest on this same tier of importance. The next factors receiving the strongest consideration include volunteer work, work experience, extracurricular activities, and character/personal qualities. Everyone is on equal footing at Berkeley as the school does not offer early admission. Becoming a Golden Bear has been highly selective process for many decades, and now it has reached its all-time high. Flawless grades in a roster of AP and honors courses is essentially a prerequisite, but there is some wiggle-room on test scores as the committee does genuinely consider demonstrated leadership and other intangibles.

Worth Your Money?

Paying $14,000 per year in tuition to attend one of the finest institutions in the country sounds like a pipe dream, particularly considering that some private schools charge four times that. For the one-quarter or so of the undergraduate student body from out of state, the annual cost of attendance will be $65,000, a far cry from the $36,000 COA for Californians (this includes the aforementioned tuition plus all direct and indirect costs). For the 47 percent of students determined eligible for need-based aid, the average award is $23,542 per year, making Berkeley a genuinely accessible place for lower-income students to attend without incurring unhealthy student loan debt.

FINANCIAL
Institutional Type: Public
In-State Tuition: $11,442
Out-of-State Tuition: $40,434
Room & Board: $16,160
Required Fees: $2,742
Books & Supplies: $850

Avg. Need-Based Aid: $23,542
Avg. % of Need Met: 83%

Avg. Merit-Based Aid: $5,979
% Receiving Merit-Based Aid: 8%

Avg. Cumulative Debt: $18,225
% of Students Borrowing: 34%

CAREER
Who Recruits
1. AlphaSights
2. Fisher Investments
3. Navigant
4. Putnam Associates
5. Western Digital

Notable Internships
1. Lyft
2. WeWork
3. Airbnb

Top Industries
1. Business
2. Education
3. Engineering
4. Research
5. Operations

Top Employers
1. Google
2. Apple
3. Facebook
4. Amazon
5. Oracle

Where Alumni Work
1. San Francisco
2. Los Angeles
3. New York City
4. Seattle
5. Boston

Median Earnings
College Scorecard (Early Career): $64,700
EOP (Early Career): $67,900
PayScale (Mid-Career): $131,800

RANKINGS
Forbes: 13
Money: 11
U.S. News: 22, National Universities
Wall Street Journal/THE: 34
Washington Monthly: 20, National Universities

#CollegesWorthYourMoney

ADMISSION
Admission Rate: 41%
Admission Rate - Men: 36%
Admission Rate - Women: 46%
EA Admission Rate: Not Offered
ED Admission Rate: Not Offered
Admission Rate (5-Year Trend): 0%
ED Admission Rate (5-Year Trend): Not Offered
% of Admits Attending (Yield): 20%
Transfer Admission Rate: 55%

Offered Wait List: 9,213
Accepted Wait List: 3,207
Admitted Wait List: 24

SAT Reading/Writing (Middle 50%): 570-670
SAT Math (Middle 50%): 580-740
ACT Composite (Middle 50%): 25-31
Testing Policy: ACT/SAT Required
SAT Superscore: No
ACT Superscore: No

% Graduated in Top 10% of HS Class: 100%
% Graduated in Top 25% of HS Class: 100%
% Graduated in Top 50% of HS Class: 100%

ENROLLMENT
Total Undergraduate Enrollment: 30,810
% Part-Time: 2%
% Male: 39%
% Female: 61%
% Out-of-State: 5%
% Fraternity: 7%
% Sorority: 11%
% On-Campus (Freshman): 92%
% On-Campus (All Undergraduate): 75%

% African-American: 2%
% Asian: 27%
% Hispanic: 22%
% White: 24%
% Other: 5%
% Race or Ethnicity Unknown: 2%
% International: 17%
% Low-Income: 37%

ACADEMICS
Student-to-Faculty Ratio: 20:1
% of Classes Under 20: 36%
% of Classes Under 40: 68%
% Full-Time Faculty: 73%
% Full-Time Faculty w/ Terminal Degree: 94%

Top Programs
Animal Science
Biological Sciences
Communication
Computer Science
Engineering
English
Political Science
Sociology

Retention Rate: 92%
4-Year Graduation Rate: 61%
6-Year Graduation Rate: 86%

Curricular Flexibility: Less Flexible
Academic Rating: ★★★✦

Inside the Classroom

Like so much growth in the annals of California state history, the story of UC-Davis is one of a post-World War II boom that saw the state's population increase by 53 percent from the 1940s to the 1950s. The school's rapid rise began in 1959 when Davis officially became a general campus of the University of California system. By 1962 it launched an engineering school, and its now prestigious law and medical schools opened in 1966 and 1968, respectively. One hundred years ago, Davis was known as the University Farm and offered no degree programs. Today, it is home to 30,000+ undergraduates alone and offers 102 undergraduate majors and roughly the same number of graduate programs. As with many UC campuses, the onset of the 2010s saw application numbers spike and acceptance rates plunge. The school that was once only a farm is, today, producing crops of graduates that line corporate offices at the leading tech companies in Silicon Valley.

There are four undergraduate schools at UCD: The College of Agricultural and Environmental Sciences, the College of Biological Sciences, the College of Engineering, and the College of Letters and Science. The university has two sets of core requirements—Topical Breadth, which mandates between twelve and twenty units in each of the arts and humanities, science and engineering, and the social sciences—and Core Literacies, which include English composition; writing experience; oral skills; visual literacy; American cultures, governance, and history; domestic diversity; world cultures; quantitative literacy; and scientific literacy. All told, that adds up to eighty-seven units of required coursework, but the categories are broad, and pretty much any course you could take fits at least one, making those curricular requirements less limiting than they first appear.

A 20:1 student-to-faculty ratio isn't terribly inspiring, especially with 7,500+ graduate students stealing their share of the spotlight. While class sizes aren't small, 63 percent of sections enroll fewer than thirty students, and 72 percent of classes are kept under fifty students. There are numerous opportunities for undergraduate research through programs like the McNair Scholars Program, the Biology Undergraduate Research Program, and Sponsored Undergraduate Research programs. A solid 41 percent of Davis seniors report having assisted a professor with research, and 50 percent engage in some type of research/creative project outside the classroom. Only 1,300 students choose to study abroad each year, but offerings do include fifty programs in thirty countries with courses taught by University of California professors.

The greatest number of degrees conferred are in biology (17 percent), the social sciences (17 percent), psychology (13 percent), engineering (11 percent), and agriculture (7 percent). Among the most heralded programs are those in animal science and all areas of engineering. In recent years Davis students have begun to capture a greater number of prestigious national awards. Twelve Fulbright Scholarships were awarded to grads and alumni in 2019, a Schwarzman Scholar was named in 2017, and the school has had a number of Rhodes Scholarship finalists since 2010.

Outside the Classroom

At 5,300 acres the Davis campus is one of the largest in the country, yet housing options are still expanding to keep up with enrollment increases. The housing capacity at the university is currently 11,000 students; freshmen are guaranteed on-campus housing, and 93 percent take advantage. In 2019, the school broke ground on a new housing project that will add 3,300 beds to the West Village section of the university. The gender disparity cannot be ignored at UC-Davis as women outnumber men by nearly a 60/40 ratio. A beautifully diverse student body is 33 percent Asian, 22 percent Hispanic, and 14 percent international. Roughly seventy Greek organizations attract 10 percent of the undergraduate population. There are approximately 800 student-run organizations, including award-winning academic teams that have captured the National Freescale Cup Autonomous Model Car Competition, the International Data Mining Cup, and the grand prize at the International Genetically Engineered Machines competition. On the subject of competition, the chance to participate in athletics exists no matter your level of skill. The Aggies field fourteen women's and nine men's Division I teams to go with twenty-seven intramural leagues and thirty-nine intercollegiate club squads. Volunteerism is strong with 600,000 hours donated annually by members of the UC-Davis community. Given the school's emphasis on environmental science, it should come as no shock that it is routinely voted one of the greener campuses in the United States, and 29 percent of dining hall food is sustainably grown. Sacramento is the nearest big city, only 15 miles from campus; San Francisco is a manageable hour-long car ride away.

Career Services

The UC-Davis Internship and Career Center (ICC) has eighteen professional employees who work with or on behalf of undergraduate students, many of whom specialize in a particular discipline such as engineering and physical sciences, health and biological sciences, agricultural and environmental sciences, and liberal arts and business. Others play roles in the areas of internship coordination, employer relations, and recruiting. Davis has a 1,706:1 student-to-staff ratio, which is among the poorest of any university profiled in this guidebook. While the staffing may be lacking for a school with over 30,000 undergraduates, there are plenty of encouraging statistics that indicate Aggies' career prospects are in good hands.

University of California, Davis

E-mail: undergraduateadmissions@ucdavis.edu | Website: www.ucdavis.edu

An admirable 80 percent of undergraduates land at least one internship; 55 percent engage in two or more internships. In total, the ICC facilitates more than 10,000 internships per year. More than 500 company recruiters visit UC Davis each year looking to hire Aggies, and many major corporations attend the six large-scale career fairs that take place each year, including the Fall/Winter/Spring Internship & Career Fair, the STEM Career Fair, and the Engineering & Tech Internship & Career Fair. There are 260,000 living Aggie alumni who are embedded at many of the top companies to work for in the country. With terrific internship and recruitment statistics, the ICC overcomes its less-than-desirable staffing to be of great assistance to job-seeking graduates.

Professional Outcomes

One year after earning their BA or BS, 14 percent of Davis grads are still unemployed. Many have found homes at Silicon Valley or other California-based juggernaut employers, including about all of the world's top tech companies. The corporations employing 200 or more Aggies include Genentech, Google, Apple, Cisco, Facebook, Oracle, Amazon, Microsoft, Salesforce, Workday, and LinkedIn. More than one hundred Aggies are presently working for Adobe and rivals Uber and Lyft. The San Francisco Bay area is home to the largest concentration of Davis alumni followed by Sacramento, Los Angeles, San Diego, and Seattle. Assisted by the large number of engineering students, recent grads take home a median starting salary of $56,000 and, by midcareer, are approaching six figures.

Within one year of graduating 39 percent of Aggies elect to continue their education, and 94 percent report that their undergraduate experience prepared them somewhere between adequately and "very well" for postgraduate study. The most popular degrees pursued are masters, MDs or other health doctorates, law, and MBA/MPA. The UC Davis School of Medicine, one of the best schools for primary care training in the country, tends to favor its own graduates, filling approximately 20 percent of its cohorts with homegrown students. The average undergraduate student who gained acceptance to at least one medical school possessed a 3.58 GPA and a 512 MCAT score. The UC Davis School of Law also draws heavily from its undergraduate schools, and many grads also find homes at other University of California schools. Currently, multiple Aggie alumni are enrolled at the likes of Harvard Law School, Duke University School of Law, and a host of other top-tier institutions.

Admission

Like all schools in the University of California system the Davis branch has experienced an influx of applicants in the last several years. It set a record in 2018-19 with 95,207 applications, 76,647 of which were from freshmen; the rest were transfers. From that pool, 41 percent were welcomed aboard to form the freshman class of 2018-19. Most had near-perfect academic transcripts as 89 percent were the proud owners of a 3.75 or higher unweighted GPA. The mid-50 percent standardized test scores were in a far wider range of 1150-1410 on the SAT and 25-31 on the ACT. A decade ago, Davis admitted 52 percent of applicants and, while grades were similarly stellar to those of the Class of 2022, standardized test scores were significantly lower.

According to admissions officers, the factors most heavily weighted in the admissions process are the rigor of one's secondary courses, GPA, standardized test scores, and the application essay. The next rung of importance is made-up of softer factors like extracurricular activities, volunteer work, talent/ability, and character/personal qualities. First-generation status is listed as a "considered" factor, but the number of students who are the first in their families to enter college suggests that this is a point of emphasis for the university. In fact, an astonishing 42 percent of current students grew up in households with parents who had not completed four-year degrees. There is no early EA or ED plan at UC-Davis—all applications are due by November 30. Getting into UC-Davis is harder than it used to be and, like other University of California campuses, it requires a fairly pristine academic transcript in a rigorous curriculum, but standardized test scores can be a bit lower than at UC-San Diego and significantly lower than at Berkeley or UCLA.

Worth Your Money?

A whopping 59 percent of those attending UC Davis receive an average need-based grant of $21,402. Considering that the estimated in-state cost of attendance is just over $35,000, the majority of undergraduates are paying a reasonable price for a valuable degree. Estimated COA for nonresidents is $64k. For the 20 percent of attendees not from California, that would be an expensive venture without any financial aid, and you likely could find a better merit aid offer from a private institution.

FINANCIAL
Institutional Type: Public
In-State Tuition: $11,442
Out-of-State Tuition: $40,434
Room & Board: $15,863
Required Fees: $3,050
Books & Supplies: $1,159

Avg. Need-Based Aid: $21,402
Avg. % of Need Met: 83%

Avg. Merit-Based Aid: $6,485
% Receiving Merit-Based Aid: 5%

Avg. Cumulative Debt: $18,575
% of Students Borrowing: 48%

CAREER
Who Recruits
1. Airbnb
2. Lyft
3. Adobe
4. LinkedIn
5. Cisco

Notable Internships
1. U.S. House of Representatives
2. Adidas
3. Credit Suisse

Top Industries
1. Business
2. Education
3. Operations
4. Research
5. Engineering

Top Employers
1. Kaiser Permanente
2. Genetech
3. Google
4. Apple
5. Facebook

Where Alumni Work
1. San Francisco
2. Sacramento
3. Los Angeles
4. San Diego
5. Orange County, CA

Median Earnings
College Scorecard (Early Career): $58,200
EOP (Early Career): $61,600
PayScale (Mid-Career): $112,600

RANKINGS
Forbes: 88
Money: 5
U.S. News: 39, National Universities
Wall Street Journal/THE: 36
Washington Monthly: 11, National Universities

#CollegesWorthYourMoney

Irvine, California | Admissions Phone: 949-824-6703

Inside the Classroom

A diverse school with a strong Asian and Hispanic representation that serves a phenomenally high percentage of first-generation college students, UC-Irvine is, like the other schools in the University of California system, becoming more selective every year. On the eve of the millennium as Y2K-mania reached its crescendo, Irvine was a school that accepted roughly half of its applicants and was primarily a safety school for those applying to the more prestigious UC campuses. Today, UCI is a top-of-the-list destination for many of the 30,000 UCI undergraduate students, half of whom are California residents, and *all* of whom proudly call themselves Anteaters. As the third decade of the 2000s kicks off, freshmen flock to Orange County not just for the school's premier location but for the eighty stellar undergraduate academic programs the university offers at a bargain price.

For a school with an overwhelming number freshmen entering its gates each year, UC-Irvine takes great care to offer first-years a soft landing. The Summer Bridge Scholars Program, Freshman Edge Program, and the Freshman Seminar Series are all designed to help new students succeed, and they are effective as 92 percent of freshmen return for their sophomore year, a retention rate on par with many highly selective private institutions. All students take a liberal arts core that involves three courses in each of science and technology, arts and humanities, and the social sciences, two writing-intensive classes, and forays into foreign language, quantitative reasoning, multicultural issues, and international/global issues. Like most California publics, UCI operates on the quarter system, which means you'll need to get used to furiously paced ten-week periods of study.

At a school with an 18:1 student-to-faculty ratio and 6,300 graduate students to serve, you might expect all classes at Irvine to be held in hundred-seat lecture halls. We are pleased to report that is not the case. In fact, 53 percent of all sections enroll nineteen or fewer students, and only 23 percent of courses contain fifty+ students. The school provides a terrific number of opportunities for undergrads to participate in some type of supervised research. More than three-fifths of students have conducted a research project, and 20 percent have assisted faculty in conducting research. The Undergraduate Research Opportunities Program helps students with proposal writing, developing research plans, and presenting their results at the annual spring UCI Undergraduate Research Symposium and/or publishing their results in the *UCI Undergraduate Research Journal*. Most students remain on campus for all four years as only about 1,000 individuals study abroad each year.

The five most popular majors at Irvine are psychology, biology, business, engineering, and computer science. The Samueli School of Engineering has a solid reputation as does the Bren School, the only dedicated computer science school in the University of California system. Programs in public health and biological sciences also earn very high marks. Between two and five graduates win Fulbright Scholarships each year, and Irvine has had an occasional Goldwater, Truman, or Marshall Scholar in the last few years, but winning prestigious national postgraduate scholarships is not a primary focus of Anteater alumni.

Outside the Classroom

It's hard to think of many more desirable locations for a college setting than Orange County, California. The Pacific Ocean is only five miles from campus, including the famed Laguna and Newport beaches. Los Angeles is within an hour's drive, and San Diego is about an hour and a half and, if you have a spare twenty-five minutes, you can head over to Disneyland for the afternoon. The suburban campus covers 1,474 acres, and 38 percent of students live in university housing. Freshmen are guaranteed two full years of housing should they choose to accept it but, at present, only 82 percent of freshmen live in the dorms. Fraternities attract 9 percent of males, and 8 percent of females join sororities. There are eighteen varsity sports teams and 400 total student-athletes. All-time, the school has produced 500 All-Americans and fifty-six Olympians. Currently, there are 677 registered campus organizations representing over nineteen categories with two notables being UCI's Circle K Chapter that dedicates 35,000 hours of service annually to the surrounding community and Kababayan (Kaba), a popular Filipino-American club. Aldrich Park, modeled after Central Park, is the beautiful centerpiece to Irvine's campus and the site of an annual spring fair. Campus-wide events like Shocktoberfest and Homecoming are well attended.

Career Services

The UCI Division of Career Pathways employs fifteen professional employees who work with or on behalf of undergraduate students as career educators, internship coordinators, or employer engagement specialists. That 1,980:1 student-to-staff ratio is among the highest of any university profiled in this guidebook. Fortunately, the school still manages to reach a significant percentage of the undergraduate population through a variety of means as evidenced by numerous impressive data points.

University of California, Irvine

E-mail: admissions@uci.edu | Website: www.uci.edu

In the 2018-19 school year career counselors conducted 4,523 one-on-one counseling sessions, and 450 companies attended the school's various career fairs that drew a collective student crowd of greater than 10,000. The UCI Division of Career Pathways not only hosts general fall and spring fairs but also gatherings for STEM careers, health jobs, and law school applicants. An additional 3,000 students attended Career Pathways Panels. In 2017-18, companies conducted on-campus interviews with 1,305 undergraduate students. The list of on-campus recruiters included Deloitte, KPMG, Ernst and Young, PricewaterhouseCoopers, Google, Amazon, Northrop Grumman, and Johnson & Johnson. A total of 46 percent of students completed internships last year; half were noncredit internships while half were for credit. The job-shadowing program, now in its fifth year, attracted 268 student participants. Career services at UCI aren't perfect; it's simply too large an operation for fifteen people to handle, but the office possesses strong enough corporate connections to assist grads in achieving positive postgraduate outcomes.

Professional Outcomes

Accounting, aerospace, internet and software, K-12 education, real estate, and retail are among the industries attracting the greatest number of Anteaters. Companies employing the greatest number of Class of 2018 members include Boeing, the Walt Disney Company, Google, EY, and Microsoft. Many also end up with nonprofit organizations like Teach for America and City Year. Looking at alumni from all years, hundreds of individuals can be found at each of Kaiser Permanente, Facebook, Apple, Edwards Lifesciences, and Deloitte. The median salary within the first couple years of entering the working world, across all disciplines, is just under $40,000; five years out the median income rises to $54k, and ten years out alumni are earning a median salary of $75k. Computer science graduates earn close to $75k right off the bat. Few grads leave the state of California; Orange County, Los Angeles, San Francisco, and San Diego soak up the vast majority.

Between 75 and 80 percent of Irvine grads plan on pursuing an advanced degree within five years of earning their bachelor's. The majority of those enrolling in graduate school do so within the state of California. Many remain at Irvine or another UC campus—Berkeley, UCLA, and San Diego are among the most popular choices. Irvine also sends graduates to Stanford and USC as well as out-of-state to the University of Washington and Georgia Tech. UC-Irvine has a strong reputation for premed. In 2018-19, the university produced the twenty-fifth most medical school applicants of any institution in the country, and Anteaters possessed higher MCAT scores than the national average. The prestigious UCI School of Medicine admitted seventeen of its own alumni in 2018, which accounted for more than 15 percent of the incoming class. The UC Irvine School of Law is only a decade old but has already skyrocketed toward the top of the rankings. In addition to remaining in Irvine for law school, undergrads often gain acceptance to other excellent law schools within the UC system and also have earned acceptances to the likes of Harvard, Georgetown, and the University of Michigan.

Admission

An almost incomprehensible deluge of 117,000+ applications rained down on the UCI admissions staff in 2019, including the greatest number of high school/nontransfer students of any school in the University of California system. In 2019, its acceptance rate fell to 26.6 percent, a far cry from only five years prior when 41 percent of high school applicants were admitted. At the time the SAT mid-50 percent range was 1040-1290; today, it is 1180-1440, quite a metamorphosis in terms of selectivity. Getting into Irvine without placing in the top decile of your high school class is nearly impossible as 98 percent of 2018-19 freshmen earned that distinction. The average GPA for attending students was 4.0.

For a school receiving six-figure application numbers each year, it still professes to hold eight factors as being of the highest importance: rigor of curriculum, GPA, class rank, standardized test scores, the essay, extracurricular activities, talent/ability, work experience, and volunteer work. Interestingly, first-generation status is listed as merely "considered," yet the school's undergraduate population is comprised of an incredible 48 percent of first-generation students. While racial/ethnic status is "not considered" in admissions, 26 percent of the student population are underrepresented minorities.

Worth Your Money?

An annual tuition of under $16,000 for California residents helps explain the rising popularity of Irvine as well as the other UC campuses. No matter your intended major, this in-state rate represents a genuine bargain. Out-of-state residents without plans to pursue computer science or engineering should think twice before committing three times that amount in tuition costs alone. You would likely be better off pursuing options in your home state or private options with merit aid.

FINANCIAL
Institutional Type: Public
In-State Tuition: $11,442
Out-of-State Tuition: $40,434
Room & Board: $16,135
Required Fees: N/A
Books & Supplies: $1,390

Avg. Need-Based Aid: $19,902
Avg. % of Need Met: 83%

Avg. Merit-Based Aid: $7,771
% Receiving Merit-Based Aid: 3%

Avg. Cumulative Debt: $19,039
% of Students Borrowing: 53%

CAREER
Who Recruits
1. Pacific Life
2. Edwards Life Sciences
3. Glidewell Laboratories
4. Western Digital
5. Northwestern Mutual

Notable Internships
1. Grant Thorton LLP
2. PlayStation
3. Yelp

Top Industries
1. Business
2. Engineering
3. Education
4. Operations
5. Research

Top Employers
1. Kaiser Permanente
2. Google
3. Amazon
4. Apple
5. Microsoft

Where Alumni Work
1. Orange County, CA
2. Los Angeles
3. San Francisco
4. San Diego
5. New York City

Median Earnings
College Scorecard (Early Career): $58,400
EOP (Early Career): $60,400
PayScale (Mid-Career): $116,000

RANKINGS
Forbes: 87
Money: 1
U.S. News: 36, National Universities
Wall Street Journal/THE: 73
Washington Monthly: 18, National Universities

#CollegesWorthYourMoney

University of California, Los Angeles

Los Angeles, California | Admissions Phone: 310-825-3101

ADMISSION

Admission Rate: 14%
Admission Rate - Men: 13%
Admission Rate - Women: 15%
EA Admission Rate: Not Offered
ED Admission Rate: Not Offered
Admission Rate (5-Year Trend): -6%
ED Admission Rate (5-Year Trend): Not Offered
% of Admits Attending (Yield): 39%
Transfer Admission Rate: 24%

Offered Wait List: N/A
Accepted Wait List: N/A
Admitted Wait List: N/A

SAT Reading/Writing (Middle 50%): 630-780
SAT Math (Middle 50%): 640-740
ACT Composite (Middle 50%): 29-35
Testing Policy: ACT/SAT Required
SAT Superscore: No
ACT Superscore: No

% Graduated in Top 10% of HS Class: 97%
% Graduated in Top 25% of HS Class: 100%
% Graduated in Top 50% of HS Class: 100%

ENROLLMENT

Total Undergraduate Enrollment: 31,505
% Part-Time: 2%
% Male: 42%
% Female: 58%
% Out-of-State: 13%
% Fraternity: 11%
% Sorority: 13%
% On-Campus (Freshman): 98%
% On-Campus (All Undergraduate): 48%

% African-American: 3%
% Asian: 28%
% Hispanic: 22%
% White: 27%
% Other: 6%
% Race or Ethnicity Unknown: 2%
% International: 12%
% Low-Income: 36%

ACADEMICS

Student-to-Faculty Ratio: 18:1
% of Classes Under 20: 51%
% of Classes Under 40: 74%
% Full-Time Faculty: 71%
% Full-Time Faculty w/ Terminal Degree: 98%

Top Programs
Computer Science
Engineering
English
Fine Arts
Mathematics
Performing Arts
Political Science
Psychology

Retention Rate: 97%
4-Year Graduation Rate: 77%
6-Year Graduation Rate: 90%

Curricular Flexibility: Somewhat Flexible
Academic Rating: ★★★★✦

Inside the Classroom

Among the most selective public universities in the country, UCLA is also the most diverse campus on the planet. The undergraduate student body is 27 percent Asian, 22 percent Hispanic, and 12 percent international, not to mention 33 percent first-generation college students, making UCLA a fascinating place to pursue one of 134 majors in 109 academic departments. More than 31,500 undergraduates enjoy a whopping 3,800 course offerings that include programs in over forty languages, many of which you won't find offered at your average university such as Armenian, Old Norse, and Sanskrit.

The general education curriculum requires that every student explore three foundational areas: the arts and humanities, society and culture, and scientific inquiry. That entails completing ten courses. Additionally, in order to graduate you'll need to meet requirements in foreign language, writing, and diversity. The school's Capstone Initiative has sought to bring a culminating senior academic endeavor to as many students as possible. As of 2018, more than sixty majors at UCLA require a capstone experience that results in the creation of a tangible product under the mentorship of faculty members.

Close to half of classrooms contain fewer than twenty Bruins, but those taking introductory courses will find themselves in a fair number of lecture halls with a hundred or more students. Professors are given impressively high marks for a research university of UCLA's size. Over 90 percent of the graduates of the College of Letters and Science rate their professors as being both intellectually challenging and accessible. By senior year, 40 percent of undergraduates have participated in a research experience. There are multiple undergraduate research journals in which students can publish their original works as well as a Research Poster Day each May when students can present. Every year one-quarter of the undergraduate population elects to study abroad, a sharp increase from only a few years ago. UCLA has 115 partner universities in forty-two countries around the globe.

By volume, the most commonly conferred degrees are in the social sciences (26 percent), biology (15 percent), engineering (7 percent), mathematics (7 percent), and interdisciplinary studies (5 percent). UCLA isn't a school where one department is ranked significantly higher than any other. Departmental rankings are high across the board in areas such as computer science, engineering, film, fine and performing arts, mathematics, political science and many more. The school also produces a reasonable number of postgraduate scholarship winners—seven graduates took home Fulbright Scholarships in 2019.

Outside the Classroom

If you can't find your niche at UCLA it can hardly be blamed on the school that offers over 1,000 clubs and student organizations. There is no shortage of opportunities to volunteer in the surrounding Los Angeles community—the Volunteer Center, Center for Community Learning, and Community Programs Office offer countless avenues for civic involvement. Greek life is readily available with more than sixty fraternities and sororities on campus, but it is hardly smothering; only 11 percent of men and 13 percent of women are Greek affiliated. UCLA's sports scene boasts storied basketball and baseball teams, big-time football, and 116 all-time championships across twenty-five Division I men's and women's sports. Ninety-eight percent of freshmen reside on campus, and 52 percent of the entire student body lives in university-owned housing. As bountiful as campus life is at UCLA, the excitement that can be found in the surrounding neighborhoods is truly limitless. Within a few miles of campus undergrads can venture to Venice Beach, Santa Monica, Malibu, or Beverley Hills. In short, you won't find too many Bruins complaining of boredom.

Career Services

With twenty-three full-time employees dedicated to undergraduates, the UCLA Career Center has a 1,373:1 student-to-counselor ratio, much higher than most of the schools featured in this guide. The university does host a number of major-specific job fairs that are attended by an impressive selection of employers. In 2018, its Engineering and Technical Fair was attended by forty organizations including the CIA, Texas Instruments, Visa, and eBay. Each academic quarter the school also hosts Hire UCLA, which is well-attended by major corporations.

When it comes to finding an internship; students are not going to have their hands held throughout the entire process. The Career Center connects students with internships via Handshake, and 60 percent of undergrads do eventually land one, but the school lacks corporate partnerships that allow for a more streamlined experience. The Career Center offers services such as an online resume critique with a five-day turnaround, and students are free to schedule an appointment or drop by for career advice, a mock interview, or graduate school exploration from 9 a.m. to 4 p.m. on weekdays. Additional events are organized by the UCLA Career Center just about every day. For example, over the course of one random week in May 2019 the center hosted a resume workshop, a consulting industry meetup, a workshop on branding oneself on LinkedIn, and a recruiting visit from the Vanderbilt University School of Medicine.

University of California, Los Angeles

E-mail: ugadm@saonet.ucla.edu | Website: www.ucla.edu

Professional Outcomes

UCLA grads flow most heavily into the education, technology, and financial services sectors. The employers that snatch up the highest number of recent Bruin grads include Disney, Google (where over 1,500 alumni presently work), EY, Teach for America, Amazon, and Oracle. Hundreds also can be found in the corporate offices of Uber, Microsoft, Facebook, Netflix, Salesforce, Airbnb, and LinkedIn. Internships definitely help students land jobs; students who had at least one internship found employment at double the rate of their peers who did not have such an experience. The average starting salary for full-time employment exceeds $52,000, a solid figure considering the vast array of degrees being conferred. A good number of students stay in L.A./Orange County after graduation, but the other most popular destination points include NYC, DC, Chicago, Seattle, and Boston.

Roughly one-quarter of graduates enroll directly in a graduate/professional school. The most attended grad schools are primarily other excellent California-based institutions including Stanford, Pepperdine, USC, Berkeley, and Loyola Marymount. UCLA students applying to medical school have experienced acceptance rates varying from 51-59 percent over recent years. The most frequently attended medical schools include Duke, Boston University, Drexel, Temple, Case Western, and NYU. Over 90 percent of Bruins applying to law school garner at least one acceptance, a clip that is roughly 15 percent better than the national average. Law schools with the highest number of UCLA grads include many of the aforementioned California universities as well Georgetown, Vanderbilt, George Washington, Duke, and American.

Admission

A decade ago, 24 percent of the roughly 50,000 applicants to UCLA received acceptance letters; today, the school receives the most applications of any college in the country with 113,761 in 2018, and the acceptance rate has fallen to 14 percent. Students from out-of-state fared better than in-state applicants and international applicants by a significant margin with out-of-staters enjoying a 23 percent acceptance rate in 2017. However, the University of California Board of Regents recently passed a measure capping out-of-state/international enrollment at 18 percent moving forward, which should curb that trend.

Those accepted straight from high school are a high-achieving bunch as a hard-to-comprehend 97 percent graduated in the top 10 percent of their high school class. The SAT 25th/75th percentile breakdown is 1270-1520 and the ACT range is 28-34. For comparison, a decade ago, the average SAT score of an admitted student was 1330; the average ACT was 29. Thus, we can say that UCLA's shrinking acceptance rate is, indeed, indicative of increasing selectivity. It's important to note that there is more than one way through these heavily guarded gates. UCLA is extremely transfer friendly, offering admission to 5,770 such students in 2018 with the vast majority coming from California's system of community colleges. UCLA has joined the ranks of the uber-selective as the pool of top-of-their-class applicants continues to grow each year. While it does employ some semblance of a holistic process that considers personal qualities, likely contributions to campus life, and challenges overcome, applicants need to bring high GPAs and test scores to the table to have a genuine shot at admission.

Worth Your Money?

The average UCLA graduate has almost $10,000 less in student loan debt than the average college graduate in the country. It helps when your in-state tuition to attend one of the finest universities around is only $13k, and the total annual cost of attendance is $34,390 for a resident but $63,382 for a nonresident. Few students receive any merit-based aid, yet over half are awarded need-based grants with a mean yearly value of $20,926. While they are rarely able to meet 100 percent of a student's demonstrated financial need, the school is priced so reasonably that graduates emerge with little debt and sky-high job prospects. Depending on your intended major and/or financial situation, UCLA can be worth your money even as an out-of-stater, despite the elevated price.

FINANCIAL
Institutional Type: Public
In-State Tuition: $11,442
Out-of-State Tuition: $40,434
Room & Board: $15,902
Required Fees: $1,784
Books & Supplies: $1,464

Avg. Need-Based Aid: $20,926
Avg. % of Need Met: 81%

Avg. Merit-Based Aid: $5,763
% Receiving Merit-Based Aid: 4%

Avg. Cumulative Debt: $22,390
% of Students Borrowing: 42%

CAREER
Who Recruits
1. Bain & Company
2. Airbnb
3. Salesforce
4. Netflix
5. Oracle

Notable Internships
1. CBRE
2. Los Angeles Magazine
3. Northrop Grumman

Top Industries
1. Business
2. Education
3. Operations
4. Engineering
5. Media

Top Employers
1. Google
2. Apple
3. Amazon
4. Facebook
5. Microsoft

Where Alumni Work
1. Los Angeles
2. San Francisco
3. Orange County, CA
4. New York City
5. San Diego

Median Earnings
College Scorecard (Early Career): $60,700
EOP (Early Career): $65,800
PayScale (Mid-Career): $116,100

RANKINGS
Forbes: 38
Money: 4
U.S. News: 20, National Universities
Wall Street Journal/THE: 25 (T)
Washington Monthly: 12, National Universities

#CollegesWorthYourMoney

University of California, San Diego

La Jolla, California | Admissions Phone: 858-534-4831

Inside the Classroom

Becoming a Triton used to be a disappointing consolation prize for applicants hoping to become a Bruin or a Golden Bear. While UCLA and Berkeley remain the crème de la crème of the UC system, the gap between those uber-elite jewels and UC-San Diego has closed significantly in recent years as applications have skyrocketed to the cusp of six-figures, and the profile of the average freshman has risen commensurately. In 2003, there were fewer than 20,000 undergraduates at the university; there are now in excess of 30,000. An extremely strong academic school, UCSD offers forty-two bachelor's degrees with many concentrations as well as fifty-five minors, all available for less than $15,000 per year in tuition.

There are six undergraduate colleges at UCSD that are meant, in the Oxford and Cambridge model, not to separate by discipline but, instead, to forge flourishing small liberal arts college communities within the larger university. Core curriculum at all of the colleges includes first- year writing, advanced writing, oral communication, mathematical reasoning, quantitative reasoning, and second language. Additionally, undergrads must complete coursework in science and technological inquiry, historical inquiry, literary inquiry, social and behavioral inquiry, artistic inquiry, theological and religious inquiry, philosophical inquiry, ethical inquiry, and diversity and social justice. Two "integration" experiences in which students make connections across disciplines also must be tackled, including one during freshman year.

Over 7,600 graduate students and a 19:1 student-to-faculty ratio are two numbers that don't bode well for those hoping for an intimate classroom experience. Yet, reality is a mixed bag. While 32 percent of course sections are held in larger lecture halls and contain fifty+ students, 43 percent of undergraduate courses sport an enrollment under twenty. Sixty percent of undergrads complete at least one research project as part of their coursework, and roughly one-quarter assist a faculty member with research outside the classroom. Study abroad numbers are approaching 1,000 undergraduates per year, which is only a sliver of the total undergraduate population. Still, opportunities in forty-two countries are available for those who desire a semester of study outside of the United States.

Altogether, the social sciences have the highest representation of all majors (29 percent) followed by biology (19 percent) and mathematics (7 percent). UCSD's computer science and engineering programs have stellar reputations in the corporate and tech communities, and programs in biology, economics, and political science are among the best anywhere. In recent years nationally competitive postgraduate fellowship programs have selected a number of Tritons, and the school has produced as many as a dozen Fulbrights per year while the Biology Department alone saw five graduates capture National Science Foundation Graduate Research Fellowships last academic year.

Outside the Classroom

Just shy of 95 percent of freshmen live on the UCSD campus, but only 44 percent of the undergraduate population live in dormitories or college-owned apartments. Fraternities and sororities have a solid but not overwhelming presence on campus, drawing 14 percent of men and women. Unlike UCLA and Berkeley, San Diego doesn't offer prime-time football or basketball teams; in fact, it hasn't fielded a football team since 1968. Rather, the twenty-three Triton squads participate in NCAA Division II and fare quite well within that less competitive environment. However, plans do exist to join Division I's Big West Conference within the next few years. A diverse student body (37 percent minority and 9 percent international) enjoy an equally diverse array of clubs. There are over 500 to choose from with many options in the areas of student government, media, and a popular intramural sports program that has a 60 percent participation rate. The 180-acre campus is situated within the wealthy beachfront town of La Jolla, a thirteen-mile highway ride from downtown San Diego. While La Jolla is not a typical college town, many students live in beachfront apartments overlooking the Pacific Ocean or Mission Bay, and few complain about the heavenly weather.

Career Services

The UC-San Diego Career Center has eighteen full-time employees who work with or on behalf of undergraduate students, many of whom specialize in a particular discipline such as pre-law, pre-health, the social sciences, the humanities, business, or engineering. UCSD's 1,683:1 student-to-counselor ratio is toward the highest of any school featured in this guide. To compensate, it puts on a multitude of annual career fairs, many of which attract 1,000+ students. Those include large-scale fairs in the fall, winter, and spring, a Graduate School Fair, an Engineering and Computing Career Fair, and an event called Impact Career Fair: Companies for a Brighter Future. Each quarter, hundreds of companies are on campus to recruit undergraduate students.

In 2017-18, the school listed 8,356 jobs/internships on Handshake, and those efforts led to 79 percent of graduates having participated in an experiential learning activity—internship, research, or community service. Thirty-minute one-on-one appointments can be scheduled, but scoring one of those appointments, particularly with a "good fit" counselor can be a challenge. Students, via op-eds in the school paper, have been clamoring for an increased number of advisors to accommodate the growing number of undergraduate students at the university. Thanks to the rising prestige of the school, UCSD students have enjoyed increasingly positive post-graduation outcomes, but there is still room to increase the level of support offered.

Professional Outcomes
A healthy 92 percent of UC-San Diego graduates are employed or in graduate school within six months of receiving their diplomas. Among the 73 percent who were employed, 95 percent had one or more job offers only three months after graduation. The most commonly entered industries were marketing/sales (14 percent), finance and banking (12 percent), accounting/auditing (11 percent), technology (9 percent) and health/medical (9 percent). Employers of 2018 graduates included the Walt Disney Company, Tesla, NBC Universal, PwC, Northrup Grumman, and EY. More than 1,000 current Google employees are UC-San Diego alumni, and Qualcomm, Amazon, and Apple all employ 500+ each. The median starting salary for San Diego grads was $55,000 in 2018. Those entering the engineering field averaged $65k, those in marketing/sales averaged $51k, and those majoring in education had a mean income of $40k. The bulk of grads remain in San Diego or relocate to Los Angeles or San Francisco.

Sixteen percent of 2018 graduates moved directly into a graduate or professional program. Remaining at UC-San Diego was the most popular choice followed by USC, San Diego State, UCLA, George Washington, NYU, the University of San Francisco, Pepperdine, and Columbia. Between 400 and 500 seniors apply to medical school each year and typically experience average to slightly below average levels of success; between 34 and 40 percent of applicants have been admitted in recent years. Pre-law students most frequently head to California-based institutions such as the University of San Diego School of Law, California Western School of Law, Thomas Jefferson School of Law, and Santa Clara University School of Law. However, Class of 2018 grads also found law school homes at the University of Chicago, Pepperdine, UCLA, Notre Dame, and Fordham.

Admission
A tsunami of 97,899 applications for a place in the Class of 2018-19 flooded the inboxes of the UC-San Diego Admissions Office, more than doubling the number of applications received a decade ago. The admit rate ten years ago was only 37 percent, not all that far from today's 30 percent. Yet, the profile of the average freshman has changed drastically in that same period. Freshmen in the Class of 2022 possessed mid-50 percent standardized test scores of a 1250-1470 on the SAT, 26-32 on the ACT, and 93 percent had an unweighted GPA higher than 3.75. A decade prior, the SAT range was 1150-1380 and "only" 84 percent had GPAs in that same range. Any way you slice it, this school has become vastly more selective in the recent past.

When you are approaching 100,000 applicants, a microscopic exploration of every application is not a realistic expectation. Thus, it makes sense that three of the four "very important" factors considered by the admissions committee are cut-and-dried: level of rigor, GPA, and standardized test scores (the SAT is submitted more often than the ACT). Class rank, interestingly, is not considered. The application essay also was assigned "very important status," and extracurricular activities, state residency, volunteer work, talent/ability, and character/personal qualities earned an "important" designation. There is no early action or early decision round at this school. If the person advising you on college admissions (counselor, parent, family friend) hasn't been paying close attention to the spike in applications and selectivity, UC-San Diego can easily become an institution that should be a "reach" or "target" school, but it could be mistakenly assigned the title of "safety school." In reality, a pristine academic transcript and test scores in the 90th percentile are prerequisites for most applicants.

Worth Your Money?
For the 24 percent of undergraduates who come from outside the state, the University of California-San Diego has an annual cost of attendance of $62,000. Residents, on the other hand, enjoy a COA of $33,000. Extremely little merit aid is distributed, making grants of the need-based variety your best bet for receiving a discount. Fortunately, 56 percent of current students receive some level of financial aid; the average award is $19,366. Staying within the UC system is always an excellent choice for residents, and while the school is getting expensive for outsiders, it may still prove to be a degree that returns your investment, particularly if you aim to work in the tech industry.

FINANCIAL
Institutional Type: Public
In-State Tuition: $11,442
Out-of-State Tuition: $40,434
Room & Board: $14,286
Required Fees: $2,728
Books & Supplies: $1,127

Avg. Need-Based Aid: $19,366
Avg. % of Need Met: 85%

Avg. Merit-Based Aid: $13,933
% Receiving Merit-Based Aid: 3%

Avg. Cumulative Debt: $21,061
% of Students Borrowing: 45%

CAREER
Who Recruits
1. Nordson Corp
2. Sherwin Williams
3. IQVIA
4. Hulu
5. Netflix

Notable Internships
1. Inuit
2. Dow Jones
3. American Express

Top Industries
1. Business
2. Engineering
3. Education
4. Research
5. Operations

Top Employers
1. Google
2. Qualcomm
3. Apple
4. Amazon
5. Illumina

Where Alumni Work
1. San Diego
2. San Francisco
3. Los Angeles
4. Orange County, CA
5. New York City

Median Earnings
College Scorecard (Early Career): $59,900
EOP (Early Career): $65,300
PayScale (Mid-Career): $123,700

RANKINGS
Forbes: 79
Money: 9
U.S. News: 37, National Universities
Wall Street Journal/THE: 37
Washington Monthly: 7, National Universities

#CollegesWorthYourMoney

ADMISSION
Admission Rate: 32%
Admission Rate - Men: 30%
Admission Rate - Women: 34%
EA Admission Rate: Not Offered
ED Admission Rate: Not Offered
Admission Rate (5-Year Trend): -8%
ED Admission Rate (5-Year Trend): Not Offered
% of Admits Attending (Yield): 18%
Transfer Admission Rate: 57%

Offered Wait List: 7,856
Accepted Wait List: 4,883
Admitted Wait List: 14

SAT Reading/Writing (Middle 50%): 620-710
SAT Math (Middle 50%): 610-770
ACT Composite (Middle 50%): 26-32
Testing Policy: ACT/SAT Required
SAT Superscore: No
ACT Superscore: No

% Graduated in Top 10% of HS Class: 100%
% Graduated in Top 25% of HS Class: 100%
% Graduated in Top 50% of HS Class: 100%

ENROLLMENT
Total Undergraduate Enrollment: 23,021
% Part-Time: 2%
% Male: 45%
% Female: 55%
% Out-of-State: 5%
% Fraternity: 9%
% Sorority: 14%
% On-Campus (Freshman): 90%
% On-Campus (All Undergraduate): 38%

% African-American: 2%
% Asian: 20%
% Hispanic: 27%
% White: 32%
% Other: 6%
% Race or Ethnicity Unknown: 1%
% International: 12%
% Low-Income: 41%

ACADEMICS
Student-to-Faculty Ratio: 17:1
% of Classes Under 20: 50%
% of Classes Under 40: 78%
% Full-Time Faculty: 86%
% Full-Time Faculty w/ Terminal Degree: 100%

Top Programs
Anthropology
Communication
Computer Science
Engineering
Environmental Studies
Global and International Studies
Performing Arts
Physics

Retention Rate: 92%
4-Year Graduation Rate: 70%
6-Year Graduation Rate: 87%

Curricular Flexibility: Somewhat Flexible
Academic Rating: ★★★★✦

Inside the Classroom

When your campus is bordered on three sides by the Pacific Ocean and the weather is 70-75 degrees virtually year around, it would be easy for academics to become an afterthought. While the University of California Santa Barbara does, indeed, have a well-earned reputation as a "party school," the approximately 23,000 undergraduate majors are, today, a higher-achieving lot than ever, and they flock to UCSB for the ninety undergraduate majors and slew of top-ranked departments every bit as much as the sand and surf.

The College of Letters and Science, the College of Engineering, and the College of Creative Studies all have different core curricular requirements. There is some crossover in terms of mandated courses in all three schools that include English, reading, and composition; literature; art; social science; and culture and thought. College of Letters and Science grads also must complete classes in foreign language and science, mathematics, and technology. Classes covering the special subject areas of European traditions, ethnicity, world cultures, and quantitative relationships are also part of some academic programs.

The student-to-faculty ratio at UC Santa Barbara is a decent 17:1, and the school does an excellent job of keeping undergraduate class sizes on the small side. In fact, more than half of sections contain fewer than twenty students, and 73 percent enroll twenty-nine or fewer. Thirty-two percent of graduates stated that they often had classes where professors knew their names, and another 41 percent responded that this occurred some of the time. An even more encouraging 89 percent of respondents said there were open channels of communication with professors either "sometimes" or "often." Undergraduate research opportunities definitely exist for those willing to forge relationships with faculty outside the classroom. A solid 57 percent of graduates report engaging in some type of independent study or research. It's not as easy to inspire Gauchos to leave their campus paradise for a semester in a foreign land—only 2 percent of students per year participate in study abroad.

The social sciences are the most popular area of study accounting for 26 percent of the total degrees conferred. Biology (10 percent), interdisciplinary studies (10 percent), math (8 percent), and journalism (7 percent) are next in popularity. The school has highly regarded programs in communication, computer science, engineering, physics, environmental science, and the performing arts. Santa Barbara graduates do not tend to apply for prestigious postgraduate fellowships in overwhelming numbers, but the school did produce four Fulbright winners in 2018.

Outside the Classroom

Freshmen live on the UCSB campus at a 90 percent clip; overall, 38 percent of the undergraduate student population resides in university-owned housing. Santa Barbara's glorious 1,000-acre campus is set against the Pacific Ocean, and multiple beaches are literally in your backyard (you can actually hear the ocean while you're studying). Of course, keeping focused is a challenge with the perfect weather, beautiful surroundings, and the fact that, no matter what rankings list you check, UCSB is one of the top party schools in the entire country. The town of Isla Vista is almost exclusively a college town with a laid back vibe full of free spirits and free-flowing hard liquor. Fraternities and sororities have a presence but do not dominate the social scene; only 9 percent of men and 14 percent of women join Greek organizations. Just about everyone on campus is involved in athletics in some way as there are twenty-nine club sports teams and a stunning 18,000 intramural participants each year. Nineteen varsity teams compete in NCAA Division I's Big West Conference. The baseball program is, perhaps, the most notable making regular tournament appearances and having produced many MLB players in its almost one-hundred-year history. There are also over 500 student clubs and numerous campus-wide events, including the famous (or infamous) annual Halloween celebration on Isla Vista. Fifty-seven percent of 2018 seniors also found time to engage in community service.

Career Services

USCB Career Services is run by nineteen professional employees who function as discipline-specific career counselors, employment specialists, graduate school counselors, and internship/experience managers. That 1,211:1 student-to-staff ratio is much higher than the average school in this guidebook, but that is not particularly alarming for a public university of Santa Barbara's size. Career services certainly keeps busy, hosting 260 workshops that, collectively, draw 2,300 students each year and also meets one-on-one with 2,565 individuals through scheduled appointments and another 3,617 through drop-ins. Four job and internship fairs held over the course of the 2017-18 school year attracted 343 employers and 4,228 students. Additionally, staff posted 38,500 jobs on Handshake for undergraduate consumption.

University of California, Santa Barbara

E-mail: admissions@sa.ucsb.edu | Website: www.ucsb.edu

This office is continuing to aggressively expand the number of employers who recruit on campus. Bain & Company, Goldman Sachs, US Bank, and Kaiser Permanente all have begun visiting Santa Barbara for information sessions, career fairs, and on-campus interviews. Internship experiences are supported through programs like the Intern Scholarship Program that issues $1,500 grants to help offset the costs of unpaid placements. An encouraging 45 percent of those who land an internship end up being hired by that organization on a full-time basis. Overall, this office does a nice job of bringing top employers to campus with regularity and hosts almost daily workshops on topics such as Engineering Boot Camp, Internships 101, So You Want to be a Researcher? and Conversations about Careers in Mental Health.

Professional Outcomes

Within six months of earning their diplomas, 84 percent of Gauchos have found employment, and only 7 percent of those seeking their first jobs have yet to nail down a position. The most popular industries entered are science/research (16 percent), engineering/computer programming (14 percent), business (13 percent) finance/accounting (11 percent), and sales (10 percent). Among the top employers of recent graduates are Google, EY, KPMG, Oracle, Amazon, IBM, and Adobe. Large numbers of UCSB alumni also can be found on the payrolls of Apple, Facebook, Microsoft, Uber, Salesforce, and Lyft. A fairly even split of Gauchos can be found in the Greater Los Angeles area and San Francisco. Many also remain in Santa Barbara or head to other Golden State locales like Sacramento, Orange County, or San Diego. Average salaries vary wildly across majors. Those joining the computer science and engineering field averaged $73,000 in compensation while those in finance took home $57,000; those entering the education, health- care, and journalism fields averaged $35k-$40k.

Seventy-five percent of Santa Barbara grads stated they intend to pursue a graduate or professional degree at some point. Of those jumping directly into an advanced degree program, 9 percent are continuing at UCSB, 23 percent at a University of California location, 16 percent at a school within the California State University System, 22 percent at a private school in California, and 36 percent go out of state. In 2018-19, there were 174 applicants to medical schools from UCSB, and acceptance rates were in line with the national average. Recent acceptances included prestigious medical schools such as Harvard, Cornell, Tufts, Georgetown, Johns Hopkins, Dartmouth, Wake Forest, UVA, UNC-Chapel Hill, and Duke. Those applying to law school or other graduate programs also gained entrance to a wide range of schools, including the most prestigious in the country.

Admission

A line 92,314 students long formed for a place in the UC Santa Barbara Class of 2022; 32 percent were admitted, and 17 percent of those accepted ultimately enrolled in the university. Those entering the university in 2018-19 earned an average high school GPA of 4.12, and 92 percent had a GPA of over 3.75. The mid-50 percent standardized test scores were a 1220-1480 on the SAT, the more commonly submitted test, and a 26-32 on the ACT. A decade ago, Santa Barbara was a much easier university to get into. At that time the average SAT score was below 1200, and the acceptance rate was close to 50 percent. It's important that current applicants do not mistake the UCSB of ten years ago for the highly selective school it is today.

For a university approaching six figures worth of applicants, it is a bit surprising that it lists the application essay as being "very important," a designation only given to two other factors: GPA and standardized test scores. Rigor of one's high school course load is ranked as "important," and factors like work experience, extracurricular activities, state residency, and first-generation status are "considered." Santa Barbara does not consider recommendations, interviews, or demonstrated interest when making admissions decisions. As is the standard with schools in the University of California System, there is no early action or early decision; rather, the regular deadline is on the early side. You must submit your application by November 30. UC Santa Barbara is a transfer-friendly institution as it accepts 57 percent of those who apply.

Worth Your Money?

Cheap tuition (sub $13k) plus expensive California living brings the overall cost of attendance to a shade under $37,000 per year. As with all of the schools in the University of California System, even if you received zero aid, UC Santa Barbara would still be a solid investment. An out-of-state student would pay $66,675 per year in tuition, meaning that budget-conscious teens and families would likely have much better private or in-state options. The school caps nonresident enrollment at 18 percent (it currently sits below that mark), but that population has been rising in recent years, so there are many people willing to spend $268,000 on a public school education—a move that we do not recommend unless financial resources are unlimited and/or you happen to be majoring in engineering or computer science.

FINANCIAL
Institutional Type: Public
In-State Tuition: $11,442
Out-of-State Tuition: $40,434
Room & Board: $15,520
Required Fees: $2,949
Books & Supplies: $1,184

Avg. Need-Based Aid: $21,635
Avg. % of Need Met: 81%

Avg. Merit-Based Aid: $8,873
% Receiving Merit-Based Aid: 2%

Avg. Cumulative Debt: $20,004
% of Students Borrowing: 50%

CAREER
Who Recruits
1. Arista Networks
2. Deckers Brands
3. Peace Corps
4. Raytheon
5. West Coast Financial, LLC

Notable Internships
1. SpaceX
2. U.S. House of Representatives
3. Telsa

Top Industries
1. Business
2. Education
3. Operations
4. Sales
5. Engineering

Top Employers
1. Google
2. Apple
3. Oracle
4. Amazon
5. Microsoft

Where Alumni Work
1. Los Angeles
2. San Francisco
3. Santa Barbara, CA
4. San Diego
5. Orange County, CA

Median Earnings
College Scorecard (Early Career): $55,300
EOP (Early Career): $58,800
PayScale (Mid-Career): $116,300

RANKINGS
Forbes: 84
Money: 30
U.S. News: 34, National Universities
Wall Street Journal/THE: 71
Washington Monthly: 21, National Universities

#CollegesWorthYourMoney

University of Chicago

Chicago, Illinois | Admissions Phone: 773-702-8650

ADMISSION
Admission Rate: 7%
Admission Rate - Men: 8%
Admission Rate - Women: 7%
EA Admission Rate: N/A
ED Admission Rate: N/A
Admission Rate (5-Year Trend): -2%
ED Admission Rate (5-Year Trend): N/A
% of Admits Attending (Yield): 77%
Transfer Admission Rate: 5%

Offered Wait List: N/A
Accepted Wait List: N/A
Admitted Wait List: N/A

SAT Reading/Writing (Middle 50%): 720-770
SAT Math (Middle 50%): 750-800
ACT Composite (Middle 50%): 33-35
Testing Policy: Test Optional
SAT Superscore: Yes
ACT Superscore: Yes

% Graduated in Top 10% of HS Class: 99%
% Graduated in Top 25% of HS Class: 100%
% Graduated in Top 50% of HS Class: 100%

ENROLLMENT
Total Undergraduate Enrollment: 6,552
% Part-Time: 0%
% Male: 51%
% Female: 49%
% Out-of-State: 71%
% Fraternity: 8%
% Sorority: 12%
% On-Campus (Freshman): 100%
% On-Campus (All Undergraduate): 55%

% African-American: 6%
% Asian: 22%
% Hispanic: 16%
% White: 46%
% Other: 8%
% Race or Ethnicity Unknown: 3%
% International: 14%
% Low-Income: 11%

ACADEMICS
Student-to-Faculty Ratio: 5:1
% of Classes Under 20: 77%
% of Classes Under 40: 92%
% Full-Time Faculty: 85%
% Full-Time Faculty w/ Terminal Degree: 85%

Top Programs
Economics
English
Environmental Studies
History
International Relations
Mathematics
Psychology
Sociology

Retention Rate: 99%
4-Year Graduation Rate: 89%
6-Year Graduation Rate: 94%

Curricular Flexibility: Less Flexible
Academic Rating: ★★★★

Inside the Classroom
Once a bastion of uncompromising intellectuals lovingly referred to as "the place where fun comes to die," the University of Chicago has undergone a transformational rebranding over the past decade. Still a destination point for an army of 6,500 brilliant young people, it now boasts an acceptance rate in the same league with Ivies like Brown and Yale (40 percent were accepted as recently as 2005) and, while still as academically rigorous as any institution in the country, it has worked to expand its previously unidimensional appeal.

There are fifty-one majors at the University of Chicago, but more than 50 percent of degrees conferred are in four concentrations: economics, biology, mathematics, and political science. Economics alone is the selection of roughly one-quarter of the undergraduate population, in large part because the university does not, for reasons of philosophy and tradition, offer a traditional business major.

The University of Chicago runs on a quarter system that equates to four ten-week sessions in which students take three or four classes at a time. Given the legendarily heavy workload at the school, the truncated terms can lead to a good deal of stress and an excessive number of all-night study sessions. All undergraduates must plow through the school's common core curriculum that requires an introduction to the tools of inquiry in every discipline: math and science (6 combined courses), humanities (6 courses), and social science (3 courses). Many elect to take nothing but core courses for their entire freshman year.

A 6:1 student-to-faculty ratio means that classrooms remain fairly intimate, and face-time with the renowned faculty is a reality. More than three-quarters of UChicago undergraduate sections have an enrollment of nineteen or fewer students. Undergraduate research opportunities are ubiquitous as 80 percent of students end up working in a research capacity alongside a faculty member. A solid 48 percent of undergrads study abroad at one of the sixty-six programs offered in thirty-two cities around the world.

No matter your area of concentration, a degree from UChicago will carry a great deal of weight in the eyes of employers and graduate/professional schools alike. All of the areas previously mentioned as the most popular majors have particularly sterling reputations with a global reach. On that topic, if you name a prestigious post-graduate award or fellowship, chances are the University of Chicago is one of the most frequent producers. In the last five years students have captured 118 Fulbright Scholarships, thirteen Goldwater Scholarships, five Marshall Scholarships, and four Rhodes Scholarships. Perhaps most astoundingly, between faculty and alumni the UChicago boasts ninety affiliated Nobel Prizes (eight are currently on faculty) over the school's illustrious history. Lastly, it also lays claim to fifty Rhodes Scholars all time, the eighth most of any university.

Outside the Classroom
With its campus based in the Hyde Park neighborhood on Chicago's South Side, students have access to a vibrant metropolis within walking distance of their dorms. Countless museums, restaurants, bookshops, parks, and theaters are never more than a stone's throw away. Given UChicago's reputation as a haven for hardcore intellectuals, it may come as a surprise that there are nineteen official Greek organizations on campus with a participation rate of 20 percent. Athletes, nicknamed the Maroons, participate in NCAA Division III. There are twenty varsity teams that are evenly split between the genders; no athletic scholarships are offered, and athletics, in general, capture a limited degree of student attention. Yet, a hard-to-comprehend 70 percent of the student body participates in the school's extensive intramural and club sports programs. Over 400 undergraduate-run clubs are active, including a number of improv and theater groups (the university is the birthplace of modern improv), community service organizations, and publications. DOC is the nation's oldest student-run film society and screens films on a daily basis. On-campus housing consists of seven residence halls divided into thirty-nine houses designed to nurture a sense of community. Freshmen are required to participate in the university housing system, but a large percentage of upperclassmen, 45 percent of the total student body, reside in off-campus housing.

Career Services
The university pours ample resources into career services, employing fifty-two full-time consultants who have highly specialized areas of expertise including business careers, law school planning, health-care careers, journalism, STEM, and start-ups. Boasting a student-to-advisor ratio of 126:1, UChicago has one of the absolute best ratios of any institution included in this book. It also puts its extensive staff to work on behalf of undergraduate students. To help quantify that statement, the staff engaged students in 12,409 one-on-one advising appointments in the 2018-19 school year.

An exceptional 80 percent of freshmen engage with the Career Advancement Office. Through the Metcalf Internship Program, massive numbers of students procure internship positions at top companies around the globe. In a given year, UChicago students secure more than 2,800 internships with more than 850 organizations. Undergraduates participate in excess of 500 employer site visits around the world that are known as Career Treks as well as 200 externships. The university forges strong connections with employers who are eager to conduct on-campus interviews with students; it currently has over one hundred full-time recruiting partners, including a laundry list of Fortune 1000 companies. Incredibly, 1,360 distinct employers recruited at the school during the 2018-19 academic year. Unmatched in terms of sheer personnel power and deeply committed to personalized, expert student counseling, UChicago Career Advancement Office is a leader in the career services realm.

Professional Outcomes

On commencement day, 93 percent of 2017 graduates already had their next step lined up, whether that involved entering the world of employment or continuing their higher education odyssey in graduate school. Business and financial services and STEM are the two sectors that scoop up the most graduates, but public policy and service and consulting also were well represented. The largest employers of 2017 grads, by volume, included Facebook, Google, JP Morgan, Goldman Sachs, McKinsey & Company, Bank of America, Citi, and Accenture. While many graduates go on to lucrative careers, the median income at age thirty-four for a UChicago alum is $62k, significantly less than graduates of many Ivy League institutions. For comparison, the median Penn grad makes $30k more.

University of Chicago grads are highly sought after by elite graduate universities. The top seven destinations for recent graduates were Yale, Columbia, Penn, MIT, Stanford, UCLA, and Johns Hopkins. Top law schools swoon at the sight of applicants from UChicago; 84 percent of applicants to Top 14 institutions gained admittance in 2017. Twenty-four grads were accepted by NYU, sixteen by UChicago itself, fourteen by Columbia, twelve by Harvard, and eight by Stanford. Med school applicants found similar success with 85 percent earning acceptance, more than double the national average. A fairly substantial 39 percent of graduates remain in the Midwest after finishing their degrees, 31 percent migrate to the Northeast, and 15 percent make the journey west.

Admission

The University of Chicago admitted a record low 7.2 percent of applicants for admission into the Class of 2022, placing the school in a selectivity stratosphere with Stanford, Yale, and Columbia. If you had predicted that figure at the turn of the millennium, sideways glances would have surely followed. In 2005 the university admitted 40 percent (not a typo) of applicants and still followed the beat of its own drummer, offering what was known as "The Uncommon App" and maintaining a reputation for welcoming waves of uber-serious bookworms. Changes in leadership and a decade of aggressive marketing practices (soliciting applications from unqualified students) led to a flood of new applicants and a sharp decline in the admit rate.

The average SAT score for admitted students is now in excess of 1500, although the school announced in 2018 that it was going test-optional. Skeptics believe that one of the motivations for the policy change was to drum up even more applicants to eventually reject, further enhancing its selectivity. Interestingly, the incoming profile of a UChicago student isn't that much different from what it was when it was "easier" to get into; the average SAT score for the Class of 2008 was in the mid-1400s, the same as a decade ago, and 99 percent of incoming students finished in the top 10 percent of their high school class. In sum, UChicago still takes similarly talented academic superstars now, accepting 7.2 percent of applicants, as it did when it accepted almost six times that figure. The difference is that instead of attracting a self-selecting pool, it now attracts hordes of applicants, the vast majority of whom are destined for rejection.

Worth Your Money?

If you are among the 43 percent of current UChicago students who qualify for financial aid, then you are in luck. The school covers 100 percent of demonstrated need, which leads to an average annual grant of $46,460. Thank goodness for that because the university has the highest cost of attendance of any school in the country at $81,531. Fortunately, if you need to pay back some epic loans, you should be able to do so by landing at one of the many top corporations to which the university funnels its graduates. If the University of Chicago is just a stop on the academic road, alumni do incredibly well in gaining acceptance into top graduate and professional schools. Either way, this school is worth your money, even at a relatively obscene price.

FINANCIAL
Institutional Type: Private
In-State Tuition: $57,642
Out-of-State Tuition: $57,642
Room & Board: $17,004
Required Fees: $1,656
Books & Supplies: $1,800

Avg. Need-Based Aid: $57,948
Avg. % of Need Met: 100%

Avg. Merit-Based Aid: N/A
% Receiving Merit-Based Aid: N/A

Avg. Cumulative Debt: $19,817
% of Students Borrowing: 29%

CAREER
Who Recruits
1. Kraft Heinz
2. Nielson
3. Boston Consulting Group
4. AQR Capital Management
5. Kaufmanm Hall & Associates

Notable Internships
1. Instagram
2. The Blackstone Group
3. Jane Street

Top Industries
1. Business
2. Education
3. Research
4. Finance
5. Media

Top Employers
1. Google
2. Goldman Sachs
3. JP Morgan
4. Facebook
5. Accenture

Where Alumni Work
1. Chicago
2. New York City
3. San Francisco
4. Washington, DC
5. Boston

Median Earnings
College Scorecard (Early Career): $68,100
EOP (Early Career): $61,700
PayScale (Mid-Career): $114,200

RANKINGS
Forbes: 16
Money: 77
U.S. News: 6 (T), National Universities
Wall Street Journal/THE: 14
Washington Monthly: 31, National Universities

#CollegesWorthYourMoney

University of Connecticut

Storrs, Connecticut | Admissions Phone: 860-486-3137

ADMISSION
Admission Rate: 49%
Admission Rate - Men: 48%
Admission Rate - Women: 50%
EA Admission Rate: Not Offered
ED Admission Rate: Not Offered
Admission Rate (5-Year Trend): -5%
ED Admission Rate (5-Year Trend): Not Offered
% of Admits Attending (Yield): 22%
Transfer Admission Rate: 61%

Offered Wait List: 2,027
Accepted Wait List: 1,249
Admitted Wait List: 502

SAT Reading/Writing (Middle 50%): 600-690
SAT Math (Middle 50%): 610-730
ACT Composite (Middle 50%): 26-31
Testing Policy: ACT/SAT Required
SAT Superscore: Yes
ACT Superscore: Yes

% Graduated in Top 10% of HS Class: 50%
% Graduated in Top 25% of HS Class: 84%
% Graduated in Top 50% of HS Class: 98%

ENROLLMENT
Total Undergraduate Enrollment: 19,133
% Part-Time: 3%
% Male: 49%
% Female: 51%
% Out-of-State: 21%
% Fraternity: 10%
% Sorority: 14%
% On-Campus (Freshman): 96%
% On-Campus (All Undergraduate): 65%

% African-American: 6%
% Asian: 11%
% Hispanic: 11%
% White: 56%
% Other: 3%
% Race or Ethnicity Unknown: 3%
% International: 10%
% Low-Income: 18%

ACADEMICS
Student-to-Faculty Ratio: 16:1
% of Classes Under 20: 52%
% of Classes Under 40: 78%
% Full-Time Faculty: 81%
% Full-Time Faculty w/ Terminal Degree: 93%

Top Programs
Accounting
Biology
Education
Exercise Science
Finance
Nursing
Pharmacy

Retention Rate: 93%
4-Year Graduation Rate: 73%
6-Year Graduation Rate: 85%

Curricular Flexibility: Somewhat Flexible
Academic Rating: ★★★↓

Inside the Classroom

New England is so overflowing with superior institutions of higher education that it is genuinely a challenge to travel more than a few miles through Massachusetts or Connecticut without accidentally bumping into one of the top colleges on the planet. However, that surplus of elite universities is balanced by a notable dearth of stellar public institutions. For applicants seeking such a school, you'll have to travel to the sleepy town of Storrs, Connecticut, a half-hour east of Hartford, where you'll find a regional giant with a national reputation. The main campus of the University of Connecticut is home to 19,000+ undergraduates, fourteen schools and colleges, and 116 undergraduate majors. While 76 percent of the student body are state residents, there are also undergraduates hailing from forty-two states and 106 countries presently enrolled, and the percentage of outsiders has been on the rise in recent years.

Whether you enter the School of Business, School of Engineering, School of Fine Arts, or other undergraduate college at Storrs you will encounter a core curriculum of basic requirements. In an effort to ensure "that a balance between professional and general education be established and maintained in which each is complementary to and compatible with the other," UConn mandates two courses in each of arts and humanities, social science, science and technology, and diversity and multiculturalism. Further, students must demonstrate competencies in information literacy, quantitative reasoning, writing, and a second language via additional coursework.

Considering the university's 16:1 student-to-faculty ratio and 8,300 graduate and professional students, one might expect all UConn courses to contain a vast sea of undergraduate faces. However, the school does a nice job of creating a balance of classroom experiences with 52 percent of sections enrolling fewer than twenty students, and only 16 percent containing more than fifty. To help forge even deeper connections with faculty, the Office of Undergraduate Research encourages students to schedule advising sessions to apply for both internal and external research posts. There are also formal programs to target including the Work-Study Research Assistant Program, the Honors Program, or the University Scholar Program that make research a centerpiece of the educational experience. Hundreds of study abroad options are on the table, and the university has taken steps to increase the rate of participation that currently sits around 15 percent.

From a sheer volume standpoint, the four most commonly conferred undergraduate degrees are in business (13 percent), health professions/nursing (12 percent), engineering (12 percent), and the social sciences (12 percent). In terms of prestige and national reputation, programs in business, pharmacy, and nursing carry a good deal of weight. Speaking of reputation, UConn's growing stature has helped its students capture an increasing number of highly competitive scholarships in 2019 including seven Fulbright Scholarships, four Goldwater Scholarships, a Udall Scholarship, and a Truman Scholarship.

Outside the Classroom

Unlike many universities of its size, a healthy 70 percent of undergraduates live on UConn's 4,100-acre campus. Freshmen are not required to live on campus, but 95 percent do. Overall, four semesters of housing are guaranteed to all entering students, and there are plenty of traditional apartments, suites, and residential learning communities available. At UConn you will be treated to one of the best college athletic programs in the country. Husky fans are a fervent bunch, and of the twenty-four varsity teams, nothing captures the attention of all of campus quite like the basketball squads. Since 1999 the men's hoops squad has captured four NCAA titles, and the women's team has won an astounding ten championships. Greek life draws 10 percent of men and 14 percent of women, adding up to 2,700 members in forty chapters. In total, there are 700 student clubs and five cultural centers. Amenities include an on-campus movie theater, ice rink, and a 191,000-square-foot recreation center that opened in 2019. Volunteer spirit is strong as students contribute a collective 1.3 million hours of community service each year. Major cities like Hartford, Providence, and Boston are close enough for a weekend jaunt.

Career Services

There are twenty-one full-time employees at the University of Connecticut Center for Career Development (CCD) who serve as career consultants, corporate relations specialists, experiential learning coordinators, and operations specialists. There are an additional six career consultants who work in the School of Business and School of Engineering, bringing the total of professional staff to twenty-seven. (That does not include the career services staff members located at UConn's branch campuses.) The CCD's 708:1 student-to-advisor ratio is higher than the average school in this guidebook, but it is fairly typical for a school with close to 20,000 undergraduates.

University of Connecticut

E-mail: beahusky@uconn.edu | Website: www.uconn.edu

Two-thirds of Huskies utilize career services at some point in their four years, and that rate is higher among students with successful postgraduate outcomes; 80 percent of 2018 graduates who found a job or graduate school within six months of receiving their diplomas had taken advantage of the CCD's services. Experiential learning—including internships—were completed by 80 percent of graduates. The school forges strong ties to national as well as local companies. In fact, the seventeen Fortune 500 companies located in Connecticut all recruit on the Storrs campus. There are number of career fairs throughout the year with the largest being the fall career fairs (All-University & STEM) that bring in 150 employers each per day and attract more than 2,000 students. Overall, the UConn CCD provides quality assistance to those it is able to reach, and its industry connections, particularly those with Connecticut-based companies, are strong.

Professional Outcomes

Eighty-eight percent of the graduating Class of 2018 had reached a positive outcome (job, grad school, military, volunteer position) within six months of earning their degrees. Among the 63 percent that had found employment, the largest numbers landed at Aetna, Cigna, Lockheed Martin, PwC, The Hartford, Travelers, and United Technologies. Historically, massive numbers of alumni also have been employed by Pratt & Whitney, Pfizer, IBM, and Deloitte. A sampling of the top job titles held by 2018 grads included financial analyst, consultant, engineer, nurse, sales consultant, and business analyst. The median midcareer salary (at age 34) is $57,000, slightly better than some higher-prestige schools within state borders like Connecticut College or Wesleyan. Huskies can be found in the largest packs in New York City and Greater Hartford—73 percent who attended a Connecticut high school remain in the state postgraduation. Boston, DC, San Francisco, and Philadelphia also have their fair share of UConn alumni.

Many of the 22 percent of 2018 graduates who immediately entered a graduate or professional program did so at their home university that caters to a total of 7,000 grad students. Based on the most recent data available, UConn grads are accepted to medical school at a 65 percent clip, a far better rate than their peers. Recent acceptances include many elite medical institutions including those at the University of Pennsylvania, Georgetown, the University of Chicago, Vanderbilt, and UVA. As many as twenty-five undergraduates per year matriculate into the University of Connecticut School of Medicine. Law acceptances in the past three years include an impressive list of the nation's top institutions such as Harvard, Yale, William & Mary, Cornell, Columbia, and Boston College.

Admission

UConn accepted 49 percent of the 34,886 Class of 2022 hopefuls, representing the lowest acceptance rate in school history and quite a departure from the UConn of a generation ago. In 2000 it received one-third as many applications and admitted more than 80 percent of in-state applicants. The mean SAT of freshmen arriving at the Storrs campus was 1306, and the mid-50 percent range was 1210-1420; a decade ago, a 1300 would have put you in the 75th percentile of attending students. Even with the changes to SAT in that time, that is still an indicator of a major jump in selectivity. Exactly half of the entering class in 2018-19 finished in the top decile of their graduating cohort, and 84 percent placed within the top quartile. That group included an astonishing 175 valedictorians and salutatorians.

For a suddenly swamped admissions office, the most important factors in evaluating applicants are the quickest to break down: standardized test scores, GPA, class rank, and the overall rigor of one's high school curriculum. First-generation status, essays, recommendations, extracurricular activities, volunteer work, character/personal qualities, and talent/ability are secondary considerations. There are no early action or early decision options at UConn; everyone faces the same January 15 deadline, but applicants should submit by the December 1 priority deadline for their best chance at merit aid offerings.

Worth Your Money?

For Constitution State residents UConn is a rock-solid deal at $13k for tuition and a total cost of attendance hovering around $30k. Those in the other New England States can attend at a discount for under $40k, but those from other states will see an annual COA of $53k. This school is a no-brainer for state residents as it's hard to get a combination of a cheaper/better education in the Northeast. For everyone else, the value of the degree would depend on the intended area of study. However, those not eligible for a discount of some kind could very likely locate better deals within their home states.

FINANCIAL
Institutional Type: Public
In-State Tuition: $13,798
Out-of-State Tuition: $36,466
Room & Board: $13,258
Required Fees: $3,428
Books & Supplies: $950

Avg. Need-Based Aid: $14,041
Avg. % of Need Met: 58%

Avg. Merit-Based Aid: $10,604
% Receiving Merit-Based Aid: 36%

Avg. Cumulative Debt: $22,208
% of Students Borrowing: 57%

CAREER
Who Recruits
1. CGI Inc.
2. ScribeAmerica
3. Mercer
4. USDA
5. Fidelity Investments

Notable Internships
1. iHeartMedia
2. UBS
3. New York Yankees

Top Industries
1. Business
2. Education
3. Operations
4. Healthcare
5. Sales

Top Employers
1. Pratt & Whitney
2. Travelers
3. The Hartford
4. Aetna
5. Cigna

Where Alumni Work
1. New York City
2. Hartford, CT
3. Boston
4. Washington, DC
5. San Francisco

Median Earnings
College Scorecard (Early Career): $58,400
EOP (Early Career): $56,700
PayScale (Mid-Career): $105,200

RANKINGS
Forbes: 130
Money: 42
U.S. News: 64, National Universities
Wall Street Journal/THE: 105 (T)
Washington Monthly: 62, National Universities

#CollegesWorthYourMoney

University of Florida

Gainesville, Florida | Admissions Phone: 352-392-1365

ADMISSION
Admission Rate: 39%
Admission Rate - Men: 36%
Admission Rate - Women: 41%
EA Admission Rate: Not Offered
ED Admission Rate: Not Offered
Admission Rate (5-Year Trend): -8%
ED Admission Rate (5-Year Trend): Not Offered
% of Admits Attending (Yield): 45%
Transfer Admission Rate: 47%

Offered Wait List: Not Offered
Accepted Wait List: Not Offered
Admitted Wait List: Not Offered

SAT Reading/Writing (Middle 50%): 640-710
SAT Math (Middle 50%): 640-730
ACT Composite (Middle 50%): 27-32
Testing Policy: ACT/SAT Required
SAT Superscore: Yes
ACT Superscore: Yes

% Graduated in Top 10% of HS Class: 77%
% Graduated in Top 25% of HS Class: 97%
% Graduated in Top 50% of HS Class: 100%

ENROLLMENT
Total Undergraduate Enrollment: 35,491
% Part-Time: 9%
% Male: 44%
% Female: 56%
% Out-of-State: 7%
% Fraternity: 17%
% Sorority: 22%
% On-Campus (Freshman): 78%
% On-Campus (All Undergraduate): 22%

% African-American: 6%
% Asian: 9%
% Hispanic: 22%
% White: 53%
% Other: 4%
% Race or Ethnicity Unknown: 3%
% International: 3%
% Low-Income: 30%

ACADEMICS
Student-to-Faculty Ratio: 18:1
% of Classes Under 20: 50%
% of Classes Under 40: 78%
% Full-Time Faculty: 84%
% Full-Time Faculty w/ Terminal Degree: 90%

Top Programs
Animal Science
Applied Physiology and Kinesiology
Biology
Business
Criminology
Education
Engineering
Journalism and Communication

Retention Rate: 97%
4-Year Graduation Rate: 68%
6-Year Graduation Rate: 90%

Curricular Flexibility: Somewhat Flexible
Academic Rating: ★★★★

Inside the Classroom

At a time when flagship state schools are being overrun by out-of-state and international students willing to pay full freight, the University of Florida stands strong as an almost exclusive landing spot for Sunshine State residents to the tune of 93 percent. Gator Nation could almost be its own small nation with 35,500 undergraduates, 16,800 graduate students, and roughly 400,000 living alumni. It's not hard to see why top Florida-based teens target UF as their number one choice. One of the top-ranked state universities in the United States can still be accessed by in-staters for an annual tuition under $7,000 at a time when many elite (and not so elite) schools are eight times higher in cost.

With sixteen colleges and one hundred undergraduate majors to choose from, the educational experiences of UF students are exceptionally diverse. That includes one of the country's largest honors programs at 3,400 students; classes within this program are capped at twenty-five. All Gators must chomp through a blend of state and university core academic requirements that include coursework in composition, humanities, mathematics, biological and physical sciences, social and behavioral sciences, and classes with "international" and "diversity" designations.

An 18:1 student-to-faculty ratio and a massive number of graduate students leads to some fairly large undergraduate course sections. Yet, the school impressively offers 50 percent of sections with an enrollment of fewer than twenty students, 36 percent have between twenty and forty-nine students, and the rest are fifty+. The Center for Undergraduate Research offers a University Research Scholars program, summer opportunities, and it hosts its own Undergraduate Research Symposium and publishes its own *UF Journal of Undergraduate Research*. The school offers 1,100 study abroad programs that are taken advantage of by more than 2,200 undergrads each year.

The Warrington College of Business and the Wertheim College of Engineering are highly respected, and a degree from either will yield one of the more absurd returns-on-investment in all of postsecondary education. Therefore, it's no surprise that those two programs confer the greatest percentage of degrees—13 percent and 12 percent, respectively. The social sciences (11 percent), biology (10 percent), and communications/journalism (8 percent) are next in popularity. The procurement of highly competitive fellowships and postgraduate scholarships is not a focal point of the university, but Gators do claim their fair share. Eight graduates of the Class of 2019 won a Fulbright Scholarship, and as many as twenty-seven students have won National Science Foundation Graduate Research Fellowships in recent years.

Outside the Classroom

Not leading off with a discussion of campus life at UF with football would be an egregious case of burying the lead. The 90,000 orange-and-blue adorned fans crammed into Ben Hill Griffin Stadium, more commonly referred to as "The Swamp," captures the lifeblood of the University of Florida. And it's not only football that is a point of athletic pride in Gainesville. UF is ranked alongside Stanford and UCLA as one of the best overall sports programs in the country. Twenty of the school's twenty-one teams compete in the ultra-competitive SEC Conference, and the Gators have earned an astounding thirty-six all-time national championships. Outside of varsity sports there are 1,000 student organizations, and 76 percent of students are engaged in campus activities for a minimum of an hour per week. There are sixty intramural sports leagues, two large fitness centers, and two lakes for swimming, boating, and relaxation. Due to a dearth of school-owned housing, only 22 percent of students live on campus, almost all freshmen. Many move into Greek houses as 17 percent of men and 22 percent of women enter fraternity and sorority life. Gainesville is constructed as a Southern college town-by-numbers experience with all the requisite components of beautiful weather, an overwhelming number of restaurants, bars, and shops, plenty of parties and, of course, the sports-crazed atmosphere.

Career Services

Unlike many schools of UF's size that have a network of smaller career services offices housed within various colleges, the centralized University of Florida Career Connections Center (C3) serves more than 54,000 current students and alumni. At C3 twenty-three professionals (not including accountants and HR personnel who work in the office) are available to assist you with career counseling, internship coordination, and networking. The university's overall student-to-counselor ratio of 1,678:1 is among the poorest of any school featured in this guidebook. Still, there are many positive, measurable things occurring at this career services center.

In 2017-18, almost 22,000 students engaged with C3 through workshops, virtually, or through one-on-one sessions; that figure represents more than three-fifths of UF's undergraduate population. Staff put on 341 professional development workshops, added 732 job and internship postings to Gator CareerLink each month, and attracted 1,130 employers and 13,453 students to career fairs. Most impressively, it facilitated over 4,600 on-campus interviews with 355 local, regional, and national employers. A solid 61 percent of 2018 graduates reported at least one non-academic internship experience during their four years of study. Twenty-three percent of employed grads reported a job fair as being a resource that helped them land their first jobs, and 10 percent cited the Career Connections Center. Despite limited staffing for individualized counseling to reach 35,000+ undergrads, UF does a nice job putting on large-scale events and bringing a vast array of companies onto campus to recruit and interview.

Professional Outcomes

Upon graduation, 60 percent of University of Florida grads planned on entering full-time employment, and 40 percent expected to enroll in a full-time graduate program. At the time they received their diplomas 55 percent had already procured a first job. The top occupation areas for 2018 graduates were engineering (13 percent), health care (11 percent), education (5 percent), computer science (5 percent), sales (4 percent), and finance (4 percent). Across the entirety of the alumni base, impressive numbers of Gators can be found at many of the nation's most desirable corporations. In fact, more than 200 UF grads are currently employed by Google, EY, Raymond James, Deloitte, Apple, Amazon, Microsoft, Oracle, PwC, and Facebook. Many graduates remain in the Gainesville area or spread out to other Florida cities including Miami, Tampa Bay, Orlando, Jacksonville, or West Palm Beach. However, substantial numbers of alumni also can be found in Atlanta, New York, DC, and San Francisco. As one would expect, starting salaries vary greatly by major. Grads of the College of Business Administration earn median starting salaries, including bonuses, of $65k, computer science majors earn $84k, English majors $31k, and psychology majors $27k; the average salary for all 2018 grads was $46k.

Of those seeking full-time graduate studies upon receiving their diplomas, 52 percent had already been admitted into a program at the time they were awarded their bachelor's. A master's degree was the most popular pursuit (48 percent) followed by degrees in the medical field (17 percent, including 6 percent working on MDs), law school (9 percent), and PhDs (6 percent). The pre-med program is solid as UF sends the second most undergrads to medical school of any university in the country, behind only UCLA. Students with strong GPAs and MCAT scores feed directly into the university's own highly ranked College of Medicine. In 2018, law school applicants enjoyed an 85 percent acceptance rate. The most commonly attended institution was UF's own law school where eighty-six graduates matriculated. Three students entered each of Harvard and the University of Chicago and two went to Yale while Columbia, NYU, and Penn all welcomed four Gators each into their prestigious law schools.

Admission

A record number 41,407 students submitted applications to the University of Florida for a spot in the 2019-20 freshman class; 14,136 were admitted, a 34 percent admit rate. The average Class of 2023 admitted student possessed a 4.45 GPA, SAT score of 1388, and ACT score of 31, all higher numbers than admitted applicants one year ago. Students tend to rank near the top of their high school class. The latest available data from the Class of 2022 shows that 78 percent placed in the top decile of their graduating cohort, and 97 percent finished in the top 25 percent. Five years ago, the acceptance rate was a far friendlier 47 percent, and the 75th percentile SAT score was lower than the average SAT score among 2023 admits, confirmation that the sinking acceptance rate is indicative of a genuine rise in the school's level of selectivity.

With such a mammoth pile of applications to weed through, one would expect the admissions committee to place the greatest value on hard numbers like standardized test scores, GPA, and class rank. However, of those three factors, the UF Admissions Office only rates GPA as being "very important" to the process. Other considerations listed as "very important" are more in line with those of an elite liberal arts school: rigor of secondary coursework, application essay, extracurricular activities, talent/ability, character/personal qualities, and volunteer work. The university does not offer any type of early action/decision plan, so all candidates are on equal footing in the regular cycle. Grades are king for Gainesville hopefuls; 98 percent had a GPA of 3.75 or above on a 4.0 scale. While standardized test scores are not advertised as "very important" or even "important" to the admissions process, they clearly play a role with 90 percent of students scoring above a 600 on the reading section of the SAT and 87 percent scoring above a 600 on the math portion.

Worth Your Money?

A $6,300 annual tuition cost in the modern era of universally exorbitant tuition looks like a misprint at first glance. Greater than half of current undergrads receive financial aid for an amount slightly *more* than cost of tuition, meaning that a good number of students are only paying housing and living expenses Amazingly, the University of Florida, even at full price—room and board and all fees—would only set you back $20k per year assuming, of course, that you qualify as a Florida resident. The sliver of students coming to Gainesville from out of state pay more than double that amount, but UF still ultimately proves a bargain. If you live in Florida and can get into the university, start packing your bags because you simply won't find a better value.

FINANCIAL
Institutional Type: Public
In-State Tuition: $4,477
Out-of-State Tuition: $25,694
Room & Board: $10,220
Required Fees: $1,904
Books & Supplies: $850

Avg. Need-Based Aid: $9,083
Avg. % of Need Met: 99%

Avg. Merit-Based Aid: $2,233
% Receiving Merit-Based Aid: 50%

Avg. Cumulative Debt: $21,800
% of Students Borrowing: 38%

CAREER
Who Recruits
1. L3 Harris Technologies
2. OMP
3. Citrix
4. Procter & Gamble
5. KPMG

Notable Internships
1. Jet Blue
2. The Walt Disney Company
3. Kellogg Company

Top Industries
1. Business
2. Education
3. Operations
4. Healthcare
5. Engineering

Top Employers
1. Amazon
2. Intel
3. Microsoft
4. Google
5. PwC

Where Alumni Work
1. Gainsville, FL
2. Miami
3. Tampa
4. Orlando
5. Jacksonville

Median Earnings
College Scorecard (Early Career): $56,000
EOP (Early Career): $56,700
PayScale (Mid-Career): $102,800

RANKINGS
Forbes: 70
Money: 21
U.S. News: 34, National Universities
Wall Street Journal/THE: 63 (T)
Washington Monthly: 16, National Universities

#CollegesWorthYourMoney

Athens, Georgia | Admissions Phone: 706-542-8776

ADMISSION

Admission Rate: 49%
Admission Rate - Men: 45%
Admission Rate - Women: 51%
EA Admission Rate: 54%
ED Admission Rate: Not Offered
Admission Rate (5-Year Trend): -6%
ED Admission Rate (5-Year Trend): Not Offered
% of Admits Attending (Yield): 45%
Transfer Admission Rate: 76%

Offered Wait List: 1,257
Accepted Wait List: 704
Admitted Wait List: 32

SAT Reading/Writing (Middle 50%): 630-700
SAT Math (Middle 50%): 610-710
ACT Composite (Middle 50%): 27-32
Testing Policy: ACT/SAT Required
SAT Superscore: Yes
ACT Superscore: Yes

% Graduated in Top 10% of HS Class: 60%
% Graduated in Top 25% of HS Class: 92%
% Graduated in Top 50% of HS Class: 99%

ENROLLMENT

Total Undergraduate Enrollment: 29,611
% Part-Time: 6%
% Male: 43%
% Female: 57%
% Out-of-State: 11%
% Fraternity: 20%
% Sorority: 31%
% On-Campus (Freshman): 98%
% On-Campus (All Undergraduate): 34%

% African-American: 8%
% Asian: 10%
% Hispanic: 6%
% White: 69%
% Other: 4%
% Race or Ethnicity Unknown: 1%
% International: 2%
% Low-Income: 21%

ACADEMICS

Student-to-Faculty Ratio: 17:1
% of Classes Under 20: 45%
% of Classes Under 40: 81%
% Full-Time Faculty: 88%
% Full-Time Faculty w/ Terminal Degree: 94%

Top Programs
Animal Science
Biology
Business
Exercise & Sport Science
International Affairs
Journalism & Mass Communication
Psychology
Public Health

Retention Rate: 95%
4-Year Graduation Rate: 66%
6-Year Graduation Rate: 86%

Curricular Flexibility: Somewhat Flexible
Academic Rating: ★★★↗

Inside the Classroom

Founded in 1785 as the first state-sponsored university in the country, UGA has since grown into a vast operation that boasts seventeen distinct colleges and schools that offer 143 majors. Those who make scenic Athens their undergraduate home are free to pursue concentrations in anything from the traditional disciplines to more exotic fields such as avian biology, furnishings and interiors, and turfgrass management. Becoming a Bulldog is infinitely more difficult than a generation ago, but that's an understandable marketplace adjustment for a school that is of extraordinarily high quality, about as sports conscious as any you'll come across, and that offers as low a tuition as you can hope to find anywhere in the country.

Students cover all of the basics through the school's core curriculum that requires two or more courses in each of English, math, science, world language/culture, and social science along with one course in quantitative reasoning. Freshmen at UGA all participate in a First-Year Odyssey seminar led by a faculty member and capped at eighteen students. Within that intimate setting, students have the opportunity to explore one of 300 thought-provoking topics including Chocolate Science, Death and Dying, Pets in Modern Society, and The Psychology of Harry Potter. Freshmen also have the choice of signing up for Residential Learning Communities, a program that allows dorm residents with similar interests to take classes together. The unique academic experience does not stop as a first-year student. The University of Georgia is the largest undergraduate institution in the country to mandate hands-on learning for every single graduate. UGA students must fulfill that requirement by completing one from a lengthy menu of internships, service options, or research opportunities.

The school's student-to-faculty ratio is 17:1 and, with 9,000 graduate students to also serve, not all of your coursework will be conducted in a cozy setting. Still, 45 percent of sections enroll fewer than twenty students compared with 11 percent of sections that enroll fifty or more. No matter your major, UGA encourages you to conduct research with a member of the school's faculty. The Center for Undergraduate Research Opportunities (CURO) awards grants to 500 students per year, and in 2018-19 a robust 550 students presented at the CURO Symposium. Meanwhile, the Office of Global Engagement helps 2,000 students annually find which of the one hundred+ study abroad programs that are led by UGA faculty is right for them.

Business is the most commonly conferred undergraduate degree, accounting for 28 percent of diplomas earned. It is followed by biology (9 percent), social sciences (9 percent), mathematics (9 percent), communication/journalism (9 percent), and psychology (6 percent). Top-ranked programs include animal science, business, communications, and public and international affairs. The school has seen an increase in its number of Fulbright Scholars, producing twenty-five over the last two years. Among public institutions, UGA also has been one of the top three producers of Rhodes Scholars over the previous two decades.

Outside the Classroom

Ninety-eight percent of freshmen, but only 34 percent of the student body, reside in university-owned housing. As you would expect at a school with over 29,000 undergraduates, there is a full smorgasbord of over 800 clubs and activities from which to choose. In 2017, The Center for Leadership and Service connected 12,500 students with over 228,000 volunteer hours. Fraternities and sororities have a strong presence with sixty-two Greek-letter organizations on campus that draw 20 percent of men and 31 percent of women. If you want to follow Division I athletics, UGA's perennial powerhouse football team draws 92,746 fans to Sanford Stadium each week in autumn. The school fields competitive men's and women's teams in a variety of other sports as well as a diverse selection of over seventy club and intramural teams. For non-athletic competitors, UGA's debate team has qualified for the National Debate Tournament for twenty-five consecutive years, and its chess team routinely wins state championships. The bottom line is that no matter your passion, you'll be able to find kindred spirits at UGA.

Career Services

The University of Georgia Career Center employs twenty-one full-time staff members including administrators, career consultants, and employer relations team members. That equates to a student-to-advisor ratio of 1,410:1, well below average compared the pool of institutions included in this book. While individualized attention is a challenge, the career center does regularly host job and internship fairs, and virtual Q&A sessions with employers are hosted on Twitter. Annually, over 1,000 companies engage in on-campus recruiting through one of the university's major-specific fairs. For example, a 2018 expo for students interested in a career in insurance/risk management was attended by sixty-five major corporations including AIG, Berkshire Hathaway, Geico, and State Farm.

Students can sign up at any time for a mock interview with a career consultant. The center also offers a more formalized series of career prep events called "Arch Ready," referencing the iconic campus landmark. Those events cover topics such as major selection, career exploration, and resume writing. The career center does engage companies to become internship partners for students, but data on the percentage of UGA undergrads that land internships is unavailable; what is known is that only 27 percent of Bulldogs who secured an internship did so through the career center. A robust alumni network will help recent grads connect with other Bulldogs anywhere in the world. Each year, close to 3,000 unique employers hire UGA grads, resulting in a wide-reaching alumni presence in business, government, and educational institutions.

Professional Outcomes

UGA's career outcomes rate (the percent of students employed or continuing their education six months after graduation) is 96 percent, 11 percent above the national average. Popular employers include Amazon, PricewaterhouseCoopers, IBM, and Deloitte. Graduate schools attended by UGA grads include many elite institutions such as Duke, Emory, UVA, UNC, Penn, and Vanderbilt. While 87 percent of students hailed originally from Georgia, many migrate to metropolitan areas around the United States with Dallas, Houston, Chicago, DC, New York City, and San Francisco among the top destinations. UGA does an excellent job of tracking graduates' starting salary data by school/major. That data allows prospective students to properly calibrate their financial expectations based on area of study. For instance, engineering grads in the Class of 2017 had a median starting salary of $60k while graduates of the Grady College of Journalism and Mass Communication reported a median income of $35k.

In 2017, a solid 20 percent of graduates elected to jump directly into a full-time advanced degree program. The most commonly attended graduate/professional schools included elite institutions such as Columbia, Duke, Emory, Georgia Tech, UNC-Chapel Hill, Penn, UVA, and Vanderbilt. In a given year, roughly half of the Bulldogs applying to medical school gain acceptance. Recent graduates are currently studying medicine at local schools, such as the Mercer University School of Medicine, as well as prestigious medical training grounds like Emory, Harvard, and Washington University.

Admission

Like many flagships around the country, the University of Georgia has grown increasingly competitive in recent years. The university received 26,027 applications in 2018, more than double the number received in 2005. The acceptance rate for a place in the Class of 2022 was 49 percent. Freshmen in 2018-19 possessed an ACT mid-50 percent score of 27-32 and 1240-1410 on the SAT. Only five years ago, the mean SAT was 1280. A strong academic profile is also essential—60 percent of successful applicants were in the top 10 percent of their class, and 92 percent were in the top quartile. Perhaps the most intimidating statistic is the average GPA of 4.0 with 95 percent of freshmen earning greater than a 3.75 over their high school careers.

A scholarship program guaranteeing any valedictorian or salutatorian from a Georgia high school free tuition has led to 4 percent of the student body being comprised of students holding those illustrious distinctions. The UGA Admissions Office says, "More than any other single factor, the grades you earn in your high school courses play the most important role in determining your competitiveness for admission to UGA." A rigorous high school course load is a must as 96 percent of admitted students took at least one AP, IB, or dual enrollment class. The school has no preference between the SAT and ACT and no longer requires the essay portion of either exam. In sum, the public jewel has become a destination point for the Peach State's top high school students. Knowledgeable applicants should use caution in underestimating the level of competition for spots on the picturesque Athens campus.

Worth Your Money?

You would be hard pressed to locate a better value for a college diploma from a highly respected institution than what you would get at UGA. In-state residents pay under $10k in tuition only and, thanks to cheap living in Athens, only $26k in total cost of attendance. Out-of-staters pay a not unreasonable total annual cost of $45k. The school offers a small amount of merit aid to 14 percent of undergrads and an average need-based grant of $11k to 42 percent of current students. It's little wonder that the average amount of debt for a University of Georgia grad is well under the national average. In short, this school is worth the money for any type of degree; even nonresidents can find a solid value here.

FINANCIAL
Institutional Type: Public
In-State Tuition: $9,790
Out-of-State Tuition: $28,830
Room & Board: $10,314
Required Fees: $2,290
Books & Supplies: $990

Avg. Need-Based Aid: $11,114
Avg. % of Need Met: 79%

Avg. Merit-Based Aid: $3,799
% Receiving Merit-Based Aid: 14%

Avg. Cumulative Debt: $22,872
% of Students Borrowing: 43%

CAREER
Who Recruits
1. Mailchimp
2. State Farm
3. Yelp
4. Boston Consulting Group
5. Home Depot

Notable Internships
1. Anthropologie
2. Delta Air Lines
3. TJX Companies

Top Industries
1. Business
2. Education
3. Operations
4. Sales
5. Healthcare

Top Employers
1. Home Depot
2. Delta
3. EY
4. Coca Cola
5. Deloitte

Where Alumni Work
1. Atlanta
2. Athens, GA
3. New York City
4. Washington, DC
5. Charlotte

Median Earnings
College Scorecard (Early Career): $50,500
EOP (Early Career): $49,900
PayScale (Mid-Career): $100,700

RANKINGS
Forbes: 99
Money: 119
U.S. News: 50, National Universities
Wall Street Journal/THE: 147
Washington Monthly: 99, National Universities

#CollegesWorthYourMoney

ADMISSION
Admission Rate: 62%
Admission Rate - Men: 56%
Admission Rate - Women: 70%
EA Admission Rate: N/A
ED Admission Rate: Not Offered
Admission Rate (5-Year Trend): 0%
ED Admission Rate (5-Year Trend): Not Offered
% of Admits Attending (Yield): 31%
Transfer Admission Rate: 51%

Offered Wait List: 2,178
Accepted Wait List: 1,479
Admitted Wait List: 39

SAT Reading/Writing (Middle 50%): 600-700
SAT Math (Middle 50%): 620-780
ACT Composite (Middle 50%): 26-32
Testing Policy: ACT/SAT Required
SAT Superscore: No
ACT Superscore: No

% Graduated in Top 10% of HS Class: 48%
% Graduated in Top 25% of HS Class: 81%
% Graduated in Top 50% of HS Class: 98%

ENROLLMENT
Total Undergraduate Enrollment: 33,915
% Part-Time: 3%
% Male: 54%
% Female: 46%
% Out-of-State: 12%
% Fraternity: 20%
% Sorority: 25%
% On-Campus (Freshman): 100%
% On-Campus (All Undergraduate): 50%

% African-American: 6%
% Asian: 19%
% Hispanic: 12%
% White: 44%
% Other: 3%
% Race or Ethnicity Unknown: 1%
% International: 16%
% Low-Income: 21%

ACADEMICS
Student-to-Faculty Ratio: 20:1
% of Classes Under 20: 38%
% of Classes Under 40: 73%
% Full-Time Faculty: 99%
% Full-Time Faculty w/ Terminal Degree: 93%

Top Programs
Agriculture
Business
Chemistry
Communication
Computer Science
Engineering
Information Sciences
Physics

Retention Rate: 93%
4-Year Graduation Rate: 70%
6-Year Graduation Rate: 84%

Curricular Flexibility: Less Flexible
Academic Rating: ★★★⯨

Inside the Classroom

The University of Illinois at Urbana-Champlain, the mammoth, highly ranked research university with an iconic Midwestern campus, serves as the beloved home to 50,000 increasingly accomplished students, including roughly 34,000 undergraduates. The university's humble beginnings as an industrial college upon its founding in 1867 are now nothing more than a distant, long-obliterated memory. Illinois' flagship institution 135 miles south of Chicago has fifteen schools and colleges, eight of which cater to undergraduate students. There are 150 academic programs including fifteen in the acclaimed Grainger College of Engineering alone.

As at many large universities, curricular mandates vary by school. The College of Liberal Arts & Sciences, by far UIUC's largest school, has a long list of must-takes including four classes in a foreign language, two English composition courses, and two courses in each of humanities and arts, natural sciences and technology, and social and behavioral sciences. In 2019-20, three cultural studies courses were added as requirements: Western Cultures, Non-Western Cultures, and US Minority Cultures.

Illinois' student-to-faculty ratio of 20:1 is among the highest of any school in this guide, and class sizes run the gamut from single-digit (12 percent) to more than fifty students (20 percent). Still, there is plenty of personalized attention available for those bold enough to seek it. A solid 32 percent of undergraduates work with a faculty member on a research project; another 20 percent have some type of fieldwork, practicum, or clinical experience. Unique opportunities for experiential learning abound at Research Park, an on-campus technology hub that hosts more than one hundred major corporations, and 2,100 employees who use the space as an incubator of innovation and a place to collaborate with Illinois faculty and students. Also strong, particularly for a school of UIUC's size, is the 24 percent participation rate for the school's study abroad programs that offers over 350 sites in fifty countries.

In sheer volume of degrees conferred, engineering is the leader at 21 percent followed by business/marketing (14 percent), the social sciences (9 percent), and communication/journalism (6 percent). The aforementioned Grainger College of Engineering, a top-ten school on any list, has a direct pipeline to top firms and tech companies. The Gies College of Business is also strong, particularly the Accounting Department, which is also a feeder to the world's best accounting firms. Prestigious scholarship competitions are similarly fond of Illinois grads— eleven of the forty-eight Fulbright Scholarship applicants from the university won awards, a performance comparable to elites such as Berkeley, Dartmouth, and Tufts. Seven seniors in the Class of 2019 captured National Science Foundation Graduate Research Fellowships.

Outside the Classroom

The University District is one of the only campuses in the United States better measured by miles than acres. The school's 354 buildings are contained on 3.3 square miles. Everything at UIUC is massive in scale. Twenty-four residence halls are home to 8,550 undergraduates, mostly freshmen, as all first-years are required to live on campus. Including private certified housing units and frat and sorority houses, approximately half of undergrads reside on campus. Student life is dominated by ninety Greek organizations that scoop up 25 percent of female and 20 percent of male undergraduates. The twenty-one NCAA Division I sports teams are also a major focal point at this school. The Fighting Illini football team plays before crowds of 60,000+ at Memorial Stadium. An unfathomable 470,000 square feet of recreational spaces offer everything from indoor tracks to a leisure pool with slide to an inline skating rink. With roughly 1,600 student-run organizations, it's hard not to find your niche somewhere. One doesn't even have to venture off university grounds to find robust cultural opportunities as the four theaters in the Krannert Center for the Performing Arts annually host more than 350 performances by students as well as touring professionals. The Krannert Art Museum boasts 10,000 original works. Those looking to road trip to a major city can reach St. Louis, Chicago, or Indianapolis in two-to-three hours by car.

Career Services

Twenty-four professional employees staff The Career Center at Illinois (TCC) with roles such as career counselor, health-career advisor, employer relations, and professional development for international students. However, additional career services supports can be found within the Gies College of Business (three professional staff); the Grainger College of Engineering (5); the School for Information Sciences (1); the Department of Economics (1); and the College of Agricultural, Consumer & Environmental Sciences (1). All told, the University of Illinois at Urbana-Champaign possesses an overall student-to-career staff ratio of 970:1, which is higher than the average university featured in this book.

Serving 34,000 undergraduate students is a monumental task, but it's one that UIUC successfully meets by offering a wide array of services and large-group activities. The TCC served one-quarter of the student population in 2017-18; 28 percent of those utilizing the office were seniors. Almost 24,000 students used Handshake to connect with alumni and potential employers. Staff also conducted 2,629 one-on-one advising sessions, completed 4,650 resume/cover letter/LinkedIn page reviews, hosted 442 employers and graduate/professional schools at career fairs, and facilitated 808 on-campus interviews. In total, 68 percent of Class of 2018 graduates completed at least one internship while at Illinois. Job shadowing, application boot camps, career fair preparation workshops, and etiquette dinners are only a small sampling of opportunities provided by the TCC to students proactive enough to take advantage. Despite the sheer numbers challenge of serving every student, UIUC Career Services provides a number of excellent programs that lead to impressive career and graduate school outcomes.

Professional Outcomes

Ninety-one percent of the members of the graduating Class of 2018 had landed at their next destination within six months of graduation. Employed (full time) graduates represented 57 percent of the total cohort, and the most popular sectors were finance, consulting, and education. Advertising/PR/marketing, computer and electronic products, health-care services and hospitals, and manufacturing were next in line. Among the corporations that landed twenty-five or more 2018 Illini grads were KPMG, Deloitte, Epic Systems, EY, PwC, Microsoft, and Amazon. More than fifteen newly minted grads landed at companies like Facebook, Google, Northrup Grumman, PepsiCo, Allstate Insurance, and Accenture. The average salary across all majors for 2018 grads was an extremely solid $61,000. Two-thirds of graduates remained in the Land of Lincoln; California, Massachusetts, Missouri, and Washington state welcomed the greatest percentages of migrating alumni.

A notably high 34 percent of Class of 2018 graduates matriculated directly into an advanced/professional degree program with 56 percent pursuing a master's degree. More than 650 students stayed put at the University of Illinois and joined the massive group of 14,500+ graduate students currently enrolled. Over twenty Class of 2018 graduates enrolled in prestigious universities such as Columbia, NYU, Northwestern, the University of Michigan, and Washington University in St. Louis, and fifteen+ continued their studies at Carnegie Mellon, Stanford, Penn, Cornell, Johns Hopkins, and the University of Chicago. Clearly, Illinois grads are extremely competitive candidates at all of the country's elite graduate programs. Medical school applicants fare decently with acceptance rates around 10 percent higher than the national average, and recent grads have trained at Rush University Medical College, Washington University School of Medicine in St. Louis, the University of Michigan Medical School, and Johns Hopkins. Law school applicants attend many fine institutions including the University of Illinois' own highly ranked law school.

Admission

The University of Illinois at Urbana-Champaign accepted 62 percent of the 39,362 applicants battling for a place in the Class of 2022. This is one of the gentler acceptance rates of any institution featured in this book, but don't let that figure mislead you; the Illini are a high-achieving lot. Those admitted for the 2018-19 school year had mid-50 percent standardized test scores of 1220-1480 (55 percent had higher than a 700 on the math portion) on the SAT and 26-32 on the ACT. Almost half (48 percent), placed in the top decile of their graduating classes, and 81 percent hailed from the top quartile. Five years ago, the percentage of top-10 percent students was actually 55 percent, but SATs were a much lower mid-50 percent range of 1160-1350, only part of which can be explained by score inflation. Applicants to UIUC's Grainger College will need to possess grades and test scores well above the aforementioned averages. Standards for entry into a computer science major are similar to those encountered at an Ivy.

The admissions committee places greatest emphasis on the rigor of one's secondary school record and the GPA earned. Standardized test scores, essays, extracurricular activities, and talent/ability are considered "important" to the decision-making process. Interestingly, the committee does not consider class rank or recommendations in an evaluative capacity. It also states that those who submit their applications by November 1 "may [have] the best chance for being admitted to our most selective programs and special attention for admission to honors programs and for merit awards." There is no reason not to apply to UIUC by the early deadline because it is a nonbinding proposition and gives you the best odds at admission. Illinois remains primarily a university for state residents as the percentage of in-staters climbed back up to 77 percent for last year's freshman class. Strong grades and SAT scores are required for serious consideration, but the admissions process is a straightforward one.

Worth Your Money?

Three-quarters of undergraduates enrolled in this university are from within the state of Illinois, entitling them to an affordable education. One of the few American schools to charge different tuition rates to business/engineering majors than education/social work majors, residents enjoy an average cost of attendance between $31k and $36k per year. Nonresidents are offered a COA of roughly $48,000, lower than most private institutions, making the University of Illinois at Urbana-Champaign a viable option for out-of-staters, especially those planning to enter the corporate or tech world. Around half of attending undergraduates are determined eligible for need-based financial aid with an average award of $16,132.

FINANCIAL
Institutional Type: Public
In-State Tuition: $12,036
Out-of-State Tuition: $29,178
Room & Board: $11,850
Required Fees: $4,174
Books & Supplies: $1,200

Avg. Need-Based Aid: $16,132
Avg. % of Need Met: 70%

Avg. Merit-Based Aid: $5,202
% Receiving Merit-Based Aid: 20%

Avg. Cumulative Debt: $23,123
% of Students Borrowing: 43%

CAREER
Who Recruits
1. Micron
2. Crowe Horwath
3. Shell
4. Phillips 66
5. BP America

Notable Internships
1. Ford Motor Company
2. Uber
3. State Farm

Top Industries
1. Business
2. Education
3. Engineering
4. Operations
5. Research

Top Employers
1. Google
2. Microsoft
3. Amazon
4. EY
5. IBM

Where Alumni Work
1. Chicago
2. Urban-Champaign, IL
3. San Francisco
4. New York City
5. Los Angeles

Median Earnings
College Scorecard (Early Career): $61,500
EOP (Early Career): $59,700
PayScale (Mid-Career): $115,300

RANKINGS
Forbes: 68
Money: 20
U.S. News: 48 (T), National Universities
Wall Street Journal/THE: 47
Washington Monthly: 17, National Universities

#CollegesWorthYourMoney

University of Maryland, College Park

College Park, Maryland | Admissions Phone: 301-314-8385

Inside the Classroom

It's a highly affordable research university with a respected name and a big-time sports program that, oh yeah, happens to be only minutes from Washington, DC, so it's no shock that the University of Maryland-College Park has become an increasingly popular college destination. A school that has been on the rise since it became the state's flagship campus in 1988, College Park today enrolls teens from all fifty states and international students from 123 countries, although three-quarters of the undergraduate population are residents. This university enrolls 41,000 total students including 30,700 undergraduates who can select from ninety-two majors across twelve colleges. Real Terrapins may be turtles that are hyper-aggressive carriers of salmonella, but the Maryland variety is an accomplished group of young scholars who, in overwhelming numbers, go on to do great things postgraduation.

Depending on which college and program you are part of, the sequence and pace at which you will fill the school's general education requirements will vary. The requirements themselves will not. There are forty-one credits of required coursework that include twelve credits in communications, six in the arts and humanities, six in behavioral and social sciences, seven in biological and physical sciences, seven in interdisciplinary or emerging issues, and three in mathematics. Maryland offers one of the best Honors Colleges, and those more able to gain acceptance (the average SAT is 1490) must complete three honors seminars and two additional honors courses.

Despite an 18:1 student-to-faculty ratio and a heavy concentration of graduate students, many undergraduate course sections at the University of Maryland are held in intimate classroom settings. In fact, 45 percent of sections enroll fewer than twenty students. Of course, you will also have your share of packed introductory lecture courses; 17 percent of classes enroll fifty or more students. Undergraduate research opportunities are within reach as 43 percent of 2018 graduates completed one, including 9 percent who completed a summer research experience. The Maryland Center for Undergraduate Research also facilitates numerous opportunities throughout the year and hosts an annual Undergraduate Research Day at which 350+ students make presentations. A reasonable number of students also pursue a semester overseas. Over 1,500 students elect to study abroad at one of 447 destinations.

Collectively, the social sciences account for 18 percent of degrees awarded by the University of Maryland with criminology, government and politics, and economics among the most popular majors. Engineering is next with 15 percent of undergraduate degrees conferred. It is followed by business (12 percent), computer science (9 percent), biology (8 percent) and journalism (6 percent). The Robert H. Smith School of Business, the A. James Clark School of Engineering, and the Merrill College of Journalism all command respect from prospective employers and graduate schools, as do programs in computer science and criminology. Maryland's reputation also helps its graduates win highly competitive national fellowships. In 2019, that haul included ten Boren Awards, nine Fulbrights, seven Critical Language Scholarships, four Goldwater Scholars, and a Churchill Scholarship.

Outside the Classroom

Campus is home to 90 percent of Terrapin freshmen and 41 percent of the overall undergraduate student body. Only first-year students are guaranteed housing. Greek life is prominent, attracting 19 percent of women and 15 percent of men. Major sports are a thriving enterprise at the University of Maryland as the school boasts twenty Division I teams that include a basketball team that won the NCAA tournament in 2002 and is playing in March Madness pretty much every year. There are 800+ clubs, including many in the realm of improv, comedy, and pre-professional as well as an intramural program so expansive it offers both competitive and recreational levels. Also notable are The Mighty Sound of Maryland, a big-time marching band, and the strength of the volunteering spirit that sees the U of M community contribute a collective two million hours per year. Suburban Maryland isn't the most exciting place you could hope for but, fortunately, Washington, DC, is only a short Metro ride away.

Career Services

There are twenty-six full-time staff members working out of the centralized University Career Center with sixteen undergraduate-focused employees stationed in the Robert H. Smith School of Business, five in the A. James Clark School of Engineering, and another five career counselors housed within other colleges and departments. That brings the grand total of professional career services staff members at College Park to fifty-two, equating to a 590:1 student-to-counselor ratio, below average compared to the average school in this book, but strong for a school with over 30,000 undergraduates.

University of Maryland, College Park

E-mail: applymaryland@umd.edu | Website: www.umd.edu

A superb 84 percent of 2018 graduates reported completing at least one internship, and more than one was the norm with 32 percent completing two internships, and 34 percent completing three. Among those who desired to turn their internship into a full-time gig postgraduation, 79 percent received an offer of employment. The jobs landed by all graduates were closely aligned with student's career goals, another testament to the work of this office. To be precise, 93 percent of job-holders reported that their position either directly aligned with their career goals or was a proper stepping-stone toward their ultimate goal. Eleven percent of graduates landed their first job via an on-campus interview with a company arranged by the University Career Center while another 13 percent made that important connection at a school-hosted job fair. On that topic, the school puts on several career fairs, including a fall event that draws 3,500 students and a Computer Science Career & Internship Fair that, alone, brings 125 companies to campus. Additionally, you can turn to the 352,000 Terrapin alumni to help you open a door into just about any hiring organization you can conjure up. Terrific internship numbers, on-campus recruiting, and overall student outcomes make this a world-class career services outfit.

Professional Outcomes

Class of 2018 graduates from the University of Maryland had, within six months of graduating, successfully found their next life step 93.5 percent of the time. Of the 72 percent of that cohort who found employment, the companies/organizations hiring the greatest number of recent grads were Deloitte (36), KPMG (29), the National Institutes of Health (29), EY (28), Accenture (22), and PwC (22). Double-digit Terrapins were also scooped up by giants including Amazon, IBM, Northrup Grumman, Capital One, and JP Morgan Chase & Co. Taking all alumni into account, more than 200 individuals with a University of Maryland affiliation presently work for Facebook, Apple, and Google. By far the most popular landing spot for alumni is the Greater Washington, DC, area with Baltimore, New York City, San Francisco, and Philadelphia next in line. The median starting salary self-report by Class of 2018 grads was $58,703; the mid-50 percent range was $41k-$69k.

Nineteen percent of Class of 2018 members headed directly to graduate and professional school to begin work on an advanced degree. Of that contingent 9 percent entered doctoral programs, 6 percent were on the path to becoming medical doctors, and 5 percent entered law school. By a wide margin, continuing at the University of Maryland was the top choice; 280 survey respondents reported remaining at their home institution. Other popular schools were George Washington University (21), Johns Hopkins (14), the University of Pennsylvania (13), Columbia (12), Georgetown (12), NYU (12), and Boston University (11). Medical school acceptance rates for Maryland students are excellent at over 60 percent between 2015 and 2017, roughly 20 points higher than the national average. In recent years the medical schools where the largest number of alumni matriculated were the University of Maryland, George Washington University, New York Medical College, and Drexel University. In that same time, law school applicants earned seventy-seven acceptances to Georgetown, twenty-seven each to Michigan and Emory, twenty-six to Cornell, eighteen to Columbia, and seventeen to Harvard.

Admission

Applicants for a spot as a freshman at College Park in 2018-19 were accepted at a rate of 47 percent; a decade earlier the admit rate was 39 percent. The mid-50 percent standardized test scores for the Class of 2022 were 1290-1480 on the SAT and 28-33 on the ACT. Three-quarters of enrolled students earned a spot in the top 10 percent of their high school class, and 93 percent were in the top quartile. The average weighted GPA was 4.28. Those class rank and GPA numbers are similar to those of ten years ago, but SAT scores are significantly higher today, even when accounting for post-2016 score inflation.

With 33,461 applicants, this admissions committee needs to look first at cold, hard numbers, which is why GPA, standardized tests, and the presence of a rigorous course load are ranked as "very important" factors. Class rank, the essay, recommendations, state residency, first-generation status, and talent/ability make up the next rung of "important" factors. There is no binding early decision option at Maryland; the early action deadline of November 1 will get you an answer by January 31. In sum, getting into Maryland's flagship university's main campus pretty much requires a 3.75 or higher GPA and standardized test scores above the 90th percentile.

Worth Your Money?

In-state tuition is under $11,000, and the total cost of attendance for those living on campus is $27k. Out-of-staters pay three times the tuition rate, which leads to a total cost of attendance of $53k+ to become a Terrapin. Getting literally any degree at the in-state rate is a no-brainer. For nonresidents, you would have to have a compelling reason to cross state lines to pay $200,000+. However, if you are eyeing the exceptional programs in business, engineering, or computer science, that sum may be worth the education and connections you will gain.

FINANCIAL
Institutional Type: Public
In-State Tuition: $8,651
Out-of-State Tuition: $33,272
Room & Board: $12,429
Required Fees: $1,944
Books & Supplies: $1,250

Avg. Need-Based Aid: $9,980
Avg. % of Need Met: 66%

Avg. Merit-Based Aid: $4,584
% Receiving Merit-Based Aid: 36%

Avg. Cumulative Debt: $28,511
% of Students Borrowing: 41%

CAREER
Who Recruits
1. AIG Retirement Services
2. Carrier Corporation
3. Corvel Corporation
4. Federal Aviation Administration
5. Lockheed Martin

Notable Internships
1. Adobe
2. Nike
3. U.S. State Department

Top Industries
1. Business
2. Education
3. Operations
4. Engineering
5. Information Technology

Top Employers
1. Booz Allen Hamilton
2. Deloitte
3. IBM
4. Capital One
5. Google

Where Alumni Work
1. Washington, DC
2. Baltimore
3. New York City
4. Philadelphia
5. San Francisco

Median Earnings
College Scorecard (Early Career): $62,900
EOP (Early Career): $53,500
PayScale (Mid-Career): $113,400

RANKINGS
Forbes: 63
Money: 43
U.S. News: 64 (T), National Universities
Wall Street Journal/THE: 75 (T)
Washington Monthly: 45, National Universities

#CollegesWorthYourMoney

University of Massachusetts Amherst

Amherst, Massachusetts | Admissions Phone: 413-545-0222

ADMISSION
Admission Rate: 60%
Admission Rate - Men: 58%
Admission Rate - Women: 62%
EA Admission Rate: 74%
ED Admission Rate: Not Offered
Admission Rate (5-Year Trend): -3%
ED Admission Rate (5-Year Trend): Not Offered
% of Admits Attending (Yield): 20%
Transfer Admission Rate: 51%

Offered Wait List: 6,250
Accepted Wait List: 2,911
Admitted Wait List: 39

SAT Reading/Writing (Middle 50%): 600-680
SAT Math (Middle 50%): 600-710
ACT Composite (Middle 50%): 26-31
Testing Policy: ACT/SAT Required
SAT Superscore: Yes
ACT Superscore: Yes

% Graduated in Top 10% of HS Class: 32%
% Graduated in Top 25% of HS Class: 71%
% Graduated in Top 50% of HS Class: 97%

ENROLLMENT
Total Undergraduate Enrollment: 23,515
% Part-Time: 7%
% Male: 50%
% Female: 50%
% Out-of-State: 18%
% Fraternity: 8%
% Sorority: 8%
% On-Campus (Freshman): 99%
% On-Campus (All Undergraduate): 62%

% African-American: 5%
% Asian: 10%
% Hispanic: 7%
% White: 62%
% Other: 3%
% Race or Ethnicity Unknown: 6%
% International: 7%
% Low-Income: 22%

ACADEMICS
Student-to-Faculty Ratio: 17:1
% of Classes Under 20: 49%
% of Classes Under 40: 77%
% Full-Time Faculty: 81%
% Full-Time Faculty w/ Terminal Degree: 94%

Top Programs
Architecture
Business
Computer Science
Nursing
Psychology
Public Health Sciences
Sociology
Sport Management

Retention Rate: 91%
4-Year Graduation Rate: 71%
6-Year Graduation Rate: 80%

Curricular Flexibility: Somewhat Flexible
Academic Rating: ★★★

Inside the Classroom

Sesame Street's iconic "One of These Things (Is Not Like the Others)" song comes to mind when examining the Five College Consortium in Western Massachusetts. The group consists of tiny, elite liberal arts schools Amherst College, Mount Holyoke, Smith, Hampshire and…UMass? That's right, UMass, a school that has 23,500 undergraduate students, another 7,000 graduate students, and 109 bachelor's degree programs that are offered across eight undergraduate colleges. While UMass Amherst students are free to cross-register in any course at the affiliated liberal arts havens, there is plenty to like on the grounds of the Commonwealth's flagship campus. The home of the Minutemen and Minutewomen boasts the highly ranked and affordable Isenberg School of Management as well as revered academic programs in sports management, architecture, computer science, and nursing.

Whether you end up in the Isenberg School of Management, the College of Engineering, or the School of Public Health and Health Sciences, you will encounter the same set of general education requirements that, fortunately, are not as overbearing as at many state universities. A ten-course, thirty-credit jaunt through writing, math, analytical reasoning, the physical sciences, and social world is all it takes to knock out the full run of nonnegotiable coursework. Those in the College of Humanities and Fine Arts and the College of Natural Sciences are required to study a foreign language; those in the Isenberg School of Management or College Engineering are not required to do so. The Commonwealth Honors College at UMass Amherst has high admissions standards (average 1386 SAT and 4.23 GPA) and even higher graduation standards, requiring additional honors coursework and the completion of a senior thesis.

The student-to-faculty ratio is 17:1, leading to undergraduate class sizes that are all over the map. You will encounter a number of smaller sections during your time at UMass as 49 percent of courses enroll fewer than twenty students; 18 percent of sections contain more than fifty students, so you also will have some larger lecture hall classes. In spite of some gigantic classes where you'll feel anonymous, a stunning 96 percent of Class of 2018 graduates reported being satisfied with their academic experience. Further, a substantial and encouraging 30 percent of that cohort reported engaging in some type of undergraduate research. For a large university, UMass also enjoys fairly wide participation in its study abroad program. Every year 1,200 students spend a semester in one of more than seventy countries.

UMass has a fairly even spread of students across its various areas of concentration. Of all degrees conferred in 2018, business/marketing diplomas accounted for 14 percent. That was followed by social sciences (12 percent), biology (10 percent), health professions (9 percent), and psychology (8 percent). Those who earn high grades find a wealth of employment and graduate school options awaiting them. UMass produces an impressive number of national postgraduate scholarship winners including fourteen Fulbright Scholars in 2018, four Goldwater Scholars in 2019, and a 2019 graduate was one of only fifteen Churchill Scholars named in the nation.

Outside the Classroom

Ninety-nine percent of freshmen live on the 1,450-acre Amherst campus, and 62 percent of the entire student body lives in university-owned housing, a relatively high figure for a state university. There are fifty-two separate residence halls. Those residing off campus typically find rentals in the surrounding towns of Amherst, Hadley, and Sunderland. Men and women both join fraternities and sororities at an 8 percent clip. Twenty-one NCAA teams compete at the Division I level, mostly within the Atlantic 10 Conference. Involvement is spread around with 38 percent of students joining at least one student-run club, 24 percent playing varsity, club, or intramural sports, and 13 percent participating in community service. There are 200+ registered student organizations, and UMass students can participate in any club or activity at the other colleges within the consortium. Amherst garners consistent praise as one the top college towns in the United States because, in its own accurate words, it offers "a perfect blend of New England natural beauty and cosmopolitan culture and energy." Even on-campus dining gets rave reviews. Road trips to Boston (90 miles) or New York City (175 miles) are possible despite the somewhat remote feel of the Western Massachusetts locale.

Career Services

There are three central career service administrators at UMass Amherst, but the majority of service providers are housed within eight career service departments in the various undergraduate colleges. Obtaining an exact count of the number of advisors was, unfortunately, not possible, but to provide some reference point for counselor availability, the business school has seven advisors and a student-to-counselor ratio of 526:1, very strong compared to the other large public universities featured in this guide. Job fair offerings are plentiful, and top employers are more than willing to make the trip to Amherst to recruit top students. The College of Engineering alone hosts six annual job fairs that cater to specialty areas like biotech jobs, environmental engineering, and tech jobs.

University of Massachusetts Amherst

E-mail: mail@admissions.umass.edu | Website: www.umass.edu

Overall, Minutemen and women feel that UMass adequately prepares them for beyond graduation; 79 percent of graduates are either "very satisfied" or "somewhat satisfied" with the way the university prepared them for the world of work. Two-thirds of 2018 graduates had some type of practicum, internship, co-op experience, or clinical assignment. Routine internship and co-op placements include the Boston Red Sox, CNN, IBM, MTV, Disney World, the Boston Globe, Sheraton, and United Technologies. With 260,000 alumni heavily concentrated in the Boston and Springfield areas, it's hard to walk down a New England street without bumping into a UMass alum. This supportive network, coupled with respected academic programs, helps the career services staff succeed in opening doors for qualified graduates.

Professional Outcomes

One year after graduating, 71 percent of UMass alumni are employed full time, 11 percent are working part time, and 18 percent are attending graduate school part time. The most populated industries are health/medical professions (13 percent), K-12 or early childhood education (8 percent), information technology (7 percent), marketing/sales (7 percent), and finance (7 percent). Companies presently employing one hundred+ Minutemen and Minutewomen include Oracle, Mass Mutual, Amazon, IBM, Google, Intel, Microsoft, PwC, Wayfair, and Apple. Boston is the most popular landing spot for graduates; it's followed by Springfield, Massachusetts; New York City; San Francisco; Washington, DC; and Los Angeles. One-third of recent graduates earn between $50-75k per year, 57 percent earn less than that range, and 9 percent take home more than $75,000 in annual income.

If you achieve stellar grades while an undergraduate at UMass, you will have a full array of graduate/professional school options awaiting you. Medical school applicants with a 3.7 GPA and an MCAT score in at least the 79th percentile are admitted to medical school more than 75 percent of the time. That rate was even higher when you include the criteria of having clinical experience *and* being open to osteopathic programs. Many recent graduates have attended medical school at UMass Medical School while others have gained acceptance to medical or dental school at Harvard, the University of Chicago, the University of Michigan, and the University of Pennsylvania. Similarly, prelaw students flock to UMass' own legal training ground or other Massachusetts-based options like Suffolk Law, but recent grads also have matriculated into elite institutions like William & Mary, Northeastern, or Boston University.

Admission

Sixty-percent of the 41,000+ applicants to UMass Amherst gained entry into the Class of 2022. A popular safety school for Massachusetts residents, only 20 percent of those who were accepted ultimately enrolled in the university. Eighty-seven percent of 2018-19 freshmen had submitted an SAT score with their applications and earned mid-50 percent scores of 1200-1390; the equivalent ACT range was 26-31. Approximately one-third of students hailed from the top 10 percent of their high school class, and 71 percent were in the top quartile. Only 3 percent finished outside the top half of their graduating cohort. Two-thirds of entering students posted high school GPAs of 3.75 or better, and only 5 percent possessed a GPA under 3.5. The university received only half as many applicants at the dawn of the new millennium. The entering Class of 2000-01 had mid-50 percent SAT scores of 1010-1240, and only 52 percent were in the top quartile of their graduating class. Clearly, admissions standards are much higher now than a generation ago.

Standardized test scores, GPA, and the level of rigor of one's coursework are the three factors weighed as "very important" by the admissions committee. Also "important" are class rank, essays, recommendations, extra-curricular activities, talent/ability, character/personal qualities, first-generation status, work experience, and the level of an applicant's interest. It is rare to see a large public university even consider demonstrated interest in admissions decisions, so make sure you take advantage by reaching out to a UMass admissions officer, visiting campus, or attending an admissions event in your area. There is an early action option in early November that will get you an admissions decision by mid-January at the latest. UMass does not offer binding early decision. Thousands apply for transfer to the Amherst campus each year, but the acceptance rate is lower than it is for freshmen.

Worth Your Money?

At full price, UMass Amherst will set a Massachusetts resident back $30,000 per year; an out-of-stater will pay just shy of $50,000. However, 73 percent of those applying for aid received an average discount of $11,478, and one-third of students received merit aid averaging close to $6k. Bay State residents are getting a terrific deal attending UMass and shouldn't hesitate to pull the trigger, regardless of their financial situation or intended academic path. With a bit of aid, it is possible to receive a four-year education at a solid institution for under six-figures in total cost of attendance. Those out of state will likely find better deals elsewhere unless they are eligible for the New England Regional Students Program that allows residents of other New England states to attend at a discount if their intended academic program is not offered by public colleges in their home state.

FINANCIAL
Institutional Type: Public
In-State Tuition: $15,791
Out-of-State Tuition: $35,112
Room & Board: $13,958
Required Fees: $1,083
Books & Supplies: $1,000

Avg. Need-Based Aid: $11,478
Avg. % of Need Met: 82%

Avg. Merit-Based Aid: $5,839
% Receiving Merit-Based Aid: 33%

Avg. Cumulative Debt: $31,897
% of Students Borrowing: 67%

CAREER
Who Recruits
1. HubSpot
2. Facebook
3. Salesforce
4. Wayfair
5. Apple

Notable Internships
1. PepsiCo
2. AIG
3. TJX Companies

Top Industries
1. Business
2. Education
3. Operations
4. Sales
5. Engineering

Top Employers
1. Oracle
2. MassMutual
3. IBM
4. Amazon
5. Google

Where Alumni Work
1. Boston
2. Springfield, MA
3. New York City
4. San Francisco
5. Washington, DC

Median Earnings
College Scorecard (Early Career): $51,400
EOP (Early Career): $51,700
PayScale (Mid-Career): $103,000

RANKINGS
Forbes: 155
Money: 109
U.S. News: 64 (T), National Universities
Wall Street Journal/THE: 160 (T)
Washington Monthly: 128, National Universities

#CollegesWorthYourMoney

University of Miami

Coral Gables, Florida | Admissions Phone: 305-284-4323

ADMISSION
Admission Rate: 32%
Admission Rate - Men: 34%
Admission Rate - Women: 31%
EA Admission Rate: 44%
ED Admission Rate: 56%
Admission Rate (5-Year Trend): -8%
ED Admission Rate (5-Year Trend): +32%
% of Admits Attending (Yield): 21%
Transfer Admission Rate: 53%

Offered Wait List: 10,405
Accepted Wait List: 4,041
Admitted Wait List: 30

SAT Reading/Writing (Middle 50%): 620-690
SAT Math (Middle 50%): 630-740
ACT Composite (Middle 50%): 29-32
Testing Policy: ACT/SAT Required
SAT Superscore: Yes
ACT Superscore: Yes

% Graduated in Top 10% of HS Class: 55%
% Graduated in Top 25% of HS Class: 83%
% Graduated in Top 50% of HS Class: 95%

ENROLLMENT
Total Undergraduate Enrollment: 11,117
% Part-Time: 6%
% Male: 47%
% Female: 53%
% Out-of-State: 60%
% Fraternity: 17%
% Sorority: 18%
% On-Campus (Freshman): 89%
% On-Campus (All Undergraduate): 38%

% African-American: 8%
% Asian: 5%
% Hispanic: 22%
% White: 41%
% Other: 3%
% Race or Ethnicity Unknown: 4%
% International: 15%
% Low-Income: 18%

ACADEMICS
Student-to-Faculty Ratio: 12:1
% of Classes Under 20: 50%
% of Classes Under 40: 83%
% Full-Time Faculty: 69%
% Full-Time Faculty w/ Terminal Degree: 86%

Top Programs
Architecture
Biology
Communication
Exercise Physiology
Marine Science
Music
Sport Administration

Retention Rate: 92%
4-Year Graduation Rate: 70%
6-Year Graduation Rate: 82%

Curricular Flexibility: Very Flexible
Academic Rating: ★★★✦

Inside the Classroom

The sunny paradise of Coral Gables, just south of Miami, is home to the University of Miami—commonly referred to as UM or "the U." It is easily identifiable by its team name, the Hurricanes, with its distinctive orange, green, and white colors. This large, private research institution that boasts a number of top academic programs and world-renowned faculty struggled to be taken seriously as a world-class institution for many decades. Having been dubbed "Sun Tan U" in the 1940s and suffering through revelations about its morally bereft football program of the 80s and 90s was a lot to overcome, yet Miami has finally arrived as an unquestioned member of higher education's elite. More selective than ever, Miami has more than gridiron glory to brag about as we enter the third decade of the millennium.

In an effort to ensure the acquisition of "essential intellectual skills and exposure to a range of intellectual perspectives and academic disciplines," UM mandates general education requirements via the Cognates Program. So-termed cognates are, at a minimum, three-course clusters that the faculty has determined share a focus or thematic elements. The three main areas of cognates are arts and humanities; people and society; and science, technology, engineering, and mathematics. Students fulfill one cognate through their major area of study and also must complete the other two broad areas. Hurricanes also must blow through two English composition courses and one quantitative skills class. Other than that, the core academic requirements at Miami are not prohibitive.

Students rate their teachers and their overall UM experience extremely favorably. A noteworthy 93 percent of graduates report being satisfied with their education while 83 percent were satisfied with their major, and 90 percent gained confidence in their own abilities over their four years of study. The student-to-faculty ratio is 12:1, and even though there are 6,000+ graduate students to serve, class sizes are reasonable. Exactly half of all course sections contain fewer than twenty students, and only 9 percent of sections sport enrollments of more than fifty undergrads. Study abroad opportunities are vast and include university-run programs in Rome, Shanghai, India, Paris, Prague, the Galapagos, Cape Town, and Buenos Aires. Undergraduate research posts can be had, but the onus is on the student to contact a professor directly, apply for placement through the Office of Research and Community Outreach, or apply for a summer research grant.

The University of Miami confers the greatest number of degrees in business/marketing (21 percent), biology (15 percent), engineering (10 percent), and the social sciences (10 percent). The Miami Business School and the College of Engineering enjoy solid national reputations, and programs in music, marine science, communications, and architecture sit high atop many rankings. UM graduates fared well at procuring highly competitive awards in 2018. The bounty included a Rhodes Scholarship, three National Science Foundation Graduate Research Fellowships, two Fulbright Scholarships, and two Goldwater Scholarships along with a Critical Language, Boren, and Gilman Scholarship.

Outside the Classroom

Eighty-nine percent of freshmen live on the University of Miami's 239-acre main campus in Coral Gables, but 62 percent of the total undergraduate student body live off campus. Fraternities attract 17 percent of male students, and sororities draw 18 percent of female students, creating a strong Greek presence within the social scene; there are close to three-dozen active Greek organizations. Of course, the U's most galvanizing force is its famous (and at times infamous) football team as well as sixteen other varsity sports squads that compete in the powerhouse Atlantic Coast Conference in NCAA Division I. Approximately 400 students participate in varsity athletics. The school is trying to move away from its "Sun Tan U" reputation, and it certainly has in terms of academic rankings, yet the South Beach atmosphere continues to earn Miami "top party school" status in many publication's rankings. For non-partiers, the school also offers 270+ clubs, thirty service organizations, an active student government, and an award-winning student-run cable channel. On-campus amenities border on luxurious with the Herbert Wellness Center being one of the finest collegiate gyms around. Students also enjoy an arboretum, the Lowe Art Museum, the Ring Theatre that launched stars like Sly Stallone and Ray Liotta, and close proximity to the beach.

Career Services

The Toppel Career Center is staffed by fifteen full-time professional employees (not counting admin assistants or office managers) who focus on employer relations, career counseling, and internship coordination. A student-to-advisor ratio of 722:1 is higher than average when set against the other institutions included in this book. Still, this office reaches the bulk of the population as 84 percent of graduates utilized Toppel at some point in their four years of study. The most utilized services were (1) resume and cover letter review, (2) career expo and fairs, (3) one-on-one career advising, and (4) job and internship listing search.

University of Miami

E-mail: admission@miami.edu | Website: www.miami.edu

A laundry list of impressive organizations/companies that visit Coral Gables to recruit and conduct on-campus interviews includes PepsiCo, American Airlines, Facebook, Adidas, EY, and the Miami Marlins. Last year, 175 companies attended the annual Career Expo, nearly 47,000 jobs and internships were posted to Handshake, 159 networking events were held, 2,251 students attended career fairs and workshops put on by Toppel staff, and 960 undergrads engaged in a one-on-one career counseling session. Career services also reviewed 2,200 resumes, conducted 863 practice interviews, and took 598 professional headshots for students to use in their job searches. That frenetic pace and strong outreach leads to mostly positive postgraduate outcomes for newly minted Hurricane alumni.

Professional Outcomes

The Hurricane Class of 2018 saw 81 percent of its members secure post-grad plans within six months with 55 percent employed full time and 34 percent in graduate school. Companies employing five or more 2018 graduates included ScribeAmerica, Citrix, Bloomingdale's, Bank of America Merrill Lynch, Citi, Morgan Stanley, and Insight Global. Across the entire alumni base, one hundred+ Canes also can be found in the offices of Google, IBM, PwC, Apple, and Microsoft. Average starting salaries were $51,000; those from the College of Engineering averaged $59k, business school grads took home $55k, and those from the College of Arts and Sciences enjoyed a mean income of $46k. Miami, New York, Boston, Chicago, and Los Angeles were the primary destinations of choice for 2018 grads.

The most frequently attended graduate schools included a mix of prestigious institutions, Miami itself, and other Sunshine State universities. In order, the schools of choice were Miami (146), Boston University (12), Columbia (10), Florida International (9), George Washington (9), NYU (9), University of Florida (9), and the University of Southern Florida (8). Premed students have the advantage of accumulating clinical hours within the University of Miami Health Systems or any of six other hospitals not far from campus. In a typical year the U's own Miller School of Medicine takes forty+ of its own exiting undergraduates, and over 90 percent of "highly recommended" applicants find a medical school home somewhere in the country.

Admission

Miami actually experienced a slight decline in applications in 2019 after receiving over 30,000 in 2018. However, the 32 percent acceptance rate for those jockeying for a spot in the 2018-19 freshman class was significantly lower than the 40 percent acceptance rate five years prior or the 44 percent rate a decade ago. The middle-50 percent ranges were 1250-1430 on the SAT and 29-32 on the ACT for current freshmen. Fifty-five percent of 2018-19 first-years earned a place in the top 10 percent of their high school class while 83 percent placed in the top quartile. The average high school GPA for attending students was 3.6. Those numbers are similar to those posted by incoming freshmen in the not-too-distant past.

Eight categories top the list of most important factors in making admissions decisions—GPA, rigor of coursework, class rank, standardized test scores, recommendations, application essays, extracurricular activities, and character/personal qualities. Due to the massive number of applicants, the university does not offer interviews as part of the evaluation process. The U offers an early decision round where 54 percent of applicants are let through the gates, but only about one-quarter of the freshman class is filled through ED. Aspiring Hurricanes will see their activities reviewed and their essays read carefully as part of a holistic process. Yet, at a school receiving so many applications, you will need to bring reasonably strong grades and within-range test scores. For reference, only 14-15 percent of attending students earned SAT reading or math scores under 600.

Worth Your Money?

The U's cost of attendance is approaching $70,000, over three times the in-state COA for the University of Florida or Florida State. To compete for the top students, the university dishes out merit aid to half of its attending undergrads at an annual average of $22,653. It also grants need-based aid to over two-fifths of students with an average annual award of almost $35,000. If your family has unlimited funds, or if you receive a solid aid package, Miami is definitely a school that can make a lot of sense from an investment standpoint. If you are on a budget, paying full freight could lead to an unpleasant financial situation early in one's adult life.

FINANCIAL
Institutional Type: Private
In-State Tuition: $50,400
Out-of-State Tuition: $50,400
Room & Board: $14,658
Required Fees: $1,530
Books & Supplies: $1,000

Avg. Need-Based Aid: $34,643
Avg. % of Need Met: 95%

Avg. Merit-Based Aid: $22,653
% Receiving Merit-Based Aid: 52%

Avg. Cumulative Debt: $22,000
% of Students Borrowing: 36%

CAREER
Who Recruits
1. SpaceX
2. Adidas
3. Hilton
4. Ball Aerospace
5. CIA

Notable Internships
1. Lincoln Financial Group
2. Cato Institute
3. Viacom

Top Industries
1. Business
2. Education
3. Healthcare
4. Arts & Design
5. Sales

Top Employers
1. Microsoft
2. IBM
3. Citi
4. Apple
5. PwC

Where Alumni Work
1. Miami
2. New York City
3. Los Angeles
4. West Palm Beach, FL
5. Washington, DC

Median Earnings
College Scorecard (Early Career): $60,100
EOP (Early Career): $54,800
PayScale (Mid-Career): $99,600

RANKINGS
Forbes: 90
Money: 378
U.S. News: 57, National Universities
Wall Street Journal/THE: 49
Washington Monthly: 222, National Universities

#CollegesWorthYourMoney

University of Michigan

Ann Arbor, Michigan | Admissions Phone: 734-764-7433

ADMISSION
Admission Rate: 23%
Admission Rate - Men: 21%
Admission Rate - Women: 25%
EA Admission Rate: N/A
ED Admission Rate: Not Offered
Admission Rate (5-Year Trend): -10%
ED Admission Rate (5-Year Trend): Not Offered
% of Admits Attending (Yield): 45%
Transfer Admission Rate: 39%

Offered Wait List: 14,783
Accepted Wait List: 6,000
Admitted Wait List: 415

SAT Reading/Writing (Middle 50%): 660-730
SAT Math (Middle 50%): 670-780
ACT Composite (Middle 50%): 30-34
Testing Policy: ACT/SAT Required
SAT Superscore: No
ACT Superscore: No

% Graduated in Top 10% of HS Class: 79%
% Graduated in Top 25% of HS Class: 96%
% Graduated in Top 50% of HS Class: 99%

ENROLLMENT
Total Undergraduate Enrollment: 30,318
% Part-Time: 4%
% Male: 50%
% Female: 50%
% Out-of-State: 41%
% Fraternity: 12%
% Sorority: 25%
% On-Campus (Freshman): 98%
% On-Campus (All Undergraduate): 31%

% African-American: 4%
% Asian: 15%
% Hispanic: 6%
% White: 58%
% Other: 4%
% Race or Ethnicity Unknown: 5%
% International: 7%
% Low-Income: 14%

ACADEMICS
Student-to-Faculty Ratio: 15:1
% of Classes Under 20: 57%
% of Classes Under 40: 78%
% Full-Time Faculty: 82%
% Full-Time Faculty w/ Terminal Degree: 91%

Top Programs
Business
Communication and Media
Computer Science
Economics
Engineering
English
Political Science
Psychology

Retention Rate: 97%
4-Year Graduation Rate: 79%
6-Year Graduation Rate: 92%

Curricular Flexibility: Somewhat Flexible
Academic Rating: ★★★★✦

Inside the Classroom

What do you get when you combine one of the best college towns in the country, one of the premier research universities in the world, and stir in a passionate sports scene? The answer is the first public university in the Northwest Territories. Originally dubbed the "Catholepistemiad of Detroit," it is now known by the catchier name of the University of Michigan. Brilliant teens flock to Ann Arbor for 263 undergraduate degree programs across fourteen schools and colleges, and their success can be measured in countless ways, whether you look at the 97 percent freshman retention rate or the fact that more current Fortune 100 CEOs are alums of the Ross School of Business than any other school on the planet.

All applicants must apply to one of the fourteen schools right off the bat. The College of Literature, Science, and the Arts (LSA) serves the majority, and those accepted are held to school-specific rather than university-wide academic requirements. However, all Wolverines ultimately end up with broad academic requirements in the areas of English, foreign language, natural sciences, and social sciences. Freshmen in the LSA take a first-year seminar that is capped at eighteen students and affords an immediate opportunity to connect with a professor in an area of academic interest. LSAers also have the option to sign up for a "theme semester" in which major topics such as India in the World or Understanding Race are explored in-and-outside the classroom through activities such as museum visits, guest lectures, and film screenings.

With almost 46,000 students on campus, including grad students, it's not surprising that undergrads will end up sitting in some large lecture halls. Michigan sports a 15:1 student-to-faculty ratio, and 18 percent of classes contain fifty or more students, but a solid 57 percent of classes offer a more intimate experience with fewer than twenty students. Opportunities to conduct independent research or work in a laboratory beside a faculty member can be found. In the 2018-19 school year 1,300 participated in the Undergraduate Research Opportunity Program. For students in all academic programs at Michigan, study abroad opportunities are taken advantage of at high rates. In fact, the university is fifth in the nation in the number of students it sends to study in foreign lands.

In general, the faculty is exceptional and overflowing with award-winning researchers. Michigan finds itself atop any ranking of best public research universities. The Ross School of Business offers highly rated programs in entrepreneurship, management, accounting, and finance. The College of Engineering is also one of the best in the country. By sheer numbers, the school confers more engineering degrees (16 percent) than in any other discipline. The social sciences are next (12 percent), and encompass incredibly strong majors in political science, economics, and psychology. Computer science, another top-notch offering, attracts 11 percent of the student body. Graduating Wolverines are routinely awarded prestigious scholarships to continue their studies. In 2019, the school produced twenty-six Fulbright Scholars, more than any other research university in the nation.

Outside the Classroom

Ann Arbor is a prototypical college town, the type you would show to a Martian who wanted to know what a quintessential American college was like. Vibrant, stimulating, and extremely safe, the 3,200-acre campus and surrounding town are ideal places to spend four years. When your football stadium seats more than 100,000, that's a pretty solid indicator that the sports scene is thriving. Donning the iconic maize and blue jerseys, Michigan's twenty-seven Division I sports teams have enjoyed a ridiculous level of success. A substantial but not overwhelming 12 percent of men and 25 percent of women belong to one of the sixty-two fraternities and sororities on campus. A hard-to-comprehend 1,600 student organizations exist. If you can conceive it, Michigan probably already offers it, and 82 percent of the student body participates in at least one club or activity. Intramural and club sports also enjoy wide participation. The Ginsberg Center for Community and Service is popular, and 54 percent of Wolverines have engaged in volunteer experiences. Only 31 percent live on campus, almost all of whom are first-year students.

Career Services

The University of Michigan Career Center employs fourteen full-time staff members as well as seven peer advisors. Only counting the full-time employees, UM has a student-to-advisor ratio of 2,166:1, one of the highest of any school featured in this guide. Thus, hand-holding is limited, but appointments with peer advisors are available for mock interviews and resume assistance. One-on-one appointments with a professional career counselor can be scheduled to discuss finding internships and jobs. The career center reaches more students through hosting workshops, putting on more than 200 per year with a total attendance exceeding 6,000 undergrads.

Staffing may be less than desired, but on the plus side, Michigan's alumni network is one of the largest and most powerful in the nation. With over half a million loyal alums spread across one hundred countries, there is always a fellow Wolverine willing to dispense advice, facilitate a job-shadowing experience or internship, or help you get your foot in the door in the industry of your choosing. Also working in the school's favor is the fact that Michigan grads are highly sought after by major employers who are happy to travel to Ann Arbor for recruiting purposes. The Ross School of Business alone arranges for hundreds of companies to recruit on campus each year, including all of the big boys: Goldman Sachs, Deutsche Bank, EY, and Morgan Stanley. At UM counselors are not going to personally hunt you down to take personality inventories and create a killer LinkedIn profile, but large-scale resources are available that will get motivated students on the right path to their next destination.

Professional Outcomes

Within three months of exiting Ann Arbor, 93 percent of the graduates of the College of Literature, Science, and the Arts are employed full time or attending graduate school. Health care, research, nonprofit work, and consulting are the four most popular sectors in which LSA alums launch their careers. Ross School of Business graduates fare quite well on the open market; within three months, 98 percent are employed with a median salary of $72k. The companies listed above that recruit on campus are among the top employers of the Class of 2017 along with PwC, Deloitte, and Amazon. Engineering grads have similar success with 96 percent employed or in grad school within six months. Computer science/engineering students, the largest group within the School of Engineering, walk into jobs averaging close to $100k. The companies employing the greatest number of alumni across all years include General Motors, Ford, Google, Microsoft, Apple, and Facebook.

As with employers, elite graduate and professional schools also hold a Michigan diploma in high esteem. University of Michigan grads applying to law school are well prepared, averaging an LSAT score in the 80th percentile and gaining acceptance at a 92 percent clip. Those aiming for medical school average MCATs above the 85th percentile and get accepted at a 54 percent clip, a rate more than 10 percent higher than the national average. In short, if you succeed at Michigan, there isn't a graduate or professional school in existence that will be beyond your reach.

Admission

After a 10 percent increase in applications in 2018, the university now has a streak of a dozen consecutive years of breaking its own record for wanna-be Wolverines. The overall acceptance rate for a place in the Class of 2022 was 23 percent, but in-state applicants fared far better, enjoying a 41 percent rate (out-of-state was 19 percent). The SAT range of current Michigan students is 1330 to 1510, and the ACT range is 30-34. For comparison, in 2014 the SAT range was 1280-1480, and the ACT range was 29-33, which tells us that admission into this popular flagship university may be a touch more difficult now than in the recent past.

The school ranks the two most important admissions factors as "rigor of secondary school record" and "GPA." Average Michigan students earned a 3.86 GPA on a 4.0 scale in the most challenging courses available to them. Standardized test scores are listed as a secondary factor alongside recommendations, personal qualities, and first-generation status. While the University of Michigan does bring a holistic approach to the process, at the end of the day the admissions staff still needs to wade through almost 65,000 applications, which means test scores are still a major selling point. However, the office means what it says about giving preference to first-generation students. First-gens make up 13 percent of the student body, and the school does not super-score the SATs or ACTs as that practice benefits the economically advantaged. The University of Michigan has more than doubled its number of applications received in the last decade, and gaining acceptance is genuinely more challenging than ever. Top students who hail from in state will face better odds than out-of-staters who need to bring an impeccable academic record to the table to garner serious consideration.

Worth Your Money?

The average amount of debt held by a University of Michigan graduate is slightly below the national average. For residents of the Great Lakes State, the school is in the "ridiculous value" category—at least by the standards of an out-of-whack marketplace. Michigan's total cost of attendance for in-state students is $30k; the out-of-state price is over $64k. Two-fifths of undergraduates receive a merit aid award, but the average amount is under $5k and is unlikely to put a huge dent in your bill. For the 38 percent of students who qualify for need-based aid, Michigan does a phenomenal job meeting most of an individual's demonstrated financial need. In fact, 78 percent of those eligible see 100 percent of their need met. The average award is $19,145. This is truly exceptional for a public institution and is only one of the many reasons this topflight university is worth your money.

FINANCIAL
Institutional Type: Public
In-State Tuition: $14,934
Out-of-State Tuition: $49,022
Room & Board: $11,534
Required Fees: $328
Books & Supplies: $1,048

Avg. Need-Based Aid: $19,145
Avg. % of Need Met: 91%

Avg. Merit-Based Aid: $4,478
% Receiving Merit-Based Aid: 41%

Avg. Cumulative Debt: $27,224
% of Students Borrowing: 37%

CAREER
Who Recruits
1. Hudson's Bay
2. BP America
3. Bain & Company
4. United Talent
5. News America Marketing

Notable Internships
1. Uber
2. Nike
3. Lockheed Martin

Top Industries
1. Business
2. Education
3. Engineering
4. Operations
5. Research

Top Employers
1. General Motors
2. Ford Motor Company
3. Google
4. Amazon
5. Microsoft

Where Alumni Work
1. Detroit
2. New York City
3. Chicago
4. San Francisco
5. Washington, DC

Median Earnings
College Scorecard (Early Career): $63,400
EOP (Early Career): $68,700
PayScale (Mid-Career): $112,200

RANKINGS
Forbes: 20
Money: 8
U.S. News: 25, National Universities
Wall Street Journal/THE: 27
Washington Monthly: 28, National Universities

#CollegesWorthYourMoney

University of Minnesota – Twin Cities

Minneapolis, Minnesota | Admissions Phone: 612-625-2008

ADMISSION

Admission Rate: 52%
Admission Rate - Men: 48%
Admission Rate - Women: 55%
EA Admission Rate: N/A
ED Admission Rate: Not Offered
Admission Rate (5-Year Trend): +7%
ED Admission Rate (5-Year Trend): Not Offered
% of Admits Attending (Yield): 27%
Transfer Admission Rate: 46%

Offered Wait List: N/A
Accepted Wait List: N/A
Admitted Wait List: N/A

SAT Reading/Writing (Middle 50%): 620-710
SAT Math (Middle 50%): 650-770
ACT Composite (Middle 50%): 26-31
Testing Policy: ACT/SAT Required
SAT Superscore: No
ACT Superscore: No

% Graduated in Top 10% of HS Class: 50%
% Graduated in Top 25% of HS Class: 85%
% Graduated in Top 50% of HS Class: 100%

ENROLLMENT

Total Undergraduate Enrollment: 34,633
% Part-Time: 13%
% Male: 47%
% Female: 53%
% Out-of-State: 28%
% Fraternity: 10%
% Sorority: 10%
% On-Campus (Freshman): 89%
% On-Campus (All Undergraduate): 22%

% African-American: 5%
% Asian: 10%
% Hispanic: 4%
% White: 65%
% Other: 4%
% Race or Ethnicity Unknown: 4%
% International: 8%
% Low-Income: 21%

ACADEMICS

Student-to-Faculty Ratio: 17:1
% of Classes Under 20: 37%
% of Classes Under 40: 73%
% Full-Time Faculty: 69%
% Full-Time Faculty w/ Terminal Degree: 80%

Top Programs
Business
Chemistry
Computer Science
Economics
Engineering
Mathematics
Political Science
Psychology

Retention Rate: 93%
4-Year Graduation Rate: 65%
6-Year Graduation Rate: 80%

Curricular Flexibility: Less Flexible
Academic Rating: ★★★

Inside the Classroom

Home to almost 35,000 undergraduates and another 16,000 graduate students, the University of Minnesota Twin Cities can easily be overshadowed by its neighboring flagships (Wisconsin, Michigan, and Illinois). Yet, UMTC deserves its fair share of the Midwestern limelight, thanks in part to a number of academic programs rising toward the top of national rankings and the university's positioning as a direct pipeline to the nineteen Fortune 500 companies located within state borders. While a 72 percent out-of-state tuition increase over the last seven years has slowed down the tidal wave of nonresident applicants, international students and out-of-staters still make up 35 percent of the undergraduate student body. The average Gopher today boasts significantly better academic credentials than previous generations at the university. In fact, four- year graduation rates have doubled since 1997, a testament to both the improved caliber of student as well as increased institutional support.

There are 150 majors on tap across seven freshman-admitting undergraduate colleges, but all students are subjected to the same twenty-three-credit Diversified Core as well as fifteen credits worth of Designated Themes. Those combined thirty-seven credits include forays into the art/humanities, social sciences, physical sciences, mathematics, literature, and history. More targeted topics include civic life and ethics, diversity and social justice in the US, the environment, global perspectives, and technology and society. All freshmen also must take a first-year writing course and one other course designated as "writing intensive" later in their educational journey. Students in the university's Honors Program must complete eight honors courses and a culminating senior thesis.

Despite a massive number of graduate students, this school generally keeps class sizes in check. A 17:1 student-to-faculty ratio is deployed effectively so that 64 percent of sections enroll twenty-nine or fewer students. On the other end of the spectrum, 20 percent of courses enroll fifty or more students, so you can expect some highly impersonal lecture-based introductory courses while in the Twin Cities. No matter your field of study, you can utilize UM's well-maintained database of upcoming faculty research projects as a way to connect directly with the professor of your choice. In the summer of 2018, more than 250 undergraduates participated in a campus-wide undergraduate research program. An outstanding 34 percent of UMTC students study abroad during their academic career with the most popular destinations being Spain, Italy, France, the United Kingdom, and Germany.

The most commonly conferred degrees at the university are in biology (12 percent), engineering (11 percent), social sciences (11 percent), business/marketing (10 percent), psychology (7 percent), and computer science (6 percent). The College of Science and Engineering and the Carlson School of Management have strong national reputations and offer top-ranked programs in accounting, business, and every branch of engineering. The quality of the chemistry, economics, psychology, and political science departments is also well-known by elite graduate schools. The school's reputation also helps those applying for prestigious postgraduate scholarships. Nine students won Fulbright Scholarships in 2019, and Minnesota also produced a number of Udall, Gilman, Critical Language, and Astronaut Scholars in recent years.

Outside the Classroom

Nine of every ten freshmen reside on the 1,200-acre Twin Cities campus in one of nine residence halls or eight apartment complexes; pretty much everyone else lives in off-campus housing as only 22 percent of the entire student body goes to sleep in university-owned domiciles. There are 3,400 students participating in Greek life, so fraternities and sororities play a fairly major role in social life. The Golden Gophers compete in twenty-three varsity sports; the most successful programs are the men's and women's ice hockey teams. Over 900 student organizations are active including nine student-run cultural centers, dozens of intramural sports, and a popular Outdoors Club. Arts and culture can be found right on campus at the school's own art, design, and natural history museums as well as the nearby Minneapolis Sculpture Garden, Guthrie Theater, Walker Art Center, and Minneapolis Institute of the Arts. Natural beauty also can be enjoyed on university grounds that contain 10,000 trees in the extensive Mississippi National River and Recreation Area, an area that also features miles of bike paths. For shopping or just hanging out, the famed Mall of America is only a fifteen-minute ride away. The Minneapolis and St. Paul campuses that together form UMTC are only three miles apart, and the best of both cities can be enjoyed from that advantageous central location.

Career Services

Instead of having one centralized career services office at the Twin Cities campus, the university has smaller offices housed within each of its undergraduate colleges. The College of Liberal Arts Career Services Office leads the way with eighteen full-time professional employees from the total of sixty-five across all colleges. That 538:1 ratio is within the average range when compared to other institutions profiled in this guidebook. However, for a school of UMTC's size, that level of support is exceptionally strong. Whether students are in the College of

Science and Engineering, the Carlson School of Management, or the School of Nursing, there will be a team of experts in the areas of career counseling, graduate/professional school advising, internship coordination, and employer relations ready to work directly on your behalf.

Career fairs are similarly segmented by discipline with annual offerings targeting those entering computer science, government, business, accounting, and health management. The College of Engineering (CSE) Career Fair draws around 3,500 students in the fall and 1,700 in the spring. The spring CSE event featured 175 companies such as Dell, Hewlett Packard, Tesla, Wells Fargo, and BAE Systems. A sampling of other career-related events in fall 2019 included a Harvard JD Admissions Information Session, a recruiting visit from Microsoft, and a staff-run Resume Writing Workshop. Having 225,000 working alumni, many of whom are local, is a huge advantage for carving out internships and other networking opportunities. The Carlson School of Management has a Long-Term Mentoring and Flash Mentoring program in which it will hand-pick a professional mentor from the business community to assist you. Between a sizable and friendly alumni base and a number of tight industry connections to Minnesota-based businesses, the Career Services Office at UMTC offers a wealth of opportunity to its undergraduates.

Professional Outcomes

The top seven companies snatching up the largest number of Gophers are all companies headquartered in the state of Minnesota: Medtronic (the largest medical device manufacturer in the world), Target, 3M, United Health Group, US Bank, Best Buy, and Cargill (the company with the highest revenue in the United States). Therefore, it is easy to see why roughly 70 percent of graduates remain in the Greater Minneapolis-St. Paul area. San Francisco, New York, Chicago, and Seattle also attract some graduates each year, and non-Minnesota-based companies like Intel, Microsoft, Amazon, Google, Apple, and Facebook all employ hundreds of Twin Cities alumni.

With 130 graduate programs in science, art, engineering, agriculture, medicine, and the humanities, the University of Minnesota retains many of its graduates as they pursue their next degrees. However, some of the top graduate programs in the country routinely welcome UM grads. For example, in 2017, alone seven architecture grads matriculated into Penn, Cornell, Columbia, and Yale. Future doctors benefit from the BA/MD program in conjunction with the University of Minnesota Medical School. The university produces 300+ applicants to medical school every year, and many go on to study within their home state but, in recent years, Gophers also have been accepted to prestigious medical institutions like Emory, the University of Wisconsin, and Columbia University.

Admission

UMTC saw 52 percent of those seeking a place in the Class of 2022 gain acceptance. Minnesota is predominately an ACT state, and 91 percent of the 2018-19 applicants submitted results from that exam, scoring a mid-50 percent range of 26-31. Those submitting SAT scores had mid-50 percent scores of 1270-1480. Half of those attending the university placed in the top 10 percent of their high school class, and 85 percent earned spots in the top quarter. The applicant pool here has grown stronger over the last decade, but admission is only slightly more competitive now than it was a decade ago.

The only factors rated as "very important" by the admissions committee are rigor of coursework, GPA, class rank, and standardized test scores. Essays, recommendations, and interviews are not considered in the process. Freshmen accepted into the University of Minnesota Twin Cities are admitted directly into one of seven undergraduate colleges. The schools requiring the highest grades and test scores are biological sciences, management, and science and engineering (CSE). In fact, the ACT range for those admitted into the CSE is 30-34 compared with the 23-28 mid-50th range for those admitted into the College of Education and Human Development. The school does offer an early action option with a November 1 deadline.

Worth Your Money?

In-state tuition of $15k and reasonable room-and-board fees make the list price approximately $29,000 for those from the Land of 10,000 Lakes. After financial and merit awards, even families making over $110,000 end up paying an average of $23,000. That makes UMTC a strong value for Minnesota teens no matter their area of academic/career pursuit. While out-of-state costs will run your four-year total bill to just under $200k, the return on investment numbers are the strongest of any school in Minnesota, including for nonresidents. The Carlson School of Management and the College of Science and Engineering are so highly regarded that a degree from either is worth a private university-level price tag.

FINANCIAL
Institutional Type: Public
In-State Tuition: $13,318
Out-of-State Tuition: $31,616
Room & Board: $10,358
Required Fees: $1,709
Books & Supplies: $1,000

Avg. Need-Based Aid: $11,360
Avg. % of Need Met: 76%

Avg. Merit-Based Aid: $5,058
% Receiving Merit-Based Aid: 19%

Avg. Cumulative Debt: $26,262
% of Students Borrowing: 57%

CAREER
Who Recruits
1. Enterprise Holdings
2. The Hertz Corporation
3. Aerotek
4. Thomson Reuters
5. Century Link

Notable Internships
1. Minnesota Timberwolves
2. Pratt & Whitney
3. U.S. State Department

Top Industries
1. Business
2. Education
3. Operations
4. Engineering
5. Research

Top Employers
1. Medtronic
2. Target
3. 3M
4. UnitedHealth Group
5. U.S. Bank

Where Alumni Work
1. Minneapolis
2. San Francisco
3. Chicago
4. New York City
5. Los Angeles

Median Earnings
College Scorecard (Early Career): $51,900
EOP (Early Career): $48,800
PayScale (Mid-Career): $104,000

RANKINGS
Forbes: 98
Money: 84
U.S. News: 70, National Universities
Wall Street Journal/THE: 95
Washington Monthly: 77, National Universities

#CollegesWorthYourMoney

University of North Carolina at Chapel Hill

Chapel Hill, North Carolina | Admissions Phone: 919-966-3621

ADMISSION
Admission Rate: 22%
Admission Rate - Men: 21%
Admission Rate - Women: 22%
EA Admission Rate: 31%
ED Admission Rate: Not Offered
Admission Rate (5-Year Trend): -5%
ED Admission Rate (5-Year Trend): Not Offered
% of Admits Attending (Yield): 45%
Transfer Admission Rate: 35%

Offered Wait List: 4,977
Accepted Wait List: 2,300
Admitted Wait List: 22

SAT Reading/Writing (Middle 50%): 640-720
SAT Math (Middle 50%): 630-750
ACT Composite (Middle 50%): 27-33
Testing Policy: ACT/SAT Required
SAT Superscore: Yes
ACT Superscore: Yes

% Graduated in Top 10% of HS Class: 78%
% Graduated in Top 25% of HS Class: 96%
% Graduated in Top 50% of HS Class: 99%

ENROLLMENT
Total Undergraduate Enrollment: 19,117
% Part-Time: 3%
% Male: 41%
% Female: 59%
% Out-of-State: 15%
% Fraternity: 20%
% Sorority: 20%
% On-Campus (Freshman): 100%
% On-Campus (All Undergraduate): 51%

% African-American: 8%
% Asian: 11%
% Hispanic: 8%
% White: 60%
% Other: 5%
% Race or Ethnicity Unknown: 4%
% International: 3%
% Low-Income: 20%

ACADEMICS
Student-to-Faculty Ratio: 13:1
% of Classes Under 20: 38%
% of Classes Under 40: 80%
% Full-Time Faculty: 72%
% Full-Time Faculty w/ Terminal Degree: 84%

Top Programs
Area Studies
Business
Chemistry
Environmental Science and Studies
Media and Journalism
Political Science
Psychology
Public Policy

Retention Rate: 97%
4-Year Graduation Rate: 82%
6-Year Graduation Rate: 90%

Curricular Flexibility: Somewhat Flexible
Academic Rating: ★★★★

Inside the Classroom

In 1789, a full thirty years before Thomas Jefferson founded UVA, our young nation's first public university was chartered. Four years later, the first cornerstone was laid smack dab in the middle of the new state of North Carolina, right next to a hill upon which sat New Hope Chapel. In that moment, simultaneously, the University of North Carolina and the town of Chapel Hill were born. Fast-forward 230 years and UNC Chapel Hill is one of the most prestigious flagship public schools in the country with 323,000+ proud alumni, the vast majority of whom were born and bred in the university's home state. That fact can be attributed to a thirty-year-old state law mandating that at least 82 percent of each freshman class be comprised of in-state students.

Massive in its scope, the lovely and affluent town of Chapel Hill is home to 19,117 undergraduates and 10,894 graduate/professional students. Undergraduates can choose from 77 bachelor's degree programs in a number of schools and colleges, the largest of which is the College of Arts & Sciences. The general education curriculum is called Making Connections and involves checking boxes in the areas of English composition and rhetoric, foreign language, quantitative reasoning, physical and life sciences, social and behavioral sciences, and the humanities and fine arts.

The student-faculty ratio is 13:1, and few courses are held in giant lecture halls; 88 percent of classes have fewer than fifty students. However, you won't have many intimate, seminar-style courses as part of your undergraduate education as only 38 percent of classes have a student enrollment under twenty. UNC sends more than one-third of graduates abroad to one of seventy countries at some point in their educational career. For a school of such massive size, an impressive 60 percent of students end up completing some type of research experience as undergraduates.

The social sciences (17 percent), media/journalism (9 percent), biology (9 percent), psychology (8 percent), business (7 percent), and parks and recreation (6 percent) are the areas in which the most degrees are conferred. The Kenan-Flager Business School is internationally renowned and requires separate admission through UNC's Assured Admission program or through an application process following freshman year. Other strong programs include those in chemistry, journalism, psychology, and political science. However, an undergraduate degree of nearly any kind from UNC will open doors in the world of employment as well as for those seeking entrance into top graduate programs around the country. In its illustrious history, UNC-Chapel Hill has produced forty-nine Rhodes Scholars and thirty-eight Luce Scholars. In 2018, ten were named Fulbright Scholars, the tenth highest total among public research universities. It also has a high rate of success in helping students procure NSF Graduate Research Fellowships.

Outside the Classroom

The University of North Carolina-Chapel Hill requires that all freshmen live in one of the school's thirty-two residence halls. However, only 51 percent of the total undergraduate population lives on campus while many others live in apartments/houses in Chapel Hill or surrounding Durham or Carrboro. Still, there are many unifying experiences that bring the campus together, none more so than UNC men's basketball. Nothing short of a local religion, it sees 22,000 pack the Dean Smith Center to root for the Tar Heels; games against rival Duke are an unforgettable experience. In sum, there are twenty-eight varsity sports teams as well as a robust network of fifty club and intramural sports. One-fifth of UNC undergrads join a fraternity or sorority, but Greek life at UNC is unusually diverse, inclusive, and service oriented. On average, its students collectively contribute 35,000 hours of community service per year. More than 800 student activities are running on the Chapel Hill campus, highlighted by the popular twenty-four-hour UNC Dance Marathon fundraiser, an involved student government, a host of cultural and professional organizations, and the widely read Daily Tar Heel, which has a distribution of 20,000.

Career Services

UNC's University Career Services Office employs fifteen full-time staff members, excluding individuals who work as administrative assistants or in IT, who work with undergraduates. That equates to a student-to-advisor ratio of 1,274:1, well below average compared to the other institutions included in this book. Other schools within the larger university do have smaller career services offices, but they primarily serve graduate students. Despite less-than-ideal personnel numbers, the staff does create solid outcomes for graduates.

Career fairs draw 600+ companies to campus per year. An impressive 297 companies recruited on campus in 2017-18 and conducted 4,238 job interviews with undergraduates. Almost 200 employers held information sessions in Chapel Hill. The Carolina Career Partners Program helps connect local companies to undergraduate job candidates. Of those students directly entering the world of employment, 80 percent landed at least one internship while at UNC and, in one-third of those cases, the internship eventually led to a job with that same organization. All of the basic career services—resume assistance, practice interviews, 1:1 career counseling, and job and internship postings through Handshake—are available to undergraduates.

University of North Carolina at Chapel Hill

E-mail: unchelp@admissions.unc.edu | Website: www.unc.edu

Professional Outcomes

Six months after leaving Chapel Hill, 97 percent of the Class of 2018 had entered employment, military service, or graduate school; only 3 percent were still seeking employment. Among the for-profit companies who hire the most graduates are Wells Fargo, IBM, Cisco, Deloitte, EY, Google, Microsoft, Amazon, Oracle, Facebook, McKinsey & Company, and Goldman Sachs. In the nonprofit sector, a large number of Tar Heels are snatched up by the AmeriCorps, NIH, Teach for America, and the Peace Corps. A sizable 56 percent of 2018 graduates hung their diplomas somewhere in the state of North Carolina while 15 percent headed elsewhere in the Southeast, 12 percent to the Northeast, and 4 percent traveled to the Pacific Coast. The average starting salary for members of the Class of 2018 was $50,000, lower than the 2017 figure of $57,000. A dozen years after graduating, alumni take home the fourth-highest median salary of any North Carolina institution.

In a typical graduating class, one-quarter of students enroll directly in graduate/professional school. Some of the most commonly attended graduate schools are other Carolina-based institutions such as East Carolina University, Appalachian State, UNC-Greensboro, or—on the elite/local front—Duke and Wake Forest. Other prestigious schools frequented by UNC alums include Columbia and Harvard. UNC-Chapel Hill had 496 applicants to medical school in 2019, the eighth highest total in the nation. Recent graduates have gone on to study medicine at institutions such as Harvard Medical School, Duke University School of Medicine, UNC School of Medicine, and the Wake Forest School of Medicine.

Admission

Gaining admission into UNC-Chapel Hill is a completely different ballgame for North Carolina residents than it is for those hailing from any of the other forty-nine states or a foreign country. In-state applicants for admission into the Class of 2022 had a 41 percent success rate; all others faced harsher competition as the overall acceptance rate was only 22 percent. While many other flagship state institutions such as Michigan, Wisconsin, and UVA have substantially increased their number of non-residents in recent years, UNC has does not have the authority to follow suit as out-of-state enrollment is capped at 18 percent.

Of those who enrolled, the middle 50 percent SAT range was 1270-1470 and 27-33 on the ACT. Over three-quarters of enrolled students placed in the top 10 percent of their high school class, and 14 percent were either the valedictorian or salutatorian. In addition to high grades, test scores, and placement toward the top of your class, the UNC admissions committee considers a number of other factors to be of highest importance: test scores, essays, recommendations, extracurricular activities, talent/ability, character/personal qualities and, of course, state residency. While in-state applicants need to be strong in all of those areas, out-of-state applicants need to be exceptional, well above the mean. In sum, the fork in the residency road sends applicants down two significantly different admissions gauntlets. For out-of-staters, higher standardized test scores and/or a "hook" can help to set you apart. In-state applicants with in-range credentials have a much friendlier but still selective process awaiting them.

Worth Your Money?

One of the most incredible bargains in all of American higher education, residents of the Tar Heel State pay less than $10k in tuition and only $23,476 in annual cost of attendance. Those from out of state pay around $50k per year, not a bad price for an education at one of the premier universities in the country. UNC-Chapel Hill only grants merit aid to 6 percent of the student body, a small percentage compared to other UNC campuses (e.g., Greensboro grants aid to 62 percent). However, UNC-Chapel Hill is, by leaps and bounds, the most generous UNC school when it comes to need-based aid. The university grants an average annual award of $16,243 to those it declares eligible, meeting 100 percent of the demonstrated need for the vast majority. Whether you are headed to Chapel Hill as a resident or out-of-stater, you will get your money's worth.

FINANCIAL
Institutional Type: Public
In-State Tuition: $7,019
Out-of-State Tuition: $34,198
Room & Board: $11,526
Required Fees: $2,027
Books & Supplies: $972

Avg. Need-Based Aid: $16,243
Avg. % of Need Met: 100%

Avg. Merit-Based Aid: $10,812
% Receiving Merit-Based Aid: 6%

Avg. Cumulative Debt: $22,466
% of Students Borrowing: 40%

CAREER
Who Recruits
1. Greystar
2. Lincoln Financial Group
3. PNC Bank
4. Comcast
5. Fidus Investments

Notable Internships
1. Vanguard
2. Adobe
3. The Walt Disney Company

Top Industries
1. Business
2. Education
3. Healthcare
4. Research
5. Operations

Top Employers
1. Wells Fargo
2. IBM
3. Cisco
4. Deloitte
5. EY

Where Alumni Work
1. Raleigh-Durham, NC
2. Charlotte
3. Winston-Salem, NC
4. New York City
5. Washington, DC

Median Earnings
College Scorecard (Early Career): $55,600
EOP (Early Career): $54,200
PayScale (Mid-Career): $100,800

RANKINGS
Forbes: 45
Money: 52
U.S. News: 29 (T), National Universities
Wall Street Journal/THE: 33
Washington Monthly: 22, National Universities

#CollegesWorthYourMoney

University of Notre Dame

Notre Dame, Indiana | Admissions Phone: 574-631-7505

Inside the Classroom

As iconic for its educational quality as for its storied gridiron glory, Notre Dame is the dream destination for Catholic students with Ivy-level academic qualifications. Four-fifths of the 8,400 undergraduate students possess a Catholic religious identity, reinforcing the school's values and traditions. Academically, a robust selection of seventy-five majors are offered across six undergraduate colleges: the School of Architecture, the College of Arts and Letters, the Mendoza School of Business, the College of Engineering, the Keough School of Global Affairs, and the College of Science (that includes a premed track).

Required coursework is comprehensive and includes four courses covering Catholic theology and philosophy. The Moreau First Year Experience is a two-semester course designed to help freshmen "integrate their academic, co-curricular, and residential experiences." Freshmen also take University Seminar, one of two writing-intensive courses mandated by the school. Six additional mandatory liberal arts courses assure that students at least dip their toes into the study of quantitative reasoning, science and technology, history, literature, and the social sciences.

A solid 62 percent of courses enroll fewer than twenty students, and 19 percent have single-digit numbers. Just under 10 percent of courses have an enrollment of more than fifty undergrads. A 10:1 student-to-faculty ratio is top notch and also represents an improvement over the 12:1 ratio of a decade ago. The Center for Undergraduate Scholarly Engagement offers hundreds of opportunities for conducting research, both individually and alongside faculty; one-third of graduates ultimately partake. One of the top universities for study abroad participation, 75 percent of Notre Dame undergrads select one of seventy-six programs in twenty-nine countries. The satisfaction rate for study abroad experiences is 93 percent.

The top six degrees conferred are computer science, mechanical engineering, sociology, international economics, marketing, and anthropology. Mendoza has a reputation as one of the country's best business schools and, to a slightly lesser extent, the College of Engineering often ranks highly on "best of" lists as well. Prestigious fellowships are won by the Irish in droves. After collecting twenty-six Fulbrights in 2018 and twenty-nine in 2017, it is one of the top producers in the whole United States. The National Science Foundation granted honors to twenty-three students and alumni in 2018, including twelve NSF Graduate Research Fellowships. The list goes on and on with five students winning Gilman Scholarships last year while others took home Gates Cambridge, Critical Language, and Truman Scholarships.

Outside the Classroom

Every single freshman and 80 percent of sophomores, juniors, and seniors live in one of the school's thirty residence halls. The focus of spiritual and recreational life, the residence halls serve a major role on a campus that is free of sororities and fraternities. Notre Dame also has no athletic program...just kidding! Sports are a way of life at the home of the Fighting Irish, whether you are a member or mere fan of one of the twenty-three NCAA Division I teams. Of course, the famed football program has a tradition unlike any other, and 81,000 pack the stands of Notre Dame Stadium each fall Saturday to cheer for the eleven-time national champions. One of the best intramural programs in the country and extensive recreational facilities ensure widespread athletic participation; the outdoor five-on-five basketball tournament draws 700 participating teams each year. If it's not sports, Irish men and women are engaged in some other meaningful activity; there are more than 500 student-run organizations active at the school. The 1,250-acre campus is as scenic as they come and includes two beautiful lakes, one famous golden dome, and all of the lush foliage one can absorb. South Bend is not a small college town but a city with a population of over 300,000. Within the immediate vicinity of campus are over fifty restaurants, seventy shops, and four museums. The beaches of Lake Michigan are sixty miles away, and Chicago is roughly a ninety-mile trip.

Career Services

The Center for Career Development (CCD) is staffed by twenty-six professional employees who work in career advising, employer relations, or event coordination and who impact undergraduate students (additional career services branches aimed at graduate students were not included in this figure). That equates to a 330:1 student-to-advisor ratio, which is in the average range when compared with other schools featured in this guide, but it is much stronger than most schools of Notre Dame's size. In short, this office works hard on behalf of its students, bringing to mind the classic Lou Holtz line, "No one has ever drowned in sweat."

More than three-quarters of students participate in at least one internship during their undergraduate years. Career fairs are attended by 450+ employers annually, including many major corporations known for employing large numbers of Fighting Irish alumni. Overall, more than 500 companies conduct approximately 7,000 job interviews on campus each academic year. The building in which the CCD is housed features forty-five interview/meeting rooms that have seen their fair share of "welcome aboard" handshakes. An alumni base 135,000 strong, many of whom have attained leadership positions in the field, are eagerly awaiting an opportunity to help current students and graduating seniors. Having one of the most connected, passionate, and loyal alumni networks in your corner is no small advantage. Tremendous corporate connections and graduate school/employment results for recent grads led to the Notre Dame CCD receiving high marks from our staff.

Professional Outcomes

A spectacular 98 percent of Notre Dame graduates are employed within six months of completing their degrees. Of the 65 percent who directly enter the world of employment, the most common industries are financial services (17 percent), consulting (13 percent), technology (8 percent), accounting (7 percent), and health services (6 percent). Massive numbers of alumni can be found in the offices of some of the nation's most desirable private employers including Deloitte, EY, PwC, IBM, Accenture, Booz Allen Hamilton, Google, Microsoft, Amazon, Goldman Sachs, JP Morgan, and McKinsey & Co. With so many entering the world's top finance/accounting/consulting firms, it isn't shocking that early career salaries tend to be high; as of 2018 the median figure was $59,000, a mark that is 32 percent higher than the national average for college grads. The highest concentration of alumni can be found in the Greater Chicago area followed by the Greater New York City area, South Bend itself, DC, San Francisco, and Boston.

Of the 22 percent of first-year alums who went directly into their graduate/professional studies, 23 percent were pursuing medical degrees, and 10 percent were studying law. Medical school applicants had a much higher rate of success than the national average; the Irish acceptance rate generally hovers around 80 percent. Class of 2018 members went on to attend institutions such as Harvard Medical School, Indiana University School of Medicine, Icahn School of Medicine at Mt. Sanai, Medical College of Wisconsin, and Albert Einstein Medical College. Presently, Notre Dame graduates can be found at some of the nation's top law schools such as Columbia, Duke, Harvard, Notre Dame, Boston College, UVA, and the University of Chicago. Those attending graduate schools for other fields can be found at comparably elite institutions all over the globe.

Admission

Of the 20,371 applicants to the Class of 2022 only 3,608 were accepted. The yield rate—admitted applicants who enrolled—was an impressively high 57 percent. Notre Dame hopefuls will need to finish at the very top of their high school class, and we don't just mean in the top decile. A hard-to-fathom 40 percent of accepted students hailed from the top 1 percent of the class, 50 percent were in the top 5 percent, and the median high school rank was in the top 2 percent. In total, 89 percent of accepted students placed in the top 10 percent. The SAT mid-50 percent range has reached similarly intimidating heights; it currently sits at 1400-1550. The ACT, which is submitted by 60 percent of applicants, has a mid-50 percent composite range of 33-35.

The admissions committee rates rigor of secondary coursework above all other factors. Class rank, GPA, standardized test scores, recommendations, essays, extracurricular activities, and talent/ability are all "important." Religious affiliation does matter at Notre Dame as 80 percent of admits identify as Catholic. Being a legacy applicant can help—22 percent of incoming 2018-19 freshmen were children of alumni. Both religious affiliation and legacy status are factors "considered" by the committee. The Fighting Irish do not offer early decision. Thanks to the extraordinary yield rate mentioned above, Notre Dame has no need to obtain binding commitments from prospective students. In recent years, the admissions standards at Notre Dame have approached Ivy League levels. Ten years ago, the acceptance rate was a much friendlier 27 percent, and the 25th percentile SAT mark was a full eighty points lower than it is today. Those with serious ambitions to spend four years in South Bend need to be in the top 1-2 percent in both academic performance and standardized test scores. Otherwise, you'll find yourself in the Rudy Ruettiger category as a long shot.

Worth Your Money?

Notre Dame has a high cost of attendance at over $73,000 per year. However, this is a school that funnels undergrads into high-paying jobs and top professional schools, leading to high lifetime earnings and the expansion and enhancement of one's personal and professional networks. The university does grant an average of $22k in merit aid to 17 percent of the student body and meets the full financial need of 48 percent of all undergraduates. Those receiving need-based aid receive an average annual grant of $40,098, helping to make the school a very worthy investment and accessible to students from all socioeconomic backgrounds.

FINANCIAL
Institutional Type: Private
In-State Tuition: $55,046
Out-of-State Tuition: $55,046
Room & Board: $15,640
Required Fees: $507
Books & Supplies: $1,050

Avg. Need-Based Aid: $40,098
Avg. % of Need Met: 100%

Avg. Merit-Based Aid: $21,626
% Receiving Merit-Based Aid: 17%

Avg. Cumulative Debt: $27,686
% of Students Borrowing: 42%

CAREER
Who Recruits
1. Salesforce
2. Boston Consulting Group
3. Facebook
4. JPMorgan Chase
5. McKinsey & Co.

Notable Internships
1. Saks Fifth Avenue
2. Citizens Bank
3. Citadel Securities

Top Industries
1. Business
2. Education
3. Operations
4. Finance
5. Research

Top Employers
1. Deloitte
2. EY
3. PwC
4. IBM
5. Accenture

Where Alumni Work
1. Chicago
2. New York City
3. South Bend, IN
4. Washington, DC
5. San Francisco

Median Earnings
College Scorecard (Early Career): $78,400
EOP (Early Career): $78,800
PayScale (Mid-Career): $130,500

RANKINGS
Forbes: 18
Money: 30
U.S. News: 15 (T), National Universities
Wall Street Journal/THE: 32
Washington Monthly: 30, National Universities

#CollegesWorthYourMoney

University of Pennsylvania

Philadelphia, Pennsylvania | Admissions Phone: 215-898-7507

ADMISSION
Admission Rate: 8%
Admission Rate - Men: 8%
Admission Rate - Women: 9%
EA Admission Rate: Not Offered
ED Admission Rate: 19%
Admission Rate (5-Year Trend): -4%
ED Admission Rate (5-Year Trend): -6%
% of Admits Attending (Yield): 67%
Transfer Admission Rate: 8%

Offered Wait List: 3,535
Accepted Wait List: 2,561
Admitted Wait List: 9

SAT Reading/Writing (Middle 50%): 700-760
SAT Math (Middle 50%): 740-800
ACT Composite (Middle 50%): 32-35
Testing Policy: ACT/SAT Required
SAT Superscore: Yes
ACT Superscore: Yes

% Graduated in Top 10% of HS Class: 96%
% Graduated in Top 25% of HS Class: 99%
% Graduated in Top 50% of HS Class: 100%

ENROLLMENT
Total Undergraduate Enrollment: 10,183
% Part-Time: 2%
% Male: 48%
% Female: 52%
% Out-of-State: 81%
% Fraternity: 30%
% Sorority: 28%
% On-Campus (Freshman): 100%
% On-Campus (All Undergraduate): 51%

% African-American: 9%
% Asian: 23%
% Hispanic: 11%
% White: 48%
% Other: 5%
% Race or Ethnicity Unknown: 4%
% International: 16%
% Low-Income: 15%

ACADEMICS
Student-to-Faculty Ratio: 6:1
% of Classes Under 20: 71%
% of Classes Under 40: 90%
% Full-Time Faculty: 77%
% Full-Time Faculty w/ Terminal Degree: 100%

Top Programs
Business
Cognitive Science
Communication
Computer Science
Engineering
English
Philosophy
Political Science

Retention Rate: 98%
4-Year Graduation Rate: 85%
6-Year Graduation Rate: 95%

Curricular Flexibility: Somewhat Flexible
Academic Rating: ★★★★★

Inside the Classroom

Once known for its insecurity over being frequently confused with Penn State and having a reputation in snooty circles as a "second-tier Ivy," the University of Pennsylvania in 2020 has long since brushed that dirt off its shoulders. Today, Penn boasts twice as many applicants as a decade ago and, with an 8.4 percent acceptance rate that is lower than Dartmouth's, it is now a dream destination for many of the brightest students around the world—and we mean *world*. Penn admits the highest percentage of international students of any Ivy by a wide margin. The 10,100+ Quaker undergrads on campus in 2018-19 are pursuing ninety distinct degrees across four schools: the College of Arts & Sciences, the College of Applied Science and Engineering, the College of Nursing and, of course, arguably the top business school anywhere—Wharton.

The Core Curriculum at UPenn is based on seven Sectors of Knowledge: society, history and tradition, arts and letters, humanities and social sciences, the living world, the physical world, and natural sciences and mathematics. In fulfilling those requirements students take mandatory courses in foreign language, writing (seminar), quantitative data analysis, formal reasoning, cross-cultural analysis, and diversity in the United States. The greatest number of students pursue degrees in business (20 percent), social sciences (15 percent), biology (11 percent), engineering (10 percent), and computer science (5 percent).

Penn has a 6:1 student-to-faculty ratio, but with a focus on research and 15,626 graduate students, not every undergraduate section is a tiny seminar. However, the university does boast an exceptional 30 percent of courses with an enrollment under ten and 71 percent with an enrollment under twenty—quite an achievement for a school of Penn's massive size. It also offers multiple ways for undergrads to conduct research, whether through independent studies or working side-by-side with faculty members. It is a testament to its focus in this area that the university publishes eleven distinct journals featuring original undergraduate research. Penn ranks first among Ivies and fourteenth among doctoral-granting institutions in study abroad participation rate; each year over 2,300 students head off to earn a semester's credit in one of eighty-five countries.

While Wharton is the ultimate name-drop, the Penn engineering program garners a more quiet respect. Outstanding programs abound throughout the university, in fields ranging from computer science to philosophy. Graduates of UPenn are, in general, met with high-paying jobs at desirable companies and entry into the best graduate and professional schools in existence. Prestigious national scholarship and fellowship programs adore Penn grads just the same. In 2017, two Penn grads won Rhodes Scholarships and another captured the distinguished award in 2019. Last year, the school produced thirty-four Fulbright Scholars, three Schwarzman Scholars, two Truman Scholars, and forty-one National Science Foundation Graduate Research Fellowships.

Outside the Classroom

Only 52 percent of students live in university-owned housing at Penn as 71 percent of juniors and 78 percent of seniors elect to live off campus. One reason for the lack of upperclassman interest in dorms is the popular Greek system that attracts over one-quarter of undergrads into one of fifty frat and sorority houses. The Quakers compete in thirty-three NCAA Division I sports in the Ivy League; over 1,000 members of the student body are varsity athletes. Many more participate in club and intramural athletics. There are multiple fitness centers including a 120,000-square-foot facility that includes an Olympic-size swimming pool, rock climbing wall, and sauna. The school also hosts the Penn Relays, the longest-running collegiate track meet in the country that draws 100,000 spectators annually. With 450+ student organizations active at Penn, there is a group that caters to wherever your talents and interests lie, whether that is in the performance, community service, or cultural identity realms. The school's newspaper, the Daily Pennsylvanian, has a staff of 250 students and has garnered many awards. Penn's West Philly campus is comprised of 215 buildings on 299 attached acres and contains plenty of green space. The urban setting affords students the benefits of walkability and easy trips to any part of the fifth-largest city in the United States.

Career Services

The University of Pennsylvania's Career Services Office has thirty professional staff members who are dedicated to undergraduate counseling, on-campus recruiting, and maintaining digital resources like Handshake. The 354:1 student-to-advisor ratio is average compared to other schools featured in this guide but strong for a school of Penn's size. Close to twenty annual career fairs are held, some of which are industry specific (engineering, finance, nursing) while others are themed such as the Common Good Career Fair; the Creative Career Fair; or the Startup, VC, and Data Analytics Fair.

Rising sophomores, juniors, and seniors find themselves in paid internships at some the world's top employers in droves. To quantify that, Class of 2018 members, between their junior and senior year, found positions at a 90 percent clip, including twenty-two at Goldman Sachs, twenty-one at Morgan Stanley, and nine at Google. Penn also excels at facilitating on-campus interviews; more than 300 companies conduct interviews on campus each year. Individualized attention is always available in the form of thirty-minute counseling appointments.

The office recommends a progression of exploration/involvement/experience/transition as undergraduates rise through their four years, and the university puts loads of resources into supporting all four phases. Ample support is also provided for those applying to medical, law, or graduate school. An equal emphasis on large-scale events such as industry-specific job fairs and one-on-one counseling leads to phenomenal graduate outcomes (more ahead).

Professional Outcomes

Seventy-two percent of Class of 2018 Quaker grads were employed six months following degree completion, another 18 percent were in graduate school, and 5 percent were still planning their next educational/career move. Finance was the sector attracting the highest percentage of grads (27 percent) followed by consulting (19 percent), technology (14 percent), and health care (7 percent). Employers hiring the greatest number of 2018 graduates included Goldman Sachs (27), Deloitte (26), JPMorgan (25), McKinsey & Company (23), Google (22), IBM (21), Capital One (20), Children's Hospital of Philadelphia (18), and Bain & Company (12). The median starting salary for all graduates is just shy of $75,000 plus an average sign-on bonus of $13,000. Among elite colleges, Penn alumni enjoy the highest midcareer salaries of any school except MIT. Unsurprisingly, the Philadelphia Metro area has the strongest concentration of alumni, but New York is a close second. San Francisco and DC also have a strong Quaker presence.

For those continuing their educational journeys, the most popular move is to remain at Penn—107 members of the Class of 2018 made that decision. The next most attended graduate schools were Columbia (15), Harvard (10), University of California (10), Oxford (8), and Yale (7). Students gain acceptance to medical school at a terrific rate—78 percent versus the national average of 43 percent. Medical schools that have taken more than five Penn grads since 2016-17 include Emory University, Temple University, Harvard Medical School, the Icahn School of Medicine at Mt. Sinai, and Penn's own uber-elite Perelman School of Medicine that sports a 4 percent acceptance rate. The acceptance rate into law school is 84 percent, which is made lower by the fact that the vast majority are aiming for top-tier schools. The most attended law schools is recent years are NYU School of Law, Penn Law School, Fordham University School of Law, Columbia University School of Law, and Harvard Law School.

Admission

Penn received close to 45,000 applications for a place in the Class of 2022, the second highest figure of any Ivy League university behind Cornell. In admitting only 3,731 prospective students (8.4 percent), 2018 was the most selective year in Penn history. The middle-50 percent SAT range for enrolled freshmen was 1420-1570, and the middle-50 percent ACT range was 32-35; similar numbers of students submitted results from each test. A nearly unanimous 96 percent of admitted Quakers earned a place in the top decile of their graduating high school class, and 85 percent possessed a GPA of 3.75 or higher on a 4.0 scale. In the past decade, the average admitted applicant's SAT scores have increased by around fifty points, and the grades/class rank have stayed the same. Back then, the school received half as many applications, and the acceptance rate was a far more forgiving 18 percent.

According to the admissions committee, rigor of secondary school record, GPA, standardized test scores, essays, recommendations, and character/personal qualities are deemed "very important" to the evaluative process. Factors classified as "important" are class rank, the interview, extracurricular activities, and talent/ability. One in seven 2018-19 freshmen were the first in their families to attend college. More than 1,300 students were admitted via early decision; the ED round saw an 18.5 percent acceptance rate, and more than half of the Class of 2022 was filled by those welcomed through a binding early acceptance. As is the case with so many top-shelf elite institutions, Penn rejects more students than ever, including thousands of teens who would have waltzed into the university a generation ago. Applying ED is a no-brainer if you want to gain a slight edge.

Worth Your Money?

Penn's total cost of attendance is $77,000+ per year and, unless you qualify for need-based financial aid, that is the price you will pay because the university does not award merit aid. It does, however, meet 100 percent of demonstrated need for all eligible students (46 percent of undergrads), awarding annual grants averaging $49k. Even if you are required to pay the full sticker price, Penn's starting salaries are such that even substantial loans will not be crippling to the vast majority of grads.

FINANCIAL
Institutional Type: Private
In-State Tuition: $51,156
Out-of-State Tuition: $51,156
Room & Board: $16,190
Required Fees: $6,614
Books & Supplies: $1,358

Avg. Need-Based Aid: $48,798
Avg. % of Need Met: 100%

Avg. Merit-Based Aid: $0
% Receiving Merit-Based Aid: 0%

Avg. Cumulative Debt: $22,103
% of Students Borrowing: 24%

CAREER
Who Recruits
1. Children's Hospital of Philadelphia
2. Teach for America
3. Facebook
4. Boston Consulting Group
5. JPMorgan Chase

Notable Internships
1. Pfizer
2. Gensler
3. HBO

Top Industries
1. Business
2. Education
3. Research
4. Operations
5. Social Services

Top Employers
1. Google
2. Amazon
3. Microsoft
4. Goldman Sachs
5. Facebook

Where Alumni Work
1. Philadelphia
2. New York City
3. San Francisco
4. Washington, DC
5. Boston

Median Earnings
College Scorecard (Early Career): $85,900
EOP (Early Career): $91,800
PayScale (Mid-Career): $133,900

RANKINGS
Forbes: 6
Money: 32
U.S. News: 6 (T), National Universities
Wall Street Journal/THE: 4
Washington Monthly: 6, National Universities

#CollegesWorthYourMoney

University of Pittsburgh – Pittsburgh Campus

Pittsburgh, Pennsylvania | Admissions Phone: 412-624-7488

ADMISSION
Admission Rate: 59%
Admission Rate - Men: 59%
Admission Rate - Women: 60%
EA Admission Rate: Not Offered
ED Admission Rate: Not Offered
Admission Rate (5-Year Trend): +5%
ED Admission Rate (5-Year Trend): Not Offered
% of Admits Attending (Yield): 23%
Transfer Admission Rate: 51%

Offered Wait List: 1,664
Accepted Wait List: 576
Admitted Wait List: 24

SAT Reading/Writing (Middle 50%): 630-700
SAT Math (Middle 50%): 640-730
ACT Composite (Middle 50%): 28-33
Testing Policy: ACT/SAT Required
SAT Superscore: Yes
ACT Superscore: Yes

% Graduated in Top 10% of HS Class: 55%
% Graduated in Top 25% of HS Class: 88%
% Graduated in Top 50% of HS Class: 99%

ENROLLMENT
Total Undergraduate Enrollment: 19,330
% Part-Time: 5%
% Male: 48%
% Female: 52%
% Out-of-State: 29%
% Fraternity: 9%
% Sorority: 11%
% On-Campus (Freshman): 96%
% On-Campus (All Undergraduate): 43%

% African-American: 5%
% Asian: 10%
% Hispanic: 4%
% White: 69%
% Other: 4%
% Race or Ethnicity Unknown: 1%
% International: 5%
% Low-Income: 16%

ACADEMICS
Student-to-Faculty Ratio: 14:1
% of Classes Under 20: 45%
% of Classes Under 40: 76%
% Full-Time Faculty: 77%
% Full-Time Faculty w/ Terminal Degree: 94%

Top Programs
Biology
Biomedical Engineering
Business
Chemistry
English
Neuroscience
Philosophy
Psychology

Retention Rate: 93%
4-Year Graduation Rate: 65%
6-Year Graduation Rate: 83%

Curricular Flexibility: Somewhat Flexible
Academic Rating: ★★★✓

Inside the Classroom

A generation ago you wouldn't see many teens from outside Pennsylvania clamoring to attend the University of Pittsburgh. In fact, for everyone other than western Pennsylvania residents, Penn State was the clear number one public university in the Keystone State. Fast-forwarding to today, Pitt attracts undergraduates from all fifty states and 102 countries. The home of the Panthers has ascended to the status of a premier public research university, and its 19,330 undergraduate students possess near-perfect transcripts and average standardized scores in the 90th percentile. Those in the Swanson School of Engineering sport SATs in the 97th percentile, and the top-ranked Honors College requires 99th percentile and above. In 2020, Pitt has become a true dream destination for massive numbers of high-achieving teens.

The university takes great care in welcoming new students to campus and ensuring a smooth transition. First-year mentors are available to help orient new students to campus life. Academic Foundations is a one-credit course that serves as an insiders' guide to Pitt, and first-year seminar classes are centered on a theme of interest with a capped enrollment of nineteen students. Pitt admits freshmen to the Dietrich School of Arts & Sciences, the College of Business Administration, the Swanson School of Engineering, and the School of Nursing. Across all undergraduate schools the university grants 104 distinct undergraduate degrees. Core coursework is mandated as follows: composition, two writing-intensive classes, algebra, quantitative and formal reasoning, two second language courses, and a class with a diversity designation. A total of nine courses in the humanities, social sciences, and natural sciences are required for all Dietrich School of Arts & Sciences students.

For a large public university, Pitt has a strong 14:1 student-to-faculty ratio and, as a result, it offers many smaller course sections to go along with some classes in large lecture halls. Forty-five percent of sections have an enrollment under twenty students, and 63 percent are capped at twenty-nine students. Plenty of personal connection with professors is available to those who seek it. Undergraduate research opportunities are granted to a healthy 52 percent of students. There are 350 study abroad programs in seventy-five countries, and many take advantage; the participation rate in the College of Business Administration is 55 percent.

The University of Pittsburgh is respected nationally by both top companies and prestigious graduate/professional institutions. Its engineering and business schools are rated top fifty in most rankings and are among the most commonly chosen fields of study. Pre-med offerings are also top-notch, with majors in the health professions, biology, and psychology rounding out the list of most popular majors. Pitt grads are no strangers to nationally competitive scholarships. In the last five years the school has produced forty-six Fulbright winners, seven Goldwater Scholars, two Churchill Scholars, and one Truman Scholar.

Outside the Classroom

A 132-acre urban campus houses 43 percent of the school's undergraduate student population. The Oakland neighborhood where the school is located is safe, walkable, and brimming with culture and fun. The Carnegie Museums of Art and Natural History and innumerable bars and eateries, including plenty of international options, are close by. The city, often rated as one of the "most livable in America," is truly an extension of campus, but campus itself isn't too shabby either. Pitt does guarantee housing to most students for three full years, and it is currently building dorms containing thousands of additional beds. Nine percent of men and 11 percent of women join Greek life, giving it a notable but not smothering presence. There are 400+ student organizations, and popular activities include the Pitt Dance Marathon that raised over $300,000 for the Children's Hospital of Pittsburgh. Intramural sports also are popular, and seemingly everyone participates. The university boasts an award-winning Robotics & Automation Society, Hillel Chapter, Hindu Students Council, and Society for Women Engineers. Pitt is an excellent school for sports fans as its nineteen varsity teams compete at the highest levels of NCAA Division I, and the football team shares a stadium with the Steelers and attracts over 41,000 fans per game.

Career Services

There are twenty-seven full-time employees at Pitt's Career Center, housed within the Office of Student Affairs. Members of the team serve as career consultants, employer development specialists, internship coordinators, and alumni engagement specialists. The office's 716:1 student-to-advisor ratio is greater than the average school in this guidebook but not alarming for a public university of its size. In fact, the University of Pittsburgh measures up well when it comes to the raw data in the areas of student engagement and employer relations.

In the 2018-19 school year, counselors conducted 4,573 one-on-one advising sessions and booked 402 total employers to attend their Fall Career + Internship Fair that includes separate days for engineering and computer science students. In total, 474 employers recruited at Pitt last year, and 760 on-campus interviews were held. Companies recruiting on campus include EY, Amazon, Epic Systems, Lockheed Martin, Vanguard, Cigna, and Deloitte. Tight employer partnerships led to internships being completed by 54 percent of graduates. However, those who complete the Internship Prep Program, a combination of workshops and individual appointments hosted by the Career Center, are guaranteed an internship or comparable experiential learning activity. With well-cultivated regional and national employer connections, Pitt students are given every opportunity to secure employment at a solid median starting salary or attend a graduate school consistent with their personal and professional goals. .

Professional Outcomes

Recent grads enter full-time employment at a 50 percent clip, 27 percent enter graduate or professional school on a full-time basis, and 9 percent are both employed and beginning their graduate studies. Only 5 percent are still seeking employment within a few months of receiving their degrees. Engineering, nursing, business, and information sciences majors were the most likely to be employed full time upon graduation. Those majors had 73-86 percent employment rates while other majors tended to flock to graduate school in large numbers. The employers scooping up the highest number of 2017 graduates included the University of Pittsburgh Medical Center (92), PNC (30), PricewaterhouseCoopers (12), BNY Mellon (11), and Deloitte (11). Actual panthers may be solitary creatures, but Pitt Panthers flock in notable quantities to major corporations. More than one hundred alumni presently work for Dick's Sporting Goods, Amazon, Google, Microsoft, and Uber.

Starting salaries fluctuate across the nine undergraduate schools. The median starting salary for Class of 2017 graduates of the Swanson School of Engineering was $65,000, College of Business Administration students earned $50,000, and Dietrich School of Arts & Sciences grads were paid just shy of $37,000. Pittsburgh, Philly, New York, and DC host the most alumni.

With so many fine graduate programs at the University of Pittsburgh itself, many newly minted grads stay put to continue their education. Among the Class of 2017, Pitt was the most popular graduate location by a wide margin, attracting 211 students. Next in popularity was Penn (11), Duquesne (10), Johns Hopkins (10), Penn State (10), and Temple (10). Five or more attended Columbia, UVA, Carnegie Mellon, and Boston University. Undergraduate applicants can apply to the Guaranteed Admissions Program that earns you conditional acceptance to the University of Pittsburgh School of Medicine, one of the best medical schools in the entire U.S. Recent Pitt graduates have gone on to attend law schools at George Washington University, the University of Chicago, and UVA as well as Pennsylvania-based options like Temple, Duquesne, and Pitt itself.

Admission

Pitt received 29,857 applications to join the Class of 2022 and allowed entrance to 59 percent. However, only 23 percent of accepted applicants ultimately entered the 2018-19 freshman class as many Pennsylvania residents applying to ultra-selective schools use Pitt as a safety school. However, there is nothing that comes close to screaming "safety school" when examining the academic credentials of current undergraduates. With a mid-50 percent SAT score of 1270-1430 (42 percent had math scores above 700) and a mid-50 percent ACT range of 28-33, today's Panthers are high achievers. Not to mention that 79 percent of the 2018-19 freshman class possessed a high school GPA above a 3.75; the average was a 4.01. Fifty-five percent hailed from their graduating class' top decile, and 88 percent placed in the top quartile.

At the top of the admissions office checklist are the rigor of one's courses, GPA, and standardized test scores. The essay is the only other factor ranking at or above the "important" level. There is no early action or early decision option at Pitt, so all applicants are following the same time line. The Pitt Honors College has become one of the premier honors programs in the country. SAT scores for admitted honors students are generally in the 1450-1500 range and the average GPA is 4.39. The school accepts between 300 and 400 students each year. Prior to the turn of the new millennium, Pitt was a school that would admit "B" students. Twenty years ago, only 29 percent of the entering Arts & Sciences students were top-10 percent finishers, and the average SAT in the nursing program was a 1060. Today, Pitt takes "A" students who took AP courses and registered strong standardized test scores; getting into the Honors College is like getting into an Ivy.

Worth Your Money?

Pitt's in-state annual cost of attendance is just over $34,000 per year; out of state that number climbs to over $48,000. Families making over $75,000 a year are not going to receive much need-based aid and will pay somewhere near full price. Only a sliver of incoming Panther freshmen net any merit aid at all. Based on that data, it is fair to say that Pitt is worth the price of admission for any Keystone State resident, no matter what degree you may be pursuing. There is a lot to like about Pitt for out-of-state and international students, but the cost will be high.

FINANCIAL
Institutional Type: Public
In-State Tuition: $18,628
Out-of-State Tuition: $32,656
Room & Board: $11,250
Required Fees: $1,090
Books & Supplies: $755

Avg. Need-Based Aid: $10,512
Avg. % of Need Met: 54%

Avg. Merit-Based Aid: $10,247
% Receiving Merit-Based Aid: 13%

Avg. Cumulative Debt: $39,462
% of Students Borrowing: 60%

CAREER
Who Recruits
1. American Eagle
2. Allegheny Health Network
3. FedEx
4. EPIC Systems
5. Norfolk Southern

Notable Internships
1. Boston Consulting Group
2. NASA Jet Propulsion Laboratory
3. CVS

Top Industries
1. Business
2. Education
3. Healthcare
4. Operations
5. Engineering

Top Employers
1. PNC
2. BNY Mellon
3. Deloitte
4. Dick'sSporting Goods
5. Amazon

Where Alumni Work
1. Pittsburgh
2. Philadelphia
3. New York City
4. Washington, DC
5. San Francisco

Median Earnings
College Scorecard (Early Career): $53,900
EOP (Early Career): $48,900
PayScale (Mid-Career): $100,400

RANKINGS
Forbes: 144
Money: 294
U.S. News: 57 (T), National Universities
Wall Street Journal/THE: 96 (T)
Washington Monthly: 174, National Universities

#CollegesWorthYourMoney

University of Richmond

Richmond, Virginia | Admissions Phone: 804-289-8640

Inside the Classroom

Considering that in 1861 many of the University of Richmond faculty went off to fight for the Confederacy whose capital was only miles from campus, it may come as a surprise that now the school is a diverse and progressive assemblage of young people from all fifty US states and more than seventy foreign countries. With roughly 3,200 undergraduates, the school is at once modest in size and robust in its academic and student life offerings; there are over sixty undergraduate majors at the university and many standout programs, including the one-of-a-kind Jepson School of Leadership Studies as well as a host of respected pre-professional pathways.

A distinctive general education curriculum includes a first-year seminar as well as the initial leg of a three-course wellness curriculum (the freshman course covers topics like alcohol education). From there, undergrads must demonstrate proficiency in a foreign language and then march through one course in each of historical studies, literary studies, natural sciences, social analysis, symbolic reasoning, and visual and performing arts. The list of required courses is relatively short, affording students a nice amount of academic freedom and exploration.

Don't let the "university" designation fool you; Richmond is all about undergraduate education. The student-to-faculty ratio is 8:1, the average class size is sixteen students, and not a single course is taught by a teaching assistant. Twenty-one percent of classes have single-digit enrollment numbers, and 70 percent of sections contain fewer than twenty students. Half of all Richmond students participate in an intensive research experience with a faculty member prior to graduation, and students can have those summer opportunities funded through the Richmond Guarantee that sees the university fund research apprenticeships as well as internships. More than 650 students receive such funding every summer. Going abroad is the norm at UR—59 percent take a semester or full year of study in one of seventy programs in thirty countries.

The highly regarded Robbins School of Business is responsible for granting 36 percent of the degrees conferred by the university, a staggering number that dwarfs any other field of study. The social sciences collectively attract 15 percent of the student body, and biology (premed is strong) accounts for 10 percent of degrees earned. The international relations, political science, and history departments also have excellent reputations. Applicants to prestigious fellowships fare quite well. In 2019, eight students won Fulbrights, three won Goldwater Scholarships, and one took home a Boren Scholarship.

Outside the Classroom

The University of Richmond's 350-acre campus houses 92 percent of the undergraduate population, and 97 percent live on campus all four years, creating a cohesive student body. Sixteen Greek organizations on campus rule the social scene with 30 percent of women joining sororities and 22 percent of men entering fraternity life. The Spiders compete in seventeen NCAA Division I sports within the highly competitive Atlantic Ten Conference, an astounding fact considering the size of the school's liberal arts college. There are 205 student-run organizations, including thirty club sports teams, fourteen religious groups, and seven honors societies. Intramural leagues are run out of the award-winning Weinstein Center for Recreation that contains a six-lane, twenty-five-yard swimming pool, racquetball/squash courts, and an indoor jogging track. UR's food services are regularly ranked high on lists of best college cuisine. School-run buses and shuttles make getting around a breeze. Campus is located only six miles from downtown Richmond, and longer road trips to DC (90 miles), the Atlantic Ocean, or the Blue Ridge Mountains make for an easy weekend getaway.

Career Services

The Office of Alumni and Career Services is staffed by fifteen full-time professional employees (not counting administrative coordinators) who hold positions like career advisor, employer relations coordinator, and director of experiential learning and assessment. That equates to a student-to-advisor ratio of 215:1, in the superior range when compared to the other institutions included in this book. It's no wonder that 99 percent of Richmond grads report being "generally satisfied" or "very satisfied" with their education one year after graduation, a good indicator of contentment with early career outcomes.

Richmond's career services office operates with a four-year plan that connects students to advisers during freshman year. A solid 78 percent of members of the Class of 2018 met with an advisor during their senior year. The SpiderConnect system and alumni connections help 70 percent of UR undergraduates land at least one internship during their four years of study. There are fifty+ regional alumni groups located around the United States and abroad, creating opportunities to build bridges and find mentorships in just about any major city. Career expos on campus typically attract fifty employers, and major corporations regularly travel to Richmond to recruit and interview current seniors. Spider Road Trips and Spider Shadowing are other avenues to hands-on job exploration opportunities. With strong industry connections, more-than-adequate staffing, and a number of innovative career exploration programs, the Office of Alumni and Career Services does well for its undergraduate students.

University of Richmond

E-mail: admission@richmond.edu | Website: www.richmond.edu

Professional Outcomes

One year after receiving their degrees, 95 percent of Richmond alums who are seeking employment have found jobs. The most popular sectors are financial services/insurance (13 percent), consulting (8 percent), technology (8 percent), teaching (5 percent), accounting (5 percent), and sales/business development (5 percent). Companies where you can find at least 50 Richmond alumni employed include Capital One (which employs 300+ Spiders), Deloitte, PwC, Wells Fargo, EY, Dominion Energy, Morgan Stanley, Altria, Google, and Accenture. The average salary range one year out of school is $50,000-$55,000. The majority of students remain in the Richmond area after finishing at the university, however large pockets of alumni can be found in New York City, DC, Philadelphia, and Boston. Richmond is a school with strong connections to industry in every region of the United States.

Within a year of graduation 28 percent of the Class of 2017 was already enrolled in a graduate or professional degree program. The school boasts an impressive list of recent acceptances into high-end law schools such as Harvard, Duke, the University of Chicago, Vanderbilt, Yale, UVA, and the University of Michigan. Even more notable is Richmond's success with helping students get accepted into medical school. Between 2013 and 2018 a phenomenal 73 percent of those who applied were accepted, a figure that blows away the national average. Medical schools attended by those students included Brown, Dartmouth, UNC, Stanford, Emory, and Harvard.

Admission

Of the 11,881 applicants for a place in the Class of 2022, only 3,584 were welcomed to the university, working out to an acceptance rate of 30 percent, an all-time low. The mid-50 percent standardized test scores also reached record levels of 1360-1490 on the SAT and 31-33 on the ACT. Fifty-six percent of entering freshmen hailed from the top 10 percent of their high school class, and 86 percent placed in the top quartile. Unweighted GPAs ranged from a 25th percentile 3.6 and a 75th percentile 3.96. A decade ago, 39 percent of applicants gained acceptance, and the SAT range was 1170-1370, a clear signal that Richmond has significantly increased its level of selectivity in recent years.

The admissions committee holds GPA and the rigor of one's secondary school courses as the two most important factors in evaluating an applicant. Seven categories make up the second tier of still "important" factors. Those are standardized test scores, class rank, essays, recommendations, extracurricular activities, character/personal qualities, and talent/ability. Leadership and engagement in high school is sincerely valued by this committee as the Class of 2022 included 268 athletic captains, twenty-three student government officials, and twenty-two editors-in-chief of school newspapers. Applying through early decision or early action is a good idea as the school is looking for applicants for whom Richmond is a genuine top choice. The school's yield rate is 23 percent, meaning 77 percent of admitted applicants head elsewhere. Thus, it's no wonder that 37 percent of the Class of 2022 was admitted via ED (those students enjoyed a 48 percent acceptance rate), 42 percent were admitted through nonbinding early action, and only a paltry 19 percent came through the regular cycle.

Worth Your Money?

Richmond's cost of attendance approaches $70,000, making a four-year degree list price of $280,000. Unlike many private universities, it only awards merit aid to 19 percent of the population, but those students receive a sizable discount of $30k, on average. UR focuses most of its generosity on those with true financial need, issuing average annual grants of $45,282 to 40 percent of the undergraduate student body. Further, Richmond meets 100 percent of the demonstrated need for those who qualify for financial aid. A uniquely intimate undergraduate setting and solid starting salaries (particularly for business grads) make Richmond worth your money, despite the high price tag.

FINANCIAL
Institutional Type: Private
In-State Tuition: $54,690
Out-of-State Tuition: $54,690
Room & Board: $12,900
Required Fees: $0
Books & Supplies: $1,100

Avg. Need-Based Aid: $45,282
Avg. % of Need Met: 100%

Avg. Merit-Based Aid: $30,325
% Receiving Merit-Based Aid: 19%

Avg. Cumulative Debt: $27,406
% of Students Borrowing: 43%

CAREER
Who Recruits
1. Baker Tilly
2. BB&T Corporation
3. Dominion Energy
4. John Hancock
5. MAXIMUS

Notable Internships
1. Cushman & Wakefield
2. The Cohen Group
3. Citi

Top Industries
1. Business
2. Education
3. Operations
4. Sales
5. Finance

Top Employers
1. Capital One
2. Deloitte
3. Wells Fargo
4. PwC
5. EY

Where Alumni Work
1. Richmond
2. New Yprk City
3. Washington, DC
4. Philadelphia
5. Boston

Median Earnings
College Scorecard (Early Career): $64,500
EOP (Early Career): $69,600
PayScale (Mid-Career): $107,500

RANKINGS
Forbes: 83
Money: 113
U.S. News: 23, Liberal Arts Colleges
Wall Street Journal/THE: 66
Washington Monthly: 32, Liberal Arts Colleges

#CollegesWorthYourMoney

University of Rochester

Rochester, New York | Admissions Phone: 585-275-3221

ADMISSION
Admission Rate: 29%
Admission Rate - Men: 28%
Admission Rate - Women: 31%
EA Admission Rate: Not Offered
ED Admission Rate: 51%
Admission Rate (5-Year Trend): -7%
ED Admission Rate (5-Year Trend): N/A
% of Admits Attending (Yield): 26%
Transfer Admission Rate: 23%

Offered Wait List: 3,203
Accepted Wait List: 1,750
Admitted Wait List: 6

SAT Reading/Writing (Middle 50%): 600-720
SAT Math (Middle 50%): 650-770
ACT Composite (Middle 50%): 29-33
Testing Policy: Test Optional
SAT Superscore: Yes
ACT Superscore: Yes

% Graduated in Top 10% of HS Class: 75%
% Graduated in Top 25% of HS Class: 94%
% Graduated in Top 50% of HS Class: 100%

ENROLLMENT
Total Undergraduate Enrollment: 6,535
% Part-Time: 4%
% Male: 50%
% Female: 50%
% Out-of-State: 59%
% Fraternity: 20%
% Sorority: 26%
% On-Campus (Freshman): 100%
% On-Campus (All Undergraduate): 90%

% African-American: 5%
% Asian: 11%
% Hispanic: 7%
% White: 41%
% Other: 3%
% Race or Ethnicity Unknown: 5%
% International: 26%
% Low-Income: 18%

ACADEMICS
Student-to-Faculty Ratio: 10:1
% of Classes Under 20: 74%
% of Classes Under 40: 88%
% Full-Time Faculty: 75%
% Full-Time Faculty w/ Terminal Degree: 94%

Top Programs
Biology
Business
Computer Science
Financial Economics
Mathematics
Music
Optics
Political Science

Retention Rate: 95%
4-Year Graduation Rate: 78%
6-Year Graduation Rate: 86%

Curricular Flexibility: Very Flexible
Academic Rating: ★★★★

Inside the Classroom

From its founding in 1850, the University of Rochester established a national reputation as a strong research university. The adoption of its Renaissance Plan in 1995 instituted a uniquely open curriculum for a STEM-focused university, smaller class sizes, and a heavy investment in modernizing campus. Paying dividends today, those changes helped the school blossom into a world-class school that is home to over 6,500 undergraduates and another 5,000 graduate students. U of R's seventy-five undergraduate majors offer students a chance at a rigorous yet flexible educational experience at a small liberal arts college within a renowned research institution.

There are literally no required subjects at the University of Rochester's College of Arts, Sciences, and Engineering. Instead, students must, over their four years of study, take one writing-focused course of their choosing and twelve-credit clusters of courses in two of the following categories (whichever two do not encompass the student's major): humanities, social sciences, and natural sciences and engineering. Those course clusters are designed to ensure "substantive and integrated study," and there are 250+ to choose from, ensuring a high degree of autonomy in selecting one's academic path. The overarching goal of the curriculum is to best reflect the school's ideals of curiosity, competence, and community.

Rochester has maintained a 10:1 student-to-faculty ratio despite graduating 500 more undergraduate students in 2018 than a decade prior. You will encounter some large lecture halls for introductory courses, but the most common class size is ten to nineteen students; 70 percent of sections enroll fewer than twenty. An impressive 77 percent of students are involved in undergraduate research, a strong indicator that opportunities for intimate learning experiences are plentiful. Approximately one-third of students take a semester abroad in one of the forty-five+ countries the university has an affiliation with.

Excellence is everywhere you look at Rochester. The Eastman School of Music is one of the best music conservatories in the United States. The Hajim School of Engineering & Applied Sciences is a top fifty institution. Other strong majors include mathematics, economics, and political science—each will open doors in their respective fields. And graduates are no strangers to prestigious fellowship programs. From 2016 to 2018 Rochester produced twenty Fulbright Scholarship winners, sixteen National Science Foundation Graduate Research Fellowship recipients, six Gilman Scholarship winners, and four Critical Language Scholarship recipients.

Outside the Classroom

Over three-quarters of undergrads reside in university-owned housing on the school's 154-acre main campus that is nestled around a bend of the Genesee River. First-years and sophomores are required to live on campus. The school's thirty-four fraternities and sororities entice 21 percent of the undergraduate student body into joining. Most Greek participants—85 percent—also are engaged with other student organizations. Twenty one NCAA Division III sports teams play as the YellowJackets while the university also boasts one of the largest club sports systems with forty registered club sports and over 1,100 members. There are more than 300 clubs with which undergrads can become involved including the *Campus Times*, a student-run newspaper in print since 1873 and a selection of top-notch a cappella groups. There are plenty of campus-wide events such as YellowJacket Weekend, a carnival that marks the start of the academic year, and great musical acts, speakers, and activists are regularly booked to provide cultural and entertainment opportunities without straying from school grounds. Harsh weather can make for long winters, but campus is always humming with some type of appealing activity. The closest major American city is Buffalo, but for the more adventurous, Toronto, Canada, is less than three hours by car.

Career Services

The Gwen M. Green Career Center for Career Education and Connections is staffed by fourteen professionals with expertise in career education and advising, employer development, and event coordination. That number does not include the eight peer advisors or administrative assistants. The University of Rochester's 450:1 student-to-advisor ratio is higher than the average school featured in this guide. Still, it manages to mostly achieve its stated aim of assisting students "in achieving their individual career goals while providing them with the resources and tools they need to develop connections between their aspirations, academic pursuits, and co-curricular experiences."

The Greene Center engages more than 500 organizations annually in recruiting and career education programs. The Spring Career and Internship Fair draws forty+ employers to campus including the US Department of State, Epic Systems, the FBI, Citi, and Johnson & Johnson. The center also offers regular events, typically multiple workshops and information sessions per week. Events in May 2019 alone included a CV and resume workshop, a night with Kraft Heinz leadership, and a virtual career conversation about innovation in the workplace. Staff is happy to meet one-on-one to help students select and secure an internship that will be meaningful to their career development process. A near-perfect 96 percent of YellowJackets complete at least one internship during their undergraduate years; 75 percent complete two or more. You can also apply for a $1,000 to $2,500 alumni grant to help fund a summer internship that might not otherwise be possible. There are a significant number of opportunities for students to engage with UR alumni through structured programs, networking, and courses offered by the Greene Center.

Professional Outcomes

Six months after receiving their diplomas, 95 percent of Class of 2018 grads had achieved positive outcomes with 51 percent employed, and a notably high 42 percent already pursuing an advanced degree. Popular industries included higher education (15 percent), internet and software (10 percent), health care (8 percent), and manufacturing (6 percent). Top employers of 2018 grads included Deloitte (11), Epic Systems (11), EY (9), and Google (7). Looking across all graduating years, significant numbers of Rochester alumni also can be found in the offices of Amazon, IBM, Apple, and Microsoft. The average starting salary for the most recent cohort of grads was an impressive $61,776; that figure was over $75k for graduates of the Hajim School of Engineering and close to $55k for those in the School of Arts and Sciences. Upstate New York, New York City, Boston, DC, San Francisco, and Philadelphia play home to the greatest number of alumni.

With over two-fifths of grads jumping directly into a graduate program, many continue their studies at the University of Rochester (207) or at other elite East Coast institutions such as Columbia (25), NYU (15), Cornell (13), and Boston University (12). The university has an excellent premed reputation, and acceptance rates into MD programs are significantly higher than the national average. Thanks to the Rochester Early Medical Scholars program, some premed students are already on an eight-year pathway toward the completion of a medical degree at the University's School of Medicine and Dentistry. Rochester's own medical school accepted four members of the Class of 2018, neighboring SUNY Buffalo took three, and SUNY Upstate welcomed two. Students matriculated into a wide range of law schools including top tier institutions like William & Mary, Emory, Boston University, the University of Wisconsin, and Indiana University.

Admission

The fight for a place in the Class of 2022 was record setting as it was the first time in the school's history that applications exceeded 20,000 and the acceptance rate dipped below 30 percent. Those accepted possessed an average GPA of 3.8 and an SAT score slightly above 1400. The mid-50 percent range for 2018-19 freshmen was 29-33 on the ACT and 1300-1500 on the SAT. This fall (2020), the university moves from test-flexible to test-optional. Undergraduate applicants to the college may now decide which exam, if any, is an accurate representation of their ability and potential for success.

Interviews are strongly recommended as part of this holistic admissions process that seeks to "identify curious, capable, and engaged students from across the globe." In addition to stellar grades in a highly rigorous academic program, the committee wants to see evidence of leadership through extracurricular involvement as well as strong character/personal qualities. Another all-time high of 476 students who were freshmen in 2018-19 were accepted via early decision, and the ED acceptance rate hovers around 50 percent, giving early applicants far better odds than those in the regular round. Those accepted through binding ED comprise 33 percent of the overall freshman class. In sum, Rochester has never been more difficult to get into, so there is far less room for error than there was a generation ago.

Worth Your Money?

Including tuition, fees, room and board, and other estimated expenses, the total projected cost of attendance at this school is $75,186 per year. The good news is that approximately 90 percent of those who apply for need-based aid see 100 percent of their financial need met. While a $300,000 sticker price for a bachelor's degree is steep, the majority of students receive sizable discounts via need-based or merit aid. The average net price paid by families, even those in the top income bracket, is $37,900; those in the lowest brackets paid far less. Further, significant starting salaries and corporate connections allow YellowJackets to get a running start toward financial stability. For those who know what they want from their education (i.e., certain about major and career oriented), the University of Rochester is worth your money.

FINANCIAL
Institutional Type: Private
In-State Tuition: $55,040
Out-of-State Tuition: $55,040
Room & Board: $16,548
Required Fees: $990
Books & Supplies: $1,310

Avg. Need-Based Aid: $52,683
Avg. % of Need Met: 95%

Avg. Merit-Based Aid: $12,483
% Receiving Merit-Based Aid: 30%

Avg. Cumulative Debt: $29,553
% of Students Borrowing: 51%

CAREER
Who Recruits
1. Instagram
2. The Martin Agency
3. Goldman Sachs
4. CarMax
5. Citi

Notable Internships
1. Wegman's Food Markets
2. Lockheed Martin
3. SpaceX

Top Industries
1. Business
2. Education
3. Research
4. Healthcare
5. Engineering

Top Employers
1. Google
2. Apple
3. IBM
4. Amazon
5. Microsoft

Where Alumni Work
1. Rochester, NY
2. New York City
3. Boston
4. Washington, DC
5. San Francisco

Median Earnings
College Scorecard (Early Career): $61,200
EOP (Early Career): $62,000
PayScale (Mid-Career): $112,700

RANKINGS
Forbes: 82
Money: 194
U.S. News: 29 (T), National Universities
Wall Street Journal/THE: 58
Washington Monthly: 43, National Universities

#CollegesWorthYourMoney

University of Southern California

Los Angeles, California | Admissions Phone: 213-740-1111

ADMISSION
Admission Rate: 13%
Admission Rate - Men: 13%
Admission Rate - Women: 13%
EA Admission Rate: Not Offered
ED Admission Rate: Not Offered
Admission Rate (5-Year Trend): -7%
ED Admission Rate (5-Year Trend): Not Offered
% of Admits Attending (Yield): 41%
Transfer Admission Rate: 25%

\# Offered Wait List: Not Offered
\# Accepted Wait List: Not Offered
\# Admitted Wait List: Not Offered

SAT Reading/Writing (Middle 50%): 660-740
SAT Math (Middle 50%): 690-790
ACT Composite (Middle 50%): 30-34
Testing Policy: ACT/SAT Required
SAT Superscore: Yes
ACT Superscore: No

% Graduated in Top 10% of HS Class: 90%
% Graduated in Top 25% of HS Class: 97%
% Graduated in Top 50% of HS Class: 100%

ENROLLMENT
Total Undergraduate Enrollment: 19,907
% Part-Time: 4%
% Male: 49%
% Female: 51%
% Out-of-State: 35%
% Fraternity: 26%
% Sorority: 27%
% On-Campus (Freshman): 98%
% On-Campus (All Undergraduate): 30%

% African-American: 5%
% Asian: 21%
% Hispanic: 15%
% White: 39%
% Other: 6%
% Race or Ethnicity Unknown: 1%
% International: 13%
% Low-Income: 19%

ACADEMICS
Student-to-Faculty Ratio: 9:1
% of Classes Under 20: 59%
% of Classes Under 40: 79%
% Full-Time Faculty: 59%
% Full-Time Faculty w/ Terminal Degree: 92%

Top Programs
Business
Cinematic Arts
Communication
Computer Science
Design
Engineering
International Relations
Performing Arts

Retention Rate: 97%
4-Year Graduation Rate: 78%
6-Year Graduation Rate: 92%

Curricular Flexibility: Somewhat Flexible
Academic Rating: ★★★★✓

Inside the Classroom

A few decades back, if you told someone in-the-know about college admissions that the University of Southern California would eventually be in the same league with UC Berkeley, they would likely have concluded that an asteroid was headed for the San Francisco Bay area. At that time, USC was stereotyped as a lily-white school for wealthy underachievers that accepted the majority of applicants. Today, the home of the Trojans is one of the premier private research universities in the country, enriched by a diverse pool of students from around the globe and sporting a lower acceptance rate than Georgetown, Tufts, Washington University in St. Louis and—to bring things full circle—Berkeley.

There are 130 undergraduate majors and minors within the Dornslife College of Arts & Sciences alone, the University's oldest and largest school. Graduation requirements are a fairly run-of-the-mill assortment of selections across the major disciplines. By degrees conferred, the most popular areas of study are business (24 percent), social sciences (12 percent), visual and performing arts (12 percent), engineering (10 percent), and communications/journalism (9 percent).

At an institution with close to 20,000 undergraduates and 27,000 graduate students you would not expect to find many tiny seminar courses with single-digit enrollments, but 14 percent of classes at USC do, in fact, meet that standard. The bulk of courses offered are in the ten to nineteen range, but you also will find yourself in a fair share of large lecture halls in your time at USC. Still, there is little anonymity in a Trojan education. Aided by a favorable 9:1 student-to-faculty ratio, the school does an excellent job facilitating undergraduate research opportunities. Each school/college has a course entitled Directed Research 490 in which students work closely with a faculty supervisor and earn between two and eight credits as well as countless opportunities to get their hands dirty in academic research.

All programs within the Marshall School of Business and Viterbi School of Engineering are highly acclaimed and have far-reaching reputations with employers and elite grad schools (more on both later). Programs in communication, the cinematic arts, and the performing arts carry sterling reputations as well. Students are quite competitive in the race for elite postgraduate fellowships. In the last decade, the university has produced ninety-eight Fulbright Student Grant Recipients. Two alumni were awarded Rhodes Scholarships in 2017. The Class of 2019 saw four Boren winners, four Critical Language Scholarship recipients, and multiple winners of NSF awards and Gilman Scholarships.

Outside the Classroom

While most Trojans live on campus as freshmen, the majority of upperclassmen reside in the surrounding neighborhoods and commute to school. That is not entirely a matter of choice; USC offers limited university-owned housing options, only enough to accommodate 30 percent of its undergraduate population. Fortunately, the school recently opened eight new residential houses which, collectively, increased its capacity by 24 percent. Greek life is thriving at USC with a 26 percent participation rate in over sixty sororities/fraternities. The Trojans beloved football team takes center stage each fall, attracting 93,000 fans each Saturday. There are nineteen additional NCAA Division I sports teams fielded by the university as well as a massive club sports operation with 2,500+ participants. Over 1,000 student organizations are active, including popular choices like student government, cultural groups, and performance troupes. Volunteer opportunities like Alternative Breaks and Friends & Neighbors Day are favorites as well with the latter drawing more than 500 students and faculty into LA for service work. USC's LA location ensures that there is never a dearth of excitement and adventure. Within a few miles of campus are countless museums, the Staples Center, multiple theaters, and all the nightlife you could desire. Being in LA has other perks—major musical acts and guest speakers from Barack Obama to alum Will Ferrell appear at the university on a regular basis. The Visions & Voices program provides free cultural events multiple times per week that draw rave reviews from the student body.

Career Services

The University of Southern California Career Center only represents a portion of the career counseling received by Trojan undergrads as additional, more specialized experts are embedded within every undergraduate college. For example, seven professionals provide counseling only to engineering students, and six work exclusively with Annenberg students. In total, there are forty-nine full-time staff members working in counseling, employer relations, and recruiting, equating to a 407:1 student-to-counselor ratio, within the average range of institutions profiled in this book. Yet, that ratio may be the only thing that could be labelled ordinary about this highly accomplished Career Center.

On-campus recruiting at USC is extraordinary with 275 employers granting on-site interviews. In 2016-17, over 3,100 students participated in 5,357 job interviews at the university. The companies recruiting on campus make for an impressive list, even if you only highlighted those that start with "A"—Adobe Systems, Accenture, Amazon, Apple, and AT&T. Outreach efforts are successful as career services engaged with 6,430 students via 1:1 counseling appointments and had just shy of 10,000 attendees at workshops and other events. Large events include the Fall Career Fair that brings 200+ employers to campus, and every school has its own concentrated fairs in areas such as architecture, engineering, and law schools. The onlineSC system also features more than 10,000 job and internship opportunities for Trojan undergrads. A strong alumni network of more than 375,000 is another useful resource for fresh graduates. USC's recruiting, engagement, and specialized career counseling offerings earn its Career Center top grades.

Professional Outcomes

USC does not release outcomes data for its graduating classes as a whole, but an examination of school-specific destinations for the Class of 2017 reveals a rosy picture. Annenberg graduates find employment at a 96-100 percent rate within six months of graduation. Alumni at the Viterbi School of Engineering are well represented at any major technology company you can name from Apple to Yahoo! In fact, USC cracked College Transitions' list of the best engineering feeder schools, sending an extremely high percentage of graduates to the most desirable employers. USC also made our list of top feeders to the tech industry alongside institutions like Caltech, MIT, and Stanford. Presently, there are between 300 and 1,500 alumni employed at each of Google, Amazon, Apple, Microsoft, Facebook, Cisco, Netflix, and Salesforce. Median salaries at age thirty-four are comparable to graduates from the nearby UC system member schools. Half of all alumni reside in the Los Angeles area while San Francisco, Orange County, and New York City are next in popularity.

Information on the graduate schools members of recent classes have attended is not published by the university (they have only recently begun to track that information). However, what can be gleaned from other sources paints a highly positive picture. College Transitions' extensive analysis of LinkedIn data revealed that the University of Southern California is one of the most prolific producers of students accepted into the T14 Law Schools. The good news doesn't stop there; the university also ranks as one of the leading producers of students accepted into top MBA programs like Wharton, Booth, and Tuck.

Admission

USC admissions (and those at several other schools) made front-page headlines for months on end in 2019 as part of the "Varsity Blues" scandal that saw famous actresses and powerful businesspeople cheating and bribing their way into the university. Interestingly, you probably wouldn't have seen people cheating their way into USC a decade ago. Admission into USC has become significantly more challenging in recent years. Five years ago, the school accepted 20 percent of those who applied. In 2018, of 64,000 wanna-be Trojans, only 8,300 were accepted, equating to an all-time low acceptance rate of 13 percent. The SAT range of the Class of 2022 was 1350-1530, and the ACT range was 30-34. On a 4.0 scale, the average high school GPA was 3.79. Those figures are slightly higher than in previous years.

To have a legitimate chance here, being in the top 10 percent of your high school class is likely a necessity as 90 percent of those in the freshman class held that distinction; 97 percent were in the top quartile. There are no unusual factors designated as "most important" by the admissions staff, but rigor of curriculum, grades, test scores, essays, and recommendations reign supreme. USC does not have an early action/early decision option, so all candidates are in the same boat. Legacy students, called "scions," make up a significant portion of the student body—19 percent. There is definitely an edge available for those with Trojan lineage. Those from a generation ago, including USC alumni now hoping to shepherd their own children into their alma mater, may find the current level of selectivity a complete and utter shock. For additional perspective, twenty years ago, 45 percent of applicants were accepted, and the average SAT score was over 200 points lower than it is for today's enrollees. Make no mistake—getting into USC is most likely for students with standardized test scores at or above the 95th percentile and a nearly flawless high school transcript.

Worth Your Money?

At almost $75,000 there is nothing shocking about the annual cost of attendance at USC; it's pretty standard these days for a private university. Where it does seem outrageously high is when you see that amount is twice the cost of any of the elite University of California schools such as Berkley or UCLA. Still, many pay less than the list price as 53 percent of current undergraduates receive merit aid awards averaging $20k per year, and 38 percent of the student population is granted need-based aid to the tune of $40k per year. Further, many USC grads go on to lucrative careers that are enhanced by the school's employer/graduate school connections as well as those of the well-connected alumni base. Those factors make this college worth your money unless, in the words of Olivia Jade Giannulli, you "don't really care about school" but "do want the experience of, like, game days, partying..." Sorry, couldn't resist.

FINANCIAL
Institutional Type: Private
In-State Tuition: $55,320
Out-of-State Tuition: $55,320
Room & Board: $15,395
Required Fees: $1,355
Books & Supplies: $1,200

Avg. Need-Based Aid: $39,568
Avg. % of Need Met: 100%

Avg. Merit-Based Aid: $20,066
% Receiving Merit-Based Aid: 53%

Avg. Cumulative Debt: $28,228
% of Students Borrowing: 35%

CAREER
Who Recruits
1. FTI Consulting
2. Moss Adams
3. Cornerstone Research
4. Nike
5. Universal Creative

Notable Internships
1. Dow Jones
2. Tesla
3. The Blackstone Group

Top Industries
1. Business
2. Education
3. Engineering
4. Operations
5. Media

Top Employers
1. Google
2. Amazon
3. Apple
4. Microsoft
5. Facebook

Where Alumni Work
1. Los Angeles
2. San Francisco
3. Orange County, CA
4. New York City
5. San Diego

Median Earnings
College Scorecard (Early Career): $74,000
EOP (Early Career): $63,700
PayScale (Mid-Career): $120,600

RANKINGS
Forbes: 30
Money: 131
U.S. News: 22, National Universities
Wall Street Journal/THE: 18
Washington Monthly: 64, National Universities

#CollegesWorthYourMoney

ADMISSION
Admission Rate: 39%
Admission Rate - Men: 35%
Admission Rate - Women: 42%
EA Admission Rate: Not Offered
ED Admission Rate: Not Offered
Admission Rate (5-Year Trend): -2%
ED Admission Rate (5-Year Trend): Not Offered
% of Admits Attending (Yield): 46%
Transfer Admission Rate: 24%

Offered Wait List: 0
Accepted Wait List: 0
Admitted Wait List: 0

SAT Reading/Writing (Middle 50%): 620-720
SAT Math (Middle 50%): 610-760
ACT Composite (Middle 50%): 27-33
Testing Policy: ACT/SAT Required
SAT Superscore: No
ACT Superscore: No

% Graduated in Top 10% of HS Class: 84%
% Graduated in Top 25% of HS Class: 95%
% Graduated in Top 50% of HS Class: 99%

ENROLLMENT
Total Undergraduate Enrollment: 40,804
% Part-Time: 7%
% Male: 46%
% Female: 54%
% Out-of-State: 6%
% Fraternity: 13%
% Sorority: 20%
% On-Campus (Freshman): 63%
% On-Campus (All Undergraduate): 18%

% African-American: 4%
% Asian: 22%
% Hispanic: 23%
% White: 40%
% Other: 4%
% Race or Ethnicity Unknown: 1%
% International: 6%
% Low-Income: 26%

ACADEMICS
Student-to-Faculty Ratio: 19:1
% of Classes Under 20: 38%
% of Classes Under 40: 68%
% Full-Time Faculty: 83%
% Full-Time Faculty w/ Terminal Degree: 91%

Top Programs
Architecture
Biochemistry
Business
Communication
Computer Science
Engineering
Geosciences
Psychology

Retention Rate: 95%
4-Year Graduation Rate: 61%
6-Year Graduation Rate: 83%

Curricular Flexibility: Somewhat Flexible
Academic Rating: ★★★↓

Inside the Classroom

A ridiculously affordable flagship university that also happens to be one of the top public schools in the United States, the University of Texas at Austin serves up a quality undergraduate education on a massive scale. The school's 40,000+ undergraduates enjoy a dizzying 156 distinct degree programs and 12,400+ annual course offerings. Austin itself is a progressive city that has wide appeal, even to coastal dwellers; however, thanks to the automatic admission granted to all Texas students in the top 6 percent of their high school class, the university remains 90 percent Texas residents.

Each year 175 freshmen are admitted into the elite Plan II Honors Program, an interdisciplinary major created in 1935. One of the best honors programs in the country, Plan II students enjoy small class sizes and are required to complete a senior thesis. The school also offers its Liberal Arts Honors Program to an additional 130 students each year. All students must complete forty-two credit hours in the statewide core curriculum. That entails a first-year Signature Course in a small seminar environment, two English composition courses, one humanities course, two classes in American and Texas government, two in US history, one in the behavioral and social sciences, one in mathematics, three in the natural sciences, and one in the visual and performing arts.

A 19:1 student-to-faculty ratio and 10,000 graduate students on campus render across-the-board tiny class sizes an impossibility. While 38 percent of course sections enroll nineteen or fewer students, more than one-quarter of classes are filled with over fifty students. Opportunities for undergraduate research vary by school. An impressive 90 percent of engineering students conduct research or intern during their four years of study; others must compete for slots in programs such as the Freshman Research Initiative, Summer Research Scholars, or use the Eureka database to find individual professors offering research assistantships. A robust study abroad program boasts 400 offerings in 103 foreign countries; 4,421 undergrads participated in 2017-18.

The Cockrell School of Engineering is one of the most heralded undergraduate engineering schools around, while The McCombs School of Business cracks just about any top ten list and dominates in the specialty areas of accounting and marketing. UT's computer science department is also top-ranked, and regularly sends graduates to the world's best tech companies (see more below). In terms of sheer volume of degrees conferred, engineering is number one (13 percent) followed by business (12 percent), social sciences (12 percent), journalism/communications (12 percent), and biology (10 percent). Prestigious fellowship organizations love UT Austin grads just as much as employers do. In its history the school has produced an impressive 112 Fulbright Scholars, thirty-one Rhodes Scholars, and twenty-three Marshall Scholars.

Outside the Classroom

You won't find many schools in this book where so few undergraduates live on campus. Only 18 percent of the total student body—63 percent of freshmen—reside on the 431-acre campus. The bulk of students live in three nearby neighborhoods: Downtown Austin, East Austin, and West Campus (which is not actually part of campus). There are more than seventy Greek organizations at UT Austin with sororities attracting 20 percent of women and fraternities enlisting 13 percent of men. Sports are a way of life at this institution. Approximately 500 student athletes compete on twenty teams in NCAA Division I competition. Since 1949 the school has captured fifty-one national championships. Texas Memorial Stadium packs in 100,000+ on football Saturdays. In excess of 1,300 student organizations includes hundreds of intramural and club sports options and a sprawling media network of newspapers, magazines, television, and radio stations to ensure that no interest goes unaccounted for. The city of Austin, a liberal enclave in a conservative state, is a perennial darling of "Best Places to Live" and "Best College Towns" lists. Few complain of boredom in a city with all the live music, good food, and culture one can handle.

Career Services

There are fifteen career centers on the UT Austin campus, eleven of which cater to undergraduate students as well as the Vick Center for Strategic Advising and Career Counseling that serves undeclared students. With fifty-two full-time employees devoted to undergrads across those eleven career centers, the university offers a 778:1 student-to-counselor ratio, higher than many of the schools featured in this guide. Some undergraduate schools offer more support than others. For example, there are twelve staff members dedicated to undergraduates in the McCombs School of Business but only two in the School of Education.

The scope of the offerings is overwhelming, as would be expected at a school with more than 40,000 undergraduates. For example, the most recent Fall Science and Technology Career Fair drew 201 employers and 2,500 students. The Spring Communication Job & Internship Fair welcomes up to eighty-five employers and 1,000 students. In 2017-18, the McCombs College of Business Career Expo featured 180+ corporations. Over one hundred employers engage in on-campus recruiting/interviewing with Texas Engineering students every year. Like many universities of its size, UT Austin cannot offer the hand-holding provided by many smaller liberal arts colleges, but it does provide plenty of on-campus networking opportunities for those bold enough to take advantage.

The University of Texas at Austin

E-mail: admissions.utexas.edu/contact | Website: www.utexas.edu

Professional Outcomes

Six months after graduating, 48 percent Longhorns are employed, 25 percent have entered graduate school, and 17 percent are still seeking their next opportunity. The for-profit sector attracts 68 percent of those employed, 18 percent pursue jobs at a nonprofit, and 14 percent enter public sector employment. At a school with nearly half a million living alumni, there is no shortage of major corporations that employ more than 500 UT Austin grads. In the tech realm Google, Facebook, Oracle, Microsoft, IBM, and Apple all meet that qualification, and giants such as Accenture, Amazon, and Uber also employ hundreds of Longhorns. Austin remains home for the largest number of graduates with the Houston, Dallas, and San Antonio areas next in popularity. Plenty of alumni also can be found in New York City and San Francisco. Starting salaries were solid and, as would be expected, fluctuated significantly by major. Business majors took home a median income of $76,000 while chemistry majors earned $46,000 and journalism majors had a median figure of $36,000.

University of Texas at Austin undergraduates go on to pursue advanced degrees in massive numbers with one-quarter electing to continue their educational journey right after completing their bachelor's. Many pursue advanced study at UT Austin itself, which offers more than one hundred graduate programs. Medical school acceptance rates hover around 55 percent, which is above the national average. The sheer volume of med school applicants is incredible; more than 700 seniors apply each year. The university's own Dell Medical School, founded in 2016, is a common destination as are other Texas-based institutions like UT-Houston, UT-San Antonio, and Baylor. Others land at premier medical schools, including Harvard, Georgetown, and UVA, each year. No matter what advanced degree you choose to pursue, an impressive UT Austin transcript can open doors to any institution in the country.

Admission

Longhorn hopefuls totaled 55,575 in the 2018 admissions cycle, almost 30,000 more than at the break of the new millennium. At that time the acceptance rate exceeded 60 percent; it is now only 35 percent. Among 2018-19 freshmen, the mid-50 percent standardized test scores were 1230-1480 on the SAT and 27-33 on the ACT. The vast majority were situated in the top 10 percent of their high school classes—85 percent earned such a distinction—and 95 percent were in the top quartile. The UT system has kept "outsiders" from making up a large percentage of the student body as 89 percent of current students hail from the Lone Star State. The school's policy of automatically accepting students from the top 6 percent of any Texas high school keeps quality home-grown freshmen pouring through the gates. There were an astounding 424 valedictorians and 284 salutatorians in the most recent cohort. Applicants to UT's business, computer science, and engineering majors will face the stiffest competition; earning entry typically requires Ivy-like credentials, especially if you're from out of state.

The university ranks pretty much every admissions factor as "very important," but it's safe to say that with such an onslaught of applications each year the hard numbers of standardized test scores, GPA, and class rank are most essential. There is no early round at UT Austin, so all applicants are in the same boat. The school has no interest in demonstrated interest on the part of applicants because it enjoys a relatively high yield rate approaching 50 percent. While the school accepts roughly 2,000 transfer students per year, that's only 24 percent of those who apply. That differs greatly from many other elite state universities where transferring is much easier than getting admitted directly out of high school. The University of Texas at Austin is the flagship school of the UT system and among the largest genuinely elite schools in the entire country. Texas residency, top-of-the-class academic performance, and solid test scores give you the best chance to get in.

Worth Your Money?

An annual in-state cost of attendance of $25,016 for a UT Austin degree is one of the best bargains anywhere in the country. In addition, almost 40 percent of undergrads qualify for need-based aid with average grants that are a hair over $10,000. Out of state, the sticker price for full COA is $52k, not an unreasonable sum for what you'll receive, particularly if you are majoring in business, engineering, or computer science. If you are a resident of Texas, there are no qualifiers—UT Austin is unquestionably worth every dollar.

FINANCIAL
Institutional Type: Public
In-State Tuition: $10,610
Out-of-State Tuition: $37,580
Room & Board: $10,804
Required Fees: N/A
Books & Supplies: $700

Avg. Need-Based Aid: $10,222
Avg. % of Need Met: 72%

Avg. Merit-Based Aid: $2,345
% Receiving Merit-Based Aid: 23%

Avg. Cumulative Debt: $24,244
% of Students Borrowing: 40%

CAREER
Who Recruits
1. Shell
2. General Electric
3. Affigen, LLC
4. Merck
5. SnapStream

Notable Internships
1. Visa
2. Uber
3. Boeing

Top Industries
1. Business
2. Education
3. Engineering
4. Operations
5. Sales

Top Employers
1. IBM
2. Google
3. Microsoft
4. Accenture
5. Amazon

Where Alumni Work
1. Austin
2. Houston
3. Dallas
4. San Antonio
5. San Francisco

Median Earnings
College Scorecard (Early Career): $58,200
EOP (Early Career): $57,900
PayScale (Mid-Career): $112,800

RANKINGS
Forbes: 76
Money: 28
U.S. News: 48, National Universities
Wall Street Journal/THE: 61 (T)
Washington Monthly: 61, National Universities

#CollegesWorthYourMoney

University of Virginia

Charlottesville, Virginia | Admissions Phone: 434-982-3200

Inside the Classroom

When Thomas Jefferson helped to found the University of Virginia in 1819, our nation's third president did more than just assist in securing the funds—he also personally designed some of the campus' now famous architecture, planned the curriculum, and recruited the first faculty members. As the so-called "father" of the school, Jefferson would undoubtedly be thrilled with what his progeny has gone on to achieve. Two hundred years after its first cornerstone was laid, UVA has become one of the most iconic public universities in the United States where state residents can get an Ivy-level education at a bargain price.

Undergrads can study within one of seven colleges/schools: the College of Arts & Sciences, the School of Engineering and Applied Science, McIntire School of Commerce, the School of Architecture, the School of Nursing, the Batten School of Leadership & Public Policy, and the Curry School of Education. Within the College of Arts & Sciences, undergraduates must complete 30 credits worth of Area Requirements broken down as follows: Natural Science and Mathematics (12), Social Sciences (6), Humanities (6), Historical Studies (3), and Non-Western Perspectives (3). Further Competency Requirements include a First Writing Requirement, Second Writing Requirement, and a Foreign Language Requirement. The 225-250 students per freshman class who are selected for the Echols Scholars Program are not bound by any competency or area requirements.

The University of Virginia sports a 15:1 student-to-faculty ration, a very strong figure for a large public institution. As such, the school is able to offer many small classes like you would find an elite liberal arts college. In fact, 17 percent of sections boast a single-digit enrollment and 55 percent contain 19 or fewer students. There will be some large lecture courses as well—15 percent of sections contain 50 or more undergrads. Undergraduate research opportunities can be challenging to uncover at any large school where graduate students get the prime spots, yet, UVA does offer a multitude of opportunities. To cite examples, every single engineering major completes one major research project, the biology department has 230 students each semester participating research, and physics students are given the chance to get their names on published work. The classroom at UVA extends well beyond Charlottesville as one-third of the Class of 2019 took a semester abroad in one of 65 countries around the world.

The two most commonly conferred degree areas of in liberal arts/general studies (17 percent) and the social sciences (16 percent). Engineering (13 percent), business/marketing (8 percent), biology (7 percent), and psychology (5 percent) are next in sheer popularity. The McIntire School of Commerce has a glowing reputation in the finance/accounting/accounting realm and the School of Engineering and Applied Science is just as highly-respected by employers in those fields. Other notable departmental strengths include computer science, economics, and political philosophy, policy, and law. Cavaliers are extremely competitive in the pursuit of prestigious national scholarships as well. The Class of 2018 produced 12 Fulbright Scholars, five Critical Language Scholars, two Marshall Scholars, a Truman Scholar, and an Astronaut Scholar.

Outside the Classroom

Just 38 percent of all students live on UVA's campus, although 100 percent of freshman do reside on school's vast 1,682-acre grounds. Greek life is popular as an equal 31 percent of men and women sign up for fraternity and sorority life. The Cavaliers compete in 27 varsity sports teams (13 men's and 14 women's) in the Atlantic Coast Conference. Approximately 2,100 students are members of 65 club sports teams and many others participate in intramural athletics. As you would expect at such a large institution, there are 1,000+ clubs available in everything from acrobatics to high powered rocketry; the process of joining some of the more competitive clubs can be fierce (i.e. the University Judiciary Committee). A cappella is beloved pastime at the school and there are countless groups to consider. Outside of being the site of a disturbing rally in 2017, Charlottesville is generally considered to be one of the most student-friendly college towns. There is no shortage of culture, craft breweries, and outdoor recreation opportunities. Plenty of Jefferson and Madison-related history can be explored nearby and a trip to the state capital of Richmond will take you just over an hour. Those looking to fly home for the holidays will enjoy the convenience of having the Charlottesville-Albemarle Airport just eight miles from campus.

Career Services

The UVA Career Center employs 43 full-time staff members giving them a student-to-advisor ration of 390:1, which is in the average range compared to schools in this guide and a very respectable level of support for a school of the University of Virginia's size. Roles of staff members include pre-health and law advisor, career counseling for public service and government community, and director of employer relations & experiential education. This well-resourced office encourages one-on-one appointments, has ample drop-in hours, daily "Coffee Chats with Career Counselors," and hosts regular "Career Communities" that help students interested in a specific field like Business & Technology or Science and Sustainability."

University of Virginia

Of the employed members of the Class of 2018, over 20 percent were connected to their job directly by career services staff/Handshake and another 8 percent heard about the opportunity at a Career Services-sponsored career fair. The University hosts large scale general career fairs in the fall and spring as well many discipline-specific events. The Engineering, Science, and Technology Career Fair attracts over 2,000 students and 230 companies each year. According to the most recent statistics available, 40 percent of undergraduates land at least one paid internship and close to 50 percent have an unpaid workplace experience. There are close to a quarter of a million Cavalier alumni and many are happy to help current students find internships, employment, or offer some level of mentorship. Each year, more than 1,000 alums return to campus for this purpose.

Professional Outcomes

Sixty-five percent of the Class of 2018 immediately joined the workforce upon receiving their degree while 16 percent headed directly to graduate school; 17 percent of graduates were still looking for their next destination. Industries attracting the greatest number of freshly-minted graduates were Internet & Software (12 percent), Healthcare (11 percent), K-12 Education (10 percent), Management Consulting (7 percent), and Higher Education (7 percent). The companies who scooped up the greatest number of 2018 graduates were Capital One (46), Deloitte (42), Oracle (29), and Microsoft (25). The average starting salary for those finding employment was a robust $66,790. Graduates of the McIntire School of Commerce had average salaries of $75k while Arts & Sciences graduates averaged $50k. Large numbers of recent graduates migrate to Washington DC and New York City and many others head to Boston, San Francisco, Seattle, Charlotte, and Atlanta.

Among the 2018 grads who decided to continue their education, 219 enrolled in an advanced degree program at UVA—the next most popular destinations were Virginia Commonwealth University (27), Columbia University (10), the University of Michigan (10), and the College of William & Mary (8). In recent years, medical school graduation for Cavaliers have beaten national averages. In the last six years, UVA applicants to MD programs have enjoyed between a 52-60 percent acceptance rate versus the national average range of 42-45 percent. Virginia grads head to a wide range of medical colleges including the nation's best like Johns Hopkins, Emory, Cornell, Harvard, Tufts, and Georgetown.

Admission

The University of Virginia received upwards of 37,000 applications for a place in their Class of 2022, more than double the number received in 2005. Just 26 percent of this this group were welcomed into the freshman class of 2018-19. Those that went on to attend the university possessed mid-50 percent SAT scores of 1330-1500; the ACT range was 30-34. Nine out of every ten freshman earned a place in top decile of their high school class and 98 percent landed in the top quartile. A stunning 96 percent of this cohort earned better than a 3.75 GPA and only 2 percent had less than a 3.5.

Six factors are rated by the UVA committee as being "very important" to the admissions process headlined by state residency. The school offers admission to 38 percent of locals but just 21 percent hailing from outside of the state. In seeking to maintain at least a two-thirds majority of Virginians, the student body is presently comprised of 69 percent state residents. Other highly-ranked factors included: rigor of secondary school record, class rank, GPA, recommendations, and character/personal qualities. Criteria ranked as still "important" includes: standardized test scores, the application essay, extracurricular activities, and talent/ability. There are no interviews offered at UVA and they do not weight demonstrated interest into their decision-making. Early decision was just added back into the equation for the 2019-20 admissions cycle so no data is yet available on how much of an edge ED applicants might receive.

Worth Your Money?

A rare public university that meets 100 percent of all students' demonstrated financial need, UVA serves up an average of $24,608 per year to qualifying students. Merit aid only goes to a sliver of students and the amount is nominal. Roughly one-third of students take out loans and the mean amount of debt for those individuals is $24k, less than the average college graduate in the country. Residents of Virginia pay an annual cost of attendance of just $33k while out-of-state undergrads are met with a COA of almost $64,000. This school, with its sparkling national reputation and strong graduate outcomes, is worth your money either way, but the real bargain is enjoyed by those whose taxes help fund the university.

FINANCIAL
Institutional Type: Public
In-State Tuition: $14,811
Out-of-State Tuition: $45,508
Room & Board: $11,590
Required Fees: $2,842
Books & Supplies: $1,350

Avg. Need-Based Aid: $24,608
Avg. % of Need Met: 100%

Avg. Merit-Based Aid: $3,815
% Receiving Merit-Based Aid: 5%

Avg. Cumulative Debt: $24,682
% of Students Borrowing: 34%

CAREER
Who Recruits
1. Yext
2. Pariveda
3. Oak Hill Advisors
4. Altria
5. Harris Williams & Co.

Notable Internships
1. Strategic Investment Group
2. NBCUniversal
3. Proctor & Gamble

Top Industries
1. Business
2. Education
3. Operations
4. Research
5. Engineering

Top Employers
1. Capital One
2. Deloitte
3. EY
4. Google
5. Accenture

Where Alumni Work
1. Washington, DC
2. Charlottesville, VA
3. New York City
4. Richmond, VA
5. San Francisco

Median Earnings
College Scorecard (Early Career): $61,200
EOP (Early Career): $71,200
PayScale (Mid-Career): $117,500

RANKINGS
Forbes: 33
Money: 10
U.S. News: 28, National Universities
Wall Street Journal/THE: 50
Washington Monthly: 52, National Universities

#CollegesWorthYourMoney

Seattle, Washington | Admissions Phone: 206-543-9686

ADMISSION
Admission Rate: 49%
Admission Rate - Men: 46%
Admission Rate - Women: 51%
EA Admission Rate: Not Offered
ED Admission Rate: Not Offered
Admission Rate (5-Year Trend): -6%
ED Admission Rate (5-Year Trend): Not Offered
% of Admits Attending (Yield): 32%
Transfer Admission Rate: 49%

Offered Wait List: Not Offered
Accepted Wait List: Not Offered
Admitted Wait List: Not Offered

SAT Reading/Writing (Middle 50%): 600-700
SAT Math (Middle 50%): 620-760
ACT Composite (Middle 50%): 27-32
Testing Policy: ACT/SAT Required
SAT Superscore: Yes
ACT Superscore: Yes

% Graduated in Top 10% of HS Class: 58%
% Graduated in Top 25% of HS Class: 88%
% Graduated in Top 50% of HS Class: 99%

ENROLLMENT
Total Undergraduate Enrollment: 32,099
% Part-Time: 8%
% Male: 47%
% Female: 53%
% Out-of-State: 19%
% Fraternity: 16%
% Sorority: 15%
% On-Campus (Freshman): 76%
% On-Campus (All Undergraduate): 29%

% African-American: 3%
% Asian: 25%
% Hispanic: 8%
% White: 38%
% Other: 7%
% Race or Ethnicity Unknown: 3%
% International: 15%
% Low-Income: 21%

ACADEMICS
Student-to-Faculty Ratio: 19:1
% of Classes Under 20: 29%
% of Classes Under 40: 67%
% Full-Time Faculty: 75%
% Full-Time Faculty w/ Terminal Degree: 80%

Top Programs
Biochemistry
Business
Communication
Computer Science
Engineering
Informatics
Psychology
Public Health

Retention Rate: 94%
4-Year Graduation Rate: 67%
6-Year Graduation Rate: 84%

Curricular Flexibility: Somewhat Flexible
Academic Rating: ★★★

Inside the Classroom

Under the perpetually rainy skies and in the birthplace of grunge, Starbucks, and modern romantic comedies rests the flagship campus of the University of Washington system, home to approximately 29,000 undergraduate students, only 63 percent of whom benefit from the uber-affordable in-state rate. International and out-of-state students have begun flocking to UW in recent years to enjoy the literally dozens of top-ranked academic programs and the deep connections to a handful of corporations located nearby that also happen to be some of the most desirable employers anywhere on the planet. With thirteen colleges/schools with undergraduate programs, 180+ majors, and 6,500 courses, UW can meet the needs of just about anyone.

UDub's quarter-based academic calendar keeps students on their toes as most students take three or four classes in each of the 10-week fall, winter, and spring quarters. A strong honors program gives students access to smaller classes, but you'll likely need a 1450+ SAT score to access the program. Core curricular requirements vary by school. Some undergraduate colleges require a foreign language, but others do not. However, all students complete coursework in three Areas of Knowledge: visual, literary, and performing arts; individual societies, and the natural world. Freshmen can enroll in First-year Interest Groups or Collegium Seminars that offer small classes and engaging topics.

The university does have a relatively high 19:1 student-to-faculty ratio that makes consistently small undergraduate class sizes a logistical impossibility. One-third of sections contain forty or more students compared to 29 percent of sections that contain fewer than twenty. Still, there are opportunities for personal connections with professors as evidenced by the fact that 55 percent of graduates complete a faculty-mentored research project. The study abroad rate of participation has climbed steadily since the turn of the millennium; roughly one-fifth now spend a semester in a foreign locale.

The most commonly earned degrees at the University of Washington are in the social sciences (15 percent), business/marketing (11 percent), biology (11 percent), engineering (9 percent), and computer science (7 percent). There are simply too many stellar majors for there to be too large a concentration in any one or two areas. The College of Engineering, which includes the revered Paul G. Allen College of Computer Science & Engineering, is one of the absolute best in the nation, but UW also boasts strong programs in everything from business to social work to environmental science. Employers adore Huskies, but so do competitive scholarship organizations. In 2019, sixteen grads and alumni were awarded Fulbrights, two won Udall Scholarships, and the school has produced thirty-five Rhodes Scholars in its illustrious history.

Outside the Classroom

A solid 83 percent of UDub students who live on campus rate the experience as "excellent." Unfortunately, only a paltry 29 percent of the undergraduate student body actually live on campus and, even among freshmen, only 68 percent reside in the dorms. Some find housing in one of the school's seventy Greek organizations that boast 4,700 members. Most live in houses and apartments in the University District of the city; downtown Seattle is a short car or bus ride away. Students come together to take part in the 850+ student organizations including the Aerial Robotics Club or the Creating a Company Club. Whatever your pleasure, the Husky Union Building (HUB) is, indeed, a great place to get involved. Heck, it even has its own bowling alley. If bowling isn't athletic enough for you, enjoy the twenty-two varsity sports teams that compete in the Pac-12 Conference. Football reigns supreme as UDub boasts the largest stadium in the Pacific Northwest, and it is known to reach deafening noise levels on fall Saturdays. Recreation is aided by state-of-the-art fitness facilities that include a pool, rock-climbing wall, driving range, and Waterfront Activities Center on Lake Washington. Gear for hiking, boating, and camping can be rented from the UWild Gear Garage.

Career Services

There are thirteen full-time employees at the Career and Internship Center that is housed within the Division of Student Life. Additional staff members serving undergraduate students can be found within the School of Engineering and School of Information Sciences to bring the total of career counselors to fifteen, a relatively small number considering that they serve more than 29,000 undergraduate students. The resulting 1933:1 student-to-advisor ratio is among the worst of any school featured in this book; however, unlike some understaffed career services offices (at schools that do make the cut for inclusion in this guide), the CIC at the University of Washington has no shortage of brag-worthy accomplishments.

UW's Career and Internship Center brings close to 400 employers to the Seattle campus each school year. In addition to the hard-to-match local corporations (chronicled in the next section), companies like Wells Fargo, Adobe Systems, Tesla, Bloomberg, Comcast, and Dell recruit and/or conduct interviews on campus. Career fairs are plentiful throughout the year and include specialty expos for data science, engineering, and business. In part due to the prime Seattle location, internships are not hard to locate; 55 percent of undergraduates complete at least one internship, 16 percent complete two, 10 percent complete three, and 38 percent complete a service-learning project. The average search time for UW grads to find employment was 9.1 weeks, and 83 percent of those who landed a job did so in a field related to their major. Thanks to some extremely impressive corporate connections and an alumni base that is embedded in some of the country's most desirable employers, UW's career services successfully overcomes its numbers disadvantage.

Professional Outcomes

Six months after graduation, 70 percent of Class of 2017 graduates had found employment, 19 percent had continued their education in graduate/professional school, and 10 percent were still hunting their first job. Of those employed, 65 percent entered the private sector, 18 percent took local, state, or federal government posts, and 17 percent joined nonprofit organizations. The most popular employers of the Class of 2017 included Google, Amazon, Microsoft, Boeing, and UW Medical Center. Including all living alumni, more than 6,000 Huskies currently work for Bill Gates, and more than 4,000 work for each of Boeing and Amazon. T-Mobile, Facebook, Apple, Nordstrom, Starbucks, and Tableau Software all employ at least 500 UDub alums. As you discern from the massive numbers of students employed by famous companies based in the state of Washington, most graduates stick around town. The Greater Seattle area is far and away the home of choice for UW grads, followed in popularity by San Francisco, Portland, Los Angeles, and New York. The mean salary for 2017 grads was a solid $52,000, but it is important to note that the response rate for the school-issued survey was quite low.

Of those headed to graduate school, just over half remain in state, mostly at the University of Washington itself to become one of the school's 12,000 graduate students. Sixty-two percent of graduate students were pursuing an MS/MA degree, 17 percent entered PhD programs, and 12 percent headed off to earn a professional degree. The University of Washington has one of the best medical schools in the country, and 95 percent of accepted med students come from Washington, Wyoming, Alaska, Montana, and Idaho, thus giving UW graduates an inside track. The University of Washington School of Law is a top fifty institution that gives UW undergrads an excellent at-home option for a legal education. However, multiple graduates have also gone on to study law at Stanford, Harvard, and Fordham in recent years.

Admission

UW-Seattle admitted 49 percent of the 45,000+ applicants desiring to join the Husky Class of 2022. On the SAT, by far the more commonly submitted test, the mid-50 percent range of 2018-19 freshmen was 1220-1360; the ACT range was 27-32. Math scores tended to be much higher, on average, than reading scores. An impressive 70 percent of attending undergrads sported high school GPAs of 3.75 and above, and the average GPA was a 3.8. Interestingly, the admissions standards for resident, out-of-staters, and international students are similar. However, differences do exist across desired majors, with applicants to programs in engineering, computer science facing the toughest odds. Other than a rise in SAT scores, not a ton has changed at UW admissions in the past decade. Back in 2009, the acceptance rate was a somewhat comparable 61 percent, the average GPA was almost identical, but the 25th percentile SAT score was 1100 compared to 1220 today.

Predictable factors like GPA and rigor of high school coursework are designated as "very important" by the admissions committee, but so is the application essay, a surprise given the volume of applications received. Standardized test scores occupy the realm of "important" factors alongside extracurricular activities, talent/ability, first-generation status, work experience, and volunteer experience. There are no legacy admissions, interviews, or consideration of demonstrated interest or class rank. The committee also recommends "taking full advantage of senior year, demonstrating a positive grade trend," and "exercising significant responsibility in a family, community, employment situation or through activities."

Worth Your Money?

With an annual in-state tuition of $11,500 and a direct pipeline to many of the world's top corporations that happen to have their headquarters in Washington state, UDub is a can't-miss option if you get the hometown discount. Many nonresidents, particularly those pursuing computer science, engineering, and business, also find a good value, even at a total cost of attendance for four years of about $200K. Students pursuing other majors may do better looking at other reputable yet less pricey options.

FINANCIAL
Institutional Type: Public
In-State Tuition: $10,127
Out-of-State Tuition: $35,508
Room & Board: $12,798
Required Fees: $1,080
Books & Supplies: $900

Avg. Need-Based Aid: $15,306
Avg. % of Need Met: 74%

Avg. Merit-Based Aid: $4,043
% Receiving Merit-Based Aid: 10%

Avg. Cumulative Debt: $20,094
% of Students Borrowing: 36%

CAREER
Who Recruits
1. Samsung
2. Vulcan Capital
3. Alaska Airlines
4. Liberty Mutual
5. HealthPoint

Notable Internships
1. Boeing
2. Nordstrom
3. United Nations

Top Industries
1. Business
2. Education
3. Engineering
4. Operations
5. Research

Top Employers
1. Microsoft
2. Boeing
3. Amazon
4. Google
5. T-Mobile

Where Alumni Work
1. Seattle
2. San Francisco
3. Portland, OR
4. Los Angeles
5. New York City

Median Earnings
College Scorecard (Early Career): $57,700
EOP (Early Career): $57,500
PayScale (Mid-Career): $112,300

RANKINGS
Forbes: 64
Money: 22
U.S. News: 62 (T), National Universities
Wall Street Journal/THE: 42
Washington Monthly: 19, National Universities

#CollegesWorthYourMoney

University of Wisconsin – Madison

ADMISSION
Admission Rate: 52%
Admission Rate - Men: 49%
Admission Rate - Women: 54%
EA Admission Rate: N/A
ED Admission Rate: Not Offered
Admission Rate (5-Year Trend): +1%
ED Admission Rate (5-Year Trend): Not Offered
% of Admits Attending (Yield): 31%
Transfer Admission Rate: 53%

Offered Wait List: Not Offered
Accepted Wait List: Not Offered
Admitted Wait List: Not Offered

SAT Reading/Writing (Middle 50%): 630-700
SAT Math (Middle 50%): 670-780
ACT Composite (Middle 50%): 27-32
Testing Policy: ACT/SAT Required
SAT Superscore: No
ACT Superscore: No

% Graduated in Top 10% of HS Class: 54%
% Graduated in Top 25% of HS Class: 90%
% Graduated in Top 50% of HS Class: 99%

ENROLLMENT
Total Undergraduate Enrollment: 32,648
% Part-Time: 10%
% Male: 49%
% Female: 51%
% Out-of-State: 35%
% Fraternity: 8%
% Sorority: 8%
% On-Campus (Freshman): 93%
% On-Campus (All Undergraduate): 25%

% African-American: 2%
% Asian: 6%
% Hispanic: 5%
% White: 70%
% Other: 3%
% Race or Ethnicity Unknown: 2%
% International: 11%
% Low-Income: 13%

ACADEMICS
Student-to-Faculty Ratio: 17:1
% of Classes Under 20: 45%
% of Classes Under 40: 72%
% Full-Time Faculty: 84%
% Full-Time Faculty w/ Terminal Degree: 91%

Top Programs
Business
Chemistry
Communication Arts
Computer Science
Economics
Engineering
Political Science
Psychology

Retention Rate: 95%
4-Year Graduation Rate: 62%
6-Year Graduation Rate: 87%

Curricular Flexibility: Somewhat Flexible
Academic Rating: ★★★✦

Inside the Classroom

One of the country's best state institutions, the University of Wisconsin-Madison has become a coveted destination for a growing number of high-caliber teens far outside Wisconsin's seventy-two counties. In fact, the undergraduate student body of approximately 33,000 is inching toward a 50/50 split between Badger State residents and out-of-staters/foreigners. The school's over 900-acre campus is less than one mile from the Wisconsin State Capital Building and rates as one of the Midwest's most gorgeous collegiate settings. Even more attractive than the scenery are the 232+ undergraduate majors and certificates as well as 9,000 courses offered. This tough-to-match selection includes an array of renowned academic programs that rank among the best in the United States.

There are eight schools and colleges that serve undergraduates: The College of Letters and Science, the Wisconsin School of Business, the College of Engineering, the School of Nursing, the School of Education, the School of Pharmacy, the School of Human Ecology, and the College of Agricultural and Life Sciences. Regardless of your home school, breadth is the goal of the university's general education requirements that all Badgers must complete. As a result, thirteen to fifteen credits must be spread over three areas: the natural sciences, the behavioral and social sciences, and the humanities and arts. Required courses in ethnic studies, communications, and quantitative reasoning round out the mandated portion of a Badger education.

At UW-Madison undergrads can expect a mix of large and small classes; 45 percent of sections enroll fewer than twenty students, but 29 percent contain more than forty students with an average class size of thirty-one. The student-to-faculty ratio is 17:1, and roughly 9,000 graduate students suck up their share of attention. Undergraduate research opportunities exist, but the onus is on the student to show initiative and procure the placement. Overall, 15 percent of undergraduates participate in research with a faculty member during their four years of study. Participation is much higher when it comes to study abroad programs. Roughly 2,300 students participate each year, which is among the highest totals of any school in the country. Overall, there are 226 programs in sixty-nine countries to choose from.

Looking for top-ranked business or engineering programs? If so, Madison is a perfect spot for you. In terms of pure percentage of degrees conferred, biology (14 percent), business (12 percent), and engineering (12 percent) are the most popular. Programs in communication, political science, and computer science also draw a sizable number of students and are very strong. The school's guiding principal known as "The Wisconsin Idea" is that a college education should influence lives outside the confines of the classroom. Thus, it is fitting that the university is the number one producer of Peace Corps volunteers. In 2019, a phenomenal forty students earned National Science Foundation Graduate Research Fellowships, eighteen graduates captured Fulbright Scholarships, three were named Goldwater Scholars, and one received a coveted Hertz Fellowship.

Outside the Classroom

One of the best college football towns in America, it would be wrong not to lead with the rowdy, joyous atmosphere inside Camp Randall Stadium on fall Saturdays. A sea of red fills the stadium as 80,000 fans rabidly root for the Badgers and create a quintessential Midwestern college experience. Football worship, along with the other twenty-two Division I Sports teams, unite a campus that is not exactly centralized. While 93 percent of freshmen reside in university-owned housing, only one-quarter of the total undergraduate population lives on campus. Fraternities and sororities are available but hardly dominate the scene as only 8 percent of Badgers join a Greek organization; still, there are sixty Greek organizations on campus with thousands of members. In excess of 900 student-run clubs and organizations are at your disposal including near-constant events hosted by the student union such as concerts, sports viewing, guest lecturers, films, and local theater productions. The spirit of volunteerism is strong as students pledge 37,000 hours annually to local charitable causes. Nature enthusiasts don't have to travel far for hiking, boating, and birdwatching because the 300-acre Lakeshore Nature Preserve is on campus and includes four miles of shoreline along Lake Mendota. Madison is consistently ranked as one of the top college towns in the entire country because it possesses a hard-to-match combination of safety, beauty, and a booming restaurant and commercial district.

Career Services

There are ten career centers on the UW-Madison campus that, collectively, employ fifty-four professionals dedicated to career advising, internship coordination, employer relations, and other career-oriented tasks. The SuccessWorks initiative caters to students in the College of Letters & Sciences (which accounts for half of enrolled undergrads) and is the largest such office with twenty-one staff members. The Career Exploration Center (CEC) is a cross-college career services office serving those who are undecided on an area of study. Wisconsin also operates career services offices dedicated to pre-law and pre-health as well as discipline-specific offices housed in each undergraduate school and college. Wisconsin's overall 554:1 student-to-counselor ratio is higher than average compared to many schools featured in this guide, but that figure is relatively strong for a school of its size.

University of Wisconsin – Madison

E-mail: onwisconsin@admissions.wisc.edu | Website: www.wisc.edu

There are some impressive statistics that elevate UW-Madison from run-of-the-mill status with regard to career services offerings. For one, 88 percent of graduates "agreed" or "strongly agreed" that UW-Madison prepared them for the next step on their career path. More tangibly, 79 percent reported completing at least one internship during their four years of study, and a stunningly high 20 percent completed three or more. Career fairs are sweeping enough to accommodate an undergraduate population of 30,000+. The Fall Career & Internship Fair draws 320+ employers, including many top corporations and over 3,600 students annually. Other fairs include a massive Spring Career & Internship Fair, the UW-Madison STEM Fair, and the Public Service Fair (also held in the spring). Thanks to plenty of targeted and accessible career guidance within every undergrad's home college and solid employment and grad school results, UW's career services are held in high regard by our staff.

Professional Outcomes

Sixty-five percent of job-seeking 2018 University of Wisconsin-Madison grads had already received and/or accepted offers when they received their diplomas. The most commonly entered sectors were health care (11 percent), financial services (5 percent), engineering (5 percent), consulting (5 percent), retail (5 percent), technology (5 percent), and insurance (5 percent). The top five employers of Class of 2018 graduates were: UW-Madison, Epic, Kohl's, Oracle, and UW Health. However, across all graduating years corporations employing a minimum of 250 Badger alumni include Google, Target, Microsoft, Amazon, Apple, PwC, Accenture, and Facebook. The bulk of grads settle in the Madison area, Milwaukee, Chicago, or the Greater Minneapolis-St. Paul area. Those who leave the Midwest head to locations such as New York City, DC, San Francisco, Los Angeles, and Denver. Starting salaries are nothing spectacular, but that is to be expected for a large school with a wide array of offerings. Those earning a bachelor's from the Wisconsin School of Business take home $59,000 in average compensation, chemical engineering majors started at a healthy $67k, and those earning degrees in communications, social work, and philosophy earned median salaries under $35k.

Of the one-quarter of the Class of 2018 who enrolled directly in graduate/professional school, 54 percent were staying at UW-Madison; more than five members of the class headed to each of the following prestigious institutions: Columbia, Duke, USC, Northwestern, Carnegie Mellon, University of Chicago, Johns Hopkins, Emory, and Stanford. Clearly, an undergraduate degree from Wisconsin will serve you well when applying to elite graduate programs across the country. An impressive 108 members of the UW 2018 cohort matriculated in medical school, and seventy-three entered law school. The University of Wisconsin-Madison's own top-ranked medical school takes a high percentage of home-grown talent as does its top-thirty law school.

Admission

Fifty-two percent of the 42,741 applicants for the Class of 2022 gained entry into UW-Madison, but that figure hardly tells the tale of how selective this flagship university has become. Enrolled freshmen possessed mid-50 percent standardized test scores of 1300-1480 on the SAT and 27-32 on the ACT, 78 percent earned a GPA of greater than 3.75 on a 4.0 scale, 54 percent placed in the top decile of their graduating class, and 90 percent were in the top quartile. Five years ago, the SAT range was a lower 1170-1410, which is partially attributable to SAT inflation; the acceptance rate was nearly identical to the 2018-19 figure.

For a school deluged with applicants, the committee still ranks the application essay as the co-leader for most important factor considered alongside rigor of one's secondary curriculum. The second tier is highlighted by in-state residency status; 53 percent of current students are from the Badger State, but that number is down 7.5 percent from a decade ago. One's GPA, recommendations, and test scores round out the list of "important" factors. There are no admissions interviews, and demonstrated interest is not considered. It's important to point out that out-of-state applicants face significantly longer odds than in-state applicants who enjoy an acceptance rate of approximately 67 percent. The number of out-of-state applications for this university has grown rapidly in recent years. As a result, nonresidents should have test scores closer to the 75th percentile and rank in the top 10 percent of their high school classes while applicants from Wisconsin can get away with less stellar academic profiles.

Worth Your Money?

Wisconsin residents pay less than $26,000 per year total cost of attendance, an incredible bargain for such a high-quality educational experience with fantastic graduate outcomes. The growing number of students who come from other states or countries help keep the UW coffers full as such students fork over $53k annually. If you come from out of state, expect to pay full price; only 10 percent of students receive any merit aid. Over one-third of students who applied for need-based aid received an average grant of $13,556. For locals, the decision to attend Wisconsin is an easy one if you are offered admission. Outsiders still can benefit from the school's stellar reputation and vast alumni networks, but they will pay a significant sum for the privilege.

FINANCIAL
Institutional Type: Public
In-State Tuition: $10,725
Out-of-State Tuition: $37,785
Room & Board: $12,200
Required Fees: N/A
Books & Supplies: $1,150

Avg. Need-Based Aid: $13,556
Avg. % of Need Met: 76%

Avg. Merit-Based Aid: $5,039
% Receiving Merit-Based Aid: 10%

Avg. Cumulative Debt: $28,229
% of Students Borrowing: 46%

CAREER
Who Recruits
1. LinkedIn
2. Facebook
3. Goldman Sachs
4. Apple
5. Accenture

Notable Internships
1. U.S. Senate
2. Ford Motor Company
3. Hasbro

Top Industries
1. Business
2. Education
3. Operations
4. Engineering
5. Research

Top Employers
1. Google
2. Target
3. Northwestern Mutual
4. Amazon
5. Microsoft

Where Alumni Work
1. Madison, WI
2. Milwaukee
3. Chicago
4. Minneapolis
5. New York City

Median Earnings
College Scorecard (Early Career): $56,200
EOP (Early Career): $44,000
PayScale (Mid-Career): $104,400

RANKINGS
Forbes: 69
Money: 46
U.S. News: 46 (T), National Universities
Wall Street Journal/THE: 67
Washington Monthly: 23, National Universities

#CollegesWorthYourMoney

Vanderbilt University

Nashville, Tennessee | Admissions Phone: 615-322-2561

ADMISSION
Admission Rate: 10%
Admission Rate - Men: 11%
Admission Rate - Women: 9%
EA Admission Rate: Not Offered
ED Admission Rate: 21%
Admission Rate (5-Year Trend): -3%
ED Admission Rate (5-Year Trend): -1%
% of Admits Attending (Yield): 49%
Transfer Admission Rate: 25%

Offered Wait List: N/A
Accepted Wait List: N/A
Admitted Wait List: 243

SAT Reading/Writing (Middle 50%): 700-760
SAT Math (Middle 50%): 750-800
ACT Composite (Middle 50%): 33-35
Testing Policy: ACT/SAT Required
SAT Superscore: Yes
ACT Superscore: No

% Graduated in Top 10% of HS Class: 89%
% Graduated in Top 25% of HS Class: 96%
% Graduated in Top 50% of HS Class: 99%

ENROLLMENT
Total Undergraduate Enrollment: 6,861
% Part-Time: 1%
% Male: 49%
% Female: 51%
% Out-of-State: 90%
% Fraternity: 30%
% Sorority: 48%
% On-Campus (Freshman): 100%
% On-Campus (All Undergraduate): 94%

% African-American: 11%
% Asian: 14%
% Hispanic: 10%
% White: 45%
% Other: 6%
% Race or Ethnicity Unknown: 5%
% International: 9%
% Low-Income: 13%

ACADEMICS
Student-to-Faculty Ratio: 7:1
% of Classes Under 20: 66%
% of Classes Under 40: 89%
% Full-Time Faculty: 77%
% Full-Time Faculty w/ Terminal Degree: 96%

Top Programs
Biology
Economics
Education
Engineering
English
Music
Political Science
Psychology

Retention Rate: 97%
4-Year Graduation Rate: 89%
6-Year Graduation Rate: 94%

Curricular Flexibility: Less Flexible
Academic Rating: ★★★★★

Inside the Classroom

With an acceptance rate that falls between Dartmouth and Cornell, Vanderbilt University in Nashville, Tennessee, has positioned itself as not only one of the South's most selective institutions but as one of the country's ultra-elite universities. Founded in 1873 by the railroad and shipping tycoon/robber baron Cornelius Vanderbilt (who had never set foot in Tennessee), this private research university is comprised of ten schools, only four of which cater to the school's 6,700+ undergraduate students. Of the sixty-seven undergraduate majors, economics, politics and government, and neuroscience are among the most popular.

Core academic requirements known as AXLE (Achieving Excellence in Liberal Arts Education) are extensive. Those in the College of Arts and Sciences must complete three or four writing-intensive courses, including a first-year writing seminar. Thirteen additional courses are mandated in foreign language, US history, social/behavioral sciences, and mathematics and natural sciences. Juniors and seniors have the option to apply to individual department's honors programs where they are then required to produce a scholarly or creative work.

With a 7:1 student-to-faculty ratio, undergraduate class sizes are kept small. In the 2018-19 school year, 28 percent of course sections contained nine or fewer students, and close to two- thirds contained nineteen or fewer; only 7 percent were large lecture hall affairs of more than fifty students. Undergraduate research opportunities can be found as part of the classroom curriculum, capstone experiences, or through the Vanderbilt University Summer Research Program that accepted eighty-seven of the 205 applicants for its 2018 cohort. Two-fifths of Commodores are adventurous enough to study abroad, and 84 percent of those who do say the experience helped them build job skills. The university offers 120 programs in forty countries.

Vanderbilt alumni are quickly scooped up by many of the world's most desirable and highest-paying corporations. Elite graduate, law, and medical schools are equally fond of those with a Vandy diploma. The School of Engineering has a particularly strong national reputation as do offerings in biology, economics, education, and music. Vanderbilt has been named a Top Producer of Fulbright Scholars, having seen fourteen students win the award in 2018. Other 2018 graduates captured Schwarzman, Boren, Critical Language, Luce, and Marshall Scholarships.

Outside the Classroom

Vanderbilt is a cohesive campus with 90 percent of all undergraduates living in the school's twenty residence halls, ten of which are exclusively for first-year students. To support its recent switch to a residential college system the school has committed $600 million to build four new facilities by 2023. The university's seventeen fraternity and fifteen sorority chapters attract 42 percent of the undergraduate student body, making Greek life a rather dominant part of the social scene. Athletics also attract a big crowd; football games draw close to 40,000 fans, and thousands of students compete at some level. The university has ten varsity women's teams and six men's that compete in NCAA Division I. Additionally, there are more than forty intramural leagues and thirty-two club sports that offer athletic participation to all students. Overall, there are 530+ student-led organizations presently active on campus, including roughly fifty that are focused on community service. Campus is situated only a mile and a half from downtown Nashville. Music City, USA, not only offers plenty of concerts but also all of the cultural, dining, entertainment, and shopping options one could desire.

Career Services

The Vanderbilt University Career Center is staffed by fifteen full-time professionals, which equates to a student-to-advisor ratio of 453:1, in the average range compared to the liberal arts schools included in this book but stronger than that when considering the university's size. The center has career coaches who specialize in areas such as fellowships, STEM, economics, and the social sciences as well as three full-time staff members devoted exclusively to employer relations. The office received rave reviews from undergrads as 98 percent rated their interactions with career services staff positively, and there is plenty of evidence as to why.

In the 2017-18 academic year the office engaged in over 2,200 coaching sessions and 1,400+ twenty-minute walk-in sessions. It hosted 534 career programs and brought 311 employers from all over the country to Nashville to conduct 1,845 on-campus interviews. Large scale events such as the Fall Career Fair attract 2,000+ students and recruiters from 140 companies including the likes of ExxonMobil, Merck, Boeing, and Booz Allen Hamilton. An abundance of legitimate internship opportunities are posted online on two platforms, HireADore and DoreWays. With more than 136,000 living alumni, many of whom remain actively connected to the school, Vanderbilt students have success networking with former Commodores. Overall, thanks to an exceptional record of guiding students into elite graduate/professional schools and tons of industry connections that help students launch their careers, it is not difficult to see why Vanderbilt's career services efforts are viewed so favorably by its own graduates.

Vanderbilt University

E-mail: admissions@vanderbilt.edu | Website: www.vanderbilt.edu

Professional Outcomes

Six months after graduating from Vandy, 83 percent of the Class of 2018 were employed or in graduate school. That is an oddly low statistic as the Class of 2017 figure was 95 percent. The 2018 cohort saw 6 percent still seeking employment and 10 percent classified vaguely as "other." The most commonly entered industry was finance (18 percent) followed by technology (14 percent), consulting (11 percent), education (11 percent), and engineering (8 percent). Graduates landed jobs with every major financial firm, consulting company, and tech giant as well as with five NFL teams. Alumni across all graduating years can be found in droves at Deloitte, Google, Microsoft, EY, Morgan Stanley, Goldman Sachs, Citi, and Facebook. The greatest number of alumni in the Greater Nashville area but large pockets also assemble in New York City, Atlanta, DC, Chicago, San Francisco, and Dallas. Midcareer median salaries for Vanderbilt graduates are number one in the state by a wide margin and rank nationally alongside Northeastern powerhouses Boston College, Tufts, and Johns Hopkins.

Among 2018 graduates who went directly on to pursue advanced degrees, 11 percent were in medical school, 11 percent in law school, and 13 percent were beginning a PhD. Institutions where recent alumni are enrolled include Oxford, MIT, Stanford, Princeton, Columbia and just about every other elite university in the world. Vanderbilt undergraduates get into med school at a solid 66 percent clip, and 2018 acceptances included Johns Hopkins, Duke, Penn, and Yale. Those pursuing a legal education from that same graduating year landed at Vanderbilt's own excellent law school as well as UVA, Harvard, Emory, and UNC-Chapel Hill. In sum, if you succeed at Vanderbilt you will have no trouble landing at a world-class graduate or professional program.

Admission

Vanderbilt not only received a record 34,313 applications for a place in the Class of 2022 and recorded the first single-digit acceptance rate in the school's history (9.6 percent), but it also set a university-best for yield rate as 49 percent of admitted students elected to enroll. For perspective, in 2000 the school received fewer than 9,000 applications and accepted 55 percent. In the 2018-19 admissions cycle the ACT was the more frequently submitted test, and the mid-50 percent range was 33-35; the range for the SAT was 1450-1560. Just a hair under 90 percent of enrolled freshmen earned places in the top 10 percent of their high school class, and 96 percent placed in the top quartile. There were 192 National Merit Scholars entering as freshmen in 2018-19. Overall, three-quarters of enrolled students had GPAs above 3.75 on a 4.0 scale; the average was 3.83.

Seven categories are deemed "very important" by this university's admissions committee: rigor of coursework, GPA, class rank, standardized test scores, application essay, character/personal qualities, and extracurricular involvement. Vandy is serious about its emphasis on extracurriculars; 100 percent of admitted Class of 2022 students held leadership positions in high school. Recommendations and talent/ability comprise the next tier of factors that are "important" to the process. Students applying early decision were admitted at a 21 percent clip, significantly higher than those applying via the regular round. In the last twenty years, Vandy has transformed from a school that accepted more than 50 percent of applicants to a single-digit dream crusher. The regional distinction in the "Southern Ivy" label is almost irrelevant these days. Rather, Vanderbilt is an Ivy-equivalent that happens to be located in the South, and only 33 percent of the student body hails from that region.

Worth Your Money?

The full cost of attendance at Vanderbilt is $71,110, but those with financial need will pay nothing near that sum. Vandy awards an average need-based grant of $49,614 per year, putting it among the endlessly endowed Ivy League schools as one of the most generous colleges in the country. It is a rare school that can meet 100 percent of demonstrated need. Unlike the Ivies, those with exceptional credentials and special talents may actually be able to procure some level of merit aid as well. Thirteen percent of undergraduates receive an average annual merit aid award of roughly $20k. However, even if you aren't fortunate enough to be counted among this relatively small group of merit aid recipients, Vanderbilt is still worth your money.

FINANCIAL
Institutional Type: Private
In-State Tuition: $50,800
Out-of-State Tuition: $50,800
Room & Board: $16,910
Required Fees: $2,106
Books & Supplies: $1,294

Avg. Need-Based Aid: $49,614
Avg. % of Need Met: 100%

Avg. Merit-Based Aid: $19,977
% Receiving Merit-Based Aid: 13%

Avg. Cumulative Debt: $22,854
% of Students Borrowing: 21%

CAREER
Who Recruits
1. Vineyard Vines
2. ExxonMobil
3. Teach for America
4. AllianceBernstein
5. Defense Intelligence Agency

Notable Internships
1. UBS
2. Lyft
3. Spotify

Top Industries
1. Business
2. Education
3. Research
4. Operations
5. Engineering

Top Employers
1. Deloitte
2. Google
3. Microsoft
4. EY
5. Amazon

Where Alumni Work
1. Nashville
2. New York City
3. Atlanta
4. Washington, DC
5. San Francisco

Median Earnings
College Scorecard (Early Career): $69,000
EOP (Early Career): $72,800
PayScale (Mid-Career): $119,100

RANKINGS
Forbes: 27
Money: 15
U.S. News: 15 (T), National Universities
Wall Street Journal/THE: 17
Washington Monthly: 44, National Universities

#CollegesWorthYourMoney

Vassar College

Poughkeepsie, New York | Admissions Phone: 845-437-7300

ADMISSION

Admission Rate: 25%
Admission Rate - Men: 33%
Admission Rate - Women: 21%
EA Admission Rate: Not Offered
ED Admission Rate: 44%
Admission Rate (5-Year Trend): 0%
ED Admission Rate (5-Year Trend): -4%
% of Admits Attending (Yield): 34%
Transfer Admission Rate: 13%

Offered Wait List: 1,138
Accepted Wait List: 566
Admitted Wait List: 48

SAT Reading/Writing (Middle 50%): 680-740
SAT Math (Middle 50%): 690-770
ACT Composite (Middle 50%): 31-33
Testing Policy: ACT/SAT Required
SAT Superscore: Yes
ACT Superscore: Yes

% Graduated in Top 10% of HS Class: 61%
% Graduated in Top 25% of HS Class: 91%
% Graduated in Top 50% of HS Class: 98%

ENROLLMENT

Total Undergraduate Enrollment: 2,456
% Part-Time: 1%
% Male: 41%
% Female: 59%
% Out-of-State: 72%
% Fraternity: Not Offered
% Sorority: Not Offered
% On-Campus (Freshman): 99%
% On-Campus (All Undergraduate): 97%

% African-American: 4%
% Asian: 12%
% Hispanic: 11%
% White: 56%
% Other: 8%
% Race or Ethnicity Unknown: 1%
% International: 9%
% Low-Income: 29%

ACADEMICS

Student-to-Faculty Ratio: 8:1
% of Classes Under 20: 67%
% of Classes Under 40: 100%
% Full-Time Faculty: 83%
% Full-Time Faculty w/ Terminal Degree: 91%

Top Programs
Art
Biology
Drama
Film
History
International Studies
Physics
Political Science

Retention Rate: 95%
4-Year Graduation Rate: 88%
6-Year Graduation Rate: 92%

Curricular Flexibility: Very Flexible
Academic Rating: ★★★★★

Inside the Classroom

A recent three-part Malcom Gladwell podcast was full of effusive praise for one college in Poughkeepsie, New York, that puts its money where its mouth is on the subject of making college affordable for low-income and first-generation students. Vassar deserves that type of attention for its commitment to creating a more egalitarian higher education world. Yet, this original member of the Seven Sisters that became coeducational in 1969 also has a well-deserved reputation for its exceptionally flexible and high-quality liberal education.

Vassar's 2,456 undergraduate students have the choice of fifty-one majors and are not beholden to a core curriculum or a murderous series of freshman- and sophomore-year requirements; instead, there are only three mandates. All freshmen must take a first-year writing seminar capped at seventeen students. The second requirement is that all students must become proficient in a foreign language; among the languages offered are Korean, Hebrew, and Old English. The last is that students must take at least one course dealing with quantitative reasoning. Other than that and, of course, one's major, there is ample room to explore electives and burgeoning intellectual passions.

The college's 336 faculty members teach every single undergraduate course offered at Vassar. An 8:1 student-to-faculty ratio leads to an average class size of seventeen students, and 20 percent of all sections have an enrollment of nine or fewer. Professors are extremely available outside the classroom as 70 percent of the faculty live on or near campus, and faculty families also live within each residence hall. Opportunities to get involved in undergraduate research are taken advantage of by 300+ students each year who work side-by-side with professors on research in the sciences, social sciences, or arts and humanities. Roughly 500 students also engage in credited community-based learning in local organizations or agencies. Vassar's Undergraduate Research Summer Institute (URSI) has been operational since 1986 and offers a plethora of ten-week research experiences in everything from astronomy to computer science to psychology. Study abroad programs are taken advantage of by two-fifths of students.

In terms of number of degrees conferred, the most popular majors are English, political science, psychology, economics, and biology. Though slightly less popular, programs in history, physics, and the fine and performing arts also receive very high marks. The lack of a core curriculum makes it easy to double major if you desire. Many grads ultimately pursue further education and find elite graduate and professional programs that respect the rigor of a Vassar education. Over the last five years Brewers also have landed forty-four Fulbright Scholarships and nineteen National Science Foundation Graduate Research Fellowships.

Outside the Classroom

Few Vassar undergraduates are eager to flee the school's idyllic 1,000-acre campus, so 98 percent of the student body remains in the residence halls all four years. Those seeking to live off campus need to request special permission. The nine traditional houses, one cooperative house, and three school-owned apartment complexes are situated on verdant grounds that have so many different tree varieties that the campus is technically branded an arboretum. Campus cohesion is further enhanced by the absence of Greek organizations. Men make up only 43 percent of the population, which can partially be attributed to the school's history as a women's college and to the realities of the demographic make-up at most liberal arts colleges. Eighteen percent of students are varsity athletes who compete as part of twenty-three NCAA Division III athletic squads. Club and intramural teams as well as facilities that include an elevated running track, a six-lane pool, a nine-hole golf course, and thirteen tennis courts ensure that opportunities for fitness are open to all. There are 145+ student-run organizations and 1,000+ annual campus events such as concerts, guest lectures, and visiting artists/performers, so there is always something to do close to home. Weekend dance parties are popular too. Poughkeepsie offers lots of natural beauty, a mall, and an array of affordable restaurants, although it won't be mistaken for a buzzing metropolis. Those seeking big-city life will have to make the two-hour trip to New York City or the three-hour ride to Boston.

Career Services

The Career Development Office (CDO) at Vassar College is staffed by eight professionals who specialize in career counseling, employer relations, law/health professions advising, and alumni outreach. That works out to a 307:1 student-to-advisor ratio, a figure superior to many schools featured in this guide. Annual events organized by this office include Career Kickoff and First Year Friday, which are designed to give freshmen an overview of the career development services available. Sophomore Career Connections and Senior Week are class-specific events intended to focus students on tasks critical to their particular place in the career development process.

In addition to hosting its own events, Vassar is a member of the Selective Liberal Arts Consortium that sponsors recruiting trips to New York City and Washington, DC. The CDO is always happy to help you with your internship, but the majority of the resources in the area are on online platforms that include Handshake. An exceptional 87 percent of Vassar grads complete at least one internship while at the college. In the 2018-19 school year the CDO conducted 3,443 one-one-one advising appointments and invited thirty-one companies to recruit on campus including NERA Economic Consulting, Teach for America, and M&T Bank. In addition to helping students find their first jobs, the CDO should be lauded for the fantastic job it does in preparing students to continue their education in medical, law, or graduate school.

Professional Outcomes

Somewhere between twenty and fifty Vassar alums can be found at highly competitive companies including Google, Facebook, EY, Deloitte, Microsoft, Citi, EY, and Amazon. Elite universities such as Harvard, Penn, NYU, and Columbia are also among the top employers of former Vassar students, many of whom earn advanced degrees and enter academia. Large contingents of Brewers can be found in the Greater New York City area as well as Boston, DC, San Francisco, Los Angeles, and Philadelphia. Average midcareer salaries are toward the bottom-of-the-pack among elite liberal arts schools, not coincidentally, in the same range as Reed, Oberlin, and Scripps that, like Vassar, produce large numbers of advanced degree earners who do not often see high remuneration early in their careers.

Within five years of graduating, the majority of Vassar alumni pursue further education, including 20 percent who enroll directly in an advanced degree program upon completing their undergraduate studies. Over the last five years medical school applicants have been admitted at an enviable 87 percent rate, over twice the national average. The most commonly attended medical schools include Dartmouth, Tufts, Columbia, and Brown. Law school applicants experienced a superb 96 percent acceptance rate. Vassar ranks in the top fifteen in the nation in percentage of undergraduates who go on to earn a PhD. It ranks particularly well in physics, political science, and sociology.

Admission

Vassar accepted 24 percent of the 8,312 applicants seeking to join the Class of 2022. The average SAT for admitted students was 1435, and the mean ACT was 32. Thirty-eight percent of those accepted were in the top 5 percent of their high school class, 61 percent were in the top decile, and 91 percent were in the top quartile. The average GPA is in the A/A- range. The number of applications has hardly increased in the past decade, and neither has the acceptance rate. (It was 25 percent in 2008-09.)

GPA and evidence of rigorous courses rests atop the list of most important factors in the eyes of the admissions committee. Standardized test scores, essays, recommendations, extracurricular activities, talent/ability, and character/personal qualities round out a holistic process as the next most important considerations. The college is extremely committed to providing need-based aid to low-income and first-generation students, and the numbers back it up. In selecting the 2018-19 freshman class, only 7 percent were legacy admits while 13 percent were first-generation college students. In addition, 24 percent of current students are Pell Grant recipients. Despite a reasonably high yield rate of 34 percent, Vassar still treasures qualified applicants who apply on a binding early-decision basis. In the 2018-19 admissions cycle ED applicants enjoyed a 44 percent acceptance rate. Vassar deserves deep admiration for its commitment to increasing access to students from all backgrounds. It has pursued those aims at the expense of hyping application numbers and, thus, increasing the perception of selectivity. As a result, those in love with this fine liberal arts institution do not face single-digit (or close to it) odds as they would at many other schools of its quality. Of course, excellent grades and test scores are still required.

Worth Your Money?

As a result of Vassar's mission to increase access to low-income students, it does not offer any merit aid, only need-based aid, which it offers in impressively generous quantities. The blow of the list price cost of attendance of $65,240 is softened by the fact that 60 percent of the undergraduate student population qualifies for aid, and the school meets 100 percent of the demonstrated need for all students. That translates to an average grant of over $51,000, making Vassar an incredibly affordable institution for those from less advantageous economic circumstances.

FINANCIAL
Institutional Type: Private
In-State Tuition: $57,910
Out-of-State Tuition: $57,910
Room & Board: $14,220
Required Fees: $940
Books & Supplies: $900

Avg. Need-Based Aid: $51,395
Avg. % of Need Met: 100%

Avg. Merit-Based Aid: $0
% Receiving Merit-Based Aid: 0%

Avg. Cumulative Debt: $21,473
% of Students Borrowing: 49%

CAREER
Who Recruits
1. NERA Economic Consulting
2. Teach for America
3. Peace Corps
4. M&T Bank
5. Shearman and Sterling

Notable Internships
1. U.S. House of Representatives
2. Major League Baseball
3. YouTube

Top Industries
1. Business
2. Education
3. Media
4. Arts & Design
5. Social Services

Top Employers
1. Google
2. IBM
3. Morgan Stanley
4. Deloitte
5. Microsoft

Where Alumni Work
1. New York City
2. Boston
3. San Francisco
4. Washington, DC
5. Los Angeles

Median Earnings
College Scorecard (Early Career): $54,600
EOP (Early Career): $46,000
PayScale (Mid-Career): $100,100

RANKINGS
Forbes: 61
Money: 134
U.S. News: 14, Liberal Arts Colleges
Wall Street Journal/THE: 56
Washington Monthly: 7, Liberal Arts Colleges

#CollegesWorthYourMoney

Villanova University

Villanova, Pennsylvania | Admissions Phone: 610-519-4000

ADMISSION
Admission Rate: 29%
Admission Rate - Men: 28%
Admission Rate - Women: 30%
EA Admission Rate: N/A
ED Admission Rate: 41%
Admission Rate (5-Year Trend): -20%
ED Admission Rate (5-Year Trend): Not Offered
% of Admits Attending (Yield): 25%
Transfer Admission Rate: 25%

Offered Wait List: 6,321
Accepted Wait List: 2,856
Admitted Wait List: 47

SAT Reading/Writing (Middle 50%): 640-710
SAT Math (Middle 50%): 660-760
ACT Composite (Middle 50%): 30-33
Testing Policy: ACT/SAT Required
SAT Superscore: Yes
ACT Superscore: Yes

% Graduated in Top 10% of HS Class: 72%
% Graduated in Top 25% of HS Class: 93%
% Graduated in Top 50% of HS Class: 99%

ENROLLMENT
Total Undergraduate Enrollment: 6,917
% Part-Time: 5%
% Male: 47%
% Female: 53%
% Out-of-State: 79%
% Fraternity: 19%
% Sorority: 39%
% On-Campus (Freshman): 99%
% On-Campus (All Undergraduate): 67%

% African-American: 5%
% Asian: 6%
% Hispanic: 8%
% White: 75%
% Other: 3%
% Race or Ethnicity Unknown: 2%
% International: 2%
% Low-Income: 14%

ACADEMICS
Student-to-Faculty Ratio: 11:1
% of Classes Under 20: 42%
% of Classes Under 40: 95%
% Full-Time Faculty: 60%
% Full-Time Faculty w/ Terminal Degree: 88%

Top Programs
Accounting
Biology
Communication
Economics
Engineering
Finance
Nursing
Political Science

Retention Rate: 96%
4-Year Graduation Rate: 87%
6-Year Graduation Rate: 91%

Curricular Flexibility: Somewhat Flexible
Academic Rating: ★★★★

Inside the Classroom

Positioned twelve miles outside of Philadelphia on the swanky Main Line is Villanova University, a school that, prior to winning an NCAA basketball title in 1985, possessed only a regional reputation. Thirty years later, the prestige of its powerhouse basketball program has launched an already renowned and highly desirable school into a whole new stratosphere. Today, this midsize Catholic research university is the proud home to 6,500 enthusiastic Wildcat undergraduates. For those who can conquer the suddenly highly-selective admissions process, Nova provides a world class educational experience in a spirited collegiate atmosphere.

Students can choose one of forty-five undergraduate programs within four schools: the College of Liberal Arts & Sciences, the Villanova School of Business, the College of Engineering, and the College of Nursing. All students must conquer the school's core curriculum that is designed to ensure a "depth of study and intellectual sophistication while recognizing that learning implies different modes of inquiry." Courses in theology, ethics, and philosophy as well as the Augustine and Culture Seminar Program comprise the Core Foundational Courses. Additional requirements include all of the usual liberal arts standards (social sciences, math, foreign language, and so on) and an upper-level theology course, a writing seminar, and a senior capstone.

The university sports a 12:1 student-to-faculty ratio and offers average undergraduate classes of twenty-two students. It is possible to receive a degree from the school without ever sitting in a giant lecture hall. In fact, only 4 percent of course sections enroll forty or more students. As a consequence, professors are unusually available in and outside of the classroom. From the start of freshman year, opportunities for meaningful undergraduate research will be within your grasp. The Villanova Match Research Programs for First Year Students allows second-semester freshmen to work as research assistants alongside distinguished faculty. The Villanova Undergraduate Research Fellows Summer Program is taken advantage of by many upperclassmen. Wildcats study abroad in impressive numbers. The 42 percent participation rate places Nova among the top ten universities in the country. There is a full menu of foreign locations with semester, year-long, and summer options.

Villanova's business, accounting, and engineering programs all receive a good deal of attention from ranking publications. The school's most popular degree is business with over one-quarter of all graduates majoring in it. Engineering and nursing are the second- and third-most commonly conferred degree areas. As the school's reputation reaches new heights, more students than ever are winning prestigious national awards. In 2018 alone, Villanova graduates earned sixteen Fulbright Scholarships, five Gilman Scholarships, three Goldwater Scholarships, and multiple National Science Foundation Graduate Research Fellowships.

Outside the Classroom

Two-thirds of the undergraduate student body currently live on a 240-acre campus that is growing more beautiful and impressive by the day. Constant progress can be observed on the university's many construction projects, and we're not talking small buildings. The school is currently erecting on-campus housing for an addition 1,135 undergrads. The newly opened Finneran Pavilion and an under-construction performing arts center are emblematic of the administration's recent splurge. The school is home to twenty-four fraternities and sororities, and roughly one-third of students participate in Greek life. Athletics, particularly basketball, are a way of life at Villanova. More than 500 student-athletes compete on the Wildcats twenty-four NCCA Division I teams, and many more participate in the forty-four club and intramural sports options. In total, there are 265 active extracurricular clubs, a fair number of which are centered on community service, which is a definite point of emphasis at Nova as students contribute a quarter million service hours annually. Radnor Township isn't cheap, but it offers tons of great hangouts and places to eat. The King of Prussia Mall, the second largest in the United States, is only a few miles away. The museums, sports, restaurants, and culture of Philly are only a straight-shot, half-hour car ride away.

Career Services

The Villanova University Career Center employs fourteen individuals who specialize in career counseling, pre-law advising, employer relations, and industry advising. The center also trains seventeen career assistants who are available to support their fellow undergraduates as well. Only counting professional employees, the office has a 468:1 student-to-counselor ratio, which is within the average range of schools profiled in this guide. However, by almost every other metric, this career center, like the university's famed basketball squad, measures up well against the competition.

Villanova University

E-mail: gotovu@villanova.edu | Website: www.villanova.edu

Including graduate students, there were 7,500 visits to the career center during the 2017-18 school year. Over 35,000 job and internship opportunities were posted online for Wildcats to explore. On campus recruiting is also strong with 365 companies making the trek to Villanova's grounds last year alone. A well-connected and passionate global network of 125,000 alumni is also available to help you make connections as you search for internships and employment. Most students are successful landing an internship as 70 percent of College of Liberal Arts and Sciences students complete at least one such experience at Nova. Large events like the Fall 2018 Career Fair drew 175+ employers to the Connelly Center. With a high level of personalized support, a robust Employer Relations Department, and excellent career outcomes for graduates (more in a moment), the Villanova University Career Center continues to do excellent work on behalf of its students.

Professional Outcomes

Within six months of commencement, Class of 2018 graduates had a placement rate of 97 percent with 74 percent entering the workforce and 17 percent matriculating into graduate or professional school. The most popular employers of members of the Class of 2018 were, not coincidentally, also companies with the largest Wildcat alumni representation. That list includes Vanguard, Verizon, PwC, JP Morgan Chase, Merck, Comcast, EY, Deloitte, and Morgan Stanley. The average starting salary across all colleges within the university was $59,500. Graduates of the business, nursing, and engineering schools all earned an average salary above $63,000 while the Colleges of Liberal Arts & Sciences figure was just a hair under $50k. Remaining in the Philadelphia Metro area is the most popular move, but large numbers also migrate to New York City, DC, Boston, Chicago, San Francisco, and Los Angeles.

Class of 2018 members went on to study at a number of topflight graduate institutions. College of Engineering grads went to schools like Northwestern, the University of Notre Dame, and Georgia Institute of Technology. Liberal arts grads entered programs at Columbia, Georgetown, Tufts, UCLA, and King's College London. Nova grads enjoyed a medical school admissions rate of 70-75 percent, far above the national average. Among the fifty-three graduates applying to law school in 2018, acceptances were earned at Fordham, the University of Michigan, Northeastern, Boston College and, of course, Villanova's own Charles Widger School of Law.

Admission

The 29 percent of successful applicants who earned a place in the Class of 2022 possessed middle-50 percent results of 1380-1490 on the SAT, 31-33 on the ACT, and a 4.10-4.48 GPA. While the profile of students who actually enrolled is a bit less intimidating, the Class of 2022 cohort was still strong. Within that group the SAT range was 1300-1470, the ACT range was 30-33, and the average weighted GPA was 4.19. In terms of class rank, 69 percent of freshmen placed in their high school class' top decile, and 88 percent earned a spot in the top quartile. For perspective, in 2015 the university admitted 43 percent of its applicants, and the 25th percentile SAT score was an even 1200.

Rigor of coursework, GPA, class rank, and standardized test scores (students evenly submit the ACT and SAT) comprise the factors deemed most important by the committee. Essays, recommendations, extracurricular activities, work experience, and volunteer work are among the areas that receive secondary consideration. There is no interview offered as part of the admissions process. Those applying through binding early decision were accepted at a 41 percent rate, providing a solid advantage over those in the regular cycle. Villanova does advertise a holistic process, but with close to 23,000 applicants these days, your SATs, GPA, class rank, and other measurables need to be within range for serious consideration. Students (and their counselors) need to be aware of the year-by-year increases in selectivity as this school has transformed in the recent past.

Worth Your Money?

Villanova rarely covers a student's full amount of need, but 47 percent of current students do receive need-based aid that averages $37k per award; only 8 percent of undergraduates are presently receiving any merit aid. The total annual cost of attendance at Nova is a hair shy of $70,000, therefore, even with aid, becoming a Wildcat is not going to come cheap. It's no wonder that teens from families in the top 10 percent of income earners make up more than half of the student body. That said, starting salaries for graduates are on the higher side, making it possible to pay back the substantial loans you may need to take out in order to attend.

FINANCIAL
Institutional Type: Private
In-State Tuition: $52,578
Out-of-State Tuition: $52,578
Room & Board: $14,020
Required Fees: $820
Books & Supplies: $1,100

Avg. Need-Based Aid: $37,141
Avg. % of Need Met: 82%

Avg. Merit-Based Aid: $19,828
% Receiving Merit-Based Aid: 8%

Avg. Cumulative Debt: $35,552
% of Students Borrowing: 53%

CAREER
Who Recruits
1. CIA
2. KPMG
3. TD Securities
4. Boston Consulting Group
5. BNY Mellon

Notable Internships
1. QVC
2. NBC Universal
3. Pratt & Whitney

Top Industries
1. Business
2. Operations
3. Sales
4. Finance
5. Information Technology

Top Employers
1. Vanguard
2. Verizon
3. PwC
4. JPMorgan Chase
5. Merck

Where Alumni Work
1. Philadelphia
2. New York City
3. Washington, DC
4. Boston
5. Chicago

Median Earnings
College Scorecard (Early Career): $77,900
EOP (Early Career): $78,300
PayScale (Mid-Career): $119,500

RANKINGS
Forbes: 72
Money: 179
U.S. News: 46 (T), National Universities
Wall Street Journal/THE: 129
Washington Monthly: 87, National Universities

#CollegesWorthYourMoney

Wake Forest University

Winston-Salem, North Carolina | Admissions Phone: 336-758-5201

ADMISSION
Admission Rate: 29%
Admission Rate - Men: 33%
Admission Rate - Women: 27%
EA Admission Rate: Not Offered
ED Admission Rate: 41%
Admission Rate (5-Year Trend): -6%
ED Admission Rate (5-Year Trend): -5%
% of Admits Attending (Yield): 37%
Transfer Admission Rate: 5%

Offered Wait List: N/A
Accepted Wait List: N/A
Admitted Wait List: N/A

SAT Reading/Writing (Middle 50%): 650-710
SAT Math (Middle 50%): 660-760
ACT Composite (Middle 50%): 29-33
Testing Policy: Test Optional
SAT Superscore: Yes
ACT Superscore: Yes

% Graduated in Top 10% of HS Class: 76%
% Graduated in Top 25% of HS Class: 92%
% Graduated in Top 50% of HS Class: 97%

ENROLLMENT
Total Undergraduate Enrollment: 5,225
% Part-Time: 1%
% Male: 47%
% Female: 53%
% Out-of-State: 78%
% Fraternity: 33%
% Sorority: 59%
% On-Campus (Freshman): 99%
% On-Campus (All Undergraduate): 75%

% African-American: 6%
% Asian: 4%
% Hispanic: 7%
% White: 69%
% Other: 3%
% Race or Ethnicity Unknown: 0%
% International: 10%
% Low-Income: 10%

ACADEMICS
Student-to-Faculty Ratio: 10:1
% of Classes Under 20: 57%
% of Classes Under 40: 96%
% Full-Time Faculty: 69%
% Full-Time Faculty w/ Terminal Degree: 94%

Top Programs
Accountancy
Chemistry
Communication
Economics
Finance
Health and Exercise Science
Politics and International Affairs
Psychology

Retention Rate: 95%
4-Year Graduation Rate: 85%
6-Year Graduation Rate: 89%

Curricular Flexibility: Somewhat Flexible
Academic Rating: ★★★★

Inside the Classroom

Founded as the Manual Labor Institute for Baptist preachers in 1834, Wake Forest has roots that sound exaggeratedly and humorously humble. Of course, the current vibe of the university could not be further from its lowly beginnings, save the retention of its Southern charm. Today's Wake Forest is generally regarded as a bubble of conservatism and wealth—the average student's parental income is over $220k—and, from an academic standpoint, this school is viewed as one of the top private research institutions outside the Northeast.

All freshmen enter the Undergraduate College that offers forty-two majors and sixty minors. Economics, biology, psychology, finance, and communications are the areas toward which the largest number of students gravitate. Those wishing to attend the School of Business apply prior to their sophomore year. All other concentrations are open to any student. Academic requirements include a freshman seminar, a four-credit writing seminar, foreign language, physical education, and one course in both quantitative reasoning and cultural diversity.

Sporting a student-to-faculty ratio of 10:1, classes are kept on the small side with 57 percent of sections enrolling fewer than twenty students. There are a fair number of courses that have twenty to thirty-nine students, but only a minuscule number that take place in large lecture halls. Close to 60 percent of Demon Deacons have the opportunity to engage in hands-on research for academic credit. Wake's robust study abroad options feature 400 semester, summer and year-long programs in 200 cities in more than seventy countries worldwide. Undergrads participate at a 63 percent rate, good enough for the seventh highest figure among doctoral degree-granting US universities.

Wake Forest is a school with strengths across a variety of disciplines, most notably chemistry, communication, accounting, finance, and international affairs. Overall, the institution has an excellent reputation across the board in both employment and academic circles, and Wake Forest grads are always considered for prestigious postgraduate fellowships. Five members of the Class of 2018 were named Fulbright Scholars, bringing the university's all-time total to 116, and it produces a Rhodes Scholar about every other year.

Outside the Classroom

Greek life gets top billing when it comes to describing the social scene at Wake. Half the student body joins a fraternity or sorority with women joining sororities at an extraordinarily high rate (59 percent). Roughly three-quarters of students live in university-owned housing with many off-campus upperclassmen flocking to nearby apartment complexes. The Demon Deacons are a powerhouse in NCAA Division I athletics, quite an achievement considering the university's modest size. Of the sixteen varsity sports teams that compete in the vaunted ACC, men's basketball and football draw the biggest crowds. The school is brimming with less serious but still dedicated athletes as a whopping 85 percent of the student body participates in intramural athletics. Many non-sports options also are available as there are more than 240 active student organizations on campus, including a full array of political, religious, and performing arts groups. The quaint Southern charm of campus extends into the surrounding small city of Winston-Salem, which offers its fair share of cultural, culinary, and shopping pursuits. However, it is worth noting that safety can be an issue as Winston-Salem has a crime rate 57 percent higher than the national average.

Career Services

The Office of Personal and Career Development (OPCD) at Wake Forest is staffed by thirty-tree full-time professional employees who serve as career coaches, employer relations specialists, and counselors who work on personal and professional development with alumni. That equates to a student-to-advisor ratio of 158:1, which ranks among the best of the institutions included in this book. The OPCD is not only generously staffed; it also operates with the clear mission of readying every single Demon Deacon for a meaningful next step in life.

In a single year, career coaches met with over 4,000 members of the student body to engage in 1:1 career planning sessions and/or small workshops. Career treks took students to New York City, San Francisco, and DC to meet with alumni in their places of business. Perhaps the office's most unique feature is that it runs a sequence of for-credit College-to-Career courses. Having an actual academic program dedicated to career prep affords the OPCD the chance to teach large numbers of students about matching their personalities to fulfilling careers, finding internships, developing cover letters, considering cost-of-living issues postgraduation, and so much more. Almost one-quarter of graduates take at least one of those courses. Employer relations at Wake are also strong, and they host a number of well-attended job fairs. Additionally, more than 12,000 job and internship postings go up each year. All freshmen are introduced to the services offered via the OPCD Orientation that alerts students to the wealth of career-prep resources available to them from the moment they step on campus. Overall, Wake Forest's career services office is held in high regard, a view backed by the fact that almost every single graduate achieves a successful outcome within months of exiting campus.

Wake Forest University

E-mail: admissions@wfu.edu | Website: www.wfu.edu

Professional Outcomes

The members of the Class of 2018 didn't take long to arrive at their next destinations. Within six months of graduation, 98 percent had either landed their first professional job or were already matriculated into a graduate program. Employers landing the highest numbers of alumni included national and multinational corporations IBM, Siemens, Volvo, Goldman Sachs, Disney, Deloitte, Dell, Gucci, PepsiCo, EY, and Nike. Over 40 percent of graduates remain south of the Mason-Dixon Line; most of those who do exit the South head to the Mid-Atlantic region and the Northeast. By the start of midcareer Wake Forest alumni earn the second-highest median salary of any school in North Carolina, behind Duke but ahead of Davidson and UNC-Chapel Hill.

Just shy of 30 percent of graduates went directly from donning their caps and gowns to pursuing advanced degrees. Students attend a wide range of schools from a selectivity standpoint, but there is a strong representation of elite institutions. As one example, an examination of recent history majors shows acceptances at elite institutions including the University of Chicago, Emory, Duke, Georgetown, Vanderbilt, Harvard, Yale, and the London School of Economics. Many biology majors headed to PhD programs or into medical school at locations such as UNC, Duke, Johns Hopkins, Tufts, and Emory; Wake Forest's medical school takes in many of its own graduates. There were 125 medical school applicants in the Class of 2018 alone.

Admission

Applicants to the Class of 2022 were accepted at a 29 percent clip, a bit lower than five years prior when 34 percent of applicants were successful. However, the average profile of an admitted student has barely changed in that time. Applications may be on the rise, but the requirements for admission have stayed fairly constant.

Wake Forest is a test-optional school, but among those attending students who submitted scores, the middle-50 percent ranges were 1310-1470 on the SAT and 29-33 on the ACT. Over three-quarters of the freshman class finished in the top 10 percent of their high school class, and 92 percent were in the top 25 percent. Those statistics jibe with factors that the admissions office self-reports as being "most important": rigor of curriculum, GPA, class, essay, and character/personal characteristics. If being a Demon Deacon has been your lifelong dream, then you should strongly consider applying early decision to gain an edge on your competition. In 2018, Wake accepted 41 percent of ED applicants compared to 27 percent in the regular round. Further, those accepted ED comprised 56 percent of the Class of 2022. Landing a spot on this gorgeous Winston-Salem campus is a straightforward proposition that is made even simpler by the university's decision to jettison standardized testing back in 2008. Nonetheless, 41 percent of applicants still submit SAT results, and 45 percent submit ACT scores. Applicants should bring stellar grades to the table, be situated among the very best of their respective high schools, and should use their ED card to their advantage.

Worth Your Money?

Wake Forest only awards need-based aid to 30 percent of its undergraduates, a low number compared to other top schools, but when it does offer aid, it does it right. One hundred percent see their full demonstrated need met for an average annual grant of $50,422. On the flip side, the school awards massive amounts of merit aid, an unusual practice for a school of its caliber. Over one-quarter of current undergraduates are recipients of merit-based awards that average $28k. The list price cost of attendance for Wake Forest is greater than $75,000, so those packages help make the school a bit more affordable for the non-wealthy. However, Wake grads still end up with debt loads that exceed the national average. Individuals required to take out a significant amount in loans should consider their career plans and other competing offers before deciding to attend Wake.

FINANCIAL
Institutional Type: Private
In-State Tuition: $54,430
Out-of-State Tuition: $54,430
Room & Board: $16,740
Required Fees: $1,010
Books & Supplies: $1,500

Avg. Need-Based Aid: $50,422
Avg. % of Need Met: 100%

Avg. Merit-Based Aid: $28,107
% Receiving Merit-Based Aid: 27%

Avg. Cumulative Debt: $36,863
% of Students Borrowing: 30%

CAREER
Who Recruits
1. MullenLowe Mediahub
2. Gap, Inc.
3. Horizon Media
4. Gartner
5. Goldman Sachs

Notable Internships
1. Bristol-Myers Squibb
2. Aramark
3. Sotheby's

Top Industries
1. Business
2. Education
3. Finance
4. Operations
5. Sales

Top Employers
1. Wells Fargo
2. EY
3. BB&T
4. PwC
5. Deloitte

Where Alumni Work
1. Winston-Salem, NC
2. New York City
3. Charlotte
4. Washington, DC
5. Raleigh-Durham, NC

Median Earnings
College Scorecard (Early Career): $63,800
EOP (Early Career): $71,500
PayScale (Mid-Career): $114,800

RANKINGS
Forbes: 56
Money: 98
U.S. News: 27 (T), National Universities
Wall Street Journal/THE: 68 (T)
Washington Monthly: 91, National Universities

#CollegesWorthYourMoney

Washington and Lee University

Lexington, Virginia | Admissions Phone: 540-458-8710

ADMISSION
Admission Rate: 21%
Admission Rate - Men: 20%
Admission Rate - Women: 22%
EA Admission Rate: Not Offered
ED Admission Rate: 50%
Admission Rate (5-Year Trend): +3%
ED Admission Rate (5-Year Trend): +11%
% of Admits Attending (Yield): 38%
Transfer Admission Rate: 5%

Offered Wait List: 1,689
Accepted Wait List: 801
Admitted Wait List: 2

SAT Reading/Writing (Middle 50%): 670-730
SAT Math (Middle 50%): 680-760
ACT Composite (Middle 50%): 31-34
Testing Policy: ACT/SAT Required
SAT Superscore: Yes
ACT Superscore: Yes

% Graduated in Top 10% of HS Class: 83%
% Graduated in Top 25% of HS Class: 97%
% Graduated in Top 50% of HS Class: 100%

ENROLLMENT
Total Undergraduate Enrollment: 1,829
% Part-Time: 0%
% Male: 50%
% Female: 50%
% Out-of-State: 84%
% Fraternity: 75%
% Sorority: 75%
% On-Campus (Freshman): 100%
% On-Campus (All Undergraduate): 76%

% African-American: 3%
% Asian: 4%
% Hispanic: 5%
% White: 81%
% Other: 4%
% Race or Ethnicity Unknown: 1%
% International: 4%
% Low-Income: 10%

ACADEMICS
Student-to-Faculty Ratio: 8:1
% of Classes Under 20: 75%
% of Classes Under 40: 100%
% Full-Time Faculty: 78%
% Full-Time Faculty w/ Terminal Degree: 95%

Top Programs
Accounting
Biology
Business Administration
Economics
English
History
Journalism and Mass Communication
Political Science

Retention Rate: 96%
4-Year Graduation Rate: 92%
6-Year Graduation Rate: 95%

Curricular Flexibility: Less Flexible
Academic Rating: ★★★★★

Inside the Classroom

The influence of two disparate figures in American history, George Washington and Robert E. Lee, helped shape a small liberal arts school known in the eighteenth century as Liberty Hall Academy and in the nineteenth century as Washington College before it evolved into Washington and Lee University that, today, is an elite liberal arts institution home to 1,800+ undergraduates. Although dubbed a "university," the only postgraduate program is its law school. Set in the small town of Lexington, Virginia, Washington and Lee is one of the premier colleges of its modest size in all of the South, and it has remained highly selective for the entirety of the twenty-first century.

W&L demands a high number of courses to fulfill its foundational and distributional requirements that collectively will take close to three full semesters to complete. Mandated coursework includes writing, foreign language, physical education, computer science, literature, fine arts, four arts and humanities classes, and two in each of the natural and social sciences. One experiential learning course that focuses on research/presentation/cultural competence rounds out the academic requirements that apply to all undergrads. The university offers thirty-seven majors and twenty-nine minors, including a fair share of interdisciplinary programs.

With an exceptionally low 8:1 student-to-faculty ratio and no graduate students to attend to, W&L undergraduates enjoy loads of attention. Three-quarters of class sections contain nineteen or fewer students, and fewer than 2 percent of courses enroll more than thirty students. Instructors earn rave reviews as 98 percent of Class of 2018 grads were either "very satisfied" or "satisfied" by the quality of their professors. Further, 87 percent were "very satisfied" with faculty's availability outside the classroom; not a single student expressed any level of dissatisfaction. Students can participate in research via the Summer Research Scholars that allows undergrads to collaborate with faculty in the field or lab. Studying abroad is a typical part of a Washington and Lee education with 70 percent of grads spending a semester or summer in a foreign land.

Altogether the various social science disciplines account for one-quarter of the degrees conferred at Washington and Lee, business (22 percent), biology (9 percent), and foreign language (6 percent) are next in popularity. The renowned Williams School of Commerce, Politics, and Economics offers outstanding business-oriented programs that feed many of the top corporations in the world. English, history, and W&L's Department of Journalism and Mass Communication are also highly respected. Given Washington and Lee's many strengths, a healthy number of students are encouraged to apply for prestigious postgraduate fellowships, and a good number are successful. In 2018, four undergrads were awarded Fulbrights while others took home a Goldwater Scholarship and a William Jefferson Clinton Scholarship to study in Dubai.

Outside the Classroom

The main campus of Washington and Lee is concentrated on fifty acres, but it has an additional forty acres of playing fields and 215 acres of green space. All first-year students are required to reside in freshman-exclusive dormitories with twelve to twenty students per floor. Sophomores and juniors primarily live in dorms, apartments, and in Greek houses. To say the Greek scene dominates social life is to grossly understate its reach on campus. The school's eight sororities attract 75 percent of female students and an identical 75 percent of males join the thirteen fraternities on campus. The Generals play twenty-four NCAA Division III sports, which means that varsity athletes comprise a sizable 25 percent of the student body; 40 percent play a varsity sport for at least one year. Twenty-five intramural sports, from flag football to Whiffle ball, attract three-quarters of the student body as well as many faculty members who are eligible to participate. An impressive 90 percent of surveyed undergraduates were satisfied with the school's extracurricular offerings. There are 120+ clubs and organizations presently operating, including the always popular Outing Club that camps and hikes around the neighboring wilderness on weekends. Lexington is a small town with a population around 7,000, but it does have its share of bars and restaurants. Richmond is a two-hour trip by car, and DC is a three-hour drive from campus.

Career Services

The Career and Professional Development Center (CPDC) is staffed by five full-time professional employees serving as pre-law advisor, international advisor, assistant director of STEM programs, and assistant director of recruitment. That equates to a student-to-advisor ratio of 366:1, which is within the average range when compared to other institutions included in this book. Excellent personalized attention is provided to the tune of 960 unique student appointments (3.3 per participating student) per year. Each year, the center staff meets one-on-one with 52 percent of the student population, including two-thirds of seniors.

The CPDC brought sixty employers to Lexington last year for information sessions, recruitment, and on-campus interviews. It also organized six career exploration trips to DC and New York City that focused on finance, the arts, advertising, marketing, and STEM fields. Staff also host more than sixty career exploration and skill-building workshops on topics such as social media, Excel, and how to write a personal statement. LexLink, the school's online job and internship platform, has roughly 1,000 postings for undergrads to pursue. A dazzling 85 percent of students complete at least one internship, fellowship, or practicum. Further, 94 percent of those completing such an experience found it "extremely helpful" or "somewhat helpful" in preparing for a career. With ample individualized attention and opportunity for hands-on experience, W&L's Career and Professional Development Center rates well in the eyes of our staff.

Professional Outcomes

In recent years 69-80 percent of graduates have found employment within six months of saying goodbye to Lexington. The most frequently entered industries have been financial services (12 percent), economics/finance (12 percent), education (8 percent), consulting (8 percent), and real estate (6 percent). With so many flocking to financial jobs, many top banks, accounting firms, and investment houses presently employ more than two dozen Generals including EY, Wells Fargo, Goldman Sachs, PwC, JP Morgan, Capital One, and Morgan Stanley. Washington and Lee is the rare college that sees the majority of its alumni relocate to cities in other states. DC, New York City, and Atlanta all draw more graduates than Roanoke or Richmond. Starting salaries for the Class of 2018 were solid with 57 percent of the cohort being paid $55,000 or more while 23 percent brought home in excess of $75,000.

Almost one-quarter of grads immediately matriculated into a graduate or professional program upon receiving their bachelor's degrees. Law school (29 percent), medical/health professional schools (22 percent), and engineering (12 percent) were the top three destinations. Recent physics and engineering students have gone on to graduate study at MIT, Carnegie Mellon, Stanford, and Vanderbilt. Law schools accepting recent grads included Wake Forest, Fordham, Georgetown, Vanderbilt, and W&L's own law school. Medical school acceptances included Rutgers Medical School, LSU School of Medicine in New Orleans, and University of Texas Medical Branch.

Admission

Of 5,855 applicants for a seat in the Class of 2022 only 1,239 were admitted for an acceptance rate of 21 percent; 474 ultimately enrolled. The mid-50 percent SAT score was 1360-1480, and the ACT range was 31-34. Most 2018-19 freshmen hailed from the very top of their high school class with 83 percent placing in the top decile and 97 percent in the top 25 percent. All of the admissions statistics are almost identical to those of a decade ago. In fact, the number of applicants, acceptance rate, and the achievement level of entering freshmen has remained relatively steady since the turn of the millennium.

The goal of the admissions committee is to "get to know you as well as possible through your application." The rigor of your high school curriculum is very important—96 percent of entering freshmen had an IB or AP background, and just shy of three-quarters studied four or more years of a foreign language. Only three other factors rated as "very important": class rank, extracurricular activities, and character/personal qualities. GPA, recommendations, essays, and standardized test scores also are considered as factors of importance in evaluating candidates. Applying early decision is a no-brainer for dedicated applicants as the acceptance rate hovers above 50 percent versus 18 percent for those in the regular cycle. In fact, the school locks in 58 percent of its freshman class via the ED round. Washington and Lee offers a genuinely holistic admissions process. Strong grades in highly rigorous courses are nonnegotiable, but qualities like leadership and what one brings to a student community also receive strong consideration.

Worth Your Money?

While a $70k+ price tag might make cost-conscious families aggressively scratch Washington and Lee off their child's college list, it is one of the most generous schools with merit aid for exceptional students. While only 22 percent receive that form of aid, the average amount is for a difference-making sum of $49,195, with as much as 10 percent of each entering class receiving the highly coveted Johnson Scholarship, which fully covers tuition, room, and board for chosen applicants. That generosity is only trumped by the school's dedication to meeting 100 percent of financial need for every qualifying student. Thanks to that level of financial assistance and excellent graduate outcomes, Washington and Lee is worth the money for most attendees.

FINANCIAL
Institutional Type: Private
In-State Tuition: $51,420
Out-of-State Tuition: $51,420
Room & Board: $13,925
Required Fees: $1,035
Books & Supplies: $1,950

Avg. Need-Based Aid: $49,195
Avg. % of Need Met: 100%

Avg. Merit-Based Aid: $45,742
% Receiving Merit-Based Aid: 23%

Avg. Cumulative Debt: $21,758
% of Students Borrowing: 31%

CAREER
Who Recruits
1. Walker & Dunlap
2. Citi
3. Merrill Lynch
4. Berkeley Research Group
5. Morgan Stanley

Notable Internships
1. Estee Lauder Companies
2. Twitter
3. North Carolina Museum of Art

Top Industries
1. Business
2. Finance
3. Education
4. Legal
5. Operations

Top Employers
1. EY
2. PwC
3. Morgan Stanley
4. Wells Fargo
5. JPMorgan Chase

Where Alumni Work
1. Washington, DC
2. New York City
3. Atlanta
4. Roanoke, VA
5. Richmond

Median Earnings
College Scorecard (Early Career): $76,100
EOP (Early Career): $78,200
PayScale (Mid-Career): $123,200

RANKINGS
Forbes: 42
Money: 26
U.S. News: 10, Liberal Arts Colleges
Wall Street Journal/THE: 70
Washington Monthly: 1, Liberal Arts Colleges

#CollegesWorthYourMoney

Washington University in St. Louis

St. Louis, Missouri | Admissions Phone: 314-935-6000

ADMISSION
Admission Rate: 15%
Admission Rate - Men: 15%
Admission Rate - Women: 15%
EA Admission Rate: Not Offered
ED Admission Rate: 42%
Admission Rate (5-Year Trend): -1%
ED Admission Rate (5-Year Trend): +15%
% of Admits Attending (Yield): 38%
Transfer Admission Rate: 20%

Offered Wait List: N/A
Accepted Wait List: N/A
Admitted Wait List: 31

SAT Reading/Writing (Middle 50%): 710-770
SAT Math (Middle 50%): 760-800
ACT Composite (Middle 50%): 32-35
Testing Policy: ACT/SAT Required
SAT Superscore: Yes
ACT Superscore: Yes

% Graduated in Top 10% of HS Class: 80%
% Graduated in Top 25% of HS Class: 97%
% Graduated in Top 50% of HS Class: 99%

ENROLLMENT
Total Undergraduate Enrollment: 7,751
% Part-Time: 8%
% Male: 47%
% Female: 53%
% Out-of-State: 90%
% Fraternity: 26%
% Sorority: 38%
% On-Campus (Freshman): 100%
% On-Campus (All Undergraduate): 74%

% African-American: 9%
% Asian: 16%
% Hispanic: 9%
% White: 51%
% Other: 5%
% Race or Ethnicity Unknown: 2%
% International: 8%
% Low-Income: 5%

ACADEMICS
Student-to-Faculty Ratio: 7:1
% of Classes Under 20: 64%
% of Classes Under 40: 81%
% Full-Time Faculty: 67%
% Full-Time Faculty w/ Terminal Degree: 94%

Top Programs
Architecture
Biology
Business
Design
Economics
Engineering
Political Science
Psychology and Brain Sciences

Retention Rate: 97%
4-Year Graduation Rate: 88%
6-Year Graduation Rate: 95%

Curricular Flexibility: Somewhat Flexible
Academic Rating: ★★★★✦

Inside the Classroom

Despite receiving consistently high rankings since *U.S. News* released its first college guide in 1983, Washington University in St. Louis is, perhaps, the finest institution that is not a household name across the nation. Yet, this Midwestern research and pre-professional powerhouse is one of the most respected institutions in the eyes of Fortune 500 employers and elite graduate schools alike. Catering to just over 7,700 undergraduates, WashU admits students into five schools: Arts & Sciences, the Olin School of Business, the School of Engineering & Applied Sciences, and the Art of Architecture programs housed within the Sam Fox School of Design and Visual Arts.

Arts & Sciences, which claims more than half the student body, offers more than eighty majors, and all are guided by the IQ Curriculum, the school's signature liberal arts course of study. As part of the IQ Curriculum students must take courses in applied numeracy, social contrasts, writing, and an additional course that is classified as "writing intensive." WashU students also must complete coursework in the humanities, social sciences, natural sciences/math, and foreign language along with three "integrations" that can be completed via multi-semester, cross-disciplinary coursework. Engineering students are not beholden to all of those curricular mandates. Special programs include the University Scholars Program in Medicine that allows students to apply for admission to both an undergraduate degree program and medical school before entering college as well as the Beyond Boundaries Program that allows students to implement a cross-disciplinary approach with the aim of solving major global and societal problems.

The university has an 8:1 student-faculty ratio, and 77 percent of classes have fewer than twenty-four students; close to one-quarter have single-digit enrollments. WUSTL students are known for being more collaborative than competitive and extremely hard working as evidenced by the fact that 75 percent double major or pursue multiple degrees. The Office of Undergraduate Research helps students land opportunities to research alongside faculty, primarily in the summers. A solid 59 percent of undergraduates report participating in a research endeavor. A relatively modest one-third of students study abroad.

Nationally recognized programs are numerous: the Olin Business School, the School of Engineering & Applied Sciences, and the College of Architecture are well-respected by employers. The Biology Department prepares many successful med school candidates, including for the university's own ultra-elite medical school. The most commonly conferred degrees are in business (15 percent), engineering (15 percent), social sciences (13 percent), biology (11 percent), and psychology (7 percent). Fulbright, Gilman, Luce, and Critical Language Scholarships all have been won by WashU grads in recent years, and two students were named Rhodes Scholars in 2018.

Outside the Classroom

It sounds trite, but by almost any metric one must conclude that Washington University students seem happy. Dorms, recreational facilities, and campus food are routinely rated well. The WashU atmosphere is known for being more laid-back and friendly than that at many of its elite peers. Seventy-four percent of the student body and 100 percent of freshmen reside on campus. WashU's ten fraternities and eight sororities draw roughly one-third of the student body into Greek participation. The Bears compete in NCCA Division II, fielding nine men's teams and ten women's squads. The athletically-inclined student body also has forty-one club teams, and a simply insane three-quarters of undergraduates participate in intramural sports. In excess of 380 student-run organizations are active at WUSTL, all under the purview of the Washington University Student Union, one of the most well-funded college student governments in the country. Each semester it funds a concert known as WILD (for Walk In Lay Down) that features a big-time musical act. Well-attended speaker events are also organized on a regular basis, and recent attendees include Mitt Romney, John Paul Stevens, and Ta-Nehisi Coates. The Campus YMCA connects over 800 students each year with twenty-eight service opportunities in the local community. Student media is popular, and *Student Life*, the school's independent newspaper, has won national awards on several occasions. In addition, the school's radio station, KWUR, is immensely popular, and not just on campus but across the St. Louis area. For those inclined to explore off campus, the university is located within a few miles of the St. Louis Zoo, multiple art museums, a host of great eateries, and the gorgeous Missouri Botanical Garden.

Career Services

The Washington University in St. Louis Career Center is staffed by twenty-one full-time professional employees who specialize in employer relations, career counseling, event planning, and pre-graduate school advising. With a student-to-advisor ratio of 367:1, WUSTL compares favorably to the other institutions included in this book. Having conducted 5,803 one-on-one advising sessions in the 2018-19 school year, the center staff does a superb job of engaging their undergraduate student population.

Washington University in St. Louis

E-mail: admissions@wustl.edu | Website: www.wustl.edu

Three large career fairs drew a collective audience of almost 2,000 individuals and 300 employers. The center also hosted over 280 low-key employer information sessions and a number of SLAMs, miniature career fairs for a particular industry where, in a bit of a role-reversal, employers pitch their companies to students. An almost hard-to-fathom 475 employers recruit on campus each year, and close to 1,114 on-campus interviews were conducted in 2018-19 (in 2016, the number of interviews was even higher—1,204). Thanks to the strong employer connections forged by career services staff, WashU students have no trouble landing internships at major companies like CBS News, Pfizer, and AT&T, and stipends are available through the university to help offset living expenses. All told, approximately 75 percent of students report completing at least one internship. With ample staffing, superior outreach, and positive student outcomes, WashU's Career Center could not be doing a better job.

Professional Outcomes

The Class of 2018 sent 74 percent of its exiting members into the workforce and 23 percent into graduate and professional schools. The thirty companies employing the highest number of WashU grads feature many of the most sought-after employers in the world including Amazon, Bain, Boeing, Deloitte, Google, IBM, Goldman Sachs, and Microsoft. Of the employed members of the Class of 2018 who reported their starting salaries, 70 percent were making over $50,000 and 18 percent were making more than $80k. By age thirty-four, alumni earn the highest median income of any undergraduate degree-granting institution in the state. Geographically, remaining in Missouri was the favored choice among fresh alums, but a fair number also resettled in New York and California.

The universities welcoming the largest number of Bears included the prestigious institutions of Carnegie Mellon, Columbia, Duke, Harvard, Penn, Princeton, and Stanford. Others were pursuing graduate degrees at non-elite schools including Case Western, Rutgers, Colorado State, and St. Louis University. In 2017, of 1,587 graduates, ninety were accepted into med school, including at WashU's own top-ranked medical school. Baylor College of Medicine attracted a large number of future physicians; students also enjoyed acceptances into Harvard Medical School, NYU School of Medicine, and the Icahn School of Medicine at Mt. Sinai.

Admission

WashU received over 31,000 applications for a place in the Class of 2022, but it admitted only 15 percent. Over 80 percent of attending students were in the top 10 percent of their high school class, and the middle 50 percent for SATs was 1470-1570 and 32-35 for the ACTs. For historical reference, in 2010, the university accepted 21 percent of applicants, and enrolling students possessed similar standardized test scores to those being accepted today.

Even with rising application numbers, the admissions committee carefully examines each application, granting "high importance" to soft factors including character/personal qualities, extracurricular activities, talent/ability, and volunteer/work experience. Essays also grace this list, and a new supplemental essay component was added for applicants in 2019. It behooves students seriously committed to WUSTL to give serious consideration to applying early. The admission rate is 42 percent in the early round compared to only 13 percent in the regular cycle, and ED entrants comprise 39 percent of the freshman class. For those applying in the regular cycle, demonstrating interest is critically important as the admissions staff is eager to know if WashU is truly one of your top choices or merely a safety school in case Harvard says "no." Formerly relegated to Ivy backup status, Washington University has stepped into the limelight as a destination point for the best and brightest from around the country. In fact, close to 65 percent of current students hail from over 500 miles away, including all fifty US states and one hundred countries. This Midwestern behemoth casts a wide net, but it only brings aboard the most brag-worthy high school fish it can find.

Worth Your Money?

A fairly standard (in the world of elite private colleges) $75,500 list price cost of attendance greets WashU freshmen. The 42 percent of undergrads who qualify for financial aid see 100 percent of that amount met by the university, which averages out to $49k in grant money each academic year. Roughly 14 percent of students also receive merit aid awards averaging roughly $10,500 per year. This school has one of the wealthiest groups of students in the country (rivaled by Colorado College and Colgate) so, for many, the price tag will not break the bank. Given that reality, WUSTL can make sense for students across a wide spectrum of socioeconomic backgrounds.

FINANCIAL
Institutional Type: Private
In-State Tuition: $54,250
Out-of-State Tuition: $54,250
Room & Board: $16,900
Required Fees: $1,042
Books & Supplies: $1,126

Avg. Need-Based Aid: $48,522
Avg. % of Need Met: 100%

Avg. Merit-Based Aid: $10,585
% Receiving Merit-Based Aid: 14%

Avg. Cumulative Debt: $22,555
% of Students Borrowing: 27%

CAREER
Who Recruits
1. Guggenheim Investments
2. Equifax
3. Cushman & Wakefield
4. Abercrombie & Fitch
5. Chicago Trading Company

Notable Internships
1. St. Louis Post-Dispatch
2. Uber
3. BlackRock

Top Industries
1. Business
2. Education
3. Engineering
4. Research
5. Operations

Top Employers
1. Boeing
2. Google
3. Microsoft
4. Amazon
5. Mastercard

Where Alumni Work
1. St. Louis
2. New York City
3. Chicago
4. San Francisco
5. Washington, DC

Median Earnings
College Scorecard (Early Career): $70,100
EOP (Early Career): $67,500
PayScale (Mid-Career): $114,900

RANKINGS
Forbes: 31
Money: 82
U.S. News: 19, National Universities
Wall Street Journal/THE: 19
Washington Monthly: 59, National Universities

#CollegesWorthYourMoney

Wellesley College

Wellesley, Massachusetts | Admissions Phone: 781-283-2270

ADMISSION
Admission Rate: 20%
Admission Rate - Men: Not Offered
Admission Rate - Women: 20%
EA Admission Rate: Not Offered
ED Admission Rate: 31%
Admission Rate (5-Year Trend): -10%
ED Admission Rate (5-Year Trend): -5%
% of Admits Attending (Yield): 47%
Transfer Admission Rate: 16%

\# Offered Wait List: 1,909
\# Accepted Wait List: 1,245
\# Admitted Wait List: 36

SAT Reading/Writing (Middle 50%): 670-740
SAT Math (Middle 50%): 660-780
ACT Composite (Middle 50%): 30-34
Testing Policy: ACT/SAT Required
SAT Superscore: Yes
ACT Superscore: Yes

% Graduated in Top 10% of HS Class: 83%
% Graduated in Top 25% of HS Class: 96%
% Graduated in Top 50% of HS Class: 99%

ENROLLMENT
Total Undergraduate Enrollment: 2,534
% Part-Time: 6%
% Male: 2%
% Female: 98%
% Out-of-State: 86%
% Fraternity: Not Offered
% Sorority: Not Offered
% On-Campus (Freshman): 100%
% On-Campus (All Undergraduate): 97%

% African-American: 6%
% Asian: 21%
% Hispanic: 13%
% White: 36%
% Other: 6%
% Race or Ethnicity Unknown: 5%
% International: 14%
% Low-Income: 20%

ACADEMICS
Student-to-Faculty Ratio: 8:1
% of Classes Under 20: 67%
% of Classes Under 40: 99%
% Full-Time Faculty: 86%
% Full-Time Faculty w/ Terminal Degree: 93%

Top Programs
Area Studies
Chemistry
Computer Science
Economics
English
History
Neuroscience
Political Science

Retention Rate: 96%
4-Year Graduation Rate: 84%
6-Year Graduation Rate: 92%

Curricular Flexibility: Somewhat Flexible
Academic Rating: ★★★★★

Inside the Classroom
In 1995, the *New York Times* proclaimed, "More than any other college—large or small— Wellesley has groomed women who shatter the glass ceiling." Twenty five years later, Barnard has surpassed Wellesley for the lowest acceptance rate among women's colleges, but Wellesley's picture-perfect campus in suburban Boston remains the premier pipeline to the boardrooms of America's most powerful companies as well as to the highest levels of politics. Students are known to be a driven bunch as committed to full engagement with campus activities as they are to the exceptionally rigorous classroom experience.

The college's 2,350 undergraduate students can select from fifty departmental and interdisciplinary majors, and economics, biology, and computer science are the most frequently conferred degrees. All freshmen must complete an expository writing course, and all seniors must demonstrate foreign language proficiency. In between, students are required to complete coursework in natural and physical science, mathematical modeling and problem solving, social and behavioral analysis, language and literature, art/music/theater/film/video, epistemology and cognition, historical studies, and religion/ethics/moral philosophy. There is also a multicultural and an uncredited physical education requirement.

The student-to-faculty ratio is only 8:1, leading to average class sizes in the seventeen- to twenty-student range. Twenty percent of course sections have single-digit enrollments while two-thirds have fewer than nineteen students. With no graduate students to compete with, opportunities for participation in research with faculty members abound. The Summer Science Research Program is cited by many graduates as the most influential part of their educational experience. Wellesley students also regularly land research positions with the National Institutes of Health, Harvard Medical School, MIT, and The Children's Hospital of Philadelphia. The Office of International Studies facilitates the overseas study of hundreds of students each year with 45 percent of juniors spending a semester in one of 160 programs worldwide.

The entire undergraduate program at Wellesley is revered by top corporations and graduate schools alike. Most programs possess sterling reputations, including chemistry, computer science, neuroscience, and political science. However, the Department of Economics appears to shine most brightly, leading many into PhD programs and high-profile careers. A large number of Wellesley graduates are awarded prestigious postgraduate scholarships each year. In 2018, the school produced four Fulbright Scholars, three Gilman Scholars, three Watson Fellows, a Critical Languages Scholar, and a Princeton in Asia Fellow.

Outside the Classroom
Approximately 97 percent of undergraduates are denizens of the school's twenty-one residence halls that range in capacity from forty to 285 students. Wellesley's 500-acre campus was described by fabled architect Frederick Olmstead as possessing "a peculiar kind of intricate beauty." Thanks to Lake Waban, a golf course, an arboretum, and botanical gardens, you will never long for gorgeous landscapes and natural beauty. There are thirteen varsity athletic teams that are members of NCAA Division III as well as eight club teams in sports that include archery, equestrian, and Nordic skiing. Athletic facilities are extensive and include the Keohane Sports Center, a pool, spin rooms, dance studios, a rock climbing wall, and just about any other fitness-related amenity one can conjure up. Wellesley women have 150 student-run organizations to choose from, including a number of dance, music, and theater groups. This is a tradition-rich school with annual events like Flower Sunday and quarterly competitions like Stepsinging, a class-vs.-class singing contest on the steps of Houghton Chapel. The town of Wellesley has coffee shops, a bookstore, and a pharmacy all within a short walk. Downtown Boston is less than half an hour away by car, but most take the T, commuter trains, or a shuttle that regularly departs from campus.

Career Services
The Wellesley Career Education Office is staffed by thirty professionals working in career counseling, internships, fellowships, experiential learning, and employer relations. For a school with 2,350 students, the size and scope of this office is remarkable. The 78:1 student-to-advisor ratio is unmatched by any institution in the country. It's no wonder that the National Association of Colleges and Employers named Wellesley the 2017 winner of the Career Service Excellence Award among small colleges; the department has been similarly recognized multiple times by national organizations for its superior career service offerings. Staff members regularly present at national conferences and publish on the topic of career preparation.

Class of 2018 members had a 98 percent satisfaction rate after in-person, one-on-one appointments; that was a dramatic improvement over the Class of 2015's satisfaction rate of 45 percent. Almost 90 percent of undergraduates complete at least one internship, including so-called Signature Internships with "leading cultural, educational, and scientific institutions; international agencies; media outlets; advocacy and community organizations; and businesses" around the globe. In the 2017-18 academic year, 80 percent of the undergraduate population engaged face-to-face with career services, and 98 percent engaged digitally. Outreach begins freshman year as 82 percent of first-years meet in person with a career counselor.

The annual total of advising sessions exceeds 6,500. There were 275 events held with a total attendance of 4,690, and thirty-three employers engaged in on-campus interviews including Google, Microsoft, Citi, and the US Department of Commerce. Unlike some of the other Seven Sister institutions, opportunities at the world's premier companies are commonplace, and salaries are higher than average. With superb resources and equally strong outcomes, the Wellesley Career Education Office deserves all of the many accolades that have been heaped upon it.

Professional Outcomes

Six months after earning their degrees, 96 percent of the Wellesley College Class of 2018 had already achieved positive outcomes. Of the three-quarters of grads who were employed, 24 percent were working in the finance/consulting/business fields, 18 percent in education, 15 percent in internet and software/technology/engineering, and 13 percent in health care/life sciences. The top employers were Accenture, Google, JP Morgan, Boston Children's Hospital, Massachusetts General Hospital, and a number of top universities that included Harvard and MIT. One hundred thirty-three members of the Class of 2018 were employed in Boston, sixty-nine in New York, fifty in California, and twenty-seven in Washington, DC. The average starting salary was a solid $59,000 with an average bonus of $11,000.

Wellesley grads almost universally go on to elite graduate programs. Of the 17 percent of 2018 grads who directly entered an advanced degree program, the top dozen most common schools attended included Ivies Harvard, Columbia, Brown, Penn, and Cornell and other upper-crust institutions at Stanford, MIT, Emory, NYU, Brandeis, Boston University, and the Olin College of Engineering. Medical school applicants are generally successful; from 2008-2018 an average of 72 percent of med school hopefuls were accepted by at least one university. Three or more recent grads have been accepted into medical school at Dartmouth, Tufts, Case Western, Boston University, and Northwestern. Law school acceptance rates hover in the low-to-mid 80s, a figure that is lowered by the caliber of law schools to which Wellesley grads typically apply. Law schools that accepted a minimum of three alumni in recent years include Yale, Duke, Harvard, Georgetown, Cornell, Penn, and UC Berkeley.

Admission

The 6,488 applications received for a place in the Class of 2023 was the second highest total in school history; the acceptance rate of 20 percent was one point higher than the previous cycle. Among admitted applicants the average SAT was 1438, the average ACT was 32, and 84 percent placed in the top decile of their graduating high school class. 2018-19 freshmen possessed similar numbers. Their mid-50 percent ranges were 1330-1520 on the SAT, 30-34 on the ACT, and 83 percent were in the top 10 percent of their class. Wellesley boasts a high yield rate of 47 percent, meaning that few apply on a whim, and nearly half of all admitted students choose to enroll in the college.

As part of its holistic review process, the admissions committee seeks "people who know that we don't know everything; who have a strong voice but listen to other voices; who have big plans but are totally open to changing them; who have taken risks, failed, and figured out a better way." As such, four factors are paramount in the evaluation process: character/personal qualities, recommendations, GPA, and rigor of one's secondary school record. The second tier of factors includes test scores, class rank, essays, talent/ability, and extracurricular activities. Applying via early decision can yield a slight advantage as 31 percent of students are accepted during the ED round. In terms of pure acceptance rate, Wellesley is the second-most selective Seven Sisters school, behind only Barnard. High grades and strong test scores are required, but many softer factors weigh heavily on admissions decisions. Applicants who are involved in their high schools and communities will fare best.

Worth Your Money?

Even at a $75,198 annual cost of attendance, Wellesley is unquestionably worth the investment. You won't receive merit aid from this school, but 56 percent of the student population does receive need-based aid, and that need is met 100 percent. That translates to an average need-based grant of close to $53,000. The quality of the education, mentorship, and professional networks make Wellesley, even at full price for non-STEM/business majors, the rare school that will return your money many times over.

FINANCIAL
Institutional Type: Private
In-State Tuition: $55,728
Out-of-State Tuition: $55,728
Room & Board: $17,096
Required Fees: $324
Books & Supplies: $800

Avg. Need-Based Aid: $52,881
Avg. % of Need Met: 100%

Avg. Merit-Based Aid: $0
% Receiving Merit-Based Aid: 0%

Avg. Cumulative Debt: $16,122
% of Students Borrowing: 52%

CAREER
Who Recruits
1. Boston Consulting Group
2. Teach for America
3. U.S. Federal Reserve
4. Massachusetts General Hospital
5. State Street

Notable Internships
1. Metropolitan Museum of Art
2. American Express
3. Dick Clark Productions

Top Industries
1. Business
2. Education
3. Research
4. Media
5. Social Services

Top Employers
1. Google
2. Microsoft
3. Accenture
4. Amazon
5. Facebook

Where Alumni Work
1. Boston
2. New York City
3. San Francisco
4. Washington, DC
5. Los Angeles

Median Earnings
College Scorecard (Early Career): $60,800
EOP (Early Career): $56,300
PayScale (Mid-Career): $106,200

RANKINGS
Forbes: 44
Money: 89
U.S. News: 3, Liberal Arts Colleges
Wall Street Journal/THE: 24
Washington Monthly: 16, Liberal Arts Colleges

#CollegesWorthYourMoney

Wesleyan University

Middletown, Connecticut | Admissions Phone: 860-685-3000

Inside the Classroom

Considered one of the "Little Ivies" and officially a member of the "Little Three" alongside Amherst and Williams, Wesleyan University in Middletown, Connecticut, has much in common with its highly selective compatriots, but it also possesses a distinctively uncompromising and independent-minded student body. One telling anecdote comes from 1998 when the administration proudly unveiled the school's new slogan, "The Independent Ivy." Many young people would love for their college to associate itself with the cache of the Ivy League, but at Wesleyan the student response was utter disgust that led to an all-out rebellion. The students launched a vocal protest, and the higher-ups quickly dropped the slogan. That's Wesleyan in a nutshell.

At 3,000 undergraduate students Wes is significantly larger than many of its elite liberal arts peers. With forty-five majors, seventeen minors, and over 1,000 classes running each academic year, the school truly has something for everyone. The academic requirements are relatively minimal, giving undergrads a high degree of intellectual freedom. There are two stages of general education courses: stage one sees students complete two courses each in the three divisions of Humanities & Arts, Social & Behavioral Sciences, and Natural Sciences & Math. Stage two is optional for most majors but may be required to receive departmental honors at graduation.

Just shy of three-quarters of class sections have fewer than twenty students, allowing for close bonds/mentorships to unfold. Students rave about the accessible faculty (the faculty-to-student ratio is 8:1), and research opportunities with professors are plentiful. The program for undergraduate Research in the Sciences funds over one hundred students per year to conduct research over the summer. The university has increased its study abroad participation in recent years to the point that almost 50 percent of students now spend a semester overseas.

There isn't one go-to major at Wes; while the social sciences (24 percent), psychology (13 percent), area/ethnic/gender studies (12 percent), and the visual and performing arts (11 percent) are the most popular, none represents a massive percentage of the total degrees conferred. Nearly every program at Wesleyan is respected in the employer/graduate school communities, with offerings in economics, English, film studies, and neuroscience receiving perhaps the most praise. Wesleyan was again named a top producer of Fulbright Scholars in 2018; six recent alums won the award after seven took home the honor in 2017.

Outside the Classroom

The unofficial but popular motto, "Keep Wes Weird," perfectly sums up this iconoclastic student body's vibe and helps describe life on campus. Those looking for wild frat parties and raucous football games would be highly disappointed (and confused) walking around the Wesleyan campus. Greek life attracts a minuscule 3 percent of students and, other than the one-quarter of undergraduates who comprise the rosters of the school's twenty-nine varsity sports teams, athletics are not a focal point for the average student. That being said, participation is high in intramural and club sports including ultimate Frisbee, kung fu, and WesClimb, which takes advantage of the schools own rock climbing wall. Wesleyan's other amenities include a 412-seat movie theater that screens films throughout the year, a fifty-meter swimming pool, a 7,500- square-foot gymnasium, and an ice skating rink. There are more than 250 active student-run groups with large numbers in the areas of activism/politics, identity, theater, comedy troupes, and a cappella. The Center for the Arts hosts more than 300 events each year from jazz concerts to one-person shows to art exhibitions. Middletown provides a nice enough small city environment with plenty of bars and restaurants to frequent, and Hartford is only a twenty-five minute drive. Just about everyone lives on campus.

Career Services

The Gordon Career Center is staffed by nine full-time staff who specialize in employer relations, general advising, health professions advising, STEM career advising, and business career advising. The 334:1 student-to-advisor ratio places it in the above-average range compared to other schools profiled in this guide. The school does not organize any large career expos/fairs; instead, it hosts events just about every day along the lines of a chat over coffee with Deloitte to a gathering entitled "Google at Wes: Laying the Foundation for Your Technical Career" featuring Wesleyan alumni who work for the tech giant.

Wes has partnered with a number of major employers to facilitate on-campus recruiting and interviews including Booz Allen, Lego (fun!), Pfizer, and Squarespace. Interested seniors participate in a job search boot camp known as Accelerate prior to engaging with those visiting companies. The WEShadow Externship programs allows current students the chance to spend anywhere from one day to one week at work with an alum. The Winter on Wyllys program is an intensive, two-week career development course available over the holidays. Data on internship participation rates and overall engagements with the career center is, at present, unavailable.

Wesleyan University

E-mail: admissions@wesleyan.edu | Website: www.wesleyan.edu

Professional Outcomes

By the end of calendar year 2018, the majority of those who received their diplomas in May had entered employment (70 percent). Graduate school was the next stop for 12 percent of new alums, and 10 percent were still seeking employment. Of those who landed jobs, the third highest number were in arts and entertainment, which isn't shocking when your school's alumni include the likes of Lin Manuel Miranda, Michael Bay, Joss Whedon, and countless Hollywood writers and producers. Tech/engineering/sciences and education took the silver and gold. The companies employing the highest numbers of Wesleyan Class of 2018 grads included Google, Epic, Analysis Group, JP Morgan Chase, Teach for America, Booz Allen Hamilton, Accenture, and Facebook. By age thirty-four Wesleyan grads have a median income of $56,500, which lags well behind the other Little Three colleges, Amherst and Williams. New York, Boston, San Francisco, and Hartford were the most popular post-college destinations.

Wes alumni are looked upon favorably by elite graduate and professional schools. From 2013-17 Wesleyan grads were accepted into medical school 55-66 percent of the time, much higher than the national average. Those with a 3.6 GPA or higher enjoyed a superior acceptance rate of 75-87 percent. In the same timespan law school applicants were successful 88-100 percent of the time and fared extremely well at the most prestigious universities. In 2016, a gasp-worthy 64 percent of law school-bound seniors found a home at a top ten law school including Yale, Harvard, Stanford, Columbia, and UChicago. Those pursuing non-professional advanced degrees enrolled in a wide range of schools from elites like MIT, Stanford, and Berkeley to state universities like Rowan, Temple, and UMass.

Admission

Wesleyan admitted 17.5 percent of its record-setting 12,788 applicants in 2018, a figure that has increased by 35 percent in the past four years. The mid-50 percent range on the SAT for members of the Class of 2022 was 1320-1500 and 30-34 on the ACT. Interestingly, this past cycle's acceptance rate was higher than 2017's 15.4 percent clip or even that of a decade ago when the university welcomed only 15 percent of applicants. Yet, somehow that is fitting because Wesleyan's admissions, like its eclectic and talented students, is not unidimensional.

Unlike some other schools of its caliber, Wesleyan does not rule out those who finished outside of the top 10 percent of their high school class. While 57 percent of the Class of 2022 earned that distinction, 85 percent finished in the top quarter, and 2 percent placed outside the top 50 percent. The No. 1 factor in admissions is the rigor of secondary school curriculum as it seeks young people who are "intellectual risk-takers" above all else. Standardized test scores have been made less important by Wesleyan's test-optional policy, but 56 percent of attending students submitted SAT scores, and 45 percent submitted ACT scores in 2018. Obviously, there's some crossover there, but we can assume the overall percentage of successful students going the test-optional route is fairly small. Applying early decision is definitely something you want to consider if Wesleyan is your top choice because it fills 51 percent of its freshman class via ED, and it has an admit rate more than double that of the regular cycle (37 percent versus 16 percent). Getting into Wesleyan is not as formulaic a process as it is at the majority of elite institutions. Essays, recommendations, first-generation status, ethnicity, personal characteristics, and performance in the classroom are all given genuine consideration. Possessing good stats is important to your admissions chances, but so is being an engaged and passionate learner.

Worth Your Money?

Wesleyan costs $75,693 annually, a price similar to its elite liberal arts kin. A tiny percentage of students receive substantial merit aid, but 97 percent receive no help of that variety. It is need-based aid that rules the day at Wes as all qualifying students (42 percent of the population) have 100 percent of their demonstrated need accounted for. The average grant for those individuals is $50,000+. Not every student who goes to this school cruises into a six-figure job, but that's the aim of a Wesleyan education. This school is worth the cost because it assists you in finding a pathway that aligns with your passions, and it makes the school affordable for those in financial need.

FINANCIAL
Institutional Type: Private
In-State Tuition: $56,704
Out-of-State Tuition: $56,704
Room & Board: $15,724
Required Fees: $300
Books & Supplies: $1,200

Avg. Need-Based Aid: $50,083
Avg. % of Need Met: 100%

Avg. Merit-Based Aid: $35,118
% Receiving Merit-Based Aid: 3%

Avg. Cumulative Debt: $23,454
% of Students Borrowing: 36%

CAREER
Who Recruits
1. MGM Resorts International
2. Pfizer
3. Analysis Group
4. McKinsey & Co.
5. Charles River Associates

Notable Internships
1. Citadel Securities
2. ABC News
3. United Nations

Top Industries
1. Business
2. Education
3. Media
4. Research
5. Social Services

Top Employers
1. Google
2. Citi
3. JPMorgan Chase
4. Accenture
5. Morgan Stanley

Where Alumni Work
1. New York City
2. Boston
3. San Francisco
4. Hartford
5. Washington, DC

Median Earnings
College Scorecard (Early Career): $54,700
EOP (Early Career): $56,500
PayScale (Mid-Career): $117,000

RANKINGS
Forbes: 40
Money: 140
U.S. News: 17, Liberal Arts Colleges
Wall Street Journal/THE: 43
Washington Monthly: 9, Liberal Arts Colleges

#CollegesWorthYourMoney

Whitman College

Walla Walla, Washington | Admissions Phone: 509-527-5176

Inside the Classroom

Due to its location in Walla Walla, Washington, there are plenty of experienced high school guidance counselors around the country who have never even heard of Whitman College. Despite a lack of instant name recognition, you'll find Whitman side-by-side in the rankings with better-known West Coast liberal arts powerhouses like Colorado College, Pitzer, and Occidental. And there's a good reason for these accolades—few colleges in the Pacific Northwest offer the intimate and supportive academic and social environment available at Whitman. The 1,475 students at Whitman, all undergrads, are a collection of high school stars who possess a median SAT score of close to 1,400 and an A/A- average in a mostly AP slate of courses. With forty-nine majors and thirty-three minors, the academic offerings at this college are robust, particularly when considering its modest size.

The Encounters Program greets freshmen with a yearlong introduction to the liberal arts. Organized around a number of themes, those courses focus on "primary sources, discussion, writing, and the construction of knowledge across academic fields." Regardless of major, all students also must pass two courses in cultural pluralism, the humanities, the social sciences, fine arts, and the sciences as well as one course in quantitative analysis. Biology, environmental studies, geology, chemistry, economics, sociology, and politics majors are all required to complete a senior research thesis.

Whitman boasts a beautifully low 9:1 student-to-faculty ratio and hosts zero graduate students, a recipe for individualized attention. Over 90 percent of sections contain fewer than twenty-nine students. The faculty has a reputation for being extremely available, attentive, and invested in undergraduate education. Undergraduate research is so embedded into the foundation of a Whitman education that the college hosts an annual Undergraduate Conference for students to present their work. The school offers ample opportunity for students to work with faculty on research projects during the year or in the summer, and it also has forged partnerships with organizations like the Fred Hutchinson Cancer Research Center in Seattle that accepts a minimum of two Whitman students for a nine-week research endeavor each summer. Greater than 40 percent of juniors study abroad in one of eighty-eight programs in forty+ countries around the globe.

By major, the greatest number of degrees are typically conferred in the social sciences (24 percent), biology (17 percent), visual and performing arts (12 percent), physical science (9 percent), and psychology (7 percent). All degree programs have solid reputations, but the biology, politics, and economics departments all have an extra shine. Whitman also does an amazing job funneling students into the most prestigious postgraduate fellowship programs. Over the last decade Whitties have captured sixty-two Fulbright Scholarships, twenty-five National Science Foundation Fellowships, twelve Watson Fellowships, and even one Rhodes Scholarship.

Outside the Classroom

One might assume that a school with fewer than 1,500 undergraduates would house just about everyone, especially with a spacious 117-acre campus. However, only 63 percent of Whitman students reside in one of the four freshman-only dorms, four upperclassmen dorms, or the eleven Interest Houses centered around commonalities like fine arts, the environment, or Asian studies. You also might expect a West Coast liberal arts school like Whitman to be Greek free, or at least to have a minimal frat/sorority presence on campus, yet that is not at all the case. Roughly 35 percent of students join fraternities and sororities, but it is important to note that they are generally viewed as inclusive and laid-back collectives in contrast to many Greek organizations at large universities. There are fifteen varsity NCAA Division III sports teams as well as ten club and sixteen intramural squads. Forty-six percent of undergrads play intramurals, and 15 percent are varsity athletes. Of the close to one hundred student organizations on campus, the Outdoor Program is one of the most popular. Many students participate in its weekend hiking, kayaking, climbing, and skiing adventures. The school also had a run of award-winning debate teams prior to 2014, although it is presently in rebuilding mode. Walla Walla is technically a city, but it's more a of quaint and charming Pacific Northwestern small town. Seattle and Portland each are over a four-hour drive.

Career Services

The Student Engagement Center (SEC) at Whitman College employs eight professional staff members and eleven undergraduate employees, many of whom serve as peer advisors. The full-time professionals serve students through career coaching, community engagement, and internship coordination. Only counting those eight professionals, the SEC still comes out with a 184:1 student-to-advisor ratio, stronger than the vast majority of colleges profiled in this guide. Thanks to that terrific level of support, Whitties can schedule up to an hour of one-on-one career counseling whenever they like. The office lays out a Four Phase Plan that, beginning freshman year, helps students begin, develop, refine, and own their stories through job shadowing, internships, alumni networking, job fairs, community service, graduate school exploration, and professional development.

Community service is a major part of the Whitman experience, and the SEC facilitates experiential opportunities in Walla Walla for 320 students per week, and 70 percent of undergraduates participate each year. Many summer internships are arranged at local organizations like the Walla Walla Public Health Department, the Walla Walla Symphony, and a local minor league baseball team. The school is supportive of those wishing to spend their summers at nonprofits and funds more than 130 such internships per year. The Whitman Connect program helps link current students with the college's 16,000+ alumni, and seventy-five alumni and parents provide job-shadowing opportunities over spring break. The key to Whitman's career service success is its genuine ability to meaningfully connect and support every single undergraduate student. Despite a dearth of national companies visiting campus and mediocre salary statistics, this office can be counted on to provide individualized nurturing and career guidance.

Professional Outcomes

When you confer fewer than 400 degrees each year, you don't expect to have massive pockets of graduates joining major corporations. However, it is worth noting that twenty or more alumni currently work for Microsoft, Amazon, Boeing, Starbucks, T-Mobile, and Nordstrom. In the last few years, students have taken interesting first jobs including as a paralegal at the US Department of Justice-Antitrust Division, audio archivist at the Smithsonian, and marketing assistant at Oxford University Press. The largest number of Whitties settle in Seattle, but Portland, San Francisco, Los Angeles, New York, and Denver are other common destinations. Midcareer median pay is on the lower side among elite liberal arts schools, in the same range as the aforementioned Occidental and Reed as well as Kenyon, Vassar, and Macalester. Part of the lower median pay figure may be attributable to the high number of Whitman alumni who are continuing their educations well into their late twenties and early thirties.

Over 60 percent of Whitman graduates continue their educations at a wide range of graduate and professional programs. Since 2009, the school has sent graduates to law schools such as Berkeley, the University of Washington, Columbia, Georgetown, Duke, the University of Pennsylvania, and the University of Chicago. In that same time, premed students have headed to elite medical programs at Northwestern, UVA, Dartmouth, and Stanford. A significant number of Whitman grads go on to earn PhDs in the sciences; the school ranks in the top fifty nationwide in that department. While many attend elite graduate/professional programs, plenty of other grads head to West Coast publics like Colorado State University, Oregon State University, and Washington State University.

Admission

Whitman's 50 percent acceptance rate for the Class of 2022 represented an average number for the college, but it should be eye-opening for any teens looking for an elite school on the West Coast. It's important to note that this applicant pool is self-selecting; the mid-50 percent test scores of attending freshmen are 1280-1440 on the SAT and 29-32 on the ACT. Fifty-two percent hail from the top decile of their high school class, and 82 percent placed in the top quartile. The average unweighted GPA was a 3.66, and 45 percent of applicants earned above a 3.75. Whitman is the rare elite college that has become slightly easier to get into in recent years. A decade ago, the acceptance rate was 46 percent, SAT/ACT scores were comparable, 72 percent earned a GPA over 3.75, and a whopping 71 percent finished in the top 10 percent of their high school cohorts.

Rigor of academic record, GPA, and the application essay form the triumvirate of "most important" factors in the eyes of the committee. Recommendations, extracurricular activities, talent/ability, and character/personal characteristics are next in order importance followed by the merely "considered" factors of standardized test scores and class rank. In 2018, the college received 179 early decision applications and welcomed 71 percent into the fold, demonstrating a clear advantage for those willing to commit through ED. The admissions committee states that it is seeking "curious, inspired, and highly engaged students with a passion for learning and a wide and eclectic range of interests; the kind of independent-minded students who are motivated to take intellectual risks in order to become the kind of leaders who can make a difference in the world." The school's admissions practices seem to support that sentiment.

Worth Your Money?

The cost of attendance at Whitman is $69,500, not an unexpected amount for a liberal arts college with such an intimate classroom and campus environment. Fortunately, approximately half of Whitman undergrads qualify for need-based aid with an average annual award of more than $36,000. For those who receive a generous merit or need-based offer, Whitman can absolutely be worth your money; at full price, this may not be the best choice for families lacking the funds to pay the costs up front.

FINANCIAL
Institutional Type: Private
In-State Tuition: $53,820
Out-of-State Tuition: $53,820
Room & Board: $13,512
Required Fees: $400
Books & Supplies: $1,400

Avg. Need-Based Aid: $36,323
Avg. % of Need Met: 92%

Avg. Merit-Based Aid: $13,429
% Receiving Merit-Based Aid: 61%

Avg. Cumulative Debt: $25,356
% of Students Borrowing: 43%

CAREER
Who Recruits
1. The Spur Group
2. Peace Corps
3. Baker Boyer Bank
4. TFA
5. Pacific Northwest National Laboratory

Notable Internships
1. WebMD
2. U.S. House of Representatives
3. Bloomsbury USA

Top Industries
1. Business
2. Education
3. Operations
4. Social Services
5. Research

Top Employers
1. Microsoft
2. Amazon
3. Boeing
4. The Spur Group
5. T-Mobile

Where Alumni Work
1. Seattle
2. Portland, OR
3. San Francisco
4. Richland, WA
5. Los Angeles

Median Earnings
College Scorecard (Early Career): $51,300
EOP (Early Career): $48,500
PayScale (Mid-Career): $102,600

RANKINGS
Forbes: 89
Money: 545
U.S. News: 46, Liberal Arts Colleges
Wall Street Journal/THE: 101 (T)
Washington Monthly: 90, Liberal Arts Colleges

#CollegesWorthYourMoney

Williams College

Williamstown, Massachusetts | Admissions Phone: 413-597-2211

ADMISSION
Admission Rate: 13%
Admission Rate - Men: 13%
Admission Rate - Women: 13%
EA Admission Rate: Not Offered
ED Admission Rate: 34%
Admission Rate (5-Year Trend): -5%
ED Admission Rate (5-Year Trend): -6%
% of Admits Attending (Yield): 43%
Transfer Admission Rate: 3%

Offered Wait List: 1,772
Accepted Wait List: 653
Admitted Wait List: 76

SAT Reading/Writing (Middle 50%): 710-760
SAT Math (Middle 50%): 700-790
ACT Composite (Middle 50%): 32-35
Testing Policy: ACT/SAT Required
SAT Superscore: Yes
ACT Superscore: Yes

% Graduated in Top 10% of HS Class: 89%
% Graduated in Top 25% of HS Class: 97%
% Graduated in Top 50% of HS Class: 100%

ENROLLMENT
Total Undergraduate Enrollment: 2,073
% Part-Time: 3%
% Male: 52%
% Female: 48%
% Out-of-State: 86%
% Fraternity: Not Offered
% Sorority: Not Offered
% On-Campus (Freshman): 100%
% On-Campus (All Undergraduate): 93%

% African-American: 8%
% Asian: 12%
% Hispanic: 13%
% White: 51%
% Other: 5%
% Race or Ethnicity Unknown: 3%
% International: 8%
% Low-Income: 19%

ACADEMICS
Student-to-Faculty Ratio: 7:1
% of Classes Under 20: 77%
% of Classes Under 40: 95%
% Full-Time Faculty: 83%
% Full-Time Faculty w/ Terminal Degree: 97%

Top Programs
Art
Biology
Computer Science
Economics
English
History
Math
Political Science

Retention Rate: 99%
4-Year Graduation Rate: 90%
6-Year Graduation Rate: 95%

Curricular Flexibility: Very Flexible
Academic Rating: ★★★★★

Inside the Classroom

Massachusetts is home to many of the finest and most historic institutions of higher learning in the United States. Starting in Boston and traveling west you would encounter many schools featured in this book—MIT, Harvard, BU, BC, Northeastern, Tufts, Brandeis, Wellesley—and, eventually, the more remote campuses of Amherst and Mount Holyoke and, lastly, tucked in the Northwest corner of the state just below Vermont you would encounter the Bay State's second-oldest school and one of the most prestigious liberal arts schools in the entire country, Williams College. Set on 450 rural acres in the Berkshires, Williams educates just over 2,000 of the brightest and most talented undergraduates one can find. The school's twenty-five academic departments offer thirty-six majors and a number of concentrations rather than minors

Students only take thirty-two total courses—four per semester—as opposed to the standard five. A Winter Study session also runs for twenty-two days in January when students can dedicate all of their attention to one course. Prior to graduation students must complete three courses in each of three Divisions: Languages and the Arts, Social Studies, and Science and Mathematics. Additionally, two writing-intensive courses and one course in quantitative reasoning are required. Rare for a liberal arts school of this caliber, no foreign language is required. Instead, the option exists to take a class exploring how different cultures interact with one another. While not quite as open as the curriculum at Brown or Amherst, Williams certainly gives its students their fair share of autonomy when it comes to course selection.

The college possesses an excellent 7:1 student-faculty ratio, and 99 percent of professorial attention goes to undergrads (they only run two small graduate programs). An unparalleled 44 percent of courses have fewer than ten students enrolled; over three-quarters have an enrollment under twenty. Thanks to relationships built with faculty through such small classes, one Williams student said, "Students often just need to talk to a professor to find a research opportunity." However, many formal opportunities to engage in undergraduate research exist in the summer, during a semester, or as part of one's senior honors thesis. Close to 50 percent of the junior class connects with the International Education and Study Away program to pinpoint the study abroad opportunity that is right for them. Included on that menu is the opportunity to study at Oxford for an entire year.

The greatest number of degrees are conferred in the social sciences (25 percent), math and statistics (12 percent), biology (9 percent), and foreign languages (8 percent). Any degree from Williams will be viewed most favorably by graduate schools and employers, but programs in economics, English, history, math and political science are especially renowned. The college also produces a massive number of highly competitive national fellowship winners. In 2018, grads and alums won twenty Fulbright Scholarships, nine NSF Graduate Research Fellowships, and a Gates Cambridge, a Watson, and a Schwarzman. In the last five years two graduates have been named Rhodes Scholars.

Outside the Classroom

For a supremely studious, tiny liberal enclave buried in the woods, Williams is unexpectedly sports-centric within the NCAA Division III. The Ephs (a shortened version of Ephraim Williams, the school's founder) compete in thirty-two varsity sports, most of which are members of the New England Small College Athletic Conference. Overall, 35 percent of the student body competes in intercollegiate sports, and many more join intramural athletic clubs. Fraternities were banished from campus more than fifty years ago, just before the school became co-educational. In the absence of Greek life, extracurriculars take on a larger social role as 96 percent of Williams undergrads are involved in at least one of the 150 outside-the-classroom organizations. Situated in the Berkshires, there is no big city that makes an easy day trip (Boston and NYC are two or three hours away), but natural beauty is ubiquitous. The largest student-run group, the Williams Outing Club, has 750 members who engage in regular hikes, campouts, and polar bear swims in the Williamstown wilderness. The vast majority of the student body—93 percent—live on campus, making the school's breathtaking residence halls the epicenter of social activity. Freshmen live together in one of two large, nearly identical residence halls that form the bustling Frosh Quad. Upperclassmen reside in one of twenty-seven more modestly sized buildings.

Career Services

The '68 Center for Career Exploration (CCE) employs thirteen full-time staff members who focus on career advising, alumni relations, and employer relations. Specialized help is available for those eying law school, a health profession, entrepreneurship, or a career in technology. The center's 160:1 student-to-advisor ratio is one of the best of any school featured in this guide. Major events hosted by the center's crew include the Fall Job and Internship Fair that is attended by seventy employers including big names like Bain, Credit Suisse, Deloitte, Epic Systems, *The New York Times*, and T. Rowe Price. The Spring Job & Internship Fair is primarily focused on nonprofit employers.

E-mail: admission@williams.edu | Website: www.williams.edu

Williams alumni are extremely available and willing to lend a hand to current students, and 65 percent of current students report consulting with an alum to plan their next steps after college. Additionally, alumni sponsored internships provide 143 undergraduates with a $3,800 stipend to pursue non-paying summer internships. The center also has introduced a new program of winter study internships with an alum. On-campus interviews are brokered through the CCE, but no data is available on the number of interviews taking place or about on-campus recruiting, although a fair amount of both definitely occur. The college recently identified its tracking of alumni outcomes as being an area of weakness, and it has begun making strides toward remedying the situation. Thanks to its superhuman work getting students into top graduate schools, the '68 Center for Career Exploration still has a glowing reputation.

Professional Outcomes

The top three areas of gain that Williams graduates self-report are thinking critically, writing clearly and effectively, and the ability to learn on their own. It's hard to name three traits that speak more to one's employability, so it shouldn't come as a shock that the most desirable employers adore the school's alumni. Companies/organizations that consistently snatch-up Williams graduates include Apple, Google, Goldman Sachs, McKinsey & Co., the Metropolitan Museum of Art, National Institutes of Health, and the New York Times Co. A significant number of students join the Peace Corps or are accepted into Teach for America. Business and education are the industries that attract the most students. At age thirty-four Williams grads earn a median income similar to Brandeis alums but a bit less than graduates of comparable Amherst. New York City, Boston, and San Francisco are the three cities most favored by Ephs post-undergrad.

For Ephs the bachelor's degrees earned at Williams are unlikely to be their last diplomas. Approximately 75 percent pursue an advanced degree within five years of leaving the college. The most frequently attended graduate programs are a not-too-shabby trio of Harvard, Columbia, and Yale. The top business, law, and medical schools attracting grads are Harvard, Columbia, and Penn. Using LinkedIn data we were able to determine that Williams College sends one of the highest percentages of graduates to prestigious medical schools of any institution in the country. It also ranked eighth overall on our list of the top producers of future PhDs and was the second-leading producer of economics PhDs.

Admission

Williams' Class of 2022 admissions data looks extremely similar to that of rival Amherst. The acceptance rate was 13 percent, and the average standardized test scores of admitted students was a 1480 on the SAT and a 33 on the ACT. Only 6 percent of those offered admission were not in the top 10 percent of their high school class. Nothing earth-shattering has occurred in Williams' admissions standards in recent years. Like many comparably ultra-selective liberal arts colleges, the admit rate has declined. In 2011, the college accepted 17 percent of the applicant pool. The profile of the average enrollee has edged closer to perfection in that time with the median freshman in 2011 possessing a 1430 SAT score; in 2018-19, the mid-50 range was 1410-1550.

The admissions office views all of the meat-and-potatoes factors as holding the most weight: rigorous schedule, test scores, class rank, and GPA, but recommendations are carefully read as well. The next tier of criteria include race/ethnicity, legacy status (roughly 14 percent of admitted students are legacies, mostly of the primary variety), first-generation status (17 percent fit that bill), and factors like volunteer and work experience. Williams seeks a racially and socioeconomically diverse group of uniquely talented students who will thrive in a close-knit academic community. However, few Hail Mary heaves end successfully here. To quantify that point, you can count on one hand the percentage of admitted applicants who scored less than 650 on a section of the SAT. Yes, it's that competitive.

Worth Your Money?

The annual cost of attendance at Williams is, in the world of elite liberal arts schools in New England, priced at the almost-standard $75,000, but those who aren't from wealthy backgrounds will pay far less. In fact, roughly half the student population qualifies for aid, and of that group all students have 100 percent of their financial need met with the average award being $57k. For the rich, the Williams bill won't sting too badly; for those in the lower-to-middle income brackets, the school will slice the cost significantly. For those in between, Williams is the caliber of school that is worth taking on debt in order to attend. Learning in seminar-style courses from some of the brightest minds around is worth paying for, and the connections you make (to peers and faculty) will stay with you for a lifetime.

FINANCIAL
Institutional Type: Private
In-State Tuition: $56,970
Out-of-State Tuition: $56,970
Room & Board: $14,990
Required Fees: $310
Books & Supplies: $800

Avg. Need-Based Aid: $56,933
Avg. % of Need Met: 100%

Avg. Merit-Based Aid: $0
% Receiving Merit-Based Aid: 0%

Avg. Cumulative Debt: $15,496
% of Students Borrowing: 41%

CAREER
Who Recruits
1. OC&C Strategy Consultants
2. Teach for America
3. M&T Bank
4. InterSystems
5. Trinity Industries

Notable Internships
1. WeWork
2. Late Night with Seth Meyers
3. Whitney Museum of American Art

Top Industries
1. Business
2. Education
3. Research
4. Finance
5. Social Services

Top Employers
1. Google
2. Goldman Sachs
3. Morgan Stanley
4. JPMorgan Chase
5. Bain & Company

Where Alumni Work
1. New York City
2. Boston
3. San Francisco
4. Washington, DC
5. Albany, NY

Median Earnings
College Scorecard (Early Career): $59,000
EOP (Early Career): $62,600
PayScale (Mid-Career): $127,500

RANKINGS
Forbes: 19
Money: 39
U.S. News: 1, Liberal Arts Colleges
Wall Street Journal/THE: 21
Washington Monthly: 12, Liberal Arts Colleges

#CollegesWorthYourMoney

Worcester Polytechnic Institute

Worcester, Massachusetts | Admissions Phone: 508-831-5286

Inside the Classroom

Worcester Polytechnic Institute, commonly referred to as WPI, is a small-to-midsize private university that is one of the fastest-growing PhD-granting schools in the United States. More than 4,300 undergraduate students and an additional 2,000+ graduate students attend school in Worcester, a city roughly fifty miles, as the crow flies, from Boston. Working on a quarter schedule, students engage in three courses for seven-week sprints as they plow through one of fifty+ rigorous degree programs, primarily in engineering.

An education at WPI is as hands-on and innovative as you will find at any university, engineering-centric or otherwise. The Interactive Qualifying Project (IPQ), often completed off campus, features work in small teams on a project that "connects science and technology with social issues and human need." The Major Qualifying Project (MQP) is a unique capstone experience in which students must identify a real-world problem and find a novel solution. A host of industry partners work with students in the MQPs. Students can participate in a four-to-eight-month paid co-op experience as part of their undergraduate experience. Core academic requirements for all undergrads also include a foray into the humanities and arts as the school seeks to produce well-rounded, team-player engineers.

With a student-to-faculty ratio of 13:1, WPI does an exceptional job keeping undergraduate classrooms cozy. In fact, a staggering 52 percent of its classes enroll fewer than ten students, creating an incredible level of academic intimacy. There are some large lecture hall courses mixed in—11 percent of sections contain more than 50 students—but WPI's level of individualized attention and small group instruction is hard to find, even at an elite liberal arts college. All students complete a minimum of two long-term research projects that are focused on solving real-world problems. That process begins freshman year, and by senior year 72 percent have engaged in off-campus research as well. Studying abroad, like most things at WPI, is not a typical experience. Many undergrads travel to one of fifty+ project centers situated on six continents where they can engage in solving real-life problems. Beginning with the Class of 2022, the school began awarding every single student $5,000 in study abroad funding with an aim toward a 90 percent participation rate within the next few years.

The undergraduate engineering program is respected worldwide and frequently graces lists of top schools for a variety of sub-disciplines. The most popular majors are mechanical engineering (19 percent), computer science (15 percent), biomedical engineering (9 percent), robotics engineering (8 percent), and chemical engineering (8 percent). Those completing all of those programs find favorable conditions as they approach graduate schools, potential employers, and prestigious national scholarship organizations. WPI undergrads have won nineteen Gilman Scholarships in the past two years and between two and five National Science Foundation Graduate Research Fellowships per year (plus many honorable mentions).

Outside the Classroom

Housing on campus is guaranteed only to freshmen; approximately three-fifths of all undergrads live on WPI's concentrated ninety-five-acre campus. Many other students reside in one of the school's nineteen fraternities and sororities; 33 percent of men and 36 percent of women go Greek. It is worth noting that women make up only 36 percent of the undergraduate student population. Twenty varsity sports teams, evenly split between men's and women's squads, compete as the Engineers in NCAA Division III. Another forty-four combined club and intramural teams and the four-floor, state-of-the-art Sports and Recreation Center that houses a pool ensure that physical activity is accessible to all. There are 225 clubs and activities that include original offerings like underwater hockey, a Rubik's Cube club, and a lock-picking club. Hey, no one would ever argue that WPI students aren't extremely creative. Of course, there are many traditional options also on the menu, including a multitude of organizations geared toward young professionals and shared academic interests. Boston is doable day trip, but there is plenty to do right in Worcester, including bustling Shrewsbury Street, museums, theaters, and loads of eateries. A growing urban area that still possesses the charm of a small-college town, Worcester can easily be navigated via public transit.

Career Services

The Career Development Center (CDC) consists of eleven professional employees, which works out to a student-to-advisor ratio of 403:1, in the average range compared to other schools featured in this guide. The staff is comprised of career counselors, corporate relations specialists, and recruiting coordinators. Students at WPI report an exceptionally high rate of satisfaction with their school's career services offerings for reasons that are obvious when you examine the basic facts.

An extraordinary 80 percent of all undergraduates, including freshmen and sophomores, interact with the CDC in some capacity each year. In the 2017-18 academic year 450 companies recruited on WPI's campus at career fairs, networking events, or on-campus job interviews. Annually, hundreds of students participate in summer internships or co-op placements that help them expand their network of career resources; the school's many corporate partners are always willing to take on WPI interns. In addition to strongly encouraging one-on-one counseling appointments, the office provides services like corporate tours, an employer-in-residence program, corporate information sessions, panel discussions, and a robust online system that allows students to connect with alumni and potential employers. Considering its highly accessible and broad array of offerings as well as positive professional and graduate school outcomes for alumni, the Worcester Polytechnic Institute's Career Development Center receives high marks from our staff.

Professional Outcomes

Within six months of graduation, 93 percent of Class of 2018 members had progressed beyond the seeking phase and had landed jobs or enrolled full time in graduate school. Companies employing literally hundreds of WPI alumni of all ages include Raytheon, Pratt & Whitney, Dell, and BAE Systems. Class of 2018 graduates found jobs at companies that included Air BNB, DraftKings, Amazon Robotics, NASA, Harvard Medical School, the US Department of Defense, and SpaceX. The average starting salary crept above $69,000 and is currently among the highest of any in the country, impressive even for a school focused entirely on STEM disciplines. Within the state of Massachusetts, only MIT sports higher graduate starting salary figures. WPI graduates most frequently remain in Greater Boston, but significant numbers relocate to New York City, Hartford, San Francisco, and Providence.

Nineteen percent of recent diploma-earners elected to immediately begin work on an advanced degree. Elite graduate schools attended by Class of 2018 grads included Duke, Columbia, Carnegie Mellon, Johns Hopkins, Harvard, Brown, Stanford, and NYU. Premed students enjoy the university's early/assured acceptance arrangements with Tufts Veterinary School, Massachusetts College of Pharmacy & Health Sciences, and Lake Erie College of Osteopathic Medicine. Recent grads have been accepted into medical school at the likes of Dartmouth, Northwestern, and Cornell.

Admission

WPI became the first top engineering university to adopt a test-optional policy in 2007, and it remains a rare breed among STEM-focused institutions. That decision has contributed to the school now receiving over 10,500 applications versus roughly 7,000 one decade ago. The acceptance rate for a place in the 2018-19 freshman class was 41.5 percent. Within that cohort 64 percent finished in the top 10 percent of their high school class while 93 percent placed in the top quartile. The average GPA was 3.89, and more than four-fifths of the group possessed a GPA above a 3.75. Among those submitting standardized test scores, the mid-50 percent on the SAT was 1300-1460, and it was 29-33 on the ACT.

Rigor of secondary school record and GPA are the only two factors deemed "very important" by the Worcester Admissions Committee. Interestingly, despite being test-optional, standardized test scores are among the factors considered "important" by the school along with class rank, recommendations, extracurricular activities, and character/personal qualities. Seventy percent of enrolled members of the Class of 2022 did, in fact, submit SAT scores and 25 percent submitted ACT scores, suggesting that only a small number of test-optional candidates are successful. It is worth noting that, as at most engineering schools, women enjoy a higher acceptance rate than men. At WPI that disparity is more pronounced than is typical; female applicants gain acceptance 53 percent of the time, and men get in at a 37.5 percent clip. There is no binding early decision option at WPI, only early action. Valuing students who are "creative and curious," who "enjoy working together to get things done," and "feel pretty sure that they're leaders, not followers," the Worcester Polytechnic Institute Admissions Committee is looking for passionate candidates who possess strong grades in AP courses and, in many cases, superior test scores.

Worth Your Money?

If your family can afford WPI, you will likely recoup a sizable portion of the $70,000 cost of attendance. Just over half of accepted students do receive a merit aid package averaging $16,235 per year, which knocks the cost down a bit. Fortunately, with such high starting salaries for recent graduates, paying $200,000 plus for an undergraduate degree from this school is not at all an unwise investment. Thirty-eight percent of students who apply for need-based aid do see 100 percent of their need met. In total, 61 percent of attending undergrads receive some level of merit-based grant that averages $24,500.

FINANCIAL
Institutional Type: Private
In-State Tuition: $51,604
Out-of-State Tuition: $51,604
Room & Board: $15,292
Required Fees: $916
Books & Supplies: $1,000

Avg. Need-Based Aid: $24,500
Avg. % of Need Met: 82%

Avg. Merit-Based Aid: $16,235
% Receiving Merit-Based Aid: 52%

Avg. Cumulative Debt: $27,000
% of Students Borrowing: N/A

CAREER
Who Recruits
1. PepsiCo
2. BAE Systems
3. General Electric
4. Travelers
5. Raytheon

Notable Internships
1. ExxonMobil
2. Dell
3. State Street

Top Industries
1. Engineering
2. Operations
3. Business
4. Information Technology
5. Research

Top Employers
1. Raytheon
2. Pratt & Whitney
3. Dell
4. National Grid
5. Google

Where Alumni Work
1. Boston
2. New York City
3. Hartford, CT
4. San Francisco
5. Providence, RI

Median Earnings
College Scorecard (Early Career): $84,900
EOP (Early Career): $85,200
PayScale (Mid-Career): $135,500

RANKINGS
Forbes: 93
Money: 148
U.S. News: 64, National Universities
Wall Street Journal/THE: 119
Washington Monthly: 116, National Universities

#CollegesWorthYourMoney

Yale University

New Haven, Connecticut | Admissions Phone: 203-432-9300

ADMISSION
Admission Rate: 6%
Admission Rate - Men: 7%
Admission Rate - Women: 6%
EA Admission Rate: N/A
ED Admission Rate: Not Offered
Admission Rate (5-Year Trend): -1%
ED Admission Rate (5-Year Trend): Not Offered
% of Admits Attending (Yield): 70%
Transfer Admission Rate: 2%

Offered Wait List: N/A
Accepted Wait List: N/A
Admitted Wait List: N/A

SAT Reading/Writing (Middle 50%): 720-770
SAT Math (Middle 50%): 730-790
ACT Composite (Middle 50%): 33-35
Testing Policy: ACT/SAT Required
SAT Superscore: Yes
ACT Superscore: Yes

% Graduated in Top 10% of HS Class: 95%
% Graduated in Top 25% of HS Class: 99%
% Graduated in Top 50% of HS Class: 100%

ENROLLMENT
Total Undergraduate Enrollment: 5,964
% Part-Time: 0%
% Male: 50%
% Female: 50%
% Out-of-State: 92%
% Fraternity: 10%
% Sorority: 10%
% On-Campus (Freshman): 100%
% On-Campus (All Undergraduate): 84%

% African-American: 8%
% Asian: 19%
% Hispanic: 13%
% White: 42%
% Other: 6%
% Race or Ethnicity Unknown: 0%
% International: 11%
% Low-Income: 13%

ACADEMICS
Student-to-Faculty Ratio: 6:1
% of Classes Under 20: 73%
% of Classes Under 40: 88%
% Full-Time Faculty: 68%
% Full-Time Faculty w/ Terminal Degree: 88%

Top Programs
Biology
Computer Science
Economics
Engineering
Global Affairs
History
Political Science
Psychology

Retention Rate: 99%
4-Year Graduation Rate: 88%
6-Year Graduation Rate: 97%

Curricular Flexibility: Somewhat Flexible
Academic Rating: ★★★★★

Inside the Classroom

World leaders, Supreme Court justices, scores of famous actors, inventors, writers, Nobel Laureates, billionaire businessmen, even fictional billionaire businessmen like The Simpsons' Mr. Burns…the list of Yale alumni fills multiple volumes of history books. Founded in 1701 as a more conservative, Puritan-rooted option to Harvard, the home of the Bulldogs is today elite, even by Ivy standards, every bit as much so as its Crimson rival of over 300 years. New Haven, Connecticut, is the destination for 5,700 undergraduates and more than 6,800 graduate students yet, thanks to the nurturing Residential College housing system, the university serves as an intimate undergraduate home while still playing the role of major private research university.

There are eighty majors and 2,000 undergraduate course offerings at Yale. Economics (13 percent), political science (9 percent), history (6 percent), biology (6 percent), and psychology (5 percent) are the university's most popular areas of concentration. In aiming to strike a balance between freedom and control, the required coursework at Yale is modest and relatively broad. Students must take courses in the natural sciences, the humanities and arts, the social sciences, foreign language, quantitative reasoning, and writing. Most majors require a one-to-two semester senior capstone experience. Depending on the major, students work closely with a professor toward the completion of an essay, portfolio, or research project.

The student-to-faculty ratio of 6:1 does translate to small class sizes, even with a larger number of graduate students on campus than undergrads. Three-quarters of classes have an enrollment of fewer than twenty students, making for a perfect environment for teaching and learning. Undergraduate research is a staple of the Yale academic experience; 95 percent of science majors participate in research with faculty and, university-wide, undergraduate research fellowships are available to 90 percent of first-years who apply. In short, you'd have to try very hard to avoid engaging in research while an undergraduate at Yale. The number of Bulldogs electing to study abroad has skyrocketed in recent years, but that explosion is relative. As with most Ivies the overall percentage who take a semester abroad remains only a sliver of the student body.

Many of Yale's undergraduate programs sit atop any major rankings list. Among the crème de la crème departments are biology, economics, global affairs, engineering, history, and computer science. Any degree from Yale will get your resume/application to employers or graduate schools on the top of the pile. The same goes for applications to competitive post-college scholarships, including the uber-prestigious Rhodes Scholarship. Yalies have captured the award 245 times, second only to Harvard in the all-time rankings. More than one hundred Yale students have captured Fulbright Scholarships, making it one of the leading producers in the country.

Outside the Classroom

With 319 years of history and a $29 billion endowment, Yale's 345-acre, tree-lined campus is a blend of beautiful stone edifices and modern amenities. Perhaps the most distinctive feature of life outside the classroom at Yale is the famed Residential College system that was imported from Oxford/Cambridge seventy years ago to facilitate a level of cohesiveness and connection typically only found at smaller liberal arts schools. Students are assigned to one of fourteen residential colleges that they will remain affiliated with for all four years. Each residence has two full-time, live-in faculty members. Greek life is not a dominant presence as only 10 percent of Yalies join a frat or sorority. So-called "secret societies," of which there are approximately forty, attract roughly half of seniors. Those include the famed Skull and Bones society, which has infiltrated American pop culture. Athletics are big-time at Yale as the Bulldogs field thirty-five NCAA Division I sports teams. An additional fifty club teams and thirty intramural sports are available for non-varsity athletes. Other student-run organizations include sixty cultural groups and fifty performance groups. Those seeking nature can canoe and camp on the 1,500 acres of the school's Outdoor Education Center or walk to the Yale Farm. Amenities and attractions include twelve dining halls, three on-campus museums, two theaters, and a library with 15 million holdings. Yale is situated in the middle of downtown New Haven, and the area is easily walkable. Boston and New York are each roughly a two-hour drive from New Haven.

Career Services

The Yale Office of Career Strategy (OCS) has thirteen professional staff members (excluding administrative assistants and counselors who only deal with graduate students) who are dedicated to tasks such as employer relations, career counseling, and summer funding opportunities. The 442:1 student-to-advisor ratio is within the average range when compared to other schools featured in this book. Still, the OCS has no shortage of brag-worthy statistics attached to its name.

For starters, in the 2017-18 academic year a staggering 13,062 current students and alumni engaged with the Office of Career Strategy, including over 4,300 one-on-one sessions with undergraduates. That same academic year the office hosted more than one hundred workshops and career exploration events that were attended by 6,300+ students. The OCS also hosted thirteen industry-specific career fairs that attracted 200 companies/organizations and close to 1,900 current students. Eighty-five top employers engaged in on-campus recruiting, and 500 students were granted interviews on Yale's grounds. The results are as impressive as the process—86 percent of Class of 2018 graduates reported that they were employed in an area directly related to their area of study. Yale students universally fill their summers with productive activities, often beginning immediately after their freshman year. By senior year 38 percent had spent the previous summer at a paid internship, 15 percent at an unpaid internship, 11 percent in laboratory research, 9 percent in academic study, and 5 percent in field research.

Professional Outcomes

Shortly after graduating 74 percent of the Yale Class of 2018 had entered the world of employment, 17 percent matriculated in graduate programs, and fewer than 2 percent were still looking for their next destination. The most common industries entered by the newly hired were finance (17 percent), education (16 percent), consulting (13 percent), technology (11 percent), and health care/medical/pharmaceutical (10 percent). Sixty-four percent of jobholders worked in the for-profit world while 35 percent worked in the nonprofit/government sectors. Starting salaries of more than $50,000 were earned by 67 percent of Class of 2018 grads, and 44 percent were awarded salaries of more than $70,000. The average starting salary was $64,642. Hundreds of Yale alums can be found at each of the world's top companies including Facebook, Google, Goldman Sachs, McKinsey & Company, Morgan Stanley, and Microsoft. Geographically, New York City has the highest concentration of alumni followed by San Francisco, Boston, DC, Los Angeles, and Chicago.

Using Class of 2017 data, among those pursuing graduate/professional programs 40 percent were pursuing a master's degree, 20 percent were in medical school, one-quarter started work on a PhD, and 6 percent went directly from undergraduate studies to law school. Unsurprisingly, given the quality of the minds admitted into Yale, medical school applicants traditionally find a home 90 percent of the time, exactly twice the national average; however, in 2018, that number was "only" 80 percent. Law school applicants do just fine as well; 87 percent were accepted into at least one school with a substantial number continuing at Yale Law School (YLS). Roughly 10 percent of YLS first-years attended Yale as undergraduates. For a complete list of where Yale alumni as a whole continue their educational journeys, simply consult a list of the best graduate/professional programs in the world.

Admission

Yale received over 35,000 applications for a place in the Class of 2022, but a meager 6.3 percent made it through the gates. Of those admitted, 95 percent placed in the top decile of their high school graduating class. The mid-50 percent range on the SAT was 1450-1560; the ACT span was 33-35. For an even better idea of the testing mastery required to become a Bulldog, look to the fact that 86 percent had an SAT Reading score of over 700, and 88 percent had an SAT Math score over 700.

You can bet a school that rejects nearly 94 percent of applicants relies on more than a few data points. The admissions committee ranks nine factors as being "most important": rigor of secondary record, GPA, class rank, standardized test scores (SAT Subject Test scores are recommended), application essay, recommendations, extracurricular activities, talent/ability, and character/personal qualities. The committee uses two overarching questions to guide its process: "Who is likely to make the most of Yale's resources?" and "Who will contribute most significantly to the Yale community?" Yale offers a unique single-choice early action (SCEA) option with a November 1 deadline. Those going that route are not bound to attend the university if accepted, but they cannot simultaneously apply ED or EA to any other school. Of the 6,016 SCEA applicants for the 2019-20 freshman cohort, 794 were admitted, a 13 percent success rate. More 2018-19 freshmen were first-generation students (18 percent) than legacy admits (11 percent). Getting into Yale is a hard-to-predict enterprise that sees many valedictorians and salutatorians bite the dust. Fantastic numbers along with a record of special talents and accomplishments that scream "future leader" will fare best.

Worth Your Money?

Yale is one of those rare schools where the contacts and networks you create while attending will make the education worth any cost. Fortunately, thanks to a $30 billion endowment, every single student who qualifies for need-based aid sees 100 percent of that need met by the university. The average grant is for $57,954, significantly reducing the sticker price cost of attendance of almost $76,000. There is no merit aid awarded by Yale, so those not in financial need will be paying full freight, but again, that will be money well spent.

FINANCIAL
Institutional Type: Private
In-State Tuition: $55,500
Out-of-State Tuition: $55,500
Room & Board: $16,600
Required Fees: N/A
Books & Supplies: $3,670

Avg. Need-Based Aid: $57,954
Avg. % of Need Met: 100%

Avg. Merit-Based Aid: $0
% Receiving Merit-Based Aid: 0%

Avg. Cumulative Debt: $14,575
% of Students Borrowing: 16%

CAREER
Who Recruits
1. The New York Times
2. Uber
3. Citi
4. Bain & Company
5. Boston Consulting Group

Notable Internships
1. Netflix
2. The Blackstone Group
3. United Nations

Top Industries
1. Business
2. Education
3. Research
4. Media
5. Operations

Top Employers
1. Google
2. McKinsey & Company
3. Goldman Sachs
4. Facebook
5. Morgan Stanley

Where Alumni Work
1. New York City
2. San Francisco
3. Boston
4. Washington, DC
5. Los Angeles

Median Earnings
College Scorecard (Early Career): $83,200
EOP (Early Career): $76,000
PayScale (Mid-Career): $138,300

RANKINGS
Forbes: 3
Money: 17
U.S. News: 3, National Universities
Wall Street Journal/THE: 3
Washington Monthly: 4, National Universities

#CollegesWorthYourMoney

Included in each school profile, we highlighted the academic programs that are among the very best on that particular campus. The next natural step is to look at top programs across all schools so that you can emerge with a bird's-eye picture of the premier American colleges in your major of interest. We included more than several dozen of the most popular areas of concentration in order to make these lists as useful and relevant to our audience as is possible.

For more useful lists, including a number of majors not covered in this book, we highly recommend visiting the College Transitions Dataverse at **www.collegetransitions.com/dataverse**. Please revisit the methodology section of this book (in the front) for an extensive explanation of how we selected the programs for inclusion.

And without further ado, we present College Transitions' Top Colleges for America's Top Majors:

Accounting
Baruch College (CUNY)
Binghamton University (SUNY)
Boston College
Brigham Young University
Bucknell University
Claremont McKenna College
Fordham University
Georgetown University
Indiana University Bloomington
Lehigh University
New York University
The Ohio State University – Columbus
Santa Clara University
University of Florida
University of Georgia
University of Illinois at Urbana-Champaign
University of Michigan
University of Notre Dame
University of Pennsylvania
University of Southern California
The University of Texas at Austin
Villanova University
Wake Forest University
Washington and Lee University
Washington University in St. Louis

Actuarial Science
Bentley University
Brigham Young University
Clemson University
Florida State University
Michigan State University
New York University
The Ohio State University – Columbus
Pennsylvania State University – University Park
Purdue University – West Lafayette
University of Notre Dame
University of California, Los Angeles
University of California, Santa Barbara
University of Florida
University of Georgia
University of Illinois at Urbana-Champaign
University of Michigan
University of Minnesota – Twin Cities
University of North Carolina at Chapel Hill
University of Pennsylvania
University of Wisconsin – Madison

Animal Science
California Polytechnic State University, San Luis Obispo
Clemson University
Cornell University
Michigan State University
North Carolina State University
The Ohio State University – Columbus
Pennsylvania State University – University Park
Purdue University – West Lafayette
Texas A&M University – College Station
University of California, Davis
University of Connecticut
University of Florida
University of Georgia
University of Illinois at Urbana-Champaign
University of Maryland, College Park
University of Massachusetts Amherst
University of Minnesota – Twin Cities
University of Wisconsin – Madison
Virginia Tech

Applied Mathematics
Brown University
California Institute of Technology
Carnegie Mellon University
Columbia University
Cornell University
Harvard University
Johns Hopkins University
Massachusetts Institute of Technology
New York University
Northwestern University
Princeton University
Stony Brook University (SUNY)
Texas A&M University – College Station
University of California, Berkeley
University of California, Los Angeles
University of California, San Diego
University of Pittsburgh – Pittsburgh Campus
University of Rochester
University of Washington – Seattle
Yale University

Architecture
California Polytechnic State University, San Luis Obispo
Carnegie Mellon University
Columbia University
The Cooper Union for the Advancement of Science and Art
Cornell University

Georgia Institute of Technology
Illinois Institute of Technology
Lehigh University
Northeastern University
Princeton University
Rensselaer Polytechnic Institute
Rice University
Syracuse University
Tulane University
University of California, Berkeley
University of Florida
University of Michigan
University of Minnesota – Twin Cities
University of Notre Dame
University of Pennsylvania
University of Southern California
The University of Texas at Austin
University of Virginia
Virginia Tech
Washington University in St. Louis

Art and/or Design
Arizona State University
Boston University
Carnegie Mellon
Columbia University
The Cooper Union for the Advancement of Science and Art
Cornell University
New York University
North Carolina State University
Northeastern University
Princeton University
Rochester Institute of Technology
Rutgers University – New Brunswick
Skidmore College
University of California, Los Angeles
University of California, San Diego
University of Notre Dame
University of Pennsylvania
University of Southern California
University of Washington – Seattle
University of Wisconsin – Madison
Vassar College
Washington University in St. Louis
Whitman College
Williams College
Yale University

Biology
Amherst College
Bowdoin College
Brandeis University
Brown University
California Institute of Technology
Carleton College
Colby College
Cornell University
Dartmouth College
Duke University
Emory University
Grinnell College
Harvard University
Haverford College
Johns Hopkins University
Macalester College
Massachusetts Institute of Technology

Pomona College
Princeton University
Reed College
Stanford University
Swarthmore College
University of California, Berkeley
University of California, Davis
University of California, Los Angeles
University of California, San Diego
University of Chicago
University of Pennsylvania
Washington University in St. Louis
Yale University

Biomedical Engineering
Boston University
Brown University
California Institute of Technology
Carnegie Mellon University
Case Western Reserve University
Columbia University
Cornell University
Duke University
Georgia Institute of Technology
Harvard University
Johns Hopkins University
Massachusetts Institute of Technology
Northwestern University
Purdue University – West Lafayette
Rice University
Stanford University
University of California, Berkeley
University of California, San Diego
University of Illinois at Urbana-Champaign
University of Michigan
University of Pennsylvania
University of Pittsburgh – Pittsburgh Campus
University of Rochester
The University of Texas at Austin
University of Washington – Seattle
University of Wisconsin – Madison
Vanderbilt University
Washington University in St. Louis
Worcester Polytechnic Institute
Yale University

Business Administration
Babson College
Bentley University
Boston College
Carnegie Mellon University
College of William & Mary
Cornell University
Emory University
Georgetown University
Georgia Institute of Technology
Indiana University Bloomington
Massachusetts Institute of Technology
New York University
Northeastern University
The Ohio State University – Columbus
Southern Methodist University
University of California, Berkeley
University of Illinois at Urbana-Champaign
University of Michigan
University of North Carolina at Chapel Hill

University of Notre Dame
University of Pennsylvania
University of Richmond
University of Southern California
The University of Texas at Austin
University of Virginia
University of Wisconsin – Madison
Villanova University
Wake Forest University
Washington and Lee University
Washington University in St. Louis

Chemistry
Bowdoin College
Bryn Mawr College
California Institute of Technology
Carleton College
College of the Holy Cross
College of William & Mary
Columbia University
Cornell University
Grinnell College
Harvard University
Harvey Mudd College
Haverford College
Macalester College
Massachusetts Institute of Technology
Northwestern University
Pomona College
Princeton University
Reed College
Rice University
St. Olaf College
Stanford University
University of California, Berkeley
University of California, San Diego
University of Chicago
University of Illinois at Urbana-Champaign
University of Minnesota – Twin Cities
University of North Carolina at Chapel Hill
Washington University in St. Louis
Wellesley College
Williams College

Chemical Engineering
Bucknell University
California Institute of Technology
Carnegie Mellon University
Colorado School of Mines
Columbia University
Cornell University
Georgia Institute of Technology
Johns Hopkins University
Lehigh University
Massachusetts Institute of Technology
North Carolina State University
Northwestern University
Princeton University
Purdue University – West Lafayette
Rensselaer Polytechnic Institute
Rice University
Stanford University
Tufts University
University of California, Berkeley
University of California, Santa Barbara
University of Illinois at Urbana-Champaign
University of Michigan
University of Minnesota – Twin Cities

University of Notre Dame
University of Pennsylvania
The University of Texas at Austin
University of Wisconsin – Madison
Washington University in St. Louis
Worcester Polytechnic Institute

Civil Engineering
Arizona State University
Bucknell University
California Institute of Technology
Carnegie Mellon University
Clarkson University
Columbia University
Cornell University
Georgia Institute of Technology
Johns Hopkins University
Lafayette College
Lehigh University
Massachusetts Institute of Technology
North Carolina State University
Northwestern University
The Ohio State University – Columbus
Pennsylvania State University – University Park
Princeton University
Purdue University – West Lafayette
Rose-Hulman Institute of Technology
Rice University
Stanford University
Texas A&M University – College Station
Tufts University
University of California, Berkeley
University of California, Davis
University of Illinois at Urbana-Champaign
University of Maryland, College Park
University of Michigan
The University of Texas at Austin
University of Wisconsin – Madison
Virginia Tech

Communication
American University
Boston College
Boston University
Cornell University
Fordham University
George Washington University
New York University
Northeastern University
Northwestern University
The Ohio State University – Columbus
Pennsylvania State University – University Park
Pepperdine University
Santa Clara University
Syracuse University
University of California, Berkeley
University of Florida
University of Georgia
University of Maryland, College Park
University of Miami
University of Minnesota – Twin Cities
University of North Carolina at Chapel Hill
University of Pennsylvania
University of Southern California
The University of Texas at Austin
University of Washington – Seattle
University of Wisconsin – Madison

Vanderbilt University
Villanova University
Wake Forest University
Washington and Lee University

Computer Science
California Institute of Technology
Carleton College
Carnegie Mellon University
Columbia University
Cornell University
Duke University
Georgia Institute of Technology
Harvard University
Harvey Mudd College
Massachusetts Institute of Technology
New York University
Northeastern University
Princeton University
Purdue University – West Lafayette
Rutgers University – New Brunswick
Stanford University
Swarthmore College
University of California, Berkeley
University of California, Los Angeles
University of California, San Diego
University of Illinois at Urbana-Champaign
University of Maryland, College Park
University of Massachusetts Amherst
University of Michigan
University of Pennsylvania
University of Southern California
The University of Texas at Austin
University of Washington – Seattle
University of Wisconsin – Madison
Virginia Tech

Criminology/Criminal Justice
American University
Arizona State University
Florida State University
George Mason University
George Washington University
Indiana University Bloomington
Marist College
Northeastern University
The Ohio State University – Columbus
Pennsylvania State University – University Park
Rutgers University – New Brunswick
San Diego State University
The College of New Jersey
University of California, Irvine
University of Georgia
University of Maryland, College Park
University of Miami
University of Pennsylvania
University of Pittsburgh – Pittsburgh Campus
University of Washington – Seattle

English
Amherst College
Barnard College
Bowdoin College
Brown University
Bryn Mawr College
College of the Holy Cross
Columbia University
Cornell University

Dartmouth College
Davidson College
Duke University
Harvard University
Haverford College
Johns Hopkins University
Kenyon College
Middlebury College
Northwestern University
Princeton University
Reed College
Stanford University
Swarthmore College
University of Michigan
University of California, Berkeley
University of California, Los Angeles
University of Chicago
University of Pennsylvania
University of Virginia
Vassar College
Williams College
Yale University

Economics
Amherst College
Bowdoin College
Brown University
Claremont McKenna College
Colby College
Columbia University
Cornell University
Dartmouth College
Duke University
Georgetown University
Grinnell College
Harvard University
Macalester College
Massachusetts Institute of Technology
Middlebury College
New York University
Northwestern University
Pomona College
Princeton University
Stanford University
Swarthmore College
University of California, Berkeley
University of California, San Diego
University of Chicago
University of Michigan
University of Pennsylvania
Vanderbilt University
Washington and Lee University
Williams College
Yale University

Education
Arizona State University
Boston College
Boston University
Brigham Young University
Brown University
Colgate University
College of William & Mary
Duke University
Emory University
Florida State University
Indiana University Bloomington
New York University

The Ohio State University – Columbus
Pennsylvania State University – University Park
Southern Methodist University
Swarthmore College
University of California, Irvine
University of Connecticut
University of Florida
University of Georgia
University of Illinois at Urbana-Champaign
University of Maryland, College Park
University of Michigan
University of Minnesota – Twin Cities
University of North Carolina at Chapel Hill
University of Pittsburgh – Pittsburgh Campus
The University of Texas at Austin
University of Washington – Seattle
University of Wisconsin – Madison
Vanderbilt University

Electrical Engineering
Bucknell University
California Institute of Technology
Carnegie Mellon University
Case Western Reserve University
Columbia University
Cornell University
Duke University
Franklin W. Olin College of Engineering
Georgia Institute of Technology
Illinois Institute of Technology
Massachusetts Institute of Technology
Northeastern University
Northwestern University
Princeton University
Purdue University – West Lafayette
Rensselaer Polytechnic Institute
Rice University
Stanford University
Stevens Institute of Technology
University of California, Berkeley
University of California, Los Angeles
University of California, San Diego
University of Illinois at Urbana-Champaign
University of Pennsylvania
University of Southern California
The University of Texas at Austin
University of Wisconsin – Madison
University of Michigan
University of Maryland, College Park
Virginia Tech
Worcester Polytechnic Institute

Environmental Engineering
Arizona State University
California Polytechnic State University, San Luis Obispo
California Institute of Technology
Carnegie Mellon University
Cornell University
Duke University
Georgia Institute of Technology
Johns Hopkins University
Massachusetts Institute of Technology
North Carolina State University
Pennsylvania State University – University Park
Purdue University – West Lafayette
Rice University
Stanford University

University at Buffalo (SUNY)
University of California, Berkeley
University of California, Davis
University of Florida
University of Illinois at Urbana-Champaign
University of Michigan
The University of Texas at Austin
University of Washington – Seattle
University of Wisconsin – Madison
Virginia Tech
Yale University

Environmental Studies
Amherst College
Bates College
Bowdoin College
Colby College
Colorado College
Cornell University
Dartmouth College
Dickinson College
Duke University
Hamilton College
Macalester College
Middlebury College
Mount Holyoke College
Oberlin College
Pitzer College
Pomona College
Tulane University
University of California, Berkeley
University of California, Davis
University of California, Santa Barbara
University of Chicago
University of North Carolina at Chapel Hill
University of Wisconsin – Madison
Williams College
Yale University

Film
American University
Binghamton University (SUNY)
Boston University
Chapman University
Columbia University
DePaul University
Drexel University
Emerson College
Florida State University
George Mason University
Ithaca College
Loyola Marymount University
New York University
Rochester Institute of Technology
Southern Methodist University
Stanford University
Syracuse University
Temple University
University of California, Los Angeles
University of Colorado Boulder
University of Miami
University of North Carolina at Wilmington
University of Southern California
The University of Texas at Austin
Wesleyan University

Finance

Arizona State University
Babson College
Baruch College (CUNY)
Bentley University
Boston College
Boston University
Carnegie Mellon University
Cornell University
Emory University
Fairfield University
Fordham University
George Washington University
Georgetown University
Indiana University Bloomington
Massachusetts Institute of Technology
New York University
The Ohio State University – Columbus
Pennsylvania State University – University Park
University of California, Berkeley
University of Illinois at Urbana-Champaign
University of Michigan
University of North Carolina at Chapel Hill
University of Notre Dame
University of Pennsylvania
University of Southern California
The University of Texas at Austin
University of Virginia
University of Washington – Seattle
University of Wisconsin – Madison
Washington University in St. Louis

Geology

Bowdoin College
Brown University
California Institute of Technology
Carleton College
College of William & Mary
Colorado School of Mines
Columbia University
Duke University
Lehigh University
Massachusetts Institute of Technology
Pennsylvania State University – University Park
Princeton University
Stanford University
Texas A&M University – College Station
Union College
University of California, Berkeley
University of California, Davis
University of California, Irvine
University of California, Santa Barbara
University of Florida
University of Michigan
University of Minnesota – Twin Cities
University of Pennsylvania
University of Pittsburgh – Pittsburgh Campus
The University of Texas at Austin
University of Washington – Seattle
University of Wisconsin – Madison
Whitman College
Yale University

History

Amherst College
Barnard College
Bowdoin College
Brown University

Carleton College
Colgate University
Columbia University
Cornell University
Dartmouth College
Georgetown University
Grinnell College
Harvard University
Haverford College
Johns Hopkins University
Kenyon College
Northwestern University
Oberlin College
Pomona College
Princeton University
Stanford University
Swarthmore College
University of California, Berkeley
University of California, Los Angeles
University of Chicago
University of Michigan
University of Pennsylvania
University of Wisconsin – Madison
Vanderbilt University
Williams College
Yale University

Industrial Engineering

Clarkson University
Clemson University
Columbia University
Cornell University
Georgia Institute of Technology
Lehigh University
North Carolina State University
Northeastern University
Northwestern University
The Ohio State University – Columbus
Pennsylvania State University – University Park
Purdue University – West Lafayette
Rensselaer Polytechnic Institute
Stanford University
Texas A&M University – College Station
University of California, Berkeley
University of Florida
University of Illinois at Urbana-Champaign
University of Michigan
University of Pittsburgh – Pittsburgh Campus
University of Southern California
The University of Texas at Austin
University of Wisconsin – Madison
Virginia Tech
Worcester Polytechnic Institute

Information Systems

Arizona State University
Bentley University
Carnegie Mellon University
Case Western Reserve University
Cornell University
Fairfield University
Georgetown University
Georgia Institute of Technology
Indiana University Bloomington
Massachusetts Institute of Technology
New York University
Northeastern University
The Ohio State University – Columbus

Purdue University – West Lafayette
Santa Clara University
University of Arizona
University of Georgia
University of Illinois at Urbana-Champaign
University of Maryland, College Park
University of Michigan
University of Minnesota – Twin Cities
University of Pennsylvania
The University of Texas at Austin
University of Washington – Seattle
University of Wisconsin – Madison

International Relations
American University
Boston University
Brown University
Claremont McKenna College
Colby College
Colgate University
College of William & Mary
Columbia University
Connecticut College
Cornell University
Dartmouth College
George Washington University
Georgetown University
Harvard University
Johns Hopkins University
Mount Holyoke College
Pomona College
Princeton University
Stanford University
Swarthmore College
Tufts University
University of California, Berkeley
University of California, San Diego
University of Chicago
University of Michigan
University of Pennsylvania
University of Southern California
University of Virginia
Williams College
Yale University

Kinesiology
Boston University
Brigham Young University
Indiana University Bloomington
Northeastern University
Occidental College
Pennsylvania State University – University Park
Rice University
San Diego State University
Syracuse University
Texas A&M University – College Station
University of Connecticut
University of Florida
University of Georgia
University of Illinois at Urbana-Champaign
University of Maryland, College Park
University of Massachusetts Amherst
University of Miami
University of Michigan
University of Minnesota – Twin Cities
University of North Carolina at Chapel Hill
University of Pittsburgh – Pittsburgh Campus

The University of Texas at Austin
University of Virginia
University of Wisconsin – Madison
Wake Forest University

Marketing
Arizona State University
Boston College
Cornell University
Emory University
Fordham University
George Washington University
Georgetown University
Indiana University Bloomington
New York University
Pennsylvania State University – University Park
Santa Clara University
Southern Methodist University
Tulane University
University of California, Berkeley
University of Florida
University of Illinois at Urbana-Champaign
University of Maryland, College Park
University of Michigan
University of Minnesota – Twin Cities
University of North Carolina at Chapel Hill
University of Notre Dame
University of Pennsylvania
University of Pittsburgh – Pittsburgh Campus
University of Southern California
The University of Texas at Austin
University of Virginia
University of Washington – Seattle
University of Wisconsin – Madison
Villanova University
Washington University in St. Louis

Materials Science and Engineering
California Institute of Technology
Carnegie Mellon University
Colorado School of Mines
Columbia University
Cornell University
Georgia Institute of Technology
Johns Hopkins University
Lehigh University
Massachusetts Institute of Technology
North Carolina State University
Northwestern University
The Ohio State University – Columbus
Pennsylvania State University – University Park
Purdue University – West Lafayette
Rensselaer Polytechnic Institute
Rice University
Stanford University
University of California, Berkeley
University of California, Los Angeles
University of California, Santa Barbara
University of Florida
University of Illinois at Urbana-Champaign
University of Michigan
University of Pennsylvania
The University of Texas at Austin
University of Washington – Seattle
University of Wisconsin – Madison
Virginia Tech

Mechanical Engineering
California Institute of Technology
Carnegie Mellon University
Case Western Reserve University
Columbia University
Cornell University
Duke University
Franklin W. Olin College of Engineering
Georgia Institute of Technology
Johns Hopkins University
Lehigh University
Massachusetts Institute of Technology
Northwestern University
The Ohio State University – Columbus
Pennsylvania State University – University Park
Princeton University
Purdue University – West Lafayette
Rensselaer Polytechnic Institute
Rice University
Rose-Hulman Institute of Technology
Stanford University
Stevens Institute of Technology
Texas A&M University – College Station
University of California, Berkeley
University of California, Los Angeles
University of Illinois at Urbana-Champaign
University of Michigan
University of Pennsylvania
The University of Texas at Austin
University of Wisconsin – Madison
Vanderbilt University
Virginia Tech
Worcester Polytechnic Institute

Neuroscience
Amherst College
Barnard College
Bates College
Boston University
Bowdoin College
Brandeis University
Brown University
Colgate University
College of William & Mary
Columbia University
Dartmouth College
Duke University
Emory University
Harvard University
Johns Hopkins University
Middlebury College
Northwestern University
Oberlin College
Pomona College
Princeton University
Tulane University
University of California, Los Angeles
University of Pennsylvania
University of Pittsburgh – Pittsburgh Campus
University of Rochester
University of Southern California
Vanderbilt University
Washington University in St. Louis
Wellesley College
Wesleyan University

Nursing
Binghamton University (SUNY)
Boston College
Brigham Young University
Case Western Reserve University
Clemson University
The College of New Jersey
Drexel University
Emory University
Fairfield University
Georgetown University
New York University
Northeastern University
The Ohio State University – Columbus
Pennsylvania State University – University Park
Rutgers University – New Brunswick
Stony Brook University (SUNY)
University of Connecticut
University of Florida
University of Massachusetts Amherst
University of Miami
University of Michigan
University of Minnesota – Twin Cities
University of North Carolina at Chapel Hill
University of Pennsylvania
University of Pittsburgh – Pittsburgh Campus
The University of Texas at Austin
University of Virginia
University of Washington – Seattle
University of Wisconsin – Madison
Villanova University

Physics
Brown University
California Institute of Technology
Carleton College
Carnegie Mellon University
Columbia University
Cornell University
Davidson College
Harvard University
Harvey Mudd College
Haverford College
Johns Hopkins University
Massachusetts Institute of Technology
Pomona College
Princeton University
Reed College
Rensselaer Polytechnic Institute
Rice University
Stanford University
University of California, Berkeley
University of California, Los Angeles
University of California, Santa Barbara
University of Chicago
University of Illinois at Urbana-Champaign
University of Maryland, College Park
University of Michigan
University of Notre Dame
University of Pennsylvania
University of Rochester
Yale University

Political Science

Bowdoin College
Brown University
College of William & Mary
Columbia University
Cornell University
Dartmouth College
Duke University
Georgetown University
Hamilton College
Harvard University
Haverford College
Macalester College
Middlebury College
Northwestern University
Princeton University
Stanford University
University of California, Berkeley
University of California, Los Angeles
University of Chicago
University of Michigan
University of North Carolina at Chapel Hill
University of Notre Dame
University of Pennsylvania
University of Rochester
Vanderbilt University
Vassar College
Washington and Lee University
Wesleyan University
Williams College
Yale University

Psychology

Barnard College
Bates College
Boston College
Brown University
Claremont McKenna College
Columbia University
Dartmouth College
Duke University
Harvard University
Haverford College
Northwestern University
Pomona College
Princeton University
Stanford University
Tufts University
University of California, Berkeley
University of California, Los Angeles
University of Chicago
University of Michigan
University of Minnesota – Twin Cities
University of North Carolina at Chapel Hill
University of Pennsylvania
University of Wisconsin – Madison
Vanderbilt University
Vassar College
Washington University in St. Louis
Wellesley College
Wesleyan University
Williams College
Yale University

Statistics

Brigham Young University
Carleton College
Carnegie Mellon University
Columbia University
Cornell University
Duke University
Harvard University
Johns Hopkins University
North Carolina State University
Northwestern University
Pennsylvania State University – University Park
Purdue University – West Lafayette
Rice University
Rutgers University – New Brunswick
Stanford University
Texas A&M University – College Station
University of California, Berkeley
University of California, Los Angeles
University of California, Santa Barbara
University of Chicago
University of Connecticut
University of Florida
University of Illinois at Urbana-Champaign
University of Michigan
University of Minnesota – Twin Cities
University of North Carolina at Chapel Hill
University of Pennsylvania
University of Washington – Seattle
University of Wisconsin – Madison
Virginia Tech

Theatre

Boston University
Brown University
Carnegie Mellon University
Chapman University
DePaul University
Elon University
Emerson College
Florida State University
Fordham University
The Juilliard School
Loyola Marymount University
Muhlenberg College
New York University
Northwestern University
Purchase College (SUNY)
Rutgers University – New Brunswick
Skidmore College
Syracuse University
University of California, Irvine
University of California, Los Angeles
University of California, San Diego
University of Connecticut
University of Illinois at Urbana-Champaign
University of Miami
University of Michigan
University of Minnesota – Twin Cities
University of Notre Dame
University of Southern California
Vassar College
Yale University

Andrew Belasco, Ph.D., a graduate of Georgetown University and Harvard University, is a higher education researcher, counselor, and CEO of College Transitions, an educational consulting firm. His work has been published in the nation's top higher education journals and featured in dozens of media outlets, including *The New York Times*, *Washington Post*, *Time*, *Boston Globe*, *Forbes*, *The Chronicle of Higher Education*, and NPR, among others. Andrew is also the co-author of *The Enlightened College Applicant: A New Approach to the Search and Admissions Process* (Rowman & Littlefield, 2016).

Dave Bergman, Ed.D., earned his doctoral degree from Temple University and has fifteen years of professional experience that includes work as a teacher, high school administrator, adjunct professor, researcher, and independent educational consultant. As a co-founder of College Transitions, Dave oversees the collegetransitions.com blog and Dataverse, reaching an audience in excess of one million readers annually. Dave is also the co-author of *The Enlightened College Applicant: A New Approach to the Search and Admission Process* (Rowman & Littlefield, 2016).

Michael Trivette, Ph.D., a graduate of the University of Georgia Institute of Higher Education, has over fifteen years of experience in the higher-education field, including college admissions, enrollment management, intercollegiate athletics, student support services, and student life. A co-founder of College Transitions, he also has experience working within the University of North Carolina System and the University System of Georgia. His research has been published in *Educational Policy*, *Review of Higher Education*, *The Journal of Higher Education*, and the *Journal of Education Finance*.

College Transitions is a college counseling firm that guides students through the undergraduate admissions and financial aid process, serving families in the U.S. and abroad.

Clinical Manual of
Substance Abuse

Clinical Manual of Substance Abuse

Second Edition

JEAN KINNEY, MSW
Executive Director, Project Cork Institute
Assistant Professor of Psychiatry
Dartmouth Medical School
Hanover, New Hampshire

 Mosby

A *Harcourt Health Sciences Company*
St. Louis   Philadelphia   London   Sydney   Toronto

M Mosby

A *Harcourt Health Sciences Company*

Publisher: Nancy L. Coon
Editor: Jeff Burnham
Associate Developmental Editor: Linda Caldwell
Project Manager: Carol Sullivan Weis

A NOTE TO THE READER:
The author and publisher have made every attempt to check pharmacological content for accuracy. Because the science of pharmacology is continually advancing, our knowledge base continues to expand. Therefore we recommend that the reader always check product information for changes in dosage or administration before administering any medication. This is particularly important with new or rarely used drugs.

Mosby, Inc.
11830 Westline Industrial Drive
St. Louis, Missouri 63146

Library of Congress Cataloging in Publication Data

Kinney, Jean
    Clinical manual of substance abuse / Jean Kinney. — 2nd ed.
        p.   cm.
    ISBN 0-8151-5092-X (softbound)
    1. Substance abuse—Treatment.   I. Title.
    [DNLM: 1. Substance Abuse—therapy.   2. Alcoholism—therapy.   WM
270 K55c 1996]
RC564.K56 1996
616.86'06—dc20
DNLM/DLC

00/9 8 7 6 5 4 3 2

Contributors

Patrick J. Abbott, MD
Assistant Professor
University of New Mexico
Senior Clinician
Center on Alcoholism, Substance Abuse, and Addictions (CASAA)
University of New Mexico
Albuquerque, New Mexico

Wendy L. Adams, MD, MPH
Assistant Professor of Medicine
Medical College of Wisconsin
Milwaukee, Wisconsin

Omowale Amuleru-Marshall, PhD, MPH
Southern Regional Director
Center for Health and Development, Inc
Atlanta, Georgia

Stuart A. Copans, MD
Associate Professor of Psychiatry
Dartmouth Medical School
Brattleboro Retreat
Brattleboro, Vermont

Christine Huff Fewell, CSW, BCD, CAC
Adjunct Faculty
Fordham University
New York University School of Social Work
New York, New York

Loretta P. Finnegan, MD
Director
Women's Health Initiative
National Institutes of Health
Bethesda, Maryland

Nancy B. Fisk, EdD, RN
Associate Professor
School of Nursing
University of Massachusetts
Amherst, Massachusetts

Heather J. Gotham, MA
Alcohol, Health & Behavior Project
University of Missouri—Columbia
Columbia, Missouri

Allan W. Graham, MD, FACP
Addiction Medicine Section
Kaiser Permanente
Denver, Colorado

Jean Kinney, MSW
Executive Director
Project Cork Institute
Assistant Professor of Psychiatry
Dartmouth Medical School
Hanover, New Hampshire

Susan McGrath Morgan, LICSW
Psychotherapist, Private Practice
Norwich, Vermont

Patrick G. O'Connor, MD, MPH
Associate Professor of Medicine
Yale University School of Medicine
Medical Director
Primary Care Center
New Haven, Connecticut

Fred C. Osher, MD
Associate Professor
University of Maryland
School of Medicine
Department of Psychiatry
Institute of Psychiatry and Human Behavior
Baltimore, Maryland

Penny Page, MLS
Director of Library
Center of Alcohol Studies
Rutgers University
New Brunswick, New Jersey

Kimberly Palma, MA
Cornell Cooperative Extension
Ithaca, New York

Virginia Rolett, MLS
Consultant
Project Cork Institute
Hanover, New Hampshire

Paula Ruth, RN, CDNS
Program Director
Addiction Recovery Service
Institute of Living
Hartford Hospitals Mental Health Network
Hartford, Connecticut

Reviewers

To my parents

Preface

WHAT TO EXPECT

Clinical Manual of Substance Abuse is intended for clinicians in primary care. It is designed to help primary care providers become more comfortable and skilled in handling the problems of substance use that are an inevitable part of their day-to-day practice. The intention is not to transform primary care practitioners into alcohol or drug abuse specialists but to facilitate managing the problems already confronting them.

Although the text is assembled to facilitate the acquisition of basic skills in identification and management, it is recognized that no text can impart clinical skills. To draw from a popular television commercial, these skills are gained the "old-fashioned way," by practice and hard work. For those already engaged in a busy clinical practice, finding the time and energy for professional development is a challenge. It is hoped that this manual will ease that task.

When compared with similar volumes, this manual may appear a bit sparse. A simple, "bare bones" approach has been adopted in defining the skills and knowledge related to management. The emphasis is on basic skills in the primary care clinician's repertoire. The standard used in identifying these has been pragmatic. *What clinical tasks fall to the primary care provider, when no one else is in a position to take them on?* Our answer to that question has defined the points of emphasis. But these should not be construed as suggesting limits to the primary care provider's role; rather, they define the starting point.

The authors and editors of a handbook or clinical manual are not afforded the luxury accorded to those who write standard texts. Manuals cannot be exhaustive; they are required to be selective. There is the need to make choices, to distinguish the important from the merely interesting, to separate the useful from the extraneous. In the attempt to synthesize a vast body of material, there is a constant struggle with what psychologists would refer to as the "figure-ground" problem. Does one see the vase or two profiles, or find that one's perceptions shift and that maintaining a consistent focus is difficult? The challenge here has been to provide sufficient context to ground the discussion without obscuring or losing sight of the foreground.

Were the old clinical truism, "to know syphilis is to know medicine," updated, it would surely be recast as, "to know alcohol and other drug use is to know medicine." Accordingly, the body of information that could be included here is truly encyclopedic. Thus, in this respect as well, considerable effort has been made to highlight the fundamentals and offer the reader a crisp, clear focus. In making decisions on inclusion vs. exclusion, the ultimate guide has been not the scientific literature but clinical practice. It comes from having been an observer of others tackling this clinical work. What are those tidbits that tend to spark an "ahhh" response? What are the frameworks that have proved useful in coalescing otherwise random facts into a coherent whole? What has facilitated clinical interactions and clinical decision making? These have been the ultimate criteria for the discussion that follows.

ORGANIZATION

The manual is organized into three parts. The first addresses the basic clinical tasks constituting the management of alcohol and drug problems. It concludes with material directed to those engaged, either formally or informally, in training and education. This first section addresses these issues from a generic perspective. Alas, there are few generic patients. Patients come to us with a specific age, gender, and cultural background. Part 2, Special Populations—Special Concerns, outlines the clinically pertinent characteristics of different segments of the population. It addresses different racial and ethnic groups, the economically disadvantaged and medically underserved segments of society, and the presentations at different points in the life cycle. It also includes a discussion of the impaired professional colleague. The third section, Appendices, offers a compilation of resources, ranging from organizations to audiovisual materials, along with information on how to acquire them.

NOTES ON THE ALCOHOL AND SUBSTANCE ABUSE LITERATURE

This alcohol and substance abuse literature is distinctive in several important respects. For one, it is multidisciplinary. The core knowledge base for the field is drawn from disparate disciplines, ranging from social sciences to medical sciences, law, economics, and political science, to the spectrum of helping professions. Thus the relevant literature is scattered through the journals of broader disciplines. Beyond its interdisciplinary nature, as a "newer" field of academic and clinical inquiry, the field is marked by a multiplicity of specialty journals. There is currently a proliferation of publications. As new ones arise, others cease publication, change publishers, or make significant changes in editorial practices. As fields "mature," the number of journals tends to decrease; a circumscribed number of well-recognized publications eventually become the major vehicle for the field's scholarly and scientific communications.

The substance abuse literature is also characterized by its relative separation and isolation from the established professional literature. The flow of information can be discerned from citation patterns, i.e., who quotes whom. Alcohol and drug journals cite materials published in the established, mainstream professional literature, but the reverse is far less common. Thus information communicated through the specialty literature does not tend to flow into the broader professional arena. A major consequence for the practitioner is that attention and effort are required not only to become informed but to remain current. The usual professional reading practices cannot be depended on to adequately accomplish that end.

There is another feature of the alcohol and drug literature that makes access to it difficult. Much of it would be described by librarians and information specialists as "fugitive" or "ephemeral" literature. Alcohol and drug journals are indexed, not from cover to cover, but only selectively by many of the established databases such as Medline. The result is that an online literature search cannot be presumed to identify the body of published work. Beyond the problems created by this pattern of selective indexing, there are several others. The biggest is that the most useful materials are often in a format that automatically excludes them from most databases, e.g., special reports commissioned by the government, national agencies, foundations, or professional associations.

As if the above did not present enough obstacles, another factor is the recent proliferation of materials directed to the general public, materials that coexist alongside the academic and scientific literature. To a large extent, these works are a mix of scientific fact and folk wisdom, punctuated by the precepts of the self-help movements. Many are written by persons with professional credentials who use that status to present themselves as authoritative. Their works are, however, wholly outside their field of established expertise, shades of Nobel Prize physicists who move on to the common cold and vitamin C. This lay body of literature is part of the growing national self-help movement. In 1988, *The New York Times* Business Section reported that these works represent an "exploding field" within publishing and accounted for tens of millions of dollars in the trade book market. As one major publishing house phrased it, "It seems as if just about every family in America is recovering from one thing or another."[7] Within a program of structured professional reading, these works may have little to recommend them. However, with literally millions of copies in cirulation, they become important because they are a source of information and misinformation for patients.

COMMENTS ON REFERENCES AND READINGS

Although many may not judge a book by its cover, they do judge it by the nature of its references and source materials. In scanning the references cited here, one may find that the cues that usually stand one in good stead, the source and the publication date, provide little assistance to judge rapidly the quality of this work or its potential usefulness. Many of the sources will be unfamiliar. Every profession has its own relatively small circle of well-respected journals. These are the primary route of professional communications. Pressed for time and faced with mountains of journals, everyone needs to zero in on a handful of publications. This means systematically overlooking work published in unfamiliar places or addressed to other professional groups.[13,15]

Unavoidably, because professionals depend primarily on the journals of their discipline to remain current, they lose out on the bulk of the published substance abuse work. Much of considerable use never comes to their attention. As was noted by a nurse educator, "Most research on alcoholism has been conducted by non-nursing health-related professionals."[3] However, the same could be said for any other health care discipline. Were the magnitude of alcohol and drug use problems inferred from the proportion of any profession's literature directed to these topics, the extent of these problems would be significantly underestimated. The need to go beyond a single professional literature to deal adequately with substance use was documented in an interesting fashion. The review of an extensive bibliography prepared by the New York University School of Nursing, as part of a major school-wide effort to enhance nursing education on alcohol and drug-related problems, showed that of the over 500 citations, approximately 90% were from sources outside of the nursing field.*

What does appear in the nursing or social work or medical primary care specialty literature is usually focused on discrete, narrowly circumscribed topics. Its primary audience consists of those with a pre-existing interest. Even fewer are addressed to fundamental topics such as screening, identification, assessment, and management.

Be prepared for a diversity of journals in this manual, many of which will be from areas outside your normal professional reading. To avoid this manual's taking on the appearance of a complex chemical formula by being peppered with footnotes, there has been an effort to show restraint. Each chapter concludes with a list of additional readings on the major topics to amplify the points covered.

We have elected also to use original sources; so some of the material, although appearing dated, reflects what are, in a number of instances, classic works. The notion that nothing of value was published more than 2 years ago is obviously erroneous. The pressure for "being current" can lead to authors citing secondary sources, ignoring the original work, and going with a more recent article that alludes to the original findings. The practice of using secondary sources is unhelpful for the readers who go to the cited work for further detail and find only an interpretation of the original data. Tracking down the original source inevitably becomes a scavenger hunt.

The practice of using secondary sources also invites distortion, sometimes with serious consequences. An excellent illustration involves the "well-established fact" that physicians and nurses have a higher prevalence of alcoholism and drug addiction than does the general population. With this "fact" in hand, multiple explanations have arisen, e.g., greater access to drugs, the pressures of the profession, and the belief that greater pharmacological knowledge may render an immunity to addiction. In a piece of interesting detective work, the often-cited physician addiction rate of 30 to 100 times the general population was tracked back through literature references to

a 1959 work on the rate of narcotic addiction in Germany in the allied medical professions for the years 1954 to 1957. This original citation was the source of current "fact."[4]

AN ALCOHOL MANUAL IN DISGUISE?

A number of similar works choose to organize the material by drug classes and have a separate chapter per drug. This method has its drawbacks—chiefly that the common features are not always apparent. They can lead the reader to sense that he or she is dealing with distinct, separate spheres of knowledge, each with its distinctive clinical approaches. The other method is to address the commonalities across substances and speak of use as a whole, under the rubric of "chemical dependency," a term sometimes used within the substance abuse field. Or the rubric may be "psychoactive substance abuse use" if one goes with the formal designation. Which approach is judged more useful may well depend on whether by inclination one is a "lumper" or a "splitter."

At the very least, most individuals, both lay and professional, conceive of at least two significant divisions, i.e., "alcohol" vs. "drugs". Beyond the obvious reasons that come to mind, this view is given credence as a logical research and clinical perspective by the organization at the national level for its research institutes. There are two institutes. One is directed to alcohol, the National Institute on Alcohol Abuse and Alcoholism (NIAAA). The other, focused on drugs, is the National Institute on Drug Abuse (NIDA). Although conducting collaborative programs, they nonetheless represent two separate domains whose efforts are far from perfectly coordinated.

For the clinician, however, there are problems with any of the aforementioned approaches to categorizing patients' presentations. Patients rarely will come to you with *a* drug problem. The notion of the pure "alcoholic" or the pure "addict" is a myth. Multiple substance use and abuse are the norm. If one substance serves as the common denominator of substance use presentations, it is alcohol. Persons dependent on other substances in substantial numbers will also be dependent on alcohol.[5]

This handbook is structured to reflect this clinical reality. If there is seemingly a weighting and overemphasis on alcohol, it is because alcohol problems provide a useful point of entry into general substance use. To be practical, one does need to start somewhere. In dealing with alcohol problems, one touches on not only the single greatest drug problem, but on what is often a solvent as well for substance use.

*Reading list undated and without attribution.

Patients with Coexisting Drug and Alcohol Problems

Type of drug use problem	Alcohol dependence at entry into drug treatment (%)
Opiates	
Patients entering treatment[2]	48
Methadone maintenance[6]	25
Residential treatment[6]	42
Outpatient drug-free treatment[6]	36
Methadone maintenance[1]	
Anglos	46
Chicanos	55
Outpatient drug-free treatment[1]	
Anglos	48
Chicanos	68
Kentucky state residents admitted[14] to	82 males
federal Lexington hospital	33 females
National sample[8]	56
Cocaine	
Cocaine, inpatient treatment[9]	73
Substance abuse, residential treatment[11]	68
Substance abuse, residential treatment[11]	89
Substance abuse, residential treatment[12]	94
Marijuana	
Substance abuse, inpatient treatment[12]	
Males	49
Females	25
Benzodiazepines[10]	95

A CLOSING COMMENT ON TERMINOLOGY: A PERSONAL NOTE

Patient . . . Client . . . Consumer . . . Customer

In this manual I have elected to retain the longstanding if somewhat out of vogue term of "patient" rather than to adopt one of the alternatives being promoted. The Mosby editors, recognizing that this might raise eyebrows, suggested that an explanation is in order. It was pointed out to me that *patient* is criticized as being "too medical" or implying "subservience."

These do not represent problems to me. For one, I do not consider medicine to be a bad word. More importantly, the meanings of *patient, nurse, physician*—*Patient,* one who suffers; *Nurse,* one who nurtures, ministers to, feeds; *Physician,* one who strives to heal or create a healing environment— evoke truths that should not be undervalued or dismissed as out-of-date.

Marketplace terminology is becoming more common in nursing, medicine, or globally, in that "thing" we now call "health care." However, the terms *client* or *consumer* or *customer* conjure up the relationship that one might have with an auto mechanic, a realtor, an insurance agent, or a used car salesman. These are not the models that I want to replicate in my dealings with physicians and nurses. Whatever its flaws or problems, my own preference is to deal with those for whom the maxim "do no harm" still has meaning, rather than the alternative, "caveat emptor."

REFERENCES

1. Anglin MD; Almog H; Fisher DG; Peters KR. Alcohol use by heroin addicts: Evidence for an inverse relationship. A study of methadone maintenance and drug free treatment samples. *American Journal of Drug Abuse* 15(2): 191-207, 1989. (27 refs.)
2. Barr HL; Cohen A. Abusers of alcohol and narcotics: Who are they? *International Journal of the Addictions* 22(6): 525-541, 1987. (23 refs.)
3. Bartek JK; et al. Nurse identified problems in the management of alcoholic patients. *Journal of Studies on Alcohol* 49(1): 62-70, 1988. (39 refs.)
4. Brewster JM. Prevalence of alcohol and other drug problems among physicians. *Journal of the American Medical Association* 255(14): 1913-1920, 1986. (95 refs.)
5. De Leon G. Alcohol—the hidden drug among substance abusers. (editorial). *British Journal of Addiction* 84(8): 837-840, 1989. (7 refs.)

6. Hubbard RL; et al. *Drug Abuse Treatment: A National Study of Effectiveness.* Chapel Hill NC: University of North Carolina Press, 1989. 213 pp. (Chapter refs.)

7. McDowell E. In land of addictions—shelves full of solace. *The New York Times.* Section D, p. 1. June 16, 1988.

8. Maddux JF; Desmond DP. Family and environment in the choice of opioid dependence or alcoholism. *American Journal of Drug Abuse* 15(2): 117-134, 1989. (42 refs.)

9. Miller NS; Gold MS. Cocaine and alcoholism: Distinct or part of a spectrum. *Psychiatric Annual* 18(9): 538-539, 1988. (10 refs.)

10. Miller NS; Gold MS. Identification and treatment of benzodiazepine abuse. *American Family Physician* 40(4): 175-183, 1989.

11. Miller NS; et al. The diagnosis of alcohol and cannabis dependence in cocaine dependents and alcohol dependence in their families. *British Journal of Addiction* 84(12): 1491-1498, 1989. (34 refs.)

12. Miller NS; et al. The diagnosis of alcohol, cocaine, and other drug dependence in an inpatient treatment population. *Journal of Substance Abuse Treatment* 6(1): 37-40, 1989. (21 refs.)

13. Rockwell DA. Readership patterns of psychiatric journals. *Archives of General Psychiatry* 29: 704-706, 1973. (2 refs.)

14. Vaillant GE. The natural history of narcotic drug addiction. *Seminars in Psychiatry* 2: 486-498, 1970. (27 refs.)

15. What journals for the physicians? (editorial). *Annals of International Medicine* 85(5): 674-676, 1976.

Contents

Detailed Contents

Clinical Manual of
Substance Abuse

PART I

Management of Substance Abuse

Substance use is one of our nation's most vexing problems. It is a concern of neighborhoods and communities and our friends and families. Civic organizations, religious bodies, national charities, and foundations focus on substance use as a major priority for action. Virtually every sector of society is touched by substance use problems—the schools, the courts, the family, and the workplace.

In this context, substance use problems have been cast in many guises; at some point they are viewed as a legal issue and at others a moral issue. Substance use has been suggested to be a statement on the zeitgeist and a commentary on our collective psychological makeup. Substance use has been approached also in terms of its relationship to social conditions, poverty, racism, and the economy. Substance use is addressed by government in the spheres of domestic policy and foreign policy. Regardless of what else substance use may represent, it is indisputably a health concern.

Substance use problems will not be resolved by any single group or strategy. Nonetheless, the health care system has a special opportunity and obligation. Unlike other groups in society, health care professionals are the least likely to be encumbered by political agendas and other competing concerns. Clinical professionals' mission is unambiguous; their patients' welfare is their first concern. Given the significant impact alcohol and other drug use can have on health, clinical personnel need no special mandate to be involved. To the contrary, as alcohol and other substance use becomes more widely recognized as a health concern, clinicians will be held accountable for the *failure* to intervene.

Unlike schools, civic groups, courts, or any other sector of society, health care professionals are in a unique position. Although there are differing views over these other groups' proper roles in dealing with substance use issues, there is no debate over the proper role of health care professionals. Prevention, early intervention, promoting treatment, and offering education are an unquestioned part of their responsibilities. As part of their routine clinical functioning, they have the data or means to acquire it, can easily acquire the skills to use this information, and have the implicit right and obligation to do so as part of their responsibility to provide care. Through these clinical activities, health care providers can promote a model for addressing substance use problems that is coherent, understood, accepted by the general population, and capable of mobilizing public action. If this seems like a Herculean task, consider the impact made by health care professionals, individually and collectively, regarding the dramatic changes in public attitudes and behavior toward smoking. This effort succeeded despite a strong, well-heeled industry lobby and widespread tobacco use, which was unthinkingly accepted and glamorized. Similarly, the role and impact of health care professionals in addressing substance use issues should not be underestimated.

Several basic questions arise for clinicians as they attempt to address their patients' substance use problems.

WHAT IS THE PROBLEM?

Anyone who uses psychoactive substances is at some risk for problems. These problems are of two

1

different types. The first are acute problems. These encompass the difficulties that can follow substance use and that typically would not have occurred in the absence of either alcohol or drug use. Acute problems can include overdoses, drug-drug interactions, accidents, altercations, an arrest for driving while impaired, date rape, or acquiring a sexually transmitted disease.

Acute problems can arise whether the agent is used recreationally, medically prescribed or self-prescribed, purchased at the drug store, at the liquor store, or on the street corner. The risk for acute problems varies with age, gender, the substance used, and the dose. The greatest risk for acute difficulties accompanies what is commonly termed *intoxication*, use that results in significant central nervous system impairment. With intoxication, there are predictable changes in perception, judgment, reaction time, concentration, and the ability to make decisions. The nature of the activities that accompany use also determines the level of risk. For example, substance use at a large party can invite different problems from those that might occur at home watching Monday night football on television.

Psychoactive substance use can also lead to chronic problems. Over time, extended heavy use of virtually any psychoactive substance leads to dependence. Dependence is marked by two phenomena. One is an increased tolerance to the effects of the substance. Larger doses are required to achieve the state that was earlier produced by lesser amounts. In addition to tolerance, there are also withdrawal symptoms. Withdrawal symptoms occur when the accustomed use is stopped abruptly or even significantly reduced. In addition to these physical phenomena, dependence is marked by personality and behavioral changes. The individual's life becomes increasingly centered around use. Alcohol or drug use dictates friends and the use of leisure time. It has a negative impact on relationships with spouse, children, and friends. Often, work performance is impaired. Financial, medical, and legal problems can become routine.

With increasing dysfunction, a number of psychological defenses emerge. These arise to protect the individual from the pain caused by the growing number and nature of life problems. The most visible and distinctive of these defenses is denial. In this respect, chronic substance use problems are not unique. Denial is common in any chronic illness. When confronted with a diagnosis of a chronic disease, patients often do not accept the diagnosis. They may look for explanations to account for a mistake, for example, by questioning the laboratory test results. Patients often attribute their symptoms to something else, usually

something more benign. Denial accompanying chronic substance use is pervasive. The patient, despite the overwhelming evidence to the contrary, genuinely does not recognize that his or her life problems are due to substance use. Without experience or training in how to respond to denial, it can become a source of frustration. Denial can evoke a sense of powerlessness in many clinicians. Many of the approaches appropriately used when a patient discredits a diagnosis or wishes to design his or her own treatment regimen—be it copper bracelets or a dose of megavitamins—are equally applicable to patients dependent on alcohol or other substances as well.

WHAT IS TREATMENT?

The term *treatment* is in many respects a misnomer. *Rehabilitation* is a more appropriate term to describe what takes place. The goal of treatment or rehabilitation is simple: to enable persons dependent on substances to live comfortably and function effectively without the use of alcohol or other drugs. There are two different components to treatment. One is directed to restoring physical health and often includes the medical supervision of withdrawal and treatment of any concomitant medical complications. However, this component is not treatment but rather preparation for treatment. It provides the possibility for a patient to participate in the rehabilitative work that lies ahead.

Treatment can be offered on either an inpatient or outpatient basis. In either setting, the common elements will be individual, group, and family counseling. Considerable effort is devoted to patient education as well, which serves a number of key functions. Education provides a rationale for abstinence. It helps patients recognize that their past behavior, much of which is guilt producing, embarrassing, and incongruent with their values, has been a symptom of an illness rather than a definition of their character. Patient education is important because, as with any other chronic disease, patients ultimately need to assume an active role in managing their illnesses and learn how to maintain health, handle stress, and avoid relapse.

Another ingredient of initial intensive treatment is preparing the patient to become involved in aftercare. For most patients there is a continuation of therapy on either an individual, family, or group basis. The focus is directed to the common pressures and problems for patients in early recovery. In addition to seeing a professional alcohol or substance abuse therapist, involvement in a self-help group is a part of many patients' aftercare. During early intensive treatment, efforts are made to introduce patients to groups such as Alcoholics Anonymous (AA), Cocaine Anonymous

(CA), or Narcotics Anonymous (NA). These groups have much to offer to patients in recovery. They provide a support group, a supportive environment, and supply a ready-made social circle of abstinent "straight" friends. The experiences of other members are a source of practical tips for coping with situations that may threaten abstinence.

A clinical response is not reserved only for dependent patients. Abuse and acute problems require attention as well. Substance abuse should be viewed as a chronic problem. It is marked by an established pattern of use that invites negative consequences. In contrast to dependence, however, there is neither physical dependence nor a life dominated by use. Thus, the goal of treatment is not necessarily abstinence. Rather the goal for treatment of abuse is to change a dangerous, high-risk pattern of use. (The exception, as will be noted, is for patients using illicit drugs.) Typically, moderation is not something that many patients can accomplish on their own with good intentions or will power. Using alcohol or drugs in a high-risk fashion is often intertwined with the patient's life, e.g., recreational and social activities and his or her means of coping with stress. For such patients, reducing the risk of future problems will entail significant major life changes. Support from professionals, patient education, and family, individual, and group counseling may be needed to accomplish a drastic life-style change.

If the patient is involved with illicit drugs, even in the absence of dependence, abstinence should still be considered as the treatment goal. Alcohol and tobacco are the only socially accepted and legal mood-altering drugs in our society. Illicit drug use entails risks that are beyond those related to their pharmacological properties. One risk results from the steps needed to procure illicit drugs, which are often of uncertain purity, strength, and composition. Some illicit drugs such as cocaine and especially crack have an exceedingly high abuse potential. For some substances, low-risk use is nonexistent.

When a problem with acute use brings someone to a health care professional, it will not be immediately apparent if the visit is prompted by an isolated incident or if a more chronic problem exists. Does the episode represent a pattern of use that invites continuing difficulties? Is it one more episode in a long history of chronic heavy use? Consequently, all incidents require evaluation. If the evaluation rules out the presence of an established problem, the intervention becomes preventive. Problems from acute use, which lead to medical attention, commonly involve adolescents and young adults. For these young people the dangers of acute problems are as great as the danger of later developing dependence.

WHAT IS MY ROLE?

The health care professional has a number of different tasks to perform with respect to patients' psychoactive substance use. These range from managing emergencies to providing medical care to patients who are in recovery. The specification of these clinical tasks has received growing attention in the alcohol and substance abuse fields. Joint collaborative efforts of federal groups, the National Institute on Alcohol Abuse and Alcoholism (NIAAA), the National Institute on Drug Abuse (NIDA), the Center for Substance Abuse Prevention (OCSAP), and professional associations within medicine and nursing have begun to delineate the core clinical responsibilities and skills pertinent to different primary care settings. Major professional organizations have also issued policy statements and position papers on this topic (see Chapter 9, Resources for Educators and Trainers). Before considering and defining your own role as a clinician, examine several of these recommendations.

Frameworks for Defining Clinical Responsibilities

American Medical Association (AMA). Over a decade ago the Council on Scientific Affairs of the AMA adopted guidelines developed by the Association's Panel on Alcoholism. These guidelines define the central requisite skills accompanying a physician's acceptance of one of three different levels of clinical responsibility for those persons with alcohol problems. These guidelines are set forth in Table 1 with slight modification to incorporate problems of other drug use.

These guidelines were the first document to address clinical skills and responsibilities. Before that time a number of reports had addressed core knowledge and attitudinal issues for those engaged in the care of alcohol-dependent and other substance-dependent persons but did not include requisite clinical competencies. Only two significant changes might be introduced if these guidelines were redrafted now, 18 years later. One such change would be recognition of the growing number of treatment programs and addiction specialists who are not organized as sole practitioners but in treatment teams. The other change would be to broaden the responsibilities for all clinicians. The approaches that have become common in addressing chronic diseases have also been applied to alcohol and other drug use problems. This has broadened basic clinical responsibilities by addressing not only the identification and management of dependence but also the need for

Table 1. Guidelines for Alcohol and Other Drug Dependency: Diagnosis, Treatment, and Referral

	Guidelines	Explanatory notes
For all with clinical responsibility: diagnosis and referral	Recognize as early as possible alcohol-induced and other drug-induced dysfunction in the biological, psychological, and social spheres.	
	Be aware of those medical conditions frequently caused by, attributed to, or aggravated by alcohol or other substance abuse.	Chronic tension states, vague somatic complaints, depression, cardiovascular and gastrointestinal disorders.
	Ensure that any complete health examination includes an in-depth history of alcohol and other drug use.	See above.
	Evaluate patient requirements and community resources so that adequate care can be prescribed according to patient needs matched to appropriate resources.	Information usually available from county medical societies, local council on alcoholism and state or local divisions on alcoholism and drug abuse.
	If there are medical needs, including severe withdrawal, make referral to a resource that provides adequate medical care.	Another physician, hospital, or alcohol or drug treatment program featuring integrated medical services.
For clinicians accepting limited treatment responsibility (restoring the patient to enable entry into long-term treatment program)	Assist the patient in becoming free of alcohol and other drugs, including management of acute withdrawal syndrome(s), commonly referred to as detoxification.	Office, hospital, or clinic may be used depending on the patient's condition.
	Recognize and treat or refer all associated complicating illnesses.	Both physical and psychiatric conditions.
	Inform the patient about the nature of the disease and the requirements for recovery.	Discuss issues relating to onset, nature, and course of illness, and prognosis, if treated or untreated.
	In collaboration with alcohol and/or substance abuse professionals:	
	1. Evaluate resources—physical health, economic, interpersonal, and social—to the degree necessary to formulate an initial recovery plan.	
	2. Determine the need for involving significant others in the initial recovery plan.	Determine clinical appropriateness, depending on ethical codes, state laws, and Health and Human Service rules and regulations concerning confidentiality. Significant others may include families (parents, siblings) and sexual partners.
	3. Develop an initial long-term recovery plan in consideration of the above standards and with the patient's participation.	This long-term recovery plan should address those factors listed in the following section. At this point, the clinician can assume the responsibilities delineated in the next section or refer to another physician or treatment program.

Table 1. Guidelines for Alcohol and Other Drug Dependency: Diagnosis, Treatment, and Referral—cont'd

	Guidelines	Explanatory notes
For clinicians accepting responsibility for long-term treatment	Acquire knowledge and skills by providing training and supervised experience in the treatment of alcohol and substance abuse problems.	Specialized programs: formal training programs, fellowships, scientific literature, visits to alcohol and drug treatment centers, and 12-step self-help programs—AA, NA, or CA.
	For the following activities conducted in collaboration with alcohol and substance abuse professionals, the responsible clinician needs to:	
	1. Establish a supportive, therapeutic, and nonjudgmental relationship.	Clinician directs, supports, and monitors the patient over a period of several years. Attempts to modify the patient's isolation, grief, and guilt, and addresses other significant psychotherapeutic issues.
	2. Within this relationship, establish specific conditions and limits under which the therapy will be conducted and carefully explain them to the patient.	Professional team members, clinician, and patient responsibilities should be carefully defined.
	3. Periodically evaluate and update the recovery plan with the patient's participation.	Evaluation should be patient-oriented and include evaluation of patient's physical health and psychological functioning.
	4. Involve the patient with an abstinent peer group when appropriate.	It is critical that referral to professionally guided or self-help groups is specific and appropriate to the patient's needs.
	5. Become knowledgeable about and be able to use various health, social, vocational, and spiritual support systems.	For example, vocational rehabilitation, educational advancement, skills training, halfway and recovery houses, recreational facilities.
	6. Evaluate significant others directly or indirectly and unless contraindicated, involve them in treatment.	Treatment may be provided by the physician and another professional, a comprehensive treatment program, or involve self-help groups such as Al-Anon.
	7. Continually monitor the patient's medication needs. After treatment of acute withdrawal, use psychoactive drugs only if there is a specific psychiatric indication in addition to alcohol or substance dependence.	Schizophrenia or major affective disorders can be treated with psychoactive substances that are not ordinarily dependence producing or subject to abuse. However, special care should be exercised in the administration or prescribing of anti-anxiety agents, benzodiazepines, or barbituates and barbituate-like drugs.
	8. Be knowledgeable about the proper use of deterrent drugs and antagonists.	Specifically disulfiram, naltrexone, and methadone.
	9. Throughout the course of treatment, continue monitoring, treating, or referring for any complicating illness or relapse.	Check for organic and psychiatric complications and inappropriate use of alcohol or other drugs, including prescribed and over-the-counter preparations.
	10. Be available to the patient as needed for an indefinite period of recovery.	

Adapted from AMA Guidelines for Alcoholism. *Diagnosis, Treatment and Referral.* Chicago: American Medical Association Council on Scientific Affairs, 1978.

prevention, risk reduction, and early intervention before dependence has been clearly established. Despite the tremendous changes that have occurred since their formulation, the levels of clinical responsibility described and their attendant responsibilities continue to be a useful point of reference.

Office of Substance Abuse Prevention and the AMA. In 1988 at the Second National Conference on Alcohol Abuse and Alcoholism, an initiative was announced to engage primary care physicians in prevention and early intervention. An educational brochure outlining essential clinician tasks was prepared and distributed nationally by the AMA to primary care providers. This pamphlet, *The Busy Physicians' Five Minute Guide to the Management of Alcohol Problems* (see pp. 7-8), like the AMA Guidelines, can be easily translated to address both alcohol and other drug use. In many ways it reiterates the AMA guidelines but with more attention to preventive efforts and the problems of dependence and acute use and abuse.

The *Busy Physician's Guide* also recognizes that management and treatment of alcohol and other drug problems requires specialized skills. It further recognizes the availability of medical and health care specialists in addiction professionals. The task of the primary care clinician is to recognize non-normative cases and make a referral for evaluation, treatment planning, and/or treatment by the appropriate specialists. Beyond this ability to screen and make an effective referral, the primary care clinician must be able to work collaboratively with these practitioners. The primary care provider is neither expected to be an addictions specialist nor function as an alcohol or drug counselor, e.g., skilled in the finer points of differential diagnosis. This model of care implicit in the *Busy Physician's Guide* is not unique to substance use problems. It applies in virtually every area of medical care, in which the role of the primary care provider is defined with respect to the presence and availability of specialists in combination with his or her own clinical expertise.

If Not Me, Who?

Consider the range of clinical needs outlined in Table 2 that are required to provide comprehensive care for substance use patients. With this range of necessary clinical activities as a reference, a central question becomes evident. "Which of these tasks, if not performed by the primary care provider, remain unaddressed because there is no one else in a strategic position to do so?" has been the measure used

Table 2. Essential Tasks in Providing Comprehensive Care to Patients with Substance Use Problems

Activity	Acute problems	Problems of chronic use
Efforts to prevent problems (primary prevention)	Community education Education of community leaders and human service workers Consultation to other service providers Patient education "Anticipatory" guidance for non-users	Community education Advocacy for informed use Identification of high-risk patients Programs for high-risk patients
Early detection (secondary prevention)	Emergency care	Routine screening Monitoring *and* follow-up of acute episodes Evaluation of suspected chronic problems Services to families Referral for treatment
Aftercare steps to maintain treatment gains and avoid relapse (tertiary prevention)	Follow-up after acute incident Risk reduction efforts Monitor efforts to moderate high-risk use	Monitoring post-treatment status Relapse prevention Supporting compliance with aftercare plan Management of routine medical care in light of recovery status

Adapted from Kinney J; Meilman P. Alcohol use and alcohol problems: Clinical approaches for the college health service. *Journal of American College of Health Associations* 36(2): 73-82, 1987.

The Busy Physician's Five Minute Guide to the Management of Alcohol and Other Drug Problems

Dimension of the Problem

Alcohol is among the most widely "self-prescribed" drugs; approximately 75% of all adults and adolescents use alcohol. Moderate alcohol use may be contraindicated with other health issues such as pregnancy or hypertension. Alcohol use may be contraindicated in the presence of prescribed medications. A safe dose or safe pattern of use is not constant across individuals nor constant for a single individual throughout his or her lifetime. In addition to complicating other conditions, alcohol use may become a primary problem—be it alcohol abuse or dependence.

A minimum of 25% of all hospitalized patients have a significant alcohol problem, regardless of admitting diagnosis or presenting problem. An estimated 20% of patients in a primary care or family practice have a significant alcohol problem. Identifying these patients is important to treat them medically and to treat the substance abuse.

Other drug use is also a national problem with multiple presentations, whether over-the-counter drug use in the elderly, the spreading use of smokable forms of cocaine, which rapidly lead to dependence, or the relationship of intravenous drug use and acquired immunodeficiency syndrome (AIDS).

Routine Screening

The CAGE questionnaire has been well documented to easily and effectively identify patients with alcohol abuse and dependence. The questions include:

Have you ever . . .

thought about	Cutting down?
felt	Annoyed when others criticize drinking?
felt	Guilty about drinking?
used alcohol as an	Eye Opener?

The CAGE questionnaire has a 4-point scoring system, ranging from 0 to 4 points. Two to three points is suggestive of alcohol dependence (especially if cutting down is included), and 4 points is diagnostic.

The Medical Record

Alcohol or drug use should be described in the medical record so that changes in use can be detected over time. Notes in the chart should include sufficient objective detail to provide meaningful data to other clinicians. Avoid one word descriptions such as "socially" or "occasionally."

The suggested format includes:
- Pattern of use.
- Problems attendant to use.
- Concern by patient's family or friends.
- CAGE score (for alcohol).

Diagnostic Criteria

The diagnosis of psychoactive substance use and dependence is made primarily on the basis of medical and social history. The earliest symptoms are always behavioral. Unlike other chronic diseases, there are no pathognomonic physical signs or symptoms to signal a transition from health to disease.

The hallmark sign is the presence of negative consequences that have resulted from use. No constellation of problems is uniquely associated with dependence; the significant problem is the multiple difficulties attributed to substance use. For example, it is probable that the individual who has had four or more problems associated with alcohol use will also meet formal criteria for diagnosis of dependence.

DSM-IV Diagnostic Criteria

Dependence is present when three of the following nine criteria have occurred for more than 1 month:
- More drinking or drug use or over a longer period than intended.
- Persistent desire or unsuccessful efforts to cut down or control use.
- Considerable time spent in getting alcohol or drugs, drinking, or recovering from effects.
- Intoxication or withdrawal when expected to fulfill major obligations.
- Important activities given up or reduced because of use.
- Marked tolerance.
- Withdrawal symptoms (for substances with withdrawal phenomena).
- Use to relieve or avoid withdrawal symptoms.

Abuse is marked by the following:
- Maladaptive pattern of use indicated by either continued use despite negative consequences or recurrent use in situations in which use is physically hazardous.

Continued.

The Busy Physician's Five Minute Guide to the Management of Alcohol and Other Drug Problems—cont'd

- Some symptoms of the disturbance have persisted for at least 1 month, or repeatedly over a longer period.
- Never having met the criteria for dependence.

Therapeutic Interventions

If uncertain as to the presence (or the extent or nature) of an alcohol or drug problem, refer for further evaluation. Proceed as with any other potentially serious medical problem. Explain the need for further evaluation or consultation. Provide reassurance and hope, noting that you are making a referral for further evaluation to someone you and the patient can trust.

If an alcohol-related incident has occurred, but there is neither abuse nor dependence, specific risk reduction-health maintenance efforts should be initiated. This effort entails that either a physician or an alcohol clinician review with the patient his or her drinking practices, health status, life-style, and activities associated with drinking to identify high-risk factors and adopt a plan to reduce risks.

For other drug use that is not socially sanctioned and entails a substantial risk for abuse or dependence, a referral is warranted. If alcohol or drug abuse or dependence is present, refer the patient for treatment.

How to Make a Referral

- *Use medical authority.* Make it clear that alcohol and drug problems are a medical concern and outside resources are necessary to treat them; that it is a condition potentially too serious to disregard; that dependence is an illness; that the patient is not to blame for having an illness; and that successful treatment is possible.
- *Provide support.* Inform the patient about the resources for help; explain that you will continue to be available.
- *Provide basic information.* Make it explicit that alcohol and other substances are drugs and their use can lead to medical problems; that they can interfere with ability to accurately perceive what is going on; that use may have serious consequences on the patient's life, e.g., physical and emotional health, academic work, social activities, and family life.
- *Inform family.*
- *Be active.*

- *Do not give only an agency name and phone number.* Have your office set up a specific appointment.

How to Select a Treatment Program

Seek a specialized alcohol/substance abuse treatment program, not a solo practitioner or psychotherapist. Treatment is generally multimodal (comprising group, individual, and family therapies and patient education), which requires a treatment team.

- Look for staff with professional training, as well as "life experience."
- Contact hospitals or mental health centers in the area for names of established programs.
- Ask colleagues for programs they have worked with and have had good patient outcomes.
- Identify a potential resource before you need it.

Collaborating in Care

- Provide support. Request a report from any treatment agency, including specific treatment recommendations and the clinician's role in the patient's care. Be prepared to reinforce the need for compliance with patient and family. Lend your medical authority to alcohol and drug abuse treatment clinicians.
- Follow-up. Schedule follow-up visits to monitor the patient's status and involvement in the treatment regimen, e.g., self-help groups, visits with a therapist.

If All Else Fails

There may be some occasions when all efforts to move the alcoholic into treatment fail. In these instances the physician:

- Provides necessary medical care for the patient, whether related or unrelated to the alcoholism.
- Explains the underlying primary problem to the patient and family, and remains ready to arrange for appropriate care and treatment.
- Encourages family members to enter formal treatment and self-help groups (Al-Anon, Alateen) to minimize their distress and handle the problems of living with the alcohol-dependent person.
- Takes steps to avoid enabling the dependent patient to continue drinking or using, e.g., not providing psychotropic medications for nerves or insomnia and not authorizing sick leave.
- Is alert to the next crisis.

Adapted from Kinney J, ed. *The Busy Physician's Five Minute Guide to Alcohol Problems.* Chicago: American Medical Association, 1988.

here to define the essential components of the primary care provider's role. The following issues are the responsibility of the primary care provider, since there are no other health care professionals able to do so.

Patient Education

Patient education is one of the strong suits of primary care. Take every available opportunity to inform patients about alcohol and other drug use. Simply discussing psychoactive substance use in the context of providing routine medical care conveys the message that substance use is a health issue. Patients are no longer surprised to be asked about smoking, exercise, diet, or other health-related habits. A goal is to have patients recognize psychoactive substance use as a health concern and a topic that they can expect to be routinely addressed. Routine discussion of use provides a greater opportunity to identify an emergent problem and helps the professional to become comfortable with the topic. Experience in discussing substance use when it is not problematic, e.g., when it is within "normal limits," just as is true for any other medical condition, makes problematic use more apparent.

Alcohol is the most commonly used substance in our society. Routine inquiry about alcohol use is further indicated because it can affect the provision of medical care. Regarding other medical conditions, alcohol use may be relatively, if not absolutely, contraindicated.

Identification of Those at Risk

A substantial proportion of patients are at risk for problems arising from psychoactive substance use. With regard to patients potentially at risk, consider both acute and chronic problems.

Acute problems. For acute problems the significant factors include:

- *Frequency of intoxication.* The more often intoxication and major impairment accompanies use, the greater the probability for untoward consequences.
- *Type of substance used.* The psychopharmacology of the substance used influences the type of problems that may occur and the extent and nature of the medical emergencies that may result.
- *The activities accompanying use.* What constitutes an ill-advised dose depends on the person's activities when drinking or using other drugs. The potential for negative consequences is greater if the activities accompanying either drinking or drug use involve using judgment, motor and perceptual skills, decision making, and the ability to maintain attention. While driving is the first activity that comes to mind, using heavy equipment or power tools can be harmful if combined with substance use. Several beers while raking the leaves may be less dangerous than the same amount consumed while chopping wood or operating a log splitter. Sports and recreational activities such as boating, swimming, or skiing when combined with "modest" use can increase the risk for acute problems. Child care, too, is an activity that cannot be overlooked.
- *General health status.* Health status is a particular risk factor for the elderly but is increasingly being recognized as a factor in other medical conditions. Heavy alcohol consumption is being linked to sudden, unexpected natural deaths and also to those deaths caused by trauma. Similarly, acute cocaine use is being identified with toxic and lethal consequences.
- *Prior experience in respect to use.* Those with little or no history of prior use are especially vulnerable to acute problems. They have less tolerance, making them more sensitive to the drug's effects. Furthermore, with inadequate information about the substance, combined with little prior experience, they are unable to anticipate the effects of the dose. Newspapers often report about adolescents who consume lethal doses of alcohol in drinking contests or as dares.
- *Age.* Two groups that need special mention are adolescents and the elderly. If the health care system's success were to be measured by life expectancy, then we would be failing with those persons 16 to 24 years of age. This is the only age group in the US with a declining life expectancy. The major causes of death for young adults are not medical causes but "social" causes, e.g., motor vehicle accidents, suicide, and homicide, in which substance use, especially alcohol, is involved.[3,6]

Discussion of substance use with adolescents is almost universally warranted. It is especially important to identify high-risk use that invites problems and negative consequences. Adolescents who do not use substances deserve attention as well. If they were to try alcohol or drugs, they would represent the naive user. Factual information can be provided without implying that they will inevitably use drugs or alcohol, thus inviting the perception of sanctioning their use. It is important to discuss adolescent alcohol and drug use generally, warning that they may at some point be confronted with another's dangerous use that could constitute a medical emergency. Alcohol and substance use is typically not an individual activity but occurs in groups. Some basic information about what constitutes medical emergencies should be imparted to all adolescents. It is important that they know the dangers of drinking contests and "chugging" drinks, mistaking coma for sleepiness, and being alert to the danger of asphyxiation from vomiting. When such situations arise, the outcome often depends on the response of others and how quickly medical attention is sought.

Another important intervention with adolescents is helping them anticipate and consider how they will handle the inevitable moment when they will be confronted with a choice of using drugs or alcohol. Adolescents often have basic facts and do not want to use drugs, but they lack the skills to decline in a way that is "face saving" for either themselves or for others who are present. Having a few "lines" to call on can be helpful.[2] Adolescents are also close to being independent health care consumers. Health care patterns adopted by adolescents and young adults will have long-term implications; stressing health maintenance and health promotion is worth the effort.

The medical problems of the elderly, combined with prescribed medications and their general sensitivity to drugs' effects as a result of aging, in addition to their tendency to use over-the-counter preparations and home remedies, make them vulnerable to drug-drug interactions. It is the elderly, not adolescents, who have the highest mortality rate from adverse drug reactions.[17]

Chronic problems. The most significant predictors for those at risk for chronic problems include:

- *A positive family history* of alcohol or other drug use. A genetic basis for some types of alcoholism and drug dependency has been established.[8,19,20] For men with a positive family history, the risk for developing alcoholism in adulthood is four times greater than for those without a positive family history.[7] This genetic predisposition appears to be of two types. One form, termed *male dominant,* is marked by earlier onset and develops without any environmental provocation. The other form, termed *milieu-limited,* requires some environmental provocation.[5]
- *A personal history* of an alcohol or substance use problem.
- *The age of onset of substance use.* There appears to be a time in adolescence during which use is initiated, which ends in the early twenties. If use of drugs, alcohol, or tobacco has not occurred by age 21, the probability of initiating drug use declines sharply. On the other hand, the earlier the use of any psychoactive substance, with alcohol and tobacco commonly being the first substances used, there is an increasing risk for the eventual use of other substances.

- *The presence of other health-compromising behaviors.* Dependence on alcohol and other substances is frequently accompanied by a pattern of health-compromising behaviors, e.g., failure to exercise, failure to use seat belts, and poor nutritional habits.[4,21]

Although this list is not complete, it includes factors that are among the most potent predictors and that can also be elicited with relative ease in a clinical setting.

Risk Reduction Efforts

Primary care has an excellent model to call on to respond to those at risk. The model is used with any chronic disease with clearly identified risk factors. Coronary disease may be an illustrative example. A young man is seen by his primary care provider. He is overweight, smokes and drinks, consumes a cholesterol-laden diet, never exercises, and has a family history of men who die of coronary artery disease before age 50. From his health team's perspective, he is a walking time bomb. It is obvious that statistically he is at risk, and the physician or nurse he sees will feel comfortable intervening even if the patient is asymptomatic. The necessary changes in life patterns for our hypothetical patient are equivalent to the changes required with substance use problems. The primary care provider might refer this patient to a specialized group and provide educational pamphlets and brochures and through continued contacts, monitor his compliance, while giving encouragement and support. It is this model that represents the optimal approach to problems of substance use. From a management perspective, the most relevant question is not "Is this patient alcoholic or drug dependent?" The important question is, "Without significant changes, is this patient at risk for future problems?" If so, then aggressive intervention is warranted.

Referral

For primary care personnel, suspected problems involving substance use can be handled the same as any other medical condition for which medical subspecialists are available for consultation or to provide a diagnostic work-up. Thus the responsibility of the health care professional is screening to identify potential problems and making referrals. In most communities there are specialists in substance abuse, who are often affiliated with a health care center. The denial that accompanies dependence may make a referral more difficult than cases involving other medical concerns, but the usual principles apply. Stress the need for an expert opinion, and if challenged, say that you are not an expert, but if there were a problem, it would be remiss to have ignored it. If the patient insists that there is not a problem, concur that that might be the case. Nonetheless, a consultation can allow both of you to be reassured. It is all right to request a consultation for your own benefit so that you can optimally manage medical care. Finally, you should not be apologetic if further investigation rules out the condition that prompted the referral.

Medical Care during Treatment

During treatment there may be a need for medical attention to manage withdrawal and any medical complication. In addition, the primary care practitioner has an important role of supporting the treatment team, providing reassurance, and expressing hopefulness about treatment outcome.

Management of Medical Emergencies

The presentation of medical emergencies will depend on the practice setting. The initial management of alcohol-related and other drug-related emergencies needs to address basic life support, identification and quantification of ingested substances, reduction of absorption, enhancement of excretion, and supportive measures to monitor and counteract possible side effects.

Medical Care after Treatment

Following treatment, the significant tasks for the primary care provider are those that occur with the management of any chronic disease: monitoring the status of patients at appropriate intervals; supporting the need for compliance with the follow-up recommendations; being alert to possible crises; and providing future medical care cognizant of the substance abuse history and adjusting standard treatment regimens as required.

WHY BE INVOLVED?

There are a number of reasons for primary care providers, nurses, physicians, and others with patient care responsibility to address substance use issues. First, it is probable that among a clinician's patients, those who are the most frustrating, requiring the most time, demonstrating low compliance, having the thickest charts and multiple complaints are also those most likely to have substance use problems. Thus one effective way of handling problem patients is to become more skilled and more comfortable treating the problems of substance use. In doing so, the clinician is not getting rid of problem patients by referring them to others, who in turn become burdened. On the contrary, patients with substance use problems who have reputations for noncompliance and resisting treatment do better than patients being treated for other chronic illnesses.

Research shows that the majority of patients with chronic diseases do not follow their prescribed treatment. Fifty percent of patients with chronic illnesses such as hypertension, diabetes, or tuberculosis drop out of care entirely within 1 year. Of those who remain under care, approximately one-third fail to take at least 65% of their medication. The end result is that less than one-third of patients with chronic illnesses who seek care benefit from modern treatment.[9] A positive outcome for only one-third of patients with chronic illnesses is a standard against which to consider outcomes for patients entering treatment for dependence on psychoactive substances.

Studies have compared the outcomes for alcohol and drug dependence treatment. For both, treatment outcomes and the factors that predict success are similar. The best outcomes are for patients whose family remains in tact, who remain employed, and often for whom a coercive factor exists such as possible job loss if they fail to enter care. Equally significant is that any treatment is better than no treatment. However, if patients are matched to treatment and those with more severe symptoms receive inpatient services, including psychiatric care as needed, the outcomes are even further improved.[13,15]

Overall, two thirds of those treated for dependence on psychoactive substances would be expected to improve. Reported success rates depend on the criteria being used, e.g., abstinence or improved functioning or some other measure such as social functioning. Success rates also depend on the interval after treatment when outcome is measured.

At 1-year post-treatment, 25% to over 60% of patients are abstinent, depending on the population. The lower rates are for older, unemployed persons with long-standing chronic problems and those treated in public facilities. The highest rates for continuing abstinence are for professionals such as nurses, physicians, or pilots for whom there is post-treatment surveillance, possible random drug testing, potential loss of license, and therefore loss of their livelihood if relapse occurs.[14]

WHY IS DEALING WITH SUBSTANCE USE DIFFICULT? OR WHAT ARE THE OBSTACLES TO PROVIDING CARE?

In the past, health care professionals were criticized for their failure to deal with substance use problems. Whether explicit or implicit, it was generally suggested that primary care professionals had poor attitudes. Consequently, there was the impression that if nurses and physicians would simply shape up, there would be no problem. This perception of the impediments of coping with patients with substance use problems is inaccurate. To understand the obstacles of clinical involvement by health care practitioners, there are factors that need to be considered.[10]

Characteristics of the Disorder

- Alcohol or drug dependency is marked by impairment of cognitive capacities, by psychological defenses to ease the emotional pain induced by the negative consequences of use, and by altered perception of events. The consequence is a failure to recognize that substance use is causing life problems.
- The onset of dependence occurs gradually. Symptomatic behavior coexists with healthy behavior.
- Gradual onset can obscure an emergent problem from recognition by the patient, family, community members, employer, and health care providers.
- The disease occurs before there is clear onset of organ pathology.
- There are no hard, objective pathognomonic markers to indicate a transition from health to illness.
- Patients and their nurses and physicians commonly share the view that alcohol and substance use problems are self-inflicted illnesses and/or willful acts. It may be helpful to remember that any number of other conditions could be similarly construed. Many of the chronic illnesses that beset modern society—some cancers, hypertension, respiratory disease—are similarly related to health habits, namely smoking, diet, lack of exercise. Also, it may be well to recognize that the question, "Is alcohol or drug dependence an illness or a bad habit?" is not an empirical one.

Patient-Based Factors

- Sense of hopelessness and feelings of shame.
- Lack of hopefulness about treatment, which may be reinforced by the clinician's own pessimism concerning treatment.
- Protection from negative consequences by friends and family members whose efforts, though well intended, can nonetheless allow an alcohol or drug problem to persist.
- Abandoning substance use may mean abandoning friends, peers, current life structure, and with illicit drugs, the income derived from either sales or marketing of drugs.

Provider-Based Factors

- Medical and nursing education and training has not adequately prepared its students to address chronic diseases in general or alcohol and substance use problems specifically.
- Hospital-based clinical settings do not make it possible for clinicians to follow patients past an acute crisis. For patients who do well, the clinician is often unaware of the outcome.
- Perceptions of poor prognosis are reinforced by a minority of patients with multiple admissions. Patients with multiple admissions, who are often memorable to the staff, can create the misleading impression that alcohol or drug dependence is a hopeless, terminal condition. This was dramatically shown in a study of admissions to a detoxification unit during a 78-month period. Of the 5000 patients seen, 2500 never returned for readmission. However, one half of one percent or 25 patients were admitted 60 times or more and accounted for almost one half of the admissions.[22]
- Treatment may be initiated at the point when the prognosis is least hopeful. This is during the latter stages of the disease or the emergence of organ pathology, when there are few social supports and serious physical dysfunctions.
- Clinicians may anticipate that patients will respond negatively if the topic of alcohol or other drug use is addressed and hesitate to intervene.
- In communities with poverty, homes headed by single women, high drop-out rates from school, and extensive unemployment and underemployment, widespread substance use can be accepted as inevitable for those living there.
- Failure to recognize the potential for an incident to be as life-threatening as dependency.
- Uncertainty about clinical skills required.

Origins of the Substance Abuse Treatment Field

- The modern treatment era can be traced to the founding of AA in 1935, which was a time when medicine considered alcoholism a terminal chronic illness not amenable to treatment.
- The field evolved outside of the mainstream of the health care system.
- Until the 1970s and the emergence of federal initiatives, there was little communication between the alcoholic treatment community and those in the health care system. At times, each viewed the other with suspicion.
- The early clinicians in alcohol and drug treatment were recovering individuals credentialed by life experiences. As professionals entered the field there was tension between the two types of clinicians and their orientations toward care.
- Despite the similarities between alcohol and drug problems, the respective treatment fields developed separately, divided by tension. Viewing problems related to alcohol and other drug use as having common denominators and referring to them jointly as substance use is a recent phenomenon.

In part, this joining of the fields reflects the reality that those dependent on either alcohol or other drugs tend to be using other substances as well and following treatment, neither can use any psychoactive substances without inviting relapse.

In addition to the formal alcohol and drug treatment fields, the late 1980s was a time of growth for self-help groups, organized and led not by professionals but lay people. Many of these groups, e.g., CA and NA, modeled themselves after AA, which has now been in existence for over 60 years. Other groups such as Adult Children of Alcoholics (ACA) and other self-help groups are more loosely structured. For professionals outside of the alcohol and drug abuse fields, separating scientific fact from the folk wisdom of self-help group members can be a difficult task.

Health Care Delivery System-Based Factors

- Third-party payment covers procedures. Care based on talking with patients, which is entailed in substance use problems, is poorly reimbursed, if at all.
- In a busy medical practice, the substance use patient initially requires more time than is usually allotted by clinic or office schedules that expect clinicians to see up to four to six patients per hour.
- In a health care setting where patients see multiple clinicians and medical records are organized by encounters, it is not easy to identify the emergence of a chronic problem, which manifests itself by continuing, subtle behavioral changes over an extended period.
- There has been no accepted standard vocabulary or format to describe substance use problems. Notes in the medical record such as "social drinker," "drinking problem," "heavy drinker," or "occasional marijuana use" provide little useful data to others.
- If health care services are not closely tied to community services, it may be difficult to organize the support systems required for treatment and early recovery.

Culturally-Based Factors

- In urban center city areas with extensive unemployment and undereducated and untrained youth, drugs may represent the most accessible occupation, providing income and status for the individual and also the family.
- Many of the social prohibitions, which served earlier as protective factors against use of substances other than alcohol, have weakened.

- There are significant segments within many communities that accept both alcohol and other substance use.
- The tobacco, liquor, and brewing industries and illicit drugs are major economic forces.
- Public policy is ambivalent and contradictory in respect to alcohol and other drug use. For example, the federal government conducts diplomacy with other countries to reduce the flow of illicit drugs, while simultaneously subsidizing tobacco farmers and threatening to invoke trade sanctions on countries that do not allow importing cigarettes.

There have been marked changes in public sentiments about substance use. The success of the antismoking campaigns and the subsequent impact on public policy and social behavior may not have seemed imaginable a generation ago. We may soon be witnessing similar societal changes in respect to alcohol and other substance use. While an absolute "no" in respect to alcohol is not likely, public opinion is clearly redefining what represents acceptable use. The problems of drinking while driving are now well recognized; "designated driver" has been introduced into our vocabularies. Public intoxication is no longer seen as humorous or acceptable public behavior. Alcoholic beverages are now required to have warning labels. Further restrictions on the advertising of alcoholic beverages are being considered. Alcohol or drug use by public officials is no longer viewed only as a private matter but has been raised as an issue in confirmation hearings for those nominated for public office. Recreational drug use is viewed as being less benign than previously and is not as widely accepted as it once was. Drug testing is being instituted as a condition of employment and is required of job applicants, including health care institutions. With primary care health team members addressing alcohol and other drug use as a health concern, they are in a position to promote long-term change in what might otherwise be a passing fad.

WHAT SKILLS ARE REQUIRED?

Addressing patients' substance use problems requires three basic skills that are included in every health professional's daily clinical efforts: data collection, building a therapeutic relationship, and patient education. In any patient encounter, these skills are intertwined. These skills can guide and simplify clinical care for substance abuse patients.

Data Collection

The amount of important data is considerable. However, at any point, the only data required are simply those needed to accomplish the clinical task immediately at hand.

Building a Therapeutic Relationship

A therapeutic relationship is the core of all patient care. A key to building a therapeutic relationship with substance abuse patients is not to respond to the person's outward behavior but to the person beneath it. Working with substance abuse patients is not unlike managing any patient with a chronic illness. While involving the chronically ill patient in managing their care, it is counterproductive to encourage them to use their will power to fight the illness. Instead, chronically ill patients need to accept the limitations of their disease, with the long-term goal of helping them learn to live with their limitations. However, before the chronically ill person accepts their limitations, there is often active grieving. Medical personnel who work with an arthritic man no longer able to use his woodworking shop or who see the young mother with multiple sclerosis dependent on others to help care for her children can empathize with their grief and frustrations.

For those just beginning to work with alcohol and drug abuse patients, empathizing with these patients' pain and grief will probably be more difficult. One natural impulse might be to expect substance abuse patients to be grateful to lay aside their addictions. It is only as one learns to understand the consequences of substance use and how central use has been in their lives that both the pain and the grief becomes intelligible. Often, despite the problems alcohol or drug use has caused, alcohol or drugs are the only thing the patient feels he or she has to count on. They depended on drugs to ease the pain that has become the core of their existence. It is safe for the clinician to assume that there is pain and also that the pain is proportional to the denial the patient shows. Denial is not to be taken personally. It is not intended to trick or manipulate the clinician but rather to trick the patient and to keep emotional pain at bay.

Patient Education

Patient education does considerably more than simply provide facts. It is not restricted to providing educational brochures or having classes for those with alcohol or other drug problems. In many clinical situations, patient education efforts are central to a successful therapeutic relationship. It helps patients recognize what treatment can provide and why it is required. To learn that their behavior has been the product of a drug or a symptom of a disease and not a definition of their character can be startling and reassuring news. Some of the most helpful forms of patient education are the clinician's brief informational comments, which allow patients a framework that renders their experiences intelligible to them.

GLOSSARY

One problem in the alcohol and substance use field has been the absence of standard terminology. Dependence and abuse are used here in accordance with the diagnostic criteria for psychoactive substance use from the American Psychiatric Association's *Diagnostic and Statistical Manual of Mental Disorders* (DSM-IV).[1]

dependence: Dependence on psychoactive substances exists when any three or more of the seven criteria below are present during a 12-month period. The criteria fall into the categories of preoccupation with use, significant life problems resulting from use, and for those substances that have addictive properties, evidence of physical dependence, tolerance, or symptoms of withdrawal.

1. Tolerance, as defined by either of the following:
   a. A need for markedly increased amounts of the substance to achieve intoxication or desired effect.
   b. Markedly diminished effect with continued use of the same amount of the substance.
2. Withdrawal, as manifested by either of the following:
   a. The characteristic withdrawal syndrome for the substance.
   b. The same (or closely related) substance is taken to relieve or avoid withdrawal symptoms.
3. The substance is often taken in larger amounts or over a longer period than was intended.
4. There is a persistent desire or unsuccessful efforts to cut down or control substance use.
5. A great deal of time is spent in activities necessary to obtain the substance, e.g., visiting multiple doctors or driving long distances, use the substance, e.g., chain-smoking, or recover from its effects.
6. Important social, occupational, or recreational activities are given up or reduced because of substance use.
7. The substance use is continued despite knowledge of having persistent or recurrent physical or psychological problems that are likely to have been caused or exacerbated by the substance, e.g., current cocaine use despite recognition of cocaine-induced depression or continued drinking despite recognition that an ulcer was made worse by alcohol consumption.

abuse: Maladaptive pattern of use that occurs during a 12-month period. This diagnosis can only be used for someone who has never been diagnosed as dependent. A maladaptive pattern is indicated by either continued use despite negative consequences, recurrent use in situations when use is physically hazardous, use that interferes with the ability to fulfill major responsibilities—at home, work, or school, or use that presents legal problems.

incident: While not a formal diagnostic category, incident refers to the problems that follow an episode of acute use, when there is not evidence of a chronic problem. As noted earlier, such episodes usually involve intoxication. As a result, the individual experiences problems that typically would not have occurred had it not been for his or her substance use.

The *Journal of the American Medical Association* reported the results of a survey of an expert panel as to the preferred definitions of various terms in the alcohol and drug fields. The definitions that follow are from that glossary.[18]

Alcoholics Anonymous (AA): An international, non-professional organization of alcohol-dependent persons devoted to the achievement and maintenance of sobriety of its members through self-help and mutual support.

detoxification: A process of safely and effectively withdrawing a person from an addictive substance.

disease concept: Recognition that chemical dependency is a chronic, progressive, and potentially fatal biogenetic and psychosocial disease characterized by tolerance and physical dependence manifested by a loss of control and diverse personality changes and social consequences.

enabling behavior: Any action by a person or institution that intentionally or unintentionally facilitates substance use or dependence.

intervention: Act of interceding on behalf of an individual who is abusing or is dependent on one or more psychoactive drugs with the goal of overcoming denial, interrupting drug-taking behavior, or inducing the individual to seek treatment.

overdose: The inadvertent or deliberate consumption of a much larger dose than that habitually used by an individual, resulting in serious toxic reactions or death.

rehabilitation: The restoration to optimum health through medical, psychological, social, and peer group support for a chemically dependent person and significant others.

relapse: Recurrence of alcohol or drug-dependent behavior in an individual who has previously achieved and maintained abstinence for a significant time beyond detoxification.

sobriety: Generally refers to complete abstinence from alcohol and other drugs of abuse in conjunction with a satisfactory quality of life.

treatment: Application of planned procedures to identify and change maladaptive, destructive, or health-injuring behaviors or to restore physical, psychological, or social functioning.

NOTE: In the literature there are several different units used in reporting blood alcohol levels. The following measures are equal: .01%, .01 g/dl, 10 mg%, and 10 mg/dl.

REFERENCES

1. American Psychiatric Association. *Diagnostic and Statistical Manual of Mental Disorders, 4th Edition.* Washington DC: American Psychiatric Association, 1994.

2. Botvin GJ. Prevention of adolescent substance abuse through the development of personal and social competence. IN: Jones CL; Battjes RJ, eds. *Etiology of Drug Abuse: Implications for Prevention. NIDA Research Monograph 56.* Rockville MD: National Institute on Drug Abuse, 1985. (43 refs.) (ADM 85-1335.)

3. Bureau of the Census. *Statistical Abstracts of the United States.* Washington DC: Government Printing Office, 1994.

4. Bush PJ; Dannoti RJ. The development of children's health orientation and behaviors: Lessons for substance abuse prevention. IN: Jones CL; Battjes RJ, eds. *Etiology of Drug Abuse: Implications for Prevention.* Rockville MD: National Institute on Drug Abuse, 1985. (35 refs.) (ADM 85-1335.)

5. Cloninger CR. Genetic and environmental factors in the development of alcoholism. *Journal of Psychiatric Treatment and Evaluation* 5: 487-496, 1983. (73 refs.)

6. Dupont RL. Teenage drug use: Opportunities for the pediatrician. *Journal of Pediatrics* 102(6): 1003-1007, 1983.

7. Goodwin DW; Schulsinger F; Hermasem L; Guze SB; Winokur S. Alcohol problems in adoptees raised apart from alcoholic biological parents. *Archives of General Psychiatry* 28(2): 238-243, 1973. (19 refs.)

8. Goplrude E. Literature review: Current state of the demand reduction field. IN: *Public Health Service Drug Demand Reduction Plan.* Washington DC: US Public Health Service, 1990. (336 refs.)

9. Haynes RB; Sackett DL; Taylor DW. How to detect and manage low patient compliance in chronic illness? *Geriatrics* 35: 91-97, 1980. (10 refs.)

10. Kinney J; Bergen B; Price TRP. Impediments to alcohol education. *Journal of Studies on Alcohol* 45(5): 453-459, 1984. (17 refs.)

11. McLellan AT; Luborsky L; O'Brien CP; Barr HL. Alcohol and drug abuse treatment in three different populations: Is there improvement and is it predictable? *American Journal of Drug and Alcohol Abuse* 12(1/2): 101-120, 1986. (21 refs.)

12. McLellan AT; Luborsky L; O'Brien CP; Woody GE; Druly KA. Is treatment for substance abuse effective? *Journal of the American Medical Association* 247(10): 1423-1427, 1982. (13 refs.)

13. McLellan AT; Woody GE; Luborasky L; O'Brien CP; Druly KA. Increased effectiveness of substance abuse treatment: A prospective study of patient-treatment "matching." *Journal of Nervous and Mental Disorders* 171(10): 597-605, 1983. (19 refs.)

14. Morse RM; Martin MA; Swenson WM; Niven RG. Prognosis of physicians treated for alcoholism and drug dependence. *Journal of the American Medical Association* 251(6): 743-746, 1984. (18 refs.)

15. National Institute on Alcohol Abuse and Alcoholism. *Sixth Special Report to the US Congress on Alcohol and Health.* Rockville MD: National Institute on Alcohol Abuse and Alcoholism, 1987.

16. National Institute on Alcohol Abuse and Alcoholism. *Eighth Special Report to the US Congress on Alcohol and Health.* Rockville MD: National Institute on Alcohol Abuse and Alcoholism, 1993.

17. Office of the Inspector General. *Drug Utilization Review.* Washington DC: Department of Health and Human Services, 1989. (95 refs.)

18. Rinaldi RC; Steindler EM; Wilford BB; Goodwin D. Clarification and standardization of substance abuse terminology. *Journal of the American Medical Association* 259(4): 555-557, 1988. (9 refs.)

19. Schuckit MA. Genetics and the risk for alcoholism. *Journal of the American Medical Association* 254(18): 2614-2617, 1985. (9 refs.)

20. Schuckit MA. Genetics and the specific dimensions of risk for alcoholism. IN: Harris LS, ed. *Problems of Drug Dependence. NIDA Research Monograph 81.* Rockville MD: National Institute on Drug Abuse, 1988.

21. Soeken KL; Bausell RB. Alcohol use and its relationship to other addictive and preventive behaviors. *Addictive Behavior* 14(4): 459-464, 1989. (11 refs.)

22. Vaillant GE. *The Natural History of Alcoholism.* Cambridge MA: Harvard University Press, 1983. 359 pp.

CHAPTER 1

An Overview of Substance Use and Abuse

DONALD A. WEST, MD
JEAN KINNEY, MSW

CLINICAL APPLICATIONS

The goals of this chapter are to assist the clinician to:

1. Appreciate the nature and dimension of substance use problems in the US.
2. Recognize the impact of substance use problems on health care delivery and health care costs.
3. Apply the public health model of etiology to substance use problems.
4. Become familiar with the major sources of morbidity associated with substance use.
5. Adopt a framework for issues related to identification and management of substance use problems.

SUBSTANCE USE AND THE HEALTH CARE SYSTEM

Among the greatest demands on the health care system are those related to chronic illness and problems involving health habits or self-care and life-style. Psychoactive substance use is a health concern in both respects. Virtually all health care indices demonstrate the impact that alcohol and other psychoactive substance use have on health. In comparison to alcohol there is far less data documenting the impact of other substances, particularly illicit substance use. However, within the US, alcohol is the most commonly used drug, as is shown in Table 1-1.

Although alcohol is the most widely used psychoactive substance, followed by nicotine, it has been recognized that individuals with alcohol problems are very likely to be using other substances as well. Commonly this phenomenon is referred to as either multiple substance use or poly-drug use. A study of the lifetime prevalence of different psychiatric disorders determined that almost one half (47%) of those with a diagnosis of alcohol abuse or dependence also had a second psychiatric diagnosis; substance abuse/dependence was the most common. Of this concomitant substance use, the preponderance of use was "hard drugs," e.g., sedatives, opiates, and hypnotics. Conversely, among those who primarily used drugs other than alcohol, a significant proportion had alcohol dependence as well. Among this group, alcohol dependence has been reported in 50% to 55% of the

Table 1-1. National Household Survey of Drug Abuse, 1993

Type of drug	Use reported for year before survey	
	Millions of people	Population (%)*
Alcohol	132.7	66.5
Cigarettes	60.9	29.4
Marijuana	18.6	9.0
Cocaine	7.5	2.2
Crack	1.0	.5
Stimulants	2.4	1.1
Analgesics†	4.6	2.2
Tranquilizers†	1.2	.6
Inhalants	2.0	1.0
Sedatives†	.8	.4
Hallucinogens	2.4	1.2

From National Institute on Drug Abuse. *The National Household Survey on Drug Abuse: Population Estimates 1993.* Rockville MD: National Institute on Drug Abuse, 1994.
*Limited to population, 14 years and older.
†Nonmedical use only.

cases.[20,36] A series of studies found that 80% to 90% of those dependent on cocaine, 50% to 60% of those dependent on marijuana, 50% to 75% of those dependent on opiates, and 25% to 50% of those dependent on benzodiazepines are also alcohol dependent.[38,39] The co-occurrence of alcohol and other drug dependence is particularly common among those under thirty. Clearly, any notion that alcohol abusers and other drug abusers are dichotomous is inaccurate.

Health Care Costs

Collectively, substance use problems have a major impact on health care expenditures. It has been estimated that alcohol and drug use, including nicotine, account for over 20%[3] of the nation's annual health care costs of $884.2 billion, which was the nation's total health care tab for 1993.[4] The total social costs associated with substance use are estimated to be $166 billion, which is considerably greater than the costs associated with other major illnesses, such as cancer—$104 billion; respiratory disease—$99 billion; AIDS—$66 billion; or coronary artery disease—$43 billion.[66] Of the $98.6 billion attributable to costs associated with alcohol-related problems,[55] approximately two-thirds represents health care costs. This total is 40% greater than the costs of drug-related problems, estimated to be $67.9 billion in 1993.[66] For 1993 the medical costs associated with smoking were estimated to be $50 billion.[7]

A disproportionate impact of substance use on hospital costs is also evident. A now-classic study examined the distribution of hospitalization costs and found that 13% of the patients had costs equivalent to the remaining 87%. The cost differential was not attributable to general health status, ethnicity, socioeconomic status, or age. The only distinguishing characteristic of the high cost group was use of alcohol and tobacco.[72] The disproportionate health care costs related to tobacco and alcohol use were examined from another perspective in a 1989 study, *Do smokers and drinkers pay their own way?*[37] This study examined the lifetime costs that smokers and drinkers impose on others, whether through collectively financed health insurance, pensions, disability insurance, group life insurance, fires, motor vehicle accidents, as well as the criminal justice system. The authors concluded that smokers do "pay their way." Although nonsmokers subsidize smokers' medical care and group life insurance, smokers subsidize nonsmokers' pensions and nursing home payments. In contrast, drinkers through excise taxes on alcohol cover barely one half of the costs imposed on others.

Another perspective on alcohol-related costs compares social costs and social benefits in terms of these costs expressed as fifths of 80 proof liquor. In 1990, the US population consumed 469,132,000 gallons of ethanol.[2] If the total volume of ethanol were converted into fifths of 80 proof liquor, that amount would be equivalent to 5,866,399,000 fifths. With the social costs estimated to be $98.6 billion and the social benefits $79.8 billion[1] the social cost per fifth is $16.80 and the social benefit per fifth $13.60.* The costs are virtually 25% higher than social benefits derived.

A Caveat

The economic costs of drug and alcohol use will grow as the costs of human immunodeficiency virus (HIV) and AIDS are calculated into the costs associated with substance use, namely intravenous drug use. For 1990, these costs were estimated to have been approximately $66.5 billion annually.[62] While education within the gay community successfully altered the high-risk practices that lead to transmission of HIV infection, there has been no similarly successful effort with intravenous substance users. The nature of drug dependence, when combined with other factors—such as societal ambivalence about an appropriate public health policy, the lack of sufficient treatment resources, and waiting lists for treatment programs—leads to a bleak prognosis.

Health Care Utilization

Those with alcohol dependence use approximately one and one-half times more health care services, have more repeated hospitalizations for the same disease, and are hospitalized four times more often than the general population.[46,72] Among hospitalized patients a minimum of 20% and as many as 35% or higher (depending on the institution, e.g., a Veterans' or urban public hospital) are estimated to have significant alcohol problems.[10,25,40,65] In an ambulatory care practice, one out of every five patients might be anticipated to have an alcohol problem. Studies of prevalence in 47 different group ambulatory practices found the incidence of problems to range from 15% to 32% for primary care practices, and up to 32% to 46% for university-based ambulatory general medicine practices.[10,14,15,33,40,63]

Patterns of health care utilization for alcohol dependence parallel those found for other chronic diseases such as hypertension, respiratory disease, diabetes, and ischemic heart disease. The health care costs dramatically increase, by as much as 500%, 6 months before diagnosis and drop sharply within the first year.[22,23,57]

Comparable data about the impact of drug use on health care utilization is not available. However,

through emergency room contacts, information collected by the Drug Abuse Warning Network (DAWN) shows that in the latter half of 1992, the last interval for which information is available, the overwhelming substance use presentations to emergency departments involve drugs other than alcohol.[67] Thus, while other drug use is much lower than that for alcohol, other drug use generates disproportionately higher rates of medical emergency contacts. Other indicators of the impact of drug use on health care delivery can be garnered from reports of increases in hospital occupancy, which is attributable to drug abuse problems and AIDS.[48]

Morbidity and Mortality[6,35]

Chronic heavy alcohol use has long been associated with excess mortality. Among studies of those with alcohol dependence, men have a 2 to 6 times greater mortality rate.[12] The rate for women has been reported as 5.1 times greater than the general population. A large portion of excess mortality is due to accidents, poisonings, and violence. In men, diseases of the circulatory system also contribute to a significant proportion of deaths. In contrast, diseases of the digestive system are a greater contributing factor to women's deaths than men's.[8] Of particular significance is that a large portion of excess mortality is centered among the young. While moderate drinking has been found to seemingly have a protective effect for cardiovascular disease, this phenomenon is limited to 2 drinks per day. In an examination of causes of cardiovascular-related deaths among the young, the overwhelming majority of patients were heavy drinkers. The lowest proportion of heavy drinkers was associated with hypertension as cause of death; the highest rate of 100% was found in aneurysms. In rheumatic and ischemic heart disease, the proportions were 87% and 74%, respectively.[17] Alcohol use has been implicated as well in sudden, unanticipated out-of-hospital deaths—50% of men and 38% of women.[51]

The National Center for Health Statistics has determined premature mortality attributable to specific alcohol-associated conditions. However, motor vehicle-related accidents, cardiomyopathy, alcoholic gastritis, suicide, and homicide are excluded from these statistics. Therefore the most significant causes of excess mortality are omitted. The result is that the years per life lost (YPLL) are significantly underestimated.[12] A major factor secondary to alcohol use that contributes to morbidity is fetal alcohol syndrome (FAS) and fetal alcohol effects (FAE). (See Chapter 16, Neonatal Effects of Alcohol and Drugs.)

Among those persons dependent on drugs other than alcohol, major causes of premature mortality are related to overdoses and a variety of medical

---

*Adjusted for inflation. Also, social benefits include tax revenues and income to restaurants and hotels associated with alcohol sales.

complications associated with use. In comparing the magnitude of mortality for alcohol and other substance use, alcohol is associated with eleven times more excess deaths per year than other substance use.[45] Again, with the impact of AIDS these proportions are changing.

Given the effects of alcohol on the central nervous system, impaired judgment, coordination, response time, and perception of events, there are problems that can occur on any drinking occasion when sufficient amounts of alcohol are consumed. Although persons with alcohol dependence are overly represented in the following statistics, roughly one-half occur in those who are not alcohol dependent. Any person who uses alcohol in high doses is at risk.

Drawing upon a review of all studies on unintentional injury, the following percentage of deaths have been found to be alcohol related:

- 27% to 47% of drownings[21]
- 35% to 77% of falls[21]
- 25% to 86% of burns[21]
- 43% of highway fatalities[42]
- 30% of suicides[46]
- 50% of homicides[44]
- 36% of pedestrian fatalities[19]

DEMOGRAPHICS OF SUBSTANCE USE
Alcohol—Per Capita Consumption

Between the early 1950s and late 1960s, US per capita consumption increased approximately 35%. Then the rate of increase began to decline. It peaked in about 1980 and has since been declining. In 1992, US-apparent alcohol consumption reached its lowest level since 1965. In 1992, the apparent per capita consumption of alcohol in the US was 2.54 gallons of pure ethanol per year for the drinking age population, defined as age 14 and above. This represents 1.29 gallons of alcohol from beer, .30 gallons from wine, and .72 gallons from liquor.[2] Not only has there been a decline in total alcohol consumption over the past few years, but there has also been a major shift in beverage preference. Since 1978, there has been a 25% drop in liquor consumption. Wine has become more popular, but the rise in its consumption has leveled off. In 1992, the average American consumed 25.8 gallons of beer, 3.5 gallons of wine, and 1.8 gallons of distilled spirits.[2]

Apparent per capita figures are deceptive, since they represent a numerical average. In fact, there is considerable variation in alcohol consumption within the US. Approximately one-third of the population does not drink. Fifty percent of the total population consumes only 20% of the alcohol. Therefore the remaining 20% of the total population consumes 80% of all alcohol. This 20% of drinkers who consume 80% of the alcohol can be further subdivided. One-third of this group—representing 7% of the total population—consumes 50% of all alcohol.[47] The implication for public policy is quite apparent. Clearly, one could reduce alcohol consumption by 50% and only inconvenience a minority of the total population.[43]

Drinking Patterns[43]

Sex. Women are more likely to be nondrinkers than men, with women being twice as likely to abstain. Men are also more than twice as likely to be heavier drinkers than women.

Age. Drinking typically begins during adolescence. By age 18 approximately 90% have used alcohol, and the proportion of regular drinkers is essentially the same as the adult population.[46,47] For both men and women, those over 44-years-old are more likely to be abstainers than those under 44 years of age. Again, the proportion of heavier drinkers is constant across all age groups at 13% of men and 3% of women.

Race. Caucasians have the highest rate of drinkers. African Americans have the lowest rate. Of African-American women, 67% are nondrinkers. Less than one-half of Hispanic women use alcohol.

Education. For both men and women there is an increase in alcohol use with higher levels of education. Those with more than 12 years of education are twice as likely to be drinkers than those with less than 12 years. However, rates of heavier drinking do not vary with educational level.

Family income. The probability of drinking alcohol rises with family income. The highest levels of drinking are for those with a family income above $50,000.

Geographical region. The South has one-third more abstainers than the remainder of the country. However, if consumption levels are recalculated based on the number of actual drinkers, then of those who *do* drink, consumption is highest in the South and lowest in the Northeast.

Marital status. For both men and women, those who are widowed have the highest rates of abstinence. Those who are married have the highest number of drinkers.

Problems of Abuse

A study to determine the relative lifetime prevalence of different psychiatric disorders (in three different locations) included alcohol and substance abuse/dependence. Table 1-2 summarizes the prevalence of substance abuse for different age groups. The study also found that substance abuse is approximately twice as high among men than women and is

Table 1-2. Lifetime Prevalence of Substance Abuse by Age-Groups

Prevalence (%)	Age-groups
13.00	18-24 years
8.00	25-44 years
.50	45-64 years
.005	>65 years

From Robins LN; Helzer JE; Weissman MM; Orraischel H; Gruenberg E; Burke JD; et al. Lifetime prevalence of specific psychiatric disorders in three sites. *Archives of General Psychiatry* 41(10): 949-958, 1984.

higher in inner cities than in rural areas. Table 1-2 suggests that substance abuse/dependence is predominantly a disorder of the young.[56]

This survey data does not include over-the-counter preparations, which are a predominant problem for the elderly or problems relating to prescribed medications, which too are more common among the elderly. A federal report on Medicare drug use expressed concern about medication mismanagement among the elderly. At that time, although those over age 60 constituted only 17% of the population, they account for 39% of all hospital drug-related admissions and 51% of all deaths from drug reactions. Mismanagement of medication is the most significant drug use problem among the elderly.[50]

Drug Use Patterns[28,29,68,69]

The National Institute on Drug Abuse (NIDA) conducts biannual surveys of substance use, the National Household Surveys and a survey of high school students and young adults. The following findings are derived from the 1993 surveys. In general, while there had been a decline in illicit substance use during the 1980s, this trend has reversed. In addition, it is apparent that use is beginning at earlier ages.

Marijuana. Marijuana use had been declining. Between 1979 and 1985, there had been a 33% decline in use among those age 18 to 25, the age group with the highest level of use. However, in 1993 there was a sharp increase in use, most notably in the young, with use beginning at an earlier age.

Marijuana use is more common among men than women, except for those under age 18. In respect to ethnicity, Hispanics have lower levels of use. Among adolescents 12 to 17 years of age, use is significantly higher in metropolitan areas than nonmetropolitan and rural areas. However, among the 25- to 34-year-old age-group there are no such differences nor are there significant differences between sections of the country. Marijuana, along with tobacco, is sometimes

considered a "gate-way" drug. Among current marijuana users and those with heaviest use, there was a significantly higher number who reported having tried cocaine. With the increasing attention to cultivation techniques, the "backyard" varieties of the 1960s have been replaced and current marijuana has virtually twice the THC of the earlier varieties.[53]

Cocaine. There had been a modest but steady rise in cocaine use since 1979. The rate of increase has however been declining. Given the low estimates of use in the general population, this rise yielded 2% of the total population in 1993. Cocaine is most common in the young and middle adult age groups, ages 18 to 34, than among younger or older age groups.

The change in the route of administration and the emergence of crack cocaine has been of particular concern. Although any method of administration is potentially lethal, the dangers increase dramatically with freebasing and smoking rather than snorting (intranasal administration). With freebasing, unlimited quantities can be ingested. The more intense effect invites repetitive use. Thus public health problems have increased, making them disproportionate to actual changes in the levels of use. While the total numbers of those reporting cocaine use in the previous year has declined, the percentage involved in freebasing or smoking has remained constant.

Cocaine use, like marijuana, is more common in men, with the exception of those under age 26, where women's use approaches that of men. Racial differences are far less marked, although rates of use are slightly higher for Hispanic males than for other groups. Cocaine use is higher in metropolitan areas, but the distinctions based on geography are not dramatic.

Heroin. Over the past decade, heroin use was primarily associated with what has been referred to as "the dinosaurs," those in their forties and fifties. However, in the past year, there has been a reemergence of heroin, with now a new generation of users, in the 13- to 23-year-old age bracket. This increase in use has been attributed to a lowering of price, greater purity, and cocaine street sellers trafficking in heroin as well.[18]

Inhalants. The use of inhalants is receiving greater attention. This attention is particularly warranted given the fact that inhalant use is concentrated among younger adolescents and preadolescents, can be associated with central nervous system damage, and also because use tends to be a group activity.

Nicotine. Since the late 1960s, when 40% of the adult population smoked, there has been a steady decline in nicotine use. Historically, men smoked more than women, however, with their higher quitting rates, the gender gap is far less marked. Among younger smokers, there is virtually no gender difference.

In respect to racial differences, Caucasians are more likely to smoke than African Americans or Hispanics. Smoking is also strongly associated with other substance use.

Other data, providing a different perspective on substance use and its problems, are provided by DAWN. This reporting system of NIDA focuses on selected drugs mentioned in emergency room episodes and medical examiner cases. Published semi-annually, this system provides clinicians and policy makers with historical data and the type and extent of current problems. Thus the DAWN network can spot difficulties such as a rise in incidents involving designer drugs or problems related to the appearance of a more potent drug than is usually available on the streets, which can lead to increased numbers of persons receiving care for overdoses. The DAWN network data have demonstrated a dramatic rise in drug-involved cases seen in emergency rooms. Cocaine-related incidents have been among the most dramatic. Between 1975 and 1985, there had been a ten-fold increase, from fewer than 1000 incidents per year to approximately 10,000.[61] By 1992, the number of emergency room incidents showed another ten-fold increase, with 119,843 emergency room episodes involving cocaine.[67] Thus, while the relative increase may not be great, the magnitude of problems associated with use have grown geometrically. This increase paralleled the emergence of crack.

WHAT ARE THE CAUSES OF SUBSTANCE USE PROBLEMS?[32]

The public health model is a useful framework to integrate the factors that give rise to alcohol and substance use problems. This framework comprises the agent, the host, and the environment.

The Agent

In our society, alcohol (the agent) is generally used in an uninformed fashion, without recognition that what constitutes a low-risk pattern of use varies with each individual and varies for a single individual throughout his or her lifetime.

The significance of the psychopharmacological properties of the agent, be it alcohol or other substances, cannot be overestimated. The abuse potential of a drug depends on its effects on the central nervous system, particularly the rapidity of action, the magnitude of the response, and the duration of its effects. These characteristics contribute to a differential abuse or addiction potential for different substances. It has been noted that in comparing cocaine and alcohol, the former generally has a much shorter time span from light use to heavy problematic use to dependence, often occurring over a period of only a few months. For alcohol, the period from light use to heavy use to chronic use more commonly occurs over a period of years.

The major drug classes and their psychopharmacological properties are presented in Table 1-3. Each major drug class is summarized in terms of its actions, the desired effects, the problems commonly associated with use, Drug Enforcement Agency (DEA) schedule, and commonly used doses.

The Host

The second element to consider is the individual (the host) who develops problems from alcohol or other drug use. More is known about individuals who develop alcohol dependence than individuals who become dependent on other drugs. For alcohol dependence, genetic factors are known to be a major determinant.[5,13,59] Those persons with a positive family history are at least four times more likely to develop alcohol dependence than those without a family history of alcohol dependence. Basic researchers have also been involved in studies conducted to identify the nature of the genetic component. Investigation of neuroreceptors has been an area of active inquiry, and the association of the D2 dopamine receptor gene has been the object of considerable attention.[49]

Much of the research on transmission of alcoholism has been centered on individuals at risk, e.g., nonalcoholic blood relatives of persons with alcohol dependence. Among the findings that distinguish family positive and family negative men are variations in alcohol dehydrogenase (ADH) and aldehyde dehydrogenase (ALDH) levels; variations in monoamine oxidase (MAO) levels; electrophysiological EEG activity and evoked and event-related potentials; neuropsychological differences in terms of perceptual characteristics and categorizing ability. One interesting phenomenon is that individuals at risk have a lower subjective response to alcohol than those individuals without a positive family history.[16,54] One interpretation is that rather than inheriting a deficiency, those individuals at risk for alcohol dependence inherit the ability to handle alcohol "too well."[52] They have greater inborn tolerance, require more alcohol to feel the effects, and are less likely to suffer physical discomfort following drinking, e.g., hangovers. Therefore they are being deprived of cues that might warn them that their consumption level places them at risk.

The home environment in which the person is reared and whether substance use problems are present does not pose further risk. Studies of half-siblings have shown that neither growing up in a home with an alcoholic parent nor being reared by an alcoholic parent increases the risk for children who do not have

---

Table 1-3. Major Classes of Commonly Abused Drugs

Sedative-hypnotics, central nervous system depressants

Action	Depression of activity at all excitable tissues. In general, act at receptors on neurons that are linked with or potentiate the γ-amino-butyric acid (GABA) system, which inhibits neuronal activity. Chloride ion flow into neurons is facilitated either by the GABA system (benzodiazepines) or directly (barbiturates), resulting in sedation.
Desired effects	Similar to alcohol—reduction of anxiety, possible elation secondary to decrease in alertness and judgment.
Common problems	Tolerance, physical dependence, and respiratory and cardiac depression with overdose (much less likely with benzodiazepines alone).
Withdrawal symptoms	Similar to those of alcohol withdrawal (but may have slower onset)—anxiety, adrenergic symptoms, tremulousness, altered perceptions, withdrawal seizures possibly leading to death (barbiturates). Severity and time of onset vary with half-life of drug.
Interaction with alcohol	Potentiation of effects, especially respiratory depression. Some degree of cross-tolerance.
Medical use	Sleep, anxiety disorders, muscle relaxation, alcohol and sedative/hypnotic withdrawal, control of seizures.

Category includes

	Usual therapeutic dose/day (adults)	Addiction risk*	DEA schedule
Benzodiazepines			
alprazolam (Xanax)	0.25-6 mg	High	IV
chlordiazepoxide (Librium)	5-100 mg	Low	IV
clonazepam (Klonopin)	1-20 mg	Low	IV
diazepam (Valium)	2-40 mg	Moderate/High	IV
flurazepam (Dalmane)	15-30 mg	Low	IV
lorazepam (Ativan)	1-10 mg	Moderate/High	IV
oxazepam (Serax)	10-120 mg	Low	IV
temazepam (Restoril)	15-30 mg	Low	IV
triazolam (Halcion)	0.125-0.5 mg	Moderate/High	IV
Barbiturates			
butabarbital (Butisol sodium)	15-120 mg	Moderate	III
butalbital (Fiorinal)	1-6 tabs	Moderate	III
pentobarbital (Nembutal)	100 mg	High	II
phenobarbital	30-400 mg	Low	IV
secobarbital (Seconal)	100 mg	High	II
Other compounds			
chloral hydrate	250-500 mg	Low	IV
meprobamate (Miltown/Equanil)	200-2400 mg	Moderate/High	IV

Stimulants

Action	*Amphetamines and methylphenidate:* Direct neuronal release of dopamine and norepinephrine and blockade of catecholamine reuptake produce euphorigenic effects. Various pharmacologically toxic sympathomimetic effects.
	Cocaine: Similar to amphetamines. Affects dopamine, norepinephrine and serotonin. Blocks reuptake of dopamine prolonging dopamine effects. May enhance dopamine transmission in mesolimbic and mesocortical areas of brain. Depletes presynaptic dopamine with prolonged use. May act on opiate system to promote addictive behavior. Toxic sympathomimetic effects particularly on cardiac, respiratory and central nervous system.

Continued.

Table 1-3. Major Classes of Commonly Abused Drugs—cont'd

Stimulants—cont'd

Desired effects	Increased alertness, feeling of well-being, euphoria, increased energy, reported heightened sexuality.
Common problems	Anxiety, confusion, irritability, weight loss, psychosis, psychological and physical dependence, social withdrawal, multiple medical problems (cardiac, central nervous system, respiratory and so on) with potential death.
Withdrawal symptoms	Depression (possibly with suicide potential), excessive need for sleep, increased appetite fatigue, anhedonia, and (especially with cocaine) craving for the drug. Usually not life threatening except for suicide potential.
Interaction with alcohol	Alcohol decreases side effects of stimulants, e.g., anxiety and withdrawal symptoms and is very commonly used with stimulants.
Medical use	Cocaine for local (ENT) anesthesia; amphetamines and methylphenidate: Attention Deficit Disorder with hyperactivity (especially in children), narcolepsy. Rarely used for depression unresponsive to other treatments.

Category includes

	Usual therapeutic dose/day (adults) (includes child's ADD dose)	Addiction risk*	DEA schedule
Cocaine (only medical use is local anesthesia)	—	High	II
dextro-amphetamine (Dexedrine)	2.5-60 mg	High	II
methamphetamine (Desoxyn)	5-25 mg	High	II
methylphenidate (Ritalin)	10-60 mg	High	II

Opioids

Action	Appear to bind to opiate receptors in specific areas in the central nervous system where they appear to mimic or block normally occurring opiate-like substances causing an altered mood state that is considered desirable and much sought after by repeated administration of the exogenous substance.
Desired effects	The "rush" or "high," a feeling of intense pleasure, often described as almost "orgasmic"; a state of decreased mental and physical awareness and of decreased physical and emotional pain.
Common problems	Rapidly acquired tolerance, physical dependence, respiratory depression secondary to accidental overdose, cellulitis, sepsis, endocarditis, increased likelihood of exposure to HIV infection and hepatitis by sharing of needles in intravenous use; risk to sexual partners of IV opiate users who have acquired HIV; legal problems related to acquiring opiates illegally.
Withdrawal symptoms	Drug craving, dysphoria, anxiety, yawning, perspiration, sleep difficulties, fever, chills, gooseflesh, abdominal cramps, nausea, diarrhea, muscle cramps, bone pain, tears.
Interaction with alcohol	Each potentiates the effects of the other in overdose situations. Possible decreased efficacy of either when taken by an individual with tolerance to the other (cross-tolerance).
Medical use	For relief of severe pain, cough suppression (codeine), anesthesia (fentanyl), addiction treatment (methadone), diarrhea (opium).

Table 1-3. Major Classes of Commonly Abused Drugs—cont'd

Opiods—cont'd

Category includes

Opiates	Usual therapeutic dose/day (Adults)	Addiction risk*	DEA schedule
codeine (multiple products)	Cough: 5-15 mg q4h	High	II
	Pain: 15-60 mg q4h		
heroin	No US medical uses	High	I
morphine	5-20 mg q4h	High	II
opium (Paregoric)	6 mg or 6 mL q4h	High	II
Opioids			
fentanyl	2-50 μg/kg	High	II
hydrocodone (Vicodan)	5-10 mg q4h		
	Limit 8/day	Moderate	III
hydromorphone (Dilaudid)	1-4 mg q4-6h	High	II
levorphanol (Levo-Dromoran)	2-3 mg q6-8h	High	II
meperidine (Demerol)	55-150 mg q3-4h	High	II
methadone (Dolophine)	Pain: 2.5-10 mg q3-4h	High	II
	Maintenance: 5-120/day		
oxycodone (Percodan, Percocet, Tylox)	1 tab q6h	High	II
propoxyphene (Darvon, Darvocet, Darvon-N)	1 tab q4h	Low	IV

Hallucinogens

Action	*LSD-like drugs* (LSD, Mescaline, psilocybin, psilocin, and probably DMA, DOT, and DMT): Structurally related to serotonin. Probably produce many of its behavioral effects by binding to serotonin receptors such as the 5HT2 receptors.
	MDMA-like drugs (MDMA, MDA): Behavioral evidence suggests that effects of this group are mediated by serotonergic binding sites, as well as alpha-2 adrenergic sites, M-1 muscarinic cholinergic, and H-1 histaminergic sites. Effects seem to be a combination of LSD-like hallucinations and amphetamine-like arousal.
Desired effects	Increased awareness of sensory input, hallucinations, perceptions of usual environment as novel, altered body image, blurring of boundaries between self and environment, temporary modification of thought processes, claims of special insights and increased empathy.
Common problems	*LSD group:* Flashbacks long after use has terminated that can lead to depression, panic attacks, or in some cases, suicide. Hallucinogenic mood disorder, psychotic (delusional) disorders with varying courses.
	MDMA group: Nausea, jaw clenching, teeth clenching, muscle tension, blurred vision, panic attacks, confusion, depression, anxiety, paranoid psychosis, hyperthermia, cardiac arrest, coagulopathy, possible degeneration of serotonergic nerve terminals (not clinically observed).
Withdrawal symptoms	There is no clinical evidence of withdrawal effects when use is terminated.
Interaction with alcohol	Not well documented.
Category includes	

LSD group	Average amount taken†	Addiction risk	DEA schedule
LSD (Acid)	10-400 μg	Low	I
Mescaline (mescal button)	100-200 mg	Low	I
psilocybin	4-10 mg	Low	I
DOM (STP)	3-5 mg	Low	I
DMT	3.3-5 mg	Low	I
MDMA group			
MDMA (Ecstasy)	110-150 mg	Low	I
MDA		Low	I

Continued.

Table 1-3. Major Classes of Commonly Abused Drugs—cont'd

Phencyclidine (PCP)

Action	Behavioral effects believed to be mediated through N-Methyl-D-Aspartate (NMDA) excitatory amino acid receptor-channel complex in the brain.
Desired effects	Visual illusions, hallucinations and distorted perceptions, feelings of strength, power, and invulnerability, depersonalization, distorted body image.
Common problems	Psychotic reactions; bizarre behavior; outbursts of hostility and violence; feelings of severe anxiety, doom, or impending death; gross incoordination; nystagmus; hypersalivation, vomiting; fever.
Withdrawal symptoms	Limited reports of withdrawal effects in humans. In other primates, symptoms include poor feeding, weight loss, irritability, bruxism, vocalizations, piloerection, preconvulsive activity, tremors, and impaired motor coordination.
Interaction with alcohol	Not well documented.
Medical use	Possible prevention of neurological damage due to ischemia (research only thus far).
Category includes	

	Average amount taken[†]	Addiction risk[‡]	DEA schedule
phencyclidine (PCP)	80-500 mg	Low	II

Cannabinoids

Action	Usually absorbed through the lungs and appears to produce effects through specific binding at endogenous THC receptor sites, sites in the brain that appear to be specific for cannabinoids.
Desired effects	Sense of relaxation and well-being euphoria, detachment modification of level of consciousness, altered perceptions, altered time sense, reported sexual arousal.
Common problems	Panic, anxiety, nausea, dizziness, difficulty in expressing thoughts, paranoid thoughts, depersonalization, visual distortions, perceptual problems, motor performance may impair driving. Impairment of ability to learn. Medical effects with prolonged use include respiratory problems, possible impaired immune function, and possible reproductive problems, including low birth-weight infants.
Withdrawal symptoms	Craving, anxiety, irritability, nausea, anorexia, agitation, restlessness, tremor, and depression.
Interaction with alcohol	Potentiates CNS depressant effects.
Medical use	Used to reduce nausea and stimulate appetite in cancer patients; possible treatment of glaucoma.
Category includes	

	Average amount taken	Addiction risk	DEA schedule
Marijuana	4-40 mg of THC per cigarette	Moderate	I
Hashish		Moderate	I
THC		Moderate	II

Table 1-3. Major Classes of Commonly Abused Drugs—cont'd

Inhalants

Action	Heterogeneous group, hydrocarbons: generally, the action is poorly understood. Absorbed by alveolar capillary beds. Presumed that inhalants disrupt neural function. Intoxication is similar to the CNS depressants. Nitrites act by vasodilation.
Desired effects	*Hydrocarbons:* the "rush," euphoria, behavioral disinhibition, sensation of floating, perceptual disturbances including hallucinations. *Nitrites:* used to postpone or enhance intercourse especially in gay male population. May cause euphoria. *Nitrous oxide:* euphoria, altered perceptions.
Common problems	*Hydrocarbons:* cardiac depressants leading to "sudden sniffing death" probably secondary to cardiac dysrythmias; aspiration or respiratory depression; atrophy of various areas of brain with attendant behavioral symptoms (with chronic use); renal complications; vehicle accidents secondary to intoxication. *Nitrites:* panic reactions, nausea, dizziness, hypotension. *Nitrous oxide:* paranoid psychosis with confusion (chronic use).
Withdrawal symptoms	Psychological symptoms documented: physical symptoms not well-established.
Interaction with alcohol	Likely to vary with substance; likely potentiations with hydrocarbons.
Medical uses	None, except for use of nitrous oxide for anesthesia.
Category includes	

	Average amount taken	Addiction risk	DEA schedule
Industrial and commercial solvents, paints, glues, other hydrocarbons, and aerosols	Variable	Moderate	NA
amyl nitrite	Variable	Unknown	NA
butyl nitrite			
nitrous oxide	Variable	Unknown	NA

Nicotine

Action	Agonist at nicotinic receptors in the central and peripheral nervous system; modulates both inhibitory and excitatory elements of number of neural pathways; may act on some of same pathways as opiates and sedative hypnotics.
Desired effects	Relaxation, stimulation, social acceptance, image.
Common problems	Cough, bronchitis, increased respiratory infections, chronic obstructive pulmonary disease, lung cancer, oral cancers, likely increase of many other cancers with use, death or injury by fire, low birth-weight babies.
Withdrawal symptoms	Craving, irritability, anxiety, possible depression.
Interaction with alcohol	Increased likelihood of use of one when the other is used; use of both greatly increases incidence of oral cancers.
Category includes	

	Average amount taken	Addiction risk	DEA schedule
Nicotine	15-20 mg/cigarette	High	NA

Continued.

Table 1-3. Major Classes of Commonly Abused Drugs—cont'd

Anabolic androgenic steroids

Action	Bind to hormone specific receptor complexes in almost every organ system in the body. Also have direct action on neuronal cell membranes mediated by specific receptors.
Desired effects	Enhancement of appearance or athletic performance with attendant self-confidence and self-esteem.
Common problems	Virilizing side effects (vary by gender) increased facial hair, deepening of voice, male pattern of baldness, acne. In women, clitoral enlargement and menstrual irregularities; feminizing effects in men, e.g., gynecomastia; reduction in HDL cholesterol; cholestatic jaundice, hepatitis, liver cancer; psychiatric side effects (hypomania, mania, depression, panic, and aggressive symptoms all reported).
Withdrawal symptoms	Depression, fatigue, decreased libido, muscle pain, headache, and craving.
Interaction with alcohol	Not well researched.
Medical use	Replacement of endogenous testosterone; increase of red blood cells and complement factor; treatment of endometriosis and fibrocystic breast disease.
Category includes	

	Average amount taken	Addiction risk	DEA schedule
Testosterone cypionate		Moderate	NA
Nandrolone decanoate	Daily doses range from 20-2000 mg		
Nandrolone phenpropionate	equivalent of testosterone/day (approximately 2-200 times the usual pharmacological dose of androgens)		
Orally active androgens (danazol, fluoxymesterone, methyltestosterone, oxymesterone, stanzolol)	Same	Moderate	NA

*Amounts significantly in excess of recommended use should be considered abuse. All risk may be higher in patients with substance abuse history.

†As there is no accepted medical use of hallucinogens, dosages listed below are the average amount taken.

‡Risk with use may be higher in patients with substance abuse history.

NA: Not applicable.

a presumed biological predisposition toward alcohol dependence.[60]

The body of research on genetic factors related to substances other than alcohol is comparatively modest. The questions that are now raising the greatest interest are whether alcohol and other substance use has a common denominator; whether individuals who are vulnerable to alcohol dependence are more vulnerable to other drugs; and the degree to which the choice of a substance is dictated by environmental factors such as relative availability, access, and opportunities for use.

Efforts to link personality traits to alcohol and drug dependence have been numerous. No personality factor and no other behaviors have reliably differentiated abusers from others. Psychological characteristics have not been found to be predictive of individuals who develop alcohol or drug dependence. Antisocial behavior and depression have been postulated by a number of researchers as predisposing characteristics. The behavior being targeted—a disre-

gard for society's rules and clinical dysphoria—is now seen as symptomatic of the illness. In most cases the depression seen in alcoholics appears to be consequent rather than antecedent to their dependence.[41]

As the result of a longitudinal prospective study of adult development, the alcoholic or addictive personality is now seen almost universally as a *symptom* of dependence. Two different groups were followed from adolescence; they are now past retirement age. One group comprised inner city working class youth, the other was a sample of Harvard students; both were initially selected for good mental health. The members of the sample were contacted periodically. In later life some of them developed alcoholism and could be compared with those who did not. The results provided no support for the theory of an alcoholic personality. Those who developed alcoholism in earlier life had not had personality or adjustment problems. The presumed predisposing personality factors or emotional problems were found to have been the result of their chronic heavy drinking. The major predictors of alcoholism were a positive family history and being raised in a culture whose norms proscribe childhood alcohol use but encourage heavy adult alcohol use and accept intoxication.[70]

In contrast to alcohol dependence, some have suggested that there is a higher rate of psychiatric disorders with illicit drug use. The hypothesis is that those persons without personality disorders may be protected by social disapproval, behaviors required to obtain and use illicit substances, and legal sanctions. Conversely, if all substances were equally available, some of those persons who become alcohol dependent might, with equal access, become dependent on other psychoactive substances. As cocaine became more widely used and available and did not evoke disapproval in social circles, a pattern of recreational use emerged. Cocaine use then began to resemble alcohol use more than other substance use. However, with the introduction of crack, its high abuse potential, and negative consequences, the acceptance of cocaine use has declined.

Family factors that have been suggested as predictive of drug abuse among adolescents are parental drug use and/or acceptance of drug use and attitudes toward self-medication in general.[11,58] In respect to familial factors and parent/child relationships, inconsistent discipline or harsh discipline with little praise and close family members with a history of criminal or antisocial behavior are found to be associated with higher rates of drug abuse.[31]

The Environment

The third factor to consider is the environment or the setting in which the individual and substances come together. For all psychoactive substance use, important factors are availability and legal sanctions and the interplay of social approval and these sanctions.[30] In general, use is least problematic when there are clear rules as to what is acceptable in respect to substance use and what is not acceptable, which explains the higher level of national problems with alcohol than other substance use. Within some communities, particularly urban areas, other substances are widely available, there is economic impetus for use, and use is correspondingly greater. Indeed, racial differences reported in patterns of use disappear when environment, i.e., area of residence, and the availability of illicit substances are considered.[34]

At the level of affiliative groups, the drug use patterns of the peer group are a predictor of an adolescent's drug use. Among those at greatest risk are more mobile children who must enter a new school and social systems. The circle of children most open to new members is the group most likely to take risks with new behavior, including sex and drugs.[11]

WHAT IS THE COURSE OF DEPENDENCE?

Although these phenomena of dependence have existed for centuries, it must be remembered that alcohol dependence or psychoactive substance use dependence, or the generic term "chemical dependency" as a disease is only a construct of the past 30 to 40 years. Much of the current thinking comes from the earliest researchers, particularly Jellinek, a pioneer in modern alcohol research. He was the first to chart the natural history of alcoholism, e.g., the sequence of symptoms of dependence.

Phases of Alcohol Addiction[26]

In 1952, Jellinek published a paper charting the signs and symptoms of alcohol addiction. This description of the natural history of alcohol dependence has been the basis of the work since his time. His data included reports of over 2000 members of Alcoholics Anonymous, in which each had set forth the symptoms that had accompanied the emergent alcohol dependence. Based on these reports, he sketched the progression of the disease of alcoholism in terms of the order and type of symptoms that appeared. This sequence is often seen as encompassing the major phenomena of any chronic substance use.

Four different stages were identified. The first is the *prealcoholic phase* in which use is socially motivated, although the individual learns he or she "feels better" with use and comes to use the substance as a means of handling stress. The second stage is the *prodromal phase* in which the substance assumes a more prominent role and may be a source of discomfort and guilt. The next stage, the *crucial phase*, is marked by loss of control and the user's inability to predict consumption once use begins. As a protection from the pain caused by use and the negative consequences it evokes, a variety of psychological defenses emerge, including denial, rationalization, minimizing, and also efforts to regain control of use by altering the environment. At this point there is increasing dysfunction and the first hospitalization is likely to occur. The final stage is the *chronic phase*, when the individual's life is centered around use, intoxication is daily, and signs of physical dependence are evident.

All observers since have noted that alcoholism is progressive and chronic; its earliest symptoms are behavioral; medical sequelae are complications of the primary condition; it is marked by both psychological and physical dependence; and that if use is resumed after a period of abstinence, problems quickly recur.

As other substance use became more prevalent, a similar progression was postulated. It has been applied generically to dependence, with the particular drug being seen as relatively less important. Within the treatment field, *chemical dependency* is the term used to describe this general phenomena.

Progression from 'Social Use' to Dependence

Another model has recently emerged. The framework, developed by clinician Vernon Johnson, addresses the subjective experience of dependence.[27] It too initially focused on alcohol but has since been used to explain the emergence of dependence on other drugs as well. This formulation views dependence as evolving out of experimental or social drinking and appeals both to learning theory and a view of alcoholism as an addiction. This model is widely used in patient education and is a successful clinical tool. It simplifies a complex topic and maximizes the role of the drug while playing down the role of emotional and social forces.

In the first of Johnson's four stages, "learning the mood swing," new drinkers or experimenters with other drugs discover that the drug makes them feel good. If moods were charted on a continuum ranging from pain to pleasure, the drug use leads to a change in mood that feels good and is experienced as positive. Inasmuch as the learning is experiential, it is also potent. Having learned that a drug such as alcohol can influence how one feels, the next step, "seeking the mood swing," becomes possible. Alcohol or other drugs can now be deliberately used for their effects. Society provides occasions when using alcohol to feel better is socially recommended to deal with unpleasant events or enhance an already good mood. Whether one has been fired or promoted, "let's have a drink" is a familiar phrase. "Seeking the mood swing" is seen as common to all drinkers.

In anyone's drinking career there are generally some unpleasant consequences as a result of either alcohol or other drug use. For social drinkers or recreational drug users, these consequences are a learning experience. The negative, unpleasant event is sufficient to alter future drinking or drug use. It is sufficient to cause the person to evaluate his or her drinking or other drug use. However, a significant minority will, for unknown reasons, continue to use alcohol or drugs despite the negative consequences. This "X" factor distinguishes those who develop chemical dependency from those who do not.

For those individuals whose drinking or drug use continues, the effect being sought—feeling better—will be followed by a less comfortable state as the negative incidents occur with increasing regularity. Johnson emphasizes that there is an emotional toll, be it embarrassment, guilt, or a lowered sense of self-worth, but because of prior learning, use continues unchanged and problems inevitably escalate. This stage is termed

"harmful dependence." The emotional pain that results is seen as the basis for the defenses that constitute many of the behavioral symptoms of alcoholism and other drug dependencies—denial, minimizing, and intellectualizing. The fourth stage is "drinking or drug use to feel normal." The dependent individual lives with constant emotional pain. The mood changes induced by alcohol or drugs are sufficient only to achieve a state of normal feeling. When physical dependence has been established, then continued use is needed to prevent withdrawal. At this point the alcohol or drug use no longer resembles the experiences of nonproblematic drinkers or their own earlier experiences.

Treatment is essential to address the emotional pain and discomfort that has been induced by dependence, including a rehabilitative regimen that will help the patient live comfortably without the use of drugs.

Natural History of Addiction, Drug Dependence

Although less well known within substance abuse circles, research has been conducted on the natural history of narcotic addiction. One of the earliest accounts is from 1970, which assessed the then current but opposing views that "once an addict, always an addict" or that addicts by age 40 tend to "mature out of addiction." It was based on two large samples. One group comprised a sample of all Kentucky state residents admitted to the state's primary treatment setting, which happened to be the Federal Narcotics Hospital. The other was a New York City hospital, which was then the principle voluntary treatment resource for the city's narcotic addicts. Based on follow-up of these admissions, the natural course of addiction was examined. Among the significant findings were that over time narcotic addicts have alternating periods of use and abstinence. This study found that narcotic addicts tend to be multiple drug users; 82% of the males and 33% of the women from the Kentucky state sample were also alcoholic. The major predictor of permanent abstinence was a stable history of employment. The therapeutic variables related to abstinence were not incarceration or hospitalization, which influenced only the short run. For the rural sample, a decrease in the availability of narcotics was the significant factor. For the urban sample, where availability was unchanged, positive influences were community-based, compulsory supervision, e.g., parole and the introduction of some substitute for narcotics use as a source of gratification and support.[71] Two more recent prospective long-term follow-up studies have further explained the natural history of drug dependence. One explores the concept of the addiction career and the initiation, duration, and cessation of drug use in terms of environmental, social and psychological influences.[64] The other has been primarily interested in the effectiveness of drug treatment and outcome.[24]

WHAT KINDS OF PROBLEMS OCCUR?

It is important to remember that two different types of problems, acute and chronic, can result from substance use. Any particular incident involving alcohol or substance use may represent a chronic problem or an isolated incident and both are of equal concern. In respect to the consequences, an acute incident can present a threat as serious as those accompanying dependence. Especially when one considers young adults, the primary concern is not dependence, but the harmful effects of the incidents of substance use. The danger of an incident is that the individual may not survive to develop a chronic problem.

HOW SHOULD THE CLINICIAN APPROACH PSYCHOACTIVE SUBSTANCE USE PROBLEMS?

Without adequate evaluation, in the absence of past history, information from collateral sources, or physical evidence, it is impossible to distinguish an isolated acute incident from one that is another episode in an ongoing pattern of problems. The approaches to manage any chronic disease process are applicable to problems of substance use. Optimal management involves prevention, risk reduction, and with subclinical manifestations more aggressive intervention that includes counseling to achieve drastic changes in health habits and life-style. If the disease state appears, the goal is to treat or refer for treatment of acute episodes, to assist the patient in making adjustments needed to reduce the severity and frequency of episodes, to enhance functional status, and to help the patient adjust to limitations that may be imposed by the illness.

Specific management tasks, which are appropriate with any chronic disease, apply to substance use problems. Box 1-1 applies these basic principles for managing chronic disease to problems related to alcohol and other drugs use.

HOW DO SUBSTANCE USE PROBLEMS PRESENT AT DIFFERENT STAGES OF LIFE?[32]

The presenting problems of substance use to the health care system are closely linked to age. Both the very young and the elderly are sensitive and physically vulnerable to the drug's effects. The substance use-induced problems experienced by young children result from parental problems and, in later life, from an increased genetic vulnerability to alcohol.

For adolescents, problems result from parental problems and also from their own use when they begin to drink and/or use other drugs. The acute problems of adolescent substance use can arise from a lack of experience and knowledge about alcohol

---

Box 1-1

Clinical Management of Chronic Disease: Application to Alcohol and Substance Use

Prevention Activities

- Provide alcohol and substance use information routinely, while providing medical care. Discuss alcohol and drug use and how it may relate to the condition being treated. Use opportunities such as school health physicals, sports physicals, or gynecological appointments to broach the subject of substance use.
- Provide anticipatory guidance, e.g., counseling and discussion before the occasions arise in which the patient must make decisions about alcohol and substance use. Especially applicable to young adolescents.

Risk Reduction Activities

- Identify patients at risk.
- Initiate a risk reduction regimen and provide patient education.
- Monitor patient's success in modifying high-risk practices.
- Make a note in the agency or medical record about risk factors and efforts to reduce risk.

Early Intervention

- Routine screening of all patients.
- If positive screening results, arrange for evaluation and further work-up.
- If patients report alcohol or substance use that is different from previously noted use, assess the implications.
- If a problem exists, arrange for treatment.

Follow-Up Care to Prevent Recurrence

- Be informed about and monitor compliance with aftercare plans.
- Include the follow-up plan in medical record or agency chart.
- Adopt a plan to respond to a relapse so that if one were to occur, important decisions do not need to be made during a crisis.

---

and other drugs, in combination with the risk-taking behavior and unseasoned judgment that is part of this developmental period. Heavy use by adolescents can interfere significantly with social and psychological maturation. Dependence in adolescents is anecdotally reported to progress more quickly than in later life.

For adults, the major problems are dependence and the eventual secondary medical problems that result from long-term, chronic heavy substance use, plus the problems their dependence creates for spouse and children.

Neonatal Period

The major influences of alcohol and other substances during the neonatal period include the following:

- Fetal effects from maternal use during pregnancy.
- Possible genetic predisposition to alcoholism if there is a positive family history.
- Possible retarded growth and development, dependent on agent and exposure.
- Problems associated with poor prenatal care of the mother.
- Risks at birth—a more difficult delivery, diminished sucking reflex, impaired maternal-infant bonding.
- Withdrawal in newborns has been found with cocaine and heroin-dependent mothers.
- Risk of HIV for infants born to HIV infected mothers.

Infancy

The risks for the infant that result from substance use problems include the following:

- Disorders arising from neonatal effects.
- Lack of stability in the family from parental abuse and dependence.
- Abuse and neglect as the result of dependence in the home.
- Nutritional deficiencies. Anecdotal reports by pediatricians note that iron deficiencies in infants from middle class families are frequently associated with parental alcoholism and "pushing" a bottle rather than introducing other foods.

Childhood

Alcohol- and substance-induced problems in childhood that result from parental abuse or dependence can present in the following ways:

Family presentations
- Greater risk of abuse and neglect.
- Family violence.
- Financial hardship.
- Parental separation and divorce.

Presentations as school problems
- Underachievement.
- Difficulty with peers.
- Truancy.
- Antisocial behavior.

Medical presentations
- Physical abuse.

- Unintentional injuries.
- Illnesses of neglect or lack of supervision.

Psychiatric presentations
- Lowered self-esteem.
- Depression.
- Attention Deficit Disorders (ADD), earlier described as hyperactivity or minimal brain dysfunction (MBD) for which there is increased risk with a positive family history of alcoholism.
- A syndrome is just now being described in children whose mothers smoked crack during pregnancy. It is marked by a variety of developmental impairments such as short attention span, an inability to be engaged by their surroundings, the absence of play, and impulsiveness.

Adolescence

Adolescent problems may occur as a result of parental substance use and also as the result of the adolescent's own use. Adolescent problems can present in the following ways:

Medical presentations
- Accidents and suicide frequently involve substance use and are the leading cause of death in this age-group.
- Unwanted pregnancy.
- Sexual assault.
- Sexually transmitted diseases.
- Alcohol/drug interactions from either substance abuse or recreational use.
- Alcohol poisoning and death, with naive drinkers at the greatest risk.
- AIDS.
- Abuse and dependence.
- Either running away or being ejected from the home.

School problems as manner of presentation
- Academic underachievement.
- Declining intellectual ability.
- Antisocial behavior.
- Truancy.
- Dropping out of school or expulsions.

Adulthood

In adults, problems result both from use as well as dependence. The common presentations include:

- Alcohol dependence—among men with a positive family history of alcoholism, there is four times greater incidence of alcoholism, which has an earlier onset than nonfamilial alcoholism.
- Medical complications secondary to chronic heavy use.
- For women there is increased risk for problems with prescription drugs because of the higher rate of prescription.

- Stress-related disorders in family members of those with dependence are more common.
- Alcohol use may substantially increase risk for other medical conditions.
- Substance use may complicate the management of other medical conditions.

Elderly

Although less prevalent in the elderly, abuse and dependence does occur, rarely with illicit drugs, but is commonly associated with alcohol, prescription drugs and over-the-counter preparations. For alcohol, this can be either the continuation of a lifelong pattern of heavy use, or be late onset heavy drinking. Of particular note among the elderly is the increased sensitivity to drug's effects. Accordingly, a drinking pattern that in earlier years was nonproblematic may, with aging, introduce risks. Similarly the elderly are sensitive to drugs of all kinds, and prescription practices need to reflect this. As a result, the following are problems unique to this age group:

- Alcohol and prescription drug interactions.
- Accidents secondary to toxicity and intoxication; fractures and other trauma secondary to falls.
- Confusion and memory impairment.
- Psychoactive substance use by caretakers is often related to elderly abuse.

No age-group is immune to alcohol and drug use problems. In Part II, identification, screening, and treatment issues for particular groups are discussed.

REFERENCES

1. Ad $ Summary. *Brand Index Leading National Advertisers.* New York: Leading National Advertisers, Inc, 1983. (NOTE: figures adjusted for inflation.)
2. Alcohol Epidemiologic Data System; Williams GD; Clem DA; Dufour MC. *Apparent Per Capita Alcohol Consumption: National, State, and Regional Trends, 1977-1992. Surveillance Report No. 31.* Rockville MD: National Institute on Alcohol Abuse and Alcoholism, 1994. (32 refs.)
3. American Medical Association. *Factors Contributing to the Health Care Cost Problem.* Chicago: American Medical Association, 1993. (66 refs.)
4. American Medical Association. Personal communication. Information provided from *Health Care Financing Review.* Chicago, 1985.
5. Anthenelli RM; Schuckit MA. Genetic studies of alcoholism (review). *International Journal of the Addictions* 25(1): 81-94, 1991. (62 refs.)
6. Archer L; Grant BF; Dawson DA. What if Americans drank less? The potential effect on the prevalence of alcohol abuse and dependence. *American Journal of Public Health* 85(1): 61-66, 1995. (32 refs.)
7. Bartlett JC; Miller LS; Rice DP; Max WB. Medical-care expenditures attributable to cigarette smoking: United States, 1993. *MMWR. Morbidity and Mortality Weekly Report* 43(26): 469-472, 1994. (7 refs.)
8. Berglund M. Mortality in alcoholics related to clinical state at first admission: A study of 537 deaths. *Acta Psychiatrica Scandinavica* 70(5): 407-416, 1984. (29 refs.)
9. Bertolucci MA; Noble J; Dufour M. Alcohol-associated premature mortality—United States, 1980. *MMWR. Morbidity and Mortality Weekly Report* 34(32): 493, 1985. (5 refs.)
10. Breitenbucher RB. The routine administration of the Michigan Alcoholism Screening Test to ambulatory patients. *Minnesota Medicine* 73(June): 425-429, 1976. (17 refs.)
11. Bush PJ; Iannoti RJ. The development of children's health orientation and behaviors: Lessons for substance abuse prevention. IN: Jones CL; Battjes RJ, eds. *Etiology of Drug Abuse: Implications for Prevention.* Rockville MD: National Institute on Drug Abuse, 1985. pp. 45-74. (74 refs.)
12. Centers for Disease Control and Prevention. Years of potential life lost before age 65: United States, 1990 and 1991. *MMWR. Morbidity and Mortality Weekly Report* 42(13): 251-253, 1993. (9 refs.)
13. Crabbe JC; Belknap JK. Genetic approaches to drug dependence (review). *Trends in Pharmacological Sciences* 13(5): 212-219, 1992. (34 refs.)
14. Cutler SF; Wallace PG; Haines AP. Assessing alcohol consumption in general practice patients: A comparison between questionnaire and interview. *Alcohol and Alcoholism* 23(6): 441-450, 1988. (13 refs.)
15. Cyr MG; Wartment SA. The effectiveness of routine screening questions in the detection of alcoholism. *Journal of the American Medical Association* 259(1): 51-54, 1988. (10 refs.)
16. Devor EJ; Cloninger CR. Genetics of alcoholism (review). *Annual Review of Genetics* 23: 19-36, 1989. (113 refs.)
17. Hanna E; DuFour M; Elliott S; Stinson F; Harford TC. Dying to be equal: Women, alcohol, and cardiovascular disease. *British Journal of Addiction* 87(11): 1593-1597, 1992. (18 refs.)
18. Hartnoll RL. Opiates: Prevalence and demographic factors. *Addiction* 89(11): 1377-1383, 1994. (38 refs.)
19. Heermann K; Syner J; Vegega ME. Motor-vehicle-related deaths involving intoxicated pedestrians: United States, 1982-1992. *MMWR. Morbidity and Mortality Weekly Report* 43(14): 249-253, 1994. (10 refs.)
20. Helzer J. Psychiatric diagnoses and substance abuse in the general population: Problems of drug dependence. IN: Harris LS, ed. *Problems of Drug Dependence, 1987. NIDA Research Monograph 81.* Rockville MD: National Institute on Drug Abuse, 1988. pp. 405-411. (10 refs.)
21. Hingson R; Howland J. Alcohol and non-traffic unintended injuries (review). *Addiction* 88(7): 877-883, 1993. (50 refs.)
22. Holder HD; Blose JO. Alcoholism treatment and total health care utilization and costs: A 4 year longitudinal analysis of federal employees. *Journal of the American Medical Association* 256(11): 1456-1460, 1986. (19 refs.)
23. Holder HD; Hallan JB. Impact of alcoholism treatment on total health care costs: A 6 year study. *Advances in Alcohol and Substance Abuse* 6(1): 1-15, 1987. (39 refs.)
24. Hubbard RL; Marsden ME; Rachal JV; Harwood HJ; Cavanaugh ER; Ginzburg HM. *Drug Abuse Treatment: A National Study of Effectiveness.* Chapel Hill NC: University of North Carolina Press, 1989. 213 pp. (Chapter refs.)
25. Jarman CM; Kellet JM. Alcoholism in the general hospital. *British Medical Journal* 2(6188): 469-472, 1979. (16 refs.)
26. Jellinek EM. Phases of alcohol addiction. *Quarterly Journal of Studies on Alcohol* 13: 673-684, 1952. (36 refs.)
27. Johnson VE. *I'll Quit Tomorrow, Revised Edition.* New York: Harper & Row, Publishers Inc, 1980. 182 pp. (11 refs.)
28. Johnston LD; O'Malley PM; Bachman JG. *National Survey Results on Drug Use from the Monitoring the Future Study, 1975-1993. Volume I: Secondary School Students.* Rockville MD: National Institute on Drug Abuse, 1994. (0 refs.)

29. Johnston LD; O'Malley PM; Bachman JG. *National Survey Results on Drug Use from the Monitoring the Future Study, 1975-1993. Volume II: College Students and Young Adults.* Rockville MD: National Institute on Drug Abuse, 1994. (0 refs.)

30. Jones CL; Battjes RJ, eds. *Etiology of Drug Abuse: Implications for Prevention, NIDA Research Monograph 56.* Rockville MD: National Institute on Drug Abuse, 1985. 283 pp. (Chapter refs.)

31. Kandel DB; Logan JA. Patterns of drug use from adolescence to young adulthood: Periods of risk for initiation, continued use and discontinuation. *American Journal of Public Health* 74(7): 660-666, 1984. (11 refs.)

32. Kinney J. Alcohol use, abuse, and dependence. IN: *Medical Consequences of Alcohol Use.* Timonium MD: Milner Fenwick, 1989. (300 refs.)

33. Leckman AL; Umlano BE; Blay M. Prevalence of alcoholism in a family practice center. *Journal of Family Practice* 18(6): 867-870, 1984. (25 refs.)

34. Lillie-Blanton M; Anthony JC; Schuster CR. Probing the meaning of racial/ethnic group comparisons in crack cocaine smoking. *Journal of the American Medical Association* 269(8): 993-997, 1993. (11 refs.)

35. McGinnis JM. Actual causes of death in the United States. *Journal of the American Medical Association.* 270(18): 2207-2212, 1993. (99 refs.)

36. Maddux JF; Desmond DP. Family and environment in the choice of opioid dependence or alcoholism. *American Journal of Drug and Alcohol Abuse* 15(2): 117-134, 1989. (42 refs.)

37. Manning WG; Keeler EB; Newhouse JP; Sloss EM; Wasserman J. The taxes of sin: Do smokers and drinkers pay their way? *Journal of the American Medical Association* 261(11): 1604-1609, 1989. (29 refs.)

38. Miller NS. Psychiatric diagnosis in drugs and alcohol addiction. *Alcoholism Treatment Quarterly* 12(2): 75-92, 1995. (85 refs.)

39. Miller NS; Summers GL; Gold MS. Cocaine dependence: Alcohol and other drug dependence and withdrawal characteristics. *Journal of Addictive Diseases* 12(1): 25-35, 1993. (15 refs.)

40. Moore RD; Bone LR; Geller G; Mamon JA; Stokes EJ; Levine DM. Prevalence, detection, and treatment of alcoholism in hospitalized patients. *Journal of the American Medical Association* 261(3): 403-407, 1989. (18 refs.)

41. Nathan PE. The addictive personality is the behavior of the addict. *Journal of Consulting and Clinical Psychology* 56(2): 183-188, 1988. (41 refs.)

42. National Highway Traffic Safety Administration. Alcohol involvement in fatal motor-vehicle crashes—United States, 1992-1993. *MMWR. Morbidity and Mortality Weekly Report* 43(47): 861-862, 1994. (2 refs.)

43. National Institute on Alcohol Abuse and Alcoholism. *Eighth Special Report to the US Congress on Alcohol and Health.* Rockville MD: National Institute on Alcohol Abuse and Alcoholism, 1993. (Chapter rcfs.)

44. National Institute on Alcohol Abuse and Alcoholism. *Fifth Special Report to the US Congress on Alcohol and Health.* Rockville MD: National Institute on Alcohol Abuse and Alcoholism, 1983. (Chapter refs.)

45. National Institute on Alcohol Abuse and Alcoholism. *Seventh Special Report to the US Congress on Alcohol and Health.* Rockville MD: National Institute on Alcohol Abuse and Alcoholism, 1990. (Chapter refs.)

46. National Institute on Alcohol Abuse and Alcoholism. *Sixth Special Report to the US Congress on Alcohol and Health.* Rockville MD: National Institute on Alcohol Abuse and Alcoholism, 1987. (Chapter refs.)

47. National Institute on Alcohol Abuse and Alcoholism. *Toward a National Plan to Combat Alcohol Abuse and Alcoholism: A Report to the United States Congress.* Rockville MD: National Institute on Alcohol Abuse and Alcoholism, 1986.

48. *The New York Times.* Section A, p 1. September 4, 1988.

49. Noble EP. The D2 dopamine receptor gene: A review of association studies in alcoholism (review). *Behavior Genetics* 23(2): 119-129, 1993. (27 refs.)

50. Office of the Inspector General. *Drug Utilization Review.* Washington DC: Department of Health and Human Services, 1989. (95 refs.)

51. Perola M; Vouri E; Penttila A. Abuse of alcohol in sudden out-of-hospital deaths in Finland. *Alcoholism: Clinical and Experimental Research* 18(2): 255-260, 1994. (11 refs.)

52. Personal communication. George E. Vaillant, 1989.

53. Pollan M. How pot has grown. The Cannabis Cup Convention. *The New York Times Magazine.* February 19, 1995. p. 30-5+ (cover story).

54. Pollock VE. Meta-analysis of subjective sensitivity to alcohol in sons of alcoholics. *American Journal of Psychiatry* 149(11): 1534-1538, 1992. (33 refs.)

55. Rice DP. The economic cost of alcohol abuse and alcohol dependence: 1990. *Alcohol Health and Research World* 17(1): 10-11, 1993. (6 refs.)

56. Robins LN; Helzer JE; Weissman MM; Orraischel H; Gruenberg E; Burke JD; et al. Lifetime prevalence of specific psychiatric disorders in three sites. *Archives of General Psychiatry* 41(10): 949-958, 1984. (25 refs.)

57. Schlesinger HJ; Mumford E; Glass GV; Patrick C; Sharfstein S. Mental health treatment and medical care utilization in a fee-for-service system: Outpatient mental health treatment following the onset of chronic disease. *American Journal of Public Health* 73: 422-449, 1983. (33 refs.)

58. Schonberg SK, ed. *Substance Abuse: A Guide for Health Professionals.* Elk Grove Village IL: American Academy of Pediatrics/Pacific Institute for Research and Evaluation, 1988.

59. Schuckit MA. Advances in understanding the vulnerability to alcoholism. IN: O'Brien CP; Jaffee JH, eds. *Addictive States.* New York: Raven Press, 1992. pp. 93-108.

60. Schuckit MA; Goodwin DW. A study of alcoholism in half siblings. *American Journal of Psychiatry* 128(9): 1132-1136, 1972. (16 refs.)

61. Schuster C. Initiatives at the National Institute on Drug Abuse. IN: LS Harris, ed. *Problems of Drug Dependence, NIDA Research Monograph 81.* Rockville MD: National Institute on Drug Abuse, 1988. (0 refs.)

62. Scitovsky A; Rice D. Estimates of the direct and indirect costs of Acquired Immune Deficiency Syndrome in the United States, 1985, 1986, 1990. *Public Health Report* 102: 5-17, 1987. (11 refs.)

63. Shute PA. Patients' alcohol drinking habits in general practice: Prevention and education. *Journal of the Royal Society of Medicine* 81(8): 450-451, 1988. (15 refs.)

64. Simpson DD; George WJ; Lehman WEK. Addiction careers: Summary of studies based on the DARP (Drug Abuse Reporting Program) 12 year follow-up. Rockville MD: National Institute on Drug Abuse, 1986. (31 refs.)

65. Smith JW. Diagnosing alcoholism. *Hospital and Community Psychiatry* 34(11): 1018-1021, 1983. (23 refs.)

66. Substance Abuse and Mental Health Services Administration. *Cost of Addictive and Mental Disorders and Effectiveness of Treatment.* Rockville MD: Substance Abuse and Mental Health Services Administration, 1994. (38 refs.)

67. Substance Abuse and Mental Health Services Administration. *Data from the Drug Abuse Warning Network (DAWN): Annual Emergency Room Data 1992, Statistical Series I, Number 12-A.* Rockville MD: Substance Abuse and Mental Health Services Administration, 1994. (0 refs.)

68. Substance Abuse and Mental Health Services Administration. *National Household Survey on Drug Abuse: Main Findings 1992.* Rockville MD: National Institute on Drug Abuse, 1995. (0 refs.)

69. Substance Abuse and Mental Health Services Administration. *National Household Survey on Drug Abuse: Population Estimates 1993.* Rockville MD: National Institute on Drug Abuse, 1994. (0 refs.)

70. Vaillant GE. *The Natural History of Alcoholism.* Cambridge MA: Harvard University Press, 1983. 378 pp. (369 refs.)

71. Vaillant GE. The natural history of narcotic drug addiction. *Seminars in Psychiatry* 2: 486-498, 1970. (27 refs.)

72. Zook CJ; Moore FD. High-cost users of medical care. *New England Journal of Medicine* 302(18): 996-1001, 1980. (12 refs.)

FURTHER READINGS
Epidemiology

Centers for Disease Control. Cigarette smoking among adults: United States, 1993. *MMWR. Morbidity and Mortality Weekly Report* 43(50): 925-930, 1994. (10 refs.)

The annual prevalence of cigarette smoking among adults in the US declined 40% during 1965-1990 but was virtually unchanged during 1990-1992. To determine the prevalence of smoking among adults, smoker interest in quitting, and the prevalence of cessation, i.e., quit ratio among adults during 1993, the Year 2000 Health Objectives Supplement of the 1993 National Health Interview Survey (NHIS-2000) collected self-reported information about cigarette smoking from a random sample of civilian, noninstitutionalized adults aged 18 years or older. This report presents the prevalence estimates for 1993 and compares them with estimates for smokers interested in quitting completely and the prevalence of cessation among ever smokers. Copyright 1995, Project Cork Institute.

Flewelling RL; Ennett ST; Rachal JV; Theisen AC. *National Household Survey on Drug Abuse: Race/Ethnicity, Socioeconomic Status, and Drug Abuse, 1991.* Rockville MD: Substance Abuse and Mental Health Services Administration, 1994. (27 refs.)

One of the two chief purposes of this report is to examine the prevalence of self-reported use of alcohol, cigarettes, and illicit drugs across subgroups of the US civilian, noninstitutionalized population aged 12 or older as defined by race/ethnicity and by other sociodemographic characteristics. Although socioeconomic factors are obvious candidates for helping to explain racial/ethnic differences, other demographic variables may also play a role. In this report, three types of sociodemographic control measures are distinguished: background demographic measures, such as age, gender, metropolitan status, and geographic region of residence; indicators of SES; and other social and lifestyle indicators, such as marital status and employment status. Public Domain.

Insurance and Health Care Reform

Arons BS; Frank RG; Goldman HH; McGuire TG; Stephens S. Mental health and substance abuse coverage under health reform. *Health Affairs* 13(1): 192-205, 1994. (23 refs.)

President Clinton's health care reform proposal articulates a complete vision for the mental health and substance abuse care system that includes a place for those traditionally served by both the public and the private sectors. Mental health and substance abuse services are to be fully integrated into health alliances under the president's proposal. If this is to occur, we must come to grips with both the history and the insurance-related problems of financing mental health/substance abuse care: (1) the ability of health plans to manage the benefit so as to alter patterns of use; (2) a payment system for health plans that addresses biased selection; and (3) preservation of the existing public investment while accommodating in a fair manner differences in funding across the 50 states. Copyright 1994, People-to-People Health Foundation, Inc.

Harwood HJ; Thomsom M; Nesmith T. *Healthcare Reform and Substance Abuse Treatment: The Cost of Financing Under Alternative Approaches. Final Report.* Fairfax VA: Lewin-VHI, Inc, 1994. (31 refs.)

The purpose of this report is to analyze five options for reforming the financing of substance abuse treatment. Estimates are presented for the cost of several "prototypical" financing reform proposals that are designed to change the organization, delivery, and access to treatment. One of the central assumptions of this report is that alcohol and drug abuse treatment is effective and should be made more widely available. Treatment effectiveness has been widely debated, and several major recent studies have concluded that the evidence for effectiveness is very good, if not definitive. Also, this report explores the cost impact of several different patterns of matching patients to types of treatment. The sections of the report briefly review what is known about the need for substance abuse treatment in the US, examine data on the economic impact of alcohol and drug abuse, present an original analysis of the current provision of substance abuse treatment in the US, describe several major approaches to reforming the financing for substance abuse treatment, and define how they have been modeled. The results are summarized for the reform options, and then some implications of these findings are briefly discussed. Copyright 1994, Lewin-VHI, Inc.

Melek S; Pyenson B. *Premium Rate Estimates for the Mental Health and Substance Abuse Benefits in the Health Security Act.* Washington DC: Milliman & Robertson, Inc, 1994. (0 refs.)

The American Psychiatric Association (APA) retained Milliman & Robertson, Inc to estimate premium rates for the alcohol, drug, and mental disease (ADM) services under the Health Security Act proposed by President Clinton. The Health Security Act refers to these as mental health and substance abuse benefits. This report presents premium rate estimates along with description of the data sources, methodology, and assumptions that were used to produce them. Copyright 1994, Milliman & Robertson, Inc.

Shaffer ER; Cutler AJ; Wellstone PD. Coverage of mental health and substance abuse services under a single-payer health care system. *Hospital and Community Psychiatry* 45(9): 916-919, 1994. (10 refs.)

Health care reform proposals based on a single-payer system of health care insurance were introduced in the US Congress in 1992 and 1993 but were superseded by the Clinton administration's health care reform proposal, which was based on managed competition. In a single-payer system, the government collects all health care funding and pays private- and public-sector providers; similar providers are paid the same rate. Other features include consumer choice of providers, distribution of risk of high utilization over the entire nation, and control of health care expenses via an annual national health care budget. Such proposals cover outpatient, inpatient, and long-term care and case management services for mental illness and substance abuse disorders, call for periodic utilization review of continuing mental health care, and eliminate the distinction between public and private services based on limits of coverage. The last provision particularly affects severely or chronically mentally ill persons who are likely to exhaust their private insurance coverage. Copyright 1994, American Psychiatric Association. Used with permission.

Impact on Health Care System

Archer L; Grant BF; Dawson DA. What if Americans drank less? The potential effect on the prevalence of alcohol abuse and dependence. *American Journal of Public Health* 85(1): 61-66, 1995. (32 refs.)

Several advisory committees have recently recommended that alcohol consumption be limited to moderate levels. Moderate drinking has been defined generally as not more than two drinks per day for healthy men and not more than one drink per day for healthy, nonpregnant women. The impact of reducing alcohol consumption to within the recommended guidelines on the prevalence of two serious alcohol-related problems was examined by modeling the relationship between average daily ethanol intake and alcohol abuse and dependence. The recommended drinking guidelines, both in their existing form and modified by a measure of impairment, were applied to the observed distribution of consumption derived from a large representative survey of the US general population. The results demonstrated that restricting drinking to the maximum allowable levels under the existing and the modified guidelines would reduce the prevalence of alcohol abuse and dependence by 14.2% and 47.1%, respectively, in the adult US general population. Implications of these findings are discussed in terms of the validity of the assumptions underlying the models and the nature and direction of future research that would form the basis of newly developed guidelines for safe drinking limits. Copyright 1995, American Public Health Association. Used with permission.

Baldwin WA; Rosenfeld BA; Breslow MJ; Buchman TG; Deutschman CS; Moore RD. Substance abuse-related admissions to adult intensive care. *Chest* 103(1): 21-25, 1993. (26 refs.)

The frequency of adult surgical and medical intensive care unit (ICU) admissions related to substance abuse was determined at a large community, trauma, and tertiary referral hospital. Of 435 ICU admissions, 14% (95% confidence interval [CI], 5% to 23%) were tobacco related, generating 16% of costs, 9% (95% CI, 0% to 18%) were alcohol related, generating 13% of costs, and 5% (95% CI, 0% to 14%) were illicit drug related, generating 10% of costs. In all, 28% (95% CI, 20% to 36%) of ICU admissions, generating 39% of costs, were substance abuse related. Substance abuse-related admissions were significantly longer and more costly than admissions not related to substance abuse (4.2 days vs. 2.8 days, $p = 0.004$; $9,610 vs. $5,890, $p = 0.001$). Frequency of substance abuse-related admission was linked with the patient's insurance status (Medicare, private insurance, uninsured). In the uninsured group, 44% of admissions were substance abuse related (95% CI, 35% to 52%), significantly higher than in the private insurance and Medicare groups, and generating 61% of all ICU costs in the uninsured group. Large fractions of adult ICU admissions and costs are substance abuse related, particularly in uninsured patients. Copyright 1993, The American College of Chest Physicians.

Bartlett JC; Miller LS; Rice DP; Max WB. Medical-care expenditures attributable to cigarette smoking: United States, 1993. *MMWR. Morbidity and Mortality Weekly Report* 43(26): 469-472, 1994. (7 refs.)

The findings in this report indicate that cigarette smoking accounts for a substantial and preventable portion of all medical-care costs in the US. For each of the approximately 24 billion packages of cigarettes sold in 1993, approximately $2.06 was spent on medical care attributable to smoking. Of the $2.06, approximately $0.89 was paid through public sources. From 1987 to 1993, the more than twofold increase in estimated direct medical-care costs attributable to smoking primarily reflect the substantial increase in medical-care expenditures during this period. In addition, the 1993 Health Care Financing Administration (HCFA) estimate of national health-care expenditures included expenses not covered by the 1987 National Medical Expenditures Survey (NMES-2), e.g., hospitalization and other medical-care costs for persons too ill to respond to NMES-2. The smoking-attributable costs described in this report are underestimated for two reasons. First, the cost estimates do not include all direct medical costs attributable to cigarette smoking, e.g., burn care resulting from cigarette smoking-related fires, perinatal care for low–birth-weight infants of mothers who smoke, and costs associated with diseases caused by exposure to environmental

tobacco smoke. Second, the indirect costs of morbidity, e.g., due to work loss and bed-disability days and loss in productivity resulting from the premature deaths of smokers and former smokers were not included in these estimates. In 1990, estimated indirect losses associated with morbidity and premature mortality were $6.9 billion and $40.3 billion, respectively; these estimates suggest that the total economic burden of cigarette smoking is more than twice as high as the direct medical costs described in this report. Public Domain.

Denmead G; Rouse BA, eds. *Financing Drug Treatment Through State Programs. Services Research Monograph No. 1.* Rockville MD: National Institute on Drug Abuse, 1994. (Chapter refs.)

This is the first volume of the planned National Institute on Drug Abuse (NIDA) series devoted to Services Research. The five papers address specific knowledge gaps and are directed to increasing the understanding of public substance abuse financing through state programs, and the related issues of reimbursement and regulation. The individual papers are directed to national patterns of Medicaid funding, variations in state Medicaid programs, a case study from the State of Washington on utilization and cost of treatment under Medicaid, a review of different programs in the New England region, and a summary of state program approaches. Public Domain.

Fox K; Merrill JC; Chang H-H; Califano JA. Estimating the costs of substance abuse to the Medicaid Hospital Care Program. *American Journal of Public Health* 85(1): 48-54, 1995. (24 refs.)

The purpose of this study was to develop a model, using the epidemiologic tool of attributable risk, for estimating the cost of substance abuse to Medicaid. Based on prior substance-use and morbidity research, population-attributable risks for substance abuse–related diseases were calculated. (These risks measure the proportion of total disease cases attributable to smoking, drinking, and drug use.) The risks for each disease were applied to Medicaid hospital discharges and days on the 1991 National Hospital Discharge Survey that had these diseases as primary diagnosis. The cost of these substance abuse–related days were added to Medicaid hospital costs for direct treatment of substance abuse. More than 60 medical conditions involving 1100 diagnosis were identified, at least in part, as attributable to substance abuse. Factoring these substance abuse–related conditions into hospital costs, 1 out of 5 Medicaid hospital days, or 4 million days, were spent on substance abuse–related care in 1991. In 1994, this would account for almost $8 billion in Medicaid expenditures. The use of tobacco, alcohol, and drugs contributes significantly to hospital costs. To address rising costs, substance abuse treatment and prevention should be an integral part of any health care reform effort. Copyright 1995, American Public Health Association. Used with permission.

Frank RG; McGuire TG; Regier DA; Manderscheid R; Woodward A. Paying for mental health and substance abuse care. *Health Affairs* 13(1): 337-342, 1994. (13 refs.)

In 1990, $54 billion was spent on alcohol/drug abuse and mental health treatment. These expenditures were concentrated in the area of inpatient psychiatric care and on persons with severe mental health and substance abuse problems. The data on expenditure patterns for mental health and substance abuse care suggest that successful health care reform in this area must implement mechanisms for controlling inpatient utilization and managing the care of persons with the most severe disorders. Copyright 1994, People-to-People Health Foundation, Inc.

Ingster LM; Cartwright WS. Drug disorders and cardiovascular disease: The impact on annual hospital length of stay for the Medicare population. *American Journal of Drug and Alcohol Abuse* 21(1): 93-110, 1995.

The authors studied 3,942,868 Medicare patients (comprised of elderly and disabled) discharged with cardiovascular disease (CVD) during 1987, of which 41,095 (1%) had a drug disorder. Among this small subgroup, the percent of those overlapping with an alcohol and/or mental disorder is 33% for the elderly and 47% for the disabled. The presence of a drug disorder-discharge diagnosis is associated with an excess of 329,650 days of hospital care and $174,498,071 in hospital charges, as illustrated by a 51% increase in average annual days in the hospital for the elderly and a similar 61% increase for the disabled. The concomitant increase in average annual discharges offers an explanation. Clinical progression in drug disorder severity (six categories were defined) is associated with increasing lengths of stay; for example, drug dependence comorbidities present longer lengths of stay than drug abuse comorbidities. Among the 12 categories of CVD defined, patients with rheumatic heart disease, hypertensive heart disease, hypertension, and other venous disorders were those whose length of stay experienced the largest percent increase when a drug disorder was present. When drug disorders compete with alcohol and/or mental disorders in a general linear model predicting average annual length of stay, they remain significant at the *P* <0.001 level. Copyright 1995, Marcel Dekker, Inc. Used with permission.

Overview of Drug Actions, Drug Effects, and Morbidity

Barber JG. *Social Work with Addictions.* New York: New York University Press, 1994. (450 refs.)

This volume, first published in Great Britain, is directed to generalist social workers who are likely to encounter substance abuse within the context of their work. The first chapter reviews the concept of addiction and summarizes the characteristics of different drug classes. The second chapter provides a social work practice model, drawing heavily on the transtheoretical model of stages of change articulated by Prochaska and DiClemente and which in the US is associated with the work of Malatt, Gordon, and Miller. The third through sixth chapters center on each of the stages of change, i.e., precontemplation, determination, action strategies, and maintenance. The final chapter deals with a variety of issues in respect to evaluation, ranging from an overview of the treatment outcome literature to addressing issues related to social policy. The work includes a number of excellent tables and figures summarizing the material. Copyright 1995, Project Cork Institute.

Brown E; Prager J; Lee HY; Ramsey RG. CNS complications of cocaine abuse: Prevalence, pathophysiology, and neuroradiology. (review). *American Journal of Roentgenology* 159(1): 137-147, 1992. (62 refs.)

The US is facing an epidemic of cocaine use by adolescents and young adults from all socioeconomic backgrounds. Epidemiological data suggest that the use of the drug continues to increase on a year-by-year basis. This is a serious public health problem because cocaine is highly addictive and is associated with a variety of serious complications. In the CNS, these complications include stroke, intracerebral hemorrhage, vascular spasm, and possibly vasculitis. Seizures and sudden death have been reported. Cocaine use during pregnancy may be associated with fetal hypoxia, intracerebral hemorrhage, and possibly congenital malformations in the neonate. Many of these complications have been recognized only in the last 5 to 10 years. For example, ischemic changes in the brains of chronic cocaine abusers have been reported only recently. Because even further increases in cocaine use are predicted by drug enforcement officials, it is expected that radiologists will encounter its complications more frequently in the future. Therefore radiologists should become familiar with the radiological manifestations of the drug's effects. This article describes the drug's pathophysiology and complications and discusses the evolving role of imaging procedures. Copyright 1992, American Roentgen Ray Society.

Dinwiddie SH. Abuse of inhalants: A review. *Addiction* 89(8): 925-939, 1994. (129 refs.)

Inhalants, a chemically heterogeneous group of psychoactive substances found in adhesives, lighter fluids, spray paints, cleaning fluids, and typewriter correction fluid, may be used by up to 10% of young people. This article reviews health effects, epidemiology, risk of other substance use and addiction, and psychiatric comorbidity associated with the practice of inhalant use. Copyright 1994, Society for the Study of Addiction to Alcohol and Other Drugs.

Edwards G; Strang J; Jaffee JH, eds. *Drugs, Alcohol, and Tobacco: Making the Science and Policy Connections.* New York: Oxford University Press, Inc, 1993. (Chapter refs.)

This edited volume with 41 contributors grew out of a conference convened in 1991 by the National Addiction Centre (London) directed to examining the connections between science and policy in the substance abuse field. The volume is organized into five major sections. The first deals with the general issues in respect to the role and limitations of science in informing public policy. The second section addresses the issues of prevention in respect to different substance abuse fields, namely alcohol, nicotine, and psychotropic substances. Section III addresses the issues related to emerging and changing policy demands. The fourth section deals with issues arising upon treatment, and the final section addresses the debate in respect to legalization. Copyright 1995, Project Cork Institute.

Fuller MG. Anabolic-androgenic steroids: Use and abuse. *Comprehensive Therapy* 19(2): 69-72, 1993. (27 refs.)

This article reviews the history of anabolic-androgenic steroids (AAS) and describes their metabolic effects, approved medical indications, and adverse consequences. The report concludes with recommendations for dealing with the current AAS problem. Copyright 1993, American Society of Contemporary Medicine and Surgery.

Gable RS. Toward a comparative overview of dependence potential and acute toxicity of psychoactive substances used nonmedically. (review). *American Journal of Drug and Alcohol Abuse* 19(3): 263-281, 1993. (158 refs.)

A procedure is outlined for comparing dependence potential and acute toxicity across a broad range of abused psychoactive substances. Tentative results, based on an extensive literature review of 20 substances, suggested that the margin of safety ("therapeutic index") varied dramatically between substances. Intravenous heroin appeared to have the greatest risk of dependence and acute lethality; oral psilocybin appeared to have the least. Hazards resulting from behavioral deficits, perceptual distortion, or chronic illness were not factored into the assessments. Copyright 1993, Marcel Dekker, Inc. Used with permission.

Greenfield TK; Weisner C. Drinking problems and self-reported criminal behavior, arrests, and convictions: 1990 US alcohol and 1989 county surveys. *Addiction* 90(3): 361-373, 1995. (37 refs.)

Use of general population surveys in addition to institutional samples is critical to disentangling the relationship between criminal behavior and alcohol problems or use of illicit drugs. Local area studies can be useful but generalizability of their results is seldom studied. Data from recent US national (*n* = 2058) and county (*n* = 3069) general population surveys are used to examine the role of alcohol problem and drug use histories in predicting self-reported criminal behavior, arrest, and conviction within a logistic regression framework. In the national and county surveys controlling for age, gender, income, marital status, employment, education, race, and drug use, lifetime drinking problems significantly predicted current criminal behavior (odds ratios 1.3 and 1.5, respectively), with slightly stronger relationships noted in equivalent models predicting arrest (odds ratios 1.7 and 1.8) and conviction (odds ratios 1.7 and 1.6). Relationships between alcohol, drugs, and criminal behavior/justice variables are discussed. Parallels between US and county results suggest that findings from intensive, articulated analyses of community-level population and institutional surveys may be cautiously generalized beyond their geographic locus. Copyright 1995, Society for the Study of Addiction to Alcohol and Other Drugs.

Hatsukami D; Nelson R; Jensen J. Smokeless tobacco: Current status and future directions. (review). *British Journal of Addiction* 86(5): 559-563, 1991. (29 refs.)

Smokeless tobacco is addicting, can cause physical dependence, and is associated with many health risks. In spite of these concerns over its use, minimal research has been conducted to understand the effects of and factors associated with smokeless tobacco use. Additionally, relatively few studies have examined potentially effective treatments for the smokeless tobacco user. This paper reviews the existing literature in this area and considers future directions for research. Copyright 1991, Society for the Study of Addiction to Alcohol and Other Drugs. Used with permission.

Lacayo A. Neurologic and psychiatric complications of cocaine abuse. (review). *Neuropsychiatry, Neuropsychology, and Behavioral Neurology* 8(1): 53-60, 1995. (110 refs.)

Cocaine abuse is a public health problem of epidemic proportions. Prominent victims, including athletes, movie stars, and businessmen, have succumbed to its use. Whether through ignorance or misinformation, many who have neglected to understand the health hazards of cocaine have paid with their life. This article presents a concise review of the complications of cocaine use as seen in both the author's practice and in the literature search, with emphasis on its impact on the nervous system because stroke and panic attacks seem to be the most frequent medical complications. This article further offers a succinct approach to the diagnosis and treatment of cocaine abuse. Copyright 1995, Raven Press, Ltd.

Lin GC; Erinoff L, eds. *Anabolic Steroid Abuse. NIDA Research Monograph 102.* Rockville MD: National Institute on Drug Abuse, 1990. (Chapter refs.)

This monograph represents a state-of-the-art information resource concerning anabolic steroid abuse and suggests future directions for research. The contents of this monograph encompass a wide range of topics beginning with the important question of whether anabolic steroids possess abuse potential and whether they play a role in the abuse of other substances. There follows an historical overview of the discovery and development of anabolic steroids, a critical evaluation of the performance-enhancing effects of anabolic steroids, and an ethnographic study of anabolic steroid abuse in New York City. Next is a summary of the epidemiological evidence on the incidence and prevalence of steroid use. To better understand the health consequences of abuse, the normal endocrine physiology and pharmacology, as well as molecular and receptor mechanisms underlying the actions of anabolic steroids, are presented, followed by an appraisal of the health risks associated with abuse. Because ado-

lescents are of special concern, a detailed account of the endocrinological effects of anabolic steroids in this special population is included. Finally, this review is completed with a discussion of the behavioral aspects of anabolic steroid use, including indications of psychological dependence and evidence for steroid-induced mental status changes and aggressive behavior. Public Domain.

Lin GC; Glennon RA, eds. *Hallucinogens: An update. NIDA Research Monograph 146.* Rockville MD: National Institute on Drug Abuse, 1994. (Chapter refs.)

This monograph represents the proceedings of a technical review conducted by NIDA, the first in 10 years directed to hallucinogens, particularly LSD. The goal was to update current knowledge; to identify preclinical and clinical research needs; to discuss issues related to human research; to ascertain what if any clinical utility is present; and finally to discuss how research in this area can contribute to treatment. The volume, organized into 13 chapters with 24 contributors, includes both qualitative and quantitative studies in both animals and humans. Topics covered include a review of the drug class; structure-activity relationships; research related to neurotransmitters, namely serotonin receptors; stimulus effects; the application of autoradiographic and electrophysiological studies; and discussion of sites of action. Copyright 1995, Project Cork Institute.

Lowinson JH; Ruiz P; Millman RB; Langford JG, eds. *Substance Abuse: A Comprehensive Textbook. Second Edition.* Baltimore MD: Williams & Wilkins, 1992. (Chapter refs.)

This is the second edition of text dealing with substance abuse issues. It has 113 contributors with 80 chapters and is organized into 11 sections. These sections address historical perspectives; determinants of substance abuse; treatment approaches; management of associated medical conditions; infection and AIDS; prevention and education; medical education and staff training; and policy issues; and review by pharmacological class, the major, different substances of abuse. Copyright 1995, Project Cork Institute.

Nelson DE; Kirkendall RS; Lawton RL; Chrismon JH; Merritt RK; Arday DA; et al. Surveillance for smoking-attributable mortality and years of potential life lost, by state: United States, 1990. *MMWR. Morbidity and Mortality Weekly Report* 43(SS-1): 1-8, 1994. (24 refs.)

This report studies mortality and years of potential life lost attributable to cigarette smoking. Mortality and years of potential life lost were estimated for each state during 1990 by using the Smoking-Attributable Mortality, Morbidity, and Economic Costs (SAMMEC) software. These estimates were based on attributable risk formulas for smoking-related causes of death. Estimates of smoking prevalence were obtained from the Behavioral Risk Factor Surveillance System and the US Bureau of the Census, and mortality data were obtained from CDC. The median estimate for the number of smoking-attributable deaths among states was 5,619 (range 402 [Alaska] to 42,574 [California]). Within each state the number of smoking-attributable deaths among males was approximately twice as high as among females. Utah had the lowest mortality rate (218 per 100,000 population) and the lowest percentage of all deaths attributable to cigarette smoking (13.4%). Nevada had the highest mortality rate (478.1 per 100,000 population) and the highest percentage of deaths from smoking (24%). The number of years of potential life lost ranged from 6,720 (Alaska) to 498,297 (California). The number of deaths attributable to cigarette smoking in 1990 remained high. Efforts are needed to control tobacco use in all states. SAMMEC data are used in many states to assist policymakers in strengthening tobacco control efforts. Public Domain.

O'Brien CP; Jaffe JH, eds. *Addictive States*. New York: Raven Press, 1992. (Chapter refs.)

This volume represents a follow-up to a volume on addiction published in 1966. Since that time the field has grown exponentially. This volume addresses the areas in which significant advances have taken place. The volume is organized into 15 chapters with 30 contributors. The topics considered include a review of epidemiology of substance use, natural history, etiology in respect to brain function and identified risk factors, and the role of drug reinforcement. There are also discussions of the relationship of psychopathology and addiction, especially in relation to antisocial personality disorder; treatment; the rationale for maintenance pharmacotherapy of opiate dependence; cost-benefit analysis; and treatment outcome. Copyright 1995, Project Cork Institute.

Patterson RE; Haines PS; Popkin BM. Health lifestyle patterns of United States adults. *Preventive Medicine* 23(4): 453-460, 1994. (46 refs.)

Reaching national health objectives depends upon our ability to encourage the performance of multiple good health behaviors. There are cognitive, social, and biological reasons for expecting health behaviors to cluster. However, few studies have found significant associations among health behaviors, with the exception of the documented link between smoking and alcohol consumption. Cluster analysis was used to identify population subgroups with similar patterns of diet quality, physical activity, alcohol consumption, and cigarette smoking. This is the first study of health behavior interrelationships to include a measure of overall diet quality and a large sample from a nationally representative survey of US adults. Seven health behavior topologies were identified: 10% of the sample (health-promoting life-style) had an overall healthy lifestyle, 25% had a good diet but sedentary activity level, 18% had fair diet but high activity level (fitness life-style). Individuals in the passive lifestyle cluster (25%) had no active health-promoting activities but did avoid risk-taking health behaviors. Of the sample, 6% were in a drinking cluster, 15% were in a smoking cluster, and 2% had a hedonic life-style characterized by heavy drinking and smoking. These life-style clusters could be characterized by demographic and socioeconomic factors. This research indicates that it is possible to identify a discrete number of health life-styles in a population sample of US adults. Understanding past, present, and changing health life-styles may provide insights for health behavior research and information for the development and targeting of public health programs that can have an impact on multifactorial diseases. Copyright 1994, Academic Press, Inc.

Sacks JJ; Nelson DE. Smoking and injuries: An overview. (review). *Preventive Medicine* 23(4): 515-520, 1994. (92 refs.)

Although the disease consequences of cigarette smoking are well documented, smoking may also be associated with increased risk of injury. The purpose of this review was to provide an overview of this potential association by conducting a literature interview. Cigarettes are the leading cause of death from fire and the second leading cause of fire-related injury. Studies estimate that compared with nonsmokers, smokers appear 1.5 times more likely to have a motor vehicle crash, 1.4 to 2.5 times more likely to be injured at work, and 2 times more likely to suffer other unintentional injuries. A variety of reasons may explain an association between cigarette smoking and injuries; these include (1) direct toxicity; (2) distractibility; (3) smoking-associated medical conditions; and (4) confounding factors, including personality or behavioral characteristics. Smoking may be an independent risk factor for thermal, motor vehicle, occupational, and other unin-

tentional injuries. Nonsmokers may be at increased risk of injury from the presence of smokers in their environments; e.g., from fires. Societal benefits from decreased smoking prevalence are likely to include reduction of both fatal and nonfatal injuries. Copyright 1994, Academic Press, Inc.

Salzman C; Balter M; Rickels K; Gillin C; Ellinwood EH, Jr; Greenblatt DJ; et al. *Benzodiazepine: Dependence, Toxicity, and Abuse*. Washington DC: American Psychiatric Association, 1990. (239 refs.)

This task force is not a comprehensive review of the pharmacology of benzodiazepines, nor is it a guide to their therapeutic indications and use. Rather, this report provides clinicians with a review of the available information on the potential hazards of benzodiazepine treatment and offers suggestions for the rational prescription of these medications, when their use can be clinically indicated. The specific goals of this report are to: (1) review patterns of prescribing clinical use of benzodiazepines; (2) identify patterns of risk for the development of physiological dependence, especially at therapeutic doses; to examine whether or not there is a clinically important difference in risk of physiological dependence among the various benzodiazepines; to characterize the discontinuance symptoms that may occur as a result of such dependence; to suggest steps for the prevention and treatment of benzodiazepine dependence; to review pharmacological factors that cause benzodiazepine dependence. (3) To describe the acute and chronic toxicity that may result from benzodiazepine administration at therapeutic doses as well as at high or toxic doses; to identify risk factors among patients that may contribute to toxicity. (4) To examine patterns of benzodiazepine use outside the context of medical practice, such as the occasional use of unsupervised therapeutic doses for symptom relief; to examine use for recreational purposes as well as use as part of polysubstance abuse pattern. (5) To place the information in a clinical context; to enable psychiatrists to weigh the relative benefit versus the risk of using benzodiazepines; to identify factors that may increase the benefit and reduce the risk of their use; and to develop prescribing guidelines for the clinically appropriate use of benzodiazepines in clinical practice. Copyright 1995, Project Cork Institute.

Schuckit MA. *Drug and Alcohol Abuse: A Clinical Guide to Diagnosis and Treatment, 4th Edition*. New York: Plenum, 1995. (Chapter refs.)

This is the fourth edition of a book directed to clinicians. It focuses on assessment, diagnosis, and treatment approaches to alcohol and other drug use. The initial chapter provides an overview, touching upon definitions, general approaches to drug mechanisms, classification of drugs and drug problems. The next 12 chapters are devoted to specific drugs, i.e., depressants, alcohol, stimulants (including cocaine), opiates and analgesics, marijuana, hallucinogens, PCP, inhalants, over-the-counter preparations, nicotine, and caffeine. The final three chapters are devoted to the phenomenon of polysubstance use; emergency management of alcohol and drug problems, including toxicity, withdrawal, organic brain syndromes, and psychiatric sequelae of use; and rehabilitation. Copyright 1995, Project Cork Institute.

Sullivan E. *Nursing Care of Clients with Substance Abuse*. St. Louis: Mosby, 1995.

This volume is directed to nurses in a wide range of clinical settings. The text focuses on nursing care for both alcohol and drug abuse. The book is outlined in three units: Understanding Substance Abuse, Nursing Care of Clients with Substance Abuse, and Opportunities and Challenges in Substance Abuse and discusses the complete cycle of abuse, treatment and recovery.

CHAPTER 2

Routine Screening and Initial Assessment

PATRICK G. O'CONNOR, MD, MPH

CLINICAL APPLICATIONS

The goals of this chapter are to assist the clinician to:

1. Introduce substance use–specific questions in a routine interview.

2. Formulate interview questions for further assessment if there has been a positive response to questions in the initial screening or when alcohol or substance use problems are immediately apparent.

3. Employ an interview style that facilitates data collection and fosters a therapeutic relationship with the patient and his or her family or significant others.

4. Document findings in the clinical record.

Despite the high prevalence of substance abuse and its many complications, primary care providers often fail to recognize and diagnose these conditions.[34] Because up to 30% of patients seen in adult primary care settings have a history of serious alcohol problems, health care professionals have an obligation to establish routine screening procedures for alcohol and substance abuse problems for all their patients so that early intervention may take place. This chapter discusses screening for substance abuse within the context of the routine medical encounter and the steps to follow when an apparent problem is identified.

SCREENING IN PRIMARY CARE

The purpose of screening is to detect the presence of a condition that may otherwise go unrecognized. There are conditions for which screening is appropriate. Screening should be targeted at diseases when the condition is widespread, when it causes significant suffering, and when it is treatable if detected in an early phase. Breast cancer represents a condition that meets these criteria, whereas a rare and less treatable malignancy, e.g., brain tumor may not. Screening tests also have ideal characteristics.[18] They should have appropriate levels of sensitivity and specificity as well as predicted value. In addition, they should be safe and with minimal side effects. Finally, they should be easy to administer and cost effective.

Alcohol dependence is an excellent example of a condition for which screening is appropriate.[17] It is highly prevalent: some studies estimate a prevalence of approximately 10% in the general population, 20% to 30% in primary care settings, and even higher in inpatient settings.[1,22] In fact, from the primary care perspective, alcohol dependence has a level of prevalence that is similar to other chronic diseases seen in primary care settings, such as hypertension and diabetes. In addition, the suffering attributed to it for both individuals and society has been well documented.[28] Finally, it has been clearly demonstrated that early intervention with alcohol-using and substance-using patients can impact the course of the disease.[1] Thus, given the need to screen for this disease, intensive efforts have been made over the last 20 years to develop appropriate screening mechanisms, which will be described below.

CHALLENGES TO SCREENING FOR SUBSTANCE ABUSE

Although substance abuse would appear to be an ideal tradition for screening activities, this problem presents special challenges that make it unique among the common chronic diseases in primary care settings. Perhaps the main obstacle to the screening and subsequent initiation of treatment is denial by the patient. Substance abuse is commonly accompanied by guilt and shame. Thus, patients frequently deny that a problem exists despite what may appear obvious to the primary care provider.[2] Care providers may perceive that even if substance abuse is identified, patients will resist a recommendation for treatment. Patients may be unwilling to be associated with other "addicts." In some communities, treatment resources may be perceived as severely limited. Thus, it may seem pointless to identify a condition for which treatment will not be accepted or for which treatment is absolutely or relatively unavailable. For example, it may seem futile to refer a patient to a methadone maintenance program with a lengthy waiting list. Another obstacle is that the health care professional may not see or appreciate the results of successful treatment. Results are best judged months after an initial encounter and referral. On the contrary, clinicians are likely to have repeated contacts with those who are untreated or for whom treatment was not successful. In combination, this leads to the inaccurate perception that treatment is ineffective. The natural history of substance abuse includes periodic relapses to drug use. As with other chronic diseases, primary care providers need to take "the long view" when evaluating treatment outcome.

Clinicians may be uncomfortable raising questions about alcohol and other substance use. This may be partially attributed to a lack of education about substance abuse in professional training.[29] In addition, clinicians may be concerned about a patient's negative response, and many fear that by broaching the topic they will threaten their relationship with the patient. To deal with these issues, clinicians need to understand the importance of screening for substance abuse disorders so that early intervention may take place. In addition, they need to understand that this is an emotionally charged issue that can be best addressed by approaching patients in a thoughtful and nonjudgmental fashion.[17] A study of general medical patients asked each patient to complete a problem list of current difficulties. The list included drug abuse. Of those who had drug abuse problems, 82% answered "yes" and/or named the drug being used. Self-reports of patient if/or when they are given the opportunity to identify a drug problem, yield more positive cases than might be expected.[41] Other studies have similarly confirmed that patients are more reliable historians when they believe the information will be treated with respect and, especially for substance abusers, in confidence.[10,11]

Finally, before considering screening for substance abuse, clinicians should consider their own attitude toward alcohol and other drug use. The notions that someone has no biases or that to be unbiased is desirable are erroneous. Alcohol and substance use problems are part of our culture. Biases identify instinctive or habitual responses and define any clinician's working hypotheses. If unexamined, they can have a subtle but significant impact on the ability to identify patients with substance use problems. Dysfunctional biases are incongruent with scientific information. On the contrary, if clinicians incorporate authoritative information from biases, they can be helpful tools for forming "clinical hunches" and discerning the cues that point to a substance use problem.

APPROACHES TO SCREENING FOR SUBSTANCE ABUSE

Screening for substance abuse should be considered within the context of the entire patient evaluation. As described earlier, all patients should be screened for substance abuse as part of an initial evaluation. It should be kept in mind that screening represents a process of early disease identification. Screening tests need to be followed by more detailed evaluations to confirm the diagnosis and to assess the severity of the diagnosis. It is well established that, when patients are screened for substance abuse, the history as documented on the patient interview is the most useful source of information. In primary care settings, the other standard patient assessment tools (physical exam and laboratory studies) play an important role in patient assessment after screening has taken place.

In screening for alcohol and substance use, it is important to remember that patients' behavioral styles and participation may be as important as the answers they give. Be aware of responses designed to convince you there is no problem. Paradoxically, the other extreme—efforts to convince you that a medical condition exists and warrants the prescription of psychoactive substances—is something to be alert to. Ironically, the health care system is used by many people as a source of drugs. Signs of drug-seeking behavior include the following:[29,39]

- *Feigning psychological distress:* For example, specific medications are sought to treat anxiety, insomnia, fatigue, or depression.
- *Deception:* "Lost" or "stolen" medication or requests for premature refills, as well as alterations or forgery of prescriptions.
- *Pressuring the physician:* Coercive tactics include trying to elicit sympathy or guilt.
- *The transient patient:* Patient from out of town who "lost" medication.
- *The patient disinterested in diagnosis:* Patient does not follow through with evaluation or is unconcerned with the diagnosis.
- *The manipulative patient:* Clinicians may sense a patient's efforts to manipulate them.

Various rapid screening instruments have been devised to detect alcohol and other drug abuse and/or dependence. Despite differing questions or formats, all screening instruments attempt to identify the following elements: (1) signs of concern about use by either the patient or others; (2) the presence of negative consequences that result from use, such as a disruption of family and interpersonal relationships; health, work-related, or legal problems; and (3) signs of physical dependence, specifically tolerance and withdrawal. When screening, it is important to be prepared to follow up and to address the findings with the patient, whether positive or negative. Following the discussion of specific screening instruments, some sample follow-up questions are listed.

Detection of abuse and dependence on alcohol and other drugs centers on the results of use, not on quantity and frequency. The basic questions being addressed in this regard are, "Is alcohol or drug use followed by consequences that are a source of concern to the individual or significant others?" and "Would these consequences most likely not have occurred if the use had not preceded them?"

The possibility of substance abuse or dependency needs to be considered in any situation in which the patient has consistent, ongoing, or deteriorating problems in the presence of continuing use. The clinician needs to develop sensitivity to the diagnostic clues of impairment of social, emotional, occupational, or psychological functioning.

Alcohol Screening

Rapid screening instruments to detect possible alcohol abuse or dependence have been most extensively evaluated.[29] Their validity and reliability have been well established in multiple populations. These instruments can be incorporated comfortably into history taking and essentially identify those for whom a more thorough assessment is indicated. The CAGE, the most commonly used instrument, has a reliability equal to other instruments and has only four questions. Following administration of the CAGE, the question, "Do you use other drugs?" can follow, given the high prevalence of polysubstance use.

CAGE. Since its introduction in 1970 by Ewing and Rouse, the CAGE has become recognized as one of the most efficient and effective screening devices for alcohol abuse/dependence.[5] It is easy to administer, only requiring about one minute to ask four questions.

- First, ask if the patient uses alcohol. If the response is "yes," proceed with the four CAGE questions.
- If the patient reports being a nondrinker, ask why, whether they ever drank in the past, and when drinking stopped.[8] Ask what the patient used to drink and how much. You may detect a past problem, a recovering person, or someone with a family history who has chosen not to drink.

Box 2-1

CAGE

"Have you ever felt you ought to	Cut down on your drinking?"
"Have people	Annoyed you by criticizing your drinking?"
"Have you ever felt bad or	Guilty about your drinking?"
"Have you ever had a drink first thing in the morning to steady your nerves or get rid of a hangover?"	Eye-opener

From Ewing J. Detecting alcoholism: The CAGE questionnaire. *Journal of the American Medical Association* 252(14): 1905–1907, 1984.

Having established that the patient drinks alcohol, the four CAGE questions can follow (Box 2-1).

Addressing other drug use. After administering the CAGE questionnaire, ask, "Do you use other drugs?" In doing so, it is important to include the use and possible misuse of illicit drugs, prescribed medications, and over-the-counter preparations.

Clinical response. Even one positive response calls for further investigation; two positive answers substantially increase the probability of alcohol dependence; and four positive responses are essentially pathognomonic for alcohol dependence.

Comments. Focusing on alcohol use to initiate assessment may be indicated on several grounds. Since alcohol is the most commonly used psychoactive substance, by starting the discussion with alcohol, the clinician is beginning with a substance that is culturally sanctioned. This can be followed by questions about prescription medication use, concluding with questions about other illicit substances, e.g., heroin, cocaine, marijuana. Patients may be less comfortable acknowledging other substance use, as they may be concerned that it is "less acceptable" to the clinician. When other substance use is present, it often involves multiple substances, including alcohol. Thus a positive result in screening for an alcohol problem does not rule out other substance use, but it does become a risk factor for other substances.

MAST. The Michigan Alcoholism Screening Test (MAST) is a more extensive screening instrument than the CAGE. It is a 25-item yes/no questionnaire devised for use by both professional and nonprofessional personnel to provide a consistent, quantifiable instrument for the detection of alcohol dependence. Variants that yield comparable results to the complete instrument have also been devised using a subset of the original 25 questions. The MAST has been widely used both within a structured interview and for self-administration. Three points or fewer indicate that dependence is unlikely, four points suggest alcohol dependence, and five or more points indicate an 80% or greater likelihood of dependence. The Brief MAST (Box 2-2) is an abbreviated version of the original 25 questions, with comparable reliability and validity.

Box 2-2

Brief MAST

Points

(2)	*1.	Do you feel you are a normal drinker?
(2)	*2.	Do friends or relatives think you are a normal drinker?
(5)	3.	Have you ever attended a meeting of Alcoholics Anonymous?
(2)	4.	Have you ever lost friends or girlfriends/boyfriends because of drinking?
(2)	5.	Have you ever gotten into trouble at work because of drinking?
(2)	6.	Have you ever neglected your obligations, your family, or your work for 2 or more days in a row because you were drinking?
(2)	7.	Have you ever had delirium tremens (DTs), severe shaking, heard voices, or seen things that weren't there after heavy drinking?
(5)	8.	Have you ever gone to anyone for help about your drinking?
(5)	9.	Have you ever been in a hospital because of drinking?
(2)	10.	Have you ever been arrested for drunk driving or driving after drinking?

Scoring:

<3 points, nonalcoholic;
4 points, suggests alcoholism;
5 or more points, indicates alcoholism.

From Selzer ML. The Michigan Alcoholism Screening Test: The quest for a new diagnostic instrument. *American Journal of Psychiatry* 27(12): 1653-1658, 1971; and Pokorny AD; Miller BA; Kaplan HB. The Brief MAST: A shortened version of the Michigan Alcoholism Screening Test. *American Journal of Psychiatry* 129(3): 342-345, 1972
*Negative responses are alcoholic responses.

Box 2-3
Trauma Scale

"Since your 18th birthday:

   Have you had any fractures or dislocations to
      your bones or joints?
   Have you been injured in a road traffic
      accident?
   Have you injured your head?
   Have you been injured in an assault or fight
      (excluding injuries during sports)?
   Have you been injured after drinking?"

Two or more positive answers are the criteria for
a positive test.

From Skinner HA; Holt S; Schuller R; Roy J; Israel Y. Identification of alcohol abuse using laboratory tests and a history
of trauma. *Annals of Internal Medicine* 101(6): 847-851,
1984. (29 refs.)

Trauma scale. The high incidence of injury
among persons who drink excessively suggests that a
history of trauma may signal the presence of alcohol
abuse or dependence. The Trauma Scale is intended
to pick up non-normative drinking, whether abuse or
dependence. Studies indicate that this brief questionnaire on the history of trauma, developed by
Skinner and others in 1984, is another highly effective screening device. It comprises five items
included in Box 2-3.

AUDIT. A newer screening instrument, the Alcohol Use Disorders Identification Test (AUDIT) developed through a collaborative project of the World
Health Organization, has shown promise as an effective tool for elucidating problem drinking in patients.[3]
The AUDIT is a 10-item questionnaire covering the
domains of alcohol consumption, drinking behavior,
and alcohol-related problems (Box 2-4).

Drug Abuse Screening

Drug abuse screening may be accomplished by
several additional questions following the administration of alcohol-specific screening instruments.
Nonetheless, there may be situations in which the
clinician wishes to specifically conduct routine drug
abuse screening, simultaneously addressing both alcohol and other drugs.

DAST. The Drug Abuse Screening Test (DAST),
first introduced in 1982, may be utilized as a broad-
based screening instrument similar to tests devised
for alcohol problems. It comprises 28 questions and

was designed to quantify the extent of drug involvement in a population seeking help (Box 2-5).

The score also offers insight into the nature of the
substance abuse problem. A DAST score of 0 to 5 is
typically associated with those individuals who only
have alcohol problems. Only 9% of patients with alcohol and drug problems, and none of those with other
substance use problems, score within that range. Thus
a score of 6 or more may indicate that drug use, in
addition to or other than alcohol, may be a problem.
For these patients, further assessment for drug and
alcohol use is needed.

Comparison of Screening Instruments

The five screening instruments described are compared in Table 2-1 in terms of formats, sensitivity, and
specificity.

The Role of the Physical Examination and Laboratory in Screening

Although the screening interview is the most
effective way to detect an alcohol or drug problem,
the physical examination and laboratory measures
can individually be useful in assessing patients with
suspected or diagnosed substance abuse, but they are
not designed for broad-based screening. With alcohol,
aside from withdrawal, no single symptom will lead to
a diagnosis of dependence. While specific physical
exam findings, e.g., signs of chronic liver disease, may
alert the clinician to possible alcohol problems, most
patients with problem drinking have a normal physical exam. Thus, strictly speaking, a physical exam has
no role in screening but rather is important in evaluating patients for complications of drug use. In the
care of alcohol dependence, the most sensitive of laboratory measures, the gamma-glutamyl transferase
(GGT), may miss up to two-thirds of the excessive
drinkers and those who are alcohol dependent. At
best, laboratory measures will detect the presence of
medical complications secondary to heavy, chronic
alcohol use, which are typically a late manifestation of
a long-standing problem.[4,36]

WHEN SCREENING IS POSITIVE: FURTHER ASSESSMENT

Screening refers to the process of identifying
individuals within a general population of patients
who may require a further, more detailed evaluation.
Thus, when patients have a positive screening for
substance abuse, they will require a more detailed
assessment to determine whether a substance abuse
problem is actually present and if so, what its
specific characteristics are. This process can be
performed by a primary care clinician or when

Box 2-4

AUDIT

1. How often do you have a drink containing alcohol?

	(Score)
[ ] Never	(0)
[ ] Monthly or less	(1)
[ ] Two to four times a month	(2)
[ ] Two to three times a week	(3)
[ ] Four or more times a week	(4)

2. How many drinks containing alcohol do you have on a typical day when you are drinking?

	(Score)
[ ] 1 or 2	(0)
[ ] 3 or 4	(1)
[ ] 5 or 6	(2)
[ ] 7 to 9	(3)
[ ] 10 or more	(4)

3. How often do you have six or more drinks on one occasion?

	(Score)
[ ] Never	(0)
[ ] Less than monthly	(1)
[ ] Monthly	(2)
[ ] Weekly	(3)
[ ] Daily or almost daily	(4)

4. How often during the last year have you not been able to stop drinking once you had started?

	(Score)
[ ] Never	(0)
[ ] Less than monthly	(1)
[ ] Monthly	(2)
[ ] Weekly	(3)
[ ] Daily or almost daily	(4)

5. How often during the last year have you failed to do what was normally expected from you because of drinking?

	(Score)
[ ] Never	(0)
[ ] Less than monthly	(1)
[ ] Monthly	(2)
[ ] Weekly	(3)
[ ] Daily or almost daily	(4)

6. How often during the last year have you needed a first drink in the morning to get yourself going after a heavy drinking session?

	(Score)
[ ] Never	(0)
[ ] Less than monthly	(1)
[ ] Monthly	(2)
[ ] Weekly	(3)
[ ] Daily or almost daily	(4)

7. How often during the last year have you had a feeling of guilt or remorse after a drink?

	(Score)
[ ] Never	(0)
[ ] Less than monthly	(1)
[ ] Monthly	(2)
[ ] Weekly	(3)
[ ] Daily or almost daily	(4)

8. How often during the last year have you been unable to remember what happened the night before because you had been drinking?

	(Score)
[ ] Never	(0)
[ ] Less than monthly	(1)
[ ] Monthly	(2)
[ ] Weekly	(3)
[ ] Daily or almost daily	(4)

9. Have you or someone else been injured as a result of your drinking?

	(Score)
[ ] No	(0)
[ ] Yes, but not in the last year	(2)
[ ] Yes, during the last year	(4)

10. Has a relative or friend, or a doctor or other health worker been concerned about your drinking or suggested you cut down?

	(Score)
[ ] No	(0)
[ ] Yes, but not in the last year	(2)
[ ] Yes, during the last year	(4)

Procedure for Scoring AUDIT

Questions 1-8 are scored 0, 1, 2, 3, or 4. Questions 9 and 10 are scored 0, 2, or 4 only. The minimum score (for nondrinkers) is 0 and the maximum possible score is 40. A score of 8 or more indicates a strong likelihood of hazardous or harmful alcohol consumption.

From Saunders JB; Aasland OG: Babor TF; de la Fuente JR; Grant M. Development of the Alcohol Use Disorders Identification Test (AUDIT): WHO collaborative project on early detection of persons with harmful alcohol consumption. II. *Addiction* 88(6): 791–804, 1993.

necessary by a substance abuse specialist. In addition to identifying patients who require more detailed evaluation, screening for substance abuse offers the opportunity to develop an effective relationship with patients so that more detailed questions can be asked with greater comfort. The clinician should be ready to ask a series of appropriate follow-up questions so that further information can be obtained to more clearly elucidate a patient's potential substance use problem.

Follow-Up Questions

When the initial rapid screening is positive, you must be prepared with follow-up questions.[8] These questions are intended to yield more information about the person's relationship with alcohol and other drugs. For example, the eight questions can be used to ascertain preoccupation.

Do you usually use drugs/ drink to get	**H**igh?
Do you sometimes drink or use drugs	**A**lone?
Have you found yourself	**L**ooking forward to drinking/using drugs?
Have you noticed an increased	**T**olerance?
Do you have memory lapses—	**B**lackouts that occurred while drinking?
Do you find yourself using/ drinking in	**U**nplanned ways?
Do you use/drink when you feel anxious, stressed, or depressed for	**M**edicinal reasons?
Do you work at	**P**rotecting your supply, having drugs or alcohol available at all times?

The mnemonics for these questions are HALT and BUMP.

Table 2-1. Comparison of Screening Tests

Screening test	Specificity % of those without	Sensitivity % of true cases	Format
CAGE			
All 4 items	100	37	4 items
3 positive items	99	66	Clinical interview
2 positive items	89	81	To detect probability of alcoholism; no cutoff score differentiating dependence and abuse
1 positive item	21	90	
Trauma scale			
	81	68	5 items
			Clinical interview
			To detect alcohol problems, not alcoholism
MAST			
Score 5 or greater	95	98	25 items
			Self-administered or clinical interview
			To detect alcoholism
AUDIT			
Score 12	97	28	10 questions
Score 8	90	61	Self-administered or clinical interview
Score 2	25	97	To assess harmful use
DAST			
Score 6 or greater	96	79	28 items
			Clinical interview or self-administration
			To detect substance abuse/dependence; drugs other than alcohol alone

Adapted from Kinney J. Medical consequences of alcohol use. IN: *Alcohol Use, Abuse, and Dependence.* Timonium MD: Milner-Fenwick, 1989.

The following set of questions can be used to ascertain important information, which includes the negative consequences that have resulted from drinking or other substance use:

- **Family** history of alcohol and/or substance use problems?
- **Alcoholics** Anonymous/other 12-step program attendance?
- **Thoughts** of having alcoholism or being drug dependent?
- **Attempts** or thoughts of suicide?
- **Legal** problems?
- **Driving** while intoxicated or using drugs?
- **Tranquilizer** or disulfiram (Antabuse) use?

The mnemonic for these questions is FATAL DT.

Look for Signs, Symptoms, Attitudes, and Behavior

While discussing alcohol or other drug use, obtaining the following information helps determine the presence of a problem: reports of family's concerns and complaints; evidence of alcohol or drug use having become a major organizing factor in the patient's life, dictating how free time is spent, how friends are chosen, and how the day is organized. Efforts by the patient to explain consequences or to characterize them as "not that serious" or as "understandable" should arouse suspicions.

Other Specific Questions

In patients who drink drugs, the presence of recent or previous withdrawal symptoms or complications should be determined. In addition, the presence of tolerance should be determined by evaluating the patient's amount of drug use over time. A complete inventory of social complications should be done, e.g., family problems such as divorce and domestic violence). In addition, an occupational history should be taken to determine if drug use has led to poor job functioning or unemployment. Finally, an inventory of legal problems should be taken, especially those that may relate to drug use, such as driving under the influence.

An inventory of potential medical symptoms and complications should also be taken. These may fall into the following three general categories: (1) complication due to the route of administration of a drug, (2) drug-specific complications, and (3) "environmental" complications of drug use.[31] For example, injection-drug use has been associated with a wide variety of infectious complications such as HIV infection, hepatitis, and bacterial endocarditis.[7] Injection-drug users are also known to be at risk for soft tissue infections, pneumonia, tuberculosis, and peripheral vascular disease. In addition to the route of administration, specific drugs may have their own unique set of associated complications. For example, alcohol dependence is associated with specific central nervous system, cardiovascular, and gastrointestinal problems.[29] Cocaine use has been associated with stroke and myocardial infarction.[32] And, heroin has been associated with renal failure.[7] Finally, various "environmental" complications related to substance abuse result from environmental or behavioral circumstances associated with substance abuse. These complications include tuberculosis and sexually transmitted diseases.[31] It is important to carefully screen for these medical conditions when substance abuse is suspected. In addition, the presence of one or more conditions should alert the clinician to the possible presence of a substance abuse disorder.

Documentation in the Medical Record

A complete substance use history will not be elicited in every clinical encounter, even when an alcohol or substance use problem is suspected. Signs and symptoms of problematic use, however, should be routinely recorded in the clinical chart. *Be specific.* Do not use descriptions such as "social drinker," "occasional use," or "recreational drug use." The basic substance use history for all patients should include the following kinds of information:[20]

Alcohol use	Yes/No
Screening	Negative/Positive
	CAGE Score (0-4)
Other substance use	Yes (indicate substances)
	No

When screening is positive, the following data should be noted as well:

Pattern of use	Frequency, amount per occasion. Number of occasions per week, circumstances, amount required to feel effect, presence of binges.
Preoccupation and efforts to control	Use when had decided not to, or more than intended; changes in circumstances of use; periods of absti-

nence or attempts to decrease amount; loss of control.

Concern by self or others	If yes, note concerned individual and basis of concern.
Problems resulting from use	Briefly describe (social, medical).
Family history	Positive/negative for alcoholism. Positive/negative for other substance dependence or abuse.
Prior treatment	If yes, when, where, and status after treatment.

False Positives

Rapid screening instruments are not diagnostic. They are intended to easily separate those who warrant further evaluation from those who do not. If further evaluation for a substance use problem is negative, this should be documented as well.

DRUG TESTING AND SCREENING

In conjunction with increasing societal concern about drug use, increasingly sophisticated laboratory methods detect drugs of abuse through analysis of body fluids.[23] For example, it is now possible to identify recent maternal cocaine use in hair samples of neonates.[16] The emergence of these drug screening techniques has evoked a number of legal and ethical questions.[13,24] Testing employees for drug use is a practice adopted by many major companies, and smaller firms may follow. The surge in drug testing during the past 10 years has raised a number of legal issues. Some of these issues focus on the validity of the testing procedures, while other issues relate to the reliability of evidence obtained.

It is important to remember that positive results only indicate recent use; they do not necessarily indicate abuse or dependence. Also, laboratory procedures are designated as either screening or confirmatory tests. The most accurate techniques are too expensive for large-scale screening. Thus, if initial screening indicates a presence of substances, it is critical to have confirmatory tests that are more specific and able to separate true positive cases from false positive results.[9,14]

SCREENING FOR PATIENTS AT RISK

Screening is indicated not only to detect an active problem but to identify those persons at risk to initiate risk reduction measures. These persons need to be consistently monitored to detect an emergent problem. Thus, as part of the screening process, it is helpful to be aware of risk factors for substance use problems and thereby identify those more likely to experience problems in the future.

Risk Factors for Acute Problems

The major factors related to acute problems are the cultural norms governing substance use, the types of activities accompanying use, and the medical status that can influence the risk of incidents.

The following societal norms related to drinking are considered predictive of acute problems[33] or harmful use and may be helpful in determining the need for intervention, education, referral, or treatment with patients:

- Solitary drinking.
- Lack of specific drinking norms.
- Tolerance of drunkenness.
- Social tolerance of negative behavior when drinking.
- "Medicinal" use of alcohol to reduce tension.
- Lack of ritualized and/or ceremonial use of alcohol.
- Alcohol use separated from overall eating patterns.
- Lack of childhood socialization into drinking patterns.
- Drinking with strangers, which increases violence.
- Drinking pursued as recreation.
- Drinking concentrated in young males.
- A cultural milieu that stresses individualism, self-reliance, and high achievement.

Virtually all drug use incorporates many of these attributes as well as the added dangers involved with illicit drug use. Cultures or settings in which alcohol or drugs are inexpensive and available throughout the day increase the risk of problems.[25,26]

The activities that accompany substance use can increase the risk of incidents. Any activities that require coordination, reaction time, and quick information processing are dangerous, e.g., driving, using heavy equipment, swimming, or boating. Thus, if use occurs with activities that require attention and judgment, such as child care, there is an increased risk for problems.[19]

Additional risk factors for substance use incidents include medical conditions in which use is absolutely or relatively contraindicated or when multiple drug use is present.[20]

Risk Factors for Dependence

Beyond the problems that arise from acute use because of central nervous system impairment, with extended heavy use there is CNS adaptation, which is evidenced by increased tolerance and by the occurrence of withdrawal syndromes with relative abstinence. These factors are presumptive evidence of alcohol or drug dependence. This may not apply for cannabis, hallucinogens, or phencyclidine (PCP).

A major risk factor for alcohol dependence is a positive family history. Children of alcoholics are at four times greater risk to develop alcohol dependence than those without a positive family history.[15] Historically, considerable effort has been devoted to identifying an "alcoholic personality." Recent research has suggested that individuals who develop alcohol dependence do not have predisposing psychological problems that distinguish them from comparable individuals who do not become alcohol dependent.[42]

Beyond a positive family history, the only other factors that render an individual more vulnerable are too little socialization to alcohol use[42] and the presence of health-compromising behaviors such as use of tobacco or failure to exercise regularly.[6,37]

INTERVIEWING GUIDELINES

Interview strategy is designed to get the essential information about substance use and determine the impairment caused by the disease if present. Ask about the person's relationship to alcohol and drugs—including prescription drugs—not simply inquire about drinking or use. Remember that substance use may be a painful subject for the dependent person; building a relationship facilitates obtaining more data in subsequent encounters.

The following interviewing tips are helpful in broaching questions about substance use problems:[8,12,20]

- *Ask highly specific, factual questions.* Use an open-ended format so that it is difficult for patients either to be evasive or to provide only a simple "yes" or "no" answer.

- *Be persistent.* If the answer to a key question is vague, ask again. Use different words or express your lack of comprehension ("I really don't understand").

- *Be matter-of-fact, as in other medical areas.* If the patient is antagonistic, recognize this as defensiveness, a symptom, not a character trait. Being matter-of-fact and straightforward is easier if you recognize that evasiveness or denial is not intended to deceive you. Instead, such behaviors are unconscious and represent a patient's self-deception and avoidance of emotional pain.

- *Be supportive by focusing on the person.* If the patient talks about others' complaints about his or her drinking, ask, "What is that like for you?" or say, "That sounds like a really difficult situation."

- *Avoid discussion of rationalizations.* This only diverts the interview.

- *Ask only the simplest questions about quantity and frequency.*

Avoid "why" questions. They seldom elicit information you are seeking. However, when problems are detected earlier, there is less impairment of judgment and less denial present. Therefore patients can respond to the situations and feelings that prompt use.

Recognize qualified answers. These can yield considerable information. If the response is "hardly at all," ask, "How often is hardly at all?" Again, with earlier intervention, there is less denial present, and patients may be able to express their own concerns and be relieved at the opportunity to do so.

Recognize attempts to persuade you that there is no problem.

Use other sources to obtain information, such as family members.

Finish the interview with less threatening material.

Research demonstrates that with skillful interviewing techniques, there is good convergence between self-report and collateral sources.[34,38,40,43]

THE FAMILY

Family members of individuals with alcohol and substance use problems are also individuals at risk. Not only does the alcohol-dependent or drug-dependent person have more contacts with health care providers, but so do family members. A study in a university-based family practice setting identified untreated alcohol dependence in 34% of the families seen. Of this group of family members, about 40% had problems that could be attributed to the family disruption, and another 20% had medical problems that might have been exacerbated by stress.[21] Problems that may bring family members to the attention of their primary care provider are stress-related disorders such as migraine headaches, ulcer disease, hypertension, or simply vague physical complaints without a clear organic basis. It is also possible to screen for those affected by the alcohol or drug use of someone else. Asking the question, "Is there anyone whose alcohol or drug use is of concern to you or troubles you?" after completing the usual screening routine can accomplish this. Embarrassment or the sense of stigma that once may have kept family members from directly bringing up concerns about a family member's substance use are now less prevalent. Therefore a family member's volunteering information about another's substance use should be anticipated. The family member just as easily may be a child, parent, or spouse. It is through a clinician's contact with family members that an alcohol or substance use problem may first come to attention.

The clinician needs to be prepared to respond to family members if screening is positive, or if they broach the issue independently. Just as the focus of an interview with the substance user is on the individual and not the drug, the same principle applies to contacts with family. Family members and clinicians tend to want to solve the problem of the substance user, but it cannot be done without the involvement of the user.

Sometimes family members strongly suspect that an alcohol or substance use problem is present, but still have doubts. They do not trust their own judgment. Their relative does not fit their stereotypic view of the alcohol or drug abuser. Furthermore, the changes in behavior that accompany substance use are slow, insidious, and often not immediately evident to others. If or when other family members voice their concerns to the dependent member, the explanations often appear logical and succeed to some degree in explaining the problem. Discussion with family members may be useful in helping them recognize the impact of substance use on their lives. The following questions can be useful in discussions with families:[42]

- Do you worry about this person's drinking or drug use?
- Have you ever been embarrassed by it?
- Are holidays more of a nightmare than a celebration because of this person's use and behavior?
- Are many of this person's friends heavy drinkers or drug users?
- Does this person often promise to quit or reduce drinking or drug use without success?
- Does this person's substance use make the atmosphere tense and anxious?
- Do you find it necessary to hide this person's alcohol or other drug use from his or her employer, other relatives, or friends?
- Has this person ever failed to remember what occurred during a period of substance use?
- Does this person avoid conversation pertaining to alcohol or substance use?
- Does this person justify his or her substance use?
- Does this person avoid social situations where alcoholic beverages will not be served or use drugs before social occasions?
- Do you ever feel guilty about this person's substance use?
- Has this person driven a vehicle while under the influence of drugs or alcohol?
- Are children afraid of this person while he or she is drinking or using drugs?
- Are you afraid of physical or verbal attack?
- Do others comment on this person's unusual drinking behavior or make comments about drug use?
- Does this person have periods of remorse after use and apologize for unacceptable behavior?

- How does the individual's alcohol or drug use affect you, e.g., by influencing the things that you now do or do not do?
- How does it make you feel?
- Has it created financial, legal, or social problems?
- Are you concerned about how this person's substance use affects other family members?

In speaking with family members, it is important to validate their concerns and acknowledge the problems that substance abuse can cause them. State that it may be useful for them to get some assistance to cope with what is typically a difficult situation. Counseling, Al-Anon, or Alateen are potential resources. Make it clear that hoping things will get better or using their other ways of coping with difficult events and stress are unlikely to be satisfactory. The techniques for making a referral discussed in the following chapter are also applicable to situations involving concerned family members.

However, there are several pitfalls in working with families. Avoid becoming the recipient of secret information, as in the call that begins, "I want to tell you something about my husband/wife/mother/daughter/son, but don't let them know I told you." This may not be as limiting a situation with other medical issues, but because the major early symptoms of alcohol and substance abuse problems are behavioral, the important data being supplied cannot be attained with a blood pressure cuff or a simple lab test. Several alternatives are open. One is to suggest the caller accompany the patient to the next appointment, then provide the patient with the opportunity to express concerns or ask questions. Another alternative is to agree not to share the details, but to request permission to inform the patient that you were contacted, by whom you were contacted, and about what concern was expressed. Avoid putting the patient on the defensive: Do not ask, prosecutor style, "Well, do you or don't you?" Take a nonthreatening stance, asking a question such as, "What has been going on that would be causing your _____'s concern?"

Primary care providers have long been aware and sensitive to the impact of chronic disease on the family, e.g., the child with asthma, the preschool-age child with serious developmental disabilities, the child with a seizure disorder that is not adequately controlled, the rapidly deteriorating older adult with Alzheimer's disease, or the juvenile diabetic. The existing expertise in dealing with chronic illness is more than adequate to enable clinicians to deal with families beset by substance abuse problems. Management of chronic disease is part of primary care practice. Many of the central issues important to working with families are related to the phenomenon of chronicity and are not substance use specific. Thus any primary care provider comes with vast experience and skills to help families with substance use problems.

THE COMMUNITY

A clinician's being informed of the community's problems with alcohol and other drugs promotes good clinical care. When there is a high incidence of drug use, it is also important that screening and assessment include sensitivity to drug-seeking behavior. Although exact data on a community's level of drug use may never be available, useful estimates can be attained from discussions with emergency room personnel, alcohol and substance abuse professionals, community workers, social service workers, and school-based personnel. An awareness of the types of substances being used in a community, and by whom, can help hone the clinician's index of suspicion and help target questioning to local patterns of substance and alcohol use.

REFERENCES

1. Babor RF; Ritson EB; Hodgson RG. Alcohol related problems in the primary health care setting: A review of early intervention strategies. (review). *British Journal of Addictions* 81(1): 23-46, 1986. (86 refs.)
2. Barnes HN. Presenting the diagnosis: Working with denial. IN: Barnes HN; Aronson MD; Delbanco TL, eds. *Alcoholism: A Guide for the Primary Care Physician.* New York: Springer-Verlag, 1987. pp. 59-65. (14 refs.)
3. Barry KL; Fleming MF. The Alcohol Use Identification Test (AUDIT) and the SMAST-13: Predictive validity in a rural primary care sample. *Alcohol and Alcoholism* 28(1): 33-42, 1993. (20 refs.)
4. Bernadt MW; Taylor C. Comparison of questionnaire and laboratory tests in the detection of excessive drinking and alcoholism. *Lancet* 1(8267): 325-328, 1982. (32 refs.)
5. Buchsbaum DG; Buchanan RG; Centor RN; Schnoll SH; Lawton MJ. Screening for alcohol abuse using CAGE scores and likelihood ratios. *Annals of Internal Medicine* 115(10): 774-777, 1991. (30 refs.)
6. Bush PJ; Iannoti RJ. The development of children's health orientation and behaviors: Lessons for substance abuse prevention. IN: Jones CL; Battjes RJ, eds. *Etiology of Drug Abuse: Implications for Prevention. NIDA Research Monograph 56.* Rockville MD: National Institute on Drug Abuse, 1985. pp. 45-74 (74 refs.)
7. Cherubin CE; Sapira JD. The medical complications of drug addiction and the medical assessment of the intravenous drug user: 25 years later. *Annals of Internal Medicine* 119: 1017-1028, 1993. (268 refs.)
8. Clark WD. The medical interview: Focus on alcohol problems. *Hospital Practice* 20(11): 59-65, 1985. (10 refs.)
9. Council on Scientific Affairs, American Medical Association. Scientific issues in drug testing. *Journal of the American Medical Association* 257(22): 3110-3114, 1987. (44 refs.)
10. Craig RJ. Diagnostic interviewing with drug abusers. *Professional Psychology* 19(1): 14-20, 1988. (49 refs.)
11. Cutler SF; Wallace PG; Haines AP. Assessing alcohol consumption in general practice patients: A comparison between questionnaire and interview. *Alcohol and Alcoholism* 23(6): 441-450, 1988. (13 refs.)

12. Devenyi P; Saunders S. *Physicians' Handbook for Medical Management of Alcohol- and Drug-Related Problems.* Toronto: Addiction Research Foundation and Ontario Medical Association, 1986. 76 pp.

13. Glantz LH. A nation of suspects: Drug testing and the Fourth Amendment. *American Journal of Public Health* 79(10): 1427-1431, 1989. (17 refs.)

14. Gold MS; Dackis CA. Role of the laboratory in the evaluation of suspected drug abuse. *Journal of Clinical Psychology* 47(Supplement 1): 17-23, 1986. (29 refs.)

15. Goodwin DW; Schulsinger F; Moler N; Hermansen L; Winokur R; Guze SB. Alcohol problems in adoptees raised apart from alcoholic biological parents. *Archives of General Psychiatry* 28(2): 238-243, 1973. (16 refs.)

16. Graham K; Koren G; Klein J; Schneiderman J; Greenwald M. Determination of gestational cocaine exposure by hair analysis. *Journal of the American Medical Association* 262(23): 3328-3330, 1989. (17 refs.)

17. Haynes JT; Spickard WA. Alcoholism. Early diagnosis and intervention. *Journal of General Internal Medicine* 2: 420-427, 1987.

18. Kerns DC; Roberts JC. Preventive medicine in ambulatory practice. IN: Barker RL; Burton JR; Zieve PD, eds. *Principles of Ambulatory Medicine, 4th Edition.* Baltimore: Williams and Wilkins, 1994. pp. 17-29.

19. Kinney J. *Weekend Program Handbook.* Hanover NH: Project Cork Institute, Dartmouth Medical School, 1987.

20. Kinney J. Alcohol use, abuse, and dependence. IN: *Medical Consequences of Alcohol Use.* Timonium MD: Milner-Fenwick, 1989. (300 refs.)

21. Leckman AL; Umland BE; Blay M. Alcoholism in the families of family practice outpatients. *Journal of Family Practice* 19(2): 205-207, 1984. (19 refs.)

22. Lewis DC; Gordan AJ. Alcoholism and the general hospital: The Roger Williams intervention program. *Bulletin of the New York Academy of Medicine* 59(2): 181, 1983. (54 refs.)

23. Montagne M; Pugh CB; Fink JL. Testing for drug use (Part 1): Analytical methods. *American Journal of Hospital Pharmacy* 45(6): 1297-1305, 1988. (65 refs.)

24. Montagne M; Pugh CB; Fink JL. Testing for drug use (Part 2): Legal, social, and ethical concerns. *American Journal of Hospital Pharmacy* 45(7): 1509-1522, 1988. (104 refs.)

25. Moore MH; Gerstein DR. *Alcohol and Public Policy: Beyond the Shadow of Prohibition.* Washington DC: National Academy Press, 1981. 463 pp. (Chapter refs.)

26. Nahas GG. Cannabis: Toxicological properties and epidemiological aspects. *Medical Journal of Australia* 145(2): 82-87, 1987. (59 refs.)

27. Nathan PE. The addictive personality is the behavior of the addict. *Journal of Consulting and Clinical Psychology* 56(2): 183-188, 1988. (41 refs.)

28. National Institute on Alcohol Abuse and Alcoholism. *8th Special Report to the US Congress on Alcohol and Health.* Rockville MD: National Institute on Alcohol Abuse and Alcoholism, 1993. 369 pp. (Chapter refs.)

29. O'Connor PG. The general internist. *Alcohol Health and Research World* 18(2): 110-116, 1994. (28 refs.)

30. O'Connor PG; Bigby J; Gallagher D. Substance abuse and AIDS: A faculty development program for primary care providers. *Journal of General Internal Medicine* 8(5): 266-268, 1993. (8 refs.)

31. O'Connor PG; Chang G; Shi J. Medical complications of cocaine use. IN: Kosten TR; Kleber HD, eds. *Clinician's Guide to Cocaine Addiction: Theory, Research and Treatment.* New York: Guilford Press, 1992. pp. 241-272.

32. O'Connor PG; Selwyn PA; Schottenfeld RS. Medical progress: Medical care for injection drug users with Human Immunodeficiency Virus infection. *New England Journal of Medicine* 331(7): 450-459, 1994.

33. Pattison EM. Cultural level interventions in the arena of alcoholism. *Alcoholism: Clinical and Experimental Research* 8(2): 160-164, 1984. (10 refs.)

34. Rydon P; Redman S; Sanson-Fisher RW; Reid AL. Detection of alcohol-related problems in general practice. *Journal of Studies on Alcoholism* 53(3): 197-202, 1992. (44 refs.)

35. Samo JA; Tucker JA; Vuchinich RE. Agreement between self-monitoring, recall, and collateral observation measures of alcohol consumption in older adults. *Behavioral Assessment* 11: 391-409, 1989. (27 refs.)

36. Skinner HA; Hold S; Sheu WJ; Israel Y. Clinical versus laboratory detection of alcohol abuse: The alcohol clinical index. *British Medical Journal* 292(6537): 1703-1708, 1986. (28 refs.)

37. Soeken KL; Bausell RB. Alcohol use and its relationship to other addictive and preventive behaviors. *Addictive Behavior* 14(4): 459-464, 1989. (11 refs.)

38. Stacy AW; Widaman KF; Hays R; DiMatteo MR. Validity of self-reports of alcohol and other drug use: A multitrait-multi-method assessment. *Journal of Personality and Social Psychology* 49(1): 219-232, 1985. (47 refs.)

39. Steering Committee on Prescription Drug Abuse, American Medical Association. *Prescribing Controlled Drugs.* Chicago: American Medical Association, 1986. 141 pp. (Chapter refs.)

40. Strecher VJ; Becker MH; Clark NM; Prasadi-Rao P. Using patients' descriptions of alcohol consumption, diet, medication compliance, and cigarette smoking: The validity of self-reports in research and practice. (review). *Journal of General Internal Medicine* 4(2): 160-166, 1989. (55 refs.)

41. Tennant FS; Day CM; Ungerleider JT. Screening for drug and alcohol abuse in a general medical population. *Journal of the American Medical Association* 242(6): 533-535, 1979. (18 refs.)

42. Vaillant GE. *The Natural History of Alcoholism.* Cambridge MA: Harvard University Press, 1983. 359 pp. (369 refs.)

43. Watson CG; Tilleskjar C; Hoodecheck-Schow EA; Pucel J; Jacobs L. Do alcoholics give valid self-reports? *Journal of Studies on Alcohol* 45(4): 344-348, 1984. (30 refs.)

FURTHER READINGS

Alexander DE; Gwyther RE. Alcoholism in adolescents and their families: Family-focused assessment and management. *Pediatric Clinics of North America* 42(1): 217-234, 1995. (102 refs.)

This article presents a family-focused approach for the assessment and management of substance abuse problems. The family-focused approach is an alternative or additive model to the individual patient approach, a different approach than that which most pediatricians are traditionally trained. This article discusses why substance abuse in adolescents may be underrecognized by physicians, as well as the importance of the family-focused approach. Clinical suggestions relevant to pediatricians also are provided. The magnitude of substance abuse problems among adolescents, with emphasis on alcohol abuse, is presented. Research findings regarding the reciprocities between family factors and alcohol are reviewed briefly, as are risk factors for alcohol problems in adolescents, family assessment techniques, and specific office screening inventories. Finally, clinical suggestions for primary care physicians are provided. Copyright 1995, Project Cork Institute.

Arborelius E; Bremberg S. Prevention in practice: How do general practitioners discuss life-style issues with their patients. *Patient Education and Counseling* 23(1): 23-31, 1994. (39 refs.)

Forty-six representative consultations in general practice were video recorded. Afterwards the patients and the General Practitioners separately reviewed the recordings and gave their spontaneous comments. A hypothetical-deductive analysis, with a starting point in current health education models, was carried out in order to characterize the health counseling discussions. Life-style issues (diet, exercise, smoking, and alcohol) were discussed in 15 sequences in eight consultations. Four types of sequences were discerned: short advice by the physician (I), a short question by the patient (II), lengthy advice by the physician (III), and a patient-centered discussion (IV). Most health education constructs studied were identified in the type IV sequence but few in type I-III. In the short and the lengthy advice sequences there were similar structures; the strategy to affect patients' life-styles involved condemning patient behaviour and exhorting patients to change. No physician commented positively on these sequences. Appropriate training might improve life-style counseling in general practice through a patient-centered approach and with guidance from constructs in health education models. Copyright 1994, Elsevier Scientific Publishers Ireland, Ltd.

Barnes HN. Listening for stories: Addiction, psychotherapy, and primary care. *Substance Abuse* 16(1): 31-38, 1995. (9 refs.)

The primary care physician can play a key psychotherapeutic role for addicted patients. This paper explores the unique opportunities in a primary care practice for addressing problems of addiction. Listening actively for patients' stories may uncover a hidden history of addiction or provide support for an addicted patient who refuses specialized treatment. Because patients seek care from a primary care clinician for many medical and psychological reasons, the primary physician may be more accessible to the addicted patient than an addiction specialist and may provide a less threatening milieu in which to raise concerns about addiction. The continuity of the primary care relationship enables the physician to bear witness to the patient's struggles with addiction over time, whether in remission or relapse. Copyright 1995, Association for Medical Education & Research in Substance Abuse.

Botelho RJ; Novak S. Dealing with substance misuse, abuse, and dependency. *Primary Care* 20(1): 51-70, 1993. (21 refs.)

This article describes a six-step model that outlines a way for primary care physicians to deal with the full spectrum of alcohol and drug problems. Each step builds on the preceding step. Using this model, clinicians can enhance skills for screening, assessing, and aiding at-risk and problem drinkers. The six-step model incorporates the transtheoretical model of behavior change and uses motivational interviewing strategies and the concept of brief, early interventions. Primary care physicians can apply this model for patients in their offices and in hospital settings where they provide continuity of care. Furthermore, physicians can also use this model to intervene successfully at both the secondary and tertiary levels of prevention. The six steps in this model are screening, assessment, education, agreement, negotiation, and follow-up. It uses a variety of strategies to aid at-risk and problem drinkers. These strategies can help patients and families overcome their ignorance about the role that alcohol plays in their lives and can motivate them toward a healthier life-style. Physicians can select strategies that range from simple advice to motivational counseling. Depending on the presenting problems and the likelihood and severity of an alcohol problem, the physician can select strategies described in this model to develop an individualized approach to motivate at-risk and problem drinkers to move through the phases of behavioral change, precontemplation, contemplation preparation, action, and maintenance. Such an approach can help patients take responsibility for changing their drinking habits. Copyright 1993, Project Cork Institute.

Braithwaite RA; Jarvie DR; Minty PSB; Simpson D; Widdop B. Screening for drugs of abuse: Opiates, amphetamines and cocaine. (review). *Annals of Clinical Biochemistry* 32(March): 123-153, 1995. (205 refs.)

The main burden of care of patients with drug abuse problems falls on specialized treatment centers. Laboratory support in the form of urine screening tests has long been recognized as an integral part of these services. When a new patient is interviewed, the doctor's first task is to diagnose drug abuse. A comprehensive urine screen for drugs carried out at the initial assessment stage is undeniably the best means of arriving at a complete picture of the drug use. Copyright 1995, Association of Clinical Biochemists.

Buchsbaum DG; Welsh J; Buchanan RG; Elswick RK. Screening for drinking problems by patient self-report: Even 'safe' levels may indicate a problem. *Archives of Internal Medicine* 155(1): 104-108, 1995. (46 refs.)

Physicians often screen their ambulatory patients for serious drinking problems by asking questions related to the quantity of alcohol that they consume. Never previously reported was whether this "quantitative" approach to screening can be used to effectively screen ambulatory patients for the presence of a serious drinking problem. The project interviewed 510 patients attending an inner city general medicine practice . . . The sensitivities of reported consumption decline with increasing drinking, while the specificities and positive predictive values rise. The report of drinking between 6 and 12 drinks per week was associated with a positive predictive value of 0.54 for an active Diagnostic and Statistical Manual of Mental Disorders, Revised 3rd Edition, diagnosis. Patient self-report of drinking can be used to screen actively drinking outpatients on the general medicine service for serious drinking problems. Further, in an urban general medicine outpatient population, even federally recommended levels of drinking may indicate a problem. Their data suggest that physicians' recommendations be adjusted for the setting in which they practice. Copyright 1995, American Medical Association.

Center for Substance Abuse Treatment. *Assessment and Treatment of Cocaine-Abusing Methadone-Maintained Patients. Treatment Improvement Protocol (TIP) Series 10.* Rockville MD: Center for Substance Abuse Treatment, 1994. (158 refs.)

This volume is a compilation of materials intended to assist state alcohol and drug abuse agencies to implement federal guidelines that require states to provide for independent review to assess the quality, appropriateness, and efficacy of treatment services receiving funding through block grants. It is particularly directed to methadone treatment services and to the increased utilization of treatment protocols and approaches demonstrated to be efficacious. Copyright 1995, Project Cork Institute.

Center for Substance Abuse Treatment. *Screening and Assessment for Alcohol and Other Drug Abuse Among Adults in the Criminal Justice System. Treatment Improvement Protocol (TIP) Series 7.* Rockville MD: Center for Substance Abuse Treatment, 1994. (41 refs.)

This Treatment Improvement Protocol (TIP) provides practical information regarding the screening and assessment of alcohol and other drug abuse in adults in the criminal justice system. It discusses screening, assessment, and treatment planning. It also examines assessment issues related to primary health care, sexually transmitted diseases, mental health, safety, and relapse. Legal and ethical issues such as the federal regulations on confidentiality are reviewed. Public Domain.

Chan AWK; Pristach EA; Welte JW. Detection by the CAGE of alcoholism or heavy drinking in primary care outpatients and the general population. *Journal of Substance Abuse* 6(2): 123-135, 1994. (44 refs.)

There is a need to improve the diagnosis of alcoholism in clinical settings because alcoholism, particularly in its early states, is often unrecognized in general medical practice and in hospitals. In this study the CAGE questionnaire was used to detect alcoholism or heavy drinking in three populations, namely, alcoholics in treatment (ALC), primary care outpatients (PC), and the general population (GP). Nearly all the ALC tested positive on the CAGE (97.8%), both for current (past year) and for lifetime alcohol-related problems. Among the PC subjects, 44.8% tested positive for lifetime alcohol problems, but the prevalence decreased to 17.2% when only past-year problems were considered. Likewise, 38.3% of the GP sample tested positive for lifetime, but half of these did not meet the 1-year recency criterion. Compared to DSM-III-R criteria during the same time intervals, the sensitivity/specificity of the lifetime CAGE was 91.2%/84% and 76.9%/85.1% in the PC and GP, respectively. The corresponding sensitivity/specificity of the past-year CAGE was 94.4%/97.0% and 74.6%/91.6%, respectively. Thus, the CAGE is an appropriate screening test for alcohol problems in these two populations, but other confirmatory tests or interviews are necessary to eliminate false positives. There were neither gender nor racial differences in the ALC sample responses to individual CAGE questions. However, there were gender differences in the PC and GP samples, with more males responding "yes" to each of the questions. The gender differences probably reflected the higher prevalence of heavy drinking and alcoholism among males. Copyright 1994, Ablex Publishing Corporation.

Cone EJ. Saliva testing for drugs of abuse. (review). *Annals of the New York Academy of Sciences* 694: 91-127, 1993. (134 refs.)

Saliva testing for drugs of abuse can provide both qualitative and quantitative information on the drug status of an individual undergoing testing. Self-administration by the oral, intranasal, and smoking routes often produces "shallow depots" of drug that contaminate the oral cavity. This depot produces elevated drug concentrations that can be detected for several hours. Thereafter, saliva drug concentrations generally reflect the free fraction of drug in blood. Also, many drugs are weak bases, and saliva concentrations may be highly dependent upon pH conditions. These factors lead to highly variable S/P ratios for many of the drugs of abuse. Table 3 provides a compilation of experimental and theoretical S/P (total) ratios determined for drugs of abuse. Estimations of the theoretical S/P (total) ratios for acidic and basic drugs were based on the Henderson-Hasselbalch equation. Saliva pH was assumed to be 6.8 unless reported otherwise by the investigators. Generally, there was a high correlation of saliva drug concentrations with plasma, especially when oral contamination was eliminated. Assay methodology varied considerably, indicating that saliva assays could be readily developed from existing methodology. There are many potential applications for saliva testing for drugs of abuse. Table 4 lists several general areas in which information from saliva testing would be useful. Clearly, saliva drug tests can reveal the presence of a pharmacologically active drug in an individual at the time of testing. Significant correlations have been found between saliva concentrations of drugs of abuse and behavioral and physiological effects. Results indicate that saliva testing can provide valuable information in diagnostics, treatment, and forensic investigations of individuals suspected of drug abuse. It is expected that saliva testing for drugs of abuse will develop over the next decade into a mature science with substantial new applications. Copyright 1993, New York Academy of Sciences.

Conigrave KM; Saunders JB; Whitfield JB. Diagnostic tests for alcohol consumption. (review). *Alcohol and Alcoholism* 30(1): 13-26, 1995. (104 refs.)

Various laboratory tests are available to assist in the diagnosis of hazardous alcohol consumption and related disorders. Standard tests such as serum gamma glutamyltransferase activity and erythrocyte mean cell volume have limited sensitivity, particularly in detecting nondependent hazardous consumption. Most also have poor specificity in that results are affected by common diseases and medications. Over the past 10 years a number of new laboratory tests have emerged. One of these, carbohydrate deficient transferrin, has high sensitivity in detecting persons with alcohol dependence and shows promise for identification of nondependent hazardous drinking; it is also highly specific. Others such as measurement of bound acetaldehyde, serum beta-hexosaminidase, and the ratio of urinary serotonin metabolites offer promise in detecting recent heavy drinking. However, many issues remain unresolved. The newest markers have often been judged by contrasting their values in patients who are clearly alcohol dependent with abstainers or very light drinkers. It is now apparent that some are relatively insensitive markers of hazardous consumption. Future research needs to examine the performance of these markers among subjects with a range of alcohol intakes to fully determine their value in assessing drinking history. In addition, assays capable of some degree of automation need to be developed for analyzing large numbers of samples. Copyright 1995, Medical Council on Alcoholism. Used with permission.

Deitz D; Rohde F; Bertolucci D; Dufour M. Prevalence of screening for alcohol use by physicians during routine physical examinations. *Alcohol Health & Research World* 18(2): 162-168, 1994. (15 refs.)

Patients who visit primary care physicians may not recognize that drinking is the source of their medical problem. Physicians, through screening for alcohol problems, must be able to make this connection if they are to prevent and/or treat the medical consequences of alcohol abuse. The authors review a survey in which primary care patients were asked whether physicians screened for alcohol consumption during routine office visits. They discuss how these results differed among demographic groups and among patients with various levels of alcohol consumption. Public Domain.

Dongier M; Hill JM; Kealey S; Joseph L. Screening for alcoholism in general hospitals. *Canadian Journal of Psychiatry* 39(1): 12-20, 1994. (32 refs.)

In a recently completed study at the North Bay Psychiatric Hospital, a tertiary resource serving a population of about 600,000 in northern Ontario, systematic screening on admission showed a very high proportion of past or present alcoholism. Fifty-seven percent of the patients were identified as having a life prevalence of (current or past) alcohol-related problems through a combination of a questionnaire and a liver function test. This figure is much higher than what is generally observed in mental hospitals. Does it reflect a widespread prevalence of alcoholism in northeastern Ontario, or is it distorted by the pattern of referral to the North Bay Psychiatric Hospital, which typically serves an underprivileged segment of the population? In an attempt to answer this question, this study was carried out in general hospitals (medical and surgical wards). It confirms a higher prevalence of alcohol-related problems (biological, psychological, and/or social) in northern Ontario general hospitals, compared with southern Ontario general hospitals, using identical methods of screening and assessment in both populations. The regional difference (odds ratio) is more evident in higher social classes. A diagnosis of alcohol abuse or dependence (currently active or in remission) was confirmed in 83.5% of the cases with positive screening who underwent the Diagnostic Interview Schedule (revised). This is a robust confirmation of the value of screening. These findings confirm the importance of systemic screening for alcoholism in general hospitals. Copyright 1994, Canadian Psychiatric Association. Used with permission.

Finn P. Addressing the needs of cultural minorities in drug treatment. *Journal of Substance Abuse Treatment* 11(4): 325-337, 1994. (52 refs.)

Many drug treatment programs have difficulty recruiting, retaining, and successfully treating minority patients. Coupled with the fact that cultural diversity among patients is likely to increase, this consideration makes it critical that counselors systematically consider the patient's ethnic and racial background during treatment. Experienced clinicians have recommended a number of approaches for counselors to increase their cultural responsiveness to minority patients, thereby improving treatment effectiveness with this population of substance abusers. Copyright 1994, Pergamon Press.

Friedman AS; Granick S. *Assessing Drug Abuse Among Adolescents and Adults: Standardized Instruments. NIDA Clinical Report Series.* Rockville MD: National Institute on Drug Abuse, 1994. (102 refs.)

This volume is intended as a reference guide to inform drug abuse treatment program staff about screening and assessment instruments for adolescents and adults. The guide is organized in three sections: introduction, assessment instruments for adolescent drug users, and assessment instrument for adult drug users. A series of four tables summarizes and compares the six instruments included. Copyright 1995, Project Cork Institute.

Klein RF; Friedman-Campbell M; Tocco RV. History taking and substance abuse counseling with the pregnant patient. *Clinical Obstetrics and Gynecology* 36(2): 338-346, 1993. (26 refs.)

The discovery of substance use disorders in pregnant patients in the obstetric and gynecologic setting requires an awareness of the importance of this matter and knowledge of the symptoms and signs. Equally important is the ability to interview patients and obtain the necessary information to reach a diagnostic impression. This article offers some practical diagnostic interviewing and counseling guidelines that will help the clinician develop an approach to screening, assessment, and referral of pregnant women with alcohol or drug use disorders. Copyright 1993, J.B. Lippincott Co.

McIntosh MC; Leigh G; Baldwin NJ. Screening for hazardous drinking using the CAGE and measures of alcohol consumption in family practice. *Canadian Family Physician* 40(September): 1546-1553, 1994. (23 refs.)

This report determines the drinking practices of a family practice population, examines the CAGE and questions about drinking as a method of screening for hazardous alcohol use, and examines the relationship between alcohol consumption and CAGE items, particularly in a subgroup of hazardous drinkers. The design is a random survey of patients representative of a clinic population, and the setting is a family practice clinic. Of 1420 patients approached while waiting to see a family physician for medical reasons, 1376 agreed to participate and 1334 turned in usable questionnaires. Drinking measures, CAGE items and CAGE questions, and levels of alcohol use were used to determine current drinking practices. A subgroup of hazardous drinkers was examined in greater detail. Forty percent of male patients and 11% of female patients reported at least one "hazardous" drinking (four or more drinks) day in the past month. Answering "yes" to CAGE items was more specific to drinking for male subjects, who also reported a greater number of maximum drinks with a CAGE score of 2 or more. This brief questionnaire was a feasible tool for identifying family practice patients who could be at risk for developing alcohol problems. All patients could be invited to complete the questionnaire while waiting for their appointments. Copyright 1994, College of Family Physicians of Canada. Used with permission.

Prevatt BC; Worchel FF. A design for conducting effective assessments: Substance abuse and sexual abuse as models. *Employee Assistance Quarterly* 9(2): 47-64, 1993. (23 refs.)

In recent years, increasingly restrictive mental health coverage by insurance companies has resulted in authorizations for shorter treatment periods. Mental health providers have been challenged to deliver briefer therapies and find other ways to reduce costs. This article presents a view that the assessment phase of therapy must become more effective in identifying the scope and severity of mental health problems, as well as become more therapeutic in nature, and therefore more cost effective. A model based on systemic questioning is introduced as a method of increasing the efficacy of initial assessments. This model combines elements of the Milan school of family therapy as well as Carl Tomm's concept of interventive interviewing. Two specific problem areas are chosen to illustrate this model: substance abuse and childhood sexual abuse. A series of interviewing questions is presented, with rationales given for particular questions. Special attention is given to creating an interview that minimizes denial, changes the perception of the problem, portrays the interviewer as nonjudgmental, and combines questioning with therapeutic progress. Copyright 1993, The Haworth Press, Inc.

Rush B; Bass M; Stewart M; McCracken E; Labreque M; Bondy S. Detecting, preventing, and managing patients' alcohol problems. *Canadian Family Physician* 40(September): 1557-1566, 1994. (28 refs.)

This report examines Canadian family physicians' attitudes, beliefs, and practices regarding alcohol use and alcohol-related problems in their patients. The design is a self-administered questionnaire mailed to a random sample of 2883 family physicians. The survey was conducted using a modified Dillman method. Participants were Canadian physicians in active office-based practice during 1989. The sample included certificated and noncertificated members of the College of Family Physicians of Canada, as well as nonmembers of the College. The main outcome measures consisted of the perceived importance of various health-promotion behaviors; the attitudes and beliefs about working with problem drinkers; the current knowledge and practices regarding identifying and managing problem drinkers; and the demographic characteristics. Respondents had a strong sense of role legitimacy in working with problem drinkers, but predominantly negative and pessimistic attitudes. Half the respondents felt they had failed in their work with problem drinkers. More physicians agreed on a psychosocial etiology for alcoholism than on a biological origin. Three quarters of respondents said they "almost always" ask patients about quantity and frequency of alcohol use, and just over one-third "almost always" ask about problems related to drinking. Data also suggest doctors have relatively few patients with alcohol problems and that they need help in responding to such patients. Physicians need more training for their role in identifying and managing patients with alcohol problems. Copyright 1994, College of Family Physicians of Canada.

Schramm W; Smith RH; Craig PA; Kidwell DA. Drugs of abuse in saliva: A review. *Journal of Analytical Toxicology* 16(1): 1-9, 1992. (101 refs.)

There has been substantial interest in the use of saliva as a diagnostic medium for drugs of abuse because it can be obtained noninvasively. Although drugs of abuse have been investigated in saliva for more than a decade, the role of saliva remains uncertain. A clear picture is difficult to obtain because of variations in (1) the analytical methods used; (2) the dose regimen of subjects, which was either unknown or differed between studies; and (3) the elapsed time between drug intake and sample collection. This communication summarizes the studies on the quantitative determination of different drugs of abuse in saliva to elucidate the current status in this area. Marijuana, cocaine, phencyclidine, opiates, barbiturates, amphetamines, and diazepines (or their metabolites) have all been detected in saliva by various analytical methods, including immunoassay, gas chromatography/mass spectrometry, and thin layer chromatography. Initial studies with cocaine and phencyclidine suggest a correlation between saliva and plasma concentrations of these drugs, indicating a dynamic equilibrium between saliva and blood. Tetrahydrocannabinol, the active component in marijuana, on the other hand, does not appear to be transferred from plasma to saliva. However, tetrahydrocannabinol is sequestered in the buccal cavity during smoking and can be detected in saliva. These findings point to the potential role of saliva in the analysis of many illicit drugs. To clearly identify the role of saliva as a diagnostic medium for drugs of abuse, research efforts should be directed towards (1) performing systematic studies on correlations between saliva, blood, and urine and (2) determining the concentrations of drugs and their metabolites in saliva as a function of dose and time after intake. Copyright 1992, Preston Publications, Inc.

Schwartz RH; Clark HW; Meek PS. Laboratory tests for rapid screening of drugs of abuse in the workplace: A review. *Journal of Addictive Diseases* 12(2): 43-56, 1993. (9 refs.)

The use of rapid, on-site drug detection devices is reviewed. These tests, which permit the detection of various psychoactive substances in urine, are easily used by nonskilled personnel. Saliva tests are available for detection of alcohol. These rapid tests have varying degrees of accuracy, and it is recommended that positive outcomes for all rapid tests be verified by standard laboratory procedures. The tests have potential use in the emergency room, doctor's office, drug treatment program, and the workplace. When access to formal laboratory testing is limited by either time or location, an easily portable test can give critical information. A number of commercially available tests are reviewed for method, accuracy, advantages, and disadvantages. Consequently, the interested practitioner should be able to find a suitable screening test from the tests reviewed. Copyright 1993, The Haworth Press, Inc.

Welsh D, ed. The primary care setting: Recognition and care of patients with alcohol problems. *Alcohol Health and Research World* 18(2): 95-168 (entire issue), 1994. (article refs.)

This topic issue with 11 articles addresses assessment in primary care settings. Individual articles focus on specific primary care sites as well as on the general issues of detection, assessment, and educational needs of different health care professions. Copyright 1994, Project Cork Institute.

Wilson DMC. Problem drinkers: Can we identify and help them? (editorial). *Canadian Medical Association Journal* 152(6): 825-828, 1995. (16 refs.)

Most people who have a drinking problem are not alcoholics. Even though problem drinkers tend to drink less than alcoholics and to have a shorter history of heavy drinking, they are still at increased risk of health problems. To significantly reduce the burden of alcohol-related problems on society, priority should be given to reducing the number of problem drinkers. Because physicians are exposed to a large adult population, and because they have credibility in diagnosing problems, they have an important role in encouraging moderation in the use of alcohol. Although the potential for physicians to make a difference is commonly viewed with skepticism, studies have demonstrated that physician interventions can be effective. By working in partnership with other professionals and making use of the community and other resources now available, physicians can optimize the effectiveness of their interventions with problem drinkers. Copyright 1995, Canadian Medical Association. Used with permission.

CHAPTER 3

Engaging the Patient in Treatment

PATRICK G. O'CONNOR, MD, MPH

CLINICAL APPLICATIONS

The goals of this chapter are to assist the clinician to:

1. Understand what motivation is and how it is perceived.

2. Understand the process of motivational interventions.

3. Identify clinician attitudes, beliefs, and behavior that can sabotage identification, confrontation, and referral.

4. Understand the clinical approaches that facilitate behavioral change.

5. Work with a patient's reactions in making referrals for consultation and/or treatment.

6. Develop strategies that effectively address a patient's resistance to entering treatment.

7. Develop management plans when attempts to initiate treatment fail.

Engaging patients in treatment represents a fundamental responsibility of primary care clinicians. Screening and subsequently making a diagnosis represent only the first steps in an often long journey of helping patients manage a health problem. This is particularly important in the management of chronic illnesses. For example, screening for and diagnosing hypertension is typically followed by an initial assessment of potential causes of hypertension along with a search for hypertension-related complications. Once this process is complete, the hard work really begins. If treatment is indicated, what are the available options? Hypertensive patients generally are asymptomatic. They may see little need to make life-style changes such as removing salt from their diet or beginning an exercise program. They may be even more reluctant to take expensive medications that may have troublesome side effects. Thus, the challenge to the primary care clinician is to motivate a hypertensive patient to accept his or her diagnosis and to become involved in treatment by convincing the patient that the benefits are in the future through the prevention of myocardial infarction or stroke.

Engaging patients in substance abuse treatment provides similar challenges. Substance-abusing patients may be "asymptomatic" or unaware of their symptoms. They may not see their substance abuse as a "problem" requiring treatment, and they may have little interest in listening to what their primary care clinician has to say. The life-style changes required to address substance abuse may be particularly "invasive." For example, patients may be asked to change their social structure to remove themselves from "high-risk" situations.

Substance abuse disorders also present a unique set of challenges that distinguishes them from other chronic diseases such as hypertension. For one, the social stigma associated with substance abuse can strengthen a patient's denial of the diagnosis. In addition, many of the "symptoms" may be "social" rather than "medical" and thus make it more difficult for patients to recognize the true problem. For example, family or employment difficulties associated with substance abuse may be less likely viewed as symptoms of a medical condition than a physical complication such as acute pancreatitis. Treatment for substance abuse may also require that a patient be referred to special treatment programs—an additional reason a patient may not follow through on a primary care provider's recommendation.

This chapter focuses on approaches suited to the primary care setting that promote a patient's involvement in substance abuse treatment. Many of these are common sense techniques that clinicians use daily for a wide variety of acute and chronic problems. Specific techniques that are especially applicable to substance abuse issues are emphasized. Primary care clinicians are in a unique position to intervene in substance abuse problems to minimize the likelihood of short- and long-term consequences.

MOTIVATION AND CHANGE

Historically, motivation has been equated with the patient's readiness to change. Until the 1970s, the dominant view was that patients with substance abuse could not be treated unless they wanted help. Treatment programs were often designed to separate motivated persons, i.e., those actively seeking help, from unmotivated ones. Unlike referrals to medical specialists, patients were often required to personally contact a substance abuse treatment program to show evidence of motivation in order to complete a referral for treatment. Perhaps most importantly, patients, family, and professionals alike assumed that "hitting bottom" was a prerequisite for successful treatment. With hindsight, this approach might be considered equivalent to waiting for a hypertensive patient to have a stroke before seeking care.

Motivation was regarded as a patient attribute. Poor motivation was considered a product of maladaptive defense mechanisms or of not being ready. Lack of motivation was often cited to explain unfavorable treatment outcomes. Research and current practice have refuted many of these assumptions.

Factors Viewed as Evidencing Motivation

The literature suggests that clinicians commonly consider various factors as they judge a patient's motivation.[1,24]

Agreement. The patient who challenges, questions, or rejects a clinician's views is often suspect. When patients disagree with a clinician concerning diagnosis or treatment, they are often viewed as "being in denial." Conversely, those who accept the clinician's views are considered not only motivated but "good patients." This simplistic view does not take into account the multiple features—medical and social—that impact patients' decision making. It also ignores the clinician's influence on how patients identify and understand their problems.

Self-labeling. The patient's acceptance or rejection of the label of "alcoholic" or "addict" is sometimes used as an index of motivation. One's willingness to categorize oneself as an addict or an alcoholic was viewed by some as evidencing a patient's recognition of the need for treatment. In the past, sometimes considerable clinical effort went into getting a patient to verbally agree with the diagnostic label. Unfortunately, this kind of pressuring can impede the acceptance of the diagnosis. While it is important to be clear with patients about diagnosis, a more effective approach may be to find areas of common ground while being explicit about the diagnosis and to avoid semantics and labels.

Desire for help. Expressing a desire for help based on recognition of a substance abuse problem is regarded as evidence of motivation.

Generally, this in fact may be an excellent indicator of motivation to change. Exploring the impetus behind help-seeking can provide useful clinical data.

Compliance. Compliant patients are generally considered motivated, whereas "noncompliant" patients are considered unmotivated.

In practice, compliance, especially that which depends on self-report, may be difficult to ascertain. In addition, noncompliant patients may be well motivated but unable to comply for various reasons such as lack of insurance, side effects, or family issues.

Distress. High levels of internal stress may contribute to motivation for treatment.

Stress, however, can be destructive as well as constructive. Distressed patients, while considered motivated, may not be able to focus clearly on the source of the stress or to consider possible solutions.

Studies of differences between individuals who entered alcohol treatment and individuals who did not found that two factors distinguished those who entered treatment. One was the level of perceived severity of illness; the other was cues from the environment. Those who entered treatment regarded themselves as more seriously ill. Also, those who entered treatment reported a higher incidence of recent events that signaled the need to do something.[2,18]

Fear alone does not prompt change. For change to occur in the presence of fear, clear actions must be recognized for escaping the threatening situation. In the absence of these actions, denial is an almost universal response.[36] Thus, for example, those threatened with a job loss are more open to treatment and have a better prognosis than those who have already sustained the loss. The latter patients cannot be directed to do something that can help them retain something of importance.

Substance abuse patients are not unique in this regard. Patients with a variety of conditions display a range of coping devices that can be functional or dysfunctional from the perspective of their primary care giver. Denial, always a response to fear and anxiety, presents difficulty for clinicians. It is not amenable to logic; it does not fade with badgering. The degree of denial is proportionate to the level of internal distress. However, it may ease in response to support. Giving emotional support, conveying hopefulness, and assuring patients that you will stand by them can provide them enough strength to constructively experience

their distress. This can enable them to cope with their emotional pain without further jeopardizing their health and general well-being.

In summary, motivation, operationally defined as an interest to change, can be viewed too simplistically. It can be seen as "present" or "absent" rather than in a spectrum that can shift and respond to a primary care clinician's efforts. In fact, primary care clinicians may play a critical role in motivating patients to change behavior and seek treatment.

The Clinician's Impact on Patients' Entry into Treatment[1,24]

When motivation is viewed primarily as an attribute of the patient, there may be too little appreciation of how primary care clinicians can both assess and enhance patients' motivation and potentially influence patient compliance and treatment outcome. Approaching motivation as a fixed, inherent patient characteristic, particularly in a patient thought to lack motivation, can create pessimism and feed into a self-defeating cycle that undermines clinical efforts. Conversely, when patients are considered motivated, clinician enthusiasm may lead to additional effort. Patients with substance abuse problems are commonly considered notoriously unmotivated and difficult to engage in treatment. This perception is further reinforced to the extent that actual symptoms of substance use problems are mistakenly viewed as evidence of the patient's intrinsic poor motivation or of moral failure.

In examining the clinician's impact on patients' entry into treatment, researchers have examined three clinician attributes:

Hostility. Hostility and moralizing can surface either overtly or covertly in confrontation, an approach commonly used with substance abuse patients. Unfortunately, patient resistance commonly follows a clinician's hostility.

Expectancies. The primary care provider's beliefs and expectations of the patient influence motivation and treatment outcome. When patients perceive professionals as genuinely wanting to help, the patient is more committed to treatment. Similarly, a clinician's beliefs about the effectiveness of substance abuse treatment may significantly impact efforts to motivate patients to seek treatment. An unduly pessimistic attitude about the benefits of treatment may result in a "why bother" attitude. However, a positive expectancy by the clinician can motivate both the clinician and patient to seek treatment.

Empathy. A supportive clinical style helps ensure the patient's acceptance of treatment goals and optimism about treatment. Important components of empathy include respect, warmth, sympathy, and active interest. Empathy requires the clinician to try to see the patients' perspective of their problems. One classic paper on the care of those with chronic illness notes that physicians who perceive problems in their relationships with patients as involving their own limitations and personal attributes are more successful in providing comprehensive care. Thus, it is important to help clinicians accept their limitations and acknowledge their negative feelings.[32] Perhaps most importantly, an empathetic approach may give patients the sense of "partnership" with their provider as they work together to solve problems.

Clinician Responses to Difficult Patient Presentations

With more attention being paid to the reciprocal nature of the patient-clinician relationship, the response of the primary care provider to difficult presentations and difficult patient types has gained importance. In difficult, stressful clinical situations, primary care clinicians' own defenses can lead to dysfunctional clinical responses.[11] There is a range of general patient types and circumstances that is particularly relevant to encounters involving substance use problems. Sometimes the clinician finds himself or herself responding not to the patient but to the patient's situation or to the symptoms that influence "how well" patients assume the traditional, expected sick role. This is communicated to the patient through the clinician's attitudes and behaviors, resulting in a vicious circle of misunderstanding and poor communication.

The characteristics presented in Table 3-1 address some situations in which clinicians may respond to patients in a dysfunctional manner.

In respect to substance use issues, the interaction of patients and clinician has also been viewed in light of the factors that deter any clinical response and decrease the likelihood of a clinician's addressing a substance use problem (Table 3-2).

Studies of nurses' responses to difficult substance abuse patients focused on hospitalized patients perceived as demanding, complaining, frustrating, time consuming, manipulating, impolite, unreasonable, and uncooperative. Several basic nurses' responses were identified—being parental, punishing, avoiding, showing anger, or explaining. These were defined as "fight or flight" responses. A key response factor was the extent to which the nurses felt the behaviors were volitional or beyond the patient's control.[33]

Table 3-1. Frequent Clinician Responses to Common Situations and Patient Types

Situation	Emotional response	Behavioral response
Terminal illness or chronic, incurable disease	Sympathy; feelings of inadequacy, low self-esteem, frustration	Denial, reluctance to discuss illness with patient, avoidance of patient
Patient in emotional crisis	Feeling helpless, out of control, inadequate; physician lacks time or skill to treat emotional aspects	Failure to consult or refer
Institutionally determined termination of relationship	Guilt, sadness	Procrastination or failure to inform patient
Patient type		
Organic brain syndrome/Dementia, or Language/Cultural differences; does not understand explanations of disease or treatment	Impatience, frustration	Hostility, rejection, abruptness, minimizing of symptoms, avoidance
Hostile or Borderline Personality	Taking responses and hostility personally; hatred, feeling threatened	Reciprocal hostility, rejection; power struggle
Overly dependent patient	Initial gratification followed by resentment, anger, impatience, guilt	Hostility, coldness, distancing
Hypochondriacal patient	Impatience, frustration, anger	Rejection, avoidance (prescription given out of exasperation)
Antisocial/Self-destructive patient	Disapproval, anger	Punitive; hostility, rejection (neglect or overtreatment)
Noncompliant patient	Sense of loss of control, threatened authority; anger; frustration	Hostility, rejection, denial (power struggle, loss of interest)

From Gorlin G; Zucker HD. Physicians' reactions to patients. *New England Journal of Medicine* 308(18): 1059-1063, 1983.

Table 3-2. Obstacles to Clinician Involvement

Characteristic	Patient	Clinician
Ignorance	of chemical dependence and its pervasive harmful consequences, e.g., stereotypes	of how narrow and biased one's perception of the illness and the victim is
Fear	of rejection by others	of rejection by patient
Fear	of being incurable and hopeless	of being incapable of managing the illness
Fear	of losing advantages of the chemical dependency	of losing the reason for the patient to visit
Anger	challenging the doctor; passive aggression	disinterest; punitive or judgmental behavior
Rationalization	alibis for substance abuse and consequences	accepting alibis or making excuses for patient's need to abuse
Projection frustration	blaming others for substance abuse and consequences	blaming patient for and showing anger at difficulty in engaging in recovery program
Impatience	desire for instant relief of consequences or recovery	to get patient into recovery program and relieve worry about impending harm
Reluctance	to begin recovery and give up chemicals	to confront patient and risk alienation of patient
Denial	wish to avoid having to change and to accept stigma	wish to avoid conflict and stigmatizing the patient and self

From Fisher JV; Whitfield CL; Liepman MR. Motivating change. IN: *Family Medicine Curriculum Guide to Substance Abuse.* Kansas City: Society for Teachers of Family Medicine, 1984.

Environmental Influences on the Patient and Clinician

To introduce further complexity, the environment of both primary care and substance abuse treatment may influence both patient and clinician motivated to address substance abuse issues. This was clearly evident in the previously described study. Nurses are aware that many environmental factors influence their ability to cope with difficult patients and their resulting frustration, e.g., the long working hours, staffing levels, and competing demands. Environmental factors, specifically identified in respect to substance abuse, entail treatment in settings that patients find embarrassing and/or unacceptable, long waiting lists for nonemergency appointments, multiple clinicians, and workers' morale.[24,34,35] Length of the waiting period before initial intake at a treatment center also predicts patients' keeping of appointments. Waiting time similarly influences patients' following through with treatment. Extended periods between initial contact and an appointment can lead a patient to reassess the severity of the problem and conclude that things "aren't that bad." There is much literature about individuals ready for change at moments of stress. However, without a therapeutic response within 2 to 4 weeks, this opportunity for change may be lost. These individuals will have accommodated for better or worse, and therefore the experience of dis-

tress and their desire and ability to use assistance will have dissipated. Other environmental factors such as distance to travel, schedules, the availability of child care, and financial costs must be considered.

THE PROCESS OF CHANGE

Rather than being considered a trait that is not easily influenced, motivation is becoming regarded as a process with identifiable stages. The natural sequence of steps in making change is pertinent to clinicians because clinical interventions can facilitate the inherent process of change. The stages of change are applicable in the health care setting to any health problem that is going to be positively or negatively affected by health habits. Examples of these include diet, exercise, smoking cessation, and adherence to medications. Proschaska and DiClemente have proposed a transtheoretical model of change that describes specific, consecutive stages through which patients may pass as they attempt to modify their behaviors (Figure 3-1). This model seemingly is particularly applicable to substance abuse. Furthermore, understanding an individual patient's stage of change may be especially relevant to primary care providers.[37]

Precontemplation. At this point the patient is not even considering change. Approximately 20% to 25% of alcohol abusers in a primary care setting in one

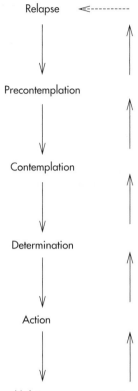

Relapse

Precontemplation

Contemplation

Determination

Action

Maintenance

Figure 3-1. Model of behavioral change process.

study were in this stage. There is no perceived need or plan to change. Patients in this stage may not be consciously aware of certain behaviors or that they have destructive or negative consequences. Instead, the problem is recognized by someone else such as a physician, family member, or co-worker. The appropriate clinical interventions at this point are predicated on the fact that the patient needs a greater awareness of the dangers of his or her present behavior. Thus, basic education followed by advice may be the most appropriate interaction at this stage. Education and advice may need to be presented in a consistent and repetitive manner, with constant reassessment of the patient's understanding of the issues being discussed. In precontemplation, "denial" is most dominant and needs to be recognized and addressed appropriately.

Contemplation. At this point the patient may begin to consider change, although he or she is often quite ambivalent. A patient may see both benefits and drawbacks to a possible change in behavior. For example, a patient might say, "I feel terrible when I wake up sick after a night of drinking, especially when I miss work. But, I enjoy being with my friends and getting out at night." To move forward from precontemplation, patients must perceive that the negative aspects of their behavior outweigh the positive ones. The clin-

ician can play a crucial role in tipping the balance in favor of change by highlighting the pluses associated with change. If the clinician emphasizes only the negative aspects of substance use, the person at this stage is likely to respond by defending the other side. One technique advocated for patients in this state is "reflective listening." This includes careful listening by the primary care clinician accompanied by reflecting or restating statements by the patient. This may help patients gain more insight into the negative aspects of their substance use behavior and help transfer ambivalence into a determination to change.

Determination. In this stage ambivalence gives way to an acknowledgment that a situation warrants action. There may be a sense of the patient's being emotionally reconciled to the need for change, even if there are some perceived losses that result, such as social contacts in the example above. For the patient at this stage, rapid, immediate intervention is important. The patient is often in a state of disequilibrium, needing some resolution. If too much time passes, the individual may return to the stage of contemplation. Thus, a potential opportunity for change has been lost. In this stage the patient needs professional assistance in selecting a course of action. For example, when a patient expresses the desire to quit smoking, the primary care clinician may discuss setting a "quit date" and plan to use a nicotine patch. The patient's task is to recognize the need for change. The clinician's task is to validate that perception and offer guidance on how to accomplish it along with support and reassurance for the changes being considered.

Action. At this stage the patient is actively changing behavior. This may be when the real "work" for both provider and patient begins. Choosing a change strategy and implementing a plan is the focus in this stage. Now, the clinical need is assistance in carrying out the plan. Without formal assistance, the patient may be left to trial and error and may not take the most helpful steps. This is also true for a number of conditions. One of the significant factors at this stage is letting others know of the plan. This increases the likelihood of following through. It also opens up avenues for support and encouragement from others.

Maintenance. Changes are sustained by continuing action. Making steps toward change encourages the desire to make further changes and demonstrates that change is possible. The process of making change is self-reinforcing. Making changes may enhance self-esteem, impart a renewed sense of competence, engender a sense of hopefulness, and prompt support from friends and family. The degree of "work" involved in maintenance may lessen with a prolonged period of abstinence, as new behaviors are more fully integrated into an individual's routines and sense of himself or herself. Obviously this does not mean, however, that relapse is not a possibility.

Relapse. Here the patient reverts back to the previous behavioral pattern. Relapse is often considered part of the "natural history" of substance abuse. If relapse occurs, the patient must once again go through the stages. It is important to be alert to the dangers of any substance use following treatment, to be vigilant to the need to maintain abstinence, and to be aware of how unlikely it is that an addicted person can resume a pattern of nonproblematic use. However, an incident or brief episode of use should not be equated with a complete relapse or viewed as treatment having been futile or progress having been lost.

Clinicians are rarely shocked by some future episode of use, termed a "break in sobriety" or a "slip." Perhaps the most significant aspect of relapse is not that there has been an episode of use, but how it is handled. Some of the most important therapeutic work for patients in treatment occurs because of a break in sobriety. Such an occurrence can be positive if handled appropriately. What has the patient learned? What were the circumstances of use? What steps can the patient take to prevent the recurrence of another episode?

Interventions to Facilitate Change

Clinical approaches to facilitate change by patients are essential in work with substance abuse/dependent patients. One challenge these patients present is that they easily perceive clinical encounters as nonsupportive attacks. Rather than prompting the process of change, this leads to a retrenchment and resistance to change. The following techniques help create an atmosphere in which change is facilitated.[25-28] In addition, Miller and Rollnick have developed an approach of motivational interviewing that has relevance for substance abuse.[27]

Giving advice. Several studies have shown that a clinician's advice can lead to a decrease in consumption of alcohol and a reduction of severity of symptoms. Advice has been described as one form of minimal or brief intervention.[5,7] One study demonstrated that a letter by the physician was sufficient to reduce benzodiazepine use.[6] Another interesting study examined the differences between internists and psychiatrists in giving advice to patients with substance use problems. Patients seen by the internists fared better. The internists made straightforward recommendations that would be given for other medical conditions. In contrast, psychiatrists used a more open-ended clinical style. They would inquire about a patient's feelings toward the recommendations, which tended to heighten the patient's ambivalence. The patients also perceived the psychiatrists' recommendations more as an elective option than as unequivocal, authoritative medical advice.

Providing feedback. The clinician's objective feedback about the nature and severity of drinking-related or drug-related problems may prompt change. This feedback can contrast sharply with the style of feedback generally offered by family or friends, which is laced with emotion and distortions, and which is global—"You always . . . !"—rather than specific. Making clear the discrepancy between a patient's present state and the patient's desired state leads to a sense of dissonance, which becomes a source of motivation. The process of developing discrepancy may be most effective when the discrepancy develops from the patients' own examination of their goals, behaviors, and the impact of their behavior in advancing their goals. Thus, a patient who says, "Why are you pestering me about my smoking? I'm here to get my cough taken care of," may be taught the impact of smoking on the immediate problem. Combining feedback with training in coping skills can further enhance effectiveness.

Setting goals. Feedback in the absence of a goal may be ineffective. Goals and feedback can enhance each other as motivational interventions. Feedback about present negative consequences may induce a discrepancy and an intention to change. Progress toward a clear goal then proceeds, influenced and reinforced by continuing feedback regarding the remaining degree of discrepancy.

Maintaining contact. Some of the most successful motivational interventions reported are relatively simple, involving continuity of contact between patient and the primary care clinician. Patients receiving a personal follow-up letter expressing concern for their welfare and inviting further consultation were found to have a significantly higher self-referral rate for substance abuse treatment. Following a missed appointment, a simple telephone call or a personal letter expressing interest in the patient increased the probability of the patient's returning.

Manipulating external consequences. Frequently those seeking treatment for substance use problems report coercion as part of the impetus to change. For patients within the same treatment program, coerced patients have successful outcomes at an equal if not higher rate than patients who report no coercive element. Those who do best in treatment, such as nurses, physicians, and pilots, are those who will be subjected to random drug screenings, who are aware of close surveillance, and who recognize the negative consequences of a return to use.[29] When the potential negative consequence is ongoing, such as loss of a job if use resumes, this is effective in maintaining change.

Providing choices. Patients benefit more when offered a choice among various intervention alternatives. This also includes eliciting a patient's views of options and the clinician's suggestions. Active participation in choice selection may make patients more invested in their treatment.

Decreasing attractiveness of substance use. Any interventions that decrease the perceived attractiveness of use and increase the immediacy of negative consequences should increase motivation for change. This technique has long been known to substance abuse clinicians as "spoiling the drinking or drug use." For this reason, after a period of intoxication or heavy use, motivation is often heightened if only briefly.

Avoiding labeling. That patients need to verbally acknowledge and accept the label of "addict" or "alcoholic" if any treatment initiated is to be successful has been proven false. Labeling creates a point for contention and argumentation where none need exist. Instead, focus on the problems the patient is having with alcohol or drugs and find a solution. Agreement on these points is all that is required to initiate treatment; a label is irrelevant.[23]

Patient Attributes

While it is often counterproductive to regard patient attributes as indicative of motivation, there are common themes that warrant a clinician's attention. Sensitivity to these following factors may facilitate working with substance use problems:

Distress. Distress is not a good indication of motivation. Even when not evident by the usual cues health care providers use to assess distress, it should be presumed. Distress by itself can lead to plans to reduce fear rather than to prompt more adaptive change. Whether distress becomes functional for prompting change depends on several factors. For one, the patients must become more conscious of their discomfort, which requires that they give up some of the psychological devices that protect them from feeling their anxiety and pain. This requires clinical maneuvers that can enhance the patient's ability to tolerate discomfort. This something can be hope, support, or assistance. It can be someone who sees the patients as ill rather than as irresponsible, self-centered, weak willed, or uncaring. In addition, it is important for the primary care clinician to clarify the sources of distress and how substance use may promote distress.

Self-esteem. Improving self-esteem is often cited by patients as a motivating force. Low self-esteem appears to hinder motivation. Initial help-seeking behavior can be undermined by a desire to avoid failure or disappointment. Generally there is a decrease in effective adaptive response and an increase in use of denial to reduce fear.

Shame. A clinician cannot address the topic of self-esteem without including a discussion of shame. Patients who feel ashamed of their illness may use one of several hiding maneuvers. Some avoid going to the clinic or fail to keep a return appointment. Others may seek care away from their home community or avoid telling family and friends of their condition. During a clinical encounter, the most common response to a perceived insult or embarrassment is for the patient to become subdued and withdrawn. The patient indirectly expresses anger and is rarely able to verbalize the feelings of shame and humiliation.[19]

Clinicians should assume that substance use disorders, just as other medical problems, induce shame, interact with a patient's vulnerabilities, and will be present in the clinical setting. In recognizing this assumption, clinicians can use their skills to manage the social context of the medical encounter. Health care workers need to diminish these feelings, avoid exacerbating them, and recognize and manage their own shame and humiliation, if present. Clinicians can experience shame and humiliation in response to at least four common situations: A failure to successfully identify the disorder; a therapeutic intervention that does not satisfy their own or colleagues' standards; disrespectful behavior by the patient or the patient's family; or their feeling shamed or humiliated through an empathic identification with the patient.

Locus of control. External orientation has been associated with increased anxiety and distress, which therefore may influence motivation for treatment. Patients with a more internal orientation may be more prone to accept and succeed in self-directed, necessary approaches and be less likely to engage in structured, directive plans.

Severity. The data on the relationship between the severity of a problem and compliance with treatment and aftercare have been mixed. This is important because severity has been difficult to measure. What may be true is that a patient's perception of a problem's severity is more crucial to success in entering treatment than the actual severity of symptoms.[2]

The Role of the Family

Within the substance abuse treatment community, considerable attention has been given to the role of the family and others close to the patient in effecting a successful referral for treatment. The technique identified with this, introduced in the mid 1970s, is referred to as "intervention," "crisis precipitation," or "social network intervention." The introduction of this clinical tool effectively countered the then-prevalent belief that an individual had to ask for help before treatment could be successfully initiated. It was also then believed that there was little to be done by family or professionals to ready a patient for treatment who had not "hit bottom." Parenthetically, it must be noted again that subsequent research has demonstrated that those who enter treatment under some coercion do as well, if not better, than those who are not.[3,13,14,38]

A family intervention to promote entry into treatment is generally undertaken under the auspices of a specially trained substance abuse professional. Primary care clinicians may be asked to participate in a family intervention being organized by the substance abuse professional. The process typically involves extensive preparation (several meetings) with the family to assess the family's situation, provide education on the nature of substance abuse problems, and allow them to deal with the considerable negative feelings, whether anger, frustration, or impotence, that have marked their lives. The premise underlying this approach is that the affected individual truly does not recognize that substance use is the source of his or her problems, and that objective feedback from family can help people recognize the nature of the problems. When the preparation is complete, a time is selected to meet with the family member. In the earlier sessions, the family had discussed and agreed on their "conditions" and on the actions they were prepared to take if the dependent family member refused their request to enter treatment. The goal of intervention is to facilitate the affected family member's entry into treatment and to allow the other family members to disengage from dysfunctional relationships with the ill member and begin to address their own needs.[36]

The family intervention was developed and has been primarily used in outpatient settings. However, there have been efforts to use the same technique with alcohol-dependent patients whose hospital admission is alcohol related. In a study of trauma patients, the technique was implemented whereby alcohol-related trauma patients were identified, their family was consulted, and an intervention conducted when the patient was ready for discharge. As part of the plan, the patient's suitcases were packed, a bed was reserved in a treatment program, and the patient's outside responsibilities were dealt with so the patient could participate in inpatient substance abuse treatment. If the patient accepted treatment, the transfer was made immediately. In a pilot study, of the patients approached, all were successfully referred, providing a model for combining treatment of alcohol-related injuries with treatment of alcoholism.[9]

More recently, a model of "Network Therapy" has been developed for the treatment of addiction. This is directed not so much in engaging individuals in treatment as it is in providing ongoing care; it recognizes that a patient's social network of family, friends, and co-workers can be an important source of support and help change patient behavior. Galanter has proposed this model as suitable to office practice.[8] Although outcome research has not been undertaken, this approach shows promise in providing enhanced support in the home and work environment.

MANAGEMENT PLANS

Management of Patients Who Are Willing to Accept Treatment

When the primary care provider has diagnosed substance abuse and the patient has agreed to engage in treatment, the primary care clinician needs to be ready to offer help immediately. There may be a small window of opportunity during which patients are willing to accept advice on changing their substance using behaviors. Thus, primary care clinicians need to "seize the moment" and offer immediate, specific, and concrete suggestions regarding substance abuse treatment. The treatment intervention should begin immediately, right in the office at the time the patient agrees to engage in treatment. Some patients may receive significant benefit from office-based interventions and suggestions and may not necessarily require referral to a substance abuse treatment specialist.

Among those patients needing referral, there may be a subpopulation who will not initially enter a formal substance abuse treatment program because of the perceived stigma attached with such programs, because of their denial, or because they have not fully accepted the implications of the diagnosis. In any case, the primary care clinician needs to offer a menu of possible options with specific guidance on how the patient should proceed. When a substance abuse referral is indicated and the patient accepts such referral, the primary care clinician needs to be aware of the treatment possibilities in the community, as well as how to access these and how to communicate effectively with programs so that care may be provided in a coordinated fashion; this keeps the primary care clinician informed and involved every step along the way.

Office-Based Interventions

It is well documented that the simple giving of advice by primary care clinicians can be a very powerful tool in the primary care setting, particularly for substance abuse. Research on both alcohol use and smoking have demonstrated that "brief" or "minimal" interventions can significantly decrease harmful behaviors associated with substance use.[4] The concept of minimal intervention is discussed in more detail in the next chapter. It is important for primary care providers to remember to keep substance abuse issues "on the table" with their patients so that they are discussed repeatedly on a longitudinal basis. Again, this is consistent with the way other chronic diseases such as hypertension or diabetes are cared for in the primary care setting. If the primary care clinician makes it clear that this is an important health-related issue, the patient is more likely to concur and perhaps accept advice.

Advice on substance abuse in primary care settings should be given in a structured fashion. This begins with informing the patient of the basis of the substance abuse diagnosis by noting the specific medical and social complications of substance use, as well as the symptoms of dependence, tolerance, and loss of control. In this context, advice should be clear on how the patient should deal with these issues. Although research hasn't fully clarified this issue, it would appear sensible to clearly recommend that the goal should be abstaining from substance use rather than setting a goal of returning to "controlled" substance use. This message should be consistent and unwavering, as patients may seek support for behaviors that fall short of abstinence.

When evaluating a substance-using patient, it is also important to carefully consider the possibility of a significant withdrawal reaction. Along with nicotine, techniques have been developed for outpatient withdrawal from alcohol and opioids that are applicable to primary care settings.[30,31] However, patients who may have more severe withdrawal, have a history of withdrawal complications such as seizures, or have significant medical or psychiatric comorbidity might be better withdrawn in an inpatient setting.

Referring Patients to Substance Abuse Treatment

Once it is clear that a patient will require services beyond those offered in an office setting, referral to substance abuse treatment programs must be considered. The process of making a referral may add greater weight to the primary care clinician's argument that something needs to be done. As stated earlier, it is critical that the primary care clinician be familiar with available treatment options in the community. For example, if the primary care clinician intends to refer patients to self-help groups such as Alcoholics Anonymous or Narcotics Anonymous, it is important that he or she be familiar with the basic principles of these programs and their locations in the community. In fact, primary care clinicians themselves are encouraged to attend "open" self-help group meetings so they can learn directly how these meetings work and can talk to their patients in a more informed fashion.

Similarly, referral to a formal substance abuse program needs to be done with a knowledge of how the program is structured and what therapies will be employed. The primary care physician should develop a working relationship with the staff of programs to which they commonly refer patients to ensure effective communication between the health care team. Finally, the primary care clinician will play an important role in supporting the work going on in substance abuse treatment programs. For example, when patients return to the office for medical or substance abuse-related problems, a discussion of the patient's progress in his or her substance abuse treatment program can greatly support the work being done in those programs.

When the patient recognizes the need for treatment, a number of steps can help ensure that a referral for treatment goes smoothly and successfully. In a referral for treatment, the following are useful guidelines.[15]

- *Use of medical authority.* Make it clear to the patient and family that substance use problems are a medical concern, that additional resources are necessary to treat them, and that it is a condition potentially too serious to disregard. Also make it clear that the patient is not to blame for having an illness and that successful treatment is possible.

- *Provide support.* Inform the patient about the resources for help; explain your continuing availability and involvement in care.

- *Provide basic information.* Use the patient's own history to explain that alcohol or other substance use can cause serious problems. Also point out that because of the pharmacological properties involved, substance use can interfere with the patient's ability to accurately perceive what is going on.

- *Inform, educate, and support family.*

- *Be active.* Do not simply provide an agency name and phone number. Have your office set up a specific appointment, with a specific program, including whom you can contact later to ensure that your patient follows through with treatment. Some agencies require the patient to schedule the initial appointment. In this case, have the patient make the call from your office. This small gesture can translate into an incredible amount of support.

- *Assure the patient of your willingness to be involved in continuing care.* Request a follow-up report or discharge summary. Define your role in the patient's ongoing care. Anticipate scheduling medical visits to monitor the patient's status as with any other disease.

In effecting a referral, there is one important caveat. *Know the referral sources.* It is helpful to have basic information available, such as names of the available programs, inclusion and exclusion criteria for admission, admission hours, name of the intake worker, costs, payment schedules, and the level of medical care provided.

How to Select a Treatment Program

In selecting a treatment program, consider the following points:[16]

- Seek a specialized substance abuse treatment program, not a solo practitioner or psychotherapist.
- Look for staff with professional training and not only "life experience."
- Determine if the program can offer the standard components of treatment; medical management; individual, group, and family therapy; introduction to self-help groups; and patient education. Does it offer both outpatient and inpatient care?
- Ask colleagues for programs with which they have worked and had good patient outcomes.
- Identify a potential resource *before* you need it.

There are no "magic bullets" and no perfect or guaranteed treatment settings or approaches. Beyond pretreatment status, family involvement and a patient's remaining in treatment are among the major determinants of outcome in program effectiveness. Through the encouragement of family and patient, you are in a position to be a positive influence.

As a primary care provider, you do not need to decide which type of substance abuse treatment is indicated. Substance abuse treatment professionals can assist with treatment planning and disposition. The factors that substance abuse clinicians will consider in developing treatment plans are summarized in Box 3-1.

Types of Treatment Programs

Various treatment programs are available for alcohol- and drug-abusing patients. The most common types of programs include detoxification services, inpatient treatment and rehabilitation outpatient therapy, long-term residential care, and self-help groups such as AA, NA, and CA. One intensive approach used primarily with drug abusers is the therapeutic community (TC), which is organized as an intensive group therapy program. Patients are closely involved with one another, with the goal of defining, instilling, and reinforcing functional behavior by peer example and peer pressure.

Box 3-1

Developing Management Plans

In Respect to the Data Base
- What is known about the patient?
- What does the patient need?
- What is the family's understanding of the problem?
- What treatment will the patient accept?
- Will concerned others continue to seek help for themselves, thus allowing for future intervention should the need arise?

In Respect to the Patient
- What is the nature of the substance use problem?
- What substances are being used and to what degree of dependence?
- What is the level of recognition of the problem?
- How does the patient conceptualize the problem?
- What is the degree of recognition of need for treatment?
- What are the community and family supports?
- What is the extent of dysfunction and in what spheres?
- Does the patient require a protected environment?

In Terms of Resources
- Who in the community and extended family can help the patient recognize the dysfunction and the need for change and promote efforts to enter care?
- What formal services are available: Evaluation, detoxification, residential, outpatient care, family counseling, special programs for women or adolescents, self-help groups?
- What are the community-based services?
- What "holes" in the formal system must be filled by creative ingenuity?

In Facilitating Referral for Treatment
- Remember movement into treatment may be an extended process.
- Provide treatment that the patient will accept, and devise strategies to monitor status.
- Use community health and human service personnel to maintain contact and reinforce need for treatment.
- If needed, develop a contract of "What if . . . ?"

From *A Curriculum for Primary Care Providers*. Hanover NH: Project Cork Institute, 1988.

Since we want to match our patients with the modality that will make the biggest impact, which strategy will work the best? For many years the 28-day inpatient substance abuse treatment was accepted as the standard for alcohol and drug dependency treatment. When these inpatient programs became the standard of alcoholism rehabilitation, both the patients and staff were different from those in programs today. In that era, by the time patients entered treatment, they were older than those patients admitted today, had late stage symptoms often accompanied by serious secondary medical complications, and were faced with the loss of family, job, and other social supports. Long-term residential rehabilitation was needed to deal with the level of dysfunction present, and further outpatient treatment simply was not available. Thus, everyone needing care had essentially two options: formal treatment limited to residential care or self-help.

It is becoming accepted that intensive and lengthy inpatient treatment may not necessarily be more effective than outpatient or brief treatment for many patients.[12,22,26] Today more patients are being identified and admitted to treatment at younger ages and in earlier stages of substance abuse.

Research on treatment outcome indicates that pairing patients to a specific treatment is significantly more effective than employing a unitary model of treatment.[10,12] In fact, one study demonstrated that the usual information regarding the amount, duration, and intensity of a patient's substance abuse problem is often the least useful for planning treatment, determining the most appropriate treatment modality in which to make a referral, or predicting the overall outcome of treatment.[21] The findings indicate that the most useful data for developing treatment plans for patients with alcohol and drug problems are those regarding pretreatment status, in terms of psychiatric status, employment, and legal problems. Whatever the treatment approach, if these issues are not addressed, the patient is at greater risk for relapse.

Through joint support of the National Alcohol and Drug Institutes (NIAAA and NIDA), a patient assessment instrument, the Addiction Severity Index (ASI), was developed to promote the matching of patients to treatment and to facilitate treatment outcome research. The ASI has proven an effective and comprehensive diagnostic tool for determining the extent and severity of alcohol and drug problems. It is a structured, 45-minute clinical interview designed to assess problem severity in seven commonly affected domains: medical condition, employment, drug use, alcohol use, illegal activity, family relations, and psychiatric condition. There is also a subjective rating of the problem areas by the patient. The design of the ASI was based on the premise that treatment must take into account problems that may have contributed to the substance use problem as well as those that have resulted from it. The Index has also been used to match patients to treatment according to the nature of their symptoms.[20] Even when the patient's treatment needs are identified, there are the issues of the patient's ability to pay for treatment, distance to treatment settings and support groups, and the importance of support for these efforts.

When Attempts to Initiate Treatment Fail

When patients with substance use problems refuse referrals for treatment, it is important to discern what the patient is actually refusing. Perhaps the patient will be willing to speak with a substance abuse specialist in the health clinic or practice site, as opposed to actually going to a new, unknown service provider. Some patients may believe that they can rid themselves of their problems by an act of will and have every intention of trying hard to do so.

When treatment is refused, the first strategy is to develop an agreement or a "contract" with the patient that specifies what the patient will do if problems continue. The clinician can offer hope that the patient does succeed, while noting that treatment of the disease is not an issue of willpower. Making comparisons with other medical conditions in which willpower would clearly be insufficient may be helpful.

From the patient's perspective, in negotiating a contract, the clinician is recognizing the patient's desire for things to get better. In such contracts the clinician lays the groundwork for evaluating the patient's hypothesis that he or she is in control of his or her substance use. If a patient finds that efforts to exert control are ineffective, the need for treatment becomes apparent and more acceptable to the patient.

The points to consider if a patient refuses treatment are summarized in Box 3-2.[17]

The prognosis with treatment is promising for patients with substance use problems. The challenge for clinicians is to foster entry into treatment. When patients with alcohol and drug use problems are regarded as any other patient having a serious illness, and when effective interventions are employed, the chances of engaging the patient in treatment are higher. If initial efforts to promote a patient's entry into treatment are unsuccessful, do not be discouraged. Substance use problems are such that there inevitably will be another crisis and another opportunity.

If Efforts to Initiate Treatment Fail

Primary Clinician's Tasks

- Negotiate an agreement with the patient about the steps to be taken if future problems arise.
- Inform and involve community health workers or other human service workers with the patient and/or family.
- Provide necessary, ongoing medical care whether related or unrelated to alcohol or substance abuse or dependence.
- Make the primary problem clear to patient, family, and others involved in general care.
- Remain ready to arrange and facilitate treatment.
- Avoid enabling the patient to continue alcohol or substance abuse. For example, do not prescribe sedative-hypnotics or anxiolytic medication or authorize "sick time," disability.
- *Be alert to the next crisis.*

Community Health and Human Service Workers' Tasks

- Be careful not to support the patient's denial by engaging in counseling for other problems. This can not only foster denial but goes against the traditional wisdom, namely that use of chemicals by those in counseling or therapy is contraindicated because patients use substances to "escape" or cope with the problems rather than use the therapy.
- Continue to point out the connection between difficulties and substance use.
- Distinguish between the patient's efforts to cope with the problem rather than the means selected to do so. Support the patient's efforts to tackle the problem in his or her own way, while pointing out that most people do not successfully treat themselves but need the assistance of treatment programs.
- Provide support to the family and support family members' efforts to get counseling as affected individuals.
- As future crises occur, encourage the patient to seek the assistance that was refused previously.

From Kinney J. Alcohol use, abuse, and dependence. IN: *Alcohol Use and Its Medical Consequences.* Timonium MD: Milner-Fenwick, 1989.

REFERENCES

1. Allan C. Seeking help for drinking problems from a community-based voluntary agency: Patterns of compliance amongst men and women. *British Journal of Addiction* 82(10): 1143-1147, 1987. (23 refs.)
2. Bardsley PE; Beckman LJ. The health belief model and entry into alcoholism treatment. *International Journal of the Addictions* 23(1): 19-28, 1988. (13 refs.)
3. Baughan DM. Crisis precipitation in alcoholism. *Western Journal of Medicine* 145(5): 680-681, 1986. (5 refs.)
4. Bien TH; Miller WR; Tonigan JS. Brief interventions for alcohol problems: A review. (review). *Addiction* 88(3): 315-336, 1993. (94 refs.)
5. Chick J; Lloyd G; Crombie E. Counseling problem drinkers in medical wards: A controlled study. *British Medical Journal* 2990(6473): 83-89, 1985. (11 refs.)
6. Cormack MA; Owens RG; Dewey ME. The effect of minimal interventions by general practitioners on long-term benzodiazepine use. *Journal of the Royal College of General Practitioners* 39(327): 408-411, 1989. (15 refs.)
7. Edwards G; Orford J; Egert S; Gutherie S; Hawker Ahensmaan C; et al. Alcoholism: A controlled trial of 'treatment' and 'advice.' *Journal of Studies on Alcohol* 38(5): 1004-1031, 1977. (39 refs.)
8. Galanter M. Network therapy for addiction: A model for office practice. *American Journal of Psychiatry* 150(1): 28-36, 1993. (72 refs.)
9. Gentilello LM; Duggan P; Drummond D; Tonnesen A; Degner EE; Fischer RP; Reed RL. Major injury as a unique opportunity to initiate treatment in the alcoholic. *American Journal of Surgery* 156(6): 558-561, 1988. (20 refs.)
10. Glaser FB. Anybody got a match? Treatment research and the matching hypothesis. IN: Edwards G; Grant M, eds. *Alcoholism Treatment in Transition.* Baltimore: University Park Press, 1980. pp. 178-196. (56 refs.)
11. Gorlin R; Zucker HD. Physicians' reactions to patients. *New England Journal of Medicine* 308(18): 1059-1063, 1983. (22 refs.)
12. Harrison PA; Hoffmann NG; Gibbs L; Hollister CD; Luxenberg MG. Determinants of chemical dependency treatment placement: Clinical, economic, and logistic factors. *Psychotherapy* 25(3): 356-364, 1988. (7 refs.)
13. Johnson Institute. *How to Use Intervention in Your Professional Practice: A Guide for Helping Professionals Who Work with Chemical Dependents and Their Families.* Minneapolis: Johnson Institute Books, 1987. 110 pp. (22 refs.)
14. Johnson VE. *I'll Quit Tomorrow, Revised Edition.* New York: Harper & Row, Publishers, Inc, 1980. 182 pp. (11 refs.)
15. Kinney J, ed. *The Busy Physician's Guide to the Management of Alcohol Problems.* Chicago: American Medical Association, 1988. 2 pp.
16. Kinney J. Alcohol use, abuse, and dependence. IN: *Alcohol Use and Its Medical Consequences.* Timonium MD: Milner-Fenwick, 1989. (300 refs.)
17. Kinney J. *Medical Student Handout.* Dartmouth-Hitchcock Weekend Program. Hanover NH: Project Cork Institute, Dartmouth Medical School, 1989.
18. Krampen G. Motivation in the treatment of alcoholism. *Addictive Behaviors* 14(2): 197-200, 1989. (7 refs.)
19. Lazare A. Shame and guilt in the medical encounter. *Archives of Internal Medicine* 147(9): 1653-1658, 1987. (48 refs.)

20. McLellan AT; Luborsky L; Cacciola J; Griffin J; McGahan P; O'Brien CP. *Guide to the Addiction Severity Index: Background, Administration, and Field Testing Results.* Rockville MD: National Institute on Drug Abuse, 1986. (34 refs.)

21. McLellan AT; Luborsky L; O'Brien CP; Barr HL. Alcohol and drug abuse treatment in three different populations: Is there improvement and is it predictable? *American Journal of Drug and Alcohol Abuse* 12(1/2): 101-120, 1986. (21 refs.)

22. Malla AK. Day treatment of alcoholism: An outcome study. *Canadian Journal of Psychiatry* 32(3): 204-210, 1987. (31 refs.)

23. Miller WR. Motivational interviewing with problem drinkers. *Behavioural Psychotherapy* 11(3): 147-172, 1983. (22 refs.)

24. Miller WR. Motivation for treatment: A review with special emphasis on alcoholism. *Psychological Bulletin* 98(1): 84-107, 1985. (272 refs.)

25. Miller WR. Increasing motivation for change. IN: Hester RK; Miller WR, eds. *Handbook of Alcoholism Treatment Approaches.* New York: Pergamon Press, Inc, 1989.

26. Miller WR; Hester RK: Inpatient alcoholism treatment, who benefits? *American Psychologist* 41(7): 794-805, 1986. (29 refs.)

27. Miller WR; Rollnick S. *Motivational Interviewing: Preparing People to Change Addictive Behavior.* New York: Guilford Press, 1991.

28. Miller WR; Sanchez VC. Motivating young adults for treatment and lifestyle change. Paper presented at the conference on Issues in Alcohol Use and Misuse by Young Adults, University of Notre Dame, South Bend IN, April 25-26, 1988.

29. Morse RM; Martin MA; Swenson WM; Niven RG. Prognosis of physicians treated for alcoholism and drug dependence. *Journal of the American Medical Association* 251(6): 743-746, 1984. (18 refs.)

30. O'Connor PG; Horwitz RI; Gottlieb LD; Kraus ML; Segal ST. The impact of gender on clinical characteristics and outcome in alcohol withdrawal. *Journal of Substance Abuse* 10(1): 59-61, 1993. (10 refs.)

31. O'Connor PG; Waugh ME; Carroll KM; Rounsaville BJ; Diagkogiannis IA; Schottenfeld RS. Primary care-based ambulatory care opioid detoxification: The results of a clinical trial. *Journal of General Internal Medicine* 10(5): 255-260, 1995. (21 refs.)

32. Ort RS; Ford AB; Liske RE; Pattishall EG. Expectation and experience in the reactions of medical students to patients with chronic illness. *Journal of Medical Education* 40(9): 840-849, 1965. (7 refs.)

33. Podrasky DL; Sexton DL. Nurses' reactions to difficult patients. *IMAGE: Journal of Nursing Scholarship* 20(1): 16-20, 1988. (48 refs.)

34. Rees DW. Prospective patients' reactions to alcoholism clinic referral. *Alcohol and Alcoholism* 21(3): 247-250, 1986. (13 refs.)

35. Rees DW; Beech HR; Hore BD. Some factors associated with compliance in the treatment of alcoholism. *Alcohol and Alcoholism* 19(4): 303-307, 1984. (18 refs.)

36. Rogers RW. A protection motivation theory of fear appeals and attitude change. *Journal of Psychology* 91:93-114, 1975. (80 refs.)

37. Samet JH; Bega M; Nuciforo S; Williams C. Assessment of readiness for behavioral change of substance abusers in primary care. *Journal of General Internal Medicine* 10(x): 48, 1995. (0 refs.)

38. Sisson RW; Azrin NH. Family member involvement to initiate and promote treatment of problem drinkers. *Journal of Behavior Therapy and Experimental Psychiatry* 17(1): 15-21, 1986. (27 refs.)

FURTHER READINGS

Anderson P. Effectiveness of general practice interventions for patients with harmful alcohol consumption. (review). *British Journal of General Practice* 43(374): 386-389, 1993. (26 refs.)

Harmful alcohol consumption can have severe consequences for both the individual and society. A review of the six published studies on the effectiveness of general practitioner intervention for individuals with harmful alcohol consumption suggests that between 5 and 10 minutes of advice leads to reductions of alcohol consumption of around 25% to 35% at follow-up 6 months or 1 year later. Two of the three studies that failed to demonstrate an intervention effect had inadequate sample sizes, and in two of the studies the control group was a comparison group that received minimal advice to reduce alcohol consumption. There was greater evidence for an intervention effect among men than woman. The methodological problems of the studies are discussed. Copyright 1993, British Journal of General Practice.

Babor TF. Avoiding the horrid and beastly sin of drunkenness: Does dissuasion make a difference? *Journal of Consulting and Clinical Psychology* 62(6): 1127-1140, 1994. (51 refs.)

Nearly 3 centuries ago, an anonymous English author prepared an educational brochure to dissuade problem drinkers from the "horrid and beastly sin of drunkenness" (Anonymous, 1705). During the past 2 decades, more than 25 randomized trials have been conducted in 12 countries to evaluate 2 basic questions: (a) Does dissuasion make a difference, and (b) What kinds of dissuasions work best? In response to the first question, studies indicate that dissuasion does make a difference with heavy drinkers who have not developed severe alcohol dependence. In response to the second question, the evidence is more equivocal because of the practical and methodological problems encountered in the comparison of different interventions. It is concluded that changes sometimes attributed to specific behavioral and psychological interventions may be due to a combination of advice, individual motivation, and nonspecific social influence. Copyright 1994, American Psychological Association, Inc.

Booth RE; Watters JK. How effective are risk reduction interventions targeting injecting drug users? (review). *AIDS* 8(11): 1515-1524, 1994. (66 refs.)

This article examines the environment and interventions that may have led IV drug users to alter behaviors and thereby reduce risk of HIV infection. It reviews 27 published studies on risk reduction efforts. The designs and their limitations are discussed and presented in tabular form. The results of each study are briefly summarized. The discussion focuses particularly upon methodological concerns. Copyright 1995, Project Cork Institute.

Buchsbaum DG. Effectiveness of treatment in general medicine patients with drinking problems. *Alcohol Health and Research World* 18(2): 140-145, 1994. (33 refs.)

Early detection of alcohol problems is vital if intervention and treatment are to be successful. The author offers ways in which primary care providers can better detect which of their patients have alcohol problems. The author reviews the evidence, which shows that even brief (5- to 15-minute) office-based interventions can positively influence patients' drinking behavior. Public Domain.

Cohen SJ; Halvorson HW; Gosselink CA. Changing physician behavior to improve disease prevention. *Preventive Medicine* 23(3): 284-291, 1994. (75 refs.)

Physicians often fail to provide nationally recommended preventive services for their patients. Addressing this, the authors have reviewed selected literature on changing physician behavior using the organizational construct of the "readiness for change" transtheoretical model. This model suggests that behavior evolves through stages from precontemplation, to contemplation, to preparation, to initiation, and to maintenance of change. Traditional continuing medical education may affect knowledge and beliefs but rarely results in behavior change. However, motivational strategies such as practice feedback reports and influential peers can foster stage change. Successful interventions aimed at physicians preparing for change frequently use an office system approach that targets not only physicians but office staff and patients. Illustrating how the readiness to change model can guide the design and implementation of interventions, the authors describe strategies being used in a state-wide randomized controlled trial to improve cancer prevention counseling and early detection by primary care physicians. The multistage interventions of Partners for Prevention include support from a medical liability carrier, a motivational videotape, a task-delineated office manual, chart flowsheets, patient activation forms, practice feedback reports, a designated prevention coordinator within each practice, and regular telephone calls and office visits by project staff. Note: The paper also comments upon the role of nonphysician office staff. Copyright 1994, Academic Press, Inc.

Cunningham JA; Sobell LC; Sobell MB; Agrawal S; Toneatto T. Barriers to treatment: Why alcohol and drug abusers delay or never seek treatment. *Addictive Behaviors* 18(3): 347-353, 1993. (15 refs.)

Reasons for delaying or not seeking treatment were compared between outpatient alcohol and drug abusers and between alcohol abusers who had either resolved their problem without treatment, were currently not resolved, or were in an outpatient treatment program. Outpatient alcohol and drug abusers exhibited few differences in their endorsed reasons for delaying seeking treatment. There were, however, several differences between resolved and nonresolved alcohol abusers who had never sought treatment and alcohol abusers in treatment, e.g., endorsing items such as "wanted to handle problem on own," or "didn't think I had a problem." Such differences may explain why some problem drinkers do not seek treatment. Treatment implications of these findings are discussed. Copyright 1993, Pergamon Press.

Cunningham JA; Sobell LC; Sobell MB; Gaskin J. Alcohol and drug abusers' reasons for seeking treatment. *Addictive Behaviors* 19(6): 691-696, 1994. (18 refs.)

Patients at two treatment facilities were asked at assessment how influential each of 10 possible reasons were in their decision to change their alcohol or drug use. Patients at both facilities most often endorsed "weighing the pros and cons of drinking or drug use" and a "warning from spouse." Patients' reasons for seeking treatment were also examined in relation to treatment compliance. Three reasons—"weighing the pros and cons," "hitting rock bottom," and experiencing a "major life-style change"—were predictive of treatment compliance. Patients who rated any of these reasons as influential were more likely to enter and complete treatment. Although more research is needed, knowledge of patients' reasons for seeking treatment might be useful in treatment matching. Copyright 1994, Pergamon Press.

Horvath AT. Enhancing motivation for treatment of addictive behavior: Guidelines for the psychotherapist. *Psychotherapy* 30(3): 473-480, 1993. (33 refs.)

Establishing sufficient motivation for treatment of addictive behavior, and maintaining this motivation, can be difficult. One method for enhancing the patient's motivation for treatment is the Cost-Benefit Analysis (CBA). The CBA is based on clinical experience and contemporary psychological research on addictive behavior, and in particular on the assumption that addictive behavior is an adaptive effort by the patient. The CBA is a generic approach suitable to psychotherapists in general practice, who may encounter various addictive behaviors at various levels of severity and who may need to enhance motivation for a variety of treatment methods and goals. Copyright 1993, American Psychological Association, Inc.

Johnson B; Clark WD. Alcoholism: A challenging physician-patient encounter. *Journal of General Internal Medicine* 4(5): 445-452, 1989. (43 refs.)

This article reviews the management of alcoholism within the framework of general medical practice. It includes the definition and characteristics of the disorder, the disease model and pathophysiology, diagnosis and screening, the denial system, and intervention treatment prognosis. Copyright 1989, Project Cork Institute.

Kiecolt KJ. Stress and the decision to change oneself: A theoretical model. *Social Psychology Quarterly* 57(1): 49-63, 1994. (89 refs.)

This paper presents a model, drawn from research on stress and on self and identity, of the decision to change oneself. In this model, the impetus for intentional self-change can be provided by a stressor-chronic role strain, a life event, or both. Stressors can implicate the self by generating unfavorable reflected appraisals, threatening competent identity performance, and generating unfavorable social comparisons. Any of these effects can reduce self-efficacy, self-esteem, and sense of authenticity, thus leading to psychological distress. Whether this impetus will lead to a resolve to change oneself is hypothesized to depend on six conditioning factors: (1) the identity-relevance of the stressor, (2) whether one attributes responsibility for a stressor to oneself, (3) awareness of and access to structural supports for self-change, (4) the belief that one can effect self-change, (5) the extent to which the benefits of changing are perceived to outweigh the costs, and (6) social support for self-change. Finally, the decision to change oneself may be precipitated by a critical event that causes persons to view their circumstances differently, usually by influencing one or more of the conditioning factors. Several types of critical events are described. Copyright 1994, American Sociological Association.

Liepman MR. Using family influences to motivate alcoholics to enter treatment: The Johnson Institute Intervention Approach. IN: O'Farrell TJ, ed. *Treating Alcohol Problems: Marital and Family Interventions.* New York: The Guilford Press, 1993. pp. 54-77. (25 refs.)

This chapter describes an approach for motivating persons who suffer from alcohol problems but are reluctant to enter treatment and begin recovery. The "Intervention" is a technique for motivating alcoholics to enter treatment through the efforts of family members and significant others directed by a skilled interventionist; it is an approach widely used by the alcoholism treatment field. Given the high human and economic costs of untreated alcoholism, this approach provides hope for concerned families when the alcoholic seems mired in denial and refuses to seek treatment. Essential ingredients for a successful Intervention are a well-trained interventionist, a family that is highly motivated to stop living with the alcoholic's drinking, and an alcoholic who attends the Intervention meeting. Copyright 1993, The Guilford Press.

Miller WR. Motivational interviewing: III. On the ethics of motivational intervention. *Behavioural and Cognitive Psychotherapy* 22(2): 111-123, 1994. (36 refs.)

This article promotes consideration and discussion of ethical issues in motivational interventions. The popular concept of patients "denial" encompasses a broad range of motivational behaviors including lying, perceptual bias, unawareness, ambivalence, resistance, and reactance. The "problem of motivation" typically arises when a therapist perceives a problem and sufficient need for change in someone who does not share this perception. In considering how to respond to such situations, one can conceive of a continuum of levels of readiness to change, and of therapeutic strategies ranging from passivity to coercion. Ethical concerns arise when there is a perceived mismatch between readiness level and intervention strategy. Motivational interviewing is a middle way between passivity and coercion, seeking to motivate change by highlighting the inconsistency of problem behavior with more valued concerns. The concern that this approach is "manipulative" combines a descriptive element and an evaluative component. Three possible descriptive meanings are discussed: that it effectively alters behavior, that it does so in persons not seeking or requesting change, and that it may operate through processes not immediately apparent. Ethical concerns regarding motivational intervention are considered within this broader context. Copyright 1994, British Association for Behavioural and Cognitive Psychotherapies.

Minicucci DS. The challenge of change: Rethinking alcohol abuse. *Archives of Psychiatric Nursing* 8(6): 373-380, 1994. (26 refs.)

Nurses usually conceptualize alcohol abuse and dependence as a progressive disease that can be managed but never cured. Yet there are millions of Americans for whom this approach is not helpful. The alcohol research community has reported impressive results with interventions guided by the assumption that many alcohol problems are learned habits that can be changed. This article reviews the clinical research in the area of brief interventions and moderation training with alcohol abusers. Nursing's vital role in advocating for and delivering such interventions is identified. Resistance to implementing alternative approaches for the treatment of alcohol problems is explored. Copyright 1994, W.B. Saunders Co.

Richmond RL; Anderson P. Research in general practice for smokers and excessive drinkers in Australia and the UK. I. Interpretation of results. (review). *Addiction* 89(1): 35-40, 1994. (for 3-part series, total of 135 refs.)

This review examines the role of the general practitioner in assisting patients to stop smoking and reduce levels of excessive drinking. After over a decade of clinical trials, the authors discuss what interventions work in general practice and interpret the results of clinical trials conducted predominantly in Australia and the UK. Studies have generally found a superiority of GPs' brief advice over that of nonintervention groups. Very brief GP advice results in smoking abstinence rates from 5% to 10%, reduction in alcohol consumption of around 25% to 35%, and reduction in proportions of excessive drinkers of around 45%. The greater investment of GPs' time and the more comprehensive interventions that include follow-up usually resulted in higher abstinence rates among smokers from between 20% to 36%, and a reduction in proportions of excessive drinkers of up to 60% to 70%. The contributions of the adjuncts—nicotine chewing gum, follow-up visits, and the personalization of health effects—are discussed. It is difficult to make comparisons between studies, and the authors examine some of the reasons. The predictors of successful outcome are presented, as they are of particular interest to GPs in terms of targeting health promotion activities. Copyright 1994, Society for the Study of Addiction to Alcohol and Other Drugs.

Richmond RL; Anderson P. Research in general practice for smokers and excessive drinkers in Australia and the UK. II. Representativeness of the results. (review). *Addiction* 89(1): 41-47, 1994. (for 3-part series, total of 135 refs.)

This paper reviews some of the issues related to the appropriateness of generalizing the results from clinical trials conducted in general practice for smokers and excessive drinkers. The authors discuss the representativeness of the results related to the method of recruitment of general practitioners and patients to the study populations. They examine methodological issues and reasons associated with general practitioners' and patients' noncompliance with maintaining the research protocols and intervention requirements that relate to the practiceworthiness and the future uptake of interventions. When assessing the applicability of interventions to general practice, there are three basic research questions relating to efficacy, effectiveness, and implementation that should be looked at quite separately. Copyright 1994, Society for the Study of Addiction to Alcohol and Other Drugs.

Sanders D; Peveler R; Mant D; Fowler G. Predictors of successful smoking cessation following advice from nurses in general practice. *Addiction* 88(12): 1699-1705, 1993. (26 refs.)

At follow-up of 751 subjects receiving a brief, nurse-administered anti-smoking intervention in general practice, 135 subjects (18%) reported stopping smoking, of whom 44 (6%) reported sustained cessation for 1 year. The demographic, social, and attitudinal characteristics of these subjects were compared with 616 subjects who continued to smoke. The most important predictors of cessation were intention to stop, personal rating of likelihood of cessation, nurse rating of likelihood of cessation, and smoking habit of partner. As practice nurses are able to distinguish likely quitters from those who are not motivated and less likely to succeed, it is important to decide whether it is more cost effective to target support at the motivated or to spend more time encouraging the less motivated. The most challenging, but possibly the most rewarding, task is to try to reduce the high proportion of new ex-smokers who relapse. Although 41.1% of those expressing a definite intention to stop smoking gave up, only 17.9% achieved sustained cessation. Copyright 1993, Society for the Study of Addiction to Alcohol and Other Drugs.

Schutz CG; Rapiti E; Vlahov D; Anthony JC. Suspected determinants of enrollment into detoxification and methadone maintenance treatment among injecting drug users. *Drug and Alcohol Dependence* 36(2): 129-138, 1994. (15 refs.)

The author's primary aim in this study has been to evaluate selected conditions thought to influence the entry of injecting drug users (IDU) into detoxification and methadone maintenance programs, making use of a prospective study design to strengthen a cross-sectional investigation of these conditions . . . they analyzed cross-sectionally gathered data on 2879 IDUs recruited through extensive community outreach efforts. . . . The authors tested their hypotheses about suspected determinants of entry into treatment by analyzing data prospectively gathered on 1039 active drug users with no recent history of being treated for drug problems. Among these 1039 IDUs . . . 144 entered a detoxification program between their recruitment interview and their next follow-up interview, conducted about 6 months after recruitment . . . and 64 entered a methadone maintenance program during that observation interval. Using multiple logistic regression analyses, they found that a recent drug overdose, a relatively higher frequency of injecting drugs, and a history of prior arrest or treatment were independent predictors of entry into detoxification. Being married or living with a partner, being female, having a lengthy duration of drug use (>10 years), and having a history of prior treatment were independent predictors of entry into methadone maintenance. These findings shed light on what appears to be a different profile of suspected determinants of entry into a detoxification treatment vs. methadone maintenance treatment; they also help clarify some potential differences between treated and untreated drug users that ought to be considered when evaluating results of investigations with IDU participants recruited solely from treatment settings. Copyright 1994, Elsevier Scientific Publishers Ireland, Ltd.

Sobell LC; Toneatto T; Sobell MB. Behavioral assessment and treatment planning for alcohol, tobacco, and other drug problems: Current status with an emphasis on clinical applications. (review). *Behavior Therapy* 25(4): 533-580, 1994. (245 refs.)

Clinical assessments serve several important functions: (1) They provide a clinical picture of the severity of the problem(s), which then can be used to develop treatment plans tailored to the needs of individual patients; (2) if change is not evident during treatment, ongoing assessment information can be used to make systematic changes in the treatment plan; and (3) progress during and after treatment can be assessed. This paper updates an earlier review, with a continuing emphasis on the clinical utility, cost minimization, and user friendliness of the instruments. The review also adds new sections on (a) clinical tools for assessing psychiatric comorbidity; (b) alcohol and drug effect expectancies questionnaires; (c) readiness/commitment to change measures; and (d) measures to assess nicotine use. This review is intended to help practitioners identify useful and expedient methods in their assessment and treatment of alcohol abusers and other drug abusers. Copyright 1994, Association for Advancement of Behavior Therapy.

Spivak K; Sanchev-Craig M; Davila R. Assisting problem drinkers to change on their own: Effect of specific and non-specific advice. *Addiction* 89(9): 1135-1142, 1994. (19 refs.)

Problem drinkers (99 males, 41 females) wishing to quit or cut down without professional help received a 60-minute session during which they were assessed and given at random one of these materials: Guidelines, a 2-page pamphlet outlining specific methods for achieving abstinence or moderate drinking; Manual, a 30-page booklet describing the methods in the Guidelines; or General Information, a package about alcohol effects. At the 12-month follow-up, subjects in the Guidelines and Manual conditions showed significantly greater reductions of heavy days (of 5+ drinks) than subjects in General Information (70% vs. 24%); in addition, significantly fewer subjects in the Guidelines and Manual conditions expressed need for professional assistance with their drinking (25% vs. 46% in General Information). No main effect of condition or gender was observed on rates of moderate drinkers. At the 12-month follow-up, 31% of the men and 43% of the women were rated as moderate drinkers. It was concluded that drinkers intending to cut down on their own derive greater benefit (in terms of their alcohol use) from materials containing specific instructions to develop moderate drinking than from

those providing general information on alcohol effects. Clinical and research implications of the findings are discussed. Copyright 1994, Society for the Study of Addiction to Alcohol and Other Drugs.

Strecher VJ; Kreuter M; Den Boer D-J; Kobrin S; Hospero HJ; Skinner CS. The effects of computer-tailored smoking cessation messages in family practice settings. *Journal of Family Practice* 39(3): 262-270, 1994. (15 refs.)

Many conventional health education materials such as pamphlets and booklets are designed to reach as wide an audience as possible; they are therefore often lengthy and contain information irrelevant to many consumers. Computer technologies allow sophisticated tailoring of messages targeted to individual patients and free of irrelevant information. In two studies in North Carolina (study 1, $n = 51$; study 2, $n = 197$), adult cigarette smokers were identified from a cohort of family practice patients. Cigarette consumption, interest in quitting smoking, perceived benefits and barriers to quitting, and other characteristics relevant to smoking cessation were collected. Based on this information, smoking cessation letters were tailored by computer to individuals. Smokers were randomly assigned to experimental (tailored health letters) or comparison groups (generic health letter in study 1, no health letter in study 2). Smoking status was assessed again at 4 months (study 1) or 6 months (study 2). Both studies found statistically significant positive effects of tailored health letters among moderate to light smokers. In study 1, 30.7% reported quitting after 6 months vs. 7.1% in the control group ($P < 0.05$); in study 2, 19.1% vs 7.3% ($P < 0.05$). Results from both studies indicate positive effects of computer-tailored smoking messages among moderate to light smokers. These findings are consistent with the focus of our computer-tailored program on psychological and behavioral factors related to smoking cessation. Smoking cessation outcomes may be enhanced by combining tailored messages with nicotine replacement therapies to treat physical dependency. Methods of tailoring health messages and incorporating the results into family practice are described. Copyright 1994, Appleton & Lange.

Washton AM; Stone-Washton N. Outpatient treatment of cocaine and crack addiction: A clinical perspective. IN: Tims FM; Leukefeld CG, eds. *Cocaine Treatment: Research and Clinical Perspectives. NIDA Research Monograph 135.* Rockville MD: National Institute on Drug Abuse, 1993. pp. 15-30 (17 refs.)

This chapter provides recommendations for treatment of cocaine addiction, particularly in respect to crack cocaine use and patterns of poly-drug use. The ingredients of an outpatient treatment program are discussed, including program design and treatment goals. There is also discussion of the extent to which cocaine addicts differ from alcoholics, and eight areas of difference seen as significant are noted. The issue of motivation is also discussed, as well as several areas of particular concern, e.g., drug screening, compulsive sexuality, management of "slips," and the role of self-help. Some data is presented on treatment outcome. Copyright 1994, Project Cork Institute.

CHAPTER 4

Substance Use Treatment

JEAN KINNEY, MSW
DONALD A. WEST, MD

CLINICAL APPLICATIONS

The goals of this chapter are to assist the clinician to:

1. Provide patient education.
2. Initiate risk reduction regimens.
3. Use minimal interventions.
4. Understand, use, and collaborate with formal treatment programs for patients with substance use problems.
5. Understand, use, and work with self-help groups.

During the initial intensive phase of substance abuse treatment, the primary care provider's main task is providing routine medical care. In this chapter the focus is on formal treatment, self-help efforts, and the role and tasks of the primary care provider during treatment. The medical management of treatment-related tasks is covered in Chapter 5.

A primary care setting has a significant percentage of patients (12% to 46%) whose use of alcohol and other drugs is problematic. However, studies have repeatedly documented that whatever the proportion, clinicians detect only a fraction of the actual cases. The detection rates range from 8% to as high as 45% to 60%.[8,53,62,81,83] Failure to recognize problematic alcohol or drug use is not the only shortcoming. In the past, even when problems were identified, the probability of a patient being referred for treatment was extremely low. One university hospital medical service only diagnosed 21% of the alcoholic patients. Even when a diagnosis was made, there was no referral for either formal treatment or AA in 79% of those cases.[61] Another study in a similar setting reported only 5% of cases being referred.[41] The best referral rate reported is 27% of those who warranted further care.[20] It is difficult to imagine any other medical condition for which a comparable low rate of detection or referral would be tolerated. Improving this situation should be a relatively modest task.

In addition, the importance of clinicians attending equally to patients with problems who do not meet the diagnostic criteria for dependence is being emphasized. This includes those who have had an acute problem, those who use substances in a high-risk fashion and meet criteria for abuse, and those individuals at risk. The rationale behind this approach is that the earlier problems are addressed, the better the outcomes. Such a broad brush approach has the greatest benefit from a public health perspective. Although the problems being addressed among those who are not dependent may be less severe, this is more than offset by the number of those affected.[51,76,78,87] The benefit of this broader perspective to both patients and the community is considerable. Of course, it is not an either/or situation. From a practical perspective, during attempts to identify the range of potential problems, those with more serious problems will be detected.

PATIENT EDUCATION

Treatment cannot be discussed without consideration of patient education. Patient education is not limited to an hour lecture during formal treatment nor should it be narrowly construed as synonymous with providing of pamphlets. It is a generic component of any intervention. Regardless of problem severity, education is a major component. It is integral to prevention, risk reduction, and early intervention. Education facilitates efforts to engage patients in treatment and begin long-term rehabilitation. Patient education is a central feature of aftercare. It underpins the skills needed to maintain abstinence and can provide the rationale for a patient to explore self-help groups. It is also a major component of relapse prevention, as it provides a cognitive structure for patients becoming attentive to the factors that may promote relapse. In addition, education provides patients with the requisite knowledge to become collaborators in long-term management.

Patient education is indicated for many different groups. All too frequently patients use medications and other substances in an uninformed fashion. This includes their efforts at self-treatment, which may involve over-the-counter preparations, or medications prescribed for previous illnesses or prescribed for a family member. Although alcohol is no longer a professionally recognized medicinal agent, the general public, to a remarkable degree, continues to act as if it were. Some use alcohol as a sleeping preparation, an anti-anxiety agent, an antidepressant, and a common cold preventative. These uses, combined with alcohol's social uses, are sufficient to make alcohol the most widely used self-prescribed agent. Those who would not hesitate to get explicit instructions regarding prescription medications may not perceive alcohol as a drug. Instead, it is viewed as a beverage. Even among otherwise sophisticated individuals, alcohol can be used without knowledge or regard for its pharmacological properties.

There are many natural opportunities to discuss use of drugs, including alcohol. Questions about substance use in the context of routine data collection make patients aware that the topic is considered an important health issue similar to smoking, exercise, or diet. Another opportunity is when discussing any prescribed medications. Such discussions should routinely include questions about other drug use, whether medically or self-prescribed, and focus on potential drug-drug interactions or alcohol-drug interactions. This promotes compliance with current treatment regimens and conveys the message that substance use is an important factor in health maintenance efforts.

Patient education is especially important in the response to an acute problem arising from either alcohol or other drug use. If an evaluation has ruled out the presence of a chronic problem, intervention is then primarily preventive and relies heavily upon educational efforts. Do not presume that the alcohol- or drug-related incident has been sufficient to teach the patient a lesson and guarantee no future problems.

It is easy to assume that the embarrassment, guilt, discomfort, or anxiety that resulted is a sufficient response. It may seem cruel to discuss it further. Those around the person may mistakenly think the polite or kind thing to do is to "just not mention it." If an adolescent is involved, the seriousness of the incident may be minimized or may even be treated by peers as a joke. Those who may have contact with the patient—emergency room personnel, police, friends, family, and health care staff—need to acknowledge the role of substance use in the incident. The actual or potential seriousness needs to be made clear. In part, the absence of feedback by others regarding incidents is what allows a problem to mushroom.

Following a substance use incident, education is central. Information is the foundation of any risk reduction efforts. Information needs to be detailed, specific, and related to the situation. The pharmacology and phenomenology have to be applied and discussed in the context of what just occurred. The underlying message is that if the individual is going to use alcohol or any other drug, he or she needs to be fully informed about it. Never assume that patients understand the potential risks associated with their alcohol or other drug use.

RISK REDUCTION EFFORTS

With an acute incident, risk reduction is the goal of education. The intent is to reduce the probability of future problems. In addition to clarification of how alcohol and drug use contributed to a particular episode, other steps such as taking an inventory of drinking and drug use practices should be taken. Review the settings in which use and associated activities take place. Inquire about a family history of alcoholism or drug abuse. Identify any medical conditions that may be adversely influenced by alcohol or other drug use. The question you and the patient are addressing is, "Are there circumstances that are likely to increase the risk of future problems?" The goal is to identify potential problems and help the patient take steps before problems arise. What might the adolescent do if faced with the decision of being a passenger in a car with an intoxicated driver? Is alcohol use going to compromise the management of diabetes or hypertension, or possibly invite adverse drug interactions with an elderly patient?

Risk reduction efforts are also indicated for those at risk for substance use problems. (See p. 49 for an overview of the risk factors for acute problems and chronic problems.) Adolescents in general, particularly those who have used alcohol but have not experimented with other substances, warrant special mention concerning risk reduction. The major causes of mortality among adolescents are accidents, suicide, and homicide. Alcohol/drug use is the major contributing factor. Adolescence is generally a healthy age. Medical care for teenagers is typically for acute illnesses or gynecological examinations for adolescent girls. In addition, there are those occasions when adolescents require medical clearance, e.g., for organized league sports, camp attendance, or school activities. These occasions need to be used to promote health maintenance and self-care, because few other opportunities are available.

In educating adolescents and preadolescents about alcohol and other drugs, different strategies are indicated depending on their prior experience with these substances. Adolescents who have not used either alcohol or other drugs need some "anticipatory" assistance to help them cope with the inevitable choices they will have to make. After age 20 to 21, the first use of illicit substances drops considerably.[46] Therefore, for adolescents who have used alcohol but have not experimented with other substances, anything that delays use represents a significant preventive measure.

Although adolescents may have a difficult time listening to their parents about issues of alcohol and drug use or may have ignored school programs concerning substance use, they usually appreciate such discussions with medical personnel. They view medical personnel as being more concerned with their health than their morals. You can offer them an opportunity to ask questions and provide a forum in which they will receive factual responses rather than lectures.

In addition to adolescents, there are parents. How well informed are they? What are their concerns? Are they members of the generation who encourage or tolerate alcohol use, rationalizing that at least it isn't drugs? Do they consider use to be inevitable and therefore allow their children to use alcohol at home, believing it is safer than having them experiment elsewhere? Many community alcohol and drug programs have programs for parents and offer support groups and literature. These programs are available to parents who want to reduce the probability of future problems and to parents whose children already have alcohol and drug problems. More schools are addressing alcohol and drug use problems by reaching out to parents and helping them develop guidelines surrounding alcohol and drug use.

At the other end of the age spectrum, alcohol and other drug use is especially problematic for the elderly. They are in the most danger for drug-drug interactions and problems related to over-the-counter products. The elderly are the segment of the population with the highest numbers of deaths from drug interactions, and are also vulnerable to a host of other complications.[1,66] Beyond the monitoring of their status, other steps can be used. To promote compliance, write out instructions. Speak with the elderly patients' primary caregivers such as their adult children or home visitors. Be sure to inquire about any misgivings or concerns patients may have. One of the myths about caring for the elderly is that they are unlikely to benefit from preventive health care efforts. The evidence is quite to the contrary. There are a number of spheres in which preventive measures definitely can pay dividends, and alcohol and drug use is one of these.[10]

MINIMAL INTERVENTIONS

Successful referral for treatment has historically been regarded as difficult. This perspective appears to have resulted from two different sets of experiences. One was the clinical experiences of the early substance abuse treatment community in an era when those services were outside of the medical care system, when early identification and treatment were not discussed, and when the majority of patients treated had long-term problems. The treatment community's view was that people needed to actively seek out treatment for it to be effective. The other source of this perception came from medical personnel whose interventions were along the order of "you really ought to cut down," "you need to do something," or "go easy on the drinking."

In the mid 1970s the substance abuse treatment community developed a technique that represented a major clinical breakthrough. This technique, known as *intervention* or *crisis precipitation*, was described in Chapter 3. It entails assembling significant people in the patient's life. They speak about the problems of use that they have personally witnessed, and they express their concerns for the patient and their hopes for the patient's entry into treatment.

The substance use treatment community and medical communities are no longer isolated from one another. Professional training has begun to attend to substance use problems. Intervention is a clinical technique to which health care professionals are being exposed during their training. Although intervention has been highly effective in moving people into treatment, paradoxically it has simultaneously reinforced the perception that referring people for treatment requires considerable effort and energy. This is not the universal experience of health care professionals. Unfortunately, the success of minimal interventions by health care professionals has been discussed far less.

Minimal interventions attest to the power of medical authority. Status as a health care practitioner can facilitate intervention and is a source of considerable leverage. It is a tool that is unavailable to those outside the health care disciplines. There have been efforts to identify the factors that help patients recognize the existence of a problem and raise their awareness of needing help. An almost universal factor is the occurrence of some event that provokes awareness of negative consequences for health and well-being. Thus, those in the healing professions are in a position to have considerable influence.[7]

Over the past decade research has consistently demonstrated the effectiveness of minimal or brief interventions. These have been found effective with a variety of drugs, settings, and populations, ranging from pregnant women, to smokers, to opiate addicts, to persons dependent upon benzodiazepines, to those with drinking problems. In many cases, simply a letter or a single counseling session has been sufficient to alter substance use patterns. For example, for patients with long-term and medically unwarranted benzodiazepine use, either a letter from the physician or a brief interview requesting that patients terminate their use was an effective intervention in 25% of the cases.[21] This is clearly not universally effective. Nonetheless, the efficacy of such minimal interventions for even a sizable minority of patients indicates the wisdom of adopting such approaches. Minimal intervention, if successful, can save time and money, and in the process, screen out those not requiring extensive efforts to prompt change.[2,5,6,9,13,16,17,28,37,45,54,73,74,77,79,91,93]

Another report that offers an example of a minimal intervention involved patients admitted to a medical unit who were identified through a routine screening as being at high risk. These patients were then invited to a follow-up interview with a nurse experienced in the management of alcohol and substance use problems. Of those approached, 97% of the patients accepted the offer of this follow-up session, which provided patients with some relevant literature and engaged them in a discussion about life-style and health; this was followed by a discussion of the screening results, with special attention directed to the specific negative consequences of continued use. This counseling session concluded with efforts to guide the patient to a decision about future use that would avoid further difficulties. Follow-up at 1 year demonstrated that those with this single session of counseling had a significantly better outcome than a matched control group without this intervention.[19,23] Bibliotherapy, another minimal intervention shown to have positive results, provides a self-help approach through a manual on the nature of alcohol problems and through specific steps the individual can take to moderate or significantly reduce drinking.[58]

Finally, the power of minimal interventions was demonstrated dramatically by a research project never conducted. An academically based primary care practice wished to study the outcome of the formal intervention in effecting referrals for treatment. The research proposal was written, submitted, and funded. The remaining step was the recruitment of patients. However, there was never the opportunity to implement the project! For the first 25 individuals whom the practice staff had identified as warranting a formal intervention, it was discovered that a physician's merely informing the patient of the concern was sufficient for the patient to agree to enter treatment. Thus, the need to initiate some special effort to promote entry into treatment proved unnecessary.[29]

FORMAL TREATMENT
Treatment of Abuse or Hazardous Use

Treatment approaches for those using alcohol or drugs in hazardous ways is a relatively new phenomenon. The origins of the modern alcohol and substance abuse treatment fields lie in self-help movements and early treatment programs staffed primarily by recovering individuals whose major credentials were their own recoveries. The focus of early formal treatment programs was on individuals who were clearly alcoholic or addicted to other drugs. Accordingly, alcohol problems were regarded exclusively from the standpoint of addiction. Each patient, regardless of his or her particular problems, was offered the same abstinence-oriented treatment.

Now, clinical approaches are devised for those whose alcohol or drug use is hazardous and who are at risk for dependence. The goal is not necessarily directed at abstinence, particularly with alcohol, but treatment efforts are targeted to reduce risk and promote moderate use. Many such efforts qualify as "minimal interventions." For example, attention is directed to helping individuals identify and moderate drinking practices that increase their risk of acute or chronic problems. The intent is to provide patients with an objective assessment of current or potential problems in a concerned but direct, sympathetic manner, along with advice directed at changing behavior.

One program, suitable for the public, was derived from a health promotion model. It offered a two-session "Drinker's Check-up," with the goal being early identification of emerging alcohol-related problems.[59] The check-up included a substance abuse treatment questionnaire, an interview, and laboratory screening, all sensitive to the early behavioral and physical effects of alcohol. The results were discussed with the participants to increase their awareness of their own risks and to discover any negative effects alcohol use might be causing them. Another approach, developed by the Minneapolis VA Medical Center's internal medicine section, was directed to reducing hazardous drinking for medically ill patients whose physical conditions were related to their alcohol use.[105] The result

was the Health Improvement Program Clinic. Its patients were those for whom standard alcohol treatment was not appropriate and who did not meet diagnostic criteria for dependence. For many patients enrolled, there had been a life-long pattern of heavy drinking, which was acceptable and not unusual in their social circles. They experienced relatively few social consequences, but they were having secondary medical problems from heavy drinking. On that basis, abstinence or dramatically reduced intake was important. The clinic has proved successful in addressing alcohol use in the context of providing routine medical care and has delivered alcohol services to many people who otherwise would have remained untreated.

Treatment of Dependence

Volumes have been written on treatment. Nonetheless, it is not a complex phenomenon. The mystery of addictions is not why people stop using, but rather, what prompts the resumption of use. The object of treatment is to intervene to reduce the probability of future use. Treatment is an intensive rehabilitative effort to enable patients to function comfortably without alcohol or drugs, to learn about the nature of dependence, to recognize the negative consequences of use, to gain alternative coping skills, and to receive emotional support. Some have compared the process of treatment with joining a special group such as a religious cult, a fraternity/sorority, or a street gang. For treatment of addictions, the new views of the world, the new identity, and the changes in habits all center around not using.

Many years ago, a health professional, referring to this new life pattern, said that the problem with alcoholism was that the cure was as bad as the disease. This perception may be shared by others; however, most people are not so bold as to voice it! This impression comes from several sources. For one, individuals in treatment, and in the earliest period following recovery, have narrow outlooks. They will not make stimulating dinner table conversation, give a synopsis of a best seller (unless it is a 12-step book on addictions), or be knowledgeable about current events. All their energies are directed to staying clean and sober. The most important part of their day will be attending an aftercare session or a 12-step group. It cannot be otherwise. It is the absence of such preoccupation that is dangerous during early recovery. It is not possible to lead a "normal" life and plan to work rehabilitation into it. Rehabilitation is needed for a normal life in the future, without substance use.

As a society, we value being autonomous and independent. These attributes, however, are not encouraged in formal substance abuse treatment nor in early recovery. Patients are urged to do as they are told and are expected to blindly follow suggestions on the basis of trust, even if or when the reasons are not immediately apparent. Patients are counseled not to make major life decisions during the first year of sobriety. As problems, questions, or concerns arise, patients are encouraged to discuss these matters in a clinical setting or within their self-help group. Considerable changes will come later during the long process of recovery.

THE NATURAL HISTORY OF RECOVERY

Compared with the natural history of untreated dependence or addiction, the process of recovery has received too little attention. However, it is a necessary point of reference when considering any treatment. It allows the clinician to look ahead and anticipate what might be on the other side. The current understanding of the natural history of recovery comes from several different sources. From the experience of clinicians in the substance abuse treatment field, a folk wisdom has evolved about the characteristics of recovery. Another source of data comes from longitudinal, prospective studies of persons who developed alcoholism or addiction and were followed-up after treatment. Insight is also provided from studies of persons who have experienced spontaneous remissions. The authors of these latter studies are always careful to note that the 'remissions' were virtually never spontaneous nor true remissions, meaning that the individuals resumed nonproblematic use of alcohol or drugs. Nevertheless, the phrase sticks and addresses the existence of successful recovery without formal treatment. Finally, biomedical research of the *subacute* or *extended* withdrawal syndrome is beginning to help explain the natural history of recovery.

Treatment Folk Wisdom

The recovery process, as discussed within the treatment community, focuses on several factors. One is the amount of time and energy required to build a solid, stable recovery. Whether it is through participation in self-help programs or involvement in a formal aftercare program, being engaged in some specific, continuing, recovery-oriented activity is regarded as important because predictably there will be difficult occasions that will threaten abstinence. Coping with these situations depends on developing and practicing protective responses. However, being forewarned is not enough. Practical tips and specific actions are suggested to reinforce the individual's commitment to sobriety and/or not using. Helpful activities might involve attending additional 12-step groups, speaking to another member either before or after an event, or arranging to be accompanied by a close friend or associate to a social event where drinking or drugs may be present. For some, it may entail taking Antabuse® (disulfiram) for a brief period.

Holidays and celebrations are often considered to represent predictably dangerous or difficult points. Patients are also cautioned about situations or individuals closely associated with past drinking or drug use. For an entire year, those in recovery will be experiencing many major events for the first time sober or straight.

One handout almost universally distributed within educational groups conducted by treatment programs depicts the signs of emergent alcoholism and the process of recovery. Its origin is unknown. It may have been developed more than 30 years ago, drawing on the work of Jellinek, who was among the first to describe the natural history of alcoholism. This view of recovery is depicted in Figure 4-1.

The scientific merits of this framework may be questioned. In fact, its use as a guide for the *exact* sequence of recovery is irrelevant. It visually conveys the message to those who are newly sober or straight that they have considerable work ahead of them. Rehabilitation is an extended process. If patients have the illusion that within 1 week or 1 month they will be functioning like a nonaddicted person, this framework effectively disavows that notion. It also helps patients handle the distress, turmoil, and confusion that they will predictably encounter. It helps patients understand what lies ahead and helps them lay aside the illusion that they 'should' be okay because they have stopped their alcohol or drug use.

Longitudinal Studies

A longitudinal, prospective study of adult development has offered the opportunity to examine the natural history of dependence, including recovery. In respect to alcohol, four factors were commonly found to be associated with recovery. One was the development of a vital interest that could replace the role of drinking. Another was the continuing presence of external reminders that drinking was and presumably would again be painful. The third was the presence of a new intimate relationship, an involvement with someone who had not been part of the earlier alcoholic drinking.* The last factor was the presence of a

---

*Given the considerable efforts now being directed to family involvement as part of substance abuse treatment, this finding has caused some consternation within treatment circles. It should be noted that Vaillant's subjects, men now in their seventies, became abstinent in an era when family treatment was uncommon. Thus, this finding may address outcomes in the absence of marital and family counseling. It similarly attests to the need for education and the considerable marital effort required to handle the many emotional responses that follow addictive behavior—guilt, remorse, anger, distrust, insecurity, vulnerability—if a marriage is to remain intact. Other research has suggested that although addicted persons often do better in groups, family members may need something different. For them, individual counseling is sometimes more important, and to some degree confirms their need for education. It is important to help them recognize that much of the addictive behavior they have encountered is a symptom and is nonwillful.[51]

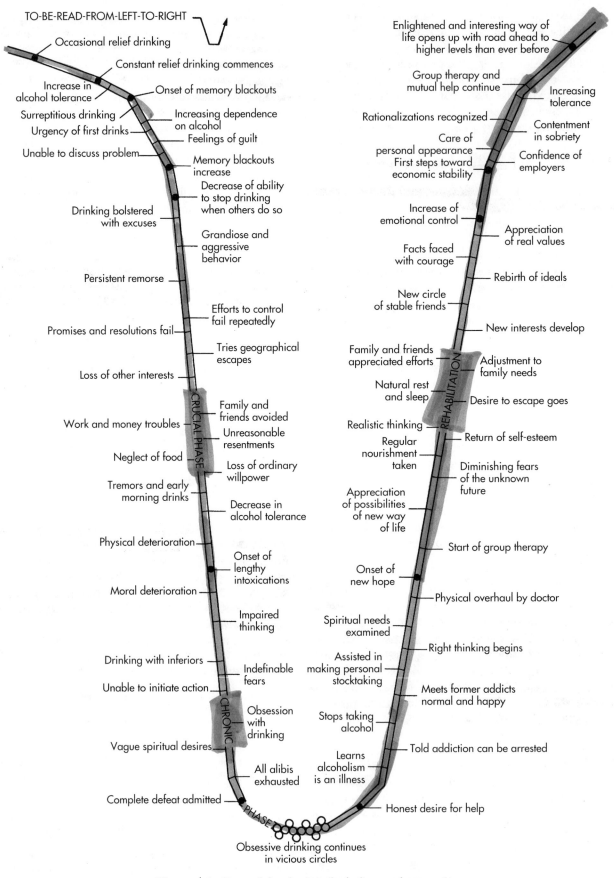

Figure 4-1. Signs of developing alcoholism and recovery.

source of inspiration, hope, and enhanced self-esteem.[98,100] For those successfully treated for drug dependence, many of the same factors apply.[84-86]

Spontaneous Remission

From a different perspective, the literature on spontaneous remission offers insight into events that promote abstinence. There are those who become sober without professional assistance or involvement in self-help efforts. Not only are there specific incidents that have prompted individuals to stop drinking, but there are explanations or meanings attached to these incidents that can offer insight. Factors cited as having prompted the cessation of alcohol use are presented in Table 4-1.[55,89,94,95,96]

Subacute or Extended Withdrawal Phenomenon (Alcohol)[3,12,14,39,70,90,92]

Until recently, recovery tended to be conceived solely in psychological terms. The nature, extent, and time for the recovery of physical functioning is only now being realized. Fifty percent of abstinent patients will experience sleep disturbances for as long as 1 year. The full recovery of cognitive and neuropsychological functioning typically occurs over 4 to 6 months. Gradually, there is improvement in many of the more subtle areas of neuropsychological functioning, e.g., the ability to abstract, which is needed to generalize and to learn from experiences, or the ability to concentrate. It is distressing but not uncommon for those in early recovery to find themselves picking up a book being read, with their place carefully marked, only to discover that the material looks wholly unfamiliar. Being reassured that such experiences are part of recovery may be exceedingly helpful.

In many instances, recent discoveries in respect to physical recovery provoke an appreciation of the treatment and self-help community's folk wisdom. The nature of extended withdrawal explains the biological basis for the treatment approaches that have evolved. The cognitive impairments found in early abstinence explain the patient's need for a highly structured, directive, and focused approach.

TREATMENT SETTINGS

Two basic settings are available for formal treatment, e.g., outpatient treatment programs or inpatient, residential care. The factors that are relevant clinically in selecting one over the other are summarized in Box 4-1. However, in the era of managed care, clinical criteria may be secondary to the status of the patient's insurance coverage.

Outpatient Treatment

The current view favors outpatient care over inpatient treatment as it is the least restrictive option available. In addition, it can offer some significant clinical advantages: It enables patients to build abstinence in their communities with existing supports; allows the patient to continue to work, provide child care, and fulfill household responsibilities; and is significantly less expensive than residential care. If a stable recovery is not possible with outpatient care, then a referral to an inpatient setting can be made. The general

Table 4-1. Factors Prompting Abstinence

Events identified as prompting abstinence	Study 1* (*n* = 51) % mention	Perceptions of events prompting abstinence	Study 2† (*n* = 29) % mention
Illness or accident	33.3	Physical illness	20.7
		Allergy or physical aversion to alcohol	9.7
Education about alcoholism	11.8		
Religious or conversion experience	25.5	Spiritual experience	13.8
Intervention by immediate family	17.7		
Intervention by friends	13.8		
Extraordinary events‡	29.4	Personal bottoms§	55.2
Alcohol-induced financial problems	21.6		
Alcohol-related death or illness of a friend	13.8		
Alcohol-related legal problems	7.8		
		Desire to change the nature of life's patterns	10.3

*From Tuchfeld BS: *Journal of Studies on Alcohol* 42(7): 626-641, 1981.
†From Ludwid AM: *Journal of Studies on Alcohol* 46(1): 53-58, 1985.
‡Includes personal humiliation, identity crisis, suicide attempt, events during pregnancy.
§Includes significant life problems such as legal difficulties, physical problems, a job loss, or an emotional crisis over disrupted interpersonal relationships.

criteria suggestive of outpatient care as the treatment of choice are summarized in Box 4-1.

There are various arrangements for outpatient care, including day treatment or evening treatment, several weekly appointments for different activities, workplace-based counseling, and use of residential halfway houses. Whatever the setting, most treatment programs include group, family, or couples therapy; efforts to refer patients to 12-step groups; and patient education through films, discussions, lectures, reading, and homework, such as self-inventories or diaries.

Box 4-1

Management of Different Diagnostic Categories

Although clinical status dictates the specific treatment recommendations, the following categories serve as general guidelines for substance abuse clinicians:

Dependence

Formal treatment is indicated.

Goals: To achieve an alcohol- or drug-free state. For opiates, methadone maintenance may be an appropriate alternative goal. Provide support and education and build skills needed to function drug-free.

Methods: Group, family, and individual counseling, patient education, and self-help organizations.

Setting: Inpatient or outpatient substance use treatment.

Indications for Inpatient Treatment
- Prior unsuccessful outpatient treatment
- Minimal social supports
- Concomitant medical problems
- Concomitant psychiatric illness
- Ambivalence about need for treatment

Indications for Outpatient Treatment
- Intact and supportive family
- No previous formal treatment
- No history of withdrawal difficulty
- Ability to use available supports
- Insights into need for treatment
- Absence of major medical problems

Abuse

Formal treatment is indicated.

Goals: To support and monitor the ability to moderate abusive patterns of use and to mobilize support systems using individual and/or group therapy. If the patient proves unable to curtail abusive use, this becomes diagnostic of dependence. The treating clinician would then be expected to initiate abstinence-oriented treatment.

Methods: Group treatment, education.

Setting: Outpatient substance abuse treatment.

Those Not Meeting Criteria for Abuse or Dependence

Intervention by primary care or community health staff is warranted. Formal treatment to achieve abstinence is not necessary.

For *alcohol* use problems.

Goals: To initiate risk reduction efforts, identify high-risk use patterns that increase the probability of future problems arising from use. Consider the domains of health status and other drug use, prescription or recreational; behavior commonly associated with use; the perceived motives for use; and family history of alcohol or drug dependence.

Setting: Outpatient. Primary care provider or substance abuse clinician.

For *drug* use problems.

Goals: For problems arising from illicit drug use, prescription medications, or other substances with a high abuse potential, non-use is the preferred treatment goal, and referral for abstinence-oriented treatment is suggested.

Setting: Outpatient. Primary care provider or substance abuse clinician.

From *Weekend Program.* Project Cork Institute, Hanover NH: Dartmouth Medical School, 1990.

Inpatient Treatment

The indications for inpatient care include being at risk for significant withdrawal, the presence of medical complications, a concurrent psychiatric illness, or a history of one or more unsuccessful outpatient treatment attempts. It is the setting of choice when there is little probability that a patient will become abstinent without the support of a structured environment. The need for this structured, protective setting can be attributed to a significant cognitive impairment, lack of social supports, or the level of impulsivity connected to drug or alcohol use.

Residential programs can be either hospital affiliated or independent. While historically, inpatient treatment tended to be organized as a rehabilitative regimen of a standard length such as 28 days, programs of fixed length are far less common. Inpatient care provides a safe, drug-free environment and intensive educational and rehabilitation efforts, with the goals of providing the skills, motivation, and knowledge needed to achieve and maintain abstinence. Efforts are directed toward cultivating a drug-free identity and helping individuals distance themselves from the behaviors associated with use, regarding them as symptoms of an illness. Patient education is a major element. It is provided through films, lectures, group discussions, reading, and "homework assignments." Patient education provides basic information about alcohol and drugs, including the pharmacological properties that invite dependence, the symptoms and etiology of dependence, common issues in recovery, and relapse prevention. The rehabilitative regimen introduces a daily routine to replace the chaos and life patterns that evolved and were predicated on securing and using substances; activity therapists are frequently members of the treatment team. Efforts are made to restore physical health and incorporate steps to promote health. One of the biggest initial reinforcements for abstinence is an enhanced sense of physical well-being. One advantage of inpatient care is that it allows patients to focus on substance use problems, which for many is a full-time job, without needing to simultaneously fulfill family and work responsibilities.

MATCHING PATIENTS TO TREATMENT

In the early days of alcohol and drug treatment, matching patients to treatment was not an issue. The only treatment available was residential care. Community-based, outpatient programs were nonexistent. This early preponderance of residential treatment has been cited as proof that residential treatment is the treatment of choice, ignoring the fact that previously there were no alternatives. Throughout the early 1970s, those entering treatment were almost exclusively persons with longstanding medical and social problems involving substance abuse. Early detection and referral simply did not occur. By definition, alcoholism was considered a disease of middle age, first appearing between the ages of 35 and 50. Such patients continue to be those for whom inpatient care is probably indicated.

More attention is now being paid to matching patients to treatment. This is due to developments in the field that allow for this possibility. Patients entering treatment today are a more heterogeneous population than those who entered treatment 1 or 2 decades ago. There are a variety of treatment options. In addition, standardized assessment instruments have been developed and have contributed to an ever-growing literature on treatment outcome. Nonetheless, definitive clinical guidelines have not yet emerged for matching patients to treatment, although there are efforts in this direction.[103] In the interim, there is considerable consensus among substance abuse clinicians about the factors suggesting a referral to either outpatient or inpatient care. These factors are summarized in Box 4-1 on p. 82.

Economic Factors in the Patient-Treatment Match

At the risk of cynicism, the most significant item in patient-treatment matching may well be matching treatment to the treatment options reimbursed by insurance. The economics of the health care system has significant bearing on the site and nature of treatment provided. This comes in two guises: The pressures created by third party payment with the accompanying utilization review, and the emergence of Health Maintenance Organizations (HMOs) and managed care. In respect to the former, third party payment requires documentation of the need for treatment and the provision of treatment. The reimbursement patterns of insurance companies are strongly biased toward outpatient care. The economic incentive is obvious. This economic bias has been supported by some of the earliest studies conducted on treatment effectiveness. Undertaken when 28-day inpatient programs were the norm, the first studies found no essential difference in outcome between inpatient and outpatient treatment.[60] Quite reasonably, as patients began to enter treatment with fewer social and medical problems, the 28-day residential care model may have represented overtreatment for many patients. The later data, which emerged from research focusing on subgroups for whom more intensive care is needed, have not been seized by the insurance industry.

Within HMOs, economic incentives also favor outpatient treatment. HMOs negotiate preferred provider status, with designated treatment programs for their members needing substance abuse treatment. In an area with 50% of the insured population enrolled in HMOs (Minneapolis-St. Paul), the emergence of HMOs has altered the delivery of substance use treatment. Over an 8-year period, there was a 100% reduction in the number of inpatient days for substance abuse treatment. Substance abuse inpatient treatment declined from 20% of all inpatient days to 9%. Another impact of HMOs, also in the Minneapolis-St. Paul area, was the emergence of new provider groups for substance abuse and mental health services.[38] HMO providers find themselves in intense competition with one another. In negotiating contracts, the incentive for each is to offer to do more for less reimbursement.

When health care reform initiatives were launched in 1993, there was considerable concern about how substance abuse and mental health treatment would fare. It was then estimated that 54 billion dollars had been expended in 1990 for alcohol/drug abuse and mental health services, overwhelmingly for inpatient care and for those with the most serious problems.[30] The accepted position was that any efforts directed at containment of health care costs would need to control inpatient utilization. A number of groups submitted proposals outlining suggested benefit packages (see policy statements in Chapter 9).

It is unfortunate that cost containment efforts are required to focus attention exclusively or even primarily on reducing access to services and reducing utilization. As one author notes, "a paradigm shift" is required to shift attention from passively responding to the development of illness to actively promoting health.[31] This is particularly true with substance abuse problems. In the meantime, capitation approaches to reimbursement have raised concerns within the treatment community. This could prompt "cookbook approaches to care" rather than care being determined by clinical status. The effort and energy being devoted to justifying and documenting the need for care are felt to be considerable. This is frustrating for clinicians because they spend as much time "treating" the medical record as the patient.[82] The inclination toward outpatient treatment models is as simplistic an approach as the earlier reliance on inpatient care.

Program Staff

The proliferation of treatment programs must become a concern to those making referrals, in that there remains a relative absence of standards for credentialing either clinical personnel or programs. General discussions of treatment may tend to obscure differences between programs. Although the components of treatment may be identical, because of differences in personnel, in practice they are not. Individual therapy or group therapy in one setting may bear little resemblance to the same activities in

another. There continue to be many differences among staff in terms of professional training and experience. Substance abuse counselors or primary therapists may not have professional training to complement life experiences or professional experience in the substance abuse field. Interest has long been the main criterion for employment in the field. Since there are no uniform standards for care or for personnel staffing treatment programs, selecting an agency for a referral becomes more difficult for community clinicians. Some factors to consider include the staff's professional credentials, the use and availability of medical and psychiatric consultations, the extent to which treatment within a standardized program can be tailored to a patient's needs, and the type and level of family involvement.

TREATMENT ACTIVITIES

Much has been written about models of addiction and treatment. One formulation postulates five supposedly different models—the learning model, the moral model, the disease model, the self-medication model, and the social model.[15] Although such discussions are interesting, they have little application to the way treatment is conducted in most treatment programs. With few exceptions, most treatment programs incorporate elements from each of these models. The content of most treatment programs, whether inpatient or outpatient, is similar.

Medical Tasks during Formal Treatment

Treatment of alcohol and substance abuse problems is typically provided by an interdisciplinary team, which includes a physician and nurses or nurse practitioners. Some of their unique, although circumscribed, responsibilities include management of withdrawal and medical complications secondary to chronic use, as well as evaluation for use of disulfiram or narcotic antagonists. In addition, the program's medical staff plays an important role in lending their medical authority to nonmedical team members, supporting the treatment program's efforts, and conveying the message that dependence or abuse is a disease and a medical issue. Medical program staff often share generic clinical responsibilities such as providing a lecture within a patient education series, conducting a group, or serving as the case manager or primary therapist for patients.

Detoxification

Residential treatment programs vary in their willingness and ability to manage withdrawal. Some have a well-trained medical staff and are able to handle detoxification. In some instances medical status may dictate a need for hospitalization. Other programs may require patients to be drug-free before entry. In addition, programs have been set up specifically to provide detoxification. Some are hospital based, but others for those who have been medically cleared are referred to as *social detox* programs, meaning they are housed outside of a medical setting and rely heavily upon a supportive milieu.

Most residential programs, although they welcome the interest of the primary care physician, require that their own medical staff assume medical responsibility during residence. This is intended to promote quality of care and a consistent treatment approach for all of a program's patients. For those being treated as outpatients, there may be the option and preference for the involvement of the patient's own health care team to offer medical care. Medical aspects of withdrawal, the management of alcohol and substance abuse emergencies, and the pros and cons of management vs. referral to treatment centers for detoxification are discussed in Chapter 5, Overview of Medical Management.

Referral: A Process

It is helpful to approach the essential data base in terms of the clinical tasks immediately at hand. There is a wealth of information that might be elicited in respect to substance use. What is important is the information required for immediate management. The data relevant at different points in management is summarized in Box 4-2.

In general it is almost irrelevant whether the patient labels himself or herself as "alcoholic" or "addicted." Energy directed to getting a patient to voice either term is generally misdirected and counterproductive because the patient's use of the label does not affect outcome. However, it is important that the patient and clinician agree about the distress the patient experiences; this distress can be attributed to the patient's inability to routinely predict consumption, or to the patient's discovery that drinking or drug use diverts him or her from previous interests, friends, and activities. In addition, there could be medical conditions exacerbated by use or problems in the patient's life, causing emotional turmoil.

In some situations, it may only take the mention of an alcohol or drug problem for the patient who is worried about the issue to cry and say, "I thought no one would ever ask." More frequently, a series of encounters is needed to establish this common framework.

At times the signs of dependence are obvious, but in other instances, the situation may be more ambiguous. Neither abuse nor dependence is a condition where speculation can be confirmed by ordering laboratory and diagnostic tests, with the

---

Box 4-2
Database for Different Clinical Tasks

Emergency Care

- Specific substances used, quantity, and interval since last administration.
- A history of alcohol or substance abuse related to emergency care.

Routine Medical Care

- Substances used, quantity, frequency, and pattern of use. This information is not helpful for the assessment of the alcohol/substance use problem but is required to make informed medical decisions about medication and medical management.

To Engage Patient in Further Evaluation

- Positive response to screening instrument.
- An alcohol or substance use incident.
- Presence of conditions that are common medical sequelae of heavy chronic use of alcohol or other substances.
- Negative consequences of alcohol or drug use.
- Concern expressed by patient, family, school, or employer.
- Factors supporting continuing use.
- Factors that provide a rationale for entry into treatment.

To Initiate Formal Treatment Planning

- Degree of dependence.
- Degree of recognition by patient of need for treatment.
- Availability of social supports and treatment sources.
- Degree of social, occupational, and family dysfunction.
- Medical status and withdrawal risk.

To Plan Aftercare

- Assessment of continuing treatment needs.
- Assessment of family's degree of support and understanding of substance use problems and treatment.
- Identification of stressors on patient and family.
- Identification of any medical limitations.
- Identification of resources in community care network to be involved in planning, to participate in management, and to assist in monitoring status.

diagnosis being made on the arrival of the laboratory slips. Alcohol and other drug use problems are diagnosed primarily by history. This includes the symptoms of the disorder which are, at least early in its history, primarily psychosocial and not medical. Therefore, the clinician must rely almost exclusively on his or her interviewing skills and an ability to forge a therapeutic alliance. Accordingly, diagnosis is best considered not as an event but as a process, which generally unfolds through a series of clinical encounters.

A hypothetical scenario might be as follows:

Mr. Pietro is new to the area. He has been treated for hypertension and is looking for a primary care provider. One stipulation for new patients is a routine screening for substance abuse. Mr. Pietro's CAGE score was 1.

On Mr. Pietro's second appointment, the focus is on monitoring his hypertension, which prompted the initial visit. His screening results are also discussed, and he is questioned about his alcohol use.

On the third appointment, Mr. Pietro is told that his hypertension is not being adequately controlled. Therefore, his alcohol use is discussed further. The nurse practitioner tries to elicit evidence of concern by Mr. Pietro or his family, as well as any other negative consequences of use. This data is significant because it may help determine the factor most likely to reinforce a patient's readiness to make changes. Patient education is provided based on the connection between alcohol use and hypertension, and the medical level is adjusted. Mr. Pietro is told that temporary abstinence from alcohol may be necessary to evaluate his hypertension, but that possibility will be discussed during his next visit.

At his fourth appointment, questioning reveals that Mr. Pietro has continued drinking. He is given an opportunity to discuss his concerns, and, as a result, a trial abstinence is ordered for a limited time.

At Mr. Pietro's fifth appointment, the nurse informs him that there has been a decrease in his systolic blood pressure. The nurse practitioner inquires about what it has been like to be abstinent (to get information about preoccupation), the amount of psychological energy required to abstain, the times when a drink has been most desired, and his mood without alcohol.

Depending on the information, the next step in the preceding scenario may be to continue to explore a possible problem with alcohol use. The patient can be given some literature and a copy of the MAST to be completed as a way of preparing for discussion at the next visit, when a plan can be adopted. Many patients may not need this intervening step and may already be willing to accept a referral.

Through several clinical contacts, the clinician elicits the necessary data. This data will formulate a diagnosis and determine the information that can be discussed with the patient, along with the recommendations for next steps. There are several options after all the necessary data are collected. For example, it is important for the clinician to make clear that with hypertension, even modest alcohol use is ill-advised. This has nothing to do with possible dependence, but abstinence that is not easily accomplished can be a warning sign. Concerns by the patient and significant others also indicate a problem. Neither the drinker nor family tend to worry needlessly. Alcohol or drug dependence is generally not a condition in which one must worry about Munchausen syndrome.

There are other ways to encourage a patient's self-evaluation, e.g., through a request for consultation and evaluation or through referral to an educational-discussion series offered by a local treatment program. The latter are programs conducted for just this type of patient. They can provide education to family members or assist the person with alcohol or drug use problems by providing facts about addiction in a setting with others who have similar concerns. The goals of such groups are to help the members recognize the stresses of use and the desire to use, and to assess the level and intensity of their involvement with substances and the extent and nature of the consequences.

Using crisis situations. There are specific exceptions to the previous approach. One is the obvious need to respond to medical emergencies. There are also the opportunities provided by emotional emergencies. A patient with a chronic problem who has just had an acute crisis requiring medical attention needs immediate, straightforward discussion of alcohol and/or other drug use. Since the patient is already in a crisis, he or she is emotionally more open to receiving this discussion. In fact, *the crisis of trauma* has been described as an opportunity not to be missed. This has been evidenced by the response to interventions of trauma patients whose injuries were alcohol-related and who were found to be alcohol dependent. In a pilot study, 100% of the patients approached about the seriousness of their accidents and the presence of alcoholism accepted a referral for treatment after discharge. The family intervention or social network approach was used during the hospital stay to effect the referral.[32] Similarly, it has been demonstrated that the threat of a job loss because of alcohol or drug use can act as a catalyst to entering treatment. On the other hand, if the loss has already occurred, the motivation dissipates because then it is too late to avoid the negative consequences.[49] When a crisis occurs, it is important to respond quickly. The rule of thumb is that within 6 weeks, the "teachable" moment or the opportunity for intervention will have disappeared.

Thus, a situation involving a crisis is unlike the example above in which the attempt is to induce or provoke a crisis by surfacing emotional discomfort, which will provide the impetus for making changes. When presented with a clear crisis related to alcohol or drug use, it is important to be direct. Even an indirect attempt to ease the distress and reduce the discomfort may indicate that the situation is not as serious as the patient had believed. It has been pointed out that no matter how serious a problem may be, objectively, if there are no perceived negative consequences, the pressure to change is virtually nonexistent.[71] In other words, "no one changes until it is too painful not to."

For a patient in a referral hospital, attention commonly is directed to the problem prompting admission, with little or no attention to a concomitant or underlying alcohol or drug problem. The rates of detection for alcohol problems are low; the rates of referral for formal treatment are even lower. The primary care physician may have to take the initiative to prompt a referral for treatment. In respect to the logistics, it is important to consider and act on this at the point of admission. Time is needed to involve family, and the patient might need to be seen by substance abuse specialists if they are available for consultation. Because of the pressure to reduce length of hospital stays, when planning is delayed, there is the risk that this effort cannot be accomplished before discharge. It is frustrating for those providing alcohol and drug consultations in hospital settings to receive a consultation request at the time of discharge. Often there is not the time available to allow the necessary work with the patient and/or family. After discharge, the patient is no longer a "captive audience." Not only is the patient no longer physically accessible, but perhaps emotionally inaccessible.

Drug Therapy[22,24,27,33–36,43,48,50,52,57,80,88,97]

Considerable research is underway in respect to the efficacy of pharmacotherapies for substance abuse problems. The literature is replete with reports of the efficacy of different agents. Despite the strides being made in understanding the pharmacological basis of addiction, the mainstay of care continues to be rehabilitative regimens and involvement in self-help efforts. The major drug therapies being used are transdermal nicotine patches for smoking cessation; methadone maintenance for heroin addiction; and disulfiram (Antabuse®) for alcohol dependence.

Considerable research has examined the efficacy of various agents in substance abuse treatment, particularly to identify agents that reduce craving. In a long series of investigations of various agents, the most recent and widely touted and marketed is naltrexone, a narcotic antagonist, which has been found to reduce relapse among alcohol-dependent persons. In late 1994 naltrexone was approved by the FDA for treatment of alcohol dependence when used in conjunction with rehabilitative regimens. However, the treatment outcome data remain limited. The maximum period of follow-up is 12 weeks.[101,102] At this time the evidence favoring naltrexone for treatment of alcohol dependence is essentially on par with similar, earlier reports for other drug therapies, none of which proved to be a universal 'magic bullet.' The safety of pharmacotherapies, especially in light of the multiple medical problems that accompany substance abuse, is always a concern. For example, although naltrexone is not associated with liver toxicity at therapeutic doses, it has been reported to diminish immune function, and its actions on the hypothalamic-pituitary-ovarian axis are well known.

TREATMENT OUTCOME

Data on the critical factors for matching patients to treatment are limited. The most accurate predictors of treatment outcome are not treatment variables but pretreatment and posttreatment factors.

The following factors have been found to be associated with positive treatment outcomes:

- *Pretreatment variables.* Good prognosticators include social stability, a stable marriage, a stable job, high socioeconomic status, and the absence of psychiatric illness.[66–68,75]
- *Posttreatment variables.* Factors in the environment associated with good outcomes are the patient's social resources, the level of environmental stressors, the patient's coping responses, and the availability of support systems.[63,98]
- *Circumstances of treatment entry.* It has been found that those referred under "coercive" conditions do as well if not somewhat better than voluntary admissions. This is clear from the evidence of referrals by employers, the experience of impaired professionals' programs, the military, or other specialized groups such as airline pilots.[85]
- *Treatment variables.* With one exception, once treatment is initiated, the nature of treatment—whether inpatient or outpatient, partial or day hospital—or the nature of the particular treatment modalities used does not greatly influence outcome. Continuing to be involved in treatment is the most important element, whatever that treatment is.[65,67]

It was once believed that recovering clinicians had an advantage over other clinical staff. It was thought that they were better able to develop a therapeutic relationship, that patients would be better able to identify with them, and that they could serve as role models. This view is no longer given much credence. Within many treatment programs, a staff member's own personal substance abuse history is no longer viewed either as a credential or as pertinent public information in clinical work. Generally, similarity between patient and therapist is not viewed as a significant factor.[4] The exception is in work with minority groups when ethnicity, familiarity with the language, and culture can ease what would otherwise be barriers to providing care.[26] (See Part II in respect to specific racial and ethnic groups and other special populations.)

The one significant treatment variable is the nature of the treatment goals and whether treatment is oriented toward abstinence or controlled drinking. The latter is likely to be ineffective with dependent persons for whom abstinence seems to be essential.[64,98] At one time controlled drinking was considered a reasonable goal, independent of the diagnosis of abuse or dependence, and received considerable attention, especially among behavioral psychologists. That view has been generally refuted, and treatment directed at teaching dependent persons to drink moderately in a nonhazardous fashion has been largely abandoned.

Beyond being challenged by many seasoned clinicians, several research studies documented the absence of moderate drinking among individuals treated for alcoholism who resumed drinking. Over time, Vaillant's longitudinal, prospective study found that one of two outcomes prevailed.[99] The active alcoholics in the study either became abstinent or they died. The number who continued drinking without accompanying problems decreased over time.[99] Another follow-up study, conducted 5 to 7 years post-treatment, found that only 1.6% of over 1200 alcoholics discharged from either medical or psychiatric facilities had developed a pattern of stable moderate drinking. It is noted that "the evolution of stable moderate drinking appears to be a rare outcome among alcoholics."[40] The research report that may have generated the most notoriety within the substance abuse treatment field involved the use of behavioral methods to promote controlled drinking. The initial report claimed the approach had been successful.[69] A subsequent follow-up by other researchers found that over time, very few of the former patients had maintained nonproblematic drinking. Complementing this treatment outcome research are other data elaborating the physiological basis and mechanisms associated with addictive states. This work too has lent support to the need for abstinence by identifying physiological factors that can account for the inability of addicted persons to resume moderate alcohol use.

Relapse Prevention

Although pretreatment variables are currently regarded as among the most accurate predictors of eventual clinical outcome, there is increasing recogni-

tion of the value of efforts to prevent relapse. Traditionally, treatment programs focused their primary efforts on assisting patients to stop drinking. This did not necessarily address the equally important issue of assisting patients to remain abstinent. There is now a growing appreciation that cessation of use and maintenance of new behaviors are two different processes.

Marlatt is the clinician/researcher who first described approaches to relapse prevention.[56] Commonly, a drinking incident or lapse of sobriety occurs in the first months following treatment. Several factors appear to be common precursors of relapse. One factor is experiencing negative emotions, e.g., frustration, anger, depression, or anxiety; another is an interpersonal conflict; another is social pressures. The latter is as likely to be internally generated (the product of patients' notions of how they believe others expect them to act,) as externally generated by actual social pressure. In each of these circumstances, without alternative coping strategies, patients easily resort to drinking or using drugs. Relapse prevention efforts provide a range of coping responses to help individuals anticipate difficult situations and rehearse effective responses. As a corollary, it is also important that patients begin to recognize their capacity to handle stress and not see themselves as always being at the mercy of external forces.

Various techniques are being used to address relapse prevention, including relaxation therapy, teaching skills of refusal, assertiveness training, and involvement in "positive addictions" that offer a sense of well-being and pleasure. The various approaches to relapse prevention should not be considered as a checklist, with everything being equally useful for a particular patient. Preferably a behavioral assessment is used that takes into account the patient's personality and the stressful, provocative situations the patient is likely to encounter. The importance of providing pleasurable activities may be obvious. Over the long term it is imperative that patients not view themselves as in a state of constant deprivation, thinking that they are not allowed to drink or use drugs. The danger of this attitude is that sooner or later these patients think they are owed a drink or drug.

PATIENT PERCEPTIONS

What clinicians consider to be therapeutic may not be viewed as such by patients. One study that involved both staff and patients rated the various elements of a clinical program as to their utility and helpfulness. The program features surveyed are presented in Table 4-2. Surprisingly, there was much less congruence between the staff's and patients' assessments than might have been anticipated. The staff tended to view the "lay" aspects of treatment, such as making contacts with

Table 4-2. Patient and Staff Ratings of Treatment Options

Program component	Patient ranking	Staff ranking
Day/Inpatient program	1	3
Initial advice from psychiatrist	2	5
Admission for detoxification	3	6
Safe "dry" environment	4	8
Talks with staff	5	9
Advice from patients	6	4
Outpatient groups	7	1
New patient groups	8	7
Relatives' involvement	9	10
AA meeting on treatment unit	10	2

Modified from Rees DW; Stone K. Patient use of treatment options at an ATU and ratings of their relative usefulness. *Alcohol and Alcoholism* 24(1): 66, 1989.

other patients and attending self-help groups, as being of greatest benefit. Conversely, patients tended to rate professionally provided services as more useful.[72] These evaluations are summarized in Table 4-2.

This data does not indicate what ultimately was and was not helpful, but it does not render the data merely interesting. It shows the importance that patients place on involvement with professional care providers, who can legitimize a problem and offer reassurance and solace. Being under care, at a point when the patient feels vulnerable, can provide reassurance that taking the risks needed to make changes will not lead to disaster.

TREATMENT PRIORITIES

The current wisdom is that substance use problems need to be treated as a priority when a patient has multiple problems. This is based on several factors. One is the recognition that the impairment accompanying active alcohol or drug dependence effectively negates a patient's ability to deal with other problems. Furthermore, as long as patients' central priorities are maintaining substance use, they are likely to sabotage or shy away from dealing with other problems, especially ones that threaten the continuation of use. The other factor is the common experience that with treatment for dependency, previously existing problems are often resolved without special efforts. This is probably because of multiple factors. For one, the individual is better able to deal with life's problems when no longer using alcohol or other drugs. Many of the problems seen are the result of alcohol and drug use. In addition, the cessation of alcohol or drug use requires tremendous personal growth and change. These changes occur rapidly; to

achieve and maintain sobriety often requires that the individual be prepared to reevaluate and reconstitute virtually every aspect of his or her life. The dramatic changes that occur in this context are comparable to those achieved only after years of psychotherapy.

A particular clinical challenge is sorting out the symptoms of dependence from concomitant psychiatric illnesses. Alcohol and drug dependency may mimic other psychiatric disorders. If a patient's presenting symptoms include alcohol or substance use, the conservative stance is to presume that any psychiatric symptomatology is derived from it and to avoid initiating treatment for a concomitant psychiatric disorder, e.g., anxiety or depression. When psychiatric illness is suspected, a referral to a treatment program that has a specific program for patients with dual diagnosis is advised. Though there are few true dual diagnosis programs, the number is increasing. For many patients, the psychiatric symptoms seen will resolve with abstinence. For other patients, psychotropic medications and psychotherapy may be necessary. With higher levels of psychiatric severity, traditional substance abuse counseling by itself has a poor outcome. However, studies have demonstrated that when substance abuse counseling is complemented by other forms of professional therapy, the prognosis is significantly improved.[106]

Sometimes the patient with an alcohol or substance use problem will be involved with other helping professionals. Some problems that bring a patient and/or family members to another professional's attention cannot be put aside until treatment for the substance use problem is completed. When simultaneous treatment is warranted, e.g., in a case involving known or suspected child abuse, it is essential that all involved have good communications during treatment planning and active treatment.

Given the nature of substance abuse problems, it is necessary that there be a consistent, single viewpoint expressed by the helping people in the system. In addition, the patient cannot be expected to be the medium of communication between different clinicians. It is useful to check in regularly with one another, but in some instances, see the patient jointly. Professionals involved should anticipate some differing perspectives among themselves. This will create tension. It is important that a patient not be caught in the middle between two service systems making incompatible demands.

SMOKING CESSATION

Primary care providers have been in the forefront of smoking cessation efforts. This trend clearly continues. Office-based interventions have been successfully combined with community-based programs, such as "stop smoking groups" and even computer-based educational initiatives, and these have been accomplished in a variety of clinical settings.[104,47]

Nonetheless, smoking was an issue long ignored by the formal alcohol and drug abuse treatment community. The view was that to expect patients to deal simultaneously with more than one addiction, namely alcohol or drugs, was unreasonable. However, substance abuse programs rarely dealt with smoking cessation at some future point, either. A comment heard in defense of not addressing nicotine was that although it is undoubtedly addictive, smoking does not make one's life unmanageable as do alcohol or drugs. For a long time patients in alcohol or drug treatment could be found chain smoking and consuming gallons of black coffee.

Over the past several years, there has been a dramatic shift within the alcohol/drug treatment community on the issue of nicotine. This is probably because of several factors: the anti-smoking lobby and increasing social disapproval and intolerance of smoking; the growing tendency within the alcohol and drug treatment communities to cease distinguishing between addictive substances and instead to view substance abuse as a single phenomenon; the growing research that attributes early cigarette use as a risk factor for future drug use; the increasing tendency of health care facilities to be smoke-free environments; the introduction within the Alcoholics Anonymous community of nonsmoking meetings; and the role of several nationally well-known treatment programs such as The Betty Ford Center becoming smoke-free and expecting patients to withdraw from nicotine as part of their treatment for substance abuse problems. With more treatment programs adopting this stance, the common perception is that smoking cessation does not compromise substance abuse treatment. On the contrary, it may assist recovery because smoking and other substance use are often intertwined behaviors. The experience has been that patients do not resist smoking cessation but perceive it as being reasonable in the context of their treatment for substance abuse. Unlike with alcohol or other drugs, most persons addicted to nicotine report that they would like to stop smoking. Regardless of whether this is accurate, patients tend to attribute any physical discomfort and withdrawal symptoms to their withdrawal from alcohol or other drugs rather than to nicotine withdrawal. Treatment outcome research confirms this perception that smoking cessation as part of substance abuse treatment does not reduce treatment effectiveness.[18,42]

However, although it represents a clear trend, smoking cessation has not yet become a universal element of substance abuse treatment. Because a treatment program's stance on nicotine has considerable importance for a patient's general health and well-being, it should be considered a relevant factor in making a referral.

WORKING WITH FAMILY MEMBERS

Not only are those with alcohol or other substance use problems an inevitable part of any primary care practice, so are their family members. Family members will have a higher rate of medical care utilization than families without alcohol or substance abuse. The recognition of the distress that other family members experience has been relatively recent. Substance abuse treatment programs have begun to offer services to family members as well. Fortunately, there are a many services available to family members in virtually any area, from self-help groups to formal treatment.

WORKING WITH MEMBERS OF 12-STEP GROUPS

12-step groups are an integral part of substance abuse treatment and recovery. They provide members a clear and simple set of steps to stay sober or straight, and they offer a social circle that is abstinent and supportive. Both inpatient and outpatient programs use the precepts of self-help as a central part of their programs. A component of treatment is introducing patients to a 12-step program (Box 4-3), which for many will become a mainstay of aftercare.

Working with members of 12-step groups begins with an understanding of the groups' traditions and guidelines. AA is the model for all other 12-step programs. The name comes from the 12 steps that were identified by the early members of AA as the sequence of actions they had taken in becoming sober. AA was formed at a time (1935) when the medical profession considered alcoholism to be essentially a terminal illness. As a lay movement, the growth of AA and the experiences of its members demonstrated that alcoholics could recover.

Box 4-3
12-Step Programs

- Alcoholics Anonymous (AA)
- Cocaine Anonymous (CA)
- Overeaters Anonymous (OA)
- Narcotics Anonymous (NA)
- Al-Anon Family Groups
- Alateen
- Adult Children of Alcoholics

In drafting the collective experience of the first members into a volume known as the "Big Book" (*Alcoholics Anonymous*), the sequence of their actions leading to sobriety is summarized. Interestingly, these actions were written in the past tense, intended not to be prescriptive but merely descriptive. Other groups that have adopted the format and experience of AA have incorporated the 12 steps as the central feature of the recovery process. Such groups are known generically as 12-step programs, changing the language of step 1 and replacing alcohol with the focus of the new fellowship.

From a therapeutic perspective, 12-step programs incorporate many of the elements considered critical for substance abuse treatment. They provide a social support system; offer a sober social circle; provide role models; accept and do not judge one another; reach out to the newest members, even describing them as the most "valuable" part of the group; rebuild members' self-esteem; and offer many practical pointers for building sobriety. In addition, they are accessible 24 hours a day in virtually any community at no cost.

Other such groups within the substance abuse field include NA (for recovering narcotic addicts), CA (for those dependent on cocaine), OA (Overeater's Anonymous) Al-Anon (for anyone affected by another's alcoholism), Alateen (for the adolescent affected by a parent's or other family member's alcoholism), and ACOA (Adult Children of Alcoholics). Attending local open meetings of 12-step groups helps the health care professional understand the usefulness of these fellowships. It imparts an understanding of an activity that recovering patients may consider vital to recovery. It is helpful to recognize that the meeting itself is the equivalent of the office visit for medical care; what happens outside of the meetings is the significant part, just as is what transpires after a patient leaves the medical clinic.

How to Make a Referral

The 12-step programs cannot be joined as other social groups nor can one make a referral of a potential member as if the group were a social service agency. The process of affiliation is best accomplished by contacts with members. Commonly, patients in treatment programs are taken to meetings as part of a formal treatment program. However, although new members are "taken," the real outreach occurs at the meeting when members seek out new persons, introduce themselves, exchange phone numbers, or make dates for coffee to talk about how the program works. Other ways of making initial contact can be through an answering service, which is available in many communities. If asked, recovering patients may agree to make themselves available to speak with someone interested in the program and take them to a meeting. With this personal, one-to-one style of becoming involved, and with patients' reticence to just go alone, the key point in referral is identifying individuals who can be the initial contact. The program will take it from there.

The Process of Affiliation

The organizational office of AA conducts a survey of the membership on a 3-year basis. The most recent survey inquired as to the source of introduction to AA. The responses appear in Table 4-3.

Approximately two-thirds of all new members to AA are introduced either by a member or through a treatment program. In either case, whatever the source of the initial contact, there are common patterns that mark the process of affiliation with AA. For those introduced via formal treatment, the patient's first attendance at meetings will occur during treatment. Meetings of 12-step groups are often provided with meeting space within treatment agencies. Programs also arrange to take patients to meetings in the community. The attention that long-term members give to newcomers is common to all meetings. Often people will linger after the meeting, drinking coffee and chatting. At that time they will make a point of introducing themselves and speaking to newcomers.

Standard advice that treatment programs give patients is to attend 60 meetings in 60 days, and in some parts of the country this has become 90 meetings in 90 days. The thinking behind this advice is that one needs an adequate exposure to a 12-step fellowship to become involved. Second, different meetings do have somewhat different qualities. By attending many meetings, potential new members have an improved chance of finding a group where they feel they belong. The period following discharge from inpatient treatment will be the most stressful. Initial intensive attendance at a 12-step group ensures that the newly sober person is in a setting to get support daily. During this period of intensive attendance, the newcomer will also be advised to seek out members informally, to make dates for coffee and conversation, or to share rides to meetings. They exchange

Table 4-3. Source of Introduction to AA

Source	Proportion (%)
An AA member	36
"On my own"	27
Formal treatment program	36
Family	19
Doctor	7

telephone numbers and are advised to call someone every day. This "reaching out" is regarded as a habit worth cultivating. It may make the difference at some later, unexpected point when the temptation to use alcohol or drugs is strong and when having someone to turn to may make the difference between using and not using. The older members make a point of telling new members that such contacts also help them as well. Thus, the new member is shown that there is built in reciprocity so one need not feel indebted, overly needy, or as a nuisance. Another aspect of this early period of involvement with a 12-step group is reading the literature of the group and making efforts to apply the group's principles in daily activities. For the individuals who feel helpless and uncertain and who question their own judgment and abilities, the self-help program can provide specific but simple approaches for rebuilding their lives.

Following this period of initial intense involvement, individuals will typically select several meetings a week to attend regularly. Also, during this period, having become familiar with many people, they will have selected a sponsor. A sponsor is a combination of mentor and big-brother or big-sister and is not viewed as a therapist or counselor. The sponsor is generally restricted to sharing his or her experience in using the tools of the 12-step program, putting the precepts of the program into practice, providing encouragement, and pointing out behaviors that may jeopardize sobriety. The new member can discuss concerns and efforts to maintain sobriety that may not be appropriate to discuss in a meeting, although they warrant attention. After 18 to 24 months, with stable abstinence established, the member may regularly attend one meeting a week. However, those who identify with this 12-step group, at times of discomfort or stress, may often increase their involvement to strengthen their coping skills, thereby getting the additional support they need and reducing the risk of a relapse.

Sources of Information and Literature

Although 12-step programs are informal organizations, each one has a national office that provides the logistical coordination required. One of the central office's primary functions is preparing and publishing literature. The addresses and telephone numbers are located in Appendix A. In addition to literature published for active members and for untreated addicted people, there is literature directed to those in the helping professions.

In addition to the national offices, there are also state or regional organizations that publish directories of meeting times and places and also make themselves available to professionals. For example, AA will put on a sample meeting for professional groups. At the community level, there is often an answering service to respond to queries or requests for assistance. Look in the white pages of the phone book under the group's name.

CONFIDENTIALITY OF ALCOHOL AND DRUG ABUSE PATIENT RECORDS[11]

In 1975 the federal government adopted rules and regulations regarding the confidentiality of all alcohol and drug abuse patient records. These regulations were revised in July of 1987.[25,68] The regulations on confidentiality should be reviewed by any provider involved in diagnosis and treatment of alcohol and substance abuse patients. They address written, informed consent, special consent for minors, and release of information in emergencies.

The confidentiality guidelines protect any information regarding alcohol and drug abuse patients obtained by any alcohol or drug abuse program receiving federal assistance. This refers to the receipt of federal funds through state and local governments and includes certification to receive Medicare funds, tax exempt status, or permission to receive tax exempt contributions. Thus, there are few medical care settings or social service settings that are exempt. The regulations define programs as those that specialize in the diagnosis, treatment, and referral for treatment for alcohol and drug abuse. The intent of the regulation is to protect the privacy of all patients, to ensure them that treatment will be completely confidential, and to ensure that patients maintain control of information regarding their care. All records pertaining to a patient's care are covered by these regulations, and written permission from the patient is required to release most information.

SOCIAL SERVICE AGENCIES

Many health care professionals are employed in social service agencies. Despite the differences in settings, many of the essential clinical tasks relating to care of substance abuse issues will be identical. This includes routine screening, early identification, patient education, and referral for specialized treatment.

However, there are several significant differences confronting those in nonmedical settings. One relates to the type of assistance patients are requesting when they turn to agencies for help. Although many patients may have health problems, people do not usually turn to social service agencies for health care. When family members catch a common cold that lingers, their teenager needs a physical to play soccer, or their first grader has fallen from a tree and requires a few sutures for a gash on the forehead, they do not make an appointment at their local mental health center or other community agency. Thus, because they are not viewed as providers of health care, those in social service agencies do not have health concerns as a clear rationale for their own intervention. Thus, discussion of alcohol or drugs may strike patients as inappropriate or intrusive.

Nonetheless, for many patients seen in community agencies, alcohol and substance abuse is often a significant problem. This is true whether the agency primarily provides therapy or counseling or offers specialized assistance, as with housing, vocational and job training for the unemployed or underemployed, meals for the elderly, or services for the homebound. In these settings, becoming comfortable and feeling entitled to broach the subject of substance use can be as much of a challenge as effectively intervening.

Increasingly, when individuals and family members recognize an alcohol or drug problem and want help, they turn directly to substance abuse treatment programs. Social service settings are unlikely to have someone coming to them specifically requesting help for alcohol or substance use. Thus, the task is identifying an alcohol or drug use problem and being aware of its contribution to the presenting problem(s). Alcohol or drug use problems are often associated with self-referrals or with people referred by others for difficulties in marriage, school, or parent/child relationships, or in suspected child abuse or mistreatment situations. In these situations, the chances are exceedingly poor that the presenting problems will be resolved as long as the substance use goes untreated.

For those providing counseling or psychotherapy, there are other reasons to be attuned to alcohol and drug use. Even when alcohol or drug use is otherwise nonproblematic, if patients in therapy use alcohol or other drugs to help them relax or unwind or to ease emotional discomfort, they are in danger of sabotaging their treatment because they are using a drug to handle things that should be addressed within therapy. Some psychotherapists recommend that anyone being seen in counseling or psychotherapy abstain from alcohol or other drug use for the duration, with the exception of a single glass of wine on a special occasion. However, drinking or using marijuana daily or drinking heavily is contraindicated.

An alcohol and drug history is recommended as part of the standard intake procedure, as well as being incorporated into the psychosocial history. Not unlike their colleagues in the health care settings, research shows social work professionals who identify a probable alcohol or substance abuse problem often fail to address it clinically. One study of clinician behavior upon reviewing charts from four different agencies found that only 5% of the patients seen were diagnosed as having an alcohol and/or drug problem for which a referral for treatment was made. Clinician interviews indicated that for an additional 30% of the cases, a substance abuse problem was suspected, but no interventions had been made. "Professional judgment" was cited as the major reason for the absence of formal diagnosis and referral. The rationale for these judgments was that substance abuse was not the core problem. The clinicians noted that the patient and/or family were not ready to deal with the substance abuse problem; or clinicians were pessimistic about the outcome of treatment; or there were organizational issues cited, such as their agency's resistance to making referrals outside the agency or the circumscribed nature of their professional roles.[44]

Common Presentations

Problems with substance use are commonly a part of the presenting symptoms regardless of whether they are immediately obvious. Frequently, the person who approaches the agency is not the substance dependent person but the spouse or other family member. The following presentations in social service agencies are those most likely to have a substance abuse component: relationship problems and problems involving children, whether centering on school problems, abuse, neglect, discipline, runaways, or children about to be cast from the home. For previously self-supporting families now beset by financial problems or legal difficulties, substance use may be an underlying problem. In counseling settings, these problems may present as stress, difficulty in coping, low self-esteem, and somatic complaints.

Screening

The CAGE and Brief MAST are suitable for broad clinical use. Their utility is not restricted to medical settings, and they can be included within intake routines. To avoid neglecting screening, especially when it may seemingly appear "unnecessary," review intake procedures and insert alcohol/substance use screening into established protocols.

Referral

When screening is positive, a referral for evaluation and treatment planning is indicated. In the case of family members, make a referral for education and treatment as affected individuals. There is no reason that education and treatment should be considered outside the range of services of the social service agency. However, in practice, beyond requiring specific clinical skills, this entails an investment of time that is often unavailable. It is on that basis that a referral to a substance abuse clinician or treatment program is suggested. The willingness of the patient to accept the referral will depend on many of the elements discussed in the previous chapter. The ability to genuinely recommend investigation of a possible problem or address the benefits of treatment is important. The potential concern that the patient may have about losing contact with the agency if the referral is accepted is also a consideration. This can be as true for family members as it is for the substance user. To the patient it may seem like an either/or situation. In addition to concern about loss of a supportive relationship, the patient may have concerns about the invaluable services provided to the family. Often patients wonder whether these services continue if a referral is accepted.

Special Challenges

One challenge is to avoid perpetuating a substance use problem by neglecting to address it, which may not always be easy to do. One cannot withhold essential services from an individual because of alcohol or substance abuse problems. Thus, the task is to provide services in a manner that continues to bring substance use problems to light. The goal is to help the family seek treatment for themselves to understand how substance use is affecting them. This enhances the family's coping skills, lessens their dependence on the family member with the alcohol or drug use problem, and reduces their own pain and dysfunction. In some instances it may enable them to set limits, which may promote treatment.

Another challenge is to avoid being too nice, nonconfrontive, and overly supportive as the basis of your therapeutic alliance with the patient. This approach is usually predicated on the erroneous notion that, later, the established relationship can provide the incentive for a patient to deal with the alcohol or substance abuse problem. In effect, the clinician could be regarded as attempting to "seduce" the patient into treatment. This strategy almost always fails. The clinician can never hope to compete with the patient's drug of choice. Failure to acknowledge the difficulties and source of a patient's problems, the dependence on alcohol or drugs, causes the patient to lose trust because the fundamental issue is being ignored. This approach also invites ambivalence and arms the patient with the ultimate weapon to resist change: to threaten to leave counseling. This can create a vicious circle. The clinician works harder on the relationship, and, at the same time, often begins to feel resentment.

REFERENCES

1. Adams WL; Yuan Z; Barboriak JJ; Rimm AA. Alcohol-related hospitalizations of elderly people: Prevalence and geographic variation in the United States. *Journal of the American Medical Association* 270(10): 1222-1225, 1993. (29 refs.)

2. Anderson P. Effectiveness of general practice interventions for patients with harmful alcohol consumption. (review). *British Journal of General Practice* 43(374): 386-389, 1993. (26 refs.)

3. Ashton H. Protracted withdrawal from benzodiazepines: The post withdrawal syndrome. *Psychiatric Annals* 25(3): 174-179, 1995. (28 refs.)

4. Atkinson DR; Schein S. Similarity in counseling. *Counseling Psychologist* 14(2): 319-354, 1986. (95 refs.)

5. Babor TF. Avoiding the horrid and beastly sin of drunkenness: Does dissuasion make a difference? *Journal of Consulting and Clinical Psychology* 62(6): 1127-1140, 1994. (51 refs.)

6. Babor TF. The WHO brief intervention study, warts and all: A response to the commentators. *Addiction* 89(6): 676-678, 1994. (2 refs.)

7. Bardsley PE; Beckman LJ. The health belief model and entry into alcoholism treatment. *International Journal of Addiction* 23(1): 19-28, 1988. (13 refs.)

8. Beresford TP; Low D; Adduci R; Goggins F. Alcoholism assessment on an orthopedic surgery service. *Journal of Bone and Joint Surgery: American Volume* 64(5): 730-733, 1982. (14 refs.)

9. Bien TH; Miller WR; Tonigan JS. Brief interventions for alcohol problems: A review. (review). *Addiction* 88(3): 315-336, 1993. (94 refs.)

10. Black JS; Kapoor W. Health promotion and disease prevention in older people: Our current state of ignorance. *American Geriatric Society* 38(2): 168-172, 1990. (42 refs.)

11. Blume SB. *Confidentiality of Patient Records in Alcoholism and Drug Treatment Programs.* New York: American Medical Society on Alcoholism and Other Drug Dependencies, Inc and National Council on Alcoholism, Inc, 1987.

12. Bokstrom K; Balldin J; Langstrom G. Individual mood profiles in alcohol withdrawal. *Alcoholism: Clinical and Experimental Research* 15(3): 508-513, 1991. (23 refs.)

13. Booth RE; Watters JK. How effective are risk reduction interventions targeting injecting drug users? (review). *AIDS* 8(11): 1515-1524, 1994. (66 refs.)

14. Brandt J; Butters N; Ryan C; Bayog R. Cognitive loss and recovery in long-term alcohol abusers. *Archives of General Psychiatry* 40(4): 435-442, 1983. (57 refs.)

15. Brower KJ; Blow FC; Beresford TP. Treatment implications of chemical dependency models: An integrative approach. *Journal of Substance Abuse Treatment* 6(3): 147-157, 1989. (41 refs.)

16. Buchsbaum DG. Effectiveness of treatment in general medicine patients with drinking problems. *Alcohol Health and Research World* 18(2): 140-145, 1994. (33 refs.)

17. Burling TA; Seidner AL; Gaither DE. A computer-directed program for smoking cessation treatment. *Journal of Substance Abuse* 6(4): 427-431, 1994. (10 refs.)

18. Campbell BK; Wander N; Stark MJ; Holbert T. Treating cigarette smoking in drug-abusing clients. *Journal of Substance Abuse Treatment* 12(2): 89-94, 1995. (28 refs.)

19. Chick J; Lloyd G; Crombie E. Counseling problem drinkers in medical wards: A controlled study. *British Medical Journal* 2990(6437): 83-89, 1985. (11 refs.)

20. Cohen M; Kern JC; Hassett C. Identifying alcoholism in medical patients. *Hospital and Community Psychiatry* 37(4): 398-400, 1986. (6 refs.)

21. Cormack MA; Owens RG; Dewey ME. The effect of minimal interventions by general practitioners on long-term benzodiazepine use. *Journal of the Royal College of General Practitioners* 39(327): 408-411, 1989. (15 refs.)

22. Crosby RD; Halikas JA; Carlson G. Pharmacotherapeutic interventions for cocaine abuse: Present practices and future directions. (review). *Journal of Addictive Diseases* 10(4): 13-30, 1991. (102 refs.)

23. Edwards G; Orford J; Egert S; Guthrie S; Hawker A; Hensman C; et al. Alcoholism: A controlled trial of "treatment" and "advice." *Journal of Studies on Alcohol* 38(5): 1004-1031, 1977. (39 refs.)

24. Farrell M; Ward J; Mattick R; Hall W; Stimson GV; des Jarlais D; et al. Methadone maintenance treatment in opiate dependence: A review. *British Medical Journal* 309(6960): 997-1001, 1994. (93 refs.)

25. Federal Register. *Confidentiality of Alcohol and Drug Abuse Patient Records, Final Rule.* Federal Register 52(110), Part II, June 9, 1987. Available from the National Clearinghouse for Alcohol and Drug Information.

26. Finn P. Addressing the needs of cultural minorities in drug treatment. *Journal of Substance Abuse Treatment* 11(4): 325-337, 1994. (52 refs.)

27. Fishbain DA; Rosomoff HL; Cutler R; Rosomoff RS. Opiate detoxification protocols: A clinical manual. *Annals of Clinical Psychiatry* 5(1): 53-65, 1993. (60 refs.)

28. Fleming MF. Personal communication, October 8, 1988.

29. Fleming MF. Screening and brief intervention for alcohol disorders. *Journal of Family Practice* 37(3): 231-234, 1993. (30 refs.)

30. Frank RG; McGuire TG; Regier DA; Manderscheid R; Woodward A. Paying for mental health and substance abuse care. *Health Affairs* 13(1): 337-342, 1994. (13 refs.)

31. Fuller MG. A new day: Strategies for managing psychiatric and substance abuse benefits. *Health Care Management Review* 19(4): 20-24, 1994. (33 refs.)

32. Gentilello LM; Duggan P; Drummond D; Tonnesen A; Degner EE; Fischer RP; Reed RL. Major injury as a unique opportunity to initiate treatment in the alcoholic. *American Journal of Surgery* 156(6): 558-561, 1988. (20 refs.)

33. Gerra G; Marcato A; Caccavari R; Fontanesi B; Delsignore R; Fertonani G; et al. Clonidine and opiate receptor antagonists in the treatment of heroin addiction. *Journal of Substance Abuse Treatment* 12(1): 35-41, 1995. (18 refs.)

34. Gold MS. Pharmacological therapies of opiate addiction. IN: Miller NS; Gold MS, eds. *Pharmacological Therapies for Drug and Alcohol Addictions.* New York: Marcel Dekker, Inc, 1995. pp. 159-174. (66 refs.)

35. Gold MS; Miller NS. Pharmacological therapies for addiction, withdrawal, and relapse: General aspects. IN: Miller NS; Gold MS, eds. *Pharmacological Therapies for Drug and Alcohol Addictions.* New York: Marcel Dekker, Inc, 1995. pp. 11-29. (78 refs.)

36. Gourlay S. The pros and cons of transdermal nicotine therapy. (review). *Medical Journal of Australia* 160(3): 152-159, 1994. (41 refs.)

37. Hamilton MR; Menkes DB; Jeffrey AK. Early intervention for alcohol misuse: Encouraging doctors to take action. *New Zealand Medical Journal* 107(989): 454-456, 1994. (30 refs.)

38. Harrison PA; Hoffmann NG; Gibbs L; Hollister CD; Luxenberg MG. Determinants of chemical dependency treatment placement: Clinical, economic, and logistic factors. *Psychotherapy* 25(3): 356-364, 1988. (7 refs.)

39. Haviland MG; Hendryx MS; Cummings MA; Shaw DG; MacMurray JP. Multidimensionality and state dependency of alexithymia in recently sober alcoholics. *Journal of Nervous and Mental Disease* 179(5): 284-290, 1991. (46 refs.)

40. Helzer JE; Robins LN; Taylor JR; Carey K; Miller RH; Combs-Orme T; et al. The extent of long-term moderate drinking among alcoholics discharged from medical and psychiatric treatment facilities. *New England Journal of Medicine* 312(26): 1678-1682, 1985. (11 refs.)

41. Hopkins TB; Zarro VJ; McCarter TG. The adequacy of screening, documenting, and treating the diseases of substance abuse. *Journal of Addictive Diseases* 13(2): 81-87, 1994. (8 refs.)

42. Hurt RD; Eberman KM; Croghan IT; Offord KP; Davis LJ Jr; Morse RM; et al. Nicotine dependence treatment during inpatient treatment for other addictions: A prospective intervention trial. *Alcoholism: Clinical and Experimental Research* 18(4): 867-872, 1994. (35 refs.)

43. Jonas JM; Gold MS. The pharmacologic treatment of alcohol and cocaine abuse: Integration of recent findings into clinical practice. (review). *Psychiatric Clinics of North America* 15(1): 179-190, 1992. (54 refs.)

44. Kagle J. Secondary prevention of substance abuse. *Social Work* 32(5): 446-448, 1987. (9 refs.)

45. Kahan M; Wilson L; Becker L. Effectiveness of physician-based interventions with problem drinkers: A review. *Canadian Medical Association Journal* 152(6): 851-859, 1995. (30 refs.)

46. Kandel DB; Logan JA. Patterns of drug use from adolescence to young adulthood: Periods of risk for initiation, continued use, and discontinuation. *American Journal of Public Health* 74(7): 660-666, 1984. (11 refs.)

47. Kendrick JS; Zahniser SC; Miller N; Salas N; Stine J; Gargiullo PM; et al. Integrating smoking cessation into routine public prenatal care: The Smoking Cessation in Pregnancy Project. *American Journal of Public Health* 85(2): 217-222, 1995. (25 refs.)

48. Kosten TA; Kosten TR. Pharmacological blocking agents for treating substance abuse. *Journal of Nervous and Mental Disease* 179(10): 583-592, 1991. (96 refs.)

49. Krampen G. Motivation in the treatment of alcoholism. *Addictive Behavior* 14(2): 197-200, 1989. (7 refs.)

50. Kreek MJ. Rationale for maintenance pharmacotherapy of opiate dependence. IN: O'Brien CP; Jaffee JH, eds. *Addictive States.* New York: Raven Press, 1992. pp. 205-230. (67 refs.)

51. Kreitman N. Alcohol consumption and the preventive paradox. *British Journal of Addiction* 81(3): 353-363, 1986. (21 refs.)

52. Lacombe S; Stanislav SW; Marken PA. Pharmacologic treatment of cocaine abuse. *DICP: The Annals of Pharmacotherapy* 25(7-8): 818-823, 1991. (51 refs.)

53. Leckman AL; Umland BE; Blay M. Prevalence of alcoholism in a family practice center. *Journal of Family Practice* 18(6): 867-870, 1984. (25 refs.)

54. Liese BS. Brief therapy, crisis intervention and the cognitive therapy of substance abuse. *Crisis Intervention* 1(1): 11-29, 1994. (40 refs.)

55. Ludwig AM. Cognitive processes associated with spontaneous recovery from alcoholism. *Journal of Studies on Alcohol* 46(1): 53-58, 1985. (12 refs.)

56. Marlatt GA; George WH. Relapse prevention: Introduction and overview of the model. *British Journal of Addiction* 79: 261-273, 1984. (40 refs.)

57. Meyer RE. New pharmacotherapies for cocaine dependence revisited. *Archives of General Psychiatry* 49(11): 900-904, 1992. (57 refs.)

58. Miller WR; Hester RK. Inpatient alcoholism treatment: Who benefits? *American Psychologist* 41(7): 794-805, 1986. (75 refs.)

59. Miller WR; Sovereign RG; Krege B. Motivational interviewing with problem drinkers: The drinkers check-up as a preventive intervention. *Behavioural Psychotherapy* 16(4): 251-268, 1988. (42 refs.)

60. Miller WR; Taylor CA. Relative effectiveness of bibliotherapy, individual, and group self-control training in the treatment of problem drinkers. *Addictive Behaviors* 5(1): 13-24, 1980. (42 refs.)

61. Mitchell WD; Thompson TL; Craig SR. Under consultation and lack of follow-up for alcohol abusers in a university hospital. *Psychosomatics* 26(6): 431-437, 1986. (29 refs.)

62. Moore RD; Malitz FE. Underdiagnosis of alcoholism by residents in an ambulatory service. *Journal of Medical Education* 61(1): 46-52, 1986. (15 refs.)

63. Moos RH; Finney JW. The process of recovery from alcoholism: Comparing alcoholic patients and matched community controls. *Journal of Studies on Alcohol* 42(5): 383-402, 1981. (45 refs.)

64. Moos RH; Finney JW. The expanding scope of alcoholism treatment evaluation. *American Journal of Psychology* 38(10): 1036-1044, 1983. (63 refs.)

65. National Institute of Alcohol Abuse and Alcoholism. *Sixth Special Report to the US Congress on Alcohol and Health.* Rockville MD: National Institute on Alcohol Abuse and Alcoholism, 1987. 147 pp. (Chapter refs.)

66. Office of the Inspector. *General Drug Utilization Review.* Washington DC: Department of Health and Human Services, 1989. (95 refs.)

67. Ornstein P; Cherepon JA. Demographic variables as predictors of alcoholism treatment outcome. *Journal of Studies on Alcohol* 46(5): 425-432, 1985. (39 refs.)

68. Pascal CB. *Revised Regulations to Protect Confidentiality of Alcohol and Drug Abuse Patient Records: Overview and Summary.* Rockville MD: Office of the General Counsel, Department of Health and Human Services, 1988.

69. Pendery ML; Maltzman IM; West LJ. Controlled drinking by alcoholics? New findings and a reevaluation of a major affirmative study. *Science* 217(4555): 169-175, 1982. (30 refs.)

70. Powell JE; Taylor D. Anger, depression, and anxiety following heroin withdrawal. *International Journal of the Addictions* 27(1): 25-35, 1992. (13 refs.)

71. Price J. Alcohol screening and early intervention: An achievable advance in management (ed.). *Medical Journal of Australia* 149(7): 345-346, 1988. (43 refs.)

72. Rees DW; Stone K. Patient use of treatment options at an ATU and ratings of their relative usefulness. *Alcohol and Alcoholism* 24(1): 63-68, 1989. (9 refs.)

73. Richmond RL; Anderson P. Research in general practice for smokers and excessive drinkers in Australia and the UK. (135 refs. for three parts)
    Part I. Interpretation of results. (review). *Addiction* 89(1): 35-40, 1994.
    Part II. Representativeness of the results. (review). *Addiction* 89(1): 41-47, 1994.
    Part III. Dissemination of interventions. *Addiction* 89(1): 49-62, 1994.

74. Richmond R; Heather N; Wodak A; Kehoe L; Webster I. Controlled evaluation of a general practice-based brief intervention for excessive drinking. *Addiction* 90(1): 119-132, 1995. (28 refs.)

75. Rounsaville BJ; Dolinsky ZS. Psychopathology as a predictor of treatment outcome in alcoholics. *Archives of General Psychiatry* 44(6): 505-513, 1987. (64 refs.)

76. Ryder D; Lenton S; Harrison S; Dorricott J. Alcohol-related problems in a general hospital and a general practice: Screening and the preventive paradox. *Medical Journal of Australia* 149(7): 355-360, 1988. (11 refs.)

77. Sanders D; Peveler R; Mant D; Fowler G. Predictors of successful smoking cessation following advice from nurses in general practice. *Addiction* 88(12): 1699-1705, 1993. (26 refs.)

78. Saunders B. Reducing overall consumption remains the key. (commentary). *Addiction* 88(5): 599-600, 1993. (4 refs.)

79. Saunders B; Wilkinson C; Phillips M. The impact of a brief motivational intervention with opiate users attending a methadone programme. *Addiction* 90(3): 415-424, 1995. (26 refs.)

80. Schwartz JL. Methods of smoking cessation. (review). *Medical Clinics of North America* 76(2): 451-476, 1992. (98 refs.)

81. Seppa K; Makela R. Heavy drinking in hospital patients. *Addiction* 88(10): 1377-1382, 1993. (23 refs.)

82. Shadle M; Christianson JB. The impact of HMO development on mental health and chemical dependency services. *Hospital and Community Psychiatry* 40(11): 1145-1151, 1989. (6 refs.)

83. Sherin KM; Piotrowski ZH; Panek SM; Doot MC. Screening for alcoholism in a community hospital. *Journal of Family Practice* 15(6): 1091-1095, 1982. (0 refs.)

84. Simpson DD. National treatment system evaluation based on the Drug Abuse Reporting Program (DARP) follow-up research. IN: Tims FM; Ludford JP, eds. *Drug Abuse Treatment Evaluation: Strategies, Progress, and Prospects. NIDA Research Monograph 51.* Rockville MD: National Institute on Drug Abuse, 1984. pp. 29-41. (21 refs.)

85. Simpson DD; Friend HJ. Legal status and long-term outcomes for addicts in the DARP follow-up project. IN: Leukefeld CG; Tims FM, eds. *Compulsory Treatment of Drug Abuse: Research and Clinical Practice. NIDA Research Monograph 86.* Rockville MD: National Institute on Drug Abuse, 1988. pp. 81-98. (23 refs.)

86. Simpson DD; George WJ; Lehman WEK. *Addiction Careers: Summary of Studies Based on the DARP (Drug Abuse Reporting Program) 12 Year Follow-up.* NIDA Treatment Research Report. Rockville MD: National Institute on Drug Abuse, 1986. (31 refs.)

87. Sinclair JD; Sillanaukee P. The preventive paradox: A critical examination. (commentary). *Addiction* 88(5): 591-595, 1993. (9 refs.)

88. Skinner MH; Thompson DA. Pharmacologic considerations in the treatment of substance abuse. (review). *Southern Medical Journal* 85(12): 1207-1219, 1992. (59 refs.)

89. Sobell LC; Sobell MB; Toneatto T; Leo GI. What triggers the resolution of alcohol problems without treatment. *Alcoholism: Clinical and Experimental Research* 17(2): 217-224, 1993. (68 refs.)

90. Sommese T; Patterson JC. Acute effects of cigarette smoking withdrawal: A review of the literature. *Aviation, Space, and Environmental Medicine* 66(2): 164-167, 1995. (27 refs.)

91. Spivak K; Sanchev-Craig M; Davila R. Assisting problem drinkers to change on their own: Effect of specific and nonspecific advice. *Addiction* 89(9): 1135-1142, 1994. (19 refs.)

92. Stockwell T. Alcohol withdrawal: An adaptation to heavy drinking of no practical significance? *Addiction* 89(11): 1447-1453, 1994. (36 refs.)

93. Strecher VJ; Kreuter M; Den Boer D-J; Kobrin S; Hospero HJ; Skinner CS. The effects of computer-tailored smoking cessation messages in family practice settings. *Journal of Family Practice* 39(3): 262-270, 1994. (15 refs.)

94. Tuchfeld BS. Spontaneous remission in alcoholics: Empirical observations and theoretical implications. *Journal of Studies on Alcohol* 42(7): 626-641, 1981. (29 refs.)

95. Tucker JA; Gladsjo JA. Help-seeking and recovery by problem drinkers: Characteristics of drinkers who attended Alcoholics Anonymous or formal treatment or who recovered without assistance. *Addictive Behaviors* 18(5): 529-542, 1993. (47 refs.)

96. Tucker JA; Vuchinich RE; Gladsjo JA. Environmental events surrounding natural recovery from alcohol-related problems. *Journal of Studies on Alcohol* 55(4): 401-411, 1994. (37 refs.)

97. Tutton CS; Crayton JW. Current pharmacotherapies for cocaine abuse: A review. *Journal of Addictive Diseases* 12(2): 109-127, 1993. (97 refs.)

98. Vaillant GE. *The Natural History of Alcoholism.* Cambridge MA: Harvard University Press, 1983. 358 pp. (369 refs.)

99. Vaillant GE. What can long-term follow-up teach us about relapse and prevention of relapse in addiction? *British Journal of Addiction* 83(10): 1147-1157, 1988. (46 refs.)

100. Vaillant GE; Clark WD. Prospective study of alcoholism treatment: Eight-year follow-up. *American Journal of Medicine* 75: 455-463, 1983. (50 refs.)

101. Volpicelli JR; Clay KL; Watson NT; Volpicelli LA. Naltrexone and the treatment of alcohol dependence. *Alcohol Health and Research World* 18(4): 272-278, 1994. (24 refs.)

102. Volpicelli JR; Watson NT; King AC; Sherman CE; O'Brien CP. Effect of naltrexone on alcohol "high" in alcoholics. *American Journal of Psychiatry* 152(4): 613-615, 1995. (7 refs.)

103. Walker RD; Howard MO; Walker PS; Lambert MD; Suchinsky R. Practice guidelines in the addictions: Recent developments. *Journal of Substance Abuse Treatment* 12(2): 63-74, 1995. (91 refs.)

104. Wiggers JH; Sanson-Fisher R. General practitioners as agents of health risk behavior change: Opportunities for behavioral science in patient smoking cessation. *Behaviour Change* 11(3): 167-176, 1994. (77 refs.)

105. Willenbring ML; Olson DH; Lathrop LA; Miller MA; Lynch JW; Sonnier E; Bielinski J; Weigenant J. *The Health Improvement Program (HIP) Clinic: A Model for Early Intervention for Hazardous Drinking in the Primary Medical Setting.* Minneapolis: Alcohol Problems Clinics, VA Medical Center, 1989. (5 refs.)

106. Woody GE; McLellan AT; O'Brien CP. Research on psychopathology and addiction: Treatment implications. *Drug and Alcohol Dependence* 25(2): 121-123, 1990. (11 refs.)

FURTHER READINGS

Braithwaite RA; Jarvie DR; Minty PSB; Simpson D; Widdop B. Screening for drugs of abuse: Opiates, amphetamines and cocaine. (review). *Annals of Clinical Biochemistry* 32(March): 123-153, 1995. (205 refs.)

The main burden of care of patients with drug abuse problems falls on specialized treatment centers. Laboratory support in the form of urine screening tests has long been recognized as an integral part of these services. When a new patient is interviewed, the doctor's first task is to diagnose drug abuse. A comprehensive urine screen for drugs carried out at the initial assessment stage is undeniably the best means of arriving at a complete picture of the drug use. Copyright 1995, Association of Clinical Biochemists.

Camacho LM; Williams ML; Vogtsberger KN; Simpson DD. Cognitive readiness of drug injectors to reduce AIDS risks. *American Journal on Addictions* 4(1): 49-55, 1995. (24 refs.)

The impact of motivational factors on AIDS high-risk behavior after participation in an AIDS intervention program was explored among 208 out-of-treatment injecting drug users (IDUs). It was hypothesized that lower-risk behavior would be evident at follow-up among IDUs who indicated higher concern about their susceptibility to AIDS before intervention. Results showed that this motivational indicator predicted lower risks 6 months after the intervention. Overall, this study indicates that psychoeducational AIDS interventions will be most beneficial to individuals with sufficient cognitive readiness to address drug- and AIDS-related issues at a personal level. Assessments of risk and motivation levels of program participants should be used to tailor intervention strategies to meet individual needs. Copyright 1995, American Academy of Psychiatrists in Alcoholism and Addictions.

Cohen SJ; Halvorson HW; Gosselink CA. Changing physician behavior to improve disease prevention. *Preventive Medicine* 23(3): 284-291, 1994. (75 refs.)

Physicians often fail to provide nationally recommended preventive services for their patients. Addressing this, the authors have reviewed selected literature on changing physician behavior

using the organizational construct of the "readiness for change" transtheoretical model. This model suggests that behavior evolves through stages from precontemplation, to contemplation, to preparation, to initiation, and to maintenance of change. Traditional continuing medical education may affect knowledge and beliefs but rarely results in behavior change. However, motivational strategies such as practice feedback reports and influential peers can foster stage change. Successful interventions aimed at physicians preparing for change frequently use an office-system approach that targets not only physicians but office staff and patients. Illustrating how the readiness to change model can guide the design and implementation of interventions, the authors describe strategies being used in a statewide randomized controlled trial to improve cancer prevention counseling and early detection by primary care physicians. The multistage interventions of Partners for Prevention include support from a medical liability carrier, a motivational videotape, a task-delineated office manual, chart flowsheets, patient activation forms, practice feedback reports, a designated prevention coordinator within each practice, and regular telephone calls and office visits by project staff. Note: The paper also comments on the role of non-physician office staff. Copyright 1994, Academic Press, Inc.

Fava JL; Velicer WF; Prochaska JO. Applying the transtheoretical model to a representative sample of smokers. *Addictive Behaviors* 20(2): 189-203, 1995. (39 refs.)

Interrelationships among key constructs of the Transtheoretical Model are examined for the first time on a large ($n = 4,144$) representative sample of smokers. The posited relationships between the early stages of change (precontemplation, contemplation, preparation) and the process of change, decisional balance, and situational temptation are generally supported. Precontemplators are found to use the processes of change the least, and those in preparation use them the most. Precontemplators also have the least negative attitudes toward their smoking behavior. Precontemplators and contemplators are tempted to smoke in more situations than those in preparation. Precontemplators are also the most addicted to smoking, followed by those in contemplation and preparation, respectively, when examined on traditional measures of smoking behavior. The implications for smoking cessation efforts are also discussed. Copyright 1995, Elsevier Science Ltd.

Miller NS. Pharmacotherapy in alcoholism. (review). *Alcoholism Treatment Quarterly* 12(2): 129-152, 1995. (102 refs.)

The pharmacological agents used in the pharmacotherapies for alcoholism (and other drug addictions) are grouped in terms of their clinical use and reviewed. The categories examined include the following: (1) Intoxication—agents that reverse the pharmacological effects of alcohol, (2) Withdrawal—agents that suppress the pharmacological withdrawal from alcohol, (3) Desire and compulsion—agents that block the preoccupation with acquiring alcohol, the desire to use or continue to use alcohol, (4) Psychiatric complications—agents that treat or ameliorate the psychiatric symptoms induced by alcohol and other drugs, (5) Psychiatric disorders—agents used in patients who have additional independent psychiatric disorders, and, (6) Concurrent drug addiction—agents used in drug addictions in addiction to alcoholism. Copyright 1995, The Haworth Press, Inc.

Miller NS; Gold MS, eds. *Pharmacological Therapies for Drug and Alcohol Addictions.* New York: Marcel Dekker, Inc, 1995. (Chapter refs.)

This volume with 36 contributors is organized into six sections. The first provides an overview discussing epidemiology, trends in drug use, and general pharmacological therapies for addiction, withdrawal, and relapse. The second section addresses the biology of addiction, with attention directed to brain reward systems, endocrine effects, and the neurobiology of drug use. The third section focuses on clinical approaches to management of withdrawal, and assessing drug-drug interactions. The fourth and fifth sections set forth the clinical and research findings in respect to pharmacological therapies with specific drug classes and their use in different clinical settings. The final section summarizes the material and discusses current approaches and clinical issues. Copyright 1995, Project Cork Institute.

Rush BR; Powell L; Crowe; Ellis K. Early intervention for alcohol use: Family physicians' motivations and perceived barriers. *Canadian Medical Association Journal* 152(6): 863-869, 1995. (26 refs.)

This study elucidates family physicians' motivations concerning early intervention for alcohol use and their perceived barriers to such intervention. This qualitative study uses focus groups and semistructured interviews. The setting is community-based, fee-for-service family medicine practices in London, Ont. Twelve focus group participants were recruited through telephone contact by two family physicians on the project team. Participants were required to be physicians in family practice in London. Twelve interview participants were recruited through a grand-rounds presentation at two local hospitals. Participants were required to be physicians in a community-based family practice in which primary care was not delivered by residents and to have agreed to participate in all phases, e.g., needs assessment, training, and evaluation of a training program on interventions to help patients reduce alcohol consumption or quit smoking. Motivations concerning early intervention for alcohol use and perceived barriers to such intervention, as identified by physicians. Physicians in the focus groups and those interviewed endorsed their role in helping patients reduce alcohol consumption and cited several reasons for the importance of that role. There was strong support for viewing alcohol use as a life-style issue to be dealt with in the context of a holistic approach to patient care. Participants cited many barriers to fulfilling their role and were particularly concerned about the appropriateness of asking all adolescent and adult patients about alcohol use, even at visits intended to discuss other issues and concerns. Physicians gave several motivations for improving their work in reduction of alcohol consumption, including their current frustration with the lack of a systematic strategy or tangible materials to help them identify and manage patients. Interventions with patients who use alcohol should be framed in the context of a holistic approach to family medicine. Qualitative knowledge of the motivations and barriers affecting physicians can inform future research and educational strategies in this area. Copyright 1995, Canadian Medical Association. Used with permission.

Sobell MB; Sobell LC. *Problem Drinkers: Guided Self-Change Treatment.* New York: The Guilford Press, 1993. (234 book refs.)

This book draws on treatment approaches described as "motivational interventions." The work is directed to practicing clinicians. The underlying philosophy is that a significant portion of individuals with alcohol problems, if sufficiently motivated, can solve these problems on their own. The initial chapters set forth the context of self-guided motivational approaches within the alcohol field. Subsequent chapters address the rationale, methods, and procedures in detail. The book addresses treatment approaches, identification of problem drinkers, and self-management strategies, including setting goals and monitoring consumption. Homework assignments, a model course of treatment, and several illustrative case studies are also included.

Thombs DL. *Introduction to Addictive Behaviors.* New York: The Guilford Press, 1994.

This book, directed to entry level substance abuse clinicians, endeavors to translate theoretical approaches and research findings. The volume is organized into eight chapters that focus on the following areas: (1) The usefulness of theory and research in understanding addictive behavior, (2) The disease model of addiction, (3) Psychoanalytic formulations of chemical dependence, (4) Conditioning theory, (5) A social learning analysis of substance abuse, (6) Family systems theory, (7) Sociocultural perspectives on alcohol and drug abuse, and (8) Implications for clinical practice.

CHAPTER 5

Medical Management

JOHN SEVERINGHAUS, MD
JEAN KINNEY, MSW

CLINICAL APPLICATIONS

The goals of this chapter are to assist the clinician to:

1. Identify the tasks related to management of alcohol and drug use.
2. Review the presentations of alcohol and other substance use problems that are common in primary care settings.
3. Review presentation of substance use-related medical emergencies.
4. Review prescribing practices related to prescription drug abuse.
5. Highlight issues pertinent to providing medical care for patients in recovery.
6. Identify core knowledge and skills for the nonmedical professional working with substance abuse patients.

OVERVIEW OF MEDICAL MANAGEMENT

This chapter reviews the medical management of patients who have problems with alcohol and other substance use. It is directed primarily to medical professionals in primary care settings—nurses, nurse practitioners, nurse clinicians, and physicians. In addition, the chapter concludes with an overview of the various medical issues of which nonmedical professionals engaged in treating alcohol and substance use problems need to be informed.

This manual does not offer specifics on the management of emergencies associated with acute or chronic use, withdrawal states, or common medical complications associated with alcohol and other substance use. It is strongly recommended that clinical settings have ready pocket references that address management of alcohol and drug use emergencies. Several are noted in *Further Readings* at the end of the chapter. Any standard medical text is the best source of information for management of the secondary medical complications of alcohol and other drug use.

ISSUES OF MEDICAL MANAGEMENT

Many specific topics related to alcohol and drug issues warrant the attention of the primary care clinician. Anyone in a primary care practice can anticipate being called on to respond to medical emergencies prompted by either acute or chronic use. Thus, it is imperative to be able to recognize the presentations of toxic states, both the physiological manifestations and the behavioral components. Similarly, it is necessary to identify withdrawal states, assess risk for withdrawal, and manage detoxification. Another important task is to become familiar with specific medical presentations frequently associated with alcohol and drug problems, as this knowledge supplements any formal screening efforts. Medical records and prescription practices can also provide clues to drug or alcohol problems. Prescription practices, too, represent another subject clearly related to alcohol and other drug use problems.

These comments are directed toward the patient with an emerging or frank substance use problem. However, they do not define the limits of appropriate attention to alcohol or drug use. Many common medical problems are now recognized as posing absolute or relative contraindications to alcohol use. Consumption and behavior considered nonproblematic or unimportant socially may no longer be regarded as medically benign. Thus, patterns of alcohol use are becoming more important in general medical care, independent of the identification of "problem drinkers" or those abusing other substances.

Common Presentations

Dramatic and unambiguous presentations occur with long-term dependence, but well-recognized secondary medical complications also signal a substance use problem. On the other hand, early identification requires focusing on more subtle behavioral indicators. The earliest symptoms of a substance use problem are behavioral. In any health care setting, be alert to changes in personality. These may be evidenced by isolation, amotivational syndrome, irritability, altered libido, decline in work or school performance, decreased concentration and memory, apathy, disinhibited behavior, or a decline in self-care. In a clinical encounter, early symptoms may appear as an inability to attend to the interviewer's questions.

Different medical settings have presentations that, in that particular setting, are commonly associated with an alcohol or drug use problem. When such presentations occur, they should create an index of suspicion.

Adult primary care. The following conditions should prompt questions about the presence of alcohol or substance use problems:

- Hypertension
- Dsyrhythmias
- Stress-exacerbated illnesses, including ulcer disease and migraine headaches
- Gastrointestinal complaints and disorders
- Sexual dysfunctions
- Sleep disturbances
- Eating disorders
- Infections
- Pulmonary problems
- Vague complaints
- Complaints of general malaise
- Bruises or burns

There is also a strong association between smoking and heavy alcohol use. Alcoholism is estimated to be 10 times more prevalent among smokers than nonsmokers. Whereas 34% of the general population smokes, over 80% of those with significant substance use problems do.[15] Among smokers who have tried to stop smoking, those with alcohol problems were found to be much less successful than those without (7% compared to 49%). Thus, ask patients who smoke more detailed questions about alcohol and drug use.

In medical encounters, the following behaviors should arouse suspicion:

- Missed appointments
- Poor compliance
- Failure to respond to standard treatment regimens
- Inappropriate affect
- Alcohol on patient's breath during medical appointment

- Explicit requests for prescriptions, or suspected drug-seeking behavior

Pediatric presentations. Parental substance use problems may be indicated by infants' failure-to-thrive in the absence of a known cause, school or adjustment problems, accidents and/or trauma, and suspected or established cases of child abuse, neglect, or maltreatment.

Similarly, behavioral clues can suggest that a parental alcohol or substance use problem be considered. These would include situations when parents fail to follow treatment plans or fail to seek medical care. Similarly, missed appointments may signal a problem.

Behavioral or developmental problems among adopted children are not often discussed but may reflect a child affected by prenatal alcohol or drug use. In such cases, alcohol- or drug-induced prenatal effects should be considered.[17]

Psychiatric presentations. Regardless of whether alcohol and substance use problems are seen in a medical setting or mental health clinic, they should be considered in the differential diagnosis in the following situations: any emergency presentation, suicidal thoughts or attempts, depressed mood that coincides with substance use, marital or family problems, and requests for prescriptions or other drug-seeking behavior.

In addition, acute or episodic periods of markedly disturbed behavior such as panic, aggression, dementia, or paranoia may indicate either recent acute use or a chronic substance use problem.

Emergency department presentations. In the emergency setting, alcohol and substance use problems may be presented in several ways. Alcohol and substance use is associated with virtually every type of trauma. As is well known, highway-related accidents often involve alcohol or drugs, including accidents involving pedestrians, bicyclists, and motorcyclists. Also, falls and accidents in the home, injuries on the job, and burn cases each have disproportionate probability of being alcohol or drug related. Commonly, in cases of assaults and domestic violence, either or both the victim and assailant is under the influence of alcohol or other drugs.

Medical emergencies that may not be immediately recognized as drug-related include apparent cardiac problems, acute neurological syndromes, and stroke.

The identification of alcohol and substance abuse problems in an emergency setting can be the basis for a referral for subsequent treatment. However, the more immediate concern is to ascertain the nature of use to guide acute management.[41] References at the end of this chapter include articles on drug and alcohol level determinations in the emergency setting. Severe agitation, paranoia, and threatening behavior

may all be behavioral indicators of acute alcohol or drug use. Generally, a hospital staff should suspect either alcohol or drug use with any patient brought to an emergency room by police. Overdoses and, to a lesser degree, withdrawal syndromes may bring people into emergency settings.

Fads and Trends

The popularity of drugs waxes and wanes. These trends are attributed to a variety of factors, some of which are economic, e.g., availability, cost, distribution networks, and street marketing tactics. In part these trends are also attributed to the level of danger and risk associated with the drug. For example, the recent rise in marijuana use among adolescents is accompanied by a rise in the perception among adolescents that the medical effects are relatively minor and that use does not pose a danger.

At the moment, reports from the DAWN system (Drug Abuse Warning Network), based on emergency room reports, suggest a significant rise in the use of heroin. Policy analysts, using an economic model, tend to speak of "supply" and "demand" characteristics. In respect to the supply side, there appear to be changes in distribution routes as well as different transportation routes for heroin into the country. In respect to the demand side, a significant issue appears to be the "absence of memory" or lack of first-hand experience among today's adolescents and young adults about the problems associated with heroin. The decline in crack cocaine use has in part been attributed to the recognition of the associated dangers; rather than being "in," crack cocaine use is now a "loser's" game.

One of the trends or fads in drug use is "designer drugs."[5,6] Designer drugs, manufactured in clandestine laboratories, by definition are chemical analogs or "cousins" of controlled substances. They are intended to offer the same psychoactive properties but to bypass federal regulation and control due to their different chemical formulations. The clearest example has been a rapid succession of fentanyl analogs on the market several years ago, each one apparently released as the Drug Enforcement Agency succeeded in identifying the previous one and adding it to the Schedule I regulatory listing. The marketer was thereby somewhat protected from dire legal consequences because each version was not *yet* technically illegal!

Anabolic Steroids[1,8,9,22,35]

Because of their perceived performance-enhancing effects, steroids invite use by athletes. During the 1950s and 1960s, their use appeared to be restricted primarily to highly trained athletes. Since then, both the popular press and medical literature have documented that anabolic steroid use has spread beyond the initial small circle of users and into the ranks of college and high school athletes and those engaged in their own conditioning programs. It was estimated in the late 1980s that 1 million Americans were spending $100 million for illicit anabolic steroids. Among high school students, 250,000 seniors are estimated to use these drugs. It should be noted that, although steroid use builds body mass, many of the benefits attributed to anabolic steroids, e.g., less fatigue, greater endurance, faster healing, and increased strength, have not been conclusively demonstrated by scientific research.

For athletic training, anabolic steroids are taken either orally or parenterally and often cyclically. Use over 4 to 18 weeks is broken by a "drug holiday."[26] The earliest reports of steroid's problems focused on the medical consequences of long-term use. There has been a growing literature on their addictive properties and on the emergence of a dependence syndrome following extended use, marked by behaviors that are consonant with diagnostic criteria for psychoactive substance dependence as defined by the DSM-IV. The following features, which are indicative of dependence, are commonly observed in anabolic steroid users: use over longer periods than intended; unsuccessful efforts to stop; continuing use despite knowledge of negative consequences; considerable effort spent to obtain these drugs or recover from their effects; withdrawal syndrome with cessation; and further use of steroids to relieve these symptoms.

The state of intoxication and withdrawal syndrome associated with anabolic steroids resembles that of cocaine and other stimulants. Intoxication is commonly marked by euphoria, a hypomanic state, disinhibition, impulsiveness, and impaired judgment. Occasionally there is a serious distortion in perceptions and in the interpretation of events in the environment, leading to episodes of panic and/or suspiciousness or paranoid thoughts. Features common to withdrawal include hyperactivity; anxiety; irritability; insomnia; loss of appetite; sweats; and increased pulse rate, temperature, and blood pressure. Acute withdrawal is reportedly followed by long-term depression, a marked contrast to the memories of euphoria associated with past use, which can thus induce craving.[8,26]

Substance Abuse Emergencies

General concerns. Specific steps are indicated in the initial management of alcohol- and substance use-related emergencies. These include attention to basic life support, identification and quantification of ingested substances, reduction of absorption, enhancement of excretion, and use of supportive measures to monitor and counteract possible side effects. The first person who makes contact with the patient may have the opportunity to gain additional history from people who accompanied the patient. This contact person should ask pertinent questions that will help assess the acute situation, particularly by getting data on relevant medical and substance use history.

Management of overdose and withdrawal is governed by the drug or combination of drugs used. Attention must be paid to the drug class and to the patient's status in assessing the risks of complicated withdrawal, the need for prophylactic drug use, and the need to alter the standard protocols.

Signs and Symptoms of Overdoses and Withdrawal Syndromes

Table 5-1 summarizes the signs and symptoms of overdoses/acute intoxication and withdrawal syndromes by drug class.

Medical emergencies of overdoses and withdrawal syndromes. The most consistent shortcoming in the response to alcohol- and drug-related emergencies is the omission of specific evaluation for a definable alcohol or drug problem and the failure to use the opportunity to address the problem and/or make a referral for treatment. As discussed in Chapter 4 (Substance Use Treatment), medical emergencies offer an opportunity for interventions. For example, patients admitted to a trauma unit have been found to be open to entering treatment at that point. Studies of spontaneous remissions have noted the occurrence of serious medical problems or accidents as factors leading to dramatic alteration of alcohol or drug use. Even in the absence of clear indications for a treatment referral, an emergency room encounter is an obvious situation in which to initiate a risk reduction regimen.

It is important to have several basic procedures in place to use emergency room events to address substance abuse problems. It is unrealistic to expect an emergency room staff to consistently gather information that might be useful in later elective steps in treatment of an underlying medical condition—including substance abuse/dependence—at the same time they are handling the primary emergency issues. This usually poses no difficulty with most transitions of care because the patient generally cooperates with further evaluation if warranted. However, with alcohol and drug problems, we cannot rely on the continued attention of the patient to such concerns once the immediate crisis is under control.

Protocols established administratively in an emergency department might include the following:
• Routine blood alcohol concentration (BAC) with other emergency laboratory work for a specified range of presentations.
• Inclusion in emergency department intake procedures of standard questions or checklist items for patient report and/or staff suspicion of alcohol or drug use.

Table 5-1. Symptoms and Signs of Drug Abuse*

Drug	Acute intoxication and overdose	Withdrawal syndromes
CNS stimulants		
Cocaine; amphetamine; dextro-amphetamine; methylphenidate; phenmetrazine; phenylpropanolamine; STP[1] MDMA[2]; Bromo-DMA[3]; diethylpropion; most amphetamine-like anti-obesity drugs	**Vital signs:** temperature elevated; heart rate increased; respirations shallow; BP elevated **Mental status:** sensorium hyperacute or confused; paranoid ideation; hallucinations; delirium; impulsivity; agitation; hyperactivity; stereotypy **Physical exam:** pupils dilated and reactive; tendon reflexes hyperactive; cardiac dysrhythmias; dry mouth; sweating; tremors; convulsions; coma; stroke	Muscular aches; abdominal pain; chills; tremors; voracious hunger; anxiety; prolonged sleep; lack of energy; profound depression, sometimes suidical; exhaustion
Opiods		
Heroin; morphine; codeine; meperidine; methadone; hydromorphone; opium; pentazocine; propoxyphene; fentanyl; sufentanil	**Vital signs:** temperature decreased; respiration depressed; BP decreased; sometimes shock **Mental status:** euphoria; stupor **Physical exam:** pupils constricted (may be dilated with meperidine or extreme hypoxia); reflexes diminished to absent; pulmonary edema; constipation; convulsions with propoxyphene or meperidine; cardiac dysrhythmias with propoxyphene; coma	Pupils dilated; pulse rapid; gooseflesh; lacrimation; abdominal cramps; muscle jerks; "flu" syndrome; vomiting, diarrhea; tremulousness; yawning; anxiety
CNS depressants		
Barbiturates; benzodiazepines; glutethimide; meprobamate; methaqualone; ethchlorvynol; chloral hydrate; methyprylon; paraldehyde	**Vital signs:** respirations depressed; BP decreased; sometimes shock **Mental status:** drowsiness or coma; confusion; delirium **Physical exam:** pupils dilated with glutethimide or in severe poisoning; tendon reflexes depressed; ataxia; slurred speech; nystagmus; convulsions or hyperirritability with methaquolone; signs of anticholinergic poisoning with glutethimide; cardiac arrhythmias with chloral hydrate	Tremulousness; insomnia; sweating; fever; clonic blink reflex; anxiety; cardiovascular collapse; agitation; delirium; hallucinations; disorientation; convulsions; shock
Hallucinogens		
LSD[4]; psilocybin; mescaline; PCP[5]	**Vital signs:** temperature elevated; heart rate increased BP elevated **Mental status:** euphoria; anxiety or panic; paranoia; sensorium often clear; affect inappropriate; illusions; time and visual distortions; visual hallucinations; depersonalization; with PCP hypertensive encephalopathy **Physical exam:** pupils dilated (normal or small with PCP); tendon reflexes hyperactive; with PCP: cyclic coma or extreme hyperactivity, drooling, blank stare, mutism, amnesia, analgesia, nystagmus (sometimes vertical), gait ataxia, muscle rigidity, impulsive or violent behavior, violent, scatological, pressured speech	None

*Mixed intoxications produce complex combinations of signs and symptoms.
[1]STP (2,5-dimethoxy-4-methylamphetamine).
[2]MDMA (3,4-methylenedioxymethamphetamine).
[3]Bromo-DMA (4-Bromo-2, 5-dimethoxyamphetamine).
[4]LSD (d-lysergic acid diethylamide).
[5]PCP (phencyclidine).

Continued.

Table 5-1. Symptoms and Signs of Drug Abuse*—cont'd

Drug	Acute intoxication and overdose	Withdrawal syndromes
Cannabis group		
Marijuana; hashish; THC[6]; hash oil; sinsemilla	**Vital signs:** heart rate increased; BP decreased on standing **Mental status:** anorexia, then increased appetite; euphoria; anxiety; sensorium often clear; dreamy; fantasy state; time-space distortions; hallucinations may be rare **Physical exam:** pupils unchanged; conjunctive injected; tachycardia; ataxia and pallor in children	Nonspecific symptoms including anorexia, nausea, insomnia, restlessness, irritability, anxiety, depression
Anticholinergics		
Atropine; belladonna; henbane; scopolamine; trihexyphenidyl; benztropine mesylate; procyuclidine; propantheline bromide; jimson weed seed	**Vital signs:** temperature elevated; heart rate increased; BP possibly decreased **Mental status:** drowsiness or coma; sensorium clouded; amnesia; disorientation; visual hallucinations; body image alterations; confusion; with propantheline restlessness, excitement **Physical exam:** pupils dilated and fixed; decreased bowel sounds; flushed, dry skin and mucous membranes; violent behavior; convulsions; with propantheline circulatory failure, respiratory failure, paralysis, coma	Gastrointestinal and musculoskeletal symptoms

From Abramowicz M, ed. Treatment of acute drug abuse reactions. *Medical Letter on Drugs & Therapeutics* 29(748): 83-86. 1987.
[6]THC (delta-9-tetrahydrocannabinol).

- Standardized "care instructions," a handout comparable to those used for other common conditions seen in emergency departments, when alcohol or other drug use is a concern.
- Standardized "supportive care instructions," a handout specifically for families and significant others when alcohol or other drug abuse/dependence is clearly present.
- Inclusion of alcohol or other drug concerns as a component of a standardized letter of information to a patient's primary care provider.

Withdrawal: Alcohol

In terms of detoxification, from history and recent use one can usually identify those who will require medical supervision and hospitalization, those who will need medication, and those who can be safely managed on an outpatient basis, with or without medication. Assessment will consider the medical history and presence of any relevant medical complications; prior withdrawal experience; any concurrent medications or other drug use; and unusual conditions (anorexia, obesity, amputations, pregnancy) that might modify the metabolism and/or excretion of drugs.

Unfortunately, withdrawal will be potentially most serious when substance use or its extent is unknown to the physician or nurse, and the patient is forced by circumstances to reduce intake or abstain. At times this may result from losing access to drugs, but in many instances it represents "miscalculation" by the dependent person. For example, patients hospitalized for elective surgery may expect to be slightly shaky but either plan to "grit their teeth" or bring enough alcohol (for a few nips) or "a few" pills. If the plan is inadequate, 1 or 2 days after surgery the patient may begin to experience withdrawal.

Similarly, a chronic heavy drinker had a withdrawal seizure on his first transcontinental flight. The flight originated in early morning when the blood concentration had already declined substantially from the previous evening's peak. In flight, the passenger was unable to match his usual daytime intake to prevent withdrawal. In such instances, individuals may be unaware of the connection between alcohol use or drug use and their experience of withdrawal; it will be up to the clinician to recognize and clarify the issue independently.

Assessing withdrawal risk. Withdrawal from opiates and stimulants may be uncomfortable and provoke anxiety in patients, but these do not present a medical risk comparable to withdrawal from alcohol and sedatives. The following checklist briefly summarizes the features relevant to assessing withdrawal risk for drugs with medically significant withdrawal syndromes such as alcohol and sedative hypnotics:

- Prior clinical status during withdrawal.
- Level of tolerance.
- Amount of alcohol or drug regularly used; maximum amount used.
- Past week's drinking or drug use history.
- Symptoms of withdrawal with a declining blood level.
- Time interval since last administration and present evidence of withdrawal phenomena.

Detoxification. Patients undergoing withdrawal may not require admission to general hospitals. Programs have been set up within the alcohol and drug treatment community to provide varying levels of clinical support during detoxification. In some instances these programs are affiliated with a hospital to provide intermediate levels of nursing care and medical supervision. Other services have been established as *social detox* programs. These settings have demonstrated that the environment in which withdrawal occurs is a significant factor in determining its medical course, and that with proper screening, many patients dependent on alcohol can be withdrawn without medications. Critical ingredients of social detox programs are a supportive environment, a staff large enough to provide interaction and reassurance, and a physical setting that provides orienting cues without sensory overload.

Sometimes primary care providers manage withdrawal directly. Commonly, they are called on to evaluate patients for detoxification programs. These may be patients who have come to the attention of a social service agency, the legal system, or a substance abuse treatment program, and for whom there are efforts in progress to initiate treatment. The primary care setting will also identify patients for whom alcohol and drug use is a significant problem and endeavor to initiate treatment.

Detoxification regimens. Withdrawal protocols have been developed and, if implemented appropriately, can provide safe, predictable withdrawal.[14,20,36] In considering detoxification, it may be useful to remember that withdrawal syndromes tend to be the opposite of the symptoms that accompany heavy, chronic use. When using medications, the goal is to manage declining blood levels of a drug without intolerable discomfort or anxiety; to avoid oversedation, therefore not achieving withdrawal or inducing respiratory depression; and to avoid undersedation, allowing emergence of major withdrawal phenomena; and preventing seizures in withdrawal from drugs with anticonvulsant properties. The specific agent used is often primarily dependent on the experience and preference of the physician. The goal is to avoid major discomfort but not mask all symptoms. In all instances, it is important to monitor status closely to identify problems early.

Independent of the drug used, there are basic options that raise particular management issues. Many concerns are similar to those confronted in general pain management, including the issue of medication schedules and of using either scheduled doses or basing doses of medication on clinical status. In terms of managing withdrawal states, the former can invite several problems. Medications will accumulate when a drug has a long half-life. Thus, they can produce delirium and somnolence and delay a patient's participa-

tion in effective substance abuse or alcohol treatment. Also, appropriate scheduled doses are based in part on the patient's stated use. There is the question of whether a patient with cognitive impairment is capable of providing accurate information. There is also the potential for manipulation by patients and some chance that use might be overreported. When there is substantial risk of severe withdrawal if patients are not adequately medicated, rote dosing may be desirable to prevent this from occurring, even at the possible expense of oversedation. Scales based on objective signs are less likely to be subject to a patient's efforts to obtain more medication. Furthermore, with assessment based on objective signs monitored at regular intervals, the patient is not made to request medication or have medication dispensed on the basis of subjective complaints.[50] In many instances prn orders may be ill-advised. These orders force patients to become engaged in drug-seeking behavior and be hypervigilant or more preoccupied by their physical states. They are placed in a situation of repeatedly deciding whether to request medication.

Management vs. referral. Most alcohol withdrawal can be managed medically by primary care providers. In many instances, detoxification can be accomplished on an outpatient basis. One report describes procedures developed to manage detoxification on an outpatient basis, which involved maintaining patients in their homes, including situations in which hospitalization would previously have been suggested.[44] In addition to concerns about safety and severe and complicated withdrawal, suggesting the need for hospitalization, the next most significant question is, "How will actual detoxification be completed sufficiently to permit movement into further treatment and recovery?" Successful outpatient management of withdrawal usually requires two critical factors: (1) the willing participation of some other concerned person to assist with medication and observe the patient's status; and (2) daily contact with a clinician, at least for the first several days, coupled with prescription of only enough withdrawal medication to get to the next clinician contact. While concern for medically severe withdrawal is warranted, immediate medical crisis is actually a low-probability outcome in outpatient withdrawal. Unsupervised patients with severe symptoms will usually "rescue" themselves with additional alcohol, sacrificing the treatment goal but preventing disaster! The likely outcomes of minimally supervised outpatient withdrawal are actually that the patient will exhaust medication early or combine it with continued alcohol use, usually resuming drinking as the precipitating crisis abates.

The final critical question is, "How will the management of detoxification be linked to the treatment services and the recovery efforts that need to follow?" Detoxification does not constitute treatment for the primary condition but is a necessary precursor: Essentially, it is the treatment of physiological withdrawal, the most common *medical complication* of alcohol dependence, and one that presents an obstacle to the actual treatment of the disorder.

The primary advantage of referring a patient to an alcohol or drug treatment program that provides detoxification, rehabilitation, and treatment does not lie in the staff's medical expertise, however impressive that may be. Rather, the advantage lies in the group milieu this setting offers. It is in the structuring of the milieu that staff expertise is apparent. It has been demonstrated that the milieu is a significant factor in determining the amounts of medication required to manage detoxification.[51] This is attributable to the nursing staff's comfort and experience managing alcohol and substance abuse problems. Also, the specialized treatment setting is much different from that of a general hospital, where the nursing staff simply does not have the opportunity to provide the intensity of interaction and attention that is required. The milieu is also a function of the support that patients afford each other. The patient being detoxified in a treatment setting can also participate in the therapeutic program to the extent that his or her condition allows, which is preferable to placement on a medical floor with little more than hospital routines and television to structure the day.

Another advantage of referral to a treatment program for detoxification is that effecting a subsequent referral after detoxification is unnecessary. The patient is already tied to a system that can provide intensive treatment for the primary condition. For the patient who is detoxified in a medical setting without being linked with some ongoing system of care, there is the danger that the restoring of physical health will be accompanied by a resurfacing of ambivalence about the need for treatment. If detoxification is managed within the larger context of treatment, the patient is confronted with only one decision and is not required to grapple with it again. Those most resistant must actively decline subsequent treatment phases rather than passively fail to follow through.

Medical Care of Recovering Patients

Primary care providers caring for substance abuse patients need to include medical factors in making aftercare plans for the patient's recovery status.

Monitoring compliance with aftercare plans. To monitor status effectively in recovery, a patient's primary care health team must be informed about the specific aftercare plans. These aftercare plans should be documented in the patient's medical record. Depending on how fragile the individual's condition,

how tenuous his or her sobriety, and the nature of life problems, some periodic contact or report by the agency may be helpful. Inasmuch as the health care providers do have considerable status with the patient, they can reinforce the efforts of the substance abuse treatment team. Unfortunately, the primary health care team cannot assume that a discharge summary will routinely be forwarded. Consequently, requesting a discharge note and treatment plan may be necessary. Substance abuse treatment programs do not automatically think of their patient's health care team as allies. An overture by the medical care staff will get their attention, possibly surprise them, and will generally convey the message of interest and availability to collaborate in aftercare.

Just as regular visits are scheduled for the patient with diabetes or hypertension, it may be appropriate, particularly in the first year of recovery, to schedule periodic appointments specifically to review the alcohol or substance use problem. Research describing the natural history of alcoholism, including the process of recovery, demonstrated that the presence of "external" reminders of the serious and chronic nature of dependence was a significant predictor of recovery.[48] Regular periodic check-ups can serve this function. Rather than considering these check-ups intrusive or unwarranted, most patients will welcome the concern and may experience it as relief and support. It also provides a forum, which may prove valuable if points of distress arise in the future.

Responding to family issues. Family members of the patient in recovery require attention. When drinking or drug use ceases, the family may have gained the capacity to deal with family problems, but they are not automatically resolved. For family members, the adjustments required in recovery can be as stressful as the period of active alcohol or drug use. Common issues that couples and families must address include the following:[49]

- *Coping with a sudden disequilibrium.* With treatment and abstinence there is sudden need to let go of old habits, reallocate responsibilities in the marriage and family, and deal with the loss of all the ground rules which can be stressful.
- *A sense of strangers "starting from scratch."* There is the need to reestablish relationships and intimacy, which can evoke apprehension. Some couples may think that the feelings of distance are wrong or abnormal rather than a common experience after treatment.
- *Attributing all problems to the family member with the substance abuse problem.* It may be difficult for others in the family to recognize that not all problems can be attributed to the family member with substance abuse problems. Placing blame impedes efforts to solve problems.

- *Discovering appropriate ways to express anger.* There is often stored anger as well as new frustrations. Many families do not know how to express negative emotions. Often families think that such feelings are unjustified, improper, or dangerous. There is apprehension about the vulnerability of the recovering spouse and a perceived need to deal with him or her delicately. Unfortunately, the failure to express negative emotions tends to block out the ability to experience and express positive feelings.
- *Loss of the fantasy that if use stops everything will be all right.* A common fantasy of family members has been that if substance use would stop, all difficulties would be remedied. Family members may not be prepared for the pressures that accompany new sobriety and the cessation of substance use.

Marriages in which one partner is involved with alcohol or drugs have a higher rate of separation and divorce. Undergoing treatment and becoming sober or drug-free does not eliminate the vulnerability to separation and divorce. The failure to satisfactorily resolve some of the issues outlined may help explain this phenomenon.

Another explanation of these findings is suggested by the study of the natural history of alcoholism and recovery. Four factors common to those who succeeded in maintaining abstinence include (1) a substitute for the dependence, e.g., jogging, religion, or involvement in work; (2) an external reminder of the painfulness of the addictive state, which could include having a painful ulcer, attending AA, or taking disulfiram; (3) support systems such as the family, church, or AA; and (4) finding a new love who was not associated with the drinking or drug use.[48] This last factor seems not to auger well for marriages. The experience of pain may have been so great as to have effectively dissolved the marital bonds. This does not only refer to the perceptions of the nonaddicted spouse but of the person in recovery. After treatment, the newly sober individual may be aware of having caused considerable pain, which induces guilt, lowers self-esteem, and destroys a marital relationship.

Prescription practices. Prescribing analgesic and psychotropic medication for recovering persons is a concern in management of medical problems (Box 5-1). Substance abuse clinicians have long been aware that use of such medications may compromise the sobriety of the recovering patient. The folk wisdom in the self-help community is that any use of psychoactive medications invites relapse. Such an absolute prohibition is unwarranted.[31] However, when such medications are required, there are several factors to bear in mind. It is important to consider the abuse potential of a drug when selecting a medication and to avoid open-ended prescriptions and prescribing on a prn basis. Use should be closely monitored.

Box 5-1

Contraindications and Indications for Psychoactive Drugs for Persons Recovering from Psychoactive Substance Abuse

Contraindicated (Likely to Precipitate Relapse and Dependence)

1. Cannabinoids
2. Hallucinogens
3. Inhalants
4. Stimulants
   Exceptions: Methylphenidate (Ritalin) possibly indicated for narcolepsy; use continues to be controversial with Attention Deficit Disorder
5. Sedatives
   Exceptions: Inpatient use in detoxification, postmyocardial infarction state, anesthesia, status epilepticus, acute delirium
6. Narcotics
   Exceptions: Inpatient use for pain relief

May Be Used Cautiously (Do Not Cause Relapse and Dependence)

1. Decongestants
   Exceptions: Use of "look-alikes" and over-the-counter diet pills that indicate a prerelapse state
2. Beverage caffeine (soda, coffee, tea)
3. Antihistamines
   Exceptions: All except terfenadine (Seldane) are contraindicated in those with a personal history of oversedation from antihistamines
4. Antidepressants
   Exceptions: Not to be used as a sedative or hypnotic
5. Nonsedative muscle relaxants
   Exceptions: Avoid when a personal history of oversedation exists; avoid use of diazepam
6. Nonnarcotic analgesics
   Exceptions: Avoid for relief of psychosomatic symptoms
7. Over-the-counter sleeping pills or bromides
   Note: Use often indicates prerelapse state

To promote compliance among patients who are apprehensive about taking any psychoactive medication, it is important to discuss why the medication is being recommended, its abuse potential, and the patient's particular concerns. Such a discussion is particularly important for patients being treated for a concomitant psychiatric disorder.[54] In some instances patients may recognize the need for medications but be concerned that their use may evoke criticism from others in the self-help community. It may be necessary to point out that the expertise of the self-help group is with substance use and not with care of other medical conditions. It may also be helpful to suggest that the patient does not need to feel obligated to discuss the care of his or her medical problems with others. Most patients committed to the self-help community will know of others who are taking psychiatric medications, and they can be encouraged to develop sober relationships with compatible individuals to share honestly this aspect of their experience.

Special considerations in the event of major illness. If a recovering patient is to be treated for a major medical illness or if there is a serious illness in the family, be alert to this as a significant source of stress. At these times, the individual's support system can be particularly useful. The immediate purpose may not be to prevent a resumption of drug use, but it can be an invaluable opportunity for patients to discover their capacity to handle tension and stress without drinking or using drugs. The additional support will also reduce anxiety. If a recovering patient is hospitalized, consider referring him or her to a substance abuse team member or contacting the patient's primary therapist if the patient is still being seen; or if the patient is actively involved in a self-help group such as AA or NA and there are meetings held in the hospital, consider arranging for the patient to be taken to a meeting. These efforts provide patients with valuable sources of support, reduce anxiety, help them handle the immediate crisis, and therefore ease management.

Review treatment regimens for preexisting medical problems. Typically, it is found that with abstinence, coexisting medical conditions are more responsive to treatment. With alcohol and other substance use problems under control, other medical problems may be managed with less medication. This is probably because of two factors: One is the removal of the direct and indirect physiological effects of psychoactive substances; the other is that with treatment and abstinence, patients are more able and more likely to comply with a prescribed treatment regimen.

Relapse prevention. The efforts directed to maintaining abstinence are significant in continuing care. After initial intensive treatment to establish sobriety, it is imperative to develop the skills and

make the life changes necessary to build a solid sobriety. The primary health care team can assist in several ways, including monitoring. In doing so there are behavior patterns to watch that are often associated with a resumption of use. One of the most common predictors of relapse is a patient's failure to continue in treatment and follow through with the agreed-on aftercare activities such as group, family, or couples therapy or involvement with a self-help group. A high level of emotional turmoil and anxiety or a continuing depressed mood, along with marked sleep disturbances, has also been found to accompany relapse.[45]

The significance of preventing relapse is that after relapse has occurred, there is generally an extended interval before a patient reenters treatment. One study reports that when patients relapsed within 2 months after treatment, they waited between 2 to 7 years before reentering care. Whether treatment was for alcohol or other substance use, alcohol was often the initial and, subsequently, the most frequently used substance. In this study the determinants of relapse were primarily interpersonal and intrapersonal situations. Antecedents to recent use were almost exclusively negative events.[38]

Management of relapse. Relapse must be regarded as a characteristic of dependence. It is not a failure of treatment or personal commitment of the patient. Managing a relapse is easier if a plan is developed, rather than trying to make plans during the crisis when use has been resumed. The plan for managing a relapse should include the steps to be taken, and by whom, to provide for evaluation and possible re-entry into treatment. The plan should be documented in the medical record. The patient who has relapsed after outpatient treatment may need the intense support of an inpatient program to regain abstinence and promote a more stable recovery. A patient who has already received residential treatment may require hospitalization for detoxification only. Any relapse is dangerous. The rapid reinstatement of the dependence syndrome and the progression of the illness ensure the emergence of even greater problems than those that preceded treatment.

SKILLS RELATED TO MEDICAL MANAGEMENT OF SUBSTANCE USE PROBLEMS
Management of the Disruptive Patient

In addition to attending to physical status as the result of injury or trauma, the emergency medical staff may also have to contend with intoxicated behavior that complicates the problems of care. Often, friends or family who accompany a patient may also be under the influence of alcohol or other drugs. There are several approaches for dealing with disruptive patients.

The disruptive patient should be anticipated when dealing with alcohol and other drug use problems: Measures can be taken to handle these predictably difficult situations. The medical director of a major treatment unit notes that this is particularly true in substance abuse treatment settings and in emergency departments, where written policies and guidelines for staff should be developed.[18] Ideally, these policies should provide as much detail as possible without restraining staff from using their clinical judgment. Procedures also need to include steps for handling violent behavior.

Guidelines for dealing with intoxicated patients include the following:[12]

- Provide information and structure: Introduce yourself, explain what is to be done, and use the patient's name.
- Communicate clearly and simply: Ask short, direct questions, one at a time; listen and be prepared to tolerate some repetition.
- Phrase responses in a positive framework: Do not explain what you cannot do; instead focus on what you can do.
- Provide a calm, reassuring atmosphere: Maintain eye contact; maintain a relaxed posture; and speak slowly and in an unpressured manner.
- Be alert to potentially violent situations: In these instances try to avoid interviewing a patient alone; avoid arguments; ask the patient to sit down; if alone, be alert to danger signals such as sweating, talkativeness, and increased agitation; get help if needed.

When confronted with an intoxicated patient, select a spot away from the main traffic area where a patient will be least disruptive to the emergency department routine and to the care of other patients. A quiet location also insulates an impaired patient from further stimulation and agitation. Do not put an intoxicated patient in an area with expensive equipment.

Substance Use–Focused History and Physical Examination

When alcohol or drug use is suspected, the history and physical examination can be used to help decide whether to rule substance abuse problems in or out of the differential diagnosis. It is essential to give importance to the patient's responses to behavioral and functional questions, which are the primary diagnostic clues before the emergence of secondary medical complications. Also, it is necessary to recognize system clusters indicative of alcohol and other drug use problems. The brief, focused history and physical examination presented beginning on p. 110 are designed to include both.

Pharmacotherapy in Treatment and Rehabilitation

Use of protective agents: disulfiram. As part of the alcohol treatment process, primary care providers may be requested to evaluate a patient for the use of disulfiram, commonly known as Antabuse®.[23,53] Antabuse® has fallen into disfavor for reasons not altogether clear; several recent articles have addressed this underutilization of a potentially helpful adjunct to therapy.[21] Disulfiram is a metabolic inhibitor or "protective" drug taken daily by mouth to deter alcohol use. If a patient is taking Antabuse, consuming alcohol leads to temporary but considerable discomfort. The symptoms of an Antabuse reaction include weakness, vertigo, decreased blood pressure, throbbing in the head and neck, labored breathing, nausea, vomiting, severe flushing of the face, and sometimes chest pains.

Antabuse acts by interfering with the usual rate of metabolism of acetaldehyde, a normal intermediate product of alcohol metabolism. Thus an Antabuse-alcohol reaction is appropriately termed an *acetaldehyde reaction*. In the presence of disulfiram, acetaldehyde rapidly accumulates in the blood stream, reaching toxic levels, rather than being rapidly transformed into acetic acid.

Disulfiram should not be considered drug therapy for treatment of alcohol dependence. It is best viewed as an adjunct to the usual forms of therapy and aftercare. For patients who frequently fight the desire to drink, it can reinforce their resolve because the consequences provide compelling reasons not to drink. Thus, disulfiram use can help provide "sober time" and allow a patient to attain the skills needed to maintain abstinence. Taking a disulfiram tablet daily requires that one daily decision be made, rather than many throughout the day. Taking disulfiram effectively postpones a drink for 5 to 7 days, the minimum period needed for clearance. Although disulfiram is most commonly used during early recovery when sobriety is tenuous, it has also been used for patients who are anticipating events where drinking might be particularly tempting, such as a vacation or business trip with many drinking occasions. Some patients have even learned to take it selectively *after* a period of extreme challenge, knowing that they are most at risk in the period of relaxation and self-congratulation that follows the completion of a major episode of stress.

Patients taking disulfiram need to avoid inadvertent consumption of alcohol, whether in the form of over-the-counter remedies or dishes cooked with alcohol. Patients need to be aware of people and situations to avoid. Thus, a patient's ability to understand and comply with these restrictions is important in

Brief, Focused Substance Use History and Physical Examination

Name _____ Age _____ Height _____ Weight _____
BAC _____ Drug Screen (if available) _____

I. Past Medical History

Have you ever been told that you had the following?

Gastritis _____	Hepatitis _____
Pancreatitis _____	Cirrhosis _____
Abnormal liver tests _____	Diabetes _____
High blood pressure _____	Delirium tremens _____
Gout _____	Anemia _____
Do you use tranquilizers? _____	Sedatives _____

Comments _____

II. Family History

High blood pressure _____   Alcoholism / drug dependence
Diabetes _____   Mother ___ / ___   Father ___ / ___
Liver disease _____   Siblings ___ / ___   Aunts/Uncles ___ / ___
                                                     Grandparents ___ / ___

Comments _____

III. Social History

Occupation _____
With whom do you live? _____
Do you have children? _____   Do you use tobacco? _____   History: Packs/day _____   Years _____
Comments _____

IV: Review of Systems	Yes	No	Explain
Fatigue	____	____	_____
Anxiety	____	____	_____
Fever, sweating	____	____	_____
HEENT			
Head trauma	____	____	_____
Headaches	____	____	_____
Epistaxis	____	____	_____
Hoarseness	____	____	_____
Vision changes	____	____	_____
Cardiovascular			
Change in exercise tolerance	____	____	_____
Shortness of breath	____	____	_____
Recurrent URI/pneumonia	____	____	_____
Chest pain/discomfort	____	____	_____
Palpitations	____	____	_____
Dizziness	____	____	_____
Gastrointestinal			
Indigestion or nausea (especially A.M.)	____	____	_____
Heavy wretching	____	____	_____
Vomiting (with blood?)	____	____	_____
Abdominal pain	____	____	_____
Jaundice	____	____	_____
Diarrhea	____	____	_____
Black, "tarry" stools	____	____	_____

Brief, Focused Substance Use History and Physical Examination—cont'd

Genitourinary	Yes	No	Explain
Trouble getting an erection	____	____	_____
Polyuria	____	____	_____
Amenorrhea	____	____	_____

Neuropsychiatric

	Yes	No	Explain
Tremors (especially A.M.)	____	____	_____
Blackouts	____	____	_____
Memory problems/changes	____	____	_____
Periods of confusion	____	____	_____
Hallucinations	____	____	_____
Staggering/balance problems	____	____	_____
Seizures (if yes, withdrawal only?)	____	____	_____
Paresthesias	____	____	_____
Muscle weakness	____	____	_____
Depression/down mood	____	____	_____
Change in appetite	____	____	_____
Decreased energy level	____	____	_____
Decreased activity level	____	____	_____
Suicide attempts/ideation	____	____	_____

Sleep (hrs) _____ EMA _____ MCA _____ TFA _____ Changes _____

V. Substance Use History

Alcohol

Do you use alcohol? _____

How often (days per week) do you drink? _____

What do you prefer? _____ How much do you drink (per day)? _____

How many drinks until you feel happy? _____ Drunk? _____

Is this more than it has taken in the past? _____

Has there been any change in your pattern over the last 6 months or 1 year? _____

What age did you begin using alcohol? _____

Have you ever drunk (in one day): Case of beer? _____ ⅕ whiskey? _____ gallon wine? _____

Have you ever used nonbeverage alcohol? _____

Longest period without alcohol? _____

Why did you stop? _____

Did you experience any discomfort? (hallucinations, tremors, fever) _____

Drugs

What drugs other than alcohol have you used? _____ How much? _____

_____   _____

When did you last use these drugs? _____

Consequences of Use

Has drinking or drug use ever caused you to miss or be late for work? _____

Has drinking or drug use ever affected your relationships or home life? _____

How do you feel about your drinking or drug use? _____

Has your physician ever told you to cut down? _____

Have you ever attended an AA meeting? _____ Why? _____

CAGE Screening Instrument

C _____ Have you ever felt the need to **C**ut down on your drinking?

A _____ Have you ever felt **A**nnoyed when others criticize your alcohol use?

G _____ Have you ever felt **G**uilty about your drinking?

E _____ Have you ever had a drink as an **E**ye opener to get going in the morning or to stop tremors?

When was your last drink? _____ How much? _____ What? _____

When was your last drug use? _____ What? _____ How much? _____

Continued.

VI. Physical Examination

General

Appearance (dress, cleanliness, etc)

Blood pressure _____ Respiratory rate _____ /min

Pulse _____ Regular _____ Irregular _____ Explain _____

Behavior	Yes	No	Explain
Anxious	____	____	_____
Irritable	____	____	_____
Uncooperative	____	____	_____
Hyperactive	____	____	_____
Alcohol on breath	____	____	_____
Dermatology			
Vascular dilation	____	____	_____
Clubbing/edema	____	____	_____
Deputyrens contractures	____	____	_____
Rhinophyma	____	____	_____
Palmar erythema	____	____	_____
Cigarette burns	____	____	_____
Spider nevi	____	____	_____
IV drug needle marks	____	____	_____

Other burns/scars not attributed to surgery? Where? _____

HEENT

Evidence of head trauma _____

Extraocular movements intact _____ Explain _____

Pupil size _____ PERRLA _____ Sclera Clear _____ Icteric _____

Nasal septum: Intact _____

Periodontal disease   Yes _____ No _____

Swollen Parotids   Yes _____ No _____

Chest

Gynecomastia _____

Lungs clear to A&P _____ Dullness _____ Rales _____ Rhonchi _____ Wheezes _____

Heart—PMI: Size and location

Rhythm regular _____ Irregular _____ Explain _____

Sounds S1 _____ S2 _____ Others? (S3, S4, Rubs, Gallops) _____

Murmur (describe if possible) _____

Abdominal Examination

Bowel sounds (+/-)

Ascites _____ Tenderness _____ Masses _____

Liver (size @ MCL) Palpable? _____ Splenomegaly _____

Neuropsychiatric

Cranial nerves intact? _____

Cerebellar: Tremor _____ Tandem walk _____ F to N _____ Romberg +/- ? _____

Extremities

Sensory (upper + lower) intact _____

Symmetrical _____

Motor (upper + lower) intact _____

Symmetrical _____

Cognition

Object retention 3 @ _____ min

World → ____ ← _____

Serial Sevens ____ ____ ____ ____ ____ ____ ____ ____

Assessment of Alcohol Use/Drug Use _____

Withdrawal Risk _____

Interviewer's Name _____ Date _____

From Noordsy D; Smith N. *Protocol for Medical Assessment.* Hanover NH: Project Cork Institute, Dartmouth-Hitchcock Weekend Impaired Driver Program, Dartmouth Medical School, 1988.

evaluating a patient for disulfiram use. General medical status and potential medical danger(s) posed by a possible reaction are further considerations when prescribing disulfiram. For a patient with severe or inadequately controlled cardiovascular illness, for example, the risk of a dangerous or even lethal reaction may mean that the drug is contraindicated: That the patient is extremely unlikely to actually drink while on disulfiram does not offset this concern. On the other hand, for a patient with less absolute contraindications who has difficulty putting together sober time, the dangers of a potential reaction need to be weighed against those of continued active alcoholism.

The level of a patient's involvement in aftercare is a significant factor. Physicians should exercise great caution in prescribing disulfiram for patients not engaged in an active recovery program. Patients may prefer to say, "I can do it myself; all I need is Antabuse!" Most often, such patients can be reminded that if the problem is sufficiently severe to warrant taking a drug with significant risks, it's also worth getting the counseling to help them best protect themselves over the long run.

Management of "craving". A new and conceptually challenging approach in the psychopharmacology of alcohol dependence is generically termed *drive reduction.* In the recent literature there are a number of studies of agents purported to reduce the subjective desire for alcohol, or "craving." The discussion has now been more specifically brought to public attention with the recent FDA approval of the long-acting opiate antagonist naltrexone (repackaged with a new trade name, ReVia®) to be used for this purpose in treating alcohol dependence. Recent antidepressant agents such as fluoxetine (Prozac®) are also being studied in this regard. The hope for these and other agents is that they will somehow ease the burden of desire for a drink in those seeking to prevent themselves from further alcohol dependence.

If clinical experience proves this approach effective, it will indeed be an important development for the treatment of alcohol problems. A number of considerations suggest caution, however, in embracing such a concept too readily, however attractive it may be. First, common sense and an awareness of history command our respect: The annals of addiction treatment are littered with examples of drugs introduced to fight the scourge of dependence on other drugs, that proved to be at best ineffective (and sometimes a source of new addiction problems). While the present new candidates are unlikely as agents of abuse, ineffective treatments still cost individuals diversion from productive recovery courses. Second, medication solutions usually have more power over the per-

ceptions of patients than other aspects of treatment and may seem to obviate the need for attention to behavior change, support, etc. This is especially true for the chemically dependent population, whose inherent vulnerability to drug-based solutions makes even the most thoughtful clinical pharmacology a two-edged sword. While this concern has been carried by some to extremes of "drug-free" thinking, with a fundamentally moral rather than scientific justification, the overall impact of medication on individuals' attitudes in recovery remains a relevant question.

Finally, the medication studies themselves suggest important *caveats.* The concept of craving has always been difficult for objective study. As the new studies show again, apparently reliable scaling methods with face validity for this wholly subjective construct do not necessarily correlate with consumption behavior. Even more unsettling are the reports that suggest these agents are most effective, not at supporting abstinence, but at *reducing consumption in those who are using alcohol at some level.* In a field where most current treatment strategies have been directed at establishing and maintaining abstinence, it will be a major conceptual challenge to incorporate medication that reduces consumption but does not eliminate the drive for alcohol altogether!

Reviewing the Medical Chart for Substance Use Problems

The medical record may offer clues that indicate a substance abuse problem. These may include a history of trauma and accidents or illnesses that are highly correlated with alcohol or drug abuse, e.g., gastrointestinal disorders or a history of strange infections, including tetanus (70% of the tetanus cases in the US are related to drug abuse). Seizures first appearing after adolescence and before age 35, subacute bacterial endocarditis or fungal infection of heart valves, or a positive tine test also suggest a substance abuse problem. The patient's failure to respond to standard treatment, or the presence of conditions that are not adequately controlled, such as diabetes, seizure disorder, and hypertension, often indicate an alcohol or drug problem.

Prescription Practices

When problems of drug use are considered, prescription drug use cannot be overlooked. The general approaches and techniques described throughout this manual are equally applicable to problems of prescription drug abuse.[33] Prescription practices can contribute to abuse of prescription drugs. The following prescribing behaviors can increase the opportunity for prescription drug misuse.[2]

Prescription writing practices. The physician's writing practices can contribute to drug misuse. This can involve prescription orders that invite alteration, e.g., by using numerals instead of writing out numbers or by using preprinted blanks with the name of a proprietary preparation. Any bank check requires both a numerical and written version of the amount involved: Prescriptions for controlled drugs deserve the same degree of attention.

Inadequate safeguards of drug supplies. Drugs stored in a site apparent to patients can invite break-ins and thefts.

Injudicious prescribing practices. Injudicious prescribing practices can include a failure to periodically review status; a failure to be sensitive to the requirement of increasing dosages; prescriptions written for a period beyond the next visit; and a failure to assess if multiple physicians are involved and if similar or contraindicated drugs are being prescribed.

Such prescribing practices may reflect several factors. In light of the many psychoactive agents currently being used, situations in which physicians question use and are aware of the abuse potential of different agents are difficult to determine. In addition to a drug's psychopharmacological properties, the patient's past history of drug or alcohol abuse is an additional risk factor. An adequate history is needed to elicit this data. Impaired professionals are a potential source for excessive prescribing. This is true especially if their own level of use serves as a benchmark for prescribing habits. If the physician is known as being impaired, there is potential for blackmail by those wanting to secure drugs. In addition, "prescription mills" exist, where drugs are prescribed for a fee, with only perfunctory consideration of a person's health or medical conditions.

The most serious prescription drug use problem involves the elderly—the group with the most fatalities related to drug overdose, and the group for whom prescription drug use is the most significant problem.[32] This problem is not attributable to the elderly extracting or altering prescriptions or engaging in behaviors commonly associated with persons having drug problems. Their problems are due to their being more likely to take multiple medications for a variety of medical problems, which predisposes them to drug-drug interactions. They are also more likely to use an array of over-the-counter products, adding one more ingredient to their pharmaceutical cornucopia. In addition, there are significant changes in drug metabolism with aging. Thus, problems resulting from prescription drug use are so common among the elderly that they should be a consideration in the differential diagnosis of virtually any problem.

DEA Guidelines for Prescribing Psychoactive Drugs[13]

Even when sound medical indications have been established for using psychoactive drugs, three additional factors should be considered in determining the dosage and duration of drug therapy.

*   *The severity of symptoms and the patient's ability to tolerate them.* Symptomatic relief is a legitimate goal of medical practice, but the use of many psychoactive drugs to achieve complete symptomatic relief requires caution because of the abuse potential and dependence liability of these drugs.
*   *The patient's reliability in taking medication, determined through observation and careful history taking.* The physician should assess the patient's susceptibility to drug abuse before prescribing any psychoactive drug and weigh the benefits against the risks. The possible development of dependence in patients in long-term therapy should be monitored through periodic check-ups and family consultations.
*   *The dependence-producing capability of the drug.* Patients should be warned about possible adverse effects caused by interactions with other drugs, including alcohol.

General guidelines for prescription practice are as follows:

*   Controlled substances have legitimate clinical usefulness, and the prescriber should not hesitate to consider prescribing them when they are indicated for the comfort and well-being of patients.
*   Prescribing controlled substances for legitimate medical use requires special caution because of the potential for abuse and dependence.
*   Good judgment should be used in administering and prescribing controlled substances so that diversion to illicit use is avoided and the development of drug dependence is minimized or prevented.
*   Physicians should guard against contributing to drug abuse through injudicious prescribing practices or by acquiescing to unwarranted demands by patients.
*   Prescribers should examine their individual prescribing practices to ensure that all prescription orders for controlled substances are written with caution.
*   Physicians should make efforts to ensure that patients are not obtaining multiple prescription orders from different prescribers.

Specific guidelines for writing prescription orders are as follows:

- The prescription order must be signed by the prescriber when it is written. The prescriber's name, address, and Drug Enforcement Agency (DEA) registration number, as well as the full name and address of the patient, must be shown on prescriptions for controlled substances.
- The written prescription order should be precise and legible to the pharmacist.
- Controlled substances prescribed without an indication for renewal cannot be renewed without authorization by the prescriber. The prescription should indicate whether it may be renewed and, if so, the number of times or duration.

DEA Schedule II. A written prescription order is required. The renewing of Schedule II prescription orders is prohibited. A dispenser may accept an oral order for Schedule II drugs only in an emergency, and such an order must be followed by a written order within 72 hours.

DEA Schedules III, IV, and V. Prescription orders may be issued either orally or in writing and may be renewed if authorized on the prescription order. The prescription order may be renewed only up to five times within 6 months after the date of issue. The quantity of a controlled substance should not exceed the amount that is needed until the next check-up. Prescription orders should be made impossible to alter. Thus, the actual amount should be written out, as well as given in Arabic or Roman numerals. Check-off boxes might be incorporated on prescription blanks to show amounts within which the prescribed amount falls, such as 1 to 25, 26 to 50, 51 to 100, and over 100. Separate prescription blanks should be used for each controlled substance. Preprinted prescription blanks with the name of a proprietary preparation should be avoided. Institutional prescription blanks should have the name, address, and DEA registration number of the prescriber printed on them.

The DEA regulations note that the prescriber has "a responsibility to inform patients of the effects of the prescribed drugs, consistent with good medical practice and professional judgment. The patient has a corresponding duty to comply with the prescriber's directions for use of the prescribed medication."

CONSIDERING SUBSTANCE USE WHEN PROVIDING GENERAL MEDICAL CARE

Among the earliest discussions about the effects of alcohol use on health status were the reports of the seemingly beneficial effects of moderate drinking related to the occurrence of coronary artery disease, the so-called J-shaped curve. Several studies using large population samples found that although those who drink heavily are more susceptible to cardiovascular disease, there is a paradoxical effect with moderate alcohol use. Individuals who consume two alcoholic beverages per day were found to have lower levels of coronary artery disease than abstainers. Two explanations have been offered for this finding. One is that modest alcohol use gives some protection against coronary artery disease. However, the basis for this is unclear. The other interpretation has been that abstainers are more likely to have other medical conditions making them more vulnerable to coronary artery disease. A history of alcohol problems may be one reason for their abstinence, or their abstinence may be related to having a rigid personality, which induces stress and therefore increases their vulnerability to alcohol abuse.

These reports that suggest that moderate alcohol use is beneficial to the heart are now being questioned. New statistical analysis of this data suggests that the protection afforded by moderate alcohol use is an artifact of the statistical methods used in the analysis, and specifically a failure to provide adequate controls for earlier alcohol use or for other unhealthy habits such as smoking.[11,27]

Contraindications to Moderate Alcohol Use

As noted earlier, medical personnel are hard pressed to "approve" the use of illicit drugs. Nonetheless, some patients may admit to recreational marijuana use. There may be no evidence of other substance abuse nor of untoward social or medical consequences. Thus, there may be little basis for recommending treatment. The intervention will be restricted to discussing drug–drug and alcohol–drug interactions and implications of drug use in situations requiring attention, reaction time, and judgment such as driving, child tending, and using power tools or heavy equipment. Monitoring for an emergent future problem is indicated. Other illicit substances that have greater abuse potential, as well as additional dangers attendant to securing drugs, e.g., unknown purity, carry a correspondingly higher risk, and, consequently, more aggressive interventions are warranted.

Were logic and scientific evidence the major determinants, a similar stance might be taken regarding alcohol use. It is often noted in substance abuse treatment circles that if alcohol were a newly discovered drug, it would not get FDA approval for its broad use in our society. It would be a controlled substance and unavailable for self-prescription. Moderate use in terms of risk for either acute problems from CNS impairment or risk for alcoholism may represent excessive use in light of existing medical conditions. The World Health Organization has introduced the term *hazardous use* for just these circumstances.[28]

The most significant example of concern about *hazardous use* is drinking during pregnancy. It is becoming more apparent that even moderate drinking during pregnancy increases the risk of abnormalities in the fetus (fetal alcohol syndrome or fetal alcohol effects). The woman planning to conceive should be equally thoughtful about not drinking. Many pregnancies are not confirmed until the middle of the first trimester. Thus, potentially harmful levels of alcohol can be consumed before a woman is aware that she is pregnant. There are other possible adverse consequences of alcohol use during pregnancy. Moderate alcohol use has been linked to an increase in spontaneous abortions. Consuming one to two drinks per day, for a total of 7 to 14 ounces of alcohol per week, doubles the risk of spontaneous abortions during the second trimester.[30]

Nursing mothers are also advised to abstain because alcohol and other drugs can be passed through breast milk to the infant.[7,16,19,25,43,46,52] Although alcohol use during breast-feeding does not affect an infant's mental development, infants whose mothers consumed one or more drinks per day have been found to have slower rates of motor development.[29] Although the mechanisms are unclear, it has been demonstrated that birth weights are related to the level of *paternal* alcohol use in the month before conception. In combination, such findings contradict the longstanding impression that alcohol is essentially benign except for individuals who develop alcoholism.

Even relatively modest alcohol use can create problems for persons with various cardiac and circulatory problems, e.g., coronary artery disease, congestive heart failure, and hypertension. Up to 10% of all hypertension is believed to be the direct result of alcohol use. For patients with established hypertension, alcohol use can make control of blood pressure more difficult. Moderate drinking has also been found to elevate the level of high-density lipoprotein (HDL). Moderate drinking may also be unwise for those with idiopathic epilepsy; diabetes mellitus; gout; osteoporosis; various skin conditions, including psoriasis; gastric and duodenal ulcers; and sleep disturbances, including sleep apnea. Although not all of these medical conditions may constitute absolute contraindication, all are included in the category of relative contraindications. A glass of wine with meals once or twice a week may not present a problem, but several drinks before and after dinner are ill-advised.

Drinking and Exercise

With the increasing interest in fitness and exercise, what are the recommendations regarding drinking and sports or exercise? Alcohol can affect performance and cause potential problems. Athletes who try to ease pregame tension with several beers may slow reaction time, impair coordination, and thus reduce their performance levels. Many endurance athletes practice carbohydrate loading before competition and may include beer as part of their pregame meal. Beer is a poor source of carbohydrates because two-thirds of its calories are from the alcohol, and thus are used as heat and are not available for energy. Drinking alcohol can affect heat tolerance and lead to dehydration because it inhibits antidiuretic hormone (ADH) and thereby invites danger of significant fluid loss. Thus, sports physicians recommend that athletes not consume alcohol for 24 hours before performance. Alcohol use during performance has essentially the same risks; but for those engaged in prolonged exercise in the cold, such as long-distance cross-country skiing or winter marathons, there is an additional risk for problems such as hypoglycemia. Finally, drinking after exercise, including champagne to celebrate or beer to quench thirst, can interfere with adequate rehydration and provide a poor source of the calories needed for bodily recovery.[10]

Relation of Intoxicating Levels of Alcohol Use to Health Status

Accidents and injuries. Along with alcohol-drug interactions, accidents and injuries are the other common medical problems associated with alcohol use. These are more likely to occur during an intoxicated state because of the nature of alcohol-induced impairment. Impaired judgment places individuals in potentially dangerous situations. Diminished judgment, along with decreased reaction and response time and reduced motor skills, decreases the ability to cope with the unexpected. The severity of injuries has also been found to rise with the level of impairment.[39]

Immune system and HIV infection. In respect to substance abuse, for the general public and health care and alcohol-substance abuse professionals, AIDS is most clearly linked with intravenous drug users, the group for whom AIDS is becoming virtually endemic. The dramatic rise of AIDS in this group is not based primarily on the pharmacological properties of the drugs but on the route of administration—intravenous use. Among intravenous drug users, human immunodeficiency virus (HIV) infection is easily transmitted via shared syringes. Given the multiple problems associated with chronic drug use, this group is not easily reached by informational and prevention efforts.

As AIDS research increases, the relationship of alcohol use and AIDS is being examined. The ability of chronic alcohol use to suppress the immune system has been established. The effects of acute use among moderate drinkers are just now being recognized. Experiments with healthy volunteers suggest that a single administration equivalent to 0.7 to 3.1 liters of beer (two to eight 12-ounce cans) had an impact on the immune system. Furthermore, these effects extended for up to 4 days after consumption, which raises the question, "Can modest alcohol consumption increase the vulnerability to infection and/or enhance the progression of latent HIV infection?"[4] On behavioral grounds alone, there is a link between intoxication and an increased risk of HIV infection. With intoxication, sexual activity is likely to be more casual and less considered, involve sexual partners determined primarily by their availability, and less likely involve contraception or safe sex practices to reduce the risk of sexually transmitted disease, including HIV infection.

Unplanned pregnancy and sexually transmitted disease. Unplanned pregnancy and sexually transmitted disease among adolescents and young adults are commonly associated with drinking situations. Intoxication often leads to increased and unprotected sexual activity because inhibitions and judgment are affected.

Unexpected and sudden natural deaths. The prevalence of positive blood alcohol concentrations (BACs) among people who have died suddenly and unexpectedly from natural causes is a recent significant finding. This relationship was based on the determination of the BAC as part of medicolegal autopsies conducted for all natural, out-of-hospital deaths occurring during a 1-year period in a large Finnish metropolitan area. Of these sudden and unexpected deaths, 36% of the men and 15% of the women had positive BACs. The BAC for approximately one-half of these men and women was 0.15 or greater. Acute consumption of alcohol by nonalcoholics was certified as being a significant contributor to 23% of the men and 8% of the women who experienced sudden, unexpected death. For men, acute alcohol use was a contributing factor for 11% of deaths from coronary artery disease, 40% from other heart disease, and 7% from all other diseases. For both sexes, the most vulnerable are those in middle age.[34]

Alcohol-drug interactions. In addition to the possibility of alcohol complicating a medical condition, there is the issue of possible interactions with medications prescribed to treat them. Alcohol-drug interactions may be the arena that makes the moderate

drinker the most vulnerable to problems arising from alcohol use. When drinking accompanies use of either prescription drugs or over-the-counter preparations, there can be undesirable and possibly dangerous alcohol–drug interactions. Although these interactions can vary between individuals, they are primarily dependent on the amount of alcohol and type of medication consumed and the person's drinking history. The moderate drinker who has not developed tolerance will have a different response than the habitual heavier drinker. In fact, the consequences may be much more serious.

Other Drugs

Clearly a number of medical conditions may be exacerbated by other drug use. Nonetheless, in this discussion, the focus has been upon alcohol, given its legal status, broad social use, and, compared to other drugs, its generally lesser addiction potential. There is after all a concept of "social drinker." On the other hand, there is no similar, broadly accepted parallel notion of "recreational" drug use. As well, there is really no comparable phenomenon of "social smoking." Although also a legal substance, in contradistinction to alcohol, the nonproblematic or nonaddictive use of nicotine is relatively rare. Research has shown that smoking as few as three to four cigarettes per day is typically associated with long-term smoking, in the neighborhood of four decades.[37] While with alcohol there may be some contraindications to moderate use, the clear stance with other substances is to counsel non-use.

The Basis for Alcohol-Drug and Drug-Drug Interactions

Two basic mechanisms can explain virtually all alcohol-drug interactions. One is that the acute presence of alcohol alters the liver's ability to metabolize other drugs. The microsomal ethanol oxidizing system (MEOS), which metabolizes a variety of other drugs as well as alcohol, may be significantly inhibited in the presence of alcohol; this may be acute in the moderate drinker. Therefore, drugs ordinarily metabolized by the liver's MEOS will not be removed as rapidly or as completely as usual. The result is that these medications will then be present in the body in higher than expected levels, which can result in unexpected toxic effects.

On the other hand, for those persons with a long history of heavy drinking, alcohol has the opposite effect on the MEOS system. The MEOS action is enhanced or speeded up through a process known as enzyme induction. Thus, certain drugs will be removed (metabolized) more quickly. The medication is removed more rapidly, hence its levels in the body will be lower than expected or desired. The net effect is that the individual will not likely be receiving the intended therapeutic effects of a given drug dosage. To compensate for this, it may be necessary to increase the dosage of the drug to achieve the therapeutic effect.

The other major source of difficulty results from the so-called additive effects. When alcohol is used in combination with another CNS depressant, the two drugs' effects are combined and may often be greater than expected. It is also important to be aware of the time interval required for metabolism. Alcohol is metabolized at the rate of approximately one drink per hour, regardless of whether the drink is a 12-ounce bottle of beer, one mixed drink with a shot of 80-proof liquor, or a 4-ounce glass of wine. Therefore, after several drinks, despite the passage of several hours, alcohol remains in the system. As long as alcohol is present, there is potential for significant additive effects, even though the other depressant drugs are taken later.

Substance Abuse and Malpractice

Malpractice suits regarding management of alcohol and substance use problems have begun to emerge. The scuttlebutt within the alcohol treatment field had been that malpractice suits have been filed based on the failure to diagnose dependence, the failure to inform the patient of a diagnosis of alcoholism, or the failure to initiate treatment. An extensive search of the published literature of the alcohol field has failed to identify such cases of malpractice. In further efforts to clarify this, the insurance broker for an academic medical center's professional liability insurance program offered suggestions for finding such information and explained why such information is difficult to acquire.[47] Until recently there has not been a central, national repository of judgments. However, individual insurance carriers who maintain in-house data bases of suits and settlements are one potential source of information. Another source of information is Jury Verdict Research, which has maintained a data base of personal injury cases, verdicts, and settlements for the past 35 years and is estimated to contain 77% of all cases for the entire period and a substantially higher proportion for the past 15 years.

St. Paul's, which is nationally the largest carrier of malpractice insurance, was unable to identify any cases of malpractice in which either undiagnosed or untreated alcoholism was the primary issue. All alcohol-related cases have focused on FAS/FAE and infants who are neurologically impaired, and such cases have been brought against family practitioners or obstetricians. In these cases, all the findings have been for the defendants. The defense has concentrated on two

premises. One is the presumption that the public is aware of the dangers associated with drinking during pregnancy. The second is that harm that may result from drinking is incurred before contact with the physician. St. Paul's noted that a successful lawsuit might be brought into a situation in which prepregnancy counseling fails to stress the potential dangers of alcohol use. However, although such an occurrence is possible, with the standardized history data bases now widely used, it is improbable that such an omission would occur.[40]

Jury Verdict Research identified 10 malpractice cases involving alcohol in settlements through the late 1980s. All cases were resolved out of court, with settlements ranging from $20,000 to $4,000,000. Again, none of these cases involved the failure to diagnose, inform, or treat alcoholism. Six of these cases involved failure to adequately treat medical conditions and failure to perform an adequate medical evaluation because the individual was believed to be alcoholic; thus, the symptoms (most often head injuries) were erroneously attributed to alcoholism, or conversely, there was a failure to identify alcoholism, which then compromised medical management of other conditions. The remaining cases included iatrogenic-induced alcohol/drug dependence, attributed to physicians inappropriately prescribing mood-altering drugs to patients known to be alcohol dependent, and also to physicians providing alcohol and drugs in exchange for sexual favors to patients known to have alcohol/drug problems.[24]

In one interesting research study, a panel of lawyers was asked to consider three scenarios regarding civil liability in an emergency department situation. Each scenario was about an impaired patient seen in an emergency department who, after receiving treatment and being released, was involved in an automobile accident. For each hypothetical situation, panel members were requested to indicate whether they would advise a patient that he or she had received potentially negative care. In one scenario, a BAC was determined, and the patient was advised not to drive; in a second scenario, the BAC was determined, but no advice was given about driving; and in the third, there was neither a determination of BAC nor any mention of the risks of operating a motor vehicle. The degree of perceived liability was related to the emergency department's behavior. Greater liability was believed to be present for the hypothetical situation in which the serum alcohol concentration was not determined and there was no mention of driving risk (the third scenario). In this situation, 43% of the panel members said they would advise about possible negligence. However, only 3.5% of the panel members indicated that they would give such advice if a serum alcohol concentration had been determined and the patient was advised to avoid driving.[42]

MEDICAL INFORMATION FOR NONMEDICAL PROFESSIONALS

Although no one would advocate that nonmedical personnel deliver medical services, there are many situations in which being informed about medical issues is important. Persons with alcohol and substance abuse problems do not present only to technically trained health care system personnel. Familiarity with emergencies and potential complications is needed so that those first identifying an alcohol or other drug problem are able to evaluate the need for medical attention. In a general assessment, medical information is part of the data base needed to assess an alcohol or substance use problem. Clinicians in the alcohol and substance abuse fields need to evaluate withdrawal risk and withdrawal phenomena and be aware of situations where medical personnel need to be involved. Patient education is another important role of substance abuse clinicians, requiring a rudimentary knowledge of the acute and chronic effects of alcohol and other drugs. Nonmedical personnel often have to reinforce, interpret, and reiterate information provided to patient and family by medical and nursing staffs.

Health History

In taking a psychosocial history, it is important that nonmedical personnel include questions related to health status.

- "Have you ever been hospitalized and for what?"
- "Do you have a history of accidents or injuries, or have you been in any fights that required medical attention?"
- "Did any of these occur when you were drinking or using drugs?"
- "Have you been under a physician's care recently or thought that you should have seen your doctor?"
- "When was the last time you were seen by a physician?"

These questions are needed in addition to the ones that establish the presence of dependence and tolerance.

Role of the Patient's Primary Care Provider

In addition to establishing if there are any problems that have led to recent medical attention, it is important to ascertain where a patient turns for medical care, who the family physician is, and whether he or she is aware of the problems that led the patient to seek help. To provide optimal clinical care and show professional courtesy, clinicians are encouraged to request permission to speak with the primary care provider whenever an alcohol or drug use problem or potential problem surfaces. Contact with the medical practice is warranted even when patients do not appear to have medical problems that indicate immediate medical evaluation.

The primary care provider has a continuing relationship with the individual and a responsibility for the individual's care, which is likely to continue beyond contact with other helping professionals. The primary care provider needs to be informed about alcohol and drug use and should document such information in the patient's medical record. Individuals with alcohol and drug problems may be seeing several care providers, none of whom has a complete picture of the individual's situation. With an alcohol or other drug problem, it is important that all care providers have the same data, agree about the goals for the patient, reinforce one another's efforts, and coordinate plans. Although the primary care provider may have been unaware of an alcohol or other drug problem before your contact, he or she is nonetheless in a position to exert considerable leverage to promote entry into treatment. Such contacts may reveal information suggestive of a chronic substance use problem. The patient's primary care provider should always be the first person considered if there are concerns about the patient's medical status or a need for medical evaluation or care. Likewise, the primary care provider is available to you if there are any medical questions. The primary care provider may become a valuable ally in dealing with a patient's resisting or minimizing the seriousness of the situation, and serve as an additional concerned voice.

Knowledge of Alcohol and Other Drug Effects

To identify behavior that may be alcohol or drug induced, it is important that the clinician have some rudimentary understanding of the behavioral effects of different drug classes and an appreciation of the dynamics of the addiction process. In the absence of basic information about drug use and its behavioral effects, there is danger of attributing drug-induced behaviors to psychiatric problems or of viewing them as maladaptive responses to life situations.

Regardless of training, no clinician will be as knowledgeable as some of their patients regarding various drug actions and the desired effects. Do not become hindered by a lack of knowledge and pretend to be informed about subjects of which you are not. Some patients who use drugs may call the different drugs by street names unknown to many clinicians. Ask the patient to define these terms. Ask what a drug does for him or her how it is administered, the duration of effects, and what it feels like as the effects wear off. There may be some disbelief about your naiveté, but generally there will be an appreciation that you bothered to ask and were well informed enough about drug use to ask the right questions.

Access to Consultation and Medical Back-Up

For the nonmedical professional dealing with patients' alcohol and substance use problems, many situations demand basic medical information, access to medical back-up, and the ability to use the medical care system.

Sometimes nonmedical personnel will have questions about the physical effects of alcohol or drug use or about the nature of patient health problems. It is important that there be medical staff to answer your general and specific case-related questions. It should be anticipated that many patients will not have an identified primary care provider and will require medical evaluation. Identify medical practices and settings to which patients can be referred either for emergency or nonemergency care. Consider which practices and settings are able to take new patients and are also comfortable and informed about alcohol and drug issues. Also consider the options available for individuals who are indigent or lack insurance.

Arranging for medical back-up. For all nonmedical professionals, easy access to medical consultation and back-up is important in several respects. There are clear, case-centered clinical questions that require medical judgments. There is also a general need to have access to someone who can translate medical literature, clarify medical information, and help incorporate it into nonmedical practice sites.

Indications for immediate medical evaluation. Many medical emergencies will be clearly recognizable. In these situations, use emergency transportation, police, or rescue squads, especially if the patient needs life support. This is evidenced by shallow, uneven breathing, rapid pulse, or fluctuating levels of consciousness, or when there is the threat of danger to others or self. When an individual is transported for emergency care, inform the emergency department of the patient's imminent arrival. Any information that can be provided to emergency staff is helpful, including current status; names of family or friends who may be with the patient and can provide information; diagnostic impressions; and relevant medical history.

Although the presentations listed may not appear to be immediately life threatening, prompt medical attention should be arranged. If the following are not adequately evaluated, serious problems could occur.

- Recent substance intake at levels that risk developing toxicity, poisoning, or organ damage even if patient is asymptomatic.
- Ingestion of unknown quantities and substances.
- Hallucinations or marked paranoia.
- Confusion or delirium.
- Severe agitation, and if efforts to quiet the patient are unsuccessful.
- Severe tremors.
- Tachycardia (>110 per minute).
- Fever (<38.0° C).
- History or evidence of trauma, especially head trauma.
- Patient is semiconscious and able to be aroused briefly, but falls asleep when stimulus is removed.

For individuals who have recently stopped drinking or have reduced their consumption significantly or intend to, the following items would suggest a significant risk for serious withdrawal.

- History of a difficult withdrawal.
- Seizures or history of seizures.
- Dependence on multiple substances.

Nonemergent indications for medical evaluation. The following considerations, which do not represent acute medical emergencies, indicate a need for medical evaluation in situations involving alcohol or drug use.

- Recent history of bleeding.
- No recent medical evaluation for these patients with heavy extended alcohol or drug use.
- Mention of general "not feeling well."
- History of chronic medical conditions for which the individual is not currently under medical care, e.g., hypertension, diabetes.

Assessing Withdrawal Risk

To assess withdrawal risks, the following information should be elicited for any patient for whom there has been a decrease in regular use or recent cessation of use.

- *Type and amounts of drugs used during the past week.* Try to elicit specific details and quantifiable amounts. When the amount is essentially unknown to the individual, make efforts to infer levels of use. The following questions may be necessary: "How often do you go to the liquor store? How much do you purchase? How long does this amount last?"

    For prescription drug abuse, ask, "How long does a prescription last? How many sources do you have for the prescription?" For illicit drugs, the key questions are, "How often do you use cocaine or crack? Daily? Weekends? How often do you purchase drugs?"

- *Level of tolerance.* "What is the amount of the alcohol/drug required to feel the effects?"

- *The interval since last alcohol or drug use and the current physical status.* This information provides a valuable means of assessing tolerance. It indicates the symptoms of withdrawal with a declining blood level. In response to this, what objective signs are there of the presence of withdrawal? Tremulousness? Agitation? Sweating? Confusion? Hypervigilance? Rapid pulse?
- *Current or past medical problems, allergies.*
- *Prior experience of either decreasing or stopping their drinking or drug use?* Prior clinical status during withdrawal is significant, especially when prior withdrawal was problematic. This is not to be limited to formal detoxification. Many individuals have had periods of relative or absolute abstinence dictated by circumstances such as conscious efforts to curtail or limit use, or hospitalizations or vacation periods that disrupt their usual source of drugs.

Interviewing considerations. When interviewing patients to assess the risk of withdrawal, attempt to get quantitative answers whenever possible. Define the terms you use so that you and the patient understand each other. Equally important, seek clarification. Ask the patient to translate unclear or ambiguous terms to ensure that you comprehend the information provided. Whenever possible, corroborate the history by speaking with someone who knows the patient, or get as much history as possible from a companion if the patient is uncommunicative, confused, or unable to talk.

Basic Emergency Medical Skills

Anyone who works in human services or helping professions should have some basic first aid or emergency medical skills, including certification in CPR and the ability to take a pulse and knowledgeably respond to a seizure. In alcohol and drug abuse settings, one should also be able to administer a simple mental status examination and know how to handle disruptive patients.

DIAGNOSIS

The emphasis in this manual is *not* on primary care clinicians making formal substance use diagnosis. The focus is on basic, essential clinical activities, highlighting the availability of substance abuse clinical personnel to make the differential diagnosis and facilitate treatment planning. This perspective is not meant to imply that diagnosing alcohol and substance use problems entails skills and knowledge beyond the primary care provider. On the contrary, when DSM-IV criteria are followed, the task of diagnosis is relatively straightforward. The one stipula-

tion is that there be an adequate data base to determine if the specified criteria are met.[3]

A checklist derived from DSM-IV that can be used clinically in making the diagnosis is found in Box 5-2 and 5-3.

The third edition of the American Psychiatric Association's *Diagnostic and Statistical Manual, Third Edition* (DSM-III), published in 1980, can be regarded as a milestone in the classification of substance use disorders. For the first time, these disorders were grouped as a distinct diagnostic entity. Previously, addictions were subsumed within the category of personality disorders. The third edition was the first also to specify diagnostic criteria for making any psychiatric diagnosis. This approach differed from the earlier formulation in which theories of etiology based on the psychodynamics presumed to be operative were the primary basis for distinguishing between disorders. Subsequent to the third edition, there have been further revisions, in 1987 (DSM-III-R) and most recently in 1994 (DSM-IV), which refine the diagnostic criteria. In the development of the DSM-IV, efforts were made to mesh the nosology with that used by the *WHO's International Classification of Disease*, now in the tenth edition (ICD-10).

Diagnostic Criteria

The DSM-IV outlines seven symptoms that may be present to diagnose substance dependence. A diagnosis is made when any three (or more) are positive, occurring at any time in the same 12-month period:

1. Tolerance, as defined by either of the following:
   a. a need for markedly increased amounts of the substance to achieve intoxication or desired effect.
   b. markedly diminished effect with continued use of the same amount of the substance.
2. Withdrawal, as manifested by either of the following:
   a. the characteristic withdrawal syndrome for the substance.
   b. the same (or closely related) substance is taken to relieve or avoid withdrawal symptoms.
3. The substance is often taken in larger amounts or over a longer period than was intended.
4. There is a persistent desire for the substance and unsuccessful efforts to cut down or control substance use.
5. Much time is spent to obtain the substance, e.g., visiting multiple doctors or driving long distances, use the substance, e.g., chain-smoking, or recover from its effects.

BOX 5-2

DSM-IV Diagnostic Checklist—Option I

Patient Name _____

Symptoms

A1. ___	Missing school/work	___	Lost time from work
	Lost job	___	Child care neglected
		___	Other
2. ___	Driving under	___	Increased tolerance
	the influence	___	Past heavy drinking
	Reckless driving		pattern
	Serious injury	___	Other ___
3. ___	DWI	___	Unpaid child support
	Domestic disputes	___	Other ___
4. ___	Friends/family		Drinking causes life problems:
	express concern	___	Relationship ___ Legal
	Guilty about use	___	Job
	Arguments about	___	Other ___
	drinking		
		___	Alcohol related arrest
		___	Blackouts
		___	Physical health
			harmed by use
		___	Intoxicated at home
		___	Use at work or school
		___	Arrests
		___	Physical fights
			or property damage
		___	Arrests
		___	License suspension

Diagnostic Criteria

| | | YES | NO |
| | | ☐ | ☐ |

ALCOHOL ABUSE:
A definite diagnosis of abuse is made when *one* of A is "yes", and both B and C are also "yes".

A. 1. Recurring failure to meet social, family, work responsibilities due to use. — —

2. Recurrent use when this is physically hazardous. — —

3. Recurring legal problems. — —

4. Continued use despite negative consequences or recurring problems due to use. — —

B. These symptoms have occurred repeatedly during a 12 month period. — —

C. Never having met the criteria for dependence. The pattern is consistent with a diagnosis of abuse. — —

ALCOHOL DEPENDENCE:
A definite diagnosis of dependence is made when any *three* of A *and* B are "yes".

YES ☐ NO ☐

A.

1. Tolerance.
   - ___ Consumed as much as one case beer, 1 gallon wine, ½ hard liquor at one time
   - ___ 4+ drinks/sitting
   - ___ Less use required to achieve intoxication
   - ___ Other

2. Withdrawal symptoms or use to avoid withdrawal symptoms.
   - ___ Morning hand tremor
   - ___ Night sweats
   - ___ Morning drinking
   - ___ Drinking before work
   - ___ Hallucinations
   - ___ Other
   - ___ Use of substitutes to self-medicate withdrawal symptoms

3. Drinking more or for longer periods than intended.
   - ___ Not a social drinker
   - ___ Drinks more than intended
   - ___ Experiences difficulty cutting down
   - ___ Greater quantity
   - ___ Other

4. A persistent desire, or one or more unsuccessful efforts to control use.
   - ___ Thoughts about cutting down
   - ___ Guilty about use
   - ___ Sees self as problem drinker
   - ___ Periods of abstinence
   - ___ Relief drinking
   - ___ Annoyed with concerns of others
   - ___ Other

5. Considerable time spent obtaining alcohol, or drinking it, or recovering from its effects.
   - ___ Daily drinking
   - ___ Binge drinking
   - ___ Drinking alone
   - ___ Needs drink
   - ___ Preoccupation with alcohol
   - ___ Other

6. Important activities (social, occupational, recreational) given up or reduced because of drinking.
   - ___ Lost friends
   - ___ Arguments about drinking
   - ___ Physical fights or property damage under the influence
   - ___ Increased isolation
   - ___ Other

7. Continued drinking despite knowledge of persistent social, psychological, or physical problems due to use.
   - ___ Prior DWI
   - ___ Other arrests
   - ___ Lost job due to alcohol
   - ___ Told drinking harming liver
   - ___ Told by MD to decrease use
   - ___ Blackouts
   - ___ Health would be better without
   - ___ Other ___
   - After drinking:
     - ___ rowdy/noisy
     - ___ courage/self-confidence
     - ___ angry/quarrelsome

B. These symptoms have occurred repeatedly during a 12 month period.
The pattern is consistent with a diagnosis of dependence. If Substance dependence: with ___ or without ___ physiological dependence

BOX 5-3
DSM-IV Diagnostic Checklist—Option II

Patient Name _____

DSM-IV Checklist for Substance Abuse and Dependence

Substance Abuse

		Yes	No
A.	Has the patient experienced the following:		
1.	Recurrent failure to meet important responsibilities due to use?	___	___
2.	Recurrent use in situations when this is likely to be physically dangerous?	___	___
3.	Recurrent legal problems arising from use?	___	___
4.	Continued to use despite recurrent problems aggravated by the substance use?	___	___

B. These symptoms have occurred within a 12 month period.   Yes ___   No ___
C. Patient had *never* met the criteria for dependence.   Yes ___   No ___

A definite diagnosis of abuse is made when any *one* of A and both B and C are "yes."

Substance Dependence

		Yes	No
A.	Has the patient experienced the following:		
1.	Tolerance (needing more to become intoxicated or having less effect with same amount)?	___	___
2.	Withdrawal* (characteristic withdrawal associated with type of drug)?	___	___
3.	Using more or for longer periods than intended?	___	___
4.	Desire to or unsuccessful efforts to cut down?	___	___
5.	Considerable time spend in obtaining the substance or using, or recovering from its effects?	___	___
6.	Important social, work, or recreational activities given up because of use?	___	___
7.	Continued use despite knowledge of problems caused by or aggravated by use?	___	___

B. These symptoms have occurred within a 12 month period.   Yes ___   No ___

*A definite diagnosis of dependence is made when any *three* of A *and* B are "yes."

6. Important social, occupational, or recreational activities are given up or reduced because of substance use.
7. The substance use is continued despite knowledge of persistent or recurrent psychical or psychological problems probably caused or exacerbated by the substance, e.g., current cocaine use despite recognition of cocaine-induced depression, or continued drinking despite recognition that an ulcer was made worse by alcohol consumption.

Specify if:

   With Physiological Dependence: evidence of tolerance or withdrawal, e.g., either Item 1 or 2 is present
   Without Physiological Dependence: no evidence of tolerance or withdrawal, e.g., neither Item 1 nor 2 is present

The criteria for substance abuse (in contrast to dependence) centers on the following two features:
1. A maladaptive pattern of substance use, leading to clinically significant impairment or distress, as manifested by one (or more) of the following, occurring within a 12-month period:
   a. recurrent substance use resulting in a failure to fulfill major role obligations at work or school; substance-related absences, suspensions, or expulsions from school; neglect of children or household.
   b. recurrent substance use in situations in which it is physically hazardous, e.g., driving an automobile or operating a machine.
   c. recurrent substance-related legal problems, e.g., arrests for substance-related disorderly conduct.

d. continued substance use despite having persistent or recurrent social or interpersonal problems caused or exacerbated by the substance (e.g., arguments with spouse and consequences of intoxication, physical fights).

2. The patient has never met the criteria for substance dependence for this class of substance.

Item 2 above is significant because of the confusion experienced by clinicians when they encounter a patient who previously met the criteria for dependence, but whose current use is seemingly under control or only slightly problematic. An incident involving alcohol or drug use may have occurred, which brings them into contact with health care or social service providers. Even when the patient's history is evident, it may be tempting, especially in light of a patient's explanations, to view the current problems as unrelated and the substance use problems as not contiguous. At this point the natural history should be regarded as a steady, although inconsistent, downward course.

In another guise, the same issue is broached by the common question, "Can alcoholics ever learn to drink safely?" One answer is found in the following analogy: The decision to resume drinking is likened to the motorist who removes the spare tire from the trunk of the car. At some point, disaster will strike. It may not be today. It may not be tomorrow. But, sure enough . . . sometime.

REFERENCES

1. Albrecht RR. Impact of medical issues on sports participation: Drug use. *Sports Medicine and Arthroscopy Review* 3(2): 95-10, 1995. (14 refs.)

2. American Medical Association. *Prescribing Controlled Drugs.* Chicago: American Medical Association, 1986. (Chapter refs.)

3. American Psychiatric Association. *Diagnostic and Statistical Manual of Mental Disorders, 4th Edition, Revised.* Washington DC: American Psychiatric Association, 1993. (0 refs.)

4. Bagasra O; Kajdacsy-Balla A; Lischner HW. Effects of alcohol ingestion on in vitro susceptibility of peripheral blood mononuclear cells to infection with HIV and of selected T-cells functions. *Alcoholism: Clinical and Experimental Research* 13(5): 636-643, 1989. (40 refs.)

5. Barnett G; Rapaka RS. Designer drugs: An overview. IN: Redda KK; Walker CA; Barnett G, eds. *Cocaine, Marijuana, Designer Drugs: Chemistry, Pharmacology and Behavior.* Boca Raton FL: CRC Press, 1989. pp. 163-174. (17 refs.)

6. Beebe DK; Walley E. Substance abuse: The designer drugs. *American Family Physician* 43(5): 1689-1698, 1991. (30 refs.)

7. Blume S. Beer and the breast feeding mom. (letter). *Journal of the American Medical Association* 258(15): 2126, 1987. (5 refs.)

8. Brower KJ; Blow FC; Hill EM. Risk factors for anabolic androgenic steroid use in men. *Journal of Psychiatric Research* 28(4): 369-380, 1994. (21 refs.)

9. Brower KJ; Blow FC; Young JP; Hill EM. Symptoms and correlates of anabolic-androgenic steroid dependence. *British Journal of Addiction* 86(6): 759-768, 1991. (27 refs.)

10. Clark N. Social drinking and athletes. *Physician and Sportsmedicine* 17(10): 95+, 1989. (14 refs.)

11. Colsher PL; Wallace RB. Is modest alcohol consumption better than none at all? An epidemiologic assessment. (review). *Annual Review of Public Health* 10: 203-219, 1989. (151 refs.)

12. Cox AE. *The Management of Intoxicated and Disruptive Patients: Emergency Department Training Manual.* Toronto: Addiction Research Foundation, 1979. (3 refs.)

13. Department of Justice. *Guidelines for Prescribers of Controlled Substances.* Washington DC: Drug Enforcement Administration, 1979.

14. Devenyi P; Saunders SJ. *Physicians' Handbook for Medical Management of Alcohol and Drug Related Problems.* Toronto: Addiction Research Foundation, 1986.

15. DiFranza JR; Guerrera MP. Alcoholism and smoking. *Journal of Studies on Alcohol* 51(2): 130-135, 1990. (28 refs.)

16. Flores-Huerta S; Hernandez-Montes H; Argote RM; Villalpando S. Effects of ethanol consumption during pregnancy and lactation on the outcome and postnatal growth of the offspring. *Annals of Nutrition and Metabolism* 36(3): 121-128, 1992. (28 refs.)

17. Frank DA; Graham JM Jr; Smith DW. Adoptive children in a dysmorphology clinic: Implications for evaluation of children before adoption. (letter). *Pediatrics* 68(5): 744-745, 1981. (10 refs.)

18. Geller A. The social, psychological and medical management of intoxication. *Journal of Substance Abuse Treatment* 1(1): 11-19, 1984. (6 refs.)

19. Goldberg HL; Nissim R. Psychotropic drugs in pregnancy and lactation. (review). *International Journal of Psychiatry in Medicine* 24(2): 129-149, 1994. (91 refs.)

20. Gross MM; Rosenblatt SM; Chartoff S; Hermann A; Schachter M; Sheinkin D; Broman M. Evaluation of acute alcoholic psychoses and related states: The Daily Clinical Course Rating Scale. *Quarterly Journal of Studies on Alcohol* 32(3): 611-619, 1971. (25 refs.)

21. Heather N. Disulfiram treatment for alcoholism: Deserves reexamination (ed.). *British Medical Journal* 299(6697): 471-472, 1989. (23 refs.)

22. Huhtaniemi I. Anabolic-androgenic steroids: A double edged sword. (review). *International Journal of Andrology* 17(2): 57-62, 1994. (32 refs.)

23. Jacobs MR; Fehr K O'B. *Drugs and Drug Abuse: A Reference Text, 2nd Edition.* Toronto: Addiction Research Foundation, 1987. (Chapter refs.)

24. Jury Verdict Research. Database search conducted for Project Cork Institute. Solon OH: Jury Verdict Research, 1989.

25. Kacew S. Adverse effects of drugs and chemicals in breast milk on the nursing infant. *Journal of Clinical Pharmacology* 33(3): 213-221, 1993. (81 refs.)

26. Kashkin KB; Kleber HD. Hooked on hormones? An anabolic steroid addiction hypothesis. *Journal of the American Medical Association* 262(22): 3166-3170, 1989. (69 refs.)

27. Kozlowski LT; Ferrence RG. Statistical control in research on alcohol and tobacco: An example from research on alcohol and mortality. (review). *British Journal of Addiction* 85(2): 271-278, 1990. (37 refs.)

28. Kranzler HR; Babor TF; Lauerman RJ. Problems associated with average alcohol consumption and frequency of intoxication in a medical population. *Alcoholism: Clinical and Experimental Research* 14(1): 119-126, 1990. (19 refs.)

29. Little RE; Anderson KW; Ervin CH; Roberts BW; Clarren SK. Maternal alcohol use during breast-feeding and infant mental and motor development at one year. *New England Journal of Medicine* 321(7): 425-430, 1989. (17 refs.)

30. Mello NK; Mendelson JH; Teoh SK. Neuroendocrine consequences of alcohol abuse in women. (review). *Annals of the New York Academy of Sciences* 562: 211-240, 1989. (150 refs.)

31. Miller SI; Frances RJ; Holmes DJ. Use of psychotropic drugs in alcoholism treatment: A summary. (review). *Hospital and Community Psychiatry* 39(12): 1251-1252, 1988. (16 refs.)

32. Office of the Inspector General. *Drug Utilization Review.* Washington DC: Department of Health & Human Services, 1989. (95 refs.)

33. Ogur B. Prescription drug abuse and dependence in clinical practice. (review). *Southern Medical Journal* 80(9): 1153-1159, 1987. (45 refs.)

34. Penttila A; Karhunen PJ; Vuori E. Blood alcohol in sudden and unexpected deaths. *Forensic Science International* 43(1/2): 95-102, 1989. (14 refs.)

35. Pope HG Jr; Katz DL. Psychiatric and medical effects of anabolic-androgenic steroid use: A controlled study of 160 athletes. *Archives of General Psychiatry* 51(5): 375-382, 1994. (47 refs.)

36. Price TRP. Withdrawal assessment scale. Hanover NH: Department of Psychiatry, Dartmouth Medical School, 1983.

37. Russell MAH. The nicotine addiction trap: A 40-year sentence for four cigarettes. *British Journal of Addiction* 85(2): 293-300, 1990. (34 refs.)

38. Schonfeld L; Rohrer GE; Dupree LW; Thomas M. Antecedents of relapse and recent substance abuse. *Community Mental Health Journal* 25(3): 245-249, 1989. (8 refs.)

39. Shepherd J; Irish M; Scully C; Leslie I. Alcohol intoxication and severity of injury in victims of assault. *British Medical Journal* 296(6632): 1299, 1988. (4 refs.)

40. Shindler N. Personal communication. September 1988.

41. Simel DL; Feussner JR. Blood alcohol measurements in the emergency department: Who needs them? *American Journal of Public Health* 78(11): 1478-1479, 1988. (10 refs.)

42. Simel DL; Feussner JR. Does determining serum alcohol concentrations in emergency department patients influence physicians civil suit liability? *Archives of Internal Medicine* 149(5): 1016-1018, 1989. (13 refs.)

43. Spigset O. Anaesthetic agents and excretion in breast milk. (review). *Acta Anaesthesiologica Scandinavica* 38(2): 94-103, 1994. (70 refs.)

44. Stockwell T; Bolt L; Milner I; Pugh P; Young I. Home detoxification for problem drinkers: Acceptability to patients, relatives, general practitioners and outcome after 60 days. *British Journal of Addiction* 85(1): 61-70, 1990. (24 refs.)

45. Svanum S; McAdoo WG. Predicting rapid relapse following treatment for chemical dependence: A matched-subjects design. *Journal of Consulting and Clinical Psychology* 57(2): 222-226, 1989. (19 refs.)

46. Tveite W. Drugs and breast feeding: A risk/benefit evaluation (review). *Veterinary and Human Toxicology* 36(Supplement 1): 1-80, 1994.

47. Vaccarino JD. Personal communication, September 1988.

48. Vaillant GE. *The Natural History of Alcoholism.* Cambridge MA: Harvard University Press, 1983. (369 refs.)

49. Vannicelli M. Treatment of alcoholic couples in outpatient group therapy. *Group* 11(4): 247-257, 1987. (12 refs.)

50. Wartenberg AA; Nirenberg TD; Liepman MR; Silvia LY; Begin AM; Monti PM. Detoxification of alcoholics: Improving care by symptom-triggered sedation. *Alcoholism: Clinical and Experimental Research* 14(1): 71-75, 1990. (27 refs.)

51. Whitfield CL; Thompson G; Lamb A; Spencer V; Pfeifer M; Browning-Ferrando M. Detoxification of 1024 alcoholics with-out psychoactive drugs. *Journal of the American Medical Association* 239(14): 1409-1410, 1978.

52. Wilton JM. Breastfeeding and the chemically dependent woman. *Clinical Issues in Perinatal and Women's Health Nursing* 3(4): 667-672, 1992. (21 refs.)

53. Wright C; Moore RD. Disulfiram treatment of alcoholism. *Annals of Internal Medicine* 111(11): 943-945, 1989. (49 refs.)

54. Zweben JE; Smith DE. Considerations in using psychotropic medication with dual diagnosis patients in recovery. *Journal of Psychoactive Drugs* 21(2): 221-228, 1989. (37 refs.)

FURTHER READINGS
Management of Withdrawal

Adinoff B; Bone GHA; Linnoila M. Acute ethanol poisoning and the ethanol withdrawal syndrome. (review). *Medical Toxicology* 3(3): 172-196, 1988. (146 refs.)

Ethanol, a highly lipid-soluble compound, appears to exert its effects through interactions with the cell membrane. Cell membrane alterations indirectly affect the functioning of membrane-associated proteins, which function as channels, carriers, enzymes, and receptors. For example, studies suggest that ethanol affects the y-aminobutyric acid (GABA)-benzodiazapine-chloride ionophore receptor complex, thereby accounting for the biochemical and clinical similarities between ethanol, benzodiazepines, and barbiturates. The patient with acute ethanol poisoning may present with symptoms ranging from slurred speech, ataxia, and incoordination to coma, potentially resulting in respiratory depression and death. At blood alcohol concentrations of greater than 250 mg% (250 mg% = 250 mg/dl = 2.5 g/L = 0.250%), the patient is usually at risk of coma. Children and alcohol-naive adults may experience severe toxicity at blood alcohol concentrations less than 100 mg%, whereas alcoholics may demonstrate significant impairment only at concentrations greater than 300 mg%. The ethanol withdrawal syndrome may be observed in the ethanol-dependent patient within 8 hours of the last drink, with blood alcohol concentrations in excess of 200 mg%. Symptoms consist of tremor, nausea and vomiting, increased blood pressure and heart rate, paroxysmal sweats, depression, and anxiety. Alterations in the GABA-benzodiazepine-chloride receptor complex, noradrenergic overactivity and hypothalamic-pituitary-adrenal axis stimulation are suggested explanations for withdrawal symptomatology. The initial evaluation of ethanol withdrawal requires doing a history of ethanol intake, an assessment of severity of past withdrawal episodes and other drug intake, and a physical examination for potential coexisting illnesses.

Erstad BI; Cotugno. Management of alcohol withdrawal. (review). *American Journal of Health-System Pharmacy* 52(3): 697-709, 1995. (138 refs.)

The diagnosis, evaluation and assessment, supportive care, and pharmacologic treatment of acute alcohol withdrawal are reviewed. Patients in alcohol withdrawal have decreased or stopped their heavy, prolonged ingestion of alcohol and have subsequently begun to have at least two of the following symptoms: autonomic hyperactivity, tremor, nausea or vomiting, hallucinations, psychomotor agitation, anxiety, and grand mal seizures. Evaluation of the patient at risk for alcohol withdrawal should include a complete history and physical examination; laboratory tests are often indicated. The patient's progress should be assessed before, during, and after therapy, preferably with a validated instrument. After the initial evaluation and assessment but before the administration of dextrose-containing solutions, a 100-mg dose of thiamine hydrochloride should be given by IM or IV injection. Routine supplementation with calcium, magnesium, and phosphate is questionable. The need for fluid and electrolyte administration varies depending on losses. Most patients in alcohol withdrawal can be managed with supportive care alone, but for more severe or complicated withdrawal, pharmacologic therapy may be necessary. Benzodiazepines, especially diazepam and chlordiazepoxide, are the drugs of choice. Barbiturates, beta-blockers, and antipsychotics are generally not recommended at first-line therapy. Several drugs in other classes, including carbamazepine and clonidine, have been shown to be about as effective as benzodiazepines in a few studies, but the studies were small, the patients were usually in mild withdrawal, and validated instruments for assessing withdrawal were often not used. Some agents such as beta-blockers may play a role as adjuncts to, not replacements for, benzodiazepine therapy. For patients in alcohol withdrawal who do not respond to supportive care, benzodiazepines are the treatment of choice. Copyright 1995, American Society of Health-System Pharmacists.

Farrell M. Opiate withdrawal. (review). *Addiction* 89(11): 1471-1475, 1994. (22 refs.)

Opiate withdrawal is one of the longest-studied and most well-described withdrawal syndromes. Opiate withdrawal has been described as akin to a moderate to severe flulike illness. Opiate withdrawal is appropriately described as subjectively severe but objectively mild. This paper describes the mechanisms of opiate dependence and withdrawal and reviews the available instruments for measuring withdrawal. The time course of assisted and unassisted withdrawal is described, as well as the range of options for managing assisted withdrawal. This review concludes that the most effective and least time- and resource-consuming approach to opiate withdrawal will substantially contribute to the overall social management of opiate dependence. Copyright 1994, Society for the Study of Addiction to Alcohol and Other Drugs.

Fishbain DA; Rosomoff HL; Cutler R. Opiate detoxification protocols. A clinical manual. *Annals of Clinical Psychiatry* 5(1): 53-65, 1993.

The purpose of any opiate detoxification protocol is to minimize or eliminate the signs and symptoms associated with opiate withdrawal, thereby decreasing the chances of relapse to opiate dependence. In the last few years, because of the development of new medications such as clonidine for the treatment of opiate withdrawal, a number of new protocols have been developed. Four types of protocols are reviewed and outlined: methadone substitution/detoxification, codeine or other opiate substitution/detoxification, opiate of choice detoxification, and buprenorphine substitution/detoxification. In addition, six protocols utilizing clonidine are presented, including a protocol utilizing opiate antagonist precipitated withdrawal. Finally, two protocols that utilize naltrexone are outlined, and adjunct medications potentially useful in opiate detoxification are reviewed. Suggestions for treating drug-seeking behavior during detoxification are summarized, as are the advantages and disadvantages of the various protocols.

O'Connor PG; Waugh ME; Schottenfeld RS; Diakogiannis IA; Rounsaville BJ. Ambulatory opiate detoxification and primary care: A role for the primary care physician. *Journal of General Internal Medicine* 7(5): 532-534, 1992.

To determine the feasibility of primary care-based ambulatory opiate detoxification (AOD) and an optimal regimen, the authors conducted a pilot study of AOD in a medical clinic comparing two regimens: clonidine and clonidine plus naltrexone. Sixty-two opiate addicts referred for AOD had the following features: mean age

was 34 years, 75% were male, 74% used cocaine, and 64% shared needles. Initially, 40 patients selected clonidine, 22 clonidine/naltrexone. The groups (clonidine and clonidine/naltrexone) were similar in baseline features, including craving scores (44/100 vs. 42/100) and withdrawal scores (20/72 vs. 17/72). Overall, 61% (38/62) of initial AODs were successful, including 43% (17/40) of those using clonidine and 95% (21/22) of those using clonidine/naltrexone (*P* less than 0.0001). Of 45 patients who ultimately completed AOD, 78% (35/45) remained in treatment for at least a month.

Blood Alcohol Determination and Drug Testing

Cone EJ. Saliva testing for drugs of abuse. (review). *Annals of the New York Academy of Sciences* 694: 91-127, 1993. (134 refs.)

Saliva testing for drugs of abuse can provide both qualitative and quantitative information on the drug status of an individual undergoing testing. Self-administration by the oral, intranasal, and smoking routes often produces "shallow depots" of drug that contaminate the oral cavity. This depot produces elevated drug concentrations that can be detected for several hours. Thereafter, saliva drug concentrations generally reflect the free fraction of drug in blood. Also, many drugs are weak bases, and saliva concentrations may be highly dependent upon pH conditions. These factors lead to highly variable S/P ratios for many of the drugs of abuse. Table 3 provides a compilation of experimental and theoretical S/P (total) ratios determined for drugs of abuse. Estimations of the theoretical S/P (total) ratios for acidic and basic drugs were based on the Henderson-Hasselbalch equation. Saliva pH was assumed to be 6.8 unless reported otherwise by the investigators. Generally, there was a high correlation of saliva drug concentrations with plasma, especially when oral contamination was eliminated. Assay methodology varied considerably, indicating that saliva assays could be readily developed from existing methodology. There are many potential applications for saliva testing for drugs of abuse. Table 4 lists several general areas in which information from saliva testing would be useful. Clearly, saliva drug tests can reveal the presence of a pharmacologically active drug in an individual at the time of testing. Significant correlations have been found between saliva concentrations of drugs of abuse and behavioral and physiological effects. Results indicate that saliva testing can provide valuable information in diagnostics, treatment, and forensic investigations of individuals suspected of drug abuse. It is expected that saliva testing for drugs of abuse will develop over the next decade into a mature science with substantial new applications. Copyright 1993, New York Academy of Sciences.

Conigrave KM; Saunders JB; Whitfield JB. Diagnostic tests for alcohol consumption. (review). *Alcohol and Alcoholism* 30(1): 13-26, 1995. (104 refs.)

Various laboratory tests are available to assist in the diagnosis of hazardous alcohol consumption and related disorders. Standard tests such as serum gamma glutamyltransferase activity and erythrocyte mean cell volume have limited sensitivity, particularly in detecting nondependent hazardous consumption. Most also have poor specificity in that results are affected by common diseases and medications. Over the past 10 years a number of new laboratory tests have emerged. One of these, carbohydrate deficient transferrin, has high sensitivity in detecting persons with alcohol dependence and shows promise for identification of nondependent hazardous drinking; it is also highly specific. Others such as measurement of bound acetaldehyde, serum beta-hexosaminidase, and the ratio of urinary serotonin metabolites offer promise in detecting recent heavy drinking. However, many issues remain unresolved. The newer markers have often been judged by contrasting their values in patients who are clearly alcohol dependent with abstainers or very light drinkers. It is now apparent that some are relatively insensitive markers of hazardous consumption. Future research needs to examine the performance of these markers among subjects with a range of alcohol intakes to fully determine their value in assessing drinking history. In addition, assays capable of some degree of automation need to be developed for analyzing large numbers of samples. Copyright 1995, Medical Council on Alcoholism. Used with permission.

Schramm W; Smith RH; Craig PA; Kidwell DA. Drugs of abuse in saliva: A review. *Journal of Analytical Toxicology* 16(1): 1-9, 1992. (101 refs.)

There has been substantial interest in the use of saliva as a diagnostic medium for drugs of abuse because it can be obtained noninvasively. Although drugs of abuse have been investigated in saliva for more than a decade, the role of saliva remains uncertain. A clear picture is difficult to obtain because of variations in (1) the analytical methods used; (2) the dose regimen of subjects, which was either unknown or differed between studies; and (3) the elapsed time between drug intake and sample collection. This communication summarizes the studies on the quantitative determination of different drugs of abuse in saliva to elucidate the current status in this area. Marijuana, cocaine, phencyclidine, opiates, barbiturates, amphetamines, and diazepines (or their metabolites) have all been detected in saliva by various analytical methods, including immunoassay, gas chromatography/mass spectrometry, and thin layer chromatography. Initial studies with cocaine and phencyclidine suggest a correlation between saliva and plasma concentrations of these drugs, indicating a dynamic equilibrium between saliva and blood. Tetrahydrocannabinol, the active component in marijuana, on the other hand, does not appear to be transferred from plasma to saliva. However, tetrahydrocannabinol is sequestered in the buccal cavity during smoking and can be detected in saliva. These findings point to the potential role of saliva in the analysis of many illicit drugs. To clearly identify the role of saliva as a diagnostic medium for drugs of abuse, research efforts should be directed towards (1) performing systematic studies on correlations between saliva, blood, and urine, and (2) determining the concentrations of drugs and their metabolites in saliva as a function of dose and time after intake. Copyright 1992, Preston Publications, Inc.

Schwartz RH; Clark HW; Meek PS. Laboratory tests for rapid screening of drugs of abuse in the workplace: A review. *Journal of Addictive Diseases* 12(2): 43-56, 1993. (9 refs.)

The use of rapid, on-site drug detection devices is reviewed. These tests permit the detection of various psychoactive substances in urine, and are easily used by nonskilled personnel. Saliva tests are available for detection of alcohol. These rapid tests have varying degrees of accuracy, and it is recommended that positive outcomes for all rapid tests be verified by standard laboratory procedures. The tests have potential use in the emergency room, doctor's office, drug treatment program, and the work place. When access to formal laboratory testing is limited by either time or location, an easily portable test can give critical information. A number of commercially available tests are reviewed for method, accuracy, advantages, and disadvantages. Consequently, the interested practitioner should be able to find a suitable screening test from among the tests reviewed. Copyright 1993, The Haworth Press, Inc.

Selavka CM; Rieders F. The determination of cocaine in hair: A review. *Forensic Science International* 70(1-3): 155-164, 1995. (69 refs.)

The explosion of literature related to the analysis of hair for cocaine and its products is reviewed. In the commonly accepted applications of hair testing for cocaine, those related to criminal or civil investigations and pharmacotoxicologic studies occupy most of the relevant published work. This review uses detailed, 'binary' (yes/no) tables to demonstrate trends in the literature, and allows researchers and caseworkers quick access to the literature most important for answering a variety of questions. Copyright 1995, Elsevier Scientific Publishers Ireland, Ltd.

CHAPTER 6

Nursing Care of the Substance-Abusing Patient

NANCY B. FISK, EdD, RN
PAULA RUTH, RN, CDNS

CLINICAL APPLICATIONS

The goals of this chapter are to assist the nurse clinician to:

1. Recognize the nurse's role in addressing substance use.

2. Recognize attitudes that may interfere with nursing care and involvement.

3. Be familiar with nursing care practices with substance abuse patients.

4. Incorporate substance use objectives into nursing assessment, diagnosis, and treatment.

Nurses are particularly well-positioned to be the first point of contact in the health care system for clients/patients with substance use problems and/or their family members. Several characteristics of nursing as a profession and nursing as a discipline contribute to this advantageous position. Among these are the variety of settings in which nurses practice, the diversity of roles which nurses can take on within these, the broad age range (entire life span) of patients with whom nurses have expertise, and the broad base of nurses' education in health and illness sciences. Additionally, professional nurses are trained and educated for health promotion activities as well as multiple levels of preventative interventions: primary, secondary, and tertiary.

While a modest but growing number of nurses work in dedicated substance abuse treatment settings—such as detoxification units, short-term residential treatment settings, partial hospitalization, or outpatient treatment units—all nurses encounter the problems of substance abuse in every setting. Nurses working in general hospital units, for example, may encounter adults with medical or surgical problems directly resulting from alcohol abuse or alcohol dependence. They may encounter elders who have used medications inappropriately because of inadequate knowledge, visual impairment, or memory deficit. They may encounter children whose parents have alcohol problems or encounter infants who have been exposed to alcohol, tobacco, or other drugs prenatally. Nurses in emergency room settings regularly encounter victims of accidents in which substance use was a factor. Household and motor vehicle accidents are often related to one's own or another's impairment from substance use. Illnesses and injuries of all kinds are associated with the long- or short-term effects of alcohol and/or other drugs. Nurses are well-informed concerning the damage-prone organs and tissues, as well as the signs and symptoms of such physiological effects.

Other nurses working in nonhospital settings regularly encounter other types of evidence of substance use problems. School nurses are able to assess children of various ages concerning their state of health and readiness for learning; they are able to see signs of abuse or neglect or of psychosocial problems that can be the red flags for a substance abuse problem in the home. They might also be the first to identify the adolescent involved with substance use. Occupational health nurses, home health nurses, psychiatric mental health nurses, hospice nurses, and nursing home nurses are just a few of the other nonhospital nurses with unique and often primary access to patients with substance abuse.

Each setting provides its own unique set of clues (based on the patient population) to which nurses become attuned. Nurses who have developed through their own experiences and interest a high index of suspicion for such problems have extraordinary opportunities to intervene. Often, the earliest possible point of intervention is available to nurses in the community setting, as no other health professional might otherwise have contact for months or even years. It is less easy to hide the clues to substance abuse from the nurse who sees individuals and families in their own homes. Thus, the importance of the nursing role cannot be overstated.

Case finding and screening, along with early intervention and prevention of complications of substance abuse, can constitute aspects of secondary and tertiary prevention that nurses have traditionally performed for all types of health conditions. Professional nurses are also well-prepared to provide teaching, counseling, and referral, as their education includes training in individual, family, and group counseling as well as courses in pharmacology, pathophysiology, and population-based health concepts.

Primary prevention strategies are also well within the purview of nursing practice, which professional nursing school curricula emphasize. An example of this is the wide variety of such strategies that can be applied by school nurses who have a broad-based, health promotion focus in their practice. Age-appropriate curricula for children and adolescents have been developed that focus on specific grades as aggregates for health promotion. Increasing self-efficacy, promoting self-esteem, building resistance techniques, and other strategies are well-utilized by professional nurses. In 1990, Sue Ann Pflum, the President of the National Nurses Society on Addictions, advised all nurses to become involved in prevention by "identifying and responding to the risk factors in our clients . . ." as automatically as "identifying risk factors for cancer, diabetes and heart disease" and "teaching our clients about [these] risk factors."[12]

The above is but a sampling of the scope of nursing practice in the addictions. It does not include the advocacy role of the nurse at the statewide and national levels. Nor does it include the administrative/policy-making levels of institutions, communities, and municipalities, which will be discussed further below. Of major importance here is that nurses represent by far the largest number of health care personnel that can be brought to bear upon this enormous health problem, which many authorities consider to be our nation's number one public health problem. By virtue of their numbers, their versatility across numerous practice settings, and the depth and breadth of nursing education, particularly with respect to the pharmacological effects of the substances of abuse, nurses are ideally suited and extremely capable of making great inroads. Furthermore, the impact of nursing upon substance abuse problems cannot only be widely accessible to persons of all ages, socioeconomic levels, and ethnic and cultural backgrounds, but also be affordable to individuals, families, communities, and state and national economies. The nurse can and should have a pivotal role in the prevention and management of substance abuse problems. However, not all nurses recognize their enormous potential to make a difference.

ATTITUDES

Much has been written about professionals' attitudes toward substance abuse and the substance-abusing patient. Nurses are no different from other health care professionals in this regard. Unless deliberately educated differently, their attitudes may be no different than those of the general population. There is no doubt that nurses encounter substance abuse concerns in every practice setting and in all aggregate populations, transcending all of the traditional "empires" and sub-specialties of nursing. However, many nurses tend to think of these problems as the exclusive domain of the psychiatric/mental health nurse specialist. At best, this is misleading. At worst, it may represent powerful, systemic denial long associated with the issues of substance abuse. The same denial is operative as well in the not atypical behavior of ignoring the clues even when they are obvious, or when considering the problem the domain of other health providers. Recalling that "denial" is not a conscious defense mechanism, these comments are made not to cast blame, but simply to point out the common pitfalls related to the nursing care of patients with potential or actual substance abuse problems.

"Nursing is the diagnosis and treatment of human responses to actual or potential health problems."[1] Who can deny, given this definition, that substance abuse for the afflicted individual and the affected family members falls within the domain of nursing practice for all nurses, not just for psychiatric/mental health nurses? For the substance abuser and all members of the family system, physical, mental, emotional, social, and spiritual health and functioning are either severely impaired or at risk. The need for professional nursing is broad and comprehensive.

THE NURSING ROLE

The *Position Statement on the Role of the Nurse in Alcoholism*, first published in 1978 by the National Nurses Society on Alcoholism, states the most basic premises of this chapter quite aptly.

The National Nurses Society on [Alcoholism] affirms its belief that [alcoholism] is a primary disease. NNSA also stresses the fact that nursing in [alcoholism] transcends the traditional dividing lines of clinical nursing specialties; that nursing care of [alcoholic] individuals and families is encompassed in every nursing specialty and not exclusively Psychiatric/Mental Health Nursing.[11]

The National Nurses Society on Alcoholism—since renamed the National Nurses Society on Addictions—

delineated five major professional activities in the role of the nurse regarding alcoholism.[11] These can appropriately be restated to encompass other drugs, including tobacco and alcohol. These five activities are as follows:
1. Identifying the problem with alcohol, tobacco, and other drugs.
2. Communicating about the problems associated with these substances.
3. Educating about substance use, abuse, and addiction/dependence.
4. Counseling the substance-using individual, family, and significant others about the addiction and its resulting problems.
5. Referring for further definitive substance abuse treatment and/or aftercare.

Identifying the Problem

Considering the variety of settings in which nurses practice, these activities encompass screening techniques. In many settings, it also involves deeper levels of assessment. Chapter 2 of this manual—Routine Screening and Initial Assessment—serves nurses well in this regard, with such instruments as the CAGE, the MAST, and DAST. A screening instrument, The Alcohol Use Disorders Identification Test (AUDIT), developed as a collaborative effort of the World Health Organization to identify harmful alcohol consumption, has been used in the training of health professionals including students of nursing. The AUDIT, appropriate for inpatient and outpatient populations, is a brief interview followed by a brief guidance/referral intervention concerning alcohol use.[4] Basic to these identification efforts is an acute level of awareness by nurses of the prevalence of the problems of alcohol, tobacco, and other drugs; their insidiousness; and their pervasiveness in every facet of life: every patient, every family, every group, every population.

Communicating about the Problem

It is appropriate nursing intervention to open communication about the substance abuse problem with the patient, with the family or significant others, and with the appropriate members of the interdisciplinary health team. Communication concerning the problem should be based on a body of knowledge and a philosophy conducive to recovery, and should be approached in a consistent, nonjudgmental manner. Essential to these efforts is a recognition of substance abuse or dependence as primary disorders in and of themselves; not blameworthy or morally tinged, but morally neutral. The substance abuser should be viewed as ill and in need of efforts to promote recovery as any other chronically ill person, rather than as being morally weak or "bad." Some nurses require the guidance of a clinical specialist to acquire the necessary knowledge, attitudes, and skills for communicating directly about the problem.

Educating about Substance Abuse

Every nurse is responsible for educating patients, families, and significant others concerning substance use and addiction. This includes general facts about these disorders and any information needed for managing their medical and psychosocial situations. Additionally, nurses with special knowledge and skills in this clinical content area should educate other members of the interdisciplinary team as well as community groups. The professional nurse is able to teach in both formal and informal settings and is able to use systematic and individualized approaches according to the needs of the learners. This is no less true for substance abuse disorders than it is for other chronic illnesses such as diabetes, heart disease, and arthritis.

Counseling the Individual, Family, and Significant Others

Nurses in all settings need a basic level of knowledge and the requisite skills to provide some initial substance abuse counseling. The use of the defense mechanism of denial by individuals, families, and significant others is a major deterrent to entering needed treatment. The inadvertent reinforcement of such denial by the nurse can be detrimental. It is crucial that nurses intervene to identify and confront it. Other psychological defense mechanisms such as projection, minimization, and rationalization, which are also commonly overused by substance abusers, also need to be recognized and addressed. In some settings, it is often appropriate that nurses assume responsibility for direct counseling, including individual and group therapy, and that they be active members of the treatment team.

Referral for Further Definitive Treatment and/or Aftercare

All nurses in any setting need to be sufficiently knowledgeable about available resources to be able to initiate an appropriate treatment referral when the substance abuse patient and/or significant others express readiness for help. Help should be sought either inside or outside the care setting if the nurse does not have adequate knowledge of the local/ regional resources. It is never appropriate to shirk the responsibility of locating a treatment resource. The importance of timing in such a referral cannot be overemphasized. Nurses at the specialist level should acquire additional knowledge of resources in order to individually match agent/agency to the need of the patient, family, and/or significant other. The clinical outcome may be greatly influenced by the appropriateness of the treatment and continuing care referral. Continuity of care and follow-up are essential nursing responsibilities in all settings.

DEFINITIVE NURSING CARE

It is always tempting, given the complexity of the diseases of addiction, to embark upon a comprehensive nursing care plan with interventions aimed at all of its physical, mental, psychoemotional, social, cultural, and spiritual complications. This would not only be beyond the scope of this chapter, but would mask or submerge the real issue: the substance abuse. In the practice world, this may be exactly what happens; the real problem is thus overlooked or buried under the myriad of nursing process rhetoric. Perhaps the first step in definitive nursing intervention is to recognize and confront nurses' own denial mechanisms with respect to substance abuse. Likewise, in keeping a family, systemic perspective, it might be tempting to focus upon the family's financial or legal problems, and in the same way deny the real problem as the probable underlying cause of these and many other family problems.

It becomes important, therefore, to follow the lead of NNSA in addressing only the definitive nursing actions here, i.e., "only those functions of the nurse which directly and specifically define the role of the nurse in relation to the problem with alcohol".[11] As the generally accepted methodology of nursing, the framework of the nursing process is used here to structure further discussion of the definitive nursing role with substance-abusing patients. This framework includes assessing the individual and family; planning nursing care; intervening, based on the plan; and evaluating outcomes and process. These steps of nursing process are roughly paralleled in the American Nurses Association publication, *Standards of Addictions Nursing Practice with Selected Diagnoses and Criteria.*[3] The standards were developed in collaboration with NNSA and take their place with a number of other documents that delineate standards for several other specialized areas of nursing practice as well as the generic standards for the profession. It is important that nurses be familiar with these documents. Nurses wishing to become more effective and comfortable in their approach to those with substance abuse disorders are well-advised to study the addictions standards that provide substantial details. Additionally, the ANA publication, *The Care of Clients With Addictions: Dimensions of Nursing Practice,* written collaboratively in 1987 by ANA, NNSA, and DANA (Drug and Alcohol Nursing Association), provides a comprehensive nursing perspective.[2] The latter includes historical threads in the development of addictions nursing; it also discusses prevention and treatment strategies for nurses, role development and role distinctions across practice settings, and levels of nursing education, to name a few topics.

Assessment

Nursing assessment of substance-abusing individuals and families draws both from nursing models and from models from other fields of study, as are those described elsewhere in this manual. In the late 1970s, Estes, Smith-DiJulio, Heinemann, and others were among the first to provide assessment guides for nursing: appraisal by interview, appraisal by physical examination, and nursing diagnosis of the alcoholic person.[7] Chychula several years later designed another instrument especially for primary care nurses.[5] Wright and Leahey have developed a comprehensive family assessment model which, while not specific for substance abuse problems, does provide an applicable family systems framework that can incorporate much of the work done in respect to the impact of substance abuse problems on the family.[14]

Nursing assessment of the individual. Understanding the role of stigma and assessing levels of denial versus levels of acceptance are a part of the assessment of the individual who is or may be a substance abuser. Estes, Smith-DiJulio, and Heinemann provide a useful description of the psychosocial traits of alcoholic patients in which they describe denial as occurring on a continuum between normal denial and psychotic denial.[7] As the disease progresses, denial of addiction and its consequences, if never addressed, is generally seen at the more pathological end of the continuum. If, however, denial is addressed, ambivalence may become apparent. While the alcohol-dependent person will tend to minimize the amount and extent of the drinking, the opposite may be true for those dependent on other drugs, particularly narcotics, when patients may exaggerate their use as a part of their drug-seeking behavior. The importance of recognizing and dealing with denial and/or ambivalence cannot be overemphasized. While these defense mechanisms may interfere with the reliability of some of the health history data, it is still necessary that a careful interview be done as a part of the nursing assessment. With strategic questioning, a history of heavy alcohol/drug use will emerge as well as other data concerning its consequences.

Assessment of the family system. The concept of "family as client" is inherent in professional nursing. The discipline's holistic and contextual perspective readily accommodates the idea that the unit of service encompasses the individual within the total context of the immediate social environment, which is the family. Family-centered nursing is now the focus of every domain of nursing, but particularly community health nursing, child and adolescent health nursing, and psychiatric/mental health nursing. Nursing educators and recent nursing texts have paid considerable attention to the application of family systems perspectives

to nursing practice.[10,14] In the case of addictions nursing, this is especially fortunate in that it seems to parallel what is happening in the larger field of addiction.

While diseases and statistics refer to individuals and head counts, addiction is increasingly conceptualized in nursing as a family systems problem. A family systems perspective yields considerably different parameters for assessment and intervention of the problem. Family intervention seeks to introduce change in the structure and/or dynamics of the family system so it will ultimately cease to foster or maintain the substance-abusing behavior.

For nursing, a particularly interesting aspect of family systems thinking is the notion of circular or mutual causality, in contrast to a linear view of causality that can easily promote explanations that deal with blame. One writer has commented that "...a systemic perspective on human problem formation and human problem resolution is holistic, collaborative, dialectical, process-oriented and circular, and as such represents a major paradigm shift from the traditional western linear perspective which is individualistic, reductionist, mechanistic, content-oriented and unidirectional."[6] In the case of substance abuse, given the negative stereotypes and nonsympathetic attitudes prevailing even (or especially) among the helping professions, nurses with a family systems perspective are provided a perspective that may help avoid the all-to-common tendency to blame the patient, and be more supportive of families of substance-abusing patients. This perspective parallels the views espoused by 12-step programs, as well as the predominant view in the addictions treatment field. It is a view also noteworthy for assisting both patient and family to resolve feelings of guilt and shame. One danger of a family perspective is that it may promote a tendency to shift blame from the individual patient onto the spouse or family. Keeping a systemic perspective is an ongoing challenge for those who wish to work effectively with families.

Nursing Diagnosis

Using the North American Nursing Diagnosis Association's list of approved diagnoses, 26 nursing diagnoses common in addictions nursing practice are identified in the ANA's *Standards of Addictions Nursing Practice*.[3,9] These include four broad diagnostic categories: the biological, the psychosocial, the cognitive, and the spiritual.[9] A few are highlighted in Table 6-1.

Planning

Nursing diagnoses established, the nurse now should set priorities and write long- and short-term goals that are realistic in terms of the capabilities and limitations of the family and the nurse's own skill and experience. Patient-centered objectives can then be written in progressive steps to meet the short-term

Table 6-1. Common Nursing Diagnosis among Substance Abuse Patients

Domains	Sample NANDA nursing diagnosis
Biological	• sensory-perceptual alteration • potential for injury • self-care deficit
Cognitive	• knowledge deficit • alteration in thought process • noncompliance
Psychosocial	• impaired communication • alteration in self-concept • anxiety
Spiritual	• spiritual distress • powerlessness • grief

goals, which must be mutually agreed upon by nurse and family. It is also important to be realistic about the designated time span of nursing service in relation to the particular family so that short-term goals can indeed be accomplished within the time frame.

Mutuality of goal-setting is both critical and problematic in substance abuse families, given the nature of the disease and the extremes of defensiveness that often characterize it. Nurse's must be alert to the level of acceptance of the disease in each family member and use their knowledge about addiction to work with the family to provide the best help possible. This is where nurses must rely on nursing experience, sense of timing, and professional judgment. Keeping the interaction open and positive rather than closed off and hopeless is of the utmost importance. Empathy and unconditional respect are essential attitudes to convey.

Each family will be different both in terms of the progression of the disease and the family's adjustment to it. Nevertheless, it is always important to plan and implement some type of intervention when a substance-abusing patient/family is under care of health professionals for other related or unrelated health problems. This may be the time when the connection between the health problems and the substance abuse will be most readily apparent to everyone.

Intervention

In this disease, nursing intervention is vital if recovery is to be achieved on a large scale. The facts about substance abuse make this quite clear. Nurses in all employment contexts have access to hundreds of these families; some at early stages of the illness, some at the middle stage, and some when it is all but too late to intervene in the fatal progression of the disease. Even at the generalist level, nurses are capable of

contributing significantly; the number of nurses must be considered an important element in their potential contribution because of the magnitude of the problem and the number of significant others also affected. A climate of hope can legitimately be established, knowing that this disease is most treatable. Many families have achieved recovery. Alcoholics Anonymous (AA) alone reports more than a million sober alcoholics. However, about 90% of alcoholic families never arrive at the doors of AA or other treatment options. Many of our most prevalent diseases are far less hopeful in prognosis for recovery.

Clear, accurate, and honest interactions concerning substance abuse and its consequences between all of the players—patient, family members, and health professionals—are vital. Also important is the straightforward and simple imparting of knowledge about the pharmacology of substances of abuse, the development of addiction, and recovery from substance abuse. The latter refers both to informal and formal didactic teaching of the scientific facts of the disease. Correction of myths and misconceptions about substance use and abuse is one of the most important therapeutic measures in recovery for all members of substance-abusing families.

A structured type of family intervention has been useful in families in which the substance abuse is actively progressing, e.g., the drinking, smoking, or taking of drugs has not yet ceased. Sometimes these are quite direct and are aimed at the singular goal (whether verbalized directly with the patient or not) of persuading the individual to enter into the appropriate specific treatment. Nurses can be instrumental as members of an intervention team or as "coaches" on the sidelines. This entails consideration of the individual's physiological status, the family's financial situation (including health insurance coverage), and miscellaneous factors such as geographic location, and family preference. Although it may seem backward to carry out discharge planning with the family and to arrange for referral, it is crucial to have the mechanisms in place to be able to act immediately whenever the patient reaches that point of acceptance/compliance when reality breaks through and substance abuse treatment is requested.

Two important considerations have been pointed out by those in the substance abuse field: 1) That health-related crises are among the best nodal points of opportunity for engaging patients into treatment and promoting change, and 2) that a multidisciplinary team approach is often most effective.[8] Back when it was universally believed that an alcoholic person "had to hit bottom" or had to independently "seek help," a clinical intervention was designed that demonstrated that those conditions were not necessary for treatment to be initiated. The approach, often termed an intervention, is based on the therapeutic use of substance use-related crises by family, friends, employers, and health team members; it focuses on providing support while expressing love and concern, and on emphasizing that the problem behaviors are part of a disease that requires treatment, not a condition that can be wished away, alleviated by willpower, waited away, or loved away. (For a description of the intervention process, see Wegscheider.)[13]

Nurses can be a part of the initiating process for such an intervention and can also individually draw upon some of the principles of the method in their work with substance-abusing individuals and families. If the crisis of illness, injury, and/or hospitalization is used constructively, the patient will be assisted in making the appropriate connections between his or her substance use and the awesome consequences. This involves what some have called "tough love": Steadfastly refusing to cover-up, smooth over, minimize, or in any way rescue the patient from the impact and emotional pain of the current crisis.

Evaluation

The Standards of Addictions Nursing Practice with Selected Diagnoses and Criteria are most useful in providing nurses with a rational and objective means for evaluating nursing care. Each standard is followed by criteria for evaluating quality of care. Three categories are included: structure criteria, process criteria, and outcome criteria. Box 6-1 shows the list of 12 standards, and Box 6-2 shows the structure, process, and outcome criteria for one of the 12 standards, Standard III—Diagnosis.

Box 6-1
Professional Practice Standards of Addictions Nursing

I. **Theory**	The nurse uses appropriate knowledge from nursing theory and related disciplines in the practice of addictions nursing.
II. **Data Collection**	Data collection is continual and systematic and is communicated effectively to the treatment team throughout each phase of the nursing process.
III. **Diagnosis**	The nurse uses nursing diagnoses congruent with accepted nursing and interprofessional classification systems of addictions and associated physiological and psychological disorders to express conclusions supported by data obtained through the nursing process.
IV. **Planning**	The nurse establishes a plan of care for the patient based upon nursing diagnoses, addresses specific goals, defines expected outcomes, and delineates nursing actions unique to each patient's needs.
V. **Intervention**	The nurse implements actions independently and/or in collaboration with peers, members of other disciplines, and patients in the prevention, intervention, and rehabilitation phases of the care of patients with health problems related to patterns of abuse and addiction.
A. Therapeutic Alliance	The nurse uses the "therapeutic self" to establish a relationship with patients and to structure nursing interventions to help patients develop the awareness, coping skills, and behavior changes that promote health.
B. Education	The nurse educates patients and communities to help them prevent and/or correct actual or potential health problems related to patterns of abuse and addiction.
C. Self-Help Groups	The nurse uses the knowledge and philosophy of self-help groups to assist patients in learning new ways to address stress, maintain self-control or sobriety, and integrate healthy coping behaviors into their life-style.
D. Pharmacological Therapies	The nurse applies knowledge of pharmacological principles in the nursing process.
E. Therapeutic Environment	The nurse provides, structures, and maintains a therapeutic environment in collaboration with the individual, family, and other professionals.
F. Counseling	The nurse uses therapeutic communication in interactions with the patient to address issues related to patterns of abuse and addiction.

Continued.

Box 6-1
Professional Practice Standards of Addictions Nursing—cont'd

VI.	**Evaluation**	The nurse evaluates the responses of the patient and revises nursing diagnoses, interventions, and the treatment plan accordingly.
VII.	**Ethical Care**	The nurse's decisions and activities on behalf of patients are in keeping with personal and professional codes of ethics and in accord with legal statutes.
VIII.	**Quality Assurance**	The nurse participates in peer review and other staff evaluation and quality assurance processes to ensure that patients with abuse and addiction problems receive quality care.
IX.	**Continuing Education**	The nurse assumes responsibility for his or her own continuing education and professional development and contributes to the professional growth of others who work with or are learning about persons with abuse and addiction problems.
X.	**Interdisciplinary Collaboration**	The nurse collaborates with the interdisciplinary treatment team and consults with other health care providers in assessing, planning, implementing, and evaluating programs and other activities related to addictions nursing.
XI.	**Use of Community Health Systems**	The nurse participates with other members of the community in assessing, planning, implementing, and evaluating community health services that attend to primary, secondary, and tertiary prevention of addictions.
XII.	**Research**	The nurse contributes to the nursing care of patients with addictions and to the addictions area of practice through the use of innovations in theory and practice and participation in research, and communicates these contributions.

From American Nurses Association and National Nurses Society on Addictions. *Standards of Addictions Nursing Practice with Selected Diagnoses and Criteria.* Kansas City MO: American Nurses Association, 1988.

Box 6-2
Example of Application of Standards of Practice

Example, Practice Standard: Diagnosis.
(See Box 6-1, Item III.)

Structure Criteria

1. The practice settings afford opportunities for collegial exchange, education, and research regarding the scientific premises upon which nursing diagnosis is based.
2. Staff education and evaluation processes assure that the nurse maintains current knowledge of nursing diagnosis development.

Process Criteria

The nurse—

1. Uses the nursing process to identify actual or potential health problems and human responses to those problems.
2. Analyzes available data according to accepted theoretical frameworks.
3. Uses nursing diagnoses congruent with and/or complementary to the diagnoses of other professional colleagues.
4. Revises nursing diagnoses in accord with new assessment data.

Outcome Criteria

1. Nursing diagnoses are documented and communicated in a manner that facilitates nursing planning, implementation, evaluation, and research.
2. Nursing diagnoses are shared with the patient (including the individual, the family, and significant others) unless contraindicated for therapeutic reasons. Affirmation of the nursing diagnosis is sought from the patient, the nurse's peers, and other professional members of the treatment team.

From American Nurses Association and National Nurses Society on Addictions. *Standards of Addictions Nursing Practice with Selected Diagnoses and Criteria.* Kansas City MO: American Nurses Association, 1988.

REFERENCES

1. American Nurses Association. *A Social Policy Statement.* Kansas City MO: American Nurses Association, 1980.

2. American Nurses Association; Drug and Alcohol Nursing Association; National Nurses Society on Addictions. *The Care of Clients with Addictions: Dimensions of Nursing Practice.* Kansas City MO: American Nurses Association, 1987.

3. American Nurses Association and National Nurses Society on Addictions. *Standards of Addictions Nursing Practice with Selected Diagnoses and Criteria.* Kansas City MO: American Nurses Association, 1988.

4. Babor TF; de la Fuente JR; Saunders J; Grant M. *The Alcohol Use Disorders Identification Test: Guidelines for Use in Primary Health Care.* Geneva Switzerland: World Health Organization, 1989.

5. Chychula N. Screening for substance abuse in a primary care setting. *The Nurse Practitioner* 13(7): 15-18+, 1984. (11 refs.)

6. Coppersmith EI. The place of family therapy in the homeostasis of larger systems. IN: Aronson M; Wolberg R, eds. *Group and Family Therapy.* New York: Brunner/Mazel, 1982.

7. Estes NJ; Smith-DiJulio K; Heinemann ME. *Nursing Diagnosis of the Alcoholic Person.* St Louis: Mosby, 1980.

8. Johnson VE. *I'll Quit Tomorrow, Revised Edition.* New York: Harper & Row Publishers, Inc, 1980. 182 pp.

9. Kim MJ; McFarland GK; McLane A, eds. *Classification of Nursing Diagnoses: Proceedings of the Fifth National Conference.* St Louis: Mosby, 1984.

10. Millers SR; Winstead-Fry P. *Family Systems Theory in Nursing Practice.* Reston VA: Reston Publishing Company, 1982.

11. National Nurses Society on Alcoholism. *The Role of the Nurse in Alcoholism.* A Position Statement Developed by the Membership at the Annual Meeting of NNSA (April 1978). Available from National Council on Alcoholism and Drug Dependence, Inc (NCADD), 12 W 21st Street, New York 10010.

12. Pflum SA. RNs can prevent, treat addiction. *American Nurse* 22(1): 5, 1990.

13. Wegscheider S. *Another Chance: Hope and Health for the Alcoholic Family.* Palo Alto CA: Science & Behavior, 1981.

14. Wright L; Leahey M. *Nurses and Families: A Guide to Family Assessment and Intervention, 2nd Edition.* Philadelphia: FA Davis, 1994.

FURTHER READINGS

NOTE: Also see Chapter 9, Resources for Educators and Trainers.

Allen K. Attitudes of registered nurses toward alcoholic patients in a general hospital population. *International Journal of the Addictions* 28(9): 923-930, 1993. (8 refs.)

The Marcus Alcoholism Questionnaire was administered to 66 registered nurses at a community hospital to ascertain their attitudes regarding alcoholic patients in a general hospital population. This was done to provide documentation on what nurses' attitudes actually are as opposed to assumptions about what they should be because of the high visibility of the problem of alcoholism. The author reports the results of the study and then contrasts them with the information about registered nurses' attitudes toward alcoholic patients at a university hospital. The article concludes with insight into contributing factors for the differences. Copyright 1993, Marcel Dekker, Inc.

Allen K. Current morale issues that impede the caregiving process of substance abuse/addictions nurses. *Issues in Mental Health Nursing* 14(3): 293-305, 1993. (17 refs.)

A telephone survey was conducted with 25 nurse managers of substance abuse/addictions programs in a metropolitan area to ascertain what morale issues impede the caregiving processes of their nursing staff. Five issues were repeatedly identified by all 25 nurse managers: (a) Lack of credibility and respect for the nurse in the eyes of other members of the multidisciplinary team; (b) lack of understanding of the role of nurses in the substance abuse/addictions program on an inpatient unit; (c) lack of adequate preparation for the role; (d) lack of acceptance of the nursing role as defined by nursing; and (e) the care of patients with concurrent diagnosis. This article analyzes these issues from the perspective of reasons for existence and possible solutions. Copyright 1993, Hemisphere Publishing Corp.

Andersen MD. Personalized nursing: An effective intervention for use with drug dependent women in an emergency room. IN: Ashery RS, ed. *Progress in the Development of Cost-Effective Treatment for Drug Abusers. NIDA Research Monograph 58.* Rockville MD: National Institute on Drug Abuse, 1985. pp. 67-82. (26 refs.)

This chapter describes a model that evaluated the effectiveness of a nursing intervention model known as "personalized nursing." This model was designed to reach treatment-resistant, drug-dependent women through emergency room contacts; those who refused referral to traditional drug treatment programs were provided personalized nursing home visits on a regular basis, with a view to reducing drug involvement. Findings indicated that nurses were able to impact the lives of women addicts, although differences between the experimental and control groups disappeared in the 6-month follow-up. Copyright 1990, Project Cork Institute.

Beebe GC. Efficacy of a substance abuse primary prevention skills conference for nurses. *Journal of Continuing Education in Nursing* 23(5): 231-234, 1992. (16 refs.)

A conference on substance abuse prevention skills was presented by the New York State Nurses Association (NYSNA) to provide nurses with skills to help patients in various practice settings. Information covered assessment, intervention, and tools for interviewing and identifying resources. A 6-month follow-up evaluation showed that the majority of the participants incorporated the skills in their nursing practice primarily in interviewing and in using assessment questions. Directions for future conferences were identified. Copyright 1992, C.B. Slack, Inc.

Bell K. Identifying the substance abuser in clinical practice. *Orthopaedic Nursing* 11(2): 29+, 1992. (7 refs.)

Illicit drugs are used regularly by 14.5 million Americans. By identifying patients who abuse substances, the nurse will be better able to provide for the treatment interventions needed and omit ineffective treatment interventions. The patient will benefit by receiving timely and appropriate care. To identify substance abusers, the nurse must know effects of commonly abused drugs, their routes of administration, withdrawal signs, and the physical assessments that should be performed. The most common drugs abused are narcotics, depressants, antidepressants, anti-anxiety drugs, stimulants, hallucinogens, and marijuana. Copyright 1992, National Association of Orthopedic Nurses.

Brogdon KE. Improving outcomes for patients experiencing alcohol withdrawal. *Journal of Nursing Care Quality* 7(3): 61-70, 1993. (14 refs.)

Nurses in acute care settings have contact with patients 24 hours a day and are in a prime position to identify withdrawal symptoms and initiate early intervention. This article looks at the effect of a nursing alcohol withdrawal protocol on decreasing patients' alcohol withdrawal symptoms. Copyright 1993, Aspen Publishers, Inc.

Burns EM; Meadows LK. *The Development, Implementation, and Evaluation of an Integrated Model Program and Curriculum in Alcohol and Other Drug Abuse for Nursing Education.* Columbus OH: Ohio State University, College of Nursing, 1988. (0 refs.)

This is a copy of a proposed model nursing curriculum for undergraduate, masters, and doctoral nursing students. This proposal was one of three contracts awarded to schools of nursing by the NIAAA as part of its larger effort to support the development of model integrated educational programs in medicine and nursing. Copyright 1990, Project Cork Institute.

Church OM; Fisk NB; Neafsey PJ, eds. *Curriculum in Nursing Education in Alcohol and Other Drug Abuse.* Storrs CT: Project NEADA. University of Connecticut, School of Nursing, 1991.

Through a federal grant contract (ADM-281-88-007) an integrated model curriculum for nursing education at the undergraduate and graduate levels as well as continuing education for faculty and graduate nurses was created. The individual modules are listed below. Each module includes complete content outlines, instructor's guide, bibliography, masters for handouts and overheads and self-efficacy pre- and post-tests as well as learning objectives, teaching strategies, and time allotments.
- Undergraduate Module I: Substance Use and Abuse: Who Do I Know and How Do I Feel about It?
- Undergraduate Module II: Understanding, Preventing and Treating Alcohol and Other Drug Abuse
- Undergraduate Module III: The Impaired Nurse—Prevention, Treatment and Ethical/Legal Implications
- Post Baccalaureate Module (Core): Continuing Education for RNs (Undergraduate Modules I, II, III accelerated)
- Graduate Module I: Primary Community Care Nursing
- Graduate Module II: Emergency/Critical Care Nursing
- Graduate Module III: Nursing Administration
- Faculty Development Module: Preparing Teachers to Teach about Alcohol and Other Drug Abuse

Crowley TJ. Contingency contracting treatment of drug-abusing physicians, nurses, and dentists. IN: Grabowski J; Stitzer ML; Henningfield JE, eds. *Behavioral Intervention Techniques in Drug Abuse Treatment. NIDA Research Monograph 46.* Rockville MD: National Institute on Drug Abuse, 1984. pp. 68-83. (21 refs.)

Substance abuse often is characterized by remissions and relapses. Relapse hazards are especially problematic among certain highly responsible professionals such as physicians, dentists, and nurses. Thus, loss of professional privilege or licensure is a common consequence of drug abuse in these professions. On the other hand, these drug-abusing professionals know that they have ingested drugs hundreds or thousands of times before without loss of license and that they probably could "get away with just one more" ingestion. Thus, their fear of future loss of licensure may not effectively induce abstinence today. This is a report of an effort to "reschedule" therapeutically the threatened loss of professional privileges or licensure with a contingency-contracting procedure among 17 drug-abusing physician, nurse, and dentist patients treated in the Halsted Clinic. Copyright 1990, Project Cork Institute.

DuPont RL; McGovern JP. Suffering in addiction: Alcoholism and drug dependence. *NLN Publication* 15(2461): 155-201, 1992. (67 refs.)

This chapter is divided into eight sections focusing on the problems of suffering, addiction, and suffering in addiction, with all sections focused on the perspective of health care workers, especially young health care professionals. The sections are the American chemical dependence problem; the nature of suffering; the nature of chemical dependence; the biology of addiction; recovery from chemical dependence; the suffering in addiction; case histories; and opportunities for young health care professionals. Copyright 1992, National League of Nursing.

Hagemaster JN; Plumlee A; Conners H; Sullivan E. Integration of substance abuse content into undergraduate and graduate curricula. *Journal of Alcohol and Drug Education* 40(1): 89-102, 1994. (10 refs.)

Nursing schools are being challenged to integrate alcohol and other drug abuse content into both their undergraduate and graduate curricula. The University of Kansas is currently involved in a coordinated approach to curriculum implementation with the support of the National Institute on Alcohol Abuse and Alcoholism (NIAAA) and the National Institute on Drug Abuse (NIDA). Copyright 1994, Alcohol and Drug Problems Association of North America.

McMahon J; Jones BT. The change process in alcoholics: Client motivation and denial in the treatment of alcoholism within the context of contemporary nursing. *Journal of Advanced Nursing* 17(2): 173-186, 1992. (60 refs.)

Although patient motivation is constantly cited as a critical intervening variable in the recovery from alcohol problems, there is a paucity of literature on it. This paper reviews the current literature that impacts motivation and its importance in treatment and develops in a stepwise manner the revised expectancy/motivation hypothesis, tentatively explaining both motivation and denial as a natural process in behavioral change. Because of the revised expectancy/motivation hypothesis's distinctly defined stages which closely relate to the process of nursing and the qualitative and quantitative measurement it entails which the nursing process demands, it offers a particularly appropriate model for treatment within nurse practice. Copyright 1992, Blackwell Scientific Publications Ltd.

Minicucci DS. The challenge of change: Rethinking alcohol abuse. *Archives of Psychiatric Nursing* 8(6): 373-380, 1994. (26 refs.)

Nurses usually conceptualize alcohol abuse and dependence as a progressive disease that can be managed but never cured. Yet there are millions of Americans for whom this approach is not helpful. Impressive results have been reported by the alcohol research community with interventions guided by the assumption that many alcohol problems are learned habits that can be changed. This article reviews the clinical research in the area of brief interventions and moderation training with alcohol abusers. Nursing's vital role in advocating for and delivering such interventions is identified. Resistance to implementing alternative approaches for the treatment of alcohol problems is explored. Copyright 1994, W.B. Saunders Co.

Naegle MA. Prescription drug regulation: Implications for nursing and health care delivery. Response of the American Nurses' Association. IN: Cooper JR; Czechowicz DJ; Molinari SP; Petersen RC, eds. *Impact of Prescription Drug Diversion Control Systems on Medical Practice and Patient Care. NIDA Research Monograph 131.* Rockville MD: National Institute on Drug Abuse, 1993. pp. 228-234. (8 refs.)

This is one of several chapters of invited comments by professional associations. It represents the position of the American Nurses' Association. In recent years an increasing number of states have granted prescribing privileges to nurses identified as advanced practitioners. "Advanced practitioners" are nurses prepared at the graduate level and/or nurses certified in particular specialties. Generally these specialty practice roles are nurse practitioner, nurse midwife, and nurse anesthetist. All nurses qualifying for prescribing privileges must validate advanced education in pharmacotherapeutics. In 1990 the Drug Enforcement Administration, which oversees and regulates controlled substances, ruled that nurses did not have plenary authority to dispense controlled substances. The objection lodged by the ANA and its rationale is summarized. It is also noted that the magnitude of diversion remains largely unknown, and that there is no reason to believe that prescription privileges of nurses are a significant factor contributing to diversion. Copyright 1994, Project Cork Institute.

Naegle MA. Substance abuse. IN: Birckhead LM, ed. *Psychiatric/ Mental Health Nursing: The Therapeutic Use of Self.* Philadelphia: Lippincott, 1989. pp. 427-464. (52 refs.)

This chapter provides an excellent overview of the issues that substance use present to the nursing professions. It covers case identification, nursing diagnosis, natural history, approaches to interviewing and management, and the family, and also addresses personal biases and attitudes towards patients with substance use problems, as well as the impaired nurse and the profession's response. Copyright 1991, Project Cork Institute.

Naegle MA. The need for alcohol abuse-related education in nursing curricula. *Alcohol Health and Research World* 18(2): 154-157, 1994. (5 refs.)

Nurses have many important and diverse roles in the primary care setting. To be effective in these roles, nurses should, as part of their education, receive clinical training on recognizing and treating patients with alcohol problems. The author describes both the history and current state of nursing curricula as it relates to the topic of substance abuse. She also reviews model curricula programs now in existence and discusses future developments in the teaching field. Public Domain.

Naegle MA; D'Arcangelo JS, eds. *Substance Abuse Education in Nursing.* New York: National League for Nursing, 1992. (Publication Number 15: 2463)

This volume is comprised of a series of eight modules. The individual titles are listed below. Each module provides an instructor's guide that includes learner objectives, recommended readings, audiovisual materials, overhead masters, handout masters, teaching strategies and sample assignments, and a bibliography.

Module 1. Gigliotti E. Fetal Effects of Maternal Alcohol and Drug Use.

Module 2. Naegle MA. Impaired Practice by Health Professionals.

Module 3. D'Arcangelo JS; Adamski T. Addictions: Nursing Diagnosis and Treatment.

Module 4. Compton M. Nursing Care in Acute Intoxication.

Module 5. Compton M. Nursing Care in Withdrawal.

Module 6. Mathwig G; D'Arcangelo JS. Drug Misuse and Dependence in the Elderly.

Module 7. Clucas AH; Clarke VP. Drug and Alcohol Problems in Special Populations.

Module 8. Clucas AH; Clarke VP. Nursing Care of Drug and Alcohol Problems in Special Populations.

Rassool GH. Nursing and substance misuse: Responding to the challenge. *Journal of Advanced Nursing* 18(9): 1401-1407, 1993. (55 refs.)

The widespread use and misuse of alcohol, drugs and other psychoactive substances are major health and social concerns that affect the lives of many. The social and health sequelae of psychoactive drugs and alcohol are preventable and manageable with minimal interventions. Nurses and other health workers can effectively respond to substance misuse problems, and their existing generic skills can be easily adapted in working with substance misusers. This article considers issues such as the extent of the problem, attitudinal considerations, and the response to substance misusers. It also offers a brief outline of the role of the nurse and addresses the urgent need for education and training in substance misuse and addictive behavior for nurse practitioners. Copyright 1993, Blackwell Scientific Publications, Ltd.

Sanders D; Peveler R; Mant D; Fowler G. Predictors of successful smoking cessation following advice from nurses in general practice. *Addiction* 88(12): 1699-1705, 1993. (26 refs.)

At follow-up of 751 subjects receiving a brief, nurse-administered anti-smoking intervention in general practice, 135 subjects (18%) reported stopping smoking, of whom 44 (6%) reported sustained cessation for 1 year. The demographic, social, and attitudinal characteristics of these subjects were compared to 616 subjects who continued to smoke. The most important predictors of cessation were intention to stop (OR 5.1, 95% CI 2.1 to 12.0), per-

sonal rating of likelihood of cessation (OR 4.9, 95% CI 2.8 to 8.5), nurse rating of likelihood of cessation (OR 4.0, 95% CI 2.2 to 7.4), and smoking habit of partner (1.9, 95% CI 1.3 to 2.9). As practice nurses are able to distinguish likely quitters from those who are not motivated and less likely to succeed, it is important to decide whether it is more cost effective to target support at the motivated or to spend more time encouraging the less motivated. The most challenging, but possibly the most rewarding, task is to try to reduce the high proportion of new ex-smokers who relapse. Although 41.1% (95% CI 28.1, 58.0) of those expressing a definite intention to stop smoking gave up, only 17.9% (95% CI 8.9, 30.4) achieved sustained cessation. However, as sustained cessation is strongly predicted by social variables such as marital status and time spent with smokers, preventing relapse may not be easy through medical intervention alone. Copyright 1993, Society for the Study of Addiction to Alcohol and Other Drugs.

Sheehan A. Nurses respond to substance abuse. *International Nursing Review* 39(5): 141-144, 1992. (0 refs.)

Because of their close contact with the community, nurses are vital in caring for substance abusers and in preventing addiction. And their roles in community and national programs in this area are increasing. This article offers an overview of the problems associated with substance abuse and how nurses are needed to provide effective care, prevention, and education. Copyright 1992, International Council of Nurses.

Sullivan E. *Nursing Care of the Substance Abusing Client.* Mosby, 1995.

Written by an expert in the field, with many expert contributors, the text focuses on nursing care for both alcohol and drug abuse. The book is outlined in three units: Understanding Substance Abuse, Nursing Care of Clients with Substance Abuse, and opportunities and Challenges in Substance Abuse, and discusses the complete cycle of abuse, treatment, and recovery.

Talashek ML; Gerace LM; Starr KL. The substance abuse pandemic: Determinants to guide interventions. *Public Health Nursing* 11(2): 131-139, 1994. (57 refs.)

The substance abuse pandemic calls for a comprehensive model from which nurses can organize the vast array of drug and alcohol knowledge required for practice in the community. The model for nursing's contributions provides a framework for organizing factors that affect health status into four determinants: biological, sociocultural, medical-technological-organizational, and environmental. The model serves as an organizing mechanism to present key information about alcohol and drug abuse. Copyright 1994, Blackwell Scientific Publications, Ltd.

Walker RD; Howard MO; Walker PS; Lambert MD; Suchinsky R. Practice guidelines in the addictions: Recent developments. *Journal of Substance Abuse Treatment* 12(2): 63-74, 1995. (91 refs.)

Consensually established principles of clinical conduct, known variously as practice guidelines, standards, protocols, or algorithms, have proliferated throughout medicine over the past decade. Institutional and disciplinary efforts to develop and promulgate guidelines for the treatment of addictive disorders have recently been initiated. The authors review guideline development activities of the American Psychiatric Association, American Psychological Association, American Society of Addiction Medicine, American Nurses Association, National Association of Social Workers, and Center for Substance Abuse Treatment of the Substance Abuse and Mental Health Services Administration. Medical care performance and outcome assessments are discussed with attention to the role they can play in evaluating and refining guidelines. Potential effects of guidelines, salutary and deleterious, on clinical practice in the addictions are delineated. Copyright 1995, Pergamon Press.

CHAPTER 7

Social Work Perspectives on Alcohol and Drug Abuse Problems

SHULAMITH LALA ASHENBERG STRAUSSNER, DSW, BCD, CEAP
CHRISTINE HUFF FEWELL, CSW, BCD, CAC

CLINICAL APPLICATIONS

The goals of this chapter are to assist the social work clinician to:

1. Address substance abuse issues within the context of social work practice.

2. Incorporate substance abuse issues as part of social work assessment with individuals and families.

3. Utilize social work skills to promote motivation, early intervention, and referral.

4. Work collaboratively with substance abuse treatment personnel.

Social workers comprise the largest number of mental health professionals in the US, with over 150,000 belonging to its professional organization, the National Association of Social Workers.[21] Given their generic training, social workers practice in a wide range of fields including health, mental health, child welfare, public welfare, vocational rehabilitation, aging, family service, education, criminal justice, and industry.

Because alcohol and drug addiction affect not only individuals' internal world but also their environment, it would seem natural, as pointed out by Petty,[23] that a profession that concerns itself with the interaction between individuals and their social environment should be interested in the treatment of alcohol and other drug abuse. Yet, until recently, few social workers were interested in the field and even fewer received training in this area as part of their professional education. Fortunately, such lack of interest is changing rapidly. Social workers are flocking to join the newly established addiction specialty section within NASW, and many schools are providing substance abuse training as part of their required or elective courses.

SOCIAL WORK APPROACHES
Historical Involvement

Social workers have contributed significantly to the development of the field of alcoholism treatment. As early as 1917, Mary Richmond, one of the major contributors to the founding of social casework, stated in her classic publication, *Social Diagnosis*, that "inebriety is a disease;" she went on to provide a description of "chronic inebriety" that was entirely consistent with the disease concept of E. M. Jellinek described almost half a century later.[14] Richmond in 1917 stated that the "disease" of inebriety does not occur in all who drink, nor even in all who get drunk. Rather, the diagnosis requires a skillful medical and physical examination and applies to "those who are habitually *overcome* by alcohol and unable to take it at all without taking it to excess."[25] She further stated that the disease is not curable in the sense that one who suffers from it cannot drink alcohol without danger of relapse. She viewed social workers as playing an important role in gathering the pertinent social data, rallying the assistance necessary to supplement the medical treatment, and providing the long period of aftercare that is usually necessary. Furthermore, Richmond included a diagnostic questionnaire for inebriety that assesses family, drinking, and medical history; the current situation; and causal factors—the same diagnostic variables used today, nearly 80 years later.

Unfortunately, few social workers followed Richmond's interest in the treatment of alcoholics until the establishment of the Yale Plan Clinics at New Haven and Hartford, Connecticut, in 1944. These clinics, staffed by an interdisciplinary team of psychiatrists, internists, psychologists, and social workers, developed a prototype of inpatient treatment that served as the model for the current alcoholism treatment programs.[5]

Between the 1940s and 1960s, three social workers emerged as leaders in the treatment of individuals with alcohol problems and their families.[18] During the 1940s, Gladys Price of the Washingtonian Center for Addictions in Boston provided the first alcoholism field placement for social work students[18] and contributed to the knowledge base regarding wives of alcoholics.[24] Around the same time, Margaret Cork at the Addiction Research Foundation in Toronto, Canada, became concerned about the problems of children of alcoholics and established a treatment program for these children. Her book, *The Forgotten Children*, based on her study of these children, remains a classic in the field.[6] Another important social work contributor was Margaret Bailey, who worked for the National Council on Alcoholism in New York City. Between 1964 and 1968, under the auspices of the Community Council of Greater New York, she headed a highly successful training project involving three agencies with family casework orientations. The resulting monograph, *Alcoholism and Family Casework*, is an excellent and still relevant contribution to the social work literature on how to work with alcoholics and their families.[1]

In 1955 the Yale (later Rutgers) Summer School of Alcohol Studies established its first formal training seminar for social workers. The faculty eventually included all three of these pioneering social workers. Margaret Bailey further contributed to social work education in alcoholism by establishing the Alcoholism Committee under the auspices of the New York City Chapter of National Association of Social Workers. Starting in 1969, and still continuing, the Committee has sponsored an annual Alcoholism Institute that has become one of the major national providers of alcoholism training, and, more recently, other drug abuse training to social workers. In addition to the Institute, the Committee (recently renamed Committee on Alcoholism and Other Chemical Dependencies) has published various journals and books (see listing at end of chapter) and provides a hotline for social workers concerned about their own, familial, or a colleague's substance abuse.

The passage by the US Congress of the Hughes Act of 1970 led to the establishment of the National Institute on Alcohol Abuse and Alcoholism (NIAAA) and the National Institute on Drug Addiction (NIDA). It also resulted in increased funding for both public and private non-profit treatment facilities, particularly for alcoholics. Consequently, numerous social workers were hired and trained in alcoholism counseling, bringing with them their knowledge base of group and family dynamics and building upon the pioneering work of Price, Cork, and Bailey.

Due to the historical evolution of the treatment of drug addiction in the US, until recently social workers have had little involvement and have made less significant contribution to the field of drug treatment. Historically, until the passage of the Harrison Narcotic Act of 1914, physicians were able to prescribe narcotics to their patients, and numerous private "sanitariums" existed under medical supervision.[3] In the years following the Harrison Act until the 1960s, few professionals were involved in treating drug addicts and no data regarding social workers as treatment providers is available. It was only during the 1980s, with the rapid escalation in cocaine dependence and polydrug abuse, that the treatment philosophy and staffing patterns of drug addiction programs and alcoholism treatment facilities began to converge.[27] Consequently, the role of the social worker as a vital member of the interdisciplinary team—with special expertise about family dynamics and an understanding of the cultural, environmental, intrapersonal, and intrapsychic influences impacting the patients—became recognized in the merging field of alcohol and other drug abuse.

Current Social Work Roles

According to national surveys, 24.4 million Americans, one in eight, used illicit drugs during 1993, and 2.7 million of them can be characterized as dependent on such drugs as cocaine and heroin, while almost 18 million Americans have a problem with alcohol.[7] It is difficult to know how many of these individuals are seen by social workers; however, due to the wide range of public and private sector settings in which social workers are employed and due to the sheer numbers of social workers throughout the various health, mental health, and welfare delivery systems, social workers are likely to come in contact with more alcohol- and other drug-abusing individuals and their family members than any other of the helping professions.

Consequently, social workers play a vital role in the assessment, motivational treatment, and referral of substance-abusing patients in various social and medical settings; furthermore, they provide individual, group, and family treatment to patients in substance abuse-specific settings. Social workers employed in nonaddiction settings such as child and family service agencies, schools, hospitals, and employee assistance programs, are often in the position to identify individuals with alcohol and other drug abuse early, before such problems become chronic and lead to multiple negative biopsychosocial consequences. To accomplish this, social workers need to view alcohol and other drug addictions as primary diseases, rather than as symptoms of other dysfunctions, and be aware that substance abuse treatment is effective.

Regardless of the setting, all social workers need to have some basic knowledge and skills to identify, intervene, treat, or refer patients with alcohol or other drug problems. Social workers need to be knowledgeable about the differential impact of various substances on a person's mood and behavior; the progressive biopsychosocial deterioration resulting from dependence on such substances as alcohol, narcotics, and stimulants; the value of the disease concept, including the nature of relapse; the crucial function of the defense of denial in addictions; and the impact of substance abuse on the family.[9,12,17,29,26,27]

ASSESSMENT

Since alcohol and other drug abuse both cause and exacerbate many physical, emotional, and social problems for individuals and their family members, and given the pervasive nature of substance abuse problems, all intake procedures need to contain questions to routinely screen for alcohol and other drug usage and resulting difficulties. Regardless of the presenting problem, all patients whose behavior is highly volatile or unpredictable or whose history indicates interpersonal, occupational, financial, and/or legal problems should be directly questioned about possible substance abuse.[27]

While some individuals may readily admit to being substance abusers, others may not. Various formal assessment instruments such as MAST and CAGE are available and should be utilized when appropriate.[27,11] It is important to keep in mind that alcohol and other drug abusers tend to rely excessively on such defense mechanisms as denial, projection, and rationalization and that such defenses are unconscious.[9,27] Thus, substance abusers are truly unaware of the full impact of the substance abuse on their lives, and it is the job of the worker to assess and label the problem for the patient, and offer help. For example,

During a parent-staff conference at the therapeutic nursery, the mother of one of the children appeared somewhat intoxicated and smelled of alcohol. Previously the staff had observed her drinking from a bottle of mineral water, which aroused suspicion as the contents appeared to look thicker than water. One of the issues of concern with the child was the need to be consistent in setting limits. The social worker matter-of-factly stated to the mother that she had observed that the mother smelled of alcohol that morning and therefore must have been drinking. She added that in her experience, when a person is drinking early in the morning, it is usually a sign of a problem with alcohol. She knew that difficulties with alcohol made it very hard to set consistent limits. The worker suggested that perhaps they needed to consider whether the drinking might be an issue they should discuss and see whether the mother would want to seek further help.

MOTIVATION

Once a substance abuse or dependence diagnosis is confirmed or even strongly suspected, the worker may need to utilize confrontation to help the patient accept the severity of the problem and/or further treatment referral. Utilizing confrontation may appear contrary to many of the teachings of social work. Social workers are taught to respect defenses and to "start where the patient is." Confrontation is thus seen as interfering with a patient's right to self-determination and as an obstacle to establishing of a working relationship with a patient. However, the use of confrontation does not mean that it has to be hostile. As pointed out by Bailey years ago, "confrontation fundamentally means a realistic evaluation of . . . (the) drinking problem with the patient. It aims to cut away denial and omnipotent fantasy and thus usually mobilizes some anxiety. It may be that the reluctance of many workers to undertake this is primarily a problem of their own discomfort . . ."[1] She went on to point out that confrontation is not unique to alcoholism and is frequently necessary in working with acting-out adolescents.

Another obstacle faced by social workers dealing with substance-abusing patients may arise from the teaching of crisis intervention theory. The traditional goal of crisis intervention is to stabilize the patient's reaction to a stressful situation and minimize anxiety in the hope of quickly returning the patient to the previous level of functioning.[10,22] However, during work with a substance-abusing patient, a crisis offers an opportunity to further diminish a patient's rigid defenses and motivate entry into treatment. For example,

Mr. S., a 35-year-old divorced man, was admitted to the hospital for the second time within a year for cellulitis and abscess of his right leg, which had not healed following surgery 8 months earlier. He was also diagnosed with cirrhosis of the liver. During his first hospitalization, he was informed that his medical problems stemmed from his excessive drinking. At that time, Mr. S. told the social worker that he drank because he worked as a bartender and "it just seemed natural with all that liquor around." He didn't think he would have any problem controlling his drinking. The social worker helped him deal with the medical and financial crises by listening to his concern about the surgery, reassuring him that everything would be okay, and helping him apply for disability benefits. During his rehospitalization,

Mr. S., who appeared extremely agitated, acknowledged that he was still drinking, but much less than before and that "it's not that big of a problem." He didn't think his physical problems were related to his drinking and now that he had used up all his savings and that his girlfriend left, he had been thinking of taking up his mother's invitation to return home in a neighboring state. Once he was home, his mother would take care of his leg. Could the social worker help arrange for his transportation to his mother?

Mr. S.'s request left the worker with two options: She could alleviate Mr. S.'s anxiety about the future and facilitate his request by arranging his discharge to his mother, or she could use the current medical crisis to break through Mr. S.'s defenses and motivate him to seek treatment for his alcohol dependence.[8] Mr. S. needed confrontation through education regarding the effect of his drinking on his physical and psychological functioning and behavior. He needed help to realize that his decreased drinking might be more of a sign of decreased tolerance than of his ability to control his drinking. Given the deadly prognosis of continued drinking for a person with cirrhosis, going along with Mr. S.'s request would mean going along with his destruction.

THE FAMILY

Social workers have long played a primary role in working with family members of alcohol and drug abusers. As indicated previously, research by Margaret Cork[6] and Margaret Bailey[1] and others provided some of the earliest understanding of the impact of alcoholism on family system. More recent work by social workers such as Claudia Black led to the growing movement focusing on young and adult children of alcoholics and the recognition of the need for specialized treatment of their own.[2]

Because each member in an addicted person's family often develops his or her own maladaptive defense system to survive, all family members must be considered, and when appropriate, included in treatment efforts.[29] Social workers must be able to recognize that the problems many nonsubstance-abusing patients present in treatment, e.g., difficulty with intimacy, poor impulse control, anxiety, chronic health disorders, or depression may result from childhood experiences with an alcohol- or drug-abusing parent, or may be due to living with an alcohol- or drug-abusing mate. The impact of drug-related AIDS on family members must also be understood and addressed.[19,20,26,27,29,30,31]

Alcohol and drug abusers rarely exist in isolation. In order to continue, an abuser usually becomes surrounded by a support system such as family members, friends, and co-workers. The people in the support system frequently take on the functions that the abuser becomes less consistently able to perform as the addiction progresses. However, this assistance has the paradoxical effect of allowing the abuser to regressively use alcohol or other drugs without suffering the debilitating consequences. This "enabling"[13,17] allows the abuser to experience secondary gains from the attention given by those in the support system; it also aids "the denial syndrome"[9] while causing the helpers to lose track of their individual needs as a merging of ego boundaries occurs.[8] For example,

Mrs. B. came to a family service agency concerned about her crying spells at work, her overwhelming sense of helplessness, and her frequent loss of temper with her three elementary school-aged children. Although she liked her job as a secretary in a small law firm, she was afraid that her bosses were getting frustrated with her crying and her frequent calls to her husband to make sure that he got to work on time and was going to pick up the children from their after-school programs. Lately he had become more forgetful and less reliable. He had missed many days of work, and she had to accept more overtime to make up for the financial loss.

She found her husband asleep with beer bottles all around him, leaving their children unsupervised, whenever she came home late from work. He claimed to be stressed at work and was always exhausted. She has tried to do more in the house to relieve some of the pressures on him, but has found it difficult to juggle all of her responsibilities. In response to the worker's questions, Mrs. B. stated that her husband always liked to listen to music and smoke pot and drink beer whenever he was home. Lately, however, she had found many more beer bottles around the house. She also noticed that he'd been taking sleeping pills whenever he woke up during the evening. What prompted her to call for an appointment at the clinic was a recent argument that she and her husband got into after she threw out some of his marijuana and beer bottles. For the first time, he hit her. Although she wasn't physically hurt, his behavior both scared her and made her feel guilty for provoking him. She also was worried that the children were being affected by the fighting, particularly her seven-year-old son, who started bed-wetting again.

In this case, it is clear that Mrs. B. exhibits behaviors typically assumed by family members of substance abusers. She is attempting to control her husband's consumption of substances by confiscating his supply and by trying to minimize stress on him. However, her behavior only leads to greater stress on her without eliminating the problem. Mrs. B. needs to be educated about the problems and consequences of substance abuse. She needs to understand that Mr. B. has lost control over his ability to stop using and that her efforts to control the situation are futile. The abuser has to assume responsibility for his own use and the negative consequences that may result. Mrs. B. needs to be supported for the efforts she has made to deal with the situation and her distress, while being given assistance in identifying her own needs

and seeking ways to deal with them. Al-Anon can be of great value in this process.

Interventions

It is also useful for social workers to have knowledge of the process called "intervention," which was developed by Vernon Johnson in the early 1970s. Because of the prevalence of denial in substance abusers, it is necessary for the effect of his or her behavior to be presented to the abuser by others in a caring, nonjudgmental way.[4] Johnson called this "presenting reality to a person out of touch with it in a receivable way."[15] Such presentation involves specific data about the impact of alcohol and other drug abuse on others and the elucidation of the actions that the others plan to take depending on the abuser's decision regarding obtaining treatment. These actions are not meant to punish but to protect the others from further harm as a result of the abuse.[16] Since conducting an intervention is a process involving specialized training, social workers can refer patients to agencies or individuals specializing in this process. They can also utilize aspects of the intervention concept in their work with family members. Therefore, the social worker treating Mrs. B. could coach her to present her concern about her husband's substance use in a clear, specific, and nonjudgmental way, and ask him to come to treatment with her or to seek some other treatment or 12-step group for himself.

Working with Children

As indicated earlier, substance abuse impacts not only adults but children of substance-abusing parents. Children often feel responsible for what happens in the family but are seldom offered any explanations of what happens to their parents or to them. Social workers need to be familiar with some of the core dynamics common to the many children of substance abusers, such as the difficulties in identifying and expressing feelings directly; and social workers should be willing to broach the subject of parental substance abuse to bring it out into the open. Because of the high correlation between child neglect, physical and sexual abuse of children and parental substance abuse, attention to this area by child welfare workers is particularly crucial.[28] The following case exemplifies some of the issues of working with children of substance abusers in a foster care setting:

Charon, a 9-year-old girl, and her 7-year-old brother Tyrone were placed in foster care after their mother was reported by school authorities for child neglect and was found to be unable to care for them because of her own increasing use of crack cocaine. Their father, who was HIV positive, was imprisoned for drug dealing. The foster care worker met with the children and foster parents to discuss the children's adjustment to their new life. While Charon appeared severely depressed, her brother was full of anger. He did not like his new school or his new "parents." He could not understand why he couldn't go home to his mother and talked about running away to find her in the old neighborhood. While the children knew that the parents used drugs, as did many people who use to come to their house, the worker assessed that they did not have a clear understanding of the nature of drugs: No one ever explained to them the power the drugs held over their parents. The worker arranged for the children to join a group for children of substance abusers at the agency; there the children received simple explanations of the nature of addictions and participated in weekly discussions of what happens to drug users, e.g., disease such as AIDS and their families. By playing various board and activity games that encouraged the labeling and sharing of feelings, the children began to realize that neither they nor their parents were "bad" but that the power of drugs made it difficult to resist them. Based on the comments made by children in various foster homes, the social worker recommended that specific substance abuse information be made available to all foster care families.

Conclusion

The abuse of alcohol and other drugs has a tremendous impact on many social work patients and their family members. While not all social workers can, or even should, become experts in this area, it is important that all social workers develop some level of competency in recognizing substance-abusing individuals, be comfortable addressing this topic with patients and their families, and make proper referrals as needed.

REFERENCES

1. Bailey MB. *Alcoholism and Family Casework: Theory and Practice.* New York: New York City Affiliate, Inc National Council on Alcoholism, 1968. 162 pp. (119 refs.)
2. Black C. *It Will Never Happen to Me.* New York: Ballantine, 1981. 178 pp. (0 refs.)
3. Brecher EM; Consumers Union of the United States. *Licit & Illicit Drugs: The Consumers Union Report on Narcotics, Stimulants, Depressants, Inhalants, Hallucinogens, and Marijuana.* Boston: Little, Brown & Co., 1972. 623 pp.
4. Casolaro V; Smith RJ. The process of intervention: Getting alcoholics and drug abusers to treatment. IN: Straussner SLA, ed. *Clinical Work with Substance-Abusing Clients.* New York: The Guilford Press, 1993. pp. 105-118. (12 refs.)
5. Cook D; Straussner SLA; Fewell CH, eds. *Psychosocial Issues in the Treatment of Alcoholism.* New York: Haworth Press, 1985. 134 pp. (Chapter refs.)
6. Cork M. *The Forgotten Children.* Toronto: Addiction Research Foundation, 1969.
7. Drug Strategies. *Keeping Score: What We Are Getting for Our Federal Drug Control Dollars?* Washington DC: Drug Strategies, 1995. 36 pp. (29 refs.)
8. Fewell C. The social work role in an inpatient alcoholism treatment team. *Social Work in Health Care* 1: 155-166, 1975-1976.
9. Fewell CH; Bissell L. The alcohol denial syndrome: An alcohol-focused approach. *Social Casework* 59(1): 6-13, 1978.
10. Golan N. *Treatment in Crisis Situations.* New York: The Free Press, 1978.
11. Gray M. Relapse prevention. IN: Straussner SLA, ed. *Clinical Social Work with Substance-Abusing Clients.* New York: The Guilford Press, 1993. pp. 351-368. (29 refs.)
12. Griffin RE. Assessing the drug-involved client. *Families in Society* 72(2): 87-94, 1991. (10 refs.)
13. Jackson JK. The adjustment of the family to the crisis of alcoholism. *Quarterly Journal of Studies on Alcohol* 15(4): 562-586, 1954. (9 refs.)
14. Jellinek EM. Phases of alcohol addiction. *Quarterly Journal of Studies on Alcohol* 13: 673-684, 1952. (36 refs.)
15. Johnson V. *I'll Quit Tomorrow, Revised Edition.* New York: Harper & Row Publishers, Inc, 1980. 183 pp. (11 refs.)
16. King BL. Decision making in the intervention process. *Alcoholism Treatment Quarterly* 3(3): 5-22, 1986. (16 refs.)
17. Levinson V; Straussner SLA. Social workers as 'enablers' in the treatment of alcoholics. *Social Casework* 59(1): 14-20, 1978.
18. Lewis DC. Addiction. IN: Turner J, ed. *Encyclopedia of Social Work, 17th Edition.* Washington DC: National Association of Social Work, 1977.
19. Markowitz R. Dynamics and treatment issues with children of drug and alcohol abusers. IN: Straussner SLA, ed. *Clinical Social Work with Substance-Abusing Clients.* New York: The Guilford Press, 1993. pp. 214-229. (17 refs.)
20. McIntyre J. Family treatment of substance abuse. IN: Straussner SLA, ed. *Clinical Social Work with Substance-Abusing Clients.* New York: The Guilford Press, 1993. pp. 171-195. (53 refs.)
21. National Association of Social Workers. *Member Records Statistical Report.* Washington DC: NASW, 1995.
22. Parad H; Parad LG. *Crisis Intervention, Book 2.* Milwaukee: Family Service of America, 1990.
23. Petty ML. Social work: The profession of choice in the treatment of alcoholism. *Smith College School of Social Work Journal* Fall: 10-14, 1975.
24. Price GM. Social casework in alcoholism. *Quarterly Journal of Studies on Alcohol* 19: 155-163, 1958.
25. Richmond ME. *Social Diagnosis.* New York: The Free Press, 1917.
26. Straussner SLA. Intervention with maltreating parents who are drug and alcohol abusers. IN: Ehrenkranz SM; Goldstein EG; Goodman L; Seinfeld J, eds. *Clinical Social Work with Maltreated Children and Their Families: An Introduction to Practice.* New York: New York University Press, 1989. pp. 149-177. (35 refs.)
27. Straussner SLA. Assessment and treatment of clients with alcohol and other drug abuse problems: An overview. IN: Straussner SLA, ed. *Clinical Social Work with Substance-Abusing Clients.* New York: The Guilford Press, 1993. pp. 3-30. (78 refs.)
28. Straussner SLA. The impact of alcohol and other drug abuse on the American family. *Drug and Alcohol Review* 13(4): 393-399, 1994.
29. Straussner SLA; Weinstein D; Hernandez R. Effect of alcoholism on the family system. *Health and Social Work* 4(4): 111-127, 1979. (45 refs.)
30. Strom DP. AIDS and intravenous drug users: Issues and treatment implications. IN: Straussner SLA, ed. *Clinical Social Work with Substance-Abusing Clients.* New York: The Guilford Press, 1993. pp. 330-350. (22 refs.)
31. Zelvin E. Treating the partners of substance abusers. IN: Straussner SLA, ed. *Clinical Social Work with Substance-Abusing Clients.* New York: The Guilford Press, 1993. pp. 196-213. (18 refs.)

FURTHER READINGS

The following books and articles have been written by the New York City Chapter, NASW Alcoholism Committee:

Cook D; Fewell CH; Riolo J, eds. *Social Work Treatment of Alcohol Problems.* New Brunswick NJ: Rutgers Center of Alcohol Studies, 1983.

Cook D; King B; Straussner SLA; Fewell CH, eds. *Health & Social Work* 4(4): entire issue, 1979.

Cook D; Straussner SLA; Fewell CH, eds. *Psychosocial Issues in the Treatment of Alcoholism.* New York: Haworth Press, 1985.

Fewell CH; King B; Weinstein D. Alcohol and other drug abuse among social workers and their families: Impact on practice. *Social Work* 38(5): 565-570, 1993. (24 refs.)

Fewell CF; Straussner SLA; Davidsen N; Dortz C; Schimmel I. *Alcohol, Tobacco and Other Substance Abuse: Social Work Policy Statement.* New York: New York City Chapter, NASW Alcoholism Committee, 1995.

Fewell CF; Straussner SLA; Dortz C. *Helping Social Workers Who Have Alcohol and Other Drug Problems: Intervening with Colleagues.* New York: New York City Chapter, NASW Alcoholism Committee, 1994.

Fewell C; Straussner SLA; Evans C; King B; Orlin A; Perone F. *Alcoholism among Social Workers: Approaching a Colleague with a Drinking Problem.* New York: New York City Chapter, NASW Alcoholism Committee. (undated.)

New York City Chapter, NASW Alcoholism Committee. *Social Casework* 59(1): entire issue, 1979-80.

Straussner SLA; Fewell CH; Cook D, eds. *Alcoholism Treatment Quarterly* 3(3): entire issue, 1986.

Straussner SLA; Panepinto W. *Alcoholism Treatment Quarterly* 5(3): entire issue, 1988.

Weinstein D; Goldberg M; Kuver J; Nadel M. Case studies. *Social Casework* September, October, November, 1988.

Other Readings

NOTE: Also see Chapter 9, Resources for Educators and Trainers.

Alaszewski A; Harrison L. Alcohol and social work: A literature review. *British Journal of Social Work* 22(3): 331-343, 1992. (44 refs.)

In the first section of this literature review, the authors examine the social and health problems associated with alcohol misuse and the ways in which social workers and other primary care workers respond to these problems. In the second section, the authors examine the nature of professional training and consider the ways in which it does and does not provide social workers and other primary care workers with the knowledge and skills to identify and help people with drinking problems. In the final section, the authors examine the ways in which training can be developed to enable social workers to respond more effectively to alcohol-related problems. Copyright 1992, British Association of Social Workers.

Barber JG. *Social Work with Addictions.* New York: New York University Press, 1994. (450 refs.)

This volume, first published in Great Britain, is directed to generalist social workers likely to encounter substance abuse within the context of their work. The first chapter reviews the concept of addiction and summarizes the characteristics of different drug classes. The second chapter provides a social work practice model, drawing heavily upon the transtheoretical model of stages of change articulated by Prochaska and DiClemente and which in the US is associated with the work of Marlatt, Gordon, and Miller. The third through sixth chapters center on each of the stages of change, i.e., precontemplation, determination, action strategies, and maintenance. The final chapter deals with a variety of issues in respect to evaluation, ranging from an overview of the treatment outcome literature to issues related to social policy. The work includes a number of excellent tables and figures summarizing the material. Copyright 1995, Project Cork Institute.

Barnea Z; Teichman M. Substance misuse and abuse among the elderly: Implications for social work intervention. (review). *Journal of Gerontological Social Work* 21(3/4): 133-148, 1994. (65 refs.)

This article reviews the literature on the misuse and abuse of psychoactive substances in the elderly. Three main patterns of abuse characteristic of this age group are identified and analyzed: Abuse of medications, alcohol, and illegal drugs. The article refers to issues such as the extent (prevalence and incidence) of the problem among the elderly, the predictors and correlates of abuse, and special dangers and effects of abuse on the elderly and their environment. The key roles that social workers should play in prevention and treatment are discussed. Copyright 1994, The Haworth Press, Inc.

Foster Z; Hirsch S; Zaske K. Social work role in developing and managing employee assistance programs in health care settings. *Social Work in Health Care* 16(2): 81-96, 1991. (17 refs.)

The hospital setting presents special needs for an Employee Assistance Program and special complications for sponsorship, development, and maintenance. What has been learned, how certain problems can be solved or avoided, and how responsibility and accountability can be negotiated are presented by a team that has successfully established such a program at a large metropolitan medical center. In addition to successes, some unsolved problems are identified for further study. Copyright 1991, The Haworth Press, Inc.

Freeman EM, ed. *Social Work Practices with Clients Who Have Alcohol Problems.* Springfield IL: Charles C. Thomas, 1985.

This is another early volume directed to social work practice with patients with alcohol problems.

Kinney J; Kurzman P. *Bibliography and Resource Guide on Alcohol and Other Drugs for Social Work Educators.* Rockville MD: OSAP, 1989. (248 refs.)

This annotated bibliography, is organized in four sections. The first section is devoted to alcohol- and substance-abuse literature from the social work professional journals. The second section is literature from the alcohol- and substance-abuse fields. The third and fourth sections are diverse resource materials. Four major content areas are covered: diagnosis and treatment, prevention, special populations, and the family. Copyright 1991, Project Cork Institute.

Malekoff A. Action research: An approach to preventing substance abuse and promoting social competency. *Health and Social Work* 19(1): 46-53, 1994. (34 refs.)

This article demonstrates the use of action research, an approach combining various social work methods to raise community consciousness, stimulate intergroup and intergenerational interaction, and motivate people to work toward change both individually and collectively. The project described represents an effort to mobilize youths and adults living in a rapidly changing, culturally pluralistic, low-income suburban community to confront the impact of drug and alcohol abuse in a context of mutual respect and support. The central theme of investigation was local youths' perceptions about drug and alcohol abuse in the context of their own lives. A group of youths, in partnership with professionals, surveyed their contemporaries with a questionnaire of their own creation. The community meeting that followed was designed to stimulate the youths through reflection, dialogue, and a plan for action. Copyright 1994, National Association of Social Workers, Inc.

Schinke SP; Bebel MY; Orlandi MA; Botvin GJ. Prevention strategies for vulnerable pupils: School social work practices to prevent substance abuse. *Urban Education* 22(4): 510-519, 1988. (13 refs.)

This article describes approaches that school social workers can use to successfully intervene with pupils at risk. It draws upon original research and data on the two recalcitrant substance abuse problems for most American schools: tobacco use and drug use. Copyright 1989, Project Cork Institute.

CHAPTER 8

Educating Yourself and Others

JEAN KINNEY, MSW

CLINICAL APPLICATIONS

The goals of this chapter are to assist the clinician to:

1. Complete a self-assessment of personal education needs.
2. Develop skills as a teacher and trainer.

The primary care provider and the community health worker have a variety of tasks beyond direct patient care. These other activities, sometimes described as indirect services, may include being involved in community education efforts, participating in professional development programs for human service workers, providing clinical consultation, and offering consultation to community groups. These activities are critical to direct patient care. Given the magnitude of alcohol and substance use problems in many communities, addressing these problems one patient at a time makes it difficult to be optimistic about the future. Ironically, it is those individuals *most* burdened by clinical responsibilities that need to become involved in nonclinical services. Through education of other professionals, the cadre of those available to care for alcohol and substance abuse problems is enlarged. Through consultation, skills are imparted that can promote earlier detection before a long-term, chronic problem is established—a problem that causes greater damage to the patient, family, and community and further burdens the health care system. Offering consultation to other health care providers prompts earlier treatment, when the prognosis is most promising. Through collaborative efforts with the community's "gatekeepers"—teachers, childcare workers, and clergy—the pool of resources to address substance use problems is extended. These individuals, if knowledgeable, encourage people to seek assistance and support those who have received treatment. These individuals are the center of an informed and caring community. Such community involvement is becoming more common for those with a commitment to primary care.

EDUCATION

The list of those who might benefit from educational efforts is virtually limitless. The old adage, "You can't give what you haven't got," suggests that the first priority is investing in one's own professional development. Start by becoming informed, polishing clinical skills, and becoming comfortable talking with patients and families affected by substance use. Perusing the professional literature or attending conferences and workshops is one way to begin.

Appreciate that enhancing clinical skills via self-study is a nontraditional approach in clinical education and training. Clinical training—whether nursing student clinical rotations, medical school clerkships, postgraduate training, time "on the floor," or social workers' field placements—is predicated on *practice* to build clinical proficiency. Ideally, training offers multiple opportunities to try out clinical tasks in a setting with good role models, with access to mentors and clinical supervisors, and where these activities are

valued. Unfortunately, this situation is not the norm for many practicing clinicians because the commodity of time and easy access to clinical experts is more limited. The practice setting is not designed for training its own staff. Therefore, one needs to work harder at organizing this, but it can be done. As a first step, review your clinical experience and identify the things that may come easily to you. Although time is always scarce, there are experts available such as colleagues and substance abuse specialists in the agency or community.

Spend Some Time Observing in a Substance Abuse Treatment Program

The opportunity to observe professionals working with substance use patients will be instructive whether it is 1 day or several days. Take an active role in negotiating observation time. Let the staff organizing the visit know what clinical tasks confront you. Select activities that most parallel the situations you encounter. If the challenge is broaching the topic of substance abuse, observe staff dealing with patients at the point of entry, e.g., staff providing consultations or conducting intake evaluations. If medical management is an issue, spend time with nursing personnel and the physician staff.

Identify a Substance Abuse Professional as a Mentor

As you use new skills, access to clinical expertise is indispensable. This can be accomplished by having a substance abuse professional join you once or twice when seeing a substance abuse patient. It may also be helpful to discuss a case ahead of time, review the possible strategies, and "walk through it." Afterward, process the encounter. How did it go? What were the difficult parts? What had not been anticipated?

Arrange for an Initial Period of Supervision

Within a few months, you will have probably experienced at least once the usual presentations and common clinical dilemmas. During this period, having someone to review clinical approaches will be helpful. After that time, consultations with supervisors on an "as needed" basis will suffice.

Staff Development and Inservice Programs

Regularly scheduled inservice or staff development programs are another method of continuing the education of you and your colleagues in your practice or agency. Being the only individual with an interest in a specialty area can be lonely. Suggest alcohol and substance abuse topics as subjects for an ongoing staff development program series or for case conferences, or take whatever occasions you have as a staff to collectively review your clinical efforts. Unless you use peer education, do not try to be the presenter at an educational program in your own agency. Regardless of your skills, almost inevitably, those from outside are more likely to be better received and more effective.

In organizing staff development programs, consider the audience. What topics interest colleagues? Regardless of whether others are aware of them, what areas do you think require attention? Do not invite persons to give presentations and leave it up to them to define the content and points of emphasis? Brief them and be specific about the points you would like addressed. The invited presenter is at your disposal; use his or her expertise to the fullest. In selecting a presenter, consider credentials and professional experience. Will the individual be perceived as an expert by the audience? Is the presenter well-informed about your practice setting so that the clinical suggestions will be appropriate and applicable?

Other Approaches

Emphasis on acquiring clinical competency is not meant to disregard other methods of professional development. Attending conferences or participating in workshops can be helpful, especially when the focus is on building clinical skills. Another possibility is to attend inservice programs conducted at alcohol/substance abuse agencies. Appendix D offers other suggestions, outlining activities that can be used individually or in small groups to polish clinical skills and consolidate them into clinical practice; skills covered in workshops and training sessions; or topics covered by readings. These suggestions employ a variety of formats. Some are paper and pencil exercises, while others are directed to introducing these approaches into patient encounters. Still others are clinical simulations to approximate the commonly encountered clinical situations.

THE HEALTH PROFESSIONAL AS EDUCATOR
Community Gatekeepers

The education of other human service workers can have many benefits. One of the most effective means of educating community gatekeepers is to provide exactly what has been suggested that you arrange for yourself. Make yourself available as a role model and extend an offer for consultation and case supervision. One of the most effective teaching methods and memorable events for a student is when an experienced clinician is readily available to assist in handling a difficult case. Anyone who has provided assistance with a problem case usually gets attention. When others have found your intervention helpful on one occasion, that increases the probability that they will seek and accept further interactions and collaboration.

In working with other professionals, do not expect or suggest that they ought to become substance abuse experts, although they deal with substance abuse problems daily. In extending assistance, recognize that the value for others in becoming more skilled with substance use is to improve their own job performance. The goal is not to search out substance abuse for its own sake. A teacher gains insight into substance issues to recognize the problems of the child in the classroom who is drained by coping with parental substance abuse and has no energy left for school work. This distinction is relevant in terms of how others identify problems and what motivates them to act.

Another route to educating helping professionals is volunteering to give a presentation. Numerous groups regularly have programs and are always looking for speakers. In your encounters with other professionals, it is important to be supportive. Be sensitive to the possibility that your own enthusiasm may come across as judgmental and as censuring others.

Frequently, the most useful information for other professionals is your knowledge about using the substance abuse service system. There is nothing more frustrating for human service personnel than to recognize a problem that needs attention, to know what needs to be done, but to be unable to effect a disposition. There is little incentive to identify a problem for which care does not seem to exist. Let others know what agencies are available to care for whom, the admission hours, and the name and telephone number of the intake worker. Identify inclusion and exclusion criteria for admissions, costs, and any other points that can facilitate disposition.

Lay Groups

Alcohol and drug problems are the major topics that currently concern citizens groups, parents, and community officials. You only have to make your availability known to acquire a long list of speaking invitations. Such activities provide good press for the medical practice or agency. Ask the person extending the invitation to suggest a topic of interest to the audience and to share his or her perceptions of the people's concerns.

Public Officials

One contribution that health care professionals can make is in functioning as "quasi" public health officers. Public officials in many communities are struggling with how they should respond to alcohol and drug problems. The felt pressure to "do something" is both internally and externally generated. For example, the criminal justice system, including police departments, probation officers, and the courts, sees the social consequences of alcohol and drug use every day—from street crime to parties of unsupervised adolescents, to sales of drugs, to possession of alcohol by minors, and to domestic violence. Similarly, the schools are concerned about the effects of students' substance use, both feeling the need and also being asked or expected to develop specialized programs. Those in different areas of public life are overwhelmed by the magnitude of problems and frustrated by the limited options available to address them. Many are interested in the formation of alternative approaches such as diversion programs for adolescents.

A not uncommon problem may be the presence of vocal citizens or community group(s) whose knowledge does not equal their level of interest. Sound public health programs do not come from forging a consensus between special interest groups. Thus, it is important that public officials have access to those who can speak from information rather than from biases and myths, who are concerned but not driven by emotions or allied with special concerns, and who command the community's respect. Their need may be for informal consultation, authoritative information, or recommendations on where information can be solicited. There may also be the need for a spokesperson willing to lend his or her professional stature to a public presentation.

TIPS FOR ORGANIZING PRESENTATIONS
Do's

In any educational endeavor, plan ahead. An effective presentation takes preparation, even if you already have developed a number of basic program offerings. Find out from those organizing the program what they have in mind for a topic. You may wish to suggest an alternative. Ask who will be in the audience, the anticipated size, how long you are expected to speak, and if there are others on the program. In choosing a topic, consider what would be of interest and ask yourself the questions mostly likely to be on the audience's mind.

Pick a subject in which you are more expert than your audience. A social worker attempting to lecture to a group of physicians about medical complications is asking for trouble. On the other hand, that therapist's presentation to physicians and nurses on practical interviewing tips might be well received.

Develop several basic talks. For any presentation, plan how you will use your allotted time. Always leave time for questions. Save some of your best information for a question-and-answer period. If these anticipated questions are not asked, you can always conclude with "one final thought . . ."

Films or videotapes can be useful in organizing a presentation. Select one appropriate to the audience, paying attention to technical quality and accuracy of information. Audio-visual materials can be an excellent vehicle for stimulating discussions. Three questions to encourage audience involvement include the following: "What kind of response did you have?" "What new information did you learn?" and "What surprised you?"

Consider audience handouts, including a summary of your talk, a list of local agencies, or general patient education literature. These are available from professional societies, community agencies, and state alcohol and drug offices. Appendix A of this manual provides a listing of different groups, many of which are sources of public information.

Don'ts

Do not be overly ambitious and try to cover everything you think someone ought to know about alcohol or other substance use. If your audience goes away understanding three or four major points, you can consider yourself successful.

Avoid crusading or telling horror stories. These approaches may interest some audiences; however, most audiences will not identify with what you are saying. The presentation will be unconnected to their experiences, and you are likely to leave them with a "not me" response. Clinical vignettes are generally inappropriate with lay audiences. With professional audiences, if case material is used, care must be taken to obscure identifying information. Avoid using jargon. Instead, look for everyday words to convey your meaning. Use examples that are relevant to the audience.

A report by members of the Harvard School of Public Health reviewed preventive efforts in the substance abuse field. It noted that scare tactics or exaggeration to emphasize the message are counterproductive. Unless information that stresses negative consequences is accompanied by clear, concrete steps outlining what can be done to reduce risk, the information will be ignored.[1] There has been a history of exaggeration in the alcohol and drug abuse field to gain people's attention. If an audience suspects this ploy, it will often discount the entire message. Furthermore, the negative consequences of alcohol and other substance use are sufficiently alarming without requiring any embellishment to generate concern. As community educators, health care professionals are in a good position to reinforce this approach in the community.

Suggested Points for Emphasis

Alcohol and substance use issues can be confusing to both professional and lay audiences. The confusion often lies, not in the absence of information, but in the absence of frameworks to assimilate the facts. Stress to lay audiences that alcohol and substance use is a health concern for reasons beyond dependence. The notion of addiction has become well understood and even popularized. For example, "choc-o-holics" or "work-a-holics" have been popularized terms. That substance use may be an acute problem because of pharmacological properties is often new information. As a culture, we have come to accept psychological explanations for many problems. Thus, it is natural to apply this to dependency. Unfortunately, the evidence suggests otherwise. The research on the role of heredity in some types of alcoholism is similarly new information.

In discussions with professional audiences, possibly the most useful approach is to use medical examples and draw on comparisons with chronic illnesses. Also, avoid terminology distinctive to the chemical dependency field that is either foreign and therefore unclear or too moralistic.[2] Consider avoiding the words "alcoholic" or "addict" as nouns, as they can easily reduce individuals to a disease entity. While not unusual in medical circles, e.g., "the diabetic," or less-accepted but still frequently heard, "the liver in room 316," there are no other conditions in which the disease state has become so universally synonymous with the patient. Furthermore, using "addict" or "alcoholic," both of which have many negative connotations, may incline the audience to distinguish themselves from "those kind of people." One factor that impedes early recognition of substance use problems is the tendency for many individuals to consider themselves immune. This is especially true if they can see no parallels between themselves and stereotypic substance abusers.

Expecting the Unexpected

Several challenges face a public speaker on alcohol and substance use topics. It is a subject about which few people in any audience will feel neutral; do not be surprised by some fervent comments. Although many people are poorly informed on the subject, they nonetheless consider themselves experts. How many people would go to a lecture on nuclear physics and feel comfortable telling the audience or the speaker "how it really is"? With alcohol and substance use, it happens all the time.

Be prepared to avoid letting someone else take over the floor. If needed, interrupt politely and firmly with a neutral comment, e.g., "That is an interesting point of view; maybe we can see if there are any other comments". You may feel the need to refute what is said, in which case an effective technique is first to agree and then to say, "Yes, many people would agree with you; however, we now understand differently." Avoid a debate. Another common situation is recovering individuals who use the opportunity to share their personal experiences, essentially taking over your job for you. A public presentation is often not the appropriate forum for these personal stories. Make a com-

ment about the prevalence of alcohol/substance use problems, pointing out the probability that many in the audience will be personally touched; this will put the emphasis back on the audience; then proceed.

Predictably, some of the audience will be troubled by a substance use problem of someone close to them, although they may not share this concern in an open forum. Therefore, answer the unasked questions. Always be sure to let people know where they can go if they are concerned about someone, providing agency names, addresses, and telephone numbers. Having such information available in a handout may be useful. Local, state, or community treatment programs can often provide copies for duplication.

PROGRAM PLANNING

Program development and planning is another area in which health care professionals may become involved. If there is any secret to planning new programs, it is to think in a systematic, disciplined fashion. Beware of the enthusiastic statement, "What we really ought to do is. . . ." Too often this involves proposing a solution to a problem not adequately defined.

When it comes to addressing a community problem, the following steps can be useful:

- Define the problem.
- Identify the information needed to consider possible solutions.
- Identify the resources available to address the problem. These include people, money, information, and influence on others.
- Develop a list of possible solutions.
- Select a plan based on the resources available and the cost benefits of different options.
- Design a strategy to implement the plan. Do not forget to incorporate who is to do what. Assign clear responsibility for coordination, different elements, and set a timetable.

There are numerous potential resources to use in any program development effort. The State Office of Alcohol and Drug Abuse may be a good place to start. State programs can assist community groups, provide materials, and be familiar with similar statewide efforts. Speaking with others who have previously tackled the problem is often a wise move. The time spent telephoning persons who have tried various approaches is a good investment. Similarly, a visit to a program may be worth the effort.

THE IMPACT ON THE MEDICAL PRACTICE

If staff of a health care center or clinic are known to be interested and informed about alcohol and substance abuse issues, they should anticipate new patients, even in this era of managed care. These new patients are not seeking assistance for their own alcohol or drug use problem. (The absence of an interested primary care provider is not what has been keeping troubled individuals from seeking treatment.) Rather, these will be persons in recovery who are seeking someone informed about a condition they view as serious.

The number of individuals in any community who are in recovery from substance use problems is significantly larger than might be anticipated. An example is a rural setting in northern New England. The largest town in the region has a population of under 10,000; most communities have only several thousand residents. Nonetheless, on any day of the week, and within 15 miles, there are at least four meetings of substance abuse self-help groups. Look at a meeting list for your own area to determine the number of AA, NA, or CA meetings each week.

Many recovering individuals perceive that their health care providers are uninformed about and disinterested in substance abuse issues. Every recovering individual has heard stories of individuals whose problems went long undiagnosed, were exacerbated, or were caused by nonjudicious prescription practices, or whose recoveries were jeopardized by the prescription of psychotropic drugs following treatment. These stories may lead recovering patients to distrust health care providers. Even when a particular patient's own personal experience does not support this perception, this may still be the case. During early recovery, this suspicion may be inadvertently confirmed if there is occasion to see their primary care provider. In early recovery, patients' lives remain as centered around substance use as before. (The focus, however, has become not using.) With this preoccupation, patients sometimes expect that everyone else should acknowledge their situation, including medical personnel. If nurses or physicians do not inquire about these patients' recovery or provide opportunity to discuss it, the patient can feel short-changed or misunderstood.

In your own practice, do not be surprised if recovering patients question the management of any problem and are especially interested in any medications prescribed. There may be a degree of antagonism or mistrust that seems to be out of place. Address this openly. Inquire about their recent treatment and efforts at abstinence, and whether they have any special concerns to which you should attend.

FUNCTIONING AS A TEAM IN A PRIMARY CARE SETTING

Substance abuse treatment is rarely provided by a single practitioner. Anyone who plans to treat substance use problems individually is making a decision to have a small clinical practice. In early treatment, the intensity of services required and the different services—patient education; support; group, family, and individual counseling; and the introduction to self-help programs—are beyond the capacity of a single person. Besides being time consuming, it is less therapeutic for the patient. The patient needs to become reconnected with people.

A team effort is equally critical for the patient not yet in formal treatment. When presented with a patient with a possible substance abuse problem, it is important to know someone who can advise you. Is there an individual within the health care center who has special expertise and responsibilities for substance use? If so, does this person function as the case manager or primary clinician in terms of the substance use problem?

Everyone working with an alcohol or substance abuse patient and the associated family members needs to agree and have the same agenda. This does not necessarily require extra time on anyone's part in providing clinical care; it is how the time is used. It means taking the time to explain how medical problems are related to substance use, and to discuss concerns with the family. In a hospital setting, the need to coordinate planning may be more apparent, such as in dealing with three nursing shifts. The same is required in primary care settings. Coordination, consistency, and clarity are essential. If everyone is talking with the patient about concerns about substance use, the nurse practitioner or physician needs to be involved, too, instead of discussing laboratory values or diagnostic tests and expecting someone else to handle the substance use as the central problem. Whoever is perceived by the patient as having overall charge of care needs to voice concern and support the other clinicians.

One obstacle to such an approach is that patient records are organized through medical encounters. To follow a theme across visits, over time, and with different clinicians is difficult.

Conclusion

Much of what has been discussed may seem ideal but difficult to implement. Few primary care providers need to be convinced of the benefits of a preventive approach to health care delivery, the value of patient education, or the need for systematic health promotion efforts. The unfortunate fact is that such activities are not reimbursed by third party insurance coverage. The schedule for payments of health care services favors procedures rather than speaking with patients. This reality has to be acknowledged. One solution at present is to use such services offered by community groups and those in the public health care system such as community health nurses or those providing prenatal care or serving families with young children. The other is to integrate health maintenance efforts into the clinical contacts with which you are presented. Finally, while lobbying to change reimbursement practices could become a full-time effort, health care providers in a community do have the opportunity to influence activities at that level. Take this role and opportunity seriously. Those for whom you would speak cannot be heard.

REFERENCES

1. DeJong W; Winsten JA. *Recommendations for Future Mass-media Campaigns to Prevent Preteen and Adolescent Substance Abuse.* Cambridge MA: Center for Health Communication, Harvard School of Public Health, 1989. (77 refs.)
2. Kinney J; Price TRP; Bergen B. Impediments to alcohol education. *Journal of Studies on Alcohol* 45(5): 453-459, 1984. (17 refs.)

FURTHER READINGS

Alaszewski A; Harrison L. Alcohol and social work: A literature review. (review). *British Journal of Social Work* 22(3): 331-343, 1992. (44 refs.)

In the first section of this literature review, the authors examine the social and health problems associated with alcohol misuse and the ways in which social workers and other primary care workers respond to these problems. In the second section, the authors examine the nature of professional training and consider the ways in which it does and does not provide social workers and other primary care workers with the knowledge and skills to identify and help people with drinking problems. In the final section, the authors examine how training can be developed to enable social workers to respond more effectively to alcohol-related problems. Copyright 1992, British Association of Social Workers.

Ashery RS. Issues in AIDS training for substance abuse workers. *Journal of Substance Abuse Treatment* 9(1): 15-19, 1992. (11 refs.)

Workers in drug treatment programs need specialized training concerning AIDS to meet the demands of their expanding roles. Initially, the treatment community failed to anticipate training needs fully, but now, comprehensive and systematic AIDS training programs must be developed. This article discusses the five steps in developing and implementing such programs: (a) assessment and information gathering, (b) curriculum development, (c) training of instructors, (d) training delivery, and (e) evaluation. Copyright 1992, Pergamon Press. Used with permission.

Beebe GC. Efficacy of a substance abuse primary prevention skills conference for nurses. *Journal of Continuing Education in Nursing* 23(5): 231-234, 1992. (16 refs.)

A conference on substance abuse prevention skills was presented by the New York State Nurses Association (NYSNA) to provide nurses with skills to help patients in various practice settings. Information covered assessment, intervention, and tools for interviewing and identifying resources. A 6-month follow-up evaluation showed that the majority of the participants incorporated the skills in their nursing practice primarily in interviewing and in using assessment questions. Directions for future conferences were identified. Copyright 1992, C.B. Slack, Inc.

Center for Substance Abuse Prevention. *Guides for Planning and Developing Your ATOD Prevention Materials. Technical Assistance Bulletins.* Rockville MD: Center for Substance Abuse Prevention, 1994. (Chapter refs.)

This is a compilation of 13 individual technical assistance bulletins designed to assist community groups and organizations in the preparation of prevention and community education materials. These bulletins address topics such as common errors, the need for pretesting, steps in designing materials, and addressing special populations. Copyright 1995, Project Cork Institute.

Center for Substance Abuse Prevention. *Prevention Primer: An Encyclopedia of Alcohol, Tobacco, and Other Drug Prevention Terms.* Rockville MD: Center for Substance Abuse Prevention, 1993. (Chapter refs.)

This publication incorporates principles of a public health approach to preventing alcohol, tobacco, and other drug problems in its discussion of issues and strategies for prevention. It is designed to provide community members the basic information and resources they need to become successful prevention practitioners. Subjects are listed in alphabetical order and include topics such as children of alcoholics, college and university students, employee assistance programs, impaired driving, parents and prevention, risk factors, and violence. Copyright 1994, Project Cork Institute.

Center for Substance Abuse Prevention. *Toward Preventing Perinatal Abuse of Alcohol, Tobacco, and Other Drugs. CSAP Technical Report 9.* Rockville MD: Center for Substance Abuse Prevention, 1993.

This report highlights the many different approaches and responses to the complex issue of perinatal alcohol, tobacco, and other drug abuse (ATOD) prevention. The report contains case studies to illustrate how theoretical frameworks and models are translated into practice and to show the various interventions that underlie a comprehensive prevention approach. The report is divided into five chapters, beginning with an introduction. Chapter 2 discusses key issues in the field that arose during discussions of prevention of perinatal ATOD abuse. Chapter 3 describes the frameworks and models used for defining problems, designing programs, and evaluating outcomes. Chapter 4 summarizes ideas and activities that can be used in various combinations to address the issue of perinatal abuse of alcohol, tobacco, and other drugs. Strategies are presented in tables for easy reference. Chapter 5 provides examples of prevention programs. Public Domain.

Chiert T; Gold SN; Taylor J. Substance abuse training in APA accredited doctoral programs in clinical psychology: A survey. *Professional Psychology: Research and Practice* 25(1): 80-84, 1994. (12 refs.)

A survey addressing substance abuse training was mailed to all 160 doctoral clinical psychology programs provisionally and fully accredited by the American Psychological Association (APA). Ninety-five replies were received, yielding a response rate of 59%. This study was conducted to ascertain whether levels of doctoral training in this area have changed appreciably since comparable surveys in 1979 and 1984. Because of the considerable increase in the number of APA-accredited PsyD programs since the previous two surveys, it was also possible to compare relative levels of training in substance abuse in PhD, PsyD, and combined PhD/PsyD programs. Survey results did not suggest that substance abuse training either has changed markedly over time or differs substantially across types of degree programs. Copyright 1994, American Psychological Association, Inc.

Cooley FB. Teaching family systems to medical students and residents for substance abuse management. *Substance Abuse* (AMERSA) 13(4): 212-218, 1993. (7 refs.)

The notion that knowledge of family systems might be useful to physicians is not universally accepted. Therefore, readiness to teach the subject requires some openness to five beliefs: (1) Practical family systems knowledge can be a helpful clinical tool; (2) this clinical tool is especially effective when patients are abusing substances liquid or solid, prescribed or not, illicit or not, swallowed, injected, snorted, or inhaled; (3) formal didactic lecture techniques are not very effective for teaching substance abuse management; (4) teaching must be done by a physician or colleague who has experience with patients struggling with addiction problems; (5) direct teaching of a family systems perspective may be less effective than other approaches. This article presents several teaching tools to facilitate the teaching of family systems to medical students and residents. Copyright 1993, Association for Medical Education & Research in Substance Abuse.

Davis AK; Parran TV Jr; Graham AV. Educational strategies for clinicians. *Primary Care* 20(1): 241-250, 1993. (25 refs.)

Largely because of a lack of training, many primary care providers are unaware of how they can prevent, detect, or manage substance abuse within their clinical practice. The educational process used to develop a teaching unit can be simplified by initially asking a few directed questions. The answers to these questions determine what needs to be taught while facilitating the subsequent steps of determining learning goals and objectives and selecting appropriate teaching materials and strategies. Evaluating the teaching unit on at least a cursory level provides useful information for planning. A variety of curriculum manuals and clinical text parts can be readily incorporated into teaching units. These same sources can alternatively be adapted to an individual's self-directed course of study. Incorporation of experiential education strategies is especially useful in substance abuse instruction. Including recovering individuals, attending self-help group meetings, or incorporating role play exercises are some experiential strategies for engaging the learner. The education process includes deciding why, what, and how to teach; developing the structure of a teaching unit; selecting educational strategies in substance abuse; selecting curriculum and clinical materials; and using organizational and networking resources. Copyright 1993, Project Cork Institute.

Durfee MF; Warren DG; Sdao-Jarvies K. A model for answering the substance abuse educational needs of health professionals: The North Carolina Governor's Institute on Alcohol and Substance Abuse. *Alcohol* 11(6): 483-487, 1994. (31 refs.)

Physicians can play an increased role in recognizing, intervening, and moderating their patients' misuse of alcohol and other drugs. This article explores the need for educational changes to permit physicians to develop skills in prevention, screening, and office-based treatment. It includes a personal account by one of the authors of recognizing deficiencies in substance abuse education both in his own medical school training and in today's health science curricula in the US. It reviews prior initiatives by the National Institutes on Alcohol Abuse and Alcoholism and on Drug Abuse (NIAAA and NIDA) to address curriculum needs and describes an innovative collaborative model in North Carolina called the Governor's Institute on Alcohol and Substance Abuse. The Governor's Institute was created in 1990 as a nonprofit corporation to promote education, research, and communication among health professionals. Some of the Institute's programs are described, including its curriculum integration project in the state's four medical schools. The article concludes that the time is right to introduce substance abuse concepts into basic and continuing education for all health professionals. Copyright 1994, Pergamon Press.

Gossop M; Birkin R. Training employment service staff to recognize and respond to clients with drug and alcohol problems. *Addictive Behaviors* 19(2): 127-134, 1994. (9 refs.)

This paper investigates the impact of a training course for Employment Service staff that is designed to provide basic level training on the identification and appropriate management of patients with drug and alcohol problems. The 2-day course was specially designed to meet the needs of staff working with unemployed people with substance abuse problems. The primary aims of the course were to help employment staff identify drug and alcohol problems, to access their severity, and where necessary, to refer patients on to more specialized agencies. The training course was attended by 145 people, with a random sample of 60 followed up 6 months later. Results showed substantial improvements in the confidence and ability of staff to deal with patients presenting with drug and alcohol problems. There was also clear improvement in the willingness of staff to intervene with such patients. Copyright 1994, Pergamon Press.

Greenfield TK; Zimmerman R, eds. *Experiences with Community Action Projects: New Research in the Prevention of Alcohol and Other Drug Problems.* CSAP Prevention Monograph 14. Rockville MD: CSAP, 1993. (Chapter refs.)

This monograph is derived from proceedings of the second international research symposium on "Experiences with Community Action Projects for the Prevention of Alcohol and Other Drug Problems." Papers in this monograph follow the format of the conference and are organized under a number of broad headings. First, conceptual issues in evaluating community action are considered. The second section reports experiences with policy adoption case studies: Licensed drinking establishments and anti-drinking-driver campaigns from Canada and Australia; two Canadian studies involving program philosophy and politics in the arenas of drunk driving prevention and tobacco regulation; the intersection of community prevention and national politics based on experiences in Israel and Poland; and strategies for implementing local policy change involving reports based on municipalities in Oxford, England, and California. Community trials design issues are the focus of the third section. Papers in the fourth section involve needs assessments or natural experiences in special settings. These naturalistic studies were related to planning environmentally based approaches. The fifth section addresses broad-based programs and their "fit" with grass-roots initiatives. These are followed by studies of cross-community differences in response to alcohol and other drug problems. The sixth section involves issues related to transferring knowledge (training) and sustaining citizen/community organization actions. Copyright 1993, Project Cork Institute.

Holder HD. Public health approaches to the reduction of alcohol problems. (review). *Substance Abuse* 15(2): 123-138, 1994. (72 refs.)

This is a review of current research concerning the prevention of alcohol-involved problems. The paper uses a public health model, i.e., the host—individual drinker, the agent—alcoholic beverages, and the environment—the drinking context to organize the scientific literature. The paper concludes with a brief summary of the effects achieved by the major prevention strategies based upon controlled studies. Copyright 1994, Association for Medical Education & Research in Substance Abuse.

Join Together. *Community Action Guide to Policies for Prevention: The Recommendations of the Join Together Policy Panel on Preventing Substance Abuse.* Boston: Join Together, 1995.

The recommendations presented in *Alcohol and Drug Abuse in America: Policies for Prevention,* the companion report to this guide, emphasizes how important community responsibility is in reducing the unlawful use of drugs and alcohol. This guide offers examples of how communities have organized around reducing unlawful drug and alcohol use, developed informed strategies to respond to this, and are taking back their communities through public action. The resources and program models outlined in this document will help readers implement the panel's recommendations, and more importantly, prepare and carry out a strategy necessary for a successful community substance abuse prevention program. Copyright 1995, Project Cork Institute.

Malekoff A. Action research: An approach to preventing substance abuse and promoting social competency. *Health and Social Work* 19(1): 46-53, 1994. (34 refs.)

This article demonstrates the use of action research, an approach combining various social work methods to raise community consciousness, stimulate intergroup and intergenerational interaction, and motivate people to work toward change both individually and collectively. The project described represents an effort to mobilize youths and adults living in a rapidly changing, culturally pluralistic, low-income suburban community to confront the impact of drug and alcohol abuse in a context of mutual respect and support. The central theme of investigation was local youths' perceptions about drug and alcohol abuse in the context of their own lives. A group of youths, in partnership with professionals, surveyed their contemporaries with a questionnaire of their own creation. The community meeting that followed was designed to stimulate the youths through reflection, dialogue, and a plan for action. Copyright 1994, National Association of Social Workers, Inc.

Wechsler R; Schnepp T. *Community Organizing for the Prevention of Problems Related to Alcohol and Other Drugs.* San Rafael CA: Marin Institute for the Prevention of Alcohol and Other Drug Problems, 1993.

This narrative has been developed as a guide for prevention professionals and activists who want to work for environmental prevention of problems related to drugs and alcohol through a community-organizing model. Part I is concerned with the ways and means of establishing an effective community organization and reviews the essential principles of community organizing. Part II details three case studies of community groups that have grappled with alcohol and other drug problems in their communities for several years. These case studies illustrate many of the community-organizing principles presented in Part I, and they also explore diverse community-based actions for prevention from which other groups may benefit. Despite their involvement in organizing for social change through agency-based activities, social service professionals can also benefit from learning more about community-based action and change. Copyright 1993, Marin Institute for the Prevention of Alcohol and Other Drug Problems.

Wilde GJ. Effects of mass media communications on health and safety habits: An overview of issues and evidence. *Addiction* 88(7): 983-996, 1993. (60 refs.)

A review is presented of factors investigated for their relevance to mass media communications specifically designed to alter health- and safety-related behaviors of the recipients. While alcohol consumption is a major concern in this paper, the evidence regarding the effective use of mass communications to modify other health and safety habits has also been incorporated. Specific topics include the choice of yardstick of effect, study methodology and the strength of conclusion this permits, and the dependency of mass communication on its four constituent components—the source, the content of the message, the channel of communication, and the characteristics of the recipients. Reference is made to using educational journalism to prevent health problems, and to increasing the educational value of traffic accident reports in daily newspapers by including information that could prevent future accidents. Copyright 1993, Society for the Study of Addiction to Alcohol and Other Drugs.

World Health Organization. *Alcohol Training in General Practice: Report on a WHO Working Group.* Copenhagen: World Health Organization, 1994. (1 ref.)

This report summarizes the efforts of a task group to ascertain the training needs of general practitioners in the European community in managing alcohol-related problems; to review existing resources; and to make recommendations about translating and/or adapting materials for dissemination. This report summarizes the discussions of the Working Group. Copyright 1994, Project Cork Institute.

CHAPTER 9

Resources for Educators and Trainers

JEAN KINNEY, MSW

CLINICAL APPLICATIONS

The goals of this chapter are to assist the clinician who provides training to:

1. Provide an overview of the central issues involved in education and training on alcohol and substance use issues.

2. Define core content.

3. Describe basic teaching methods.

4. Provide practical tips for planning educational and training sessions.

Education is frequently one of the many responsibilities of health care professionals. Nonetheless, given its importance, it is an activity for which few have had any formal training or supervision. Most individuals find themselves learning on the job.

This chapter suggests material to assist those involved in educational endeavors. This is organized in terms of basic topics essential to any educational enterprise. Any presentation and its particular emphasis will differ, depending on the audience. However, the topics covered here represent those that alcohol and substance professionals consider core knowledge. Different teaching methods are reviewed, along with their relative limitations and advantages. As examples, several sample programs are presented. Further resources for trainers and educators are also noted.

CONCEPTUAL FRAMEWORKS

One of the problems in substance abuse education is the tendency to present too much information without a conceptual framework that allows participants to organize and synthesize the material. In such instances students often feel inundated, and are without the tools to distinguish the significant from the trivial. This is particularly true when a presentation covers multiple drug classes, focusing on their distinctive characteristics in terms of drug actions, the at-risk patient populations, specific risk factors, and management of overdose and withdrawal.

In organizing a presentation, try to highlight common features and basic principles, and provide frameworks for assimilating the material. It is also useful to give some thought to the topics that can easily be found in reference materials whenever specific clinical questions arise, in contrast to general constructs that do not lend themselves to that route of acquiring information. Pay attention to the latter.

Defining the Clinician's Responsibilities

It is important to provide the audience with an outline and definition of the clinical tasks to be covered in an educational session. It is also important to define the tasks considered obligatory for all primary care clinicians as compared to those that are elective or more specialized and thus relegated to substance abuse specialists. This manual focuses on essential clinical tasks.

In making distinctions between essential versus elective clinical responsibilities, one touches upon recurring points of tension: "What *is* and what *is not* within the area of primary care?" and "What is the relationship of primary care providers to subspecialty care?" These issues are commonly discussed as if there were unambiguous reference points, which is rarely the case. What a primary care setting can appropriately manage varies for different medical conditions and across practice sites. It is a function of the staff's prior experience and training, the diagnostic and treatment procedures required, the numbers of cases routinely seen, the competing demands for clinicians' attention, and the availability of specialists. In this era of managed care, the health insurance also is a defining factor.

Primary care providers vary in their desire and comfort in using subspecialists and specialists. In some cases, this clearly reflects professionals' pride in their ability to care for a variety of medical problems. In some cases, it is prompted by what often happens when making referrals to academic medical centers or tertiary care settings: Some primary care practitioners find that it is not unusual to lose a patient entirely or to be disregarded and neither informed nor consulted about management. Consequently, in workshops and training, when emphasis is placed on the model used here, e.g., screening, identification, and referral for formal treatment, a common response of primary care providers is, "What if I don't want to refer my patient to a treatment program but want to provide treatment myself?" Such comments often reflect clinicians' sensitivity to this larger issue of their roles in relation to specialists and the pressures placed upon them by managed care. On the other hand, the question may reflect a naiveté and lack of experience about what alcohol and substance abuse treatment entails. Unfortunately, the mention of a referral may lead some practitioners to consider that their own skills are being viewed as inadequate.

In responding to such comments, experienced substance abuse educators have found that it is usually pointless to debate whether primary care providers should provide treatment. The most significant limitation generally confronting primary care providers is their ability to offer the diversity of services that substance use treatment entails. There are more helpful responses than issuing dictums and making individuals feel unskilled or that their competence is being challenged. A better approach is for substance abuse educators to ask primary care providers to consider which tasks fit into their own practices and which are better viewed as collaborative efforts. The answers may vary with providers or be determined by patients' clinical status and social situations. Point out also that the term *treatment* may not be the best way to describe the needed care. *Rehabilitation* is a more accurate term. Draw parallels from rehabilitative medicine and the variety and intensity of evaluation, assessment, and treatment planning with efforts to restore and maximize functioning, whether with stroke victims or with those with other physical impairments.

Clarifying the Skill Being Addressed

Pay attention to how any presentation of skills is structured. Within this manual, the essential skills are described as those directed toward building a therapeutic alliance, providing patient education, and collecting data, all of which are already components of clinical practice. Convey the message that trainees will use their existing skills and that the task is to refine these skills and apply them to the situations presented by substance use patients.

Applying the Framework of Chronic Disease to Alcohol and Substance Abuse Problems

The requirements for early intervention and management of alcohol and substance use problems will only make sense within the framework of substance use problems as a chronic disease process. The only major distinction between dependence on psychoactive substances and other chronic illnesses is that the early symptoms are behavioral, with no biological indices that signal the transition from health to disease.

CORE INFORMATION IN EDUCATIONAL PROGRAMS
The Impact of Alcohol/Substance Use on the Health Care System

Certain information should be included to emphasize that alcohol and substance use is a health care issue for individuals, while making a significant impact on the health care system. This includes information on health care costs related to alcohol and substance use, the impact of alcohol and substance use on health care utilization, morbidity and mortality associated with alcohol and substance use, and of alcohol and other substances as major causes of death.

The Impact of Alcohol and Substance Abuse Patients in Participants' Own Clinical Setting

Although some universal good might be achieved by health care professionals becoming more attuned to alcohol and substance abuse problems, it is important to address what the individual professional benefits will be for trainees. It may be necessary to make explicit that attending to alcohol and drug problems does not entail outreach to new patients. On the contrary, every primary care practice already has a substantial number of alcohol and substance abusers needing intervention. In doing so, clinicians are apt to discover that rather than creating more work, many of their existing efforts will be more successful. The number of problem patients—those who represent ongoing management problems, who do not respond to standard care, or who have poor compliance and may require multiple visits for the same problem—is likely to decline when their unrecognized substance abuse problems are addressed.

It is important to tell patients that having an alcohol or substance use problem is not their fault. The same kind of affirmation must also be made of clinicians' prior efforts. They have not personally been deficient. Inadequate education and training is the problem, which is partially attributable to substance abuse being a new field and to the long-term separation of alcohol treatment from the medical mainstream. Society's broad views about alcohol and drug problems, views that are now changing, have also been instrumental in defining substance issues as a nonmedical concern.

Demographics of Substance Use

Classifying different patterns of alcohol and substance abuse according to basic demographic variables such as sex, age, race, education, and socioeconomic class is important. The purpose is to have clinicians recognize that alcohol and substance use problems are not limited to any single age group, social class, racial group, or geographical area. This provides an index of suspicion based on data. Emphasis also needs to be placed on multiple substance abuse to dispel the perception that "pure" alcoholics and "pure" drug addicts are dichotomous.

Etiology of Substance Use Problems

The public health framework of the agent, host, and environment is a useful model to incorporate the factors that influence alcohol and substance use problems. Emphasis needs to be placed on distinguishing between acute and chronic problems because each has different risk factors.

Natural History of Dependence on Psychoactive Substances

For considering the natural history of dependency on psychoactive substances, two different but complementary models are available. The first, noted for its historic importance and subsequent influence on later work, is the four-stage progression described by Jellinek.

The second is often referred to as "the Johnson model." Postulating a four-step progression from an initial experience with alcohol or drugs to later dependence, it is often a useful vehicle in demonstrating that dependence is not chosen and that those who initially become dependent are not fundamentally different psychologically from the population. This simple formulation places more weight on pharmacological factors than on other elements. The model has proven useful in patient education for those touched by chemical dependency; it often has the same impact with professional audiences. The model may provide a basis for identifying with and thereby empathizing with substance abuse patients.

Vaillant's research outlining the natural history of alcoholism, in conjunction with the research findings on the role of heredity, dispelled many of the myths long shared by lay people and professionals, such as beliefs in an addictive personality and that psychological problems are the major factor in the emergence of alcoholism and drug dependence.

Psychopharmacology of Major Drug Classes

Attempting to treat patients' alcohol and drug problems without understanding the various drug class' psychopharmacology is a handicap. The elements of behavioral pharmacology must be understood, including the major acute and chronic actions, the effects desired by drug users, and the associated withdrawal syndromes.

ATTITUDES

The view of alcohol and substance use problems as either self-inflicted illnesses and/or willful acts must be addressed in any training. Challenging these directly often precipitates resistance. It may be more helpful to point out other conditions similarly related to health habits, including some cancers, hypertension, and respiratory disease—which are due to smoking, poor diet, and lack of exercise. The question, "Is psychoactive substance dependence an illness or a bad habit?" is not an empirical one.

There is much literature about how the "bad" attitudes of helping professionals toward alcohol and substance abuse patients result in inadequate patient care. In this literature, substance abuse educators are encouraged to urge their students to be nonjudgmental and empathic. Educational research views the problem differently. The problem, according to this formulation, is not negative attitudes but physicians' general devaluing of the importance of providing the kind of care that substance abuse patients and other chronic patients require, i.e., support, education, and counseling, which are not technological procedures or somatic interventions. Such tasks are commonly delegated to nonmedical personnel.[1]

To attribute failure to engage patients in treatment to clinicians' bad attitudes is a disservice to clinicians. Accordingly, to view the instilling of "good" attitudes as a goal of training, and therefore a topic of a session, although common, is not encouraged. Most people do not identify with sermons and assume that the message is intended for someone else. Ultimately, the best way to instill functional attitudes is by modeling them. Do not lecture about being empathetic; demonstrate the desired behavior in a simulated interview. To speak about the importance of a team approach solely from one discipline is not convincing. Instead, encourage the use of an interdisciplinary mix of faculty to demonstrate teamwork.

PLANNING EDUCATIONAL PROGRAMS

When planning educational programs, be specific about the program's objectives and the intended audience, and how these affect the recruitment of faculty, the program schedule, and the organization of individual sessions.

Establishing Program Goals

Educational programs are often described as workshops, conferences, symposia, or training sessions. The distinctions between these are ambiguous. In practice, programs fall into one of two groups. Some programs, whether for experts or novices, conducted primarily in a lecture or panel format, either introduce or update the audience about information relevant to practice and offer an overview of clinical implications. Other programs introduce and/or enhance clinical skills.

For participants, the satisfaction with a program is often determined by the fit between their expectations and what takes place. For faculty and participants, a precise statement about the goals and objectives is imperative. The essential question you should consider is, "In what way will participants be different as the result of attendance?" The answer will dictate the selection and number of faculty, educational methods, program design, and space requirements.

Recruiting Faculty

In selecting faculty, seeking competence in the content area is a given. Another factor is the discipline of the audience. Faculty whose training and credentials parallel those of the audience are more likely to be perceived as knowledgeable. Also, these faculty, familiar and sensitive to discipline-specific issues, are better able to translate the information for the audience.

In the alcohol and substance use fields, many of the experts are practitioners outside of the traditional health care system. Thus, their professional training is not in a health care discipline. In using these clinicians as faculty, it is imperative that their professional experience is not restricted to treatment or rehabilitation settings outside or marginal to the medical care system. There are several dangers in selecting faculty who are uninformed about the health care setting. They may not appreciate the demands on health care workers; they may not have been forced to process their own biases and possible antagonism toward health care professionals; and their professional vocabulary may be confusing and unfamiliar to the audience.

Few models for management of alcohol and substance use problems do not use a treatment team and interdisciplinary efforts. A lecture on the importance of collaboration and team building within education programs should incorporate faculty of different backgrounds and stress team teaching whenever possible.

Identifying Training and Educational Methods

Clinical training requires educational methods beyond lecture, presentation, and discussion. It requires "doing," e.g., experientially based methods with supervision and feedback. The more the training framework resembles actual clinical encounters, the greater its probability of being effective. Simulated or practice patients, "scripted" role plays, and critiqued role play of problem clinical situations, combined with expert demonstrations of clinical encounters, are effective training methods. In all cases, feedback to participants is essential. All of these methods are experientially based, requiring participants' active involvement.

Experiential Approaches

Educational research has consistently demonstrated that knowledge and attitudes are poor predictors of clinical performance; this has implications for the design of continuing educational programs and professional education. Presenting information and/ or shaping attitudes with the expectation that this will promote the desired clinical behavior is an approach that cannot be justified.

Experiential methods can be incorporated into virtually any workshop session. When group activities are used, any formal presentations should be brief and used to introduce and highlight the main points or topical areas. As part of the discussion following the activity, the major points should be reiterated and reinforced using examples from the exercise.

Any experiential activity—role play, simulated or practice interviews, or problem-solving discussions— needs to be processed. In presenting and processing activities, group leaders should include the three identified major skill areas that are components of virtually any clinical task, e.g., data collection, relationship building, and patient education.

If the participants are asked to focus on particular points, develop a worksheet for the exercises.

Patient Management Problems

A paper and pencil format used in clinical teaching settings is Patient Management Problems (PMPs). After a brief case presentation, the trainee indicates the clinical steps that he or she would take in management of the patient. Feedback is given based on the clinical decisions made. The format is a "branching decision tree," with future choices dictated by prior decisions. Beyond the immediate comments on the outcome of steps taken, there is a separate scoring system, with clinical actions designated as negative, positive, or neutral. Within workshops, PMPs promote self-assessment and the assimilation of the knowledge base. They are not intended for nor well suited to teaching interactional skills.

Clinical Training

Clinical training is labor intensive. While an individual faculty member may make formal introductory remarks, additional faculty will be required when the session turns to skill building. Ideally, in clinical training, the maximum ratio of trainees to faculty is 5:1. Training techniques can include role play and simulated/practice patients. Both of the latter formats require careful training of those taking the patient role; this is a preworkshop task. In addition to feedback from faculty or the practice patient, videotaping is another means of helping trainees assess their performances. Videotaped encounters can be jointly critiqued by faculty, "patient," and trainee, with the opportunity to stop the action and go over "rough spots."

Program Schedules

There are two biases for those who design educational programs. One bias is that it is important to allow for leisure time. The other bias is that it is important to use available time intensively. The latter bias, shared by the editor, presumes that clinicians have full, busy schedules. Participants' time should be considered valuable. A workshop or conference usually requires additional demands both before and after it occurs. Clinicians may need to reschedule patients or possibly close a practice. For some clinicians, attending a conference represents a loss of income. All clinicians will have to arrange coverage. Educational programs are not perceived as social opportunities. The use of time and the relevance of topics must justify attendance. Furthermore, clinicians receive many educational offerings, so a program competes with many others.

Audience Composition

The homogeneity or heterogeneity of the audience is a significant factor in designing and structuring educational programs. The heterogeneous audience presents special challenges to the conference organizer. Faculty are appreciative when the program announcement clearly specifies for whom the program is intended, including content, experience, and disciplines. When there is preregistration, faculty should be informed of numbers and audience composition.

If the participants at a workshop represent a diverse and heterogeneous group, this can best be addressed by concurrent sessions. When this is not done, to allow adequate preparation, the faculty member is forced to select an audience out of the whole group. The result may be that for some the presentation is too sophisticated, while for others it is too elementary. In such instances, for the benefit of participants and faculty members it is usually helpful to acknowledge the disparate backgrounds and the subsequent problems. A brief poll of the audience can confirm this for everyone. In a formal presentation, if there is a diverse audience, if possible, incorporate the "extremes" within the audience through brief efforts to translate material, i.e., clarifying terms and concepts and using examples from this minority's clinical settings. Paradoxically, when experiential techniques are used, a heterogeneous audience can be less of a problem. The participants can be subdivided by the natural groupings present, or small groups can be designed to have a mixture of backgrounds, and the more experienced individuals can help coach their less experienced colleagues.

Most professionals need continuing education to maintain licensure. Arrange to have a program approved for continuing education credits by the professional groups whose members you hope to attract. If the program is interdisciplinary and includes physicians, other professional groups such as nursing, alcohol, and substance abuse clinician associations are sensitive to their members being considered second-level participants. Many groups awarding credits will expect that someone from their discipline be involved in the planning and be someone on the faculty.

In program planning the provision of continuing education credits is something to attend to early so that the information can be included on program announcements.

Evaluation

Program evaluation is a requirement for most continuing education programs. There is the suspicion that many programs' evaluation efforts are primarily directed to complying with this requirement for certification. Less effort appears directed to ascertain the responses of participants to help guide future program development. Spend some time considering what questions you have, the concerns in planning the program, and feedback you would like from participants.

SAMPLE PROGRAMS

The following five sample programs can be developed using this manual as a faculty source book and/or as a participant's text.

I. Training of Primary Care Practitioners in Clinical Care of Alcohol and Substance Use Problems

GOAL: To impart core clinical skills to physicians and nurse clinicians/nurse practitioners in the management of alcohol and substance use problems. These include routine screening, risk reduction regimens, referral for further assessment and/or treatment, patient education, management of withdrawal, management of medical sequelae, and management of medical care after treatment to foster sobriety.

CONTENT: Overview of alcohol and substance use issues as a health care concern; basic frameworks for approaching alcohol and substance use problems; screening techniques; interviewing approaches; engaging the patient in treatment; management of withdrawal; description of treatment; and the primary care practitioner's role in pretreatment, during formal treatment, and in aftercare.

METHODS: Preworkshop assignments. Workshop: lecture, small-group discussion, audio-visual presentations, clinical teaching exercises, simulated patients, role play. Postworkshop assignments.

FACULTY: A faculty team with experience as trainers and teachers using different disciplines would be assembled. These include physicians with expertise in alcohol and substance use and with strong internal medicine backgrounds; nurses with experience in alcohol and substance use, medical management, and interviewing and interactive skills; and alcohol-substance abuse clinicians with backgrounds in consultation and/or practice in a medical setting. Supplementing this faculty are trained simulated patients to assist in clinical teaching exercises.

FORMAT: 2 days, 20 hours

SCHEDULE: Preworkshop activities distributed 3 weeks before workshop.
2 hours: Introduction to substance use.
3 hours: Routine screening and initial assessment.
3 hours: Engaging the patient in treatment.
2 hours: The health care worker's role.
3 hours: Medical issues (two concurrent sessions, for medical and nonmedical professionals).
3 hours: Special populations (three 1-hour concurrent sessions).
2 hours: Strategies for implementation.
1 hour: Information services.

FACILITIES: Lecture hall for 50 people, 10 rooms to accommodate small-group discussion, area for display and demonstration of resources and information services.

COST: Per 50 trainees: $13,200 (total = 7 faculty × $500/day, 2 additional small-group leaders × $350/day, 13 simulated patients × $75/session × 2 sessions). Instructional cost/person: $264.

II. Introduction to Alcohol and Substance Use Issues for Primary Care Providers

GOAL: To review alcohol and substance use problems as they present in primary care practices, and the role of the clinician in addressing these problems.

CONTENT: Dimensions and nature of alcohol and substance use problems, their presentations through the life cycle, etiology of alcohol and substance abuse problems, and natural history of disease and recovery; overview of treatment, tasks of the clinician in responding to alcohol and substance use issues.

METHODS: Workshop: lecture, small-group discussion, audio-visual presentations.

FACULTY: 6 total; substance abuse clinicians (4); physician with experience in alcohol and substance use and with strong background in internal medicine (1); nurse (1).

FORMAT: 1 day

SCHEDULE: 1 hour: Introduction to alcohol and substance use as a health care issue.
              1 hour: Etiology, natural history of alcohol-substance use problems.
              1 hour: Treatment and the role of the primary care provider.
              1 hour: Introduction to screening.
              1 hour: Interviewing skills.
              1 hour: Engaging patient in treatment: the process of referral.
              1 hour: Overview of issues in medical management.

FACILITIES: Lecture hall to accommodate 50 people; for small-group discussion, 6 small rooms to hold 10 people (9 participants, 1 faculty).

COST: Per 50 trainees: $3000 (6 faculty at $500/day). Instructional cost/person: $60.

III. Alcohol and Substance Abuse Training for Human Service Workers

GOAL: To impart core clinical skills to nonmedical human service workers, e.g., screening, referral for assessment, care of persons in treatment.

CONTENT: Dimensions and nature of alcohol and substance use problems, their presentations through the life cycle, etiology of alcohol and substance abuse problems, and natural history of disease and recovery; overview of

treatment, screening instruments, the process of initiating a referral, collaborating with treatment personnel.

METHODS: Preworkshop assignments. Workshop: lecture, small-group discussion, audio-visual presentations, clinical demonstrations, role play, simulated/practice patients. Postworkshop assignments.

FACULTY: 20 total; alcohol-substance abuse clinicians (8); physician or nurse (2); simulated patients (10).

FORMAT: 1 day

SCHEDULE: 1 hour: Overview of alcohol and substance use problems.
              1 hour: Etiology and natural history of chemical dependency.
              1 hour: Introduction to treatment and role of human service worker.
              1½ hours: Screening.
              1 hour: Interviewing skills.
              1½ hours: Engaging patient in treatment: the process of referral.
              1 hour: Incorporating alcohol and substance issues in practice.

FACILITIES: Lecture hall to accommodate 50 people; for small groups, 10 rooms to accommodate 8 people (5 trainees, 2 faculty, 1 simulated patient).

COST: Per 50 trainees: $6000 (10 faculty at $500/day; 10 simulated patients at $100). Instructional cost/person: $120.

IV. Advanced Topics for Alcohol and Substance Abuse Clinicians

GOAL: To update alcohol and substance abuse clinicians on current topics in the field.

CONTENT: Frameworks for approaching alcohol and substance use issues; special populations; medical issues for nonmedical personnel.

METHODS: Preworkshop assignments. Workshop: lecture, small-group discussion, audio-visual presentations. Postworkshop assignments.

FACULTY: Physician or nurse practitioner in alcohol and substance abuse field from academic medicine, alcohol-substance abuse clinicians in health care settings. 10 total (5 presenters/small-group leaders, 5 small-group leaders).

FORMAT: 1 day

SCHEDULE: 3 hours: Medical aspects.
              3 hours: Special populations.

FACILITIES: Lecture hall to accommodate 50 people; for small-group discussion, 5 small rooms to hold 12 people each.

COST: Per 50 participants: $4250 (5 × $500/day presenters, 5 × $350/small-group leaders). Instructional cost/person: $85.

V. Alcohol and Substance Abuse Clinicians Providing Consultation to Health Care Settings

GOAL: To provide skills to alcohol and substance abuse clinicians for consulting with health care providers.

CONTENT: Alcohol and substance use as a health care issue; frameworks for approaching alcohol and substance use; the health care worker's role in the management of alcohol and substance use problems; working in an interdisciplinary setting.

METHODS: Preworkshop assignments. Program: lecture, small-group discussion, audiovisual presentations, case presentations, other. Postworkshop assignments.

FACULTY: Physician, nurse in alcohol and substance abuse field (2); alcohol-substance abuse clinicians in health care settings (3).

FORMAT: 1 day

SCHEDULE: 3 hours: Update on medical issues.
2 hours: Consultation skills.
1 hour: Staff interactions.

FACILITIES: Large room (60 people), 5 small-group rooms.

COST: Per 50 trainees: $2500 (total = 5 faculty × $500/day). Instructional cost/person: $50.

RESOURCES
Professional Education Projects

Improving the care of patients with alcohol and other drug problems has been fostered through programs to train nurses, physicians, and other health care professionals. The first initiative was the Career Teacher Program sponsored by the NIDA and NIAAA. It was initiated in the early 1970s to train faculty from various medical schools who could foster curriculum development in their institutions. Following this initiative, several programs were initiated by private foundations: The Kroc Foundation (Project Cork, Dartmouth Medical School, and Morehouse Medical School), the Commonwealth Foundation (CHART Program at Harvard Medical School), and the Pew Foundation (The Johns Hopkins Medical School and The Johns Hopkins Hospital). With the growing activity in medical education, a professional society, AMERSA, emerged, whose membership comprises those in academic medicine with primary interests in medical education and research on alcohol and substance abuse.

Consensus Meeting, November 13-15, 1985, Rancho Mirage, CA. Sponsored by AMERSA, National Institute on Drug Abuse, and National Institute on Alcohol Abuse and Alcoholism.

The meeting was attended by more than 100 leaders from national professional organizations. The purpose was to define minimal knowledge and skills that primary care physicians need to recognize and successfully diagnose, intervene, and treat those with alcohol and drug problems. The session also recommended steps to enhance medical education in this topical area, particularly in the primary care disciplines, and to identify priorities for future efforts. Consistent with the recommendations of the Consensus Conference, new federal initiatives emerged for nursing education and medical education (and, in the wake of these, social work education); these initiatives focused on the primary care disciplines.

NIDA- AND NIAAA-SPONSORED HEALTH PROFESSIONS CURRICULUM DEMONSTRATION PROGRAMS[2]
Schools of Nursing

Case Western Reserve University, School of Nursing

10900 Euclid Avenue, Cleveland OH 44104-4904.
Project Director: Diane Morris, PhD, RN.
Telephone: (216) 368-5907. Fax: (216) 368-3542.

The focus of curriculum development is upon community nursing, infusing substance abuse content throughout the curriculum, as well as focusing on nurses as a high-risk group. The project is developing curriculum materials that address the special needs of families and special populations such as the elderly, adolescents, women of childbearing age, and acute and chronically ill patients. The project has five faculty fellows in the area of acute and critical care, medical-surgical, maternity, geriatric, and community health nursing.

City College of New York (CUNY), Lehman College, Division of Nursing

250 Bedford Park Boulevard, West, Bronx NY 10468.
Project Director: Sarah Beaton, PhD, RN.
Telephone: (718) 960-8790. Fax: (718) 960-8488.

The faculty development efforts are directed to both baccalaureate- and Master's-level nurses. Special attention is directed to serving various cultural groups; a systematic approach to instruction that reflects multicultural needs is being developed. Attention will be directed to the following clinical skills: assessment, identification of risk factors, screening, treatment, and referral, especially in the areas of community health, maternal health, and psychiatric-mental health areas. The project is preparing curriculum materials and specialized resources to augment training efforts.

New York University, Division of Nursing

Shimkin Hall, Room 429, 50 West Fourth Street, New York NY 10003.

Project Director: Madeline A. Naegle, PhD, RN.

Telephone: (212) 998-5300. Fax: (212) 995-4359.

Nursing and other health discipline faculty of New York University's School of Education, Health, Nursing and Arts Professions will develop, implement, and evaluate a model nursing curriculum and educational program. Content and clinical skills essential to nursing education at baccalaureate and Master's degree levels will be identified and incorporated into experiential and classroom teaching, including simulated and actual clinical situations. A working committee of faculty with expertise in alcohol and other drug problems and in curriculum development will study the structure and content of major courses with goals of expanding content hours and skills for students prepared as generalist practitioners of nursing. Representatives of student groups will be members of the committee. Relevant content will also be integrated into core courses at the Master's degree level. Faculty development is central to the project. The incorporation of research approaches and findings will promote research by faculty and encourage such interests in Master's degree students. Learning outcomes for faculty and students, assessment criteria for teaching strategies, and applicability of the model to other programs will be evaluated.

The Ohio State University, College of Nursing

1585 Neil Avenue, Columbus OH 43210.

Project Directors: Elizabeth M. Burns, PhD, RN, and Arlene Thompson, PhD, RN.

Telephone: (614) 292-4746 or 614/292-4578. Fax: (614) 293-3163.

The project will use an interdisciplinary working committee to plan and develop a model program and curriculum that comprise minimum knowledge and clinical skills for alcohol and other drug abuse nursing care. Undergraduate, Master's, and doctoral levels are targeted for pilot testing and subsequent revision and implementation. Alcohol and other drug abuse curriculum content will be incorporated into courses relating to 1) the assessment and diagnosis for infants, children, and adults experiencing physical, psychiatric, and/or mental health problems; 2) advanced nursing for acute care and long-term care of children and adults; prevention and intervention strategies for school-age children and adolescents; and 3) nursing science, nursing research, and selected areas of advanced study, including individual, family, and community systems. Faculty development will include a survey to determine faculty knowledge, attitudes, instructional skills, and clinical competencies

required to implement the model curriculum and program, as well as the content and strategies necessary to acquire those competencies. Guidelines for the implementation by other institutions will be included. The evaluation design will include an assessment of the overall curriculum effectiveness, including assessment of student outcomes related to knowledge, skills, attitudes, and practice behavior.

University of Cincinnati, College of Nursing and Health

3110 Vine Street, Cincinnati OH 45221-0038.

Project Director: Janice Dyehouse, PhD, RN.

Telephone: (513) 558-5269. Fax: (513) 558-7523.

The faculty development program is addressing both undergraduate and graduate curricula. The emphasis is upon culturally diverse groups. The clinical training sites being used include the major institutions, both public and private, in the Cincinnati area. The faculty fellows are drawn from the areas of parent-child, community health, mental health, and medical-surgical nursing.

University of Connecticut, School of Nursing

147 Courtyard Lane, U-59, Storrs CT 06268.

Project Director: Olga Church, PhD, RN.

Telephone: (203) 486-3713. Fax: (203) 486-0512.

A model training program that includes an integrated curriculum in alcohol and other drug abuse will be developed, implemented, and evaluated. An interdisciplinary working committee will be responsible for program development. The program will incorporate prevention, acute care, and postcrisis care content and interventions for patients with alcohol and other drug abuse problems. The target groups for the program are nursing faculty, undergraduate nursing students, and graduate nursing students with majors in primary community care nursing, critical care nursing, and nursing administration. Computer-assisted instruction will be evaluated formatively and summatively, using standardized instruments and research-designed assessments to determine attitudes, values, behavioral changes, and overall program outcomes.

University of Illinois at Chicago, College of Nursing

845 South Damen Avenue, Chicago IL 60612.

Project Director: Laina Gerace, PhD, RN.

Telephone: (312) 996-9174. Fax: (312) 996-8066.

Alcohol and other drug abuse is one of the school's priority health problems. The curriculum development initiative has three goals: faculty development, expansion of curricular offerings, and strengthening area resources to address community service and training needs. There are four faculty fellows from the areas of public health, maternal-child health, medical-surgical, and psychiatric nursing.

University of Kansas Medical Center, School of Nursing

3901 Rainbow Boulevard, Kansas City KS 66160-7500.

Project Director: Eleanor Sullivan, PhD, RN.
Telephone: (913) 588-1601. Fax: (913) 588-1605.

Expansion of current course offerings will be directed toward the areas of intervention and/or referral, as well as assessment of societal attitudes; other efforts are directed at developing a faculty mentorship program, providing general faculty workshops, integrating the ANA Nursing Association standards, incorporating ethical and legal issues, and assessing the specialized needs of each clinical area. The faculty fellows have participated in one of the national summer school of alcohol/drug abuse study programs.

University of South Florida, College of Nursing

12901 Bruce B. Downs Boulevard, MDC-Box 22, Tampa FL 33612-4799.

Project Director: Ona Z. Riggin, EdD, RN.
Telephone: (813) 974-2191. Fax: (813) 974-5418.

This project involves five faculty fellows drawn from the areas of maternal/child health, medical-surgical, geropsychiatric, adult, and family health nursing. The projects goals are to provide faculty development (both didactic and ongoing clinical training), integrate alcohol and other drug teaching throughout the curriculum, offer continuing education programs for practicing nurses, and develop and implement specialized teaching modules. Beyond local facilities, the fellows will be involved in off-site clinical programs and national conferences.

University of Texas at Houston, Health Science Center, School of Nursing

1100 Holcombe Boulevard, Suite 5.518, Houston TX 77030.

Project Director: Marianne Marcus, EdD, RN.
Telephone: (713) 792-7893. Fax: (713) 794-4690.

The curriculum development efforts are directed particularly to meeting the needs of ethnic and minority populations served in the Southwest region of the US. Each of the four major clinical specialty areas has a faculty fellow: Adult health, parent-infant health, community health, and psychiatric mental health nursing. The curriculum is being designed for both undergraduate and graduate nursing students.

University of Washington, School of Nursing

Department of Psychosocial Nursing, SC-76, Seattle WA 98915.

Project Director: Shirley Ann Murphy, PhD, RN.
Telephone: (206) 543-8569. Fax: (206) 543-3625.

This faculty development program is being directed to the school's four major clinical departments. The faculty fellows will be selected from each of these areas, and individually designed professional development programs will be created for each, drawing upon local and national resources.

Schools of Medicine

Boston University, School of Medicine

Division of Psychiatry, 818 Harrison Avenue, Boston MA 02118.

Project Director: Laurence Miller, MD.
Telephone: (617) 534-4230. Fax: (617) 534-4517.

This faculty development program, affiliated with one of the major urban public hospitals, is organized in recognition that 50% of that institution's patients have alcohol or other substance abuse as a primary or secondary diagnosis. The program has four faculty fellows from the areas of psychiatry, pediatrics, emergency medicine, and internal medicine. The goals of this program are to measurably increase curriculum efforts in both basic science and clinical teaching, to enhance skills in prevention, treatment and diagnosis, and to promote efforts by fellows in substance abuse research.

Brown University School of Medicine, Center for Alcohol and Addiction Studies

Brown University, Box G, Providence RI 02912.
Project Director: David C. Lewis, MD.
Telephone: (401) 863-1109. Fax: (401) 863-3510.

This project involves the active participation of 14 faculty representing departments of internal medicine, family medicine, community medicine, pediatrics, psychiatry, and obstetrics/gynecology (ob/gyn). This faculty has established minimum knowledge and skill competencies across all six disciplines and has identified instructional modules addressing such areas as assessment and diagnosis, prevention, treatment options/referral, family issues, withdrawal, physiology and pharmacology, intoxication and overdose, substance abuse, and AIDS. The instructional modules are designed as a learning hierarchy so that they can be implemented in a sequential manner across different disciplines and trainee levels. During the implementation, a program evaluation is being conducted and a research design is being developed for conducting an outcome evaluation of the training program.

Case Western Reserve University, School of Medicine

Department of Family Medicine, 10900 Euclid Avenue, Cleveland OH 44106-4950.

Project Director: Antonnette Graham, PhD.
Telephone: (216) 844-3791. Fax: (216) 844-3791.

The objectives of this faculty development effort are directed to general curriculum development, with special attention to understanding and intervening with special populations, especially inner-city African Americans, the elderly, and women. The project is utilizing seminars and journal clubs as educational vehicles. The five fellows are from the departments of psychiatry, family medicine, emergency medicine, geriatrics, and internal medicine. The primary curriculum materials used are those developed by Project Adept from Brown University.

The Johns Hopkins Hospital, Department of Pediatrics

Park Building, Room 301, 600 North Wolfe Street, Baltimore MD 21205.
Project Director: Hoover Adger Jr, MD.
Telephone: (301) 955-2910.

A working committee of pediatric faculty has assisted in meeting the substance abuse teaching needs within the existing curriculum and has prioritized teaching objectives and content. Substance abuse instruction is being integrated into the department's ongoing clinical teaching program, including two core lecture series, a noon Conference Series, and Grand Rounds. Pediatric faculty involved in implementing the curriculum have participated in a faculty development program to improve their knowledge and clinical teaching skills. Educational methods include role playing, videotaped interviews, case management problems, and lectures. Outcome evaluation measures for the program will assess changes in the prevalence of substance abuse problems in the pediatric population and in the detection rate of house staff and residents.

The Johns Hopkins University School of Medicine

600 North Wolfe Street, Baltimore MD 21205.
Project Director: David C. Levine, MD.
Telephone: (301) 955-8131.

The model program design, developed by a working committee of internal medicine faculty, is based on educational-behavioral principles, including the use of such teaching methods as small-group discussion, performance feedback, and role play with simulated patients. Evaluation of the effectiveness of the curriculum will include assessment of changes in trainees' knowledge, attitudes, skills, and practice behavior. Baseline studies on trainee practice patterns with respect to identification and intervention with alcohol and drug abuse problems have been conducted. Curriculum components designed for faculty, house staff, and medical students will emphasize early identification, state-of-the-art screening approaches, motivation into care, intervention and counseling skills, and referral to treatment.

Medical College of Virginia

Box 109, MCV Station, Richmond VA 23298.
Project Director: Sidney Schnoll, MD, PhD.
Telephone: (804) 786-9914.

This project involves faculty from the departments of primary care—internal medicine, pediatrics, psychiatry, and ob/gyn—in the design of a curriculum in alcohol and drug abuse that links the clinical research and clinical teaching expertise in these departments. A team of 20 faculty participated in a 2-day workshop designed to identify curriculum needs in alcohol and drug abuse and to develop interdisciplinary clinical research projects that could be implemented in the drug abuse content and determine how a revised curriculum could address current overlaps and gaps. Teaching strategies will include special projects relevant to the interdisciplinary clinical research program. Each stage of curriculum development and implementation will be evaluated and carefully documented to facilitate replication efforts by other medical institutions.

Society of Teachers of Family Medicine (STFM)

University of California Irvine Medical Center, Building 29A, Route 81, 101 The City Drive South, Orange CA 92668.
Project Director: Peter Coggan, MD.
Telephone: (714) 634-5171.

The STFM received a faculty development award. Ten family medicine physicians from different medical schools across the country were identified to participate in a 2-year faculty development training program. The curriculum involved a combination of group workshops conducted by STFM and targeted educational activities within each fellow's own medical institution. The focus of training is achievement of knowledge and clinical skill competencies in alcohol and drug abuse and development of teaching materials and teaching strategies. Individual fellows will be evaluated, using pretest and posttest measures of substance abuse attitudes, mastery of knowledge, and skill-learning objectives. (See Bibliography for publications and materials.)

University of Alabama at Birmingham

Medical Education Facility, Suite 609, University Station, Birmingham AL 35294.
Project Director: William D. Lerner, MD.
Telephone: (205) 934-4451.

An integrated curriculum in alcohol and other drug abuse is being developed in the departments of medicine, psychiatry, and family medicine. The proposed curriculum will include an expansion of the current preclinical curriculum and the development of a 1-month intensive clinical experience in the newly established Center for Impaired Health Professionals. This clinical rotation is offered as part of the Acting Internship Program to undergraduate students. Residents and faculty from the three participating specialty departments will rotate through this clinical teaching site. Evaluation of the proposed curriculum will assess trainee knowledge and skills as well as the impact of the model curriculum on other teaching departments who receive consultation and assistance from the alcohol and drug abuse program faculty.

University of California at Los Angeles, School of Medicine

UCLA Neuropsychiatric Institute, 760 Westwood Plaza, Los Angeles CA 90024.

Project Director: J. Thomas Ungerleider, MD.

Telephone: (310) 825-0293. Fax: (310) 825-6792.

This faculty development program is coordinated with the Charles R. Drew University of Medicine and Science. In addition to medical education, a major focus is upon law enforcement and public policy as these relate to health professions. An interdisciplinary faculty team represents the departments of family medicine, pediatrics, obstetrics/gynecology, anesthesiology, psychiatry, and emergency medicine. The program relies upon field placements in both university and community settings. A major emphasis is upon acquisition of interactive, clinical skills.

University of Massachusetts Medical School

Chemical Dependency Service, MCCM Memorial Hospital, 119 Belmont Street, Worcester MA 01605.

Project Director: Michael R. Leipman, MD.

Telephone: (508) 793-6170. Fax: (508) 793-6394.

This project, completed in 1994, was directed to training primary care physicians. A weekly seminar and self-guided study were the major means for approaching faculty education. The project utilized simulated patients to assess curriculum changes.

University of Nevada, at Reno, School of Medicine

Department of Psychiatry and Behavioral Sciences, Reno NV 89557-0046.

Project Director: John Chappel, MD.

Telephone: (702) 938-8265. Fax: (702) 938-8265.

There are four faculty fellows from the departments of family and community medicine, pediatrics, internal medicine, and obstetrics and gyne-

cology. While substance abuse teaching was introduced in 1975, heretofore it has been conducted within the department of psychiatry. A major goal of the program will be to extend teaching beyond that department.

University of North Carolina at Chapel Hill

Center for Alcohol Studies, CB #7175, Medical School Wing A, Chapel Hill NC 27599.

Project Director: David S. Janowsky, MD.

Telephone: (919) 966-0617. Fax: (919) 966-0617.

The project was completed in 1994. The broad goals of the faculty development effort were to increase faculty fellows' skills in clinical teaching, patient care, and research in substance abuse; to strengthen existing programs of substance abuse teaching; and to move toward an integrated curriculum approach. Among the disciplines included as fellows are family medicine, psychiatry, internal medicine, emergency medicine, obstetrics and gynecology, and student health. The evaluation design has relied upon a case study method format.

University of North Dakota School of Medicine

Southwest Campus, University of North Dakota, 515 East Broadway, Bismarck ND 58501.

Project Directors: Keith Foster, MD, and Richard L. Davidson, EdD.

Telephone: (701) 224-2549.

A working committee of representatives of the basic sciences, internal medicine, family medicine, psychiatry, and clinical faculty will assess substance abuse needs within the existing curriculum and develop objectives for each level of training within the medical school. This core group, through the input of selected subcommittees, will establish alcohol and drug knowledge and skill competencies that trainees are to attain and include the curriculum objectives for each instructional level. Selected full-time faculty and part-time clinical preceptors throughout the state will participate in a week-long professional training program at a treatment center as part of the faculty development component of the project. Outcome evaluation measures will include preattitude, postattitude, and skill-learning objectives. This curriculum model will address teaching strategies effective in rural communities and will be implemented in four regional teaching sites throughout the state.

University of Southern California, School of Medicine

1975 Zonal Avenue KAM 500, Los Angeles CA 90033.

Project Director: Dale C. Garell, MD.

Telephone: (213) 342-2279. Fax: (213) 342-2722.

This faculty development program was directed toward faculty fellows developing skills to initiate a specialty-specific curricula directed to training undergraduates and postgraduates, and to continuing professional development efforts. The faculty development enterprise relied heavily upon the use of experiential teaching methods, observation, and participation in treatment programs. The USC Medical Center does not have a comprehensive substance abuse treatment program; thus, faculty fellows relied heavily upon community resources.

University of Texas Health Science Center at San Antonio

Department of Family Practice, Audie Murphy VA Hospital, 7400 Merton Minter Boulevard, San Antonio TX 78284.

Project Director: Demmie Mayfield, MD.

Telephone: (512) 617-5195. Fax: (512) 617-5195.

This project, completed in 1994, focused upon creating an interdisciplinary team of faculty able to provide clinically based training for residents and other faculty within their affiliated departments. The fellows all participated in a regularly scheduled seminar series, two off-site intensive workshops, and national and regional meetings. The departments represented in the training included internal medicine, pediatrics, psychiatry, and family medicine. An annual CME program (to which the school sends trainees) was also developed and offered to adjunct faculty teaching in family practice in a four-state area.

University of Virginia, School of Medicine

Department of Behavioral Medicine and Psychiatry, Blue Ridge Hospital, Drawer D, Charlottesville VA 22901.

Project Director: R.J. Canterbury, MD.

Telephone: (804) 924-2241. Fax: (804) 982-1853.

The purpose of the project is to develop a comprehensive educational program in substance abuse at the University of Virginia School of Medicine. The program is intended to promote the interaction between basic science and clinical faculty across disciplines and enhance the development of a systematic and interdisciplinary approach. A primary feature of the program is the development of eight modules on substance abuse education for integration into the preclinical curriculum, pediatric and psychiatry clerkships, and interdisciplinary fourth-year electives. Additionally, an interdisciplinary series of lectures, using the modules, will be offered on a quarterly basis for residents and faculty. Project staff will serve as resources for the medical school, the university, and the community, and as consultants to other schools interested in developing programs at their own institutions. The educational modules and accompanying instructor's manual will be presented at national meetings and be available for dissemination to other schools and residency programs throughout the country.

University of Wisconsin, School of Medicine

777 South Mills Street, Madison WI, 53715.

Project Director: Michael Fleming, MD, MPH.

Telephone: (608) 263-9953. Fax: (608) 263-5813.

This faculty development project, completed in 1994, centered upon providing a longitudinal, multi-level learning experience that incorporated clinical, educational, and research components. The curriculum for fellows included the following four elements: a 2-month placement in a community-based alcohol/drug program; three off-site, week-long immersion experiences in three different treatment settings; regular didactic seminars; and the development of a subspecialty substance abuse clinic conducted by the fellow. In addition, there was an ongoing seminar directed to curriculum development.

Yale University

Connecticut Mental Health Center, 34 Park Street, New Haven CT 06519.

Project Director: Richard S. Schottenfeld, MD.

Telephone: (203) 789-7079. Fax: (203) 789-7088.

The acronym for this faculty development program is CADRE (Clinical Alcohol and Drug Research and Education). The faculty fellows, following training in diagnosis, intervention, treatment, and research, will be primarily engaged in developing a required clinical clerkship component for each of the four target departments from which the fellows are drawn. The school is in the process of curriculum reform under a major grant from the Robert Wood Johnson Foundation, and faculty fellows' efforts to evaluate the need for curriculum change will be meshed with this other project.

Vanderbilt University

Vanderbilt Medical Center North, Box 23106, Nashville TN 37232.

Project Director: Peter Martin, MD.

Telephone: (615) 322-3527. Fax: (615) 343-8639.

This project involves faculty from the departments of internal medicine, psychiatry, pediatrics, and ob/gyn in the design of the model alcohol and drug abuse curriculum. A working committee has established minimum knowledge and skill competencies for primary care specialties and developed a matrix of teaching objectives for each of the four disciplines. Following an assessment of the existing preclinical, clinical, and residency curriculum, faculty are developing curriculum components for each level of training. Curriculum modules for residency and faculty training are being developed separately for each of the four disciplines. Evaluation of the curriculum will include knowledge, skill, and attitude assessments for each level of training and an assessment of the process of developing and implementing changes in the curriculum.

Wake Forest University, Bowman Gray School of Medicine

Department of Psychiatry and Human Behavior, Medical Center Boulevard, Winston-Salem NC 27157.
Project Director: Loretta Y. Silva, PhD.
Telephone: (919) 716-4558. Fax: (919) 716-6380.

This program is being conducted in collaboration with the North Carolina Governor's Institute project, a project directed at promoting collaborative efforts among the state's medical schools in the area of substance abuse education. The faculty development activities include creating and using organized problem- or case-based experiences, providing assistance in integrating this into teaching activities, providing mechanisms of ongoing communication and collaboration, and devising an integrated curriculum model.

Wayne State University, School of Medicine

Addiction Research Institute, 4201 At. Antoine Boulevard, Suite 9-A, Detroit MI 48201.
Project Director: Eugene P. Schoener, PhD.
Telephone: (313) 577-1388. Fax: (313) 577-6685.

This faculty development program, completed in 1994, focused upon enhancing training in the areas of prevention, assessment, diagnosis, intervention, treatment, and referral. The project hosted an annual retreat for faculty fellows, monthly group work sessions, quarterly seminars, and workshops. The project also designed and offered the CME program. The program had three faculty fellows from the departments of psychiatry, pediatrics, and internal medicine.

Schools of Social Work

Boston University, School of Social Work

Alcohol and Drug Institute, One University Road, Room 216, Boston MA 02215.
Project Director: MaryAnn Amodeo, PhD.
Telephone: (617) 353-3763. Fax: (617) 353-3763.

The faculty development efforts will build upon the efforts of the Alcohol and Drug Institute for Policy, Training, and Research. It will offer faculty development seminars, help develop clinical placements and internships, and introduce 10 new content modules within the undergraduate curriculum.

Case Western Reserve University, Mandel School of Applied Social Science

11235 Bellflower Road, Cleveland OH 44106-7164.
Project Director: Lenore Kola, PhD.

Telephone: (216) 368-8670. Fax: (216) 368-8670.

The project's efforts are centered upon the implementation of a training model that will emphasize group instruction, network development, and collaborative efforts in assessment, development, and implementation of social work curricula. Three fellows from the areas of family prevention, substance abuse in criminal justice, and women's addiction and treatment are involved. Fellows will be engaged in curriculum review, needs assessment, review of literature and pedagogical methods, and the creation of resource materials.

University of Connecticut, School of Social Work

1798 Asylum Avenue, West Hartford CT 06117-2698.
Project Director: Michie N. Hesselbrock, PhD.
Telephone: (203) 241-4768. Fax: (203) 241-4786.

The faculty development effort is directed toward the development of a course of four faculty who will be able to plan and promote the integration of substance abuse material into the social work practice sequences of casework, group work, community organization, policy planning, and administration. Efforts are also directed to creating substance abuse as a substantive area of concentration for students. A long-range goal is the creation of a series of continuing education courses for practitioners in the state. Faculty development for fellows will include an inservice seminar and site visits to treatment programs.

University of Denver, Graduate School of Social Work

Spruce Hall South, Room 333, 2148 South High Street, Denver CO 80208.
Project Director: William Cloud, PhD.
Telephone: (303) 871-2921. Fax: (303) 871-2845.

The goal of this program is to introduce a concentration in substance abuse. The focus of the faculty development program is to prepare curriculum materials, provide faculty seminars, and develop field placements in substance abuse settings. Four faculty fellows are enrolled, whose areas of interest include women; AIDS victims; and mental health and drug problems among Hispanics, the elderly, and Native Americans.

University of Maryland at Baltimore, School of Social Work

525 West Redwood Street, Baltimore MD 21201.
Project Director: Dale Masi, PhD.
Telephone: (410) 706-3636. Fax: (410) 706-6046.

The program has the goal of initiating a concentration area in substance abuse, as well as integrating substance abuse material throughout the curriculum to enable students to be able to recognize, intervene, treat, or refer substance abuse patients. Fellows participating in the program come from the following areas: relapse prevention, women, aging, and minorities.

Rutgers, The State University of New Jersey, School of Social Work

PO Box 1133, New Brunswick NJ 08903.
Project Director: Eileen M. Corrigan, DSW.
Telephone: (908) 932-7194. Fax: (908) 932-8181.

The goals of this project are to develop what is currently an alcohol-substance abuse minor into a substance abuse minor, to adapt curriculum models to incorporate them into the school's programs, and to develop a well-trained pool of substance abuse clinical faculty. The faculty development efforts for the five fellows will involve attendance at summer schools, guided readings, short-term clinical experiences, and an ongoing seminar series.

Virginia Commonwealth University, School of Social Work

1001 West Franklin Street, Richmond VA 23284-2027.
Project Director: Sanford Swhwartz, PhD.
Telephone: (804) 828-0458. Fax: (804) 828-0716.

The faculty development efforts proposed include creating current awareness service for substance abuse literature, dealing with attitudes and practice patterns that mitigate against social workers' involvement with substance abuse patients, and familiarizing social workers with principles of case management. Fellows will be involved in the design of the first-year course of studies within the Master's level program to incorporate substance abuse material.

Doctoral Programs in Clinical Psychology

University of New Mexico, Department of Psychology

Albuquerque NM 87131-1161.
Project Director: William R. Miller, PhD.
Telephone: (505) 277-2805. Fax: (505) 277-1394.

This program involves four faculty members, whose activities will be directed to incorporating more substance abuse–related material within the doctoral program. The areas of faculty include cross-cultural psychology, community treatment evaluation, interpersonal communications, and family therapy. The goal is to ensure consistent training for all doctoral students in the areas of assessment, treatment, screening, cross-cultural issues, prevention, and early interventions. Efforts will also be directed to developing resources for training of related professionals such as school counselors, pastoral counselors, and substance abuse clinicians.

RESOLUTIONS AND POLICY STATEMENTS BY PRIMARY CARE DISCIPLINES ON ALCOHOL AND SUBSTANCE USE

Professional associations have passed resolutions or issued policy statements related to the obligations and/or need for members to be involved in the areas of alcohol and other substance use. The following have been set forth and/or adopted by various primary care disciplines.

American Academy of Pediatrics

- Alcohol use and abuse: A pediatric concern. *Pediatrics* 79(3): 450-453, 1987.
- Resolution on the harmful effects of alcohol consumption during pregnancy (adopted 1986).
- Selection of substance abuse treatment programs. *Pediatrics* 86(1): 139-140, 1990.
- Drug-exposed infants. *Pediatrics* 86(4): 639-642, 1990.
- Policy statement: Alcohol consumption in relation to pregnancy. *Journal of Pediatrics and Child Health* 28(3): 219, 1992.
- Role of the pediatrician in prevention and management of substance abuse. *Pediatrics* 91(5): 1010-1013, 1993.
- Fetal alcohol syndrome and fetal alcohol effects. *Pediatrics* 91(5): 1004-1006, 1993.
- Reducing the risk of human immunodeficiency virus infection associated with illicit drug use. *Pediatrics* 94(6): 945-947, 1994.
- Financing of substance abuse treatment for children and adolescents. *Pediatrics* 95(2): 308-310, 1995.

American Academy of Psychiatrists in Alcoholism & Addictions (aaPaa)

- Addressing substance abuse: A priority in health care reform. *American Journal on Addictions* 3(1): 87, 1994.
- Position statement on nicotine dependence. *American Journal on Addictions* 4(2): 179-181, 1995.

American College Health Association (ACHA)

- Statement on college alcohol and drug abuse. *Journal of the American College Health Association* 34: 228, 1986.
- Statement on college alcohol and drug abuse. *Rockville MD: American College Health Association, 1984.*

American College of Emergency Physicians

- Motor vehicle safety, position paper. *Annals of Emergency Medicine* 14: 822-823, 1985.

American College of Obstetricians and Gynecologists

- Cocaine abuse: Implications for pregnancy. *International Journal of Gynecology and Obstetrics* 36(2): 164-166, 1991.

American College of Physicians

- Position paper on chemical dependence. *Annals of Internal Medicine* 102: 405-408, 1985.

American College of Sports Medicine

- Position statement on the use of alcohol in sports. *Medicine and Science in Sports and Exercise* 14(6): R9-R11, 1982.
- Position statement on the use of anabolic androgenic steroids in sports. *Medicine and Science in Sports and Exercise* 19(5): 534-539, 1987.

American Hospital Association (AHA)

- Admission to general hospitals of patients with alcohol and other drug problems: Policy and statement, 1957. Revised 1983.
- Substance abuse policies for health care institutions. Chicago IL: American Hospital Association, 1992.

American Medical Association (AMA)

- House of Delegates. *Reaffirmation of the 1956 statement recognizing alcoholism as a disease.* Chicago: American Medical Association, 1966.
- Guidelines for alcoholism: Diagnosis, treatment, and referral (adopted 1979).
- Policy statement on alcoholism as a disability (adopted 1981).
- Council on Scientific Affairs. Fetal effects of maternal alcohol use. *Journal of the American Medical Association* 249(18): 2517-2521, 1983.
- Consensus Development Panel. Consensus Report: Drug concentrations and driving impairment. *Journal of the American Medical Association* 254(18): 2618-2621, 1985.
- Council on Scientific Affairs. Report: Alcohol and the driver. *Journal of the American Medical Association* 255: 522-527, 1986.
- Board of Trustees. Alcohol: Advertising, counter-advertising, and depiction in the public media. *Journal of the American Medical Association* 256(11): 1485-1488, 1986.
- Council on Scientific Affairs: Drug abuse in athletes. *Journal of the American Medical Association* 259(11): 1703-1705, 1986.

- Council on Scientific Affairs. Issues in employee drug testing. *Journal of the American Medical Association* 258(15): 2089-2095, 1987.
- Council on Scientific Affairs. Scientific issues in drug testing. *Journal of the American Medical Association* 257(22): 3110-3114, 1987.
- Board of Trustees. Interim Report: Prevention and control of AIDS (issued 1987).
- Council on Ethical and Judicial Affairs. *Ethical Issues Involved in the Growing AIDS Crisis* (adopted 1987).
- House of Delegates. Resolution #113: *Drug Dependencies as Diseases* (adopted June 1987).
- Board of Trustees. *Drug Abuse Epidemic in the United States: An Epidemiological Report.* Chicago: American Medical Association, 1988.
- Board of Trustees. *Drug Abuse in the United States: A Policy Statement.* Chicago: American Medical Association, 1988.
- Council on Scientific Affairs. *Reducing Transmission of Human Immunodeficiency Virus (HIV) among Intravenous Drug Abusers.* Chicago: American Medical Association, 1988.

American Medical Society on Alcoholism and Other Drug Dependencies (AMSAOD)

- Policy recommendations on highway safety in relation to alcoholism and other drug dependencies (adopted March 3, 1987).
- Position statement on drug dependencies as diseases (adopted March 24, 1987).
- Position statement on nicotine dependence and tobacco (adopted April 20, 1988).
- Affirmation of position statement on alcoholism as a complex primary physiological disease (adopted April 24, 1988).

American Nurses' Association (ANA)

- American Nurses' Association. *Addictions And Psychological Dysfunctions in Nursing: The Profession's Response to the Problem.* Kansas City MO: American Nurses' Association. Division on Psychiatric and Mental Health Nursing Practice, 1984.
- American Nurses' Association; Drug and Alcohol Nursing Association; National Nurses Society on Addictions. *The Care of Clients with Addictions: Dimensions of Nursing Practice.* Kansas City MO: American Nurses' Association, 1987.
- American Nurses' Association; National Nurses Society on Addictions. *Standards of Addictions Nursing Practice with Selected Diagnoses and*

Criteria. Kansas City MO: American Nurses' Association, 1988.

American Osteopathic Academy of Sports Medicine

- Policy statement and position paper: Anabolic androgenic steroids and substance abuse in sport, 1989. Middleton WI, May 1989.

American Society of Preventive Oncology

- Position statement on tobacco and nicotine dependence.
  Cancer Epidemiology, Biomarkers & Prevention 1(4): 255-256, 1992.

American Public Health Association (APHA)

- Advertising and promotion of alcohol and tobacco products to youth.
  American Journal of Public Health 83(3): 468-472, 1993.

American Psychiatric Association (APA)

- Position statement on substance abuse.
  American Journal of Psychiatry 138(6): 874-875, 1981.
- *AIDs Primer.* APA AIDS Education Project: Washington DC, 1988.
- Position statement on methadone maintenance treatment.
  American Journal of Psychiatry 151(5): 792-794, 1994.
- Position statement on the need for improved training for treatment of patients with combined substance use and other psychiatric disorders.
  American Journal of Psychiatry 151(5): 795-796, 1994.

American Society of Addiction Medicine (ASAM)

- Public policy statement on prevention.
  Journal of Addictive Diseases 11(3): 117-120, 1992.
- Public policy statement on the use of alcohol and other drugs during pregnancy.
  Journal of Addictive Diseases 11(4): 125-127, 1992 (adopted Nov. 6, 1988).
- Public policy statement on chemically dependent women and pregnancy.
  Journal of Addictive Diseases 11(4): 127-130, 1992.
- Public policy statement on nicotine dependence and tobacco.
  Journal of Addictive Diseases 12(1): 141-143, 1993.
- Public policy statement on reimbursement for the treatment of nicotine dependence.
  Journal of Addictive Diseases 12(1): 143-145, 1993.
- Public policy statement on nicotine dependence: Documentation of nicotine dependence on death certificates and hospital discharge sheets.
  Journal of Addictive Diseases 12(1): 145-146, 1993.
- Public policy statement on addiction medicine and health insurance reform.
  Journal of Addictive Diseases 12(2): 161-163, 1993.
- Public policy statement on the role of medical review officers.
  Journal of Addictive Diseases 12(2): 155-60, 1993.
- Public policy statement on clinical applications of the nicotine patch.
  Journal of Addictive Diseases 12(4): 161, 1993.
- Public policy statement on core benefit for primary care and specialty treatment and prevention of alcohol, nicotine and other drug abuse and dependence.
  Journal of Addictive Diseases 12(4): 162-166, 1993.
- Public policy statement on principles of medical ethics.
  Journal of Addictive Diseases 13(1): 125-30, 1994.
- Public policy statement on medical care in recovery.
  Journal of Addictive Diseases 13(2): 124-125, 1994.
- Public policy statement on the definition of alcoholism.
  Journal of Addictive Diseases 13(2): 123-124, 1994.

Association of Program Directors in Internal Medicine

- Alcohol and other substance abuse and impairment among physicians in residency training.
  Annals of Internal Medicine 116(3): 245-254, 1992.

National Association of Social Workers (NASW)

- Policy statement on alcohol- and other substance-related problems.
  NASW Policy Statements. Silver Spring MD: NASW, June 1988.

Statements on Health Care Reform and Substance Abuse Treatment

- Bigby JA; Butynski W; Elam LC; Geller A; Graham A; Kinney J; Koop CE; et al. Statement to the President's Task Force on National Health Care Reform. Hanover NH: Project Cork Institute, 1993.

- Center on Addiction and Substance Abuse, Columbia University; Brown University Center for Alcohol and Addiction Studies Recommendations on Substance Abuse Coverage and Health Care Reform. New York: Center on Addiction and Substance Abuse, 1993.
- Consortium of Medical Educators in Substance Abuse Essential Requirements for Medical Education in Substance Abuse. Los Angeles: University of California, 1993.
- Legal Action Center. *Model Legislation Mandating National Health Insurance Benefit for Treatment for Alcoholism and Drug Addiction*. Washington DC: Legal Action Center, 1993.
- Society of Americans for Recovery. *SOAR Proposes Criteria for Addiction Treatment*. Washington DC: SOAR, 1993.

REFERENCES

1. Kinney J; Price TRP; Bergen BJ. Impediments to alcohol education. *Journal of Studies on Alcohol* 45(5): 453-459, 1984. (17 refs.)
2. Center for Substance Abuse Prevention. *Directory of Projects: Faculty Development Program in Alcohol and Other Drug Abuse*. Rockville MD: Center for Substance Abuse Prevention, 1994.

FURTHER READINGS

Adger H Jr; McDonald EM; Duggan AK. Evaluation of a CME workshop on alcohol and other drug use. *Substance Abuse* (AMERSA) 13(3): 129-138, 1992. (17 refs.)

This paper reports on evaluation results from a 3-hour workshop, "Substance Abuse: What the Pediatrician Should Know and Do." The workshop was organized into three major components: a didactic session on general concepts of alcohol and other drug (AOD) abuse, a case discussion of the pediatrician's role, and an interactive skillsbuilding session on AOD interviewing involving videotaped observation and participant role plays. The evaluation plan was designed to examine the workshop's impact on pediatric health care providers' knowledge and practice in the timely identification and treatment of AOD abuse among patients and their families. This paper examines the evaluation results. Copyright 1993, Project Cork Institute.

Alaszewski A; Harrison L. Alcohol and social work: A literature review. (review). *British Journal of Social Work* 22(3): 331-343, 1992. (44 refs.)

In the first section of this literature review, the authors examine the social and health problems associated with alcohol misuse and the ways in which social workers and other primary care workers respond to these problems. In the second section, the authors examine the nature of professional training and consider the ways in which it does and does not provide social workers and other primary care workers with the knowledge and skills to identify and help people with drinking problems. In the final section, the authors examine the ways in which training can be developed to enable social workers to respond more effectively to alcohol-related problems. Copyright 1992, British Association of Social Workers.

American Association of Dental Schools. Curriculum guidelines for education in substance abuse, alcoholism, and other chemical dependencies. *Journal of Dental Education* 56(6): 405-408, 1992. (13 refs.)

The American Association of Dental Schools, the American Dental Association, and the American Student Dental Association have recognized alcoholism and other chemical dependencies collectively as a pervasive disease and social problem. They have adopted resolutions relative to the disease of chemical dependency as it affects dentists, dental and allied dental students, their families, patients, and other members of the dental family. This article outlines curriculum guidelines designed to enhance student and dental practitioner understanding of the etiology, prevention, and recovery process related to substance abuse, alcoholism, and chemical dependency so that they may help themselves, "at risk" patients, families, and fellow colleagues. Copyright 1992, American Association of Dental Schools.

Ashley MJ; Brewster JM; Chow YC; Rankin JG; Single E; Skinner HA. An agenda for action. *Canadian Medical Association Journal* 143(10): 1097-1098, 1991. (0 refs.)

Participants at the October 1989 Canadian national conference, "Preventing Alcohol Problems: The Challenge for Medical Education," reached a consensus on several key issues, providing the basis for an ambitious agenda for action. First, there was consensus that the current educational experiences of medical students and residents relating to alcohol problems are inadequate. Second, there was general agreement on the range of material that should be taught. Third, it was clear that appropriate teaching vehicles of several kinds are already in place, although modifications may be required. Fourth, it was agreed that agencies outside the medical schools have specific roles to play in ensuring the adequacy and appropriateness of professional education in this area. The participants identified a number of steps: (1) Each Canadian medical school should examine the current situation regarding professional education on alcohol problems. (2) If the review indicates inadequacies in professional education in this area, it is essential to obtain the commitment of key faculty members for change. (3) Recognizing that commitment to change must be accompanied by both leadership and coordination of the effort to change, the participants stressed the need for each medical school to ensure these key components. (4) The building of a multidisciplinary network of people with interest and skills in the alcohol field should be undertaken systematically. (5) Specific educational objectives for undergraduate and postgraduate training should be developed. (6) Basic science and community health elements in the undergraduate curriculum may require strengthening. (7) Each Canadian medical school should establish policies of low-risk alcohol consumption at school functions. Copyright 1991, Project Cork Institute.

Baldwin JN; Light KE; Stock C; Ives TJ; Crabtree BL; Miederhoff PA; et al. Curricular guidelines for pharmacy education: Substance abuse and addictive disease. *American Journal of Pharmaceutical Education* 55(4): 311-316, 1991. (27 refs.)

According to several recent surveys, substance abuse education is an area of instructional deficiency at colleges of pharmacy. Faculty and students responding to these surveys favored required lectures, guest speakers, and elective courses for such education over adding required courses, although some colleges successfully utilize such a course. This paper has been prepared by members of the American Association of Colleges of Pharmacy Substance Abuse Education and Assistance Special Interest Group to suggest required and elective courses on substance abuse for pharmacy students. Suggested content areas include the following: psychosocial aspects of alcohol and other drug use; pharmacology and toxicology of abused substances; identification, intervention, and treatment of people with addictive disease; and legal issues. Within each area, objectives, suggested curricular location, resources, and potential elective experiences are identified. Copyright 1991, American Association of Colleges of Pharmacy.

Bell JR. Lessons from a training program for methadone prescribers. *Medical Journal of Australia* 162(3): 143-144, 1995. (5 refs.)

This report describes the key lessons from evaluation of the training program to date. The training program comprised a methadone prescribers' manual; a small-group interactive workshop designed to challenge attitudes and assumptions that are the major obstacles to delivering effective treatment; and a clinical placement designed to assess clinical skills. Copyright 1995, Project Cork Institute.

Bigby J; Barnes HN. Evaluation of a faculty development program in substance abuse education. *Journal of General Internal Medicine* 8(6): 301-305, 1993. (16 refs.)

This study's objective is to determine whether a faculty development program was effective in increasing clinical skills and the amount of substance abuse teaching of individual medical faculty. Program participants were evaluated with a structured assessment before and several months after participating in a faculty development program in substance abuse education. Eighty percent of participants were general internal medicine faculty who on average devoted 25% of their time to teaching. The remainder of the participants were family medicine, psychiatry, or other internal medicine faculty and nonphysician teachers. The participants attended a learner-centered, largely experiential faculty development program in substance abuse education to improve their clinical and teaching skills with patients in the general medical setting. Eighty-six percent of the participants completed the evaluation. The participants reported increased confidence in their clinical skills in recognizing substance abuse, presenting the problem to the patient, and referring the patient for treatment. The participants also reported improved attitudes toward patients and increased teaching about the management of the primary problem of substance abuse, but not at the expense of teaching about medical complications. Copyright 1993, Hanley & Belfus, Inc.

Blume SB. *Identification and Referral of Children of Alcoholics: A Training Program for Medical Professionals*. New York: Children of Alcoholics Foundation, 1992. (0 refs.)

This manual is designed as an implementation guide to train medical professionals in the identification and referral of children of alcoholics. The book is divided into four sections: (1) What you need to know about children of alcoholics, (2) developing a resource list for patients, (3) identification and referral, and (4) evaluation. The manual provides overhead masters and questions to accompany the video vignettes, which are provided on the training video and publicity materials. Copyright 1993, Project Cork Institute.

Burger MC; Spickard WA. Integrating substance abuse education in the medical student curriculum. *American Journal of the Medical Sciences* 302(3): 181-184, 1991. (11 refs.)

Physicians miss the diagnosis of substance abuse in significant numbers of patients, partly because of a lack of education about identifying and treating those patients. This article describes an attempt to integrate substance abuse into the curriculum of a traditionally organized medical school. Faculty selection, determination of the skills and knowledge needed, and methods for enriching the curriculum to include substance abuse are described. Problems encountered during the project, benefits of implementing the curriculum changes, and recommendations for other medical schools choosing to implement such a program also are provided. Copyright 1991, Lea & Febiger.

Chiert T; Gold SN; Taylor J. Substance abuse training in APA accredited doctoral programs in clinical psychology: A survey. *Professional Psychology: Research and Practice* 25(1): 80-84, 1994. (12 refs.)

A survey addressing training in substance abuse was mailed to all 160 doctoral clinical psychology programs provisionally and fully accredited by the American Psychological Association (APA). Ninety-five replies were received, yielding a response rate of 59%. This study was conducted to ascertain whether levels of doctoral training in this area have changed appreciably since comparable surveys in 1979 and 1984. Because of the considerable increase in the number of APA-accredited PsyD programs since the previous two surveys, it was also possible to compare relative levels of training in substance abuse in PhD, PsyD, and combined PhD/PsyD programs. Survey results did not suggest that substance abuse training either has changed markedly over time or differs substantially across types of degree programs. Copyright 1994, American Psychological Association, Inc.

Davis AK; Parran TV Jr; Graham AV. Educational strategies for clinicians. *Primary Care* 20(1): 241-250, 1993. (25 refs.)

Largely because of a lack of training, many primary care physicians are unaware of how they can prevent, detect, or manage substance abuse within their clinical practice. The educational process used to develop a teaching unit can be simplified by initially asking a few directed questions. The answers to these questions determine what needs to be taught while facilitating the subsequent steps of determining learning goals and objectives and selecting appropriate teaching materials and strategies. Evaluating the teaching unit on at least a cursory level provides useful information for planning. A variety of curriculum manuals and clinical text parts can be readily incorporated into teaching units. These same sources can alternatively be adapted to an individual's own self-directed course of study. Incorporation of experiential education strategies is especially useful in substance abuse instruction. Including recovering individuals, encouraging attendance at self-help group meetings, and using role play exercises are all useful experiential strategies for engaging the learner. The education process includes the following: deciding why, what, and how to teach; developing the structure of a teaching unit; selecting educational strategies in substance abuse; selecting curriculum and clinical materials; and using organizational and networking resources. Copyright 1993, Project Cork Institute.

Durfee MF; Warren DG; Sdao-Jarvies K. A model for answering the substance abuse educational needs of health professionals: The North Carolina Governor's Institute on Alcohol and Substance Abuse. *Alcohol* 11(6): 483-487, 1994. (31 refs.)

Physicians can play an increased role in recognizing, intervening, and moderating their patients' misuse of alcohol and other drugs. This article explores the need for educational changes to permit physicians to develop skills in prevention, screening, and office-based treatment. It includes a personal account by one of the authors of recognizing deficiencies in substance abuse education both in his own medical school training and in today's health science curricula in the US. It reviews prior initiatives by NIDA/NIAAA to address curriculum needs and describes an innovative collaborative model in North Carolina called the Governor's Institute on Alcohol and Substance Abuse. The Institute was created in 1990 as a nonprofit corporation to promote education, research, and communication among health professionals. Some of the Institute's programs are described, including its curriculum integration project in the state's four medical schools. The article concludes that the time is right to introduce substance abuse concepts into basic and continuing education for all health professionals. Copyright 1994, Pergamon Press.

Felton G. An opinion piece: The consensus conference. *Journal of Professional Nursing* 7(3): 184-187, 1991. (4 refs.)

In the spring of 1989, the Alcohol, Drug Abuse, and Mental Health Administration (ADAMHA), through the National Institute on Drug Abuse (NIDA) and the National Institute on Alcohol Abuse and Alcoholism (NIAAA), added nursing to its consensus development programs by organizing a 3-day meeting to prepare a consensus statement on the minimum knowledge, scientific information, training, skills, and attitudes that baccalaureate nursing graduates need in the prevention, diagnosis, treatment, and management of the use and abuse of alcohol and other drugs (AODA). There are some obvious and some not-so-obvious reasons for concern about AODA. One is the growing effects of drug dependence and addiction on society including increased criminal behavior, as well as the direct consequences of drugs and long-term changes on individual health and their associated social burdens and costs. Another startling concern is that attention and resources for AODA disorders and drug-taking behavior have most often been focused on treatment after addiction rather than on effective preventive strategies. Nurses spend more time with individuals and families than any other health professionals. Copyright 1992, Project Cork Institute.

Hagemaster JN; Plumlee A; Conners H; Sullivan E. Integration of substance abuse content into undergraduate and graduate curricula. *Journal of Alcohol and Drug Education* 40(1): 89-102, 1994. (10 refs.)

Nursing schools are being challenged to integrate alcohol and other drug abuse content into both their undergraduate and graduate curricula. The University of Kansas is currently involved in a coordinated approach to curriculum implementation with the support of the National Institute on Alcohol Abuse and Alcoholism (NIAAA) and the National Institute on Drug Abuse (NIDA). Copyright 1994, Alcohol and Drug Problems Association of North America.

Klein RF; Foucek SM; Hunter SD. Recovering alcoholics as patient instructors in medical education. *Substance Abuse* (AMERSA) 12(2): 82-89, 1991. (9 refs.)

This article describes the use of recovering alcoholics as patient instructors to teach third-year medical students behavioral counseling skills related to interviewing, conveying the diagnosis, and initiating treatment for substance abuse problems. It addresses the training of patient instructors and the interview exercise, and reports the initial results of the curriculum innovation. Copyright 1991, Association for Medical Education & Research in Substance Abuse.

Long P; Gelfand G; McGill D. Inclusion of alcoholism and drug abuse content in curricula of varied health care professionals. *Journal of the New York State Nurses Association* 22(1): 9-12, 1991. (20 refs.)

Alcoholism and drug abuse are prevalent health problems in the US. Practitioners in nursing, medicine, and dentistry need to be cognizant of the insidious signs of chemical dependency. A descriptive survey using a researcher-designed questionnaire yielded a sample that consisted of 11 medical schools, 2 dental schools, 25 baccalaureate and higher-degree nursing programs, and 38 associate degree nursing programs. The survey findings indicated that the curricula for nursing, medicine, and dentistry were inadequate in chemical dependency content. This survey evidenced the need for a stronger educational effort addressing both knowledge of alcoholism/drug abuse and impaired professional practice in the curricula of the health professional programs examined. Copyright 1991, New York State Nurses Association.

National Institute on Alcohol Abuse and Alcoholism; National Institute on Drug Abuse. *Project Descriptions: Model Curricula for Alcohol and Other Drug Abuse Physician and Nurse Education.* Rockville MD: NIAAA and NIDA, 1989. (0 refs.)

The NIAAA and NIDA are jointly sponsoring a program to develop and demonstrate effective models for integrating alcohol and other drug abuse teaching into the medical and nurse education curricula. Descriptions of the 12-model curriculum projects are presented in this publication. The model curricula are based upon discipline-specific knowledge and skill objectives and address undergraduate, graduate, residency, and faculty training needs. Each project includes the following components: (1) Use of a faculty working committee to assess alcohol and other drug abuse instructional needs and to develop curriculum objectives, (2) development of curriculum materials and pilot testing of a selected segment of the curriculum, and (3) a 14-month implementation and evaluation phase. Public Domain.

O'Connor PG; Bigby JA; Gallagher D. Faculty development in substance abuse and AIDS: A curriculum for primary care providers. *Substance Abuse* (AMERSA) 13(3): 105-111, 1992. (8 refs.)

The onset of the AIDS epidemic in the 1980s has resulted in a new and rapidly growing body of clinical knowledge that needs to be assimilated by health care personnel. Care of patients with human immunodeficiency virus (HIV) infection has come increasingly under the auspices of primary care providers as the number of these patients has grown and new therapeutic approaches have been developed. Substance abuse has been identified as a major risk factor for HIV infection and appears to be increasing in importance relative to other risk factors. Primary care providers for those with HIV infection thus frequently find themselves needing to have expertise in substance abuse as well. Various models have been employed to help educate primary care providers to better care for persons with the dual problem of substance abuse and HIV infection, including continuing medical education, training fellowships, institutional-based programs, and practice-based interventions. The faculty development approach is commonly employed as a way to disseminate knowledge, teach skills, and explore attitudes concerning clinical topics by "teaching the teachers" of other health care providers. The authors developed an intensive 3-day faculty development program for primary care providers that focuses on the interface of substance abuse and AIDS. In this report, the authors give an overview of their curriculum and program objectives. Copyright 1992, Association for Medical Education & Research in Substance Abuse.

RESOURCES
Center for Substance Abuse Treatment:
Treatment Improvement Protocols

The Center for Substance Abuse Treatment publishes a series of treatment improvement protocols. The series to date includes the following:

Barthwell AG; Gibert CL. *Screening for Infectious Diseases among Substance Abusers. Treatment Improvement Protocol (TIP) Series 6.* Rockville MD: Center for Substance Abuse Treatment, 1993. (Chapter refs.)

Center for Substance Abuse Treatment. *Assessment and Treatment of Cocaine-Abusing Methadone-Maintained Patients. Treatment Improvement Protocol (TIP) Series 10.* Rockville MD: Center for Substance Abuse Treatment, 1994. (158 refs.)

Center for Substance Abuse Treatment. *Assessment and Treatment of Patients with Coexisting Mental Illness and Alcohol and Other Drug Abuse. Treatment Improvement Protocol (TIP) Series 9.* Rockville MD: Center for Substance Abuse Treatment, 1994. (105 refs.)

Center for Substance Abuse Treatment. *Screening and Assessment for Alcohol and Other Drug Abuse among Adults in the Criminal Justice System. Treatment Improvement Protocol (TIP) Series 7*. Rockville MD: Center for Substance Abuse Treatment, 1994. (41 refs.)

Center for Substance Abuse Treatment. *Simple Screening Instruments for Outreach for Alcohol and Other Drug Abuse and Infectious Diseases: Treatment Improvement Protocol (TIP) Series 11*. Rockville MD: Center for Substance Abuse Treatment, 1994. (7 refs.)

Davis C; Henderson R. *Combining Substance Abuse Treatment with Intermediate Sanctions for Adults in the Criminal Justice System. Treatment Improvement Protocol (TIP) Series 12*. Rockville MD: Center for Substance Abuse Treatment, 1994. (16 refs.)

Kandall SR. *Improving Treatment for Drug-Exposed Infants: Treatment Improvement Protocol (TIP) Series 5*. Rockville MD: Center for Substance Abuse Treatment, 1993. (210 refs.)

McLellan AT; Dembo R. *Screening and Assessment of Alcohol- and Other Drug-Abusing Adolescents: Treatment Improvement Protocol (TIP) Series 3*. Rockville MD: Center for Substance Abuse Treatment, 1993. (Chapter refs.)

Mitchell JL. *Pregnant, Substance-Using Women: Treatment Improvement Protocol (TIP) Series 2*. Rockville MD: Center for Substance Abuse Treatment, 1993. (92 refs.)

Nagy PD. *Intensive Outpatient Treatment for Alcohol and Other Drug Abuse. Treatment Improvement Protocol (TIP) Series 8*. Rockville MD: Center for Substance Abuse Treatment, 1994. (39 refs.)

Parrino MW. *State Methadone Treatment Guidelines: Treatment Improvement Protocol (TIP) Series 1*. Rockville MD: Center for Substance Abuse Treatment, 1993. (Chapter refs.)

Schonberg SK. *Guidelines for the Treatment of Alcohol- and Other Drug-Abusing Adolescents: Treatment Improvement Protocol (TIP) Series 4*. Rockville MD: Center for Substance Abuse Treatment, 1993. (70 refs.)

National League of Nursing, Curriculum Materials

A series of 8 modules has been publish by the National League for Nursing, edited by MA Naegle and JS D'Arcangelo. *Substance Abuse Education in Nursing*. New York: National League for Nursing 1992. (Publication Number 15: 2463)

The individual titles are listed below. Each module provides an instructor's guide that includes learner objectives, recommended readings, audio-visual materials, overhead masters, handout masters, teaching strategies and sample assignments, and a bibliography.

Module 1. Gigliotti E. Fetal Effects of Maternal Alcohol and Drug Use.

Module 2. Naegle MA. Impaired Practice by Health Professionals.

Module 3. D'Arcangelo JS; Adamski T. Addictions: Nursing Diagnosis and Treatment.

Module 4. Compton M. Nursing Care in Acute Intoxication.

Module 5. Compton M. Nursing Care in Withdrawal.

Module 6. Mathwig G; D'Arcangelo JS. Drug Misuse and Dependence in the Elderly.

Module 7. Clucas AH; Clarke VP. Drug and Alcohol Problems in Special Populations.

Module 8. Clucas AH; Clarke VP. Nursing Care of Drug and Alcohol Problems in Special Populations.

Office for Substance Abuse Prevention

The Physician Does Make a Difference: Recognizing the Faces of Alcohol and Drug Abuse. Trainer/Educator Guide. Rockville MD: Office for Substance Abuse Prevention, 1991. (0 refs.)

These two videotapes of approximately 20 minutes each, with an accompanying teacher's guide, were developed to promote health professionals' training. The major sections of the tape are directed to overcoming barriers to diagnosis, signs and symptoms, clinical interviewing, early intervention, and preventive efforts.

Project ADEPT Curriculum Materials

The Brown University School of Medicine, Center for Alcohol and Addiction Studies has developed a series of curriculum materials for primary care medical education. The series includes 5 units: Core Modules; Special Topics; AIDS & Substance Abuse; Special Populations; Race, Culture & Ethnicity.

Address: Center for Alcohol and Addiction Studies, Brown University, Box G, Providence RI 02912.

Project CORK Slide-Lecture Series: *Alcohol Use and Its Medical Consequences*

Each unit in the series contains a set of professionally rendered slides, accompanied by a brief legend, and key references. Ten units deal with alcohol and another addresses cocaine. The series was originally intended as a curriculum aid for faculty to use in presentations and lectures. The series can also be used for independent study, and is suited for education in the health professions. Address: Milner-Fenwick, Inc 2125 Greenspring Drive, Timonium MD 21093-3100.

Unit 1. Biochemistry, Pharmacology and Toxicology of Alcohol. 2nd Edition. (53 slides, 31 pp. text) by RP Smith, PhD.

Unit 2. Alcohol and the Liver. (59 slides, 31 pp. text) by HL Bonkowsky, MD.

Unit 3. Hematologic Complications of Alcohol. (40 slides, 18 pp. text) by GG Cornwell, MD; JR McArthur, MD.

Unit 4. The Alimentary Tract and Pancreas. (67 slides, 33 pp. text) by PR Anderson, MD; HL Bonkowsky, MD.

Unit 5. Alcohol, Pregnancy, and the Fetal Alcohol Syndrome. 2nd Edition. (79 slides, 61 pp. text) by AP Streissguth, PhD; RE Little, PhD.

Unit 6. Endocrine and Metabolic Effects of Alcohol. (25 slides, 13 pp. text) by R Adler, MD, PhD.

Unit 7. The Neurological Complications of Alcohol and Alcoholism. 2nd Edition (64 slides, 47 pp. text) by JL Bernat, MD; M Victor, MD.

Unit 8. Overview of Medical Complications. (60 slides, 28 pp. text) by TRP Price, MD.

Unit 9. Alcohol Use, Abuse, and Dependence. (93 slides, 83 pp. text) by J Kinney, MSW.

Unit 10. Native American Alcohol and Substance Abuse. (37 slides, 26 pp. text) by J Kinney, MSW.

Unit 11. Cocaine Use and Its Medical Consequences. (62 slides, 55 pp. text) by M Fuller, MD.

Social Work Education Modules

The National Association of Social Workers (NASW), in collaboration with the Council on Social Work Education (CSWE), under a grant from the Center for Substance Abuse Prevention, has developed five substance abuse training modules. These are now in press and will be distributed by NCADI, as well as available from NASW. The topics of the modules are (1) policy, (2) practice, (3) human behavior, (4) field practice, and (5) special populations. The racial and ethnic groups in this fifth module are Native Americans, Pacific Islanders, African Americans, Hispanics, Asians, and also gays and lesbians.

Project Coordinator: Norma Taylor, NASW. Telephone: (202) 408-8600.

CSAP Project Officer: Armando Pollock, CSAP. Telephone: (301) 443-1845.

PART II

Special Populations— Special Concerns

This manual provides a grounding in general alcohol and substance use issues. In clinical practice the generic patient is nonexistent. American society is an amalgam of cultural and ethnic groups. There are significant cultural minorities—African Americans, Hispanics, and Native Americans. Although characteristics distinctive of other groups are less dramatic, they are just as real. The Vermont farmer, the Franco-American, the Portuguese who live along the New England seacoast, the person who lives in the hills of Appalachia, the person from the rural deep South, the acculturated Asian, the newly arrived Asian, or the dislocated blue collar worker from the North Central industrial belt—all have distinctive cultural attributes.

In the literature on ethnic minority groups, there are several common refrains. One is the relative absence of adequate research. Data are often drawn from national surveys in which minority groups are under-represented. In addition to "overlooking" minority groups, these national reports have often ignored significant differences within minority groups. This is most apparent in studies that discuss Native Americans or Hispanics. Language is the feature that usually underscores the definition of *Hispanic*. Within the Hispanic community, there is diversity based on geographical location, the Southwest versus urban inner cities of the Northeast; country of origin; and the period of migration, or, for many Mexican Americans, being native peoples.

In addition to ethnicity, other patient attributes are becoming recognized as significant for the clinician. Different age groups, women, and family members of those with substance use problems (especially children in the home, as well as adult children) are likely to have special needs. Similar attention needs to be paid to these ethnic or cultural subgroups. Since there is little research, information available on these ethnic subgroups tends to be speculative. It often represents untested theoretical extrapolation from the larger culture. For the clinician, the best advice is to be alert to the special needs of these patients, recognizing that a full set of "how to's" remains to be developed. In the interim, thoughtful reflection needs to substitute for firm data.

ETHNIC AND CULTURAL CONSIDERATIONS

Cultural aspects are relevant for the clinician. In significant ways, culture defines the acceptable and unacceptable drinking and drug use practices in the community. Culture influences what behaviors are viewed as problems. In this way, culture influences the factors that promote concern and pressure to seek assistance. Cultural factors influence patients' use of available care and from whom they seek help. To ignore or underestimate the role of culture can unwittingly create a population of noncompliant, frustrated patients.

Of particular importance for the clinician is a minority group member's relationship to his or her cultural history and majority culture. Different schema have been developed to consider an individual's cultural self-identification. However, for the practitioner, there are limited cultural perspectives to consider. Some primarily identify with the ethnic culture, its values, world view, and institutions, while others primarily identify with the majority culture. These latter individuals espouse the values of the larger culture and its ways of thinking and doing things. Some may be uninformed about their cultural history while others are informed but disinterested, individuals sometimes described as *assimilated*. Individuals who can move between the native culture and the majority American culture comfortably and are equally adept at functioning in either are called *bi-cultural*. Finally, some individuals find themselves estranged from both cultural groups because they are not comfortable in either. These latter individuals often do not have a clear sense of the community to which they belong and are likely to experience difficulty as a result.

Social scientists, as well as other members of the population, hold a variety of views about the importance of cultural orientation, and especially which cultural orientation is good for an individual or for society. These perspectives are manifested in numerous ways, such as what is proper or improper for schools in terms of bilingual education, how health services should be organized, and the language(s) used in printing voter ballots. For the health care field, these perspectives are reflected in discussions of how health care services should be organized and delivered; the importance of having staff of similar cultural and ethnic backgrounds to the patients they care for; discussions about the need for separate vs. integrated treatment programs; and, from a clinician's stance, the importance of incorporating or collaborating with nontraditional healers. For those who care for patients in ethnic communities in which the traditional culture is maintained, it is helpful to remember that the nurse or physician is a nontraditional healer from the perspective of that community. There is a small but articulate group of academics, social scientists, and clinicians, many of whom are members of minority groups, particularly African Americans, who view an individual's cultural identity as vital to any discussion of health. They maintain that the various cultural orientations are not simply interchangeable individual choices without any implications. It is their view that African Americans who are primarily identified with the majority white culture attempt and indeed are encouraged by that culture to reject and disavow their history, roots, and identity. However, the identity they hope to achieve cannot be theirs. They maintain that to be non-white in American society is *not* a neutral attribute. For African Americans, the collective experience of slavery and its continuing legacy needs to always be in the foreground. Thus, it is imperative to be fully aware of the larger political and economic factors that continue to oppress minorities and hit black Americans hardest.

In caring for patients of ethnic groups, having a sense of their cultural orientation is important. This can be ascertained by considering the basic dimensions listed in the box, which are a part of everyone's life.

Becoming Acquainted with the Culture

In providing health care and clinical services in any community, it is necessary to become familiar with the community and its members. It is often useful to start by considering the nature and source of any preconceived notions. They will serve as the *(Special Populations—Special Concerns)* operating assumptions for your work. If thoughtfully considered, they can be put to the test of experience.

Some of the means by which you can familiarize yourself with the community include the following:
- Exploring the community's history and cultural traditions.

Cultural Orientation

	Traditional or Culture of Origin	Majority Culture
Social	• Close friends from same ethnic background	• Close friends not restricted to ethnic group
	• Leisure activities within ethnic community	• Leisure activities not primarily within ethnic community
Language	• Fluent in native language, or	• Not fluent in native language, or
	• Uses primarily the idiom of the ethnic group	• Does not speak native language
Spiritual/Religious	• Familiar with and participates in ethnic ceremonies and celebrations	• Unfamiliar with, or
		• Does not participate in festivities of the ethnic community
Family	• Defined by frame of reference of the ethnic culture	• Primarily considers family as the spouse and children, the nuclear family unit

From Babor TF; Mendelson JH. *Annals of the New York Academy of Sciences* 472: 46-59, 1986. (29 refs.)

- Identifying its socioeconomic characteristics.
- Identifying the community's leaders—the formal leaders and the informal leaders whose opinions are valued and who are influential in community life. Is the community homogeneous or heterogeneous? If the community is heterogeneous, what tensions does this generate?
- Speaking with members of the community.
- Speaking with clinicians in the health center.
- Attending community functions.

In the course of these contacts, consider the following questions:
- Who are the community's influential members?
- What are the community's significant concerns?
- To whom do individuals turn for help, under what circumstances, and with what expectations?
- What are the dominant views of the health care center or social service agency; or what expectations are likely to be attributed to you?
- How does the group view health, disease, and illness?

- What are the strengths of the culture? What supports or promotes health care?
- What do they believe about the causes of drinking, the role of drinking, and the impact of drinking on the community?
- What are the definitions of drinking problems? Drug problems? Dependence?

CLINICAL ENCOUNTERS

When caring for patients who are members of an ethnic or racial minority or culture other than their own, clinicians must attend to many additional points. The clinician should be sensitive to nonverbal cues that can indicate what is comfortable or uncomfortable interaction in clinical settings. The clinician should not be surprised if he or she is watched closely for evidence of prejudice or disinterest. As necessary, the clinician should acknowledge the limits of personal knowledge or experience. Sage advice remains, "The patient is the best instructor."

CHAPTER 10

African Americans

OMOWALE AMULERU-MARSHALL, PhD, MPH

CLINICAL APPLICATIONS

The goals of this chapter are to assist the clinician to:

1. Be aware of the patterns of alcohol and other drug use among African Americans.

2. Become familiar with morbidity and mortality associated with African-American substance use.

3. Be familiar with factors related to the etiology of substance use problems within the African-American community.

4. Be knowledgeable about special clinical approaches to treating African Americans.

5. Be familiar with approaches to prevention of substance abuse among African Americans.

Almost 20 years ago, it was demonstrated that very little serious study of African-American substance abuse, in its own right, was ever attempted. Historically, there had been few studies on alcohol consumption patterns and consequences among African-American populations. In 1976, 30 years of scientific literature on alcoholism was reviewed, from 1944 to 1974.[15] Of the 16,000 articles published, only 77 contained any discussion of alcohol use by African Americans. Furthermore, only 11 articles reported studies in which African Americans were targeted exclusively. This provides a useful context in which to consider alcohol and other drug use among Americans of African descent.

Although since then, there has been some improvement in the dearth of studies about African Americans, the more recent studies have had considerable methodological problems. The data that began to emerge on the prevalence and consequences of substance abuse among African Americans was usually found in general population surveys with small and geographically skewed samples of African-American respondents.[25] There continue to the present time to be few studies focusing on African Americans.[29,73,68,37,23] The consequence is a lack of adequate or valid information on substance abuse among African-American populations, especially as it relates to issues beyond mere incidence and prevalence.

EPIDEMIOLOGY
Alcohol Use and Related Problems

Available studies indicate that African Americans experience significant problems from alcohol use.[38] Such findings had led to a traditional perception that African Americans drank more than any other group in the US. However, this view was challenged by the results of the first national survey of African and Hispanic American drinking patterns, in which black men and white men were found to have similar drinking patterns.[38] With respect to black women, nearly one-half (46%) were described as abstainers, compared with approximately one-third (34%) of white women. The 1984 survey revealed that twice as many white women as black women (8% vs. 4%) were classified as frequent heavy drinkers, and that the proportion of black women in the heaviest drinking category was slightly less than that of white women. These findings seemed to conflict with earlier findings from national surveys that black women were more likely than white women to drink heavily.[53]

More recent reports indicate that available results are still inconclusive.[8] In 1990 white males in the 18 to 44 age range as well as the 45 and over age range drank more than black males in the same age cohorts. The percentages of current white female drinkers also

dwarfed the equivalent proportions of black females in the same age ranges (Table 10-1). In 1992, 37% of European Americans as opposed to almost half (49%) of African Americans in the age range of 18 to 25 reported abstention from the use of alcohol.[52]

The heavier drinking category offers inconsistent patterns by age and gender. Black males in the 18 to 44 age range reported a slightly greater proportion of heavier drinkers than do white males in the same age cohort. However, a higher percentage of white males in the 45 years and over range reported being heavier drinkers than did black males. Among females, for whom comparative data was only available for the 18 to 44 age range, black females reported a higher proportion of heavier drinkers than did white females (Table 10-2).[52]

While the data on drinking patterns continues to be inconclusive, there is no controversy about the fact that African Americans, especially African-American males, experience comparatively excessive rates of problems associated with drinking.[11,72] This is true for every type of problem except drinking and driving. Significantly, the excess in African-American rates exists for both acute and chronic alcohol-related health problems. More black than white persons are reported to have experienced symptoms of alcohol withdrawal.[34,38,71] Among the most tragic alcohol-related health problems that affect American Africans are cirrhosis and esophageal cancer. In 1950 cirrhosis

Table 10-1. Percentage of Current Drinkers by Sex, Race, and Age: United States, 1990

Age	Males		Females	
	Black	White	Black	White
18-44 years	65.5	80.4	44.0	65.1
45 years and over	51.3	68.1	24.5	37.9

From National Center for Health Statistics. *Health, United States, 1993.* Hyattsville MD: Public Health Service, 1994.

Table 10-2. Percentage of Heavier Drinkers among Current Drinkers by Sex, Race, and Age: United States, 1990

Age	Males		Females	
	Black	White	Black	White
18-44 years	14.7	13.2	3.9	2.8
45 years and over	10.01	15.0	*	4.7

From National Center for Health Statistics. *Health, United States, 1993.* Hyattsville MD: Public Health Service, 1994.
* Too small to calculate.

death rates were greater among white than black Americans. Over the next 30 years, cirrhosis death rates more than tripled among black men, while increasing only slightly among white men. During the same period, black women's cirrhosis death rates more than doubled, while there was a negligible increase among white women.[51]

In 1991, the cirrhosis death rate for black males was 17.4, far greater than the 11.2 which was the rate for white males. In fact, although the cirrhosis death rates for black males have been steadily declining since 1970, the rate in 1991 was still almost twice the 1950 rate. This is in contrast to the rate for white males which, after also peaking in 1970, had fallen below the 1950 level by 1991. While black and white females both also experienced peaks in cirrhosis death rates in 1970, the 1991 rate of 4.8 for white females was significantly less than it was in 1950 and about half as much as the black female rate of 8.2 in 1991. This 1991 rate for black females dwarfed their 1950 rate of 5.7.[52] While cirrhosis death in African Americans has been primarily attributed to alcohol consumption, their excess mortality underscores a special and complex vulnerability that extends beyond the mere consumption of alcohol and suggests an interactive etiology.[60]

Alcohol consumption also contributes to cancer of the esophagus. Between 1979 and 1981, the incidence rate of esophageal cancer among black men aged 25 to 34 was 10 times greater than it was among white men of the same age group.[11] In 1991 the incidence rate of 15.1 for black males of all ages was still almost three times the rate of 5.6 for all ages of white males. Conversely, the five-year esophageal cancer survival rate, during the period 1983 to 1990 in selected geographic areas in the US, was 5.5 for black males and 9.9 for white males.[52] Given the consistent finding that black males consume alcohol at largely equivalent or lower rates than white males, these differentials would seem to confirm that there are certain cofactors, peculiar to the African-American experience, that synergistically interact with alcohol in the etiology of these problems.[72,66]

Other Drug Use and Related Problems

The information about other drug use in the African-American community is even less reliable than it is regarding alcohol use. The typical observation is that illegal drug use is a highly prevalent and widely pervasive problem in African-American communities across the nation. By the use of indirect and controversial indices such as arrest records, admissions for treatment, emergency room episodes, and medical examiner data, the proportion of African Americans among drug abusers has been placed above 22%.[25] In particular localities, this proportion

may be considerably higher. In the 23 cities contributing to the Drug Use Forecasting Annual Report in 1993, the proportions of booked African-American male arrestees testing positive for drugs ranged from 60% to 86%, while the proportions for African-American females ranged from 46% to 87%.[54]

Alcohol is joined in popularity by heroin, cocaine (crack), marijuana, and PCP among African Americans. Because heroin or cocaine is involved in two-thirds of drug-related deaths, it should be no surprise that black men are more than twice as likely as white men to die from the direct effects of illicit drugs. Similarly, black women are nearly twice as likely as white women to die from drug use. In the 10-year period between 1979 and 1989, for example, the drug-related death rate for black men rose 133% compared to a 50-percent increase for both white men and black women and a decline in the rate for white women.[41]

In 1992 African-American males represented 38.4% while African-American females represented 18.9% of nonfatal emergency room episodes related to cocaine use, far in excess of their proportions in the national population. For African-American males, this proportion is 6.5 times their proportion in the national population, and for African-American females, 2.9 times their proportion in the national population.[52] Table 10-3 indicates that these rates have grown since 1985 for both African-American males and African-American females, signaling increases in problems with the use, if not increases in the use, of cocaine. Significantly, although the numbers of cocaine-related emergency room episodes have increased for every group, the proportions for both white males and white females have declined since 1985.[54]

In contrast to these indices, the reported use of both marijuana and cocaine by African-American respondents to household surveys in 1992, in the age range 18 to 25, is lower than that of white respondents: 12% and 11% for marijuana and 2.0% and 1.4% for cocaine.[52] Note that although only 1.4% of African-American respondents reported cocaine use in 1992,

Table 10-3. Cocaine-Related Emergency Room Episodes by Sex and Race: United States, 1985-1992

Selected years	Males		Females	
	Black	White	Black	White
1985	28.3	26.2	13.7	14.3
1987	31.7	23.0	17.0	11.9
1989	30.0	22.5	16.0	12.0
1992	38.4	17.8	18.9	8.4

From National Center for Health Statistics. *Health, United States, 1993.* Hyattsville MD: Public Health Service, 1994.

the same age cohort, in the same year, represented 8.8% of cocaine-related emergency episodes; an even greater proportion than white respondents who had reported more cocaine use.[52] These inconsistencies have been explained by recognizing that household surveys miss significant groups of high-risk, marginal African Americans in this society, such as homeless, institutionalized, and incarcerated persons.[41,22,68,57]

Given the types of drugs that American Africans seem to prefer, there is a greater risk for hepatitis B, infectious endocarditis, and HIV/AIDS. In fact, the black male death rate from AIDS of 52.9 per 100,000 is more than three times higher than the white male death rate of 16.7, while the black female death rate of 12.0 is also more than nine times higher than the white female death rate of 1.3. Note that this is an exploding problem, particularly for Americans of African descent. In the 12-month period ending on September 30, 1993, the relative incidence rates of AIDS cases should be alarming. For every 100,000 African-American males over the age of 13 years, there were 244.3 cases diagnosed during that period. This was more than four times the equivalent rate of 54.3 for white males. Still more disconcerting was the incidence rate of black females, which at 64.3 was almost 14 times the rate of white women at 4.6.[52] The considerable contributions of injecting and other drug use, including alcohol consumption, to these incidence and mortality rates have been acknowledged.[41,68,64]

Another cause of death for which African-American males had excessive rates in 1991 is homicide. The homicide rate among black males was almost eight times in excess of the rate among white males, while black females had almost five times the homicide rate of white females. This differential is most arresting in the 15 to 24 age cohort, where the black male rate is more than nine times the white male rate.[52] The use and/or distribution of alcohol and other drugs have been implicated in more than 70% of African-American homicide incidents.

Typically, in discussions of substance abuse, tobacco abuse and addiction are benefited by a conspiracy of silence. As addictive as this substance is, its use tends to be treated as quasi-acceptable. Even in substance abuse treatment and self-help recovery settings, tobacco is accorded a benign character. Its contribution to the excess mortality of African Americans qualifies it as one of the most dangerous drugs used by them. Indeed, African Americans smoke more and quit less than European Americans. In 1992, 35.3% of black males and 26.8% of black females, contrasted with 27.6% of white males and 25.1% of white females, over age 25, were current smokers. The slightly greater consumption of tobacco still does not seem to explain the differentials in death rates from cancer of the respiratory system and diseases of the heart, particularly disfavoring

Table 10-4. Death Rates from Respiratory Cancer and Heart Disease According to Sex and Race: United States, 1991

Cause of death	Males		Females	
	Black	White	Black	White
Respiratory cancer	88.4	58.1	27.4	26.8
Heart disease	272.7	196.1	165.5	100.7

From National Center for Health Statistics. *Health, United States, 1993.* Hyattsville MD: Public Health Service, 1994.

African-American males.[52] Table 10-4 depicts the pertinent rates.

Urban African-American Youth

The realities of race and class in the US have left their impact on the contemporary American city. Thus, the terms *urban youth* or *urban adolescent* are almost interchangeable with the term *national minority youth.* In 1991 the total US population was a little more than 252 million, of which approximately 12.4% were African Americans.[52] The majority of these, some 31 million African Americans, live in urban areas; and with white flight to the suburbs, more large cities have gained a majority African-American population.[33] When the increasing Hispanic American and Asian American populations are added, the majority of urban youth are found to be from ethnic groups outside the ethnic and cultural mainstream of this society.[25]

As a consequence, these young people and the communities they represent are beset by a variety of social problems.[10] They constitute a disproportionately large number of America's indigent youth. In 1992 more than 46% of African-American children under age 18 lived in families that exist on the "precipice of desperation," below the Federal poverty level.[52,47] Their educational and employment records are profiles of failure and underdevelopment. The school dropout rate among African-American urban youth is estimated to be 50%. Unemployment among African-American adolescents hovers around 40%. Many of these young people are confronted with idleness, gang membership, crime, violence, pregnancy, drug use, and drug distribution, all of which ironically appear to be more feasible in their communities than education and gainful employment.[11]

However, there are major consequences. Over the past 5 years, juvenile drug arrests more than tripled in many of the nation's largest cities. In 5 out of 12 cities sampled for juvenile drug use forecasting in 1993, African-American males had the highest proportions of juvenile arrestees. The proportions ranged from a high of 96% in Washington DC to a low of 53% in Indianapolis. In the remaining seven cities, all but one reflect the disproportionate involvement of Hispanic male youth.[55] While these reported patterns are undoubtedly an artifact of the cities selected, the dominance of national minority youth in juvenile arrests is a national shame.

Even more alarming is the escalation of violent and homicidal episodes that are clearly driven by the proliferation of retail drug sales in inner-city neighborhoods. Uzi submachine guns, 357 Magnums, and MAC 10s, easily acquired from huge drug sale profits, have recently become associated with a frightening increase in juvenile murder. As competing gangs engage in open combat over drug sales territory, many innocent bystanders become homicide statistics.[16] Homicide is the number one cause of death among young African-American men aged 15 to 24, and as observed earlier, the African-American mortality rate is almost eight times the white rate in this age cohort.[52] Although it is generally acknowledged that alcohol and other drugs are implicated in the majority of homicides, the multiple ways in which the use and distribution of alcohol and other drugs facilitate homicide incidents are still mystifying.

These patterns of increase in adolescent drug arrests and violence indirectly indicate that the number of urban youth who are being inducted into drug use must also be increasing. Many of the adolescent crack dealers' clients are young people, themselves. Since a vial of crack is cheap in many places, there is easy access to an instantaneous high and almost certain addiction.

The patterns of crack distribution and use that characterize the nation's central cities have been widely reported in the popular press, but the abuse of other substances, particularly heroin, marijuana, PCP, nicotine, and alcohol, should be equally alarming. The concern about nicotine and alcohol should not be limited to viewing them as gate-way drugs. Although there is some support for this gate-way hypothesis, nicotine and alcohol are dangerous drugs in their own right.[45] The addictive potential, health consequences, and excess mortality of alcohol and nicotine qualify these substances as among the most dangerous.

The effects of alcohol are often mistakenly considered to be primarily protracted and felt over the long term. However, alcohol takes an immediate toll on the nation's youth. Between 1989 and 1991, the 15 to 24 age range had the highest death rate from motor vehicle crashes in the general population. Among African Americans, this age cohort similarly had the highest death rate from motor vehicle crashes.[52] While between 1990 and 1991, the number of alcohol-related traffic fatalities dropped 10%, traffic crashes remain the single greatest cause of death among American youth, and almost half of all traffic fatalities are alcohol related.[41]

Table 10-5. Past-Month Drug Use by 8th and 12th Graders by Specific Substance, Race, and Sex: United States, 1992

Drugs	8th graders		12th graders	
	Black	White	Black	White
Marijuana	3.7	4.6	10.8	16.7
Cocaine	0.3	0.5	0.4	1.2
Inhalants	2.9	5.8	1.3	2.7
Alcohol	20.6	26.7	38.9	54.8
Cigarettes	7.7	18.1	10.9	34.6

From National Center for Health Statistics. *Health, United States, 1993.* Hyattsville MD: Public Health Service, 1994.

In 1992 household interviews regarding the use of selected substances in the past month by people aged 12 to 17 revealed that except in the case of cocaine, white respondents reported higher proportions than black respondents. Even in the case of cocaine, the differential was negligible: 0.2% for black respondents and 0.1% for white respondents. However, in the cases of alcohol, marijuana, and cigarettes, the white proportions (17%, 4%, and 12%) were consistently higher than the black proportions (13%, 3%, and 3%) respectively.[52] In focusing on the past-month use by eighth and twelfth graders, this dominant pattern of greater use among white young people persists (Table 10-5).[52]

Despite the consistent findings regarding greater use among white youth,[63,2,18,57,21,17] in the minds of many the drug use/distribution problem is the most significant one confronting African-American urban communities.[57] The recognition that the high school and household surveys fail to capture the prevalence of drug use among certain higher-risk populations (e.g., school dropouts, juvenile delinquents, and homeless people) helps to foster this popular view.[41,22,68,57] These subpopulations have been reported to have higher rates of prevalence.[57,59] The perception of a dramatic escalation of drug use and the proliferation of associated problems had also been fostered by the significant attention given to this face of the problem in the popular press.[16,44,48] The value of these articles lies in their focus on the social environments from which drug involvement emerges.

ETIOLOGY: A DIFFERENT PERSPECTIVE

The level of devastation of African Americans associated with substance abuse demands that professional attention be directed at deciphering the factors that combine to create this special vulnerability. Health care professionals generally use etiological models that are person-centered. This tendency is a product of their training and the fact that interventions with individuals are easier to accomplish than interventions in social systems. However, person-centered approaches to the etiology of drug abuse, especially those that emphasize biological factors, fail to explain the over-representation of African Americans among drug-abusing populations. They also do not acknowledge the racially and culturally differentiated conditions that influence the onset of substance abuse.[65,23,40] Moreover, such approaches fail to account for the relatively recent nature of these excessive use patterns.

Many analysts of substance abuse among African-descended Americans assert that, while there are both biogenetic and person-specific psychological contributors, the environment in which African Americans are sequestered offers the primary causes of substance abuse.[9,10,38,43,56,62,67,68] Frantz Fanon was a psychiatrist who, years after his death, has continued to receive wide recognition in some circles for his insightful analysis of behavioral disorders in the context of oppressive social systems. Fanon[27] chided those seeking to "explain everything by movements of the psyche, deliberately leaving out of account the special character of the social situation." He argued that, " . . . the events giving rise to the disorder are chiefly the bloodthirsty and pitiless atmosphere and the firm impression that people have of being caught up in a veritable apocalypse."[27]

This perspective is central to a reconsideration of the causes of substance abuse in African Americans. It is relevant to any attempt to enhance the effectiveness of health care professionals with African-American patients. Undoubtedly, substance abuse among African Americans is symptomatic of a larger societal dilemma. Most Americans of African ancestry live their lives in what has been called the "mundane extreme environment."[61] These environments are viewed as the products of sociostructural racism, which is being defined as the historical and systematic arrangement of productive and social relations in this society so that they, without extraordinary intervention, develop a certain racial group and, dialectically, underdevelop other racial groups.[5] This form of racism is the most lethal because it gives the overwhelming impression of representing the "natural order of things." It is the least discernible, although it imposes the greatest hardships on the largest number of persons, and it is a major contributor to premature deaths.[15]

In turn, this sociostructural arrangement yields institutional, interpersonal, and intrapersonal racism. It pervades the prevailing values, social relations, the entire environment; indeed, even individual psyches.[15] The extreme environments in which most American Africans live are characterized by poverty in a society with a materialistic ethic; by unemployment and underemployment; by lack of education or miseduca-

tion; by dense clustering of persons in inadequate housing; by inadequate or unavailable health care; by disempowerment and dependency; and by environmental pollutants, including the relatively excessive availability of alcohol, tobacco, and other drugs.[61]

The following excerpt illustrates life in the extreme environment:

Like most young American people, they are material girls and boys. They crave the glamorous clothes, cars and jewelry they see advertised on TV, the beautiful things that only big money can buy. But many have grown up in fatherless homes, watching their mothers labor at low paying jobs or struggle to stretch a welfare check. With the unemployment rate for African-American teenagers at 37%, little work is available to unskilled, poorly educated youths. The handful of jobs that are open—flipping burgers, packing groceries—pay only minimum wages or "chump change," in the street vernacular. So these youngsters can turn to the most lucrative option they can find. In rapidly growing numbers, they are becoming the new criminal recruits of the inner city, the children who deal crack.[44]

The fact is that many urban adolescents, caught up in the drug world, are enticed by the big money associated with the trade but not by the drugs.[12] In a major market like New York City, an aggressive teenage dealer can make as much as $3000 a day. Even the entry-level 9- and 10-year-old lookouts make $100 a day.[44]

Added to these socioeconomic challenges, these young people live their lives in a profound cultural, psychological, and spiritual crisis with features and dimensions that interplay to create a synergistic vulnerability.[4] It is perhaps this phenomenon, more than any other, that predisposes African-American adolescents to excessive rates of self-destructive behaviors, including substance abuse.[15] Despite the possibility of a causal relationship between these factors and substance abuse, there is very little elaboration, beyond mere acknowledgment, of this etiological complex in establishment mental health literature and clinical practice.

It has been suggested that the most visible signs of endemic societal inequity such as sociostructural racism are when differential rates of mortality, morbidity, and incarceration disfavor certain groups (e.g., races) in the same society.[16] African Americans, particularly African-American men, in this society, live with a comparatively higher risk than do white people not only of incarceration but of morbidity and premature death. It was reported that in the US, there are at least 30 states where African-American prisoners constitute 25% to 95% of the total prison population. Yet there are only seven states and the District of

Columbia where African-American citizens represent 20% or more of the total population.[13] In 1991, African-American men, who constitute only about 5.9% of the nation's population, represented 45.5% of male state prison inmates. African-American women, 6.5% of the national population, represented 46% of female state prison inmates. In the Federal system, African Americans contributed 33.8% of prisoners in 1993.[46] Table 10-6 illustrates the racially correlated disparity, which also holds true for illness and death.

Indices of morbidity such as "limitation of activity caused by chronic conditions" and "respondent-assessed health status" conform to the established pattern of excessive African-American health problems. Of course, black men and women have the highest rates of hypertension and obesity, respectively, in comparison with each other and with white men and women.[52] It is, therefore, consistent that when death rates from 15 leading causes are compared among black and white Americans, black men are found to have the highest rate for each major cause and for all causes combined except diabetes mellitus, chronic obstructive pulmonary diseases, and suicide. Black women have the highest mortality rates for diabetes mellitus, and white men die more as a result of the other two causes. In fact, black males' combined death rate from all causes, the highest rate of excessive mortality of any race/sex group in the US, is 1.7 times greater than the next highest combined death rate (white males), while black females' combined death rate from all causes is 1.6 times greater than the next highest female rate (white females) (Table 10-7).[51]

The tendency to single-mindedly focus on a preferred problem in a social vacuum needs to be resisted. This preferred problem myopia prevents health care professionals from recognizing that a sinister and consistent pattern emerges in infancy and continues throughout the tragically abbreviated lives of African-descended people in America. The emergence of the same pattern in almost every case, disfa-

Table 10-6. Percentage of National Population, 1991, State and Federal Prisoners According to Race and Sex: United States, 1993

Race/Sex	National population	State prison population	Federal population
White males	40.9	35.4	
White females	42.7	36.2	
Black males	5.9	45.5	33.8
Black females	6.5	46.0	

From Maguire K; Pastore AL, eds. *Source Book of Criminal Justice Statistics 1993*. Washington DC: Department of Justice, 1994.

Table 10-7. Death Rates for All Causes by Race and Sex: United States, 1989-1991

	Death rate per 100,000	
	Male	Female
African Americans	1062.0	582.4
Asians	369.0	222.2
Europeans	642.7	370.3
Hispanics	521.3	284.5
Native Americans	582.6	340.6

From National Center for Health Statistics. *Health, United States, 1986*. Washington DC: Government Printing Office, 1986.

voring African-American people, and especially African-American males, could not simply be a function of chance. In particular cases such as homicide, the differential between young black and white males is so large that it demands analysis of the sociostructural context in which these problems emerge.

Thus, the approach to etiology being advanced here requires a multi-factorial, multigenerational, and interactive understanding of causes.[1] It resists precise, linear, cause-effect models and favors a willingness to view some causes as effects, themselves.[17] A useful analogy might be an etiological tree with the "root" or primary causes being historical and sociostructural factors. These then give rise to "trunk" or secondary causes composed of microecological factors. These, in turn, give rise to "branch" or tertiary causes that are familial and person-specific factors. This approach is consistent with the public health paradigm that simultaneously locates causes in the environment, in the disease-bearing vector or agent, and in the host, and attempts to attenuate risk in each of these dimensions. To limit one's attention and interventions only to the tertiary end with individuals and their immediate families, however successful one's efforts are, is to co-exist, and tacitly collaborate with, the very conditions that spawn the malformations that one is attempting to remediate. Health professionals are, therefore, obligated to evolve a professional balance between prevention and treatment.

PREVENTION ISSUES

To address the substance abuse problem in youth, communities should be helped to decide precisely what it is they wish to prevent. Clearly, pathogenic environments could be targeted as efforts are made to contribute to the development of humanizing ecologies. Interventions might also be directed at the availability and promotion of the agents—the various mood-altering substances—themselves. These categories of activities require social policy correctives and demand different skills from prevention professionals. Even when the focus is on the host, decisions still might be made to clarify the specific targets of prevention efforts. Is it "any drug use" (experimental or recreational) that should be prevented? Or is it "drug abuse" (problematic or addictive) that should be prevented? The more democratic or inclusive the discussion of these and related questions, the larger the constituency that will adopt the clarified policies and boundaries.

Ultimately, efforts to prevent substance abuse problems among African Americans must target fundamental social change. Specifically, it will require that adequate education, full employment, adequate housing, universal health care, and political empowerment be among the targets of prevention programs. These targets, concerned as they are with the environment, can seem less intimidating to individual health care professionals if they are conceptualized within a traditional public health framework that distinguishes the host, the agent, and the environment from each other. Although the boundaries between these dimensions are fluid, the model has been generally accepted and useful. The attainment of public health objectives is significantly hampered in any environment characterized by social injustice.

Unfortunately, most drug abuse prevention activities are targeted at the *host* (the individual); but while it is important to understand and manipulate the dynamics of innate or acquired individual vulnerability, expending the bulk of prevention resources on individual-centered activities can hardly be defended. Social policy prevention strategies targeted at the *agent* (drugs) are certainly more defensible. These efforts to reduce drug availability, including tobacco and alcohol, have not enjoyed a great deal of official favor. They have been overshadowed by demand-reduction initiatives, which tend to be focused on individual behavioral change. Moreover, the distinction between supply and demand is, in many ways, spurious, especially in the case of the African-American colony. When policymakers do not recognize this, the result is simplistic "Just Say No" demand-reduction strategies, in contempt of African-Americans' objective victimization.

Minimizing the importance of targeting the production and distribution of mood-altering substances is particularly cynical when the host or the victim is African American and is virtually absent from the upper echelon of the narco-industry. The supply/demand transaction is all too reminiscent of the master/slave relationship in that the significant decisions about the production and distribution of legal and illegal drugs are made by others. The power to deploy ships, planes, and 18-wheelers; to provide warehousing; and to corrupt governments—like the power to establish and license liquor outlets and to selectively inundate African-American communities with pro-drug advertisement—is not possessed by many African Americans. At best, the participation of the African-American community is at the level of collaboration.[35] Therefore, the easy accessibility of mood-altering substances in African-American communities must be a target for prevention activities.

The relatively recent entry of the term *high-risk youth* in the lexicon of substance abuse professionals was spearheaded by the US Center for Substance Abuse Prevention. Although the potential for labeling individual youth, by situating the "risk" in them, is there, the term does represent federal acknowledgement that certain segments of this society do experience a differential vulnerability to substance abuse problems.[12] Given the social injustice historically developed in this society, targeting particular prevention trials to identified high-risk youth has resulted in the over-representation of national minority, particularly African Americans, youth in these projects. Although there is little reliable information about the exact extent of drug use among high-risk urban youth, anyone who lives or works in their communities can attest to the presence and magnitude of the drug-related problems that exacerbate their already-complicated lives.

Success at the level of inoculating or "drug-proofing" African Americans—interventions directed at the *host*—will be enhanced if the special psychocultural malady of African-American psyches is addressed. Theorists of African psychology suggest that cultural domination is *the* fundamental crisis facing African Americans.[42] The increasingly excessive prevalence of substance abuse problems among African-descended persons must be understood as a function of the gradual erosion of their cultural insulation.

While this cultural erosion has been a protracted, historical process, its pace was accelerated by desegregation and assimilation. The dismantling of the Jim Crow arrangements, as desirable as that was, is now regarded by some as a bitter-sweet victory. Significant elements of cultural identity and other factors that tended to insulate African Americans from social pathogens have been deserted for "Americanism," which places a high value on material wealth and individualism. The reality is that materialism, even if it were healthy, is the exclusive domain of the favored, and individualism in a racially unjust society constitutes defection.

Most African Americans exist in a cultural wilderness in which material voyeurism and self-deprecation are the norms. Hilliard, one of America's leading scholars of African psychology, cautions, "No people can be liberated who are cultural neuters. Individuals may survive as shooting stars with temporary spurts of speed but with a curved path that ends in darkness. It is the group that survives as an eternal galaxy."[39] The survival of the group is now seriously threatened, in that African-American men are frequently referred to as an endangered species. By the year 2000, one analyst estimated, 70% of all African-American men in the US will be dead, in jail, on drugs, or in the throes of alcoholism.[36] Another calculated that if criminal justice patterns in place in 1992 continued, 40% of all African-American males between the ages of 18 and 35 will be incarcerated by the year 2000. And by the year 2010, three-quarters of all young African-American men in this nation will be in prison on an average day.[49] This collective condition, and particularly the pandemic rates of avoidable mortality discussed earlier, could well be interpreted as the final stage of a historical process that " . . . first killed the being spiritually and culturally before seeking to destroy it physically."[26]

If this dismal prospect for the masses of African Americans is to be avoided, in the absence of major social correctives, certain dynamic psychocultural processes have to be reversed. The protracted, multigenerational inculcation of dependency on others for life-support arrangements, as well as for group and personal definitions, must be reversed. Cultural distortions derived from self-deprecation and the slavish imitation of others must be interrupted. Moreover, the adoption of values that glamorize individualism, materialism, and assimilation must be challenged.

Prevention programs developed for African-American populations must pursue the following objectives: The restoration of historical memory; the reclamation of cultural identity; the redevelopment of psychocultural self-determination; the resumption of autonomous control over African children's socialization; the resurrection of communalism in African-American communities; the redevelopment of economic self-reliance; and the restoration of spirituality.

Some of the most fundamental tenets of an African-centered worldview include communalism or the notion that the group's survival is more valued than the individual's and that individuals are not only defined by their group's collective experience but are responsible to it. Hence the practice of mutual aid and interdependence follows and is derived, in part, from cosmological ideas of universal order and interdependence as well as intergenerational connectedness. Additionally, a value orientation based on a transcendental relationship with the Divine and on submission to divine purposes is a prominent residual of pre-European-African cultural instincts.

Intervening with Youth

With youth, as with other age groups, intervention strategies must be informed by the sociocultural and historical background of those involved.[15] Addressing such issues as housing, vocational training, remedial education, job development, cultural integrity, and group self-esteem may be more valuable than personal counseling.[30] Additionally, culturally tailored activities can be most effectively implemented in ethnically and culturally homogeneous groups. Not only should the content be tailored to reflect the particular historical and collective experiences of the specific group, but the effectiveness of the tasks of preparation and intervention presupposes the participation of like-kind professionals.

Prevention or even treatment activities that incorporate the themes and issues presented here will have maximum effectiveness if they are directed at youth who are either not yet initiated into the use or distribution of drugs (especially crack-cocaine) or whose use has progressed to an advanced stage with harmful consequences. Unfortunately, the harsh realities of life for many African-American adolescents almost predispose their involvement in the lucrative drug trade. The prospect of interrupting the drug distribution or recreational drug use of inner-city youth is remote. In the absence of major social correctives, it is particularly unlikely when involvement is weighted toward drug distribution. The bizarre consequences that follow the involvement of African and other national minority youth in the drug economy make the question of legalization an appropriate and timely issue for debate, at least in those arenas where their lives are given the highest priority.

TREATMENT ISSUES

Treatment presupposes that an individual's drug use has progressed to the point of compulsive or addictive use. The question must be asked, "What distinguishes the African-American addict from other 'at risk' African Americans?" A Fanonian analysis is also useful in this context. He asserted that the "mummification of individual thinking [merely reflected], the cultural mummification, every neurosis, every abnormal manifestation in a . . . [African-American person] is the product of his or her cultural situation. [Pathology in] an individual is simply the elaboration, the formation, the eruption within the [psyche] of conflictual clusters arising in part out of the environment and in part, out of the purely personal way in which the individual reacts to these influences."[28] Thus, addictive disorders in African Americans are essentially individual reactions to a pathogenic environment.

The vulnerability of the individual includes innate and acquired attributes. It expresses itself both in terms of who gets introduced and recruited into drug use and in the duration and intensity of the drug use career. As stated before, it is important for health care professionals to have an interactive approach to substance abuse etiology. Also, in clinical encounters with African-American patients, they cannot ignore or minimize salient features of the traditional microcosmic understanding of addictive disease or the sociocultural context in which the disease emerges.

This two-pronged approach acknowledges that societal and cultural factors are implicated in the onset of substance abuse problems and must be manipulated to prevent them. However, it also acknowledges that once addiction has been established, its treatment requires specific interventions that respond to its primacy. In other words, providing an alcohol-dependent person with a job will merely result in a working alcoholic if the alcoholism is not arrested. While ultimately having a job will influence the recovering alcoholic's ability to maintain sobriety, addictive disorders must be accorded clinical primacy in recognition of their ability to undermine any other corrective interventions until they are treated in their own right.

An analogous argument is that the cessation of smoking does not cure lung cancer once it has developed. Like addictive disorders, the cure rate is unacceptably low and almost requires early onset diagnosis. The improvement of sociostructural deficits—unemployment, subhuman housing, and disempowerment—for a given African-American addict/alcoholic will not resolve his or her addiction, as such. However, these improvements will ultimately forestall relapse and support treatment gains. To the extent that these improvements also benefit the family and the microcommunity, they can potentially help inoculate the next generation against substance abuse.

The best predictors of treatment success in the mainstream addiction field include the following variables: An unalienating employment situation that the patient can re-enter after treatment; an intact, drug-free family willing to participate in the patient's treatment; and an accessible, culturally comfortable, self-help group of recovering individuals with whom the patient can affiliate for long-term support. These components are usually not present by the time African Americans come to professional attention. By that time, typically, the first two conditions are almost never present. In the third case, the level of African-American participation in traditional 12-step groups continues to be low.[71] This may occur because these groups, except under conditions of significant African-American participation and control, fail to acknowledge themes that are peculiar to the African-American collision. Similarly, cultural alienation may account both for restricted access to, and abortive experiences in, mainstream treatment programs.

Recognizing that these traditions and practices offered limited general application because they were developed to help persons whose class and cultural origins were quite dissimilar from those of most African Americans, the traditional 12 Steps were modified to be more consistent with an Africentric view of the world. The following modifications were developed as part of an Africentric treatment model.[6]

The Africentric 12-Steps

Step 1. We admitted that we were powerless over our condition in the world as African-American individuals and that our lives were unmanageable by us alone.

Step 2. We came to believe that a power and a purpose greater than our own could restore us to health and sanity.

Step 3. We made a decision to turn our will and our lives over to the Creator, whose divine purpose we seek to find through service to our group.

Step 4. We made a searching and fearless moral inventory of the condition of our group and our contribution to it.

Step 5. We admitted to the Creator, to ourselves, and to others of our group, the exact ways in which we have contributed to the condition of our group.

Step 6. We were entirely ready to have the Creator remove these defects of character and practice.

Step 7. We humbly asked the Creator to remove our shortcomings.

Step 8. We made a list of the specific ways in which we can make amends to our ancestors, family, and community, and to our children still unborn.

Step 9. We continue to make amends wherever and whenever possible except when to do so would bring injury and/or harm to our group.

Step 10. We continue to take daily inventory of our contribution to the condition of our group and promptly admit and correct any negative behaviors.

Step 11. We seek through meditation, study, and work to improve our conscious contact with the Creator, our group, and the world, seeking only for knowledge of the Creator's will for the African experience and the power to find and execute our individual purpose in it.

Step 12. Having had a spiritual and cultural awakening as a result of these steps, we try to carry this message to other impaired African Americans and practice these principles in all our affairs.

A comparison of these Africanized steps with the more conventional ones should clearly reveal the cultural differences between them. This comparison should also expose the cultural bias that is an essential part of the conventional 12 steps used in AA or NA.; their underlying values reflect a Eurocentric worldview.

It is important to point out that African Americans can be expected to react differently to the cultural assaults of white supremacy. This heterogeneity among African Americans is often noted, as it has become fashionable to emphasize these intrablack differences and thereby discredit and ignore the overwhelmingly common experiences that influence all African-American people's self-definitions.[9] The reality is that these differences are merely different reactions to the same phenomenon of racial (cultural) domination.

As an illustration of this point, the terms *assimilated, nomadic, habitual,* and *Africentric* are being substituted to represent four cultural styles identified by Bell and Evans as *acculturated, bicultural, traditional,* and *culturally-immersed.*[9] The assimilated (acculturated) African American is seen as someone in flight from his/her Africanity and locked in a desperate imitation of whites. The nomadic (bicultural) African American lives in an in-between state and is psychoculturally preoccupied with transitions and translations. The habitual (traditional) African American is comfortably expressive of the cultural habits of the American black experience. The Africentric (culturally-immersed) African American is psychoculturally oriented to the nurturance and celebration of African history, culture, values, and self-determination.

Although the fluidity of these styles, as well as the absence of pure types, is conceded, they are still significant to clinical practice because individuals primarily anchored in one or another of these styles will respond differently to white providers or to Eurocentric, mainstream treatment settings. Both the assimilated and the nomadic African American will benefit from and, in the first case, may actually prefer such therapeutic settings. Conversely, the habitual and the Africentric African American will tend to do poorly in settings that do not, at the very least, provide culturally comfortable, African-American providers in familiar settings serving African-American patients. Since the "habitual" category probably contains the most African Americans, the probability of treatment failure in the typical mainstream setting is not insignificant. Further refinement of these basic four styles has been attempted and offers interesting alternative perspectives on the heterogeneity of American Africans.[7,4]

Models of identity formation, postulated several years ago, still have clinical relevance. They underline the psychologically pivotal nature of cultural domination. One such model identifies capitulation, revitalization, and radicalization as three stages of identity formation that depict the culturaly victimized African person.[15] The first stage, capitulation, is characterized by identification with the majority oppressor culture. The second stage, revitalization, is characterized by repudiation of the dominant culture and a simultaneous romanticizing of African/black culture. The third stage, radicalization, is characterized by a critical synthesis and an unambivalent commitment to a humanizing praxis.

Another compatible model of identity formation, offering five stages, overlaps the one just described. The first of these is "pre-encounter" and is equivalent to the capitulation stage. The second stage, "encounter," represents a psychologically painful and disruptive confrontation with racism. This leads to the third stage, "immersion-emersion," comparable to the revitalization stage in the other model. The fourth stage, "internalization," is a reflective and transitional one leading to the fifth stage, "radicalization."[20] These stages articulate psychocultural themes that may define some African Americans generally or at different points in their lives. These are issues that should be taken into account when African-American patients are being engaged in therapy.[15,20]

Another similar but differently structured scheme, developed some years ago, also confirms the centrality of cultural domination to African-American psychological functioning. Rather than stages, this scheme articulates the following six styles of adaptation:[35]

- *Continued apathy*, marked by passive submission to racial inequity.
- The *counter-culture solution*, an adaptive style that adopts an exotic life-style to transcend the entire African-American struggle.
- *Seeking a piece of the action*, characterized by a high motivation to achieve competence and personal gain without regard for other African Americans.
- The *black nationalist alternative*, predicated on seeking distance from white institutions.
- The *authoritarian solution*, focused on the identification with disciplined groups such as the Nation of Islam.
- *Aware cognitive flexibility*, a commitment and posture to create new approaches and embrace a life-affirming ideology and hope.

The preceding models are highlighted to illustrate the various ways African psyches can be contorted by European cultural domination. It has been suggested by African-American psychologists that the experience of chattel slavery, the "Maafa," served as an incubator that has given rise to multigenerational, pathological adjustments.[3] It has been proposed that therapeutic interventions directed at African-American alcohol-dependent and other drug-dependent persons might be potentiated by cultivating an educated analysis of slavery and its consequences.[6] Moreover, it is crucial that health care personnel be willing to acknowledge racially engendered inequity as a reality that presents a major challenge to African-American health.[65,23] Ultimately, treatment requires the reconnection of African Americans with an African world view and spiritual ethos that predate the advent of slavery.[50]

These suggestions form a basis for tailoring treatment to the cultural needs of African-descended people. They should not, however, be construed as a replacement for conventional practices in chemical-dependency treatment. They are intended to augment traditional treatment programs which, while somewhat effective with predominantly white, middle-class patients, have a more uneven record with black and other culturally different patients.[31] The effectiveness of these programs with African-American patients will increase when health care providers confront the fact that black Americans are not "honorary whites." Africentric modifications to the standard interventions must be incorporated.

Additional issues concerning the process of treatment or counseling distinguish black patients from the white patients for whom these conventional practices were developed. Events such as the way patients are addressed, eye contact, physical proximity, touching, tone, language, and humor represent just the first level of cultural negotiation. More complex issues such as patient-role expectations, concreteness, self-disclosure, reticence, authenticity, trust, and counseling duration should all be reconsidered when the patient is consciously or unconsciously African. This is not simply because the patient's life experiences fall outside the cultural mainstream, but particularly because the patient has been oppressed by the cultural mainstream.

From Cultural Specificity to Cultural Appropriateness

What does all of this mean for the health care provider? It means that health care providers who choose to attempt to catalyze the psychological well-being of African-descended people must not merely encourage them to "Just Say No" to drugs. African-American patients must be taught to say "Yes" to their name, to their racial heritage, to the reality of racial inequity, to their history, to the need for self-determination, to their culture, to their spirituality, and to their traditional values. The African notion—"I am because we are, and because we are, therefore I am"—underscores the fact that the nurturing of individual self-esteem cannot really be accomplished without the cultivation of collective self-esteem. Strategies to inoculate African Americans from the development of substance abuse disorders must include the restoration of historical memory.

Unless this occurs, the demise of their group will not cease. As Diop asserts, "When we talk about personality . . . we can only mean a cultural personality. And what is the basis of the cultural personality of a people, African or otherwise, if not a historical and psychic . . . self-consciousness? . . . Rather than deal in generalities, we must know what the black soul is because it is our soul."[26]

Population groups in this country differ in the nature of life experiences, and they reflect different historical, socioeconomic, and cultural events, which in turn have an impact on risk factors and resiliency. Accordingly, the importance of culturally competent interventions is now being acknowledged.[70,58] As the role of culture in illness and health promotion has been increasingly considered, there has been an evolution in the definition of cultural competence. Initially, it was defined as a set of academic and interpersonal skills that allows individuals to increase their understanding and appreciation of cultural differences and similarities within, among, and between groups.[58] Others have extended the definition to incorporate a continuum that ranges from cultural destructiveness, cultural incapacity, cultural blindness, cultural precompetence, cultural competence, to cultural proficiency.[19] These terms were each given specific definitions.

Current practitioners in the field tend to use an array of terms interchangeably, e.g., "culturally relevant," "culturally specific," or "culturally sensitive". As a result, this practice has tended to introduce confusion to the attempts to fully appreciate the complex role that culture plays in the natural history and psychosocial development of substance use behavior.[58]

The lack of precision in terminology fails to highlight differences in approaches that are significant and need to be made explicit. A bizarre but certainly very clear example of cultural sensitivity is the alcohol and tobacco industries' production, marketing, and sales of particular products in African-American communities. The targeted advertising, using outdoor, electronic, and print media, reflects an exquisite sensitivity to, and exploitation of, tastes, styles, and values which, though they inhere in the culture, lend themselves to pathological behavior and dependencies.

Working primarily within the complex of African-American experiences, and ignoring the additional challenges of cross-cultural interventions, the author has been developing a typology of cultural competence with respect to interventions.[5] The framework suggests that a program could have varying degrees of cultural competence. The first level is *cultural specificity*. It refers to activities that merely target a particular cultural group, in recognition of its cultural integrity. The second level, *cultural sensitivity*, refers to programs whose interventions accommodate the cultural styles, habits, values, and preferences of the targeted group. Unfortunately, a number of programs hold this out as the desired level of cultural competence; in the process they inadvertently inculcate, into their efforts to promote health, features that are in fact pathogenic and pathological. Especially under conditions of oppression, cultural habits develop and cultural practices are adopted which reflect, if not extend, the cultural assaults a given group has historically received. It is necessary, therefore, for programs to move to a level of cultural competence for which the term *culturally appropriate* has been reserved. This level incorporates those efforts that can heal the particular cultural traumas that a given group's history presents. These might even be said to be culturally therapeutic interventions or programs. They do not merely seek to concede to certain cultural features but to transform the culture's capacity to cultivate and support healthy human development.[5]

It has been argued that interventions that qualify as culturally appropriate or therapeutic for American Africans should result in the Critical C's:

- Africentric *Consciousness* or racial self-knowledge,
- Africentric *Commitment* or racial self-preference, and
- Africentric *Conduct* or racial self-maintenance.[5]

This is because of the peculiar cultural victimization that African people have historically suffered in the US.

Attention on the Critical C's does not suggest that prevention or treatment activities directed at African-American individuals should not include information about the types of drugs used, the ways in which they are used, and their psychopharmacological effects. There is no intention to de-emphasize the need to present the progression from experimental to recreational, and then to problematic and addictive use, with their attendant physical, psychological, and social problems. There is no intention to discourage the use of the disease concept of addiction to an extent that does not medically absolve the individual of all responsibility. There is no intention to ignore that drug addiction, with its biological and psychosocial categories of dependence, requires that certain individual and familial high-risk features be clearly presented and apprehended. Finally, there is no intention to discourage the presentation of the litany of costs—whether legal, financial, health, occupational, familial, etc.—that are associated with drug use.

There is, however, the intention of suggesting that substance abuse epidemiology, highlighted by the excessive prevalence of drug-related problems among African Americans, should be subsumed within a larger picture of avoidable and excessive African-American mortality. There is every intention to recommend that the historical emergence of African-American substance abuse, introduced during slavery, be viewed as an extension of the master/slave relationship. This drama of cultivated demand and managed supply is equally prominent, irrespective of the legality of the substance. It is intended to advocate that the narco-industry, including alcohol and tobacco, with its African-American petite-dealers, advertisers, factors, and collaborators, must be exposed by our interventions.

These interventions will be appropriate opportunities to highlight high-risk considerations that affect the entire African-American community as a consequence of macro and micro racism, including intrapersonal racism or self-hatred. A cost-benefit analysis of drug distribution and use, at the level of the individual, the family, the community, and the race, creates an opportunity for introducing an Africentric axiological orientation that places the well-being of the group above that of the individual. Finally, individualized decision-making exercises, focusing on the psychological and political choices of resistance of, or collaboration in, the demise of one's own people, should be the basis of a contract to cultivate appropriate life skills. The objectives of this cultural augmentation are, as stated before, Africentric Consciousness, Africentric Commitment, and Africentric Conduct.

REFERENCES

1. Abbey A; Smith MJ; Scott RO. The relationship between reasons for drinking alcohol and alcohol consumption: An interactional approach. *Addictive Behaviors* 18(6): 659-670, 1993. (42 refs.)
2. Abma JC; Mott FL. Substance use and prenatal care during pregnancy among young women. *Family Planning Perspectives* 23 (3): 117-122. (10 refs.)
3. Akbar N. *Chains and Images of Psychological Slavery*. Jersey City NJ: New Mind Productions, 1984.
4. Amuleru-Marshall O. *Cultural Polemics on African Americans*. Washington DC: Macro Systems, Inc, 1991. (OSAP National Training System Trainers Manual)
5. Amuleru-Marshall O. *Uhuru Recovery Model: An Africentric Treatment Program*. Atlanta GA: unpublished manual, 1991.
6. Amuleru-Marshall O. Nurturing the black adolescent male: Culture, ethnicity and race. IN: Abramczyk LW; Ross JW, eds. *Nurturing the Black Adolescent Male in the Family Context: A Public Health Responsibility*. Columbia SC: University of South Carolina, 1992.
7. Amuleru-Marshall O. Political and economic implications of drugs in the African-American community. IN: Goddard LL, ed. *An African-centered Model of Prevention for High Risk Youth*. Rockville MD: Center for Substance Abuse Prevention, 1993. (27 refs.)
8. Barr KEM; Farrell, MP; Barnes GM. Race, class and gender differences in substance abuse: Evidence of middle-class/underclass polarization among black males. *Social Problems* 40(3): 314-327, 1993. (17 refs.)

9. Bell P; Evans J. *Counseling the Black Client: Alcohol Use and Abuse in Black America*. Center City MN: Hazelden Foundation, 1981.

10. Beverly C. The limitations of prevention in addiction services. IN: Wright R; Watts TD, eds. *Prevention of Black Alcoholism: Issues and Strategies*. Springfield IL: Charles C. Thomas, 1985. (21 refs.)

11. Billingsley A. Black families in a changing society. IN: Dewart J, ed. *The State of Black America 1987*. New York: National Urban League Inc, 1987. (34 refs.)

12. Black MM; Ricardo IB. Drug use, drug trafficking, and weapon carrying among low-income, African-American, early adolescent boys. *Pediatrics* 93(6): 1065-1072, 1994. (43 refs.)

13. Brickhouse WJ. *Black Men in Prison: What Might the Over-Representation in Numbers Mean?* Presented at the American Psychological Association 96th Annual Meeting, August 12-16, Atlanta GA, 1988.

14. Brown LP. Crime in the black community. IN: Dewart J, ed. *The State of Black America 1988*. New York: National Urban League Inc, 1988. (61 refs.)

15. Bulhan HA. *Frantz Fanon and the Psychology of Oppression*. New York: Plenum Press, 1985.

16. Church GJ. Thinking the unthinkable. *Time*, May 30, 1988.

17. Cooper ML; Peirce RS; Huselid RF. Substance use and sexual risk taking among black adolescents and white adolescents. *Health Psychology* 13(3): 251-262, 1994. (40 refs.)

18. Cornelius MD; Day NL; Cornelius JR; Geva D; Taylor PM; Richardson GA. Drinking patterns and correlates of drinking among pregnant teenagers. *Alcoholism: Clinical and Experimental Research* 17(2): 290-294, 1993. (24 refs.)

19. Cross TL; et al. *Towards a Culturally Competent System of Care. Volume I: A Monograph on Effective Services for Minority Children Who Are Severely Emotionally Disturbed*. Washington DC: Georgetown University Child Development Center, 1989.

20. Cross WE. The Thomas and Cross models of psychological nigrescence: A review. *Journal of Black Psychology* 5: 13-31, 1978.

21. Crowley JE. Educational status and drinking patterns: How representative are college students? *Journal of Studies on Alcohol* 52(1): 10-16, 1991. (26 refs.)

22. Curtiss MA; Lenz KM; Frei NR. Medical evaluation of African-American women entering treatment. *Journal of Addictive Diseases* 12(4): 29-43, 1993. (30 refs.)

23. Darrow SL; Russell M; Cooper ML; Mudar P; Frone MR. Sociodemographic correlates of alcohol consumption among African-American and white women. *Women and Health* 18(4): 35-49, 1992. (25 refs)

24. Dembo R; Schmeidler J; Burgos W; Taylor R. Environmental setting and early drug involvement among inner-city junior high school youths. *International Journal of the Addictions* 20(8): 1239-1255, 1985. (37 refs.)

25. Department of Health and Human Services, Subcommittee on Chemical Dependency. *Report of the Secretary's Task Force on Black and Minority Health, Volume VII. Chemical Dependency and Diabetes*. Washington DC: Department of Health and Human Services, 1985. (170 refs.)

26. Diop CA. Civilization or barbarism: An authentic anthropology. IN: Van Sertima I, ed. *Great African Thinkers, Volume 1*. New Brunswick NJ: Transaction Books, 1986. (107 refs.)

27. Fanon F. *The Wretched of the Earth*. New York: Random House Inc, 1968.

28. Fanon F. *Toward the African Revolution*. New York: Grove Press, 1969.

29. Farrell AD; Anchors DM; Danish SJ; Howard CW. Risk factors for drug use in urban adolescents: Identification and cross validation. *American Journal of Community Psychology* 20(3): 263-285, 1992. (19 refs.)

30. Ford DS. Factors related to the anticipated use of drugs by urban junior high school students. *Journal of Drug Education* 13(2): 187-197, 1983. (8 refs.)

31. Groves GA; Amuleru-Marshall O. Chemical use and dependency among African Americans. IN: Livingston LL, ed. *Handbook of Black American Health: The Mosaic of Conditions, Issues, Policies and Prospects*. Westport CT: The Greenwood Publishing Group, 1994. (32 refs.)

32. Hare BR. Black youth at risk. IN: Dewart J, ed. *The State of Black America*, 1988. New York: National Urban League Inc, 1988. (20 refs.)

33. Harper FD. Alcohol use and alcoholism among black Americans: A review. IN: Watts TD; Wright R, eds. *Black Alcoholism: Toward a Comprehensive Understanding*. Springfield IL: Charles C. Thomas, 1983. (50 refs.)

34. Harper FD; Dawkins MP. Alcohol and blacks: Survey of the periodical literature. *British Journal of Addiction* 71(2): 327-334, 1976. (13 refs)

35. Harrell JP. Analyzing black coping styles: A supplemental diagnostic system. *Journal of Black Psychology* 5: 99-108, 1979.

36. Herbers J. More blacks slip into poverty. *San Francisco Chronicle*, January 28, 1987.

37. Herd D. We cannot stagger to freedom: A history of blacks and alcohol in American politics. IN: Brill L; Winick C, eds. *Yearbook of Substance Use and Abuse, Volume 3*. New York: Human Sciences Press, 1985. (102 refs.)

38. Herd D; Grube J. Drinking contexts and drinking problems among black and white women. *Addiction* 88(8): 1101-1110, 1993. (13 refs.)

39. Hilliard AG. The cultural unity of black Africa: The domains of patriarchy and matriarchy in classical antiquity. IN: Van Sertima I; Williams L, eds. *Great African Thinkers, Volume 1*. New Brunswick NJ: Transaction Books, 1986. (28 refs.)

40. Huselid RF; Cooper ML. Gender roles as mediators of sex differences in adolescent alcohol use and abuse. *Journal of Health and Social Behavior* 33(December): 348-362, 1992. (48 refs.)

41. Institute for Health Policy. *Substance Abuse: The Nation's Number One Health Problem*. Princeton NJ: Robert Wood Johnson Foundation, 1993.

42. Jahannes JA. Substance abuse and the legacy of racism. *Journal of the National Medical Association* 79(5): 473-475, 1987.

43. King L. Alcoholism: Studies regarding black Americans. IN: NIAAA. *Alcohol and Health Monograph 4: Special Population Issues*. Rockville MD: National Institute on Alcohol Abuse and Alcoholism, 1982. (101 refs.)

44. Lamar JV. Kids who sell crack. *Time*, May 9, 1988.

45. Maddahian E; Newcomb MD; Bentler PM. Single and multiple patterns of adolescent substance use: Longitudinal comparisons of four ethnic groups. *Journal of Drug Education* 15(4): 311-326, 1985. (21 refs.)

46. Maguire K; Pastore AL, eds. *Source Book of Criminal Justice Statistics 1993*. Washington DC: Department of Justice, 1994.

47. Marable M. *How Capitalism Underdeveloped Black America*. Boston MA: South End Press, 1983.

48. Media statement delivered by LD Johnston at a news conference. Washington DC: Office of the Secretary of Health and Human Services, January 13, 1988.

49. Miller JG. *Search and Destroy: The Plight of African-American Males in the Criminal Justice System*. Alexandria VA: National Center on Institutions and Alternatives, 1992.

50. Myers LJ. *Understanding an Afrocentric World View: Introduction to an Optimal Psychology*. Dubuque IA: Kendall/Hunt Publishing Company, 1988.

51. National Center for Health Statistics. *Health, US, 1986*. Washington DC: Government Printing Office, 1987.

52. National Center for Health Statistics. *Health, US, 1993*. Hyattsville MD: Public Health Service, 1994.

53. National Institute on Alcohol Abuse and Alcoholism. *Sixth Special Report to the U.S. Congress on Alcohol and Health*. Rockville MD: National Institute on Alcohol Abuse and Alcoholism, 1987. (Chapter refs.)

54. National Institute of Justice. *Drug Use Forecasting: 1993 Annual Report on Adult Arrestees: Drugs and Crime in America's Cities*. Washington DC: Government Printing Office, 1994.

55. Nobles WW; et al. *The Culture of Drugs in the Black Community*. Oakland CA: A Black Family Institute Publication, 1987.

56. Oetting ER; Beauvais F. Adolescent drug use: Findings of national and local surveys. *Journal of Consulting and Clinical Psychology* 58(4): 385-394, 1990. (40 refs.)

57. Orlandi MA. The challenge of evaluating community-based prevention programs: A cross cultural perspective. IN: Orlandi MA; Weston R; LG Epstein, eds. *Cultural Competence for Evaluators: A Guide for Alcohol and other Drug Abuse Prevention Practitioners Working with Ethnic/Racial Minorities*. Rockville MD: Office for Substance Abuse Prevention, 1992. (44 refs.)

58. Padgett D; Struening EL; Andrews H. Factors affecting the use of medical, mental health, alcohol, and drug treatment services for homeless adults. *Medical Care* 28(9): 805-821, 1990. (36 refs.)

59. Parrish KM; Dufour MC; Stinson FS; Harford TC. Average daily alcohol consumption during adult life among decedents with and without cirrhosis: The 1986 National Mortality Followback Survey. *Journal of Studies on Alcohol* 54(4): 450-456, 1983. (21 refs.)

60. Pierce CM. The ghetto: An extreme sleep environment. *Journal of the American Medial Association* 67(2): 162-166, 1975. (10 refs.)

61. Primm BJ. Drug use: Special implications for black America. IN: Dewart J, ed. *The State of Black America 1987*. New York: National Urban League Inc, 1987. (40 refs.)

62. Ringwalt CL; Palmer JH. Differences between white and black youth who drink heavily. *Addictive Behaviors* 15(5): 455-460, 1990. (14 refs.)

63. Rotheram-Borus MJ; Rosario M; Meyer-Bahlburg HFL; Koopman C; Dopkins SC; Davies M. Sexual and substance use acts of gay and bisexual male adolescents in New York City. *The Journal of Sex Research* 31(1): 47-57, 1994. (50 refs.)

64. Russell M; Cooper ML; Frone MR. The influence of sociodemographic characteristics of familial alcohol problems: Data from a community sample. *Alcoholism: Clinical and Experimental Research* 14(2): 221-226, 1990. (19 refs.)

65. Taylor J; Jackson B. Factors affecting alcohol consumption in black women, Part II. *International Journal of the Addictions* 25(12): 1415-1427, 1990. (15 refs.)

66. Thornton CI; Carter JH. Treating the black female alcoholic: Clinical observations of black therapists. *Journal of the National Medical Association* 80(6): 644-647, 1988. (17 refs.)

67. Van Hasselt VB; Hersen M; Null JA; Ammerman RT; Bukstein OG; McGillivray J; et al. Drug abuse prevention for high-risk African-American children and their families: A review and model program. *Addictive Behaviors* 18(2): 213-234, 1993. (118 refs.)

68. Wash H. *Cultural Specific Treatment: A Model for the Treatment of African-American Alcoholics*. Chicago: Jetpro Graphics, 1988.

69. Wells EA; Morrison DM; Gillmore MR; Catalano RF; Iritani B; Hawkins JD. Race differences in antisocial behaviors and attitudes and early initiation of substance use. *Journal of Drug Education* 22(2): 115-130, 1992. (27 refs.)

70. Williams M. Blacks and alcoholism: Issues in the 1980s. *Alcohol Health and Research World* 6(4): 31-40, 1982. (5 refs.)

71. York JL; Biederman I. Hand movement speed and accuracy in detoxified alcoholics. *Alcoholism: Clinical and Experimental Research* 15(6): 982-990, 1991. (30 refs.)

72. Zimmerman MA; Maton KI. Life-style and substance use among male African-American urban adolescents: A cluster analytic approach. *American Journal of Community Psychology* 20(1): 121-137, 1992. (35 refs.)

FURTHER READINGS

Beatty LA. Issues in drug abuse prevention intervention research with African Americans. IN: Cazares A; Beatty LA, eds. *Scientific Methods for Prevention Intervention Research. NIDA Research Monograph 139*. Rockville MD: National Institute on Drug Abuse, 1994. pp. 171-201. (68 refs.)

Drug use and abuse arguably are the most widespread and devastating social problems affecting the American population, contributing significantly to the incidence of crime, illness, and premature death. The consequences of the abuse of licit and illicit drugs in the African-American population, however, are disproportionately more severe, with comparatively higher crime, morbidity, mortality, and family disruptions caused by drug involvement. The purpose of this chapter is to present issues that affect drug abuse prevention research with African Americans. The focus is on diversity in the African-American population; ideologic concerns; theory development; and methodology and design concerns. Copyright 1994, Project Cork Institute.

Burston BW; Jones D; Roberson-Saunders P. Drug use and African Americans: Myth versus reality. *Journal of Alcohol and Drug Education* 40(2): 19-39, 1995. (57 refs.)

The need for accurate data regarding drug use is not a necessity merely for those who are directly involved in the anti-drug movement. Accurate theory and data are needed by youth, their parents, and the general population to prevent accelerated drug use among some groups as part of a self-fulfilling prophecy. Beliefs about who uses and who does not use drugs may enhance susceptibility levels of those who are part of a stereotypical demographic segment. Similarly, beliefs about who uses and who does not use drugs may subject some groups to greater scrutiny by employers and/or by the criminal justice system. Accordingly, this paper analyzes several common beliefs about drug use in the African-American community reflected in the literature. Additionally, the paper explores the implications of such beliefs for treatment, intervention, and public policy. Copyright 1995, Project Cork Institute.

Christmon K. Historical overview of alcohol in the African-American community. *Journal of Black Studies* 25(3): 319-330, 1995. (26 refs.)

This article provides a historical overview of the use of alcohol in the African-American community. To address the issue of alcoholism in the African-American community, four dimensions of the issue are addressed: The use of alcohol in Africa, views of Africans on drunken behavior, involvement of alcohol in the enslavement of Africans, and the establishment of drinking patterns in the US among African Americans. Copyright 1995, Sage Publications, Inc.

Flewelling RL; Ennett ST; Rachal JV; Theisen AC. *National Household Survey on Drug Abuse: Race/Ethnicity, Socioeconomic Status, and Drug Abuse, 1991*. Rockville MD: Substance Abuse and Mental Health Services Administration, 1994. (27 refs.)

One of the two chief purposes of this report is to examine the prevalence of self-reported use of alcohol, cigarettes, and illicit drugs across subgroups of the US civilian, noninstitutionalized population aged 12 or older as defined by race/ethnicity and by other sociodemographic characteristics. A second purpose is to demonstrate the extent to which racial/ethnic differences in drug use prevalence may be influenced by differences in other sociodemographic characteristics measured in the NHSDA, particularly socioeconomic status (SES). Because race/ethnicity is associated with some types of drug use and also with numerous other demographic characteristics, it is likely that observed differences across racial/ethnic subgroups are attributable to other sociodemographic differences among groups. Although socioeconomic factors are obvious candidates for helping to explain racial/ethnic differences, other demographic variables may also play a role. In this report, three types of sociodemographic control measures are distinguished: Background demographic measures such as age, gender, metropolitan status, and geographic region of residence; indicators of SES; and other social and lifestyle indicators such as marital status and employment status. Public Domain.

Herd D. Predicting drinking problems among black and white men: Results from a national survey. *Journal of Studies on Alcohol* 55(1): 61-71, 1994. (31 refs.)

Abstract: This study describes the prevalence of alcohol-related problems and develops predictive models to explain racial differences in subsamples of 494 black and 568 white men from a national probability survey of drinking patterns and problems. The results showed that although black men exhibited higher mean scores on many types of alcohol-related problems, they did not report significantly higher rates of heavier behavior drinking and drunkenness, nor did they score higher on a scale of permissiveness of drinking norms. A hierarchical regression analysis indicated that race independently predicts problem scores, even when controlling for other social and demographic factors. Moreover, an interactive model showed that race interacts significantly with the frequency of heavier drinking and some sociodemographic characteristics. As frequency of heavier drinking increases, rates of drinking problems rise faster among black men than white men. Religion and unemployment also had different effects on rates of alcohol-related problems in each group of men. These findings suggest that racial differences in the prevalence of drinking problems might be related to differences in sociocultural context of drinking and in the material condition under which black and white men live. Copyright 1994, Alcohol Research Documentation, Inc.

Johnson KA; Jennison KM. Stressful loss and the buffering effect of social support on drinking behavior among African Americans: Results of a national survey. *Journal of Alcohol and Drug Education* 39(2): 1-24, 1994. (65 refs.)

This article is an analysis of stressful loss both for the individual and extended kinship network members, the buffering hypothesis, and utilitarian drinking in a national probability sample of 1478 African Americans. Multiple logistic regression analysis indicates that respondents who experienced stressful losses, or whose extended family members experienced such losses, are significantly more likely to drink excessively. Utilitarian drinking by African Americans may, therefore, in part be a reaction to life circumstances in which alcohol represents an attempt to cope with traumatic social and psychological stress. The results also indicate that supportive social resources, particularly the extended kinship network and African-American church, can attenuate or buffer the effects of negative life stressors on drinking. These important resources could be utilized more than they presently are in education prevention and treatment programs for the African-American alcoholic and problem drinker. Copyright 1994, Alcohol and Drug Problems Association of North America.

Kogan MD; Kotelchuck M; Alexander GR; Johnson WE. Racial disparities in reported prenatal care advice from health care providers. *American Journal of Public Health* 84(1): 82-88, 1994. (31 refs.)

The relationship between certain maternal behaviors and adverse pregnancy outcomes has been well documented. One method to alter these behaviors is through the advice of women's health care providers. Advice from providers may be particularly important in minority populations, who have higher rates of infant mortality and prematurity. This study examines racial disparities according to women's self-reports of advice received from health care providers during pregnancy in four areas: tobacco use, alcohol consumption, drug use, and breast-feeding. Health care providers' advice to 8310 white, non-Hispanic, and black women was obtained from the National Maternal and Infant Health Survey. After controlling for sociodemographic, utilization, and medical factors, the study indicates that African-American women were more likely to report not receiving advice from their prenatal care providers about smoking cessation and alcohol use. The difference between African Americans and Caucasians also approached significance for breast-feeding. No overall difference was noted in advice regarding cessation of drug use, although there was a significant interaction between race and marital status. These data suggest that African-American women may be at greater risk for not receiving information that could reduce their chances of having an adverse pregnancy outcome. Copyright 1994, American Public Health Association.

Lusane C, ed. *Pipe Dream Blues: Racism and the War on Drugs*. Boston: South End Press, 1991.

In 1989 the National Urban League in "The State of Black America" stated, "Substance abuse is the single major leading social, economic, and health problem confronting the African-American community." This work describes the toll that substance abuse has taken, and that has disproportionately impacted communities of color; the economic and political realities that have maintained this problem; and the gross ineffectiveness of the "war on drugs" and the manner in which this approach has obscured the roots of the illicit drug problem. The book pays particular attention to the historical and political context between the issues of drugs and racism. The work is divided into three parts. The first describes the impact of illicit drugs on communities of color; discusses how racism has influenced public policy and perceptions; describes the nature of illegal and legal drug profits, and who benefits; and examines the international side of the drug crisis and how US foreign policy has contributed to it. The second section uses the District of Columbia as a case study, the relationship to the political issues attendant to statehood for the district, and the emergence of the drug trafficking from WWII to the present. The third section sets forth a number of policy recommendations and programs that provide a basis for a more straightforward discussion of public policy initiatives regarding drugs and racism. Copyright 1994, Project Cork Institute.

Rubin RH; Billingsley A; Caldwell CH. The role of the Black church in working with Black adolescents. *Adolescence* 29(114): 251-266, 1994. (50 refs.)

Some 635 Northern African-American churches were surveyed regarding the offering of youth support programs. Of these, 176 reported having at least one program directed at adolescent non-members of the church, primarily from low-income homes. The most common programs consisted of Christian fellowships, ministry, counseling, group discussions, rap sessions, seminars, and workshops. Sports activities were second in frequency. Least common were services related to AIDS and youth health. It appears the greatest interest in youth programs is in churches that are Methodist, older, middle class, large in membership, owned or mortgaged, and with more paid clergy and staff. Characteristics of youth-oriented pastors are discussed. Generally, it was found that some of the most prominent issues facing

African-American adolescents are not being adequately addressed by African-American churches. Suggestions for improving this situation are made, as well as citations of promising programs. Copyright 1994, Libra Publishers. Used with permission.

Stanton B; Galbraith J. Drug trafficking among African-American early adolescents: Prevalence, consequences, and associated behaviors and beliefs. *Pediatrics* 93(6): 1039-1043, 1994. (22 refs.)

Drug trafficking by minority youths in low-income, urban areas has received considerable publicity from the mass media in the past half-decade. However, there has been correspondingly little exposition of this problem in the medical literature. This review provides an overview of the epidemiology and consequences of drug trafficking among urban youths and describe factors associated with drug trafficking. Existing data indicate that approximately 10% of male, urban, African-American early adolescents report having engaged in drug trafficking, with a higher percentage of youths reporting having been asked to sell drugs and/or indicating that they expect to become involved in drug trafficking. Rates increase with advancing age. Reported rates of drug trafficking are comparable to rates of tobacco and alcohol use among early adolescents and are substantially higher than use rates of illegal drugs. Drug trafficking is associated with increased mortality, accounting for one-third to one-half of homicide-related deaths in some studies. The practice is also associated with other health-risk behaviors, including nonfatal violence, substance use, and incarceration. Perceived social pressures by family members and/or peers to engage in drug trafficking and the belief that a youth's wage-earning potential is limited to drug trafficking are highly correlated with involvement in this activity. In summary, drug trafficking is a prevalent risk behavior among adolescents that has several negative health consequences. Copyright 1994, American Academy of Pediatrics.

Whitehead TL; Peterson J; Kaljee L. The "hustle": Socioeconomic deprivation, urban drug trafficking, and low-income, African-American male gender identity. *Pediatrics* 93(6): 1050-1054, 1994. (32 refs.).

Drug trafficking seems to be both prevalent and associated with considerable morbidity and mortality among inner-city African-American males. Survey data have indicated the possible importance of economic need in the rapid emergence of drug trafficking in this population. In the present study, an historical-cultural approach is used to examine this economic relationship further and to explore the role that drug trafficking plays in a society that has permitted its successful and rapid growth. Data were obtained from interviews of approximately 600 African Americans residing in inner-city neighborhoods in Washington, DC and Baltimore during nine drug- and AIDS-related studies conducted over 4 years. From the perspective of the study participants, the needs to provide economic support for one's family and to achieve some sense of status, respect, and reputation among one's peers are two core constructs of masculine identity in the US. The historical and worsening inequities in access to economic resources and power by African-American males are viewed as significantly reducing the opportunity for economic success through more social or legal enterprises. Nonmainstream activities (such as drug trafficking) are perceived as opportunities for becoming economically successful and for establishing a power base for individuals denied access to mainstream opportunities. Copyright 1994, American Academy of Pediatrics.

CHAPTER 11

Hispanics

PATRICK J. ABBOTT, MD
MARGIE TRUJILLO, PhD

CLINICAL APPLICATIONS

The goals of this chapter are to assist the clinician to:

1. Recognize the diversity and characteristics of the US Hispanic population.
2. Be familiar with the substance use patterns and attendant problems.
3. Be familiar with cultural factors that impact access to and utilization of treatment, as well as mediate the course of care.

The Hispanic population is the second largest minority population in the US, following African Americans. In the 1990 census, Hispanics numbered 22.4 million, representing 9% of the total population.[49] It is presently the fastest-growing minority group and is predicted to be the largest minority by the year 2010. Other notable characteristics of this population include a larger family size, younger median age, and less favorable socioeconomic status than the majority population.[62,47] Hispanic-American income is below the poverty level in approximately 14.9% of families vs. 9.5% of non-Hispanic families.[20,47]

Hispanic, formerly "Latino," is a term that represents a diverse and heterogeneous population, including Mexican Americans, Puerto Ricans, Cubans, and South and Central Americans. The 1990 Census reported the following breakdown according to national origin: 60% Mexican Americans, 12% Puerto Ricans, 5% Cubans, 23% origins in other countries.[47] The majority of US Hispanics live in five Southwestern states: Arizona, California, Colorado, New Mexico, and Texas. The largest segment of this population in these five states is Mexican American. Approximately 60% of the Cuban population live in Florida. Most Puerto Ricans live in the Northeast, and Central and South Americans live predominantly in East Coast cities.[25] Hispanic populations tend to cluster in large US cities. For example, Miami's Cuban population, approximately 500,000, is second only to Havana's, and Los Angeles has the second largest Hispanic population (mainly Mexican Americans) next to Mexico City. New York City's population of Puerto Ricans actually exceeds that of San Juan, Puerto Rico.

The various Hispanic ethnic groups differ widely in education, health, cultural background, income level, and language. For example, Cuban Americans have college education rates almost three times the rate of other Hispanics.[20] As a result of this tremendous cultural diversity, generalizations across populations and geography are not possible. Large epidemiologic; surveys focusing on Hispanic alcohol drug use and abuse are rare, and even more scarce are comparative studies of intra-ethnic or regional differences. However, some patterns can be established for certain populations. From both national and regional data, there appears to be higher problematic use of alcohol, heroin, inhalants, and cocaine.[10,46,53]

PATTERNS OF ALCOHOL USE
National Surveys

Two large national samples of alcohol use (1969, 1979) have been published for the entire US population.[12,20] Within these surveys of national drinking practices, Hispanics, especially men, demonstrate a greater percentage of heavy drinking. However, the sample of Hispanics was too small to generate data on intra-ethnic differences.

The first large-scale national survey of Hispanic drinking practices was conducted in 1984,[10] the result of 1453 personal interviews with respondents in their homes. The following patterns emerged:

- Among Hispanic men, 22% are abstainers and 36% drink heavily or moderately heavy.
- Hispanic men drink more heavily in their thirties than in their twenties, with consumption decreasing after age 40. This contrasts with the US general population data that shows a decrease of consumption almost a decade earlier.
- Among groups of national origin, Mexican-American men have a higher rate of abstinence and frequent heavy drinking than other Hispanic males. About 44% of Mexican Americans are in the heavy drinking category compared with 24% of Puerto Ricans, 6% of Cubans, and 24% others.
- Hispanic men drink heavier than women, and women abstain proportionally more than men, approximately 2:1.
- Most Hispanic women either abstain (47%) or drink minimally; Mexican-American women drink more than women of other Hispanic groups.
- With Hispanics of both sexes, drinking decreases after age 60, and there is an increase in those who abstain.
- For both sexes, drinking levels increase with rising levels of income and education.
- First generations born in the US drink more but do not have more alcohol-related problems.

Regional Surveys

Additionally, regional surveys of Hispanic drinking practices have been conducted.[1,8,24,32,41,46] A study of drinking patterns in San Francisco identified a higher frequency of heavier drinking and problem drinking among Hispanic men compared with blacks and whites, and found that Hispanic women have higher rates of abstinence than men and women from other groups.[8] Community surveys in Texas generally found lower rates of drinking than surveys in California and again found high rates of abstinence among women.[24,32,41,46]

Surveys conducted in New York City of Puerto Ricans found that drinking primarily occurs in socioeconomically deprived men and that Puerto Ricans had the highest ratio of men-to-women drinkers.[28,29,30]

The consistent finding of lower consumption and high rates of abstinence among Hispanic women is most likely related to the strong negative cultural sanctions against drinking.[1,8,28,29,30] However, with higher education, there is a trend of increasing consumption rates. The higher prevalence of drinking by Hispanic men is because drinking by Hispanic men does not taper off significantly after age 30, in contrast to the black and white population.

PATTERNS OF OTHER DRUG USE

In the past (in addition to alcohol), heroin and inhalants have been viewed as problem drugs within the Hispanic community. In the last decade, however, the use of cocaine has grown exponentially.

National Surveys

Both national surveys and scattered regional reports document the extent of use and abuse of drugs other than alcohol. National data has been provided by the inclusion of drug use patterns within the Hispanic Health and Nutrition Examination Survey (HHANES), conducted between 1982 and 1984.[19] Information was gathered on marijuana, cocaine, inhalants, and sedative use for a sample of persons between ages 12 and 44. Efforts were made to identify intra-ethnic variability.

Some of the relevant findings from the national HHANES study about drug abuse are as follows:

- Lifetime use and current use of the four drugs surveyed were equally as high for Mexican Americans and Puerto Ricans as compared with lower rates for Cubans.
- Inhalants and sedatives were not widely used by any group.
- Puerto Ricans were more likely to have used and to be current users of cocaine than either Mexican Americans or Cubans. Lifetime cocaine use among Puerto Ricans was 21.5%, compared to 11.1% for Mexican Americans and 9.2% for Cuban Americans. Current cocaine use was 8.9% for Puerto Ricans, 3.8% for Cuban Americans, and 2.4% for Mexican Americans.
- Among Mexican Americans and Puerto Ricans, inhalants tended to be used initially, before use of either marijuana or cocaine.
- Men were always more likely to have used the surveyed substances.
- Individuals preferring to speak English rather than Spanish during the interview were more likely to have used or to be current users.

The 1991 National Household Survey on Drug Abuse showed the following estimates of Hispanic abuse of illicit drugs: Ever used—31%; used in the past year—12%; and used in the past month—6.4%.[49] These rates were all lower than in white and black populations, except that use in the past year was higher than in whites. However, frequency of use of cocaine and abuse of cocaine in the past year and month were higher for Hispanics than whites. This was also true for heroin use. These rates must be interpreted with caution because they are not corrected for social and environmental risks. One study that corrected for these factors found that the racial/ethnic differences disappeared.[38]

Other national data are provided by the Client Oriented Data Acquisition Process (CODAP) and the Drug Abuse Warning Network (DAWN). These surveys suggest higher use of heroin among Hispanics.[40,55] While offering insights into the nature and magnitude of drug problems, these surveys do not reflect the true incidence in the community but in the delivery of treatment and emergency services.

The National Survey Results on Drug Use from The Monitoring the Future Study, 1993, shows that Hispanics in the eighth grade have the highest rates of use for nearly all drugs.[34] Hispanics in their senior year continue to have the highest usage rates for cocaine, crack, other cocaine, and heroin, but not for other drugs. The drop in drug use rates in twelfth grade is thought to be due to differential school dropout rates. These findings were nearly identical in another study that compared substance use between Mexican-American and white non-Hispanic eighth- and twelfth-grade students.[13]

Regional Surveys

A survey of heroin use among Mexican Americans in southern Texas found that Mexican Americans were second to African Americans as the largest ethnic minority among the opiate addict population. In addition, Mexican Americans tended to use fewer illicit drugs, had a higher arrest record than a comparable black or white population, and were voluntarily abstinent or employed a greater proportion of the time. Typically the onset of abuse was age 20 or older.[17]

Surveys also have found high rates of heroin use among Puerto Ricans.[39] In 1978 it was estimated that one of every 14 Hispanics in metropolitan New York City was either a drug addict or abuser.[36] This was at a time when Hispanics constituted 12% of the population of New York City but accounted for 20% of the estimated 125,000 addicts in the area.

In 1986 the State of New York conducted a statewide household survey of the following abused substances: marijuana, cocaine, phencyclidine, hallucinogens, inhalants, and illicit methadone.[51] Differences for lifetime use between Hispanics and non-Hispanics emerged for cocaine (14% Hispanics, 9% non-Hispanics), heroin (5% Hispanics, 1% non-Hispanics), and illicit methadone (2% Hispanics, 0.5% non-Hispanics). Recent substance use, over the past 6 months, showed the following differences: marijuana (12% Hispanics, 9% non-Hispanics), cocaine

(7% Hispanics, 4% non-Hispanics), and any drug use (14% Hispanics, 10% non-Hispanics).

Although the HHANES general population survey did not show wide use of inhalants, certain Hispanic subpopulations appear to be at risk. Regional studies have examined inhalant use by socially deprived youth.[44,48,53] A Texas drug abuse prevention program found that 47% of Mexican Americans have tried inhalants as compared with 17% for the white population and 10% for the black population.[53] In the Los Angeles area, a survey using adolescents as peer interviewers found rates of current inhalant use that were 14 times greater than in comparative national data.[44]

Efforts have been made to identify the natural history of inhalant use. Grades 6 and 12 were surveyed in a small, rural southern Texas community.[42] Of those using inhalants, 80% started on or before their fourteenth birthday. Inhalant use often preceded all other drug use, including tobacco and cigarette use. Another survey of seventh through twelfth graders in New York found differences in inhalant use between students living inside and outside of New York City.[21] Within New York City, the prevalence was highest for white non-Hispanic students. However, outside of New York City, the prevalence was highest among Hispanic students. For those Hispanic students who lived outside of the city, more than one in five had used inhalants in the preceding 6 months.

Perinatal substance use is of grave concern because of its relationship to neonatal and obstetrical complications. A large survey in California showed the following prevalence of perinatal drug exposure in Hispanic women: alcohol 6.87%, any drug 2.75%, cannabinoids 0.61%, cocaine 0.55%, opiates 1.06%, amphetamines 0.35%, and tobacco 3.29%.[61] Hispanic women had the second highest prevalence rate for alcohol, but lower prevalence rates for other drug use than other ethnic groups except Asians.

PROBLEMS RELATED TO SUBSTANCE USE

A survey in the Los Angeles area that was part of the larger National Epidemiology Catchment Area survey examined 6-month and lifetime prevalence of alcohol and drug abuse/dependence in East Los Angeles.[6,7,35] The Los Angeles area predominantly comprises Hispanics of Mexican-American origin. Findings included the following:

- Hispanic men had higher prevalence of alcohol abuse/dependence, particularly in the older age group, than non-Hispanic men; in fact, the highest rates of any national site surveyed.
- No major differences were found in the severity of alcohol abuse/dependence between Hispanics and non-Hispanics.

- The prevalence of drug abuse/dependence was higher for non-Hispanic whites than Hispanics, again highest of any national site.
- Hispanic women infrequently abuse or become dependent on drugs or alcohol.

Prior national surveys of the general population have shown increased problems with alcohol among the Hispanic population.[12,10] However, it was not until recently that a careful survey designed to ascertain intra-ethnic differences was conducted with a Hispanic population.[10] Data from that survey show that for men, the prevalence of one or more alcohol-related problems was 22% for Mexican Americans, 8% for Puerto Ricans, and 4% for Cubans. The most common problems among Hispanic men were salience (attention-getting quality) of drink-seeking behavior (7%), impaired control over drinking (6%), problems with other people (7%), and health problems (6%).

The prevalence of one or more alcohol-related problems in women was found to be low in all populations: 7% for Mexican Americans, 7% for Puerto Ricans, and 2% for Cubans. The types of problems found were salience (attention-getting quality) of drink-seeking behavior (3%), belligerence (3%), health problems (3%), and problems with people other than spouse (3%).

Other surveys of specific regional Hispanic groups have noted higher arrests for DWIs, increased death rates directly related to alcohol, and increased mortality from cirrhosis of the liver.[37,44] Reports of the Los Angeles Medical Examiner's office from 1970 to 1979 show higher rates of blood alcohol level in Hispanic victims of homicide than in a black or white population.[26]

One large study examined age, race/ethnicity, and marital status of a large group ($n = 62,829$) of alcoholic men receiving inpatient care at Veterans Affair Hospitals throughout the country.[4] This study found that Hispanic men were significantly less likely to complete treatment or attend detoxification and more likely to be hospitalized for other primary diagnosis. They concluded that young Hispanic men are in need of special treatment interventions that focus on early identification of alcohol problems, encourage initiation into treatment, and reduce attrition.

A number of problems related to heroin abuse among Hispanics have been noted, including high death rates, increased crime rates, and alcohol abuse.[17,65] Serious health problems have been reported among Puerto Ricans in New York City; drug dependence was the second greatest cause of death in this population.[2] The annual death rate from drug abuse was 37.9 per 100,000, compared with 23.2 per 100,000 for the total population.

Inhalant abuse causes a variety of problems, including organic brain syndrome, anemia, cardiac dysrhythmia, lead poisoning, and liver and kidney damage.[58] Inhalant abuse can have a significant negative impact in a range of social spheres. Inhalant use is of special concern; it appears to be the drug of choice with young, economically deprived adolescents and is often the first drug used.[19,58] Inhalant use is often associated with Hispanic adolescents in the Southwest. A study of Cuban immigrants found that inhalant users were exclusively young males from low socioeconomic levels and disrupted families. Their performance in school was poor; they had serious antisocial behavior; and their use of inhalants was part of a pattern of polysubstance use and abuse.

The acquired immunodeficiency syndrome (AIDS) rates for Hispanic adolescents/adults and children in 1991 were 2.5 to 7.5 times higher than for non-Hispanic whites.[18] In 1991 the overall incidence for AIDS in the US was 31.6 per 100,000 for Hispanics, and 11.8 per 100,000 for non-Hispanic whites. The rates for Hispanics vary widely by geographic area. Likewise, the mode of transmission varies dramatically depending on place of birth.

CULTURAL FACTORS

A number of culturally related issues affect both alcohol and drug use. These include the manner in which problems manifest themselves and the tendency to use or avoid health care facilities, which ultimately affects the outcome of treatment and the ability to promote prevention. There is a growing literature that points to the level of acculturation as a significant factor. Precisely how acculturation impacts the use and abuse of alcohol and drugs remains unclear. Is it a factor that promotes stress? If so, what is the interrelationship of cultural attributes and stress, and for whom? Does the degree of acculturation represent a problem of adaptation? Is it related to a deterioration of immigrants' social institutions?[23,28]

Acculturation appears to alter attitudes toward alcohol use and heavy drinking. Women in particular are sensitive to changes in the degree of acculturation. With increased acculturation, women tend to become more tolerant of alcohol use and increase levels of consumption.[9] This has been described in Puerto Rican, Cuban-American, and Mexican-American women.[3] One of the dangers described in California associated with acculturation is the dangerous mixture of high-peak drinking (Mexican) and increased-frequency drinking (American) among Mexican Americans.[24] As a consequence of acculturation, the infrequent periods of heavy drinking typical of Mexican drinking became more frequent as the individual adopted an indigenous style of American drinking.

In a study completed in a Northern California emergency room, Hispanic males were more likely than non-Hispanics to have positive alcohol breathalyzer readings and report drinking before the event that led to their admission to the emergency room.[14] They also reported a causal relationship between their drinking and the event. These findings were strongest among the moderate and high acculturation groups.

In recent years a number of concepts have been described in the literature pertaining to intrinsic personal and cultural values of Hispanics. For example, the term *machismo*, which has a variety of connotations and generally refers to strength, masculinity, independence, dignity, and responsibility, has been applied to drinking situations. In this context, machismo has been used to represent less desirable traits, including the implied meanings that the Hispanic man is not a "man" if he cannot hold his liquor or that by seeking treatment, he is weak. However, there is no evidence that this is tied directly to drinking or drug-using practices.[28,50] In addition, the clinical use of the construct has been questioned. While it is important for clinicians to be informed about subtle sociocultural issues, generalizations about the meaning and usefulness of nonspecific terms should not be made in assessing or treating Hispanics.

Another area of cultural significance is the role of the family in the presentation of substance abuse and in treatment. Hispanics are stereotypically viewed as being more involved with both their immediate and extended family. Traditionally, the family is viewed as a buffer against both alcohol and drug use. Another impression of Hispanic families is that they are difficult to engage in treatment and tend to cover up substance abuse.[52] However, there is no comparative data to suggest that this is unique to Hispanic families. Now, because of the severe deterioration and disorganization of the traditional Hispanic family, its role as a protection against alcohol and drug abuse seems to have diminished. Additionally, Hispanic families tend to be younger and have more children.[62] They have a lower median income than the general population and have accelerated divorce rates.[24] Immigrant families entering the US for the first time may experience severe erosion of their social milieu and family system, which leaves them vulnerable to alcohol and drug abuse.[24,58]

There are tremendous cultural variations between different Hispanic ethnic groups. Thus, generalizations about Hispanics have little use. For example, in three Hispanic subgroups (Dominicans, Puerto Ricans, and Guatemalans) in the New England area, there was considerable variation both in drinking practices and in the resources to which they turned for assistance.[27] Dominicans drank less, Guatemalans drank more, and Puerto Ricans drank the same as before their arrival to this country. The indigenous therapy selected by each group also varied: Dominicans actively participated in the Catholic church, which revitalized community spirit, emphasized the importance of family, and discouraged excessive drinking; Guatemalans initiated an AA group; and Puerto Ricans joined the Pentecostal church. Thus, religious and spiritual healing practices can be effectively incorporated into and used in conjunction with formal treatment.[28,54]

Another study described variation among drinking patterns of Mexican Americans according to location and whether their migration to the US was recent or more remote.[1] This study compared Mexican Americans in California with those in Texas.[24] In the latter, both Anglo and Hispanic men were found to drink less, and gender differences were less marked.[24] Other studies have shown that even in a particular setting, there can be considerable divergence of drinking styles.[59]

TREATMENT CONSIDERATIONS

The ideal content and organization of a treatment program for Hispanics are unknown.[11] Research examining treatment effectiveness for Hispanics is minimal. Most of what is currently recommended is based on clinical impressions rather than confirmed by controlled outcome studies. It is unknown whether general treatment outcome research can be applied to Hispanics or how it needs to be modified. This highlights the need to direct more resources into research examining various culturally based treatment options for minority populations.

Evaluation

Certainly a thorough evaluation of the patient—including level of acculturation, time elapsed since migration, language preference, alcohol/drug use patterns, and emotional, sociocultural, and health-related issues—is the first step in matching the patient with appropriate treatment. Padilla and Salgado de Synder have summarized critical information for the "culturally informed evaluation."[44] Since the degree of acculturation has been shown to correspond with drinking patterns (particularly in women), some measure of this would be useful during the initial evaluation.[9] Several scales are available to measure this concept; these scales can be filled out by patients during their initial evaluation.[9,16]

Staffing Patterns

It has been recognized that matching patients' and therapists' culture and ethnicity may improve entry into treatment, retention, and outcome.[33] Ideally, staffing patterns need to provide bilingual, bicultural therapists in the treatment setting. Unfortunately, most treatment programs lack experienced and qualified Hispanic counselors. While there is little data to suggest that treatment outcome is better if ethnic matching occurs, it may increase the probability of patients initiating and following through with treatment.[60,63] A group of investigators reported improved outcome in treating Puerto Rican heroin addicts when the treatment program emphasized education, cultural sensitivity, and employment of bilingual/bicultural staff.[36] One program found that their Hispanic referrals increased fivefold by simply adding a Hispanic interviewer to their intake staff.[65] Another outpatient substance abuse program discovered that whenever a specific ethnic group included 75% of the treatment population, these patients were retained in treatment significantly longer.[5,60]

Family

Substance abuse can erode important family and social ties. Thus, restorative efforts to repair an individual's familial/social network can buffer the effects of alcohol/drug abuse. Family involvement is an important focus in working with Hispanics.[22] Generally, both the Hispanic patient's immediate family and extended family are significant and should be involved in the intervention process. Two studies have provided preliminary evidence on the effectiveness of family therapy in a Cuban-American Hispanic population.[56] Szapocznik developed brief strategic family therapy (BSFT) based on structural family therapy.[56,57] He found BSFT well suited for the Cuban-American adolescent population he treated in Miami. Szapocznik conducted a series of clinical trials with adolescents comparing conjoint and one-person family therapy. His results demonstrate that one-person family therapy is as effective as conjoint family therapy in bringing about and sustaining improvement in drug-abusing adolescents and their families.

The second major contribution by Szapocznik et al. was the development of procedures to engage resistant families in therapy.[57] The procedures, based on strategic structural systems concepts, were highly effective. Patients in the experimental group were engaged in treatment at a rate of 93% as compared to 42% in the control group. And the difference in treatment completion was equally as significant: 77% as compared to 25% in the control group.

Self-Help Groups

Alcoholics Anonymous (AA) and Narcotics Anonymous (NA) programs have been adapted to Spanish-speaking populations. Most large cities have several Spanish-speaking AA or NA groups. For many Hispanics

AA is the most affordable treatment and recovery resource. Hoffman[31] described two models of Hispanic AA in Los Angeles, one using "terapia dura" (tough therapy) and the other being less confrontive. He describes how "terapia dura" transforms the machismo complex into more appropriate social alternatives for young male immigrants from Central America. These social alternatives include sobriety and being head of the family. Clear efficacy of these self-help programs, both in minority and majority populations, has not been demonstrated. However, they provide an established social milieu for those individuals whose social ties have been severed by alcohol and drug abuse.

Folk/Religious Beliefs

In providing treatment to Hispanics, the clinician should be aware of various folk beliefs and practices. Indigenous or folk healing practices can vary widely. For example, the etiology of alcohol and drug abuse may be viewed as related to numerous psychosocial stressors such as vices, hexes, or spells.[59] In Mexican-American populations, treatment prescribed by the folk healer (Curandero) may be a combination of counseling and herbal cures such as *haba de San Ignacio*, which causes nausea and vomiting when consumed.

The European Spiritism philosophy of Alan Kardec has heavily influenced Cuban Americans and Puerto Ricans.[51] Cuban Americans may also believe in Santeria and Brujeria, religious beliefs brought to the Caribbean from Africa. Finally, more traditional religious affiliations are often critical in the Hispanic individual's social network and can play a key role in treatment.[51]

Special Populations

Demographic and acculturation data suggest that the special needs of Hispanic youth, elderly, and women should be addressed.[9] Treatment programs must modify their approaches for these special populations. Since these subpopulations traditionally are reluctant to come into clinics, aggressive outreach must be integrated into treatment programs.

REFERENCES

1. Alcocer A. Quantitative study. IN: Technical Systems Research Institute. *Drinking Practices and Alcohol Related Problems of Spanish Speaking Persons in Three California Locales.* Sacramento CA: Office of Alcohol and Drug Programs, 1979.
2. Alers JO. *Puerto Ricans and Health.* New York: Hispanic Research Center, Fordham University, 1982.
3. Black SA; Markides KS. Acculturation and alcohol consumption in Puerto Rican, Cuban-American, and Mexican-American women in the United States. *American Journal of Public Health* 83(6): 890-893, 1983. (9 refs.)
4. Booth BM; Blow FC; Cook CAL; Bunn JY; Fortney JC. Age and ethnicity among hospitalized alcoholics: A nationwide study. *Alcoholism: Clinical and Experimental Research* 16(6): 1029-1034, 1992. (38 refs.)
5. Brown BS; Joe GW; Thompson P. Minority group status and treatment retention. *International Journal of the Addictions* 20(2): 319-335, 1986. (42 refs.)
6. Burnam MA; Hough RL; Escobar JI; Karno M; Timbers DM; Telles CA; et al. Six-month prevalence of specific psychiatric disorders among Mexican Americans and non-Hispanic whites in Los Angeles. *Archives of General Psychiatry* 44(8): 687-694, 1987. (42 refs.)
7. Burnam MA. Prevalence of alcohol abuse and dependence among Mexican-Americans and non-Hispanic whites in the community. IN: Spiegler D; Tate D; Aitken S; Christian C, eds. *Alcohol Use Among US Ethnic Minorities. NIAAA Research Monograph 18.* Rockville MD: National Institute on Alcohol Abuse and Alcoholism, 1989. pp. 163-177. (37 refs.)
8. Caetano R. Self-reported intoxication among Hispanics in Northern California. *Journal of Studies on Alcohol* 45(4): 349-354, 1984. (7 refs.)
9. Caetano R. Acculturation and drinking patterns among US Hispanics. *British Journal of Addiction* 82(7): 789-799, 1987. (42 refs.)
10. Caetano R. Drinking patterns and alcohol problems in a national sample of US Hispanics. IN: Spiegler D; Tate D; Aitken S; Christian C, eds. *Alcohol Use Among US Ethnic Minorities. NIAAA Research Monograph 18.* Rockville MD: National Institute on Alcohol Abuse and Alcoholism, 1989. pp. 147-162. (18 refs.)
11. Caetano R. Priorities for alcohol treatment research among US Hispanics. *Journal of Psychoactive Drugs* 25(1): 53-60, 1993. (40 refs.)
12. Calahan D; Room R. *Problem Drinking Among American Men. Rutgers Center of Alcohol Studies, Monograph No. 7.* New Brunswick NJ: College and University Press, 1974.
13. Chavez EL; Swain RC. An epidemiological comparison of Mexican-American and White non-Hispanic 8th- and 12th-grade students' substance abuse. *American Journal of Public Health* 82(3): 445-447, 1992. (10 refs.)
14. Cherpitel CJ. Acculturation, alcohol consumption, and casualties among United States Hispanics in the emergency room. *International Journal of the Addictions* 27(9): 1067-1077, 1992. (18 refs.)
15. Clark B; Midanik L. Alcohol use and alcohol problems among US adults: Results of the 1979 national survey. IN: National Institute on Alcohol Abuse and Alcoholism, *Alcohol Consumption and Related Problems, Alcohol and Health Monograph No. 1.* Rockville MD: National Institute on Alcohol Abuse and Alcoholism, 1982. pp. 3-52. (40 refs.)
16. Cuellar I; et al. An acculturation scale for Mexican-American normal clinical populations. *Hispanic Journal of Behavioral Science* 2: 199-217, 1980.
17. Desmond D; Maddux J. Mexican-American heroin addicts. *American Journal of Drug and Alcohol Abuse* 10(3): 317-346, 1984. (90 refs.)
18. Diaz T; Buehler JW; Castro KG; Ward JW. AIDS trends among Hispanics in the United States. *American Journal of Public Health* 83(4): 504-509, 1993. (29 refs.)
19. Division of Epidemiology and Statistical Analysis, US Department of Health and Human Services. *Findings from the Hispanic Health and Nutrition Examination Survey: Use of Selected Drugs Among Hispanics: Mexican-Americans, Puerto Ricans, Cuban Americans.* Rockville MD: National Institute on Drug Abuse, 1987.

20. Eden SL; Aguilar RJ. The Hispanic chemically dependent patient: Considerations for diagnosis and treatment. IN: Lawson GW; Lawson AW, eds. *Alcoholism and Substance Abuse in Special Populations*. Rockville MD: Aspen Publishers, Inc, 1989. pp. 205-222. (32 refs.)

21. Frank B; Marel R; Schmeidler J. The continuing problem of solvent abuse in New York State. IN: Crider RA; Rouse BA, eds. *Epidemiology of Inhalant Abuse: An Update, Research Monograph 85*. Rockville MD: National Institute on Drug Abuse, 1988. pp. 77-105. (7 refs.)

22. Gilbert MJ. Alcohol consumption patterns in immigrant and later generation Mexican-American women. *Hispanic Journal of Behavioral Sciences* 9(3): 299-313, 1987. (46 refs.)

23. Gilbert MJ. Alcohol-related practices, problems, and norms among Mexican Americans: An overview. IN: Spiegler D; Tate D; Aitken S; Christian C, eds. *Alcohol Use Among US Ethnic Minorities. NIAAA Research Monograph 18*. Rockville MD: National Institute on Alcohol Abuse and Alcoholism, 1989. pp. 115-134. (58 refs.)

24. Gilbert M; Cervantes R. Alcohol services for Mexican-Americans: A review of utilization patterns, treatment considerations, and prevention activities. *Hispanic Journal of Behavioral Sciences* 8(3): 191-223, 1986. (70 refs.)

25. Gomez AG; Vega DM. The Hispanic Addict. IN: Lowinson JH; Ruiz P, eds. *Substance Abuse: Clinical Problems and Perspectives*. Baltimore: Williams & Wilkins, 1981.

26. Goodman RA; Mercy JA; Rosenberg ML. Alcohol use and homicide victimization: An examination of racial/ethnic differences. IN: Spiegler D; Tate D; Aitken S; Christian C, eds. *Alcohol Use Among US Ethnic Minorities. NIAAA Research Monograph 18*. Rockville MD: National Institute on Alcohol Abuse and Alcoholism, 1989. pp. 191-204. (35 refs.)

27. Gordon AJ. The cultural context of drinking and indigenous therapy for alcohol problems in three migrant Hispanic cultures. *Journal of Studies on Alcohol* Supplement 9: 217-240, 1981. (13 refs.)

28. Gordon AJ. State-of-the-art review: Caribbean Hispanics and their alcohol use. IN: Spiegler D; Tate D; Aitken S; Christian C, eds. *Alcohol Use Among US Ethnic Minorities. NIAAA Research Monograph 18*. Rockville MD: National Institute on Alcohol Abuse and Alcoholism, 1989. pp. 135-146. (38 refs.)

29. Haberman PW. Denial of drinking in a household survey. *Quarterly Journal of Studies on Alcohol* 31(3): 710-717, 1970. (8 refs.)

30. Haberman PW; Sheinberg J. Implicative drinking reported in a household survey: A corroborative note on subgroup differences. *Quarterly Journal of Studies on Alcohol* 28(3): 538-543, 1967. (4 refs.)

31. Hoffman F. Cultural adaptations of Alcoholics Anonymous to serve Hispanic populations. *International Journal on the Addictions* 29(4): 445-460, 1994. (24 refs.)

32. Holck SE; Warren CW; Smith JC; Rochat RW. Alcohol consumption among Mexican American and Anglo women: Results of a survey along the US-Mexico border. *Journal of Studies on Alcohol* 45(2): 149-154, 1984. (16 refs.)

33. Institute of Medicine. *Broadening the Base of Treatment for Alcohol Problems*. Washington DC: National Academy of Science, 1990.

34. Johnston LD; O'Malley PM; Bachman JG. *National Survey Results on Drug Use from the Monitoring the Future Study, 1975-1993. Volume II: College Students and Young Adults*. Rockville MD: National Institute on Drug Abuse, 1994.

35. Karno M; Hough RL; Burnam A; Escobar JI; Timbers DM; Santana F; Boyd JH. Lifetime prevalence of specific psychiatric disorders among Mexican Americans and non-Hispanic whites in Los Angeles. *Archives of General Psychiatry* 44(9): 695-700, 1987. (30 refs.)

36. Langrod J; Alksne L; Lowinson J; Ruiz P. Rehabilitation of the Puerto Rican addict: A cultural perspective. *International Journal of the Addictions* 16(5): 841-847, 1981. (6 refs.)

37. Lex B. Review of alcohol problems in ethnic minority groups. *Journal of Consulting Clinical Psychology* 55(3): 293-300, 1987. (66 refs.)

38. Lillie-Blanton M; Anthony JC; Schuster CR. Probing the meaning of racial/ethnic group comparisons in crack-cocaine smoking. *Journal of the American Medical Association* 269(8): 993-997, 1993. (11 refs.)

39. Lukoff IF. *Some Aspects of the Epidemiology of Heroin Use in a Ghetto Community: A Preliminary Report*. Washington DC: Government Printing Office, 1972.

40. Mandel J; Bordaho V. DAWN: A second look: Its impact on minorities and public policy. *American Journal of Drug Alcohol Abuse* 7(3/4): 361-377, 1980. (16 refs.)

41. Maril RL; Zavaleta AN. Drinking patterns of low-income Mexican-American women. *Journal of Studies on Alcohol* 40(5): 480-484, 1979. (8 refs.)

42. Mata A; Rodriguez SA. Inhalant abuse in a small rural south Texas community: A social epidemiological overview. IN: Crider RA; Rouse BA, eds. *Epidemiology of Inhalant Abuse: An Update. NIDA Research Monograph 85*. Rockville MD: National Institute on Drug Abuse, 1988. pp. 49-76. (55 refs.)

43. Orford J. Critical conditions for change in the addictive behaviors. IN: Miller WE; Heather N, eds. *Treating Addictive Behaviors*. New York: Plenum Press, 1986. pp. 91-108. (42 refs.)

44. Padilla AM; Salgado de Snyder VN. Hispanics: What the culturally informed evaluator needs to know. IN: Orlandi MA; Weston R; Epstein LG, eds. *Cultural Competence for Evaluators: A Guide for Alcohol and Other Drug Abuse Prevention Practitioners Working with Ethnic/Racial Communities. OSAP Cultural Competence Series I*. Rockville MD: OSAP, 1992. pp. 117-146. (50 refs.)

45. Padilla ER; Padilla AM; Morales A; Olmedo E. Inhalant, marijuana, and alcohol abuse among Barrio children and adolescents. *International Journal of the Addictions* 14(7): 945-964, 1979. (21 refs.)

46. Paine HJ. Attitudes and patterns of alcohol use among Mexican Americans: Implications for service delivery. *Journal of Studies on Alcohol* 38(3): 544-553, 1977. (6 refs.)

47. Peterson JL; Marin G. Issues in the prevention of AIDS among black and Hispanic men. *American Psychologist* 43(11): 871-877, 1988. (66 refs.)

48. Reddy MA. *Statistical Record of Hispanic Americans*. Detroit: Gale Research Inc, 1993.

49. Reed B; May P. Inhalant abuse and juvenile delinquency: A control study in Albuquerque, New Mexico. *International Journal of the Addictions* 19(7): 789-803, 1984. (25 refs.)

50. Ruiz P; Langrod JG. IN: Lowinson JH; Ruiz P; Millman RB; Langford JG, eds. *Substance Abuse: A Comprehensive Textbook, 2nd Edition*. Baltimore: Williams & Wilkins, 1992.

51. Ruiz R; Padilla A. Counseling Latinos. *Personnel and Guidance Journal* 55: 401-408, 1977.

52. Sanchez A, ed. Drug abuse and treatment of the "Tecato" or Mexican-American junkie. IN: *A Multi-Cultural View of Drug Abuse*. Cambridge MA: Schenkman Books Inc, 1978.

53. Santos De Barona M; Simpson D. Inhalant users in drug abuse prevention programs. *American Journal of Drug and Alcohol Abuse* 10(4): 503-518, 1984. (47 refs.)

54. Simpson D; Curtis B; Butler MC. Description of drug users in treatment: 1971-1972 DARP admissions. *American Journal of Drug and Alcohol Abuse* 2(1): 15-28, 1975. (2 refs.)

55. Singer M; Borrero MG. Indigenous treatment for alcoholism: The case of Puerto Rican spiritism. *Medical Anthropology* 8: 246-273, 1984. (74 refs.)

56. Szapocznik J; Daruna P; Scopetta MA; Aranalde MDL. The characteristics of Cuban immigrant inhalant abusers. *American Journal of Drug and Alcohol Abuse* 4(3): 377-389, 1977. (31 refs.)

57. Szapocznik J; Kurtines W; Foote F; Perez-Vidal A; Hervis O. Conjoint versus one person family therapy: Further evidence for the effectiveness of conducting family therapy through one person with drug-abusing adolescents. *Journal of Consulting and Clinical Psychology* 54(3): 395-397, 1986. (6 refs.)

58. Szapocznik J; Perez-Vidal A; Brickman AL; Foote FH; Santisteban D; Hervis O; Kurtines WM. Engaging adolescent drug abusers and their families into treatment. A strategic structural systems approach. *Journal of Consulting and Clinical Psychology* 56(4): 552-557, 1988. (22 refs.)

59. Trotter RT. Evidence of an ethno-medical form of aversion therapy on the United States-Mexico Border. *Journal of Ethnopharmacology* 1: 279-284, 1979.

60. Tucker BM. US ethnic minorities and drug abuse: An assessment of the science and practice. *International Journal of the Addictions* 20(6/7): 1021-1047, 1985. (139 refs.)

61. US Bureau of the Census. *Persons of Spanish Origin in the United States, March 1982: Series p-20, No. 396.* Washington DC: Bureau of the Census, 1985.

62. Vega WA; Kolody B; Hwang J; Noble A. Prevalence and magnitude of perinatal substance exposures in California. *New England Journal of Medicine* 329(12): 850-854, 1993. (16 refs.)

63. Westermeyer J. Research on treatment of drinking problems. *Journal of Studies on Alcohol Supplement* 9: 44-59, 1981. (79 refs.)

64. Westermeyer J. The psychiatrist and solvent-inhalant abuse: Recognition, assessment, and treatment. *American Journal of Psychiatry* 144(7): 903-1606, 1987. (94 refs.)

65. Wurzman I; Rounsaville BJ; Kleber HD. Cultural values of Puerto Rican opiate addicts: An exploratory study. *American Journal of Drug Alcohol Abuse* 9(20): 141-153, 1982. (20 refs.)

FURTHER READINGS

Black SA; Markides KS. Aging and generational patterns of alcohol consumption among Mexican Americans, Cuban Americans and mainland Puerto Ricans. *International Journal of Aging and Human Development* 39(2): 97-103, 1994. (23 refs.)

The relationship between aging and drinking among US Hispanics is not well understood. The present study used data from the Hispanic Health and Nutrition Examination Survey to describe life-course patterns of alcohol consumption among Mexican Americans, Cuban Americans, and Puerto Ricans residing in the mainland US. Age differences in patterns of consumption among Mexican-American and Puerto Rican males were found to reflect aging effects, as evidenced by increasing percentages of former drinkers coupled with consistently low percentages of abstainers at all ages. Among Cuban males, cohort effects were evidenced for middle-aged and older men by a continuation of low rates from younger years, as well as a sharp difference between the rates of the middle-aged and older cohorts and those of the younger cohort. Age differences in all three groups of females were found to reflect cohort effects, as evidenced by large proportions of lifelong abstainers across all age cohorts. Copyright 1994, Baywood Publishing Co., Inc.

Boles S; Casas JM; Furlong M; Gonzalez G; Morrison G. Alcohol and other drug use patterns among Mexican-American, Mexican, and Caucasian adolescents: New directions for assessment and research. *Journal of Clinical Child Psychology* 23(1): 39-46, 1994. (30 refs.)

This report examines substance abuse rates among subgroups of Mexican-American students by comparing alcohol and drug use rates of Mexican-American adolescents born in the US to those of Mexican-American students born in Mexico and to those of Caucasian students attending the same schools. A total of 3404 ninth- and eleventh-grade students were surveyed by the California Substance Use Survey (Skager, Austin, & Firth, 1991; Skager, Firth, & Maddahian, 1989). It was found that Mexican females abstain the most from drug and alcohol use. Mexican males also reported lower drug and alcohol use than their Mexican-American and Caucasian counterparts, who had similar rates of alcohol use. In terms of prevention and intervention, Caucasian ninth graders reported the highest percentages receiving a substance abuse prevention program for at least part of a semester. Mexican-American students, however, were more likely to report not having received any prevention programming in school. Implications for assessment and prevention are discussed. Copyright 1994, *Journal of Clinical Child Psychology.*

Caetano R. Drinking and alcohol-related problems among minority women. *Alcohol Health and Research World* 18(3): 233-241, 1994. (28 refs.)

Although drinking by African-American and Hispanic women in the US differs from that of white women in terms of prevalence rates and incidence of alcohol-related problems, factors such as age and employment status have similar effects on drinking in each group. However, influences on drinking among minority women are complex and must be thought of as an interaction of cultural, personal, and historical factors. This interplay is beginning to emerge from ethnic studies. Public Domain.

Caetano R. Priorities for alcohol treatment research among US Hispanics. (review). *Journal of Psychoactive Drugs* 25(1): 53-60, 1993. (40 refs.)

This article reviews the clinical research conducted with US Hispanics and discusses priorities for alcohol treatment research in this ethnic group. Specific areas in which research is needed include epidemiological descriptions of patient characteristics, access and utilization of alcohol treatment, the structure of alcohol programs, pathways to treatment, alcohol dependence and treatment effectiveness, and treatment matching in alcohol treatment. Methodological requirements, research funding strategies, and professional training needed for implementing the research needs identified in the article are also discussed. A concerted effort by funding institutions is needed to emphasize the importance of this research, and an increased commitment of funds for research and professional training is necessary. Such funds should be earmarked for research with minorities and training for minority professionals. Copyright 1993, Haight-Ashbury Publications.

Canino G. Alcohol use and misuse among Hispanic women: Selected factors, processes, and studies. *International Journal of the Addictions* 29(9): 1083-1100, 1994. (37 refs.)

This paper presents a critical review of epidemiologic studies of the use and misuse of alcohol on Hispanic women. Although there is a wide variation in alcohol use among different Hispanic groups, there is some uniformity. The findings of most studies indicate that drinking, drunkenness, and "excessive drinking" are predominately male activities. Abstention rates are high among Hispanic women, and a pattern of infrequent "light" drinking and low prevalence rates of alcoholism is usually observed in most groups of Hispanic women. The role of societal mores and culture in shaping these patterns of alcohol use is discussed. Recommendations for needed future research with Hispanic women are also made. Copyright 1994, Marcel Dekker, Inc.

Center for Substance Abuse Prevention. *Prevention Material Available in Spanish.* Rockville MD: Center for Substance Abuse Prevention, 1994. (0 refs.)

This bibliography consists of 97 entries of prevention materials available in Spanish. For each entry the following information is provided: title; author; organization address; year; format; length;

context; topics; mode of delivery; target audience; setting; language; readability; availability; and description. Public Domain.

De La Rosa MR; Adrados JLR, eds. *Drug Abuse Among Minority Youth: Methodological Issues and Recent Research Advances. NIDA Research Monograph 130*. Rockville MD: National Institute on Drug Abuse, 1993. (Chapter refs.)

Advances have been made in understanding the nature and extent of drug abuse problems encountered by minority youth. Despite these advances, little is known about the patterns, causes, and consequences of illicit and licit drug use and abuse among minority youth. The limited literature suggests that because of cultural influences, unique economic situations, and formal and informal social network systems, the drug-abusing behavior of minority youth may vary significantly from that of nonminority youth. The paucity of research can be attributed to several factors: (1) The inadequate exploration of the important role that ethnic and racial factors play in drug abuse behavior, (2) inaccessibility of these populations to researchers, (3) lack of trained minority drug abuse researchers, (4) lack of well-designed community-based research projects, and (5) lack of resources to conduct needed research. The papers in this volume fall into three categories: Review of theory-driven research findings, methodological and other research problems, and needs for future research. Specific chapters address research with Puerto Rican youth, links between cultural identification and substance use, acculturation scales, interactional theory applied both to African-American and Puerto Rican youth, network theory and its application to African-American and Hispanic youth, and use among Native Americans. In respect to methodological issues, the following are considered: The validity of self-report; acculturation strain theory; the methodological issues around studies of gangs; tracking urban elementary school students' drug use; social and community policies in African-American communities; and substance use among refugee populations. Public Domain.

Delgado M. Hispanic natural support systems and alcohol and other drug services: Challenges and rewards for practice. *Alcoholism Treatment Quarterly* 12(1): 17-31, 1995. (20 refs.)

The professional literature suggests that natural support systems are an important ingredient of Hispanic culture and a key factor that should be integrated into all aspects of AOD practice. This article seeks to help AOD practitioners better identify and utilize Hispanic natural support systems in their efforts to provide culture-specific services to an ever-increasing population. Copyright 1995, The Haworth Press, Inc.

Felix-Ortiz M; Munoz R; Newcomb MD. The role of emotional distress in drug use among Latino adolescents. *Journal of Child and Adolescent Substance Abuse* 3(4): 1-22, 1994. (70 refs.)

The Latino (Hispanic) population is one of the fastest growing in the country and, relative to other groups, it is a population that must cope with a number of immigration-related stressors. As a result, Latino adolescents may be at special risk for emotional distress and drug use. This paper reviews issues around emotional distress and drug use in Latino adolescents. Issues addressed include comorbidity of emotional distress and drug use; the question of whether emotional distress is an antecedent or consequence of drug use; assessment issues; and the relationship between emotional distress, drug use, and high-risk behaviors. In a survey of primarily ninth and tenth grade immigrant Mexican students, emotional distress was assessed using three abbreviated scales of depression, hostility, and anxiety based on the Hopkins Symptom checklist; a history of suicide attempts was also assessed. Frequency and quantity of 10 substances including alcohol, cigarettes, and hard drugs also were assessed. Most types of

drug use were significantly correlated with emotional distress and positive history of suicide attempts. A high frequency of alcohol use and inhalant use were associated with emotional distress and a positive history of suicide attempts. Hostility was most strongly correlated with drug use. It is suggested that hostility as well as moderate to high depression symptom levels be considered risk factors for drug use and suicidality in Latino adolescents. It is also recommended that emotional distress be explicitly addressed in the treatment of drug abuse and other problem behaviors in Latino adolescents. Copyright 1994, The Haworth Press.

Flannery DJ; Vazsonyi AT; Torquati J; Fridrich A. Ethnic and gender differences in risk for early adolescent substance use. *Journal of Youth and Adolescence* 23(2): 195-213, 1994. (30 refs.)

This study examined interpersonal and intrapersonal risk for substance use in a sample of Caucasian and Hispanic early adolescents. A total of 1170 sixth and seventh graders, equally divided by gender, participated. Interpersonal risk was assessed by susceptibility to peer pressure, parental monitoring, peer substance use, parent-child involvement, and school adjustment. Intrapersonal risk was measured via self-efficacy, impulsivity, aggression, depression, and academic achievement. As expected, mean level of use did not differ between ethnic groups. Regression analyses indicated that susceptibility to peer pressure and peer alcohol use was the best predictor of individual substance use. These findings were consistent across gender and ethnicity. In all groups, interpersonal variables accounted for more variance in predicting risk (49% for Hispanic males) than did intrapersonal variables (0% for Hispanic females). Findings are discussed (1) in terms of examining mean levels vs. the underlying pattern predicting substance use, and (2) regarding implications for prevention efforts in early adolescence. Copyright 1994, Plenum Press.

Flewelling RL; Ennett ST; Rachal JV; Theisen AC. *National Household Survey on Drug Abuse: Race/Ethnicity, Socioeconomic Status, and Drug Abuse, 1991*. Rockville MD: Substance Abuse and Mental Health Services Administration, 1994. (27 refs.)

One of the two chief purposes of this report is to examine the prevalence of self-reported use of alcohol, cigarettes, and illicit drugs across subgroups of the US civilian, noninstitutionalized population aged 12 or older as defined by race/ethnicity and by other sociodemographic characteristics. A second purpose is to demonstrate the extent to which racial/ethnic differences in drug use prevalence may be influenced by differences in other sociodemographic characteristics measured in the NHSDA, particularly socioeconomic status (SES). Because race/ethnicity is associated with some types of drug use and also with numerous other demographic characteristics, it is likely that observed differences across racial/ethnic subgroups are attributable to other sociodemographic differences among groups. Although socioeconomic factors are obvious candidates for helping to explain racial/ethnic differences, other demographic variables may also play a role. In this report, three types of sociodemographic control measures are distinguished: Background demographic measures such as age, gender, metropolitan status, and geographic region of residence; indicators of SES; and other social and lifestyle indicators such as marital status and employment status. Public Domain.

Gfroerer JC; De La Rosa M. Protective and risk factors associated with drug use among Hispanic youth. *Journal of Addictive Diseases* 12(2): 87-107, 1993. (38 refs.)

Analysis of data from a nationally representative sample of Hispanic youths, age 12 to 17 and their parents, was done to investigate the impact of a number of variables on youths' drug-using behavior. The significance of youth, household, and parental characteristics were tested using the measures of youth drug use as dependent variables in regression models. Parents' attitudes and use of licit and illicit drugs were found to play an important role in their children's drug use behavior. The results also provide some support for the hypothesis that Hispanic children whose parents are more acculturated into American society are at higher risk of using drugs. Youths of Mexican origin, youths living outside large metropolitan areas, and females were found to be more likely to use drugs. The results provide supportive evidence that for drug prevention education programs to be effective with Hispanic youths, they must be family oriented. Copyright 1993, The Haworth Press, Inc.

Glick R; Moore J, eds. *Drugs in Hispanic Communities*. New Brunswick NJ: Rutgers University Press, 1990.

This volume deals with the extent and nature of substance use problems in Hispanic communities, highlighting the sociocultural and political issues that give rise to and maintain these problems. Copyright 1990, Project Cork Institute. (actually only on DC cat)

Hoffman F. Cultural adaptations of Alcoholics Anonymous to serve Hispanic populations. *International Journal of the Addictions* 29(4): 445-460, 1994. (24 refs.)

Hispanic AA groups in Los Angeles operate with two different models, one involving "terapia dura" (rough therapy) and the other employing less confrontive methods. "Terapia dura" adapts expressions of the machismo value complex to produce social alternatives for young male immigrants from Central America. In the less confrontational version, machismo is muted. Hispanic AA groups make little provision for the problems of women, and gays are stigmatized. Members' economic status, ethnicity, and level of acculturation condition the style and content of meetings and strategies for group survival. Copyright 1994, Marcel Dekker, Inc.

Marcell AV. Understanding ethnicity, identity formation, and risk behavior among adolescents of Mexican descent. *Journal of School Health* 64(8): 323-327, 1994. (33 refs.)

The population of adolescents of Mexican descent is growing rapidly in the US. However, the health needs of this group are not being adequately addressed by the health care system. Understanding the factors contributing to risk behavior in adolescents of Mexican descent may help improve service delivery and use. This article presents a sociodemographic profile of this group as well as a description of how one's degree of ethnic identification, acculturation, and other risk factors may contribute to problem behavior. Recommendations are provided to increase culturally appropriate prevention programs for youth of Mexican descent. Copyright 1994, American School Health Association.

Mayers RS; Kail BL; Watts TD, eds. *Hispanic Substance Abuse*. Springfield IL: Charles C. Thomas, 1993. 258 pp.

This multiauthored volume addresses substance abuse issues in the various Hispanic populations. It includes information on epidemiology, treatment, and cultural barriers and approaches to promoting treatment. Copyright, 1993, Project Cork Institute.

Szapocznik J, ed. *A Hispanic/Latino Family Approach to Substance Abuse Prevention. CSAP Cultural Competence Series*. Rockville MD: Center for Substance Abuse Prevention, 1994. (Chapter refs.)

This monograph deals with the role of the family in respect to substance use and prevention within the Hispanic community. Individual chapters deal with the nature of the substance abuse problem, the role of the family in intervention, community initiatives, and school-based programs. Included within the discussion are descriptions of a variety of prevention and early intervention programs. Copyright 1995, Project Cork Institute.

Vega WA; Gil AG; Zimmerman RS. Patterns of drug use among Cuban-American, African-American, and white non-Hispanic boys. *American Journal of Public Health* 83(2): 257-259, 1993. (14 refs.)

This study examined initiation into drug use during grade school years in a sample of Cuban-American, black, and white non-Hispanic students in the greater Miami, Florida, area. Findings indicate that first use of alcohol occurs in fifth grade and cigarettes in sixth grade for all subgroups except white non-Hispanics, who peak in the fifth grade. White non-Hispanics had the highest lifetime levels of alcohol and cigarette use. Foreign-born Cuban Americans had a lower lifetime prevalence of alcohol and cigarette use than US-born Cuban Americans. Higher acculturation level was related to first use of alcohol. One important implication of this study is that alcohol interventions should begin no later than third grade and smoking interventions no later than fourth grade. Copyright 1993, American Public Health Association.

Vega WA; Zimmerman RS; Warheit GJ; Apospori E; Gil AG. Risk factors for early adolescent drug use in four ethnic and racial groups. *American Journal of Public Health* 83(2): 185-189, 1993. (35 refs.)

It is widely believed that risk factors identified in previous epidemiological studies accurately predict adolescent drug use. Comparative studies are needed to determine how risk factors vary in prevalence, distribution, sensitivity, and pattern across the major US ethnic/racial groups. Baseline questionnaire data from a 3-year epidemiological study of early adolescent development and drug use were used to conduct bivariate and multivariate risk factor analyses. Respondents ($n = 6760$) were sixth and seventh grade Cuban, other Hispanic, black, and white non-Hispanic boys in the 48 middle schools of the greater Miami (Dade County) area. Findings indicate 5% lifetime illicit drug use, 4% lifetime inhalant use, 37% lifetime alcohol use, and 21% lifetime tobacco use, with important intergroup differences. Monotonic relationships were found between 10 risk factors and alcohol and illicit drug use. Individual risk factors were distributed disproportionately, and sensitivity and patterning of risk factors varied widely by ethnic/racial subsample. While the cumulative prevalence of risk factors bears a monotonic relationship to drug use, ethnic/racial differences in risk factor profiles, especially for African Americans, suggest differential predictive value based on cultural differences. Copyright 1993, American Public Health Association.

Zapata JT; Katims DS. Antecedents of substance use among Mexican-American school-age children. *Journal of Drug Education* 24(3): 233-251, 1994. (46 refs.)

This article describes a study designed to examine the association of demographic, psychological, and environmental characteristics of a sample of Mexican-American students of low socioeconomic status in elementary and middle school and their reported use of nine substances. Students in grades four, five, and six ($n = 2295$; males 52% and females 48%) located in a metropolitan school district in South Texas were surveyed to ascertain information pertaining to the initiation and/or ongoing use of substances. Regression analyses were employed to determine the relative contribution of variables measured to lifetime use of both minor and major substances. Results indicate that a specific combination of variables was predictive of both minor and major substance use for the subjects surveyed. Implications for future research and substance intervention are included. Copyright 1994, Baywood Publishing Co., Inc.

CHAPTER 12

Migrant Workers

KIMBERLY PALMA, MA

CLINICAL APPLICATIONS

The goals of this chapter are to assist the clinician to:

1. Increase understanding of the migrant culture.

2. Ascertain the extent of the substance abuse problem in migrant farmworkers in the US, while understanding the limits of data available on this subject.

3. Understand the implications of the migrant life situation and its impact on intervention strategies for substance abusers.

4. Identify interventions with the highest probability of success with the population.

5. Understand the importance of coordinating services, both locally and between states.

6. Identify the policies that impact on migrant workers and substance use problems.

7. Identify critical areas that require further study to improve delivery of services to migrant workers.

Why have migrant farmworkers been identified as needing special attention when dealing with substance abuse? On the surface, it may seem obvious, in that we are all aware of the stereotype of migrant workers who have nothing better to do than drink all day, then fight in the evening. Such anecdotal evidence indicates that there is a high incidence of substance abuse among migrants. However, data to substantiate subjective observation are minimal. While it is difficult to ascertain the exact degree of the problem among migrants, it is undeniably an issue that needs to be addressed. More important for clinicians, however, is understanding migrants life situation and the implications for service delivery. The subculture and living conditions of the migrants make them a population requiring extraordinary intervention.

MIGRANT CULTURE
Demographics

Depending on the definition used and the agency supplying the data, estimates of the number of migrant and seasonal farmworkers and their dependents range from 2½ to 4½ million. Numbers have been gradually declining, with a more dramatic drop in certain regions. This change is primarily because of mechanization, increasing costs of hiring migrant labor, and decline in the number of farms.

There is less demand for migrant labor; consequently, it has become harder to earn even a subsistence through farm work. Annual earnings can be difficult to document, but even with several members

working, a typical family's wages fall well below the poverty level. Mechanization and poor crops have resulted in shortened harvest seasons and more "down time" on any given day. Thus, it has become less feasible for entire families to travel together, which contributes to an increasing proportion of single men in the migrant stream. Although it varies by ethnic group, fewer than one-third of migrants in the US are now women and children. This demographic trend affects the culture of the population, which in turn impacts in several ways on the incidence and characteristics of substance use.

The ethnic composition of the migrant population has also changed over the years. It comprises Mexican Americans, the largest ethnic group within the migrant population; African Americans; Puerto Ricans; Native Americans; Caucasians; and to a lesser extent, Haitians, Filipinos, Vietnamese, Jamaicans, and Central Americans. The concept of migrants as both an ethnic and cultural minority is important. Although most migrants are members of minority ethnic cultures, they also belong to a unique subculture dictated by their migrancy.

Migrant life is characterized by frequent moves to follow the crops. The true interstate migrant moves 2 to 11 times in 1 year. Historical movement patterns are illustrated in Figure 12-1 and are given the names Eastern, Central, and Western streams. However, these streams are becoming less well defined, as agricultural, economic, and natural forces converge to require farmworkers to travel anywhere they can find work, for however short a duration.

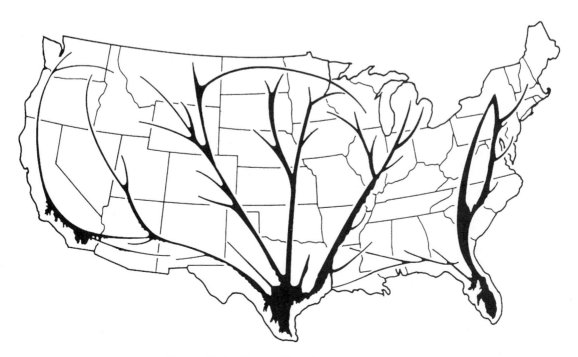

Figure 12-1. Migrant lifestyle movement patterns.

Ethnically, Hispanics predominate in the Central and Western streams. African Americans have historically been dominant in the Eastern stream, but increasing numbers of Mexican Americans have been traveling the East as well. Additionally, various Caribbean, Latin American, and East Asian peoples have been joining the farmworker ranks. For several years in the 1980s, for example, Haitians were an important part of the East Coast migrant force, but most quickly moved on to other areas of the economy. In the 1990s, there is a trend for migrants to originate from farther south in Mexico, as well as from Central America. Contrary to popular thought, 81% of foreign-born farmworkers are legally authorized to work in the US.

Health and Living Conditions

The middle man who connects the farmer with the farmworker is integral to the system. This person (usually a former laborer), called a crewleader or contractor, matches labor with jobs; negotiates the nature of the work, wages, and dates of employment; and usually arranges for transportation, shelter, and meals for the workers. Opportunities for abuse of this position abound, and abuse does occur although arguably less so than in the past. Recruitment practices are sometimes unscrupulous, with terms of employment being misrepresented.

Once an individual or family signs on with a contractor, they lose their autonomy. They may be transported interstate by bus, with the result that they then have no way to leave their camp other than by the transportation that the crewleader agrees to provide at a charge. Costs for housing, meals, alcohol, cigarettes, and other services are typically deducted from the paycheck by the crewleader, often at exorbitant prices. Thus, a laborer may see little of his paycheck, and he frequently may find himself in increasing debt to the crewleader. This system of continuous indebtedness is a major factor in the exploitation of the migrant worker.

In the 1990s there is a trend for some growers to negotiate directly with laborers, especially when they have worked for the grower for many years. This arrangement increases the potential for autonomy, particularly if the farmworkers have their own transportation.

Physical violence and alcohol may also be used to subjugate migrants. In 1984 documented cases of involuntary servitude were reported in the US. The provision of alcohol by the crewleader is also a point for emphasis. Alcohol has been described as "part of the lubricant that makes the system operate." In their proposal for funds to study alcohol abuse among migrants, Mattera et al. of the State University of New York at Geneseo describe a typical situation where the crewleader illegally sells liquor, increasing the price by as much as 100% to workers who may be recruited for their weakness for alcohol. Local officials tolerate this practice because it prevents the migrants from going to community establishments. As Mattera et al. state, "The tedium and uncertainty of camp life, the downward drift of unattached men into migrant labor, and the economic rewards accruing to the crewleader all work to make alcohol consumption an integral part of the system."

Migrants often live in squalid labor camps furnished by the grower. The camp may be comprised of cinderblock buildings, trailers, or houses. Outhouses and inside facilities tend to be poorly maintained. There may be no hot water, and the only running water may be an outside faucet. There are rarely laundry facilities. Overcrowded conditions are common: Entire families often live in one small room, and single men may be housed in dormitory style rooms called "bullpens." In many cases, a room called the commissary serves as kitchen, dining area, and the social center for the entire camp. Camps are often adjacent to the fields, subjecting the inhabitants to pesticide drift or direct spray. Similar living conditions are difficult to find elsewhere in the US. Some camps boast more humane conditions; however, most of the housing is substandard.

Migrant camp life is also one of physical and social isolation. Even those individuals who have their own transportation are often unwelcome in the rural communities near their camps. Positive stimulation is rare on the camp and chiefly arises from social interaction among workers. Boredom often contributes to substance abuse.

But migrant workers face problems worse than boredom. In 1986 the federal government mandated that migrants have sanitary facilities and drinking water at the worksite; however, enforcement is behind legislation. Migrant workers are the only workers in the US not protected against toxic substances by OSHA and are virtually the only workers excluded from national labor laws and denied the right to organize and bargain collectively. California, Arizona, and New Jersey are the only states that allow collective bargaining.

Consequently, migrants suffer from health problems directly attributable to their working conditions. In fact, the health status of migrants is comparable to third world populations. The average life expectancy among migrant workers is 52 years, and the infant mortality rate is two to three times the national average. The incidence of tuberculosis is 17 times that of the general US population. Occupational diseases include skin and lung damage from pesticide and weather exposure, fractures, loss of limbs and nails, and muscle damage from stoop labor. There is a high incidence of sanitary diseases such as urinary tract infections (stemming from chronic urine retention caused by lack of toilets at the workplace), hepatitis, diarrhea, food poisoning from inadequate refrigeration, and rodent and insect bites. Migrants also have a high incidence of hypertension, malnutrition, and anxiety and other mental health problems. The rate of alcoholism is controversial and will be discussed at length later.

Farm work is one of the most dangerous occupations. The work itself leads to severe physical and emotional stress on migrant farmworkers.

A recent and growing threat to the health of migrants is human immunodeficiency virus (HIV) infection. A 1992 Centers for Disease Control and Prevention study of farmworkers in Immokalee, Florida, found the rate of HIV infection to be 5%—10 times that of the general population. Reasons for the higher prevalence are many and complex. They include high rates of risk factors such as sexually transmitted diseases, tuberculosis, and substance abuse; limited familiarity with and understanding of HIV prevention measures; and restricted access to resources to prevent and treat HIV and AIDS.

There are some culture-specific risk factors for certain members of the migrant population. One is the self-administration of therapeutic drugs, particularly among people who come from areas of Mexico where most drugs are available over-the-counter. This practice leads to inexpensive access to needles, which can later be shared for illicit drug use. Another danger is sexual intercourse with multiple partners. In some growers' large camps in California and Florida, prostitutes are brought in as "entertainment." Several men will share the same prostitute, calling themselves "milk brothers."

Mobility is a major factor in the educational status of migrants. The dropout rate for migrant students is 50%, which is not surprising in that these children change schools many times within a year. Educational continuity is almost impossible to attain, although national programs such as the Migrant Student Records Transfer System and tutorial and adult education projects attempt to track and provide educational supplements for migrant children. These students are often needed in the field at a young age, and conditions for studying are poor at labor camps. Social isolation and the trauma of constantly moving are additional impediments to their education. However, there are those migrants who do persevere in their educational endeavors.

Psychosocial Characteristics

Some unique psychosocial characteristics can be attributed to the migrant subculture. Most migrants have a strong work ethic, which is integral to the existence of the system. The average migrant family would fare better economically if it remained in one place and collected social services benefits, yet each year millions of people suffer the intolerable living and working conditions of the migrant system to have the dignity of earning their own living. Although their work is often called unskilled labor, migrants are specialists who take great pride in their techniques.

The migrant is at the mercy of the crewleader and grower for whom he works. Migrants often see themselves as having few choices and being either the victims or beneficiaries of a fate beyond their control. Migrants have a weak political voice and few powerful advocates. Continuous exploitation and abuse inhibit trust among migrants and lower their expectations of achievement in life. In numerous surveys, migrants have indicated that they do not expect to ever become successful, and the most they hope for is a better life at their next destination. This seems to be particularly true of older people with a longer familial history of migrancy. Low expectations contribute to being oriented in the present. To strive toward long-term goals such as education (or substance abuse recovery) takes extraordinary motivation.

Low self-esteem is a chronic problem among migrants, who receive little social acceptance or encouragement, and whose labor holds the lowest status in our society. Emotional and physical stress are evident in many of the health complaints of migrants. Some crewleaders purposely recruit the deinstitutionalized mentally ill and alcoholic. Because of economic factors mentioned earlier, more and more families are forced to separate for long periods of time, leading to depression and isolation. Occupants of a camp often become one another's surrogate family, which has implications for substance abuse interventions.

SUBSTANCE ABUSE AMONG MIGRANTS
Alcohol

In 1978 the President's Commission on Mental Health received a report from its task panel on migrant and seasonal farmworkers, stating that "by all measures of economic disadvantage and social disorganization, the (migrant) farmworker population would be most at risk for mental disorder within the US." Furthermore, it quoted studies of the effects of occupational status on alcoholism and substance abuse that indicate that the probability of problems related to drinking among farmworkers is the highest of all occupational categories, including unemployed persons.

When attempting to determine whether migrants fulfill these dire predictions, the panel encountered difficulties in data collection. A questionnaire was distributed to directors of 96 migrant health clinics, 66 community mental health centers (CMHCs) located in the stream, and 33 National Institute on Alcohol Abuse and Alcoholism (NIAAA) projects in the stream. Twenty-four percent of the CMHCs and 36% of the migrant health centers returned the questionnaire, although many forms were incomplete. Only three of the NIAAA projects responded and therefore were not included in the analysis. Of the 37 responses from CMHCs, only seven directors had any contact with the population.

With this limited response, generalizing is difficult. However, project directors cited alcoholism as the most significant mental health problem of migrants, followed by anxiety and depression. While this is useful information, the more important implication for the panel was the realization that there was little information on migrants. The recommendation to the President's Commission was that "immediate efforts should be made to gather statistically reliable data to determine the extent of alcoholism, alcohol-related problems, and substance abuse problems within this population so that innovative models can be developed for the treatment and prevention of these mental health problems."

To date this charge remains largely unmet. A 1982 report for Tulare, California, County Department of Health concluded that alcohol consumption was a visible sign of severe mental stress. In 1983 Mattera et al. conducted personal interviews with 121 African-American men living on labor camps in western New York and found that the migrants in their sample did not drink more frequently or more heavily than their national sample counterparts (African-American males). They also found that unattached, older African-American men accounted for much of the heavy drinking in migrant camps and for most of the serious medical consequences of excessive alcohol consumption. This is important to note because current trends show an increasing proportion of these men in the migrant stream.

The Mattera study addressed why migrants have a reputation as heavy drinkers and found that episodic weekend drinking, drinking during work 'down times,' and the appearance of doing nothing all conspire to reinforce the image of the migrant as shiftless, drunken, and irresponsible. This pattern of migrant drinking differs from mainstream America and is also more visible because of the communal living conditions. Yet those interviewed consistently emphasized that they would never drink on a workday.

A migrant health survey conducted in 1978 among Mexican-American workers in Wisconsin found that 44% of those interviewed claimed that they never drank, and that only 2.8% drank often. These percent-

ages may be different today, as increasing numbers of young, male Mexican Americans travel and work together. In this setting, there are often weekend beer-drinking episodes similar to those found among other members of this age group in the US.

The 1986 Annual Report to the Maryland Governor's Commission on Migratory and Seasonal Farm Labor listed the problems cited by most health department providers in five counties. Increasing use of illicit drugs and excessive use of alcohol were the fifth and sixth most prevalent concerns mentioned. Richard Cervantes of the University of California at Los Angeles, who specializes in Hispanic mental health issues, explained in a recent *Philadelphia Inquirer* article that Mexicans do not drink regularly but do drink in large quantities, while the opposite is true of American drinking patterns. As Mexicans migrate, the two patterns blend, causing high rates of alcoholism. These and other reports contain important anecdotal information, but more conclusive data are needed to document the actual extent of the substance abuse problem among migrants.

Illegal Drugs

While alcohol remains the drug of choice for most migrants, as in the rest of the population, other drugs have increased in prevalence in recent years. Drug choice is dependent on such factors as ethnicity, age, proximity to urban areas, exposure to different lifestyles, and of course, cost. Crack cocaine use has increased among African-American migrants. Heroin is also a problem, especially where there is easy access to needles.

IMPLICATIONS OF MIGRANCY FOR SUBSTANCE ABUSE INTERVENTIONS
Barriers to Service

One of the most difficult problems for a migrant seeking any type of health care is cost. Few can afford to purchase their own health insurance, and most have problems meeting Medicaid eligibility guidelines because of residency and income requirements. It is also financially difficult for them to take time away from work to visit a health care site. Such visits are usually restricted to emergencies. There is also the question of obtaining permission from the grower or crewleader to miss work.

Access is another issue; many migrants do not have their own vehicles, making them reliant on the crewleader or the service provider to arrange for transportation. The schedule of most organizations does not accommodate the schedule of the farmworker; during peak harvest time laborers are often expected to work 6 or 7 days a week, often for 12 or more hours a day. Additionally, rural areas have relatively few health care services, and migrants tend to be housed in the most isolated areas.

Other barriers include lack of child care, and language and cultural differences. Although many substance abuse centers, particularly in rural areas, have difficulty finding practitioners who speak Spanish, this problem is minor compared with trying to find staff fluent in Haitian, Creole, or Vietnamese. Migrants are often unfamiliar with the bureaucratic process and are hesitant participants in formal procedures. Those migrants who are either working in this country illegally or who are uncertain of their legal status are especially reluctant.

The itinerancy of the migrant is the most important factor affecting delivery of service. Not only is it difficult for migrants to establish eligibility for Medicaid and similar benefits, they may also be excluded from local- or state-funded substance abuse programs. If eligibility is not a problem, hesitancy by the practitioner to invest effort and scarce resources in someone who will be gone in 2 months is likely to be one. Those programs that do reach out to the migrant population will have the challenge of attempting to ensure some degree of continuity once the patient has moved on to the next destination.

Cultural Barriers

Because of the migrant's experience with exploitation, trust must be painstakingly established by the practitioner. Although visitors to a migrant camp are typically treated with courtesy, any attitude of superiority or patronization is recognized immediately. Bureaucrats and "enforcers" are regarded with suspicion, especially if a migrant is living or working in this country illegally or hiding from society for other reasons; any official-looking person with a briefcase full of forms to be completed will likely be met with resistance. Because general health care is so difficult and costly to obtain, it has been well documented that migrants do not use services until a problem is life threatening. Additionally, many ethnic groups in the migrant stream rely heavily on more accessible folk cures. This low utilization of health care includes substance abuse programs as well. It should also be considered that there is a stigma attached to the disease of substance abuse among migrants, as well as in the general population. Because drinking is an integral part of the migrancy system, it is less probable that an individual laborer will recognize that his or her alcohol use is problematic. Finally, the individual who does attempt recovery will find little support in the camp environment. Their communal life-style is not conducive to recovery because others do not understand what the recovering abuser is struggling with, and much of the camp's social life revolves around alcohol

and sometimes other drug use. Inpatient treatment programs are helpful; however, these programs are often unfeasible for the migrant.

RECOMMENDATIONS FOR INTERVENTION
Model Programs

As research has lagged far behind need, so has activity in prevention and treatment. We need to look at both current and former strategies to find viable options for intervention.

For several years the BOCES Geneseo Migrant Center in New York ran a weekend program that provided alternative activities to drinking. The full-day program offered educational, athletic, creative, and cultural activities outside the camp to sober migrants. If a migrant had been drinking, he was not allowed to attend that day, but participation the next week was offered as an incentive to maintain sobriety. While this sort of programming does not address treatment for the alcoholic, it was effective for those who would drink because of boredom. This successful project ended when funding was terminated.

A task force in Chester County, Pennsylvania, was formed in 1988 to address the alcoholism problems among Mexican mushroom pickers in the area. It has been recognized that service providers had not focused on Hispanic populations in the past and that farmworkers are an even more challenging population to reach. Juan Rodriguez is one of the few people to have reached out to the mushroom workers. He did outreach efforts from 1982 to 1986 and talked with hundreds of workers, but conceded that the intensive therapy needed was unavailable in that area. None of the residential treatment centers were designed to serve Spanish-speaking patients, and the nearest regular meeting of Alcoholics Anonymous for Spanish speakers was in Wilmington, Delaware. The situation documented in Chester County is typical of most of the country.

The Sandusky County Alcohol/Drug Program in Ohio has coordinated outreach efforts with migrants since 1985. This project uses sober alcoholics, all current or former farmworkers, to do outreach and counseling in area migrant camps. The only migrants required to visit the program's headquarters were those who were court-referred following an alcohol-related arrest. The outreach workers have visited nearly 100 camps with a total of approximately 10,000 residents. They found few migrants who considered themselves alcoholics, even fewer who sought help, and only several who had been able to maintain sobriety. Difficulties cited by this program include the fact that migrants are not in contact with an outreach worker often enough for the outreach worker to break through the alcoholics' resistance before they must move on to find new work.

In 1994 two new programs that focus on outreach were funded. One is the "Farmers in Prevention" Substance Abuse Outreach Program, sponsored by the Tri-County Community Mental Health Center in Newton Grove, North Carolina. The other, funded by the US Department of Health and Human Services, serves seven counties in upstate New York. The lead agency is the Cornell Migrant Program, and five other providers make up the remainder of a service consortium. Taking a holistic approach, this project will focus its efforts in two areas: Education, prevention, and referral services for farmworkers; and staff training and collaboration among service providers. Outreach workers will conduct prevention programs for workers and provide support services during and after treatment.

Characteristics of Successful Programs

Although there are few examples to follow when designing intervention strategies with migrants, there are lessons to be learned from these and other programs designed for this special population. Whenever possible, personnel for any substance abuse program should be as similar as possible to the patient when working with an isolated group such as the migrants. Practitioners should speak the same language and share the same ethnic characteristics. Ideally, former or current farmworkers should be used. The peer counseling and educational models have historically been effective in the substance abuse field across the population. Role models can have a significant impact on migrant farmworkers, who see themselves as different from mainstream Americans. A recovered addict who also shares the migrant culture is a powerful role model to the migrant whose low self-esteem limits his expectations for himself. These guidelines for selection of personnel are admittedly difficult to attain, but their importance cannot be overestimated.

The concept of outreach is equally important, although this is rarely a component of traditional substance abuse treatment programs. Many practitioners would maintain that if a patient is not motivated enough to seek treatment voluntarily, the prognosis for recovery is bleak. Yet the barriers between the migrant and the service delivery system are so significant that outreach to engage the patient is essential. The individual must still take responsibility for choosing recovery, but extra efforts are necessary to help the migrant realize that a new way of life is possible. Outreach cannot, nor should not, take the place of more intensive strategies, but it must be a precursor.

Other deviations from traditional approaches are also indicated. It can be invaluable to work closely with professionals who have had experience with migrants, including migrant program staff, public health, and labor and legal personnel who have already established credibility with the target population. Although it requires more coordination, a multidisciplinary team approach has consistently proven to be most effective.

The intervention should also consider the unique social system in which the migrant exists. It will be of limited effectiveness to treat the individual without addressing the problem in the context of his communal living situation that encourages drug abuse. Therefore, a system-wide approach that uses several modes of intervention is recommended. For example, education could be offered to all residents of a camp, starting with children but including adults. The need for basic information at all ages must be recognized; many migrants lack a fundamental understanding of health-related issues, including substance abuse. This points to another possible strategy, one that integrates drug education with other essential information such as health education and life skills. Role models can be used to encourage exploration of alternative behaviors. Activities that take the migrant off the camp and offer positive stimulation can be extremely effective in discouraging drug use before it reaches the point of addiction. At the most severe degree of abuse, traditional treatment modes can be used but must be adapted to address the special needs of the population.

Practitioners are likely to find resistance if they initially approach the substance abuse issue alone. It may be beneficial if they are able to integrate their program with health and education services that address needs the migrants consider more critical. It is not necessary that an alcoholism treatment center, for instance, become a primary health care provider; in fact, such a tactic might result in duplication of services. However, it may be advisable to work closely with others already providing these services. An example would be to offer to run drug education programs for those in the waiting area at a migrant health center or at least have an established referral system in place within the center. Such an approach would result not only in easier access to the migrant population, but also in more efficient use of scarce resources.

It is important that any intervention attempts have realistic goals, or extreme frustration will inevitably occur. The recovery of any addict is a difficult struggle, and especially so for the migrant. It may take years before there is any visible sign of impact, a fact the practitioner must be prepared for. The Sandusky, Ohio, project, which used indigenous personnel and extensive outreach, found that it took 3 years before the outreach workers were accepted and trusted.

It should be obvious by now that the practitioner cannot hope to be successful with the migrant by working in a vacuum. Whatever progress is made must be maintained and followed up by others because soon the patient will be moving.

CONTINUITY
Local Coordination of Services

The importance of a multidisciplinary approach has already been emphasized. Networking with experts in the migrant field is crucial. Coalitions of all involved with direct services to migrants can be helpful because of the isolation of the patient's experience. Such issues as transportation and child care can be more easily handled by a team than by several independent agencies.

Another issue is documentation. While this would seem to be an obvious need with any patient, in practice it is a difficult task with migrants. Records tend to be kept in a less formal manner than with "regular" patients because of several factors: Difficulty in obtaining complete information from the patient, the fact that a practitioner may only see the patient a few times before he moves, and because outreach to migrant camps may not be the usual business for an agency. Therefore, record-keeping may be poor. Yet complete and consistent documentation is perhaps even more crucial with the migrant than with the typical patient because more practitioners are likely to be involved with the migrant.

Interstate Coordination of Services

The challenge of ensuring continued services once a patient has moved is a momentous one. Others in the migrant field have established interstate networks that may be of some assistance. The National Migrant Health Program has been in existence since 1963. The purposes of the program include service coordination, policy formulation, technical assistance, and evaluation. The Migrant Student Record Transfer System (legislatively authorized through June of 1995) tracks school-age migrants, while the Migrant Dropout Reconnection Program maintains a data base of high school dropouts up to age 21. These projects are the most advanced for migrant tracking among service providers. While these projects can be helpful in maintaining continuity in treatment, it is important that clinicians and programs in the substance abuse field develop their own interstate network. In addition to networking, a unique approach would be to develop a pilot project where the feasibility of "traveling intervention" is tested. Methods of maintaining ongoing counseling with a group of people who travel together on the season should be experimented

with. With the support of progressive crewleaders and growers, it may be possible to establish "recovering" crews who live and work together and who work on their addictions together. Although this may seem an unlikely approach, it is precisely this type of innovative thinking that has proven most successful with migrants.

RELEVANT MACROPOLICIES
Limits of Traditional Interventions

It is evident that practitioners in the substance abuse field and in other disciplines face an enormous task when trying to provide adequate services to migrants. The goal of this chapter is to provide practical information that will be immediately helpful to the clinician who encounters the migrant patient. However, it is impossible to give recommendations without touching on the systemic factors that affect service delivery.

Systemic Changes Needed

Unless the migrant can afford to pay for services and can get time off work to undergo treatment, improvements within the substance abuse service community will be of small value. Therefore, efforts to create a migrant health insurance program should be supported. Education of employers should be undertaken to reinforce the value of having a sober work force and perhaps increase their willingness to take steps to support that goal.

More generally, significant improvements must be made in the living conditions of migrants. Housing and working conditions must be brought up to at least minimal standards. The strict enforcement of existing regulations alone would have an important impact. Assurance of the right to collective bargaining would put migrants on a comparable level of power with other workers in the US. Opportunities for educational and vocational advancement must be improved, as well as assistance for those who would like to settle outside of the migrant stream. Migrants need to be allowed the essentials of life so that they can empower themselves as individuals and as a unique and valuable culture.

AREAS FOR FURTHER STUDY

As we have seen, data on substance abuse among migrants is extremely limited. When addressing any social problem, compiling of information on the subject is an important task. Perhaps no other segment of modern American society is so little understood as the migrant farmworkers. Funds should be made available, and substance abuse experts should take the initiative to conduct empirical studies of this issue.

Similarly, documentation of all service initiatives with the population is important. Suitability of programs for replication should be considered, and information concerning both successes and failures should be shared freely. The treatment of substance abuse problems among migrants is a new field with exciting possibilities for those who would take the challenge.

This provides some basic information on migrancy and its implications for the substance abuse field. For those individuals serious about working with migrants, there is much more to learn. More importantly, do your learning in a personal way. Reading the suggested materials listed here will be helpful, but visiting a migrant camp would teach you things you would never learn from a book. Second, once you do begin your work with migrants, expect to have disappointments and frustrations, but persevere. Realistic expectations and the realization that you are contributing in an area that few have attempted will help maintain your efforts. Finally, realize that there will be many rewards for your work. Travelers of the migrant stream are a special group who will demonstrate sincere appreciation for those who have earned their respect. For yourself, you will know that you are contributing to the well-being of those millions of "invisible" people who produce the food for our tables.

PROGRAMS FOR MIGRANT SUBSTANCE ABUSERS

The following programs have provided substance abuse services to migrant farmworkers. Because so little has been done in this field, this is not a list of current model programs. It should serve instead as a sample of the exploratory efforts made in the field.

Sandusky County Alcohol/Drug Program

Fremont OH 43420.

Funded for 3 years (1985 to 1987) to provide outreach to migrant workers in Sandusky and Wood counties in Ohio, the program used sober alcoholics who were either current or former farmworkers. Outreach workers provided educational, referral, and support services. The program also had a court-mandated educational component for migrants arrested for alcohol-related offenses.

Weekend Program, BOCES Geneseo Migrant Center

Geneseo NY 14420.

This program, funded from 1972 through 1980, provided alternative activities for migrants of all ages on weekends. Workers had to be sober to participate. Educational, cultural, and athletic programming was offered as incentive for migrants to remain sober on weekends.

REFERENCES

Bustos SR. Alcohol abuse among Hispanics. *The Philadelphia Inquirer*, July 17: 2-4 CC, 1988.

Dement EF. *Out of Sight, Out of Mind: An Update on Migrant Farmworker Issues in Today's Agricultural Labor Market*. Raleigh NC: National Governor's Association, 1985.

Harper D; et al. Migrant farm workers: Social conditions, adaptive belief systems, and psychiatric care. *Psychiatric Quarterly* 51(1): 28-8, 1979.

Johnston HL. *Health for the Nation's Harvesters*. Farmington Hills MI: National Migrant Worker Council Inc, 1985.

Krauth L. Program to provide help for alcoholic migrants making gains. *Blade,* December 1987.

Interviews with Robert Lynch. Director, BOCES Geneseo Migrant Center, Geneseo NY, November 1994.

Interview with Dr. James Watson. Professor of Sociology, SUNY, Geneseo NY, November 1994.

Maryland Advisory Committee to the United States Commission on Civil Rights. *Migrant Workers on Maryland's Eastern Shore*. Washington DC: Maryland Advisory Committee, 1983.

Mattera G; et al. *Alcohol Use among Migrant Laborers*. Geneseo NY: New York State Health Research Council, 1983.

Mines R; Kearney M. *The Health of Tulare County Farmworkers: A Report for the Tulare County Department of Health*. Visalia CA: Tulare County Department of Health, 1983.

National Commission to Prevent Infant Mortality. *HIV/AIDS: A Growing Crisis among Migrant and Seasonal Farmworker Families*. Washington DC: National Commission to Prevent Infant Mortality, 1993.

National Rural Health Care Association. *The Occupational Health of Migrant and Seasonal Farmworkers in the United States*. Kansas City MO: NRHCA, 1985.

Slesinger DP. *Health Needs of Migrant Workers in Wisconsin*. Madison WI: Bureau of Community Health, 1979.

Task Panel on Migrant and Seasonal Farmworkers. *Report Submitted to the President's Commission on Mental Health*. Washington DC: Government Printing Office, 1979.

FURTHER READINGS

Friedland W; Nelkin D. *Migrant Agricultural Workers in America's Northeast*. New York: Holt, Rinehart & Winston, Inc, 1971.

This book provides a good overview of life on the migrant stream. While it explores national issues, it is more valuable for its anecdotal style, which allows the reader to get an idea about what it is like to be a migrant. Some conditions have changed since the book was published, but not enough to alter its usefulness today.

Hoff W. *Use of Health Aides in Migrant Health Projects*. Rockville MD: Community Health Service, 1972.

This report offers practical suggestions for using indigenous workers in a health program. Considerations for recruitment, training, supervision, and evaluation are given.

Johnston HL. *Health for the Nation's Harvesters*. Farmington Hills MI: National Migrant Worker Council Inc, 1972.

This is a history and analysis of the national Migrant Health Program and the relevant issues that affect migrant health care. It is important reading for anyone who is seeking to design new service delivery systems.

Mattera G; Lynch R. *Our Nation's Migrant Farmworkers*. MDNM Geneseo NY: National Migrant Referral Project Inc, 1972.

This is a multimedia resource kit that provides an experiential format for learning about migrant farmworkers. Components contain information on migrancy in general and on four ethnic groups in the migrant stream: African-Americans, Indians, Mexican Americans, and Haitians. Materials include a slide/audiocassette presentation, annotated bibliography, discussion photos, games, migrant autobiographies, poetry, several booklets and articles, and a user's guide.

Shankin BN. *Health Care for Migrant Workers: Policies and Politics*. Cambridge MA: Ballinger Publishing Company, 1974.

This is a detailed policy analysis of migrant health care as it was in the mid 1970s. Although the book is slightly dated, it offers relevant assistance in planning and evaluating intervention strategies. It contains some creative ideas while remaining practical.

Task Panel on Migrant and Seasonal Farmworkers. *Report Submitted to the President's Commission on Mental Health*. Washington DC: Government Printing Office, 1974.

The report summarizes an extensive analysis of the state of migrant mental health and related issues of the early 1970s. It is valuable as a general framework for understanding the migrant condition and how it affects mental health, including substance abuse problems.

CHAPTER 13

Native Americans

JEAN KINNEY, MSW

CLINICAL APPLICATIONS

The goals of this chapter are to assist the clinician to:

1. Recognize the diversity among Native Americans.

2. Be familiar with the factors that contribute to substance use.

3. Be familiar with the health problems and the social and economic conditions that beset Native American people.

4. Be familiar with cultural factors that influence access to and utilization of substance abuse services.

A common but inaccurate perception is that Native Americans are a homogeneous group and that differences between tribes are negligible. On the contrary, differences between Native American groups are often marked by differing languages, customs, ceremonies, and world views. In addition, significant differences exist in the legal systems, the economic status, and the social problems that confront a tribe. Therefore, although statements are made about Native Americans as a group, they often represent averages and do not adequately describe most Native Americans. The 2 million Native Americans in the US are members of over 500 tribes and Alaskan Native villages. Many of the issues that confront Native Americans are common across tribes—dislocation, economic development, relationship to the federal government, and urban migration—but how these issues have been experienced and the responses to them vary.

Beyond the cultural diversity among tribes, there is often equal diversity within tribes. Some members live in rural settings and others in urban settings. There are Native Americans whose primary orientation is to the traditional culture; others to the majority culture. There are also bicultural individuals and those whose identity is not firmly grounded in either culture. Patterns and problems of alcohol and other substance use also vary.

Becoming Acquainted with the Culture

To become acquainted with a particular community, consider the following steps: Become informed about the tribe's history and cultural traditions, its socioeconomic characteristics, and the relationship of the tribe and community to the federal government. Identify social roles in the community, skills taught, and values transmitted. Speak with elders, community leaders, and tribal members who actively practice traditional medicine and with colleagues in health centers who serve the community. Also attend community functions.

In respect to alcohol and drug use, consider the following questions: What is the role of alcohol and other drug use in the community? What are the operational definitions of alcohol or drug problems? What are perceived as the causes of alcohol and other drug use problems? Who are the abstinent members of the tribe, and what is the basis for abstinence?

Historical Notes

To be informed about contemporary Native American society requires a knowledge of the histories of native peoples—a history unknown to most European Americans, except in the most superficial details. A recurring theme in this history is the relationship of Native Americans to the federal government in regard to treaties made and broken, dislocation and isolation on reservations, and Native Americans' status as "wards" of the government. The term *ward* implies that Native Americans have been regarded as being dependent on the federal government and as needing governmental oversight and assistance in managing their affairs. This historical relationship has considerable bearing on current efforts of Native Americans to effect self-determination and revitalize community life through a return to traditional ways and values.[4,30]

Alcohol use and alcohol problems are also intertwined with this history. Alcohol was not used by Native Americans until it was introduced by the Europeans, after which it was frequently the primary medium of exchange. Problems among Native Americans developed rapidly. Several tribal chiefs, concerned about the impact of alcohol on community life, petitioned President Thomas Jefferson to ban the sale of liquor to Native Americans. In 1802 a federal law was enacted that authorized the president to stop the traffic of liquor to Native Americans. This was followed in 1832 by formal legal prohibition of sales to and among Native Americans. There were periodic updates to further elaborate fines, rules, and other restrictions such as the application of the law to Native Americans serving in the military. Even when Native Americans were granted full citizenship in 1924, prohibition still remained in effect until 1953.[42]

With the repeal of this prohibition, Native Americans could drink legally off the reservations. However, the reservations were free to establish whatever controls and prohibitions they wished. Most continued to restrict sales significantly. Although the initial impetus for prohibiting alcohol use by Native Americans was in part humanitarian and a response to the concerned elders, it was also consonant with the racist view of Native Americans held by Europeans. In this instance, as in numerous others, Native Americans were regarded and treated as less capable of controlling their behavior and making independent decisions than other citizens and thus in need of the government to protect them from their presumed "childish impulses."[4,42]

ETIOLOGY OF ALCOHOL PROBLEMS

Since the introduction of alcohol by Europeans, there have been problems resulting from use. Some problems are to be anticipated; any culture incurs some costs when it sanctions drinking. Given the psychopharmacological properties of ethanol, no cultural group using alcohol can anticipate getting by unscathed. Alcohol problems are greater in Native Americans than in other groups within the US, but, the extent to which this has always been true is unknown. The cause of this disproportionately higher level of alcohol problems has received considerable attention from social scientists. The various theses and hypotheses have included the following:[47]

- *Genetic vulnerability.* This hypothesis was given credence in the early 1970s by the supposed discovery of a slower metabolism rate in Native Americans than in whites.[9] Criticized for its methodological flaws, the research was challenged shortly after publication. Efforts to replicate the original work found no differences in either the rate of metabolism or the level of liver alcohol dehydrogenase (ADH).[6,25] It also needs to be recognized that the alcohol and drug abuse fields, when using racial groups to designate a cultural or special subset of the population, often use the term *racial* improperly. There are greater genetic differences within racial groups than between them.[15]

- *Sociocultural perspectives.* Within this framework, several themes prevail, such as loss of historical traditions, the stresses of acculturation, the degree of dependency instilled by the federal government, and the forced relocation to reservations which were unable to support those living there. The historical context in which alcohol was introduced has also been cited. Attention has been given to the cultural stress present when alcohol was first introduced, as well as to the first models of drinking—the heavy drinking style of trappers, traders, and frontiersmen. Alcohol use has also been viewed symbolically as "the world's oldest protest movement."[18]

- *Economic factors.* The economies of most reservations are chronically depressed. Despite some improvements, poverty, poor health, and inadequate health care, housing, and transportation remain common. Youth have a future that promises them little. In this setting, the short-term relief of drinking or drugs may outweigh any perceived long-term damage that may result.[4]

Significant differences exist between tribes; at the same time, considering the social and economic characteristics of Native Americans as a group provides a useful context for health care providers and others concerned about alcohol and substance use problems. Among the basic parameters that influence health status—family income, the proportion of families below the poverty level, education level, and unemployment rates—there are significant differences between Native Americans and the rest of the population. These are summarized in Table 13-1.

There are marked differences as well between mortality rates of Native Americans/Alaskan Natives and the total population. These are summarized in Table 13-2. Sources of premature mortality are summarized in Table 13-3.

Table 13-1. Social Characteristics

	Native peoples	Total US population
Median age (years)	24.2	32.9
Median family income	19,886	30,056
Persons below poverty level (%)	31.6	13.1
High school graduates (%)	65.3	75.2
Unemployment rate (males)	16.2	6.4
(females)	13.5	6.2

From Indian Health Service. *Trends in Indian Health, 1994.* Rockville MD: Indian Health Service, 1995.

Table 13-2. Distribution of Death by Age Group

Age	Rate per 100,000	
	Native peoples	Total US population
Under 1 year	1085.9	971.9
1-4 years	73.2	46.8
5-24 years	199.3	99.2
25-34 years	252.5	139.2
35-44 years	369.2	223.2
45-54 years	664.3	473.4
55-64 years	1347.1	1196.9
65-74 years	2555.9	2648.6

From Indian Health Service. *Trends in Indian Health, 1994.* Rockville MD: Indian Health Service, 1995.

Table 13-3. Premature Mortality in Indian Health Service Areas (1989-1991)

	Indian Health Service areas*	US all races
Years of productive life lost years/1000 population	109.2	56.2
Age-adjusted mortality, rate per 1,000,000		
All causes	713.9	520.2
Injury & poisoning	159.3	55.1
Accident mortality	116.9	37.0
Suicide	21.3	11.5
Homicide	18.4	10.2
Tuberculosis	3.4	0.05

From Indian Health Service. *Regional Differences in Indian Health, 1994.* Rockville MD: Indian Health Service, 1995.
*Excludes 3 of the 12 IHS areas, which have a problem of underreporting Native American race on death certificates.

ALCOHOL/SUBSTANCE USE AND THE NATIVE AMERICAN

Tribal Variations in Use Patterns

There is considerable tribal variation in drinking patterns.[19] For some tribes, there is virtually no tradition of moderate drinking. To drink is to drink to intoxication. In other tribes, intoxication is less accepted, drinking is less criticized, and "social drinking" is present. It has been reported that in more highly structured tribal societies, there are more negative sanctions placed on drinking. Among these tribes, drinking is less public, with more in-home and private drinking and fewer alcohol-related arrests. When a problem occurs, it evokes more shame and guilt over the accompanying medical sequelae. It must be remembered that much Native American drinking is more properly considered problem drinking or alcohol abuse than alcohol dependence. After age 40, there is a sharp decline in drinking, a greater decline than occurs in the general population.

The drinking patterns of the tribe and community influence the definitions of behaviors that are deemed deviant and dysfunctional. These, in turn, influence the pressures on individuals to enter treatment and the selection of treatment goals.

Half of Native Americans live in urban areas. The percentage of abstainers in this group, about 30%, is the same as in the general US population. However, among Native Americans who drink, there are significantly fewer infrequent, light, or moderate drinkers and over twice as many heavy drinkers.[43]

Many tribes are found in the urban setting. The drinking pattern is an amalgam of practices brought from different rural areas and reservations of different tribes, translated into the urban setting. In part, these patterns also reflect drinking practices common in some nonurban areas. Men drink more frequently and more heavily than women. Drinking is associated with social situations; there is little solitary drinking. Men often drink in groups and pass the bottle; it is considered discourteous or even insulting to refuse the offer of a drink. The alcohol is usually drunk rapidly with the intent of becoming intoxicated. Drinking often continues until the supply is exhausted or until the drinkers become stuporous. Since alcohol is shared in drinking groups, money is not necessary to drink. In contrast to the quiet and reserved demeanor typical in sober states, loud and boisterous behavior occurs during drinking, with exaggerated symptoms of drunkenness displayed. Overt, aggressive, and sexual behaviors are frequently associated with drinking. Binge drinking is also common. Although sometimes there is verbal disapproval, there are few social sanctions against drinking. There is little interference with or open condemnation of an individual's behavior during drinking.[43]

Drinking as Defined by Native Americans

Among Native Americans, problem drinking tends to be defined in respect to the social group, rather than in terms of individual clinical markers or negative consequences for the individual. Behaviors that Native Americans would consider indicative of problematic use include the following:[43]

- Drinking heavily and overtly at urban pow wows.
- Drinking at the drum or dancing while intoxicated at urban or rural pow wows.
- Community leaders regularly drinking in low-status bars.
- Asking direct and personal questions while under the influence of alcohol.
- Drinking alone.
- Not eating during a drinking session.
- Drinking wine rather than beer or hard liquor.
- Drinking at serious business events (community meetings).
- Drinking in areas designated as sacred space.
- Making uninvited sexual overtures while under the influence of alcohol.
- Drinking while participating in athletic contests.
- Not being able to defend oneself in a fight because of level of intoxication.
- Not providing adequate financial support for family because of the expenses of drinking.

Interestingly, there is virtually no mention of medical sequelae, accidents, suicide, or homicide as indices of a problem, despite their disproportionate numbers among Native Americans.

Risk Factors for Alcohol Problems

Different types of alcohol and substance use problems have different associated risk factors. For groups with a higher incidence of intoxication and its associated impairment, there is a higher incidence of acute problems associated with use. In respect to dependence, having a positive family history of alcoholism, of drug dependence, and for the medical sequelae from chronic heavy drinking are significant. Just as there is a genetic component for alcohol dependence, there appears to be a genetic basis for having or being spared the medical consequences of heavy alcohol use. Other risk factors include membership in a tribe that tolerates and accepts intoxication and does not have a pattern of moderate use.

By the definitions of substance abuse professionals, there are many negative medical and social consequences of alcohol use among Native Americans. This raises the question, Is dependence as high as such figures would indicate?[5] Thirty years ago, the early modern alcohol researcher, Jellinek, described several distinct types of alcoholism.[23] He noted that the

French variant of alcoholism for that era was marked by medical sequelae related to the high level of alcohol consumed. However, high consumption was culturally acceptable and heavy drinking was prescribed. That type of alcoholism was not marked by either psychological dependence or loss of control. In assessing alcohol use and the associated problems in some Native Americans, the question must be considered: Is heavy drinking culturally prescribed and essentially normative? Although there are severe negative consequences, Native American problem drinking is not wholly synonymous with alcohol dependence, as it is recognized in white middle class American culture.[11,44] This not only raises problems for screening in clinical situations, but for epidemiological research. An initial field test of the Diagnostic Interview Schedule (DIS) proved it to be a promising instrument with this population, although there were problematic areas. For example, the common practice of "passing the bottle" does fit with efforts to measure a "standard drink."[36]

PROBLEMS ASSOCIATED WITH ALCOHOL AND SUBSTANCE USE
Health Indices Related to Alcohol and Substance Use

From 1981 to 1983, 13 conditions were identified in Native Americans as accounting for 92% of the total years per life lost (YPLL) before age 55. These are summarized in Table 13-4. These same conditions represented 46% of all IHS outpatient visits and 73% of the total IHS hospital days. These reflect the relationship between morbidity and mortality and socioeconomic and environmental conditions. To reduce the mortal-

ity rate, living conditions, environment, and personal behavior need to be addressed.[37] While mortality has dramatically improved in Native Americans since the 1970s, the level of mortality continues to exceed other portions of the US population (Table 13-5).

Of particular concern is Native Americans in the 15 to 45-year age group. The rates of productive years lost are approximately two times that of the general population. Furthermore, the causes from death in this group—unintentional injuries, homicides, and suicides—are essentially nondisease causes.[21,22]

Alcohol-Associated Premature Mortality

Using Multiple Cause of Mortality tapes produced by the National Center for Health Statistics, premature mortality attributable to specific alcohol-associated conditions has been determined for Native Americans. These may appear as either the underlying cause or as a contributing cause of death. The data is presented in YPLL. The most significant causes of excess mortality are excluded—motor vehicle-related, cardiomyopathy, alcoholic gastritis, suicide, and homicide that are due to alcohol use. Thus, the YPLL are significantly underestimated. This is summarized in Table 13-3 and 13-4.

The differences in alcohol-related causes of premature mortality are significant between Caucasians, African Americans, and Native Americans, as a group and by sex. The rates of alcohol-related YPLL parallel that of total YPLL from all causes in the US in being higher in men than women. However, there are some important differences. Generally, African Americans have the highest rates of premature mortality, followed by Native Americans and then Caucasians, but this is not the case for alcohol-related premature

Table 13-4. Health Indices Related to Alcohol and Substance Use

	Total productive life lost (%)	Deaths (rate per 100,000)
IHS total (all causes)	100.0	695.1
Unintentional injuries	32.9	116.5
Infant mortality	18.7	12.6
Violence	13.5	43.1
Cardiovascular diseases	7.0	192.3
Alcoholism	6.5	52.7
Cancer	4.3	92.9
Respiratory diseases	3.6	42.2
Digestive diseases	2.3	24.2
Infectious diseases	1.8	13.6
Diabetes mellitus	0.9	25.5
Chronic renal failure	0.7	11.7
Pregnancy and childbirth	0.1	0.0
All other	7.8	60.4

From Rhoades ER; et al: The Indian burden of illness and future health intervention. *Public Health Report* 102(4): 361-367, 1987.

Table 13-5. Alcohol-Associated Premature Mortality

Alcohol-associated condition	Group	Male (rates per 100,000)	Female (rates per 100,000)
Alcohol abuse	White	372.9	19.7
	Black	131.5	32.2
	Native American	548.8	97.3
Alcohol dependence	White	117.2	32.8
	Black	459.1	158.8
	Native American	769.8	372.0
Alcoholic cirrhosis	White	98.6	39.5
	Black	253.3	120.5
	Native American	527.3	349.1

From Rhoades ER: et al: The Indian burden of illness and future health intervention. *Public Health Report* 102(4): 361-367, 1987.

deaths. Native Americans have the highest rate of alcohol-associated YPLL. Native American women have greater premature mortality from cirrhosis than either black or white males (see Table 13-5).[8] Premature mortality is higher in Native Americans than in the general population for all causes except respiratory diseases, cancer, and cardiovascular disease, for which the rates are essentially the same.[37]

Tribal Comparisons

As a result of differences in drinking practices, there are corresponding differences between tribes in the types and rates of medical consequences of alcohol and substance use. The marked differences between tribes should make suspect any generalizations of the findings based on the examination of specific tribal group. For example, in the aggregate, the incidence of FAS for Native Americans is significantly higher than in the majority culture. However, there is considerable variation in the rates for different tribes, with an overall range from 4/1000 to 33/1000 live births; the 4/1000 incidence is similar to that of the majority culture.[32] Of significance is the presence of a minority (25%) of women with multiple FAS–affected children.[37] Differences are found in the reported rates for cirrhosis, e.g., one tribe has a rate four times the national average, and another a rate only slightly higher than the national average.[24,27] The proportion of abstainers also varies by tribe, e.g., over half of Navajo women are reported to be nondrinkers.[43]

THE IMPACT OF CULTURE ON CLINICAL CARE

Clinicians need to be aware that behaviors they think define the clinician/patient encounter and the Western model of medical care may be incongruent with Native American patients' beliefs and perceptions. The perceptions of the illness and disease, etiology, and factors used to categorize physical problems may be quite different from that of the clinician. When this is the case, it may alter the medical encounter.[29,40]

Views of Illness and Disease

Illness and disease within traditional Native American culture is not considered due to biological factors. Rather, there is the perception that illness arises from fundamental imbalances or disharmonies in the relationship of spirit, body, the ancient traditions, and relationship to the physical universe. Some tribes have views of healing that differentiate between "Indian" illness and "Whiteman" sickness. If the causative agents are deemed to be spiritual, it is an "Indian illness;" traditional medicine, healing, and cleansing ceremonies would be viewed as appropriate. If the causative agents are attributed to Western influences, then individuals would use the IHS medical care system.

In respect to alcohol and substance abuse, the clinician and the Native American patient may agree on the *dysfunctions* resulting from use. The disease concept may not be the model used by Native Americans to understand the phenomena. This is in opposition to the usual view that acceptance of the disease concept is important for recovery and is necessary to help relieve guilt. Incorporation of traditional methods of healing and purifying are important ingredients of treatment, especially for those who strongly identify with traditional culture. Thus, the primary care provider might prescribe traditional means of healing.

Clinical Interactions

The manner of personal presentation by Native Americans may be misunderstood by clinicians. There is reservation and reticence about self-disclosure; therefore, the clinician's history taking may arouse discomfort. Personal matters are traditionally handled within the immediate and extended family. Sharing such information may be regarded as inappropriate or as burdening health care or human service workers. The Native American patient may discuss peripheral issues at first as a way of getting a sense of the clinician, the clinician's orientation, and the level of concern. Direct eye contact is viewed by many Native Americans as rude and intimidating, contrary to the majority culture's view.

The extended family is an important part of Native American life, providing a source of nurturance, support, and identity. For those persons oriented to the tribal culture, use of cultural resources is important in developing treatment plans.

Cultural Orientation

Finally, a patient's orientation to the traditional culture and the majority culture will be a significant factor in matching patients with appropriate treatment. There are essentially four groups: Those with a traditional orientation, those whose major identification is with the majority culture, those who are bicultural, and those whose identity is not grounded in either the majority or Native American traditional culture. Table 13-6 is a guide in assessing cultural orientation.[46]

Not only will the patient's present cultural orientation affect the encounter, but the cultural orientation of childhood may become significant in light of the stresses accompanying illness. For the acculturated adult reared in the traditional culture, there may be a need for the comfort, solace, and healing of traditional medicine to supplement Western "white" medicine.

TREATMENT CONSIDERATIONS
Natural History

As is true for the general population, there is some evidence of a significant level of "spontaneous remission" that may be better considered as amelioration of problems in the absence of formal treatment. A number of studies have found that the proportion of Native Americans who have quit using alcohol by age 30 and 40 exceeds the proportion in the general population. One study has examined the natural history of alcohol problems in a native village in the Pacific northwest, a village that was studied twice in 19 years. Three-quarters of the males had a lifetime history of alcohol dependence, with the problem blossoming in the early twenties. However, of these, approximately half stopped drinking after an average of 15 years. This was almost always in the absence of treatment and in response to a specific, personal reason such as financial, family, or health problems. Within the village, two drinking styles were predominate, abstinence or heavy drinking consistent with a diagnosis of abuse or dependence. At the same time, the village had a lower rate of alcohol problems at the end point of follow-up. The prevalence rate in the village had declined, and both public drunkenness and assaultive behavior were less common. In respect to community life, during this period there was improvement in the economic conditions and educational levels. Within the village, there was also a revitalized tribal council and an increased interest in the tribal heritage.[26]

Use of AA

Alcoholics Anonymous has become a mainstay of treatment. It has also been widely used as an aspect of treatment of Native Americans although the literature is not universally positive as to its utility or acceptance by Native Americans. One writer has described AA as the most controversial treatment modality, being incongruent with Native Americans' cultural orientation. A major problem is the "confessional" public style of AA, which is contrary to the private, family-centered setting traditionally used for handling problems. On the other hand, Native Americans acculturated to the majority culture do well in AA.[27]

The General Service Board of the AA Fellowship has developed a pamphlet for Native Americans with "stories" by Native Americans to translate the AA experience.[17] Other groups have already attempted to translate the 12 steps of AA, using language and phrasing better suited and more congenial to Native Americans who identify with the traditional culture.[34]

Use of Traditional Healing

The potential value of using traditional methods of healing and other indigenous practices as components of alcohol and drug treatment is receiving more recognition. Although their rationales may differ, many clinicians who work with Native Americans agree that some cultural resurgence and tradition-enhancing efforts are important in providing alcohol and drug treatment. For programs that serve many Native Americans, the medicine man and the sweat lodge are aspects of the traditional culture most commonly incorporated into the standard treatment regimen. The Native American Church is found to a lesser degree. Although the forms of ritual vary, the sweat lodge is common in many tribal traditions. As generally practiced, therapeutic sweats may last for several hours. After the sprinkling of water on hot rocks, the leader of the sweats evokes prayers that are continued by the participants in turn. The ceremony is generally structured into sequences called "rounds." The ceremony is a cleansing ritual that reestablishes harmony between an individual and the universe and involves making a commitment to Native American heritage. Those participating in a sweat lodge are a cross-section of community members. This can facilitate the reintegration of the estranged individual back into the

Table 13-6. Assessing Cultural Orientation

TRADITIONAL			
Spiritual	**Social**	**Training**	**Family**
Attends ceremonies, sweats, or other functions of tribal belief system.	Spends leisure time with native people. Prefers activities centered around Indian community.	Prefers to learn in an unstructured setting. Uses extended periods for listening and observing. Places greater emphasis on learning from elders.	Perceives relationships as extended family, encompassing all relations. Maintains continual contact with all family members. Ultimately includes individual's tribe.
Has knowledge of the ceremonies, sweats, or other outward signs of tribal belief system, but does not actively participate on a regular basis.	Spends leisure time with native people. Prefers activities centered around Indian community. Enjoys contemporary activities within the context of the "all-Indian" teams, rodeos, or tournaments.	Prefers to learn in an unstructured setting. Uses extended listening and observation. Places greater emphasis on learning from grandparents. Has received some formal education.	Perceives relationships as extended family. Maintains continual contact with all family members. Strong identification with tribal background.
Believes in a church doctrine or has participated in an organized religion, but does not actively attend on a regular basis.	Spends most leisure time outside Indian community. Prefers activities in general community. Occasionally attends pow wows or other Indian community activities.	Prefers to learn in a structured classroom setting. Is assisted by movies and speakers. Has had minor exposure to grandparents' and elders' teachings. Somewhat uncomfortable with assessment of skills and knowledge through written evaluation.	Perceives family relationships as restricted to parents, brothers, sisters, spouse, and children. Maintains occasional contact with grandparents and other relatives. Identifies with tribe. Has had minimal contact with ancestral people or land.
Attends church or organized religious activities such as Bible study.	Spends leisure time outside Indian community. Prefers activities centered around general community events and social gatherings.	Prefers to learn in a structured classroom setting. Is assisted by process through formal lectures, didactics and assessment of skill, and knowledge through written evaluation.	Perceives relationships as primarily family. Focuses on relationship to spouse and children, occasionally encompassing brothers, sisters, and grandparents.
CONTEMPORARY			
Religion	**Recreation**	**Education**	**Self**

From Cox WM. *Treatment and Prevention of Alcohol Problems: A Resource Manual.* Orlando FL: Academic Press Inc, 1987.

community. The leaders of the sweat lodge, as well as other healers within the community, are often among the most vocal spokesmen *for* sobriety and regard drunkenness as incompatible with traditional ways.[16]

Treatment Outcome

The results of Native American alcohol treatment programs have been described as "mixed" and "disappointing." A recurrent observation by treatment evaluators is the need for treatment programs that are sensitive to tribal, cultural, age, and sex differences. It has also been widely noted that the treatment model used is predominantly the Western medical model. This model has not worked for patients who see themselves as neither sick nor diseased. The cultural differences between staff and patients produce tension and contribute to low staff morale and high patient recidivism. It has also been observed that treatment programs prepare patients to return to a world that does not exist for them, e.g., resuming the role of wage earner, having sober acquaintances, and resuming social and recreational activities not organized around drinking.[16,44]

The lack of common, basic services for Native Americans and the absence of standards for staffing and training lead to poor treatment outcome. With the absence of these services, there is an inability to match patients with the most clinically appropriate treatment services. In part, this is due to mixed funding sources. Some services are provided by tribes through contracts they negotiate; others are provided by the IHS. Other factors handicapping treatment are tension between recovering individuals and those who are not; tension between workers with formal training and those with nontraditional training; and tension between Native Americans and those who are not.[36]

There has been almost no formal evaluation of programs sponsored by the IHS, the major provider of specialized services for Native Americans. However, from the limited data available, it appears that at least for Native American men, treatment outcome is related to the same factors that are significant for the general population. Treatment outcome has been found to be largely associated with pretreatment variables. Those with the best outcomes are younger, employed, have intact families and readily available social supports, are of higher socioeconomic status, and enter treatment with fewer physical and social dysfunctions and less chronicity.[41] If the treatment is not cultural specific, the patients who would do better most resemble the general majority population.

In respect to Native Americans in general programs, some reports suggest that the outcome is as good or better than in other minority group members. A study of patients of alcohol/substance abuse programs conducted by the Veterans Affairs found that Native American patients were among those most likely to complete treatment.[10]

The Family

The involvement of family has become accepted as essential in alcohol and substance abuse treatment, including with Native Americans. However, "family" cannot be considered synonymous with "nuclear family." Family should be viewed as the extended family or the kinship network. The family is the traditional setting in which problems are to be addressed. A therapeutic challenge for the primary care practitioner is functioning as an outsider in a closed family system. It is important to be patient, promote the family's problem-solving abilities, and recognize that decisions will be made in the family. This avoids thinking of the physician or nurse as the expert or advice giver and presuming that compliance ensues in deference to technical expertise and medical authority. Paradoxically, in recognizing and accepting the authority of the family, the clinician increases the probability that medical opinions and recommendations will be seriously considered.[28,29] Men may find candid discussion of problems in front of wives or children uncomfortable and resist.

Women

There is considerable discussion in the literature of alcohol use among Native American women. The absence of treatment programs specifically for Native American women is frequently mentioned as a problem. However, because of the nature and limitations of the demographic studies conducted, the data are open to question. Nonetheless, the following appear to be common features of drinking among Native American women.[8,9,27,37,46] Considerable diversity exists for drinking patterns by women of different tribes. For instance, among the Navajo over 50% of the women are reported to be nondrinkers. Women typically drink less than men.

Women's drinking is likely to arouse more disapproval than men's drinking. Although they represent the minority of cases of alcohol dependence, women are overly represented in treatment facilities. This may reflect a greater impetus for Native American women to enter treatment, a pressure attributable to the greater community disapproval of women's drinking and the greater impact of women's drinking on the family with the inability to fulfill caretaking functions.

Native American women may be able to enter treatment facilities more conveniently because they may have resources less available in the majority culture. For instance, the extended family is available to assume responsibilities such as child care. Other explanations are that women's heavy drinking leads to medical complications more quickly, and that women's drinking creates more dysfunction in the home and family than does comparable drinking in men. Unlike the shared drinking of men, women's alcohol use is more likely to take place in the home and in the company of the spouse. Native American women have the highest rate of cirrhosis in the US. This is speculated to be the result of two factors: Women's apparent increased vulnerability to liver disease, and the significant minority of women who drink heavily.

In treatment, special attention needs be given to the woman whose spouse is a heavy drinker because this is a significant risk factor for relapse. It is important to develop specific plans for coping with the spouse's drinking. Promote the development of alternative support systems from the extended family and the community. Sobriety is consonant with traditional values; therefore, involvement in traditional activities can affirm and support abstinence.

Adolescents

Adolescents typically have a higher rate of alcohol/ substance use than older persons, with an accompanying heightened risk for problems. In Native American adolescents, the rates of use are higher than for non-native teens. This has been a consistent finding over the past 20 years.[3] Of Native youth, reservation youth are more involved with drugs than those off the reservation.[2,25]

Although alcohol was the primary psychoactive agent 20 years ago, multiple drug use has since become the norm for Native American teenagers. Native American youth have higher rates of use for nearly every drug category. Rural isolation appears to provide no protection. In some sites, less accessibility to alcohol may increase the use of other substances. To a significant degree, Native American youth are younger when they begin to use alcohol and first become intoxicated, usually before adolescence.

Inhalants are also commonly used by Native American adolescents. In some tribes up to 30% of all young adults have used volatile substances. Because inhalant use is a group behavior, the potential for problems is increased.[5]

Tobacco is often overlooked in discussions of substance use, including smokeless products such as chewing tobacco and snuff. One recent study found that in a sample of Native American sixth graders, 28% currently used smokeless tobacco, while the general population figure is 3.3%. Among the experimenters, the proportion of girls approached that of boys, and was virtually eight times that of girls in the general population. For boys the rate was doubled. Of those who used smokeless tobacco, more than half also reported having tried cigarettes.[1] The prevalence of substance use is presented in Table 13-7.

There has been a general downward trend in substance use among Native American adolescents, which mirrors the trend nationally. However, surveys of Native adolescents have found that there has been a small but continuing increase of cocaine and psychedelics. (In speculating about the reasons for this, the researchers note that marijuana use is common and that the same supply line may well also handle cocaine and psychedelics).[3]

The same study found that while the rates of use have been declining, the proportion of adolescents at high risk has remained in the 17% to 20% range over the past 20 years. Another area of interest is use among younger teens and preadolescents. Among fourth through sixth graders, the numbers who report any use of alcohol or marijuana has declined over the past decade. However, the proportion who have used inhalants and nicotine remains relatively constant (Table 13-8).

Table 13-7. Prevalence of Substance Use in Native American Youth

Drug	Percent of those surveyed			
	1975	1980-81	1984-85	1988-90
Alcohol	76	85	79	74
Getting drunk	—	—	46	51
Marijuana	41	74	57	54
Inhalants	16	30	21	23
Cocaine	6	11	7	9
Stimulants	10	24	21	16
Heroin	3	5	5	4
Psychedelics	7	9	9	12
Tranquilizers	—	6	7	3
PCP	—	—	10	7
Cigarettes	—	—	79	67
Smokeless tobacco	—	—	—	51
N	1235	2159	1510	5768

From Beauvais F. Trends in adolescent drug and alcohol use. *American Indian and Alaska Native Mental Health Research* 5(1): 1-12, 1992.

Table 13-8. 4th-6th Grade Students' Lifetime Substance Use

	Percentage reporting use		
	1980-81	1987-88	1989-90
Alcohol	33	22	21
Marijuana	23	16	10
Inhalants	14	14	15
Cigarettes	34	33	32

From Beauvais F. Trends in adolescent drug and alcohol use. *American Indian and Alaska Native Mental Health Research* 5(1): 1-12, 1992.

For Native American adolescents, the major causes of death are accidents, suicide, and homicide. The mortality rates for Native American adolescents are significantly higher than for comparable age groups in the total population. For children ages 5 to 14 years, the mortality rate for Native American children is 50% higher. Between the ages of 15 to 24 years, the mortality rate is 2.7 times higher for Native American youth.[12]

Tribal rates for adolescent suicide, auto accidents, child abuse and neglect, and spouse abuse are proportional to the tribe's alcohol and drug use. Of Native American adolescent suicides, approximately 90% are considered related to heavy alcohol use, with the majority occurring under the influence of alcohol. Postmortem interviews with immediate and extended family members, friends, and teachers of adolescents who committed suicide identified patterns of chronic and acute stressors related to suicide. The chronic stressors included having had more than one significant caretaker before age 15; having had a higher percentage of caretakers with five or more arrests; having experienced two or more losses through divorce or desertion; having a history of arrests before age 15; and having attended a boarding school. An important cultural factor related to adolescent suicide is the degree of tribal stability in terms of religion and traditions, and the presence or absence of pressures on children to acculturate.[7]

Culture-Based Risk Factors

Cultural identification affects the levels of drug and alcohol use. Among older youth, identification with native culture is somewhat of a protective factor. Those with a native cultural identification use fewer drugs but more alcohol. Bicultural youth have the least alcohol and drug use.[3]

It is postulated that the increased use of alcohol and other substances by Native American youth is related to several factors. For one, schooling typically occurs in either boarding schools or in community schools in which Native Americans are the minority. Both settings have problems and are considered far from ideal by either educators or experts in adolescent development. For Native American youth there is some evidence that higher rates of alcohol and other drug use accompany boarding school attendance. Men who had attended boarding school appear to be at greater risk for serious alcohol and drug problems in adulthood than those who have not.[41] Recent studies suggest that the level of stress, the level of perceived family support, and family members' acceptance of rejection of alcohol use are also related to levels of adolescent drinking.[13]

Another risk factor for youths is that the adult role models often drink heavily and drink with peers. For Native Americans, adolescent drinking is not culturally opposed. Historically, prohibition on reservations has encouraged traveling to drink and thus increases the risk of accidents. Finally, in some tribes bootlegging is common, thus condoning illegal consumption.[46]

The impact of conflicting cultural orientations on adolescents, as they are faced with normal developmental tasks, has been questioned. The four developmental tasks include the following: The acceptance of the biological role; the struggle to become comfortable with one's sexuality; the choice of an occupational identity; and the struggle toward independence (see Chapter 18, Adolescents). The nor-

mally anticipated difficulties in accomplishing these tasks is compounded for Native American adolescents. The Native American traditional culture is unknown and devalued by the majority culture. There is an absence of low-risk drinkers as role models within the immediate tribe. The attributes of "good" role models by traditional standards are not similarly defined by the majority culture. Developing a vocational identity is difficult given the average 9-year education, limited work skills, and few job opportunities unless youth are willing to relocate to an urban area. Beyond alcohol's use in easing the emotional pain of cultural conflict, drinking has assumed a major role as a rite of passage to adulthood. In addition, the values implicit in the traditional Native American culture are in conflict with those of the majority culture.[33]

The following treatment guidelines are suggested in working with Native American adolescents at any point in the progression of an alcohol or substance use problem: Provide education on the relationship of alcohol and substance use to driving accidents, unwanted pregnancies, sexually transmitted diseases, human immunodeficiency virus (HIV) infection, and suicides and homicides; involve nuclear and extended family; promote an abstinent peer support system; promote activities to build ties to the traditional culture, including traditional healing and cleansing ceremonies; encourage alcohol- and substance-free recreational activities; consider an assessment for educational supports and vocational training; identify stressors for relapse; lend support; and focus on the universal need of adolescents to develop coping strategies and problem-solving skills, both of which translate into the need for choices and for a time-limited frame of reference.[38]

General Clinical Guidelines

- Admit your ignorance or the limits of your knowledge of the Native American experience.
- Know that you will be watched closely for inconsistencies, e.g., stereotypical, "government," or "white" behavior.
- Offer medical advice as something to be considered as part of a holistic scheme.
- Understand that many Native Americans believe that medicine men give patients power and that Western physicians keep power.
- Tell patients what you are doing and why.
- Be prepared to listen more and devote more attention to patients.
- Offer patients choices, especially children.
- Involve family members, immediate and extended.
- Be patient.

REFERENCES

1. Backinger CL; Bruerd B; Kinney MB; Szpunar SM. Knowledge, intent to use, and use of smokeless tobacco among sixth grade school children in six selected US sites. *Public Health Report* 108(5): 637-642, 1993. (48 refs.)

2. Beauvais F. The consequences of drug and alcohol use for Indian youth. *American Indian and Alaska Native Mental Health Research* 5(1): 32-37, 1992. (1 ref.)

3. Beauvais F. Trends in adolescent drug and alcohol use. *American Indian and Alaska Native Mental Health Research* 5(1): 1-12, 1992. (18 refs.)

4. Beauvais F; LaBoueff S. Drug and alcohol abuse intervention in American Indian communities. *International Journal of the Addictions* 20(1): 139-171, 1985. (47 refs.)

5. Beauvais F; Oetting ER. Indian youth and inhalants: An update. IN: Crider RA; Rouse B, eds. *Epidemiology of Inhalant Use.* Rockville MD: National Institute on Drug Abuse, 1989. pp. 30-34. (18 refs.)

6. Bennion L; Li TK. Alcohol metabolism in American Indians and whites. *New England Journal of Medicine* 294(1): 9-13, 1976. (15 refs.)

7. Berlin IN. Suicide among American Indian adolescents: An overview. *Suicide and Life Threatening Behavior* 17(3): 218-232, 1987. (66 refs.)

8. Bertolucci MA; Noble J; Dufour M. Alcohol-related premature mortality—1980. *MMWR. Morbidity and Mortality Weekly Report* 34(32): 31-32, 1985. (5 refs.)

9. Blume SB. Women and alcohol: A review. *Journal of the American Medical Association* 256(11): 1467-1469, 1986. (51 refs.)

10. Booth BM; Blow FC; Cook CAL; Bunn JY; Fortney JC. Age and ethnicity among hospitalized alcoholics: A nationwide study. *Alcoholism: Clinical and Experimental Research* 16(6): 1029-1034, 1992. (38 refs.)

11. Community Training and Resource Center. Underserved populations: American Indians and alcohol. *CTRC Update* Spring 1983.

12. Davis SM; Hunt K; Kitzes JM. Improving the health of Indian teenagers: A demonstration program in rural New Mexico. *Public Health Report* 104(3): 271-278, 1989. (26 refs.)

13. Dick RW; Manson SM; Beals J. Alcohol use among male and female Native American adolescents: Patterns and correlates of student drinking in a boarding school. *Journal of Studies on Alcohol* 54(2): 172-177, 1993. (28 refs.)

14. Fenna D; Mix L; Schaeffer O; Gilbert JAL. Ethanol metabolism in various racial groups. *Canadian Medical Association Journal* 105(September): 472-475, 1971. (24 refs.)

15. Fisher AD. Alcoholism and race: The misapplication of both concepts to North American Indians. *Canadian Review of Sociology and Anthropology* 24(1): 81-98, 1987. (47 refs.)

16. Flores PJ. Alcoholism treatment and the relationship of Native American cultural values to recovery. *International Journal of the Addictions* 20(11-12): 1707-1726, 1985-86. (25 refs.)

17. General Services Board (Alcoholics Anonymous). *AA for Native North Americans.* New York: General Services Board (Alcoholics Anonymous), 1989. (Pamphlet, publication number P21-406)

18. Hall RL. Alcohol treatment in American Indian populations: An indigenous treatment modality compared with traditional approaches. IN: Babor T, ed. Alcohol and culture: Comparative perspectives from Europe and America. *Annals of the New York Academy of Sciences* 472: 168-178, 1986. (46 refs.)

19. Heath DB. American Indians and alcohol: Epidemiological and sociocultural relevance. IN: Spiegler D; Tate D; Aitken S; Christianson C, eds. *Alcohol Use among US Ethnic Minorities. NIAAA Research Monograph 18.* Rockville MD: National Institute on Alcohol Abuse and Alcoholism, 1989. pp. 206-222. (63 refs.)

20. Indian Health Service. *Chart Series Book.* Rockville MD: IHS, 1988.

21. Indian Health Service. *Regional Differences in Indian Health, 1994.* Rockville MD: Indian Health Service, 1995. 93 pp. (0 refs.)

22. Indian Health Service. *Trends in Indian Health, 1994.* Rockville MD: Indian Health Service, 1995. 123 pp. (0 refs.)

23. Jellinek EM. *The Disease Concept of Alcoholism.* New Haven CT: Hillhouse Press, 1960. 246 pp. (468 refs.)

24. Kunitz SJ; Levy JE; Odoroff CL; Bollinger J. The epidemiology of alcoholic cirrhosis in two Southwestern Indian tribes. *Quarterly Journal of the Studies on Alcohol* 32(3A): 706-720, 1971. (22 refs.)

25. Leiber CS. Metabolism of ethanol and alcoholism: Racial and acquired factors. *Annals of Internal Medicine* 76(2): 326-327, 1972. (10 refs.)

26. Leung PK; Kinzie JD; Boehnlein JK; Shore JH. A prospective study of the natural course of alcoholism in a native American village. *Journal of Studies on Alcohol* 54(6): 733-738, 1993. (28 refs.)

27. Lewis RG. Alcoholism and the Native American: A review of the literature. IN: National Institute on Alcohol Abuse and Alcoholism. *Alcohol and Health: Special Population Issue.* Rockville MD: National Institute on Alcohol Abuse and Alcoholism, 1982. pp. 315-328. (42 refs.)

28. Lewis RG; Ho MK. Social work with Native Americans. *Social Work* 20(5): 379-382, 1975. (15 refs.)

29. Lockhart B. Historic distrust and the counseling of American Indians and Alaskan Natives. *White Cloud Journal* 2(3): 31-34, 1981. (7 refs.)

30. Mail PD; Johnson S. Boozing, sniffing, and toking: An overview of the past, present, and future of substance use by American Indians. *American Indian and Alaska Native Mental Health Research* 5(2): 1-33, 1993. (86 refs.)

31. Manson SM; Shore JH; Baron AE; Neligh G. Alcohol abuse and dependence among American Indians. IN: Helzer JE; Canino GJ, eds. *Alcoholism in North America, Europe, and Asia.* London: Oxford University Press, 1992. pp. 113-130. (41 refs.)

32. May PA; Hymbaugh KJ; Aase JM; Samet JM. Epidemiology of fetal alcohol syndrome among American Indians of the Southwest. *Social Biology* 30(4): 374-387, 1983 (47 refs.)

33. National Institute on Alcohol Abuse and Alcoholism. *A Growing Concern: How to Provide Services for Children from Alcoholic Families.* Rockville MD: NIAAA, 1985.

34. National Native Alcohol Abuse Program. *Help for Ourselves.* (pamphlet). Ottawa Ontario: Northwest Indian Training Institute. (undated)

35. Oetting ER; Beauvais F. Epidemiology and correlates of alcohol use among Indian adolescents living on reservations. IN: Spiegler D; Tate D; Aitken S; Christian C, eds. *Alcohol Use among Ethnic Minorities.* Rockville MD: National Institute on Alcohol Abuse and Alcoholism, 1989. pp. 239-267. (23 refs.)

36. Query JN. Comparative admission and follow-up study of American Indians and whites in a youth chemical dependency unit on the north central plains. *International Journal of the Addictions* 200(3): 489-502, 1985. (32 refs.)

37. Rhoades ER; Hammond J; Welty TK; Handler AO; Amler RW. The Indian burden of illness and future health intervention. *Public Health Report* 102(4): 361-367, 1987. (8 refs.)

38. Rooney T. Adolescents, Unit 13. In: Kinney J, ed. *Alcohol and Substance Use: Curriculum and Resource Materials.* Hanover NH: Project Cork Institute, 1988.

39. Schinke S; Gilchrist L; Schilling RF; Walker RD; Locklear VS; Kitajima E. Smokeless tobacco use among Native American adolescents. (letter). *New England Journal of Medicine* 314(16): 1051-1052, 1986. (7 refs.)

40. Tracks JG. Native American noninterference. *Social Work* 18: 30-34, 1973. (9 refs.)

41. Walker RD; Benjamin GA; Kivlahan D; Walker PS. American Indian alcohol misuse. IN: Spiegler D; Tate D; Aitken S; Christian C, eds. *Alcohol Use among Ethnic Minorities.* Rockville MD: National Institute on Alcohol Abuse and Alcoholism, 1989. pp. 301-311. (12 refs.)

42. Watts TD; Lewis RG. Alcoholism and Native American youth: An overview. *Journal of Drug Issues* 18(1): 69-86, 1988. (63 refs.)

43. Weibel JC. American Indians, urbanization, and alcohol: A developing urban Indian drinking ethos. IN: National Institute on Alcohol Abuse and Alcoholism. *Alcohol and Health: Special Population Issues.* Rockville MD: National Institute on Alcohol Abuse and Alcoholism, 1982. pp. 331-358. (118 refs.)

44. Weibel-Orlando JC. Indian alcoholism treatment programs as flawed rites of passage. *Medical Anthropology Quarterly* 15(3): 63-69, 1984. (25 refs.)

45. Weibel-Orlando JC. Substance abuse among American Indian youth: A continuing crisis. *Journal of Drug Issues* 14(2): 313-335, 1984. (74 refs.)

46. Weibel-Orlando JC. Culture-specific treatment modalities: Assessing client-to-treatment fit in Indian alcoholism programs. IN: Cox WM, ed. *Treatment and Prevention of Alcohol problems: A Resource Manual.* Orlando FL: Academic Press, Inc, 1987. pp. 262-283. (52 refs.)

47. Young TJ. Substance use and abuse among Native Americans. *Clinical Psychological Review* 8(2): 125-138, 1988. (85 refs.)

FURTHER READINGS

American Indian and Alaska Native Mental Health Research 4(3): 1-132 (entire issue), 1992.

The 12 articles in this issue examine different aspects of government and social policy in respect to alcohol policy and Native Americans. Particular attention is directed to reservation and border communities, the role of community development in policy development, and the potential impact of various control strategies, with particular attention to actions to reduce mortality. Copyright 1994, Project Cork Institute.

Austin GA. Substance abuse among minority youth: Native Americans. (review). *Prevention Research Update* 2(Winter): 1-28, 1988. (108 refs.)

This is the first of several issues that abstract and review recent research on minority and other youth at high risk of substance abuse. This issue addresses the problem in general and then focuses specifically on Native Americans. The report provides an overview of the nature and extent of substance use and its associated problems, correlates of use, and prevention approaches. In addition, abstracts are provided for recent literature, addresses of the first authors, and a listing of other sources of information. Copyright 1990, Project Cork Institute.

Cheadle A; Pearson D; Wagner E; Psaty BM; Diehr P; Koepsell T. Relationship between socioeconomic status, health status, and life-style practices of American Indians: Evidence from a Plains reservation population. *Public Health Reports* 109(3): 405-413, 1994. (19 refs.)

This paper presents information on the prevalence of a variety of health behaviors and health conditions on an American Indian reservation in the Plains region of the western US. In addition, data from two non-Indian comparison groups were used to examine the extent to which differences in health status and health behaviors between Indians and non-Indians could be explained by differences in socioeconomic status. The American Indian data were from a survey conducted in 1988 during an evaluation of a local community-based health promotion program, part of the Kaiser Family Foundation's Community Health Promotion Grants Program. The comparison groups were 12 communities in California surveyed in evaluating the Community Health Promotion Grants Program and three Plains states participating in the Behavioral Risk Factor Surveillance Survey. The results show that the higher prevalences of risk-taking behavior in Indians and their poorer self-reported health status remained after adjustment for socioeconomic status. Also, for Indians, higher levels of income and education were not associated with improved self-reported health status and lower prevalence of tobacco use, as was the case in the comparison groups. The higher prevalence of risk-taking behaviors and ill health for American Indians residing on one reservation, even for those with higher socioeconomic status, suggests a need for investigating other social and environmental influences. Public Domain.

Fleming CM. American Indians and Alaska Natives: Changing societies past and present. IN: Orlandi MA; Weston R; Epstein LG, eds. *Cultural Competence for Evaluators: A Guide for Alcohol and Other Drug Abuse Prevention Practitioners Working with Ethnic/ Racial Communities. OSAP Cultural Competence Series I.* Rockville MD: OSAP, 1992. pp. 147-171. (38 refs.)

As with American society as a whole, contemporary American Indian and Alaska Native communities are facing a host of life-threatening ills including racism, poverty, AIDS, child abuse, and alcohol and other drug use. Many of these threats have resulted from centuries of change forced on Indian and Native societies. For many people in these societies, such change has meant tremendous losses of culture, dignity, and life. In an attempt to depart from life-styles and situations that compromise well-being, Indians and Natives have begun to identify for themselves culturally congruent values and behaviors that enhance life for the individual, the family, and the community. New programs seeking to change individual and collective attitudes and behaviors are being developed and implemented in "Indian country." And with the lives of individuals, families, and tribes at stake, Indians and Natives have welcomed the evaluation of these programs. However, evaluation approaches that do not consider the history and culture of each Indian and Native group may impede progress toward the goals that these communities so urgently seek. This chapter provides an overview of the major cultural dimensions of Indian and Native societies, past and present. These dimensions address individual, family, and societal issues, and illustrate the rich diversity of American Indian and Alaska Native culture. Public Domain.

King J; Thayer JF. Examining conceptual models for understanding drug use behavior among American Indian youth. IN: De La Rosa MR; Adrados JLR, eds. *Drug Abuse Among Minority Youth: Methodological Issues and Recent Research Advances. NIDA Research Monograph 130.* Rockville MD: National Institute on Drug Abuse, 1993. pp. 129-143. (44 refs.)

This chapter examines two promising theoretical models that may explain substance use among American Indian youth. One is a life stress model, the other a modified peer cluster model. According to the authors, the former proposes that the primary predictive factors of substance abuse are life stress, availability of social support form family, and other formal and informal social institutions. The latter model hypothesizes that the strongest predictive factor for substance abuse is peer influence, particularly association with deviant peers. Both models were tested for their relative ability to predict rates of substance use in the youth interviewed. Goodness-of-fit indicators demonstrated that both models were of equal quality in accounting for the patterns among factors hypothesized to relate to substance use. Public Domain.

LeMaster PL; Connell CM. Health education interventions among Native Americans: A review and analysis. *Health Education Quarterly* 21(4): 521-538, 1994. (61 refs.)

Relatively few health education interventions directed at preventing health behaviors and managing chronic illness in Native Americans have been reported in the literature. This article provides a selective review of health education interventions in Native Americans that address the prevention and management of chronic illnesses/conditions and preventive health behaviors. For each intervention included in the review, a description of its cultural relevance, sample, design, and evaluation is provided. Limitations are noted, as well as implications for research and practice. Alcohol, including FAS, and substance use are among the topics discussed. Copyright 1994, SOPHE.

Lobb ML; Watts TD. *Native American Youth and Alcohol: An Annotated Bibliography.* New York: Greenwood Press, 1989. (365 refs.)
The introduction to this annotated bibliography provides an overview of the literature in the 11 major topical areas incorporated. These major topical areas are accidental death, biomedical factors, crime, etiology, gender, policy and prevention, reservations, sociological factors, suicide, treatment, and urban vs. rural settings. A subject index and author index are provided. Copyright 1990, Project Cork Institute.

Snipp CM. Sociological perspectives on American Indians. (review). *Annual Review of Sociology* 18: 351-371, 1992. (142 refs.)
The sociology of American Indians incorporates perspectives from across the social sciences. Recently, sociologists have taken a greater interest in American Indians, perhaps because American Indians have become increasingly visible in the diverse ethnic mosaic of American society. This review focuses on the position of American Indians in the US socioeconomic hierarchy: Their numbers, where they live, and their social and economic well-being. The collapse and revitalization of the Indian population has been a central issue within American Indian demography. The recent growth in the population has been accompanied by increasing urbanization. These developments have significant implications for the socioeconomic well-being of American Indians in contemporary society. Alcohol use, crime, and mental illness are discussed. Copyright 1992, Annual Reviews, Inc.

Swaim RC; Oetting ER; Thurman PJ; Beauvais F; Edwards RW. American Indian adolescent drug use and socializing characteristics. *Journal of Cross-Cultural Psychology* 24(1): 53-70, 1993. (56 refs.)
The socialization variables of family strength, religious identification, school adjustment, family sanctions against drug use, and peer associations correlate with youth drug abuse. A path model testing the relationships between these variables among Anglo youths has shown that peer drug associations mediate the influence of the other factors and that with minor exceptions peers are likely to be the dominating force in youth drug abuse. The current study applied the same path model to a group of American Indian youths, and the findings were replicated with two important exceptions. Peer drug associations, although still dominant in the model, were not as highly correlated with drug use for Indian youths, and family sanctions against drugs had a direct and indirect influence on drug use. Differences in family dynamics in American Indian youths may account for the findings; they may associate more with and learn about drug use from same-aged siblings and other relatives in the extended family, and they may have a greater number of adult family figures to apply sanctions against drug use. Copyright 1993, Western Washington University.

Weisner TS; Weibel-Orlando JC; Long G. "Serious Drinking," "White Man's Drinking" and "Teetotaling": Drinking levels and styles in an urban American Indian population. *Journal of Studies on Alcohol* 45(3): 237-250, 1984. (69 refs.)

RESOURCES

Association on American Indian Affairs (AAIA)
Jerry Flute, Executive Director. PO Box 268, Tekakwitha Complex, Agency Road #7, Sisseton SD 57262. (605) 698-3998. A private, nonprofit organization founded in the 1920s, the AAIA is supported by voluntary contributions. It provides technical assistance to Indian tribes and organizations working in health, education, legal matters, economic and community development, and Indian child welfare. *Indian Affairs.* Newsletter: Three issues/year. Free to Indians and organizations. Information about Association activities and activities in the Indian world.

Fetal Alcohol Syndrome Project (1979-1985)
Philip May, PhD, Project Director, CASA. 2350 Alamo SE, University of New Mexico, Albuquerque NM 87131. (505) 768-0107. The Fetal Alcohol Syndrome (FAS) Project was funded by the Indian Health Service in 1979 as a pilot prevention program on FAS among American Indians. A team of experts designed a comprehensive program to meet the treatment needs of the Indian people, provide staff training to physicians and outreach workers, and answer fundamental research questions about the occurrences of FAS in the Indian population. The project was developed to directly serve the American Indian population in New Mexico and parts of Colorado, Utah, and Arizona. In 1980 about 240,000 Indians lived on 26 reservations in these areas. Major funding for this project ended in 1982. *Fetal Alcohol Syndrome Resource Guide, 3rd Edition, Revised, 1985.* Developed by The National Indian FAS Prevention Program, Albuquerque NM 87102. Provides information on materials and resources available for prevention activities in FAS. Also lists programs working in the field of FAS/Effects prevention, and lists films, slide presentations, and curricula, books, posters, printed materials, and prevention programs. Available from the Indian Health Service (see below). *Patient Education Pamphlets on FAS and Native Americans.* Developed by The National Indian FAS Prevention Program. All Indian Pueblo Council. Albuquerque NM 87102. Available from the Indian Health Service.

The Indian Drinking Practices Project (1978-1985)
Joan Weibel-Orlando, PhD, Project Director. The Neuropsychiatric Institute, UCLA, Los Angeles CA 90024. Current address: Department of Anthropology, 3502 Trousdale Parkway, University of Southern California, Los Angeles CA 90089-0032. (213) 740-1900. From 1978 to 1985 a research team of anthropologists, statisticians, and American Indian community specialists worked on the factors that influence drinking behavior and/or provide support for those Indians who want to stop drinking. Copies of the papers, chapters, and journal articles that resulted from the project are available from the library of the National Clearinghouse for Alcohol and Drug Information (NCADI), PO Box 2345, Rockville MD 20847. (800) 729-6686 or (301) 468-2600.

Indian Health Service (IHS), Alcoholism and Substance Abuse Programs Branch
Johanna Cledenger, MD, Chief. 5600 Fishers Lane, Rm 5A20, Rockville MD 20857. (301) 443-4297. The Indian Health Service (IHS) is a comprehensive health care program for American Indians and Alaska Natives. Presently the IHS operates 46 general hospitals and funds five tribally operated hospitals and 300 health centers/stations. The IHS also funds approximately 300 Tribal/Native, Corporate/Urban Organization-managed Alcohol and Substance Abuse Programs. The estimated number of Indian and Alaska Natives eligible for IHS services in 1986 was approximately 1 million. The Alcoholism and Substance Abuse Programs

Branch conducts 3-day symposium/training sessions on alcohol abuse for IHS providers. Community-based youth programs for every service unit are being developed.

National Association for Native American Children of Alcoholics (NANACoA)

Anna M. Latimer, Executive Director. 1402 Third Avenue, Suite 1110, Seattle WA 98101. (206) 324-9360. Organized at the 1988 Annual Convention of the National Association for Children of Alcoholics by more than 70 Indian people from 30 different tribes, NANACoA is a national, nonprofit organization offering information and support for Native American children of alcoholics. Activities include planning a national conference for Native American children of alcoholics in 1989, establishing a national network and newsletter, and increasing community awareness and recognition of the needs of Native American children of alcoholics.

National Center for American Indian and Alaska Native Mental Health Research (NCAIANMHR)

Spero M. Manson, PhD, Director. Department of Psychiatry, University of Colorado, Health Sciences Center, 4455 East Ninth Avenue, Denver CO 80220. (303) 372-3232. The National Center for American Indian and Alaska Native Mental Health Research is funded by the National Institute of Mental Health with additional support from the National Institute of Alcohol Abuse and Alcoholism. The Center focuses on research, research training, information dissemination, and technical assistance. Its primary objectives are identifying psychiatric and psychological problems affecting Native American and Alaska Native populations; promoting and coordinating research projects designed to improve mental health service delivery systems; and providing clearinghouse information to individuals interested in mental health, alcoholism, and drug abuse among American Indians and Alaska Natives. *American Indian and Alaska Native Mental Health Research: The Journal of the National Center.* Published three times annually. A scientific journal containing empirical research, program evaluations, case studies, unpublished dissertations, and other articles relating behavioral and social sciences and Native Americans. Subscription rates: $35/volume. *Bibliographic Retrieval System.* Collects, indexes, and disseminates information about journal articles, dissertations, professional papers, and research reports on American Indian and Alaska Native mental health. In 1987 it included 2300 entries.

Native American Research Information Service (NARIS)

American Indian Institute, The University of Oklahoma, 555 Constitution Avenue, Norman OK 73072. (405) 325-4127. NARIS is a computerized database focusing on Native American and Native Alaskan issues. The database includes over 15,000 citations. Most citations include complete bibliographic information, funding sources, document location, tribe, geographic location, index terms, and a brief abstract of the study. NARIS includes ongoing research and studies that have not been published or widely distributed. NARIS services are available without charge to IHS offices, agencies, and tribal and Indian organizational programs funded by IHS. *Descriptors by Selected Generic Topics.* A controlled vocabulary developed by NARIS. 60 pages.

Native American Women's Health Education Resource Center

Charon Asetoyer, Executive Director. PO Box 572, Lake Andes SD 57356. (605) 487-7072. Opened in February 1988 by the Native American Community Board Health Education Project, the Center is the first Native American Women's Health Education Resource Center based on a reservation. It offers information to raise Native American women's consciousness levels about fetal alcohol birth defects, family planning, reproductive rights, AIDS and other sexually transmitted diseases, prenatal care, nutrition, menopause, and child development. The Center offers support groups and acts as a facility for organizing women around issues of concern and social change. *Wicozanni Wowapi: Good Health Newsletter.* Quarterly. Suggested donation: $5 to $10/year. *Fetal Alcohol Syndrome: A Global Issue.* Native American Community Board, 1987. 32 minutes. $38. Audience: School children, families, health care providers. Fetal alcohol syndrome brochure and poster. Free.

Seattle Veterans Administration Hospital, Alcohol and Drug Dependence Program

R. Dale Walker, MD, Chief. 1660 South Colombian Way, Seattle WA 98108. (206) 764-2113. Numerous studies have been published on screening Native Americans and on doing Native follow-up studies after treatment.

Western Behavioral Studies

Fred Beauvais, PhD, Department of Psychology, Colorado State University, Fort Collins CO 80523. (303) 491-6827. Funded by the National Institute on Drug Abuse (NIDA), the Western Behavioral Studies at Colorado State University has been tracking the epidemiology of drug use among American Indian adolescents since 1975. The data for their studies are gathered from surveys administered to Indian youth from reservations across the country. Numerous articles regarding prevalence have been published, with statistical tables showing trends from 1975 to 1987.

CHAPTER 14

Rural Residents

ALLAN W. GRAHAM, MD, FACP

CLINICAL APPLICATIONS

The goals of this chapter are to assist the clinician to:

1. Recognize the factors that define rural areas.
2. Be aware of the stresses upon and features that distinguish health care services in rural areas.
3. Be aware of the features that characterize substance use problems.
4. Be aware of the factors that may limit treatment and provide obstacles to treatment.
5. Become familiar with sources of care.

DEFINITIONS

The problems of substance use display characteristic signs and symptoms, whether in rural or urban dwellers, the wealthy or the impoverished, the highly or the poorly educated. However, the rural environment presents special combinations of economic, geographical, cultural, and political problems that further shape the manifestations of substance abuse. The most influential factors are low population densities, low incomes, specialized regional economic activities, relative scarcity of health professionals, and strong cultural biases. Rural counties tend to be quite diverse. Providing medical care in rural areas, which includes addressing substance abuse, requires sensitivity to the unique locale.

The US Census Bureau defines rural populations as those towns of fewer than 2500 persons or in the open country. With the 1950 census, new terminology was introduced—metropolitan and nonmetropolitan. To qualify as a metropolitan area, a county had to have a population center of 50,000 or more. Counties contiguous to metropolitan centers were included in the metropolitan area. In 1960, 30% of Americans were classified as living in nonmetropolitan areas. That proportion has continued to decline. In 1980 the nonmetropolitan population was 26%, and the 1990 census shows a further small decline to 25%. Of this group, less than 10% live on farms. These rural residents are distributed across 84% of the land area.[4]

The US Department of Agriculture (USDA) has further categorized nonmetropolitan counties, depending on their specialized regional economic activities, into one of seven groups: (1) farming-dependent, (2) manufacturing-dependent, (3) mining-dependent, (4) specialized government activities, (5) persistent poverty, (6) federal lands, and (7) destination-retirement. USDA studies demonstrate that most nonmetropolitan counties are characterized by specialization rather than diversity, making them more fragile to economic change than more heterogeneous metropolitan areas.[6]

ECONOMIC CHARACTERISTICS

Underemployment characterizes most rural labor markets. Proportionately more workers in nonmetropolitan areas are underemployed, whether because of lack of hours, few employment alternatives, or discouragement from looking for work. Likewise, unemployment is higher in rural areas. The consequent effect on incomes is predictable: The average income outside of urban areas is 75% of that for workers in the urban area.

Growth of new jobs is similarly more sluggish. Historically, two-thirds of the nation's new jobs have been in the service industry; only 12% of those jobs are located outside of urban areas.[6]

Poverty, too, is more prominent in rural sections. Nonurban areas have 25% of the population, but 38% of the nation's poor (incomes below the federally defined poverty level). In rural areas, temporary poverty attributed to prolonged job loss is also greater than in urban areas.[4] Job retraining is particularly important in dealing with this problem.[36] In rural areas, this is less easily accomplished because fewer jobs are created, which is attributed to the specialized nature of most rural economies. If the key industry in a rural area is doing poorly, the entire community tends to suffer, as the alternatives for its residents are limited.

HEALTH CARE SERVICES

The health care system is an important route for identification, treatment, and referral for substance use problems. Unfortunately, rural health professionals are relatively scarce per capita compared with their urban counterparts. Rural areas have 12% of the nation's physicians and 25% of the population. The doctor/patient ratio in rural areas is only one-third if what it is in urban areas, in the vicinity of 50 per 100,000 in rural areas and 160 per 100,000 in urban settings. This discrepancy continues to grow. Over the past 10 years, the number of rural physicians has grown by 14%. In urban areas the increase is more than twice that amount (32%).[29]

The dismantling and subsequent reimplementation of the National Health Service Corps, a program that many rural communities have depended on for health care personnel, will further reduce the stream of newly trained physicians to rural clinics. Rural physicians receive lower reimbursement rates than their urban counterparts for performing identical procedures. The heavy mix of Medicare and Medicaid patients in rural areas is also an economic barrier to new physician influx.[31] Health care financing changes are needed to redress some of these serious financial disincentives; an excellent current initiative is the Health Care Financing Administration's (HCFA) Rural Health Clinics Program, which is improving the economic incentives for primary care delivery to Medicare and Medicaid recipients.

Community and migrant health centers and certified rural health centers have been important resources for primary health care, particularly for lower-income patients. However, federal funding makes these programs ever vulnerable to political currents, and the regulatory requirements are often onerous. In recent years, inflation has increased more rapidly than funding; and hoped-for ancillary services such as dental care, pharmacies, and substance abuse counseling have failed to materialize.[30]

Nurses and allied health professionals are in similar states of shortage. Of the country's RNs, 18% practice in rural areas and care for 25% of the population. Recruitment of nurses is impaired by lower pay scales, less flexibility in scheduling, and less variety of social experiences and contacts.

Rural hospitals, too, have been inequitably treated. The federal Medicare policy has routinely set reimbursement for rural services at rates lower than those for similar urban services. In addition, many state and federal planners have ideas of consolidating hospitals in hopes of achieving economies of scale and cost savings. However, rarely have such savings occurred. Frequently, communities are threatened with the closure of the only community hospital within 25 or 50 miles. Thus, access to medical care would be further reduced.

Community mental health centers have experienced the same difficulties. In respect to substance abuse, these centers probably represent the most important entry point into care for those with lower incomes. However, funding priorities at both the state and federal levels have generally gone toward services for care of the chronic mentally ill and those previously served by state hospitals, rather than for outpatient services for alcohol and substance abuses. Evaluation of the effects of these priorities is rarely a component of the programs themselves; this leads to treatment by "politics" and an undermining of professional and community leadership.[27]

Federal funding is consistently lower per capita for health services in rural America: 42% less for health services and 50% less for social services. This is particularly damaging to alcohol and substance abusers. Similarly, 9% of the funding for programs for the homeless goes to rural areas, which have 18% of the homeless persons. Forty-four percent more rural residents are uninsured than urban residents.[30]

SUBSTANCE USE PROBLEMS
Prevalence and Rural-Urban Differences

The aforementioned rural and urban differences highlight some of the realities that make alcohol and substance abuse treatment more difficult in rural areas. The lack of data concerning unique populations is a constant frustration. The variability of alcohol consumption from one rural region to another is striking. For example, both the highest and the lowest levels of alcohol consumption are found in predominantly rural states. The highest levels of alcohol consumption per capita occur in Alaska, Nevada, New Hampshire, and Vermont; the lowest rates of consumption in Kentucky, West Virginia, Tennessee, and North Carolina. But per capita consumption levels do not predict the levels of alcohol problems; rather, they indicate regional differences in the number of abstainers. While regionally the South has a lower per capita consumption, of those who do drink, consumption is higher than in the seemingly "wetter" regions. Highway spot-checks of breath alcohol fail to show any consistent patterns of rural/urban predominance; in Vermont, a study found the rates consistent with those in urban areas.[7]

Reports in the 1980's had indicated that rates of depression and drug dependence were higher in urban areas; on the other hand, alcohol dependence appeared to be somewhat higher in rural areas.[2,3] For interviewees in the 1985 National Household Survey on Drug Abuse, no differences were found for alcohol use between rural and urban persons, but a lower usage for marijuana and cocaine did appear in the rural group.[23] Recent studies of youth show essentially equal use of alcohol, inhalants, and stimulants; somewhat lower use of hard drugs by rural adolescents; and a narrowing gap between rural use of marijuana and the somewhat higher urban use.[8, 10, 19, 34] Anabolic steroid use even appears to be used equally in rural and urban areas.[40]

For women of child-bearing age, studies in 1989 in Alabama found no differences between rural and urban use of marijuana, cocaine, opiates, amphetamines, and barbiturates as assessed by systematic urine drug testing.[13]

Treatment Services

Low-population densities in rural areas necessitate special efforts to coordinate state and federal agencies, often revealing striking levels of interagency animosity, competitiveness, and sovereignty.[18,24] Availability of AA meetings within reasonable distances decreases proportionately with decreasing population density. Similarly, intensive outpatient programs, which require daily commuting, are difficult to provide; if offered, they may require special transportation arrangements. In rural areas, public transportation is uniformly less adequate; distances traveled are greater; and the impediments of adverse weather are more significant.[10, 11] The empirical literature on rural services is limited and generally descriptive in nature, focusing on perceived service needs.[23] A study in the mid-1980's of rural, hospital-based chemical dependency treatment showed that only 18.7% of 797 nonmetropolitan hospitals in the US offered any alcohol or chemical abuse services. Further, few hospitals not offering these services planned to offer them in the immediate future. Chemical dependency treatment was more likely to be found in hospitals in areas with greater population density, higher per capita income, more physicians per capita and more psychiatric services.[25]

Nationally, services typically are sparser in rural areas. In respect to substance abuse treatment, some important ancillary supports for persons in early

Notes on Being a Country Doctor

The following remarks are the objective observations of a country doctor who lives in the town where Dr. Bob, cofounder of Alcoholics Anonymous, was born. These comments have been spawned by early morning runs in crisp autumn air in front of Dr. Bob's modest, clapboard house; by walks through the grocery, greeting patients and friends over summer squash; and by worship in the Victorian church where Dr. Bob sat with his mother almost a century ago. The remarks will undoubtedly show a naive enthusiasm for sharing in the lives of other people. These comments depict something of the uniqueness of rural practice.

"For me the greatest joy of practicing medicine in a rural community is the personal experience of belonging to a wondrous network of human relationships, an unbelievably rich fabric of life that I witness, study, and help create daily. Generations of family relationships and genetics weave their results in ever-new patterns before me. And I, for my small part, try to alter some of the patterns that have shown themselves to be harmful over the generations and to encourage the development of new patterns that will reflect health. My part as a country doctor is to bring together in a caring way the science of medicine, the politics of rural agencies, the economics of governmental programs, and the emotions of sick persons. Expressing love and concern in this way is for me the art of medicine.

"As a family physician in a small town, I have a privileged vantage point that allows me to watch families with substance abuse create and recreate their unmistakable patterns of confusion, suffering, and loss. I see my patients—alcoholics, cocaine addicts, adult children of alcoholics, and their families—all play their roles in this real-life network, giving painful vitality to the otherwise sterile data of rural health care delivery. Multigenerational families stay largely intact in my rural community, since population change is slow. I personally know patients from the same family spanning multiple generations. These family databases are further enriched by the formal and informal sharing of information among our town's two dozen physicians. Even the local newspaper does its share to augment the data by providing weekly highlights in the form of *The Court News* and *The Police Log*, detailing names and ages of all alleged offenders of disorderly conduct charges, DWIs, and domestic violence calls. Anonymity is clearly harder to maintain in small towns than in urban areas. Paradoxically, the only reliable place to find anonymity in our town is an AA meeting."

recovery (e.g., day care for children, halfway houses, "safe houses," and trained social service personnel) are often difficult to find. As traditionally organized, many of these services require a minimal population density to be economically feasible. Mental health centers commonly have long waiting lists, especially for uninsured patients. Certified alcohol and drug counselors, and physicians and nurses with specialized expertise in addiction treatment are few. Furthermore, financial incentives are minimal for developing new free-standing counseling and rehabilitation services for most of these patients. For a time in the 1980s and early 1990s, a growth area emerged in the rural health economy for providing substance abuse treatment to affluent or insured urban residents. The lower wage scales in rural areas allowed these treatment programs to position themselves competitively. However, managed health care's restrictions on residential care and state health care financial difficulties have caused many of the programs to close.

Community Values and the Social Environment

A comparison of loggers in New Hampshire, Sioux Indians in South Dakota, retired elderly persons in Arizona, African Americans in North Carolina, and coal miners in West Virginia would highlight regional differences in cultural values. However, the influence of these regional differences in treatment outcome has not been well investigated. Distinctive regional biases may exist. A striking example of ingrained regional bias comes from an unpublished, National Institute on Alcohol Abuse and Alcoholism-funded study conducted in a rural Vermont county in 1979. It revealed that of 225 randomly selected residents, 68% believed "problem drinking" to be an emotional problem, 62% thought it a mental health problem, and 50% felt it was an individual right.[33] This did not reflect the then-current national views. If the dominant beliefs and biases of a community are not congruent with current substance abuse treatment programs, this may be a significant impediment. The ability to change belief systems, particularly to educate people about the disease concept of alcoholism, appears to be difficult.[20,22,39]

A study of rural Alaskan Native youth showed high levels of drug use compared to other rural populations in the US; however, closer analysis of the non-Native youth in rural Alaska also revealed similarly increased rates of drug use compared to US rural

Vignette from a Family Practice*

Picture yourself hearing this family history, told by two rural physicians, Dr. Hammond and Dr. Clifford, as you comfortably rock in a white wicker chair on the front porch of one of their homes on Main Street. This brick, post-Civil War, Victorian home treats you to an expansive view of the town's tree-lined central residential area. You are enjoying the late summer breeze, which gently encourages a mood of relaxation and reminiscence. The doctors begin with enthusiastic comments about the sobriety of a patient they have both recently seen in the office. Their remembrances reveal a mutual respect for the patient, a person they have come to know over a decade as he has traveled the difficult path to recovery. Their musings spread like ripples in the pond of collective memory, first one then the other touching on the various high points of the patient's history and that of his family. Memories come forward with an unexpected vitality and enthusiasm, delighting even the physicians. It seems as if we are sitting together with the patient himself. Dr. Hammond begins the story.

"Tom Colby, a 68-year-old widower and retired roofer, came in for a check-up. His blood pressure and heart have given him trouble over the past decade, but since he's sober these past 20 months, he has been much healthier. We doctors used to tell him that alcohol produced hypertension for many people and that cardiac rhythm problems were a common effect of heavy drinking and withdrawal. Tom didn't quite hear the message for a long time. Now that his blood pressure and heart are under control, he has developed a new problem: swollen ankles. He complains about his varicose veins making his legs feel heavy and his ankles puffy; but Tom's almost proud, since the swollen legs are a consequence of helping others. You see, Tom now volunteers at the meals site for the elderly, and his legs swell when he stands for a long time. He accepts the swelling graciously, knowing that by helping other people he feels worthwhile.

"Sharing his own experience of recovery has changed Tom's self-esteem and personal goals. He now shares a personal vision that someday he would like to become an alcohol counselor. This kind of talk is very different from that of 2 years ago, when he refused to accept further treatment for his alcoholism. Over the previous decade, Tom had been treated several times at Serenity House, a residential facility based on the principles of AA. However, he could never "get with the program" after leaving residential care. He could never relate to AA meetings and never felt comfortable sharing his feelings in groups. However, 2 years ago, following a hospitalization for alcoholism and suicidal thoughts, something "clicked" in Tom, and the AA program had taken root.

"He says he's now going to three AA meetings a week and enjoying the fellowship more than ever before. The sense of boredom that filled his first few "dry" months has given way to a sense of inner peace and fulfillment. I encouraged him during this time of boredom 1 year ago to get some part-time work, to try some volunteering, and to reach out with some "12th step" visiting. I guess Tom got the message from the program, since he is now doing all three of those activities and loving every minute of it."

The doctors recall a time 3 years ago and share thoughts about the circumstances that led to Tom's last hospitalization for alcoholism. At the beginning of that period, Tom had been in Founders' Hall, the community's treatment center located within the community hospital, where one of the doctors had worked with him. During his treatment, Tom was unable to bond to the AA program. Grudgingly, he had gone to AA meetings while in treatment and then for the first couple of months after discharge. Gradually, he left the Fellowship and slipped deeper into loneliness and self-pity. He then resumed drinking within weeks. His depression worsened dramatically when a love relationship with the widow of a drinking buddy went sour. For a couple of weeks he became increasingly despondent and then violent toward himself and others. Dr. Clifford picks up the story.

"Everyone was trying to control him, but no one could as long as the alcohol was influencing his cognition. Everyone felt so helpless because nothing they did appeared to work. They were angry because he had now lost the abstinence he had narrowly maintained for several months. His older daughter stopped me on the street and pleaded his case, wondering what she could do next. I suggested that she go to Al-Anon. She wasn't happy with that reply. Two weeks later his family brought him into the office, requesting hospitalization for detoxification. He was admitted, but signed out "against medical advice" the next morning, saying he had "other more important things to do." Within days, matters became even worse. Tom bought a handgun and appeared at the door of his younger daughter's home. He made threats to kill his granddaughter and then himself. The police were called and managed to get Tom and the gun out of the house. His daughter felt terribly

Continued.

Vignette from a Family Practice*—cont'd

guilty and responsible for the whole affair. She insisted that she and her disabled child had brought on the problem of Tom's drinking. Another 2 days passed, and Tom finally agreed to his family's wishes and again re-entered the hospital for medical detoxification. This time something had changed. Nobody knew quite what, but 4 days later when Tom left the hospital, he had a different attitude and spirit. This time he started going to AA regularly, staying sober 'a day at a time' and amazing his doctors that his AA program had finally worked."

You are drawn away from the conversation and notice that clouds are now building over the rooftops of the houses to the north and west. The wind has stirred considerably, and leaves are being tossed about in the maple trees lining the driveway. The telephone rings, and Dr. Clifford goes inside to answer it. Being "on call" requires him to stay close to either his phone or beeper much of the time. He soon returns, having settled a matter of refilling someone's prescription, which ran out on this Saturday afternoon, "all of a sudden." Dr. Clifford begins to reminisce again, but this time portrays a picture of Tom's extended family and the trouble his drinking caused the people around him.

"Tom's wife died years ago in an automobile accident. Her drinking never seemed to the family to be out of control, although I had always suspected a problem because of her difficult-to-control hypertension. The older daughter, Sheila, became the caretaker of the family. She single-handedly raised her younger sister, Margaret, did the housework before going to school, and kept a part-time job on weekends. Sheila became a legal secretary and, subsequently, the office manager of a large law firm. She always had a knack for managing affairs skillfully, although she tended to be intolerant of other people's shortcomings. She came to my office, too, until last year when I misdiagnosed an ailment, thereby proving her long-suspected suspicion that I was incompetent. She had symptoms of a viral syndrome—muscle aches, sore bones, and fatigue. What looked like a viral syndrome turned out to be Lyme disease, which was pretty evident 1 week later when the characteristic skin lesions appeared. However, by that time, Sheila had sought the opinion of another doctor in town. Sheila continued to seek opinions from additional specialists; however, she was never satisfied with any one person's competence. After 6 months she called me and asked about high-dose penicillin therapy for Lyme disease. It seems the arthritis consultants she saw at the medical school didn't recommend starting penicillin, and she

thought that it would be helpful. She now wanted another opinion. Sometimes it's hard to satisfy patients." He stops and shakes his head, and Dr. Hammond resumes the family history.

"Margaret, the younger daughter, is a patient at our office, too. She works in a local department store now. She's had a rough time with depression and alcoholism, just like her father. Her last suicide attempt 4 years ago was brought on by feelings of inadequacy and guilt from being unable to care for her three children. Giving them up voluntarily to foster care was more than she could stand. She drank until stuporous and was brought to the hospital unconscious, and then remained for detoxification. She refused further alcoholism treatment and signed out of the hospital against medical advice after 72 hours. She was ultimately committed to a psychiatric hospital for persisting suicidal ideation. After a year of outpatient counseling for both alcoholism and depression, she has put her life back together. Much hard work on her part and much patient assistance by counselors and AA members helped her achieve sobriety. Occasionally she had a slip and binged a day or so, but so far, each time she was able to pull herself back to the AA program and her support community. She now has been totally abstinent for a couple of years. Although she is in recovery from alcoholism, Margaret's medical problems still persist. She now suffers from irritable bowel syndrome; I think this is a somatic manifestation of her current emotional stress. Because of her persistent complaints of pain, I've evaluated her intestinal tract from end to end, always finding a normal-looking bowel. Her mucosal biopsies verify these observations, showing 'mild, chronic, nonspecific inflammation.'"

The wind has settled down, and a flock of pigeons draws your attention to the North Congregational Church. As the birds take to the air and leave their perches on the spires of Dr. Bob's boyhood church, the doctors' attention is diverted, too, toward a discussion about the exact location of the house in which Dr. Bob really grew up. Was it the humble, clapboard house at the corner of Central and Summer Streets as Claire Dunn affirms, or was it pediatrician Dave Toll's building on Main Street?

"Birds of a feather flock together" is the overt message of this flight of pigeons, and so it would seem with Tom's extended family. Dr. Clifford shares his insight about the alcoholic patterns he has observed in the spouses.

"Sheila's husband used to go to Al-Anon, and I would visit with him after meetings. But he found his

---

Vignette from a Family Practice*—cont'd

own drinking was more of a problem than he thought. He began attending AA meetings and realized that he needed AA for his own alcoholism. Unfortunately, he hasn't found the time to go to both Al-Anon and AA. Margaret's husband, a machinist, is also a recovering alcoholic. He doesn't know who his parents were; he was adopted. He understands that a high percentage of adopted children have biological parents who were alcoholic. Sometimes he, too, feels guilty and blames himself for making his parents' life so difficult that they had to give him up for adoption.

His alcohol counselor has tried to help him understand the situation differently, but his feelings don't change just because reason is given."

The setting sun casts a warm light on you, the doctors, and the pedestrians on Main Street. The stories of Tom's family are reminders that each person has his own walk to make in life and recovery. In a small town, people often walk together, their lives intertwined. Small towns have unique and special charms.

*This history provides an illustration, in real-life terms, of the previously discussed points, both objective and subjective. This history does not describe any specific person but is a composite drawn from a number of different patients and families. Hopefully, it will vitalize the image of substance abuse treatment in a rural area.

---

norms. The authors suggest that other, non-ethnic factors in social environment were probably contributing to the usage patterns; these include uncertain economic conditions, family instability, and lack of access to cultural values.[1] This study and another from the same group illustrate the need for care in interpreting national and ethnic data in the context of specific locales and amidst ethnic subgroups.[32]

A view commonly voiced by rural clinicians is that geographical isolation and the frontier spirit of "doing it yourself" contribute adversely to entry into substance abuse treatment. The ethos of the rural community is embodied in personal independence, pride of self-sufficient survival, and satisfaction in helping neighbors. Belonging to a community is an important aspect of a person's life. Taking pride in community organizations, participating in service activities, and, in the process, accepting some loss of personal anonymity are essential attributes of most rural persons.

A study conducted in Quebec comparing a small sample of rural and urban alcoholics found borderline personality disorder in almost half of the urban alcoholics but in none of the rural alcoholics. Several possible explanations were given. One was that there may be less borderline personality disorder in rural areas than in urban areas. In one particular rural area, drinking was more integrated into the everyday rituals and patterns of community life than it is in urban areas. Both drunkenness and heavy drinking may, in fact, be less dysfunctional in a rural area in which people know one another, and it may be less likely to bring people into contact with the police or authorities. Thus, the alcohol-dependent person may be more tolerated and be less likely placed in marginal status.[38]

Sources of Assistance

In rural communities it appears that help is sought first from family, nuclear and extended, and then from friends or neighbors. The last recourse is professionals. Health advice from a relative, hairdresser, or neighbor is generally solicited and followed before resorting to a physician's counsel. For substance abuse, help is generally forced on the individual by whichever social agency he or she has offended: (1) The court for DWIs, theft, physical abuse, and divorce proceedings; (2) social and rehabilitative services for child neglect or personal unmanageability; and (3) the employer for impaired work performance.

Rarely does the physician focus enough pressure to get a patient into substance abuse treatment (5% of referrals to residential care).[12] However, the physician often misses his best opportunities to "coerce" patients into treatment by ignoring the reality that 20% of acute hospitalizations are related to alcohol and substance abuse.[28] These hospital stays can permit the physician to deal with a sober patient by the third hospital day if a systematic identification process brings these at-risk patients to the physician's attention.[14] He or she will find the family constellation available and generally of great assistance with historical facts and observations. The physician will have the physical realities of medical disease to offset the denial of illness and resistance to care. Any newly arrived health care professionals in a rural community would do well to focus most of their attention on these moments for intervention, doing their best to emphasize the biological abnormalities that are clearly present.[15]

Television has been identified as an important and effective source of drug education for adolescents both in urban and more recently in rural areas. In a

Advice to Rural Care Providers

Rural areas, by virtue of smallness, provide unique opportunities for people to experience human closeness. These opportunities abound in our own "backyards" and are commonly brought to fruition through our sharing personal information with our medical partners, reading the town newspaper, and listening to our staff grapevine for clues to our patient's substance abuse problems. Small is beautiful, but it has its consequences and its increased responsibilities. A small community has relatively few professionals to initiate positive change in the community's social institutions and in patients' lives.[1] If a professional sees something that ought to be done, then he or she is likely the person who needs to do it. Fewer people to help do a job means more personal initiative is necessary to get tasks done. However, fewer people in a community also means positive change can often be accomplished more quickly and may be easier to initiate.

A healthy respect for the interrelatedness of all available service persons will be one of the rural physician's best assets. When involved with problems of substance abuse, the practitioner will need to place cooperation ahead of solo virtuosity in delivering care; he or she will need to work in consort with local mental health agencies and various state and local institutions instead of independently. Careful planning with all available substance abuse professionals is essential given the marked limitations of resources. Those with a special interest in addictions medicine will have to practice that specialty part-time because of the lack of patient volume to do it full-time. These practice limitations are inextricably woven together with the special rewards of rural medical practice that come from sharing life and sharing the bonds of community.

1. Schumacher EF. *Small Is Beautiful.* New York: Harper & Row, Publishers, Inc, 1973.

---

study from small- and medium-sized Texas school districts, 1023 eighth and tenth graders identified television as their primary source of drug information, followed by parents and print media in second and third place, and friends and teachers in fourth and fifth.[26]

Special Populations

Groups with special needs exist in rural areas as elsewhere. In nonurban areas the problem begins with the difficulty of bringing enough people together to mount a program that will inevitably use group process as a central feature. Potential benefits of homogeneous grouping include improved rates of retention in treatment; this was demonstrated in a small study of elderly patients.[21] A few other characteristic rural subgroups described in the medical literature include court offenders in Alabama,[35] retired elderly in Florida[9] and Arizona,[5] adolescents in Idaho,[22] and Native Americans in California.[39] In the long run, as with all substance abuse dependency treatment, tailoring care to patient needs and patient uniqueness will provide the best outcomes.

Pedestrians are a special group of persons who, interestingly, demonstrate a higher fatality rate in rural than urban areas. In 1992 national data showed that 12% of all pedestrian deaths involved an intoxicated driver and 36% an intoxicated pedestrian, and of the intoxicated pedestrians 60% had blood alcohol concentrations greater than 0.20 grams/100 mL.[16] Roads with higher speed limits showed higher fatality rates, probably owing to the lack of pedestrian barriers and sidewalks adjacent to locations of service and sale of alcohol.

Stress and Alcohol Use

To examine the effect of economic crisis on referrals for substance abuse services, a 10-year period in Nebraska was reviewed during which a severe economic downturn occurred. The economic problems included a 100% increase in business closings over 4 years, a 24% increase in farm bankruptcy between 1985 and 1986, and a decrease of 31% in the state's farm assets from 1981 to 1984. Interestingly, not only was there *not* an increase in farmers with substance abuse problems, but there was a 5% decrease per year from 1983 to 1987, the last year of the study. Furthermore, during that same period of turmoil in Nebraska, there was a decrease in school dropouts, no increase in divorces, and no increase in farm suicides.[17] This suggests that a link between alcohol problems and stress is not universal. It also attests to rural residents' considerable capacity to cope with stress and problems.

Confidentiality

Confidentiality is a special problem in rural areas. Word-of-mouth travels quickly along the rural routes.

The small, stable population provides short feedback loops that are helpful for giving doctors information about family networks, but these short loops can also transmit breaches of confidentiality quickly. The small population makes it more likely that staff members at the hospital or office will know relatives, neighbors, or friends of patients. The closeness of these associations increases the opportunity for breaches of confidence. On the other hand, patient collusion and family denial is a bit more difficult to carry off successfully in a rural area. Doctors and office staffs have more contacts with the impaired person's employer, friends, neighbors, and relatives. Reports about impaired behaviors are therefore more readily available to doctors seeking confirmation of a suspected substance use problem. The availability of these reports, however, may offend the impaired person and alienate him or her further from the health care system. The alcohol- or drug-dependent person, skillful at side-stepping personal responsibility, may take offense at his physician's well-intended efforts to identify the addiction, blame him for invasion of privacy, and go to another doctor. This may be a particularly sensitive problem for specialty surgeons, who may adopt the position of avoiding the most obvious alcohol- or drug-related behavior to maintain a superficial cordiality.

Practice Principles for Rural Care Providers

1. Recognize that the lack of personal anonymity is a double-edged sword that may work for and against you.
2. Listen to what your patients are trying to tell you.
3. Be attuned to a patient's concerns that are not exclusively physical.
4. Accept people and they will accept you.

REFERENCES

1. Beauvais F; Segal B. Drug use patterns among American Indian and Alaskan Native youth: Special rural populations. *Drugs & Society* 7(1/2): 77-94, 1992. (21 refs.)
2. Blazer D; Crowell BA; George LK. Alcohol abuse and dependence in the rural south. *Archives of General Psychiatry* 44(8): 736-740, 1987. (30 refs.)
3. Blazer D; et al: Psychiatric disorders: A rural/urban comparison. *Archives of General Psychiatry* 42(7): 651-656, 1985.
4. Bureau of the Census. *Statistical Abstract of the United States, Edition 114.* Washington DC: Bureau of the Census, 1994.
5. Christopherson VA; Escher MC; Bainton B. Reasons for drinking among the elderly in rural Arizona. *Journal of Studies on Alcohol* 45(5): 417-423, 1984. (24 refs.)
6. Cordes SM. *The changing rural environment and the relationship between health services and rural development.* Paper presented at San Diego, Rural Health Services Research Agenda Conference, 1987.
7. Damkot DK. Alcohol incidence in rural drivers: Characteristics of a population and clues for countermeasures. *Drug and Alcohol Dependence* 9(4): 305-324, 1982. (28 refs.)

8. Donnermeyer JF. The use of alcohol, marijuana, and hard drugs by rural adolescents: A review of recent research. (review). *Drugs & Society* 7(1/2): 31-75, 1992. (79 refs.)
9. Dupree LW; et al. The Gerontology Alcohol Project: A behavioral treatment program for elderly alcohol abusers. *The Gerontologist* 24(5): 510-516, 1984.
10. Edwards RW. Drug and alcohol use by youth in rural America: An introduction. *Drugs & Society* 7(1/2): 1-8, 1992. (0 refs.)
11. Ford TD; Sarvela PD. Adolescent substance prevention education network: A rural-based pilot program for preventing alcohol and other drug use among pregnant adolescents. IN: Marcus CE; Swisher JD, eds. *Working with Youth in High-Risk Environments: Experiences in Prevention. OSAP Prevention Monograph 12.* Rockville MD: Office of Substance Abuse Prevention, 1992. pp. 31-42. (12 refs.)
12. Founders Hall. Personal communication. St Johnsbury VT, 1989.
13. George SK; Price J; Hauth JC; Barnette DM; Preston P. Drug abuse screening of childbearing-age women in Alabama public health clinics. *American Journal of Obstetrics and Gynecology* 165(4): 924-927, 1991. (15 refs.)
14. Graham AW. Screening for alcoholism by life-style risk assessment in a community hospital. *Archives of Internal Medicine* 151(5): 958-964, 1991. (50 refs.)
15. Graham AW. Brief intervention. IN: Miller NS, ed. *Principles of Addiction.* Chevy Chase MD: American Society of Addiction Medicine, 1994. Section IV. pp. 1-7.
16. Heermann K; Syner J; Vegega ME. Motor-vehicle–related deaths involving intoxicated pedestrians: United States, 1982-1992. *MMWR. Morbidity and Mortality Weekly Report* 43(14): 249-253, 1994. (10 refs.)
17. Hsieh HH; Cheng SC; Sharma A; Sanders RA; Thiessen C. The relation of rural alcoholism to farm economy. *Community Mental Health Journal* 25(4): 341-347, 1989.
18. Jeffrey MJ; Reeve RE. Community mental health services in rural areas: Some practical issues. *Community Mental Health Journal* 14(1): 54-62, 1978.
19. Kelleher KJ; Rickert VI; Hardin BH; Pope SK; Farmer FL. Rurality and gender: Effects on early adolescent alcohol use. *American Journal of Diseases of Children* 146(3): 317-322, 1992. (34 refs.)
20. Kilty KM. Longitudinal analysis of a demonstration rural outreach alcoholism program. *Journal of Studies on Alcohol* 45(2): 124-130, 1984. (14 refs.)
21. Kofoed LL; Tolson RL; Atkinson RM; Toth RL; Turner JA. Treatment compliance of older alcoholics: An elder-specific approach is superior to "mainstreaming." *Journal of Studies on Alcohol* 48(1): 47-51, 1987. (12 refs.)
22. Lassey ML; Carlson JE. Drinking among rural youth: The dynamics of parental and peer influence. *International Journal of the Addictions* 15(1): 61-75, 1980. (16 refs.)
23. Leukefeld CG; Clayton RR; Myers JA. Rural drug and alcohol treatment. (review). *Drugs & Society* 7(1/2): 95-116, 1992. (45 refs.)
24. Maypole DE. Alcoholism detoxification services in a rural community: A formal development approach. *Alcohol Health and Research World* 5(4): 43-47, 1981. (11 refs.)
25. Mick SS; Morlock LL; Salkever D; de Lissovoy G; Malitz FE; Jones AS. Rural hospital-based alcohol and chemical abuse services: Availability and adoption, 1983-1988. *Journal of Studies on Alcohol* 54(4): 488-501, 1993. (32 refs.)
26. Mirzaee E; Kingery PM; Pruitt BE; Heuberger G; Hurley RS. Sources of drug information among adolescent students. *Journal of Drug Education* 21(2): 95-106, 1991. (12 refs.)
27. Mollica RF. From asylum to community: The threatened disintegration of public psychiatry. *New England Journal of Medicine* 308(7): 367-373, 1983.

28. Moore RD; Bone LR; Geller G; Mamon JA; Stokes EJ; Levine DM. Prevalence, detection, and treatment of alcoholism in hospitalized patients. *Journal of the American Medical Association* 261(3): 403-407, 1989. (18 refs.)

29. Movassaghi H; et al. Selected characteristics of Wisconsin physicians: Young physicians, foreign medical graduates, and medical school graduates. *Wisconsin Medical Journal* 86(1): 22-25, 1987.

30. National Association of Community Health Centers and the National Rural Health Association. *Health Care in Rural America: The Crisis Unfolds.* Washington DC: NACHC and NRHA, 1988.

31. Norton CH; McManus MA. *Rural Health Research Agenda Conference: Background Tables on Demographic Characteristics, Health Status and Health Services Utilization.* Washington DC: McManus Health Policy Inc, 1987.

32. Oetting ER; Beauvais F. Adolescent drug use: Findings of national and local surveys. *Journal of Consulting and Clinical Psychology* 58(4): 385-394, 1990. (40 refs.)

33. Pandiani J. Personal communication, 1979.

34. Peters VJ; Oetting ER; Edwards RW. Drug use in rural communities: An epidemiology. *Drugs & Society* 7(1/2): 9-29, 1992. (10 refs.)

35. Poole JE. Reducing repeat alcohol related offenses and other treatment management problems: A pilot project conducted in a rural southeastern county. *Journal of Alcohol and Drug Education* 32(2): 32-44, 1987. (30 refs.)

36. Ross PJ; Morrissey ES. Two types of rural poor need different kinds of help. *Rural Development Perspective* (October): 7-45, 1987.

37. Smith CJ; Hanham RQ. *Alcohol Abuse, Geographical Perspectives.* Washington DC: Association of American Geographers, 1982.

38. Tousignant M; Kovess V. Borderline traits among community alcoholics and problem drinkers: Rural-urban differences *Canadian Journal of Psychiatry* 34(8): 796-799, 1989. (18 refs.)

39. Weibel-Orlando JC. Drinking patterns of urban and rural American Indians. *Alcohol Health and Research World* 11(2): 8-12, 1986-1987. (18 refs.)

40. Whitehead R; Chillag S; Elliott D. Anabolic steroid use among adolescents in a rural state. *Journal of Family Practice* 35(4): 401-405, 1992. (16 refs.)

FURTHER READINGS

Abbey A; Scott RO; Smith MJ. Physical, subjective, and social availability: Their relationship to alcohol consumption in rural and urban areas. *Addiction* 88(4): 489-499, 1993. (21 refs.)

The alcohol availability literature indicates that under some conditions, physical availability is positively associated with per capita alcohol consumption. Smart (1980) suggested that at the individual level, subjective and social aspects of availability may mediate and outweigh the influence of physical availability. The study described here examined the simultaneous effects of physical, subjective, and social availability on alcohol consumption. Standardized telephone interviews were conducted with 781 adult drinkers. As hypothesized, physical availability was not a significant multivariate predictor of alcohol consumption for residents of Michigan counties with high, medium, and low alcohol outlet densities. Subjective and social availability indicators were significant predictors of alcohol consumption. Similar patterns of results were found in multiple regression analyses for African Americans and Caucasians and women and men, although African Americans and women consumed less alcohol than did Caucasians and men. The theoretical and practical implications of these results are discussed. Copyright 1993, Society for the Study of Addiction to Alcohol and Other Drugs.

Barry KL; Fleming MF. The Alcohol Use Disorders Identification Test (AUDIT) and the SMAST-13: Predictive validity in a rural primary care sample. *Alcohol and Alcoholism* 28(1): 33-42, 1993. (20 refs.)

This study compares the validity of a new screening instrument developed by the World Health Organization, the Alcohol Use Disorders Identification Test (AUDIT), to the short version of the MAST in 287 primary care patients. Subjects were classified as meeting a lifetime or current DSM-III diagnosis of alcohol misuse and/or dependence based on the DIS-R interview schedule. Based on the original WHO guidelines (score of 11 or more), 37 (13%) scored positive on the AUDIT and 103 (36%) had a weighted score of 5 or more on the SMAST-13. The internal reliability of the AUDIT was 0.86, compared to the SMAST-13 at 0.85. Cut-off scores in this sample for current alcohol problems, utilizing Receiver Operating Curves, were 7-8 for the AUDIT and 5 for the SMAST. This study confirms the utility of the AUDIT for current alcohol problems and the SMAST-13 for lifetime or past problems in a rural clinical sample. Copyright 1993, Medical Council on Alcoholism. Used with permission.

Behnke M; Eyler FD; Conlon M; Woods NS; Casanova OQ. Multiple risk factors do not identify cocaine use in rural obstetrical patients. *Neurotoxicology and Teratology* 16(5): 479-484, 1994. (14 refs.)

This nonconcurrent, cohort study of consecutive admissions to one of three hospital units—labor and delivery ($n = 474$), well-born nursery ($n = 100$), and the neonatal intensive care unit ($n = 100$)—was designed to determine the prevalence of cocaine exposure in a rural obstetrical sample and to determine the relationship between exposure and perinatal variables. Urines were analyzed for benzoylecgonine, and the Obstetrical Complications Scale was completed for each mother-infant pair. Elementary comparisons were made using Chi Square analyses and Student's t-test. Stepwise discriminant and discriminant function analyses were performed. The prevalence of exposure in the three groups of subjects ranged from 5% to 7%. No significant differences in perinatal variables were found between users and nonusers in either of the newborn samples. In the maternal sample, the groups differed on 12 mother or infant factors. However, no single variable or set of variables predicted use vs. nonuse in any of the groups. Copyright 1994, Pergamon Press.

Braithwaite RL. Challenges to evaluation in rural coalitions. *Journal of Community Psychology (CSAP Special Issue):* 188-200, 1994. (21 refs.)

This article explores methodological and practical evaluation issues when formative assessments are conducted on predominantly rural African-American communities. An overview of the nature of alcohol, tobacco, and other drugs (ATOD) in rural areas is presented. Attention is given to a community organization and development (COD) approach to coalition formation for community-based health promotion programming. Principles based on Freezer's (1989) conceptualization of community level are noted. The application and dynamics of third-party evaluation in rural settings to support coalition maintenance and sustainability for ATOD are discussed. The establishment and role of an Evaluation Planning Team (EPT) are also noted. Based on programmatic and process evaluations of 35 coalitions organized between 1989 and 1993 in rural counties in Georgia, the lessons learned through an action-oriented evaluation methodology are detailed. This evaluation approach encourages coalition members to maintain a major role in the design, execution, and interpretation of all assessment activities. Copyright 1994, Clinical Psychology Publishing Co.

Bray JH; Rogers JC. Linking psychologists and family physicians for collaborative practice. *Professional Psychology: Research and Practice* 26(2): 132-138, 1995. (36 refs.)

This article describes a pilot, demonstration project that linked psychologists and family physicians to improve the care of patients with alcohol and other drug abuse problems. The project facilitated collaborative practice between family physicians and psychologists to enhance treatment of patients with alcohol and other drug abuse as well as other psychosocial problems in rural America. Ten pairs of psychologists and family physicians in rural Texas and Wyoming participated in the project. The training successfully established linkages between psychologists and family physicians for the care of a broad range of medical and psychological problems. This article discusses the linkage training, the factors that facilitated and hindered collaboration, and the implications for future training and collaborative health care practice. Copyright 1995, American Psychological Association, Inc.

Center for Substance Abuse Treatment. *Rural Issues in Alcohol and Other Drug Abuse Treatment: Award for Excellence Papers. Technical Assistance Publication Series 10.* Rockville MD: Center for Substance Abuse Treatment, 1994. (Chapter refs.)

To help focus attention on the special service delivery problems of rural areas, the Center for Substance Abuse Treatment (CSAT) and the National Rural Institute on Alcohol and Drug Abuse (NRI-ADA) sponsored an "Award for Excellence" competition in the Fall of 1992. Individuals and agencies from rural areas across the country were invited to submit papers describing their efforts to provide services to those with alcohol and other drug problems. The goal of the competition was to elicit—and then publicize—the innovative and unusual strategies, approaches, and research findings from rural programs. The submitted papers are printed in this volume: Some describe local programs, while others concern entire regions. Public Domain.

Deffenbaugh KB; Hutchinson RL; Blankschen MP. Substance use among youth (grades 4-12) in rural Indiana: Students' reported use vs. parents' perceptions of students' use. *Journal of Alcohol and Drug Education* 39(1): 19-33, 1993. (28 refs.)

The purposes of this study were to (1) assess the substance use by 2125 youth (grades 4-12) in rural Indiana and (2) explore the differences between students' reported use of substances and the parents' perception of students' use. While all parents believed that some students were using substances (i.e., cigarettes, alcohol, and marijuana), they underestimated the percentage of students in their child's grade who reported the use of a variety of substances, especially alcohol. If parents are to be allies in the fight against drugs, it is imperative that they be aware of the dimensions of the problem. Copyright 1993, Alcohol and Drug Problems Association of North America.

Donnermeyer JF; Park DS. Alcohol use among rural adolescents: Predictive and situational factors. *International Journal of the Addictions* 30(4): 459-479, 1995. (74 refs.)

This study tests the effects of predictive and situational factors on alcohol use in a sample of rural youth. Five predictive factors accounted for 57% of the variance in frequency of alcohol use in the total sample, based on stepwise regression analysis. The predictive factors also accounted for 38% of the variance in frequency of drinking when the regression analysis was restricted only to those who drink. Controlling for these and entering situational factors into the regression analysis accounted for an additional 16% of the variance. Six situational factors were statistically significant, five of which concerned various locations for drinking. Copyright 1995, Marcel Dekker, Inc. Used with permission.

Haugland G; Siegel C; Alexander MJ; Galanter M. A survey of hospitals in New York State treating psychiatric patients with chemical abuse disorders. *Hospital and Community Psychiatry* 42(12): 1215-1220, 1991. (39 refs.)

In New York State, 88 of 143 hospitals providing psychiatric inpatient treatment responded to a mailed questionnaire designed to determine the size of three subgroups of chemical abusers—alcohol abusers, drug abusers, and polychemical abusers—in inpatients with psychiatric diagnosis, as well as the availability of services for these patients. Data for New York City and its metropolitan area were analyzed separately. In 1987 almost one-third of psychiatric admissions both in and outside the metropolitan area had comorbid chemical abuse disorders. Of patients in the metropolitan area with comorbid chemical abuse, 75% had a drug abuse disorder; in rural areas 88% of patients with chemical abuse disorders abused alcohol. Both hospital- and community-based aftercare services, especially in the metropolitan area, were less available to psychiatric patients with chemical abuse than to patients without these disorders. Copyright 1991, American Psychiatric Association. Used with permission.

Howland RH. The treatment of persons with dual diagnoses in a rural community. *Psychiatric Quarterly* 66(1): 33-49, 1995. (50 refs.)

Persons with dual diagnosis of psychiatric illness and substance abuse represent a large subpopulation within the mental health system, but mental health service delivery systems typically do not adequately address their special needs. The literature on dual diagnosis is marked by the paucity of information on rural settings. This paper describes the characteristics of a rural community mental health system, which illustrate the difficulties in treating persons with dual diagnosis in rural communities. These problems include a fragmented system of services, centralized services in a large geographic area, overly restrictive regulations, conceptual differences in treatment approaches, confidentiality and stigma in a rural culture, and the academic and professional isolation of mental health workers, leading to high turnover and a shortage of staff with sufficient training and experience to work with persons with dual diagnosis. Some recommendations to address these problems and to improve the delivery of services to persons with dual diagnosis are suggested. Copyright 1995, Human Sciences Press, Inc.

Long KA; Boik RJ. Predicting alcohol use in rural children: A longitudinal study. *Nursing Research* 42(2): 79-86, 1993. (49 refs.)

This study describes the prevalence and correlates of alcohol use and examines the ability to predict alcohol use in rural sixth and seventh grade children. The sample consisted of 625 children from six schools in small Montana towns. Self-administered questionnaires contained measures of sociodemographic characteristics, self-concept, school attitudes, beliefs about the effects of alcohol, and alcohol use. Fifty-eight percent of the children reported using alcohol. Children's beliefs about alcohol were significantly correlated with alcohol use. Logistic regression analysis failed to identify a model having adequate sensitivity and specificity for classifying sixth and seventh grade students as "users" and "nonusers" based on variables assessed in grades 3 and 4. Nevertheless, with other variables held constant, children who displayed both negative self-concept and negative school attitudes in grades 3 and 4 were most likely to use alcohol in grades 6 and 7. Copyright 1993, American Journal of Nursing Co.

Metz GJ. Substance abuse prevention in rural areas: Project LIFE. *Alcoholism Treatment Quarterly* 12(3): 121-130, 1995. (15 refs.)

Project LIFE was comprised of two training efforts: A 3-day program (Living in Freedom Everyday) and a 5-day program (Living in Freedom Early). The project was a response to the need for more substance abuse prevention education in school districts. During its first year of implementation, the project was successful in meeting its objectives. Eighty-eight schools and 12 community agency personnel participated in an intensive training program. A central aspect of the program was teams of participants developing, implementing, and evaluating action plans. The plans comprised strategies directed toward the school district's drug-free policies, classroom curricula, staff inservice sessions, and community/parent awareness programs. Site visits to 22 participating school districts took place 3 months after the training. Of the proposed 77 strategies, 71 were achieved as reported by participants. These results along with the methodology of action planning are described. Project LIFE represents a promising effort to assist rural school personnel in substance abuse prevention education. Copyright 1995, The Haworth Press, Inc.

Moxley RL. US rural drug abuse research needs and research policy. (review). *Drugs & Society* 7(1/2): 117-139, 1992. (26 refs.)
This article is the result of a literature review and assessment of US rural drug abuse research and drug research policy formation by government agencies. It also presents results of a participant observation study of one of the major research institutes, the National Institute on Drug Abuse (NIDA), and its linkages with groups influential to its research policies. NIDA also has linkages that influence its other activities such as service and drug testing oversight functions, but these activities were not studied. This review reveals a decade of relative inattention to the job of obtaining a national assessment of the rural drug situation, especially with regard to prevalence and impact of drugs in the adult population, efficacy of prevention efforts by rural institutions and workplaces, effectiveness of treatment programs, and drugs and crime. There have also been relatively few individual subnational or regional research efforts or even rural-urban case study comparisons aimed at these research topics. Various influences on drug research policy were discovered; rural drug research advocates need to know about these influences to use them to stimulate support for rural drug research. The main influences were found to be in certain committees and offices in the legislative and executive branches of the federal government. Cases were also identified, however, in which nongovernmental organizations were found to be influential and, in certain cases, even individuals were found to have some impact on research policy. Copyright 1992, The Haworth Press, Inc.

National Rural Health Association; Office of Rural Health Policy. *Rural Mental Health and Substance Abuse Resources Directory, 1993.* Rockville MD: Office of Rural Health Policy, 1993. (0 refs.)
This directory is a compilation of up-to-date agencies and programs designed to address the mental health and substance abuse issues faced by rural communities. The categories included are federal agencies, regional federal agencies, national organizations, regional organizations, state agencies and organizations, rural health research centers, foundations, and other resources including clearinghouses, toll-free numbers, directories, and publications. Copyright 1993, Project Cork Institute.

Osher FC; Drake RE; Noordsy DL; Teague GB; Hurlbut SC; Biesanz JC; et al. Correlates and outcomes of alcohol use disorder among rural outpatients with schizophrenia. *Journal of Clinical Psychiatry* 55(3): 109-113, 1994. (49 refs.)
Alcohol use by persons with schizophrenia is common and has been associated with increased severity of psychiatric symptoms, multiple psychosocial problems, abuse of other drugs, and poor treatment outcomes. Most of the previous research in this area has been with urban patients. The authors examined the correlates and outcomes of alcohol use in a rural sample of 75 DSM-III-R outpatients with schizophrenia. Based on multiple measures, 25% ($n = 19$) of 75 rural patients with schizophrenia were diagnosed with current co-occurring alcohol use disorders. Clinicians' ratings and self-reported symptoms were used to examine correlates of alcohol use, and the study group was followed prospectively for 1 year to identify all episodes of rehospitalization, incarceration, or literal homelessness. Alcohol use disorder was statistically significantly associated with unstable housing, conceptual disorganization, denial of mental illness, and rehospitalization during 1-year follow-up. Several trends suggested that alcohol use was also related to positive symptoms of psychosis. In rural patients with schizophrenia, alcohol use appears to play a significant role in destabilizing psychosocial adjustment. These results replicate similar findings in urban settings. Copyright 1994, Physicians Postgraduate Press, Inc. Used with permission.

Smith MG; Hill GC. An alcohol and drug education needs assessment survey among 4-H youth in isolated, rural northeast Nevada. *Journal of Alcohol and Drug Education* 40(1): 69-88, 1994. (26 refs.)
Data assessing the extent of drug and alcohol use among 4-H members were collected in the Fall of 1990 from 255 youth in a three-county area of rural northeastern Nevada. The results were compared to a similar survey conducted in local schools by the Nevada State Department of Education. No statistically significant differences in drug and alcohol use were found between the 4-H members and the students in the school survey. Of the 4-H members, 70% indicated that 4-H had made a difference in their attitudes about drug and alcohol use. Yet, school was the most reported source of their current information about drugs and alcohol. Recommendations for 4-H programs wanting to implement contemporary programs are included. Copyright 1994, Alcohol and Drug Problems Association of North America.

Stevens MM; Freeman DH Jr; Mott LA; Youells FE; Linsey SC. Smokeless tobacco use among children: The New Hampshire Study. *American Journal of Preventive Medicine* 9(3): 160-167, 1993. (41 refs.)
Rural public school children initially in grades 4, 5, and 6 participated in a 36-month follow-up study of substance abuse prevention. Children completed self-report questionnaires at baseline and annually for 3 years after the introduction of prevention programs. The authors compared outcomes of (1) a comprehensive school curriculum ("Here's Looking at You, 2000"), (2) the curriculum plus a parenting course ("Parent Communication Course") and a community task force (Johnson Institute Model), and (3) control condition. Neither the curriculum nor the curriculum plus parent and community intervention had any effect on smokeless tobacco use by this preadolescent and young adolescent population. The authors used stepwise logistic regression to determine prediction models for smokeless tobacco use. Initiation of smokeless tobacco use is associated with sex, grade, and having friends who use drugs. Although regular use increases with grade, poor family relations, and low school satisfaction, the greatest risk factor was the individual's ever trying smokeless tobacco. The authors describe the culture of smokeless tobacco use in this population, and they discuss the implications of their research for smokeless tobacco use prevention. Copyright 1993, American College of Preventive Medicine.

CHAPTER 15

Dual Diagnosis

FRED C. OSHER, MD

CLINICAL APPLICATIONS

The goals of this chapter are to assist the clinician to:

1. Appreciate the historic division between the substance abuse and mental health fields and their impact on service delivery to, and outcomes for, the dual diagnosis population.

2. Identify the clinical characteristics of substance abuse and mental illness in the general population; be familiar with DSM-IV terminology.

3. Appreciate the heterogeneity of the dual diagnosis population, yet identify some common clinical features.

4. Identify the data needed to diagnose a separate psychiatric disorder in the presence of known substance abuse; identify the data needed to diagnose substance-related disorders in the presence of a chronic psychiatric disorder and to assess the dual diagnosis population; and be aware of the strengths and limitations of existing assessment tools.

5. Be aware of a variety of techniques needed to treat the dually diagnosed, including detoxification, crisis stabilization during the acute phases, counseling and motivational interventions, case management, and psychopharmacology for the chronic phase.

6. Develop individualized treatment plans based on assessment of the severity and type of mental illness and substance-related disorder.

7. Be tolerant and flexible about the concepts of self-help, psychotherapy, pharmacotherapy, and abstinence, with treatment approaches dictated by patient needs rather than by a particular philosophy; and feel comfortable working with staff of other professional disciplines, lay personnel, and family.

8. Develop empathy for the dually diagnosed individual, offering a realistic yet optimistic expectation of treatment outcomes.

A HISTORICAL CLINICAL DILEMMA

One of the most significant complicating factors in working with substance abusers can be the presence of a co-occurring psychiatric disorder. These patients are often well known to a treatment system and have generally been characterized as problematic and treatment resistant. Sensitivity to this issue is essential because of the high incidence of psychiatric symptoms in the substance abuse population, as well as the high incidence of substance-related disorders in the psychiatric population. Historically, failure to recognize co-occurring conditions and appropriately intervene have contributed to the disastrous morbidity and mortality associated with having dual diagnosis. These patients can also be seen as victims of the long history of mistrust, misunderstanding, and disrespect between the psychiatric and chemical dependency professions. Often their exclusion from treatment settings is the product of narrow-mindedness toward one or the other disciplines. Fortunately, the willingness of the systems involved to work cooperatively on behalf of persons with dual diagnosis is improving. These patients have promoted an important "bridging of the gap" between mental health and substance abuse providers.

HOW TO CONSIDER THE POPULATION WITH DUAL DIAGNOSIS

In discussing the dual diagnosis population, it is important to understand what distinguishes this group from anyone who uses psychoactive substances and displays abnormal moods or behaviors. Figure 15-1 conceptualizes these patients.

The two intersecting circles represent the populations of individuals with mental and addictive disorders. These circles are divided in half because this approximates the percentage of psychiatric patients who have symptoms related to psychoactive substance use and of substance abusers who have psy-

chiatric symptoms. The acute clinical presentations of patients within the shaded area can look identical. The clinician's task is to identify where the patient fits within this area and develop treatment strategies based on that assessment.

Within shaded area **1** are patients with primary psychiatric disorders and whose symptoms are exacerbated by the use of psychoactive substances, but who do not meet DSM-IV criteria for a substance-related disorder. The prevalence of substance use contributing to psychiatric symptoms is so high that it is essential to screen for this use in all psychiatric patients. The reasons for psychiatric patients' use of substances must be understood. Within this area are patients who may be self-medicating to modify their intolerable moods, thoughts, or behaviors or to ameliorate the side effects of medications. They may also be using drugs for the same reasons as the general population—peer acceptance and perceived normalization. While abstinence is not necessary for everyone with a psychiatric disorder, we must realize, and communicate, the increased vulnerability of psychiatric patients to the negative consequences of substance use.

Within shaded area **2** are patients who have a primary substance-related disorder with signs and symptoms of a co-occurring mood or behavior disorder. Within DSM-IV, these have been called substance-induced disorders. The high rates of suicide and homicide found in this patient population make identification of these symptoms essential. Clinical intervention must initially focus on withdrawing the psychoactive substance and closely monitoring the symptoms. The duration of abstinence required will vary among individuals, depending on their drugs of abuse and psychiatric symptomatology. This period of abstinence is needed to avoid mislabeling these patients as mentally ill and exposing them to inappropriate care and unwarranted treatment risks.

This chapter focuses primarily on those patients within shaded area **3**. These are people with two separate chronic relapsing illnesses. While each illness exacerbates the other, they are driven by different genetic, biochemical, and social factors. Having defined the core qualifications for inclusion in this subgroup, it is necessary to appreciate the heterogeneity that exists within this group. This is true of their psychiatric diagnosis, which include large percentages of thought disorders, mood disorders, and personality disorders. It is true of their substances of abuse, which include all known psychoactive agents. Polysubstance abuse is frequently reported within this group. Their choice of drug is as dependent on availability as on a specific desired change in consciousness. Heterogeneity is also seen in the range of

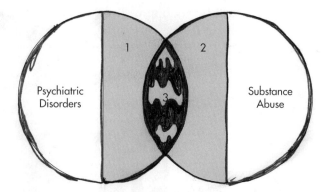

Figure 15-1. Populations of psychiatrically ill and chemically dependent persons.

dysfunction the dual diagnosis patients experience. While some dual diagnosis patients have the semblance of a productive life, it is common for others to have chaotic backgrounds, florid symptomatology, and an apparent deteriorating course. The young man with schizophrenia who regularly uses cocaine has different needs than the elderly woman with recurrent depressive episodes who abuses alcohol. Combining these patients into specific programming or treatment strategies will invariably lead to failure. Careful assessment and thoughtful individualized treatment planning are needed.

CHARACTERISTICS OF THE DUAL DIAGNOSIS POPULATION

In a review of the existing literature on the dual diagnosis population, several limitations become obvious: The terminology is different between published articles, making comparisons difficult; the definitions of various mental illnesses and substance abuse disorders have changed over time; sampling bias introduced by inadequate assessments and different clinical settings may limit generalizability; and a wide variety of assessment instruments and techniques has been used to define and treat this population. The lack of longitudinal studies for two sets of disorders known to have a chronic and fluctuating course is also an important limiting factor. Nonetheless, several associated factors can be identified within the dual diagnosis population.

The literature on dually diagnosed populations has generally characterized them as young males with a wide variety of psychiatric diagnosis. Factors contributing to the relative youth of this group have included the demographics of our country, in which a postwar "baby boom" exists; the widespread increase in alcohol and drug use since the 1960s; and the high visibility of young persons with mental illnesses who are not being admitted to state institutions due to restricted admission policies. However, youth is becoming less of a common denominator as the baby boomer cohort enters its forties and continues to have co-occurring disorders. Recent reviews have also identified the prevalence of dual disorders in adolescents to be quite high, with approximately half of all adolescents receiving mental health services having dual diagnosis. Other recent studies have reported no gender differences in the prevalence of dual diagnosis, suggesting that women with either a mental or addictive disorder are at as high a risk to develop a co-occurring disorder as their male counterparts. Once more, the heterogeneity of persons with dual disorders must be appreciated in assessment and treatment planning.

Regardless of how defined and measured, co-occurring disorders are associated with a wide array of negative outcomes. These include a greater incidence of mood disorders and suicidality; more frequent hospitalization and use of emergency services; more episodes of violent behavior and incarceration; more noncompliance with treatment plans; and increased housing instability and homelessness. The effects of having two disorders on everyday functioning is pervasive, and the patient's prognosis is poorer than with having either a mental illness or an addictive disorder. These tragic consequences of having two disorders compel a more adequate response to the needs of these individuals.

CLINICAL APPROACHES
Assessment

The assessment of the dually diagnosed patient relies heavily on careful history taking. When the mental status of patients can look identical between different subgroups of either psychiatric or substance abuse individuals, data collection becomes paramount. It is important to remember, however, that while the presence of co-occurring disorders increases the use of treatment services, a greater detection of the contributing factors does not necessarily result. These patients are notoriously poor historians, with all the denial and minimization of any substance abuser and often the additional cognitive impairments of their mental illness. Third party information is essential. Clinicians should anticipate difficulties with engaging these patients into treatment and should develop a concept of longitudinal assessment in which data collection may occur over a series of brief contacts. The clinician attempts to determine the temporal relationships between psychiatric symptoms and the use of psychoactive substances. Identifying possible periods of abstinence, e.g., hospitalizations, jail time, treatment programs and determining mental function during those periods is useful. A detailed family history is needed, with attention to possible genetic contributions to either psychiatric illness or substance abuse.

Objective rating scales, useful in the general population, have limited application for diagnosing the dually diagnosed patient. Most of these screening and assessment instruments have not been validated in this group, which leads to a high percentage of both false positives and false negatives. Specific tests such as scales of depression or cognition can be useful in monitoring symptoms but not in determining the etiology of those symptoms. Current research suggests that the Addiction Severity Index may be valid and reliable in assessing the severity of dysfunction, the presence of less severe psychiatric illnesses, and the degree of drug and alcohol dependence in these patients. Quality of life measurements are important for planning treatment and determining outcome.

self medication!

Laboratory testing can be useful in assessing acute presentations of bizarre behavior, disordered thinking, or disturbances in mood secondary to psychoactive substances. Urine or blood toxicologic screens can determine evidence of alcohol or drug use that can aid diagnosis. In addition, blood chemistries including liver profiles and complete blood counts can provide clues to ongoing heavy use of psychoactive agents. Testing may also help in monitoring compliance and abstinence and in providing external support for treatment goals. Many tests are costly, and ability to pay is frequently a factor in this underinsured population.

In summary, the data needed to assess the relative contributions of substance use and psychiatric illness to a patient's presentation include the following: A careful history from both the patient and collateral informants; a review of medical records for evidence of alcohol and other drug use complications, as well as previous psychiatric contacts; a complete physical examination to identify physical manifestations of heavy alcohol or drug use; and laboratory tests to discover evidence of alcohol or drug use and to rule out organic explanations of psychiatric symptoms. No existing testing method can absolutely diagnose either a psychiatric or substance use disorder and should not be overly relied on. There is no substitute for a longitudinal empathic effort to understand the patient's presentation in treatment settings.

Treatment

In considering the treatment of the dually diagnosed individual, the clinician must have accurately assessed the relative contribution of each disorder to the clinical presentation and also be able to provide a treatment environment conducive to recovery. Replacing frustration with hopefulness is essential and requires an *integrated* treatment approach available in a continuum of care sites. Rather than the development of new intervention techniques, a better understanding and application of existing ones is necessary. Because the routine application of either mental health or chemical dependency interventions is not indicated, an integration of these principles must be used. The burden of integrating different philosophies, recovery models, and interventions should not fall on the patient. Each treatment provider must have an understanding and respect for mental health and addiction principles. The patient should not be shuffled from one type of treatment to another, and the message he or she receives should be consistent with management of the two disorders.

Over the past decade, a number of articles have been written espousing the principles of integrated treatment, and numerous clinical models have been developed. In addition to integrating mental health and substance abuse treatments, many programs have emphasized flexibility, comprehensiveness, case management, and long-term approaches. In a review of over 30 studies of integrated treatment approaches, Drake et al. have identified the following consistent findings: Decreased utilization of inpatient services; global improvements in functional status; and the capacity of programs to engage their target population in meaningful treatment.

Many models of treatment of the dually diagnosed patient are viewed as occurring in separate phases. In one model, four treatment phases have been identified—engagement, persuasion, active treatment, and relapse prevention. Progression through these phases is slow and may require some repetition, but the goals of decreasing dependence on addictive substances and increasing autonomy are universal. Recent efforts have attempted to match motivational interventions to the patient's phase in treatment.

Engagement

For engagement into treatment to be effective, the patient must be attracted to and retained in programs. This engagement is essential because chronic illnesses require chronic care management. Programs have to offer something the patient wants, ranging from relief of troubling symptoms to the provision of adequate food or shelter. Often, young chronic adult patients have vocational expectations, and programs that provide job counseling and work opportunities can maintain a connection to these people. A primary ongoing therapeutic relationship is necessary. The more severely disabled patients require a case manager. Higher-functioning patients may benefit from a counselor, and in relapse prevention phases, a self-help sponsor. Given the volatile nature of this group, 24-hour crisis stabilization should be available. The goal of engagement is to form a trusting relationship to allow treatment providers to support the patient throughout the treatment process.

Persuasion

Convincing patients to accept abstinence-oriented treatment is called persuasion. The dual diagnosis patient's increased vulnerability to the consequences of drug use should be emphasized. Peer groups can reinforce the clinician's message that uncontrolled substance use is serious. Hospitalization can be an opportune time for persuasion. It is critical that the patient achieve optional control of the co-occurring psychiatric disorder during this phase. When patients acknowledge that a change in substance use behavior is in their best interest, primary treatment can be pursued. The goal of persuasion is to prepare the patient for active change interventions.

meet them where they are at! Find out what they want.

Thou shall not should on oneself! — Ellis

Active Treatment

The active treatment phase has many components. Group therapies and peer interaction form the basis of most interventions, but leaders will have to actively control the level of confrontation based on their assessment of the members' fragility. Tolerance and flexibility must be built into all treatment plans. The types of interventions and their timing or intensity will be determined by an assessment of the person's illness and needs. While specific treatment interventions are not included in this summary, the steps toward recovery for dually diagnosed patients parallel those of traditional chemical dependency programs. Medications will be needed to treat underlying psychiatric conditions. Disulfiram can be helpful in maintaining patients in therapy. Laboratory monitoring is essential to ensure a credible program and help patients resist compulsion to use drugs. Self-help groups will not be tolerated by all dually diagnosed patients, and creative alternatives to this support network must be developed. Good examples are AA-oriented groups with a specific dual diagnosis focus, such as Double Trudgers in Los Angeles or Double Trouble in New Jersey. Day treatment programs need to be seen as viable alternatives to bars or street corners. Eventually, effectively managed patients with higher-quality lives will inspire those in earlier stages of recovery. The management of co-occurring chronic conditions requires long-term plans.

Relapse Prevention

A relapse prevention model is applicable for treatment of the dually diagnosed patient. Relapse and slips are to be anticipated, and patients in general are to be welcomed back rather than extruded from treatment settings. There is a fine line between engagement and enabling, i.e., unintentionally facilitating the continuing use of substances. This should be regularly addressed by treatment providers. Despite temporary setbacks, realistic expectations for changes in behavior and eventual recovery should be high if the patient is to remain hopeful. The goal of this phase is to identify risk factors for returning to substance abuse and to develop strategies to minimize the risks and reinforce positive behavioral change. Family involvement is an important component of the intervention strategy. Those closest to the dually diagnosed patient are often the most aware of the relationship between the patient's two disorders. In addition, they too have heard contradictory advice on how best to respond to their loved one's problems and are often confused and angry. The term *family* should be interpreted broadly, and significant others should be included in treatment planning.

Conclusion

Regardless of proposed assessment and treatment strategies for the dually diagnosed, little will be done until the historic divisions between the mental health and chemical dependency fields are addressed. Sadly, the current barriers to identification and treatment perpetuate the myth of the dually diagnosed as untreatable. Recent federal initiatives for research and treatment of this population have promoted cooperation between the two disciplines, which should be commended, but more training and development of integrated programming is needed. Successful efforts to provide services to the dually diagnosed may have positive ramifications for all mentally and chemically impaired individuals.

REFERENCES

American Psychiatric Association. *Diagnostic and Statistical Manual of Mental Disorders, 4th Edition.* Washington DC: American Psychiatric Association, 1994.

Bachrach LL. Young adult chronic patients: An analytical review of the literature. *Hospital and Community Psychiatry* 33(3): 189-197, 1982. (65 refs.)

Center for Substance Abuse Treatment. *Assessment and Treatment of Patients with Coexisting Mental Illness and Alcohol and Other Drug Abuse. Treatment Improvement Protocol (TIP) Series 9.* Rockville MD: Center for Substance Abuse Treatment, 1994. DHHS Publication No. (SMA) 94-2078, 1994. (105 refs.)

Drake RE; McLaughlin P; Pepper B; Minkoff K. Dual diagnosis of major mental illness and substance disorder: An overview. *New Directions for Mental Health Services* 50(Summer): 3-12, 1991. (54 refs.)

Drake RE; Noordsy DL. Case management for people with coexisting severe mental disorder and substance use disorder. *Psychiatric Annals* 24(8): 427-431, 1994. (20 refs.)

Drake RE; Osher FC. Alcohol use and abuse in schizophrenia: A prospective community study. *Journal of Nervous and Mental Disease* 177(7): 408-414, 1989. (30 refs.)

Drake RE; Osher FC; Wallach MA. Homelessness and dual diagnosis. *American Psychologist* 46(11): 1149-1158, 1991. (88 refs.)

Freed EX. Alcoholism and schizophrenia: The search for perspectives: A review. *Journal of Studies on Alcohol* 36(7): 853-881, 1975. (186 refs.)

Galanter M; Castaneda R; Ferman J. Substance abuse among general psychiatric patients: Place of presentation diagnosis and treatment. *American Journal of Drug and Alcohol Abuse* 14(2): 219-244, 1988.

Helzer JE; Pryzbeck TR. The co-occurrence of alcoholism with other psychiatric disorders in the general population and its impact on treatment. *Journal of Studies on Alcohol* 49(3): 219-224, 1988. (14 refs.)

Lehman AF; Myers CP; Corty E. Assessment and classification of patients with psychiatric and substance abuse syndromes. *Hospital and Community Psychiatry* 40(10): 1019-1025, 1989. (51 refs.)

McLellan AT. New data from the Addiction Severity Index. *Journal of Nervous and Mental Disorders* 173(7): 412-423, 1985. (26 refs.)

Mueser KT; Bellack AS; Blanchard JJ. Comorbidity of schizophrenia and substance abuse: Implications for treatment. *Journal of Consulting and Clinical Psychology* 60(6): 845-856, 1992. (133 refs.)

Osher FC; Kofoed LL. Treatment of patients with psychiatric and psychoactive substance abuse disorders. *Hospital and Community Psychiatry* 40(10): 1025-1030, 1989. (52 refs.)

Pepper B; Ryglewicz H. The young adult chronic patient and substance abuse. *TIE Quarterly Bulletin* 1(3):1-8 1984. (15 refs.)

Regier DA; Farmer ME; Rae DS. Comorbidity of mental disorders with alcohol and other drug abuse: Results from the Epidemiologic Catchment Area (ECA) study. *Journal of the American Medical Association* 264(19): 2511-2518, 1990. (55 refs.)

Richardson MA; Craig RJ; Haugland G. Treatment patterns of young chronic schizophrenics in the era of deinstitutionalization. *Psychiatric Quarterly* 57(2): 243-249, 1985. (40 refs.)

Ridgely MS; Osher FC; Talbott JA. *Chronically Mentally Ill Young Adults with Substance Abuse Problems: Treatment and Training Issues.* Rockville MD: Alcohol, Drug Abuse, and Mental Health Administration, 1987. (60 refs.)

Safer D. Substance abuse by young adult chronic patients. *Hospital and Community Psychiatry* 38(5): 511-514, 1987. (33 refs.)

Schneier FR; Siris SG. A review of psychoactive substance use and abuse in schizophrenia: Patterns of choice. *Journal of Nervous and Mental Disease* 175 (11): 641-652, 1987. (94 refs.)

Schuckit MA. Genetic and clinical implications of alcoholism and affective disorder. *American Journal of Psychiatry* 143(2): 140-147, 1986. (27 refs.)

Talbott JA. *Chronic Mentally Ill Young Adults With Substance Abuse Problems: A Review of Relevant Literature and Creation of a Research Agenda.* Rockville MD: Alcohol, Drug Abuse, and Mental Health Administration, 1986. (155 refs.)

Weiss RD; Mirin SM; Griffin ML. Methodological considerations in the diagnosis of coexisting psychiatric disorders in substance abusers. *British Journal of Addiction* 87(2): 179-187, 1992. (47 refs.)

Ziedonis DM; Fisher W. Assessment and treatment of comorbid substance abuse in individuals with schizophrenia. *Psychiatric Annals* 24(9): 477-483, 1994. (26 refs.)

FURTHER READINGS

Baigent M; Holme G; Hafner RJ. Self reports of the interaction between substance abuse and schizophrenia. *Australian and New Zealand Journal of Psychiatry* 29(11): 69-74, 1995. (19 refs.)

Fifty-three psychiatric hospital inpatients with a dual diagnosis of substance abuse and schizophrenia were given the Brief Symptom Inventory and the Schizophrenia/Substance Abuse Interview Schedule. Mean age was 29; 49 were men. Only 11% were employed. Forty percent abused mainly alcohol, 40% cannabis and 8% amphetamines; 20% abused more than one substance. Mean onset age of drug abuse was 16 years; schizophrenia was diagnosed a mean of 5 years later, and subjects had been admitted to hospital an average of 7 times since then. Most believed that drug abuse initiated or exacerbated their schizophrenia; 80% took drugs primarily to relieve dysphoria and anxiety. Amphetamines improved subjective well-being significantly more than alcohol, but choice of drugs was determined mainly by price and availability. Only cannabis increased positive symptoms of schizophrenia and only amphetamines reduced negative ones. Effectively treating this population requires an integration of psychiatric and drug treatment services, ideally in a community context. Copyright 1995, Royal Australian and New Zealand College of Psychiatrists. Used with permission.

Brady KT; Roberts JM. The pharmacotherapy of dual diagnosis. *Psychiatric Annals* 25(6): 344-352, 1995. (33 refs.)

This article provides an overview of the issues related to pharmacotherapy of dual diagnosis. The authors address the process of differential diagnosis and the task of assessment, the pharma-cotherapeutic agents available, and the role of psychosocial treatment. The review addresses pharmacotherapeutic strategies for patients with dual diagnosis, Axis I psychiatric disorder and a substance abuse disorder. Prevalence estimates are reviewed to define the scope of the problem, and specific issues concerning diagnosis discussed. Current pharmacologic treatment are reviewed. Where specific pharmacologic treatment studies are absent, guidelines based on general principles of clinical psychopharmacology are offered. Copyright 1995, Slack, Inc.

Caton CLM; Wyatt RJ; Felix A; Grunberg J; Dominguez B. Follow-up of chronically homeless mentally ill men. *American Journal of Psychiatry* 150(11): 1639-1642, 1993. (13 refs.)

To supply information on the efficacy of on-site day treatment for homeless mentally ill men in shelters, the authors followed up homeless mentally ill men 18 months after placement in community housing. By the 18-month follow-up, the positive effects of the program at 6 months had deteriorated: 44% of the men had returned to shelters at some point during the follow-up period, and the number of men with criminal justice contacts had increased to a proportion exceeding that before the program. A concurrent diagnosis of substance abuse increased the risk of homelessness during follow-up. These findings underscore the need for innovative treatment and support services for the homeless mentally ill who have concurrent substance abuse. Copyright 1993, American Psychiatric Association. Used with permission.

Clark RE. Family costs associated with severe mental illness and substance abuse. *Hospital and Community Psychiatry* 45(8): 808-813, 1994. (15 refs.)

The study documents the economic assistance in the form of money, in-kind contributions, and time spent in caregiving by families of adults with both severe mental illness and substance abuse disorders. Parents of adults with dual disorders reported that family members gave significantly more money and time to the adult child than did parents of adults with no chronic illness. The estimated value of family assistance in the dual disorder group was $9703 using the opportunity-cost method and $13,891 using the substitution method, compared with $2421 and $3547 for the group with no chronic illnesses. Dual disorders impose a significant economic burden on families. Direct support that families provide to adult children with dual disorders should be considered carefully in treatment planning and policy decisions. Copyright 1994, American Psychiatric Association. Used with permission.

Clark RE; Drake RE. Expenditures of time and money by families of people with severe mental illness and substance use disorders. *Community Mental Health Journal* 30(2): 145-163, 1994. (36 refs.)

Families are typically a major source of support for people with mental illness, but substance abuse places an additional burden on family relations and could reduce the amount of direct support they give. Data from families of 169 people with co-occurring mental illness and substance abuse indicate that they give substantial time and money to their relatives with dual disorders. More severe current substance abuse appeared to reduce family spending but not direct caregiving. Patients with more severe alcohol problems were more likely to live with parents than with other family members. Copyright 1994, Human Sciences Press, Inc.

Comtois KA; Ries RK. Sex differences in dually diagnosed severely mentally ill clients in dual diagnosis outpatient treatment. *American Journal on Addictions* 4(3): 245-253, 1995. (38 refs.)

The authors explored gender differences among clients enrolled in an integrated outpatient program for dually diagnosed severely mentally ill patients. A total of 338 clients (36% women) were evaluated in several clinical areas. Women were more often diagnosed with affective disorders and men with schizophrenia. Women were more often single vs. polydrug users, showed lower levels of substance use, and had higher overall functioning. Women, however, attended groups less often than men despite comparable individual attendance and compliance. The authors discuss results in terms of program evaluation and future research. Copyright 1995, American Academy of Psychiatrists in Alcoholism and Addictions.

Drake RE; Bartels SJ; Teague GB; Noordsy DL; Clark RE. Treatment of substance abuse in severely mentally ill patients. *Journal of Nervous and Mental Disease* 181(10): 606-611, 1993. (63 refs.)

Substance abuse is the most common comorbid complication of severe mental illness. Current clinical research converges on several emerging principles of treatment that address the scope, pace, intensity, and structure of dual diagnosis programs. They include the following: (a) Assertive outreach to facilitate engagement and participation in substance abuse treatment, (b) close monitoring to provide structure and social reinforcement, (c) integration of substance abuse and mental health interventions in the same program, (d) comprehensive, broad-based services to address other problems of adjustment, (e) safe and protective living environments, (f) flexibility of clinicians and programs, (g) stage-wise treatment to ensure the appropriate timing of interventions, (h) a longitudinal perspective congruent with the chronicity of dual disorders, and (i) optimism. Copyright 1993, Williams & Wilkins, Inc.

Drake RE; Noordsy DL. Case management for people with coexisting severe mental disorder and substance use disorder. *Psychiatric Annals* 24(8): 427-431, 1994. (20 refs.)

Case management for dually disordered patients integrates substance abuse treatment into the comprehensive community support program model. The approach to substance abuse intervention proceeds through stages of engagement, persuasion, active treatment, and relapse prevention, with a variety of specific interventions in each stage. The interventions are flexible, individualized, and determined in part by patients' preferences. Based on a biopsychosocial model, individual, patient-specific factors that sustain substance abuse are identified and targeted for intervention. Treatment includes empirical trials and reviews of progress at each step until stable abstinence is achieved. All stakeholders are involved in the process of identifying targets and implementing intervention. Copyright 1994, Slack, Inc.

Drake RE; Wallach MA. Moderate drinking among people with severe mental illness. *Hospital and Community Psychiatry* 44(8): 780-782, 1993. (10 refs.)

This report evaluates the long-term stability and consequences of moderate drinking among severely mentally ill persons by examining longitudinal ratings of alcohol use from two independent clinical groups. The clinical controversy about moderate drinking was conceptualized in terms of competing hypotheses. If moderate drinking is a realistic life-style choice for severely mentally ill persons, a large proportion of moderate drinkers should be able to sustain regular drinking without adverse consequences over time. If moderate alcohol consumption is an unrealistic choice, only a small proportion should stay at that level of drinking over time; many who appear to be moderate drinkers should show evidence of abuse over longitudinal follow-up. The data indicate that moderate drinking is only rarely a stable long-term strategy; what in a cross-sectional study appears to be nonproblematic drinking often becomes an alcohol use disorder when viewed over the long term. Patients seem to become aware of this risk

over time, and many adopt abstinence. Copyright 1993, American Psychiatric Association. Used with permission.

Fanco H. Combining behavioral and self-help approaches in the inpatient management of dually diagnosed patients. *Journal of Substance Abuse Treatment* 12(3): 227-232, 1995. (20 refs.)

The combination of a token economy and a self-help model make it feasible to organize and maintain an intensive dual-diagnosis treatment program in a public municipal hospital acute psychiatric ward. The program described here, which integrates the token economy and 12-step approaches, fosters voluntary and active patient participation in the process of simultaneous recovery from mental illness and addiction; it also networks the patient with community resources. Implementation of the clinical program involved addressing multiple clinical and organizational obstacles, including a multihandicapped and often nonmotivated patient population, a lack of psychiatric staff trained in managing substance abuse, and the need to integrate mental health with substance abuse clinical interventions. The program has been operating more than 5 years and has treated more than 1,000 patients. As the token economy became an integral part of the ward routine, violence on the ward declined substantially, and patient participation in group activities increased significantly. Copyright 1995, Pergamon Press.

Jerrell JM; Hu T; Ridgely MS. Cost effectiveness of substance disorder interventions for people with severe mental illness. *Journal of Mental Health Administration* 21(3): 283-297, 1994. (42 refs.)

This study examines the cost effectiveness of three intervention strategies for people with severe mental illness who are dually diagnosed patients in terms of service use and costs. The interventions represent three primary approaches to treating these disorders: 12-step recovery, case management, and behavioral skills training. The study suggests that all three approaches are reducing acute and subacute service use and increasing involvement with outpatient and case management treatments. However, both the case management and behavioral skills approaches reduce costs more than the 12-step recovery approach, although not to a statistically significant degree in the data collected thus far. Overall, the societal costs for these patients are reduced by 43% without increasing the burden on patient families or on the criminal justice system. Copyright 1994, Association of Mental Health Administrators.

Kozaric-Kovacic D; Folnegovic-Smalc V; Folnegovic Z; Marusic A. Influence of alcoholism on the prognosis of schizophrenic patients. *Journal of Studies on Alcohol* 56(6): 622-627, 1995 (35 refs.)

Objective: This study was undertaken to investigate possible difference in clinical, social and hospital prognosis in schizophrenics with or without codiagnosed alcoholism. Method: A representative sample was selected by a two-stage random sample of sets from the total of 10,569 schizophrenic patients registered in the Croatian Psychotic Case Register in the period of 1962-71. The resulting 449 schizophrenic patients were psychiatrically examined in 1973-75 wherever they were found—at home, in a hospital or in a social-health institution. Of these original patients, 312 with or without a dual diagnosis of schizophrenia and alcoholism who were found at home were followed up until the final examination in 1990-91. Results: Rate changes in 37 patients with the dual diagnosis were signitifcant in the following characteristics: they were more often men, married, with a paranoid-hullicinatory disease form, were aggressive during examination, and were without psychiatric aftercare or regular psychopharmacotherapy (P <.01); they came from rural areas, had a mixed clinical picture with a deteriorating disease course and were less communicative and socially functional, and were without work self-initiative and personal income (*P* <.05). Conclusions: Schizophrenic patients found at home with codiagnosed alcoholism have poorer clinical, hospital, social and life prognosis and need longer hospitalization. They represent a special subgroup of schizophrenics requiring special therapeutic approach and early identification, inasmuch as their course of the disease has a tendency toward rapid deterioration. Prevention of alcoholism and its adequate treatment have far reaching implications for the prognosis of schizophrenic illness. Copyright 1995, Alcohol Research Documentation, Inc. Used with permission.

Lehman AF; Cordray DS. Prevalence of alcohol, drug, and mental disorders among the homeless: One more time. *Contemporary Drug Problems* 20(3): 355-383, 1993. (28 refs.)

> With meta-analysis of the 16 epidemiological studies of the homeless with adequate samples and diagnostic methods, considerable variation in prevalences was found, with better methodology associated with lower estimates. Weighted estimates of rates were 18% for current severe mental disorder, 28% for current alcohol disorder, and 10% for current drug use disorder. Copyright 1993, Federal Legal Publications, Inc.

Lyman SR; Pulice RT; McCormick LL. Developing strategies for providing services to the mentally ill-chemically abusing population. *Administration in Social Work* 17(4): 97-108, 1993. (25 refs.)

> This study resulted from a request from state and local government in one county in New York State who were concerned about the availability of services and the interrelationship between agencies charged with providing services to this patient group. Anecdotal information suggested that this patient group was large in number, had a primary mental illness, and was very disruptive to the service systems. Recommendations were expected to create changes in service delivery to mentally ill-chemically abusing individuals at a reasonable cost. Copyright 1993, The Haworth Press, Inc.

Minkoff K; Drake RE, eds. Dual diagnosis of major mental illness and substance disorder. *New Directions for Mental Health Services* 50(Summer): entire issue, 1991.

> This volume concerns the issue of coexisting chronic mental illness and substance abuse. Topics include epidemiology, assessment, case management, psychotherapy, treatment models and treatment systems, legal issues, and health care needs.

Mueser KT; Bellack AS; Blanchard JJ. Comorbidity of schizophrenia and substance abuse: Implications for treatment. *Journal of Consulting and Clinical Psychology* 60(6): 845-856, 1992. (133 refs.)

> The problem of substance abuse disorders in schizophrenia patients is reviewed, including the prevalence of comorbid disorders, assessment, hypothesized mechanisms underlying abuse, and the clinical effects of abuse on the course of illness and functioning. The principles of treatment for dual diagnosis schizophrenia patients are outlined, and the limitations of existing interventions are noted. Gaps are identified in current knowledge about the impact of substance abuse on schizophrenia and its treatment. Copyright 1992, American Psychological Association, Inc.

Mueser KT; Pallavi N; Tracy JI; DeGirolamo J; Molinaro M. Expectancies and motives for substance use in schizophrenia. *Schizophrenia Bulletin* 21(3): 367-378, 1995. (29 refs.)

> The study examined the internal reliability of standardized measures of substance use expectancies and motives in a schizophrenia population (*n* = 70) and the relationship of these expectancies and motives to alcohol and drug use disorders. Internal reliabilities were uniformly high for the subscales of the expectancy and motive measures. Analyses of the relationship between substance use disorders and expectancies revealed strong substance-specific expectations. Alcohol expectancies were related to alcohol disorders but not to drug disorders, cocaine expectancies were related to drug but not to alcohol disorders; and marijuana expectancies were more strongly related to drug than to alcohol use disorder. In contrast, motives were related to substance use disorders, and self-reported substance use problems were related to expectancies and motives in nonspecific manner. These results suggest that expectancy and motive questionnaires developed for the primary substance abuse population may be valid for psychiatric populations. Research on motives and expectancies may help to clarity the functions of substance abuse in person with schizophrenia. Public Domain.

Nunes EV; McGrath PJ; Quitkin FM. Treating anxiety in patients with alcoholism. *Journal of Clinical Psychiatry* 56(Supplement 2): 3-9, 1995. (49 refs.)

> The clinical management of patients who present with anxiety syndromes combined with alcohol abuse or dependence is reviewed. A critical step is to make the differential diagnosis between alcohol-induced anxiety (principally alcohol withdrawal) and anxiety disorders per se. Interview and examination techniques useful in making this differential are presented. Clinical management of and pharmacotherapy for alcohol withdrawal are outlines. Anxiety disorders that can be comorbid with alcoholism include panic disorder, social phobia, obsessive compulsive disorder, generalized anxiety disorder, and posttraumatic stress disorder. Psychotherapeutic and pharmacotherapeutic measures for each of these in the setting of alcoholism are suggested, and various possible interrelationships between anxiety disorders and alcoholism are considered. Although anxiety disorders may contribute to the underlying etiology of alcoholism in some cases, alcohol abuse tends to take on a life of its own. Treatment of an anxiety disorder can rarely, if ever, be expected to cure alcoholism. Therefore, the need to institute simultaneous treatment aimed at establishing and maintaining sobriety is emphasized. Research on anxiety disorders and alcoholism is as yet inadequate to fully answer many clinical questions about their relationship and their appropriate diagnosis and management. More research is needed in this area. Copyright 1995, Physicians Postgraduate Press, Inc. Used with permission.

Pulice RT; Lyman SR; McCormick LL. A study of provider perceptions of individuals with dual disorders. *Journal of Mental Health Administration* 21(1): 92-99, 1994. (25 refs.)

> Human service workers devote much time in preparing to serve patients. The majority of this preparation is focused in one direction, with exposure to a limited type of patient. The growing population of individuals with dual disorders of mental illness and substance abuse challenges this tradition in training, in that these patients pose unique, multiple, and overlapping characteristics, symptomatology, and behaviors requiring a synthesis of training approaches. Based on survey data collected in a county in New York, this study discusses how providers from various agencies view individuals with dual disorders and proposes coordination and training efforts to respond to providers' treatment concerns. Copyright 1994, Association of Mental Health Administrators.

Quimby E. Homeless clients' perspectives on recovery in the Washington DC, Dual diagnosis project. *Contemporary Drug Problems* 22(2): 265-289, 1995 (12 refs.)

> Dually diagnosed homeless persons remain homeless longer, live under more desolate circumstances, and need more specialized services. Treatment for mentally ill abusers of alcohol and other drugs tends to be fragmented rather than integrated. This report

examines a three year (110-1993) research demonstration for homeless substance abusers with severe mental disorders. It involved a collaboration between the New Hampshire-Dartmouth Psychiatric Research Center, Community Connections, and Howard University. The project studied two case management models within Community Connections and a comparison group that received traditional treatment from DC community mental health centers. Quantitative and qualitative data were collected. A study of factors seen as promoting or retarding treatment by 50 demonstration project clients found that issues of autonomy and control were central in their relation to treatment. On the one hand, case, management needed to be assertive; but on the other, the client needed to feel in control. Copyright 1995, Federal Legal Publications, Inc.

Ridgely MS; Goldman HH; Willenbring M. Barriers to the care of persons with dual diagnosis: Organizational and financial issues. *Schizophrenia Bulletin* 16(1): 123-132, 1990. (39 refs.)

Among the frustrations of managing the dual disorders of chronic mental illness and alcohol and drug abuse is that simply knowing what to do (by way of special programming) is insufficient to address the problem. The system problems are at least as intractable as the chronic illnesses themselves. Organizing and financing care of patients with comorbidities is complicated. At issue are the ways in which we administer and finance mental health and alcohol and drug. Separate administrative divisions and funding pools have compounded the problems inherent in serving persons with multiple disabilities. Arbitrary service divisions and categorical boundaries at the state level prevent local governments and programs from organizing joint projects or creatively managing patients across service boundaries. When patients cannot adapt to the way services are organized, we risk reinforcing their overuse of inpatient and emergency services. This article reviews the barriers in organizing and financing care (categoric and third party financing, including the special problem of diagnosis-related groups limitations) and proposes strategies to enhance the delivery of appropriate treatment. Public Domain.

Ries R; Mullen M; Cox G. Symptom severity and utilization of treatment resources among dually diagnosed inpatients. *Hospital and Community Psychiatry* 45(6): 562-568, 1994. (21 refs.)

The authors' goal was to determine the clinical characteristics of patients admitted to an acute voluntary psychiatric unit with a dual diagnosis treatment program. Psychiatric patients with a past substance use disorder, like those with a current substance use disorder, may be at risk for increased symptom severity and increased utilization of treatment resources and may need specialized treatment planning. The needs of dually diagnosed patients with mood disorders and of those with chronic psychotic conditions should be considered in local and national mental health care planning. Copyright 1994, American Psychiatric Association. Used with permission.

Selzer JA; Lieberman JA. Schizophrenia and substance abuse. *Psychiatric Clinics of North America* 16(2): 401-412, 1993. (56 refs.)

Although lifetime, annual, and current use of drugs of abuse have decreased in surveys of students, drug use has become concentrated and perhaps even increased in the socially disadvantaged and perhaps in persons with schizophrenia. In schizophrenia, the vulnerability to substance abuse may be caused by efforts to self-medicate or because many individuals with schizophrenia live in economically poor areas where substance abuse is endemic. Substance abuse and dependence represent an increasingly frequent challenge for clinicians who care for patients with schizophrenia. Because drugs of abuse are characterized by psychotic organic mental disorders as part of the phenomenology of intoxication or withdrawal, diagnostic clarity is often difficult to achieve. Furthermore, once in treatment (often involuntarily), these patients can frustrate clinicians through the patient's denial of having one or both types of disorder. There is a scarcity of long-term treatment and residential settings. Exploration of what needs are fulfilled by drugs of abuse also may give clinicians a better sense of what patients with schizophrenia perceive as unmet needs (for example, for affliction) and enable clinicians to tailor treatment plans accordingly. Copyright 1993, WB Saunders Co.

Weinberg D; Koegel P. Impediments to recovery in treatment programs for dually diagnosed homeless adults: An ethnographic analysis. *Contemporary Drug Problems* 22(2): 193-236, 1995. (30 refs.)

This article draws on the authors; ethnographic data to describe factors that hindered the ability of dually diagnosed homeless individuals to negotiate and complete treatment in each of the study's treatment settings. The authors begin with a description of the authors' ethnographic data collection and analysis. The authors next describe the two programs in which the authors' study population was involved. The authors then turn to a discussion of three practical tensions that chronically interfered with many clients' ability to participate in these treatment programs: (1) the antithetical demands placed on people by social life in the programs and social life as a homeless person on the streets; (2) the challenge of participating in treatment while struggling to meet immediate subsistence needs; and (3) the difficulties that arose for homeless dually diagnosed individuals as they came to recognize that many of their problems could not be resolved through participation in treatment. The authors conclude by highlighting the implications of their observations for those concerned with providing services to dually diagnosed homeless individuals. Copyright 1995, Federal Legal Publications, Inc.

CHAPTER 16

Effects of Prenatal Alcohol and Drugs

ANN P. STREISSGUTH, PhD
LORETTA P. FINNEGAN, MD

CLINICAL APPLICATIONS

The goals of this chapter are to assist the clinician to:

1. Understand the physical and social implications of fetal alcohol effects.
2. Be familiar with the three P's of prevention.
3. Be aware of necessary intervention and the need for professional referrals.
4. Understand the methodological issues related to study of prenatal drug exposure.
5. Be familiar with the epidemiology of substance use by pregnant women.
6. Be able to make a referral for substance use treatment and to recognize the impediments to entering treatment.
7. Be familiar with the outcomes for children who have been prenatally exposed to drugs and the roles of environment.

PRENATAL ALCOHOL EXPOSURE

by Ann P. Streissguth

Alcoholism is a major public health problem in the US, and fetal alcohol syndrome (FAS) is one of its most devastating sequelae. FAS is among the leading known causes of mental retardation; some estimates place it first. It is the only one entirely preventable. FAS is caused by heavy maternal alcohol use during pregnancy. The alcohol ingested by the mother can have a direct toxic effect on the developing embryo and fetus. Individual genetic factors are also involved. About one-third of the children born to alcoholic mothers have the full FAS. Others have only partial effects, while some may be unaffected.

FAS can be diagnosed at birth or at any time in life, but the physical characteristics are easier to identify in infancy and early childhood. The physical birth defects are often rather mild in children with FAS. Their significance derives from their prognosis for later developmental disabilities, which may be severe. These developmental disabilities do not go away, and, even as adults, these patients are often disabled and need special care and programming. About 1 to 3 babies in every 1000 born have the full FAS; many more have partial effects. In communities where alcohol abuse is prevalent in women, as many as 1 in 100 babies may be affected. The cost to society is enormous, estimated at $596,000 to $1.4 million per FAS child throughout his or her lifetime.[23,25]

Fetal Alcohol Syndrome

The FAS diagnosis is usually given by dysmorphologists. Unlike Down syndrome or Turner's syndrome, for which laboratory tests provide a definitive diagnosis, FAS is diagnosed by clinical symptoms alone. A diagnosis of FAS is warranted when a child heavily exposed to alcohol in utero has a cluster of three kinds of symptoms: Growth deficiency, certain dysmorphic features, and some CNS effects. The pattern of facial characteristics is distinctive and includes short palpebral fissures (eye slits), indistinct and/or long philtrum (the ridges running between the nose and mouth), narrow upper lip, small chin, and/or flat midface. Flat nasal bridge, epicanthic folds, and other eye and ear anomalies are also seen with increased frequency, as well as minor anomalies of the hands and arms. Heart defects occur in 30% to 40% of patients with FAS.[4,5,6]

The growth deficiency occurs both prenatally and postnatally for weight and/or height. The CNS manifestations depend somewhat on the child's age, although microcephaly, with the implication of small brain, is noted throughout life except in cases where macrocephaly is noted. The latter is probably attributed to an arrested hydrocephalus. Other CNS characteristics in infancy include tremulousness, weak suck, hypotonia (and sometimes hypertonia), and slow development.

Hyperactivity and mental retardation are often noted during preschool years. Attention deficits, memory problems, learning problems, and impulsivity are noted throughout life. The diagnosis can often be made at birth, but the best time is between 8 months and 8 years, when the facial and growth characteristics are most notable. The facial characteristics are recognizable but somewhat different during adolescence and adulthood because of excessive growth of the nose and chin in some patients.[3,13,24,26,27,31]

Fetal Alcohol Effects

Patients with a history of excessive prenatal alcohol exposure, but without enough characteristics to warrant a diagnosis of FAS, are often categorized as having possible fetal alcohol effects (FAE). This is a descriptive term and not a real diagnosis because no clear diagnostic criteria currently exist. In the absence of a clear prenatal alcohol exposure history, such a term is meaningless because only the characteristics of the full FAS are unique to alcohol. Children with FAE may be just as disabled as children with FAS and just as in need of services, even though fewer of them are clearly mentally retarded. Children with FAE are frequently at additional risks because they often appear fairly normal. Thus, their cognitive deficits go unrecognized as birth defects and are mistaken for poor motivation. Accordingly, they often do not receive the help they need to reach their full potential.[1,20]

In large epidemiological studies (that can adjust statistically for other causes of poor outcome), prenatal alcohol exposure, even at moderate levels, has been linked to developmental problems, motor problems, IQ decrements, attentional deficits, and memory problems. Difficulty with concentration, organization, persistence, and flexible problem solving, and a variety of adverse effects on offspring, even in the absence of physical manifestations of FAE or FAS, are also common. These alcohol-related behavioral problems, often termed *minimal brain damage,* may occur even in the absence of the physical effects of prenatal alcohol exposure and at lower doses.[28,29]

Through such large-scale epidemiological studies, we know that prenatal alcohol exposure, even at moderate levels or what is commonly called "social drinking," can increase the rate of spontaneous abortions, stillbirths, low birth weight, and/or developmental deviations. Binge patterns of consumption (four or five drinks at a time, even if only occasionally) are among the most damaging in terms of long-term behavioral effects. Prenatal alcohol exposure can cause a variety of neurobehavioral effects, even in the absence of FAS/FAE, including tremulousness, weak suck, and poor state control in newborns. Mild developmental delays, delayed reaction time, attentional deficits, memory problems, learning problems, and difficulty with organization, persistence, and impulsivity are also common. The long-term implications of these subtle cognitive deficits observable in preschool and young school-age children have now been examined into the adolescent years. Arithmetic disabilities and problems with adaptive behavior continue to be measurable as long-term outcomes associated with prenatal alcohol exposure, even after adjustment for other risk factors.[28,29]

Prevention

FAS is an entirely preventable form of mental retardation. All of the other alcohol-related effects associated with moderate drinking levels could also be prevented if women abstained from drinking during pregnancy. The Surgeon General of the US has issued a warning recommending that all pregnant women and those planning a pregnancy should abstain from drinking alcoholic beverages. This includes beer, wine, and liquor, including wine coolers, light beer, and other drinks that contain alcohol in any form.

When a pregnant woman drinks any of these beverages, alcohol quickly circulates from the mother's blood to the baby's blood. Since the fetus is more vulnerable than the mother, alcohol can cause irreparable damage, particularly to the developing brain. Unfortunately, one of the times when the fetus is the most vulnerable is right around the time of conception, even before the mother knows that she is pregnant. That is why the Surgeon General has warned women not to drink when they are planning a pregnancy. There is neither an established safe dose of alcohol during pregnancy nor a safe time to drink. The fetus can be affected by amounts of alcohol that have no distinguishable effects on the mother.[10,12,14,18,19,22]

To prevent FAS and other alcohol-related effects, we need the "3 P's": **P**ublic education campaigns, **P**rofessional training, and the **P**rovision of clinical services for mothers and children at risk. Families can help women by supporting their abstinence, sharing nonalcoholic beverages, and letting them know that they appreciate their responsible behavior. Health care agencies can help by passing on the message to all patients, e.g., women who are not yet pregnant, husbands, grandparents, and children. Communities can pass on the message through signs at locations where alcoholic beverages are sold, public health spots on radio and television, and legislation to mandate warning labels on alcoholic beverage advertising. Schools can help by providing curriculums on the health risks of drinking during pregnancy to students

of all ages. The protection of our next generation is all of our responsibility.[23,25]

Several model programs exist that include public awareness campaigns with such components as warning notices at stores that sell alcohol, bus signs, public service announcements on television, and newspaper articles. Crisis phone lines, posters, brochures, and pamphlets for both general and specific audiences have also been developed. Special alcohol and drug treatment programs targeted to pregnant women and mothers with young children are urgently needed in most communities.[15,16]

In Seattle a model advocacy program for the highest-risk women in the community has been developed. This model of advocacy was demonstrated through a project known locally as "Birth to 3," which involved women who had abused drugs and alcohol heavily during pregnancy and were relatively unconnected with community services including prenatal care. Although, because of the demonstration nature of this project, women were enrolled at delivery, advocacy could begin at any point during the pregnancy. The program selects and trains a small group of paraprofessional "advocates" to work one-to-one with a mother for the first 3 years after the birth of the baby. Each advocate carries a caseload of only 12 to 15 of these highest-risk mothers, thus allowing the approach to be holistic and individualized to each mother's expressed needs, goals, capabilities, and situation. The work focuses on the advocate helping each mother begin to deal successfully with the problems she faces, which may include obtaining safe housing, terminating abusive relationships, obtaining community support, obtaining alcohol and drug treatment, and utilizing effective family planning techniques including pregnancy terminations. Classes in parenting, anger management, and personal growth are encouraged as appropriate. Results to date have been encouraging, and training modules are available.[8,9]

Professional education should include the variety of professionals who may come in contact with pregnant women, families with alcohol problems, and/or disabled children. These include public health nurses, pediatricians, obstetricians, physical and occupational therapists, preschool and other school teachers, judges, ministers, psychologists, psychiatrists, speech and language specialists, developmental disabilities specialists, child protective workers, and probation and parole officers. Professional awareness of FAS/FAE will ensure that the community can protect its children from the adverse effects of prenatal alcohol exposure and from the compounding postnatal effects of growing up in alcoholic families, where the children are at risk for neglect, physical and sexual abuse, and alcohol and drug dependence. Some states have mandated professional training, e.g., Missouri.

Intervention

Despite our best prevention efforts, children with FAS continue to be born. Because children with birth defects such as FAS can be further compromised by postnatal trauma, it is also important to think of ways to help affected children escape further damage. Studies of children of alcoholic parents show that the longer the children remain in alcoholic households, the more emotional and psychosocial problems the children have. Children born with FAS should be signals to the health care team and to the community that theirs is a family in distress. Mothers who give birth to children with FAS are themselves at risk for major health problems, psychosocial problems, and early death.[27]

Child advocates can represent the interests of young children in these high-risk environments. All of the helping professions need to consider the welfare of the children in high-risk alcohol and drug-dependent settings. Of all the children in these settings, those with FAS and FAE are likely to be among those with the highest risk for poor outcome. Schools must recognize the needs of children and adolescents with FAS and FAE and develop intervention programs based on their specific cognitive needs, which are different from children with other birth defects such as Down syndrome.[2,3]

Communities must provide structured residential facilities for such patients as they reach older adolescence and adulthood, because protective environments are often needed throughout their lives, and appropriate foster and adoptive homes are not available for all.

It is the right of every handicapped child to develop to his/her own fullest potential, and it is the responsibility of the community to provide the appropriate opportunities. Communities need to identify and assist alcohol-affected children in need of special services. As many children with FAS are unable to be cared for by their biological families, the community ultimately assumes the burden of care. If communities do not provide physical and emotional protection and appropriate educational and vocational experiences for these vulnerable children, the problems will be compounded in the next generation.[7,11,21]

Some states are already mobilizing toward these aims, and a variety of model programs already exist, but unless specific regional FAS/FAE prevention/intervention programs are established to monitor and coordinate these activities, it is unlikely that these issues will be properly addressed. Prevention of alcohol-related birth defects and intervention with affected children need to be important goals of health care practitioners.

Comments for Primary Care Providers

In contacts with adolescents of both sexes, there are numerous reasons to broach the issue of alcohol use. There is the issue of drinking and driving, both as the operator of a vehicle or as a passenger. The relationship of alcohol use to unprotected and unwanted intercourse, to date or acquaintance rape, to sexually transmitted disease, and to unplanned pregnancy is well established. It is helpful to point out that alcohol use is a lifelong concern, not just an issue for adolescents. In this context, the relationship of drinking to birth defects, and the importance of abstinence in pregnancy, can easily be made. As with any major issue, be prepared to reiterate this message.

As noted, some of the most serious neonatal effects of alcohol consumption may occur in the first trimester, even before a woman is aware of her pregnancy. However, this is no reason to avoid helping women who continue to drink during their pregnancies. The children born to heavy-drinking women who were successful in reducing their intake, even if not achieving complete abstinence, had a reduced incidence of FAS. Some women will be able to stop alcohol use during pregnancy merely because of a clear educational statement from a health care provider; others will need referrals to women-oriented alcohol treatment programs. All women should be queried about alcohol use habits at their first prenatal visit, given some educational intervention, and told to refrain from alcohol use during pregnancy and lactation.

In adopted children, there may be a higher prevalence of FAS or FAE which was either not suspected or diagnosed, or of which the adoptive parents were uninformed. In assessments of developmental disabilities in adopted children, FAS or FAE needs to be considered in the evaluation, and subsidized adoptions and extended services should be available to such families, as needed.

PRENATAL DRUG EXPOSURE

by Loretta P. Finnegan

Much concern has been expressed over the last several decades about the effects of licit and illicit drugs upon pregnancy, the fetus, the newborn, and child. Numerous research studies have undertaken the difficult task of determining the effects of alcohol, cocaine, and opiates from a physiological and developmental standpoint. Many issues have been clearly defined with regard to the effects of alcohol on pregnancy, the fetus, and the newborn, and its relationship to long-term development. FAS has been described, as well as FAE. Long-term studies of infants prenatally exposed to alcohol have been ongoing over the last decade, as discussed in the first portion of this chapter.

Despite a growing number of studies that have investigated the reproductive effects of maternal cocaine use, a homogeneous pattern of fetal effects has not been established, and there is little consensus on the adverse effects of the drug. Although considerable concern has been expressed about the high rate of cocaine use in pregnant women, a rush to judgment has occurred about the extent and permanency of specific effects of intrauterine cocaine exposure. Many predictions about adverse developmental outcomes for children prenatally exposed to cocaine have been promulgated by the scientific and lay communities, despite the lack of supportive scientific evidence. Many have been concerned about the potential severity and universality of cocaine effects, but premature conclusions may be potentially harmful to children.

Infants have been exposed to opiates for centuries. Only in the last two decades have researchers evaluated the short- and long-term effects. The neonatal abstinence syndrome has been defined, and recommendations for treatment have been published. However, studies on long-term effects are limited, and, as in the research on cocaine effects, numerous confounding factors exist in respect to pregnant opiate-dependent mothers.

Research studies on prenatal exposure to alcohol, cocaine, and opiates have defined a number of structural and behavioral effects upon the fetus and newborn. It is clear, from a pharmacological basis and animal research, that many of these effects are biologically plausible through direct or indirect mechanisms. However, the research to date has not clearly defined specific independent effects. In fact, few studies exist on the effects of long-term opiate and cocaine exposure.

Research on prenatal exposure to licit and illicit drugs is of key public health importance. Moreover, researchers and funding agencies must work diligently to advance the research from the methodological weaknesses of the past and to define the risks and nature of structural and behavioral outcomes. While defining these effects, researchers, clinicians, and public policymakers must also develop intervention services for both mothers and children and be advocates for improved health care and drug treatment services for women dependent upon cocaine, opiates, or alcohol.

Epidemiology

Estimates of drug use during pregnancy in the US vary according to the location evaluated, the populations studied, and the methodologies used. The National Institute on Drug Abuse (NIDA) presented the results of the first representative survey on the prevalence of drug use in pregnant women in the US at its 1994 Conference—Drug Addiction Research and the Health of Women. The study design of this National Pregnancy and Health Survey involved a two-stage process. First, a probability sample of private and public hospitals was selected. Only hospitals with more than 20 annual births in the 48 contiguous states were eligible. All federal government hospitals except for large Indian Health Service hospitals were excluded. A probability sample was then derived of mothers delivering liveborns at these hospitals who met survey eligibility criteria. There were 2613 women in 52 hospitals in both metropolitan and non-metropolitan areas. The survey found that 5.5%, or 221,000 of the 4 million women who give birth every year used some illicit drug during pregnancy. The survey also estimated that the number of babies born to women who used drugs during pregnancy was 222,000, a close parallel to the estimates for the number of mothers. These estimates show that, at some time during their pregnancy, 119,000 women (2.9%) reported use of marijuana and 45,000 women (1.1%) reported use of cocaine. These are the two most frequently used illicit drugs. The survey also found that 757,000 women (18.8%) used alcohol and 820,000 women (20.4%) smoked cigarettes at some time during pregnancy.

Overall estimated rates of drug use during pregnancy were higher for African Americans than for Caucasians and Hispanics. The survey found that 11.3% (75,000) of African-American women, 4.5% (28,000) of Hispanic women, and 4.4% (113,000) of Caucasian women used an illicit drug during pregnancy. While the rates of use were higher for African Americans, it must be emphasized that the total estimated number of Caucasians using drugs during pregnancy was much larger than the number of African Americans or Hispanics.

Rates of marijuana use during pregnancy were highest for African-American women, 4.5% compared with 3.0% for Caucasian women, and 1.5% for Hispanic women. The population estimates for marijuana use were 30,800 African-American women, 77,500 Caucasian women, and 9100 Hispanic women. Rates of cocaine use during pregnancy were higher for African-American women, 4.5% (30,000), than for Caucasian women, 0.4% (9200), or for Hispanic women, 0.7% (4400). "Crack" was the predominant form of cocaine used by African-American women, and it accounted for the much higher rate of overall use of cocaine in African Americans.

Drug use prevalence breakdowns solely by race/ethnicity groups do not and cannot represent the full spectrum of the interplay of multiple factors in the problem of drug abuse. Socioeconomic differences are obvious factors. This study found that in general, rates of any illicit drug use were higher in women who were not married, had less than 16 years of formal education, were not working, and relied on some public source of funding to pay for their hospital stay. The magnitude of the differences in rates among race/ethnicity groups further varied when sociodemographic variables were taken into account. Some of the significant differences in any illicit drug use between Caucasians and African Americans, and between African Americans and Hispanics, disappeared when sociodemographic variables were also considered, e.g., African-American vs. Caucasian rates for those who were not married, or African-American vs. Caucasian rates for those receiving some public aid for their hospital stay. This study shows that drug use is a serious problem for women of all races, with race/ethnicity-specific preferences for particular drugs. Interventions should therefore be targeted to meet the needs of the specific subpopulation.

Cocaine

Many reports have expounded on the detrimental effects of cocaine on infant morbidity. However, many of these have not been substantiated by repeated studies. Assessments of the organic impact of cocaine on the human pregnancy have not always considered confounding factors. These include, associated variables such as poverty, hopelessness, inadequate prenatal and postnatal care, and deficient nutrition; types of cocaine use; multiple drug use; sexually transmitted diseases; and toxic adulterants mixed with, or used to process, cocaine.

Despite these shortcomings, consistent findings include the impact of maternal morbidity upon the neonate, e.g., infections, impaired growth, smaller head circumference, and prematurity. Inconsistent findings include the occurrence of congenital abnormalities and abnormal neurobehavior. Transient findings include electrocephalographic abnormalities[11] and tortuous iris vasculature in the eye grounds.[23] More extensive reports concerning infant morbidity related to cocaine are elaborated elsewhere.[6,10,20 25,27,29,35,36,37,38]

Cocaine's low molecular weight and high solubility in both water and lipids allow it to pass easily cross the placenta and enter fetal compartments. This transplacental passage is enhanced with intravenous or freebase use of cocaine. In addition, the relatively low pH of fetal blood (cocaine is a weak base) and the low fetal level of plasma esterases, which usually metabolize this drug, may lead to accumulation of cocaine in the fetus. Furthermore, the "binge" pattern commonly associated with cocaine use may lead to even higher levels of cocaine in the fetus. Transfer of cocaine appears to be greater in the first and third trimesters of pregnancy. Cocaine has such potent vasoconstrictive properties that the constriction of uterine, placental, and umbilical vessels may retard somewhat the transfer of cocaine from mother to fetus. There is a concomitant deleterious effect of this vasoconstriction, namely fetal deprivation of essential gas and nutrient exchange resulting in fetal hypoxia.[39] In addition to an acute hypoxic insult, long cocaine use may produce a chronic decrease in transplacental nutrient and oxygen flow, leading to intrauterine growth retardation. Although the relationship of cocaine use to congenital malformations is still controversial, a decrease in fetal blood supply during critical periods of morphogenesis and growth may result in organ malformations.[3,5,12,22,28,30] Studies in sheep have shown that maternal cocaine administration results in dose-dependent, catecholamine-mediated increase in maternal blood pressure and a decrease in uterine blood flow, with a significant reduction in uterine blood flow for at least 15 minutes.[2,32]

The course of labor may also be affected by maternal cocaine use. Intravenous administration of a local anesthetic such as cocaine may cause a direct increase in uterine muscle tone. "Crack" also appears to directly increase uterine contractility and may thus precipitate the onset of premature labor. Higher rates of early pregnancy losses and third trimester placental abruptions appear to be major complications of maternal cocaine use. Several investigators have reported increased stillbirth rates in cocaine-using women.[1,4,21] It is currently postulated that increased levels of catecholamines, increased blood pressure, and increased body temperature, whether in combination or alone, may play etiologic roles in early fetal loss and later abruptio placentae.

With regard to the teratogenic potential of cocaine in humans, there are conflicting reports in the literature. Animal studies have provided some answers regarding cocaine's effects by controlling for many of the confounding variables found in the human literature. The animal studies, as with the human literature, have produced evidence of growth retardation, placental abruption, cerebral infarctions, increased prenatal and postnatal mortality, limb/digit reductions, and eye anomalies. But as with the human literature, the teratogenic risk seems low in animal models and seems to require high doses and individual susceptibility.[7]

Several literature reviews and analyses deserve comment. Koren has done an extensive review on the potential teratogenic effects of cocaine and has published a meta-analysis with Lutiger.[29] He proposes a hypothesis regarding maternal-fetal toxicology of cocaine,[25] based on his analysis of published data and experimental evidence in their laboratory. Cocaine is used by pregnant women in two distinct modes. Social cocaine users consume cocaine as part of a mixed socioeconomic class, maintain reasonable medical care, and tend to discontinue cocaine use once pregnancy is detected. There is no evidence that this mode of exposure increases the reproductive risk of such pregnancies in terms of perinatal complications, dysmorphology, or neurobehavioral development.[20] Addicted women use cocaine throughout pregnancy, and in addition to cocaine, they have clustering of other reproductive risk factors, including cigarette smoking, alcohol consumption, a tendency to lower socioeconomic classes, shorter education, poor prenatal/medical care, use of other drugs of abuse, younger age, being single parents, and having sexually transmitted diseases. Analysis of all available studies conducted with this population suggests that cocaine is not a major human teratogen and that most children are likely to be normal both morphologically and neurodevelopmentally. Koren and Lutiger hypothesize, however, that there is a subgroup of fetuses susceptible to the adverse effects of cocaine because of the following: Variability in placental transfer of cocaine, variability in placental-vascular response to cocaine, and variability in fetal pharmacodynamics.

Opiates

It is well known that the physical problems encountered by the pregnant drug-dependent mother are enormous. For one, medical complications abound from the frequent use of dirty needles. Moreover, the women are extremely sexually active and have a history of sexually transmitted diseases. Living conditions are poor, and many infections are transmitted within these settings. Because these women are poorly nourished, they frequently have vitamin deficiencies such as in vitamin C (associated with nicotine smoking) and the B vitamins (associated with cocaine use). In addition, iron deficiency anemia and folic acid deficiency anemia occur during pregnancy. From the frequent use of needles, the women have abscesses, ulcers, thrombophlebitis, bacterial endocarditis, hepatitis, and urinary tract infection. Sexually transmitted diseases such as gonorrhea, syphilis, herpes, and AIDS are common.

The most common obstetrical complication in opiate-dependent women with no prenatal care is preterm birth. The incidence of low birth weight may approach 50%. These infants have the expected complications seen in preterm infants, discussed later. If the infants are born at term, they may have pneumonia or meconium aspiration syndrome. In both premature and term infants, withdrawal from opiates may occur. Appropriate assessment and rapid treatment are essential so that the infants may recover without incident.[13,14]

Treatment of Opiate-Dependent Women

Medical treatment for pregnant drug-dependent women must include perinatal services, pharmacotherapy, health education, and referral. Perinatal services encompass evaluation and treatment by a perinatologist and a perinatal nurse clinician. Antenatal testing is performed. Human immunodeficiency virus (HIV) counseling and testing and nutritional counseling are provided. The mother should deliver in a hospital where emergency services are readily available in case of complications. Infants are frequently small and many need intensive care.

Methadone maintenance has proved efficacious in the treatment of pregnant opiate-dependent women. Doses range from 10 to 90 milligrams with a mean of 50 milligrams. It is clear that methadone is safe for pregnant women. The only major problem encountered is withdrawal symptoms in the neonate. Appropriate methadone use, coupled with comprehensive prenatal care, can decrease the complications of pregnancy, childbirth, and infant development.[8,16,17]

Medical withdrawal of pregnant opiate-dependent women from methadone generally is *not* indicated. Methadone doses should not be decreased, but provided at a level that comforts the mother and decreases the chances of withdrawal of the mother and the fetus. In the third trimester, many women will need an increase in methadone dose because of various physiological changes and weight gain. If the mother has any specific psychiatric illnesses, appropriate psychotropic medication should be provided with the methadone.[16]

If a pregnant woman has any specific medical complications such as hyperthyroidism or diabetes, appropriate medical consultation is essential. Additionally, because of the poverty in which many of the women live, many medical complications occur. A good clinical history can frequently determine the background of the patient and lead to a clearer understanding of the addictive process in this woman. Therefore, the treatment team must provide an appropriate environment so that the woman may stay in a healthy physical and psychological state.

Utilizing perinatologists' current techniques, methadone maintenance and pharmacological treatment as needed, and psychosocial counseling, opiate-dependent women can have a healthy pregnancy and a good gestational outcome.[16,17]

Opiate-Exposed Infants

The extremely high-risk environment of the pregnant drug-dependent woman predisposes her to a host of neonatal problems. In heroin-dependent women, many of their nenates' medical complications are due to low birth weight and prematurity. As a consequence, conditions such as asphyxia neonatorum, intracranial hemorrhage, hyaline membrane disease, intrauterine growth retardation, hypoglycemia, hypocalcemia, septicemia, and hyperbilirubinemia are common in opiate-exposed, low-birth-weight babies. Because infants born to women who receive methadone maintenance are more apt to have higher birth weights and a decreased incidence of premature birth, medical complications generally reflect the following: (a) The amount of prenatal care the mother has received; (b) whether she has suffered any particular obstetrical or medical complications, including toxemia of pregnancy, hypertension, or infection; and, most importantly, (c) multiple drug use that may produce an unstable intrauterine milieu complicated by withdrawal and overdose. This last situation is extremely hazardous because it predisposes the neonate to meconium staining and subsequent aspiration pneumonia, which may cause significant morbidity and increased mortality.[19]

Narcotic abstinence contributes considerably to neonatal morbidity. However, not all infants born to drug-dependent mothers show withdrawal symptomatology. Several investigators have reported that between 60% and 90% of infants show symptoms.[32,33,34] Because the biochemical and physiological processes governing withdrawal are still poorly understood, and because of polydrug abuse, erratic drug taking, and vague and inaccurate maternal histories, it is not surprising to find varying descriptions and experiences in reports from different centers.

Neonatal narcotic abstinence syndrome is described as a generalized disorder characterized by signs and symptoms of central nervous system hyperirritability, gastrointestinal dysfunction, respiratory distress, and vague autonomic symptoms that include yawning, sneezing, mottling, and fever.[9,13,15] The infants initially develop mild, high-frequency, low-amplitude tremors that progress in severity. High-pitched cry, increased muscle tone, irritability, increased deep tendon reflexes, and an exaggerated Moro reflex are all characteristic of this syndrome. The rooting reflex is increased, and sucking of fists or thumbs is common; yet when feedings are administered, the infants have extreme difficulty and regurgitate frequently.

The feeding difficulty occurs because of an uncoordinated and ineffectual sucking reflex. The infants may develop loose stools; therefore, they are susceptible to dehydration and electrolyte imbalance. Time of onset of symptoms is variable. Following delivery, serum and tissue levels of the drug(s) used by the mother begin to fall. The newborn continues to metabolize and excrete the drug, and withdrawal or abstinence signs occur when critically low tissue levels have been reached.

Because of the variation in time of onset and in degree of severity, a spectrum of abstinence patterns may be observed. Withdrawal may be mild and transient, delayed in onset, have a stepwise increase in severity, be intermittently present, or have a biphasic course that includes acute neonatal withdrawal followed by improvement and then an exacerbation of acute withdrawal.[9]

More severe withdrawal seems to occur in infants whose mothers have taken large amounts of drugs for a long time. Usually the closer to delivery a mother takes a narcotic, the greater the delay in the onset of withdrawal and the more severe the symptoms in her baby. As noted, the maturity of the infant's own metabolic and excretory mechanism plays an important role after delivery. Due to the variable severity of the withdrawal, the duration of symptoms may be anywhere from 6 days to 8 weeks. Although the infants are discharged from the hospital after drug therapy is stopped, their symptoms or irritability may persist for more than 3 to 4 months.[9]

Behavior of Drug-Exposed Infants

Previous data document the adverse effects of common correlates of drug use on developmental outcomes. There are, however, many other factors in the environments of pregnant women, also present throughout the infancy and early childhood of their children, that may also impact on development and behavior. Furthermore, these may be differentially distributed between cocaine users and nonusers. These include parenting difficulty, family violence, nutrition, health status, housing, unemployment, stress, alcohol, and other social and environmental variables. Tobacco is but one important example of a confounding factor in this area of research.[33]

Cocaine is not innocuous in its effects. Its intoxicating actions may impair the parent-child relationship. Other behaviors related to drug dependency may also compromise the health of the fetus and child. However, studies to date seem to show that only a small proportion of cocaine-exposed pregnancies result in negative outcomes of clinical significance. Further research with improved methodology and longer follow-up are needed to clarify the gestational effects of cocaine on humans.[33]

What are the consequences of overestimating the risks of intrauterine cocaine exposure? Blaming this exposure alone for adverse infant outcomes may have negative maternal consequences such as unnecessary termination of pregnancy, as demonstrated recently by Koren and co-workers.[26] Additionally, the labeling of cocaine-exposed children who have developmental impairments as children who are irreparably damaged may confer a self-fulfilling prophecy of failure. This may also lead to inattention to other sources of developmental risk.[31,34] Cocaine users and their children have many other risks, and these need more accurate consideration for research to advance in this area.

Research

The methodological problems in studying consequences of illicit drug use in human populations may never allow final conclusions regarding effects on child behavior and development. However, further research with improved methodology is imperative to shed light on some of the complex interrelationships of substance exposure, as well as on social and biological factors in determining such outcomes. Some considerations in improving methodological control of confounding in this area of research include the following: (a) Improved identification of confounders, (b) more precise measurement of confounders, (c) control for confounding effects via group or individual matching in study design, or by analytic statistical techniques such as stratification or multivariable analysis.

Parenting Skills

Being a parent and a drug-dependent woman presents many conflicts. Research studies conducted under the auspices of the National Institute on Drug Abuse (NIDA) and others have defined the characteristics of parenting behavior in cocaine-using women. Current research is directed toward defining, through assessment of maternal lifestyles, the potential for adequate parenting by drug-dependent women.[18] The literature on the effects of prenatal drug exposure and child outcome is inconclusive because of a paucity of methodologically sound studies and because models to date have failed to consider the role of parenting and the larger caregiving environment.

One of the basic premises of childrearing and intervention models is that infant behavior is part of a communication system within the caregiving environment. This is a dyadic and dynamic system in which feedback from one partner to the other is used to regulate this system and in most cases ensure normal developmental outcome.[18] In early work with drug-exposed infants, this complexity was not appreciated, and main effect or linear models were used. As a consequence, it was believed that drug exposure per se led to poor developmental outcome. If the mother was considered at all, it was thought that she could only lower the developmental outcome of the child. The Maternal Lifestyles Study, a multicenter, prospective longitudinal study funded by National Institute of Child Health and Human Development, NIDA, Administration for Children, Youth and Family, and the Center for Substance Abuse Treatment, is attempting to address these issues by studying the effects of prenatal drug exposure on the interplay between the neurobehavioral and regulatory capacities of the child and the parenting and environment factors. In this study, four centers have screened over 16,000 newborn deliveries for prenatal exposure to cocaine and/or opiates and are following a group of exposed infants (subdivided into birth weight categories) and a comparison group at developmentally appropriate ages for at least the first 3 years of life. With the results of such methodologically sound studies, and with adequate numbers of subjects, the chance of defining more precisely the outcomes of infants exposed to drugs in utero has markedly increased.[18]

Treatment Issues

The need to address parenting within treatment programs has been recognized for the past 20 years; however, it has only recently been widely implemented. There is a need to include parenting services to (a) address the risk of developmental and behavioral problems for children born to substance-abusing mothers, and (b) attempt to reduce barriers to women's participation in treatment related to the presence of other dependent children.[18]

Parenting services may take many forms and combinations such as dyadic prevention/intervention, developmental day care/child care, therapeutic child care, parent support groups, parent-child activity, parent education, and parenting curriculums. Whatever form is used, parenting services should reflect a developmental model that assesses mothers' and infants' behavioral strengths and weaknesses and emphasizes sensitive, responsive parent-child interaction as an essential element to both the child's and parent's development.[18]

To integrate parenting services within a treatment program, a family-centered treatment model is recommended. Central elements to this approach are honoring the racial, ethnic, cultural, and socioeconomic diversity of families; building on the strengths unique to each family; and respecting different methods of coping. A family-centered approach enables parenting services for substance-abusing women and to recognize that each mother-child dyad embodies a unique configuration of both strengths and vulnerabilities; to be driven by collaborative strategies that consider personal, familial, and social factors; and to be provided within a multidisciplinary team that includes treatment clinicians and child development specialists in partnership. Until we can provide such services for drug-dependent parenting women, current attitudes and legal practices should be tempered.[18]

Those concerned about child welfare and those who provide clinical care have identified special needs to respond to the number of children affected by drug use during pregnancy. Important steps include the following:[24]

1. Anonymous prevalence studies of positive urine screens for drugs in various populations to identify high-risk pregnant drug abusers so that treatment services can be offered.

2. Prenatal care programs designed specifically for pregnant addicts.
3. Improved screening techniques for mothers and infants, e.g., meconium and hair analysis to provide information about previous exposure so that counseling and support for the mother can be provided.
4. Outreach programs to identify addicted women of childbearing age before pregnancy occurs in order to offer treatment options.
5. Shelters for pregnant addicts with appropriate day care centers that are away from sources.
6. Effective educational programs about drug addiction in schools.
7. Intervention programs for toddlers who exhibit behavioral abnormalities, with follow-up into the school years.
8. Investigation of the relative contribution of lifestyles vs. drug exposure in the production of intrauterine growth retardation, obstetric complications, and infant behavior.

Social Policy Issues

In respect to social policy, various approaches have been suggested to protect children of drug-dependent mothers. These include getting systematic and massive public education and support by community leaders to stress that no drugs be used during pregnancy; giving hospitals the legal power and financial resources to care for babies until they are medically ready for discharge and the home environment is ready to care for them; the placing of children of drug-dependent parents who cannot care for them; and facilitating the adoption process when parents anticipate little chance for improvement.[24]

Special programs for children affected by prenatal drug exposure remain limited. Such programs are needed to address and prevent any developmental disabilities; to provide supportive services to parents or other caretakers such as foster parents or guardians caring for the child because of the mother's continued drug use; and to help parents or caretakers cope with behavioral problems.[24]

There are special considerations for children who remain in the home. Drug abuse treatment is necessary for drug-dependent mothers. Some of the most alarming statistics in terms of outcome for children born to mothers addicted to cocaine are those associated with child abuse and neglect. Child abandonment is common with infants who require extended care at birth or are later hospitalized. Intoxication from crack is associated with outbursts of violence, which increase the risk for battering. In many urban areas, where crack use is prevalent, treatment programs have long waiting lists. Facilities that will accept pregnant women or women with infants are few. Unfortunately, even if treatment is provided, outcome studies suggest that compared with alcohol and opiate dependence, individuals dependent on cocaine, especially in the form of crack, have much more difficulty maintaining abstinence. Thus, some oversight of children in the home is imperative. However, in urban areas in which child welfare systems are already overburdened, the probability of oversight to identify problems and intervene on the child's behalf is low.[24]

Legal Measures

A disturbing social development—the emergence of court actions filed against pregnant women dependent on cocaine—has received national attention. Women are now being charged with child abuse for administering cocaine to the fetus through the umbilical cord.

In this context, unfortunately, judges, legislators, and prosecutors, like the public in general, have obtained most of their information about drug-dependent pregnant and parenting women from the popular press. The coverage of the so-called "crack epidemic" and "crack baby" has been, to a large extent, inaccurate and alarmist. Careful research and measured responses have not been widely covered, and the prevailing assumption is that children exposed prenatally to crack are inevitably and irremediably damaged.

The reaction to the problems of drug addicted pregnant women has thus been largely punitive. Hundreds of women have been prosecuted on unprecedented theories of fetal abuse and drug delivery through the umbilical cord. These prosecutions continue, even though no appellate court in the country has upheld one. Thousands of women have also been reported under civil child neglect laws and investigated for being neglectful or abusive parents based solely on a positive urine toxicology specimen at the birth of the child. African-American women have been arrested and reported disproportionately to authorities despite evidence that Caucasian and African-American women use illegal substances at approximately the same rate. Judges often assume, incorrectly, that drug-dependent pregnant women have access to appropriate drug treatment, to contraceptive and abortion services, and to prenatal care. Moreover, they do not view addiction as a disease nor understand that relapse may be part of recovery. The public policy statements of leading medical and public health organizations opposing punitive responses have helped. Continued prosecution of pregnant women, cutbacks in services for pregnant and parenting drug users, and the continued belief of many leaders that children's physical and emotional health problems can be blamed exclusively on cocaine or other drugs suggest the need for extensive judicial and public education and organized opposition to punitive approaches to this health problem.[18]

REFERENCES
Prenatal Alcohol Exposure

1. Aronson M; Olegard R. Children of alcoholic mothers. *Pediatrician* 14(1/2): 57-61, 1987. (12 refs.)
2. Burgess DM; Streissguth AP. Fetal alcohol syndrome and fetal alcohol effects: Principles for educators. IN: Special Section. "Children at Risk." *Phi Delta KAPPAN* 74(1): 24-30, 1992.
3. Carmichael Olson H; Burgess DM; Streissguth AP. Fetal alcohol syndrome (FAS) and fetal alcohol effects (FAE): A lifespan view, with implications for early intervention. *ZERO TO THREE/ National Center for Clinical Infant Programs* 13(1): 24-29, 1992.
4. Clarren SK. Recognition of fetal alcohol syndrome. *Journal of the American Medical Association* 245(23): 2436-2439, 1981. (28 refs.)
5. Clarren SK; Smith DW. The fetal alcohol syndrome. *New England Journal of Medicine* 298(19): 1063-1067, 1978. (17 refs.)
6. Dorris M. *The Broken Cord.* New York: Harper Collins, 1989.
7. Giunta CT; Streissguth AP. Patients with fetal alcohol syndrome and their caretakers. *Social Casework* 69(7): 453-459, 1988. (15 refs.)
8. Grant TM; Ernst CC; Streissguth AP; Phipps P; Gendler B. When case management isn't enough: A model of paraprofessional advocacy for substance-abusing mothers. *Journal of Case Management* (in press).
9. Grant TM; Ernst CC; Streissguth AP. Intervention with high-risk mothers abusing alcohol and drugs: The Seattle Birth to Three advocacy model. *American Journal of Public Health* (in press).
10. Halmesmaki E. Alcohol counseling of 85 pregnant problem drinkers: Effect on drinking and fetal outcome. *British Journal of Obstetrics and Gynaecology* 95(3): 243-247, 1988. (15 refs.)
11. Kleinfeld JS; Wescott S, eds. *Fantastic Antone Succeeds! Experiences in Educating Children with Fetal Alcohol Syndrome.* Fairbanks AK: University of Alaska Press, 1989. 368 pp.
12. Kopera-Frye K; Tswelnaldin P; Streissguth AP; LaDue RA. Preventing FAS by empowering Native American chemical dependency counselors. *IHS Provider* 19(4): 66-69, 1994. (11 refs.)
13. LaDue RA; Streissguth AP; Randels SP. Clinical considerations pertaining to adolescents and adults with fetal alcohol syndrome. IN: TB Sonderegger, ed. *Perinatal Substance Abuse: Research Findings and Clinical Implications.* Baltimore: The Johns Hopkins University Press, 1992. pp. 104-131. (7 refs.)
14. Larsson G; Bohlin AB. Fetal alcohol syndrome and preventive strategies. *Pediatrician* 14(1/2): 51-56, 1987. (54 refs.)
15. Little RE; Streissguth AP; Guzinski GM; Uhl CN; Paulozzi L; Mann SL; et al. An evaluation of the pregnancy and health program. *Alcohol Health and Research World* 10(1): 45-53, 1985. (23 refs.)
16. Little RE; Young A; Streissguth AP; Uhl CN. Preventing fetal alcohol effects: Effectiveness of a demonstration project. *Ciba Foundation Symposium* 105: 254-270, 1984. (10 refs.)
17. National Institute on Alcohol Abuse and Alcoholism. *Alcohol & Health: 8th Special Report to the US Congress. From the Secretary of Health & Human Services, US Department of Health & Human Services.* Washington DC: Public Health Service, National Institute of Health, 1993.
18. Robinson GC; Armstrong RW, eds. *Alcohol and Child/Family Health: The Proceeding of a Conference with Particular Reference to the Prevention of Alcohol-Related Birth Defects.* Vancouver British Columbia: British Columbia FAS Resource Group, 1988.
19. Rosett HL; Weiner; Edelin KC. Treatment experience with pregnant problem drinkers. *Journal of the American Medical Association* 249(15): 2029-2033, 1983. (20 refs.)
20. Russell M; Henderson C; Blume SB. *Children of Alcoholics: A Review of the Literature.* New York: Children of Alcoholics Foundation, 1985. (498 refs.)
21. Streissguth AP. Fetal Alcohol Syndrome: An overview and implications for patient management. IN: Estes NJ; Heinemen ME, eds. *Alcoholism: Development, Consequences, and Interventions.* St Louis: The CV Mosby Co, 1986. (75 refs.)
22. Streissguth AP. Today I visited an Aleut village. Observations on preventing fetal alcohol syndrome. *IHS Provider* 15: 125-127, 1990. (5 refs.)
23. Streissguth AP. The 1990 Betty Ford Lecture: What every community should know about drinking during pregnancy and the life-long consequences for society. *Substance Abuse* 12(3): 114-127, 1991. (26 refs.)
24. Streissguth AP. Fetal alcohol syndrome and fetal alcohol effects: A clinical perspective of later developmental consequences. IN: Zagon IS; Slotkin TA, eds. *Maternal Substance Abuse and the Developing Nervous System.* San Diego: Academic Press, Inc, 1992. pp. 5-25. (55 refs.)
25. Streissguth AP. Fetal alcohol syndrome: Understanding the problem; understanding the solution. What Indian communities can do. *American Indian Culture and Research Journal* 18(3): 45-83, 1994. (65 refs.)
26. Streissguth AP. A long-term perspective of FAS. *Alcohol Health and Research World* 18(1): 74-81, 1994. (9 refs.)
27. Streissguth AP; Aase JM; Clarren SK; Randels SP; LaDue RA; Smith DF. Fetal alcohol syndrome in adolescents and adults. *Journal of the American Medical Association* 265(15): 1961-1967, 1991. (39 refs.)
28. Streissguth AP; Barr HM; Bookstein FL; Sampson PD. *The Enduring Effects of Prenatal Alcohol Exposure on Child Development: Birth through 7 Years, a Partial Least Squares Solution.* Ann Arbor MI: University of Michigan Press, 1993. pp. 300 (290 refs.)
29. Streissguth AP; Barr HM; Sampson PD; Bookstein FL. Prenatal alcohol and offspring development: The first 14 years. *Drug and Alcohol Dependence* 36(2): 89-99, 1994. (52 refs.)
30. Streissguth AP; Grant TM; Ernst CC. Preventing fetal alcohol syndrome by working with high risk and other strategies: The Seattle Advocacy Model. *Proceedings for the 1994 NIAAA FAS Prevention Conference* (in press). (27 refs.)
31. Streissguth AP; LaDue RA; Randels SP. *A Manual on Adolescents and Adults with Fetal Alcohol Syndrome with Special Reference to American Indians, 2nd Edition.* Albuquerque NM: Indian Health Service, 1989.
    [Available free from the Indian Health Service Fetal Alcohol Syndrome Information Office at Indian Health Service, Headquarters West, 5300 Homestead Road NE, Albuquerque NM 87110. Phone: (505) 837-4121.
32. US Surgeon General: Surgeon General's advisory on alcohol and pregnancy. *FDA Drug Bulletin* 11(2): July 1981.

Prenatal Drug Exposure

1. Acker D; Sachs B; Tracey KJ. Abruptio placentae associated with cocaine use. *American Journal of Obstetrics and Gynecology* 146(2): 220-232, 1983. (2 refs.)
2. Baxi LV; Petrie R. Pharmacologic effects on labor: Effect of drugs on dystocia, labor and uterine activity. *Clinical Obstetrics and Gynecology* 30(1): 19-32, 1987. (71 refs.)

3. Bingol N; Fuchs M; Diaz V; Stone RK; Gromisch DS. Teratogenicity of cocaine in humans. *Journal of Pediatrics* 110 (1): 93-96, 1987. (16 refs.)

4. Chasnoff IJ; Burns WJ; Schnoll SH; Burns KA. Cocaine use in pregnancy. *New England Journal of Medicine* 313(11): 666-669, 1985. (17 refs.)

5. Chasnoff IJ; Chisum GM; Kaplan WE. Maternal cocaine use and genitourinary malformations. *Teratology* 37(2): 201-204, 1988. (23 refs.)

6. Chasnoff IJ; Griffith DR; MacGregor S; Dirkes K; Burns KA. Temporal patterns of cocaine use in pregnancy: Perinatal outcome. *Journal of the American Medical Association* 261(12): 1741-1744, 1989. (22 refs.)

7. Church MW. Does cocaine cause birth defects? (commentary). *Neurotoxicology and Teratology* 15(5): 289, 1993. (0 refs.)

8. Connaughton JF; et al. Perinatal addiction: Outcome and management. *American Journal of Gynecology* 129: 679, 1977.

9. Desmond MM; Wilson GS. Neonatal abstinence syndrome: Recognition and diagnosis. *Addictive Diseases* 2: 1975.

10. Dixon SD; Bejar R. Echoencephalographic findings in neonates associated with maternal cocaine and methamphetamine use: Incidence and clinical correlates. *Journal of Pediatrics* 115 (5 Pt 1): 770-778, 1989. (53 refs.)

11. Doberczak TM; et al. Neonatal neurologic and encephalographic effects of intrauterine cocaine exposure. *Journal of Pediatrics* 113(2): 354-358, 1988. (28 refs.)

12. Fantel AF; MacPhail BJ. The teratogenicity of cocaine. *Teratology* 26(1): 17-19, 1982. (23 refs.)

13. Finnegan LF; Kaltenbach K. Neonatal abstinence syndrome. IN: Hoekelman RA; Nelson N, eds. *Primary Pediatric Care.* St Louis: Mosby-Year Book, 1992. pp. 1367-1378.

14. Finnegan LF; Wapner RJ. Narcotic addiction in pregnancy. IN: Neibyl JR, eds. *Drug Use In Pregnancy.* Philadelphia: Lea and Febiger, 1987. pp. 203-222, Chapter 16.

15. Finnegan LP. Neonatal abstinence syndrome: Assessment and pharmacotherapy. IN: Rubaltelli FF; Granati B, eds. *Neonatal Therapy: An Update.* New York: Elsevier Science Publishers BV (Biomedical Division), 1986.

16. Finnegan LP. Treatment issues for opioid-dependent women during the perinatal period. *Journal of Psychoactive Drugs* 23(2): 191-201, 1991.

17. Finnegan LP; Hagan T; Kaltenbach KA. Scientific foundation of clinical practice: Opiate use in pregnant women. *Bulletin of the New York Academy of Medicine* 67(3): 223-239, 1991. (20 refs.)

18. Finnegan LP; Kaltenbach K; Kandall SR; Lester B; Mayes LC; Paltrow LM. The conflicts for parenting drug dependent women—what does research show us? IN: Harris L, ed. *Problems of Drug Dependence*, 1995. Rockville MD: National Institute on Drug Abuse, 1996 (in press).

19. Finnegan LP; Resser DS; Connaughton JF. The effects of maternal drug dependence on neonatal mortality. *Drug and Alcohol Dependence* 2: 131-140, 1977.

20. Graham K; Koren G. Characteristics of pregnant women exposed to cocaine in Toronto between 1985 and 1990. *Canadian Medical Association Journal* 144(5): 563-568, 1991. (21 refs.)

21. Hadeed AJ; Siegel SR. Maternal cocaine use during pregnancy: Effect on the newborn infant. *Pediatrics* 84(2): 205-210, 1989. (28 refs.)

22. Hoyme HE; Jones KL; Dixon SD; Jewett T; Hanson JW; Robinson LK; Msall ME; Allanson JE. Prenatal cocaine exposure and fetal vascular disruption. *Pediatrics* 85(5): 743-747, 1990. (41 refs.)

23. Isenberg SJ; et al. Ocular signs of cocaine intoxication in neonates. *American Journal of Opthalmology* 103: 211, 1987.

24. Kinney J. Other Special Populations. IN: Kinney J, ed. *Clinical Manual of Substance Abuse.* St Louis: Mosby-Year Book, 1991. pp. 245-284. (93 refs.)

25. Koren G; Bologa M; Long D; Feldman Y; Shear NH. Perception of teratogenic risk by pregnant women exposed to drugs and chemicals during the first trimester. *American Journal of Obstetrics and Gynecology* 160(5 Pt 1): 1190-1194, 1989. (15 refs.)

26. Koren G; Gladstone D; Robeson C; Robieux I. The perception of teratogenic risk of cocaine. *Teratology* 46(6): 567-571, 1992. (11 refs.)

27. Kramer LD; Locke GE; Ogunyemi A; Nelson L. Neonatal cocaine-related seizures. *Journal of Child Neurology* 5(1): 60-64, 1990.

28. Lipshultz SE; Frassica JJ; Orav EJ. Cardiovascular abnormalities in infants prenatally exposed to cocaine. *Journal of Pediatrics* 118(1): 44-51, 1991. (44 refs.)

29. Lutiger B; Graham K; Einarson TR; Koren G. Relationship between gestational cocaine use and pregnancy outcome: A meta-analysis. *Teratology* 44(4): 405-414, 1991. (77 refs.)

30. Mahalik MP; et al. Teratogenic potential of cocaine hydrochloride in CF-1 mice. *Journal of Pharmacology and Science* 69: 703, 1980.

31. Mayes LC; Granger RH; Bornstein MH; Zuckerman B. The problem of prenatal cocaine exposure: A rush to judgment. (editorial). *Journal of the American Medical Association* 267(3): 406-408, 1992. (43 refs.)

32. Moore TR; Sorg J; Miller L; Key TC; Resnick R. Hemodynamic effects of intravenous cocaine on the pregnant ewe and fetus. *American Journal of Obstetrics and Gynecology* 155(4): 883-893, 1986. (16 refs.)

33. Neuspiel DR. Cocaine and the fetus: Mythology of severe risk. (commentary). *Neurotoxicology and Teratology* 15(5): 305-306, 1993. (11 refs.)

34. Neuspiel DR. On pejorative labeling of cocaine exposed children. (editorial). *Journal of Substance Abuse Treatment* 10(4): 407, 1993. (2 refs.)

35. Salamy A; Eldredge L; Anderson J; Bull D. Brain-stem transmission time in infants exposed to cocaine in utero. *Journal of Pediatrics* 117(4): 627-629, 1990. (13 refs.)

36. Shih L; et al. Effects of maternal cocaine abuse on the neonatal auditory system. *International Journal of Pediatric Otorhinolaryngology* 15: 245, 1988.

37. Teske MP; Trese MT. Retinopathy of prematurity-like fundus and persistent hyperplastic primary vitreous associated with maternal cocaine use. *American Journal of Ophthalmology* 103(5): 719-720, 1987. (5 refs.)

38. van de Bor M; Walther FJ; Sims ME. Increased cerebral blood flow velocity in infants of mothers who abuse cocaine. *Pediatrics* 85(5): 733-736, 1990. (25 refs.)

39. Woods JR; Plessinger MA; Clark KE. Effect of cocaine on uterine blood flow and fetal oxygenation. *Journal of the American Medical Association* 257(7): 956-957, 1987. (18 refs.)

40. Zelson C; Rubio E; Wasserman E. Neonatal narcotic addiction: Ten year observation. *Pediatrics* 48(2): 178-189, 1971. (20 refs.)

FURTHER READINGS

Barr GA; Jones K. Opiate withdrawal in the infant. (review). *Neurotoxicology and Teratology* 16(2): 219-225, 1994. (112 refs.)
Many infants are exposed in utero to illicit opiate drugs such as heroin and to prescribed opiates such as methadone. It is therefore important to understand the effects of acute and chronic exposure to such drugs on the immature organism. A necessary step in understanding the long-term effects of early drug exposure is to describe fully how the drug acts on neurobehavioral systems in

the neonate. Because infants typically experience withdrawal from opiates, either in utero or shortly after parturition, a fuller understanding of the consequences of opiate withdrawal in the immature animal is an important but largely unexplored area of research. Although there has been some question as to whether infants undergo withdrawal, more recent experiments demonstrate that the rat neonate experiences clear behavioral changes during opiate abstinence, including the induction of "dysphoric" states on cessation of drug exposure. It is proposed that the infant organism undergoes withdrawal but that the signs and symptoms differ from those in the adult. Copyright 1994, Pergamon Press.

Behnke M; Eyler FD. The consequences of prenatal substance use for the developing fetus, newborn, and young child. (review). *International Journal of the Addictions* 28(13): 1341-1391, 1993. (338 refs.)

Although substance use has been a worldwide problem at all levels of society since ancient times, recent attention has been focused on the use of legal and illegal substances by pregnant women. Almost all drugs taken by pregnant women are known to cross the placenta and affect the fetus. This article reviews the effects on the fetus and neonate of the drugs most frequently used by pregnant women in the US—nicotine, alcohol, marijuana, opiates, and cocaine. When possible, information regarding long-term medical problems is included. Copyright 1993, Marcel Dekker, Inc. Used with permission.

Bell GL; Lau K. Perinatal and neonatal issues of substance abuse. (review). *Pediatric Clinics of North America* 42(2): 181-261, 1995. (185 refs.)

Substance abuse during pregnancy can be teratogenic for the fetus and can cause decreased growth parameters in the newborn. Short-term and long-term neurobehavioral problems also have been documented in babies born to substance-abusing mothers. The problem of substance abuse during pregnancy and its effects on the fetus is unique in medicine in that it is 100% preventable. Physicians need to lead society to take action in preventing substance abuse during pregnancy, with emphasis on abstinence long before pregnany. Until medical schools and residency programs take responsibility for teaching the importance of preventing substance abuse and of identifying the substance abuser, drug and alcohol use will continue to exact its tragic toll on future generations. Copyright 1995, WB Saunders Co.

Coles CD; Platzman KA. Behavioral development in children prenatally exposed to drugs and alcohol. (review). *International Journal of the Addictions* 28(13): 1393-1433, 1993. (157 refs.)

Empirical research on the behavioral consequences to the offspring of use of recreational and addictive drugs and alcohol by pregnant women is reviewed. The current epidemic of cocaine use has raised the specter of a host of "cocaine babies" whose prenatally induced impairments will interfere with social and academic functioning and constitute an immense social burden. In fact, examination of effects of drug exposure on infant behavior and subsequent development suggests a much more subtle and complicated process that must take into account not only the child's prenatal exposure but the various other environmental factors. These other factors include caregiving competence and social environment. Copyright 1993, Marcel Dekker, Inc. Used with permission.

Floyd RL; Rimer BK; Giovino GA; Mullen PD; Sullivan SE. A review of smoking in pregnancy: Effects on pregnancy outcomes and cessation efforts. (review). *Annual Review of Public Health* 14: 379-411, 1993. (103 refs.)

Prenatal smoking has become one of the most-studied risk factors in contemporary obstetrics. This article provides an overview of the problems related to smoking during pregnancy and a discussion of the research trials conducted to promote prenatal smoking cessation. The authors pay particular attention to intervention approaches, emerging issues, and implications for policy and practice. Copyright 1993, Annual Reviews, Inc.

Goldberg HL; Nissim R. Psychotropic drugs in pregnancy and lactation. (review). *International Journal of Psychiatry in Medicine* 24(2): 129-149, 1994. (91 refs.)

This article reviews the literature on the use of psychotropic drugs in pregnancy and lactation. Medline search yielded more than five hundred titles of which 91 were selected for reference. Fetal physiology and teratogenicity are discussed, and the effects of specific drugs on the fetus and newborn are presented. When possible, recommendations for use or nonuse are presented. Though no controlled studies have been done in pregnant women to truly prove their safety, it appears that most current psychotropic drugs appear fairly safe for use in pregnancy. Copyright 1994, Baywood Publishing Co, Inc.

Hutchings DE. The puzzle of cocaine's effects following maternal use during pregnancy: Are there reconcilable differences? (review). *Neurotoxicology and Teratology* 15(5): 281-286, 1993. (21 refs.)

This is a selective review of the clinical and epidemiological literature. It attempts to reconcile disparate and contradictory findings dealing with the morphologic, growth, and neurobehavioral effects in neonates and young children from prenatal exposure to cocaine. A history of cocaine use in the US is briefly presented, followed by impressionistic observations of some of the events during the cocaine epidemic of the 1980s. Based on the collective research findings, it is tentatively suggested that the teratogenic effects of prenatal cocaine may be produced only in those infants exposed to the highest doses reported in the literature. It remains unknown, however, whether these effects may be dependent on the concurrent abuse of alcohol and/or cigarettes. As to growth and neurobehavioral outcomes, effects attributable primarily to cocaine appear to be only marginal and transitory. The data to support these conclusions are particularly tenuous and are thus offered only as working hypotheses. Because of the intractable methodological and interpretive problems inherent in human developmental research on substance abuse, any attempt to draw definitive conclusions is admittedly premature. Because these methodological problems also complicate the efforts of ongoing studies, answers to these persistent questions may not be readily forthcoming. Copyright 1993, Pergamon Press.

Kain ZN; Rimar S; Barash PG. Cocaine abuse in the parturient and effects on the fetus and neonate. (review). *Anesthesia and Analgesia* 77(4):835-845, 1993 (135 refs.)

In the last decade, cocaine abuse has reached epidemic proportions. Approximately 30 million people or 15% of the US population have tried cocaine at least once, and 5 million are regular users. The prevalence of cocaine abuse in the obstetric population ranges from 7.5% to 45%. The wide-spread use of cocaine has resulted in an increase in both maternal and neonatal morbidity and mortality. Because pregnant patients who use cocaine may require anesthesia more frequently than those who do not, a thorough understanding of the consequences of cocaine abuse is essential. This review describes the pharmacology of cocaine abuse in pregnancy, the different effects of cocaine on the parturient, fetus, and neonate, and the anesthetic considerations in these patients. Copyright 1993, International Anesthesia Research Society.

Robins LN; Mills JL; Krulewitch C; Herman AA; Brison K; Brooks-Gunn J; et al. Effects of in utero exposure to street drugs. *American Journal of Public Health* 83(Supplement): 9-32, 1993. (116 refs.)

The concern about the effects of drugs during pregnancy has prompted a host of studies in the last 10 years. This report summarizes what is now known and considers what types of studies might improve our understanding of the short- and long-term consequences of illicit drug exposure in utero. The authors then consider whether the studies that, scientifically, seem the next logical step are feasible in terms of current research tools for assessing exposure and its effects; the probable cost and difficulty of completing such studies; the length of time it would take to achieve results; and the ethical and legal considerations that impede funding for such studies and getting access to study subjects and their records. Copyright 1993, American Public Health Association. Used with permission.

Rosen TS; Johnson HL. Prenatal methadone maintenance: Its effects on fetus, neonate, and child. (review). *Developmental Brain Dysfunction* 6(6): 317-323, 1993. (39 refs.)

Methadone maintenance has been the treatment of choice for heroin addiction for the past several years. It blocks the craving and euphoric effects of heroin and can be administered once a day. Methadone maintenance during pregnancy is associated with better prenatal care and life-style, but the effects on neonate and child have reportedly been problematic. The mean gestational age and birth weight have been reported to be lower, with a higher incidence of small-for-gestational-age. A higher incidence of small head circumferences as compared with weight, which frequently persists into childhood, has also been reported. The incidence of abstinence symptoms varies between 70% and 90% with increased severity and duration and a higher incidence of late-occurring seizures. The incidence of sudden infant death syndrome has reportedly been increased in these infants. Follow-up studies during the first 2 years have reported from no abnormalities to problems with tone, coordination, hyperactivity, short attention span, and developmental delays. Bayley Mental Developmental Index and Psychomotor Developmental Index mean scores have been similar in both methadone and control children—however, with a disproportionate number of low scores in the methadone children. On further data analysis, maternal drug abuse, maternal functioning, and family environmental conditions were important predictors of the child's neurodevelopmental outcome. In summary, children born to mothers on methadone maintenance with a suboptimal intrauterine environment are at high risk for neurodevelopmental problems when raised in a high-risk environment associated with the drug culture. However, these same infants raised in an optimal nurturing and stable situation have a good prognosis. Copyright 1993, S Karger AG, Basel.

Singer L; Arendt R; Minnes S. Neurodevelopmental effects of cocaine. *Clinics in Perinatology* 20(1): 245-262, 1993. (113 refs.)

The US has recently been compelled to acknowledge and to cope with an alarming increase in drug exposure in newborns owing to a new cocaine epidemic. Perhaps because of the sudden national recognition of the problem, the lack of knowledge about the effects of cocaine on child development, and the sheer magnitude of the problem in urban areas, the issue of cocaine exposure in children has been characterized by medical, legal, and social policy controversies. This article elucidates what is and what is not known about cocaine's neurodevelopmental effects and informs perinatologists about the complex issues associated with understanding and caring for the cocaine-exposed newborn. Copyright 1993, WB Saunders Co.

Smith GH. Intervention strategies for children vulnerable for school failure due to exposure to drugs and alcohol. (review). *International Journal of the Addictions* 28(13): 1435-1470, 1993. (97 refs.)

Children exposed in utero to drugs and alcohol and/or who grow up in a family in which these substances are misused are vulnerable to failure at all age levels, prenatally through adulthood. This article reviews developmental issues presented by children vulnerable to school failure because of the biological effects of prenatal exposure to drugs and/or the environmental problems in growing up in a family in which misuse of drugs and alcohol occurs. Characteristics and needs of these students are discussed, along with recommendations for education and community-based systems of services to them and their families. Model programs serving children prenatally through school age are identified. Copyright 1993, Marcel Dekker, Inc. Used with permission.

Snodgrass SR. Cocaine babies: A result of multiple teratogenic influences. *Journal of Child Neurology* 9(3): 227-233, 1994. (56 refs.)

The history of cocaine use is reviewed. Cocaine teratogenesis has only recently been studied, and initial human studies had serious methodological flaws. These flaws included ascertainment bias, publication bias (studies finding cocaine effects have been more likely to be presented or published), and overemphasis on the perinatal period. Comparison with alcohol teratogenesis shows that alcohol is a more potent teratogen, which, however, produces major and specific effects (fetal alcohol syndrome) in less than 10% of offspring with heavy alcohol exposure during pregnancy. Nonspecific minor congenital anomalies or fetal alcohol effects are seen in a larger number. Personal experience with two groups of children exposed to cocaine in utero is reviewed. Insurance patients gained weight and took vitamins, and generally, their children did well in spite of cocaine use. Indigent patients were usually unmarried and often "street people," probably used more cocaine, generally used other drugs as well, often did not gain weight during pregnancy, and were much more likely to have children with problems. Surveys show that most cocaine users also use alcohol, often simultaneously. Those who use both agents are more likely to have troubled backgrounds and antisocial behavior and to drop out of treatment programs than those who use only alcohol. Cocaethylene or ethylbenzoylecgonine is formed in the liver when cocaine and alcohol are simultaneously ingested. It is a potent stimulant and dopamine uptake blocker that is more toxic to myocardial cells than is cocaine. Good nutrition is now known to be very important in preventing congenital anomalies and fetal death. A multihit model of neurologic handicap, which stresses the importance of a good postnatal environment, is briefly outlined. This model explains why cocaine use during pregnancy is more dangerous to the street person who uses multiple drugs than to the middle class mother who takes prenatal vitamins. Copyright 1994, Decker Periodicals.

Woods JR Jr. Clinical management of drug dependency in pregnancy. IN: Chiang CN; Finnegan LP, eds. *Medications Development for the Treatment of Pregnant Addicts and Their Infants. NIDA Research Monograph 149.* Rockville MD: National Institute on Drug Abuse, 1995. pp. 39-57. (28 refs.)

The urgency of substance abuse treatment in pregnancy is underscored by current estimates of substance usage. Formulating solutions to this widespread, largely unaddressed problem in obstetrics requires a clear understanding of barriers to care for pregnant substance abusers. The three most relevant barriers are the attitudes and behavior of substance-abusing women, the attitudes and lack of understanding of the pregnant addict by obstetric care providers, and the lack of coordination between obstetric care providers and those professionals involved in mental health and drug abuse treatment. This chapter discusses these barriers and suggests ways to remove them. Copyright 1995, Project Cork Institute.

Legal Readings

Batey R; Garcia SA. Prosecution of the pregnant addict: Does the cruel and unusual punishment clause apply? *Criminal Law Bulletin* 27(2): 99-113, 1991.

> Responding to the growing tendency of prosecutors to file criminal charges against pregnant drug addicts, the authors argue that any such prosecution may amount to the imposition of cruel and unusual punishment. Analysis of this constitutional question requires consideration of *Robinson vs. California* and *Powell vs. Texas,* US Supreme Court decisions rendered more than 20 years ago. The authors contend that, despite lower court misreadings of these opinions (Powell in particular) these constitutional decisions, until modified or overruled, bar criminal penalties for child or fetal abuse by pregnant addicts. Copyright 1991, Warren, Gorham & Lamont, Inc.

Glink SB. The prosecution of maternal fetal abuse: Is this the answer? *University of Illinois Law Review* 1991(2): 533-580, 1991. (341 legal refs.)

> At least 11% of all women in labor today will test positive for the presence of illegal drugs in their bloodstream. This note briefly addresses the various constitutional, social, moral, and ethical issues raised by the criminal prosecution of pregnant women for what professionals dub "fetal abuse." The central focus of this note, however, concerns the concrete realities and current status of criminal liability for pregnant women whose illegal substance abuse causes prenatal injuries to the fetus. Because it appears that imposing criminal liability is the current trend, the concern of this note is the pressing question of how to limit the use of criminal sanctions to best serve the interests and protect the rights of all parties involved—not the theoretical question of whether criminal sanctions are the best solution to the problem. Part II of this note discusses the historical development of fetal rights and the various forces that have led states to criminally prosecute women who give birth to drug-dependent babies. Part III examines the criminal statutes that prosecutors currently are using to impose liability on drug-dependent mothers. Part IV analyzes these statutes and discusses the reasons why their use in the fetal rights/substance abuse context is inappropriate. Part V proposes a possible statute and sentencing scheme that must accompany any statute that attempts to criminalize maternal conduct causing injury to the fetus. Copyright 1991, University of Illinois College of Law.

Golden MR. When pregnancy discrimination is gender discrimination: The constitutionality of excluding pregnant women from drug treatment programs. *New York University Law Review* 66(6): 1832-1880, 1991. (260 legal refs.)

> This article presents examples to demonstrate that drug treatment programs are reluctant to admit pregnant women, often with painfully ironic consequences. Punishing women for using drugs during pregnancy—by prosecuting them under drug trafficking or criminal child protection statutes, depriving them of custody of their children, or holding them civilly liable for prenatal damage—has become an increasingly popular response to the crisis of drug addiction in pregnant women. Not only do these punitive measures raise constitutional and policy concerns, they also fail to address the underlying problem: Experience has shown that the threat of punishment will not prevent many women from becoming addicted to drugs, nor will it cure those currently addicted. A more direct and rational answer to the

problem of maternal drug abuse is drug treatment. Part I of this article discusses the current status of drug abuse and drug treatment for pregnant women; Part II asserts that exclusion of women on the basis of pregnancy from a service benefiting both men and women is gender discrimination; and Part III applies equal protection analysis to drug treatment programs' exclusion of pregnant women. Copyright 1991, New York University School of Law.

Greene DL. Abusive prosecutors: Gender, race and class discretion and the prosecution of drug-addicted mothers. *Buffalo Law Review* 39(Fall): 737-802, 1991. (274 legal notes.)

> This article addresses the issue of prosecutor discretion, particularly in the area of alcohol and drugs and addicted pregnant women. The article addresses possible procedural controls of prosecutors and the institution of review boards to provide oversight of prosecutor discretionary behavior. The article is organized into four parts. The first discusses prosecutor discretion and its potential abuse. The second part surveys the justification for allowing prosecutors wide latitude, and the current inadequate constraints. It also discusses how demographics, pluralistic ignorance, and ideology may play a role. Part three discusses how gender, color, and class may influence prosecutors, and how feminist critiques can expose these biases. The final section discusses potential reforms. Copyright 1994, Project Cork Institute.

McGinnis DM. Prosecution of mothers of drug-exposed babies: Constitutional and criminal theory. *University of Pennsylvania Law Review* 139(2): 505-539, 1990. (169 legal notes.)

> During the late 1980s, a new prosecutorial trend developed: Women who had used drugs during pregnancy and subsequently delivered drug-exposed babies were charged with a variety of crimes including criminal neglect, delivery of drugs to a minor, and involuntary manslaughter. It was estimated that 18 such cases were pending nationwide as of October 1989, representing an abrupt increase in the wake of the Supreme Court's July 1989 decision in *Webster vs. Reproductive Health Services.* Early in 1990 the American Civil Liberties Union counted at least 35 cases across the country as this prosecutorial trend continued into the new decade. This comment first discusses the constitutional ramifications of these prosecutions. It then analyzes the prosecutions in the context of criminal legal theory. Finally, it discusses the prosecutions in the context of the national debates on abortion and drug abuse. This comment concludes that the criminal justice system is ill-suited to intervene in the complex medical and sociological problems associated with drug use and pregnancy, which may be more effectively and humanely addressed by drug treatment programs for pregnant addicts. Copyright 1990, University of Pennsylvania Law School.

Moss KL. Substance dependency during pregnancy: The limits of the law. *Women's Health Issues* 1(3): 120-126, 1991. (41 refs.)

> The incidence of fetuses exposed to drugs and alcohol in utero has generated increasing nationwide attention from the media, social service agencies, state prosecutors, state legislatures, and Congress. What is now clear is that women who use drugs during pregnancy are being singled out and punished for their behavior in unprecedented ways. The phenomenon of punishing pregnant women for being "bad mommies" because they did not behave "properly" while pregnant is not new. In the past, courts have authorized Cesarean sections against the mother's wishes or have taken guardianship of a fetus away from the mother, but these cases were rare. Today's drug problem, however, has provided a new context in which state intervention in the lives of pregnant women seems more acceptable because of the danger that excessive drug use can pose to the fetus. Some prosecutors,

courts, and legislatures seem to believe that pregnant women may be punished and their rights curtailed because of "fetal rights." Yet if upheld in this context, states will be free to intrude in the lives of all pregnant women, even when they do not engage in illegal behavior. The consequence will be to drive women away from health and prenatal care to the detriment of their health and that of their children. This article reviews the recent developments in this area, including the most major criminal cases and state legislative efforts undertaken in the past year. The legal problems and implications of these developments will be explored and several alternative responses proposed. Copyright 1991, Jacobs Institute of Women's Health.

Peak K; Del Papa FS. Criminal justice enters the womb: Enforcing the "right" to be born drug-free. (review). *Journal of Criminal Justice* 21(3): 245-263, 1993. (76 refs.)
With simultaneous increases in drug-addicted newborns and convictions of women who delivered illegal drugs to their children in utero, a legal and moral dilemma has ensued: Whose "rights" should prevail—those of the infant to be born healthy and drug-free, or those of the mother to privacy, bodily integrity, and equal protection under the law? This article examines this dilemma and the developing role of law and criminal justice regarding such behaviors. It discusses the effects of illegal drugs on fetuses, the punishment of improper maternal behavior generally, the rights of the unborn, and predominant arguments for and against such prosecutions. Also considered are equity issues and possible alternative means for addressing this problem. Copyright 1993, Pergamon Press.

Petrow J. Addicted mothers, drug-exposed babies: The unprecedented prosecution of mothers under drug-trafficking statutes. *New York Law School Law Review* 36(4): 573-607, 1991. (264 legal refs.)
Since the mid-1980s, state prosecutors have been prosecuting an increasing number of women under unprecedented interpretations of child abuse and drug-trafficking statutes. Part II of this note presents a brief background of the cases involving criminal prosecutions of drug-addicted women who have exposed their babies to drugs, along with an overview of recent attempts by state legislatures to pass legislation in this area. Part III of this note discusses constitutional issues related to the criminal prosecution of drug-addicted women under drug-trafficking statutes, including the novel application of existing state drug laws to women who give birth to drug-exposed babies. It argues that the use of drug-delivery statutes to punish the mothers of drug-exposed babies violates the mothers' due process right to fair notice under the Fourteenth Amendment, the mothers' fundamental right to privacy, and the mothers' right to autonomy in decision making about reproduction. It also argues that using these state statutes to prosecute drug-addicted pregnant women amounts to ex post facto legislation. Last, this part asserts that the application of the existing state criminal laws to addicted mothers runs afoul of the constitutional requirements of evidentiary support in criminal prosecutions, the guarantees of equal protection under the law, and the protections against cruel and unusual punishment. Part IV examines whether any of the traditional justifications of criminal punishment are applicable, because "no questions of criminal justice are more fundamental than the bases for imposing criminal punishment." A review of the different theories demonstrates that rehabilitation is the most plausible justification for imposing criminal sanctions. Part V concludes that rehabilitation should be provided not as a justification for, but in place of, criminal penalties. This section argues that drug treatment programs designed to meet the needs of pregnant women must be made available, accessible, and affordable. According to the drug treatment programs that combine medical and therapeutic treatment in the form of obstetric, pediatric, and postpartum gynecologic care, positive results have been reported. Copyright 1991, New York Law School.

Roberts DE. Punishing drug addicts who have babies: Women of color, equality, and the right of privacy. *Harvard Law Review* 104(7): 1419-1482, 1991. (307 legal refs.)
Women increasingly face criminal charges for giving birth to infants who test positive for drugs. Most of the women prosecuted are poor, African American, and addicted to crack cocaine. In this article, the author seeks to add the perspective of poor African-American women to the current debate over protecting fetal rights at the expense of women's rights. Based on the presumption that African-American women experience several forms of oppression simultaneously, the author argues that punishing drug addicts who choose to carry their pregnancies to term violates their constitutional rights to equal protection and privacy regarding their choices about reproduction. The author begins by placing these prosecutions in the context of the historical devaluation of African-American women as mothers. After presenting the view of prosecutions as punishing drug-addicted women for having babies, the author argues that this punishment violates the equal protection clause because it stems from and perpetuates African-American subordination. Finally, the author argues that the prosecutions violate women's constitutional rights to autonomy and freedom from invidious government standards for childbearing. In presenting the view that the prosecutions violate women's privacy rights, the author critiques the liberal, "negative" conception of privacy rooted in freedom-from-government constraints. She concludes by advocating a progressive concept of privacy that places an affirmative obligation on the government to guarantee individual rights and recognizes the connection between the right of privacy and racial equality. Copyright 1991, Harvard University Law School.

RESOURCES

Alcohol: Pregnancy and the Fetal Alcohol Syndrome, 2nd Edition, 1994
(Unit 5 of the Project Cork Institute curriculum, *Alcohol Use and Its Medical Consequences,* a slide lecture series, 2nd Edition, 1994.) Authors: Ann P. Streissguth and Ruth E. Little Produced by Project Cork Institute, Dartmouth Medical School. Available through Milner-Fenwick, Inc, 2125 Greenspring Drive, Timonium MD 21093. To order, call 1(800) 432-8433. Cost: $180. This extensive, 79-unit slide presentation is now available in its second edition. With its 62 pages of accompanying text, this unit gives a comprehensive overview of alcohol as a teratogenic drug and shows the major effects of ethanol by trimester of pregnancy. The slides illustrate the clinical perspective of FAS/FAE, current experimental and clinical research on FAS-related behavior problems, and issues of public health. Authors include Ann P. Streissguth, professor of Psychiatry and Behavioral Sciences, University of Washington School of Medicine, Seattle, Washington, and Ruth E. Little, ScD, epidemiologist, National Institute of Environmental Health Sciences, Research Triangle Park, North Carolina.

Slide Teaching Unit on FAS
Author: Karen Hymbaugh for the National Indian FAS Prevention Program. Available from Vicki Garcia, Mental Health Programs Branch IHS, 5300 Homestead Road NE, Albuquerque NM 87110. Phone: (505) 837-4121. This set of 20 slides with written text aimed at American Indians describes FAS and some community-based prevention ideas. Available free on loan to any Indian community and may be reproduced at cost.

FAS Fetal Alcohol Syndrome

Authors: Geoffrey B. Robinson, MD, and colleagues. Available from Perennial Education, Inc, 930 Pitner Avenue, Evanston IL 60202.Toll-free telephone: 1(800) 323-9084. Fax: (312) 328-6706. Price: $345 per program *Program 1.What is FAS?* This 24-minute video for families, educators, and health professionals examines the cause, treatment, and prevention of alcohol-related birth defects. It features interviews with mothers and families of FAS children and commentaries from international experts. *Program 2. Preventing FAS.* This 21-minute video focuses on primary and secondary prevention, e.g., reducing alcohol consumption, raising public awareness, identifying high-risk women, and helping them stop drinking.

Circle of Life, Part II

Author: Diane Pittman, MD, Indian Health Service, MCH Coordinator, Bemidji Area, Bemidji MN. Available from the Indian Health Service Unit, Bemidji MN. Phone: (218) 759-3414. Cost: $45 per set. This 32-minute video deals with the effects of alcohol and drugs on pregnancy, abusive relationships, teen pregnancy, and teen parenting. It has a Native American focus and includes interviews with teenage parents. (Part I is 43 minutes, focusing primarily on teen pregnancy and Native American spirituality.)

Preventing Fetal Alcohol Syndrome and Other Alcohol-Related Birth Defects

Authors: Elizabeth Howard, MAT, Deanie Kepler, MS, and Jerry Adams, PhD. Produced by the Association for Retarded Citizens of the United States. Available from ARC: 2501 Avenue, J/PO Box 6109, Arlington TX 76005. Phone: 1(800) 433-5255.This includes a teacher's manual and student's manual for high school classes. The teacher's manual includes lesson plans, class activities for above-average and below-average students, and guidelines for class discussions, role playing, compositions, duplication masters, worksheets, and evaluations. A cartoon booklet and a student manual for 10 community involvement projects for prevention activities are also included.

Fetal Alcohol Syndrome In-Service Training Manual

Produced by the California Urban Indian Health Council, 2422 Arden Way, Suite A32, Sacramento CA 95925. Phone: (916) 920-0313. This 37-page curriculum is designed to help health programs intervene with pregnant women who may be using or abusing alcohol, and to raise the community's awareness of the results of drinking during pregnancy. In addition to educating about FAS, this program identifies Indian women of childbearing age whose drinking creates a risk for the unborn, and it helps communities set up a service referral system for high-risk infants. Although it offers special information for Indian communities, it is also useful for developing such programs in a more general context. The kit includes flip chart display information, and educational resources, including lists of available movies, test questions, discussion topics, and background information.

Right from the Start

Produced by the Pregnancy and Health Program, University of Washington Medical School and media services of the Child Development and Mental Retardation Center, University of Washington, Seattle WA 98195. Phone: (206) 543-5017. This is available in two forms: A 90-minute VHS video cassette and a 78-slide, synchronized slide tape presentation. Each one costs $38/week to rent. Purchase price of the VHS is $123.00; the synchronized slide-tape presentation is $185. This innovative presentation discusses a healthy pregnancy from the newborn's point of view. It cautions pregnant women against the use of alcohol, cigarettes, and other potentially harmful drugs, and stresses the importance of good nutrition, sufficient rest, and regular exercise. Hundreds of copies of this presentation have been purchased by the State of Pennsylvania to meet a legislative mandate for healthy pregnancy education for all high school students.

FAS Films

Available from Mental Health Programs Branch IHS, 5300 Hornstead Road NE, Albuquerque NM 87110. Phone: (505) 837-4121.

FAS Video

Produced by Dr. Jon Aase, Clinical Professor Pediatrics, University of New Mexico. Available from Flora and Company, PO Box 8263, Albuquerque NM 87198-8263. Phone: (505) 255-9988. Video for healthcare professionals, doctors and others, on diagnosis of FAS. Cost $150, 32 minutes.

The Fabulous FAS Quiz Show

Coproduced by the Washington State Department of Health and the Western Washington Chapter of the March of Dimes. To purchase, contact the March of Dimes, 1904 3rd Avenue, #230, Seattle WA 98101. Or call Nancy White or Ruth Francis at (206) 624-1373. Cost is $35 plus tax for video and guide. Guide and video can also be purchased separately. This fetal alcohol syndrome prevention video is designed to educate middle school students. Fast paced and entertaining, the 15-minute video uses a game show format to emphasize the theme, "Knowledge plus choice equals power." The lively video is designed to be used with an interactive teacher's guide that outlines suggested activities and resources. The video not only reveals the damage caused by prenatal alcohol exposure but touches on relevant teenage topics such as the relationship between alcohol consumption, sexual activity, and alcohol-related birth defects.

ORGANIZATIONS

Association for Retarded Citizens

PO Box 6109, Arlington TX 76005. Administrative National Offices. For services, refer to state or local chapters.

Center for Science in the Public Interest

1501 16th Street NW, Washington DC 20036. Phone: (202) 332-9110. This useful 52-page booklet by Deborah M. Schecher, JD, is available: *Alcohol warning signs: how to get legislation passed in your city.*

Children of Alcoholics Foundation

555 Madison Avenue, 20th floor, New York NY 10027. Phone: (212) 754-0656 or 1(800) 359-COAF. Fax: (212) 754-0664. Brochures, reports, educational curricula, fact sheets, and videos are available. Charge for some materials; some brochures are free.

March of Dimes Birth Defects Foundation

1275 Mamaroneck Avenue, White Plains NY 10605. Phone: (914) 428-7100. Pamphlets and films are available on alcohol and pregnancy and alcohol-related birth defects.

National Council on Alcoholism and Drug Dependence, Inc.

12 West 21st Street, New York NY 10010. Phone: (212) 206-6700, and 1511 K Street NW, Washington DC 20005. Phone: (202) 737-8122. Pamphlets and fact sheets are available on alcohol-related birth defects; alcoholism and alcohol-related problems among women; alcoholism and other alcohol-related problems among children and youth; and facts on alcoholism and alcohol-related problems.

NOFAS: National Organization on Fetal Alcohol Syndrome

Contact Patti Munter, Executive Director, 1815 H Street NW, Suite 1000, Washington DC 20006. Phone: (202) 785-4585. Newsletter, brochures, state by state resources guides.

National Clearinghouse for Alcohol Information

National Institute on Alcohol Abuse and Alcoholism, PO Box 2345, Rockville MD 20847-2345. Phone: 1(800) 729-6686. A selected, annotated resource guide on fetal alcohol effects is available, including state prevention contacts, booklets, pamphlets, films, slides, bumper stickers, posters, and FAE program contacts. Many items are free.

PUBLICATIONS

A Baby Brother is Born to_____

Produced by the National Organization on Fetal Alcohol Syndrome (NOFAS), and Heartsprings Inc. To purchase, write to NOFAS, 1815 H Street NW, Suite 1000, Washington DC 20006. Phone: (202) 785-4585. Cost is $10.95 including shipping and handling. A little, interactive book about welcoming a baby brother into the world. The book is designed to be customized with the name of the child awaiting the birth of his or her baby brother. It is best read as a story/workbook; it presents why drinking during pregnancy is dangerous, in a simple yet beautiful way. In English and Spanish, with drawings by the celebrated Native American artist Sam English and text by Native American poet Luci Tapahonso.

Alcohol & Health: 8th Special Report to the US Congress

US Department of Health & Human Services, National Institute on Alcohol Abuse and Alcoholism, Public Health Service, National Institute of Health, 1993. Very informative, includes a chapter on the effects of alcohol on fetal and postnatal development, pp. 203-232. Available free: National Clearinghouse for Alcohol and Drug Information, PO Box 2345, Rockville MD 20852. Maryland and DC metro area, call (301)468-2600. Toll free: 1(800) 729-6686.

Alcohol, Tobacco, and Other Drugs May Harm the Unborn

US Department of Health & Human Services, 1990. Office for Substance Abuse Prevention, DHHS Publication No. (ADM) 90-1711, Rockville MD. This booklet is intended for women of childbearing age and their partners. It is also written for health care providers and others working with young women of childbearing age. It is addressed to volunteers active in the prevention and early intervention of drug abuse, including the abuse of beer, wine, distilled spirits, tobacco, and other drugs, be they illicit, prescribed, or over-the-counter. Available free: National Clearinghouse for Alcohol and Drug Information, PO Box 2345, Rockville MD 20852. Maryland and DC metro area, call: (301) 468-2600. Toll free: 1(800) 729-6686.

Alcohol-Related Impairment

Free publication. Write to NIAAA, Alcohol Alert Office of Scientific Affairs, Scientific Communications Branch, Room 409, Willco Building, 6000 Executive Boulevard, Rockville MD 20892-7003. Offered by the National Institute on Alcohol Abuse and Alcoholism, this free publication explores alcohol's acute impairment ability, reveals how alcohol affects complex mental and motor functions, and discusses approaches to impairment testing.

The Broken Cord

Michael Dorris. HarperCollins: New York, 1989. With a forward by Louise Erdrich. A family's ongoing struggle with fetal alcohol syndrome (FAS), this is the true story of one American Indian child adopted from a reservation. The boy develops slowly and has a wide range of physical, behavioral, and mental problems that his adoptive father, despite all his loving efforts, cannot alleviate. Searching to understand why, he learns the hard facts of fetal alcohol syndrome. Can be purchased in paperback, $9.95; hardback, $18.95; or inquire at your local library. HarperCollins, 10 E 53rd Street, New York NY 10022.

Fantastic Antone Succeeds! Experiences in Educating Children with Fetal Alcohol Syndrome

Kleinfeld JS; Westcott S, eds. Fairbanks AK. University of Alaska Press, 1989, pp. 368. Descriptive experiences of family members and educators as they work to develop to their fullest potential. Available from University of Alaska Press, Fairbanks, AK. Phone: (907) 474-6389 or from NOFAS (the National Organization on Fetal Alcohol Syndrome). Hardcover $30.00 or paper cover $20.00 (plus $3.50 for shipping and handling).

FEN Pen, Family Empowerment Network Newsletter

A newsletter providing support for families affected by FAS/FAE. Annual subscription available for $5.00 (Family) or $10.00 (Professional) from: *FEN Pen,* University of Wisconsin-Madison, 521 Lowell Hall, 610 Langdon Street, Madison WI 53703-1195. Phone: (608) 262-6590.

Fetal Alcohol Syndrome: The Impact on Children's Ability to Learn

Karen B. Troccoli. National/Education Consortium (NHEC) Occasional Paper #10, 1994. Produced in collaboration with Children of Alcoholics Foundation. National Health/Education Consortium, c/o Institute for Educational Leadership, 1001 Connecticut Avenue NW, Suite 310, Washington DC 20036. Phone: (202) 822-8405. Fax: (202) 872-4050. Available also from the Children of Alcoholics Foundation, 555 Madison Avenue, 20th floor, New York NY 10027. Phone: (212) 754-0656 or 1(800) 359-COAF. Fax: (212) 754-0664. Cost: $5. Designed to provide health care professionals, educators, and public policy-makers the information they need to help youngsters born with fetal alcohol syndrome (FAS) or fetal alcohol effects (FAE), this report addresses the importance of identifying these children early and providing them services tailored to their special needs. A useful resource also for parents and family members.

Iceberg

Published by FASIS (Fetal Alcohol Syndrome Information Service), a federally recognized 501(c)3 nonprofit, community organization. A quarterly educational newsletter for people concerned about fetal alcohol syndrome (FAS) and fetal alcohol effects (FAE). Subscriptions are available on a prepaid basis, $20/year professional rates; $10/year family rates. Contact Iceberg, PO Box 95597, Seattle WA 98145-2597 for more information.

CHAPTER 17

Children of Alcoholics

HEATHER J. GOTHAM, MA
KENNETH J. SHER, PhD

CLINICAL APPLICATIONS

The goals of this chapter are to assist the clinician to:

1. Recognize the limits of knowledge about children of alcoholics and to critically consider the popular beliefs.

2. Understand the diversity of problems among children associated with parental alcohol problems.

3. Understand factors that place children at risk.

4. Be familiar with treatment approaches toward children of alcoholics and different targets of intervention.

The topic of children of alcoholics (COAs) has received considerable attention in the popular media. In these accounts, and in some of the academic literature, COAs are at risk for a host of difficulties—such as physical and developmental abnormalities, school problems, anxiety and depression, being victims of child abuse, and being more likely themselves to develop alcohol or other substance use problems. The media attention is important because COAs are a large subgroup of the population. It has been estimated that one in eight Americans is the child of an alcoholic. This represents 28.6 million individuals in the US, 6.5 million of whom are under age 18.[157]

However, what needs to be said at the outset is that having a parent with an alcohol use disorder does not necessarily mean that a child will develop the adverse outcomes suggested in the popular literature. It may be surprising that the empirical research on the negative consequences for children of alcoholics is quite limited. All appearances to the contrary, much of the discussion of the effects of parental alcoholism on children is largely anecdotal, and largely derived from clinical impressions. Although there is a growing body of research, in 1990 the National Institute on Alcohol Abuse and Alcoholism (NIAAA) characterized this work as being "in its infancy."[95] The studies conducted tend to have a number of limitations. Most are retrospective and cross-sectional in nature, meaning that they measure characteristics of COAs at only one point in time. This limits the generalizations that can be made about the functioning of COAs and does not allow one to pinpoint parental alcoholism as *the* explanation for the behaviors attributed to COAs. Few studies of COAs have used longitudinal designs necessary to disentangle the issues of causality.

The higher rates of problems among COAs suggest that they are at *higher risk* for various problems. There are several pathways (called mediating mechanisms) by which parental alcohol abuse might be translated into problems in a child. One research group notes three possible pathways: Genetic predispositions; teratogenic effects of maternal drinking during pregnancy or paternal drinking before conception; and lastly, family environment.[97] There are also several factors (called moderating variables) that might interact with parental alcoholism to either attenuate or exacerbate the effect of parental alcoholism on a child. For example, self-esteem may be a moderating variable, in that children who have high self-esteem may be less likely to develop problems

even if their parents are alcohol dependent.[149] Moderating variables are sometimes called protective or resiliency factors.

This chapter provides an overview of the research being conducted on children of alcoholics. It discusses the biological, psychological, and social impact of parental alcoholism on children across the life span. It considers the pathways that may mediate or transmit problems in a parent to problems in a child, and also the factors that moderate or change the relation between parental alcohol dependence and child problems. It also discusses clinical approaches health care professionals can use with COAs.

SOME CAVEATS
Differences among Alcoholics

Before discussing children of alcoholics, it is important to note that alcohol dependence is a heterogeneous category. Not all alcoholics are alike. This heterogeneity is emphasized because it can affect research dealing with COAs.

As discussed earlier in this manual, various people have endeavored to identify subtypes of alcohol dependence. One typology categorizes alcohol dependence into Type I and Type II: Type I alcoholics have a later age of onset, feel a "loss of control" about drinking, and feel guilt and fear about dependence. In distinction, Type II alcoholics have an earlier age of onset, feel an "inability to abstain" from alcohol, and engage in antisocial behavior when drinking.[25] Another typology describes Type A drinkers who show a later onset, fewer childhood risk factors, less psychopathological dysfunction, and fewer symptoms of dependence; also, Type B drinkers whose dependence is more chronic, are more likely to have a family history of alcoholism, use several drugs, have psychopathological dysfunctions, and experience life stress.[1] A third scheme adopts a three-part typology—Types A, B, and C. Type A drinkers are early-stage problem drinkers with alcohol-related problems but not dependence; Type B drinkers show moderate dependence, drink daily, and are socially oriented; and Type C drinkers have severe dependence, are socially isolated, and drink in binges.[93]

Several other factors distinguish among alcoholics. Location of drinking seems to be important, as research has shown that marital satisfaction was higher if drinking took place in the home rather than out of the home.[38,64,129] Another factor is drinking style or pattern—daily, binge, weekend heavy drinking, or abstinence—and its impact on family life.[135] Finally, a high comorbidity of alcoholism with other major psychiatric illnesses—such as other substance abuse, antisocial personality disorder, depression, and anxiety disorders—is also an important factor in considering

(NOTE: Although within the popular literature adult children of alcoholics (ACOAs) are distinguished from younger children of alcoholics (COAs), for the purposes of this chapter, except where noted, the term "children of alcoholics" (COAs) refers to all offspring of alcoholics, regardless of age.)

differences among alcoholics.[56,112,121] These other parental problems may be as significant in determining what happens to the child as the alcoholism.[67] For example, a child's depression may be related to an alcoholic parent's depression rather than to the alcoholism per se.

This variety of characteristics among drinkers or alcoholics suggests that different behavior patterns may in turn have different impacts upon children in the family. Quite reasonably, a central question may prove to be, "Children of what type of alcoholic?"

Child Development

When possible outcomes for children of alcoholics are considered, the developmental trajectory of the child needs to be examined.[66] Throughout the life span, each period can be thought of as a platform for subsequent stages, and children go through developmental stages differently. It may be that COAs experience developmental lags that put them behind others in their growth. Alternately, it may be that COAs experience deficits or differences in functioning that continue, at least in part, throughout life.

Risk Not Destiny

As noted previously, not all—and probably not most—COAs are negatively affected. This is true despite statements such as, "ALL CHILDREN RAISED IN ALCOHOLIC HOMES NEED TO BE ADDRESSED. ALL CHILDREN ARE AFFECTED" (capitalization from original source).[8] Some children are exposed to fewer disruptions, and some may have less genetic loading for problems. It is also possible that other factors or moderating variables may alter the outcomes; in the discussion below, both vulnerability and protective factors are considered.

Alcohol vs. Family Dysfunction

It is important to be aware of whether effects attributed to parental alcoholism are specific to COAs or are in fact associated with growing up in fragile families, e.g., families with parental psychopathology, marital discord, or considerable stress. Teasing apart these factors requires rigorous research strategies with adequate control groups.

BIOPSYCHOSOCIAL OUTCOMES OF PARENTAL ALCOHOLISM ON CHILDREN ACROSS THE LIFE SPAN

As mentioned above, the number of parents with an alcohol use disorder is distressing. National research data suggest a lifetime prevalence rate for alcohol dependence of 25% in men and 4% to 5% in women.[112] Moreover, it has been estimated that in the US there are 6.6 million COAs below age 18, and 22 million COAs

aged 18 and above.[123] These figures indicate that not only is alcoholism a major problem in society, but that children of alcoholics represent a substantial proportion of the population. The following is a review of the research findings on biological, psychological, and social outcomes in COAs of all ages.[39,131,154]

FAS/FAE

As noted in the Neonatal Effects of Alcohol and Drugs chapter in this volume, perhaps the most blatant and damaging outcome of parental alcohol use is fetal alcohol syndrome (FAS) or fetal alcohol effects (FAE). Maternal alcohol consumption can result in a syndrome of symptoms such as cognitive dysfunctions, abnormal facial features, behavioral deficits, and growth deficiency, some of which continue through adolescence and into adulthood (see Chapter 16, Neonatal Effects of Alcohol and Drugs).

Cognitive and Motor Functioning

More generally than in work regarding FAS/FAE, researchers have studied potential cognitive and motor functioning differences in COAs from birth to adulthood. The evidence suggests that COAs have deficits relative to non-COAs on tests of abstraction/conceptual reasoning, and that COAs have lower mean verbal ability (although still well within the normal range) than non-COAs.[107,131,141] Mixed evidence has been found regarding deficits in visual-spatial learning and performance.[48,126,127,139] Furthermore, in at least one study, taking the age of the child and the home environment into account attenuated cognitive and motor differences between COAs and non-COAs.[97]

Psychophysiological Characteristics

Research examining whether there are psychophysiological differences between COAs and non-COAs has generally been aimed at identifying biological markers for an inherited vulnerability to alcoholism.[131] For example, spontaneous brain wave activity, e.g., EEG patterns has been studied, but there is inconsistent evidence for differences between COAs and non-COAs.[47,69,110]

Another more promising line of research examines event-related potentials (ERPs—brain wave forms elicited by presenting subjects with direct sensory stimulation or a cognitive task). A meta-analysis of this research has concluded that there are deficits in the P3 waves of male children of alcoholic fathers. However, P3 wave deficits have been found in other disorders such as attention deficit/hyperactivity disorder and schizophrenia, and they are seen more reliably in male children of alcoholic fathers than in other groups of COAs. On these bases, the diagnostic specificity of P3 wave deficits is questioned.[108]

A final area of psychophysiological research has examined measures of autonomic activity. Although COAs are not different from non-COAs on many resting measures, e.g., heart rate, skin conductance, differences have been found on several measures of reactivity to external stimuli. For example, compared to non-COAs, male COAs had increased heart rate reactivity to aversive stimuli while sober.[106] Also, multigenerational COAs, e.g., alcoholic males with alcoholic fathers and paternal grandfathers were shown to have smaller skin conductance responses to impending shocks.[45] It has been suggested that this reflects "poor conditioning to signals for punishment," a pattern similar to that found in antisocial personality disorder.[45]

It seems that studies of psychophysiological differences between COAs and non-COAs have had both positive and negative results. This area of research is important because if reliable biological or psychophysiological markers for alcoholism are found, early education and intervention strategies can be aimed at children who may be at higher risk.

Child Physical and Sexual Abuse

It has frequently been suggested that child physical and sexual abuse is higher among COAs. While this might seem intuitive and has been advanced by clinicians, there is little empirical research in this area, and the results are contradictory.[76,88] Too often the studies are characterized by methodological limitations such as biased samples and inaccurate/imprecise definitions of both abuse and alcoholism.[136] Nonetheless, several studies suggest that the prevalence of alcoholism in parents who physically abuse their children is higher than in those who do not abuse their children.[51,158] One study, for example, reported that sons of alcoholic fathers were six times as likely to have been physically abused by their fathers than were sons of nonalcoholic fathers.[138] Again, whether this association is more strongly related to parental alcohol abuse or to other confounding variables such as family conflict or socioeconomic status is not certain. Another important area of focus for this research stems from the suggestion that alcoholism, combined with someone's having been abused as a child, makes the transmission of child-abusing behavior more likely.[136]

The rates of alcoholism in parents who sexually abuse their children have also been reported as high.[123] Again, little research has been conducted. Also, sexual abuse of COAs by non-family members may be more likely if alcohol use affects parental monitoring. For example, one study found that nonoffending mothers' substance abuse was significantly related to more sexual abuse incidents in their daughters.[75]

A more general effect of growing up with an alcoholic parent appears to be increased risk for injury. One study found that sons of alcoholic fathers were seven times as likely to have lost consciousness due to traumatic head injury than sons of nonalcoholic fathers.[138] Another found that children of problem-drinking mothers had 2.1 times the risk of serious injury as children of nondrinking mothers. Furthermore, children of problem-drinking mothers married to moderate- or heavy-drinking fathers had 2.7 times the risk of serious injury as children of nondrinkers.[7]

Academic Problems

Consistently, studies have found more academic difficulties in COAs than in non-COAs. This includes COAs having poorer school attendance and lower standardized test scores, and being more likely to repeat a grade and fail to graduate.[29,60,73,89] One recent study found that adolescent children of "alcohol misusers" had lower grade point averages, skipped more school days and classes, and were more likely to be at risk for dropping out than the general sample of junior and senior high school students.[20] While school problems are consistently associated with parental alcohol problems, the direct causal factors are not clear. A number of scenarios are possible. It could be that children, because of genetic and/or teratogenic effects of alcohol, are beset with cognitive deficits or a conduct disorder that interfere with active learning in a classroom environment. Or, an absence of family monitoring and active support and encouragement may erode school performance. These scenarios may also be combined.

Psychopathology

As a preface to reviewing studies of psychopathology in COAs, two points should be made. Alcohol use disorders are not the only conditions in parents associated with their children's problems. Other parental psychiatric disorders are related to negative child outcomes, as well. Also, as noted above, alcoholism can co-occur with other disorders. Therefore, these comorbid disorders could be responsible for increased rates of various syndromes in COAs.

Attention Deficit/Hyperactivity Disorder (ADHD). ADHD (characterized by distractibility, fidgeting, impulsivity, and attention problems) in childhood has been linked to parental alcoholism in many studies. However, the link is not as clear and as strong as has been suggested. Some research has not found a higher rate of attention deficits in COAs than in non-COAs.[113] Equally important, the quality of studies reporting a positive association is being questioned because many of these studies failed to separate hyperactive children from those who express hyperactive and aggressive or undersocialized behavior. Also, it has been suggested that children of parents with other psychiatric disorders also have higher rates of hyperactivity. Thus, an increased risk for ADHD may not be specific to COAs.[150] Given equivocal study findings, methodological problems, and perhaps problems with diagnostic specificity, a definitive statement of the relation between hyperactivity and parental alcoholism is not currently justified.

Conduct disorders. Similarly, numerous studies have suggested that COAs are more likely than children of nonalcoholic parents to have conduct problems.[150] COAs are purportedly more likely to engage in physical aggressiveness, lying, fighting, and school truancy; have other behavior problems; or be referred to a school psychologist.[5,144] The relation between conduct disorders and parental alcoholism might be attributable to a genetic transmission of a predisposition for developing a conduct disorder and/or to a disruption in the child's environment, e.g., parental divorce. Research suggests that when disruption in the family environment is controlled for, the relationship between conduct disorders and parental alcoholism is attenuated or eliminated.[103]

Antisocial Personality Disorder (ASP). A related issue is the risk for ASP in adult COAs. An excess of COAs is diagnosed with ASP.[123] However, the relation between alcoholism in parents and ASP in COAs is more complicated than it might seem. Studies suggesting an increased risk for ASP in COAs may have failed to control for ASP in parents. Furthermore, the disorder may have several dimensions or subtypes,[53] only one or some of which may be related to alcoholism.[134]

Depression and anxiety. Associations between family history of alcoholism and both depression and anxiety disorders have been examined in COAs of all ages. In their review of childhood psychopathology in COAs, West and Prinz[150] reported that COAs may be more likely to have depressive and anxiety disorders than non-COAs. However, some studies have found conflicting results. For example, one study that compared a group of COAs from families with multigenerational alcoholism—an average of four alcoholic relatives—to a control group did not find significant differences in rates of depressive or anxiety disorders.[57]

Even in studies showing higher rates of childhood psychopathology in COAs, the chronicity of these emotional problems is unclear. In a comparison of families of recovering alcoholics to families without alcoholism, the rate of emotional problems in the children was similar. On the other hand, children of relapsed alcoholics had twice as many problems.[90] This suggests that heightened levels of psychological problems, whether anxiety or depression, might be somewhat transient and tied to a parent's active alcohol problem—or as another study suggests, to parental psychopathology in general rather than to alcoholism in particular.[63]

Regarding adults, in data from a large community sample, the current prevalence rates of simple phobia and agoraphobia, and lifetime prevalence rates of dysthymia, generalized anxiety disorder, panic disorder, simple phobia, and agoraphobia were significantly higher in adult COAs than in non-COAs.[83] Depression also seems related to COA status,[123] although at least one study[83] did not find a significantly higher prevalence of depression in COAs. It had been suggested that alcoholism and depression share a genetic diathesis[155] such that being the child of an alcoholic could be expressed as alcoholism in male COAs and depression in female COAs; however, more recent data calls this theory into question.[86] Nonetheless, the relation between family history and depression is probably complex and may involve family and environmental stressors and depressive comorbidity in the parents.[123]

Alcohol and Other Substance Use Disorders

A main concern of both empirical research and clinical literature concerning COAs has been measuring the transmission of alcoholism from parent to offspring. The prevalence of alcoholism is higher in all first-degree relatives of alcoholics, and on average, COAs are three to five times more likely to develop alcoholism than non-COAs.[31] Studies have shown relationships between familial alcohol abuse and adolescent alcohol abuse, both from the perspectives of more alcoholism in parents of alcoholic adolescents than of nonalcoholic adolescents and of higher rates of alcohol abuse in COAs than in non-COAs.[150] Researchers are now attempting to determine the nature of the relationship more precisely. For example, there may be different risks for sons or daughters of alcoholic mothers or fathers. A meta-analysis suggested that paternal alcoholism is related to increased rates of alcoholism in sons and daughters, while maternal alcoholism is related to increased rates of alcoholism only in daughters.[109] Other factors also may be important, as a combination of family history of alcoholism and antisocial behaviors most strongly predicted alcohol dependence 10 years later.[54] In addition to increased risk for alcoholism, several studies have suggested COAs are also at increased risk for other drug use or abuse.[22,68,132]

Personality and Temperament

Recently, a review of research regarding COAs and personality attributes[153] concluded that there is no clear evidence that COAs have higher levels of neuroticism (negative affect such as anxious and depressive feelings) or positive affect (happiness, extraversion) than non-COAs. However, there seems to be more consistent evidence that behavioral undercontrol is related to COA status.[131] Behavioral undercontrol is somewhat of an umbrella category, encompassing traits such as impulsivity, risk taking, and hyperactivity.[153] Further specification of this concept is needed, especially because it seems to be related to ADHD and conduct disorders. However, evidence that sons of alcohol-abusing or alcohol-dependent fathers scored higher on a measure of behavioral activity than sons of nonalcoholic fathers suggests that this may indeed be a personality or temperamental trait found differently in COAs.[140]

Interpersonal Relationships

Although the topic of interpersonal functioning in COA's has recently become popular with the national media and within clinical writings, a major review of the empirical literature concluded that relevant data was sparse and equivocal.[150] Many interpersonal deficits have been suggested as being linked to a family history of alcoholism. For example, some studies have found that more COAs than non-COAs report problems such as difficulty trusting people, inability to identify and express feelings and needs, more marital conflict, less social support, less family cohesion, and less marital satisfaction.[10,37] Differences in adult attachment styles have also been found, suggesting that COAs might be more likely to have avoidant or anxious styles,[13] or that female but not male COAs have dysfunctional attachment styles.[40] However, research in this area is plagued by limitations and a lack of objective measurement techniques.

Perhaps the most discussed potential interpersonal problem in COAs is codependency. Codependency has been described as an addiction, personality disorder, psychosocial condition, and/or interpersonal style characterized by denial, constriction of emotions, depression, hypervigilance, compulsions, anxiety, substance abuse, and stress-related medical complications related to living with or growing up with an alcohol-abusing individual.[19] Despite the popularity of the codependency issue in clinical writing and the public media, little empirical research has been conducted on it. A recent study suggested that results from one measure of codependency were largely explained by negative affectivity (depression and anxiety) and general psychological distress.[50] Furthermore, several studies have not found strong associations between codependency and family history of alcoholism.[46,98] When such a relationship is found, it may be that the effect is caused by pathological aspects of family life such as emotional and physical abuse related to having an addicted family member, rather than by having an addicted family member per se.[116] Future research regarding codependency needs both to explain the concept and to explore its relationship to family members with substance addictions.

Another interpersonal outcome currently popular in the mass media and clinical literature is the notion of children's roles. Popular clinical lore has suggested that many COAs develop roles in the family to maintain family homeostasis. As Black noted,

> The oldest child often becomes a 'responsible child' who takes on many of the household and parenting responsibilities; the younger child often becomes an 'adjuster,' who finds it much easier to exist by simply adjusting to whatever happens. Other children may become the 'placator' who becomes very skilled at listening and showing empathy. However, some other children act out and display delinquent behavior which typifies the state of the family.[9]

Despite the popularity of family roles and the development of several instruments to assess them,[111,114] there is little empirical support for this theory. Family roles are highly correlated with family disorganization variables of intimacy, cohesiveness, and deliberateness. Furthermore, several studies have found no or few differences between COAs and non-COAs.[111,114] In addition, when roles were found to discriminate between children from alcoholic and nonalcoholic homes, family disruption was sometimes a better predictor of roles than family alcoholism.[33] Thus, the specificity of role development in COAs, and hence its usefulness, appears highly questionable.

Summary

A number of potential outcomes in COAs have been reviewed. They cover a broad range of problems, have varying levels of severity, and are associated with all phases of the life span. The most compelling evidence seems to indicate that COAs are more likely than non-COAs to develop alcoholism or other psychopathological disorders themselves; are at risk for a range of cognitive deficits, especially related to verbal ability; and are more likely to be physically or sexually abused. Despite what may seem like a long list of potentially noxious outcomes, most children of parents who abuse alcohol do not suffer these outcomes.[149] Furthermore, some effects seem to be situationally tied to parents' use of alcohol or are found in children of families with other problems, e.g., other parental psychopathology.

POTENTIAL MEDIATORS TO THE RELATION BETWEEN FAMILY HISTORY OF ALCOHOLISM AND PROBLEMS IN CHILDREN

Given the above-noted associations between familial alcoholism and problems in children, how might we explain them? That is, what are the most specific factors or pathways by which parental alcoholism transmits problems to children? Factors such as biological differences (including genetic effects) and patterns of family functioning may mediate (account for) the relation between parental alcoholism and unfavorable outcomes in children.

Biological and Genetic Factors

Genetic transmission of alcoholism. A number of biological and genetic factors have been hypothesized as mediators of the relationship between parental alcoholism and children's problems, especially alcoholism. For example, the increased risk for COAs to develop alcohol dependence could be caused by their genetic makeup. Family, twin, and adoption studies have suggested that alcohol dependence has a strong genetic component.[17,31,80] As noted earlier, the risk for first-degree relatives of alcoholics to develop alcoholism has been reported as between four and seven times that for first-degree relatives of nonalcoholics.[31,85] Historically, the genetic link has been suggested as stronger in men than women, and also to vary as a function of subtype of alcoholism.[81] However, other work suggests a genetic relation to development of alcoholism in women,[72] as well as a specific relationship between maternal alcoholism and alcoholism in daughters.[109]

Individual responses to alcohol. It is important to note that COAs do not appear different than non-COAs in their ability to metabolize and eliminate alcohol from their systems.[131] However, research suggests that COAs, especially male children of male alcoholics, react and respond to alcohol differently than children of nonalcoholics, which may affect their vulnerability to develop alcoholism and other problems. COAs may be more sensitive to the positive effects of alcohol (being stimulated) and less sensitive to the negative effects of alcohol (feeling intoxicated), which may in turn lead to increased levels of drinking in COAs.[96] Also, male children of male alcoholics have an increased stress-dampening effect.[107,131] That is, after consuming alcohol, male COAs show smaller changes in heart rate than do non-COAs when presented with an aversive or novel situation. These differences in response to alcohol may be important, as a study has found that males who responded to a dose of alcohol with less body sway and fewer subjective feelings of intoxication were four times more likely to develop alcoholism 10 years later than those with more normative responses.[128]

Psychosocial and Family Environment Factors

Children of alcoholics are also considered at risk for a number of negative outcomes because of the psychosocial experiences that accompany growing up in an environment of alcohol dependence. For example, divorce, poverty, and parental criminality occur more frequently in families with an alcohol-abusing member.[150] Other factors including a child's attachment style, general family interaction patterns, and parental monitoring will be examined in more detail below. However, it needs to be stressed that even when mediating familial variables can be recognized, causal directions cannot be assumed. Although it might appear that parental alcoholism leads to poor parental modeling that leads to problems in children, there are several other possible scenarios. A third variable might be at work. For example, parental antisocial personality may "cause" alcoholism in the parent and poor rearing conditions and thus be the critical variable in explaining the association between a parent's drinking and family conditions. Or, there might be reverse causation, in that a child's psychopathology may contribute to or maintain alcoholism. Evidence suggests that men and women drink more after interacting with a child acting as if he or she had an attention deficit disorder than with a normally behaving child.[105]

Furthermore, researchers have proposed that alcohol may have an adaptive effect in some families, e.g., allow for the expression of emotion, force other family members to join together and take action, and restore equilibrium in the family because behavior of steady drinkers is predictable.[135] Marital satisfaction has been positively correlated to the husband's alcohol consumption in several studies.[38,62] Also, others have noted that the effects of parents' drinking level on children's satisfaction with parent-child relationships are not always negative.[130] This reasoning does not attempt to diminish the negative effects that alcoholism can have on a family. Instead, it highlights the interactive and systemic nature of families as groups of people acting and reacting to one another, rather than focusing on the individual alcoholic family member and his or her effects on the family.

Childhood attachment. A variable that might explain part of the relationship between family history of alcoholism and children's outcomes is attachment style in infancy. A recent study found that mothers of insecure infants drank significantly more than mothers of secure infants.[99] This suggests that insecure attachment style might be an effect of maternal drinking. However, disrupted attachment behavior, although usually assumed to be related to a transaction between the child and mother, may primarily reflect temperamental differences in the child.[32] Regardless of the causal relation, infants with insecure attachment styles may be more likely to develop socioemotional problems later in childhood and adulthood.[12]

General family milieu. Numerous studies have suggested that familial interaction patterns and the overall family milieu of COAs are more likely to be noxious and have characteristics such as the following: Increased conflict; decreased cohesion, expressiveness, independence, and intellectual/cultural awareness; impaired problem solving; and more hostile communications among family members.[65,131,136] As noted above, these patterns may also change with the alcoholic family member's current drinking status.[135]

Family rituals. A more specific example of family factors that influence the later development of alcoholism in COAs are family rituals, e.g., dinner time, holidays, vacations, evenings, weekends, and when there are visitors.[4,156] Families are described as having either distinctive rituals, where the family ensures that the alcoholic's behavior does not disrupt the ritual, or subsumptive rituals, which are often disrupted. While family rituals may not be related to alcoholism in adolescent COAs,[44] there is some evidence that alcoholic families with subsumptive rituals produce more children who will become alcoholics than those with distinctive rituals.[4,156]

Parenting styles. Another way of explaining the relationship between parental alcoholism and negative outcomes in children is that alcohol actively interferes with the parenting role. As mentioned previously, COAs seem to be at increased risk for being abused and neglected by their parents, and child abuse and neglect have been shown to have severe effects on children's well-being and development.[71] Furthermore, a lack of parental monitoring (especially paternal) has been related to adolescents' association with drug-using peers and adolescent drug use.[21,35] Deficits in parental monitoring are also implied by some studies, such as research showing that children of heavy-drinking mothers are more likely to have injuries[7] and that COAs may be at higher risk for physical and sexual abuse by nonfamily members.[123]

Parental modeling. Parental modeling of alcohol use has also been linked to poor outcomes in children. Parents' current alcohol and other drug use has been associated with adolescents' alcohol and other drug use.[21,35] Modeling effects may be especially salient in some situations, such as in sex-specific (father-son, mother-daughter) families,[52] for young adult male COAs,[23] and when the alcoholic father is highly regarded by the mother.[78]

Life events. Another potential mediator of the relation between parental alcoholism and negative outcomes in children is life events.[26] Life stress is predictive of alcohol use in adolescents,[27] and children living with an alcoholic parent may be exposed to more life stress or negative life events. Consequently, COAs may be more likely to develop negative outcomes such as substance use. Several studies have found that COAs experience more negative life events than do non-COAs,[55,118,119] and that negative life events are related to anxiety and depression. However, whether COAs experience fewer positive life events and more negative life events than non-COAs is not entirely clear.[15,118,120]

Labeling effects. Although being labeled the offspring of an alcoholic as a COA may help that person find needed support or appropriate interventions, it can also have a stigmatizing effect.[16] In one study, adolescents labeled as COAs were rated by their peers as significantly more deviant than normal adolescents and as similar to mentally ill teenagers in some respects. Furthermore, mental health professionals judged the behavior of an adolescent labeled a COA in a taped interview as more pathological than the same behaviors in the same adolescent not so labeled. Being labeled a COA may lead to rejection by peers, differential treatment by teachers, or unwarranted counseling or help from mental health professionals. Caution needs to be taken before singling out an individual as a child of an alcoholic, especially if the individual is not showing signs of problems.

Summary

Thus, there may not be a direct causal relationship between parental alcoholism and problems in children. Rather, several genetic and biological factors, as well as several family- and social-functioning factors spawned by parental alcoholism, may cause some of the negative outcomes that occur more often in COAs than in non-COAs.

POTENTIAL MODERATORS OF THE RELATIONSHIP BETWEEN FAMILY HISTORY OF ALCOHOLISM AND PROBLEMS IN CHILDREN

The preceding section described variables that appear to directly affect children's outcomes, and that potentially mediate or transmit the relationship between parental alcoholism and poor outcomes in the child. However, other variables may interact with or moderate the impact of parental alcoholism or other mediators on the child by either attenuating or exacerbating their effects. For example, it seems that only some children with an alcohol-dependent parent encounter difficulties in childhood or adulthood.[3,63,95] Even for children from problem families, e.g., those marked by an intergenerational cycle of poverty, despair, criminality, or emotional illness where parental alcohol dependence could contribute to a troubled adulthood, protective factors such as the degree of severity of family crises, the level of isolation from or integration into the community, and the child's self-esteem may attenuate the potential negative effects of growing up in that family. A general caution is needed here. Although many findings are touted as representing protective or resiliency factors, the experimental designs used to generate these data are generally incapable of distinguishing such effects due to lack of prospective studies, lack of adequate control groups, and failure to test for interactions.[131]

Individual-Level Protective Factors

Identifying protective factors that may help insulate COAs from potential negative effects is of particular interest to clinicians. Several potential factors have been identified, such as higher IQ, higher self-esteem, not being separated from a primary caretaker during the first year, and lack of family conflict.[149] In addition, self-awareness might be important in predicting alcohol-related problems and alcohol use in adolescents.[117]

Interpersonal and Social Protective Factors

Several interpersonal and social factors may moderate the effects of familial alcoholism on child outcomes. As noted above, lower rates of alcoholism have been found in adult COAs from families who have maintained traditions such as celebrating holidays and having meals together and thus keep intact some of the symbolic functions of the family.[4]

Social support, both familial and nonfamilial, may also be a moderator or protective factor.[24,131] Several studies have found that levels of familial support are lower in COAs vs. non-COAs.[6,59] Furthermore, the impact of parental psychopathology (alcoholism and other mental illnesses) seems to be attenuated in adult offspring with larger social support networks.[104,152]

CLINICAL APPROACHES FOR HEALTH CARE PROFESSIONALS

Due to the increased attention that society has given both to treating alcoholism and recognizing that families and friends of alcohol abusers can be negatively affected, health care professionals now have a wide variety of interventions and treatments from which to choose. However, given that many adverse effects in children are situationally tied to parents' active alcoholism, perhaps the most important intervention involves direct treatment of a parent's alcoholism. Several studies have found that families with a recovering member function either better than those with currently drinking family members[115] or not significantly different from families without an alcohol-dependent member.[91] More specifically, differences in children's externalizing and internalizing behaviors (based on mother and father's ratings) between control, recovered alcoholic, and currently

alcoholic families have been reported.[22] COAs of recovered alcoholics may get better (or may never have been as bad) after their parent stops drinking. While interventions designed to treat parental alcoholism may be the first and most important step, efforts are also directed at the family as a whole and at COAs as individuals.

Efforts Directed at Parents

As several chapters of this manual are geared toward individual treatment of alcohol abuse, strategies will not be discussed at length. However, it is interesting to note a growing trend toward diversity in treatment. The Institute of Medicine recently published a report, *Broadening the Base of Treatment for Alcohol Problems,* suggesting that treatment be broadened beyond traditional AA-oriented inpatient strategies for "alcoholics."[61] The report states that treatment should (a) encompass a wide variety of modalities, e.g., pharmacological, behavioral, family-oriented; (b) be provided by many levels of professionals, from community programs and social service agencies to work place health plans and individual health care workers; and (c) be aimed at individuals with a full range of alcohol use and abuse problems. Furthermore, an emphasis is being placed on enhancing primary care health workers' awareness of alcohol use in their patients, including ways in which physicians and nurses can screen for problems, refer for treatment, and provide brief interventions that effect changes in alcohol use in their patients.[148]

Efforts Directed at the Family

In a review of family therapy outcome studies, O'Farrell discusses three main areas in which family therapy can be effective: "(a) initial commitment to change—recognizing that a problem exists and deciding to do something about it; (b) the change itself—stopping abusive drinking and stabilizing this change for at least a few months; and (c) the long-term maintenance of change."[101] Although treatment schemes focusing on the whole family of an alcoholic member have been gaining popularity over the past several decades, they are not considered a prototypical treatment strategy. A review of Veterans Administration treatment services for alcohol-involved families found that family-oriented programs were not frequently utilized.[125] However, a number of family-oriented treatment schemes based on family systems theory[135] and on social learning theory[79] (incorporating behavioral techniques) have been developed. Actually, although referred to as "family therapy for alcoholism," most treatment approaches have been aimed at the marital dyad rather than at the entire family.

Until recently, research studying the effectiveness of family-oriented treatments has been lacking.[28] Because, as just noted, most approaches are actually aimed at partners, generally the existing outcome research also has been limited to marital interactions and functioning. Behavioral techniques—such as having spouses provide positive and negative consequences for drinking behavior,[133] and contracting with the alcoholic for compliance with Antabuse[70]— have been used and been found more effective than control conditions using traditional methods, e.g., alcohol education, supportive counseling. In addition, behavioral marital therapy, a more systematized treatment strategy, has been used with alcoholic families and been found to be effective in several studies.[100,101,102] Treatment outcome studies need to be conducted on current family treatment strategies, and new strategies may need to be developed. One group of researchers outlined guidelines for the development of family-oriented intervention programs for at-risk (COA) and/or drug-involved adolescents.[36] Based on empirical studies of families of COAs and non-COAs, they suggested that family interventions designed to prevent and limit drug use in children target changes in parenting such as parental monitoring of children and parental modeling of drug use.

Community and state agencies also provide assistance to families with an alcohol-abusing member. One example is the Emergency Services Child Abuse Prevention Program (ESCAPP).[11] This program coordinates services for families such as self-help for treatment of the alcohol problem, and any work, housing, and medical needs of the family. The short-term goal of the ESCAPP is to prevent physical abuse and neglect of the children, and the long-term goal is to engender a broad base of social and environmental support for the entire family. Programs such as this, which take into consideration a wide range of family needs rather than just the alcohol or other substance abuse problem, are more likely to help stabilize a family and foster lifelong changes in family members, particularly in their problem-solving ability.

Efforts Directed at COAs

Regardless of age, the first step in dealing with the child of an alcoholic is to determine the nature of the problem. Careful assessment is needed, as problems may be best treated with empirically recognized techniques rather than with treatments specific to COAs. Outcome studies have noted the efficacy of treatments for many disorders, including cognitive therapy for depression,[2] behavior modification for enuresis/encopresis,[74] exposure treatment for phobias and PTSD,[84,143] parent training for children with oppositional disorders,[147] and cognitive behavior therapy

and interpersonal therapy for bulimia.[42] Thus, while growing up in a family with an alcoholic member may contribute to a problem, the solution may not need to be directed primarily at familial alcoholism. To date there is no evidence to suggest that using standard techniques with COAs would be different than with non-COAs.

However, if the family member continues to abuse alcohol, and/or there appear to be problems in the offspring specifically related to the family member's alcoholism, there are treatment programs targeted directly at COAs. These programs tend to focus on providing education on alcohol and other substance abuse, skills-training to enhance coping behaviors, and social support via peer groups. As with the family treatment literature, empirical data regarding the efficacy of such programs are limited. The following is a short review of four formats of COA-specific treatment programs: Bibliotherapy, group psychotherapy, individual psychotherapy, and school-based interventions.

Bibliotherapy. A common need for COAs dealing with an alcohol problem in the family is basic information about alcohol as a drug and an addiction. Such information can help reassure the COA that she or he is not responsible for the parent's behavior or illness. There are many developmentally appropriate fiction and nonfiction books and pamphlets to help COAs deal with alcoholism in the family and other alcohol-related family disruptions such as divorce, chronic illness, and death and dying.[82,94]

Group psychotherapy. Psychoeducational groups for COAs are perhaps the most popular format for treatment, and they have been designed for COAs of all ages.[145] For instance, one group of researchers described a psychoeducational group treatment approach for young children (their patients were aged 5 to 8) that educates children about alcohol and alcoholism using books, films, lectures and toys; helps the children share feelings and experiences; and problem solves for difficult situations involving the alcoholic parent.[49] Several studies have found that group treatment with child and adolescent COAs has resulted in more positive coping skills and social skills and increased knowledge about alcoholism;[151] however, results vary widely across groups. An empirical study of a COA group for college students has also been published.[30] Topics of COA group sessions included the alcoholic family system, codependency, denial, control issues, and psychic numbing. Also, several studies have shown that after a structured or semistructured group treatment program, adult COAs had reduced symptoms of anxiety and depression and healthier coping attitudes.[30,41,122]

Al-Anon and Al-Ateen are self-help groups for relatives of alcoholics that follow the model of Alcoholics

Anonymous. Unfortunately, empirical research on Al-Ateen is not sufficient to determine its effectiveness.[151] The same can be said for Al-Anon, although one study found that wives of alcoholics who had attended Al-Anon reported better alcohol-related coping skills than wives of alcoholics who had not attended Al-Anon.[124] However, whether involvement in Al-Anon has more positive effects than other group treatments is unknown, and several studies have found that length of attendance in an alcohol problem-related group is an important determinant of outcome.[77,142] Empirical studies of group treatments are needed.

Individual psychotherapy. Individual therapy strategies for treatment of COAs have been based on numerous theoretical models such as developmental and systems perspectives[14] and rational-emotive therapy.[43] Also, a cognitive behavior therapy intervention for school psychologists to use with COAs has been outlined that includes modeling normal interpersonal functioning, thought-stopping worrisome or self-defeating thoughts, and cognitive restructuring.[146] Unfortunately, systematic descriptions of therapy treatment plans and treatment outcome research are severely lacking in this area.

School-based programs. Many schools and community agencies are beginning to offer programs or services for children of alcoholics. Prevention programs such as the Cambridge and Somerville Program for Alcoholism Rehabilitation (CASPAR) attempt to provide education about alcoholism and alcoholic families to all children in the public schools.[34] Referrals can then be made to after-school programs or to individual support staff. Support or psychoeducational group formats are probably the most common, and although outcome data are rare, they do suggest some effectiveness.[151] Individual and group counseling was provided in the Student Assistance Program, a school-based prevention program for high school COAs designed to provide information regarding alcoholism, improve students' coping skills, and reduce feelings of stigma and isolation.[92]

A major obstacle to school-based programs can be selection and recruitment of COAs. One study found that self-selection and parental consent procedures for a school-based prevention program for fourth through sixth grade COAs did not result in a group of children whose families had alcohol-abusing members.[87] This reticence of children to self-select into a treatment program may be caused by worries about being stigmatized.[16] It is encouraging to note that another study found that college and high school COAs were interested in participating in an educational and support group.[137]

One way that young COAs who are unwilling or unable to identify themselves can mobilize alternative sources of support is through school-based programs aimed at assisting all children. An example is the Phone-A-Friend service, in which children at home after school can call high school students for support or help with homework.[11] Parents can also request the service to call their children at home alone after school. Another school-based intervention is the ESCAPE (Enhancing Social Competence and Personal Efficacy) program. This comprehensive program is designed for "developing self-efficacy, social interaction skills, and interpersonal problem solving strategies" in all children in all grade levels.[94] The authors of the ESCAPE program provide examples of literature, films, creative writing assignments, group discussion topics, and other forms of cooperative learning that can be incorporated into any curriculum to promote understanding of alcohol-related topics and problems as well as of coping skills.

Summary

In cases of children living in the home, treatment for the alcoholic parent should be the priority, and family-oriented treatment may be a way to provide attention to all potentially affected family members. Treatment specific to COAs should be based on the nature of the problem and should follow empirically supported treatment plans. Beyond these strategies are treatments specifically focused on COA status. For example, a great deal of literature designed to help children of alcoholics is currently popular. Support groups can be safe, comfortable forums in which people's stressful experiences are affirmed. Short-term psychotherapy or counseling may also be useful, and school-based prevention and treatment plans are available in some communities. Contacting a substance abuse treatment program can be an efficient way of identifying a community's resources. Substance abuse treatment programs may offer counseling for adult COAs, conduct time-limited support groups, and be informed about the self-help network. If they do not offer all of these services, they can be a guide to the necessary connections.

Although COAs may seek treatment for problems specifically related to growing up with an alcoholic parent, it would behoove clinicians and health care providers to consider first the nature of the presenting problem. As seen in this review, many problems in current functioning are associated with having a family history of alcoholism; however, as one group of researchers suggested, help seeking by COAs may be more related to *personal* emotional or psychological adjustment than to "characteristics of parents or caregivers."[58]

REFERENCES

1. Babor TF; Hofmann M; Del Boca FK; Hesselbrock VM; Meyer RE; Dolinsky ZS; et al. Types of alcoholics: I. Evidence for an empirically derived typology based on indicators of vulnerability and severity. *Archives of General Psychiatry* 49(8): 599-608, 1992. (49 refs.)

2. Beck AT; Rush AJ; Shaw BF; Emery G. *Cognitive Therapy of Depression.* New York: The Guilford Press, 1979.

3. Beidler RJ. Adult children of alcoholics: Is it really a separate field for study? *Drugs & Society* 3(3/4): 133-141, 1989. (16 refs.)

4. Bennett LA; Wolin SJ. Family culture and alcohol transmission. IN: Collins RL; Leonard KE; Searles JS, eds. *Alcohol and the Family: Research and Clinical Perspectives.* New York: The Guilford Press, 1992. pp. 194-219.

5. Bennett LA; Wolin SJ; Reiss D. Cognitive, behavioral, and emotional problems among school-age children of alcoholic parents. *American Journal of Psychiatry* 145(2): 185-190, 1988. (38 refs.)

6. Benson CS; Heller K. Factors in the current adjustment of young adult daughters of alcoholic and problem drinking fathers. *Journal of Abnormal Psychology* 96(4): 305-312, 1987. (38 refs.)

7. Bijur PE; Kurzon M; Overpeck MD; Scheidt PC. Parental alcohol use, problem drinking, and children's injuries. *Journal of the American Medical Association* 267(23): 3166-3171, 1992. (28 refs.)

8. Black C. *It Will Never Happen to Me.* Denver CO: MAC Printing & Publications, 1982.

9. Black C. Effects of family alcoholism. IN: Saitoh S; Steinglass P; Schuckit MA, eds. *Alcoholism and the Family.* New York: Brunner/Mazel, 1992. pp. 272-281. (0 refs.)

10. Black C; Bucky SF; Wilder-Padilla S. The interpersonal and emotional consequences of being an adult child of an alcoholic. *International Journal of the Addictions* 21(2): 213-231, 1986. (22 refs.)

11. Blau GM; Whewell MC; Gullotta TP; Bloom M. The prevention and treatment of child abuse in households of substance abusers: A research demonstration progress report. *Child Welfare* 73(1): 83-94, 1994. (17 refs.)

12. Bowlby J. *Attachment and Loss: Volume 1. Attachment.* New York: Basic Books, 1969.

13. Brennan KA; Shaver PR; Tobey AE. Attachment styles, gender and parental problem drinking. *Journal of Social and Personal Relationships* 8(4): 451-466, 1991. (26 refs.)

14. Brown SA. *Treating Adult Children of Alcoholics: A Developmental Perspective.* New York: John Wiley & Sons, 1988.

15. Brown SA. Life events of adolescents in relation to personal and parental substance abuse. *American Journal of Psychiatry* 146: 484-489, 1989. (23 refs.)

16. Burk JP; Sher KJ. Labeling the child of an alcoholic: Negative stereotyping by mental health professionals and peers. *Journal of Studies on Alcohol* 51(2): 156-163, 1990. (26 refs.)

17. Cadoret RJ. Genetics of alcoholism. IN: Collins RL; Leonard KE; Searles JS, eds. *Alcohol and the Family: Research and Clinical Perspectives.* New York: The Guilford Press, 1990. pp. 39-78. (123 refs.)

18. Callan VJ; Jackson D. Children of alcoholic fathers and recovered alcoholic fathers: Personal and family functioning. *Journal of Studies on Alcohol* 47(2): 180-182, 1986. (10 refs.)

19. Cermak TL. Diagnostic criteria for co-dependency. *Journal of Psychoactive Drugs* 18(1): 15-20, 1986.

20. Chandy JM; Harris L; Blum RW; Resnick MD. Children of alcohol misusers and school performance outcomes. *Children and Youth Services Review* 15(6): 507-519, 1993. (36 refs.)

21. Chassin L; Pillow DR; Curran PJ; Molina BSG; Barrera M Jr. Relation of parental alcoholism to early adolescent substance use: A test of three mediating mechanisms. *Journal of Abnormal Psychology* 102(1): 3-19, 1993. (61 refs.)

22. Chassin L; Rogosch F; Barrera M. Substance use and symptomatology among adolescent COAs. *Journal of Abnormal Psychology* 100: 449-463, 1991.

23. Chipperfield B; Vogel-Sprott M. Family history of problem drinking among young male social drinkers: Modeling effects on alcohol consumption. *Journal of Abnormal Psychology* 97(November): 423-438, 1988.

24. Clair D; Genest M. Variables associated with the adjustment of offspring of alcoholic fathers. *Journal of Studies on Alcohol* 48(4): 345-355, 1987. (48 refs.)

25. Cloninger CR. Neurogenetic adaptive mechanisms in alcoholism. *Science* 236(4800): 410-416, 1987. (55 refs.)

26. Cohen S; Wills TA. Stress, social support, and the buffering hypothesis. *Psychological Bulletin* 98(2): 310-357, 1985.

27. Colder CR; Chassin L. The stress and negative affect model of adolescent alcohol use and the moderating effects of behavioral undercontrol. *Journal of Studies on Alcohol* 54(3): 326-333, 1993. (39 refs.)

28. Collins RL. Family treatment of alcohol abuse: Behavioral and systems perspectives. IN: Collins RL; Leonard KE; Searles JS, eds. *Alcohol and the Family: Research and Clinical Perspectives.* New York: The Guilford Press, 1990. pp. 285-308. (59 refs.)

29. Connolly GM; Casswell S; Stewart J; Silva PA; O'Brien MK. The effect of parents' alcohol problems on children's behaviour as reported by parents and by teachers. *Addiction* 88(10): 1383-1390, 1993. (28 refs.)

30. Cooper A; McCormack WA. Short-term group treatment for adult children of alcoholics. *Journal of Counseling Psychology* 39(3): 350-355, 1992. (35 refs.)

31. Cotton NS. The familial incidence of alcoholism: Review. *Journal of Studies on Alcohol* 40(1): 89-116, 1979. (84 refs.)

32. Davidson RJ; Fox NA. Frontal brain asymmetry predicts infants' response to maternal separation. *Journal of Abnormal Psychology* 98(May): 127-131, 1989.

33. Devine C; Braithwaite V. The survival roles of children of alcoholics: Their measurement and validity. *Addiction* 8(1): 69-78, 1993. (33 refs.)

34. DiCicco L. Children of alcoholic parents: Issues in identification. IN: Matlins SM; Walker WW; Waite BJ, eds. *Services for Children of Alcoholics. NIAAA Research Monograph 4.* Rockville MD: National Institute on Alcohol Abuse and Alcoholism, 1981. pp. 44-59. (21 refs.)

35. Dishion TJ; Patterson GR; Reid JR. Parent and peer factors associated with drug sampling in early adolescence: Implications for treatment. IN: Rahdert ER; Grabowski J, eds. *Adolescent Drug Abuse: Analyses of Treatment Research. NIDA Research Monograph 77.* Rockville MD: National Institute on Drug Abuse, 1988. pp. 69-93. (47 refs.)

36. Dishion TJ; Reid JB; Patterson GR. Empirical guidelines for a family intervention for adolescent drug use. *Journal of Chemical Dependency Treatment* 1: 189-224, 1988.

37. Domenico D; Windle M. Intrapersonal and interpersonal functioning among middle-aged female adult children of alcoholics. *Journal of Consulting and Clinical Psychology* 61, 659-666, 1993.

38. Dunn NJ; Jacob T; Hummon N; Seilhamer RA. Marital stability in alcoholic-spouse relationships as a function of drinking pattern and location. *Journal of Abnormal Psychology* 96(2): 99-107, 1987.

39. El-Guebaly N; Offord DR. The offspring of alcoholics: A critical review. *American Journal of Psychiatry* 134: 357-365, 1977.

40. El-Guebaly N; West M; Maticka-Tyndale E; Pool M. Attachment among adult children of alcoholics. *Addiction* 88(10): 1405-1411, 1993. (29 refs.)

41. Emshoff JG. A preventive intervention with children of alcoholics. *Prevention in Human Services* 7(1): 225-253, 1989.

42. Fairburn CG; Jones R; Peveler RC; Hope RA; O'Connor M. Psychotherapy and bulimia nervosa: Longer-term effects of interpersonal psychotherapy, behavior therapy, and cognitive behavior therapy. *Archives of General Psychiatry* 50(6): 419-428, 1993.

43. Ferstein ME; Whiston SC. Utilizing RET for effective treatment of adult children of alcoholics. *Journal of Rational Emotive and Cognitive Behavior Therapy* 9(1): 39-49, 1991.

44. Fiese BH. Family rituals in alcoholic and nonalcoholic households: Relations to adolescent health symptomatology and problem drinking. *Family Relations* 42(2): 187-192, 1993. (41 refs.)

45. Finn PR; Kessler DN; Hussong AM. Risk for alcoholism and classical conditioning to signals for punishment: Evidence for a weak behavioral inhibition system. *Journal of Abnormal Psychology* 103(2): 293-301, 1994. (53 refs.)

46. Fischer JL; Wampler R; Lyness K; Thomas EM. Offspring codependency: Blocking the impact of the family of origin. *Family Dynamics of Addiction Quarterly* 2(1): 20-32, 1994.

47. Gabrielli WF; Mednick SA; et al. Electroencephalograms in children of alcoholic fathers. *Psychophysiology* 191(4): 404-407, 1982. (26 refs.)

48. Garland MA; Parsons OA; Nixon SJ. Visual-spatial learning in nonalcoholic young adults with and those without a family history of alcoholism. *Journal of Studies on Alcohol* 54(2): 219-224, 1993. (27 refs.)

49. Goldman BM; Rossland S. Young children of alcoholics: A group treatment model. *Social Work in Health Care* 16(3): 53-65, 1992. (34 refs.)

50. Gotham HJ; Sher KJ; Raskin G. Do co-dependent traits involve more than basic dimensions of personality and psychopathology? *Journal of Studies on Alcohol* (in press).

51. Hamilton CJ; Collins JJ Jr. The role of alcohol in wife beating and child abuse: A review of the literature. IN: Collins JJ, ed. *Drinking and Crime: Perspectives on the Relationship between Alcohol Consumption and Criminal Behavior.* New York: The Guilford Press, 1985. pp. 253-287.

52. Harburg E; Davis DR; Caplan R. Parent and offspring alcohol use: Imitative and aversive transmission. *Journal of Studies on Alcohol* 43(5): 497-516, 1982. (29 refs.)

53. Hare RD. *Psychopathy: Theory and Research.* New York: John Wiley & Sons, 1970.

54. Harford TC; Parker DA. Antisocial behavior, family history, and alcohol dependence symptoms. *Alcoholism: Clinical and Experimental Research* 18(2): 265-268, 1994. (24 refs.)

55. Havey JM; Dodd DK. Environmental and personality differences between children of alcoholics and their peers. *Journal of Drug Education* 22(3): 215-222, 1992. (19 refs.)

56. Helzer JE; Pryzbeck TR. The co-occurrence of alcoholism with other psychiatric disorders in the general population and its impact on treatment. *Journal of Studies on Alcohol* 49(3): 219-224, 1988. (14 refs.)

57. Hill SY; Hruska DR. Childhood psychopathology in families with multigenerational alcoholism. *Journal of the American Academy of Child and Adolescent Psychiatry* 31(6): 1024-1030, 1992. (43 refs.)

58. Hinson RC; Becker LS; Handal PJ; Katz BM. The heterogeneity of children of alcoholics: Emotional needs and help-seeking propensity. *Journal of College Student Development* 34(1): 47-52, 1993.

59. Holden MG; Brown SA; Mott MA. Social support network of adolescents: Relation to family alcohol abuse. *American Journal of Drug and Alcohol Abuse* 14(4): 487-498, 1988. (33 refs.)

60. Hyphantis T; Koutras V; Liakos A; Marselos M. Alcohol and drug use, family situation and school performance in adolescent children of alcoholics. *International Journal of Social Psychiatry* 37(1): 35-42, 1991. (22 refs.)

61. Institute of Medicine. *Broadening the Base of Treatment for Alcohol Problems: Report of a Study by a Committee of the Institute of Medicine Division of Mental Health and Behavioral Medicine.* Washington DC: National Academy Press, 1990.

62. Jacob T; Dunn NJ; Leonard K. Patterns of alcohol-abuse and family stability. *Alcoholism: Clinical and Experimental Research* 7(4): 382-385, 1983. (29 refs.)

63. Jacob T; Leonard K. Psychosocial functioning in children of alcoholic fathers, depressed fathers and control fathers. *Journal of Studies on Alcohol* 47(5): 373-380, 1986. (25 refs.)

64. Jacob T; Leonard K. Alcohol-spouse interaction as a function of alcoholism subtype and alcohol consumption interaction. *Journal of Abnormal Psychology* 97(2): 231-237, 1988.

65. Jacob T; Seilhamer RA. Alcoholism and family interaction. IN: Jacob T, ed. *Family Interaction and Psychopathology: Theories, Methods, and Findings.* New York: Plenum Press, 1987. pp. 535-580.

66. Johnson JL; Rolf JE. When children change: Research perspectives on children of alcoholics. IN: Collins RL; Leonard KE; Searles JS, eds. *Alcohol and the Family: Research and Clinical Perspectives.* New York: The Guilford Press, 1990. pp. 162-193. (120 refs.)

67. Johnson JL; Sher KJ; Rolf JE. Models of vulnerability to psychopathology in children of alcoholics. *Alcohol Health and Research World* 15(1): 33-42, 1991. (96 refs.)

68. Johnson S; Leonard KE; Jacob T. Drinking, drinking styles and drug use in children of alcoholics, depressives, and controls. *Journal of Studies on Alcohol* 50(5): 427-431, 1989. (28 refs.)

69. Kaplan RF; Hesselbrock VM; O'Connor S; DePalma N. Behavioral and EEG responses to alcohol in nonalcoholic men with a family history of alcoholism. *Progress in Neuro-Psychopharmacology & Biological Psychiatry* 12(6): 873-885, 1988. (22 refs.)

70. Keane TM; Foy D; Nunn B; Rychtarik RG. Spouse contracting to increase Antabuse compliance in alcoholic veterans. *Journal of Clinical Psychology* 40(1): 340-344, 1984.

71. Kendall-Tackett KA; Williams LM; Finkelhor D. Impact of sexual abuse on children: A review and synthesis of recent empirical studies. *Psychological Bulletin* 113(1): 164-180, 1993.

72. Kendler KS; Heath AC; Neale MC; Kessler RC; Eaves LJ. A population-based twin study of alcoholism in women. *Journal of the American Medical Association* 268(14): 1877-1882, 1992. (50 refs.)

73. Knop J; Teasdale TW; Schulsinger F; Goodwin DW. A prospective study of young men at high-risk for alcoholism: School behavior and achievement. *Journal of Studies on Alcohol* 46(4): 273-278, 1985. (28 refs.)

74. Kupfersmid J. Treatment of nocturnal enuresis: A status report. *The Psychiatric Forum* 14(2): 37-46, 1989.

75. Leifer M; Shapiro JP; Kassem L. The impact of maternal history and behavior upon foster placement and adjustment in sexually abused girls. *Child Abuse and Neglect* 17(6): 755-766, 1993. (48 refs.)

76. Leonard KE; Jacob T. Alcohol, alcoholism, and family violence. IN: VanHasselt VB; Morrison RL; Bellack AS; Herson M, eds. *Handbook of Family Violence.* New York: Plenum Press, 1990. pp. 383-406.

77. McBride JL. Assessing the Al-Anon component of Alcoholics Anonymous. *Alcoholism Treatment Quarterly* 8(4): 57-65, 1991. (16 refs.)

78. McCord J. Identifying developmental paradigms leading to alcoholism. IN: Pittman DJ; White HR, eds. *Society, Culture, and Drinking Patterns Reexamined.* New Brunswick NJ: Rutgers Center of Alcohol Studies, 1991. pp. 480-491. (27 refs.)

79. McCrady BS; Noel NE; Abrams DB; Stout RL; Nelson HF; Hay WM. Comparative effectiveness of three types of spouse involvement in outpatient behavioral alcoholism treatment. *Journal of Studies on Alcohol* 47(6): 459-467, 1986. (33 refs.)

80. McGue M. Genes, environment, and the etiology of alcoholism. IN: Zucker R; Boyd G; Howard J, eds. *The Development of Alcohol Problems: Exploring the Biopsychosocial Matrix of Risk. NIAAA Research Monograph 26.* Rockville MD: National Institute on Alcohol Abuse and Alcoholism, 1994. pp. 1-40. (15 refs.)

81. McGue M; Pickens RW; Svikis DS. Sex and age effects on the inheritance of alcohol problems: A twin study. *Journal of Abnormal Psychology* 101(1): 3-17, 1992. (61 refs.)

82. Manning DT. Books as therapy for children of alcoholics. *Child Welfare* 66(1): 35-43, 1987. (43 refs.)

83. Mathew RJ; Wilson WH; Blazer DG; George LK. Psychiatric disorders in adult children of alcoholics: Data from the Epidemiologic Catchment Area project. *American Journal of Psychiatry* 150(5): 793-800, 1993. (53 refs.)

84. Mattick RP; Andrews G; Hadzi-Pavlovic; Christensen H. Treatment of panic and agoraphobia: An integrative review. *Journal of Nervous and Mental Disease* 178(9): 567-576, 1990.

85. Merikangas KR. The genetic epidemiology of alcoholism. (editorial). *Psychological Medicine* 20(1): 11-22, 1990. (80 refs.)

86. Merikangas KR; Leckman JF; Prusoff BA; Pauls DL; Weissman MM. Familial transmission of depression and alcoholism. *Archives of General Psychiatry* 42(4): 367-372, 1985. (27 refs.)

87. Michaels ML; Roosa MW; Gensheimer LK. Family characteristics of children who self-select into a prevention program for children of alcoholics. *American Journal of Community Psychology* 20(5): 663-672, 1992. (30 refs.)

88. Miller BA. The interrelationships between alcohol and drugs and family violence. IN: De La Rosa M; Lambert EY; Gropper B, eds. *Drugs and Violence: Causes, Correlates, and Consequences. NIDA Research Monograph 103.* Rockville MD: National Institute on Drug Abuse, 1990. pp. 177-207. (91 refs.)

89. Miller D; Jang M. Children of alcoholics: A 20-year longitudinal study. *Social Work Research & Abstracts* 13(4): 23-29, 1977. (5 refs.)

90. Moos RH; Billings AG. Children of alcoholics during the recovery process: Alcoholic and matched control families. *Addictive Behaviors* 7(2): 155-163, 1982. (21 refs.)

91. Moos RH; Moos BS. The process of recovery from alcoholism: III. Comparing functioning in families of alcoholics and matched control families. *Journal of Studies on Alcohol* 45(2): 111-118, 1984. (32 refs.)

92. Morehouse ER. Working with children of alcoholic parents in an outpatient alcoholism treatment facility and in the schools. IN: Matlins SM; Walker WW; Waite BJ, eds. *Services for Children of Alcoholics. NIDA Monograph 4.* Rockville MD: National Institute on Alcohol Abuse and Alcoholism, 1981. pp. 138-145.

93. Morey LC; Skinner HA; Balshfield RK. A typology of alcohol abusers: Correlates and implications. *Journal of Abnormal Psychology* 93(4): 408-417, 1984. (44 refs.)

94. Nastasi BK; DeZolt DM. *School Interventions for Children of Alcoholics.* New York: The Guilford Press, 1994. (307 refs.)

95. National Institute on Alcohol Abuse and Alcoholism. Children of alcoholics: Are they different? *Alcohol Alert* 9: 1-4, 1990.

96. Newlin DB; Thomson JB. Alcohol challenge with sons of alcoholics: A critical review and analysis. (review). *Psychological Bulletin* 108(3): 383-402, 1990. (96 refs.)

97. Noll RB; Zucker RA; Fitzgerald HE; Curtis WJ. Cognitive and motoric functioning of sons of alcoholic fathers and controls: The early childhood years. *Developmental Psychology* 28(4): 665-675, 1992. (91 refs.)

98. O'Brien PE; Gaborit M. Codependency: A disorder separate from chemical dependency. *Journal of Clinical Psychology* 48(1): 129-136, 1992. (34 refs.)

99. O'Conner MJ; Sigman M; Brill N. Disorganization of attachment in relation to maternal alcohol consumption. *Journal of Consulting and Clinical Psychology* 55(6): 831-836, 1987. (33 refs.)

100. O'Farrell TJ. Marital and family therapy in alcoholism treatment. *Journal of Substance Abuse Treatment* 6(1): 23-29, 1989. (42 refs.)

101. O'Farrell TJ. Families and alcohol problems: An overview of treatment research. *Journal of Family Psychology* 5: 339-359, 1992.

102. O'Farrell TJ; Cutter HSG. Behavioral marital therapy couples groups for male alcoholics and their wives. *Journal of Substance Abuse Treatment* 1(3): 191-204, 1984. (50 refs.)

103. Offord D; Allen M; Abrams M. Parental psychiatric illness. *Journal of the American Academy of Child and Adolescent Psychiatry* 17(2): 224-238, 1978.

104. Ohannessian CM; Hesselbrock VM. The influence of perceived social support on the relationship between family history of alcoholism and drinking behaviors. *Addiction* 88(12): 1651-1658, 1993. (27 refs.)

105. Pelham WE; Lang AR. Parental alcohol consumption and deviant child behavior: Laboratory studies of reciprocal effects. *Clinical Psychology Review* 13(8): 763-784, 1993. (98 refs.)

106. Peterson JB; Pihl RO; Seguin JR; Finn PR; Stewart SH. Heart-rate reactivity and alcohol consumption among sons of male alcoholics and sons of non-alcoholics. *Journal of Psychiatry & Neuroscience* 18(4): 190-198, 1993. (58 refs.)

107. Pihl RO; Peterson J; Finn P. Inherited predisposition to alcoholism: Characteristics of sons of male alcoholics. *Journal of Abnormal Psychology* 99(3): 291-301, 1991. (195 refs.)

108. Polich J; Pollock VE; Bloom FE. Meta-analysis of P300 amplitude from males at risk for alcoholism. (review). *Psychological Bulletin* 115(1): 55-73, 1994. (153 refs.)

109. Pollock VE; Schneide LS; Gabriell WF; Goodwin DW. Sex of parent and offspring in the transmission of alcoholism: A meta-analysis. (review). *Journal of Nervous and Mental Disease* 175(11): 668-673, 1987. (58 refs.)

110. Pollock VE; Volavka J; Goodwin DW; Mednick SA; Gabrielli WF; Knop J; et al. The EEG after alcohol administration in men at risk for alcoholism. *Archives of General Psychiatry* 40(8): 857-861, 1983. (28 refs.)

111. Potter AE; Williams DE. Development of a measure examining children's roles in alcoholic families. *Journal of Studies on Alcohol* 52(1): 70-77, 1991. (18 refs.)

112. Regier DA; Farmer ME; Rae DS; Locke BZ; Keith SJ; Judd LL; et al. Comorbidity of mental disorders with alcohol and other drug abuse: Results from the Epidemiologic Catchment Area (ECA) Study. *Journal of the American Medical Association* 264(19): 2511-2518, 1990. (55 refs.)

113. Reich W; Earls F; Frankel O; Shayka JJ. Psychopathology in children of alcoholics. *Journal of the American Academy of Child and Adolescent Psychiatry* 32(5): 995-1002, 1993. (42 refs.)

114. Rhodes J; Blackham GJ. Differences in character roles between adolescents from alcoholic and nonalcoholic homes. *American Journal of Drug and Alcohol Abuse* 13(1/2): 145-155, 1987.

115. Roberts MCF; Floyd FJ; O'Farrell TJ; Cutter HSG. Marital interactions and the duration of alcoholic husbands' sobriety. *American Journal of Drug and Alcohol Abuse* 11(3/4): 303-313, 1985. (24 refs.)

116. Roehling PV; DeYoung J; Bosker M; Schut LJ. Parental abuse as a mediator of codependence among alcoholics' offspring. Paper presented at the annual American Psychological Association convention, Toronto, August 1993.

117. Rogosch F; Chassin L; Sher KJ. Personality variables as mediators and moderators of family history risk for alcoholism: Conceptual and methodological issues. *Journal of Studies on Alcohol* 51(4): 310-318, 1990. (38 refs.)

118. Roosa MW; Beals J; Sandler IN; Pillow DR. The role of risk and protective factors in predicting symptomatology in adolescent self-identified children of alcoholic parents. *American Journal of Community Psychology* 18(5): 725-741, 1990. (40 refs.)

119. Roosa MW; Sandler IN; Beals J; Short JL. Risk status of adolescent children of problem drinking parents. *American Journal of Community Psychology* 16(2): 225-239, 1988. (39 refs.)

120. Roosa MW; Sandler IN; Gehring M; Beals J; Cappo L. The Children of Alcoholics Life-Events Schedule: A stress scale for children of alcohol-abusing parents. *Journal of Studies on Alcohol* 49(5): 422-429, 1988. (38 refs.)

121. Ross HE; Glaser FB; Germanson T. The prevalence of psychiatric disorders in patients with alcohol and other drug problems. *Archives of General Psychiatry* 45(11): 1023-1031, 1988. (41 refs.)

122. Roush KL; DeBlassie RR. Structured group counseling for college students of alcoholic parents. (technical note). *Journal of College Student Development* 30(3): 276-277, 1989. (6 refs.)

123. Russell M; Henderson C; Blume S. *Children of Alcoholics: A Review of the Literature.* New York: Children of Alcoholics Foundation, Inc, 1985. (498 refs.)

124. Rychtarik RG; Carstensen LL; Alford GS; Schlundt DG; Scott W. Situational assessment of alcohol-related coping skills in wives of alcoholics. *Psychology of Addictive Behaviors* 2(2): 66-73, 1988.

125. Salinas RC; O'Farrell TJ; Jones WC; Cutter HSG. Services for families of alcoholics: A national survey of Veterans Affairs treatment programs. *Journal of Studies on Alcohol* 52(6): 541-546, 1991. (13 refs.)

126. Schandler SL; Brannock JC; Cohen MJ; Mendez J. Spatial learning deficits in adolescent children of alcoholics. *Experimental and Clinical Psychopharmacology* 1: 207-214, 1993.

127. Schandler SL; Cohen MJ; McArthur DL; Antick JR; Brannock JC. Spatial learning deficits in adult children of alcoholic parents. *Journal of Consulting and Clinical Psychology* 59(2): 312-317, 1991. (38 refs.)

128. Schuckit MA. Low level of response to alcohol as a predictor of future alcoholism. *American Journal of Psychiatry* 151(2): 184-189, 1994. (48 refs.)

129. Seilhamer RA; Jacob T. Family factors and adjustment of children of alcoholics. IN: Windle M; Searles JS, eds. *Children of Alcoholics: Critical Perspectives.* New York: The Guilford Press, 1990. pp. 168-186. (88 refs.)

130. Seilhamer RA; Jacob T; Dunn NJ. The impact of alcohol consumption on parent-child relationships in families of alcoholics. *Journal of Studies on Alcohol* 54(2): 189-198, 1993. (46 refs.)

131. Sher KJ. *Children of Alcoholics: A Critical Appraisal of Theory and Research.* Chicago: University of Chicago Press, 1991. (615 refs.)

132. Sher KJ; Walitzer KS; Wood PK; Brent EE. Characteristics of children of alcoholics: Putative risk factors, substance use and abuse, and psychopathology. *Journal of Abnormal Psychology* 100(4): 427-448, 1991.

133. Sisson RW; Azrin NH. Family member involvement to initiate and promote treatment of problem drinkers. *Journal of Behavior Therapy and Experimental Psychiatry* 17(1): 15-21, 1986. (27 refs.)

134. Smith SS; Newman JP. Alcohol and drug abuse-dependence disorders in psychopathic and nonpsychopathic criminal offenders. *Journal of Abnormal Psychology* 99(November): 430-439, 1990.

135. Steinglass P; Bennett LA; Wolin SJ; Reiss D. *The Alcoholic Family.* New York: Basic Books, Inc, 1987. (Chapter refs.)

136. Steinglass P; Robertson A. The alcoholic family. IN: Kissin B; Begleiter H, eds. *The Biology of Alcoholism: Volume 6. The Pathogenesis of Alcoholism: Psychosocial Factors.* New York: Plenum Press, 1983.

137. Stratton PD; Penney A. High school and college student children of alcoholics: A pilot educational program and assessment of readiness for assistance. *Journal of Alcohol and Drug Education* 38(2): 100-112, 1993. (51 refs.)

138. Tarter RE; Hegedus AM; Goldstein G; Shelly C; Alterman A. Adolescent sons of alcoholics: Neuropsychological and personality characteristics. *Alcoholism: Clinical and Experimental Research* 8(2): 216-222, 1984. (44 refs.)

139. Tarter RE; Jacob T; Bremer DA. Cognitive status of sons of alcoholic men. *Alcoholism: Clinical and Experimental Research* 13(2): 232-235, 1989. (16 refs.)

140. Tarter RE; Kabene M; Escallier EA; Laird SB; Jacob T. Temperament deviation and risk for alcoholism. *Alcoholism: Clinical and Experimental Research* 14(3): 380-382, 1990. (22 refs.)

141. Tarter RE; Laird SB; Moss HB. Neuropsychological and neurophysiological characteristics of children of alcoholics. IN: Windle M; Searles JS, eds. *Children of Alcoholics: Critical Perspectives.* New York: The Guilford Press, 1990. pp. 73-98. (126 refs.)

142. Trama JA; Newman BM. A comparison of the impact of an alcohol education program with Al-Anon on knowledge and attitudes about alcoholism. *Journal of Alcohol and Drug Education* 34(1): 1-16, 1988. (23 refs.)

143. Trull TJ; Nietzel MT; Main A. The use of meta-analysis to assess the clinical significance of behavior therapy for agoraphobia. *Behavior Therapy* 19(4): 527-538, 1988.

144. Tubman JG. Family risk factors, parental alcohol use, and problem behaviors among school-age children. *Family Relations* 42(1): 81-86, 1993. (48 refs.)

145. Vannicelli M. *Group Psychotherapy with Adult Children of Alcoholics.* New York: The Guilford Press, 1989. (155 refs.)

146. Webb W. Cognitive behavior therapy with children of alcoholics. *School Counselor* 40(3): 170-177, 1993.

147. Wells KC; Egan J. Social learning and systems family therapy for childhood oppositional disorder: Comparative treatment outcome. *Comprehensive Psychiatry* 29(2): 138-146, 1988.

148. Welsh DM, ed. The primary care setting: Recognition and care of patients with alcohol problems. (topical issue). *Alcohol Health and Research World* 18(2): entire volume, 1994.

149. Werner EE. Resilient offspring of alcoholics: A longitudinal study from birth to age 18. *Journal of Studies on Alcohol* 47(1): 34-40, 1986. (19 refs.)

150. West MO; Prinz RJ. Parental alcoholism and childhood psychopathology. (review). *Psychological Bulletin* 102(2): 204-218, 1987. (106 refs.)

151. Williams CN. Prevention and treatment approaches for children of alcoholics. IN: Windle M; Searles JS, eds. *Children of Alcoholics: Critical Perspectives.* New York: The Guilford Press, 1990. pp. 187-216. (119 refs.)

152. Williams OB; Corrigan PW. The differential effects of parental alcoholism and mental illness on their adult children. *Journal of Clinical Psychology* 48(3): 406-414, 1992. (42 refs.)

153. Windle M. Temperament and personality attributes of children of alcoholics. IN: Windle M; Searles JS, eds. *Children of Alcoholics: Critical Perspectives*. New York: The Guilford Press, 1990. pp. 129-167. (129 refs.)

154. Windle M; Searles JS, eds. *Children of Alcoholics: Critical Perspectives*. New York: The Guilford Press, 1990. (Chapter refs.)

155. Winokur G; Reich T; Rimmer J; Pitts FN. Alcoholism: III. Diagnosis and familial illness in 259 alcoholic probands. *Archives of General Psychiatry* 23(2): 104-111, 1970.

156. Wolin SJ; Bennett LA; Noonan DL. Family rituals and the recurrence of alcoholism over generations. *American Journal of Psychiatry* 136(4B): 589-593, 1979.

157. Woodside M. Research on children of alcoholics: Past and future. *British Journal of Addiction* 83(7): 785-792, 1988. (38 refs.)

158. Yama MF; Fogas BS; Teegarden LA; Hastings B. Childhood sexual abuse and parental alcoholism: Interactive effects in adult women. *American Journal of Orthopsychiatry* 63(2): 300-305, 1993.

CHAPTER 18

Adolescents

STUART A. COPANS, MD
JEAN KINNEY, MSW

CLINICAL APPLICATIONS

The goals of this chapter are to assist the clinician to:

1. Recognize the developmental factors with implications for substance use and problems.
2. Be familiar with signs and symptoms of adolescent substance use.
3. Be familiar with the natural history of adolescent substance use.
4. Conduct an assessment of the adolescent and family members.
5. Be able to make a referral for treatment.

Adolescence is a special period, during which more physical and emotional changes occur than at any other time in life. While the onset of adolescence is defined by physical changes, the transition to adulthood is defined by changes in role. In America this consists of a series of increasing privileges associated with age—as in the right to vote, marry, purchase cigarettes or alcohol, or even be President. It also is defined by age along with specific training, as in the right to drive a car; or with specific legal events, as in being an emancipated minor or in being tried as an adult rather than as a juvenile for certain crimes. The physical changes that indicate the beginning of adolescence may appear as early as age 7 or as late as the mid- or late teens. The social changes that signal the end of adolescence and the onset of adulthood may occur as young as 14, with marriage, pregnancy, and emancipation, or may not occur until the mid-20's in the case of graduate or medical students who remain financially dependent on their parents until they graduate.

Health Issues

Although most adolescents are healthy, this is the age group in which mortality rates have increased most dramatically in recent decades.[3] Many adolescents engage in risky behaviors that can affect health. Unintentional injury, homicide, and suicide are the leading causes of death. As many as one in four adolescents are at risk for substance abuse problems, sexually transmitted diseases, unintended pregnancy, and school problems. Adolescents as a group encounter barriers to health care. Along with young adults, they are the group most likely to be uninsured or underinsured.

CHARACTERISTICS OF ADOLESCENCE

There are several distinctive and predictable characteristics of adolescence. While adolescence is typically a healthy time, the rapidity of physical changes tends to produce an almost physiological confusion for many adolescents. They commonly become self-preoccupied and overly concerned about their health, in some instances almost hypochondriacal. Adolescents' complaints may appear minor to adults. However, their concern is real and should not be ignored. Often physical complaints are a clue to emotional stresses that the adolescent may find it harder to talk about.

The three most common causes of deaths during adolescence are nonmedical—accidents, homicide, and suicide—which have been closely linked to alcohol and drug use. When adolescents present us with physical complaints that appear trivial, it is important to also check for signs of depression or for self-endangering or self-destructive behaviors.

A tremendous need to conform to their peers is another characteristic of adolescence. This is reflected in the desire to dress alike, wear the same hairstyle, listen to the same music, and even think alike. A perpetual concern for adolescents is being *different*. Being different is a particular concern for adolescents who may want or need professional help, in that adolescents will not seek help unless it is "peer acceptable." They often avoid professional care because of the fear that if they do go, something really wrong will be found, which would officially certify that they are different from their peers.

Fluctuating behavior is common in adolescence. It frequently alternates between agitation and acquiescence. Sometimes their thinking only makes sense to themselves and their friends. For example, not being selected for a role in a school play may "prove" to the adolescent that he or she will always be a failure. If use of the family car is denied for Friday, adolescents may overreact and even accuse their parents of never letting them have the car even as they stand with the keys, ready to drive off.

Adolescence is usually a continuing, yet uneven, move toward maturity. Most adolescents have periods when they are depressed and confused and believe they are going crazy, and think they are the only ones who have ever felt this way. Despite all that adolescents seem to share with one another, these thoughts and feelings frequently go unspoken. Combined with this developmental despair are psychological defenses that lead to feelings of omnipotence. Adolescents often practice massive denial, blame others, and rationalize themselves out of being responsible for their actions.

Another important point is that in early adolescence girls are developmentally more mature than boys. At the onset of puberty, girls are about 2 years ahead, physically. This creates a difference in social functioning because social and physical development coincide. This can cause problems in social interactions for boys and girls of the same age, because their ideas of what constitutes a good party or appropriate behavior may differ dramatically. Girls may consider their boy peers "dweebs." Hence boys, aware of these assessments, may be distressed, but girls feel displaced also. Therefore, because of this developmental difference, girls have an advantage in school. For example, girls may be a year ahead of boys in reading skills. Remember this disparity when dealing with younger adolescents.

Four Tasks of Adolescence

From a developmental perspective, the goal of adolescence is to accomplish four tasks. One task is acceptance of the biological role, which means adolescents become comfortable with their identities as either boys or girls. This is primarily an intellectual effort that has nothing to do with sexuality or experimentation with sex. A second task is the struggle to become comfortable with sexuality. The concept of being heterosexual—able to engage in social and eventually sexual activities with someone of the opposite sex—or of being homosexual does not come easily. Adolescence is a time of insecurity and considerable self-consciousness. Another task is choosing an occupational identity. It becomes important to find an answer to, "What am I going to do (be)?" Adolescents require some time to work this out, which can entail considerable indecision. The fourth task is the struggle toward independence. This entails real conflict, balancing both the internal push to break away from home and parents and the need to be cared for. This conflict appears as rebellion because it is difficult to feel independent while living at home and being cared for by parents. Rebellion of some type is so common during this period that adolescents who do not rebel in some fashion should be suspect.

Rebellion can be evident in style of dress and appearance. It is usually the opposite of what the parents' generation accepts. Being late from a date, buying something without permission, and arguing with parents are some ways that adolescents test their independence. Adolescents are aware of their dependence and often feel shame as a result. It is important that parents recognize the rebellion and respond to it. Some well-meaning parents accept almost any behavior from their teenagers. Often such teenagers will try anything to get their parents angry. Drinking with friends, drastically changing their hair, piercing their bodies, not cleaning their rooms, or helping the neighbors but not their parents are all common ways of testing and asserting independence. Rebellion can be destructive and most commonly occurs when the parents either do not recognize the rebellion or do not respond to it. It can take many forms such as running out of the house after an argument and driving off recklessly, getting really drunk, running away, or for girls, getting pregnant despite frequent warnings from their overprotective parents.

There are many hindrances to completion of the four basic tasks. One results from the social paradox that adolescents are physically ready for adult roles long before contemporary society allows it. Instead, our society dictates that young people stay adolescents throughout junior high school, high school, college, and, in some cases, graduate school. Another social paradox comes from mixed messages such as "Be heterosexual, get a date, get a job, and grow up" and conversely, "Be home on time, save money for college, and don't argue with me." The confusion of messages such as "Grow up, but stay under my control" can cause tension. In our society, messages about sex-

uality are particularly confusing, with violent conflicts in our society about same-sex behaviors, birth control, premarital sex, and abortions.

Parental Alcohol and Drug Use

Parental alcohol and drug use can be another hindrance. Some adolescents find it difficult to leave home until things are all right with their parents. Despite threats to leave home prematurely, adolescents of alcoholic families may stay and be dependent for many years.

Adolescents constitute the group most likely to be involved with drugs other than alcohol. Thus, it is imperative for parents to think broadly, in terms of substance use, abuse, and chemical dependency rather than just in terms of drinking and alcohol dependence.

As we have learned more about alcoholic family systems and have realized that we must focus not just on the effect of an alcoholic parent's behavior on their offspring but on the effects of the family as a whole on the adolescent's behavior and belief system, our understanding of the effects of parental substance abuse have broadened. Fossum and Mason's description of shame-bound belief systems can help us understand the variety of psychiatric and behavior problems of adolescents from substance-abusing families.[4] Steinglass's work on the phases of the substance abusing family can help us understand why it is often after a parent stops drinking that an adolescent will come to medical or psychiatric attention; and Riess's work on the role of ritual in the transmission and interruption of intergenerational substance abuse can help us understand the variations we see among substance-abusing adolescents.[10,12]

Destructive rebellion may occur more often in teenagers who have parents with alcohol or drug problems. In these cases, adolescents often wonder whether they share their parent's propensity to use alcohol or drugs excessively. These adolescents may try to prove to themselves that they can drink to intoxication Friday and not need to drink for the rest of the week. Thus, they hope to demonstrate that they can control alcohol or drugs better than their parents. Adolescents tend to live in the present. They rationalize that the ability to resist use every day predicts their future behavior, but they may also realize that this is not the case. Thus, they continue to test themselves with alcohol or drugs, buffering the healthy anxiety that would propel them into more mature behavior. These adolescents often miss the emotional and social opportunities that increase self-confidence, which is something all adolescents need.

The Emergence of Alcohol and Drug Use Patterns

Studies of alcohol use and drinking patterns of adolescents consistently show that by age 13 approximately 30% of boys and 22% of girls are drinkers. By 18, 92% of boys and 73% of girls drink alcohol. Sex differences are present in all age groups, but regardless of age, boys are more likely to drink than girls and tend to be heavier drinkers by the time they are 18. In respect to demographic characteristics, adolescent drinking reflects adult drinking patterns. Northeasterners are more likely to be drinkers than those from other areas of the country. In respect to religion, Catholics are least likely to be nondrinkers. Caucasians are more likely to be drinkers than members of other racial groups. The National Institute on Drug Abuse (NIDA), in reporting substance use trends, noted that sex differences appear to have narrowed, although drinking and heavy drinking continue to be disproportionately concentrated in men. The differences between geographical regions continue.[7]

Risk Factors and Protective Factors

Over a decade ago, 10 risk factors were identified for adolescent substance abuse: Poor parent/child relationships; low self-esteem; psychological disturbances such as depression; low academic motivation; other problem behaviors; absence of religion; high experience-seeking behavior; high family and peer substance use; and early cigarette use. Two separate studies have demonstrated that the risk of alcohol/substance abuse increased in proportion to the number of risk factors present, with a 100% risk with five factors.[5]

Other factors also influence adolescent substance use. Family constitution is one. Adolescents from single parent or stepparent families have a higher prevalence of alcohol use than those with intact families when parental use and parental education levels are controlled. The level of adolescent alcohol use also appears to be related to the number of stressful events experienced by the family.[1] Finally, it is recognized that a general pattern of health-compromising behavior, e.g., failing to exercise and use seat belts, and smoking cigarettes, is associated with adolescent substance use.[5]

ADOLESCENT ALCOHOL AND DRUG USE PROBLEMS
Dimension of Problems

Approximately three-fourths of the more than 40,000 deaths each year in persons aged 10 to 24 years in the US are related to preventable causes such as motor vehicle crashes (37%), homicide (14%), suicide (12%), and other injuries, e.g., drowning, poisoning, or being burned (12%).[2] To a significant extent, these causes of death are alcohol or other drug related.

- In the 13- to 17-year age group, it is estimated that there are 3 million problem drinkers and over 300,000 teenagers dependent on alcohol.[6,11]

- Drinking is a significant problem for 10% to 20% of adolescents.[7]
- Of adolescent cases in a pediatric trauma center, 34% involved alcohol or other drug use.[8]
- 97% of adolescents who abuse drugs also use alcohol.[11]
- Over the last 20 years, life expectancy has increased for all age groups except for ages 15 to 24. The three leading causes of death in this age group are accidents, suicide, and homicide, all closely linked to alcohol and drug use.[7]
- Drivers aged 16 to 24 constitute 17% of the population, yet they are involved in 48% of fatal accidents.[7]
- Daily, 14 adolescents aged 15 to 19 die, and 360 are injured in alcohol-related traffic accidents.[8]
- Of adolescents admitted for substance abuse treatment, 96% are polysubstance abusers.[9]
- In 1992 more than half of high school seniors used alcohol in the previous month; 28% reported binge drinking; and less than half felt there was great risk in consuming five or more drinks at least once during a weekend.[9,11]

One way to understand the prevalence of substance abuse problems in adolescence is through the framework of the adolescent developmental tasks cited earlier. The transition to adulthood is difficult for most adolescents. In contemporary American society, knowing when you are an adult is often difficult to determine. For many adolescents, drinking and drug use is a rite of passage. It is not only an adult activity, but one way to be accepted by peers. It can offer entry to a particular group of peers. Even adults often encourage other adults to drink and imply that not drinking is antisocial. For adolescents, with their conformist ideals and increased vulnerability to peer pressure, not drinking at a party where others are drinking is often harder for them than for adults.

Learning to be intimate with someone of the opposite sex can be threatening to many adolescents. Alcohol can be used to avoid intimacy or to seek intimacy without responsibility. "I wasn't myself last night; I was really plastered" is something boys or girls will say to disavow what happened the night before. Sexual experimentation can be excused during intoxication. In our society, being drunk has long provided a "way out" or an excuse. Often people are not held accountable for actions that occur when they are intoxicated. Thus, getting drunk can often help adolescents express these increasingly powerful impulses without taking direct responsibility for their behavior.

To attain independence is to learn to set limits for yourself and develop self-control, which is more difficult for some adolescents than for others. It is particularly difficult concerning issues such as drinking when societal messages and alcohol advertising suggest that having more than one drink is appropriate adult behavior. In the process of learning self-control, adolescents react negatively to adults setting limits for them. If parents are too aggressive in forbidding alcohol use, it may backfire. Adolescent development is characterized by changes in thinking patterns. Before age 13, adolescents generally adhere to concrete rules for behavior. From ages 13 to 15, adolescents are likely to question the justification of set rules. They feel that conventions are arbitrary, thus rules supporting them are invalid. By age 16, most of them begin to realize that some rules are necessary.

The development of identity is another important task that involves experimentation. Adolescents may use alcohol to experiment with different roles and identities. Risk taking is closely connected to experimentation, and some risk taking involves physical danger, which explains why adolescents are labeled as having a sense of invulnerability. Unfortunately, alcohol can further increase this sense of invulnerability and lead to risk taking with dangerous consequences. It is not surprising that accidents are the leading cause of death in adolescents and that alcohol use and abuse is heavily implicated in fatal accidents from all causes.

As adolescents accomplish these developmental tasks, the number of problem drinkers decreases, but for a significant proportion of problem drinkers, these problems will persist and worsen. However, for many, problem drinking may end in death or disability long before either outcome.

CLINICAL MANAGEMENT OF ADOLESCENT ALCOHOL/SUBSTANCE ABUSE

In dealing with adolescents, apply the same clinical tasks as with older patients. Guidelines for interviewing adolescents are set forth in Box 18-1.

Signs of Adolescent Substance Use Problems

The following behaviors are often warning signs of problems related to alcohol or substance use, although they are not linked exclusively to alcohol or drug use problems. If an initial evaluation rules out substance use, further evaluation is indicated to identify and address the behaviors of concern, whatever the origin.

School activities
- Drop in school performance.
- Irregular school attendance.
- Unexplained drop in grades.

Health indicators
- Feelings of loneliness, paranoia, and depression.
- Frequent accidents.
- Frequent "flu" episodes, chronic cough, chest pains, and "allergy" symptoms.
- Impaired ability to fight off common infections, fatigue, and loss of vitality.
- Impaired short-term memory.
- Inexplicable mood changes, e.g., irritability, hostility.
- Change in health or grooming.

Family relationships
- Decreased interest in school or family social activities, sports, and hobbies.
- Failure to provide specific answers to questions about activities.
- Not bringing friends home.
- Not returning home after school.
- Personal time that is unaccounted for.
- Strange phone calls.
- Unexplained disappearance of possessions in the home.
- Verbal (or physical) mistreatment of younger siblings.
- Desire to be secretive or isolated.
- Increased money or poor justification of how money was spent.

Relationships with peers
- Dropping old friends.
- New group of friends.
- Attending parties where parents are not home to monitor behavior.

Personal issues
- Change in personal priorities.
- Collecting beer cans or drug paraphernalia.
- Possession of "drug" materials.
- Wearing clothing or jewelry symbolic of the drug culture.

NATURAL HISTORY OF SUBSTANCE USE PROBLEMS

Adolescent substance use can be regarded as occurring along a spectrum. The four categories are experimentation; regular, although largely nonproblematic use; abuse; and dependence. The stages of adolescent substance abuse are described in Table 18-1, and are consistent with the Johnson model for the progression of alcohol use to alcohol dependence experimentation, seeking the mood swing, preoccupation with the mood swing, and use of drugs to feel normal.

In the assessment of adolescent substance use, the signs and symptoms will vary with the level of use, the degree of preoccupation with use, and how central use is to the adolescent's life. In assessing the effects, consider the impact of use in respect to relationships with peers, school activities, the family, and self.

Box 18-1

Interviewing Guidelines

The Setting

This part of an interview with an adolescent patient should be held in a private setting without parents. It is helpful to have related pamphlets prominently displayed and multiple copies to give away. Pamphlets should include information about alcohol and drug use and other health-related risk-taking behaviors. The setting for the interview should have age-appropriate decor.

Confidentiality

____ Reassure the patient that your discussion is confidential and that you will not disclose the details of your conversation with parents without the patient's permission unless a serious health risk exists.

Assessing Risk

____ Family relationships: Relationship with parents and siblings.

____ School performance: Academic performance, attendance, relationship with teachers, and personal goals.

____ Leisure activities: "What are some of the things you like to do when you're not in school?"

____ Self-esteem: "Describe yourself. What are your strengths?"

____ Other health risk behaviors (e.g., sexual activity and cigarette smoking).

Bringing Up the Topic of Drugs and Alcohol

____ Nonjudgmental: Introduce the topic of drug and alcohol use in a nonjudgmental way: "I know a lot of kids your age use drugs and alcohol."

____ Health context: Introduce the topic of substance use in the context of concern for the patient's health. "I'd like to know a little about what you do in this regard because it's important to your health."

Screening for Substance Use (RAFFT)

____ "Do you drink or use drugs to **RELAX**, feel better about yourself, or to fit in?"

____ "Do you ever drink alcohol or use drugs when you are **ALONE**?"

____ "Do you or any of your closest **FRIENDS** drink or use drugs?"

____ "Does a close **FAMILY** member have a problem with alcohol or drug use?"

____ "Have you ever gotten into **TROUBLE** from drinking or drug use (e.g., skipping school, bad grades, or trouble with the law or parents)?"

For Identified Substance Use Problems, Assess Problem Severity

____ Drinking frequency: "Do you drink regularly?" How often: Every day? Once or twice a week?" Get specifics.

____ Drinking quantity: "How much did you drink the last time you got drunk? How much do you usually drink? Do you ever drink specifically to pass out?"

____ Drug use frequency: "About how often do you use drugs? Every day? Once or twice a week?" Get specifics.

____ Context: "Where do you drink/take drugs? Parties only? With friends in cars? Home? School? By yourself, at home or in school?"

____ Dependence: "Do your social activities always involve alcohol/drugs? What would happen if you couldn't have any alcohol/drugs?"

____ Social consequences: "What kind of trouble have you gotten into because of alcohol/drugs? Do your parents suspect that you drink or take drugs?"

For Identified Substance Use Problems, Negotiate Follow-Up

____ Allow the patient to describe his/her understanding of his/her alcohol and drug use. "How would you describe your alcohol or drug use? Do you think it has become a problem for you or dangerous to your health?"

Continued.

Box 18-1

Interviewing Guidelines—cont'd

For Identified Substance Use Problems, Negotiate Follow-Up—cont'd

___ State clearly that the patient has a problem with substance use. Provide concrete, health-related and psychosocial evidence.

___ Stress the importance of working with the patient's parents to address the substance use problem. "I'd like to have your permission to talk to your parents about this. It's important that we involve them because, for us to provide the best treatment for your problem, we will need their support."

___ Negotiate for a follow-up appointment, ideally with parents present.

___ Assume responsibility for acting as intermediary between the patient and his/her parents: "At one of our next visits I can meet with you and your parents and explain this to your parents in a way that they can understand. Then we can all work together to help you."

___ Solicit the patient's verbal agreement to involve parents.

___ Solicit the patient's verbal agreement to come for a follow-up.

___ Schedule a follow-up appointment.

For Those Who Have Never Used Alcohol or Drugs, Prevention/Anticipatory Guidance

___ Assess exposure: "Have you ever been tempted to try alcohol or drugs because of your friends?"

___ Intentions and attitudes: "If your friends offered you alcohol or drugs, would you try them? Why or why not?"

___ Express concern about health problems related to alcohol and drug use.

___ Allow the patient to describe his or her understanding of the problems of alcohol and drug use.

___ Correct misunderstandings.

___ Provide valid factual information about alcohol and drug use. Offer pamphlets.

___ Reinforce positive attitudes expressed by the patient regarding avoidance of alcohol and drug use.

___ Suggest strategies for avoiding alcohol or drugs.

Modified from Project ADEPT, Brown University Center for Alcohol and Addiction Studies, Providence RI, 1990.

As a general rule, consider any drug use that affects school activities or performance in school to be indicative of a serious problem.

GENERAL CONSIDERATIONS IN WORKING WITH ADOLESCENTS

In working with adolescents, avoid obvious authority symbols such as white coats, numerous and framed diplomas, and a remote clinical attitude. The adolescent may already have some difficulty with authority figures. Informal dress and setting can remove one barrier. On the other hand, a clinician with spiked hair who plays rock music will not be appreciated either. Adolescents want you to know about those things but not be involved in them. An attempt to deceive the adolescent will fail. They are a hard group to fool, and they expect honesty. Respect them and be yourself. This means asking for a translation of their vocabulary if you are not familiar with the lingo. The clinician should be more empathetic than sympathetic. This is true of all therapeutic relationships. Sympathy is feeling as another person does. Empathy is knowing and understanding how a person feels but not having the same feelings at the time. For example, it is not helpful for the clinician to be depressed with the person seeking help.

Generally, there are three types of therapy for adolescents. One involves manipulation of the environment, which can include arranging for the father to spend more time with his child, obtaining a different school program for the child unhappy in the present one, or organizing temporary placement for the child whose parents are unavailable to them at the time. Standard insight therapy—psychological, psychodynamically oriented, traditional therapy—is not often used. Not many adolescents are ready for or could even benefit from this kind of therapy. Those who can benefit from it tend to be bright, advantaged young people who seem more capable and older than their chronological ages.

Commonly the most productive therapy is a relational approach. This requires time for the clinician and adolescent to become well acquainted and for the adolescent to feel comfortable. The clinician is a supportive, neutral person who is available to the adolescent in a different way than parents or peers.

Table 18-1. Natural History of Substance Use Problems: Signs and Symptoms of Adolescent Substance Use

Stage	Pattern of use	School	Peers	Family	Self
Experimentation	Occasional		← Few effects →		
Regular use					
(Seeking the mood swing)	Weekends Occasional weekdays	Grades may become erratic	Hanging around drug-using crowd	Some increase in family conflict	Changes in dress and choice of music; may be increased mood swings
Abuse					
(Preoccupation with use)	Occasional weekdays (e.g., before or after school)	Decreased school performance	Avoids straight friends	Verbal and physical fights	Depression, stealing, fabrication, and misperception of events
Dependence					
(Use to feel normal or as a requisite for functioning)	Daily, instead of usual activities	May drop out or be expelled	Alienation from original friends; antisocial behavior, sexual acting out	Increased shame and conflict	Guilt, remorse, depression, anger, paranoia, physical deterioration

Modified from Kinney J; Alcohol use and its medical consequences. In *Alcohol Use, Abuse, and Dependence.* Timonium MD: Milner-Fenwick, 1989.

The issue of confidentiality is always mentioned. It can be a mistake for the clinician to guarantee that nothing said will ever be repeated. The therapist is responsible for the safety of others as well as the adolescent patient. Pediatrician and child psychiatrist Dr. Hugh MacNamee told everyone he treated that although most of what they said would be confidential, if they told him anything that would cause harm to themselves or others, he would "blow the whistle." He made it clear that he would not do so without first telling them, but nonetheless, he would do it. From his experience, adolescents accept this stipulation, maybe even with relief. It may help to know that someone else is going to exert some control, especially if they are unsure about their own capabilities at the time.

MacNamee suggested keeping the adolescent informed about any contacts with others about him or her. If a parent calls, start off the next session by telling the adolescent about the telephone call. If a letter needs to be written to a school, probation officer, or someone else, share what you have written with the adolescent. It is probable that what he or she imagines you might say is worse than anything you would say, regardless of the problem. Because trust is such an issue with adolescents, it is important that you tell them what you would say about them to others.

Although this is a good approach to the issue of confidentiality, the clinician needs to be aware of other complicating factors, including the legal issues of a child's right to care vs. a parent's right to be informed. There may be circumstances in which an adolescent has a legal right to be treated without parental knowledge or consent. In any case, the rules you follow must be clear to the adolescent patient.

ALCOHOL AND DRUG USE ASSESSMENT

It is important to take a family history and ask about alcohol or drug problems and prescription or nonprescription drug use. Include grandparents, uncles, aunts, brothers, sisters, cousins, and parents. Ask the adolescent how he or she spends free time and to describe a typical day. Ask about a typical weekend night. Ask about his or her peer group, their ages, activities, and drug and alcohol use. Ask how they are regarded and described by other high school groups, and then ask about his or her own drug and alcohol use. Ask about parental relationship, sleep, appetite, and depression.

Undiagnosed adolescent alcohol abuse for as long as 6 years is caused by adolescents' ability to hide their problems, parents' failure to recognize their children's problems, and school systems' choice to ignore or expel problem children. It is not unusual for parents to actively protect, rescue, and take care of an adolescent who abuses alcohol and/or drugs without realizing that this supports and prolongs the abuse. Such parents pay for forged checks, hire lawyers to get legal charges dropped, intervene for their children at school, or blame school authorities for problems.

When asking about drug and alcohol use, ask about the first time the adolescent was drunk, how much the adolescent drinks now, how often, and if he or she has ever tried to stop or cut down. Ask about blackouts and school and legal problems. Finally, do not assume that an adolescent is providing a completely accurate history. Denial is a common characteristic of adolescent alcohol or drug abuse. It is important to obtain information from parents and teachers about an adolescent's alcohol or drug problems.

CONSULTATION AND TREATMENT REFERRALS

Although adolescents will occasionally request treatment, more often they come under some duress. It is important for clinicians to stress that their task is to help them and that they are not agents of their parents, the law, or the school system. However, part of helping them may involve intervention, which involves confrontation. Thus, total confidentiality cannot be assured.

The importance of working with the family cannot be overemphasized. The parents need to deal with their child's alcohol/substance abuse, and they must consider efforts that may have protected, hidden, or excused the problem. When it is clear that there is a significant problem and that all efforts to involve the adolescent into treatment have failed, the parents may need to seek legal help. Most states allow for parents to request state assistance if they feel they cannot enforce safe limits for their children. Although this is a drastic and difficult step, it can be important when adolescents who abuse alcohol or drugs act in ways that endanger themselves or others. Parental participation in Al-Anon has been shown to correlate with adolescent recovery.

Probation can also be a way to mandate treatment for adolescents, but it only works if parents stop protecting them from the consequences of their behavior.

COMMENTS ON TREATMENT

Once it has been determined that an adolescent needs treatment and he or she has agreed to it, it is important to proceed carefully. Because medical and psychiatric complications frequently accompany adolescent substance abuse, a thorough medical and psychiatric evaluation should precede or be an early part of any treatment plan. Treatment options include out-

patient, residential, or hospital-based care and can involve individual, group, and family counseling, plus self-help groups such as AA or NA. Halfway houses or group homes may also be helpful for adolescents who are not ready to return home from a hospital-based program but who no longer need the structure of a hospital.

Some good alcohol/drug treatment programs exist for adolescents, but some are less concerned with therapeutics than with making profits. Do not forget to consider these questions before referring an adolescent to any program:

- Does the program work?
- Is the program drug free?
- Is there a strong family component?
- Is there a strong therapeutic component?
- Is there a strong educational component?
- Is the adolescent involved in treatment planning?
- Is there a peer component?
- Are there provisions for aftercare?
- What are the costs and risks of treatment, including financial and time costs?
- What beliefs are instilled?
- What are the staff's credentials, including training, experience, licensure, and certification?
- Is there a full range of services, including pediatric, psychiatric, educational, psychological, and substance abuse therapists?
- Is there involvement with AA?
- How do the program's staff regard visitors?
- Is the program internally evaluated?
- Is the program accredited? If so, by whom?

When referring an adolescent for treatment, it is important to remember that psychoactive substance dependence is a chronic disease, and that treatment does not end with discharge. The conceptual model to use is not that of an acute illness such as appendicitis, for which an appendectomy will end the problem. It is a chronic illness like asthma or arthritis; ongoing monitoring is always essential. Some cases are mild and only require outpatient treatment, but others may require hospitalization.

INVOLVEMENT IN SELF-HELP GROUPS

How might AA be useful for adolescents with alcohol/substance problems? How would adolescents be able to identify with a group of 35- to 55-year-olds? In some locales there are now young people's groups where the average age is the low to mid-20s. Even if there are no young people's groups in your vicinity, age should not be a barrier to adolescents joining AA. On the contrary, several features of AA might appeal to them. This group of adults will definitely not preach to them. Furthermore, given the collective life experiences within AA, the members are not likely to be shocked, outraged, or impressed by any adolescent's behavior. The members will treat adolescents as adults capable of making responsible choices. The adults in AA could be potential surrogate parents, aunts, uncles, and grandparents. The intergenerational contact, which often is not available elsewhere to adolescents, can be a benefit. Because being alcoholic or abusing drugs is still a stigmatized condition, parents may be more uncomfortable than their children about AA attendance for adolescents. The therapist may need to help parents with this. In making a referral, the same guidelines outlined in the section on AA would apply.

PREVENTION

One important task for anyone working with adolescents is to be aware of the potential problems that virtually any adolescent may encounter in respect to alcohol and drugs. Even if adolescents are not currently into drugs or alcohol, anticipatory discussion with them about how they might handle the situation when it inevitably arises can be helpful. For the adolescent having any kind of problem, an alcohol/drug history is imperative. In many communities, efforts are already being made through parent and adolescent groups to develop healthy peer values and norms about alcohol/drug use.

Among the important stressors for adolescents that may contribute to, precipitate or exacerbate a substance abuse problem are a history of physical or sexual abuse, the death of close family members or friends, and relocation to a new town, neighborhood, or school district. It is particularly important to provide support, and, when indicated, counseling for adolescents falling into these categories.

MINORITY YOUTH

Unfortunately, much of what has been said about the presentation and treatment of substance abuse does not capture the problems of many urban minority youth. Regardless of whether these youths are African American, Hispanic, or Native American, they are far more likely to live in substandard housing, be in families with fewer economic resources, have less access to medical care, attend substandard schools, or be dropouts. If they live in urban areas, they are more likely than their Caucasian peers to live in areas in which drug use is prevalent and accompanied by violence.

The problems of minority adolescents are more prevalent and pernicious, and therefore need to be a special concern for health care professionals. See the chapters on African Americans, Hispanics, and Native Americans for discussion of special concerns and approaches to working with these minority groups.

REFERENCES

1. Burnside MA; Baer PE; McLaughlin RJ; Pokorny AD. Alcohol use by adolescents in disrupted families. *Alcoholism: Clinical and Experimental Research* 10(3): 274-278, 1986. (16 refs.)
2. Centers for Disease Control and Prevention. Mortality trends and leading causes of death among adolescents and young adults: United States, 1979-1988. *MMWR. Morbidity and Mortality Weekly Report* 42(23): 459-462, 1993. (5 refs.)
3. Cheng TL; Klein JD. The adolescent viewpoint. *Journal of the American Medical Association* 273(24): 1957-1958, 1995. (13 refs.)
4. Fossum MA; Mason MJ. *Facing Shame.* New York: Norton, 1989.
5. Glynn TJ; Leukefeld CG; Ludford JP, eds. *Preventing Adolescent Drug Abuse: Intervention Strategies. NIDA Research Monograph 47.* Rockville MD: National Institute on Drug Abuse, 1983. (Chapter refs.)
6. Johnston LD; O'Malley PM; Bachman JG. *National Survey Results on Drug Use from the Monitoring the Future Study, 1975-1993. Volume I: Secondary School Students.* Rockville MD: National Institute on Drug Abuse, 1994. (0 refs.)
7. Kinney J. Alcohol use, abuse, and dependence. IN: *Alcohol Use and Its Medical Consequences.* Timonium MD: Milner-Fenwick, 1989. (199 refs.)
8. Loiselle JM; Baker MD; Templeton JM Jr; Schwartz G; Drott H. Substance abuse in adolescent trauma. *Annals of Emergency Medicine* 22(10): 1530-1534, 1993. (16 refs.)
9. Martin CS; Arria AM; Mezzich AC; Bukstein OG. Patterns of polydrug use in adolescent alcohol abusers. *American Journal of Drug and Alcohol Abuse* 19(4): 511-521, 1993. (21 refs.)
10. Saitoh S; Steinglass P; Schuckit MA, eds. *Alcoholism and the Family.* New York: Brunner/Mazel, 1992. (Chapter refs.)
11. Statistical Bulletin. Trends in drug and alcohol use by youth in the USA. *Statistical Bulletin* 74(3): 19-27, 1993. (14 refs.)
12. Steinglass P; Bennett LA; Wolin SJ; Reiss D. *The Alcoholic Family.* New York: Basic Books, Inc, 1987.

FURTHER READINGS

Alexander DE; Gwyther RE. Alcoholism in adolescents and their families: Family-focused assessment and management. *Pediatric Clinics of North America* 42(1): 217-234, 1995. (102 refs.)

This article presents a family-focused approach for assessing and managing substance abuse problems. The family-focused approach is an alternative or additive model to the individual patient approach, a different approach than that in which most pediatricians are traditionally trained. This article discusses why substance abuse in adolescents may be underrecognized by physicians, as well as the importance of the family-focused approach. Clinical suggestions relevant to pediatricians also are provided. The magnitude of substance abuse problems among adolescents, with emphasis on alcohol abuse, is presented. Research findings regarding the reciprocities between family factors and alcohol are reviewed briefly, as are risk factors for alcohol problems in adolescents, family assessment techniques, and specific office screening inventories. Finally, clinical suggestions for primary care physicians are provided. Copyright 1995, Project Cork Institute.

Augustyn M; Simons-Morton BG. Adolescent drinking and driving: Etiology and interpretation. *Journal of Drug Education* 25(1): 41-59, 1995. (87 refs.)

In adolescents, drinking and driving is an important cause of injury, disability, and premature death. A literature review of the demographics and etiology of drinking and drinking/driving reveals the following: (1) which subgroups of the adolescent population are more likely to drink and drink/drive; (2) where and why adolescents drink and drink/drive; (3) peer and family issues associated with adolescent drinking and drinking/driving; (4) adolescent expectancies and perceived efficacies associated with drinking and drinking/driving. A discussion of the role of theory and the use of etiologic data in intervention research precedes an overview of several types of school-based alcohol-prevention programs and recommendations for more theory-based interventions. Copyright 1995, Baywood Publishing Co, Inc.

Bergmann PE; Smith MB; Hoffmann NG. Adolescent treatment: Implications for assessment, practice guidelines, and outcome management. *Pediatric Clinics of North America* 42(2): 453-472, 1995. (11 refs.)

Treatment for adolescent substance abuse does work. Not only are there clear improvements in substance use frequency and in the number of substances used 1 year after treatment, but also sharp reductions in school and legal problems. Improvements in treatment and the continuum of care can be made, however. Substance abuse treatment cannot end with the formal treatment episode. Continuing attendance at support groups, family support, and proactive re-entry plans at school all help to ensure continued recovery after treatment. Many adolescents receive much medical care in the year before admission; however, very few adolescents or their parents list physicians as referral sources at admission. Adolescent substance abuse should be identified by physicians and thereby treated sooner. Through the use of a three-item screen, physicians can reliably identify high-risk adolescents and confidently refer them for a formal chemical dependency evaluation. The use of Formal Inference-Based Recursive Modeling (FIRM) has provided a means of understanding how the interactions of certain pretreatment characteristics best predict treatment outcome. Based on such analyses, patient needs can be identified and practice guidelines can be empirically derived through an iterative process of implementation and evaluation. As the variability of treatment elements increases, treatment process data will become richer. This trend will enable providers to further refine the patient-treatment match by determining the amounts of exposure to specific treatment elements that are most predictive of a positive outcome for a particular group of patients. Efforts have been made to classify chemically dependent patients through the use of factor and cluster analytic techniques. After identification of discrete types of patients and then assessment of how the many services in the treatment experience interact to produce favorable outcomes, optimal treatment guidelines could potentially be derived for each patient type. More research in this area would further strengthen the bridge between the domains of clinical assessment, practice guidelines, and treatment outcome, setting the stage for even more effective patient-treatment matching and improved outcomes. 1995, WB Saunders Co.

Botvin GJ; Botvin EM. Adolescent tobacco, alcohol, and drug abuse: Prevention strategies, empirical findings, and assessment issues. (review). *Developmental and Behavioral Pediatrics* 13(4): 290-301, 1992. (83 refs.)

Use of psychoactive substances is higher in the US than anywhere else in the industrialized world. Community leaders, health professionals, and policymakers are searching eagerly for new approaches to an old problem. As drug-related crime affects more and more people, the public has become increasingly fixated on finding effective solutions. For the past few years, drug abuse has ranked as the number one problem facing America, according to

most public opinion surveys. In addition to longstanding concerns about the health, social, and legal consequences of drug abuse, new urgency exists for developing better methods of treating and preventing drug abuse because of its role in the transmission of AIDS. This article summarizes the evidence for prevention. The authors begin by discussing issues related to the etiology of substance use and the theoretical perspectives that appear to have heuristic value in developing potentially efficacious prevention strategies. Traditional and more recently developed preventive interventions are described, with an emphasis on the most promising approaches. Several key issues relating to prevention research methodology are discussed. The authors conclude with suggestions about prevention research that warrant further study. Copyright 1992, Williams & Wilkins.

Cromer BA; McLean CS; Heald FP. A critical review of comprehensive health screening in adolescents: Psychosocial screening. (review). *Journal of Adolescent Health* 13(2): 52-57, 1992. (67 refs.)

A crucial part of an adolescent's health status is his or her function within the psychosocial realm. Dramatic changes can occur over relatively short periods of time, and annual comprehensive assessments are indicated. Preventive education and timely intervention can improve psychosocial outcomes in teenagers. The authors review five areas of pressing national concern: depression, school problems, sexual abuse, substance abuse, and somatoform disorders. Depression as a syndrome with cognitive, psychomotor, and biologic manifestations must be distinguished from sadness as a transient affective symptom. School problems include attention deficit/hyperactivity disorder, learning disorders, and school absence. Sexual and substance abuse may lead to behavioral or psychological problems. The symptoms of somatoform disorders may be related to psychological distress or conflict. Copyright 1992, Society for Adolescent Medicine.

Denton RE; Kampfe CM. The relationship between family variables and adolescent substance abuse: A literature review. (review). *Adolescence* 29(114): 475-495, 1994. (27 refs.)

Adolescent substance abuse has been the focus of nationwide attention, and researchers have examined an assortment of variables relating to this disease. One area of interest has been the relationship between adolescent chemical dependency and family factors. A review of the current literature yields two broad categories: (1) family drug usage patterns, and (2) family atmosphere. In general, there seems to be a significant relationship between family variables and teenage substance abuse; however, the strength of the relationship differs with the substance used. Specifically, research has shown a strong relationship between adolescent substance abuse and family drug usage, family composition, family interaction patterns, and discrepancies in family perceptions. Findings and their implications for practitioners are discussed. Copyright 1994, Libra Publishers. Used with permission.

Donovan C; McEwan R. A review of the literature examining the relationship between alcohol use and HIV-related sexual risk-taking in young people. (review). *Addiction* 90(3): 319-328, 1995. (35 refs.)

Young people are a potentially vulnerable population for the spread of HIV. The influence of alcohol on sexual behavior is common knowledge. More recently, studies have attempted to illuminate the relationship between alcohol use and sexual risk taking in relation to HIV transmission. In their review of the literature, the authors highlight three important points. First, methodological problems make establishing any relationship extremely difficult. Secondly, the concept of sexual risk taking has to include acknowledging the context in which sex takes place rather than defining risk only in terms of sexual acts.

Finally, populations of gay men and lesbians are sufficiently different from heterosexuals, with regard to the influence of alcohol on sexual behavior, to make generalizations about one population inappropriate for another. Copyright 1995, Society for the Study of Addiction to Alcohol and Other Drugs.

Epps RP; Manley MW; Glynn TJ. Tobacco use among adolescents: Strategies for prevention. *Pediatric Clinics of North America* 42(2): 389-402, 1995. (67 refs.)

Tobacco use is a major public health problem that has its onset during childhood and adolescence. To prevent the onset, physicians can reach children and their parents in their offices beginning in the prenatal period and continuing through adulthood. For pediatricians and other physicians who care for children, NCI recommends five office-based activities that begin with the letter "A." The 5 A's include Anticipatory guidance, Ask, Advise, Assist, and Arrange follow-up visits. Elimination of tobacco use requires a comprehensive strategy that includes health professional interventions, policy changes, advertising restrictions, comprehensive school-based programs, community activities, and advocacy approaches. Physicians and health professionals have major roles to play in each of these interventions. Copyright 1995, WB Saunders Co.

Farrell M; Strang J. Substance use and misuse in childhood and adolescence. (review). *Journal of Clinical Psychiatry* 32(1): 109-128, 1991. (139 refs.)

Substance abuse has particular implications for the developing fetus in utero, for the child in a family with an ongoing pattern of substance misuse, and for the teenager using a variety of substances. Additionally, there are now forms of drug abuse related almost entirely to children and adolescents (notably volatile substance abuse). In many countries over the past decade, the age of initiation into substance abuse has gradually decreased. This review assesses pertinent research developments in the field of substance abuse in the young, including which research attempts to draw clinically applicable conclusions. The paucity of research is such that few data exist on many important areas within the substance abuse literature pertinent to the young. The review covers assessment, classification, epidemiology, biological factors, psychological factors, outcome, and treatment. Copyright 1991, Physicians Postgraduate Press, Inc. Used with permission.

Hawkins JD; Catalano RF; Miller JY. Risk and protective factors for alcohol and other drug problems in adolescence and early adulthood: Implications for substance abuse prevention. (review). *Psychological Bulletin* 112(1): 6-105, 1992. (308 refs.)

The authors suggest that the most promising route to effective strategies for the prevention of adolescent alcohol and other drug problems is through a risk-focused approach. This approach requires identifying risk factors for drug abuse and effective methods for addressing risk factors, then applying these methods to appropriate high-risk and general population samples in controlled studies. The authors review risk and protective factors for drug abuse, assess a number of approaches for drug abuse prevention potential with high-risk groups, and make recommendations for research and practice. Copyright 1992, American Psychological Association, Inc.

Hennessy M. Adolescent syndromes of risk for HIV infection. (review). *Evaluation Review* 18(3): 312-341, 1994. (126 refs.)

Some risk factors result from predominantly social processes, others from the biological disposition of the host. The distinction between the two is not altogether satisfactory. We exist in a world where human and natural processes are inextricably bound. In one sense, biological changes are social: They happen in social beings and are the processes of social factors. But they

are not socially produced in the same sense that poverty is. Despite these several methodological limitations in epidemiologic research, attention given to the study of subgroups has tended unwittingly to give high visibility to research on AIDS conducted by epidemiologists. This perpetuates the image of the disease as a medical problem, and thus marginalizes social-cultural factors and social scientists in its search for ways of combating AIDS. When we decontextualize individual behavior, we make assumptions about the situation: That it is stable, yet has no contextual history; that it operates in a normative manner; and that our assumptions about the normative manner are correct. We do not measure sources of variance in a person's actions caused by the situation or by person-situation interaction. Nor do we allow for the history of dynamic processes that are a part of long-term role relationships. Copyright 1994, Sage Publications, Inc.

Kress JS; Elias MJ. Substance abuse prevention in special education populations: Review and recommendations. (review). *Journal of Special Education* 27(1): 35-51, 1993. (86 refs.)

Special education populations are a high-risk group for the development of future substance abuse for a number of reasons. Students with emotional disturbances and learning disabilities face unique risk factors and skills deficits. Such students are at a considerable disadvantage for successfully negotiating peer pressure and high-stress situations. However, very few prevention programs target specifically this population. An overview of the risk factors and skills deficits unique to special education students is used to evaluate existing approaches to prevention and to make recommendations for future efforts. Copyright 1993, Grune & Stratton.

Lamminpaa A. Alcohol intoxication in childhood and adolescence. (review). *Alcohol and Alcoholism* 30(1): 5-12, 1995. (78 refs.)

Coma and vomiting are the most common symptoms in young teenagers intoxicated by alcohol. Severe toxicity, manifested as coma, occurs at lower blood alcohol concentrations in young teenagers than in adults. The effect of ethanol on the state of consciousness is directly proportional to blood alcohol concentration. In children under 5 years of age, the risk of hypoglycaemia is increased. A significant risk in acute alcohol intoxication is the rapid development of coma, which in cold environments could lead to fatal hypothermia. Preschool children reportedly eliminate ethanol twice as fast as adults, whereas young teenagers eliminate it at the adult rate. The biochemical disturbances in children 11 to 16 years of age with alcohol intoxication resemble those of adults. Mild acidosis of a respiratory or metabolic origin and mild hypokalaemia are common findings in young teenagers. Fluid replacement with glucose-containing fluids and follow-up are generally the only treatments needed for complete recovery. Motives for alcohol intoxication are a wish to get drunk or experiment, problems in human relations, and attempted suicide. The underlying problems are often family related, such as divorce, an alcoholic parent, or a lower socioeconomic status. Copyright 1995, Medical Council on Alcoholism. Used with permission.

Leccese M; Waldron HB. Assessing adolescent substance use: A critique of current measurement instruments. (review). *Journal of Substance Abuse Treatment* 11(6): 553-563, 1994. (67 refs.)

Various instruments are available to screen for and assess adolescent substance abuse and aid in planning appropriate interventions. Assessment practices in treatment facilities for adolescents have tended to rely on unstandardized, local measures or on measures developed for adults with unknown reliability and validity for adolescents. This review is a resource for health professionals regarding the assessment of adolescent substance involvement and the type of instruments available. Conceptual issues relevant to the evaluation of adolescent substance use are discussed. Then, standardized, adolescent-specific assessment tools are briefly summarized, including screening questionnaires, comprehensive instruments, and several other substance-related instruments. Copyright 1994, Pergamon Press.

Peterson L; Brown D. Integrating child injury and abuse-neglect research: Common histories, etiologies, and solutions. (review). *Psychological Bulletin* 116(2): 293-315, 1994. (202 refs.)

Research on injuries, the leading health threat to children in the US, has been infrequent and badly fragmented. Research on unintentional injuries and on abuse-neglect have similar histories, including recent rapprochement with behavioral interventions, and reveal similar etiologies for child injury. Furthermore, recent studies document difficulties in discriminating between unintentional and abuse-neglect–related injuries. The areas also face similar methodological and conceptual challenges. Finally, the same interventions may prevent negative outcomes in both areas. A working model to summarize a more integrated approach to injury prevention is offered. Increasing societal awareness of the threat posed by injuries and strengthening mutually applicable strategies of injury prevention would be desired results of unifying efforts in these historically isolated arenas. NB. Alcohol/substance abuse is noted as one of many potential contributors to accidents in children. Copyright 1994, American Psychological Association, Inc.

Rotunda RJ; Scherer DG; Imm PS. Family systems and alcohol misuse: Research on the effects of alcoholism on family functioning and effective family interventions. (review). *Professional Psychology: Research and Practice* 26(1): 95-104, 1995. (106 refs.)

This article reviews the most prominent research at the interface between studies of alcohol addiction and family systems psychology. The review addresses the general effects of alcohol misuse on family functioning as determined in empirical studies comparing healthy families, alcohol-afflicted families, and otherwise troubled families. Three factors ("dry" vs. "wet" families, family development and the progression of alcoholism, and family structure) are identified as particularly relevant to understanding the treatment needs of families affected by alcohol misuse. Research examining the general efficacy of family interventions in the treatment of alcoholism, and specific treatment considerations unique to treating families coping with alcohol misuse, are reviewed. Copyright 1995, American Psychological Association, Inc.

Weissberg RP; Caplan M; Harwood RL. Promoting competent young people in competence-enhancing environments: A systems-based perspective on primary prevention. (review). *Journal of Consulting and Clinical Psychology* 59(6): 830-841, 1991. (99 refs.)

Recent studies indicate that 15% to 22% of American children and adolescents suffer from diagnosable mental disorders. Researchers estimate that 25% to 50% engage in risk behaviors leading to negative health and behavior outcomes such as drug abuse, unwanted pregnancy, AIDS, delinquency, and school dropout. The prevalence of problem behaviors, as well as current social trends, demands that effective primary prevention programs be developed and disseminated. This article reviews successful family-, school-, and community-based prevention efforts for reducing the incidence and severity of children's psychosocial problems. High-quality, comprehensive, competence-promotion programs that focus on both children and their socializing environments represent the state-of-the-art in prevention. Establishing enduring, effective preventive interventions requires increased attention to program design, implementation, and institutionalization. Copyright 1991, American Psychological Association, Inc.

Wodarski JS; Smyth NJ. Adolescent substance abuse: A comprehensive approach to prevention intervention. (review). *Journal of Child & Adolescent Substance Abuse* 3(3): 33-58, 1994. (74 refs.)

Adolescent substance abuse remains a significant problem confronting the nation. This paper addresses the state of practice in adolescent substance abuse prevention intervention. Data on the extent, nature, and consequences of adolescent substance use are presented, and problems with the definition of substance abuse in this population are considered. Primary and secondary prevention programs are discussed, including programs targeting high-risk youth, school and peer groups, families, and communities. Tertiary prevention intervention efforts are outlined, and the need for further treatment research highlighted. In addition, the importance of intervention across multiple populations and systems is emphasized. Copyright 1994, The Haworth Press.

CHAPTER 19

College Students and Campus Programs

JEAN KINNEY, MSW

CLINICAL APPLICATIONS

The goals of this chapter are to assist the clinician to:

1. Recognize the patterns of substance use in college students.
2. Participate in the development of campus programs.
3. Recognize the impediments to developing campus programs.
4. Be aware of central elements of campus-wide substance use programs.

SUBSTANCE USE PATTERNS

Alcohol and drug use on the college campus has received considerable attention over the past decade.[10,19] The most recent national survey of college students and young adults, conducted on a regular basis by the National Institute on Drug Abuse (NIDA), shows that, with a few significant exceptions, college students' substance use patterns are generally similar to those of their age peers not attending college. Data from this survey describing annual prevalence rates are summarized in Table 19-1.

SUBSTANCE USE BY YOUNG ADULTS

Interestingly, it is for licit drugs—nicotine and alcohol—that one finds the most significant differences between students and nonstudents. College students are only slightly more likely to be drinkers, but they are far more likely to drink heavily. In the NIDA study, virtually half of male college students (49%) and a third of female students (33%) reported drinking five or more drinks in a row in a prior two-week period. Other recent large surveys have also documented a pattern of heavy drinking by a significant portion of students. On the other hand, college students, are far less likely to be smokers than those not attending college.[11]

The higher rates of both college student drinking and heavy drinking may, in part, be attributable to two demographic factors. One, alcohol use increases when young adults move away from their parents and begin living independently. Secondly, drinking declines after marriage for both men and women. Those who do not go to college are more likely to live at home or be married, both of which are associated with less drinking. In combination, these two factors may explain the differences in drinking patterns.[11]

Gender Differences

In general the gender differences present during high school continue into college. Women are less likely to use illicit substances, although their use of tranquilizers is on par with that of male students. The proportion of women who drink approximates that of men, but they are less likely to be heavy drinkers or daily drinkers. Previously, sex differences were negligible in respect to smoking. The 1993 survey shows that for the first time, the proportion of women who report daily smoking exceeds that of men, 16% vs. 14%.[11]

Trends in Substance Use Patterns

As is apparent from Figure 19-1, there has been a general overall decline in illicit drug use since 1980. However, the college community has reason for concern if it looks to the use patterns of current middle school and high school students. The long-term pattern of declining use that began in the 1980s is no longer evident. Annual prevalence rates have leveled out, followed by a sharp increase in the use of illicit drugs in 1993, including marijuana, LSD, inhalants, and stimulants. Furthermore, many of the attitudes and beliefs about substance use that would provide protection and reduce use seemingly have "softened." For example, only 53% of eighth grade students consider a pack a day smoker to be inviting health risks.[11]

The most dramatic change in substance use is the increase in students who report heavy drinking. Along with this, more students cite "drinking to get drunk" as the motive for drinking. In this respect, the college campus does not reflect the general population's drop in alcohol consumption, which includes a decline in heavy drinking by age peers.

Seemingly, students' drinking practices did not change substantially following the changes in the legal drinking age in the 1980s. There was an immediate decrease in consumption, but with time the numbers of students drinking returned to the previous levels.[5] Why do college students differ from other sectors of society? It has been suggested that campuses provide some insulation from the effects of the

Table 19-1. Substance Use by Young Adults

Substance	Annual prevalence (%)	
	College students	Non-students
Any illicit drug use*	31.0	30.0
Illicit drug use other than		
marijuana*	13.0	15.0
Marijuana	28.0	26.0
Cocaine	2.7	4.6
Crack	0.6	1.7
Stimulants*	4.2	6.0
LSD	5.1	5.5
Inhalants	3.8	2.7
Heroin	0.1	0.3
Other opiates	2.5	2.8
MDMA (ecstasy)	0.8	0.9
Tranquilizers*	2.4	2.7
Licit drugs		
Alcohol	87.0	84.0
5 drinks/occasion* during prior 2 weeks	40.0	34.0
Nicotine (daily)	15.0	27.0

From Johnston LD; O'Malley PM; Bachman JG. *National Survey Results on Drug Use from The Monitoring the Future Study, 1975-1993. Volume II: College Students and Young Adults.* Rockville MD: National Institute on Drug Abuse, 1994.
*Does not include medically prescribed drug use.

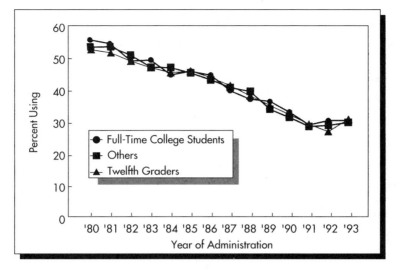

Figure 19-1. Any Illicit Drug: Trends in Annual Prevalence among College Students vs. Others. (Johnston LD; O'Malley PM; Bachman JF. *National Survey Results on Drug Use from The Monitoring the Future Study, 1975-1993. Volume II: College Students and Young Adults.* Rockville MD: National Institute on Drug Abuse, 1994.)

change in drinking age, and that students and student organizations are major targets for alcohol advertising.

Problems Related to Use

Data on the magnitude and nature of problems related to alcohol and substance use on college campuses have long been scant, although two recent, large surveys of college students have significantly remedied this.[20,21,29] Colleges individually have not systematically gathered data on different campus problems that would allow them to identify the contributory role of alcohol or drugs. When such data has been gathered, it has generally been treated as confidential and has not been published in professional literature. There has been concern that if such findings became available to the press, the institution might be viewed less favorably by the public, alumni, prospective students and their parents, potential donors, and for public institutions, the state legislature, which controls funds.

A wide-spread perception within campus-related professional associations, college health service personnel, and deans of student life has been that substance use, predominantly alcohol, is the major factor in almost any significant campus problem. Invariably, drinking is a factor in vandalism of college property, altercations, date rape, and incidents of intolerance directed toward women and minorities.[15,18] Alcohol has consistently been reported to be a factor in over 50% of untoward incidents.[4] Drinking behavior is also considered a major factor in problems related to academic life, e.g., class attendance and academic achievement.[18,25] Student health services report that alcohol is a major factor in accidents, health center utilization, and the general health problems of students.

The percentage of students who report various types of problems is summarized in Table 19-2.

Significant factors for risk of problems are how frequently an individual student engages in heavy drinking, and the proportion of students within the school with these heavy drinking patterns. A 1994 study by Wechsler, involving 140 institutions with a sample of 17,592 students, explored the occurrence of negative consequences and drinking patterns, particularly the frequency of "binge" drinking. In the study, "binge" drinking for males was defined as five or more drinks per occasion; for females, four or more drinks. "Frequent binge drinkers" had binged three or more times in the proceeding 2 weeks; "infrequent binge drinkers" had binged 1 or 2 times in the 2-week period; and "non-binge drinkers" were those with no such incidents.[29]

The relative risk of different problems is clearly a factor of the presence and frequency of binge drinking, as evidenced in Table 19-3.

Beyond differences among students, there are also differences among schools. Colleges/universities were found to vary in the proportion of their students who reported such heavy drinking incidents. While 44% of the total sample of students reported binge drinking, the percentages for institutions ranged from a low of only 1% of students at one school to a high of 70% of students at another.

Negative consequences associated with drinking do not fall solely upon those who drink heavily. Schools with higher levels of heavy-drinking students are more likely to have other students reporting a problem from someone else's drinking (Table 19-4).

While the research has tended to focus on the negative outcomes for individuals, alcohol use also impacts

Table 19-2. Student Reports of Alcohol-Related Problems

Drinking problem	Percentage of drinkers who reported a problem during 1985[a]	Percentage in 1990-1991[*,b]	
		Under age 21[**]	Over age 21[***]
Acute effects			
Hangover	75.7	65.9	59.1
Vomiting	37.1	57.0	41.6
Driving			
Drove a car after several drinks	34	34.9	36.6
Drove a car knowing they had drunk too much	49.2	—	—
Drove a car while drinking	37.3	—	—
Was arrested for driving while intoxicated (DWI)	1.6	1.4	2.0
Academic			
Attended class after several drinks	8.4	—	—
"Cut" class after several drinks	9.1	—	—
Missed class because of hangover	26.5	32.7	26.1
Low grade because of too much drinking	5.4	26.6	19.5
Interpersonal problems			
Criticized by someone they were dating because of drinking	13.4	—	—
Fought after drinking	14.7	26.6	19.5
Problems with community			
Legal troubles because of drinking	6.2	—	—
Lost job because of drinking	1.0	—	—
Difficulties with administration because to drinking	2.9	11.7	8.3
Damaged property or acted with malice after drinking	11.3	9.8	5.3
Self-perception of drinking			
Thought they might have a drinking problem	9.9	11.7	11.8

[a]Modified from Engs RC; Hanson DJ. University students' drinking patterns and problems: Examining the effects of raising the purchase age. *Public Health Report* 133(6): 647-673, 1985.

[b]From Data from Core Alcohol and Drug Survey as reported by Presley CA; Meilman PW; Padgett JF. Facts and myths. *New Directions for Student Services* 67(Fall): 15-27, 1994.

[*]Of the total sample (3375 students from 56 institutions), 21% were abstainers and 78% were drinkers who reported these problems.

[**]n = 29,970. Of the sample of 55,670 students, slightly over half were under age 21.

[***]n = 25,673.

on the quality and nature of campus life. One outcome too frequently overlooked is the role of alcohol in campus violence, either as perpetrator or victim.[19]

Origins of Institutional Attention

The earliest pressure to address alcohol and substance use problems came from recovering alumni. Many campus alumni magazines have printed first person accounts by recovering alumni. Typically these individuals do not blame the alma mater for causing their alcohol dependence, but they claim that the campus environment provided fertile ground for its later emergence. Also, in the 1970s there were federally funded pilot demonstration educational programs specifically targeted to college students.

Much of the attention to alcohol problems on college campuses is a manifestation of society's increasing awareness of alcohol and substance use problems. However, some factors have been unique to the campus community, such as concern about institutional liability. Although the number of litigated cases has been small, they have received considerable attention.[8] Under its "duty to care," a college is responsible for the well-being of its students. Although the institution's obligation to supervise student conduct may be limited, it cannot claim a total absence of responsibility. It is important to differentiate between student activities that are wholly personal and those the institution sponsors and/or regulates. The institution also has potential liability in its

Table 19-3. Percentage of Students Reporting Alcohol-Related Problems by Respondents' Drinking Patterns

	Binge drinking		
Problem	None	Infrequently	Most frequent binge drinkers
Have a hangover	30	75	90
Do something you regret	14	37	63
Miss a class	8	30	54
Forget where you were or what you did	8	26	54
Get behind in school work	6	21	46
Argue with friends	8	22	42
Engage in unplanned sexual activity	8	20	41
Get hurt or injured	2	9	23
Damage property	2	8	22
Have unprotected sex	4	10	22
Have trouble with campus or local police	1	4	11
Require medical Tx for alcohol overdose	<1	<1	
Have had five or more alcohol-related problems since start of the school year	3	14	47

From Wechsler H; Davenport A; Dowdall G; Moeykens B; Castillo S. Health and behavioral consequences of binge drinking in college: A national survey of students at 140 campuses. *Journal of the American Medical Association* 272(21): 1672-1677, 1994.

Table 19-4. Secondary Effects of Others' Drinking

Problem reported by non-binge drinkers	Percentage of students reporting by instititional ranking of levels of binge drinking		
	Low binge	Middle	High
Was insulted or humiliated	21	30	34
Had serious argument or quarrel	13	18	20
Was pushed, hit, or assaulted	7	10	13
Had property destroyed	6	13	15
Had to care for drunken student	31	47	54
Studying or sleep interrupted	42	64	68
Unwanted sexual advance	15	21	26
Victim of sexual assault or date rape	2	1	2
Experienced at least one of above	62	82	87

From Wechsler H; Davenport A; Dowdall G; Moeykens B; Castillo S. Health and behavioral consequences of binge drinking in college: A national survey of students at 140 campuses. *Journal of the American Medical Association* 272(21): 1672-1677, 1994.

role as proprietor, with the duty to maintain safe premises. This includes controling rowdiness at football games or parties or protecting others from a student known to be abusive.[8,26] The rise in the legal drinking age highlighted the issue of institutional liability.

Colleges must also contend with the issues of organized sports, such as the National Collegiate Athletic Association's (NCAA) mandatory drug testing to establish a student's or team's eligibility. The NCAA's mandatory drug testing is, in theory, only one component of a larger substance use educational and prevention effort. However, testing has received the most attention and institutional resources. In addition, federal initiatives to establish drug-free campuses have prompted further institutional action. The *drug-free campus* legislation has made distribution of federal funds contingent on colleges establishing programs to promote nonuse among students and employees. These mandated programs are to include clearly established disciplinary actions for those violating the campus policy.

The Role of the Campus Health Service

The college health service plays a central role in addressing campus alcohol and drug use problems.

The American College Health Association, the professional association for student health centers, has adopted guidelines for substance abuse services provided by student health services.[27] For those in the student health service, the most vexing problems may prove not to be clinical issues, but the responsibility for coordinating campus-wide efforts. Thus, in the discussion that follows the emphasis is upon campus programs.

IMPEDIMENTS TO ORGANIZING CAMPUS PROGRAMS

Although campus efforts to address student alcohol and substance use are no longer foreign to colleges and universities, they are still a recent phenomenon. For example, the American College Health Association (ACHA), which has a reputation for its progressive stance toward health care issues, did not create standards for member institutions until 1987.[27] The history of this is worth recounting for the light it sheds on the impediments to organizing campus programs.

Although it no longer formally accredits health services, the ACHA has continued to promulgate guidelines for health center efforts. These guidelines incorporate standards for clinical care, record keeping, health promotion, ethics, confidentiality, and the role of the student health service as a "public health officer" within the institution. The ACHA has long been recognized for its advocacy of health care maintenance and health promotion. Indeed, one of the most interesting examples of this stance was the recommendation, in the fourth edition of its guideline published in 1984, that rabies vaccine be administered prophylactically to students doing biological field work. This recommendation was made at a time when the Centers for Disease Control indicated that the incidence of rabies was 0:100,000 persons. Yet at the same time, in this issue of the guidelines, there was no mention of alcohol or other substances.[2]

In hindsight, failing to deal with substance use while attending to rabies is incongruous. Conversations with those involved in drafting the 1984 guidelines that did not address substance use provide some telling comments. While no longer reflecting the thinking of the ACHA, these comments shed light on attitudes that may persist in some quarters in respect to campus substance use issues. One explanation provided for the failure to deal with substance use was that alcohol and other drug use was not considered a health center issue, and furthermore, it was handled by deans' offices or other campus groups. Another explanation was that alcohol abuse treatment was not effective; therefore, it was considered unfair to burden member schools with delivery of services of undemonstrated value. Finally, it was noted that alcohol abuse/dependence was really symptomatic of other, more basic issues such as stress or adjustment problems, common problems addressed by counseling services.[12]

Common Misperceptions

Although they are not disinterested, many campus administrators have little sophistication about alcohol and substance use problems. Accordingly, personal biases and impressions often substitute for information and data. The following are several myths common to campuses that should be countered by the student health service.

Heavy drinking is just a stage. The perspective that heavy drinking is just a stage could be called the developmental hypothesis of spontaneous remission. This is the belief that a diploma, a little more maturity, and some adult responsibilities will cause a developmental phase marked by excessive alcohol consumption to pass. Therefore, no intervention is required. One flaw in this stance is that alcohol problems can be serious enough that the individual may not survive to have a spontaneous remission.

Often accompanying this perspective is the belief that alcohol problems in adolescence or early adulthood are the result of psychological problems. Accordingly, if treatment were to be offered, it would be geared toward dealing with the presumed underlying issues being expressed by alcohol abuse. While studying adult psychological development, Vaillant found that alcohol-dependent individuals were indistinguishable from their nonalcohol-dependent counterparts in respect to psychological well-being in earlier life.[28] Vaillant's research also supported the well-documented finding of the genetic basis for alcoholism in men. Research has typically shown that those with a positive family history have a four times greater risk of developing alcoholism.

Substance use problems respond to education. That substance use problems respond to education is another common stance and could be considered the educational deficit approach. In this framework, students are considered uninformed about alcohol or other drugs; therefore, education becomes the primary intervention. This ignores several realities, an important one being that students arriving on college campuses have already been targets of educational programs in their high schools and communities. Educational efforts are often simplistic and insufficient. There is ample data showing that change in knowledge does not necessarily lead to changes in behavior.

Substance use problems as cases of bad manners. Competing with the educational deficit model is the approach that substance use problems are cases of bad manners, which is essentially a moral issue. Those with alcohol problems are regarded as having poor attitudes and questionable values. The challenge of programming becomes having students "shape up." Discussion of "responsible drinking" can reinforce this orientation. The obvious unspoken counterpoint to responsible drinking is irresponsible drinking. Many students may be at substantial risk but do not view themselves, nor are they viewed by their peers, as being irresponsible.

Nondrinkers thrust into a drinking culture. Another misconception is that students are commonly and mistakenly viewed as nondrinkers thrust into a drinking culture. On the contrary, the majority of students enter college with an established drinking pattern. Not only do they arrive on campus as drinkers, but many qualify as heavy drinkers, having more than five drinks per occasion. This pattern is reported by 48% of men and 30% of women who are high school seniors.[11]

Student drinking is fun. Finally, it is widely assumed that student drinking is fun. If so, there is a reluctance to take away students' pleasures, or it is considered puritanical to recommend moderation or elimination of alcohol and drug use. This myth is easily supported if one's own experience with moderate alcohol use is projected onto students, presuming that the student experience parallels that of adults, if in an exaggerated form. For a significant minority, drinking is not fun. Blackouts are frightening, and hangovers are unpleasant. Finding that one's roommate has vomited on the floor is disgusting and strains the relationship. Waking up the next morning in a stranger's bed is demeaning, embarrassing, and a violation of values. When this reality is not addressed, we invite students to repress and distort their perceptions of their drinking behavior because the truth may be too painful. In the process, distorted, drugged memories of events go uncorrected. One of the tasks for campus health care providers is to select and circulate to colleagues pertinent literature on misconceptions and important concepts.

Other myths and beliefs. A survey of colleges that have received money for prevention programming from the US Department of Education's Fund for the Improvement of Secondary Education (FIPSE) has also identified misconceptions and frequently held myths.[22] These include the beliefs that "everyone drinks to excess" and that "the consequences of college drinking and drug use are minor." In response to this latter belief, the researchers noted that a large number of students have had negative consequences. While a hangover, which slightly over 60% of students reported, an argument or fight (30%), or nausea or vomiting (50%) might be termed unfortunate and conceivably not serious, other events go beyond simply being untoward. These include trouble with authorities, 14%; doing something later regretted, 36%; sexual misconduct, 15%; injury, 15%; vandalism, 8%; suicide attempt or thoughts, 5%; and unsuccessful efforts to stop using, 6%.

History of Substance Abuse Field

The history of the alcohol/substance abuse field has itself been an impediment. Historically, the modern alcohol treatment field is rooted in the self-help movement of AA, founded in 1935. The initial and virtually exclusive focus of the early alcohol field was on alcohol dependence and its treatment. This was true through the early 1970s when the NIAAA was founded, which then provided an impetus to research and training. As a consequence of attention directed primarily to alcohol dependence, virtually all alcohol problems were viewed as part of the progression of alcoholism. Accordingly all those with alcohol problems were offered similar treatment—inpatient and abstinence-oriented. No other options were available. If treatment were refused, the individual was regarded as being "in denial" or not amenable to care. If the individual later developed clear-cut dependence, that confirmed the perception that if one waits long enough, all alcohol problems lead to alcohol dependence.

When the above model for treating alcohol problems was introduced to college campuses, it was met with suspicion. By responding to all clinical problems in an identical fashion, alcohol counselors and professionals became suspect. Often they were viewed as technicians or functioning out of an ideological stance. The myths and misbeliefs common in the campus community, combined with the orientation of alcohol treatment personnel, led to a strained truce.

In addition, in the early days of campus programming, recovering alumni were those most vocal about issues concerning alcohol and other substance abuse. They pleaded for educational efforts to prevent future student alcoholism. On campus, the concerns of alumni regarding alcohol issues were reinforced by those administrators, staff, and faculty who were similarly personally affected. The earliest campus programs relied almost exclusively on educational efforts such as "alcohol days" or alcohol "awareness weeks" marked by special programs, outreach programs to living groups, and panels of recovering alumni. These were targeted at all students in hope of reaching the subgroup who might become dependent on alcohol in the future. Since there was no recognition of different types of substance use problems, it was presumed that for the rest of the student population drinking was essentially self-regulated, nonproblematic, and thus required no intervention.

CORE COMPONENTS IN A CAMPUS PROGRAM
Public Health Model

The public health model is a good framework to consider approaches to alcohol and substance use problems on the college campus. Descriptions of the components of the public health model in respect to college alcohol and substance use are as follows:

The agent. The use of alcohol and other drugs (the agent) can lead to two types of problems. There are acute problems that follow a single drinking episode, which are a consequence of drug-induced effects. There are also chronic problems that develop over time and are related to tolerance, physical dependence, and the pattern of use. Chronic problems of use have received the most attention on college campuses; however, acute problems may be more significant for this population.

The host. An individual's (the host) risk for alcohol dependence has been well documented. The major risk factors include a positive family history, compounded by growing up in a culture without clear prescriptions and proscriptions for alcohol use. The risk factors for acute problems are less commonly recognized but are primarily products of environmental factors.

There are several groups of students at greatest risk for acute problems. Those with less drinking experience are at the greatest risk. Many student health services find that freshmen are those most likely to be seen for overdoses and acute alcohol poisoning. Of the typical freshmen class, 16% describe themselves as nondrinkers.[6] Most of these nondrinkers become drinkers during their first year of college. Many problems accompany this transition from nondrinker to drinker or other transitions in drinking status, such as light or infrequent drinkers becoming more regular and/or heavier drinkers. During their freshmen year, students report an increase in the frequency of drinking-related problems.[7] Fraternity members are another group at special risk for acute problems. Many of the rituals and aspects of fraternity life focus on drinking. In respect to acute problems, special campus events such as homecoming, fraternity pledge week, or special campus weekends should be of concern. These events are likely to involve heavier drinking and are accompanied by more alcohol-related problems.

A study conducted at the University of Pennsylvania found that the best predictor of alcohol problems during college was the frequency of drinking to intoxication reported by incoming students.[25] Incoming freshmen who were the heaviest drinkers in their class and who had had a prior alcohol-related incident were found to be at higher risk for future problems. By the end of their sophomore year, these students had more overall visits to the health center, more alcohol-related visits to the health center, and a lower grade point average.

The environment. Cultural and environmental norms that are predictive of acute problems provide an accurate description of college drinking practices. The drinking norms associated with acute problems include solitary drinking; over-permissive norms of drinking; lack of specific drinking norms; tolerance of drunkenness; adverse social behavior tolerated during drinking; utilitarian use of alcohol to reduce tension and anxiety; lack of ritualized and/or ceremonial use of alcohol; alcohol use apart from family and social functions; alcohol use separated from overall eating patterns; lack of child socialization into drinking patterns; drinking with strangers, which increases violence; drinking pursued as recreation; drinking concentrated in young men; and a cultural milieu that stresses individualism, self-reliance, and high achievement.[17] In summary, these factors describe college alcohol use.

The college community has also been the target of extensive marketing efforts by the brewing industry, for obvious reasons. This segment of the population is among the heaviest beer drinkers. Sales to fraternities are significant. For example, one college of 7500 students, in auditing the fraternity system's fiscal records, noted $250,000 of expenditures for the combined social budgets, most of which went toward the purchase of beer. Promotional efforts on the college campus involve a long-range investment by the beer producers. If new drinkers develop "brand loyalty," which continues throughout a lifetime, and especially if these drinkers are heavy drinkers, the cost of promotion is easily recouped.

Promotional efforts directed to campuses have included providing kegs of beer as prizes for campus events such as blood drives. Some students are compensated for being campus promotional representatives, distributing advertising paraphernalia such as caps, posters, and napkins with the brewer's logo. Beer companies are major advertisers in campus newspapers and other campus publications. Many associations of college professionals have passed marketing guidelines for promotion of alcoholic beverages and have requested that their members not allow alcohol beverage promotion on campus unless the marketers abide by the guidelines.

In terms of general advertising, women and minorities have become targets of special campaigns. Although spokesmen for the liquor and brewing industries describe the advertising as an effort to increase "market share," some are suspicious. In that females and minorities drink less than white males, it is hard to imagine that special advertisements to these groups are not also intended to increase the total market by recruiting more and heavier drinkers.

The Public Health Framework and Intervention

The public health framework offers a functional and coherent approach to campus alcohol and substance use problems. As one of the most knowledgeable sources in the community, the health service can be a resource and model for others who need to become more informed and involved. The public health model is well suited as an organizing framework; it is an easily understood approach. Also, by adopting a model adaptable across campus settings, the health service can "squeeze out" less functional alternative frameworks. The following are the major phenomena of concern: A college-age population is essentially a healthy population. (The college health service is the primary care setting in which acute disease predominates.) However, if a student were to encounter a major health problem resulting in death or disability, the odds are extremely high that alcohol use would be implicated. Recall that the only segment of the population with a declining life expectancy is the 18 to 24 year age group. When medical causes are separated from social causes, then social causes—accidents, suicide, and homicides—are major contributors to this decline in life expectancy. Alcohol/substance use figures prominently in these causes of mortality.

A study of lifetime prevalence of major psychiatric disorders indicates that alcohol/substance abuse is the most common psychiatric disorder among 18 to 45 year olds. Alcohol/substance abuse is virtually twice as common as the second most common disorder. This finding is independent of education or social class. Thus, the idea that these individuals are not in the college population is unfounded.[23]

Statistically, deaths from alcohol and substance overdoses remain relatively infrequent. However, the possibility of such an occurrence is the nightmare of every campus health service staff and college administrator. Less dramatic but more significant is the role of alcohol use and to a lesser degree other drug use in the problems encountered daily. According to health service staff, alcohol use is a prominent feature of accidents and injuries, requests for the morning-after pill, unwanted pregnancy, and sexually transmitted disease. It also contributes significantly to acquaintance rape, vandalism, and academic failure.

Classifying alcohol/substance use as a public health problem has certain treatment advantages: It fosters an integrated approach, underscores the need for multiple types of intervention, and prevents the tendency to look for the "magic bullet." This model can also provide leverage for intervention, as well as a rationale and imperative to act. Making alcohol abuse a public health issue can reduce opposition because it is hard to be against health. On the other hand, segments of the campus community may become divided among other approaches.

Features of a Comprehensive Program

In the introduction to the draft of Rutgers University's first campus alcohol policy, the observation was made that "the hard part was determining how to think about the topic," and once that had been worked through, the task was relatively easy. Published in 1981, that document was one of the earliest efforts to articulate a comprehensive campus program.[3] It remains commendable for its scope, the process it sets forth, and the recognition that it is essential to establish both prescriptions and proscriptions for behavior. Activities that should be institutional efforts are mentioned below.[3,13,27]

Health services. The health service provides direct clinical services or facilitates referral for care, as well as provides a health education role. In these capacities the health service may serve as the institution's "public health officer," bringing potentially harmful drinking and drug use practices to the attention of appropriate groups; developing emergency procedures, with guidelines for handling intoxicated persons and defining medical emergencies; and providing consultation. The following activities warrant consideration:

- *Establishing individualized patient education.* Provide every student with individual patient education related to his or her alcohol use, blood alcohol content (BAC), drinking patterns, and any absolute or relative contraindication for alcohol use.
- *Developing outreach programs for students at risk.* Develop programs specifically to meet the needs of different populations such as children of alcoholics; those who enter school with a history of alcohol or drug treatment; individuals who have been treated while at college and require support to maintain abstinence in a heavy-drinking environment; or those with a positive family history who are at higher risk for future alcohol problems.
- *Providing clinical care.* Implement routine screening, evaluation, interventions, referral for treatment, monitoring of students with acute problems, and monitoring of persons in treatment or recently out of treatment to help prevent relapse. Organize an AA and/or NA meeting on campus that is easily accessible to students, faculty, and staff. Develop protocols that specify clinical encounters warranting routine alcohol evaluation.
- *Maintaining health center medical records.* A health history should be completed by all incoming students, including information on family history, alcohol and drug use patterns, and treatment for substance abuse. Methods should be instituted to allow identification of an emergent alcohol or substance use problem. Such identification is difficult when medical records only include clinical encounters.

- *Providing assistance and serving as a consultant to others involved in campus-wide program planning.* Although it may offer leadership and administer a campus program, the College Health Service is not the only campus group that needs to address alcohol and substance use issues. Other college groups have significant roles that cannot be delegated to others. Some of the potential program activities that each might offer include:

Office of residential life. Various initiatives might be incorporated within an Office of Residential Life. These include establishing norms for living groups and thereby articulating normative behavior, and involving students in living units for defining the drinking-related behaviors that they consider unacceptable and offensive. Risk management groups might be used to review any alcohol-related incident and consider alternative actions that might have been taken and that might reduce future risk. Protocols for residence hall advisors are essential to clearly define the steps to be taken if concern arises about a student. In a similar fashion, the steps that students should take in alcohol/drug-related emergency situations should be spelled out. Finally, a number of schools have established designated substance-free living areas, which serve both recovering students and others wishing to minimize contact with alcohol and drug use.

Greek organizations. Membership in a Greek organization is commonly associated with drinking and substance use problems. Programmatic efforts with fraternities and sororities might be directed to items such as their securing consultation about drinking practices. This is sometimes termed the "fire marshal" approach—helping the student organization review and eliminate potential dangerous or problematic drinking practices. "Required" drinking, while possibly less common and generally covered by institutional regulations, has still not wholly disappeared. This includes drinking games and contests and mandatory drinking as part of pledging. It is also important for Greek groups to develop guidelines for serving alcoholic beverages. These might include labeling the alcohol content of premixed beverages, establishing hours for serving beverages, and training bartenders. Also in some schools, the Greek organization and other student groups sponsoring social events are required to provide monitors who do not drink at social events.

University administration. Clearly the school administration is a major factor is setting the tone of a school's response to substance use. The following are important considerations in developing its alcohol and drug policy: Offering programs for impaired faculty; mandating clinical evaluation for students with suspected alcohol problems, for alcohol- or other drug-related disciplinary offenses, or in cases of academic failure; and reviewing the institution's insurance coverage for students, faculty, and staff to ensure adequate access to alcohol/substance use evaluation and treatment.

Faculty. Faculty are often the neglected group in campus substance use programs. The following activities are appropriately targeted to them: Educational initiatives about the relationship between substance use and academic performance, and suggested protocols for action when confronted with a suspected substance use problem. In addition, it may be useful to include alcohol and other drug issues as illustrative examples within the intellectual life of the community. Substance use-related issues can provide good course material, e.g., public policy, history of social movements, and women's studies. Substance use-related topics may also be well suited for student research papers. In addition, it is important to deal with impaired faculty. An "impaired professors program" should be able to deal with issues beyond alcohol-substance use, such as Alzheimer's disease or mood disorders. In line with this, information on resources for dealing with a substance use problem in the family can be helpful.

Athletic department. Athletic departments are well aware that they need to be attentive to policies of the NCAA and their own athletic conferences. General education of coaches and trainers can be an important element of campus-wide efforts. Other possible efforts include the following: (1) Conducting team educational programs that relate the effects of alcohol and other substance use (including "performance-enhancing" drugs) on performance. (2) Helping athletic teams set standards for team members. This entails discussing use that is acceptable to the team and that which is not, and specifying ways in which the team will enforce its collective decision. (3) Incorporating alcohol and drug information within health education and fitness programs. Whether these programs are conducted for the community or only for the students, they should incorporate information on alcohol and drug use. (4) Developing policies about alcoholic beverages at sporting events.

Alumni. Activities directed to faculty should provide information and education about campus efforts. In addition, some policies about alcohol use at alumni gatherings might be considered. Alcohol use at alumni social functions needs to be consistent with norms promoted on campus. Other programmatic efforts might involve providing visiting alumni with information about area AA meetings or providing a meeting place for recovering alums.

Other campus groups. Other campus groups also need to consider their role in establishing a campus-wide effort. The campus police need training and guidance in responding to alcohol- or other substance use-related emergencies. The campus chaplaincy should be able to address issues of substance use as a pastoral concern with individuals, as well as the impact on the spiritual life of the community. Student supportive services can include staff in study skills centers who stay alert to substance use problems, make referrals for evaluation, and provide information on the impact of alcohol use on academic performance.

Many of the above items can simultaneously serve different levels of prevention. For example, designating alcohol-free housing may be a primary prevention for acute problems as well as a tertiary prevention for a recovering student.

Establishing a Program

A major combined problem for those in developing campus alcohol and drug programs is conceptualizing and then organizing the task. First, the focus should be on the institution's commitment to addressing alcohol problems. Next, help should be given to the institution to assess what will be entailed and to recognize the need for substantial internal support. Accomplishing this requires more than meeting once with senior administrators, polling faculty for opinions, or making a cursory presentation to trustees. It requires informing others so that not to act becomes impossible. Key administrators must be informed of the scope of the problem and acquire a realistic appreciation of what will be required to respond effectively. Preparation of a "white paper" or something similar for the institution's consideration may facilitate this appreciation.

Planning. Having decided to address alcohol and substance use issues, the next step is *not* to hire a coordinator, delegate the alcohol issue to him or her, and allow everyone else to go about their business as usual. Making a difference in community norms, drinking practices, and attitudes is not easily achieved or accomplished by decree. Consider the planning that goes into a presidential search, a major and multiple-year fund-raising effort, or curriculum revision. Outside consultants are called in, other institutions are contacted, and a plan for action is sketched out. For change of the magnitude desired in drinking and drug use practices, strategic planning for a multiple-year time frame is necessary. Remember that although considered the last bastions of tradition, institutions of higher education can be remade over a very brief period. In a 4-year period, the student body turns over. Quickly the institutional memory can be reshaped and new patterns defined as "that's how

we always have done it." A concerted effort will also require fiscal resources.

The effective campus program requires sophisticated leadership. Analytical and community development skills are a plus. Knowledge of and experience with adolescent development is also helpful. How does one factor alcohol use into the developmental process? What functions is the current alcohol use pattern serving? The writing on this topic in the alcohol literature is fairly narrow, focusing on adolescents' experimentation with alcohol, their sense of being invulnerable, or their risk-taking characteristics. But this certainly is not the whole picture. How does alcohol use fit into developmental tasks? It appears to relate to experimentation not with alcohol, but with intimacy, or means of trying on roles, without needing to assume responsibility for the outcome and other larger issues.

An important early step in planning and implementing a program is collecting basic descriptive data about actual alcohol use patterns on the campus. Without some sense of the distribution of drinking practices among students, we may unwittingly adopt a distorted perception of campus alcohol use. By way of comparison, consider alcohol use patterns in the general population. Of adults over age 21, 30% are essentially nondrinkers, consuming less than one drink per year. Of the remainder of the adult population, 50% drink but as a group consume only 20% of all the alcohol. That leaves only one-fifth of the population, or 20%, consuming 80% of all alcoholic beverages. Even in that group of heavy drinkers, 50% of all alcohol is consumed by 7% of the population.[16]

What is found on the college campus? Presumably there will be fewer abstainers than in the general population, but similarly there appears to be a heavy-drinking subgroup. A survey of alcohol use at a New England private college is shown in Table 19-5.

This information also provides a different but equally striking picture of the considerable differences in drinking. In the typical week, 57% of the

Table 19-5. Distribution of Alcohol Consumption among Students

Quartile	Proportion of alcohol consumed in typical week (%)
1st	1.5
2nd	11.5
3rd	23.0
4th	64.0

From Meilman P. Survey of Dartmouth College Drinking Patterns. Dartmouth College Student Health Service: Hanover NH, 1989.

students report having from 0 to 6 drinks. At the other end of the continuum is the 2.3% of the students who report having between 40 to 50 drinks per typical week. The impact of this on the pattern of total alcohol consumption is that a small group of heavy drinkers, less than 3% of all students, consumes an amount of alcohol equal to *all* the alcohol consumed by 57% of their peers in combination.[14]

Information on the spectrum of drinking practices is also useful in the clinical realm in identifying those who are heavy drinkers by the campus's norms. With the tendency not to be aware of the number of light-drinking students, it is easy to accept a student's assertion, "Everyone drinks just like me."[1]

An important component of an institutional effort is an alcohol policy. An alcohol policy should not read like a penal code. It should set forth a clear, direct statement of the institution's stance toward alcohol use and the means it intends to use in addressing these. Consider as a parallel, the institutional statements on academic honesty. In such statements, the institution's stance is clear. The standards set for members' behavior are unambiguous. There is not, however, an effort to establish comprehensive policing efforts to ensure compliance. However, if violations of the honor code come to attention, they will be treated without hesitation as serious breeches of the ethos underpinning the community's intellectual life.

A question that commonly comes to light when alcohol policies are discussed is, "Can we enforce the policy?" One response is opting to go no further than creating "all the policy we think we can enforce," which often is little. There has been the perception that more limited statements would reduce liability, which is not the case.[5] No institution can protect itself from suit in our litigious society. The institution is often the deep pocket. The best protection for the institution if litigation occurs is a comprehensive student education and treatment referral program.

Implementation. A comprehensive program needs to involve all sectors of the community. This does not mean that every one need be a "true believer" in the same fashion. People will have different concerns: Public relations; institutional liability; the record on the playing field or not jeopardizing the school's status with the NCAA by coming up with positive urine screens; the quality of life or academic life; health concerns; or personal identification with the issues of children of alcoholics or alcohol dependence. A model program can encompass all of these motives, not deeming some more legitimate and noble than others. Ultimately, campus-wide involvement occurs when alcohol issues are recognized as intruding on each of us.

It is important to avoid the common practice of labeling people as deficient, remiss, or showing poor attitudes by not having been involved with the topic of alcohol. Developing campus programs should not be perceived as a campaign to have people shape up.[13]

In definitions of the need for change, one segment of the community often overlooked initially is the students. Others formulate policy, make the basic decisions, and put it to the students for some review and comment, which is often unfavorable. Those charged with planning often become bogged down in attempting to determine how to engineer students' acceptance. Students' negative responses may say as much about their exclusion from the process as about the program efforts proposed. There is the strong suspicion that if students are engaged in the process, they become informed about the issues, recognize the need for action, perceive any proposed actions as reasonable and intrinsically inevitable in light of the data, and support any actions eventually proposed.

Education is a common element of programs. But too often education is nothing more than slogans, operationally defined by whatever information fits on a lapel button. Education is a continuous process; there isn't *the* event that will do it once and for all. Education efforts need to be tailored to specific groups and employ a variety of different modalities. A limited but significant number of emergency responses need to be part of everyone's fund of knowledge in a campus community. These responses might be considered the alcohol use equivalent of CPR.

Every campus alcohol program will need to determine the threshold of concern for individuals. Or phrased another way, what is the institution prepared to overlook? The threshold for concern should be low. Whether an alcohol incident represents an isolated event or a chronic problem will never be immediately apparent. The consequences of acute problems can be as disastrous as those connected with alcohol dependence. The accepted stance is always to err on the conservative side.

There may be the tendency to "finally" take a stand. Unfortunately, this often occurs after a lengthy period of vacillating behavior. Finally, something dramatic is done, which may not be well thought out. For example, several years ago there was a growing awareness and concern about alcohol use by the local high school students. There were the usual incidents for the age group—unchaperoned parties with drinking, parents allowing alcohol to be served in their homes, drinking and driving, bringing alcohol to school dances, or coming to dances after drinking. That year the soccer team had an outstanding season and made it to the play-offs for the state championship. A parent put a bottle of champagne on the bus. The team subsequently won. In the course of the celebrating, someone remembered the champagne on the bus, and the players proceeded to pour it over one another. This led to a public uproar. In the aftermath, the team members refused to tell who got it from the bus. Interestingly, the parent who provided the champagne never confessed, either. As a result, the next year's team was not allowed to participate in any post-season games, regardless of their playing record. Beyond the questions of delaying punishment for such an extended period or penalizing players who may not have been present, there was a further irony. Not only were the students following a well-established tradition witnessed at the conclusion of every professional championship series, but this incident may have represented the most appropriate, nondestructive use of alcohol ever displayed in the school. But, this was the time to "put the foot down." Although an extreme example, this points out the capacity to undermine one's efforts if action is taken precipitously.

In conclusion, consider how campus efforts may be evaluated. Various parameters can be used to measure program impact, such as levels of dorm damage, the numbers of emergency visits to the local hospital emergency department, the number of cases involving alcohol or other drug use that come before the campus judiciary system, and how each of these is handled. However, there is another dimension. It does not easily lend itself to measurement but is also important. This is captured by the following incident, related by a colleague who learned of it only by chance:

At the prodding of concerned friends, a fraternity member was seen by a substance use counselor and eventually entered residential treatment. This set off a wave of referrals from the student's fraternity, one of which turned out to be the current president. This student was treated as an outpatient on campus and became active in AA as part of continuing treatment. Following that year's fraternity rush, the first house meeting with the new pledge class was held. Of those present, each in turn introduced himself. In a parody of introductions at AA meetings, one of the first pledges to introduce himself, after giving his name, added, "and I'm an alcoholic." This was met with by tittering and laughter. Each subsequent pledge introduced himself in a similar fashion, concluding with, "and I'm an alcoholic." Finally, it was the president's turn. He looked around at each person and introduced himself in a quiet but forthright way—"I'm Joe, and I really *am* an alcoholic." Dead silence.

Ultimately, the goal is for change to permeate the community so that everyday encounters between persons, of the sort that go unnoticed by others, will embody increased awareness and appreciation of the problems accompanying alcohol use. Such moments as described, in this case taking 10 seconds, represent the outcome of many years' work and are among the most eloquent testimonies to a campus's efforts.

CLINICAL SERVICES

In respect to clinical care, the general approaches outlined throughout the manual are also applicable to a college population. There are several points worth noting.

Screening

Several studies of the use of the traditional screening tests, namely, the CAGE (see Chapter 2, Routine Screening and Initial Assessment), have raised some questions about its utility with a college population.[9,24,30,31] One possible difficulty with the usual screening tools is that the questions focus upon identifying behaviors that may *not* be deviant or unacceptable in campus circles. A student may have had a number of negative consequences or have had several close calls from a safety standpoint; but the student may consider this normal, therefore not "feel guilty," nor ever have been in a situation where anyone questioned the drinking or expressed concern.

In respect to screening, the point is not simply to screen for dependence or abuse, but also to identify essentially dangerous, high-risk drinking patterns. One of the best indices in this population is the frequency of intoxication. This is also effective in identifying those with ongoing alcohol problems.[25]

Protocols

A colleague often comments that a major obstacle to asking about alcohol and/or other drug use is the "fear of a positive response." One solution is to have clear protocols in place to facilitate evaluations and to promote referrals. In many institutions, full-time and interdisciplinary staff with a several-bed infirmary is a thing of the past. In this situation, having clear-cut guidelines is even more important; there is not the luxury of conferring with colleagues, nor necessarily the time to do so.

Brief Interventions

This is a population for which brief treatment models or brief interventions are particularly timely and efficacious, especially for at-risk drinkers.[10] For example, a recent report noted the positive results of simply informing high-consumption students by letter that their drinking was greater than that of most other students. At follow-up a year later, the students getting this informational letter had reduced consumption, while those drinking in a similar fashion who had not received this feedback had no alteration in drinking.[1] Abuse and at-risk use is far more common than dependence. This is a group for which efforts to moderate drinking patterns are appropriate and successful.

Recovering Students

Every campus needs to recognize that some of its students probably will enter college as recovering alcohol- or drug-dependent individuals. The college health and counseling service needs to be sensitive to their needs. One of the obvious requisite steps is to ascertain this information. Understandably, it may not be information that a student includes on an admission application, but any health service forms need to ask this question. As with any other chronic medical condition, there may be some role in monitoring and supporting aftercare plans, in being alert to these students' continuing involvement in 12-step programs, or in involving them in campus-convened support groups. Some schools also have substance-free dorms or houses that, while not restricted to recovering students, may be an important environmental support for their maintaining abstinence.

REFERENCES

1. Agostinelli G; Brown JM; Miller WR. Effects of normative feedback on consumption among heavy drinking college students. *Journal of Drug Education* 25(1): 31-40, 1995. (38 refs.)

2. American College Health Association. Recommended Standards and Practices for a College Health Program, 4th Edition, 1983. *Journal of American College Health* 32(4): entire issue, 1984.

3. Burns WD. *Report of the Rutgers University Committee on the Use of Alcohol.* New Brunswick NJ: Rutgers University, 1981.

4. Chassey RA; Clifford DA. Responsibility versus choice: A different approach to alcohol education. (technical note). *Journal of College Student Personnel* 29(3): 275-276, 1988. (4 refs.)

5. Engs RC; Hanson DJ. University students drinking patterns and problems: Examining the effects of raising the purchase age. *Public Health Report* 133(6): 647-673, 1988. (61 refs.)

6. Friend KE; Koushki PA. Student substance use: Stability and change across college years. *International Journal of the Addictions* 19(5): 571-575, 1984. (4 refs.)

7. Glicksman L. Consequences of alcohol use: Behavior changes and problems during first year of university. *International Journal of the Addiction* 23(12): 1281-1295, 1988. (24 refs.)

8. Gullard ED; Flouney AC. Universities, colleges and alcohol: An overview of tort liability issues. IN: BACCHUS of the United States, Inc and The Inter-Association Task Force on Campus Alcohol Issues. *First National Conference on Campus Alcohol Policy Initiatives.* Distributed by BACCHUS of the United States, Inc and The Inter-Association Task Force on Campus Alcohol Issues, 1986. pp. 63-74. (14 refs.)

9. Heck EJ; Williams MD. Using the CAGE to screen for drinking-related problems in college students. *Journal of Studies on Alcohol* 56(3): 282-286, 1995. (23 refs.)

10. Howard GS; Nathan PE, eds. *Alcohol Use and Misuse by Young Adults.* Notre Dame IN: University of Notre Dame Press, 1994. pp. 198. (Chapter refs.)

11. Johnston LD; O'Malley PM; Bachman JG. *National Survey Results on Drug Use from The Monitoring the Future Study, 1975-1993. Volume II: College Students and Young Adults.* Rockville MD: National Institute on Drug Abuse, 1994.

12. Kinney J; Peltier D. *Model Alcohol Program for the Campus Health Service.* Paper presented Annual Conference, National Council on Alcoholism, Washington DC, April 1985.

13. Kinney J; Peltier D. A model alcohol program for the college health service. *Journal of American College Health* 34(4): 229-233, 1986. (14 refs.)

14. Meilman P. *Survey of Dartmouth College Drinking Patterns.* Hanover NH: Student Health Service, Dartmouth College, 1989.

15. Meilman PW. Alcohol-induced sexual behavior on campus. *Journal of American College Health* 42(1): 27-31, 1993. (19 refs.)

16. National Institute on Alcohol Abuse and Alcoholism. *Toward a National Plan to Combat Alcohol Abuse and Alcoholism: A Report to the United States Congress.* Rockville MD: National Institute on Alcohol Abuse and Alcoholism, 1986.

17. Pattison EM. Cultural level interventions in the arena of alcoholism. *Alcoholism: Clinical and Experimental Research* 8(2):160-164, 1984. (39 refs.)

18. Pezza PE; Bellotti A. College campus violence: Origins, impacts, and responses. *Educational Psychology Review* 7(1): 105-123, 1995. (53 refs.)

19. Prendergast ML. Substance use and abuse among college students: A review of recent literature. (review). *Journal of American College Health* 43(3): 99-113, 1994. (86 refs.)

20. Presley CA; Meilman PW; Lyerla R. *Alcohol and Drugs on American College Campuses: Use, Consequences, and Perceptions of the Campus Environment. Volume I. 1989-1991.* Carbondale IL: Southern Illinois University, 1993. 105 pp. (6 refs.)

21. Presley CA; Meilman PW; Lyerla R. *Alcohol and Drugs on American College Campuses: Use, Consequences, and Perceptions of the Campus Environment. Volume II: 1990-1992.* Carbondale IL: Southern Illinois University, 1995. 123 pp. (0 refs.)

22. Presley CA; Meilman PW; Padgett JF. Facts and myths. *New Directions for Student Services* 67(Fall): 15-27, 1994. (15 refs.)

23. Robins LN; Helzer J; Weissman MM; Orraischel H; Gruenberg E; Burke JD; et al. Lifetime prevalence of specific psychiatric disorders in three sites. *Archives of General Psychiatry* 41(10): 949-958, 1984. (25 refs.)

24. Ross HE; Tisdall GW. Identification of alcohol disorders at a university mental health centre using the CAGE. *Journal of Alcohol and Drug Education* 39(3): 119-126, 1994. (14 refs.)

25. Smith DS. *Screening for problem drinking in college students.* Paper presented American College Health Association annual meeting, New Orleans, May 1986.

26. Smith MC. Students, suds and summons: Strategies for coping with campus alcohol abuse. *Journal of College Student Development* 30(2): 118-122, 1989. (14 refs.)

27. Task Force on Alcohol and Drugs, American College Health Association. Standards on Alcohol and Substance Use, Misuse, and Dependency. *Journal of American College Health* 36(2): 60-63, 1987. (0 refs.)

28. Vaillant GE. *Natural History of Alcoholism.* Cambridge MA: Harvard University Press, 1983. 378 pp. (369 refs.)

29. Wechsler H; Davenport A; Dowdall G; Moeykens B; Castillo S. Health and behavioral consequences of binge drinking in college: A national survey of students at 140 campuses. *Journal of the American Medical Association* 272(21): 1672-1677, 1994. (26 refs.)

30. Werner MJ; Walker LS; Greene JW. Longitudinal evaluation of a screening measure for problem drinking among female college freshmen. *Archives of Pediatrics & Adolescent Medicine* 148 (12): 1331-1337, 1994. (35 refs.)

31. Werner MJ; Walker LS; Greene JW. Screening for problem drinking among college freshmen. *Journal of Adolescent Health* 15(4): 303-310, 1994. (34 refs.)

FURTHER READINGS

Anderson DS; Gadaleto AF. *1994 College Alcohol Survey. Preliminary Results.* Fairfax VA: David S. Anderson and Angelo F. Gadaleto, 1994. (0 refs.)

The College Alcohol Survey is sent to a representative sample of 330 colleges and universities offering at least the BA or BS degree. This sample is selected from each of the 50 states and the District of Columbia. The survey is mailed to Vice Presidents of Student Affairs, who are requested to direct the survey to the most appropriate person(s) on their campuses. Nonrespondents are sent a reminder 4 weeks after the initial mailing. This same procedure was followed in 1979, 1982, 1985, 1988, 1991, and 1994. Response rates have ranged from 50% to 72%. These 1994 Preliminary Results were based on 200 responses, representing a rate of 61%. Final results with additional returns and comparisons with 1991 and baseline years will be prepared and formally released. Copyright 1994, Project Cork Institute.

Baer JS; Kivlahan DR; Marlatt GA. High-risk drinking across the transition from high school to college. *Alcoholism: Clinical and Experimental Research* 19(1): 54-61, 1995. (27 refs.)

Alcohol use and related problems were studied from the senior year in high school to the first autumn in college for 366 heavy-drinking students. Four risk factors—subject sex, family history of drinking problems, prior conduct problems, and type of college residence—were evaluated as predictors of (1) differential changes in drinking rates, (2) differential changes in alcohol-related problems, and (3) alcohol dependence symptoms during the first college term. Results suggest that both dispositional and environmental factors are associated with changes in drinking rates and the existence of dependence symptoms. Increases in the frequency of drinking were specifically and strongly associated with residence in a fraternity (men) or sorority (women). Three risk factors were associated with increased quantity of drinking: male gender, residence in a fraternity or sorority, and a history of conduct problems. Prior conduct problems were also consistently associated with dependence symptoms during the first term in college. A family history of alcohol problems was not consistently related to changes in use rates or problems, although some analyses suggest interactive effects. Early interventions on college campuses should target individuals using additive risk profiles. Copyright 1995, Research Society on Alcoholism. Used with permission.

Center on Addiction and Substance Abuse at Columbia University. *Rethinking Rites of Passage: Substance Abuse on America's Campuses.* A Report by the Commission on Substance Abuse at Colleges and Universities. New York: Center on Addiction and Substance Abuse at Columbia University, 1994. (73 refs.)

This report, by a task force that commissioned itself as the Commission on Substance Abuse at Colleges and Universities, is the second in a series of reports that focuses upon alcohol use on campuses. In particular it directs attention to patterns of high-risk use, namely, consumption of more than five drinks per occasion, which is characterized as having reached "epidemic proportions." Following an Executive Summary and Background Papers, the report is organized into five sections. The first is the nature of the problem; the second, the explanations set forth for college student alcohol use; the third, the relationship between the school and the student; the fourth, a review of programs to date and their lack of success in addressing campus alcohol problems; the final section, recommendations for action. Copyright 1994, Project Cork Institute.

Keller DS; Bennett ME; McCrady BS; Paulus MD; Frankenstein W. Treating college substance abusers: The New Jersey Collegiate Substance Abuse Program. *Journal of Substance Abuse Treatment* 11(6): 569-581, 1994. (20 refs.)

University students with serious substance abuse disorders may require specialized treatment. The New Jersey Collegiate Substance Abuse Program (NJCSAP) was a treatment center developed for this population that allowed students to receive treatment while remaining in the university environment. NJCSAP was structured into three levels of care so that patients could be matched to treatment of appropriate intensity. In addition, NJCSAP helped students develop a network of supportive recovering peers and activities on the Rutgers University campus. An evaluation of the patient population revealed a group of students with a history of severe substance use and related problems. Implications of the evaluation results are discussed. Copyright 1994, Pergamon Press.

Meilman P; Presley CA; Lyerla R. Black college students and binge drinking. *Journal of Blacks in Higher Education* 4(Summer): 70-71, 1994. (0 refs.)

A large percentage of colleges and universities in the US are "party schools." Even the most academically serious institutions have alcohol- and drug-related partying as a dominant extracurricular activity. A recent report from the Center on Addiction and Substance Abuse at Columbia University concluded that "binge drinking is the number one substance abuse problem in American college life." The study found that 90% of the reported rapes on campus occurred when either the victim or the assailant had been drinking. Nearly 70% of all suicide victims on campus were legally intoxicated when they took their lives. When they drink, some 20% of all college students abandon their usual safe sex practices. While alcohol abuse is rampant on college campuses, research reported here reveals that black college students are far less likely to use and abuse alcohol than are white college students. Copyright 1994, CH II Publishers.

Ryan BE; Colthurst T; Segars L. *College Alcohol Risk Assessment Guide: Environmental Approaches to Prevention.* La Jolla CA: University of California at San Diego, 1994. (41 refs.)

This guide, directed to college personnel, describes steps to gather and evaluate information on alcohol problems in the campus setting. It has a particular focus upon environmental issues, i.e., college policies and the community in which the institution is located. Five appendices include work sheets to assist in assessment. Copyright 1995, Project Cork Institute.

Ryan BE; Mosher JF. *Progress Report: Alcohol Promotion on Campus.* San Rafael CA: Marin Institute, 1991. 89 pp. (106 refs.)

This study documents the significant progress made in the last 2 years in tempering the aggressive marketing practices of the alcoholic beverage industry on college campuses. The marketing reforms are a response to pressure put on the industry by students, college administrators, public health activists, governmental officials, and local communities. Despite the recent progress, the alcohol industry maintains a major marketing presence on campus. As a result, it continues to exacerbate what campus health officials describe as the number one health problem of college students. Based on these findings, the study concludes with six recommendations to reduce the toll of alcohol-related problems on college campuses and to address the continuing abuses of the alcohol beverage industry in its college marketing program. Copyright 1991, Marin Institute.

Single E. The impact of social and regulatory policy on drinking behavior. IN: Zucker R; Boyd G; Howard J, eds. *The Development of Alcohol Problems: Exploring the Biopsychosocial Matrix of Risk.*

NIAAA Research Monograph 26. Rockville MD: National Institute on Alcohol Abuse and Alcoholism, 1994. pp. 209-248. (166 refs.)

The author presents a thorough review of the literature on alcohol control and its relationship to the prevalence of alcohol-related problems. He explores the theoretical linkages between control policy, alcohol consumption, and adverse consequences, and he summarizes the research literature on the impact of the minimum legal drinking age, density of outlets, restrictions on days and hours of sale, price and taxation policies, warning labels, and other control policies. The author also discusses the impact of alcohol advertising and situational features of drinking venues. He concludes that, in general, easing restrictions on alcohol availability results in increased consumption by both moderate and heavy drinkers. Public Domain.

Wechsler H; Isaac NE; Grodsrein F; Sellers DE. Continuation and initiation of alcohol use from the first to the second year of college. *Journal of Studies on Alcohol* 55(1): 41-45, 1994. (17 refs.)

Wide-spread and heavy alcohol use by American college students is a concern to college administrators and public health officials. This study surveyed a cohort of 611 college students during their first and second year of college to examine the development of alcohol use behaviors in college. Almost every student who used alcohol during the first year continued to do so during the second year. Similarly, many of the students who were binge drinkers the first year continued binge drinking the second year. One-third of male freshmen who had not binged the first year initiated this behavior during the second year, although relatively few female students did so. Compared to continued users, the students who initiated alcohol use during the second year were light users. In addition, students who drank more heavily in high school were more likely to be binge drinkers in college. Consequently, programs that address alcohol use by college students need to focus on early detection and intervention rather than on primary prevention. Copyright 1994, Alcohol Research Documentation, Inc. Used with permission.

RESOURCES

American College Health Association Task Force on Alcohol and Substance Use

Contact   PO Box 28937, Baltimore MD 21240-8937.

Description Organized in 1985, the Task Force prepared standards on substance abuse, misuse, and dependence that were approved by the ACHA Board in September 1987 and published that month in the *Journal of American College Health*. In collaboration with the ACHA national office, the task force arranges for and provides professional development opportunities for persons in the college health field to deal effectively with the issues of alcohol and other substance use, misuse, and dependence on campus.

Materials   The ACHA publishes four pamphlets on alcohol and other drugs: *Adult Children of Alcohol Abusers; Alcohol and Other Drugs: Risky Business; Alcohol: Decisions on Tap;* and *How to Help a Friend with a Drinking Problem.*

The BACCHUS and GAMMA Peer Education Network

Contact   Drew Hunter, Executive Director, PO Box 10430, Denver CO 80250-0430. (303) 871-3068.

Description The BACCHUS and GAMMA Peer Education Network is an international association of college and university-based peer education programs focusing on alcohol abuse prevention and other related student health and safety issues. It is the mission of the association to actively promote peer education as a useful element of campus health education and wellness efforts. To do so, the professional and volunteer staff devote most of their activities to the following:

- To develop and maintain a thriving student network.
- To provide resources that promote and support peer education activities.
- To provide high-quality training opportunities locally, regionally, and nationally.
- To promote a national forum on student alcohol abuse prevention and on other student health or safety concerns.
- To create, promote, and disseminate new research on alcohol and other student health or safety issues.

The BACCHUS and GAMMA Peer Education Network was established in 1975 and is comprised of over 700 campus-based chapters. The organization is the founding member of the Inter-Association Task Force on Alcohol and Other Substance Abuse Issues.

Materials   The BACCHUS and GAMMA Peer Education Network offers a wide variety of educational materials for college students, such as pamphlets, posters, videos, and training programs, including a 17-module Certified Peer Educator Training program. An educational materials catalog can be received by contacting the National Headquarters at (303)871-3068.

A monthly newsletter, *The BACCHUS Beat,* contains current information, program ideas from other schools, and resource information. The Network also hosts a national educational conference each November, the General Assembly, and 12 Spring regional conferences across the country.

Inter-Association Task Force on Alcohol and Other Substance Abuse Issues

Contact   Drew Hunter, Executive Director, The BACCHUS and GAMMA Peer Education Network, PO Box 10430, Denver CO 80250-0430. (303) 871-3068.

Description Founded in 1983, the task force is a 20-member coalition of associations representing nearly all student leaders and administrators involved in student affairs work in higher education. It seeks to eradicate the abuse of alcohol, tobacco, legal and illegal drugs, and other substance by college students. It strives to inspire students to review their life-styles and make informed decisions regarding these substances. The IATF supports teaching college students life skills that will enable them to be successful in college and afterwards.

Materials   Each year the Task Force publishes a program-planning calendar and National Collegiate Awareness Week manual.

The association sponsors awards to campuses with outstanding NCAAW programs, promotes an NCAAW campaign poster competition, and consults with the alcohol beverage industry to ensure the most responsible standards of marketing and product orientation. The IATF also hosts a national training conference, the National Collegiate Conference on Life Skills, each February.

National Association of Student Personnel Administrators, Inc (NASPA)

Contact   1875 Connecticut Avenue NW, Suite 416, Washington DC 20009-5728. (202) 265-7500.

Description   NASPA provides leadership and professional growth opportunities for the chief student affairs officer and other professionals who consider higher education and student affairs issues from an institutional perspective.

Materials   *Alcohol Policies and Procedures on College and University Campuses,* 1987. 99 pp. J. Sherwood, Editor. $7.50, plus $3.50 shipping/handling charge.

This monograph addresses one of the nation's most serious problems: substance abuse. Not only does the book initiate useful dialogue on campuses, it suggests how to establish effective policies. By pointing out issues of legal liability, the book gives every college and university an opportunity to examine its role in responding to substance abuse.

Developing Effective and Legally Sound Alcohol Policies, 1994. 14 pp. E.D. Gulland, Author. $5.00, plus $3.50 shipping/handling charge.

Five years after the passage of the Drug-Free Schools and Communities Act Amendments, which required all institutions to implement substance abuse policies, alcohol use and the development of effective alcohol policies continue to be major concerns on college campuses. This white paper, published by United Educators Insurance Risk Retention Group, Inc, reviews the current legal climate and how it affects the development and administration of sound alcohol policies, with comments from college and university administrators on their experiences in implementing institutional alcohol policies.

National Collegiate Athletic Association (NCAA)

Contact   Frank D. Uryasz, Director of Sports Sciences and Primary Staff Liaison, NCAA Committee on Competitive Safeguards and Medical Aspects of Sports 6201 College Boulevard, Overland Park KS 66211-2422. (913) 339-1906.

Description   The NCAA sponsors programs in drug use prevention, intervention, and education that reach out to college student-athletes, coaches, and athletics administrators, as well as to grade school and high school youth. The NCAA provides a number of programs either dealing exclusively with drug education or having significant drug education components.

Rutgers University Student Services

Contacts   Alcohol & Other Drug Assistance Program for Students. Lisa Laitman, Program Director. (908) 932-

7976. Student Health Service. Dr. Robert H. Bierman, Medical Director. (908) 932-8429.

Address   Hurtado Health Center, 11 Bishop Place, Rutgers University, New Brunswick NJ 08903. (908) 932-7401.

Description   Rutgers University has been in the forefront of developing and implementing a comprehensive campus alcohol policy, as well as prevention and treatment programs. In 1980 the Committee on the Use of Alcohol issued a 44-page recommendation report, which has been subsequently used as a model for policy development and prevention programs on other campuses; and in 1984 a policy statement and regulations were adopted. The Alcohol & Other Drug Assistance Program for Students (ADAPS) was developed to assist the university community in the early identification of students with alcohol- and other drug-related problems that interfere with their ability to perform academically, maintain their health, and develop mature relationships. The program provides services to high-risk students; those who are abusing substances and developing problems; students from families where there is addiction; and active and recovering addicts. Individual counseling, group counseling, assessment, consultation, family therapy, and intensive outpatient treatment are among the services offered. The ADAPS also operates on-campus housing units for recovering students with the support of the University Housing Office.

Materials   *Regulations Concerning the Use of Alcohol Beverages, 1984. Revised University Policy Statement on the Use of Alcoholic Beverages,* 1984.

Network of Colleges and Universities Committed to the Elimination of Drug and Alcohol Abuse

Contacts   Vonnie Voltri, Senior Associate, US Department of Education, 555 NW New Jersey Avenue, Washington DC. (202) 219-2265, and Dr. Edward Hammond, President, Fort Hays State University, Hays KS 67601. (913) 628-4231.

Description   A planning group of 15 college and university presidents and high-level administrators was convened by the US Department of Education in October 1987. They proposed a set of standards for the network and have subsequently met to develop a self-assessment checklist and implementation guidelines. Network membership is open to all 4-year colleges and universities. Members will attend an annual national forum and have access to advisory services and other resources. Institutions will be recognized for their membership. Other sources of information and materials are the national offices of fraternities and sororities.

CHAPTER 20

SUSAN McGRATH MORGAN, LICSW
JEAN KINNEY, MSW

CLINICAL APPLICATIONS

The goals of this chapter are to assist the clinician to:

1. Be familiar with gender differences in substance use patterns and morbidity.

2. Be familiar with the physiological factors that contribute to differences in the effects of alcohol on women.

3. Understand the obstacles to treatment for women and factors that may increase access to treatment.

4. Understand the treatment needs of special populations of women.

The traditional assumption in the substance abuse treatment field had been that alcohol dependence is alcohol dependence and drug dependence is drug dependence, regardless of gender. Indeed, research on substance abuse problems in women was very limited. In respect to alcohol problems, a literature review indicated that only 28 English language studies of women with alcoholism were published between 1928 and 1970. This traditional wisdom is now being questioned. Currently research is examining the physiologically based differences between male and female substance use. Similarly, the treatment community is becoming sensitive to sociocultural factors that affect treatment approaches and access to treatment. Research and clinical experience also indicate that women concerned about substance abuse issues also are touched deeply by general women's issues in our society.[58]

Despite the growing attention to women's problems, the available data are not easily synthesized. One difficulty is that researchers frequently study women who enter treatment; this limits what can be said about the extent, nature, and magnitude of problems in the general population. Further complicating the situation is that those being studied seemingly represent all of the possible combinations of alcohol and other substance use. Subjects of research studies range from alcohol-dependent women, to women with drug dependence, to women with alcohol dependence who use/abuse/are dependent on other substances, to female substance users who drink/drink heavily/are alcohol dependent. The extent to which these populations are discrete or overlapping is unknown. Again, generalizations from any of these individual studies is difficult. In addition, the research to date has used relatively small samples and has focused on narrow topics. Thus, although facts and truth proliferate, there is not always greater understanding.

GENDER DIFFERENCES IN SUBSTANCE USE

Women represent a growing percentage of drinkers, those with alcohol problems and those with alcohol dependence. For younger women in the general population, the proportion of drinkers is beginning to approximate that of men. That men, as a group, are statistically more likely to be drinkers is primarily because of the greater number of abstainers among older women. These older women, born on the heels of Prohibition, are of an era in which women's drinking was less socially acceptable and far less prevalent. The behavior of their granddaughters is quite different.

In respect to other drug use, the same pattern is generally true, with the notable exception of prescription drugs for nonmedical purposes. Table 20-1

Table 20-1. Substance Use in the Past Year by Gender, 1993

Substance	Men (%)	Women (%)
Alcohol	71.7	61.7
Nicotine	32.4	26.6
Any illicit drug	14.2	9.6
Marijuana	11.7	6.5
Cocaine	3.2	1.3
Crack	0.8	0.2
Inhalants	1.4	0.6
Hallucinogens	1.7	0.6
Prescription*	3.9	3.7
Stimulants	1.5	0.9
Sedatives	0.7	0.8
Tranquilizers*	1.1	1.3
Analgesics	2.2	2.2

From Substance Abuse and Mental Health Services Administration. *National Household Survey on Drug Abuse: Population Estimates 1993.* Rockville MD: Substance Abuse and Mental Health Services Administration, 1994. (0 refs.)
*Nonmedical use.

summarizes the substance use patterns of women vs. men, and Table 20-2 highlights the differences for different age groups. The information is drawn from the most recently published Household Survey, conducted regularly on behalf of the National Institute on Drug Abuse. The table includes the proportion of the population over age 14, who report use within the past year. It should be noted that the Household Survey does not include incarcerated persons or the homeless, two groups with a high prevalence of substance use.

Patterns of Use

Women's use patterns appear to differ from men's in several ways. Middle to late adolescence is the time of greatest risk to initiate drug use. Young men are more likely than young women to experiment with a variety of different drugs. The one exception is prescribed psychoactives. In women, psychoactive substance use is more likely to begin with prescription drugs.[40] In general, women use more prescription medications for nonmedical purposes, as evidenced by the Household Survey. Women are prescribed psychotropic drugs more frequently than men. Thus, they have greater access to prescribed substances that alone or in combination with alcohol can cause problems. Women also use medicinal, mood-altering, legal drugs more than men.[51]

Associated Problems

Studies of treatment populations suggest that the nature of problems associated with dependence and

Table 20-2. Substance Use in the Past Year for Women of Different Ages, 1993

Substance	All women (%)	Age groups (%)		
		18-25 yrs	26-34 yrs	>34 yrs
Alcohol	61.7	77.5	77.5	57.6
Nicotine	26.6	35.3	33.6	23.7
Any illicit drug	9.6	22.0	13.2	5.1
Marijuana	6.5	17.2	10.2	2.5
Cocaine	1.3	3.7	2.4	0.5
Crack	0.2	0.5	0.4	**
Inhalants	0.6	1.5	0.2	0.1
Hallucinogens	0.6	3.0	0.4	**
Prescription*	3.7	6.2	4.8	2.9
Stimulants	0.9	1.6	1.2	0.5
Sedatives*	0.8	0.6	0.7	0.8
Tranquilizers*	1.3	2.0	1.6	1.2
Analgesics	2.2	3.7	3.1	1.5

From Substance Abuse and Mental Health Services Administration. *National Household Survey on Drug Abuse: Population Estimates 1993.* Rockville MD: Substance Abuse and Mental Health Services Administration, 1994. (0 refs.)
*Nonmedical use.
**Too low to estimate.

substance use problems distinguishes men from women. One study of women with alcohol dependence found that 70% had a history of using prescribed psychoactive drugs, a rate 1.5 times greater than for alcoholic men. Of the women prescribed psychoactive drugs, one-half could recall at least one occasion of having used alcohol in combination with the medication; also, one-half had been prescribed more than one category of drug.[6] Women with substance dependence are more likely than men to have a cyclical substance use history, marked by periods of alternating high-drug or high-alcohol use.[51] Women are also more likely than men to use other drugs in combination with alcohol.[51] Of those with alcohol dependence, women were more likely to simultaneously abuse sedatives, minor tranquilizers, and legal substances; men were more likely to abuse cannabis and tobacco.[63]

In patients admitted to private hospitals for cocaine treatment, despite many similarities between the sexes, several significant differences have been identified. Women start to use cocaine at a younger age than the men. This is in contrast to what is generally found in opiate users and in those with alcohol problems. The introduction of crack-cocaine seemingly changed some of the traditionally anticipated differences between men and women. With the emergence of crack, women's use rivaled, and in some cities exceeded, use by men.[56]

In respect to psychiatric illness, dependent women are more likely to experience affective disorders, while men are more likely to have anti-social personality disorders.[10,41,58] There is also an increased incidence of eating disorders in women.[12] Women experience greater levels of guilt, shame, depression, and anxiety than men.[58] It has been suggested that genetic factors may predispose women to comorbidity between major depression and alcohol dependence.[44]

Psychosocial and Cultural Issues

Studies of treatment populations suggest other gender-based differences. Women with dependence are reported to have lower expectations for their lives than men with dependence, and also to express more concern with survival and minimizing discomfort.[58,62] Within treatment populations, women are more likely to be socially disadvantaged than men. Female patients are less likely to be employed, to hold high-status jobs, to be self-supporting, and to be financing their own drug use. In these circumstances, women may support their addiction with petty larceny, shoplifting, and prostitution.[58,76] Women have been found to be more likely than men to cite specific reasons for their substance use, although no differences existed between the men's and women's reasons. In addition, there may well be gender differences in the feelings associated with substance use.[29]

In cocaine use, women have noted the desirable effect of a reduction in feelings of guilt; on the other hand, men reported experiencing more guilt. Also, women and men may differ in the course and response to treatment. Women were more frequently diagnosed with depression, and their depressive symptoms took longer to resolve than those of men.

The women in the study demonstrated a slower recovery and had more residual problems after treatment. This raises several significant questions. Do the guilt-reducing properties of cocaine make this a particularly reinforcing drug for some women? Is there a difference in the severity of the withdrawal syndrome for men and women? If so, what implications may this have for differential effectiveness of pharmacological intervention?[29]

Relational and Family Patterns

There are gender-based differences in women's relationships to family and to spouse or partner. Women who come from families where drugs were commonly used as a primary coping strategy are more likely to themselves become addicted.[58] Women with substance use problems have often experienced greater familial disruption than men, and often exhibit a pattern of over-responsibility in their families.

Women are usually the primary caretakers of children. Some have suggested that family members may discourage women from seeking help, as it can be perceived as a threat to their caretaking responsibilities[3,58] However, studies on women's perceptions of the impetus for their entry into treatment have found that pressure/encouragement from family members is often noted.[52] At the same time, women are less likely than men to have a male counterpart supporting them in treatment.[41] In fact, women with alcohol and/or other drug problems (cocaine and opiates) are more likely than men to be involved with a drug-dependent partner.[51] Unlike men, women heroin users are less commonly involved in a stable intimate relationship or marriage; are more likely to have their children living with them; and are largely dependent on their mothers for child care.[51]

In contrast to men, both alcohol- or opiate-involved women come from drug-abusing and disorganized families.[51] Female heroin addicts are more likely than male heroin addicts to have first been introduced to heroin by family members or others close to them. The development of dependence is linked to the family's approval of use or the absence of clear disapproval of use, in combination with easy access to the drug.[51]

Vocational and Employment Patterns

In the work place and vocational spheres, differences between men and women are evident. Women with substance use problems—just as women in the general population—are less likely than men to be employed. They also have fewer vocational skills and training.[51] Women with alcohol or other drug problems are more likely to be dependent on a family member or on public assistance for survival than men, as well as more likely to be the primary caretakers of children.[52,58]

DIFFERENCES AMONG WOMEN
Ethnic Considerations

Ethnicity would be anticipated to be an important basis for differences among women. While data remain limited, there are differences in patterns of use. Caucasian women are more likely than either Hispanic or African-American women to be drinkers, to be smokers, and to have used illicit drugs in the past year. Table 20-3 summarizes the use of selected substances by women from different ethnic/racial groups.

Sexual Orientation

With the limited attention to substance use problems of women generally, it is not surprising that there

Table 20-3. Women's Substance Use in the Past Year by Race and Ethnicity

Substance	Percent of women reporting use in past year			
	All women	Caucasian	African American	Hispanic
Alcohol	61.7	65.8	47.8	53.2
Nicotine	26.6	27.3	26.4	22.8
Any illicit drug	9.6	11.8	8.9	9.1
Marijuana	6.5	6.4	7.4	6.4
Cocaine	1.3	1.2	1.4	2.0
Crack	0.2	0.1	0.7	0.3
Inhalants	0.6	0.6	0.3	0.8
Prescription	3.7	4.1	2.5	3.2

From Substance Abuse and Mental Health Services Administration. *National Household Survey on Drug Abuse: Population Estimates 1993.* Rockville MD: Substance Abuse and Mental Health Services Administration, 1994. (0 refs.)

has been little discussion of lesbian and bisexual women. Beyond sexism, lesbian addiction goes unaddressed because of homophobia and the attendant societal stigma. Research is exceedingly limited, although work is being done.[39] Treatment programs for women are among those most sensitive to the needs of this population.

It has been repeatedly reported that lesbians and bisexual women are at greater risk for substance use problems. Various studies have spawned estimates that 25% to 35% of lesbians have a serious substance use problem. This elevated level has been in part attributed to the "fact" that much of lesbian social life revolves around bars.[79] However, in truth it appears that this elevated risk has been an artifact of the research methodology employed. A recent study, the first that used *random* sampling methods rather than *convenience* samples, failed to support this contention. No significant differences were apparent between the lesbian/bisexual women and heterosexual women, either for drinking patterns or for rates of alcohol problems.[8] Another study published about the same time, which primarily focused upon the similarities and differences in substance use patterns of lesbians and gay men, while plagued by a small response rate, nonetheless had some findings of note. In general the substance use patterns of gays and lesbians were similar. The one striking difference was the high levels of smoking by lesbians, not only in comparison to gays but to women generally. The proportion of lesbians who were current smokers was 48%.[73]

A subgroup of lesbians that may be particularly vulnerable to substance use problems is adolescents. A common theme in empirical studies and clinical reports of lesbian, gay, and bisexual youth is the chronic stress created by the verbal and physical abuse they receive from peers and adults. This can lead to a number of problems, including difficulties at school, running away or being ejected from home, encounters with the law, prostitution, substance abuse, and suicide attempts.[66]

Even though the rates of problems may not be as high as had been presumed, there are unique treatment issues. Lesbian/bisexual women entering treatment will confront special issues such as when and how to reveal lesbian identity and how to deal with homophobia.[79] There is a small but rich literature on treatment issues, both in formal treatment and in self-help groups.[7,19,32,37,38] There has been some recognition, too, of the special problems that face a partner of a lesbian with a substance use problem.[23]

The toll of AIDS in the gay community is well known. Lesbians are also at elevated risk for human immunodeficiency virus (HIV)/AIDS if sexually active with a partner who is an intravenous drug user. Sur-

veillance data for 1980 to 1989 found that 95% of all AIDS cases reported by women with only female partners involved intravenous use by the partner.[15]

Age-Related Differences

Although age has not received particular attention, it is repeatedly cited as *the* factor related to the differences that are identified among women. For example, in alcoholic women, younger women have been reported at greater risk for other drug use and at substantially higher risk for attempted or completed suicide.[27]

One study of the effects of age demonstrated considerable differences between women under and over age 35.[35] Age 35 was chosen as the point for separating age groups to divide the sample into those who had reached adulthood before or after the early 1970s, a period of dramatic cultural changes. The question was, "Have shifts in cultural norms and behavior in respect to substance use, as well as women's roles, influenced the natural history of those who enter treatment?" This seemed to be the case. The age-related differences identified among women included the following:

Substance use patterns. Younger women (under age 35) were more likely than older women to use marijuana, cocaine, stimulants, opiates, and hallucinogens on a weekly basis. One-third of younger women reported weekly use of marijuana, and one-third reported weekly use of cocaine. While 16% of younger women reported daily drinking, this was 2.5 times more common in older women, (40%).

Onset of use. Over half of the younger women (56%) had started drinking before age 16, compared to 14% of the older women. If age 18 is the point of adulthood, 83% of the younger women, compared with 46% of the older women, had spent their entire adult lives as drinkers. The differences for drug use during adulthood are even more extreme. For the older women, 14% had been using drugs since age 18, compared to 74% for the younger women.

Settings for use. Women's drinking has frequently been characterized as solitary, private, and hidden. This is less true of younger women; slightly over half reported that their drinking or drug use occurred primarily with others, compared to 20% of older women. Thus, the pattern of solitary, private use is more true of older women.

Correlates of use. Despite the lower percentage reporting daily drinking, younger women were not likely to have experienced binges and have suffered signs of serious withdrawal, and they were more likely to have used alcohol or drugs during pregnancy. They were also more likely to have consumed about a fifth of liquor per day and to have been violent toward others. Younger women had a 2.5 higher incidence of eating disorders, with 25% reporting either anorexia or bulimia or alternating periods of starving and bingeing and purging. Rates of depression were similar across age groups. In comparison with older women, the younger group had considerably more work-related problems, e.g., in relationships with supervisors and co-workers, the quality of work, time off the job, and injuries on the job. Younger women were also more likely to have been the driver in a motor vehicle accident, to have been arrested, or to have been jailed overnight. In the year before treatment, younger women had more hospitalizations for psychiatric care and received more emergency room medical treatment, while their hospitalization and outpatient medical care was similar to that of the older women.

Violence and abuse. Younger women also had a history of greater physical abuse as children (36%). As adults, the prevalence of abuse escalated, with 48% of younger women reporting physical abuse and 32% reporting rape or coerced sexual intercourse. This is in contrast to older women, of whom 23% reported a history of physical abuse before age 18, rising to 35% after age 18. For younger women, relationships with boyfriends and spouses were marked by domestic violence and abuse. Of married women, younger women were 2.5 times more likely than older women to have a spouse with an alcohol or substance abuse problem.

Past history. Younger women demonstrated a wider range of problems and more incidents of social difficulties before age 15. These included truancy (30%), suspensions or expulsions from school (23%), being arrested (14%), running away from home more than once (28%), vandalism (19%), shoplifting and stealing (53%), and starting physical fights (27%). Younger women reported being more sexually active in early adolescence, with 20% having had sexual intercourse with more than one person before age 15.

The widowed. Although elderly widows have not been identified as a subgroup at special risk, the question of the relationship of grief, bereavement, and the subsequent use of alcohol was examined in women admitted for substance abuse treatment. Tranquilizer use reportedly is greater for widows, even in the absence of a therapeutic effect. Three-fourths of the widows had a history of heavy alcohol use before the deaths of their husbands. There was a significant subgroup who did appear to be at increased risk for an alcohol problem after the death of their husbands. These were women who had no family history of alcohol problems but whose deceased husbands had been alcohol dependent and had not been treated. Alcohol problems emerged in these women in response to pathological grief, which was the legacy of the alcoholic marriage.[5]

NATURAL HISTORY

In terms of the symptoms of alcohol problems, there are several notable differences between men and women. Though less true of younger women, as a group, women more frequently drink at home and drink alone and are still more likely to hide their drinking. Whether treated or untreated, women are more likely to encounter family disruption, with higher rates of divorce and separation. Generally they have fewer social supports available and describe their primary relationships as being neither satisfactory nor supportive. Women are more likely than men to lose their jobs. Suicide attempts and depression are more common in women. Women are more vulnerable to affective disorders than men. This makes the differential diagnosis between the depression and dysphoria associated with heavy alcohol use a clinical challenge.[9]

Medical complications from chronic, heavy drinking are more likely to appear earlier and with less lifetime consumption in women. This phenomenon is referred to as a telescoped progression. The interval between the onset of heavy drinking and a referral for treatment is likely to be shorter for women. Women alcoholics come into treatment earlier than men. This is attributable to higher rates of medical complications, the exhaustion of social supports and resources needed to continue alcohol use, and a greater number of alcohol-related problems.[9,10,11,70] Women have more alcohol-induced problems than men when the length of alcohol abuse history, antisocial personality disorder, and employment status are taken into account. However, men outnumber women entering treatment by almost four to one.[14]

Little is known about personality factors that may predate the emergence of alcohol dependence in women. A follow-up in later life of a sample of women college students found that factors predictive of alcohol dependence in later life were considerably different from those in men. The best predictor for alcohol dependence in women might be termed *purposeful drinking*—that is, drinking to relieve shyness, to get high, to be happy, and to get along better.[9] Research also indicates that women who are heavy social drinkers expect drinking to relieve worries, nervousness, and tension. Studies have demonstrated that these are actually not the effects produced in social drinkers. There is initial euphoria as the blood alcohol level rises, but this is often followed by greater dysphoria.[49]

BIOLOGICAL FACTORS

Men and women handle alcohol differently too. With a standard dose of alcohol, women will have higher blood alcohol levels than men for several reasons. The first obvious factor is the weight differential.

Women achieve a higher blood alcohol concentration than men of comparable weight because of their higher proportions of body fat and because alcohol is not fat soluble. Also, the rate of absorption of alcohol varies for women at different phases of the menstrual cycle, presumably in response to changes in hormonal levels. Premenstrually, women absorb alcohol more rapidly than in other phases of the menstrual cycle, which leads to higher blood alcohol levels.[76]

Another difference between men and women is termed *first pass metabolism*—metabolism of alcohol in the stomach because of alcohol dehydrogenase (ADH) produced by the gastric lining. There are significant differences in the relative amounts of gastric ADH found in men and women. For nonalcoholic men, up to 20% of alcohol consumed may be metabolized in the stomach. For nonalcoholic women, the gastric first pass metabolism is only 23% that of men. Therefore, of the alcohol consumed, women have more available to them to enter their circulation. With chronic heavy drinking, at a level commensurate with alcohol dependence, the amounts of ADH found in the stomach lining are reduced in both men and women. For alcoholic women, the gastric ADH activity and first pass metabolism become negligible.[24]

GENETIC FACTORS

Alcohol dependence in many cases is said to be genetic, based on research conducted on men. Distinguishing familial from nonfamilial alcoholism has clinical significance and importance for research efforts. Nonfamilial alcoholism (in men) is characterized by the absence of a positive family history, later onset, fewer early-life antisocial problems, higher education, occupational achievement, and fewer alcohol-related difficulties.[71] Familial alcoholism, again in men, is marked not only by a positive family history but also by earlier onset, more early-life antisocial problems, and more severe symptoms that necessitate and/or lead to earlier recognition and treatment. Familial alcoholism is not associated with increased psychiatric illnesses.[16,26,28]

Furthermore, two variants of familial alcoholism have been postulated, based on the Swedish adoption studies. The more common variety is termed *milieu-limited* (Type I) alcoholism. This type accounts for most cases and is common in both men and women. It is less severe and is associated with adult-onset alcohol abuse in either biological parent. It is called milieu-limited because its occurrence and severity in the adoptee has been influenced by the postnatal environment. Thus, it requires both genetic predisposition and environmental provocation. If only one of these factors is present, the rate of alcoholism is no greater than for the general population. However, for

"male-limited" (Type II) alcoholism, said to account for 25% of all male alcoholism, transmission appears unaffected by the environment. When such susceptibility is present, alcohol abuse in sons is nine times greater independent of environment. It is related to severe alcoholism in the father, usually developed in adolescence.[16] The earliest genetic studies with women subjects suggested several differences. Women adoptees in families with a milieu-limited pattern of alcoholism, in contrast to men from these families, were found to be more vulnerable to the environment. The outcome was not necessarily increased risk of alcohol problems. In families with a positive history of male-limited alcoholism, although daughters show no increase in alcohol problems, an increased rate of somatic complaints was identified.[28] The results of the earliest twin studies involving women were somewhat equivocal. A face-to-face population study published in 1992 using female twins from a national registry concluded that there is a strong genetic component to alcohol dependence in women, as strong as that found in men. The findings suggest that inheritance to liability for alcoholism is in the range of 50% to 60%.[43] Further analysis suggests that there is no substantial environmental transmission and that transmission is equivalent from both mothers and fathers to offspring.[45]

Other studies have suggested that there is an environmental factor. A study of adoptees suggests that women more than men are sensitive to environmental issues, and that while genetics may be the singular risk factor for males, for women there is also an environmental factor. Early family conflict, psychopathology in the adoptive family, and a biological predisposition seem to interact to increase the risk of alcoholism.[18]

Beyond being associated with alcohol dependence, a positive family history is predictive of other health problems in alcoholic and nonalcoholic family members. The effects of alcohol abuse and a positive family history of alcoholism on health appear to be independent and additive.[26] Research has also suggested that women in families with multigenerational, male-limited alcoholism have an apparent increased risk of hypertension. Earlier research had strongly suggested that men from multigenerational male-limited alcoholic families, independent of the presence or absence of alcoholism, displayed cardiovascular hyperactivity stress, which has been identified as a risk factor for cardiovascular disease. This also appears to be true of women family members.[55]

MEDICAL CONSEQUENCES

It has long been recognized that women are more vulnerable than men to liver damage from alcohol use. Liver damage in women is produced with shorter periods of heavy drinking and at lower levels of alcohol consumption. Excess mortality for women is 5.1 times that of men.[4] Liver disease and other digestive disorders are the primary causes. The difference in metabolism, especially the increased bioavailability of ethanol resulting from decreased gastric oxidation, is considered the major contributor to the enhanced vulnerability of women to acute and chronic complications of alcoholism.[24] Somewhat unexpectedly, in women increased mortality has also been associated with binge drinking. This suggests that women may be very sensitive to short periods of high levels of alcohol.[74]

Beyond being more vulnerable to liver disease, women are generally more illness-prone than men. Women are more vulnerable to adverse effects of alcohol, having more serious health consequences.[26,69] An effort was made to identify the medical problems associated with different levels of average consumption, as well as the relationship of problems to high levels of intake, for both men and women. In women, regular drinking that exceeds 25 g per day is linked to a significant increase in alcohol-related medical and psychosocial problems. For women, as with men, frequent consumption of six or more drinks per occasion is also significantly related to an increase in problems. In women, in contrast to men, problems are a function of the frequency of consuming large amounts of alcohol, rather than of daily high consumption.[47]

Despite a formal policy to include equal numbers of men and women in studies conducted by the National Institutes of Health (NIH), the major agency supporting biomedical research, few strides have been made. According to a report by the US General Accounting Office, the NIH has failed to keep the required records of the number of women included in studies to allow monitoring of compliance, and has continued to approve research proposals that exclude women without a rationale for doing so.[22,46,61] In respect to medical sequelae associated with substance use, the studies on the effects on women remain limited. The situation is likely to continue until the larger issue of routinely involving women in biomedical research is addressed.

Hypertension

The relationship between alcohol use and hypertension has received considerable attention. The studies have found the strongest associations between alcohol use and hypertension to be in men. For example, an examination of the effects of moderate use noted the following: "Women drank less than men and did not have a positive relationship between alcohol intake and blood pressure. However, systolic blood pressure was inversely associated with a spirit intake of 1 to 9 drinks per week (but not more than 10 drinks per week)."[13] In women, there are more complex interactions and intervening variables regarding the association between alcohol consumption and hypertension.

Data from a large-scale study of hypertension was analyzed with regard to alcohol consumption and blood pressure. Although an association was found between hypertension and alcohol use in women, it was a more complex relationship than in men. For men, consumption of 40 g of alcohol per day led to increases in both systolic and diastolic pressure (of 5 to 6 mm Hg and 4 to 5 mm Hg). For men, 7% of hypertension was due to alcohol consumption ≥40 g/day. In women, hypertension was related to age, alcohol consumption, and smoking. For younger women (30 to 44 years), there was no significant relationship between alcohol consumption and blood pressure. However, for older women (ages 45 to 69 years), there was a strong correlation between alcohol consumption and smoking. Women smokers showed steep increases in the adjusted mean diastolic (5.2 mm Hg) and systolic (9.6 mm Hg) blood pressure with alcohol consumption of ≥20 g/day. For women nonsmokers, there was no such relationship.[42]

Pulmonary Function

In respect to smoking, it might be noted that in both women and men, pulmonary function is affected by heavy alcohol consumption. Weekly consumption to 350 g of alcohol has an effect on FEV comparable to the effect of daily smoking of 15 g of tobacco.[48] As noted in Chapters 2 and 4, drinking and smoking co-occur. Also of particular concern is the failure of older women to quit smoking at a rate comparable to that of men, and also the high percentage of adolescent girls who are beginning to smoke despite public health campaigns. This is one area with a marked difference between ethnic groups, with African-American adolescents, especially females, being far less likely than their Caucasian peers to begin using tobacco.[57]

Breast Cancer

In 1987, two major studies first reported that alcohol consumption increases the risk of breast cancer for women already at risk.[59,67] Women at risk for breast cancer were reported to have a 50% elevation in risk with one drink per week, rising to a 100% increase in risk with more than three drinks per week. These levels of alcohol consumption are typically considered moderate and nonproblematic. A review of the initial data raised questions about the relationships reported. A 1989 review article noted, "Although three prospective studies show a slightly increased risk of breast cancer for drinkers versus nondrinkers, the results of correlation studies and case control studies have been inconsistent. At present, it seems premature to consider such a drastic recommendation, i.e., suggesting a reduction in drinking until further information becomes available."[50] A recent review article, "Alcohol and breast cancer: Where are we now and where do we go from here?" responds to some of those questions. The article reports upon a meta-analysis of over 50 epidemiological studies. The importance of the topic is also highlighted, namely, that (1) breast cancer is a major source of morbidity and mortality, (2) alcohol consumption is common, and (3) drinking is modifiable. Despite the methodological problems, the authors conclude that while causality remains unknown, the data suggest that a modest but positive association does exist: The risk is dose related, with a 25% increase in risk with daily intake of the equivalent of two drinks, though risk may be modified by factors such as age, weight, and estrogen use.[68]

Reproductive and Related Endocrine Dysfunction

In women with a history of heavy alcohol use, there is decreased gonadal mass, infertility, and obstetric and gonadal problems. Not all problems are restricted to heavy drinkers, they also involve women social drinkers. These include luteal phase dysfunction, anovulation, and persistent hyperprolactinemia. For reasons that are unclear, alcohol use does not affect first trimester miscarriages. However, during the second trimester, there is an increase in spontaneous abortion rates both for moderate drinkers (one or two drinks per day), who have a 100% greater risk than occasional drinkers, and for heavier drinkers (three or more drinks per day), who have a 350% percent greater risk.[53]

AIDS

A problem of growing concern is the rise of HIV infection and AIDS in women, primarily related to their own intravenous drug use or to having a sexual partner with AIDS. It would appear that young women with alcohol and multiple substance use problems are at particular risk.[82] While a 3:1 ratio of male to female intravenous drug users has been frequently cited, in younger women this disparity is disappearing.[36] Women appear to have a faster transition from drug use inititiation to dependence; tend to be introduced to drug use by partners; have drug-using partners, which promotes access to drugs; are more likely to engage in needle-sharing; and with the potential for prostitution are likely to have greater ease in maintaining a steady supply of drugs. All of

these factors contribute to an increased risk of HIV/AIDS infection.[1,2,36,60] Beyond the risk to these women, the other issue of concern is perinatal transmission in pregnancy. A public health priority is intervention to reduce the spread of HIV/AIDS in this population.[20]

Medical Emergencies

In relation to the drinking population, women are overly represented in emergency room visits, as indicated by data drawn from the *Drug Abuse Warning Network* (DAWN).[56] It is speculated that this is because of women's greater vulnerability to overdoses at lower levels of consumption and of their greater likelihood of using alcohol in combination with other drugs. With many overdoses reported as accidental, one important intervention is education about the effects of alcohol and other drugs, alone and in combination.[17]

Alcohol problems in women greatly increase the risk for suicide. A recent study determined that alcoholic women have a history of suicide attempts five times greater than that of nonalcoholic women, with 40% of the alcoholic women in this study reporting a suicide attempt. Furthermore, close to 50% who make one attempt will make a future suicide attempt. Youth and alcohol/drug use and abuse in women is a high-risk combination.[27]

PSYCHOSOCIAL CONSEQUENCES
Emotional Distress

Data initially collected by the National Institute of Mental Health as part of a major longitudinal epidemiologic study on the incidence of psychiatric illness in the general population was analyzed to determine the role of current and past alcohol use as a predictor of functioning 1 year later on re-interview. For both men and women, current heavy drinking, along with higher levels of psychiatric distress at the initial interview, was associated with higher levels of psychiatric distress at one-year follow-up. For women, a history of heavy alcohol use was an additional predictor of psychiatric distress 1 year later.[21]

Violence

A number of studies indicate that women with substance use problems are at an increased risk for verbal abuse, as well as for moderate and severe physical violence.[25,41,79] The level of violence by a spouse has proven to be an effective predictor of whether the woman was part of the alcoholic sample. This was true even after controlling a variety of factors such as the presence of alcohol problems in the spouse, income levels, parental violence, and parental alcohol problems.[54] Incidences of incest and rape are also found to be higher and have been cited by women as leading to drug use.[80] Because of the levels of violence being reported, the importance of routinely evaluating women who enter substance abuse treatment for posttraumatic stress disorder is being emphasized.[25,62]

Marital Status

Women alcoholics are more likely to have alcoholic spouses. There is a dramatic difference in marriage outcomes depending on the sex of the alcoholic spouse; women alcoholics are more likely than men alcoholics to be divorced.[9] Nine out of ten marriages in which the wife is alcoholic end in divorce, whereas only one of ten marriages in which the husband is alcoholic ends in divorce.

CLINICAL CONSIDERATIONS
Risk Factors

Factors associated with a higher risk for alcohol or drug problems in women include early onset of alcohol and/or other drug use, being divorced or separated, gynecological problems, eating disorders, smoking, and a history of being prescribed psychoactive drugs.

Entry into Treatment

In terms of what prompts treatment and the perceptions of problems when entering care, women have been found to differ from men in several ways. Generally, women report more depression, anxiety, sense of powerlessness, hopelessness, and guilt,[51,78] although these are not associated with greater rates of psychiatric illness. In addition, women entering treatment often had recent episodes of violence. Their husbands, in contrast to the wives of male patients, were generally less supportive and more frequently had their own alcohol or drug problems. Nevertheless, while reporting less support for entry into treatment, women, more than men, cited pressure from others as a major precipitating factor. Children, other relatives, work colleagues, and their general practitioners were noted. A concern unique to women is fear of losing custody of the children. More commonly, women did not see either alcohol or drug use as their primary problem. Thus, they often expressed concern about the ability of a substance abuse program to assist them.[52,77]

Screening

Routine screening for alcohol and drug use problems, as described in Chapter 2, is indicated for women as well as for men. There is some question as to the utility of several of the common screening instruments, including laboratory measures and interview methods. Carbohydrate-deficient transferrin, for example, while a good marker for hazardous alcohol

consumption in men, is not as reliable an indicator in women.[31] Despite these potential problems, different research groups recommend the CAGE for broad-based screening with women.[72]

For women, there are special opportunities for screening.

* Annually in the US, it is estimated, there are over 35 million gynecological office visits. This provides an opportunity for screening and case identification of women who may have not had any other health care contact. In addition, this represents a population of women with a known increased prevalence both for heavy drinking and for nonmedical psychoactive drug use.[64]

* The strong relationship between domestic violence and alcoholism and/or alcohol or drug abuse in women suggests screening for spousal violence and for alcohol- and drug-related problems.[25,54]

Patient Education

* Women, especially adolescent women, badly need factual information on the effects of alcohol and drugs. For example, there is the danger of women modeling their drinking to that of their companions in a social setting, with potentially disastrous results. In a social setting, the tendency is for the heaviest drinker to set the pace for the entire group's drinking rate. Everyone tends to accommodate the heaviest drinker, e.g., in ordering another round of drinks or in having drinks "topped off".

* The educational materials available, which describe the blood alcohol content (BAC) produced by different numbers of drinks for persons of different weight (Table 20-4), never incorporate the significant differences between men and women, which have a bearing on blood alcohol concentrations.

* Women's greater psychotropic drug use and misuse warrants careful review of prescribing practices for

Table 20-4. Number of Drinks to Produce a Given BAC Level for the Hypothetical Average Male and Female Drinker

BAC	Number of drinks 150-pound average male	Number of drinks 120-pound average female
.02	1	½
.05	2½	1½
.10	5	<2
.20	10	<5
.25	12½	6¼
.30-.40	15-20	7½-10

From Project Cork Institute, Dartmouth Medical School, Hanover those at risk. The question as to whether the potential risks outweigh the desired benefits needs to be considered. Potentially more stringent criteria are appropriate for prescribing psychotropic medications to high-risk women, and extra effort to monitor compliance is needed.[6]

Diagnosis and Intervention

In respect to diagnosis, the dysfunctions resulting from alcohol or other drug use should be the major factor. Women may consume significantly less alcohol than men, perhaps 45% less, but experience difficulties of similar magnitude.[9]

It is important to recognize the value of interventions for pregnant women who are drinking or engaged in drug use. For example, some practitioners in an academic medical center hesitate to follow the Surgeon General's advice and recommend total abstinence during pregnancy.[75] Instead, medical staff have suggested that with under two drinks per day there is no statistically increased frequency of fetal alcohol syndrome (FAS) and fetal alcohol effects (FAE). This stance is attributed to not wishing to induce guilt about consumption that has already occurred during the pregnancy. Although this is well intended, for many women, no risk is acceptable. This one-drink limit could be misinterpreted as meaning that one drink constitutes safe use.

Intervention with pregnant women who are heavy drinkers is warranted by the results. To presume that whatever damage has occurred to the fetus is irreversible or that the women's use cannot be moderated is erroneous. Even a reduced intake by heavy drinkers unable to achieve abstinence has been associated with significant reduction in the occurrence of FAS and FAE. Alcohol abuse was associated in a dose-dependent manner with fetal growth retardation detectable by ultrasonography from 27 weeks of gestation. Of the women with continuous alcohol abuse, 89% gave birth to infants with at least one feature of FAE, compared with only 40% of those who decreased their alcohol consumption.[34]

Note: See Chapter 16 for a discussion of prenatal effects of alcohol and substance use.

Management and Treatment

There has been virtually no systematic research indicating that outcomes differ by gender. Both males and females with similar demographic characteristics, in comparable stages of their illness, are presumed to do equally well in similar treatment settings.[9] A few recent studies do suggest that women may have more satisfactory outcomes 1 year post-treatment than men.[65]

However, some studies show that women's rates of entrance, retention, and completion of treatment are significantly lower than for men.[58]

Access to treatment may be a dimension on which men and women differ. For women there are the issues of child care and affording treatment because women have a greater chance of losing their jobs, having lower wages and benefits, and being their children's sole source of support. Women may need more ancillary supports and services because they are single mothers, are victims of domestic violence, or have fewer supportive people in their environment.[9,10,11]

AA remains the primary treatment for alcohol dependence, and the rate of women entering AA continues to increase.[81]

Here are some factors suggested as being important in women's treatment:

Provision of child care facilitates recovery.

Pregnancy and childbirth are points where intervention is often effective with chemically dependent women.[34]

Training in and skillful application of women's issues minimize distrust of social service system providers.[58,83] Attitudes toward addicted women are often negative, and chemically dependent women are often subjected to sexual harassment.[52,58]

Most treatment programs have been designed primarily by men or male-oriented institutions and are informed by research on male populations. A not-uncommon criticism of Alcoholics Anonymous and 12-step programs is that they foster continuing female dependence. This, however, is not a universally accepted view. As one feminist author commented, "Those I see going into 12-Step programs are basically trying to stay alive. They are not the people that one would see at political meetings. Without recovery they would probably be dead, and dead women don't have any politics."[33]

Treatment models based on the Self-in-Relation theory of women's development and other feminist theories that account for women's psychosocial and environmental realities require exploration in terms of substance abuse treatment.[58]

REFERENCES

1. Allen K. Female drug abusers and the context of their HIV transmission risk behaviors. IN: Battjes RJ; Sloboda Z; Grace WC, eds. *The Context of HIV Risk among Drug Users and Their Sexual Partners. NIDA Research Monograph 143.* Rockville MD: National Institute on Drug Abuse, 1994. pp. 48-63. (14 refs.)

2. Astemborski J; Vlahov D; Warren D; Solomon L; Nelson KE. The trading of sex for drugs or money and HIV seropositivity

among female intravenous drug users. *American Journal of Public Health* 84(3): 382-387, 1994. (28 refs.)

3. Bepko C. Disorders of power: Women and addiction in the family. IN: McGoldrick M; Anderson C; Walsh F, eds. *Women in Families.* New York: Norton, 1989. pp. 406-426.

4. Berglund M. Mortality in alcoholics related to clinical state at first admission: A study of 537 deaths. *Acta Psychiatrica Scandinavica* 70(5): 407-416, 1984. (29 refs.)

5. Blankfield A. Grief, alcohol dependence, and women. *Drug and Alcohol Dependence* 24(1): 45-49, 1989. (20 refs.)

6. Blankfield A. Female alcoholics: Alcohol dependence and problems associated with prescribed psychotropic drug use. *Acta Psychiatrica Scandinavica* 82(6): 445-450, 1990. (58 refs.)

7. Bloomfield KA. *Community in Recovery: A Study of Social Support, Spirituality, and Voluntarism among Gay and Lesbian Members of Alcoholics Anonymous.* Berkeley CA: University of California at Berkeley, 1990. Note: Doctoral Dissertation, Public Health, on file with university.

8. Bloomfield KA. A comparison of alcohol consumption between lesbians and heterosexual women in an urban population. *Drug and Alcohol Dependence* 33(3): 257-269, 1993. (40 refs.)

9. Blume SB. Women and alcohol: A review. *Journal of the American Medical Association* 256(11): 1467-1469, 1986. (49 refs.)

10. Blume SB. Chemical dependency in women: Important issues. *American Journal of Drug and Alcohol Abuse* 16(3/4): 297-307, 1990. (52 refs.)

11. Blume SB. Gender differences in alcohol-related disorders. *Harvard Review of Psychiatry* 2(1): 7-14, 1994. (93 refs.)

12. Bullick ICM. Drug and alcohol abuse by bulimic women and their families. *American Journal of Psychiatry* 44(12): 1604-1606, 1987.

13. Bulpitt CJ; Shipley MJ; Semmence A. The contribution of a moderate intake of alcohol to the presence of hypertension. *Journal of Hypertension* 5(1): 85-91, 1987. (21 refs.)

14. Butynski W; Canova DM. Alcohol problem resources and services in state supported programs. *Public Health Report* 103(6): 611-620, 1988. (6 refs.)

15. Chu SY; Buehler JW; Fleming PL; Berkelman RL. Epidemiology of reported cases of AIDS in lesbians, United States 1980-89. *American Journal of Public Health* 80(11): 1380-1381, 1990. (6 refs.)

16. Cloninger CR. Genetic and environmental factors in the development of alcoholism. *Journal of Psychiatric Treatment and Evaluation* 5(5): 487-496, 1983. (73 refs.)

17. Corrigan EM. Gender differences in alcohol and other drug use. *Addictive Behaviors* 10(3): 313-317, 1985. (21 refs.)

18. Cutrona CE; Cadoret RJ; Suhr JA; Richards CC; Troughton E; Schutte K; et al. Interpersonal variables in the prediction of alcoholism among adoptees: Evidence for gene-environment interactions. *Comprehensive Psychiatry* 35(3): 171-179, 1994. (40 refs.)

19. Deevey S; Wall LJ. How do lesbian women develop serenity? *Health Care for Women International* 13(2): 199-208, 1992. (20 refs.)

20. Des Jarlais DC; Friedman SR; Ward TP. Harm reduction: A public health response to the AIDS epidemic among injecting drug users. (review). *Annual Review of Public Health* 14: 413-450, 1993. (110 refs.)

21. Dryman A; Anthony JC. An epidemiologic study of alcohol use as a predictor of psychiatric distress over time. *Acta Psychiatrica Scandinavica* 80(4): 315-321, 1989. (22 refs.)

22. Dubois MY; Burris JF. Inclusion of women in clinical research. *Academic Medicine* 69(9): 693-694, 1994.

23. Finnegan DG; McNally EB. The lonely journey: Lesbians and gay men who are co-dependent. *Alcoholism Treatment Quarterly* 6(1): 121-134, 1989. (7 refs.)

24. Frezza M; diPadova C; Pozzato G; Terpin M; Baraona E; Lieber CS. High blood alcohol levels in women: The role of decreased gastric alcohol dehydrogenase activity and first-pass metabolism. *New England Journal of Medicine* 322(2): 95-99, 1990. (31 refs.)

25. Fullilove MT; Fullilove III RE; Smith M; Winkler K; Michael C; Panzer PG; et al. Violence, trauma, and post-traumatic stress disorder among women drug users. *Journal of Traumatic Stress* 6(4): 533-543, 1993. (34 refs.)

26. Glenn SW; Parsons OA; Stevens L. Effects of alcohol abuse and familial alcoholism on physical health in men and women. *Health Psychology* 8(3): 325-341, 1989. (32 refs.)

27. Gomberg ESL. Suicide risk among women with alcohol problems. *American Journal of Public Health* 79(10): 1363-1365, 1989. (25 refs.)

28. Goodwin DW. Studies of familial alcoholism: A review. *Journal of Clinical Psychiatry* 45(12): 14-17, 1984. (29 refs.)

29. Griffin ML; Weiss RD; Mirin SM; Lange U. A comparison of male and female cocaine abusers. *Archives of General Psychiatry* 46(2): 122-126, 1989. (49 refs.)

30. Grilo CM; Levy KN; Becker DF; Edell WS; McGlashan TH. Eating disorders in female inpatients with versus without substance use disorders. *Addictive Behaviors* 20(2): 255-260, 1995. (20 refs.)

31. Gronhoek M; Henriksen JH; Becker U. Carbohydrate-deficient transferrin: A valid marker of alcoholism in population studies: Results from the Copenhagen City Heart Study. *Alcoholism: Clinical and Experimental Research* 19(2): 457-461, 1995. (19 refs.)

32. Hall JM. An exploration of lesbians' images of recovery from alcohol problems. *Health Care for Women International* 13(2): 181-198, 1992. (42 refs.)

33. Hall JM. Lesbians and alcohol: Patterns and paradoxes in medical notions and lesbians' beliefs. *Journal of Psychoactive Drugs* 25(2): 109-119, 1993. (109 refs.).

34. Halmesmaki E. Alcohol counseling of 85 pregnant problem drinkers: Effect on drinking and fetal outcome. *British Journal of Obstetrics and Gynaecology* 95(3): 243-247, 1988. (15 refs.)

35. Harrison AP. Women in treatment: Changing over time. *International Journal of the Addictions* 24(7): 655-673, 1989. (12 refs.)

36. Hartel D. Context of HIV risk behavior among female injecting drug users and female sexual partners of injecting drug users. IN: Battjes RJ; Sloboda Z; Grace WC, eds. *The Context of HIV Risk among Drug Users and Their Sexual Partners. NIDA Research Monograph 143.* Rockville MD: National Institute on Drug Abuse, 1994. pp. 41-47. (31 refs.)

37. Herbert JT; Hunt B; Dell G. Counseling gay men and lesbians with alcohol problems. *Journal of Rehabilitation* 60(2): 52-57, 1994. (59 refs.)

38. Holleran PR; Novak AH. Support choices and abstinence in gay/lesbian and heterosexual alcoholics. *Alcoholism Treatment Quarterly* 6(2): 71-83, 1989. (6 refs.)

39. Hughes TL; Wilsnack SC. Research on lesbians and alcohol: Gaps and implications. *Alcohol Health and Research World* 18(3): 202-205, 1994. (20 refs.)

40. Kandel DB; Logan JA. Patterns of drug use from adolescence to young adulthood: Periods of risk for initiation, continued use, and discontinuation. *American Journal of Public Health* 74(7): 660-666, 1984. (11 refs.)

41. Kane-Cavaiola C; Rullo-Cooney D. Addicted women: Their families' effect on treatment outcome. IN: Isaacson EB, ed. *Chemical Dependency: Theoretical Approaches and Strategies Working with Individuals and Families.* Binghamton NY: The Haworth Press, Inc, 1991. pp. 111-119. (8 refs.)

42. Keil U; Chambless L; Remmers A. Alcohol and blood pressure: Results from the Luebeck Blood Pressure Study. *Preventive Medicine* 18(1): 1-10, 1989. (21 refs.)

43. Kendler KS; Heath AC; Neale MC; Kessler RC; Eaves LJ. A population-based twin study of alcoholism in women. *Journal of the American Medical Association* 268(14): 1877-1882, 1992. (50 refs.)

44. Kendler KS; Heath AC; Neale MC; Kessler RC; Eaves LJ. Alcoholism and major depression in women: A twin study of the causes of comorbidity. *Archives of General Psychiatry* 50(9): 690-698, 1993. (43 refs.)

45. Kendler KS; Neale MC; Heath AC; Kessler RC; Eaves LJ. A twin-family study of alcoholism in women. *American Journal of Psychiatry* 151(5): 707-715, 1994. (56 refs.)

46. Kolata G. NIH neglects women, study says. *The New York Times,* Section B, p. 4, June 19, 1990.

47. Kranzler HR; Babor TF; Lauerman RJ. Problems associated with average alcohol consumption and frequency of intoxication in a medical population. *Alcoholism: Clinical and Experimental Research* 14(1): 119-126, 1990. (19 refs.)

48. Lange P; Groth S; Mortensen J; Appleyard M; Nyboe J; Jensen G; Schnohr P. Pulmonary function is influenced by heavy alcohol consumption. *American Review of Respiratory Disease* 137(5): 1119-1123, 1988. (26 refs.)

49. Lex BW; Mello NK; Mendelson JH; Babor TF. Reasons for alcohol use by female heavy, moderate, and occasional social drinkers. *Alcoholism: Clinical and Experimental Research* 6(4): 281-287, 1989. (44 refs.)

50. Lownfels AB; Zevola SA. Alcohol and breast cancer: An overview. *Alcoholism: Clinical and Experimental Research* 13(1): 109-111, 1989. (23 refs.)

51. Marsh JC; Miller NA. Female clients in substance abuse treatment. *International Journal of the Addictions* 20(6/7): 995-1019, 1985. (94 refs.)

52. Marsh K; Simpson D. Sex differences in opiate addiction careers. *American Journal of Alcohol Abuse* 12: 309-329, 1986. (38 refs.)

53. Mello NK; Mendelson JH; Teoh S. Neuroendocrine consequences of alcohol abuse in women. *Annals of the New York Academy of Sciences* 562(6): 211-240, 1989. (150 refs.)

54. Miller BA; Downs WR; Gondoli DM. Spousal violence among alcoholic women as compared to a random household sample of women. *Journal of Studies on Alcohol* 50(6): 533-540, 1989. (30 refs.)

55. Miller SB; Finn PR; Ditto B; Pihl RO. Risk for hypertension in female members of multigenerational male-limited alcoholic families. *Alcoholism: Clinical and Experimental Research* 13(4): 505-507, 1989. (8 refs.)

56. National Institute on Drug Abuse. *Data from the Drug Abuse Warning Network (DAWN): Annual Emergency Room Data 1992, Statistical Series I, Number 12-A.* Rockville MD: Substance Abuse and Mental Health Services Administration, 1994. (0 refs.)

57. Nelson DE; Giovino GA; Shopland DR; Mowery PD; Mills SL; Eriksen MP. Trends in cigarette smoking among US adolescents, 1974 through 1991. *American Journal of Public Health* 85(1): 34-40, 1995. (83 refs.)

58. Nelson-Zlupko L; Kauffman LE; Dore MM. Gender differences in drug addiction and treatment: Implications for social work intervention in the substance-abusing woman. *Social Work* 40(1): 45-54, 1995. (55 refs.)

59. O'Connell DL; Hulka BS; Chambless LE; Wilkinson WE; Deubner DC. Cigarette smoking, alcohol consumption, and breast cancer risk. *Journal of the National Cancer Institute* 78(2): 229-234, 1987. (31 refs.)

60. O'Leary A. Factors associated with sexual risk of AIDS in women. IN: Battjes RJ; Sloboda Z; Grace WC, eds. *The Context of HIV Risk among Drug Users and Their Sexual Partners. NIDA Research Monograph 143.* Rockville MD: National Institute on Drug Abuse, 1994. pp. 64-81. (82 refs.)

61. Pinn VW. The role of the NIH's Office of Research on Women's Health. *Academic Medicine* 69(9): 698-702, 1994.

62. Root MPP. Treatment failures: The role of sexual victimization in women's addictive behavior. *American Journal of Orthopsychiatry* 59(4): 542-549, 1989. (29 refs.)

63. Ross HE. Alcohol and drug abuse in treated alcoholics: A comparison of men and women. *Alcoholism: Clinical and Experimental Research* 13(6): 810-816, 1989. (32 refs.)

64. Russell M; Coviello D. Heavy drinking and regular psychoactive drug use among gynecological outpatients. *Alcoholism: Clinical and Experimental Research* 12(3): 400-406, 1988. (60 refs.)

65. Sanchez-Craig M; Leigh G; Spivak K; Lei H. Superior outcome of females over males after brief treatment for the reduction of heavy drinking. *British Journal of Addiction* 84(4): 335-340, 1989. (18 refs.)

66. Savin-Williams RC. Verbal and physical abuse as stressors in the lives of lesbian, gay male, and bisexual youths: Associations with school problems, running away, substance abuse, prostitution, and suicide. *Journal of Consulting and Clinical Psychology* 62(2): 261-269, 1994. (61 refs.)

67. Schatzkin A; Jones DV; Hoover RN; Taylor PR; Brinton LA; Ziegler RG; Harvey EB; Carter CL; Licitra LM; Dufour MC; Larson DB. Alcohol consumption and breast cancer in the epidemiological follow-up study of the first health and nutrition examination survey. *New England Journal of Medicine* 316(19): 1169-1173, 1987. (112 refs.)

68. Schatzkin A; Longnecker MP. Alcohol and breast cancer: Where are we now and where do we go from here? (review). *Cancer* 74(3): 1101-1110, 1994. (112 refs.)

69. Schenker S; Speeg KV. The risk of alcohol intake in men and women: All may not be equal. (editorial). *New England Journal of Medicine* 322(2): 127-129, 1990. (10 refs.)

70. Schilit R; Gomberg E. Social support structures of women in treatment for alcoholism. *Health and Social Work* 12(3): 187-195, 1987. (18 refs.)

71. Schuckit MA. Relationship between the course of primary alcoholism in men and family history. *Journal of Studies on Alcohol* 45(4): 334-338, 1984. (23 refs.)

72. Seppa K; Koivula T; Sillanaukee P. Drinking habits and detection of heavy drinking among middle-aged women. *British Journal of Addiction* 87(12): 1703-1709, 1992. (33 refs.)

73. Skinner WF. The prevalence and demographic predictors of illicit and licit drug use among lesbians and gay men. *American Journal of Public Health* 84(8): 1307-1310, 1994. (23 refs.)

74. Smith EM; Lewis CE; Kercher C; Spitznagel E. Predictors of mortality in alcoholic women: A 20-year follow-up study. *Alcoholism: Clinical and Experimental Research* 18(5): 1177-1186, 1994. (37 refs.)

75. Surgeon General advisory on alcohol and pregnancy. *FDA Drug Bulletin* 11(2): July 1981. (0 refs.)

76. Sutker PB; Goist KC; King AR. Acute alcohol intoxication in women: Relationship to dose and menstrual cycle phase. *Alcoholism: Clinical and Experimental Research* 11(1): 74-79, 1987. (18 refs.)

77. Thom B. Sex differences in help-seeking for alcohol problems: 1. The barriers to help-seeking. *British Journal of Addiction* 81(5): 777-788, 1986. (13 refs.)

78. Thom B. Sex differences in help-seeking for alcohol problems: 2. Entry into treatment. *British Journal of Addiction* 82(9): 987-989, 1987. (7 refs.)

79. Underhill BL. *Providing Lesbian-Sensitive and Lesbian-Specific Alcoholism Recovery Services.* Los Angeles: Alcoholism Center for Women, 1993. (121 refs.)

80. Volpe J; Hamilton G. How women recover: Experience and research observations. *Alcohol Health and Research World* 7(2): 28-39, 1982-1983.

81. Weisner C; Greenfield T; Room R. Trends in the treatment of alcohol problems in the US general population, 1979 through 1990. *American Journal of Public Health* 85(1): 55-60, 1995. (43 refs.)

82. Windle M. High-risk behaviors for AIDS among heterosexual alcoholics: A pilot study. *Journal of Studies on Alcohol* 50(6): 503-507, 1989. (23 refs.)

83. Zankowski GL. Responsive programming: Meeting the needs of chemically dependent women. *Alcoholism Treatment Quarterly* 4(4): 53-65. (16 refs.)

FURTHER READINGS

Abbott AA. A feminist approach to substance abuse treatment and service delivery. *Social Work in Health Care* 19(3/4): 67-83, 1994. (70 refs.)

A major concern of service providers and policymakers has been the increased number of individuals and families entering the health care system either using or abusing alcohol and other drugs or suffering from the ramifications of a significant family member's substance abuse. An additional concern involves a lack of adequate understanding of these patients and a lag in the development of appropriate treatment strategies, especially in relation to women. This article pays particular attention to substance use among women; the identification of deficits in current mainstream treatment efforts, which historically have been developed primarily by male providers for male substance abusers; and the advantages and specifics of treatment based on a feminist perspective, and their application to other at-risk populations. Copyright 1994, The Haworth Press, Inc.

Aldrich MR. Historical notes on women addicts. *Journal of Psychoactive Drugs* 26(1): 61-64, 1994. (18 refs.)

This brief communication highlights some of the historical phenomena related to addiction in women. When opium was more readily available, with or without prescription, women were more likely to be addicts than men. Addicted women tended to be white, upper- or middle-class women. While some were among the most famous women authors and artists, most were housewives. Women associated with the medical profession—nurses and doctors' wives—had higher rates of addiction. Female addiction spread in the early nineteenth century with the widespread use of laudanum compounds for "female troubles." In many cases, addiction was iatrogenic. Victorian customs are also cited as contributing to addiction in women. As the consequences of addiction became more apparent, the upper classes were instrumental in passing laws to regulate access. With the passage of the Harrison Act in 1914, patterns of addiction changed. In addition to addiction among women, "infant doping" had also been common and contributed to increased infant mortality. Copyright 1994, Project Cork Institute.

Bepko C, ed. *Feminism and Addiction.* New York: The Haworth Press, Inc, 1991. (Chapter refs.)

The field of family therapy is undergoing a radical revision as feminist clinicians and theorists stimulate and expand understanding of the ways gender issues impact on work in families. This collection attempts to redress the imbalance of focus in mainstream treatment paradigms by exploring women's issues in detail and by looking at constructs about addiction while challenging constructs about gender. It struggles with theoretical, social, and clinical issues that are the focus of current debate by therapists, feminists, the addiction treatment community, and patients who struggle to integrate their self-help recovery programs with therapy. This book represents an intersection of the struggles of men's experience vs. women's, therapy vs. self-help, and systems therapy vs. the more linear approaches of addictions treatment models. It questions whether power is a construct clinically relevant to women affected by addiction; if so, in what ways? The volume offers a sampling of current work by family therapists in areas that are critical to women and therefore to families. Many of the authors use constructivist approaches to understanding and treating women's experience. Constructivist theory is a philosophical framework for treatment that allows for the interactive recreating and "restorying" of experience in ways that are collaborative, internal, and organic rather that external, hierarchical, and imposed. This book is divided into three parts. First is theory, research, and social issues. The second part deals with feminist approaches to training and to treatment of the addictions. Part three is directed to special issues in treatment and recovery. Copyright 1993, Project Cork Institute.

Biron LL; Brochu S; Desjardins L. The issue of drugs and crime among a sample of incarcerated women. *Deviant Behavior: An Interdisciplinary Journal* 16(1): 25-43, 1995. (43 refs.)

Based on a sample of incarcerated women in Quebec prisons in 1989, this study focuses on drug use and abuse and its relation to crime, with a special concern for age of onset, nature of conviction, previous criminal activities, motivation, and other related variables. The emerging profile of these subjects is one of drug-related problems rather than of a deep involvement in criminality. Within this population of women prisoners, a strong link between drugs and crime is still difficult to establish. In conclusion, it is suggested that future research rely more on qualitative analyses to gather a better understanding of the operating processes. Copyright 1995, Taylor & Francis.

Center for Substance Abuse Treatment. *Practical Approaches in the Treatment of Women Who Abuse Alcohol and Other Drugs.* Rockville MD: Center for Substance Abuse Treatment, 1994. (Chapter refs.)

This manual helps treatment program personnel meet the specific needs of women with substance abuse problems. It is for substance abuse treatment staff who work in programs that serve both men and women and for staff who serve women only. Although written for a wide audience, the manual is most relevant to federally funded programs that mainly serve low-income populations. The manual is presented in eight chapters, including the introductory chapter. These focus upon the following topics: The current epidemiology of substance use among women; approaches to the treatment; barriers to engaging women in treatment and outreach strategies to deal with those barriers; models of comprehensive care in each stage of the treatment process as well as in continuing care; and program management issues. Copyright 1995, Project Cork Institute.

Chou SP. Sex differences in morbidity among respondents classified as alcohol abusers and/or dependent: Results of a national survey. *Addiction* 89(1): 87-93, 1994. (15 refs.)

To date, none of the studies on gender differences in physical morbidity have focused on persons classified as DSM-III-R alcohol abusers and/or dependent in the general population. This data note presents data from a nationally representative survey on drinking practices and related problems examining gender differences in physical morbidity in respondents receiving these diagnoses. Results indicated that for certain major sociodemographic subgroups of the population, gender differences in morbidity were significant. The female-to-male odds ratios of these subgroups generally varied within the range of 1.5 and 2.0, reflecting about two times greater odds of females experiencing morbid conditions than males. Copyright 1994, Society for the Study of Addiction to Alcohol and Other Drugs.

Evans C; Lacey JH. Multiple self-damaging behaviour among alcoholic women: A prevalence study. *British Journal of Psychiatry* 161(November): 643-647, 1992. (24 refs.)

In patients being treated for specific behavior-control problems, there exists an important subgroup of "multi-impulsive" patients whose treatment might be facilitated if the full range of their problems were recognized and dealt with as one general issue of impulse control. In women in particular, loss of control of eating may be prevalent and easily concealed from staff, and may thwart treatment. This survey of 50 women attending an alcoholic treatment unit explored the prevalence of behavior-control problems other than those of alcohol. Three-quarters of the women also had other behavioral problems. Over half the sample had thought of taking an overdose, and just under half had actually taken one; about one-fourth had cut themselves deliberately; half described impulsive physical violence; half acknowledged a period of "promiscuity;" and at least 16% had had a clinically diagnosable eating disorder. More research is needed, but the authors believe that all self-damaging behavior should be addressed simultaneously to prevent "revolving door" relapses as emotional distress is transferred from one behavior to another. Copyright 1992, Royal Society of Medicine.

Kendrick JS; Zahniser SC; Miller N; Salas N; Stine J; Gargiullo PM; et al. Integrating smoking cessation into routine public prenatal care: The Smoking Cessation in Pregnancy Project. *American Journal of Public Health* 85(2): 217-222, 1995.(25 refs.)

In 1986 the state health departments of Colorado, Maryland, and Missouri conducted a federally funded demonstration project to increase smoking cessation in pregnant women receiving prenatal care and services from the Women, Infants, and Children (WIC) program in public clinics. Low-intensity interventions were designed to be integrated into routine prenatal care. Clinics were randomly assigned to intervention or control status; pregnant smokers filled out questionnaires and gave urine specimens at enrollment, in the eighth month of pregnancy, and postpartum. Urine cotinine concentrations were determined at CDC by enzyme-linked immunosorbent assay and were used to verify self-reported smoking status. At the eighth month of pregnancy, self-reported quitting was higher for intervention clinics than for control clinics in all three states. However, the cotinine-verified quit rates were not significantly different. Biochemical verification of self-reported quitting is essential to the evaluation of smoking cessation interventions. Achieving changes in smoking behavior in pregnant women with low-intensity interventions is difficult. Copyright 1995, American Public Health Association. Used with permission.

Roth P, ed. *Alcohol and Drug Issues Are Women's Issues.* Metuchen NJ: Women's Action Alliance and The Scarecrow Press, Inc, 1991. (Chapter refs.) *Volume One: A Review of the Issues. Volume Two: The Model Program Guide.*

This first of this two-volume series reviews and summarizes the major issues related to alcohol, drugs, women and their lives. It has 24 chapters and 30 contributors. Chapters are devoted to recent biomedical research pertinent to women; sociocultural phenomena; effects of alcohol and drug use during pregnancy; and special populations. The special population groups specifi-

cally discussed include those related to ethnicity and race, i.e., Native Americans, Asian Americans, lesbians, African Americans, and Latinos; sexual orientation; relationships and status, i.e., as children, mothers, single parents, or being homeless. The volume concludes with a review of prevention and treatment approaches sensitive to women's needs. The second volume, on model programs, addresses program development and how to conceptualize and follow through with women-sensitive programs. It covers initial planning, staffing, needs assessment, program content, staff development and training, a curriculum for participants, and evaluation. It also describes the experiences of six women's service organizations as case studies and examples. The final chapter provides a broad and annotated compendium of resources, including audiovisual aids; reading lists; organizations and funding sources, both public and private; materials such as protocols; and evaluation instruments. Copyright 1992, Project Cork Institute.

Schneider KM; Kviz FJ; Isola ML; Filstead WJ. Evaluating multiple outcomes and gender differences in alcoholism treatment. *Addictive Behaviors* 20(1): 1-21, 1995. (62 refs.)

This study followed 592 alcoholics (180 women and 412 men) after discharge from inpatient treatment. Multiple measures of treatment outcome were used to broaden the authors' understanding of the process of recovery from alcohol abuse and how that process differs for men and women. Patients were interviewed by telephone 3 to 15 months after discharge to gather information about posttreatment experiences including relationships with family, role performance, psychological impairment, and effort toward recovery. Additionally, if any alcohol use took place after treatment, information was collected about the pattern of alcohol consumption. Results indicated being married is consistently related to less drinking for men, while for women, being married contributes to relapse in the short term. The determinants of each measure of outcome were different for women and men, indicating that the process of recovery is not the same for both genders. The study confirms that drinking is related to other adverse outcomes for men, but not necessarily for women. It is evidence that women and men have different posttreatment functioning and that different characteristics are predictive of these outcomes. Copyright 1995, Elsevier Science Ltd.

Turner S. Alcoholic women's self-esteem. *Alcoholism Treatment Quarterly* 12(4): 109-116, 1995. (25 refs.)

American women in general and women alcoholics in particular suffer from low self-esteem, characterized by a discrepancy between one's ideal self-concept and actual self-concept. For many, this discrepancy begins in adolescence. For alcoholic women, it is difficult to ascertain whether their gender or their alcoholism is more damaging to self-esteem. However, some alcoholic women have low self-esteem that is so entrenched that even achieving abstinence or making improvement in drinking behavior does not help raise it. This paper examines the relationship between the fall of self-esteem in adolescent females and persistent low self-esteem in some alcoholic women. Copyright 1995, The Haworth Press, Inc.

Welsh DM, ed. *Alcohol Health and Research World* 18(3): entire issue, 1994.

This topical issue is directed to the issue of women and alcohol. Articles focus upon epidemiology of drinking, endocrine factors, genetics, sexuality, treatment needs, risk factors across the life span, alcohol-related problems of minority women, and alcohol and other drug abuse.

CHAPTER 21

The Elderly

WENDY L. ADAMS, MD, MPH
JEAN KINNEY, MSW

CLINICAL APPLICATIONS

The goals of this chapter are to assist the clinician to:

1. Recognize the demographic changes that lead to increases in the elderly population.
2. Increase awareness of factors that heighten the risk of substance use problems in the elderly.
3. Be familiar with the presentations of substance use problems in the elderly.
4. Be able to initiate screening, intervention, and prevention efforts with the elderly.

DEMOGRAPHIC CHARACTERISTICS

The US is witnessing a phenomenon known as the *graying of America*. This refers to the increasingly large proportion of older persons in the total population and the corresponding rise in the average age. In 1970 the average age was 28 years. By 1992 that had increased to 33.5 years. Increased longevity and a declining birth rate have contributed to this change—along with the aging of the post-World War II baby boom generation, now in its forties and fifties.

A larger percentage of the population than ever before is age 65 or older. Between 1900 and 1975, the proportion of elderly people increased sevenfold, while the total population increased only by a factor of 2.5. Of the approximately 255 million people in the US, 31 million are age 65 or older.[6] This is the group arbitrarily defined as the elderly or aged. Each day, 3000 people die and 4000 people reach age 65, so that there is a net gain of 1000 in the elderly population. The proportion of the population age 65 and older is the fastest-growing segment of the population.

The problems of elderly people are a growing concern for our society. The health care system is increasingly confronted by the demands of caring for those persons with chronic illness and the related need for home health and social services. For example, with a more mobile population and fewer intergenerational households, there is a demand for low- and moderate-priced housing with supportive social services.

STRESSES OF AGING*

In dealing with elderly people, it is important to keep in mind that they have different stresses than do younger people. Stresses may arise from social, psychological, or physical factors. Iatrogenic stresses can also occur as the helping professions serve (or inadequately serve) elderly people.

Social Factors

One's role in society contributes greatly to one's self-esteem and sense of identity. Modern American culture seems addicted to youth, and there is a national preoccupation with disguising signs of aging. Elderly people are not revered or valued in our culture. As one's social role changes with aging, self-esteem may suffer. Retirement often brings with it, besides a change in societal role, a plunge in social and financial status. Younger family members may not be available to help with these problems because of geographic distance or personal disinclination. Fortu-

*Adapted from Kinney J; Leaton G. *Loosening the Grip: A Handbook of Alcohol Information, 5th Edition*. St. Louis: Mosby-Year Book, Inc, 1995.

nately, however, the increase in numbers of healthy, active elderly people has occasioned the rise of such organizations as the American Association of Retired Persons, which do much to combat stereotypes and to voice the needs and concerns of older people.

Social policy has also neglected the needs of older people. Despite the growth of the elderly population, for instance, the National Institute of Mental Health spent a mere 1.1% of its budget for research on problems of the elderly only 1 decade ago. Only 1% of its budget for services went to provide care for the elderly. This figure is now changing, but it suggests an underlying attitude of disinterest in older people's needs.

In advanced age, physical and/or cognitive disability and medical illness often develop. Family and friends, as well as health care professionals and other helpers, are sometimes overwhelmed by the multiplicity, chronicity, and confusing nature of the disorders of the aging. Caregivers often feel helpless with older people, doubting whether they can contribute. Few clinicians volunteer to take elderly patients. If an elderly patient comes into a helping agency, the clinician will probably transfer the case to someone more "appropriate" or refer the patient to another agency. Reimbursement for social and medical services is often inadequate, further discouraging clinicians from taking older patients. Family members may feel frustrated, angry, guilty, and generally helpless. The older person may end up feeling like a nuisance and may be lonely. Education of health and social service providers about the needs of frail elderly people, resources available, and appropriate standards for measuring change and improvement is needed.

Receiving medical care and paying medical bills can in themselves be stressors for older people. Elderly people have twice as many visits to a physician, and their average hospital stay is 3.5 times longer and 5 times more costly than for persons under age 65. Insurance coverage (including Medicare) is often inadequate, especially for preventive services. The chronic illnesses older people suffer often require much time and few "high tech" interventions; our present insurance system reimburses especially poorly for this type of care.

Psychological Factors

Self-esteem and life satisfaction are usually quite stable over the life course and generally are well preserved in old age. The stressors most likely to decrease life satisfaction and self-esteem appear to be health or financial problems. Loss is one common experience of aging, particularly from illnesses and deaths of family and friends. Loss of loved ones means loss of support and companionship and often leads to questioning about loss of self and anticipating one's own death. There is often a sense of loss from geographical separations of family. Fifty percent of all grandparents do not have their grandchildren living close by. As new generations are born, they are not accessible to the older generation whose lives are coming to an end. There is also the loss of money from earned income; elderly people usually do not have an income equivalent to that earlier in their lives. Lack of money has obvious implications in vital areas of self-esteem. Losses also accompany retirement; there is the loss of status, gratification, and often most importantly, professional identity. There is sometimes also the loss of body functions and skills, leading to a loss of the ability to do things that were formerly rewarding. With aging, some senses become less acute. Elderly people can thereby be deprived of accurate cues from their environment, which sometimes leads to suspiciousness in older persons. The most feared loss is probably of cognitive ability; to lose one's mind is the ultimate indignity.

Elderly people may cope with losses in a number of ways. When they are able to cope with losses, they will not come to the attention of helping professionals. Sometimes, however, people respond to losses in maladaptive ways, as in *denial*. For example, in response to a doctor's observation that a patient's hand is more swollen, the patient may say, "Oh no, it's no different than it's always been." Another common way of handling loss is by *somatization*. Older people often feel it is not acceptable to complain of emotional pains. Having something wrong physically or "mechanically" is socially more acceptable. Helping professionals need to be alert to physical complaints substituting for emotional ones and to find creative approaches to alleviate the discomfort without lowering the patient's self-esteem. Another maladaptive way of handling loss is *restricting affect*. Instead of saying it does not exist, as with denial, there is withdrawal from the world in an attempt to be less vulnerable. When people use withdrawal as a coping mechanism, they may see others reciprocally withdrawing and lose additional sources of affection, interest, and caring. They, in turn, interpret this as dislike, and they may feel their initial withdrawal is justified. Therefore, it is important to reach out to isolated older people, even when they seem initially uninterested in social contact. *Alcohol or drug use* may also be a maladaptive way of coping with age-related loss. To be effective, treatment plans must help such patients find alternative coping strategies.

Depression and Suicide

Depressive symptoms are common in older people, though only 2% to 4% suffer from a diagnosable depressive syndrome. In health care settings and especially in nursing homes, the prevalence is much higher. Mood changes can also signify the onset of physical illness or cognitive impairment in elderly people; so the differential diagnosis is broad, and great skill may be required to sort out the many factors involved.

Depression in elderly people may not present like depression in younger persons, with tearfulness, inability to sleep, or loss of appetite. Some tips for recognizing depression in elderly people are an increased sensitivity to pain, refusal to get out of bed when physical problems do not require bed rest, poor concentration, a marked narrowing of coping style, and more physical complaints. Often the poor concentration leads to absentmindedness and inattentiveness, which may be misdiagnosed as dementia. More often, however, dementia and depression occur concomitantly. In either case, recognition and treatment of depression will improve the quality of life. Because so many things are likely to be going on in the surrounding environment for elderly people, it is too easy to forget the potential benefits of judiciously prescribed antidepressants.

Recognizing and treating depression in elderly people is of tremendous importance, partly because of the quality of life for these patients, but also because of the increased risk of suicide in this age group. Of those who commit suicide, 25% are over age 65. The rate of suicide for those over 65 is five times that of the general population. After age 75, the rate is eight times higher. Heavy alcohol use markedly increases the risk of suicide.[30]

Physical Changes with Aging

The physical changes from normal aging generally do not cause impairment of function. However, with increased longevity comes increased vulnerability to disease. Chronic illness becomes more common as we age and may bring with it disability. Chronic pain and loss of vision, hearing, mobility, or other functions are stresses with which many older people must cope. Nonetheless, only 5% of people age 65 or older are institutionalized in nursing homes, convalescent centers, or similar facilities.

Normal aging does cause physiological changes that have an important effect on how our bodies handle drugs. As we age, there is a decrease in lean body mass and total body water and an increase in body fat.[17] A result is an increase in the blood levels of drugs that are largely water soluble, such as alcohol. Other drugs such as the fat-soluble benzodiazepines remain in the body longer because of these changes. Most people also experience a decline in the excretion of drugs by the kidney.

These changes, along with increases in the frequency of illness and in the number of medications used, generally contribute to an increased sensitivity to lower levels of drugs, a greater vulnerability to drug toxicity, and an increased risk of adverse interactions between drugs. This applies to prescription drugs, over-the-counter drugs, illicit drugs, and beverage alcohol. A level of use that is not problematic in a middle-aged person may cause serious difficulties for someone who is older.

Also, the aging process probably makes the elderly more vulnerable to the acute effects of alcohol, although research on this subject has been limited. Those with some existing impairment in balance or in cognitive functioning are particularly susceptible to the adverse CNS side effects of alcohol.[5]

USE OF ALCOHOL AND OTHER SUBSTANCES

The substance use patterns of the elderly differ considerably from other portions of the population, as are summarized below.

Alcohol

Elderly people generally have a somewhat lower rate of alcohol use than middle-aged and young adults. Nonetheless, several studies have shown that more than half of older people do use some alcohol. In the large National Institute on Aging study, known as the Established Populations for Epidemiologic Studies in the Elderly (EPESE) study, thousands of older adults were questioned about their drinking. The prevalence of alcohol use varied considerably by geographic location, but on average, 73% of men and 56% of women 65 and older used some alcohol.[10a] Depending on location, between 7% and 10% of women and 22% and 36% of men used 1 ounce or more of alcohol per day. As in other studies, men at all ages and in all locations were more likely than women to drink. The frequency of drinking decreased with increasing age. Nonetheless, even in women in Iowa 75 and older, the age group with the lowest frequency of drinking, 30% still used some alcohol. Other surveys generally show similar results, though they vary some with the geographic location, age range, sex ratio, and socioeconomic status of the population studied.

Studies that have followed people over time have generally found a decrease in drinking with increasing age.[1,14,15] Those who used alcohol when younger are unlikely to become complete abstainers unless health problems intervene.

Even if it does not qualify as "alcohol abuse," drinking in older people is important to health care professionals for two reasons. First, safe levels of use have not been established. For instance, we know that, in middle-aged people, two drinks per day are enough to

contribute to high blood pressure.[11] In older people who obtain higher blood alcohol levels per drink, the amount required to affect blood pressure is probably lower. Some research has suggested that women who drink one drink a day or more are at a substantially increased risk of developing breast cancer.[8] The risk of hip fracture is also increased in heavy social drinkers.[19] Secondly, nonabusive drinking can also become problematic if medications are used concurrently (see below).

Little is known about the relationship of alcohol use to life stresses and changes, although there has been conjecture. The advent of retirement communities has provided an interesting opportunity to examine some aspects of these questions. It appears that in these settings, which offer their residents a variety of leisure activities such as golf, swimming, crafts classes, and discussion groups, social isolation is not tied to higher levels of alcohol use. On the contrary, the heaviest drinkers, defined as drinking at least two drinks per day, who constituted 20% of those studied, were also socially more active. Since entering the community, one-third of the individuals noted a change in drinking patterns, with three-fourths reducing their alcohol use. But that leaves one-fourth who reported increased drinking. One question raised is whether social activity in retirement communities may facilitate or even promote heavier drinking by some individuals.[3]

Over-the-Counter (OTC) Preparations

For many people, use of OTC medications is the first response to an illness or a medical problem. Self-prescribed preparations are used more extensively than prescription medications. The typical American household is estimated to have an average of 17 OTC products. In response to the question of how they handle everyday health problems, 35% of elderly people report they do not treat the problem, 35% use an OTC medication, 15% use prescription medications available in the home, 11% use some other home remedy, and 13% contact their doctor or dentist.[9] If elderly people take any action for a health problem, they probably will use an OTC preparation.

When chronic illness accompanies aging, there is an impetus to find preparations to ease discomfort. Thus, the elderly take seven times more OTC drugs than any other age group.[21] One study of healthy elderly people identified 54% as regularly using OTC drugs. Of that group, 50% reported that they typically used analgesics, laxatives, or antacids four to six times per week.[9] Of those who use OTC drugs daily, 80% are believed to simultaneously use prescribed drugs, alcohol, or both.[21] Some may often use six or more preparations.

The number of OTC preparations is growing. Potent medications that previously required a doctor's prescription, e.g., ibuprofen and naproxen, are now available without one. In addition, an issue of growing importance is that, of the major sources of information about OTC preparations, health care professionals do not rank high. When asked about their primary source of information on OTC drugs, 23% of the elderly surveyed identified advertising; 20% identified friends, relatives, and neighbors; 20% identified pharmacists; only 14% identified physicians; and 13% identified labels on products.[9]

Prescription Drugs

Although accounting for only 13% of the population, elderly people use approximately 31% of prescribed medications. Upward of 60% of elderly people do use some prescription medication; in many studies more than 80% do. Some of the drugs most commonly prescribed also have high potential for adverse drug reactions. Nonsteroidal anti-inflammatory drugs, for example, increase the risk of gastrointestinal bleeding, especially for older people. Central nervous system depressants, especially long-acting benzodiazepines, increase the risk of falls and hip fracture and have high addictive potential. When use of addictive drugs is sanctioned by physicians, defining "abuse" can be difficult. In such circumstances, it may be more useful to identify functional or social impairments that the use is causing than to identify criteria for "abuse."

Adverse Drug Reactions

Adverse drug reactions are more common in elderly people, largely because they use more drugs. Because of multiple chronic illnesses, they may be under the care of more than one physician, none of whom may be fully informed about the extent of the patient's drug regimen. As drug regimens become more complex, there is a greater probability of error by the patient as well as greater potential for metabolic interactions between drugs. Concurrent use of drugs, even 10 or more hours apart, can significantly affect absorption, distribution, metabolism, and toxicity.[29,31,32] The unique physiological changes that accompany aging and affect drug distribution and metabolism also contribute to the increased risk of drug-alcohol interactions. The risk of an adverse drug reaction in those in their fifties may be as much as 33% greater than for those in their forties. Above age 60, there appears to be a further twofold to threefold increase. Diagnosis of adverse drug reactions may be hampered because of their resemblance to illnesses common in old age, such as gait disturbances and cognitive impairment. Analysis of Medicare hospital bills suggests that in 1987, 200,000 elderly people were hospitalized because of adverse drug reactions or experienced an adverse drug reaction when hospitalized; annually, 32,000 elderly people incur hip fractures from drug-induced falls. Twice that number (approximately 63,000) have serious mental impairments either induced or aggravated by drug use; and 2 million elderly people are addicted or at risk of addiction to minor tranquilizers or sleeping pills because of daily use for at least 1 year.[24]

Alcohol-Drug Interactions[33]

Many commonly prescribed drugs can interact with alcohol, by several mechanisms. The effects of aging and alcohol on commonly prescribed drugs with hepatic metabolism are summarized in Table 21-1. Nonhepatic interactions between drugs and alcohol can also occur. For example, the anti-ulcer drugs cimetidine, ranitidine, and famotidine inhibit alcohol metabolism in the stomach, resulting in greater absorption of alcohol and higher blood alcohol levels per drink. Because elderly people already attain higher blood alcohol levels per drink because of age-related changes in drug distribution, this effect is probably of even more importance to this group. Aspirin also increases blood alcohol levels when used concurrently with alcohol. It is imperative that elderly people be warned about the increased effects of alcohol if they drink while on these medications. Alcohol used concurrently with nonsteroidal anti-inflammatory drugs may substantially increase the risk of the gastrointestinal inflammation and bleeding that these drugs cause. The increased sedation, delirium, and psychomotor impairment that can occur when alcohol is used concurrently with benzodiazepines and other CNS depressant drugs has been mentioned.

Illicit Drug Use

What in the vernacular is termed *illicit* drug use is rare in elderly people. The lifetime prevalence of drug abuse in those 65 years and older is about one-half of 1% (0.005%).[29] Little information is available about older persons involved in illicit drug use or about older street addicts. A study of methadone maintenance patients in New York found 2% were over age 60. However, it is highly likely that the number of older persons with illicit drug use problems will increase dramatically over the next decade. Studies have found that within methadone maintenance programs, one-third of the patients are over age 40 and one-fourth are between ages 40 and 49. It has been estimated that given the drug use patterns of those now in middle age, within the next 10 years the number of those over age 60 with an illicit drug problem will quadruple.[28]

Table 21-1. Aging and Alcohol Effects on Drugs with Hepatic Metabolism

Drug	Aging effects	Alcohol effects
Acetaminophen	Normal or decreased Cl*	Enhanced toxicity in heavy drinkers Overall Cl unchanged
Aspirin	Normal or decreased Cl	Prolongs bleeding time Aggravates chronic GI blood loss
Oral anticoagulants	Pharmacokinetics normal Increased effect on aging liver	Potentiates effects acutely Chronic alcohol increases Cl
Heparin	Increased bleeding, especially in elderly women	
Tolbutamide	Decreased hypoglycemic response	Acute alcohol increases half-life Alcohol may exaggerate hypoglycemia
Antidepressants	Increased blood levels (Imipramine) Generally increased CNS effect	Potentiates effects acutely Increased risk of hypothermia

Benzodiazepines	Diazepam and chlordiazepoxide
	    Normal to decreased Cl
	    Half-life increased
	Increased plasma levels
	Generally increased sedation and
	    psychomotor impairment
	Lorazepam and oxazepam Cl affected little
	    or none
		Diazepam: Acute alcohol decreases Cl
		Lorazepam: Pharmacokinetics normal
		Generally increased sedation

Chloral hydrate	Increased sedation	Acute alcohol decreases Cl Enhanced CNS effects
Barbiturates	Increased CNS effects Half-life increased	Potentiation Acute alcohol increases half-life Chronic alcohol increases Cl
Antihistamines	Increased sedation	Potentiation
Phenothiazines	Increased blood levels	Increased extrapyramidal effects Decreases alcohol metabolism
Cimetidine	Decreased (renal) Cl Mental confusion more common	Slight increase in peak blood alcohol level
Propranolol	Normal to decreased Cl Decreased heart rate response	Acute alcohol decreases Cl
Phenytoin	Increased Cl Hydroxylation rate decreased	Acute alcohol decreases Cl Chronic alcohol increases Cl
Opiates	Decreased plasma binding increases blood level	Acute alcohol decreases Cl Chronic alcohol increases Cl

From Scott RB; Mitchell MC. Aging, alcohol, and the liver. *Journal of the American Geriatrics Society* 36(3): 225-265, 1988.
*Plasma clearance.

Not only do the patterns of substance use vary among elderly people, but so do the associated problems and presentations.

ALCOHOL PROBLEMS

Between 2% and 4% of elderly people meet DSM-III criteria for alcohol abuse or alcoholism.[25] Approximately 10% have problems related to drinking that are not severe enough to meet DSM-III criteria. In general, men have a much higher likelihood of being problem drinkers than women; the prevalence decreases with increasing age; and there is considerable geographic variation in the prevalence of alcoholism. In medical settings, the prevalence is higher and appears to increase with increasing levels of care. In primary care settings, 10% to 15% of elderly patients are alcohol abusers or dependents, while up to 25% of hospitalized elderly people are. Studies have found alcohol problems in 10% to 58% of medical and psychiatric patients.[18] An analysis of Medicare billing data showed that elderly people nationally are hospitalized more often for alcohol-related problems than for heart attack.[2] Recognizing alcohol problems in elderly people in medical settings can be challenging, and generally physicians have recognized and intervened with only a small proportion of these patients. Since alcoholic patients most often present initially to their primary care physicians, improving recognition of alcohol problems in medical settings and devising successful interventions for primary care doctors should be a major focus of future research. Studies of treatment populations consistently find that about 10% of patients entering alcohol treatment programs are age 65 and older.[4,12]

Types of Alcohol Dependence

Alcohol problems make their initial appearance at different points in life.[4] Most elderly alcoholics have had a long history of alcohol use and abuse. Although these people have been relatively resistant to alcohol-related morbidity through middle age, they often begin to experience deterioration of physical and cognitive functioning as they reach their sixties and seventies. There is also a group of people who develop alcoholism in old age. For some of these people, the stresses of aging may have been too great or have come too fast or at the wrong time. They turned to alcohol as a coping mechanism. Reflecting these two different patterns, alcoholism in elderly people is commonly described either as *early onset* or *late onset*. Researchers have adopted different age cutoff points to distinguish these two varieties, falling anywhere between ages 40 to 60. Despite the differences between the two varieties, there is general agreement that of elderly people with alcohol dependence, approximately one-half began drinking heavily before age 40; and approximately two-thirds before age 60.[5] Thus, the ratio of early onset to late onset alcoholism is around 2:1.

Some differences identified between those with early and late onset alcohol dependence are summarized in Table 21-2.

Many factors may contribute to the development of late onset alcohol dependence. Problems from alcohol use sometimes emerge in later life with minimal changes in alcohol consumption. Because of the normal aging process, what had pre-

Table 21-2. Characteristics of Early and Late Onset Alcohol Dependence

Characteristics	Early onset (%)	Late onset (%)
Separated or divorced	22	55
Widowed	33	9
Time spent in jail	78	55
Organic mental syndrome	11	36
Serious health problems	44	91
Family history of alcoholism	86	40

From Bienenfeld D. Alcoholism in the elderly. *American Family Physician* 36(2): 163-169, 1987.

viously been a benign "heavy social" drinking pattern for some individuals becomes problematic. Some elderly people, however, seem to develop drinking problems as a maladaptive response to social stresses. These include retirement, loss of a spouse or others, economic hardships, social isolation, and changes in living situations. The view that changing life circumstances and social isolation are specific factors that provoke alcohol problems in elderly people is largely speculative. At any age, alcohol may be used to cope with major life stresses. For elderly people, these stressors are predictable and more numerous.

For the clinician, awareness of differences between early and late onset alcoholism is important both for screening and for treatment. For those with early onset alcoholism, the odds are greater that some of the usual social indicators of alcoholism can be elicited via past medical and social history. For those with a history of an identified alcohol problem, any current drinking should be of concern. Of those with significant alcohol problems, the number who return to nonproblematic social drinking is small.[36] There is also a greater probability of prior alcohol treatment in early onset alcoholics. One treatment program found that slightly over one-third of early onset patients had had prior treatment. Even of those with late onset alcohol dependence, however, 17% had some prior treatment.[20] In treatment programs, emphasis on developing alternative coping strategies is of particular importance for late onset alcoholics.

Presentations

Alcohol problems in elderly people often have nonspecific presentations. Many of the negative consequences of alcohol and/or drug abuse in younger persons, such as job, family, and legal problems, are less common in elderly people. Although there is little information on the nature and magnitude of medical problems found in alcohol-dependent elderly people, elderly alcoholics probably present more commonly with medical complications of their drinking. Because multiple medical problems are common in elderly people, the clinician must have a high index of suspicion to recognize alcohol-related medical problems in this group. In elderly people, some of the presentations commonly mistaken for age-related illness are malnutrition, falls, other accidents, incontinence, mood swings, depression, confusion, less attention to self-care, and unexpected reactions to prescribed medications. The results of one study of 216 patients, age 65 and above, admitted to the Mayo Clinic's substance abuse treatment service are summarized in Table 21-3.[36]

Table 21-3. Current and Past Medical Diagnoses in Elderly Patients with Alcoholism

Diagnosis	Current diagnoses Number	Past diagnoses Number	Total Number	Total (%)
Alcoholic liver disease				
Abnormal hepatic enzyme values	37	2	39	18.1
Fatty liver	18	0	18	8.3
Alcoholic hepatitis	11	5	16	7.4
Alcoholic cirrhosis	17	5	20	9.3
Hypertension	71	2	73	33.3
Chronic obstructive pulmonary disease	65	1	66	30.6
Cardiovascular disease				
Coronary artery disease	36	5	41	19.0
Valvular heart disease	12	0	12	5.6
Arteriosclerosis obliterans	9	2	11	5.1
Cardiomyopathy	6	0	6	2.8
Neurological disease				
Organic brain syndrome	52	2	54	25.0
Cerebrovascular disease	12	2	14	6.5
Peripheral neuropathy	20	1	21	9.7
Cerebellar degeneration	13	0	13	6.0
Cerebellar ataxia	11	0	11	5.1
Essential tremor	6	0	6	2.8
Diabetes mellitus	17	1	18	8.3
Peptic ulcer disease	4	29	33	15.3
Alcoholic gastritis	6	3	9	4.2
Pancreatitis	1	6	7	3.2
Colonic polyps	4	10	14	6.5
Benign prostatic hypertrophy	16	19	35	23.2*
Psoriasis	8	3	11	5.1
Degenerative joint disease	38	6	44	20.4

From Hurt RD; et al. Alcoholism in elderly persons: Medical aspects and prognosis of 216 inpatients. *Mayo Clinic Proceedings* 63: 756, 1988.
*Of men.

Screening

The importance of taking an alcohol and drug use history does not decline with aging of the patient. One goal of history taking is to identify alcohol or drug dependence. An additional goal of history taking that assumes greater importance with increasing age is to identify medically hazardous alcohol use, including potential alcohol-drug interactions. Asking about quantity and frequency of use is therefore as important as asking about adverse consequences of drinking. Several techniques enhance the accuracy of self-reported quantity and frequency of drinking. Asking about each type of alcoholic beverage separately will increase the accuracy of reporting. The "Timeline follow-back" procedure uses a calendar and visual aids to enhance reporting of alcohol consumption.[35] This procedure asks about drinking on each specific day of the week for as far back as the interviewer deems important. Heavy drinking determined by this method is a good indicator of problem drinking. In older people, daily drinking is more common than binge drinking for those with alcohol problems.[4,5,12] If a standardized way of asking about problem drinking is needed, the CAGE questionnaire* is probably especially useful for older people in medical settings. It is brief and avoids questions about social consequences of drinking that don't apply to older people. Recently a version of the Michigan Alcohol Screening Test more applicable to older people has been developed, which may prove useful in screening for alcohol problems in this population.

For those who have actual or potential medical complications of their drinking but are not dependent on alcohol, appropriate levels of drinking will need to be determined individually in the context of the patient's medical status. For instance, people on warfarin will essentially need to abstain. Those with

*From Kinney J; Leaton G. *Loosening the Grip: A Handbook of Alcohol Information, 5th Edition.* St Louis: Mosby-Year Book, Inc, 1995.

hypertension exacerbated by heavy drinking can probably have two or three drinks a week without ill effects. Heavy drinkers not dependent on alcohol will often respond to physician advice to cut down on drinking. For those who are dependent, involvement in a formal treatment program or self-help group such as Alcoholics Anonymous will usually be required to attain abstinence. It is important, however, that the primary care physician not give up on those who do not respond to efforts at traditional treatment programs. Recent work by Willenbring and colleagues[38] suggests that ongoing treatment in the primary care setting with attention to social and medical complications of alcoholism can be successful at reducing hospital days and 2-year mortality in medically ill alcoholics refractory to traditional treatment. Ultimately, the central factor in distinguishing between a heavy nondependent drinker and an alcoholic may be the patient's response to the information that his or her current alcohol use is hazardous. Those unable to moderate or abstain in the face of recognized alcohol-related medical problems are highly likely to be dependent on alcohol.

Obstacles to Identification and Intervention

Many of the screening instruments in common use are based on the behavior of young men and do not transfer well to older people.[16] Because older people are often retired, for instance, they will not have problems at work. Because they often live alone, they are less likely to have alcohol-induced marital problems. It is particularly challenging to identify problem drinking in people with cognitive impairment. Family, friends, and neighbors are important sources of information about those who are unable to give a good history themselves.

Other factors also contribute to poor recognition of alcohol problems in older people. Classic signs of alcohol dependence may be obscure. Tolerance, manifest by requiring more alcohol to achieve the same effect, is one classic component of alcohol dependence. Older people, who attain higher blood alcohol levels per drink, may honestly report requiring less alcohol intake to get the same effect as before. Withdrawal, though its signs and symptoms are little different in older people, may not be recognized until late in the course. Many other possible causes of the tachycardia, hypertension, delirium, and so on will be thought of first in elderly people. Social decline is often marked by nonspecific features, described above, and differs from the presentation in younger people. A high index of suspicion is required to diagnose alcohol problems in older people when signs and symptoms are nonspecific.

Elderly people, as well as other segments of the population, are likely to be protected by family, friends, or caretakers. They may fail to see the problem, ignore what they suspect, or justify not intervening in an alcohol problem because no one wants to take away someone's "last pleasure." Thinking "What do they have to live for, anyway? They have been drinking all these years, they'll never stop now, and I don't want to be the one who asks them to give up the bottle" is also common. "Enabling" the drinking of an alcoholic is not unique to situations involving elderly people. It is probably more common, though, for those persons closest to an elderly problem drinker to actively facilitate the continuation of drinking. For example, a neighbor or housekeeper may ensure access to alcohol by purchasing it for the homebound person and thereby circumvent and sabotage others' efforts to intervene. In situations where family members or friends support problem drinking or are reluctant to intervene, it is important to point out that problem drinking is not pleasurable drinking. Such complications of heavy drinking as cognitive impairment, gait disturbances, and other physical dependencies are greatly feared by most older people. These impairments often lead to nursing home placement, which most elderly people wish to avoid at almost any cost.

Detoxification and Treatment

Detoxification protocols need to be adjusted for elderly people. Generally, because of autonomic and cardiovascular instability, detoxification is better managed in a hospital than on an outpatient basis. Although the general strategy is similar for managing withdrawal in younger patients, there are several caveats. Withdrawal is likely to take longer for elderly people, especially those with cognitive impairment. Prophylactic use of benzodiazepines in the absence of withdrawal symptoms is contraindicated because it might provoke delirium. It is generally recommended that their use be delayed and prescribed in response to specific signs and symptoms of withdrawal. Drugs with a short half-life are preferable to longer-acting agents. It should be anticipated that dosages can be reduced by one-half to two-thirds.[5] In a person also dependent on benzodiazepines, withdrawal may take considerably longer than alcohol withdrawal alone.

The use of Antabuse (disulfiram) has been suggested by some, although with careful consideration to the risks and potential benefits. In elderly people, the risks may be considerable. Physically they are more frail, and their metabolic ability to handle disulfiram is a factor. They may be less able to comply with the restrictions because of cognitive impairments. Furthermore, their greater use of over-the-counter preparations increases the probability of inadvertent drug reactions. An uncomfortable disulfiram reaction for someone younger may be a medical crisis and even lethal for someone elderly.[5]

Elderly people need the same type of rehabilitation services as younger persons—education, counseling, and involvement in self-help groups. Treatment programs typically incorporate elderly people into their general programs. The prognosis is at least as good for elderly people as for younger persons. In addition to the treatment program's standard regimen, elderly people also require a thorough medical evaluation and potentially more extensive social service involvement at discharge and as a part of aftercare.[20]

Research in the early 1980s indicated that elderly alcoholics had comparable treatment outcomes to younger patients, which was interpreted as refuting the need for specially focused programs for older persons. However, more recent research has demonstrated that programs tailored to elderly people enhance outcome by reducing treatment drop-out; by increasing rates of aftercare; and by dealing with relapses without losing these patients in treatment.[22]

For most clinicians, the issue of specialized vs. standard programs is likely to be nothing more than an academic interest because so few programs have been developed for elderly people. However, some of the benefits of programs designed for elderly people may be achieved within the standard programs, with some inventiveness. Referring agencies and health care providers need to be sensitive to the accommodations that might be made to serve elderly people better. It can be beneficial to match patients with clinicians who are knowledgeable about and comfortable in treating elderly people within standard programs and who are able to work at a slower, gentler pace.[22] Abrasive confrontation, which is used in some programs, is not likely to be effective with elderly persons. Supportive groups are important to elderly people in reducing the sense of isolation, enhancing communication skills, providing a forum for problem solving, and dealing with denial. Small-group sessions or individual therapy within a general treatment program can help develop special skills for coping with losses, enjoying leisure time, and developing new relationships after the loss of loved ones. An important element for elderly people is referred to as *life review*. Groups need to allow for the elderly person's reminiscence and processing of the past, as it allows them to see their lives as a whole. For those in treatment for alcohol problems, incorporating this process without diminishing self-esteem or devaluing the elderly person's life is important. This is not only important in formal alcohol treatment but in contacts with health care and social service professionals.[31]

Treatment of the cognitively impaired alcoholic is especially difficult. Often a prolonged period of enforced abstinence from alcohol will be needed to determine if the person will recover sufficient cognitive function to pursue cognitively oriented treatment options. If not, a permanently supervised living situation such as a nursing home or group home where alcohol is not available will probably be needed.

Referrals

Contacting local agencies that serve elderly people may be a useful step in identifying potential treatment programs for an elderly patient. Such agencies have undoubtedly had patients who have received alcohol treatment. Based on these experiences, such agencies can help identify those programs that are most successful in involving older people, and equally important, that are sensitive to and able to work effectively with community agencies in organizing aftercare. In selection of a treatment program, another important factor will be the patient's physical and cognitive status. The facility must be equipped to manage the withdrawal symptoms and medical problems that arise.

DRUG USE PROBLEMS

Illicit drug use, as mentioned above, is uncommon in elderly people, although prescription and OTC drug use is often problematic. A major report mandated by 1988 legislation reviewed and made recommendations on drug use in the Medicare program. Among its findings was that those age 60 and above, though constituting only 17% of the population, account for 51% of all deaths from drug reactions. A significant portion of these result from drug mismanagement.[26]

Benzodiazepines and narcotics are among the most commonly prescribed drugs for elderly people. Dependence on benzodiazepines is particularly problematic. Though there are few data on diagnosing and treating benzodiazepine dependence in elderly people, physicians should be aware of the addiction potential of these drugs and be alert to the possibility of dependence in patients who request them repeatedly.

Concurrent use of drugs, even 10 or more hours apart, can significantly affect absorption, distribution, metabolism, and toxicity.[31,33,34] With more drugs being used, including alcohol, there is also greater potential for adverse interactions. A study of hospitalized patients found that all patients taking more than eight drugs had at least one interacting pair of drugs in the therapeutic regimen.[20] Drug mismanagement and overmedication can easily occur in retirement and nursing homes.[10]

Screening

Taking a medication history at each patient visit is probably the best screening mechanism for problematic use of medications. This can be done in the office by nonphysician staff and recorded in the chart in a place the physician will check at each visit. Designating a special place in the chart for a medication list that is regularly updated will help keep track of the fluctuations in medication use. Asking people to bring their medications with them on each office visit is helpful and often enlightening. Asking specifically about visits to other physicians and about medications prescribed at those visits will improve completeness of drug use information. Specific questioning about OTC medication use is also important. A color code or other mechanism for highlighting medication with addiction potential can help keep the physician alert to potential addiciton problems.

Some of the diagnostic clues to misuse of OTC preparations are summarized in Table 21-4.

Intervention

When benzodiazepine addiction is suspected, successful intervention requires an individualized approach. Some patients will recognize the undesired complications of the addiction and be motivated to taper the drug as outpatients or to attend traditional treatment programs. Many will not be willing to do this: In this case, attention to complications of the drug use can still improve the patient's status. For example, changing to a shorter-acting drug such as lorazepam will decrease the risk of hip fracture and excessive sedation.

When narcotic use is excessive, it is important to consider alternative approaches to pain management.

Pain clinics have evolved in recent years and often can use nonpharmacologic approaches such as biofeedback, relaxation, and physical therapy to decrease the need for narcotics. Alternative medication is also often possible.

For potential problems resulting from polypharmacy and drug-drug interactions, the most useful steps entail the use of office routines and clinical protocols that can help spot potential medication misuse. Even the most elaborate efforts by a medical practice will never be able to eliminate drug misuse. Thus, it is important to have a high index of suspicion for drug problems when caring for elderly people.

Prevention

Prevention of medication problems can occur both in health care settings and in the community. Nurses have an important role in health care settings. Setting aside time for nurses to educate patients about taking medications and about their potential side effects and interactions with other drugs or alcohol is appropriate whenever a new drug is prescribed, but especially when major changes in the regimen have been made. Improving office protocols and medical record keeping to better track medication use can also prevent medication problems.

Today's middle-aged patient is tomorrow's elderly patient for some other clinician. Today's adolescent is establishing a framework for making independent decisions about health care, self-care, and life-style, which will have a bearing on life-long health habits. What questions should any individual consider before

Table 21-4. Diagnostic Clues to Over-the-Counter Drug-Induced Problems

Drug class	Diagnostic clues
OTC analgesics	Gastritis
	Heme-positive stools
	Nephropathy
	Elevated alkaline phosphatase
Laxatives	Continuing diarrhea
	Metabolic abnormalities (hypokalemia, hypocalcemia)
	Nonspecific inflammatory changes at rectal biopsy
Antihistamines and anticholinergics	Mental status abnormalities
	Unusual reactions to prescription psychotropic medications
Alcohol-based OTCs	Elevated liver enzymes
	Worsening of preexisting chronic conditions
	History of alcohol abuse
Caffeine	Anxiety
	Insomnia
	Tachydysrrhythmias
Nicotine	Stigmata of smoking or oral tobacco use
	History of alcohol abuse

From Kofoed LL. OTC drug overuse in the elderly: What to watch for. *Geriatrics* 40(10): 55-60, 1985.

taking medication? What specific questions are important for the particular patient? Physicians, nurses, pharmacists, and health care reporters all have opportunities to educate younger people on these issues, which may have a positive impact on their future drug use habits.

Patients rarely consult their primary care provider before making decisions about self-care or using OTC preparations, nor does any practitioner wish to be contacted on that basis. Patients are not frequently advised to discuss their OTC medication purchases with the pharmacist. However, the pharmacist is an underused resource and ally for the clinician. The pharmacist is almost always available; one of his or her roles is public education and information. Patients need instruction about the kind of questions to ask: "Are there any contraindications when using this product? If taking prescription medications, is there a need for concern about interactions? Are there any side effects?"

GENERAL SUGGESTIONS FOR WORKING WITH ELDERLY PEOPLE

Remember that elderly people are survivors of hard times. Getting through the Depression and two world wars required strength. Survivors have a wealth of experience to bring to coping with the stresses of aging. Make it clear that you respect their strengths and experience and that you have high expectations for their ability to overcome their problems.

Because many elderly persons are reluctant to seek or receive help, a family member often makes the initial contact. Family members' views of the situation, their ideas and fears, need to be discussed. Whatever the problem, the chances are good that something can be done to improve the picture. It often surprises families that there is hope for recovery. Professionals can help the family, too, as they cope with a difficult situation, e.g., arranging for Meals-on-Wheels or making simple suggestions about how to make routines easier.

In conversation with elderly people, do not always stick with neutral topics like the weather. Discuss common interests such as gardening or baseball, as well as some controversial topic, something appealing. You can enhance self-esteem by letting the person know that you not only want their opinions, you want them to listen to yours.

Multiple resources may be needed to assist elderly people. In many instances older adults with alcohol problems need to become reinvolved in the world. Meaningful contacts can come from a variety of people, not just from professional helpers. The janitor in the client's apartment building, a neighbor, or a crossing guard at the street corner may all be potential allies. If the person was once active in a church group, civic organization, or other community group, but has lost contact, recommend that he or she get in touch with the organization. Often a member will visit or assist in other ways. Many communities have senior citizen centers that offer social programs, Meals-on-Wheels, counseling on Social Security and Medicare, and transportation.

When cognitive impairment is a factor, providing cues to orient the person may be helpful. Mention dates, days of the week, and current events. Do not, however, expect a cognitively impaired person to retain such information or to learn new skills. Since remote memory is usually preserved longer than recent memory, discussing past life events and interests may be socially rewarding.

Beware of those who arrange trivial activities for older people to occupy their time. Crafts classes, for instance, ought to teach real skills, not just keep people busy. Many elderly people also have something they can teach others. For example, the carpenter no longer steady enough to use tools can advise people who want to remodel their homes. Elderly people have a richness of life experiences and much to contribute.

Finally, appreciate what is entailed in approaching medical and social services. Are there long waits at several different offices? Does it require using stairs, elevators, and hallways? Are there certain times of day when using public transportation is easier? Any adjustments that make using services as uncomplicated, convenient, and economical as possible are worth the effort.

REFERENCES

1. Adams WL; Garry PJ; Rhyne R; Hunt WC; Goodwin JS. Alcohol intake in the healthy elderly. *Journal of the American Geriatrics Society* 38(3): 211-216, 1990.
2. Adams WL; Yuan Z; Barboriak JJ; Rimm AA. Alcohol-related hospitalizations in elderly people: Prevalence and geographic variation in the United States. *Journal of the American Medical Association* 270(10): 1222-1225, 1993. (29 refs.)
3. Alexander F; Duff RW. Drinking in retirement communities. *The Gerontologist* 28(5): 632-636, 1988. (27 refs.)
4. Atkinson RM. Substance use and abuse in later life. IN: Atkinson RM, ed. *Alcohol and Drug Abuse in Old Age: Clinical Insights.* Washington DC: American Psychiatric Press, 1984. pp. 2-21.
5. Bienenfeld D. Alcoholism in the elderly. *American Family Physician* 36(2): 163-169, 1987. (10 refs.)
6. Bureau of the Census. *Statistical Abstract of the United States, Edition 114.* Washington DC: Bureau of the Census, 1994.
7. Cohen S. Alcoholism in the elderly. *Canadian Family Physician* 34(3): 723-731, 1988.
8. Colditz GA. Epidemiology of breast cancer: Findings from the Nurses' Health Study. *Cancer* 71(Supplement 4): 1480-1489, 1993.
9. Coons SJ; Hendricks J; Sheahan S. Self-medication with nonprescription drugs. *Generations* 12(4): 22-26, 1988. (30 refs.)
10. Cooper JW. Medication misuse in nursing homes. *Generations* 14(2): 56-57, 1988. (6 refs.)

10a. Coruoney-Huntley J; Brock DB; Ostfeld AM; Taylor JO; Wallace RB. *Established Populations for Epidemiologic Studies in the Elderly.* Washington DC: Department of Health and Human Services NIH Publication No. 86-2443: 196-199, 1986.

11. Criqui MH. Alcohol and hypertension: New insights from population studies. *European Heart Journal* 8(Supplement B): 19-26, 1987.

12. Dunne FJ; Schipperheijn JA. Alcohol and the elderly. *British Medical Journal* 298(6689): 1660-1661, 1989. (21 refs.)

13. Eisdorfer C. Care of the aged: The barriers of tradition. *Annals of Internal Medicine* 94(3): 256-260, 1981.

14. Fillmore KM. Prevalence, incidence, and chronicity of drinking patterns and problems among men as a function of age: A longitudinal and cohort analysis. *British Journal of Addiction* 82(1): 77-83, 1987. (16 refs.)

15. Glynn RL; Bouchard GR; Lo Castro JS; Laird NM. Aging and generational effects on drinking behaviors in men: Results from the Normative Aging Study. *American Journal of Public Health* 75(12): 1413-1419, 1985. (36 refs.)

16. Graham K. Identifying and measuring alcohol abuse among the elderly: Serious problems with existing instrumentation. *Journal of Studies on Alcohol* 47(4): 322-326, 1986. (21 refs.)

17. Greenblatt DJ; Sellers EM; Shader RI. Drug disposition in old age. *New England Journal of Medicine* 306: 1081-1088, 1982.

18. Gurnack AM; Thomas JL. Behavioral factors related to elderly alcohol abuse: Research and policy issues. *International Journal of the Addictions* 24(7): 641-654, 1989. (12 refs.)

19. Hernandeq-Avila M; Colditz GA; Stampfer MJ; Rosner B; Speizer FE; Willett WC. Caffeine, moderate alcohol intake, and risk of fractures of the hip and forearm in middle-aged women. *American Journal of Clinical Nutrition* 54(1): 157-63, 1982.

20. Hurt RD; Finlayson RE; Morse RM; Davis IJ. Alcoholism in elderly persons: Medical aspects and prognosis of 216 inpatients. *Mayo Clinic Proceedings* 63(9): 753-760, 1988. (31 refs.)

21. Kofoed LL. OTC drug overuse in the elderly: What to watch for. *Geriatrics* 40(10): 55-60, 1985. (0 refs.)

22. Kofoed LL; Tolson RL; Atkinson RM; Toth RL; Turner JA. Treatment compliance of older alcoholics: An elder specific approach is superior to mainstreaming. *Journal of Studies on Alcohol* 48(1): 47-51, 1987. (12 refs.)

23. Lesage J; Zwygart-Staucher M. Detection of medication misuse in elders. *Generations* 12(4): 32-36, 1988. (5 refs.)

24. Mitchell GW; Stanaszek WF; Nichols NB. Documenting drug-drug interactions in ambulatory patients. *American Journal of Hospital Pharmacy* 36(5): 653-657, 1987.

25. Myers JK; Weissman MM; Tischler GL; Helzer CE; Leaf PJ; Orvaschel H; Anthony JC; et al. Six month prevalence of psychiatric disorders in three communities. *Archives of General Psychiatry* 41(10): 959-967, 1984.

26. Office of the Inspector General. *Drug Utilization Review.* Washington DC: Department of Health and Human Services, 1989. (95 refs.)

27. Ogur B. Prescription drug abuse and dependence in clinical practice. *Southern Medical Journal* 80(9): 1153-1159, 1987. (45 refs.)

28. Petersen DM. Substance abuse, criminal behavior, and older people. *Generations* 12(4): 63-67, 1988. (19 refs.)

29. Robins LN; Helzer JE. Lifetime prevalence of specific psychiatric disorders in three sites. *Archives of General Psychiatry* 41(10): 949-958, 1984. (25 refs.)

30. Ross RK; Bernstein L; Trent L; Henderson BE; Paganini-Hill A. A prospective study of risk factors for traumatic deaths in a retirement community. *Preventive Medicine* 19(3): 323-334, 1990.

31. Schiff SM. Treatment approaches for older alcoholics. *Generations* 12(4): 41-45, 1988. (13 refs.)

32. Schuckit MA, ed. Alcohol, drugs and the elderly. *Drug Abuse and Alcoholism Newsletter* (Vista Hill Foundation) 18(3): 1-4, 1989.

33. Scott RB; Mitchell MC. Aging, alcohol, and the liver. *Journal of the American Geriatrics Society* 36(3): 225-265, 1988. (110 refs.)

34. Shimp LA; Ascione FJ. Causes of medication misuse and error. *Generations* 12(4): 17-22, 1988. (28 refs.)

35. Sobell LC; Sobell MB. Timeline Followback: A technique for assessing self-reported alcohol consumption. IN: Litten R, Allen J, eds. *Measuring Alcohol Consumption.* Totowa NJ: The Humana Press, 1992.

36. Vaillant GE. *The Natural History of Alcoholism.* Cambridge MA: Harvard University Press, 1983.

37. Willenbring ML; Christensen KJ; Spring WD; Rasmussen R. Alcoholism screening in the elderly. *Journal of the American Geriatrics Society* 35(9): 864-869, 1987. (15 refs.)

38. Willenbring ML; Olson DH; Bielinski J. Integrated outpatient treatment for medically ill alcoholic men: Results from a quasi-experimental study. *Journal of Studies on Alcohol* (in press).

39. Williams GD; Dufour M; Bertolucci D. Drinking levels, knowledge, and associated characteristics. 1985 NHIS Findings. *Public Health Report* 101(6): 593-598, 1986. (16 refs.)

FURTHER READINGS

Adams WL; Yuan Z; Barboriak JJ; Rimm AA. Alcohol-related hospitalizations of elderly people: Prevalence and geographic variation in the United States. *Journal of the American Medical Association* 270(10): 1222-1225, 1993. (29 refs.)

This study determines the prevalence, geographic variation, and charges to Medicare using 1989 hospital claims data from the Health Care Financing Administration (HCFA). Rates were determined using (1) hospital claims records form the HCFA's Medicare Provider Analysis and Review Record (MEDPAR) database for all Medicare Part A beneficiaries aged 65 years and older; (2) county population estimates for 1985 from the Bureau of the Census; and (3) per capita consumption of alcohol by state in 1989 as estimated by the US Department of Health and Human Services. Data include all hospital inpatient Medicare Part A beneficiaries aged 65 years and older in the US in 1989. The prevalence of alcohol-related hospitalizations in people aged 65 years and older nationally in 1989 was 54.7 per 10,000 for men and 14.8 per 10,000 for women. Comparison with hospital records showed that MEDPAR data had a sensitivity of 77% to detect alcohol-related hospitalizations. There was considerable geographic variation; prevalence ranged from 18.9 per 10,000 in Arkansas to 77.0 per 10,000 in Alaska. A strong correlation existed between alcohol-related hospitalizations and per capita consumption of alcohol by state (Spearman correlation coefficient, 0.64; $P < .0001$). In 1989 the hospital-associated charges to Medicare for all admissions where the primary diagnosis was alcohol related ($n = 33,039$) totaled $233,543,500. Median charge per hospital stay was $4514. Alcohol-related hospitalizations for elderly people are common; rates were similar to those for myocardial infarction as detected by the same method. The charges to Medicare for this preventable problem are considerable. Ecological analysis suggests that per capita consumption in the total US population predicts alcohol-related hospitalizations in the elderly population. Copyright 1993, American Medical Association

Atkinson RM. Late onset problem drinking in older adults. (review). *International Journal of Geriatric Psychiatry* 9(4): 321-326, 1994. (28 refs.)

After the first descriptions of late onset alcoholism in the early 1970s, no systematic attention followed for more than a decade.

In the past 10 years, however, that has changed, and this report summarizes recently acquired knowledge about late onset problem drinking, including the author's own work. The incidence of new alcoholism cases does decline with age but remains appreciable in the late sixties. Samples of aging alcoholics in treatment show that as many as one-fourth to two-thirds of cases had onset after age 60. Risk factors for late onset alcoholism include female gender, higher socioeconomic status, and (in some but not all studies) life stressors; however, neither psychiatric comorbidity nor positive family history of alcoholism appears to contribute in most cases. Compared to longstanding alcoholics, late onset cases tend to be milder and more circumscribed, and they may also fluctuate more, with an apparently high likelihood of spontaneous remission, at least over the short term. These characteristics have implications for the use of brief and informal interventions to prevent and reduce late onset problem drinking, but also suggest caution in interpreting the response of late onset cases to treatment in uncontrolled studies. Present knowledge of late onset alcoholism is fragmentary; more systematic clinical research on its characteristics and treatment is needed. Copyright 1994, John Wiley & Sons, Ltd.

Atkinson RM; Tolson RL; Turner JA. Factors affecting outpatient treatment compliance of older male problem drinkers. *Journal of Studies on Alcohol* 54(1): 102-106, 1993. (31 refs.)

This study identifies predictors of outpatient treatment compliance in a cohort of 205 male problem drinkers, age 55 to 79 years. Patients agreed to attend a weekly outpatient therapy group designed for older persons and abstain from using alcohol for 1 year. Patients who were drinking-driving offenders, who had later onset of alcohol-related problems, and/or whose spouses also participated in counseling were more likely than others to comply with outpatient requirements. Copyright 1993, Alcohol Research Documentation, Inc. Used with permission.

Ayd FJ Jr. Prescribing anxiolytics and hypnotics for the elderly. *Psychiatric Annals* 24(2): 91-97, 1994. (19 refs.)

The author describes problems related to inappropriate prescribing of anxiolytics and hypnotics to the elderly. Physiological changes associated with aging that make the elderly more susceptible to the benzodiazepines are noted. Withdrawal phenomenon and its management are described. Alternative agents are discussed. Copyright 1994, Project Cork Institute.

Barnea Z; Teichman M. Substance misuse and abuse among the elderly: Implications for social work intervention. (review). *Journal of Gerontological Social Work* 21(3/4): 133-148, 1994. (65 refs.)

This article reviews the literature on the misuse and abuse of psychoactive substances in the elderly. Three main patterns of abuse characteristic of this age group are identified and analyzed: abuse of medications, of alcohol, and of illegal drugs. The article refers to issues such as the extent (prevalence and incidence) of the problem in the elderly, the predictors and correlates of abuse, and its special dangers and effects on the elderly and their environment. The key roles that social workers should play in prevention and treatment are discussed. Copyright 1994, The Haworth Press, Inc.

Brennan PL; Moos RH; Mertens JR. Personal and environmental risk factors as predictors of alcohol use, depression, and treatment-seeking: A longitudinal analysis of late-life problem drinkers. *Journal of Substance Abuse* 6(2): 191-208, 1994. (39 refs.)

This study examines how personal risk factors (prior functioning, male, unmarried, early onset of drinking problems, and avoidance coping) and environmental risk factors (negative life events, chronic stressors, and friends' approval of drinking) predicted changes in older problem drinkers' (*n* = 659) adaptation over a

1-year interval. Personal risk factors independently predictive of poorer outcomes included poorer prior functioning, being male, and making more use of avoidance coping strategies. Of environmental risk factors, negative life events, chronic health and spouse stressors, and having more friends who approved of drinking were independent predictors of poorer follow-up functioning and treatment seeking. Interactions between personal and environmental risk factors helped predict subsequent alcohol consumption and treatment seeking. For example, lighter drinkers were more likely than heavier drinkers to curtail alcohol use in response to new health events; friends more strongly influenced the treatment seeking of unmarried problem drinkers and individuals who used more avoidance coping strategies. Copyright 1994, Ablex Publishing Corp.

Brower KJ; Mudd S; Blow FC; Young JP; Hill EM. Severity and treatment of alcohol withdrawal in elderly vs. younger patients. *Alcoholism: Clinical and Experimental Research* 18(1): 196-201, 1994. (12 refs.)

The authors conducted a retrospective chart review of older (*n* = 48; mean age = 69) and younger (*n* = 36; mean = 30) patients admitted to residential/inpatient treatment for alcohol withdrawal and dependence. Although the two age groups did not differ in terms of recent drinking history, the elderly group had significantly more withdrawal symptoms for a longer duration than the younger group. The elderly group also had more symptoms of cognitive impairment, daytime sleepiness, weakness, and high blood pressure. Finally, no significant differences were found between age groups in either the dosage or number of days of detoxification medication, although a trend was found for more days of medication in the elderly. The authors conclude that alcohol withdrawal may be more severe in elderly than in younger persons. Accordingly, treatment may take longer and should target the specific profile of symptoms that characterize alcohol withdrawal in the elderly. Copyright 1994, Research Society on Alcoholism. Used with permission.

Egbert AM. The older alcoholic: Recognizing the subtle clinical clues. *Geriatrics* 48(7): 63-69, 1993. (25 refs.)

Alcoholism is a common disease in older patients, affecting up to 10% of those living at home and as many as 40% of those in nursing homes. Symptoms tend to be nonspecific, including "failure to thrive," insomnia, diarrhea, and dementia. Morbidity and increased mortality can occur with no more than one or two drinks daily because of altered pharmacokinetics with aging. Recognizing alcohol-induced brain injury, which can resemble Alzheimer's disease, is particularly important in the management of older patients and may require the judicious use of benzodiazepine therapy. Copyright 1993, CIBA.

Forster LE; Pollow R; Stoller EP. Alcohol use and potential risk for alcohol-related adverse drug reactions among community-based elderly. *Journal of Community Health* 18(4): 225-239, 1993. (38 refs.)

This paper documents the frequency of alcohol consumption and concurrent use of alcohol and medications in a random sample of elderly community dwellers. Further, a profile of older persons likely to drink alcohol is developed, and the extent to which they are at potential clinical risk from their concurrent use of alcohol with prescription and OTC medications is explored. While approximately 43% are abstainers, most older respondents reported using alcohol. Older drinkers who take one or more drugs that place them at potential risk for negative drug-alcohol interactions represent one-quarter of this sample but are often overlooked in estimating the extent of alcohol problems in the elderly. By far the most common risk was from the combined use of OTC pain medications and alcohol (19%). The multivariate analyses revealed that sex, educational attainment, and religious affiliation are important factors to consider in developing a profile of older people at risk for alcohol-related adverse drug reactions. Implications for health care and social service professionals who work with elderly community dwellers are discussed. Copyright 1993, Human Sciences Press, Inc.

Jones TV; Lindsey BA; Yount P; Soltys R; Farani-Enayat B. Alcoholism screening questionnaires: Are they valid in elderly medical outpatients. *Journal of General Internal Medicine* 8(12): 674-678, 1993. (23 refs.)

This paper assesses the validity of the CAGE (cut down, annoyed, guilty feelings, eye-opener) questionnaire and the Michigan Alcoholism Screening Test (MAST) in distinguishing between elderly patients with and without alcohol abuse or dependence disorders. In this cross-sectional study, patients were interviewed with a "gold standard," the alcohol module of the Revised Diagnostic Interview Schedule (DIS-III-R), and two screening questionnaires (the CAGE and the MAST). The study was conducted in the outpatient medical practice of a university teaching hospital. All English-speaking continuity patients 65 years of age or older able to participate were eligible; complete data were available for 154 (91%) of the 170 people who agreed to participate. Sixty-seven patients (44%) were active drinkers, whereas 87 (56%) reported abstinence. Twenty-five patients (16%) met Diagnostic and Statistical Manual of Mental Disorders-III-Revised (DSM-III-R) criteria for alcohol abuse or dependence. A CAGE score of 2, the conventional cutoff point, had a sensitivity and a specificity of 48% and 99%, respectively. A MAST score of 5, the originally recommended cutoff point, had a sensitivity and a specificity of 52% and 91%, respectively. The areas under the receiver operating characteristic (ROC) curves were 0.91 for the CAGE and 0.61 for the MAST. The CAGE and the MAST were both characterized by low sensitivities at conventional cutoff points, but the CAGE was significantly more effective than the MAST in discriminating between elderly medical outpatients with and without alcohol abuse or dependence. Copyright 1993, Hanley & Belfus, Inc.

Jonsson B; Sernbo I; Kristensson H; Johnell O. Hip fractures in middle-aged men: A consequence of early retirement and alcohol misuse. *Alcohol and Alcoholism* 28(6): 709-714, 1993. (35 refs.)

From the 1950s to the 1980s, the incidence of hip fractures in women aged 50 to 64 and of cervical fractures in men of the same ages in Malmo did not increase, whereas the incidence of trochanteric fractures in men aged 50 to 64 increased significantly. Significant background factors in men were alcohol misuse, living alone, early retirement, previous fractures, low weight/height ratio, and less severe trauma—more in men with trochanteric than cervical fractures. The deviant life-style and suspected physical inertia in this group of middle-aged men probably predisposes them to osteoporosis and increased fracture risk. Copyright 1993, Medical Council on Alcoholism. Used with permission.

King CJ; Van Hasselt VB; Segal DL; Hersen M. Diagnosis and assessment of substance abuse in older adults: Current strategies and issues. *Addictive Behaviors* 19(1): 41-55, 1994. (63 refs.)

Alcohol and substance abuse in older adults until recently has received little empirical attention in the literature. However, in light of the increasing number of older adults in the population, clinicians and researchers alike are recognizing the importance of evaluating specific assessment and treatment strategies for such older substance abusers. Because distinctive biological, cognitive, and psychosocial variables appear to be correlated with substance abuse in older adults, evaluation and intervention methods employed with younger cohorts may be inappropriate or ineffective with individuals 55 or over. This article examines these characteristics as they pertain to the unique problems and service needs of the elderly. Relevant diagnostic and assessment

strategies are reviewed. Finally, suggestions for future work in this area are outlined. Copyright 1994, Pergamon Press.

Marcus MT. Alcohol and other drug abuse in elders. *Journal of Enterostomy Nursing* 20(3): 106-110, 1993. (15 refs.)

With the growing population of older persons, ET nurses can expect more elderly patients in their practice setting. Elderly persons are not immune to alcohol and other drug abuse. Detection of substance abuse in this population is complex and often missed. The purposes of this article are as follows: (1) Examine barriers that may prevent nurses from addressing substance abuse in the elderly; (2) suggest risks for psychoactive substance abuse in this population; (3) identify warning signs that should alert nurses to the problem; and (4) outline treatment options for substance-abusing patients. Copyright 1993, *Journal of Ostomy and Continence Nurses Society.*

Moos RH; Brennan PL; Mertens JR. Diagnostic subgroups and predictors of one-year re-admission among late-middle-aged and older substance abuse patients. *Journal of Studies on Alcohol* 55(2): 173-183, 1994. (42 refs.)

This naturalistic study uses data based on clinical records to examine treatment utilization and 1-year re-admission rates for three diagnostic subgroups of late-middle-aged and older substance abuse inpatients in Department of Veterans Affairs (VA) Medical Centers: Inpatients with an alcohol or drug dependence diagnosis (*n* = 11,652); inpatients with an alcohol or drug psychosis (*n* = 3510); and inpatients with an alcohol or drug disorder and a concomitant psychiatric disorder (*n* = 5977). As expected, substance abuse patients in the latter two subgroups received more treatment before, during, and after an index episode of care than did patients with only an alcohol or drug dependence diagnosis. From a broad perspective, these results indicate a match between treatment services and patients' needs. However, relatively few older substance abuse patients received outpatient mental outpatient aftercare, especially patients with alcohol or drug diagnosis psychoses. The 1-year re-admission rate in the group overall was higher than that usually reported in younger and mixed-age groups of substance abuse patients. Re-admission was predicted by unmarried status (a predisposing factor) and need, as indexed by several diagnostic and treatment characteristics. Copyright 1994, Alcohol Research Documentation, Inc. Used with permission.

Pompei P; Foreman M; Rudberg MA; Inouye SK; Braund V; Cassel CK. Delirium in hospitalized older persons: Outcomes and predictors. *Journal of the American Geriatrics Society* 42(8): 809-815, 1994. (47 refs.)

The purpose of this study was fourfold: To determine the rate of delirium in hospitalized older persons, to contrast the clinical outcomes of patients with and without delirium, to identify clinical predictors of delirium, and to validate the predictive model in an independent sample of patients. Two prospective cohort studies were conducted in medical and surgical wards of two university teaching hospitals. In the derivation cohort, 432 patients were enrolled from the University of Chicago Hospitals. Patients 65 years or older admitted to one of four wards were eligible. Subjects were excluded if they were discharged within 48 hours of admission, unavailable to the research assistants during the first 2 days of hospitalization, or judged too impaired to participate in the daily interviews. In the test cohort, 323 patients 70 years or older admitted to Yale-New Haven Hospital were studied. Subjects were screened for delirium daily and referred to experienced clinician investigators if acute mental status changes were observed. The clinician investigators assessed the patient for delirium based on DSM-III-R criteria. Duration of hospitalization was adjusted for diagnosis-related groups (DRG), and mortality rates were determined at discharge and 90 days after discharge. Sociodemographic characteristics, cognitive and functional status, comorbidity, depression, and alcoholism were examined as predictors of delirium. The rate of delirium in the derivation cohort was 15%; subjects with delirium had longer hospital stays and an increased risk of in-hospital death. Cognitive impairment, burden of comorbidity, depression, and alcoholism were found to be independent predictors of delirium. The ability of the model to stratify patients as low, moderate, or high risk for developing delirium was validated in the test cohort in which the rate of delirium was 26%. This study confirms the high rate of delirium in hospitalized older persons and the associated adverse outcomes of prolonged hospital stays and increased risk of death. Patients can be stratified according to their risk for developing delirium using relatively few clinical characteristics which should be assessed on all hospitalized older persons. Copyright 1994, Journal of the American Geriatrics Society.

Rains VS; Ditzler TF. Alcohol use disorders in cognitively impaired patients referred for geriatric assessment. *Journal of Addictive Diseases* 12(1): 55-64, 1993. (23 refs.)

Alcohol use disorders (AUD) are thought to be underdiagnosed in the geriatric population. A retrospective medical record review was performed on 383 patients who presented for outpatient geriatric assessment from 1985 to 1990. The record review included data on the alcohol consumption history, age, sex, presence of alcoholic beverages in the home, geriatric psychiatry evaluation, and alcohol-related diagnoses. AUD were recognized as contributing to medical problems in 10% of patients with a mean age of 78 years. All except one patient were found to be cognitively impaired. In addition, 9% of patients regularly consumed alcohol, and this consumption was not considered in the diagnosis despite the presence of cognitive impairment. Of cognitively impaired patients, 25% were consuming alcohol at the time of evaluation. These results indicate that alcohol consumption and AUD are common in cognitively impaired patients presenting for geriatric assessment. Recognition of AUD is essential, as chronic alcohol toxicity represents one cause of potentially reversible dementia. Because there are no validated instruments for alcoholism screening of cognitively impaired elderly patients, evaluation should include a past and present consumption history, a search for alcoholic beverages at the home visit, and possible psychiatric referral. Copyright 1993, The Haworth Press, Inc.

Shorr RI; Robin DW. Rational use of benzodiazepines in the elderly. (review). *Drugs & Aging* 4(1): 9-20, 1994. (105 refs.)

In the 40-year introduction of benzodiazepines into clinical practice, considerable controversy has surrounded their use. While there is little evidence to suggest wide-spread abuse or long-term use in most age groups, benzodiazepines continue to be widely prescribed to older adults in both community and long-term care settings. Several studies have described an increased sensitivity to the clinical effects and toxicity of benzodiazepines in older adults. However, it is unclear whether these observations are attributable to age-related changes in benzodiazepine pharmacokinetics or pharmacodynamics. Benzodiazepines are the safest and most effective agents available for the pharmacological management of symptoms of anxiety and insomnia. However, the acute administration of benzodiazepines is associated with impairments in cognition, memory, coordination, and balance; and long-term use, even at therapeutic dosages, has been associated with symptoms of withdrawal upon abrupt discontinuation. Therefore, it is essential that the practitioner develop a treatment plan when utilizing these agents to treat older patients. This plan may also involve psychotherapy or other nonpharmacological modalities in the management of anxiety or insomnia. Although the authors recommend initiating benzodiazepines using lowest available dosage, older patients should be treated with enough drug to produce a therapeutic response. For most clinical situations of anxiety or insomnia, the authors recommend prescribing limited quantities, e.g., a 2-week supply with a return visit for re-evaluation of effectiveness and adverse effects of a drug with a short elimination half-life. Persistent anxiety or insomnia in the elderly may require a medical and possibly psychiatric evaluation. If benzodiazepines are used continuously for 6 weeks or longer, the authors recommend a gradual taper over 2 to 12 weeks with frequent follow-up to evaluate for signs of withdrawal or the return of symptoms. Copyright 1994, Adis International Ltd.

Sitar DS. Metabolism and pharmacokinetics of drugs in the aging population. *Clinical Biochemistry* 26(6): 437-438, 1993. (5 refs.)

Persons over age 65 represent the most rapidly growing segment of the population. In fact, for the next 20 years, it is projected that the most rapidly growing cohort will be persons older than 85 years. The prevalence of diseases increases substantially as persons age, and the diseases tend to be chronic and multiple. Drug therapy is a widely used intervention to ameliorate signs and symptoms of these diseases. Polypharmacy is a common consequence of this situation, and the elderly are perceived to be at increased risk of drug-related adverse patient events. However, our understanding of the mechanisms contributing to these observations is incomplete, and a review of our present understanding of this situation is useful in an attempt to optimize drug therapy in the older patient. Copyright 1993, The Canadian Society of Clinical Chemists.

CHAPTER 22

Impaired Health Care Professionals

JEAN KINNEY, MSW

CLINICAL APPLICATIONS

The goals of this chapter are to assist the clinician to:

1. Recognize the dimension of problems of substance use in health care professionals.
2. Be familiar with risk factors.
3. Be able to recognize factors that may indicate a substance use problem in a professional colleague.
4. Be able to utilize impaired professionals programs for intervention.

Health care professionals are not only confronted by the alcohol and substance use problems of their patients. Because one in four individuals is directly touched by an alcohol or drug problem, a significant minority of health care personnel also will be touched as family members. This may be either through their family of origin or through the problems of a spouse or children. In addition, health care professionals may be touched by the problems of a colleague.

The alcohol and substance use problems presented by colleagues may invite the greatest confusion and be those most difficult to confront and respond to effectively. Under any circumstance, relationships with colleagues are complex. None of us works in a vacuum. Inevitably, we are interdependent in our professional functioning. Professional self-esteem is tied to the performance of others. Colleagues who work together closely develop a shared history, and many of us spend more hours with colleagues than with family or friends. Often colleagues are not merely professional associates but are friends or like family. Accordingly, a colleague's suspected substance use problem is not simply an issue of professional performance: Personal relationships invite confusion and ambivalence and make dealing with the problem all the more difficult.

DIMENSIONS OF THE PROBLEM

There is a growing literature on professional impairment resulting from drug and/or alcohol use. This literature has tended to be alarmist. It has, for example, been widely and repeatedly reported that health care professionals have a higher incidence of alcohol and drug use problems than the general population. A commonly cited figure has been physicians' purported risk of addiction as 30 to 100 times that of the general population. By extension the same is said to be true of nurses and other health care providers. Authors have referred to alcoholism and drug addiction as occupational hazards.

Much of the literature on the impaired professional is devoted to explanations of the phenomenon. A variety of factors are commonly cited, such as the health professional's access to drugs and the nature and magnitude of the stresses associated with the health professions. Another is a hypothesized false sense of invulnerability to substance use problems because professionals think they know how to use drugs in an "informed" or "safe" fashion. Also, the general independence of professions is seen as a contributing factor. There are fewer formal controls in the sense of "supervision" or monitoring of performance than, for example, in the industrial workplace. The literature has now begun to question these assumptions about occupational hazards for drug or alcohol abuse.

Physician Impairment

A 1986 review article examined the literature on physician impairment, including the nature of the supporting documentation. This data was drawn from licensure and disciplinary actions, mortality rates, the proportion of physicians in treatment populations, the percentage of physicians in psychiatric treatment with an alcohol-drug diagnosis, and surveys of physicians about past treatment of alcohol or drug problems.[8] In addition, the author traced the original source of the widely quoted physician addiction rate of 30 to 100 times the rate for the general population. This entailed meticulous follow-up of the references and citations provided to support that figure. Interestingly, the original source proved to be a 1959 work on narcotic addiction in the allied medical professions of Germany for the years 1954 to 1957. The conclusion based on the literature was that although writings about physician impairment have grown dramatically, most of the statistics presented on prevalence are alleged and without supporting data. Thus, the prevalence of practicing physicians with alcohol or drug problems is unknown. It was suggested that it may well be no higher than the general population. Indeed, more recent studies support that supposition.[24,27]

Nurse Impairment

For nurses, too, reliable direct data are unavailable. Estimates based on general population figures for women suggest that 5% of nurses are alcohol dependent and 1% to 2% drug dependent. The American Nurses' Association in 1984 estimated that 6% to 8% of nurses have a substance use problem.[3] This figure was interpolated from disciplinary actions taken by regulatory boards. Such data are not a wholly adequate measure. For one, they include only those whose problems are so severe as to result in disciplinary action. What is evident, however, is that alcohol and drug use problems are the basis for most disciplinary cases. A survey of State Boards of Nursing found that two-thirds of cases coming before the Boards were the result of substance use.[15]

More recent population-based studies suggest that, similarly to physicians, nurses do not appear more prone to substance abuse problems than their counterparts outside of the nursing field.[16,31] The profession as a whole may not have a disproportionate number of persons with substance abuse problems. Nonetheless, there may be differences within the profession related to the type of clinical setting. One report found that there appeared to be greater use of controlled substances by nurses in critical care settings than in noncritical care areas. The supposition is that such settings provide enhanced access to drugs.[32]

Other Health Professionals

Impairment in other health professionals and social service professionals has received far less scrutiny than have the problems of nurses and physicians. While there has been concern about impaired members within the professional organizations, e.g., of social workers, psychologists, pharmacists, and dentists, the research to date on these other professional groups is very limited (see Further Readings).

Health Professionals' Substance Use Patterns

In 1984-85 a major study of the drug use of 500 practicing physicians and 500 medical students was reported. The type of use was categorized either as recreational, self-treatment, or instrumental use. The results are summarized in Table 22-1.

For the physicians, recreational use most often involved marijuana and cocaine; self-treatment most frequently involved tranquilizers and opiates. Of the 3% (11) of physicians reporting a history of drug dependence, six had used the drug recreationally, two for self-treatment, one for treatment under another provider's direction, and two were unidentified. A subsequent study found essentially the same phenomena.[17] This latter study is noteworthy because the sample was selected so as to allow direct comparisons to the general population. The findings showed no difference in levels of experimentation in past use. In respect to current use, physicians had lower levels of illicit drug use than did the general population. One factor did distinguish physicians' substance use—the higher levels of self-medication with controlled substances. This supports an earlier finding that psychoactive drug use by physicians and medical students exceeded that of a comparable sample of pharmacists and pharmacy students.[21]

Similar findings are reported for nurses. A number of studies have examined the traditional wisdom that nurses are more vulnerable to substance use problems. One study employed a subset of nurses interviewed as part of a national study on the incidence of psychiatric illness, the Epidemiological Catchment Area study. The researchers found that the nurses were no more likely to have used illicit drugs than their non-nursing counterparts. They were, in fact, less likely to have a history of alcohol abuse.[31]

Students

The use patterns for medical students are summarized in Table 22-1. For the 5% reporting a history of drug dependence, the bulk (70%) represented drug dependence that arose from recreational drug use. For the students reporting dependence, one-fourth were currently abstaining; the remainder were still actively using.[21]

A study of alcohol use in medical students found that men drank more heavily than women in preclinical training, but that male intake dropped at the point of clinical training. Within the study, excessive drinking and alcohol abuse were defined as two separate dimensions. Excessive use was defined in terms of the drinking norms for the medical student's class. Abuse was defined according to the research interview schedule to assign DSM-III criteria (Diagnostic Interview Schedule). During medical school, 11% of students met criteria for excessive drinking for at least one 6-month interval, and 18% met criteria for alcohol abuse. Of particular significance was that two-thirds of those characterized as alcohol abusers, which involved the occurrence of negative consequences, did *not* also meet criteria for excessive drinking. This reinforces the point that abuse is not adequately predicted by quantity and frequency of drinking. Of further interest was that 27% of the students had entered medical school having met criteria for abuse at some earlier point. Of those, a significant proportion (two-thirds) were found to have "retired from abuse" without any abuse evident during the 4 years of medical school. On the other hand, 7% of the class were identified as "first time abusers" during medical school. Excessive drinkers and abusers were not distinguishable from their counterparts along any of the usual sociodemographic variables, mood variables, or use of counseling variables. Abusers did receive significantly higher grades during the first year but not in subsequent years of medical school.[11]

There is relatively little research directed to substance use by nursing students. One study, however, examined the drinking during the course of training and found an increase. This increase is not from

Table 22-1. Physician and Medical Student Substance Use (Percentage)

	Physicians	Medical students
Lifetime psychoactive drug use	59.2	77.2
Current use		
Past year	33.3	43.6
Regular (1+ times/month)	9.5	16.1
Type of use		
Recreational (ever)	35.0	73.0
Self-treatment (ever)	42.0	33.0
Self-treatment (current)	25.0	15.0
Instrumental (ever)	16.0	17.0
Instrumental (current)	0.0	0.0
Use via another's prescription (any time)		
Daily (a month or more)	5.7	2.5
Drug dependent, at any time	3.3	5.2

From McAuliffe WE; et al. Psychoactive drug use among practicing physicians and medical students. *New England Journal of Medicine* 315(13): 805-809, 1986.

drinking more per drinking occasion, but from drinking more frequently.[16] Not mentioned is the potential confounding factor of legal drinking age. Women, who comprise 90% of all nursing students, may be less inclined than men to use falsified identification and drink in public facilities when under the legal drinking age. Also, in an institution with a predominance of women, there may be fewer opportunities to drink when legally under age. Of student nurses, 14% were identified as impaired, having work- or school-related problems resulting from their alcohol or drug use.[16]

RISK FACTORS

Several studies have suggested risk factors or at least identified characteristics of impaired health professionals. As a recent review of the impaired physician literature notes, the popular wisdom on the etiology of physician and nursing substance abuse largely has not been borne out.[10] The current consensus is that what may appear as reasonable hypotheses, e.g., increased access to drugs, occupational stress, are not necessarily distinctive risk factors.

When stress is implicated, it is only significant in the presence of other mediating factors. An early study of physician addiction found that although physicians are subject to stress, only those with an inadequate childhood become vulnerable to addiction.[34] Other studies have confirmed that in the absence of other contributory factors, stress in itself does not predispose to substance abuse. Some of the contributory factors identified include an unsatisfactory marriage;[13,34] the absence or inability to use the support of family and close friends;[16,34] for men, a heavy-drinking spouse;[13] and attributional style, i.e., when the source of stress is viewed as something wholly external, subject to events beyond one's control and nonresponsive to one's actions.[16] Or put another way, as several investigators note, the greater the history of disruption or disturbance in general, in diverse life areas, the higher the risk.[9]

The degree of direct patient contact has been suggested as increasing vulnerability to substance use problems for nurses and physicians.[15,20] For physicians, medical specialty has been suggested as a risk factor. To the extent that the incidence of self-treatment with psychoactive substances is associated with increased risk, there are significantly different rates of reported current self-treatment for different specialties. The respective rates are as follows: psychiatrists, 48%; anesthesiologists, 44%; primary care, 24%; surgery and surgical subspecialties, 23%; other medical specialties, 22%; and ob-gyn, 17%.[21]

Various medical specialties are now examining the problems in their members. Anesthesiology has taken a lead in this. One of the earliest reports by a treat-ment program for impaired physicians found that anesthesiologists were disproportionately represented in the physician patients.[30] More recent studies, however, have not found anesthesiologists to have higher levels of substance abuse problems generally. It has been suggested that the disproportionate number in treatment may in part have been the result of higher levels of detection and referral. At the same time, special issues related to opioid addiction confront those in anesthesiology, whether physicians or nurse anesthetists, because of the nature of the setting. There is some thought that addicted members of anesthesiology may be more subject to relapse given the nature of the clinical setting.[28,35]

In a comparison of impaired nurses with their nonimpaired colleagues, a number of potential identifying characteristics have been reported.[29] These are summarized in Table 22-2.

In terms of physical health, impaired nurses had more hospitalizations in the prior 5-year period, excluding substance abuse treatment admissions, and had 25% more physician visits, excluding routine examinations and hospitalizations.

In terms of gender, men had disproportionately higher rates of impairment, accounting for 12% of the impaired group but only 2% of the nonimpaired nurses. Substances of dependence for the impaired nurses are summarized in Table 22-3.

SIGNS OF IMPAIRMENT

Beyond the anticipated marital problems or disturbances in family life, impaired health care professionals will show impairment in their professional performance. Suggestive signs and symptoms of substance use problems in health care professionals are outlined below.

Physicians

The list of possible warning signs, (Box 22-1) first set forth in 1979 by Breiner, continue to be useful.[7] Other authors meanwhile have developed lists of warning signs and symptoms; while the general elements are similar, certain factors are emphasized in specific settings (see, for example, Silverstein JH; et al., 1994, who address opioid use and controlled medication use by anesthesiologists).

Nurses

A number of authors have suggested behaviors that may indicate a substance use problem in nurses. The following list includes general signs and symptoms as well as performance-related factors:[18]

- Odor of alcohol on breath.
- Excessive use of mouthwash or mints to mask evidence of alcohol use.
- Tremulousness.

Table 22-2. Characteristics of Impaired and Nonimpaired Nurses

Characteristics	Prevalence in nurses (%)	
	Impaired	Nonimpaired
Family of origin		
Assuming parental responsibilities in childhood	22	48
Heavy drinking	32	10
Death of one or both parents from alcoholism	16	2
Parental death from drug addiction	5	—
Alcoholic family member	62	28
Depression in family member	55	36
Sexuality*		
Sexual dysfunction	54	25
Homosexual sexual preference	13	2
Current life circumstances		
Marriage of 10+ years	14	49
Divorce	59	—
Children living with them	28	56
Spouse alcohol dependent†	16	3

From Sullivan EJ. Comparison of chemically dependent and nondependent nurses on familial, personal and professional characteristics. *Journal of Studies on Alcohol* 48(6): 563-568, 1987.
*Significantly greater numbers of impaired nurses report single parenthood, incest, sexual molestation, miscarriage, and abortions.
†Impaired nurses are more likely to be married to a spouse with alcoholism; however, the spouses of impaired nurses are more likely to be recovering than are the alcohol-dependent spouses of nonimpaired nurses.

Table 22-3. Substances of Abuse of Impaired Nurses

Substance	Percent
Alcohol alone	43
Narcotics alone	23
Alcohol in combination with narcotics or other drugs	32
Other drugs	2

From Sullivan EJ. Comparison of chemically dependent and nondependent nurses on familial, personal and professional characteristics. *Journal of Studies on Alcohol* 48(6): 563-568, 1987.

- Excessive sick time.
- Emotional lability; mood may swing from irritableness and tenseness to calmness or euphoria.
- Absent or late to work, especially after several days off. Late in returning from breaks during work, often with elaborate explanations.
- Sleeping or dozing on duty.
- Social isolation, possibly a change to the night shift, eating alone, avoiding informal gatherings with colleagues.
- Frequent trips to the bathroom (women taking purse). Addicts may go to the bathroom immediately after being in the narcotic cabinet.
- Evidence of personal problems, especially with spouse or children or financially.

Clues in job performance
- Sloppy, illegible handwriting.
- Errors in charting.
- Errors in patient care.
- Lapses in memory, or confusion.
- Shunning job assignments, or job "shrinkage."
- Evidence of diversion.

Clues in job interviews
- Vague references.
- History of frequent job changes.
- Physical appearance.

Drug diversion is one method of acquiring drugs by substance users that may distinguish them from others. The following are warning signs of drug diversion by nursing personnel.

Clues to nurse diversion of drugs from the unit
- Extreme interest in giving medications and carrying the narcotic keys.
- Being on the unit when off duty.
- Use of maximum prn doses when other nurses use less.
- Patient complaints of not receiving sedatives, when the records indicate they were administered.
- Physical changes in multiple dose vials, indicating a substitution of saline or water.
- Frequent wastage such as spillage or of drawing blood into a syringe.

Box 22-1

Warning Signs of Substance Abuse

Medical Student

- Any failure of the student to any degree in any area of medical education.
- Few or no friends in class.
- Functioning socially as an isolate or misfit.
- Lack of ability to laugh at oneself and at one's condition of being a student; lack of the usual students' jocularity about classes and professors.
- Any regular use of mind-altering medication, including alcohol, to the point of mild inebriation, or repeated or occasional episodes of marked excess of such drugs or alcohol.
- Irregular or inconsistent grades even without failure.
- Irregular or poor class attendance.
- Friction with the professor. Even when the professor is the cause of the difficulty, the question must be asked, "Why did *this* student become the target of that professor?"

Resident

- Repeated intellectual errors—not just isolated instances but repeated intellectual difficulties in the residency.
- Numerous careless mistakes such as repeatedly writing milligram instead of gram.
- Friction with personnel or patients.
- Markedly too much or too little time devoted to studies, work in hospital, or recreational activity.
- Unusual social or financial difficulties.
- More than one change of career choice during a 3-year residency.
- Plans to go into a particular area of endeavor but purposely avoiding being thoroughly trained in that area.
- Avoidance in general internship or residency of a particular area of exposure such as pediatrics, urology, or pathology.
- More than a rare use of mind- or mood-altering medication.

Young Physician (5 to 10 Years Postresidency)

- At the end of the 5-year period not married or not in some serious relationship.
- During the first 2 years of private practice, money placed first and student's idealism left behind.
- Any inappropriate use of drugs or alcohol.
- Friction with any colleagues in private practice.
- Any social or professional isolation.
- Impairment in professional functioning

   Office behavior: Disorganized schedule, inaccessible to patients and staff, excessive drug use and prescription supply, frequent absences.

   Hospital behavior: Often late, absent, or ill; decreased work and chart performance; inappropriate orders; being unavailable; subject of hospital gossip; heavy drinking at staff functions.

   Clues from curriculum vitae: Frequent job changes or relocation, unusual medical history, decline in professional productivity, vague letters of reference, inappropriate qualifications.

- Emergency room supplies appear to be missing; these are more easily diverted because of less accurate records.
- Entire stock of a drug from pharmacy is missing, as well as the sign-out sheet. This is sometimes dismissed as an accounting error.

IMPAIRED PROFESSIONALS PROGRAMS

Several landmarks can be identified in the emergence of formal efforts to address impairment in the health professions.[26] In 1972 the American Medical Association's Council on Mental Health issued *The Sick Physician,* which spoke to the effect of suicide, psychiatric illness, alcoholism, and drug addiction on both the profession and its members.[2] The following year, the AMA adopted the recommendations set forth in that report, which became the basis for the medical profession's future efforts. Another significant factor was the series of publications that emerged from a longitudinal study of alcoholism and drug addiction, detailing the emergence, treatment, and process of recovery in physicians, nurses, social workers, and lawyers.[4,5,6] These publications, by reporting the finding of favorable treatment outcomes, documented the potential for good resolutions when a diagnosis is made and appropriate treatment initiated.

Also helping the movement gain momentum was the emergence of groups of recovering members of AA who formed allied organizations such as Doctors or Lawyers in AA. In addition, the professions responded to impairment through grass roots activities of its members. For example, within nursing, groups of professionals emerged with a specific interest in the field of addictions nursing, which subsumed the issue of impairment. These groups, such as the National Nurses' Society on Addictions, which have remained autonomous, took on the roles of educator and advocate to the larger profession. The formal efforts of the American Nurses' Association were undertaken in collaboration with this specialty organization.[5]

Efforts to deal with impaired professionals now fall into three major areas: Employee assistance programs of institutions, programs conducted by professional associations, and programs of state licensure boards. Programs endeavor to promote early recognition, intervention, and rehabilitation of those suffering from impairment from substance abuse problems, as well as impairment from physical and mental illness or aging. The underlying premise of these programs is that impaired professionals are often unable to seek help spontaneously because of the nature of the illness; therefore, their colleagues have a special obligation to encourage voluntary treatment.

Impaired professionals programs conducted by professional associations commonly incorporate the following activities:

- Maintain a liaison with appropriate officials of county medical societies, specialty professional societies, hospital medical staff, and state boards of registration and licensure.
- Conduct educational programs on professional impairment directed to their members, their families, the professional staff of hospitals, county and state level professional associations, and other interested groups.
- Establish a registry of the appropriate resources for treatment of alcoholism (including AA resources specific in most communities for the physicians, nurses, or health care personnel), other drug dependence, mental health, geriatrics, and other problems leading to impairment.
- Receive requests to investigate questions of specific impairment.
- Provide appropriate intervention when necessary.

- Seek assistance for those who need financial aid during treatment or rehabilitation, an effort to allow maintaining a practice.

Beyond helping members voluntarily seek treatment, these groups have a relationship to state licensing and registration boards, who have independent and separate mechanisms for responding to concerns about professional performance. While program structure varies from state to state, in general, state boards of registration or licensure are prepared to respond to "concerns" brought to their attention by the lay public, family members, or professional colleagues. These individuals are assured that they will not be identified in the nonprejudicial inquiry that such reports generate. The focus of the inquiry is to ascertain if a problem exists and, if so, to take steps to ensure an adequate assessment and to initiate rehabilitative measures.

Impaired professionals programs, since instituted, have tended to treat individuals whose problems are among the most serious and longstanding. When first initiated, despite the rhetoric, in practice impaired professionals programs were synonymous with substance abuse. This may now be changing. The experience of the Colorado Physician Health Program is of note. It has functioned for 7 years as a free-standing, not-for-profit corporation. Since it was founded, there has been a steady increase of referrals for problems other than substance abuse. Also, the proportion of self-referrals has risen.[12]

A thoughtful essay on the health professions' response to impairment, which is noted as being aptly described as a "profession self-help effort," raises important and provocative ethical issues.[22] Among the points addressed is the delicate tension that always exists when there are simultaneous efforts to protect the public welfare and to respect individual rights. While not alleging that state boards established to identify and respond to impaired professionals have acted capriciously, the process is deemed not wholly nonprejudicial. Potential harm is inherent when initiating an investigation. With a disease presumed to have impaired judgment and impaired perception of essential events, a professional's response to allegations becomes suspect. Another issue is that in the interest of promoting care and protecting the professional's right to privacy, these proceedings are without public scrutiny. What is the public's right to know? This is not an irrelevant question for current or former patients. Without such mechanisms, the professions are always subject to charges of covering up, protecting their members at others' expense, being engaged in a "whitewash," and having a double standard in respect to addictions. The latter is particularly true in light of the professions' documented shortcomings in diagnosing and ensuring treatment of addictions in their patients. Thus, the alternative question must also be raised, "Can a profession adequately address its members' impairment as long as its current standards of patient care remain unacceptable?"

Entry into Treatment

As in the general population, studies of impaired professionals show that for those who enter treatment, there has been some precipitating factor. This may have been a personal crisis such as threatened or actual divorce or separation, or an intrapersonal crisis such as overwhelming feelings of despair, thoughts of suicide, or suicide attempts. In addition, many report that they were confronted by peers about their professional performance.

What also stands out in the histories of recovering professionals is the number of missed opportunities for earlier diagnosis.[4] Many recovering professionals noted that during the period that their addiction was well established, they had been under medical or psychiatric care but that a diagnosis was not made. Several individuals reported having been reassured by medical practitioners that they were *not* alcoholic or drug addicted.

Treatment Outcome

A number of studies have reported treatment outcome data for impaired professionals.[2,5,26] It appears that the prognosis is as good, if not better, for health care professionals than for the general population.[23] Some treatment programs are directed specifically to physicians and other health care providers. However, the general clinical wisdom is that there is no intrinsic reason that such special treatment programs are necessary. Some would make the case that clinical gains may be made when a health care professional becomes simply another individual in treatment rather than being a doctor or nurse in treatment. The general treatment principles apply equally to nurses and physicians, although some special considerations might be anticipated related to aftercare and monitoring as a condition for a return to clinical practice.

Although treatment of health care professionals does not significantly differ, there are some useful ideas about the phenomena associated with dependence and how these interact with treatment.[20] Khantzian provides some thoughtful observations on the treatment of impaired physicians. A common denominator of the phenomena commonly associated with addiction can be conceived as "difficulty in self-regulation," particularly in the domains of feelings, self-esteem, and self-care. In respect to feelings, Khantzian points out that often what is sought in drug use is not an "altered" state of consciousness but an altered state of feeling, which is not "pleasure" or "euphoria" but a relief from displeasure and dysphoria. He observes

that some who use drugs find that they help them contain or master painful feelings or a host of overwhelming feelings. In terms of self-esteem and self-care, a reported common observation is that those who come to be identified as impaired have had an excellent reputation with colleagues and patients. Thus, in some important respect, impaired clinicians have not been able to provide for themselves what they have been able to give to their patients. A tendency to devalue oneself is not uncommon. While success as a student, clinician, healer, teacher, or researcher provides some compensation, these external sources of recognition cannot substitute for an inner sense of confidence and self-worth. Also, although much has been written about addiction as "suicide by installment," considering the other side of the coin may be more useful and accurate, i.e., seeing the behavior as not motivated by self-destructive impulses but as a lack of skill in self-care.

Khantzian concludes with the ways in which the standard treatment approaches may help remedy the failures in self-regulation. One important, although unappreciated, function of an impaired professional committee is advocating for those who have shown too little capacity to care for themselves even though devoted to others. It is also noted that aggressive efforts to achieve sobriety, along with confinement in residential care, may be important in setting controls for some individuals. Placing the professional clearly under someone else's care halts the professional's futile efforts at self-care. For the impaired professional, one benefit of becoming involved in self-help efforts such as AA or NA is the group's demonstrated ability to assist its members in learning to live with their vulnerabilities. This is a significant contributor to self-acceptance, which, in turn, is an important aspect of self-esteem. This call to promote self-care was echoed in a 1992 editorial, "Physician—Cherish Thyself," which accompanied a *JAMA* article on physician drug use and self-treatment.[33] Some of these same points have been addressed in discussion of the recovery process of nurses with substance use disorders. Incorporating a number of constructs that are part of the self-help effort is suggested as vital to the process of self-integration.[19]

Re-entry to Practice

Rather than being professionally banished from their professions, impaired professionals are returning to work following treatment. Although clearly important to the treated individual, it also has important implications for the health care professions. The conditions imposed for a return to practice depend on the circumstances under which treatment was initiated. Almost universally, some monitoring is required. This may involve a return-to-work contract, which specifies the monitoring activities and action that will be taken in the event of a relapse. One program requests a preaddressed letter of resignation to the licensing board, to be sent in the event of a future positive urine screen. Random urine screens are often required, as is documentation of involvement in a formal aftercare program or use of disulfiram or naltrexone.

Regarding the return to the work place, there are several situations unique to nurses. For one, there may be stringent restrictions on access to narcotics keys. If an institution is small, this restriction may affect the ability to maintain or find a job. If a nurse has been fired, finding a new job may be difficult. Nurses may find that sleep problems, common in recovery, may be aggravated by working rotating shifts.

Professional Education and Training

In addition to establishing peer efforts to identify and assist impaired members, attention has been directed to including the topic in professional education and training.[14] Professional associations, in collaboration with their education counterparts, have developed and introduced curriculum modules on professional impairment. Continuing education programs and sessions within professional meetings have become common, with some formal programs for impaired students.[1,25] Clearly, however, there is more to be done. A 1994 survey of over 200 nursing schools nationwide found that fewer than half of those who responded had policies on student impairment. Also of concern is that virtually half of the schools who reported an instance of a suspected substance abuse report also reported having taken no action, i.e., essentially they "looked the other way".

Various surveys have been conducted on professionals' attitudes toward impairment of colleagues. The general findings indicate that those who are younger, i.e., more recently trained consider themselves better informed generally on issues related to substance use. They are also more likely to be accepting and comfortable with the current approaches to impaired professionals that focus on treatment instead of disciplinary measures. Of course, these findings may say as much about the evolution of drug use in the general culture—with the emergence and broader acceptance of "recreational" use and with greater recreational drug use within that age group—than they say about the success of educational efforts.

One difficulty in professional training on substance abuse is that clinicians are sometimes knowledgeable and informed in the abstract but unable to apply this to a patient's care. When a patient has a substance use problem, there is the tendency to view the patient as an aberrant case, an exception, and, despite evidence to the contrary, not a "real" substance abuser. A similar set of dynamics may apply to confronting a colleague's impairment, as suggested in a study of recovering nurses. Despite their own successful treatment and viewing themselves as professionals in recovery, when confronted with a hypothetical scenario asking how they would respond to an impaired colleague, a substantial number noted that they would not feel equipped to intervene and would likely do nothing. Nurses are seemingly not unique in this regard. Ironically, both anecdotal accounts, as well as a few published articles, indicate that the substance abuse professionals also encounter difficulty in addressing the impairment of substance abuse clinicians, whether impairment results from relapse or a previously undiagnosed condition.

OTHER SOURCES OF SUBSTANCE-RELATED IMPAIRMENT

Another potential source of alcohol and substance use impairments in professional performance is unrelated to the professional's own use of alcohol or drugs. Rather, it comes from being an affected family member, whether having been raised in a home with substance abuse problems or in being the spouse or parent of someone with a substance use problem.

The prevalence of alcohol problems suggests that a significant number of health care professionals will be children of alcoholics. That experience may color the expectations and perceptions of the prognosis for patients. Furthermore, one's patients' substance use problems likely will have an emotional charge. As the significant symptoms of substance use disorders are behavioral, the dynamics in clinical interactions may strike an all-too-responsive and familiar chord.

Data support the observation that the helping professions have a large share of children from alcoholic families. A study of the characteristics of impaired nurses found that 62% had an alcoholic family member and 16% had one or two parents who died of alcoholism.[29] More importantly, a percentage of the nonimpaired nurses were also touched by alcoholism. In the control group, of nonimpaired nurses 10% reported heavy drinking, 2% reported a parental death from alcoholism, and 28% reported alcoholism in a family member. Another study of alcoholism in different professions found that for all the subjects, 35% had at least one alcoholic parent.[4] Unexpectedly, the proportion of women professionals with an alcoholic parent was markedly higher than the proportion reported by men: 41% compared to 29%. Percentages reporting an alcoholic parent for the different professions are summarized in Table 22-4.

The ways in which children cope with substance use in a dysfunctional family may have some bearing on the perceived overrepresentation of children of alcoholics in the helping professions. Not only are the roles functional within the family, they may predispose

Table 22-4. Parental Alcoholism
in Impaired Professionals

Profession	Parental alcoholism (%)
Physicians	29
Attorneys	27
Dentists	24
Nurses	46
Social workers	38

From Bissell L; Haberman P. *Alcoholism in the Professions.* New York: Oxford University Press, 1984.

individuals to certain professions or to roles such as the family hero, the responsible one, and the placater.

The impact of being a family member and the potential for this leading to professional dysfunction is most vividly seen in the course of training. Many students are still closely tied to their families of origin, not only emotionally but financially. They are just beginning to establish homes and families of their own. They may also have younger siblings who remain in the home who are a source of concern. Another factor is the structure of professional training, which provides opportunities for observation. As novices in the clinical realm, students have not yet acquired sophistication in responding to difficult clinical situations, so their responses are both more "raw" and more forthright.

Faculty have observed that clinical encounters involving a patient with substance abuse can be difficult for some students. In the most extreme and obvious cases, students may become overly involved or conversely distance themselves by limiting or rebuffing contacts with the patient. Stress in a student's personal life may appear related to a parental alcohol problem, but this may not affect their performance of clinical responsibilities. The faculty member may have personal opinions as to the potential benefits of counseling or psychotherapy, but in this instance this is clearly outside the realm of student supervision and the student-faculty relationship. Clinical supervision is not therapy. However, there are times when these personal experiences clearly affect clinical encounters with patients and become the source of professional dysfunction. It is difficult to justify overlooking something that can seriously threaten competence in dealing with potentially one-third of a student's future patients. It is improbable that a student will enter an arena of professional practice that will negate the need to deal with substance use issues.

Students encountering difficulties working with substance use patients should not automatically be presumed to be children of alcoholics. There are developmental stages that influence a student's ability to handle difficult types of clinical encounters. Aside from their personal life experiences, students are forced by patients with substance use problems to face basic issues that are part of acquiring a professional identity. With only an emerging appreciation of the limits any clinician encounters, the student must ponder, "What is the professional's ability to 'make' people well?" and "To what extent is an individual clinician responsible for ultimate patient outcomes?"

REFERENCES

1. American Medical Association. *Primer on Medical Student Impairment.* Chicago: American Medical Association, 1986.
2. AMA Council on Mental Health. The sick physician: Impairment by psychiatric disorders, including alcoholism, and drug dependence. *Journal of the American Medical Association* 223(6): 684-687, 1973. (9 refs.)
3. American Nurses' Association. *Addictions and Psychological Dysfunctions in Nursing: The Profession's Response.* Kansas City MO: The American Nurses' Association, 1984.
4. Bissell L; Haberman P. *Alcoholism in the Professions.* New York: Oxford University Press, 1984. 214 pp. (Chapter refs.)
5. Bissell L; Jones RW. The alcoholic physician: A survey. *American Journal of Psychiatry* 133(10): 1142-1146, 1976. (23 refs.)
6. Bissell L; Skorina JK. One hundred alcoholic women in medicine: An interview study. *Journal of the American Medical Association* 257(21): 2939-2944, 1987. (15 refs.)
7. Breiner SJ. The impaired physician. (letter). *Journal of Medical Education* 54(8): 673, 1979.
8. Brewster JM. Prevalence of alcohol and other drug problems among physicians. *Journal of the American Medical Association* 255(14): 1913-1920, 1986. (95 refs.)
9. Brooke D; Edwards G; Taylor C. Addiction as an occupational hazard: 144 doctors with drug and alcohol problems. *British Journal of Addiction* 86(8): 1011-1016, 1991. (28 refs.)
10. Centrella M. Physician addiction and impairment—current thinking: A review. *Journal of Addictive Diseases* 13(1): 91-105, 1994. (31 refs.)
11. Clark DC; Eckenfels EJ; Daugherty SR; Fawcett J. Alcohol use patterns through medical school. *Journal of the American Medical Association* 257(21): 2921-2926, 1987. (18 refs.)
12. Dilts SL; Gendel M; Lepoff R; Clark C; Radcliff S. The Colorado Physician Health Program: Observations at 7 years. *American Journal on Addictions* 3(4): 337-345, 1994. (9 refs.)
13. Estep R; Novack JA; Helsel DG. Impaired small town physicians and their spouses. *Journal of Drug Issues* 19(3): 351-367, 1989. (46 refs.)
14. Gorovitz S. Preparing for the perils of practice. *Hastings Center Report* 14(6): 38-41, 1984. (11 refs.)
15. Green P. The chemically dependent nurse. *Nursing Clinics of North America* 23(1): 81-94, 1989. (24 refs.)
16. Haack MR. Stress and impairment among nursing students. *Research in Nursing and Health* 11(2): 125-134, 1988. (43 refs.)
17. Hughes PH; Brandenburg N; Baldwin DC; Storr CL; Williams KM; Anthony JC; et al. Prevalence of substance use among US physicians. *Journal of the American Medical Association* 267(17): 2333-2339, 1992. (33 refs.)
18. Hughes TL; Smith LL. Is your colleague chemically dependent? *American Journal of Nursing* 94(9): 30-35, 1994. (7 refs.)
19. Hutchinson SA. Toward self-integration: The recovery process of chemically dependent nurses. *Nursing Research* 36(6): 339-343, 1987. (24 refs.)
20. Khantzian EJ. The injured self, addiction, and our call to medicine. *Journal of the American Medical Association* 254(2): 249-252, 1985. (14 refs.)
21. McAuliffe WE; Rohman M; Santangelo S; Feldman B; Magnuson E; Sobol A; et al. Psychoactive drug use among practicing physicians and medical students. *New England Journal of Medicine* 315(13): 805-810, 1986. (86 refs.)

22. Morrow CK. How the profession treats impairment: Doctors helping doctors. *Hastings Center Report* 14(6): 32-38, 1984. (21 refs.)

23. Morse RM; Martin MA; Swenson WM; Niven RG. Prognosis of physicians treated for alcoholism and drug dependence. *Journal of the American Medical Association* 251(6): 743-746, 1984. (18 refs.)

24. Niven RG; Hurt RD; et al. Alcoholism in physicians. *Mayo Clinic Proceedings* 59(1): 12-16, 1984. (31 refs.)

25. Polk D; Glendon K; DeVore C. The chemically dependent student nurse: Guidelines for policy development. *Nursing Outlook* 41(4): 166-170, 1993. (24 refs.)

26. Sargent DA. The impaired physician movement: An interim report. *Hospital and Community Psychiatry* 36(3): 294-297, 1985. (19 refs.)

27. Siegel BJ; Fitzgerald FT. A survey on the prevalence of alcoholism among the faculty and house staff of an academic teaching hospital. *Western Journal of Medicine* 148(5): 593-595, 1988. (13 refs.)

28. Silverstein JH; Silva DA; Iberti TJ. Opioid addiction in anesthesiology. (review). *Anesthesiology* 79(2): 354-375, 1993. (79 refs.)

29. Sullivan EJ. Comparison of chemically dependent and nondependent nurses on familial, personal and professional characteristics. *Journal of Studies on Alcohol* 48(6): 563-568, 1987. (12 refs.)

30. Talbott GD; Gallegos KV; Wilson PO; Porter TL. The Medical Association of Georgia's Impaired Physicians Program: Review of the first 1000 physicians. Analysis of specialty. *Journal of the American Medical Association* 257(21): 2927-2930, 1987. (22 refs.)

31. Trinkoff AM; Eaton WW; Anthony JC. The prevalence of substance abuse among registered nurses. *Nursing Research* 40(3): 172-175, 1991. (29 refs.)

32. Trinkoff AM; Storr CL. Relationship of specialty and access to substance use among registered nurses: An exploratory analysis. *Drug and Alcohol Dependence* 36(3): 215-219, 1994. (12 refs.)

33. Vaillant GE. Physician, cherish thyself: The hazards of self-prescribing. *Journal of the American Medical Association* 267(17): 2373-2374, 1992. (6 refs.)

34. Vaillant GE; et al. Physicians' use of mood-altering drugs: A 20-year follow-up report. *New England Journal of Medicine* 282(7): 365-370, 1970. (41 refs.)

35. Weeks AM; Buckland MR; Morgan EB; Myles PS. Chemical dependence in anaesthetic registrars in Australia and New Zealand. *Anaesthesia and Intensive Care* 21(2): 151-155, 1993. (19 refs.)

FURTHER READINGS

Aach RD; Girard DE; Humphrey H; McCue JD; Reuben DB; Smith JW; et al. Alcohol and other substance abuse and impairment among physicians in residency training. *Annals of Internal Medicine* 116(3): 245-254, 1992. (29 refs.)

Substance abuse and impairment are serious societal problems. Physicians have historically had high rates of substance abuse, which has been viewed as an occupational hazard. Most authorities agree that the rate of alcoholism in practicing physicians is similar to that in control populations and that the rates of other substance abuse are greater, although some studies have shown no difference. Data about substance abuse by residents in training are limited but suggest that the use of benzodiazepines is greater than that by aged-matched peers, whereas the use of alcohol is similar between the two groups. Medical institutions, including those with teaching programs, have legal and ethical responsibilities concerning substance abuse by current and future physicians. Many training programs, however, do not provide educational programs on this subject, do not have faculty trained in substance abuse medicine, and do not have a formal system to address the problem of residents who are suspected or known to be substance abusers. This position paper examines the extent of substance abuse, including alcohol abuse, in physicians in residency training. It outlines approaches to the problem and delineates responsibilities of institutions and residency program directors. Recommendations are made to establish an informational program and a clearly defined, organized process to address the problems of substance abuse in residents. Careful and humane approaches can be used to identify and treat residents with substance abuse problems, allowing them to complete their training as competent and drug-free professionals. An appendix provides the names and addresses for Impaired Physicians Programs by state. Copyright 1992, American College of Physicians.

Blazer LK; Mansfield PK. A comparison of substance use rates among female nurses, clerical workers, and blue collar workers. *Journal of Advanced Nursing* 21(2): 305-313, 1995. (28 refs.)

The issue of impairment of practicing professional nurses by alcohol and other drugs has become a critical concern since the 1980s. The literature abounds with conjectures about the many nurses who are impaired, often without valid data to support the claims that the problem in nursing is greater than in the general population. This study compares the reported substance use of employed female nurses with that of two other groups of working females. Survey data from 920 nurses, 405 clerical workers, and 200 females employed in nontraditional trades jobs in two large eastern states revealed that there was little evidence of "abuse" of any of 15 substances; that nurses did not report higher rates of substance use than the other two groups; and that most reported substance use occurred in the younger age groups, reflecting the national trend. The need for continuing research efforts and confirmation of valid data, and primary prevention efforts with young female workers, including at-risk student nurses, is made evident. Copyright 1995, Blackwell Scientific Publications, Ltd.

Blondell RD. Impaired physicians. *Primary Care* 20(1): 209-220, 1993. (39 refs.)

The prevalence of chemical dependency in physicians in the US is probably the same as for the general population, about 8% to 12%. Organized medicine has responded by establishing programs to help these impaired physicians. Chemically impaired physicians can be treated and followed by structured programs with favorable results. To prevent untreated physician impairment due to chemical dependency, nonimpaired physicians must learn about this problem and take appropriate actions. To lessen the effects of substance abuse in physicians, proactive strategies of prevention should be adopted by medical schools, hospital staffs, and similar physician organizations. This chapter discusses the following: The chemically impaired physician (prevalence, etiology and natural history, signs and symptoms); responding to impaired physicians (professional responses and barriers to treatment); how the impaired physician is helped (collecting information, preparing for an intervention, and interventing); rehabilitation of the impaired physician (initial treatment, extended care, and continuing care); outcomes (treatment outcomes and program outcomes); and prevention (primary, secondary and tertiary).

Brennan SJ. Recognizing and assisting the impaired nurse: Recommendations for nurse managers. *Nursing Forum* 26(2): 12-16, 1991. (15 refs.)

Substance abuse by nursing professionals has increased considerably, according to the literature and statistics of the States' Boards of Nursing. The role expectation of "nurse infallibility" promoted by health care professionals contributes and leads to denial of problems by nurses in health care settings from the nurse manager's perspective. The author discusses ways to identify the chemically dependent nurse and considers some legal/ethical implications regarding the impaired nurse. Copyright 1991, Nursing Publications.

Fewell CH; King BL; Weinstein DL. Alcohol and other drug abuse among social work colleagues and their families: Impact on practice. *Social Work* 38(5): 565-570, 1993. (24 refs.)

This article presents data from a 1987 random sample survey mailed to the membership of the New York City chapter of the National Association of Social Workers. The purpose of the study was to determine the prevalence of alcohol and other drug problems as perceived by social workers in their colleagues, family members, and friends. Of the 198 respondents, 43% said that they had known at least one social worker who had a problem with alcohol or other drugs. The large number of social workers with close personal involvement with substance abuse was significant: 60% had close friends or family members with a problem, 39% had a nuclear family member with a problem, and 11% were adult children of alcoholics. The latter group reported a significantly higher impact on job functioning than did the other groups. Implications of these findings and recommendations for dealing with them are discussed.

Flaherty JA; Richman JA. Substance use and addiction among medical students, residents, and physicians. (review). *Psychiatric Clinics of North America* 16(1): 189-197, 1993. (29 refs.)

This literature review examines the existing data on alcoholism and drug addiction and substance usage by physicians. Questions examined include the following: What is the true prevalence of substance abuse and alcohol problems in medical students, physicians in training, and practicing physicians? Do these rates change over the course of training and entry into practice? Are the rates greater or less than those for the general population or specific control populations such as nurses or lawyers? What are the risk factors that determine which physicians become substance abusers or alcoholics? What is the relative role of family history compared with other psychosocial factors? Do medical students bring to medical school a risk for alcoholism or do they become at-risk from the incumbent demands of their training? Are there gender differences in substance abuse and alcohol problems in medical students and physicians? If so, are these different from their general population age cohorts? What is the prognosis over time and the effects of treatment on maintaining abstinence rates?

Handley SM; Plumlee AA; Thompson NC. The impaired nurse: Organizational and professional models of response. *AAOHN Journal* 39(10): 478-482, 1991. (8 refs.)

Two models of response, organizational and professional, affect the impaired nurse, who is both an employee and a professional. The organizational model of response uses an Employee Assistance Program (EAP) to detect and intervene with impaired employees. The professional model of response involves mechanisms established through the board of nursing, including post-treatment monitoring. When both models are available, linking mechanisms such as coordinators, policies, and re-entry practices can combine the strengths of each model. Copyright 1991, American Association of Occupational Health Nurses.

Hughes PH; Baldwin DC Jr; Sheehan DV; Conard S; Storr CL. Resident physician substance use, by specialty. *American Journal of Psychiatry* 149(10): 1348-1354, 1992. (25 refs.)

This study compares substance use by medical specialty among resident physicians. The authors estimated the prevalence of substance use of 11 medical specialties from a national sample of 1754 US resident physicians. Emergency medicine and psychiatry residents showed higher rates of substance use than residents in other specialties. Emergency medicine residents reported more current use of cocaine and marijuana, and psychiatry residents reported more current use of benzodiazepines and marijuana. Contrary to recent concerns, anesthesiology residents did not

show high rates of substance use. Family/general practice, internal medicine, and obstetrics/gynecology were not among the higher or lower use groups for most substances. Surgeons had lower rates of substance use except for alcohol. Pediatric and pathology residents were least likely to be substance users. The authors' previous research indicates that residents overall have lower rates of substance use than their age peers in society. Yet resident substance use patterns do differ by specialty. Residents in some specialties are more likely to use specific classes of drugs, to use a greater number of drug classes, and to be daily users of alcohol or cigarettes.

Hughes PH; Conard SE; Baldwin DC Jr; Storr CL; Sheehan DV. Resident physician substance use in the United States. *Journal of the American Medical Association* 265(16): 2069-2073, 1991. (14 refs.)

A national survey was conducted to determine patterns of drug use in 3000 American resident physicians. Sixty percent (1785) of the residents surveyed responded. This report evaluates the prevalence of drug use by the respondents, when they initiated drug use, and their reasons for current use. Substance use rates are compared with those of other studies of resident physicians and with a sample of their nonphysical age peers surveyed the same year. Heavy substance use patterns were not observed in resident physicians. They had significantly lower rates of use for most psychoactive substances than their peers in the general population but did report higher rates of past-month use of alcohol and benzodiazepines. A sizable minority began using benzodiazepines and prescription opiates during their residency years—the stage in physicians' training when they first receive prescribing privileges. Current users of benzodiazepines and opiates used these drugs primarily for self-treatment rather than for recreation. These two substances are often associated with impairment at later stages in the physician's career. Copyright 1991, American Medical Association.

Lewy RM. Pre-employment drug testing of housestaff physicians at a large urban hospital. *Academic Medicine* 66(10): 618-619, 1991. (8 refs.)

To address drug use and abuse by physicians beginning their graduate medical education, the Presbyterian Hospital at Columbia-Presbyterian Medical Center began a pre-employment drug testing program for housestaff physicians in 1987. Between 1987 and 1990, each of the 791 housestaff physicians beginning training at the hospital received a pre-employment urine toxicology examination. Despite the limitations of pre-employment drug testing, two physicians did test positive for illegal drugs. Based upon their test results and individual clinical evaluations, both physicians were denied a clinical appointment at the hospital. Their clinical training was temporarily interrupted while they received indicated treatment. The author suggests that the main value of the program is to provide a focus for addressing issues related to substance abuse during graduate medical education. Copyright 1991, Journal of the Association of American Medical Colleges.

Logan AP. Impairment: To report or not to report. Is there a choice? *New Jersey Nurse* 22(7): 7, 1992. (2 refs.)

Most action taken by state boards of nursing or licensure is for violations of the Nurse Practice Act involving substance abuse. This article describes the guidelines recommended by the New Jersey Board of Nursing for reporting suspicions of a colleague's chemical dependency.

Lutsky I; Hopwood M; Abram SE; Cerletty JM; Hoffman RG; Kampine JP. Use of psychoactive substances in three medical specialties: Anesthesia, medicine and surgery. *Canadian Journal of Anaesthesia* 41(7): 561-567, 1994. (25 refs.)

To determine the prevalence of psychoactive substance use in three specialty groupings, 1624 questionnaires were sent to physicians in medicine, surgery, and anaesthesia; all had trained at the same academic institution. A response rate of 57.8% was achieved. Comparison of prevalence of impairment rates showed no differences between surgery (14.4%), medicine (19.9%) and anaesthesia (16.8%). Substance abuse was clearly associated with a family history of abuse: 32.1% of the abusers had a family history of such abuse compared with 11.7% of the nonabusers. Increased stress at various career stages did not appear to increase substance abuse; problem areas during medical lifetimes were similar for each specialty. Substances most frequently used were marijuana (54.7%), amphetamines (32.9%); and benzodiazepines (25.1%). Seventy-three used nonprescribed psychoactive drugs. Drug counseling programs were judged inadequate by most. Use of alcohol and drugs by faculty members was reported by a number of respondents.

Nace EP, ed. *Achievement and Addiction: A Guide to the Treatment of Professionals.* New York: Brunner/Mazel, 1995. 245 pp. (Chapter refs.)

Beyond providing a general orientation to substance abuse issues, this volume addresses issues related to the substance abuse treatment of human service professionals. Specifically it deals with the professions of practicing physicians, as well as of residents and medical students, nurses, pharmacists, attorneys, and business executives.

Naegle MA. Impaired practice by health professionals. Module II.2. IN: Naegle MA; D'Arcangelo JS, eds. *Substance Abuse Education in Nursing.* New York: National League for Nursing, 1992. pp. 117-219. (35 refs.)

This curriculum module deals with impaired health professionals. The first portion provides an outline of the materials included. Topics include data on prevalence, co-worker and institutional behaviors that perpetuate the problem, legal and regulatory actions, ethical concerns, and programs to address the problem. The instructor's guide, which forms the bulk of the module, includes learner objectives, recommended readings, audio-visual materials, overhead masters, handout masters, teaching strategies, and sample assignments, plus a bibliography.

Reamer FG. The impaired social worker. *Social Work* 37(2): 165-170, 1992. (43 refs.)

The social work literature contains little about the impaired professional, despite increased attention to the problem by other professions. This article discusses the concept of the impaired professional; reviews research on the various types of impairment, the prevalence and causes of impairment, and responses to it; and outlines a model assessment and action plan for social workers who encounter an impaired colleague. Copyright 1992, National Association of Social Workers, Inc.

Richman JA. Occupational stress, psychological vulnerability and alcohol-related problems over time in future physicians. *Alcoholism: Clinical and Experimental Research* 16(2): 166-171, 1992. (36 refs.)

This paper elaborates the conceptual frameworks and major results to date from an ongoing longitudinal study of alcohol problems in male and female future physicians. A medical student cohort was surveyed at medical school entrance and in the second and third years of training. Relative to life span developmental orientations, a sizable proportion of premedical school problem drinkers "matured out" of their earlier patterns after entrance into occupational training roles. Relative to occupational selection vs. stress perspectives, medical school problem drinkers were equally divided between those manifesting onset before training and those manifesting onset during medical training. Overall, both male and female problem drinking declined during the preclinical years (in contrast to premedical school levels) but manifested a trend toward a reversal of the previous decline after the initiation of clinical training. The major psychosocial predictor of alcohol abuse during clinical training involved social-relational deficits or narcissistic personality styles. Moreover, this relationship was mediated by social support deficits and patient care-related stressors. This cohort is currently being resurveyed in the last year of medical school and will be followed again during residency training. Copyright 1992, Research Society on Alcoholism. Used with permission.

Sullivan EJ; Handley SM. Alcohol and drug abuse in nurses. (review). *Annual Review of Nursing Research* 10: 113-125, 1992. (34 refs.)

This article reviews the research on alcohol and drug abuse in nurses published between 1980 and 1990. The research was divided into three thematic categories: (a) The prevalence of alcohol and drug abuse in nurses and student nurses; (b) characteristics of nurses who abuse alcohol and drugs; and (c) nurses' attitudes toward colleagues with alcohol or drug dependence problems.

RESOURCES
Audio-Visual

Our Brothers' Keeper

Video or 16-mm film, 57 minutes or 35 minutes condensed version. Includes study guide. San Diego: Operation Cork, 1980. Available from the Hazelden Publications, Center City MN. The film dramatizes the story of a practicing physician who develops alcohol dependence and its impact on family, practice, and patient care.

Organizations

American Nurses' Association

600 Maryland Avenue SW, Washington DC 20024-2571. (202) 651-7000.

Materials   American Nurses' Association. *Addictions and Psychological Dysfunction in Nursing: The Profession's Response to the Problem.* Kansas City MO, 1984. ANA, 60 pp.

Drug and Alcohol Nursing Association, Inc.

660 Lonely Cottage Drive, Upper Black Eddy PA 18972-9313. (610)847-5396.

A professional organization for nurses involved in alcohol and other drug use fields. The annual conference offers continuing education and networking opportunities.

National Nurses' Society on Addictions

Kim Bains, Executive Director. (919) 787-5181.
Resources:
• *The Role of Nurses in Alcoholism, The Impaired Nurse, Educating Nurses on Addiction.*
• *Standards of Addictions Nursing Practice with Selected Diagnoses and Criteria,* 58 pp., 1988, published with the American Nurses' Association.
• *The Care of Clients with Addictions: The Dimensions of Nursing Practice,* 32 pp., 1987, published with the American Nurses' Association.
• *Nursing Care Planning with the Addicted Client,* 1989.

Social Workers Helping Social Workers

John F. Fitzgerald, Route #63, Goshen CT 06756. (203) 489-3808.

Alcohol and Drug Organizations[1]

VIRGINIA ROLETT, MLS

The organizations are listed in alphabetical order. A series of indexes is located at the end of this appendix, beginning on page 381. The indexes allow locating an organization by the type of audience served or the nature of the organization. The categories include the following:

- Clearinghouses
- Special focus of group by population
- Hotlines
- Self-help groups
- Library organizations
- Professional organizations
- Canadian-based
- US-based

For each organization the following information is provided: Name or the office of a contact person; postal address; telephone number as well as Fax number and E-Mail addresses if available; a brief description; and a selection of publications of particular interest.

Addiction Research Foundation, Library (ARF)

Address: 33 Russell Street, Toronto ON M56 251, Canada
Phone: 416/595-6144
Fax: 416/595-6601
Description: Organized in 1949 as an agency of the government of Ontario, the ARF provides treatment, conducts research, and disseminates information about alcoholism and drug addiction. The ARF is a collaborating center for research and training on drug dependence of the World Health Organization. The Foundation is significant to those beyond the province for its research, educational materials, and information services.

Publications: *Product Catalogue.* 80 pp. Free. (Phone: 800/661-1111 US and Canada).
Guide to Substance Abuse Resources on the Internet, by Sheila Lacroix.
The Journal. Bimonthly. Canada $15/$19. Covers provincial events and international issues in the addictions field. Excellent reviews of books and audio-visual materials.
Projection. Bimonthly. Canada $18/$23. An objective audio-visual review service. (See Appendix D.)

Addictions Foundation of Manitoba, William Potoroka Memorial Library

Address: 1031 Portage Avenue, Winnipeg MB R3G OR8, Canada
Phone: 204/944-6233
Fax: 204/772-0225
Description: The library has almost 4000 books, about 400 videotapes and films, and an in-house database. It collects and disseminates alcohol and drug information on behalf of the Foundation and serves professionals, students, and the general public throughout the province. It responds to short queries from others.

Publications: *Directions.* Quarterly. Newsletter for provincial addictions professionals,

[1]From Center for Substance Abuse Prevention. *How to Organize and Operate an Information Center on Alcohol, Tobacco and Other Drugs: A Guide.* Rolett V; Kinney J, eds. Rockville MD: Center for Substance Abuse Prevention (in press).

educators, and interested members of the public. Free.

Audiovisual Resource Catalog. 42 pp. Free.

Directory of Manitoba Addictions Services and Programs. Irregular. Free.

Directory of Services: Addictions Foundation of Manitoba. Irregular. Free.

Pamphlets, booklets, and reports are free to Manitoba residents.

Alberta Alcohol and Drug Abuse Commission Library (AADAC)

Address: 2nd Floor, 10909 Jasper Avenue, Edmonton AB T5J 3M9, Canada
Phone: 403/427-4275 (Library)
Fax: 403/427-2352 (Library)
E-Mail: INET 2000: AADAC.LTBR
Description: For over 40 years, AADAC has been providing prevention and treatment services for alcohol and other drug problems. Its library collection contains 5000 books and reports and 120 journals. Information services are available to the public.
Publications: *AADAC Library New Resources List.* Available to libraries.
Developments. Newsletter. 10 issues/year. Free.

Association of Canadian Distillers

Address: Suite 1100-90, Sparks Street, Ottawa ON K1P 5T8, Canada
Phone: 613/238-8444
Fax: 613/238-3411
Description: The Association of Canadian Distillers is a national trade association established to protect and advance the interests of its 10 members, all of whom are licensed manufacturers and marketers of distilled spirits products. The Association's mandate involves promoting and protecting the viability of the Canadian distilled spirits industry and proactively encouraging more socially responsible attitudes toward consumption.
Publications: Annual Report
Brochure. Provides history of distilleries and describes the Association.

Brewers Association of Canada Information Resource Centre (IRC)

Address: 155 Queen Street, Suite 1200, Ottawa ON K1P 6L1, Canada
Phone: 613/232-9601
Fax: 613/232-2283
Description: National trade association for Canadian brewing companies, both conventional and microbreweries. Information Resource Centre primarily serves organizational members.
Publications: *Publications Catalog.* Free.
Legislation Digest. Irregular. Canada $100/volume.

Adult Children of Alcoholics, World Service Organization (ACA)

Address: PO Box 3216, 2522 W Sepulveda Boulevard, Torrance CA 90510
Phone: 310/534-1815
Description: ACA is a 12-step program for adults who grew up in an alcohol-troubled home. The World Service Organization provides information about and referral to meetings throughout the country and offers assistance to those organizing new groups.

Al-Anon Family Group Headquarters, Inc.

Address: Box 862, Midtown Station, New York NY 10018-0862
Phone: 212/302-7240
Fax: 212/869-3757
Description: Al-Anon is a self-help program for family members and friends of those with an alcohol problem. It serves both Al-Anon and Alateen. Alateen is directed to teenagers with an alcoholic parent. In 1994 Al-Anon included about 30,000 groups in more than 100 countries, including 3200 Alateen groups. Al-Anon was founded by Lois Wilson and was originally known as AA Auxiliary.
Publications: *Publications Catalog.* Free.
Directory. Lists worldwide offices. Free.
Al-Anon Speaks Out. Quarterly newsletter for professionals. Free.

Alcohol Research Information Service (ARIS)

Contact: Robert L. Hammond, Director
Address: 1106 East Oakland Avenue, Lansing MI 48906
Phone: 517/485-9900
Fax: 517/485-1928
Description: The Alcohol Research Information Service is a nonprofit organization whose purpose is to collect, correlate, and disseminate information regarding alcohol and alcoholic products—their manufacture; sale and use for

beverage, industrial, or other purposes; and their impact on health and well-being in the US. The organization admits to a bias, namely, that the use of beverage alcohol, individually and collectively, has a net harmful effect. ARIS invites walk-in visitors and phone queries from 9 AM to 5 PM.

Publications: *The Bottom Line on Alcohol and Society.* Quarterly journal. Subscription. *Monday Morning Report.* Bimonthly newsletter. Free. *The Globe.* Journal. Subscription.

Alcoholic Beverage Medical Research Foundation (ABMRF)

Contact: Mack C. Mitchell Jr, MD, President
Address: 2013 East Monument Street, Baltimore MD 21205
Phone 410/327-0361
Fax: 410/327-0597
Description: Established in 1982 with support from the malt beverage industries of the US and Canada, it supports medical, behavioral, and social research and information dissemination on the use of alcoholic beverages and the prevention of alcohol-related problems. Grant recipients are from US and Canadian academic institutions. Resource Center on moderate drinking provides literature searches on request.
Publications: *Journal of the ABMRF.* Quarterly. Free. Abstracts of current literature on the psychosocial and medical effects of moderate drinking, news about the Foundation, and selected statistical tables.

Alcoholics Anonymous General Services Office (AA)

Address: Box 459, Grand Central Station, New York NY 10163
Phone: 212/870-3400
Fax: 212/870-3003
Description: The General Services Office responds to inquiries about the Fellowship, prepares and distributes literature including lists of the thousands of AA groups around the world, and maintains links with each AA group. AA literature and audio-visual materials are directed to alcoholics, AA members, and human service and health care professionals.
Publications: *Catalog.* Free.

American Academy of Health Care Providers in the Addictive Disorders

Contact: Richard E. Rogers, Executive Director
Address: 260 Beacon Street, Somerville MA 02143
Phone: 617/661-6248
Fax: 617/868-4840
Description: Founded to determine standards of training and clinical experience in the field of addiction treatment, the Academy requires these standards for health care providers who receive certification, regardless of discipline. The Academy recognizes those who have satisfied the training and experience requirements necessary to be qualified health care providers in the addictive disorders. The Academy's Information and Referral Service for professionals and managed care companies provides information about specialty providers.
Publications: *International Register of Health Care Providers in the Addictive Disorders.* Semiannual. $15 members; $25 nonmembers.

American Academy of Psychiatrists in Alcoholism & Addictions (aaPaa)

Contact: Alice Conde, Executive Director
Address: PO Box 376, Greenbelt MD 20768
Phone: 301/220-0951
Fax: 301/474-0219
Description: Founded in 1985 to improve education, prevention, treatment, and research in the field of alcoholism and addictions and to strengthen the training of psychiatrists in the addiction field, the Academy holds annual meetings in conjunction with the American Psychiatric Association and edits a peer-reviewed journal.
Publications: *The American Journal on Addictions.* Quarterly. Subscription.

American Council for Drug Education (ACDE)

Address: 136 East 64th Street, New York NY 10021
Phone: 212/758-8060; 800/488-3784
Description: Founded in 1977, the ACDE provides information on health hazards associated with the use of tobacco, alcohol, marijuana, cocaine, crack, and other psychoactive drugs. It prepares and publishes educational materials for

employees and employers, parents, children, educators, students, policymakers, and constituents.

Publications: *Publications Catalog.* Free.
The Drug Educator. Quarterly membership newsletter.

American Medical Association (AMA)

Contact: John J. Ambre, MD, PhD, Director, Department of Toxicology and Drug Abuse

Address: 515 North State Street, Chicago IL 60610

Phone: 312/464-4559 (Department of Toxicology and Drug Abuse)

Fax: 312/464-5842 (Department of Toxicology and Drug Abuse)

Description: The AMA's Department of Toxicology and Drug Abuse has successfully pressed for recognition of alcoholism as a major public health problem. It continues its work defining the physician's responsibilities in caring for addicted persons, promoting physician education, tackling the problem of the impaired physician, and advocating enlightened public policy toward addictions.

Publications: *The Busy Physician's Guide to the Management of Alcohol Problems.* Pamphlet. Free.
AMA's Guidelines for Physician Involvement in the Care of Substance Abuse Patients. Free.
Special Reports
AMA Policy Statements

American Public Health Association (APHA)

Address: 1015 Fifteenth Street NW, Washington DC 20005

Phone: 202/789-5600 (Ask for chairperson of Section on Alcohol and Drugs)

Fax: 202/789-5661

Description: The Alcohol and Drugs Section of APHA aims to enhance the visibility and effectiveness of public health policy relating to AOD prevention and treatment. The Section initiates policy resolutions for APHA adoption, sponsors sessions at the annual meeting, and contributes to the review of the scientific basis for public health policies and programs involving alcohol, tobacco, and other drugs. Founded in 1872, APHA is the largest organization

of public health professionals in the world, representing more than 32,000 members from 77 occupations of public health.

Publications: *American Journal of Public Health.* Monthly.
The Nation's Health. Newspaper. Monthly.
Publications Catalog. Free.

American Society of Addiction Medicine (ASAM)

Contact: James F. Callahan, DPA, Executive Vice President

Address: 5225 Wisconsin Avenue NW, Suite 409, Washington DC 20015

Phone: 202/244-8948

Fax: 202/537-7252

Description: ASAM is a national medical specialty society of physicians in the field of alcohol and other drug dependencies. It was admitted to the American Medical Association's House of Delegates as a voting member in June 1988, and in June 1990 the AMA added addiction medicine (ADM) to its list of self-designated specialties. Members encompass all medical specialties and subspecialties. Physician certification is offered.

Publications: *ASAM News.* Membership newsletter. Bimonthly.
Healthcare Reform Alert. Newsletter. Bimonthly.
Journal of Addictive Diseases. Subscription. Quarterly.
ASAM Membership Directory
Position Statements and Guidelines
Syllabi for Certification Program Review Course

Association for Medical Education and Research in Substance Abuse (AMERSA)

Contact: Kathryn Cates-Wessel

Address: Center for Alcohol and Addiction Studies Box G, Brown University, Providence RI 02912

Phone: 401/863-7791

Fax: 401/863-3510

Description: Started in 1976 by the federally funded Career Teachers in Alcohol and Drug Abuse, AMERSA is a national organization directed to education of health professionals in the field of alcohol and drug abuse. Full membership is available to those holding faculty appointments as well as others as determined by the membership committee. AMERSA arranges field placements for students and trainees who desire experience in alcohol and drug abuse treatment, research, and education.

Publications: *Substance Abuse.* Quarterly. Institutions $150; $170 foreign; $48 individuals.

British Columbia Prevention Resource Centre

Address: 211-96 E Broadway, Vancouver BC V5T 1V6, Canada
Phone: 604/874-8452; In BC only, 800/663-1880
Fax: 604/874-9348
Description: The British Columbia Prevention Resource Centre is funded by the Ministry of Health and is operated under contract. The Centre provides toll-free information services to residents of the province seeking information about prevention, organizations, programs, materials, and research in the area of substance misuse. In addition, the Resource Centre has a collection of materials available for on-site use.
Publications: *Frontline.* Quarterly.
Resource Catalogue
Video Catalogue. Describes over 350 videos on prevention and treatment. Videos are available for loan to organizations within the province.

Brown University Center for Alcohol and Addiction Studies

Contact: David Lewis, MD, Director
Address: Brown University, Box G, Providence RI 02912
Phone: 401/863-3173
Fax: 401/863-3510
Description: Established in 1982 with assistance from NIAAA and NIDA, the Center is directed to research, education and training, and the development of public health policy. In addition to curriculum materials, it offers a postdoctoral training program for physicians and doctoral-level professionals in human services and education.
Publications: *Project ADEPT.* Curriculum and associated materials for primary care physicians and other health care professionals.

Canadian Centre on Substance Abuse (CCSA)

Address: 75 Albert Street, Suite 300, Ottawa ON K1P 5E7, Canada
Phone: 613/235-4048
Fax: 613/235-8101
E-Mail: INET 2000: NCSA.NET; CSAP PREV-LINE: JAUSTIN
WWW: http:; www.ccsa.ca
Description: NCSA is the coordinating office of the Canadian Substance Abuse Information Network (CSAIN), a nationwide consortium of resource-sharing partners linked electronically. It is a World Wide Web (WWW) Site on the Internet. The Web site provides information on treatment and prevention efforts in Canada, as well as policy documents, statistics, and general information related to alcohol, tobacco, and other drugs. The NCSA fulfills information requests or directs them to an appropriate source. It develops and produces electronic and printed information products including databases, directories, inventories, and bibliographies.
Publications: *Directory of Substance Abuse Organizations in Canada*
Canadian Profile: Alcohol, Tobacco and Other Drugs
Treatment-Canadian Directory of Substance Abuse Services
CCSA Publications. Publications list.
Action News/Action Nouvelles. (CCSA) newsletter.

Center for Medical Fellowships in Alcoholism and Drug Abuse

Contact: Marc Galanter, MD, Director
Address: Division of Alcoholism and Drug Abuse, NB20N31, Department of Psychiatry, NYU School of Medicine, 550 First Avenue, New York NY 10016
Phone: 212/263-6960
Fax: 212/263-8285
Description: The Center is jointly sponsored by the American Academy of Psychiatrists in Alcoholism and Addictions (aaPaa), the Association for Medical Education in Substance Abuse (AMERSA), and the American Society of Addiction Medicine (ASAM). It promotes postgraduate medical training in the addictions; establishes training standards for medical training in the addictions; disseminates information on existing postgraduate programs; and promotes the establishment of new programs in qualified medical training centers.

Publications: *Postgraduate Medical Fellowships in Alcoholism and Drug Abuse.* Annual. Approximately 60 pp. Describes training programs in the US.
Division of Alcoholism and Drug Abuse, Department of Psychiatry, NYU School of Medicine, 1993. 22 pp. Describes programs and projects.

Center for Substance Abuse Prevention (CSAP)

Contact: Elaine Johnson, PhD, Director
Address: 5600 Fishers Lane, Rockwall II Building, 9th floor, Rockville MD 20857
Phone: 301/443-0365
Fax: 301/443-5447
Description: CSAP, a part of the Substance Abuse and Mental Health Services Administration (SAMHSA) of the Public Health Service, US Department of Health and Human Services, was created by the Anti-Drug Abuse Act of 1986. It oversees and coordinates national drug prevention efforts, funds demonstration grant programs, coordinates a national training system for prevention, and manages an information clearinghouse. It also runs a regionally-based network of programs to promote prevention at the state level, the RADAR (Regional Alcohol and Drug Awareness Resources) Network.
Publications: *Catalog.* Available from the National Clearinghouse for Alcohol and Drug Information (NCADI). Phone: 800/729-6686

Center for Substance Abuse Treatment (CSAT)

Contact: David Mactas, Director
Address: Rockwall II Building, Suite 618, 5600 Fishers Lane, Rockville MD 20857
Phone: 301/443-5052
Hotline: 800/662-HELP; Drug Information & Treatment
Fax: 301/594-6762
Description: The Center for Substance Abuse Treatment (CSAT), within the Substance Abuse and Mental Health Services Administration of the US Department of Health and Human Services, was established to direct and coordinate federal efforts to promote treatment of alcohol and other drug problems.
Publications: *CSAT Treatment Improvement Protocols (TIPS).* Order from NCADI. Free.

Center on Addiction and Substance Abuse at Columbia University (CASA)

Contact: Hila Richardson, Deputy Director of Research; Sharon Gray, MLS, Librarian
Address: 152 West 57th Street, New York NY 10019
Phone: 212/841-5200
Fax: 212/956-8020
E-Mail: SG202@Columbia.edu
Description: Founded in 1992, CASA is an independent, nonprofit corporation affiliated with Columbia University. It works with experts in medicine, law enforcement, business, law, economics, communications, teaching, social work, and the clergy. Its goals are to explain the social and economic cost of substance abuse; identify what prevention and treatment programs work for whom and under what circumstances; and encourage individuals and institutions to take responsibility to prevent and combat substance abuse. The library will respond to questions from professionals with an interest in the field.
Publications: *Catalog of Publications.* Free.
Cigarettes, Alcohol, Marijuana: Gateways to Illicit Drug Use, 1994. 64 pp. $8.

Children of Alcoholics Foundation, Inc.

Contact: Director of Public Information
Address: PO Box 4185, Grand Central Station, New York NY 10163-4185
Phone: 212/754-0656; 800/359-COAF
Fax: 212/754-0664
Description: A voluntary, nonprofit organization established in 1982. Primary purposes are to reach, help, and offer hope to young and adult children of alcoholics; inform and educate the public and professionals about this group; disseminate research and new data on the effects of family alcoholism on children; and encourage federal, state, and local decision makers to respond to the needs of this high-risk group.
Publications: *Catalog.* Free.

Cocaine Anonymous World Service Office, Inc. (CA)

Address: 3740 Overland Avenue, Suite G, Culver City CA 90034
Phone: 310/559-5833, Administrative office; 800/347-8998, 24-hour referral line
Fax: 310/559-2554

Description: Founded in 1982, CA is a fellowship of people who help each other recover from their addiction to cocaine and other mind-altering substances. Its structure is similar to that of AA, with meetings held throughout the US. The World Service Office maintains a 24-hour referral line. The Co-Anon program is available for affected family members.

Publications: *Fact File.* Free.

CSAP National Resource Center for the Prevention of Perinatal Abuse of Alcohol and Other Drugs

Contact: Information Specialist
Address: 9302 Lee Highway, Fairfax VA 22031
Phone: 703/218-5600; 800/354-8824
Fax: 703/218-5701
Description: The Center offers information and referral services on fetal and perinatal consequences of maternal alcohol, tobacco, and other drug abuse for physicians and allied health care professionals. The Library is a national information repository that collects, catalogues, and abstracts documents and makes information available on an online database. It responds to queries with bibliographies, reprints, and other information. *PREMIS* offers direct access to a database, an electronic bulletin board, electronic teleconferencing, and an E-mail system. The database includes information on programs, organizations, funding sources, professionals and resource persons, resource centers and clearinghouses, and state laws and current legislative activity, as well as current literature and research. The Center also provides training and technical assistance to community professionals, legislators, and the media.

Publications: Information Packet. Publications also available from NCADI.
                Healthy Delivery. Newsletter. Quarterly. Free.
                PREMIS. An online information system with toll-free access. Starter kit with a user manual and demo disk. $25.

CSAP Workplace Helpline

Phone: 800/843-4971
Description: Operated by the Center for Substance Abuse Prevention, the Helpline is answered by a person, not a machine, Monday through Friday 9 AM to 8 PM. It offers telephone consultation, resource referrals, and publications to business, industry, and unions to assist in planning, developing, and implementing comprehensive drug-free work place programs.

Distilled Spirits Council of the United States (DISCUS)

Contact: Matthew Vellucci, Librarian
Address: 1250 Eye Street NW, Washington DC 20005
Phone: 202/628-3544
Fax: 202/682-8888
Description: This trade association for liquor producers and marketers in the US monitors national, state, and local alcohol legislation; maintains statistics on production and sales; maintains a library; and welcomes inquiries from the general public.

Publications: *Legislative Summary.* Organized by state. Free.
                Pamphlets and brochures.

Drug and Alcohol Nursing Association, Inc. (DANA)

Contact: Susan Piscator, Executive Director
Address: 660 Lonely Cottage Drive, Upper Black Eddy PA 18972-9313
Phone: 610/847-5396
Fax: 610/847-5063
Description: Established in 1979 as a professional organization for nurses involved in alcohol and other drug use fields, DANA is concerned with standards of practice, quality of care, and standards of specialty practice. The annual conference offers continuing education and networking opportunities.

Publications: *Dana.* Newsletter for members.

Drug Dependency Services, Nova Scotia Department of Health Library (DDS)

Address: Lord Nelson Building, 5675 Spring Garden Road, 6th Floor, Halifax NS B3J 1H1, Canada
Phone: 902/424-7214
Fax: 902/424-0550
Description: DDS, formerly the Nova Scotia Commission on Drug Dependency, develops and delivers services in community education, prevention, assessment,

and treatment throughout Nova Scotia. The library offers information services to residents of the province and responds to brief questions for those beyond.

Publications: *Audiovisual Catalogue.* Information on alcohol, drugs, and gambling.

Drug Dependency Services Library, Newfoundland Department of Health

Address: Southcott Hall, 8th Floor, Forest Road, PO Box 8700, St John's NF A1B 4J6, Canada
Phone: 709/729-0732
Fax: 709/738-4920
Description: The agency coordinates alcohol/drug education, prevention, and treatment services within Newfoundland and Labrador. Its library offers information services to residents of the province and responds to brief questions for those from beyond.
Publications: *Audiovisual Catalog*
Audiovisuals for Youth Catalogue
Book Catalogue
Journal Catalogue
Reports Catalogue
DDS Information
Family Series. Brochures.

Drugs & Crime Clearinghouse, Office of National Drug Control Policy

Address: 1600 Research Boulevard, Rockville MD 20850
Phone: 800/666-3332
Description: Funded by the Office of National Drug Control Policy (ONDCP) and managed by the Bureau of Justice Statistics (DOJ), the clearinghouse distributes data on drugs and crime. In 1994 it became a part of the National Criminal Justice Reference Service. The Clearinghouse focuses on serving the data needs of federal, state, and local government agencies and policymakers. The Clearinghouse can arrange access to Bureau of Justice Statistics data sets and other criminal justice data available on public computer tapes, CD-ROMs, and disks.
Publications: *Catalog of Selected Federal Publications on Illegal Drug and Alcohol Abuse.* Free.
Drugs, Crime, and the Justice System. 1992. National report compiling drug data from various sources.

Drug Policy Foundation (DPF)

Address: 4455 Connecticut Avenue NW, Suite B-500, Washington DC 20008-2302
Phone: 202/537-5005
Fax: 202/537-3007
E-Mail: 76546.215@compuserve.com or DPFwashDC@aol.com
Description: The DPF is an independent, nonprofit organization with more than 18,000 members. Its goal is to educate on alternatives to current drug control strategies. DPF believes that current drug policies are expensive, create a new class of criminals, and do not address the health aspects of the drug control issue. DPF aims to educate political leaders and the public about alternative policies and programs that exist both abroad and in the US. It has a large, uncatalogued collection of drug policy print and audio-visual materials that is open to the public for on-site use. Library services are not available. DPF hosts an annual conference for policymakers and medical and legal professionals.
Publications: *Book and Video Catalog.* Free.
Drug Policy Letter. Quarterly. Free to members. $25/year to media, government officials, libraries, and educational institutions.

Employee Assistance Professionals Association (EAPA)

Contact: Michael L. Benjamin, Chief Operating Officer
Address: 2101 Wilson Boulevard, Suite 500, Arlington VA 22201
Phone: 703/522-6272
Fax: 703/522-4585
Description: Founded in 1971 as the Association of Labor-Management Administrators and Consultants on Alcoholism (ALMACA), the organization changed its name in 1989. It currently has almost 7000 members engaged directly in providing employee assistance services. In 1987 it established a Certification Commission for certification of EAP professionals under an examination system. The Association publishes an extensive selection of brochures, books, and research publications on prevention, treatment, and education. The Resource Center responds to

professional information requests without charge.

Publications: *Publications Catalog.* Free.

Federal Drug, Alcohol and Crime Clearinghouse Network

Phone: 800/788-2800

Description: The Network was established by the Office of Drug Control Policy to enhance access to federal drug clearinghouses. Callers are linked directly to a clearinghouse of their choice: National Clearinghouse for Alcohol and Drug Information; Drugs and Crime Data Center & Clearinghouse; Drug Abuse Information and Treatment Referral Line: Drug Free Workplace Helpline; CDC National AIDS Clearinghouse; National Criminal Justice Reference Service; HUD Drug Information and Strategy Clearinghouse.

Fetal Alcohol Education Program, Boston University School of Medicine

Contact: Lyn Weiner, MPH, Executive Director

Address: 7 Kent Street, Brookline MA 02146

Phone: 617/739-1424

Description: Founded in 1974 by Henry L. Rosett, MD, and Lyn Weiner, MPH, the Program conducts research and provides professional education on prevention, identification, and treatment of alcohol-related birth defects. It develops teaching materials and conducts professional on-site training, conferences, and workshops. The program provides training and support groups for biological, foster, and adoptive parents of children with FAS. The program has a library collection, and program staff will respond to phone and mail requests for information.

Publications: *Publications Catalog.* Free.
Alcohol, Drugs and the Fetus: A Teaching Package. A manual and 84 slides organized into modules. Directed to physicians and allied health professionals.
Here's to Healthy Babies. Community education curriculum; presenter's manual and 19 slides.
FAS: Parent and Child. Handbook answering the most commonly asked questions about sleeping, eating, growth, behavior, and learning problems in children with FAS.

Hazelden Foundation

Contact: Barbara Weiner, Librarian

Address: Box 11, Center City MN 55012

Phone: Library: 612/257-4010
Educational Materials: 800/328-9000

Description: Founded in 1949 as a residential treatment program, the Foundation now includes education and training at its Minnesota Center as well as at other sites throughout the country. Of special note is a week-long "Professionals in Residence Program," which offers experiential learning in addition to lectures and discussions with program staff. Hazelden also offers comprehensive prevention training to teachers, counselors, and community leaders working with at-risk youth. Hazelden is a major publisher in the alcohol-drug field. The library will respond to questions from professionals.

Publications: *Educational Materials Catalog.* Free.
Calendar of Continuing Education Opportunities. Workshop descriptions. Free.
Hazelden News and Professional Update. Newsletter for professionals. Free.

Health Canada

Address: Departmental Library, Jeanne Mance Building, Room 500, Ottawa ON K1A 0K9, Canada

Phone: 613/954-8593

Fax: 613/957-3379

Description: Health Canada (Federal Department of Health) assists Canadians to maintain and advance their physical and mental well-being. The departmental library was established in 1991. Its collections focus on health policy, health promotion, health financing and service delivery, mental health, and health and well-being of specific populations, e.g., aged, children, natives. All library services are available to the public. Online services are only available to Health Canada employees.

Publications: *Health Canada Publications List.* Free. Publications on a variety of topics including alcohol and drugs.

HUD Drug Information & Strategy Clearinghouse (DISC)

Address: PO Box 6424, Rockville MD 20850
Phone: 800/578-3472
Fax: 301/251-5747
Description: DISC provides housing officials, residents, and community leaders with information and assistance on drug abuse prevention and drug trafficking control techniques. It operates and maintains databases with information about national and community antidrug programs. The Clearinghouse acquires and reviews more than 1500 reports, articles, news items, videos, grant applications, and other materials annually. Information specialists conduct searches of specialized databases for materials about antidrug programs and strategies.
Publications: Information packages. Information on drug-free work places, eviction legislation, grantsmanship, and technical assistance for Public Housing Drug Elimination Program grant applicants. Resource Lists. Other public and private information sources.
"How-to" brochures. Explain strategies and resources for drug prevention, drug treatment, law enforcement and security, and housing management.
Fliers. New HUD regulations and funding opportunities.

Institute on Black Chemical Abuse (IBCA)

Contact: Librarian
Address: 2616 Nicollet Avenue South, Minneapolis MN 55408
Phone: 612/871-7878
Fax: 612/871-2567
Description: IBCA responds to phone or mail requests with photocopies of articles and bibliographies. It provides a range of substance abuse treatment, education, prevention, and professional training services.
Publications: *ICBA Scope.* Newsletter. Quarterly. Free.
Catalog of Publications. Free.

International Lawyers in Alcoholics Anonymous (ILAA)

Contact: Eliseo D.W. Guana
Address: 14643 Sylvan Street, Van Nuys CA 91411-2327
Phone: 818/785-6541
Description: ILAA serves as a clearinghouse to assist attorneys seeking help for alcohol and other drug problems. It also holds an annual convention.

International Nurses Anonymous (INA)

Contact: Pat Green, RN
Address: 1020 Sunset Drive, Lawrence KS 66044
Phone: Home: 913/842-3893
             Work: 913/749-2626
Description: INA is comprised of nurses involved in any 12-step program such as Alcoholics Anonymous, Narcotics Anonymous, Overeaters Anonymous, and/or Al-Anon. INA is not affiliated with any other organization. Its purpose is to provide a mechanism for networking and mutual support, especially among newly recovering nurses.

Johnson Institute

Contact: Bud Remboldt, CEO
Address: 7205 Olms Lane, Minneapolis MN 55439
Phone: 800/231-5165
Fax: 612/831-1631
Description: Established in 1966, the Institute conducts educational and training programs, offers consultation services, and is a major producer of films, videos, and printed materials for training professionals and educating the general public.
Publications: *Catalog.* Publications, videos, and training programs. Free.
Observer. Newsletter. Quarterly. Free.

Join Together

Address: 441 Stuart Street, Sixth Floor, Boston MA 02116
Phone: 617/437-1500
Fax: 617/437-9394
E-Mail: info@jointogether.org
Description: Started in 1991, Join Together is a national program to help communities fight substance abuse. It is funded by a grant from the Robert Wood Johnson Foundation to the Boston University School of Public Health. Program components include public policy panels, a National Leadership Fellows Program, a National Computer Network, a Communications Program, and technical assistance to community programs. Although Join Together does not have a formal information service,

professionals respond to phone queries. Its National Computer Network, a part of *Handsnet,* is available to the public by subscription. (See Appendix F.)

Publications: *Reports and Recommendations of Policy Panels.*
Community Action Guides to accompany recommendations
Annual Survey of Community Substance Abuse Prevention Activity
FASA Update. Newsletter. Quarterly. Free.

Lesbian, Gay, Bisexual and Transgender Specialty Center at the Lesbian and Gay Community Services Center

Address: 208 West 13th Street, New York NY 10011
Phone: 212/620-7310
Description: Founded in 1994, the Center is a RADAR Specialty Center. It responds to questions through its E-Mail on the *PREVline* network. The hours are Monday, Wednesday, Thursday, 6 to 9 PM and Saturday 1 to 4 PM. (See Appendix F.)

Marin Institute

Contact: Nancy Humphreys, Associate Director, Resource Center
Address: 24 Belvedere Street, San Rafael CA 94901
Phone: 415/456-5692
Fax: 415/456-0491
Description: Established in 1987 and designated to receive long-term core funding from the Beryl Buck Trust, the Institute's goal is to reduce the toll of alcohol and other drug problems on Marin County and on society in general. The Institute develops, implements, evaluates, and disseminates innovative approaches to prevention locally, nationally, and internationally. The Resource Center is a state of the art information system designed to support the work of the Institute staff and their constituencies. It has two major collections: The *Industry Database,* a unique collection of nearly 8000 abstracts by and about the alcoholic beverage industry; and the *Online Catalog,* which contains about 3000 items on prevention of alcohol, tobacco, and other drug problems. The *Thesaurus* developed by the Institute includes more than 1000 alcohol and other drug prevention terms in the social sciences, business, and health fields.

Publications: *Marin Institute Thesaurus.* Print $50. ASCII (must be ordered with print version) $10.
Alcohol Industry Database Report. Quarterly. $32/year.

Midwest Regional Center for Drug Free Schools and Communities

Contact: Donna Wagner, Dissemination Coordinator
Address: 1900 Spring Road, Suite 300, Oakbrook IL 60521-1480
Phone: 708/571-4710; 800/252-0283
Fax: 708/571-4718
Description: The Midwest Regional Center is one of five regional centers in a national network established by the US Department of Education. It provides training, technical assistance, planning, and information resources to help schools develop strategies to prevent the use and abuse of alcohol and other drugs.

Publications: *Products Catalog.* Free.

Narcotics Anonymous World Service Office, Inc. (NA)

Contact: Carl E. Prescott, Public Information
Address: PO Box 9999, Van Nuys CA 91409
Phone: 818/780-3951
Fax: 818/785-0923
Description: Narcotics Anonymous is a 12-step program, modeled after AA for persons involved with drugs other than alcohol.

Publications: *Products Listing.* Free.
NA Update. Semiannual newsletter for professionals. Free.

National AIDS Information Clearinghouse, CDC (CDC NAC)

Address: PO Box 6003, Rockville MD 20849-6003
Phone: 800/458-5231; TTY/TDD 800/243-7012
Hotline: 800/342-AIDS (English)
Hotline: 800/344-SIDA (Spanish)
Fax: 301/738-6616
E-Mail: aidsinfo@cdcnac.aspensys.com
Description: A reference, referral, and publication distribution service for HIV and AIDS information, the Clearinghouse offers information on all aspects of HIV/AIDS prevention, care, and social support. Its collection includes descriptions of

over 19,000 AIDS-related programs and over 11,000 materials on topics ranging from general information to education and training programs in over 50 languages. The bilingual, multidisciplinary staff of the Clearinghouse offers reference and referral services and document delivery. Services are accessible by phone, by Internet services, by FAX, and by mail. The Internet services include E-Mail (see above) and a listserv that is a read-only mailing list for those who wish to receive AIDS-related documents from CDC.

Address: listserv@cdcnac.aspensys.com
To subscribe send the following message:
subscribe aidsnews (enter your) first name last name to the above address. Available to anyone with E-mail access. File Transfer Protocol (FTP) site address: cdcnac.aspensys.com.
URL address using Mosaic or similar software: ft://cdcnac.aspensys.com
Gopher address: cdcnac.aspensys.com

Publications: Brochure. Describes services.

National AIDS Clearinghouse

Address: Canadian Public Health Association, 1565 Carling Avenue, 4th Floor, Ottawa ON K1Z 8R1, Canada
Phone: 613/725-3769
Fax: 613/725-9826
Description: The Clearinghouse serves AIDS educators throughout Canada and the world. It is the central Canadian documentation centre on AIDS/HIV in Canada. The Clearinghouse offers distribution of free materials, a lending library, and information and referral services in English and French.
Publications: *Canadian AIDS News*. Bimonthly. Free.
Catalogue of Videos. Videos available for loan within Canada. Free.

National Association for Children of Alcoholics (NACoA)

Address: 1426 Rockville Pike, Suite #100, Rockville MD 20852
Phone: 301/468-0985
Fax: 301/468-0987
Description: Founded in 1983, the National Association for Children of Alcoholics (NACoA) provides public and professional information, education, advocacy, and community networking on behalf of children and families affected by alcoholism and other drug dependencies. NACoA programs and members work to increase public awareness and services for children of alcoholics.
Publications: *NACoA NETWORK Newsletter*. Bimonthly membership newsletter.
Poor Jennifer . . . She's Always Losing Her Hat. Educational video with trainer's guide, posters, and audio cassette.

National Association for Native American Children of Alcoholics (NANACOA)

Contact: Anna M. Latimer, Executive Director
Address: 1402 Third Avenue, Suite 1110, Seattle WA 98101
Phone: 206/467-7686
Fax: 206/467-7689
Description: NANACOA was organized at the 1988 Annual Convention of the National Association for Children of Alcoholics by more than 70 Native Americans from 30 different tribes. It serves as a source of information, training, and support for Native American communities around the needs of children of alcoholics. Activities include planning a National Conference for Native American Children of Alcoholics and regional training programs and increasing community awareness and recognition of the needs of Native American children of alcoholics.
Publications: Newsletter

National Association of Alcoholism and Drug Abuse Counselors (NAADAC)

Address: 3717 Columbia Pike, Suite 300, Arlington VA 22204
Phone: 703-920-4644; 800/548-0497
Fax: 703/920-4672
Description: NAADAC is a national professional organization for alcoholism and drug abuse professionals with over 17,000 members. It runs a credentialing program with two levels of certification for counselors certified in their states. Certification requirements include education, clinical experience, and successful completion of an exam, which is offered two times a year.
Publications: *The Counselor*. Bimonthly journal.

NAADAC Newsletter
Study Guide (for certification exam), $25 members/$45 others.

National Association of Lesbian and Gay Alcoholism Professionals (NALGAP)

Contact: Caroline Ritter
Address: 1147 South Alvarado Street, Los Angeles CA 90006
Phone: 213/381-8524
Fax: 213/381-8525
Description: NALGAP is a national membership organization comprised of professionals and other concerned individuals. Its mission is to address and counteract the effect of heterosexual bias and homophobia on those affected by alcoholism and other drug addictions through advocacy, training, networking, and resource development. NALGAP sponsors an annual conference specifically for members.
Publications: *NALGAP Annotated Bibliography: Alcoholism, Substance Abuse and Lesbians/Gay Men,* 1987. 900 entries, 259 pp. $10.
                Newsletter. Quarterly. Free to members.

National Association of Perinatal Addiction Research and Education (NAPARE)

Contact: Judith C. Burnison, Executive Director
Address: 11 East Hubbard Street, Suite 200, Chicago IL 60611
Phone: 312/541-1272
Hotline: 800/638-BABY
Fax: 312-541-1271
Description: NAPARE was founded in 1987 by clinicians, researchers, social service professionals, educators, and attorneys to respond to the need for an interdisciplinary forum to address the problem of perinatal addiction. NAPARE trains physicians, nurses, child welfare workers, therapists, and case workers to recognize symptoms of drug abuse. It also holds an annual conference. NAPARE responds to information requests from professionals.
Publications: *Publications Catalog.* Free.
                Update on Perinatal Addiction Research and Education. Newsletter. Quarterly.

National Association of State Alcohol and Drug Abuse Directors (NASADAD)

Contact: Public Policy Director
Address: 444 North Capitol Street NW, Suite 642, Washington DC 20001
Phone: 202/783-6868
Fax: 202/783-2704
Description: NASADAD coordinates and encourages cooperative efforts between the federal government and state agencies on alcohol and drug abuse. It serves as a resource on state drug programs and on state legislative information.
Publications: *Publications Catalog.* Free. Selected NASADAD publications are distributed free by NCADI.

National Clearinghouse for Alcohol and Drug Information (NCADI)

Address: PO Box 2345, Rockville MD 20847
Phone: 301/468-2600; 800/729-6686
Fax: 301/468-6433
Description: NCADI is the information service of the Center for Substance Abuse Prevention of the US Dept. of Health and Human Services. It acts as the central point within the federal government for current print and audio-visual materials about alcohol, tobacco, and other drug problems. Information specialists respond to more than 18,000 alcohol- and other drug-related inquiries each month. They distribute bibliographies and publications, posters, videotapes, and prevention curricula. NCADI maintains an extensive full-service library. It coordinates the Regional Alcohol and Drug Awareness Network (RADAR), which facilitates access to state and local sources of information about alcohol and other drugs.
Publications: *Publications Catalog.* Free.
                Prevention Pipeline. Alcohol and drug current awareness service. Bimonthly.
                RADAR Network Alert. Excerpts from *PREVline.* Monthly.
                CSAP Acquisitions List. Bimonthly. Materials entered into CSAP's in-house database.
                NCADI News Monitor. Monthly.

National Consortium of Chemical Dependency Nurses, Inc. (NCCDN)

Contact:	Randy Bryson, Executive Director
Address:	1720 Willow Creek Circle, Suite 519, Eugene OR 97402
Phone:	503/485-4421; 800/87-NCCDN
Fax:	503/485-7372
Description:	A nonprofit corporation, the Consortium is an association of RNs and LPNs engaged in the practice of, or interested in, chemical dependency nursing. The Consortium also supports and advocates for the recovery and reinstatement of the impaired professional. NCCDN offers certification for nurses practicing in the field of chemical dependency.
Publications:	*CD Nurse Briefing.* Newsletter.

National Clearinghouse on Family Violence

Address:	Family Violence Prevention Division, Health Canada, #1109 Finance Building, Ottawa ON K1A 1B5, Canada
Phone:	613/957-2938; 800/267-1291
Fax:	613/941-8930
Description:	Established in 1982 as a resource center for information and solutions to violence in the family, the clearinghouse provides information to frontline workers, researchers, and community groups across Canada.
Publications:	Brochures and pamphlets. Free. *The Family Violence Film and Video Catalogue.* Films and videos available for rental through the offices of the National Film Board of Canada.

National Clearinghouse on Substance Abuse (NCSA)

Address:	75 Albert Street, Suite 300, Ottawa ON K1P 5E7, Canada
Phone:	613/235-4048
Fax:	613/235-8101
E-Mail:	INET 2000: NCSA.NET; CSAP PREV-LINE: JAUSTIN
WWW:	http:; www.ccsa.ca
Description:	NCSA is the coordinating office of the Canadian Substance Abuse Information Network (CSAIN), a nationwide consortium of resource-sharing partners linked electronically. It is a World Wide Web (WWW) Site on the Internet. The Web site provides information on treatment and prevention efforts in Canada,

as well as policy documents, statistics, and general information related to alcohol, tobacco, and other drugs. The NCSA fulfills information requests or directs them to an appropriate source. It develops and produces electronic and printed information products including databases, directories, inventories, and bibliographies.

Publications:	*Directory of Substance Abuse Organizations in Canada* *Canadian Profile: Alcohol, Tobacco and Other Drugs* *Treatment-Canadian Directory of Substance Abuse Services* *CCSA Publications.* Publications list. *Action News/Action Nouvelles.* (CCSA) newsletter.

National Clearinghouse on Tobacco and Health, Canadian Council on Smoking and Health

Address:	170 Laurier Avenue West, Suite 1000, Ottawa ON K1P 5V5, Canada
Phone:	613/567-3050
Fax:	613/567-5695
Description:	Founded in 1989, the Clearinghouse provides information on tobacco use, prevention, and reduction issues, programs, resources, and initiatives to eligible professionals. It is an integral component of the National Strategy to Reduce Tobacco Use in Canada.
Publications:	*Update on Smoking and Health.* Three issues/year. *Youth and Tobacco Fact Sheet Series.* Single copies free. *Tobacco and Health Network Directory.* Canada $20.

National Council on Alcoholism and Drug Dependence, Inc. (NCADD)

Contact:	Hamilton Beazley, President
Address:	12 West 21st Street, New York NY 10010
Phone:	212/206-6770
Hotline:	(for referrals) 800/NCA-CALL
Fax:	212/645-1690
Description:	Founded in 1944, NCADD currently works in partnership with nearly 200 affiliates throughout the nation. It actively advocates government policies to reduce alcohol and other drug addictions and to provide for the treatment needs and rights of affected people. Its

annual meetings and publications are excellent continuing education opportunities and information resources.

Publications: *Catalog of Publications.* Free.
NCADD Amethyst. Newsletter. Quarterly. $50/year.

National Institute on Alcohol Abuse and Alcoholism (NIAAA)

Contact: Enoch Gordis, MD, Director
Address: 6000 Executive Boulevard, MSC 7003, Rockville MD 20892-7003
Phone: 301/443-3885
Fax: 301/443-6077
Description: NIAAA is one of 16 research institutes that comprise the National Institutes of Health. NIAAA conducts and supports biomedical and behavioral research, health services research, research training, and health information dissemination regarding the prevention of alcohol abuse and the treatment of alcoholism. The National Clearinghouse for Alcohol and Drug Abuse responds to questions about the NIAAA and distributes its publications. Its database is available from CDP Online, a commercial database vendor.
Publications: *Alcohol Health and Research World.* Quarterly. $13/year; $16.50/year foreign.
Research Monograph Series
ETOH. Alcohol and Alcohol Problems Science. Bibliographic database. (See Appendix F.)

National Institute on Drug Abuse (NIDA)

Contact: Alan I. Leshner, Director
Address: Parklawn Building, 5600 Fishers Lane, Rockville MD 20857
Phone: 301/443-6480
Description: One of 16 research institutes overseen by the National Institutes of Health. NIDA conducts and supports biomedical and behavioral research, health services research, research training, and health information dissemination regarding the prevention and treatment of drug abuse. The Institute is organized into five divisions: Intramural Research, Extramural Research, Education and Research Training, Research Dissemination, and Epidemiological Studies.
Publications: *NIDA Notes.* Newsletter for professionals. Quarterly.
NIDA Capsules. Newsletter. Irregular.

Publications Catalog. Available from the National Clearinghouse for Alcohol and Drug Information (NCADI).

National Nurses' Society on Addictions (NNSA)

Contact: Kim Bains, Executive Director
Phone: 919/787-5181
Description: NNSA is a professional organization for nurses whose field of practice is substance abuse/addictions nursing, including clinicians, educators, managers, and researchers. Full membership is available to registered professional nurses; others may become associate members. The organization is dedicated to providing quality comprehensive care to addicted persons and their families. Certification for nurses in the specialty was developed in collaboration with the National Consortium of Chemical Dependency Nurses.
Publications: Quarterly newsletter.
NNSA position papers, including the following:
The Role of Nurses in Alcoholism, The Impaired Nurse, Educating Nurses on Addiction
Standards of Addictions Nursing Practice with Selected Diagnoses and Criteria, 1988. 58 pp. Published with the American Nurses' Association.
The Care of Clients with Addictions: The Dimensions of Nursing Practice, 1987. 32 pp. Published with the American Nurses' Association.
Nursing Care Planning with the Addicted Client, 1989.

National Rural Institute on Alcohol and Drug Abuse

Contact: Douglas Stevens, Outreach Program Coordinator
Address: School of Arts and Sciences Outreach, UW-Eau Claire, Eau Claire WI 54702-4004
Phone: 715/836-2031
Fax: 715/836-2380
Publications: The Institute is a program of the University of Wisconsin-Eau Claire's School of Arts and Sciences Outreach Office. The Institute arranges an annual conference and professional development seminars to present innovative programs and policies important to rural alcohol and drug abuse. The

programs are self-supporting and include violence, gaming, policymaking, health delivery, and medical issues. The presented papers are not published but are available at the Institute library, which is a part of the RADAR Rural Specialty Center.

National Self-Help Clearinghouse

Address: 25 West 43rd Street, Room 620, New York NY 10036
Phone: 212/642-2944
Fax: 212/642-1956
Description: The Clearinghouse conducts training for professional and lay people about self-help methods, carries out research activities, maintains an information and referral databank, publishes materials, and addresses professional audiences about policies affecting self-help groups.
Publications: *Self-Help Reporter.* Quarterly.
                How to Organize a Self-Help Group
                Organizing a Self-Help Clearinghouse
                New Dimensions in Self-Help
                Directory of Regional Self-Help Clearinghouses

New Jersey Alcohol/Drug Resource Center and Clearinghouse

Contact: Penny Page, MLS, Director
Address: Center of Alcohol Studies, Smithers Hall-Busch Campus, Rutgers University, Piscataway NJ 08855-0969
Phone: 908/445-0787
Fax: 908/445-0790
Description: The Clearinghouse is housed at the library of the Rutgers Center of Alcohol Studies. It serves institutions of higher education, state agencies, communities, and school districts throughout the state by providing technical assistance, training, and resources in alcohol and other drug abuse education and prevention. It responds to information requests from the general public in New Jersey and beyond with subject bibliographies, fact sheets resource guides, videos on loan, copies of articles, prepared handouts, and more.
Publications: *Publications List.* Free.

Northeast Regional Center for Drug-Free Schools and Communities

Contacts: Gerald Edwards, EdD, Director

                Larry McCullough, Director of Dissemination
Address: 12 Overtone Avenue, Sayville NY 11782-0403
Phone: 516/589-7022
Fax: 516/589-7894
Description: The Northeast Regional Center is one of five regional centers in a national network established by the US Department of Education. It helps schools and communities develop prevention and early intervention programs designed to combat the multifaceted problems facing today's youth. The Center disseminates information throughout the region on effective prevention and on educational programs and strategies.
Publications: *Products Catalog*

Office of Minority Health Resource Center (OMHRC)

Contact: Odette Wynter-Tuckson
Address: PO Box 37337, Washington DC 20013-7337
Phone: 301/565-4020; 800/444-6472
Fax: 301/565-5112
Description: The Office of Minority Health (OMH) established the OMH Resource Center as a national resource for minority health information. The Resource Center facilitates access to minority health information, health promotion activities, preventive health services, and public health education. It offers assistance in the analysis of issues and problems that relate to minority health, and it provides assistance to organizations and individuals working in minority health professions. The Center maintains information, resources, and publications on health-specific topics that target African Americans, Asian Americans, Alaska Natives, Hispanics/Latinos, Native Americans, and Pacific Islander. It provides information services and maintains five minority health databases.
Publications: *Publications List*

Office on Smoking and Health (OSH)

Contacts: Michael P. Eriksen, ScD, Director
                Steve DePaul, Manager, Technical Information Center
                Jennifer Michaels and Bill Marx, Information Specialists

Address: 1600 Clifton Road NE, Mail Stop K-50, Atlanta GA 30333.

Phone: 404/488-5705; 404/488-5708

Fax: 404/332-2552; Information Service. Request a FAX directory of information 24 hours/day.

Hotline: 800/CDC-1311, for promotional materials.

Fax: 404/488-5939

Description: The Office on Smoking and Health (OSH) is a division of the Centers for Disease Control, National Center for Chronic Disease Prevention and Health Promotion. It coordinates strategic efforts aimed at the prevention and cessation of tobacco use and the protection of nonsmokers throughout the US and worldwide. It includes a small information center, which can provide assistance beyond the printed, faxed, and recorded information messages available through the phone numbers above. The OSH develops and distributes the *Surgeon General's Report on Smoking and Health;* coordinates a public information and education program on tobacco use and health; coordinates tobacco education and research efforts within the Department of Health and Human Services (DHHS); and funds, implements, and monitors state tobacco control plans and a tobacco control coalition. The *Smoking and Health Database* is available as a part of *CDP File,* a CD-ROM produced by the National Center for Chronic Disease Prevention and Health Promotion. The *Smoking and Health Database* can also be accessed on CDC WONDER, a public health information network, and as a part of the *Combined Health Information Database (CHID)* available on CDP Online, a commercial database service. (See Appendix F for information about database access.)

Publications: *Catalog of Publications.* Free.
Annual Bibliography with abstracts. Free.
Smoking and Health Database. (See Appendix F.)

Parents' Resource Institute for Drug Free Education (PRIDE)

Contact: Thomas Gleaton, EdD, President

Address: The Hurt Building, Suite 210, 50 Hurt Plaza, Atlanta GA 30303

Phone: 404/577-4500; 800/67PRIDE

Fax: 404/688-6937

Description: A nonprofit organization devoted to alcohol, tobacco, and other drug prevention, the Institute offers information to the public and programs for parents, youth, educators, businesses, and governments.

Publications: *Catalog.* Free.

Project Cork Institute

Contact: Jean Kinney, MSW, Executive Director

Address: 14 South Main Street, Suite F, Hanover NH 03750-2015

Phone: 603/646-3935

Fax: 603/646-2068

E-Mail: cork@Dartmouth.edu

WWW: http://www.dartmouth.edu/dms/cork/

Description: The Institute was founded in 1978, initially as part of a medical education curriculum development effort. In 1982 its role was expanded to promote education of health care professionals in substance abuse, particularly through the provision of academic support services. The Institute produces *CORK,* an online database of 25,000 items, available via Internet and the Dartmouth College Library System. It also produces curriculum materials and informational/ resource materials and provides current awareness services.

Resource Center on Substance Abuse, Prevention and Disability

Contact: Information Specialist

Address: 1331 F Street NW, Suite 800, Washington DC 20004

Phone: 202/783-2900

TDD: 202/737-0725

Fax: 202/628-3812

Description: The Center develops educational resources and responds to questions related to alcohol and other drug abuse prevention and treatment issues for people with disabilities. Its services include database searches of the center's collection, reprints of relevant articles, references, and referrals to other organizations.

Publications: General Information Packet

Resource Centre, Addictions and Community Funded Programs (ACFP), Indian and Northern Health Services, Medical Services Branch, Health Canada

Address: Room 1189, Jeanne Mance Building, Tunney's Pasture, Ottawa ON K1A 0L3, Canada

Phone: 613/957-3389

Fax: 613/957-9969

Description: ACFP supports First Nations and Inuit people and their communities in establishing and running programs to arrest and offset high levels of alcohol, drug, and solvent abuse in their populations.

Publications: *Resource Centre Catalogue.* Free.

Rutgers University Center of Alcohol Studies, Library

Contact: Penny Page, MLS, Library Director

Address: Smithers Hall, Busch Campus, Piscataway NJ 08855-0969

Phone: 908/445-4442

Fax: 908/445-5944

Description: The Center is internationally recognized for its research, education, clinical services, and information. The Center's library houses the world's largest collection of alcohol information and can provide individualized information services, specialized bibliographies, and document delivery services.

Publications: *Publications Catalog.* Free.

Saskatchewan Health Resource Centre

Address: 3475 Albert Street, Regina SA 54S 6X6, Canada

Phone: 306/787-3090

Fax: 306/787-3823

Description: The Resource Centre collection of approximately 8000 books, 500 journals, 600 audio-visuals, and a pamphlet resource file reflects current health policies as well as prevention, treatment, and program support. It includes extensive holdings in the addictions field. The Resource Centre provides interlibrary loans and information services. The audio-visual collection is available for loan within the province.

Publications: *Profile.* Newsletter. Quarterly.
Alcohol and Other Drug Services Directory. Annual. Overview of alcohol- and other drug-related community resources in Saskatchewan.
Film and Video Directory on Alcohol and Other Drugs. Video titles in the Resource Centre.

Smokers Anonymous World Services (SA)

Address: PO Box 591777, San Francisco CA 94123

Phone: 415/750-0328

Description: SA helps members and others to live without smoking using the 12-step self-help program model adapted from Alcoholics Anonymous.

Publications: *Seven Minutes: A Forum for Smokers Who Don't Smoke.* Newsletter. Quarterly.
National list of meeting places and contacts
Information pamphlets
Starter kits for new meetings

Society of Teachers of Family Medicine (STFM)

Contact: Executive Director

Address: PO Box 8729, Kansas City MO 64114

Phone: 800/274-2237

Fax: 816/333-3884

E-Mail: stfm@mcimail.com

Description: Founded in 1967 to support family medicine as an academic discipline, STFM holds annual meetings and workshops for its 3700 members. *A Group on Substance Abuse* presents at meetings and works with the US Center for Substance Abuse Prevention.

Publications: *Family Medicine.* Bimonthly journal. Subscription.
STFM Publications List. Free.

Southeast Regional Center for Drug-Free Schools and Communities (SERC)

Contact: Brian W. Buford

Address: Spencerian Office Plaza, Suite 350, University of Louisville, Louisville KY 40292

Phone: 502/588-0052; 800/621-7372

Fax: 502/852-1782

E-Mail: BW.BUFO0I@ULKYVM.LOUISVILLE.EDU

Description: SERC is one of five regional centers in a national network established by the US Department of Education. SERC offers training, consultation, dissemination of information, and technical support to schools, communities, and states. The Center facilitates school-community cooperation and evaluates and disseminates information on effective alcohol and other drug education prevention programs and strategies.

Publications: *Products Catalog.* Free.

Southwest Regional Center for Drug-Free Schools and Communities (SWERC)

Contact: Margretta Bartlett
Address: University of Oklahoma, 555 Constitution Avenue, Room 138, Norman OK 73037
Phone: 405/325-1454; 800/234-SWRC
Description: SWERC was established in 1987 in response to the passage of the Drug-Free Schools and Communities Act. SWERC serves as a catalyst for planned social change by helping individuals, families, schools, and communities create environments supportive of healthy life choices regarding alcohol and other drugs and related high-risk behaviors. Technical assistance, information, and consultation services are provided to state and local educational agencies and to institutions of higher education. SWERC provides printed materials, training modules, and an online computer information system, *Teachers' Information Network.*
Publications: *Products Catalog.* Free.
                Southwest Regional Center for Drug-Free Schools and Communities NEWS. Newsletter. Quarterly. Free.

Substance Abuse Librarians and Information Specialists (SALIS)

Address: PO Box 9513, Berkeley CA 94709-0513
Phone: 510/642-5208 (Andrea Mitchell)
Description: SALIS is an international association of individuals and organizations with special interests in the exchange and dissemination of alcohol, tobacco, and other drug information. Created in 1978, SALIS annual meetings offer members opportunities for professional development, information exchange, and networking. SALIS is an

affiliate member of the International Council on Alcohol and Addictions (ICAA). It actively collaborates with the Center for Substance Abuse Prevention (CSAP) RADAR Network and the NIAAA-CSAP Alcohol and Other Drug Thesaurus Project.

Publications: *SALIS News.* Bimonthly newsletter. Includes reviews of reference books and videos.
                SALIS Directory.

Trauma Foundation

Contact: Robin Tremblay-McGaw, Information Specialist
Address: Building One, Room 306, San Francisco General Hospital, San Francisco CA 94110
Phone: 415/821-8209
Fax: 415/282-2363
E-Mail: emcl@itsa.ucsf.edu
Description: The Trauma Foundation is the home office for the San Francisco Injury Center and The Pacific Center for Violence Prevention. It houses a special library on injury and violence prevention, which includes a wealth of alcohol and drug information. The library offers full reference services.
Publications: *Resources for Injury and Alcohol Problem Prevention*

Western Center for Drug-Free Schools and Communities

Contact: Information Specialist
Address: 101 SW Main Street, Suite 500, Portland OR 97204-3212
Phone: 503/275-9479
Fax: 503/275-9489
Description: One of five regional centers in a national network established by the US Department of Education, the Center offers training, consultation, dissemination of information, and technical support to schools, communities, and states.
Publications: *Products Catalog.* Free.

INDEX ORGANIZATION NAMES

National Consortium of Chemical Dependency
  Nurses, Inc.
National Council on Alcoholism and Drug
  Dependence, Inc.
National Institute on Alcohol Abuse and Alcoholism
National Institute on Drug Abuse
National Nurses' Society on Addictions
National Rural Institute on Alcohol and Drug Abuse
National Self-Help Clearinghouse
New Jersey Alcohol/Drug Resource Center
  and Clearinghouse
Northeast Regional Center for Drug-Free Schools
  and Communities

O
Office of Minority Health Resource Center
Office on Smoking and Health

P
Parents' Resource Institute for Drug Free Education
Project Cork Institute

R
Resource Center on Substance Abuse, Prevention
  and Disability
Resource Centre, Addictions and Community Funded
  Programs
Rutgers University Center of Alcohol Studies, Library

S
Saskatchewan Health Resource Centre
Smokers Anonymous
Society of Teachers of Family Medicine
Southeast Regional Center for Drug-Free Schools
  and Communities
Southwest Regional Center for Drug-Free Schools
  and Communities
Substance Abuse Librarians and Information Specialists

T
Trauma Foundation

W
Western Center for Drug-Free Schools and Communities

CANADIAN AND US

Canadian
Addiction Research Foundation Library
Addictions Foundation of Manitoba
Alberta Alcohol and Drug Abuse Commission Library
Association of Canadian Distillers
Brewers Association of Canada Information Resource
  Centre

British Columbia Prevention Resource Centre
Canadian Centre on Substance Abuse
Drug Dependency Services, Nova Scotia Department
  of Health Library
Drug Dependency Services Library, Newfoundland
  Department of Health Library
Health Canada
National AIDS Clearinghouse
National Clearinghouse on Family Violence
National Clearinghouse on Substance Abuse
National Clearinghouse on Tobacco and Health.
  Canadian Council on Smoking and Health
Resource Centre, Addictions and Community Funded
  Programs. Indian and Northern Health Services,
  Medical Services Branch, Health Canada
Saskatchewan Health Resource Centre

US
Adult Children of Alcoholics, World Service
  Organization
Al-Anon Family Group Headquarters, Inc.
Alcohol Research Information Service
Alcoholic Beverage Medical Research Foundation
Alcoholics Anonymous General Services Office
American Academy of Health Care Providers in the
  Addictive Disorders
American Academy of Psychiatrists in Alcoholism
  & Addictions
American Council for Drug Education
American Medical Association, Department of
  Toxicology and Drug Abuse
American Public Health Association Section on
  Alcohol and Drugs
American Society of Addiction Medicine
Association for Medical Education and Research
  in Substance Abuse
Brown University Center for Alcohol and Addiction
  Studies
CDC National AIDS Information Clearinghouse
Center for Medical Fellowships in Alcoholism
  and Drug Abuse
Center for Substance Abuse Prevention
Center for Substance Abuse Treatment
Center on Addiction and Substance Abuse at
  Columbia University
Children of Alcoholics Foundation, Inc.
Cocaine Anonymous World Service Office, Inc.
CSAP National Resource Center for the Prevention
  of Perinatal Abuse of Alcohol and Other Drugs
CSAP Workplace Helpline
Distilled Spirits Council of the United States
Drug and Alcohol Nursing Association, Inc.
Drug Policy Foundation
Employee Assistance Professionals Association

Federal Drug, Alcohol and Crime Clearinghouse
  Network
Fetal Alcohol Education Program, Boston University
  School of Medicine
Hazelden Foundation
HUD Drug Information & Strategy Clearinghouse
Institute on Black Chemical Abuse
International Lawyers in Alcoholics Anonymous
International Nurses Anonymous
Johnson Institute
Join Together
Lesbian, Gay, Bisexual and Transgender Specialty
  Center at the Lesbian and Gay Community
  Services Center
Marin Institute
Midwest Regional Center for Drug Free Schools
  and Communities
Narcotics Anonymous World Service Office, Inc.
National Association for Children of Alcoholics
National Association for Native American Children
  of Alcoholics
National Association of Alcoholism and Drug Abuse
  Counselors
National Association of Lesbian and Gay Alcoholism
  Professionals
National Association of Perinatal Addiction Research
  and Education
National Association of State Alcohol and Drug Abuse
  Directors
National Clearinghouse for Alcohol and Drug
  Information
National Consortium of Chemical Dependency
  Nurses, Inc.
National Council on Alcoholism and Drug
  Dependence, Inc.
National Institute on Alcohol Abuse and Alcoholism
National Institute on Drug Abuse
National Nurses' Society on Addictions
National Rural Institute on Alcohol and Drug Abuse
National Self-Help Clearinghouse
New Jersey Alcohol/Drug Resource Center and
  Clearinghouse
Northeast Regional Center for Drug-Free Schools
  and Communities
Office of Minority Health Resource Center
Office on Smoking and Health
ONDCP Drugs & Crime Clearinghouse
Parents' Resource Institute for Drug Free Education
Project Cork Institute
Resource Center on Substance Abuse Prevention
  and Disability
Rutgers University Center of Alcohol Studies,
  Library
Smokers Anonymous
Society of Teachers of Family Medicine

Southeast Regional Center for Drug-Free Schools
  and Communities
Southwest Regional Center for Drug-Free Schools
  and Communities Trauma Foundation
Trauma Foundation
Western Center for Drug-Free Schools and
  Communities

INDEX OF ORGANIZATIONAL FOCUS AND TYPE

Clearinghouses

National AIDS Information Clearinghouse
Federal Drug, Alcohol and Crime Clearinghouse
  Network
HUD Drug Information & Strategy Clearinghouse
National AIDS Clearinghouse
National Clearinghouse for Alcohol and Drug
  Information
National Clearinghouse on Family Violence
National Clearinghouse on Tobacco and Health.
  Canadian Council on Smoking and Health
National Self-Help Clearinghouse
New Jersey Alcohol/Drug Resource Center
  and Clearinghouse
ONDCP Drugs & Crime Clearinghouse

Hotlines

CDC National AIDS Information Clearinghouse
Center for Substance Abuse Treatment
Cocaine Anonymous World Service Office, Inc.
CSAP Workplace Helpline
National Association of Perinatal Addiction Research
  and Education
National Council on Alcoholism and Drug
  Dependence, Inc.
Resource Center on Substance Abuse Prevention
  and Disability

Industry

Alcoholic Beverage Medical Research Foundation
Association of Canadian Distillers
Brewers Association of Canada Information Resource
  Centre
Distilled Spirits Council of the United States
Marin Institute

Providers of Information to Professionals

Addiction Research Foundation, Library
Addictions Foundation of Manitoba, Library
Alberta Alcohol and Drug Abuse Commission Library
Alcohol Research Information Service
British Columbia Prevention Resource Centre
Brown University Center for Alcohol and Addiction
  Studies
CDC National AIDS Information Clearinghouse

Center for Medical Fellowships in Alcoholism
and Drug Abuse
Center for Substance Abuse Prevention
Center for Substance Abuse Treatment
Center on Addiction and Substance Abuse at
Columbia University
Children of Alcoholics Foundation, Inc.
CSAP National Resource Center for the Prevention
of Perinatal Abuse of Alcohol and Other Drugs
CSAP Workplace Helpline
Drug Dependency Services, Nova Scotia Department
of Health Library
Drug Dependency Services Library, Newfoundland
Department of Health
Drug Policy Foundation
Fetal Alcohol Education Program, Boston University
School of Medicine
Hazelden Foundation
Health Canada
Institute on Black Chemical Abuse
Johnson Institute
Join Together
Marin Institute
Midwest Regional Center for Drug Free Schools
and Communities
National AIDS Clearinghouse
National Association for Children of Alcoholics
National Association for Native American Children
of Alcoholics
National Association of Perinatal Addiction Research
and Education
National Clearinghouse for Alcohol and Drug
Information
National Clearinghouse on Family Violence
National Clearinghouse on Substance Abuse,
Canadian Centre on Substance Abuse
National Clearinghouse on Tobacco and Health.
Canadian Council on Smoking and Health
National Council on Alcoholism and Drug
Dependence, Inc.
National Institute on Alcohol Abuse and Alcoholism
National Institute on Drug Abuse
National Rural Institute on Alcohol and Drug Abuse
New Jersey Alcohol/Drug Resource Center
and Clearinghouse
Northeast Regional Center for Drug-Free Schools
and Communities
Office of Minority Health Resource Center
Office on Smoking and Health
ONDCP Drugs & Crime Clearinghouse
Project Cork Institute
Resource Center on Substance Abuse Prevention
and Disability
Resource Centre, Addictions and Community Funded
Programs, Indian and Northern Health Services,
Medical Services Branch, Health Canada

Rutgers University Center of Alcohol Studies, Library
Saskatchewan Health Resource Centre
Southeast Regional Center for Drug-Free Schools
and Communities
Southwest Regional Center for Drug-Free Schools
and Communities
Trauma Foundation
Western Center for Drug-Free Schools and
Communities

Professional Organizations

American Academy of Health Care Providers in the
Addictive Disorders
American Academy of Psychiatrists in Alcoholism
& Addictions
American Medical Association
American Public Health Association Section
on Alcohol and Drugs
American Society of Addiction Medicine (ASAM)
Association for Medical Education and Research
in Substance Abuse
Drug and Alcohol Nursing Association, Inc.
Employee Assistance Professionals Association
National Association of Alcoholism and Drug Abuse
Counselors
National Association of Lesbian and Gay Alcoholism
Professionals
National Association of State Alcohol and Drug Abuse
Directors
National Consortium of Chemical Dependency
Nurses, Inc.
National Nurses' Society on Addictions
Society of Teachers of Family Medicine

Self-Help

Adult Children of Alcoholics
Al-Anon
Alcoholics Anonymous
Cocaine Anonymous
International Lawyers in Alcoholics Anonymous
International Nurses Anonymous
Narcotics Anonymous
National Self-Help Clearinghouse
Smokers Anonymous

Special Populations

Adult Children of Alcoholics
Children of Alcoholics Foundation
CSAP National Resource Center for the Prevention
of Perinatal Abuse of Alcohol and Other Drugs
Health Canada
HUD Drug Information & Strategy Clearinghouse
Institute on Black Chemical Abuse
Midwest Regional Center for Drug Free Schools
and Communities
National AIDS Information Clearinghouse

National Association for Children of Alcoholics

National Association for Native American Children of Alcoholics

National Association of Lesbian and Gay Alcoholism Professionals

National Clearinghouse for Alcohol and Drug Information

National Rural Institute on Alcohol and Drug Abuse

Northeast Regional Center for Drug-Free Schools and Communities

Office of Minority Health Resource Center

Resource Center on Substance Abuse Prevention and Disability

Resource Centre, Addictions and Community Funded Programs, Indian and Northern Health Services, Medical Services Branch, Health Canada

Southeast Regional Center for Drug-Free Schools and Communities

Southwest Regional Center for Drug-Free Schools and Communities

Western Center for Drug-Free Schools and Communities

Alcohol and Drug Periodicals[1]

PENNY PAGE, MLS

The list of periodicals below focuses specifically on alcohol and other drug issues. Although some periodicals, especially the research journals, are expensive, many are low-cost or free and serve as excellent sources of current information on alcohol and other drugs.

The entries are listed alphabetically by title, and each entry provides complete publication information, if available. All publications are in English, and subscription prices are quoted in US dollars at the 1994 rates. Special Canadian rates are provided, if known; rates for other foreign subscribers are not included.

Most of the research and clinical journals are indexed by the major indexing services and online databases that cover alcohol and other drug topics, including *Medline, Current Contents, Excerpta Medica, PsychInfo, ETOH (Alcohol and Alcohol Problems Science Database), DrugInfo, and CORK (Alcohol Information for Clinicians and Educators Database).*

The focus of each periodical is shown in parentheses (Current Awareness, General Interest, Prevention and Education, Public Policy, Research, or Treatment). Items marked with an asterisk (*) are especially recommended for small nonresearch collections. These publications focus on education, treatment, or prevention issues or offer summaries of important research projects and findings.

*Action News/Action Nouvelles

Canadian Centre on Substance Abuse, 75 Albert Street, Suite 300, Ottawa ON K1P 5E7, Canada. ISSN 1183-8280 (English), ISSN 0846-9954 (French)

Bimonthly. Canada $15 (GST included) foreign $20.

National newsletter on substance abuse issues in Canada, with international coverage. Analyzes drug policy, reports on conferences, and special events. Read by health care professionals, treatment workers, educators, policymakers, politicians, police, and media. (Current Awareness, Public Policy, Research, Treatment)

Addiction

Carfax Publishing Co, PO Box 25, Abingdon Oxford-shire OX143UE, England, or PO Box 2025, Dunnellon FL 34430-2025. Phone: 44-0-235-521154; Fax: 44-0-235-553559. ISSN 0965-2140

Monthly. $726 institutions; $262 individuals.

International multidisciplinary journal with special interest in third world alcohol and drug problems. Includes research studies, review articles, book reviews, and reports from research centers around the world. Formerly *British Journal of Addiction* (until 1993). Annual index. (Public Policy, Research)

*Addiction Letter

Manisses Communications Group, Inc, 205 Governor Street, Box 3357, Providence RI 02906-0757. Phone: 800-333-7771; Fax: 401-861-6370. ISSN 8756-405X

Monthly. $137 institutions; $97 individuals.

Articles on prevention and treatment of alcohol and other drug abuse. Includes book reviews and brief updates of research studies. (Prevention and Education, Treatment)

Addictive Behaviors: An International Journal

Pergamon Press, Inc, Journals Division, 660 White Plains Road, Tarrytown NY 10591-5153. Phone: 914-524-9200; Fax: 914-333-2444. ISSN 0306-4603

Six times/year. $400 institutions; $94 individuals.

[1] From Center for Substance Abuse Prevention. *How to Organize and Operate an Information Center on Alcohol, Tobacco and Other Drugs: A Guide.* Rolett V; Kinney J, eds. Rockville MD: Center for Substance Abuse Prevention (in press).

Research studies, theoretical papers, and reviews on problems associated with alcohol, tobacco, other drug use or eating disorders. Emphasis on factors associated with addictive disorders as well as treatment strategies and outcome. Annual author index. (Research)

Adolescence Magazine

A & D Publications Corp, 3201 SW 15th Street, Deerfield Beach FL 33442-8190. Phone: 800-851-9500; Fax: 305-360-0034. ISSN 1042-7589

Bimonthly. $26.

Provides information for counselors about alcohol and other drug addictions and eating disorders in youth. Includes brief book and video reviews, a listing of treatment resources, and a calendar of education and training programs. Formerly *Adolescent Counselor* (until 1992). (Treatment)

Alcohol

Pergamon Press, Inc, Journals Division, 660 White Plains Road, Tarrytown NY 10591-5153. Phone: 914-524-9200; Fax: 914-333-2444. ISSN 0741-8329

Bimonthly. $590 institutions; $96 individuals.

Publishes laboratory and clinical studies of the biological and medical effects of alcohol. Annual author and subject indexes. (Research)

*Alcohol Alert

National Institute on Alcohol Abuse and Alcoholism, Office of Scientific Affairs, Scientific Communications Branch, 6000 Executive Boulevard, Room 409, Rockville MD 20892-7003. Phone: 301-443-3860.

Quarterly. Free.

Provides current information on alcohol research and treatment for health professionals and other interested persons. Each issue focuses on a specific topic. (Research, Treatment)

Alcohol and Alcoholism: International Journal of the Medical Council on Alcoholism

Pergamon Press, Inc, Journals Division, 660 White Plains Road, Tarrytown NY 10591-5153. Phone: 914-524-9200; Fax: 914-333-2444. ISSN 0735-0414

Six times/year. $355 institutions; $250 individuals.

Research on biomedical, psychological, and sociological aspects of alcohol use and alcoholism; includes experimental and clinical studies. Book reviews. (Research)

Alcohol, Drugs and Driving

Brain Information Service, Brain Research Institute, University of California, Los Angeles CA 90024-1746. Phone: 310-825-3417; Fax: 310-206-3499. ISSN 0891-7086

Quarterly. Free.

Abstracts and original research studies on effects of alcohol and other drugs on driving skills. International coverage of biomedical and psychosocial studies as well as of educational and law enforcement programs. Keyword and author indexes for each issue. Cosponsored by Anhauser-Busch Foundation. (Current Awareness, Prevention and Education, Public Policy, Research)

Alcohol, Drugs and Traffic Safety: Current Research Literature

BTJ Tryck Ltd, Traktor Vagen 13, S-226 60 Lund, Sweden. Phone: 46-46 180380; Fax: 46 46 304400. ISSN 0280-7645

Quarterly. $105.

English abstracts of biomedical and social science literature on all aspects of alcohol or other drug use and traffic safety. Online database available: Dalctraf. Author, title, and subject indexes for each issue. (Current Awareness, Public Policy, Research)

*Alcohol Health and Research World

Superintendent of Documents, Mail Stop SSOM, US Government Printing Office, Washington DC. 20402-9375. Phone: 202-783-3238. ISSN 0090-838X

Quarterly. $13.

Published by the National Institute on Alcohol Abuse and Alcoholism. Provides in-depth overviews of current research, treatment, and policy issues related to alcohol problems. Each issue has special focus. Annual author and subject indexes. (Public Policy, Research, Treatment)

Alcoholism: Clinical and Experimental Research

Williams & Wilkins, 428 East Preston Street, Baltimore MD 21202-3993. Phone: 410-528-4000; Fax: 410-528-4312. ISSN 0145-6008

Bimonthly. $265 institutions; $135 individuals.

Official journal of the Research Society on Alcoholism and the International Society for Biomedical Research on Alcoholism. Publishes research and clinical studies of the biomedical, physiological, and psychological effects of alcohol and alcoholism, as well as studies of treatment approaches. Includes abstracts of papers presented at the annual meeting of the Research Society on Alcoholism. Annual author and subject indexes. (Research)

*The Alcoholism Report

National Council on Alcoholism and Drug Dependence, PO Box 11318, Birmingham AL 35202-1319. Phone: 800-633-4931; Fax: 205-995-1588. ISSN 0276-3613

Monthly. $97.

Newsletter on professionals in the alcohol and other drugs field. Provides current information on policies and funding issues, federal alcohol/drug program and activities, and other public and private agencies and organizations. Includes a calendar of professional workshops and meetings. (Current Awareness, Public Policy)

*Alcoholism Treatment Quarterly

The Haworth Press, 10 Alice Street, Binghamton NY 13904-1580. Phone: 800-342-9678; Fax: 607-722-1424. ISSN 0734-7324

Quarterly. $150 institutions; $185 libraries; $35 individuals; Canadian rates 30% above US rates.

Original studies and reviews of treatment models, techniques, and outcomes. (Treatment)

Alcologia

Editrice Compositori, Via Stalingrado 97/2, 40128 Bologna, Italy. Phone: 051/32.78.37-32.78.11; Fax: 0039-51-32.50.23. ISSN 0394-9826

Three times/year. $50.

Research and clinical articles on biomedical and psychosocial aspects of alcohol use. Also features a regular "alcoholic beverages" section covering topics such as composition of beverages, consumption patterns, and labeling regulations. Although published in Italy for the Italian Society of Alcohology; all main articles are in English. (Research, Treatment)

American Journal of Drug and Alcohol Abuse

Marcel Dekker Journals, PO Box 5017, Monticello NY 12701-5176. Phone: 212-696-9000; Fax: 212-685-4540. ISSN 0095-2990

Quarterly. $395 institutions; $197.50 individuals.

Biomedical and psychosocial research studies on treatment and problems associated with alcohol and other drug abuse. Annual author/subject index. (Research)

*Behavioral Health Management

Medquest Communications, Inc, 629 Euclid Avenue, Suite 500, Cleveland OH 44114. Phone: 216-522-9700; Fax: 216-522-9707. ISSN 1052-4614

Bimonthly, plus one extra issue in August. $40 US; $55 Canada. Articles on research, intervention and treatment, prevention and education, and recovery from alcohol and other drug problems. Most issues focus on a special topic. Also includes brief book and audio-visual reviews and updates about programs and professionals in the alcohol/drug field. Formerly *Alcoholism and Addiction Magazine* (until 1990), incorporating *Addiction and Recovery* (from 1994). (Prevention and Education, Treatment)

*The Bottom Line on Alcohol in Society

Alcohol Research Information Service, 1106 East Oakland, Lansing MI 48906. Phone: 517-485-9900; Fax: 517-485-1928. ISSN 0161-1267

Quarterly. $20.

Good source of statistics on alcohol production, consumption, and problems. Also covers alcohol policy and legislation. Generally a US focus, but there is frequently a section on alcohol problems around the world that presents consumption statistics as well as policy and programs on alcohol abuse in other countries. (General Interest, Public Policy)

*Box 1980: AA Grapevine

Alcoholics Anonymous Grapevine, Inc, 475 Riverside Drive, New York NY 10115. ISSN 0362-2584

Monthly. $12 US; $14 Canada.

The international journal of Alcoholics Anonymous. Recounts experiences and opinions of Alcoholics Anonymous participants and news of AA programs; includes a calendar of events. (General Interest)

*Changes: The Magazine for Personal Growth

US Journal, Inc, and Health Communications, Inc, 3201 SW 15th Street, Deerfield Beach FL 33442-8190. Phone: 305-360-0909. ISSN 0892-1504

Bimonthly. $42 US; $36.50 Canada.

Articles for people recovering from chemical dependence, codependency, or related dysfunctions. (General Interest)

Contemporary Drug Problems

Federal Legal Publications, Inc, 157 Chambers Street, New York NY 10007. Phone: 212-619-4949. ISSN 0091-4509

Quarterly. $45 institutions; $36 individuals.

Research studies that focus on the medical, legal, social, and policy issues related to alcohol and other drug abuse. Includes reviews of prevention and control measures in US and other countries. Book reviews; annual author, title, and subject indexes. (Public Policy, Research)

*Counselor

National Association of Alcoholism and Drug Abuse Counselors, 3717 Columbia Pike, Suite 300, Arlington VA 22204-4254. Phone: 703-920-4644; Fax: 703-920-4672

Bimonthly. $36.

Focuses on intervention and treatment issues related to alcohol and other drug problems. Each issue has special theme. Includes a calendar of training events and employment classifieds for counselors. (Treatment)

Current Contents: Life Sciences and Social and Behavioral Sciences

Institute for Scientific Information (ISI), 3501 Market Street, Philadelphia PA 19104. Phone: 800-523-1850 or 215-386-0100. ISSN 0011-3409 (Life Sciences) and 0092-6361 (Social and Behavioral Sciences)

Weekly. $460/section.

Current awareness service for worldwide research information in specific disciplines. Each issue contains the tables of contents from books and journals in related disciplines, as well as author, publisher, and title keyword indexes. Two sections include good coverage of alcohol and other drug literature. The Life Sciences edition covers biochemistry, biomedical research, neuroscience, physiology, and pharmacology. The Social and Behavioral Sciences edition includes psychology, public health, social issues, social work, and sociology. Copies of articles are also available from ISI. Expensive but an excellent resource for keeping up with the international research literature. Also available on diskette and as an online database, Current Contents Search. (Current Awareness, Research)

*DATA—Brown University Digest of Addiction Theory and Application

Manisses Communications Group, Inc, 205 Governor Street, PO Box 3357, Providence RI 02906-0757. Phone: 800-333-7771 or 401-831-6020; Fax: 401-861-6370. ISSN 1040-6328

Monthly. $197.

Digests of selected research and clinical articles from scholarly journals. Covers broad range of psychoactive substances and treatment approaches to chemical dependencies, including prevention issues. Digests contain abbreviated bibliographies, full citations to the original article, and reprint information. Each issue also includes a section of abstracts, covering additional substance abuse literature. (Current Awareness, Research, Treatment)

Dram Shop and Alcohol Reporter

PO Box 590, Falmouth MA 02541

Monthly. $95.

Newsletter containing summaries of legal cases and findings regarding social host liability and alcohol-related incidents (crime, accidents, etc.). Covers cases throughout the US. (Public Policy)

Drug Abuse: Current Research on Alcohol and Drug Dependence

Swedish Council for Information on Alcohol and Other Drugs (CAN), Information and Documentation Centre, Box 27302, S-102 54 Stockholm, Sweden. ISSN 0283-8117

Quarterly. Price not available (contact publisher).

Abstracts of biomedical and social science research literature on effects of alcohol and other drugs; traffic accidents not included. Covers English language and foreign language documents (with English abstracts). Author, title, and subject indexes in each issue. Available as an online database, NORDRUG (contact CAN for information). (Current Awareness, Research)

*Drug Abuse Update

National Families in Action, 2296 Henderson Mill Road, Suite 300, Atlanta GA 30345. Phone: 404-934-6364; Fax: 404-934-7137. ISSN 0739-6562

Quarterly. $30.

Provides summaries of current research studies as well as prevention and treatment efforts related to alcohol and other drug use by youth. Book and video reviews. Annual index available separately for $5. (Prevention and Education, Public Policy, Research, Treatment)

Drug and Alcohol Dependence: An International Journal on Biomedical and Psychosocial Approaches

Elsevier Science Publishing Co, Box 882 Madison Square Station, New York NY 10059. Phone: 212-989-5800; Fax: 212-633-3990. ISSN 0376-8716

Six times/year (in three volumes). $604.

Multidisciplinary journal that publishes original studies, preliminary notes, and review articles in the areas of biomedical, clinical, sociocultural, educational, and medico-legal research. Subject and author indexes for each complete volume. (Research)

Drug and Alcohol Review

Carfax Publishing Co, PO Box 25, Abingdon Oxfordshire OX143UE, England, or PO Box 2025, Dunnellon FL 34430-2025. Phone: 44-0-235-521154; Fax: 44-0-235-553559. ISSN 0959-5236

Quarterly. $298 institutions; $98 individuals.

Publishes original papers and reviews articles for professionals in the alcohol/drug field. Covers the biomedical, clinical, psychological, and sociological aspects of alcohol, other drug, and tobacco use. Official journal of the Australian Medical and Professional Society on Alcohol and Other Drugs, but it is not limited to a specific regional focus. Book reviews; annual author index. (Research, Treatment)

Drug Information Services Update

Drug Information Services, University of Minnesota, Health Sciences Unit F, Room 3-160, 308 Harvard Street, SE, Minneapolis MN 55455. Phone: 612-624-6492.

Quarterly. $20.

Provides short abstracts of current journal articles on alcohol and other drug issues, including prevention programs and strategies, impaired driving, drug testing, and problems in special populations. Available as an online database, DRUGINFO, through the Internet (database thesaurus also available). (Current Awareness)

Drugs and Society: A Journal of Contemporary Issues

The Haworth Press, 10 Alice Street, Binghamton NY 13904-1580. Phone: 800-342-9678; Fax: 607-722-1424. ISSN 8756-8233

Quarterly. $90 institutions; $125 libraries; $38 individuals.

Provides a forum for information about various drug-related issues. Includes research studies as well as review and discussion articles on topics such as drug control, etiology and epidemiology of drug use, and treatment of drug abuse (including alcoholism). (Public Policy, Research, Treatment)

EAP Digest

Performance Resource Press, Inc, 1863 Technology Drive, Suite 200, Troy MI 48083-4244. Phone: 313-588-7733; Fax: 313-588-6633. ISSN 0273-8910

Bimonthly. $56.

Articles for employee assistance professionals on identification, treatment, and policy related to alcohol and other drug problems in the work place. Issues include classified ads, treatment directory, consultants directory, and brief reviews of new publications and audio-visuals. (Public Policy, Treatment)

EAP Quarterly

The Haworth Press, 10 Alice Street, Binghamton NY 13904-1580. Phone: 800-342-9678; Fax: 607-722-1424. ISSN 0749-0003

Quarterly. $130 institutions; $185 libraries; $38 individuals.

Includes research and scholarly articles on work place programs dealing with alcohol and other drug problems. Book reviews; video/movie reviews. (Public Policy, Research, Treatment)

*Employee Assistance

Stevens Publishing Corp, 3630 J.H. Kultgen Freeway, Waco TX 76706. Phone: 817-776-9000. ISSN 1042-1963

Monthly. $77 US; $97 Canada.

Covers issues of concern to employee assistance professionals, such as managed care, intervention, and work site safety. Includes a list of upcoming conferences and workshops as well as classified ads and a referral/consultant directory. (Public Policy, Treatment)

Excerpta Medica. Section 40: Drug Dependence, Alcohol Abuse and Alcoholism

Elsevier Science Publishing Co, 655 Avenue of the Americas, New York NY 10010. Phone: 212-989-5800; Fax: 212-633-3990. ISSN 0925-5958

Six times/year. $539.

Abstracting service covering a selective survey of international literature pertaining to the nonmedical use of alcohol, other drugs, and organic solvents. Entries are arranged under broad subject headings with annual author and subject indexes; each entry contains full citation and English language abstract. Available online (EMBASE) through several commercial vendors including Dialog and CDP; also available on CD-ROM (compact disk) from Silver Platter. (Current Awareness)

*The Forum

Al-Anon Family Group Headquarters, Box 862 Midtown Station, New York NY 10018-0862. Phone: 212-302-7240; Fax: 212-869-3757. ISSN 0194-8121

Monthly. $9 US; $10 Canada.

Magazine for family members and friends of alcoholics to share personal experiences related to family alcoholism, coping, and recovery via a 12-step format. (General Interest)

International Journal of the Addictions[†]

Marcel Dekker Journals, PO Box 5017, Monticello NY 12701-5176. Phone: 212-696-9000; Fax: 212-685-4540. ISSN 0020-773X

Monthly. $1150 institutions; $575 individuals.

International focus on research, training, and treatment issues in the field of addiction and substance abuse. Strong in public policy and consumption patterns in specific populations. Annual author/subject index. (Public Policy, Research, Treatment)

*The Journal: Addictions News for Professionals

Addiction Research Foundation, 33 Russell Street, Toronto, ON M5S 2S1, Canada. Phone: 800-661-1111.

Bimonthly. US $15; Canada $19.

Newspaper format featuring articles of current interest on alcohol, other drug, and tobacco use. Covers substance use, related problems, and policies in Canada, the US, and around the world. Also provides summaries of recent alcohol and other drug research. Includes a calendar of upcoming conferences and brief book and audio-visual reviews.

[†]As of January 19, 1996 titled Substance Use & Misuse.

(Current Awareness, General Interest, Prevention and Education, Public Policy)

Journal of Addictive Diseases

The Haworth Press, 10 Alice Street, Binghamton NY 13904-1580. Phone: 800-342-9678; Fax: 607-722-1424. ISSN 1055-0887

Quarterly. $180 institutions; $235 libraries; $48 individuals; Canadian rates 30% above US rates.

Basic and clinical research studies on alcohol and other drug abuse; each issue has special theme and includes a guide to resources on that topic. Also covers treatment and public policy issues. Official journal of the American Society of Addiction Medicine. Formerly *Advances in Alcohol and Substance Abuse* (until 1991). (Public Policy, Research, Treatment)

*Journal of Alcohol and Drug Education

Alcohol and Drug Problems Association of North America, Allen B. Rice II, Journal Executive, 1120 East Oakland, PO Box 10212, Lansing MI 48901-0212. Phone: 517-484-0016; Fax: 517-484-0444. ISSN 0090-1482

Three times/year. $25 ADPA members; $40 others; $50 outside US.

Articles dealing with aspects of alcohol and other drug education in schools, colleges and universities, and community settings. Covers educational philosophies, approaches, techniques, and evaluation. Book reviews. (Prevention and Education)

*Journal of Chemical Dependency Treatment

The Haworth Press, 10 Alice Street, Binghamton NY 13904-1580. Phone: 800-342-9678; Fax: 607-722-1424. ISSN 0885-4734

Semiannually. $90 institutions; $1125 libraries; $34 individuals.

Articles for counselors, health professionals, and social service personnel who treat chemically dependent patients and their families. Focuses on clinical issues but also includes theory and research in support of clinical practice. Each issue has specific theme. (Research, Treatment)

*Journal of Child and Adolescent Substance Abuse

The Haworth Press, 10 Alice Street, Binghamton NY 13904-1580. Phone: 800-342-9678; Fax: 607-722-1424. ISSN 0896-7768

Quarterly. $40 institutions; $75 libraries; $34 individuals; Canadian rates 30% above US rates.

Includes articles on clinical and research issues related to treatment of adolescent substance abusers. Book reviews. Formerly *Journal of Adolescent Chemical Dependency* (until 1993). (Research, Treatment)

*Journal of Drug Education

Baywood Publishing Co, 26 Austin Avenue, Box 337, Amityville NY 11701. Phone: 516-691-1270; Fax: 516-691-1770. ISSN 0047-2379

Quarterly. $112 institutions; $36 individuals.

Research and practical articles covering a wide range of issues related to drug education and prevention. Includes literature on prevalence and risk factors. Book reviews; annual author index. (Prevention and Education, Research)

Journal of Drug Issues

PO Box 4021, Tallahassee FL 32315-4021. ISSN 0022-0426

Quarterly. $80 institutions; $55 individuals.

Original research and commentary on drug policy issues, covering all psychoactive substances. Viewpoints range through social, legal, political, economic, historical, and medical ramifications of public policy. Issues often have unifying theme. Brief book reviews; annual author/title index. (Public Policy, Research)

Journal of Psychoactive Drugs

Haight-Ashbury Publications, 409 Clayton Street, San Francisco CA 94117-1911. Phone: 415-565-1904; Fax: 415-621-7354. ISSN 0279-1072

Quarterly. $140 institutions; $80 individuals.

Each issue usually features cohesive theme dealing with particular aspect of drug abuse treatment, public policy, or drug use by a specific population. Covers all types of chemical use and/or dependency. Includes book reviews and short communications, which allow a general exchange of ideas among the professional population. Annual author and subject indexes. (Public Policy, Research, Treatment)

Journal of Studies on Alcohol

Alcohol Research Documentation, Inc, Rutgers Center of Alcohol Studies, PO Box 969, Piscataway NJ 08855-0969. Phone: 908-445-2190; Fax: 908-932-5944. ISSN 0096-882X

Bimonthly. $120 US; $130 Canada.

Original research articles dealing with biomedical, behavioral, and sociocultural aspects of alcohol and its use. Includes human and animal studies, as well as literature review articles and book reviews. Annual subject and author indexes. (Research)

Journal of Substance Abuse

Ablex Publishing Corp, 355 Chestnut Street, Norwood NJ 07648. Phone: 201-767-8450; Fax: 201-767-6717. ISSN 0899-3289

Quarterly. $115 institutions; $40 individuals.

Presents research, literature reviews, and brief reports on studies of biological or psychosocial aspects of alcohol abuse, other drug abuse (including smoking), and obesity and eating disorders. Annual author index. (Research)

Journal of Substance Abuse Treatment

Pergamon Press, Inc, Journals Division, 660 White Plains Road, Tarrytown NY 10591-5153. Phone: 914-524-9200; Fax: 914-333-2444. ISSN 0740-5472

Bimonthly. $235 institutions; $110 individuals.

International interdisciplinary journal with focus on clinical treatment of alcoholism and other drug abuse. Book reviews; annual author and keyword indexes. (Public Policy, Treatment)

Pharmacology, Biochemistry and Behavior

Pergamon Press, Inc, Journals Division, 660 White Plains Road, Tarrytown NY 10591-5153. Phone: 914-524-9200; Fax: 914-333-2444. ISSN 0091-3057

Monthly; three volumes/year. $1440 institutions; $104 individuals (if library already subscribes).

Publishes original research (primarily animal studies) on pharmacological, biochemical, and behavioral effects of alcohol and other drug use. Author and subject indexes for each volume.

*Prevention Pipeline

National Clearinghouse for Alcohol and Drug Information, Department PP, PO Box 2345, Rockville MD 20847-2345. Phone: 800-729-6686; Fax: 301-468-6433

Bimonthly. $20.

Current awareness service designed for professionals and researchers as well as the lay public. Includes announcements of new school and community prevention programs in the US, upcoming conferences and meetings (national and international), funding sources, abstracts of recently published research studies and articles and audio-visual materials dealing with a variety of alcohol and drug use issues. Many cited items are available from NCADI free. (Current Awareness, Prevention and Education)

*Professional Counselor

A&D Publications Corp, 3201 SW 15th Street, Deerfield Beach FL 33442-9879. Phone: 800-851-9100; Fax: 305-360-0034. ISSN 1042-7570

Bimonthly. $26.

Publishes articles for professionals who treat alcohol and other drug problems or other types of compulsive disorders (eating disorders, sexual abuse, codependence). Includes news highlights from the field, brief book and audio-visual reviews, a list of upcoming conferences and meetings, a referral directory of treatment services, and classified ads. (Treatment)

Psychology of Addictive Behaviors

Educational Publishing Foundation, 750 First Street NE, Washington DC 20002-4242. Phone: 708-578-3720. ISSN 0893-164X

Quarterly. $60 institutions; $45 members.

Official journal of the Society of Psychologists in Addictive Behaviors. Publishes original research and review articles on the psychological aspects of addictive behavior. Covers alcohol use and alcoholism, other drug use and abuse, eating disorders, smoking and nicotine addiction, and other compulsive disorders. Book reviews; annual author index. (Research, Treatment)

Research Communications in Substances of Abuse

PJD Publications Ltd, PO Box 966, Westbury NY 11590. Phone: 516-626-0650. ISSN 0193-0818

Quarterly. $80.

Basic and clinical studies on the use and abuse of alcohol and other drugs and substances of abuse. Focus is on biochemical, physiological, and pharmacological aspects. Book reviews; annual author and subject indexes. (Research)

*SALIS News

Substance Abuse Librarians and Information Specialists, PO Box 9513, Berkeley CA 94709-0513. ISSN 1072-4567

Quarterly. $20 US, Canada, and Mexico; free to SALIS members.

Official newsletter of the Substance Abuse Librarians and Information Specialists. Provides information on new reference sources, periodicals, and audio-visuals on alcohol and other drugs as well as on related conferences and programs of interest. (Current Awareness)

*Student Assistance Journal

Performance Resource Press, 5615 West Cermak Road, Cicero IL 60650-2290. Phone: 800-593-2193. ISSN 1042-6388

Five times/year. $46 US; $55 Canada.

Official journal of the National Association of Leadership for Student Assistance Programs. Publishes information on problems experienced by students, focusing on alcohol and other drug misuse. Covers student assistance programs and techniques for prevention and intervention. Book and media reviews. (Prevention and Education, Treatment)

Substance Abuse

Manisses Communications Group, Inc, 205 Governor Street, Box 3357, Providence RI 02906-0757. Phone: 401-831-6020; Fax: 401-861-6370. ISSN 0889-7077

Four times/year. $97 institutions; $69 individuals.

Journal of the Association for Medical Education and Research in Substance Abuse. Publishes articles related to clinical issues and to content and techniques of substance abuse education for health care professionals. (Prevention and Education, Treatment)

Substance Abuse Report

Business Research Publications, 1333 H Street NW, Washington DC 20005. Phone: 202-822-6338. ISSN 1040-4163

Semimonthly. $275.

Current news on alcohol and other drug abuse treatment. Covers federal policies and funding for programs. (Public Policy, Treatment)

Directory of Substance Abuse Databases, Networks, and Bulletin Board Systems[1]

VIRGINIA ROLETT, MLS

These databases, networks, and bulletin board systems can provide a wealth of information to users about alcohol and drugs. Their numbers are changing rapidly as funding from private and public sources waxes and wanes. This *Directory* offers an introduction to database networks and BBS available in early 1995. Contact the producers for current information packets.

There is wide variation in the ease with which different databases, networks, and BBSs can be searched. Some have particularly user-friendly access, while others are reputedly more difficult to use.

DATABASES OF ALCOHOL AND/OR DRUG INFORMATION
Alcohol and Alcohol Problems
Science Database (ETOH)

Description: ETOH aims to provide complete and current coverage of the scientific alcohol research literature. It includes more than 85,000 records of materials drawn from biomedical, psychosocial, legal, and public policy literature and is updated with about 400 new records monthly. It is indexed with a controlled vocabulary of descriptors selected from the *AOD Thesaurus*,

Second Edition. US Department of Health and Human Services, Washington DC, 1995. Available from NCADI (Appendix A).

Availability: CDP Online, a commercial vendor, by subscription. National Clearinghouse for Alcohol and Drug Information (NCADI) performs searches at a reduced fee. (See Appendix A.)

Producer: Office of Scientific Affairs, National Institute on Alcohol Abuse and Alcoholism, Willco Building, Suite 409, 6000 Executive Boulevard, Bethesda MD 20892-7003.
Documentation: Quick *Reference Guide to ETOH.*
Phone: 301/443-3860.

Alcohol and Other Drug Information
for Clinicians and Educators (CORK)

Description: An interdisciplinary bibliographic database of alcohol and drug information for clinicians and educators, *CORK* contains more than 22,000 selected records including journal articles, books, book chapters, and reports. It is updated quarterly. *CORK* excludes basic science literature, animal studies, non-English language materials, and articles that focus on medical management of sequelae of substance abuse rather than on substance abuse per se.

[1]From Center for Substance Abuse Prevention. *How to Organize and Operate an Information Center on Alcohol, Tobacco and Other Drugs: A Guide.* Rolett V; Kinney J, eds. Rockville MD: Center for Substance Abuse Prevention (in press).

Availability:
- PREVline (see below).
- Internet access
  TELNET: lib.Dartmouth.edu
  GOPHER.Dartmouth. edu
  http://WWW.Dartmouth.edu
- Direct phone to Dartmouth Online Catalog: 603/643-6310 (2400 baud) or 603/643-6300 (9600 baud); 603/643-6000 (14.4 baud)
- Those without Internet access can contact Project Cork for searches. Results can be sent via E-Mail.

Searching Guide and Descriptor List. Free.

Producer: Project Cork Institute at Dartmouth Medical School, 14 South Main Street, Suite 2F, Hanover NH 03755.
E-Mail: Project.Cork@Dartmouth.EDU
Phone: 603/646-3935; Fax: 603/646-2068.

Information on Drugs and Alcohol (IDA)

Description: An alcohol and other drug prevention file developed by the Center for Substance Abuse Prevention and NCADI. The focus is on prevention. *IDA* includes journal articles, state, federal, and international reports, book chapters, and newsletters.

Availability: Ask an information specialist at NCADI to search it. Not available for direct online searching.
Phone: 800/729-6686; 301/468-2600 to request a search.

Producer: National Clearinghouse for Alcohol & Drug Information, PO Box 2345, Rockville MD 20847.

NCADI's Prevention Materials Database

Description: Produced for the Center for Substance Abuse Prevention by the National Clearinghouse for Alcohol and Drug Information (NCADI), the database includes a current collection of primary prevention materials. It includes, but is not limited to, prevention products such as videos, posters, pamphlets, booklets, board games, buttons, curricula, comic books, coloring books, computer software, and fact sheets.

Availability: IBM-compatible discs and *User Manual.* Free to RADAR Network members; $12 to others.
Phone: 800/729-6686; 301/468-2600.

Producer: National Clearinghouse for Alcohol and Drug Information, PO Box 2345, Rockville MD 20852.

Prenatal Smoking Cessation Database (PSCD)

Description: PSCD contains information on the application of effective prenatal smoking cessation program activities and risk reduction efforts. It includes bibliographic citations and abstracts for journal articles, book chapters, technical reports, proceedings, papers, policy documents, legislation, monographs, and educational materials. The information is directed to health professionals and health educators.

Availability: One of seven databases on *CDP File,* a CD-ROM available for $44/year for two releases (March and August) from the Government Printing Office, Superintendent of Documents, PO Box 37194, Pittsburgh PA 15250-7954.
Request CDP File, CD-ROM Subscription, Stock # 717-145-00000-3.
One of 25 subfiles on Combined Health Information Database (CHID), CHID is available via a commercial database vendor, CDP Online. CHID is a group of 25 computerized bibliographic databases developed and managed by health-related agencies of the federal government.
Phone: 301/468-6555, x4300.
Order copies of the *CHID Search Reference Guide* and the *CHID Word List* from CHID, PO Box 1917, Rockville MD 20849-1917.

Producer: Centers for Disease Control and Prevention, National Center for Chronic Disease Prevention and Health Promotion, Rhodes Building, Suite 1100, 4770 Buford Highway NE (Mail Stop K-13), Atlanta GA 30341-3724.
Phone: 404/488-5080.
Contact the Center directly for information about reference resource tools for searching the PSCD database.

Quick Facts

Description: Operated by Cygnus Corp. under contract with NIAAA's Alcohol Epidemiologic Data System, this is an electronic bulletin board system. It contains the text of current NIAAA reports and statistical data on the scope and consequences of alcohol use and abuse. *Quick Facts* includes consumption, patterns of alcohol use, projections of alcohol abuse, mortality from cirrhosis of the liver, alcohol-related fatal traffic accidents, alcohol-related morbidity, criminal offenses, and attitudes and perceptions concerning alcohol. It is updated monthly.

Availability: Free. For information and an instructional brochure, phone: 202/289-4992.
- Direct computer access. Phone: 202/289-4112.
- On-line time is free. Only cost is that of the long distance phone call.
- *FedWorld Network* (see below).

Producer: Cygnus Corporation, 1400 Eye Street NW, Suite 1275, Washington DC 20005.

Smoking and Health Database

Description: A bibliographic database of scientific and technical information about smoking and tobacco use that covers more than 30 years and contains abstracts for over 60,000 items. The information is international and is obtained from professional journals, books, and technical reports. Citations are indexed and abstracted.

Availability:
- One of seven databases on *CDP File,* a CD-ROM available for $44/year/ two releases (March and August) from the Government Printing Office, Superintendent of Documents, PO Box 37194, Pittsburgh PA 15250-7954. Request *CDP File— CD-ROM Subscription,* Stock # 717-145-00000-3.
- Through the CDC WONDER Network (see below).

Producer: Developed by the Centers for Disease Control's Office on Smoking and Health, Technical Information Center. (See Appendix A.)

Substance Abuse Information Database (SAID)

Description: SAID is directed at employers. It provides information on work place substance abuse programs, laws, and resources. It includes sample work place policies and program descriptions, sample employee awareness programs and supervisory training programs, information on establishing a drug testing program, abstracts of federal and state legislation relevant to work place laws, relevant findings, studies and surveys, abstracts of books, and journal articles.

Availability: Free on two IBM-compatible discs with *User's Manual.* Updated irregularly, once or twice a year.
Phone: 800/808-0965; 301/913-2816.

Producer: Department of Labor, Substance Abuse Information Database Support Center, 4915 St. Elmo Avenue, Suite 505, Bethesda MD 20814.

SELECTED DATABASES WITH SIGNIFICANT ALCOHOL AND OTHER DRUG INFORMATION

These large and complex databases are regularly searched at large public and university research libraries by professional librarians with extensive searching expertise.

Many public, academic, and special libraries offer database searching on a cost-recovery basis or provide end-user access to the databases on CD-ROM. Small information centers may find it cost effective to use the access offered by neighboring libraries rather than to purchase direct access from commercial vendors. All information centers should know which databases may be useful for them to search and should consider obtaining direct access to databases that are used regularly.

Some databases are free, some involve a fee, some are directly accessible, and others are only available through commercial vendors. The major commercial database vendors are listed at the close of the appendix.

Combined Health Information Database (CHID)

Description: CHID is a computerized bibliographic database developed and managed by health-related agencies of the federal government. It contains references to health information and health education resources. In addition to two subfiles, described above, that focus on smoking information, CHID includes 23 additional subfiles directed to health professionals, health educators, patients, and the public. Among the 25 subfiles with more than 115,000 abstracted items are a number of subfiles relevant to addictions, such as *AIDS Education; Cancer Prevention and Control; Comprehensive School Health; Disease Prevention/Health Promotion; and Prenatal Smoking*

Cessation. The searcher may choose to search the subfiles separately, in groups of subfiles, or the entire file.

Availability: CHID is available on CDP Online, a commercial database vendor.

Producer: Each subfile is produced by a different agency and has its own selection, cataloging, indexing, and processing rules. Information about each producer and copies of the *CHID Search Reference Guide* and the *CHID Word List* for all 25 subfiles can be ordered from: CHID, PO Box 1917, Rockville MD 20849-1917.
Phone: 301/468-6555, x4300; Fax: 301/770-5164.

Educational Resources Information Center (ERIC)

Description: Bibliographic database with abstracts and full text documents. Includes many prevention materials relating to school and universities. Updated monthly.

Availability: • CDP Online and Knight-Ridder Information, Inc by subscription.
• Without charge via the Internet at University of Syracuse and University of North Carolina at Chapel Hill.
• Available in print and on CD-ROM at most research libraries.

Producer: Produced for the US Department of Education by ERIC Processing and Reference Facility, Information Systems Division, 1301 Piccard Drive, Rockville MD 20850-4305. Phone: 301/258-5500.

Psychological Abstracts (PsycINFO)

Description: Bibliographic citations and abstracts. Covers world literature in psychology and related disciplines. Updated monthly.

Availability: • CDP Online and Knight-Ridder by subscription.
• Available in print and on CD-ROM at most research libraries.

Producer: American Psychological Association, 750 First Street NE, Washington DC 20002-4242. Phone: 800/374-2722.

MEDLINE

Description: Provides bibliographic citations and abstracts of the biomedical literature. MEDLINE is a computerized version of Index Medicus, International Nursing Index, and Index to Dental Literature. Updated monthly. Specialized files and backfiles available.

Availability: • CDP Online and Knight-Ridder by subscription.
• MEDLINE and specialized subfiles are available in CD-ROM and online formats directly from the National Library of Medicine.
• Available in print and on CD-ROM at most medical libraries.

Producer: National Library of Medicine, MEDLARS Management Section, 8600 Rockville Pike, Bethesda MD 20894.
Phone: 800/638-8480.
Canadian Coordinator: Health Sciences Resource Center (HSRC). Canada Institute for Scientific and Technical Information (CISTI), National Research Council of Canada, Ottawa ON K1A 0S2, Canada. Phone: 613/993-1604.

NETWORKS AND BULLETIN BOARD SYSTEMS (BBS)

The networks and bulletin board systems described below offer valuable resources. On a database, a user can conduct an interactive search for information compiled by the database producer. On a network or BBS, the user can actually participate in bulletin boards and discussion groups in addition to searching databases and sending messages via E-Mail. *Section 3* describes networks and BBSs and the many ways in which they have rapidly become of major importance to all information centers.

CDC Wonder

Description: CDC Wonder is an online public health information and communications system accessible to IBM-PC–compatible computers with special software. The software allows users to access datasets; analyze data, create, and print presentation-quality graphics; send E-Mail and transmit data files. The system offers menu-driven access to 24 databases with information on mortality, hospital discharges, cancer incidence, and AIDS, including the *Smoking and Health Database and Morbidity and Mortality Weekly Report.*
Data can be accessed and analyzed through "fill-in-the-blank" request screens. Full text of public health reports and CDC guidelines can be identified and downloaded. E-Mail can

be exchanged with CDC staff using an online index of the names and numbers. The index includes the areas of expertise of CDC personnel. Those beyond the CDC may send to and receive E-Mail from registered users. In this way CDC Wonder can serve as a "gateway" to the E-Mail portion of the Internet.

Availability: Free registration and toll-free phone access for users. The required CDC Wonder Software package is available only for IBM-PC–compatible computers. The software and users' guide costs $49.50 from NTIS, Springfield VA 22161. Phone: 703/487-4650; Fax: 703/321-8547.

Plans are in process to have the system directly accessible on the Internet (World Wide Web) by the end of 1997.

Producer: Centers for Disease Control and Prevention (CDC), 1600 Clifton Road NE, Mailstop F-51, Atlanta GA 30333.

Customer Support Hotline Phone: 404/332-4569 then press 2, 2, 1 or contact John Macke at 404/488-7509.

FedWorld

Description: NTIS' FedWorld is a project that connects users electronically to many federal departments and agencies. From *FedWorld* one can access more than 100 computer bulletin board/database systems operated by the US Government, including *Quick Facts* (see above) and other systems relating to children and families, medical and health services, and more.

Availability:
- Direct phone access. Using a computer and a modem with a communications software package, dial *FedWorld* Phone: 703/321-8020 (Set Parity=NONE, Data Bits=8, Stop Bit=1, Terminal Emulation=ANSI).
- On the Internet Telnet to: fedworld.gov@internet.

Producer: National Technical Information Service. Phone: 703/487-4608.

Handsnet

Description: A commercial, electronic network that connects users with more than 3500 health and human service organizations. Its *Information Forums* offer human services news as well as policy, program, and management information. The forums are updated daily by experts from national organizations in the field. Forums include the following:

Alerts: Urgent notices and calls for action on public policy and legislation.

Federal Budget & Policy: In-depth analysis and discussion of *hot* topics.

Children, Youth & Families: Research, programs, and policies.

Resources: Directory of Congressional and media contacts, announcements of funding opportunities, conferences, and more.

Legal Services: Case developments of relevant law; same-day, full-text Supreme Court decisions; network's legal services attorneys and specialized litigation support centers.

News and Blues: Online clipping service provides daily briefs from major newspapers and wire services on human service issues. Handsnet offers an E-Mail connection for users that extends to all users of the Internet. Other Internet access is not available.

Availability: Introductory package includes software and 1 month's subscription for $50. Additional months $25/ month or $270/year including free software. Additional monthly charges of $10 minimum includes 2 hours online time and limited data transfer. Average monthly costs including all fees = $38.50/month. Software provides an easy-to-use graphic interface.

Producer: Handsnet, 20195 Stevens Creek Boulevard, Suite 120, Cupertino CA 95014. Phone: 408/257-4500; Fax: 408/ 257-4560; E-Mail: HN0012@handsnet.org

Join Together

Description: A substance abuse resource center and a national electronic mail exchange for community leaders and activists. Searchable databases include the following: *Funding news.* Public and private sources of money with full text of relevant notices from the Federal Register. *Hot off the press.* Summaries of newspaper articles written daily. *Public policy.* Results of expert policy panels and updates on pending substance abuse legislation.

Events calendar.

National forum. Publications from other organizations.

Other related internet sites. The Internet connection can be used to access resources around the world.

Availability:
- Internet: Gopher site: gopher.jointogether.org
  URL: http://www.jointogether.org/jointogether.html
- Registered users of PREVline (see below) have access to Join Together as a part of PREVline.
  Although Join Together Online is free, some users may pay a fee for access to the Internet. Lists of Internet providers and free software for one of them (America Online) is included in the free *Join Together Introductory Kit.* The *Kit* also offers an excellent explanation of relative pros and cons of some options for gaining access to the Internet.
- Join Together is also stored on HANDSNET, a nonprofit network (see above) not connected to the Internet.

Producer: Join Together, 441 Stuart Street, Sixth Floor, Boston MA 02166.
Phone: 617/437-1500; Fax: 617/437-9394; E-Mail: info@jointogether.org

Partnerships Against Violence NETwork (PAVNET)

Description: PAVNET is an interagency electronic resource on the Internet. It was created by the Departments of Agriculture, Justice, Education, Labor, Health and Human Services, and Housing and Urban Development and directed to state and local officials. PAVNET offers information about techniques for combating violence in America. It includes descriptions and contacts for more than 600 programs around issues of community, youth and family violence, substance abuse, and victims' rights. Descriptions and contacts for programs of prevention, enforcement, and treatment/rehabilitation, along with foundation and federal funding sources, are also listed. PAVNET provides Gopher links on the Internet to other federal and clearinghouse databases, as well as points to access to other violence prevention information and community information.

Availability:
- Through PREVline (see below).
- Directly on the Internet. Gopher to: pavnet.esusda.gov
- PAVNET. Online files on violence prevention programs, funding, and technical support can also be accessed via E-Mail for those who do have only E-Mail access to the Internet.

Send a message to: almanac@ra.esusda.gov with the command

send pavent catalog or send pavent-funding catalog or send pavnet-programs catalog or send pavent-infosource catalog

Producer: John Gladstone, Youth Development Information Center, National Agricultural Library, 10301 Baltimore Boulevard, Room 304, Beltsville MD 20705-2351. Phone: 301/504-5462; Fax: 301/504-6409; E-Mail: jgladsto@nalusda.gov

PREVline

Description: An electronic community dedicated to exchanging ideas and information concerning ATOD problem prevention. Public access is available to *Public Plaza* with E-Mail, bulletin boards, downloadable files, and selected databases. Full Internet access is provided at no charge to RADAR Associates and Specialty Centers, CSAP grantees, and to others by special arrangement. Full access provides easy, direct connections to the following databases and networks on the Internet:

World Health Organization. Geneva, Switzerland

MARVEL, Library of Congress

This includes the membership of Congressional committees, and a phone and Fax directory for all Congressional members

NIH Library. National Institutes of Health

CORK, Alcohol and Drug Abuse Information for Health Care Professionals, Dartmouth College

Cornell University Library

Join Together Network

PAVNET, Partnerships Against Violence Network

Availability: • PREVline can be accessed through the Internet via telnet (path: telnet ncadi.health.org/login: prevline)
                  • Directly via modem and telephone to 301/770-0850, login: prevline

Producer: Center for Substance Abuse Prevention (CSAP), National Clearinghouse for Alcohol and Drug Information (NCADI), PO Box 2345, Rockville MD 20847-2345. Phone: 800/729-6686 or 301/468-2600.

DATABASE VENDORS

The following vendors provide access to multiple information databases through large computer systems and user-friendly software. Each system includes databases with significant information about alcohol and other drugs. Organizations that wish direct access to databases should contact vendors for information about their specific databases, services, and fees.

CDP Online Formerly BRS Information Technologies, Inc. 333 Seventh Avenue, New York NY 10001. Phone: 800/950-2035, 212/563-3006; Fax: 212/563-3784; Internet: cdplus@cdplus.com

Knight-Ridder Information, Inc. Formerly DIALOG Information Services, Inc. 2440 El Camino Real, Mountain View CA 94040. Phone: 800/334-2564.

National Library of Medicine, MEDLARS Management Section 8600 Rockville Pike, Bethesda MD 20894. Phone: 800/638-8480.

Government Printing Office (US) Superintendent of Documents, Washington DC 20402. Phone: 202/512-1800.

Activities for Professional Development

JEAN KINNEY, MSW

This section can be a tool box for professional development. There are various activities in diverse formats, including paper and pencil checklists, individual clinical exercises, small-group clinical exercises, and guided observations. There are instruments to help assess current levels of clinical skill and the degree of comfort in performing them, instruments to help assess the clinician's assumptions of patients with alcohol and substance use problems, and methods of auditing current clinical work. These can be used to identify needs and goals for professional development.

Mention of professional development brings to mind attendance at workshops, seminars, or training programs. The materials here supplement such efforts. Some of the clinical exercises assess current clinical activities, while others can help incorporate or polish skills. They were designed to assist practitioners to take advantage of resources within their communities and within their own clinical practices.

The checklist below correlates different practice areas related to alcohol and substance use problems. For each item there is a scale for rating your comfort in performing the identified task. Thus, you are able to identify areas of strength and weakness. In regard to which tasks may be targets for professional education efforts, clearly not all these listed will be of equal importance within a particular setting.

CHECKLIST—CONFIDENCE IN CLINICAL SKILLS

Instructions: On a scale of 1 to 5, rate your confidence in performing the following tasks. "1" indicates low confidence and "5" indicates high confidence.

Not Confident   **Very Confident**

Taking an alcohol/drug use history.
1   2   3   4   5

Treating major medical complications.
1   2   3   4   5

Informing the patient of the diagnosis.
1   2   3   4   5

Working with substance abuse professionals.
1   2   3   4   5

Diagnosing withdrawal syndromes.
1   2   3   4   5

Managing withdrawal states.
1   2   3   4   5

Assessing alcohol-drug and drug-drug interactions.
1   2   3   4   5

Recognizing legal issues related to alcohol and other drug use.
1   2   3   4   5

Dealing with a colleague's possible drinking or drug use problem.
1   2   3   4   5

Diagnosing complications of chronic alcohol and drug use.
1   2   3   4   5

Not Confident   **Very Confident**

Diagnosing abuse and dependence.
1   2   3   4   5

Formulating a treatment plan.
1   2   3   4   5

Making a referral to self-help groups.
1   2   3   4   5

Providing patient education about alcohol and other drugs.
1   2   3   4   5

Working with the family members or significant others.
1   2   3   4   5

Assessing a patient's risk for developing alcohol or other drug problem.
1   2   3   4   5

Making a referral for treatment.
1   2   3   4   5

Identifying problems of abuse through problems exhibited by other family members.
1   2   3   4   5

Using consultation.
1   2   3   4   5

From Hanover, NH: Project Cork Institute, 1979.

SELF-ASSESSMENT OF PERCEPTIONS OF PATIENTS WITH SUBSTANCE USE PROBLEMS

The Seaman-Manello Scale was developed in the late 1970s as an attitude scale for nurses. Some items are outdated. Its inclusion here is not as a scale of attitudes but as a means of identifying the clinician's operating assumptions and hypotheses about dependence on alcohol and other drugs.

Directions

The following 30 statements concern alcohol and alcoholism. Please read each statement carefully and then decide how strongly you agree or disagree with each statement. You may feel that a particular statement does not describe all of those persons who are alcoholic. Answer the questions as they apply to most individuals with alcoholism. Also, there may be some questions about experiences you have not had. If so, answer those questions with what you believe to be true. Answer every question. There are no right or wrong answers. These statements are not designed to tell how good a nurse or clinician you are.

Indicate your level of agreement or disagreement with each of the following statements by entering a number on the line to the right of each statement, using the following scoring system:

1. STRONGLY DISAGREE
2. DISAGREE
3. NEITHER AGREE NOR DISAGREE
4. AGREE
5. STRONGLY AGREE

1. The life of an alcoholic is not a very pleasant one. _____

2. I feel I work best with alcoholic patients. _____

3. Alcoholics are not just concerned with their own happiness. _____

4. Alcoholics are very sensitive people. _____

5. Alcohol in moderate amounts can actually be beneficial to a healthy person. _____

6. Alcoholics are usually in poor physical health. _____

7. I prefer to work with alcoholics rather than other patients. _____

8. Alcoholics respect their families. _____

9. The alcoholic suffers from feelings of inferiority. _____

10. There is nothing wrong with drinking moderate amounts of alcohol. _____

11. I think that it is unfortunate that alcoholics often suffer from delirium tremors. _____

12. Alcoholics deserve hospital space just like any other patients. _____

13. Alcoholics want to stop drinking. _____

14. Alcoholics were driven to drink by other problems. _____

15. Alcoholic beverages are harmless when used in moderation. _____

16. Alcoholic patients need psychiatric consultation. _____

17. I don't think that my patients would become angry if I discussed their excessive drinking with them. _____

18. Alcoholics who do not obey nurse's orders should be treated anyway. _____

19. Alcoholics feel they are bad people because of their drinking. _____

20. People should drink alcoholic beverages if they wish to. _____

21. Alcoholics should receive medical treatment. _____

22. I feel comfortable when working with alcoholics. _____

23. Most alcoholics do not like being alcoholics. _____

24. An alcoholic is lonely. _____

25. When used wisely, alcoholic beverages are no more harmful to normal adults than nonalcoholic beverages. _____

26. Alcoholism is an illness. _____

27. It does not embarrass me to talk to alcoholics. _____

28. I can help an alcoholic even if he or she will not stop drinking. _____

29. Alcoholics usually have severe emotional difficulties. _____

30. The consumption of alcoholic beverages cannot make normal people weak and silly. _____

SCORING SHEET

Transfer your answers from your answer sheet to the appropriate spaces on this sheet.

1 ___	2 ___	3 ___	4 ___	5 ___
6 ___	7 ___	8 ___	9 ___	10 ___
11 ___	12 ___	13 ___	14 ___	15 ___
16 ___	17 ___	18 ___	19 ___	20 ___
21 ___	22 ___	23 ___	24 ___	25 ___
26 ___	27 ___	28 ___	29 ___	30 ___
___ (Subscale Q)	___ (Subscale R)	___ (Subscale S)	___ (Subscale T)	___ (Subscale U)

Total the items for each subset of questions. Each subset is related to one of five attributes or scales.

Guide to Interpretation of Scores

Subscale I (Q). Case disposition: Therapy versus punishment.

A high score on this scale, calculated as "Q" on the scoring sheet, indicates a belief that alcoholics are physically ill and that medical treatment is warranted. A low score indicates a belief that alcoholics are in good physical health and should be punished for their alcoholism.

Subscale II (R). Personal/professional satisfaction in work with alcoholics.

A high score on this scale, calculated as "R" on the scoring sheet, indicates that the clinician is likely to find work with alcoholics rewarding, enjoys having them as patients, and is comfortable treating them. A low score indicates feelings of discomfort and embarrassment when dealing with people with drinking problems. Those with low scores question their ability to successfully treat alcoholic people.

Subscale III (S). Inclination to identify: Ability to help alcoholic patients.

Those who score high on this scale, calculated as "S" on the scoring sheet, tend to see alcoholics as potentially respectable citizens who can be helped to resume normal lives. They are likely to believe that alcoholics want to be cured and that the nurse can help them attain this goal. Nurses who score low tend to believe that alcoholics are selfish and do not want to be helped. The nurse is likely to believe that if the patient does not try, the nurse does not have to.

Subscale IV (T). Perceptions of personal characteristics of alcoholic persons.

Those who score high on this scale, calculated as "T" on the scoring sheet, tend to see alcoholics as basically unhappy people—lonely, sensitive, doubting their own worth, and having severe emotional difficulties. The nurse who scores low on this scale tends to see alcoholics as simply excessive drinkers without psychological problems.

Subscale V (U). Personal attitudes toward drinking.

High scores on this scale, calculated as "U" on the scoring sheet, indicate a probable belief that alcohol is not bad and that moderate consumption of alcohol may actually be beneficial. Those who score low on this scale probably believe that the danger is in the alcohol and not in the person, and that the consumption of alcohol in any quantity is harmful, if not morally wrong.

From National Institute of Alcohol Abuse and Alcoholism. *The Community Health Nurse and Alcohol Related Problems.* Rockville MD: NIAA, 1978.

SELF-ASSESSMENT OF CLINICAL PRACTICE

CLINICAL CASE AUDIT

Auditing all patients seen for a specified period can be instructive. It offers some useful baseline information about a clinician's current practice; determines the present level of identification of alcohol or drug problems; and can help in identifying problematic alcohol or other drug use.

For each person seen, during a set period, note the following information:

a. Whether the patient definitely has or is suspected of having an alcohol or other substance use problem.

b. The basis for either a definite "yes" or the factors that create a suspicion of substance use problems.

c. The substances involved.

d. The nature of presenting complaints.

e. Any associated medical problems.

Conduct such an audit periodically. Compare the results at different times. Are there differences in the proportions of patients identified? Are there differences in the proportions of those suspected to the proportions confirmed? How have the factors that alert you to a problem changed?

CLINICAL CASE AUDIT

Directions: For 2 to 3 days keep a brief record of each clinical contact, noting if substance use problems are present or suspected, and the data that informs that assessment.

Name	Substance Abuse Present/Suspected	Significant Data
1.		
2.		
3.		
4.		
5.		
6.		
7.		
8.		
9.		
10.		
11.		
12.		
13.		
14.		
15.		
16.		
17.		
18.		
19.		
20.		
21.		

GOALS FOR PROFESSIONAL DEVELOPMENT

The worksheet below can be helpful in identifying goals for professional development activities.

A. As part of your current professional situation, what are the five most common clinical tasks you foresee in respect to alcohol and substance use problems?

1. _____
2. _____
3. _____
4. _____
5. _____

B. Of the above activities, rank these along three different dimensions—your level of comfort, your sense of proficiency in performing them, and your assessment of their relative importance in providing clinical care in your clinical setting?

Comfort in performance. List the task with which you are most at ease first.

1. _____
2. _____
3. _____
4. _____
5. _____

Assessment of proficiency. List the task with which you feel you are most proficient first.

1. _____
2. _____
3. _____
4. _____
5. _____

Perceived importance. List the task you consider most important in providing clinical care first.

1. _____
2. _____
3. _____
4. _____
5. _____

C. Are there particular age groups of concern? Are there ethnic or minority populations for whom your practice setting provides medical care? List these below.

_____   _____
_____   _____
_____   _____

Of these special patient groups, are any of special interest or concern? Do any have special needs of which you are aware in respect to alcohol and substance use problems? Circle them.

D. Compare your ratings and responses with the above questions. Are there any patterns? Do some items fall at the top of each list and others toward the bottom? Taking all this information into account, list these five tasks as the focus for your professional development activities. Also identify the most effective methods in handling these tasks. How might workshops, visits to treatment programs, case supervision, or guided readings be helpful?

Priorities for professional development and possible methods.

1. _____   _____
                   _____
                   _____
2. _____   _____
                   _____
                   _____
3. _____   _____
                   _____
                   _____
4. _____   _____
                   _____
                   _____
5. _____   _____
                   _____
                   _____

BECOMING FAMILIAR WITH COMMUNITY RESOURCES

Treatment Programs

In working with someone with an alcohol or other drug use problem, the clinician needs to use community treatment resources. The following information for different agencies will help:

- Name, address, telephone numbers.
- Types of treatment offered.
- Telephone number of staff person who handles intake.
- Admission hours, if applicable.
- Information routinely needed to evaluate a referral.
- Any financial or income guidelines:
    Does the agency serve low-income patients?
    Does the agency accept self-payment, with an initial deposit and payment plan?
    Must patients have health insurance?
- Exclusion criteria:
    Medical?
    Psychiatric?

Consider creating a resource file, using either a rolodex, file cards, or a notebook so that the information is easily accessible to all clinical staff.

Self-Help Groups

Attend a meeting

If you have never attended a meeting of a self-help group, do so. For a listing of times and places, contact a local treatment program or local hospital, both of which are likely to have a listing of local meetings. For AA, many areas have answering services. The telephone number is listed under "AA" in the white pages of the telephone directory.

In attending the meeting, consider the following questions:

- What is transpiring that is therapeutic?
- In addition to attending meetings, what are the factors that seem key to being engaged in a self-help group?
- What attitudes are expressed about health care professionals?
- What feature(s) of the meeting did you least expect?

Speak with a member

Ask someone you know who has a contact in AA or NA to identify someone willing to speak with you—someone in recovery, active in the program, and had substance abuse–related medical problems.

In your discussions with that person, ask about

- Interactions with the medical community.
- Attitudes of medical personnel toward them.
- Attitudes expressed about medical professionals.
- Number of emergency room visits or medical visits.
- Medical encounters and how often he or she was asked about substance abuse.
- What helped prompt the decision to enter a rehabilitation program.
- How his or her medical conditions have changed with abstinence.
- Concerns about medical care that may have arisen during recovery.

INDIVIDUAL CLINICAL ACTIVITIES

The following activities can be used to practice skills addressed in this manual.

Introducing the CAGE

For your next 10 to 25 patients, even if you do not suspect substance abuse, ask screening questions and any indicated follow-up questions. Record the results of the questions and note your ease in asking them. Review the results. Identify the patients with whom you are most uncomfortable in broaching the topic. (These patients are among the most likely to be misdiagnosed because you will be least likely to ask them questions in a related way.)

Practice the screening instrument with a recovering alcoholic or drug user as a sample patient. Then adopt a start date to initiate a "trial run." Again, use the screening instrument routinely even if use seems inappropriate or uncomfortable.

Review the CAGE and decide where to insert it in the history and data collection format that you routinely use.

Discussing Positive Findings with Patients

Prepare a list of potential questions to ask when there is a positive response to screening.

What steps would you routinely consider as options available to you following a positive finding? Review the following scenarios:

Scenario 1. The results of routine screening for alcohol problems are negative. The patient has made some comments about occasional episodes of heavy drinking. There is also a positive family history of alcohol dependence.
• What are the patient's risk factors?
• How would you broach the topic of high-risk alcohol use?
• What kind of follow-up or monitoring would be appropriate?

Scenario 2. The daughter of a 64-year-old patient comes in to ask your help in confronting her father about his drinking. She goes into great detail about her father's long history of alcohol abuse. You have discussed alcohol use with this patient, who has consistently denied frequent consumption or any problem related to drinking.
• How do you define your role in this case?
• What options do you foresee for intervening?

Developing a risk reduction checklist

Compile a list of topics or of actual questions that you consider important when screening is positive. Draft a parallel list of points that you think are important to convey to a patient when screening is positive.

File this in an accessible spot so that you can use it as the need arises until it becomes second nature.

Relapse

Consider the following scenarios.

Scenario 1. A patient who has recently completed residential treatment comes in for his scheduled visit for monitoring and follow-up of hypertension.

What services might be provided by the primary care setting to reduce the probability of relapse? What information do you wish to elicit from the patient?

Scenario 2. A recovering patient with stable abstinence for slightly over 1 year is scheduled for hip replacement surgery.
• What concerns might the patient have?
• What steps can be taken to prepare the patient?
• What supports can potentially be mobilized?
• What are the options for sedation and management of postoperative pain.

Scenario 3. You are contacted by a family member of a patient you thought was doing well. The spouse reports that the patient has resumed drug use.
• How can you use this information.
• What are the alternatives for intervening?

For your practice, develop a protocol for relapse prevention and management of relapse as if one were to occur. What elements might be included in respect to frequency of visits, the essential components of the database, indicators for concern, agreements you might wish to make with the patient and family, and information from treatment personnel?

Medical Management

To review pertinent issues within your clinical practice, consider the following:
• Generate a list of the addictive drugs you prescribe. What is a safe dosage that you feel comfortable dispensing?
• Keep a record of the new patients you see; note which, if any, questions that you ask them relate to substance use/abuse.
• Create problem lists for 10 patients in your practice. Record how long this takes. Record how long it takes you to review nonproblematic list charts as you follow these patients on return visits. Consider constructing problem lists for all return visits for 1 month.

- Consult with other team members to discuss selection of standardized protocols, e.g., screening for withdrawal to detect patients with special medical indications for different dosages or medications.

SMALL-GROUP CLINICAL EXERCISES

The following exercises might be used within the context of a staff in-service program or might be organized informally as a peer education activity. In using these, it is helpful for someone knowledgeable about alcohol and substance use to help process the experience, pointing out what is effective and ineffective and tailoring these to clinical practice.

Administering the CAGE

Group size: Two or three people.

Task: Have one member of the group administer the CAGE to a second member, with a third person as an observer. Exchange places so that everyone has an opportunity to administer the CAGE.

Processing: Provide feedback to one another.

Follow-Up Questions When Screening Is Positive

Group size: Three or four people.

Setting: The assigned roles are clinician, patient, and one or two "coaches." Coaches are assigned to the clinician and the patient, or a single coach works with both. The role of the coach is to be available for consultation. The coach may also judiciously interrupt the interview to make suggestions to his or her associate.

Task: The member simulating the patient selects a persona and offers a short précis of the situation. The clinician administers the CAGE and continues with follow-up questions.

Processing: Provide feedback to one another. Focus on effective and counterproductive strategies and the emotional responses of both the clinician and the patient in the simulated encounter.

Interviewing, Personal Challenges

Group size: Three or four people.

Setting: The assigned roles are clinician, patient, and one or two coaches, with one assigned to the clinician and the other to the patient, with a single coach assigned to both.

Task: The trainee simulating the clinician establishes the scenario and briefs the "patient." Participants are encouraged

to select situations with which they are uncomfortable or that represent their worst fear, e.g., the angry patient, the patient who threatens to bolt, the passively resistant patient, or the patient who denies a problem.

Processing: Provide feedback. The clinician should seek clarification from the patient about the cues and approaches that provoked particular responses.

Engaging the Patient

Group size: Three to four members.

Setting: Simulate the following scenarios. Have one member simulate the patient, another the clinician, and the remainder serve as coaches.

Scenario 1: An elderly patient comes to your clinic for an ongoing routine check-up. He has had problems with elevated blood pressure, which has not consistently responded to medication. The patient's wife died 7 years ago, and now he lives only with a pet dog. The patient (Mr. Smith) has a strong odor of alcohol on his breath, and looking through his medical file, you realize that this has been noted on several occasions. In fact, 1 year ago another worker asked Mr. Smith about his drinking, which resulted in the patient screaming at the worker and threatening never to come back. The chart further indicates that Mr. Smith was given benzodiazepines following his last visit to help with sleep difficulties. Today the patient has a large bump on his forehead and a cut that has just begun to heal under his right eye.

Scenario 2: Mr. and Mrs. Jones are waiting to see you. Mr. Jones's recurring chief complaint has been an upset stomach. A co-worker informs you that Mrs. Jones has been loudly blaming the patient for wasting her and the clinic's time for a silly headache. When they both come into the office and are interviewed, it becomes apparent that Mr. Jones's recent headache began the night before following a cocktail party at their house. Mrs. Jones blurts out, "One drink and he gets a hangover. I told him to have a Bloody Mary . . . worked great for me." Mr. Jones turns to his wife and softly replies that he gets headaches because he worries what she will do once she starts drinking. "Damn it. Don't you start again; I am not an alcoholic," replies Mrs. Jones. Quietly, Mr. Jones apologizes. He then tells you that it is not a serious headache, and maybe he should just take some more aspirin. Mrs. Jones says, "Yeah, go ahead and take some more aspirin. You call me an alcoholic and you're addicted to aspirin. You've had over six already, and it's not even 10 AM."

Scenario 3: Joe Doe is a 30-year-old man recently hospitalized for alcoholic hepatitis. He has been seen at your clinic for both alcohol-related physical and emotional difficulties and has been treated in the local hospital emergency room following a brawl related to using phencyclidine hydrochloride (PCP) and amphetamines. Today he states that although he had been sober for 3 weeks, he began drinking again 5 days ago after breaking up with his girlfriend. The patient is observed to be quite tremulous; however, he states that he will not go to a detoxification center. He complains, "The nurses are mean there, and besides I don't think I'm an alcoholic, anyway." Mr. Doe states that if he could have something for his nerves, he could go through withdrawal at home, stay sober this time for good, and be able to return to work in 2 days. He also requests that you write a medical excuse to his supervisor because he had to miss work for the past 5 days. At first he appeared polite, but now he is asking personal questions and if you would like to have dinner with him.

Scenario 4: Jane Doe is a co-worker you do not know well but see everyday. She is always fun to be around. She tells hilarious stories and has a positive outlook. Lately she has been late for work with increasing frequency. What in the past seemed like a positive attitude now appears to be inadequate excuses. You feel a little embarrassed to say something to her, especially because her daughter socializes and goes to school with your children. At a recent going-away party for a co-worker, Jane was observed drinking her cocktails in close succession, even after others had stopped drinking. One year ago, on New Year's Eve, Jane was arrested for drinking

while intoxicated (DWI), but the charges were dropped. However, you remember how your co-workers all agreed how unfair the arrest was and believed that the police were waiting outside the lounge trying to "make their quota." One day Jane's daughter, accompanied by your daughter, asks to speak to you. Her daughter states that her mother has a drinking problem and has been using pot; and because her mother has always spoken highly of you, Jane's daughter requests that you talk with her mother.

Processing: Participants provide feedback to one another. Focus on effective and counterproductive strategies. Focus on emotional responses in the simulated interview.

Common Presentations and Clinician Responses

Group size: Three or four people.

Setting: The assigned roles are clinician, patient, and one or two coaches, with one assigned to the clinician and the other to the patient, or a single coach assigned to both.

Task: For the role play scenario, adapt the commonly encountered patient types and clinician responses described in Chapter 3. These include the patient with a chronic, incurable disease; the patient in emotional crisis; the patient with dementia; the patient with language or cultural differences; the hostile patient; the overly dependent patient; the antisocial patient; the self-destructive patient; and the noncompliant patient. Have one member be the clinician who wishes to discuss a possible chemical dependency problem with a "patient," played by another participant. The third person is the observer and coach for the clinician. Try to focus on the three major clinical tasks: data collection, relationship building, and patient education.

Processing: Provide feedback. Identify effective and ineffective approaches to these patient types and presentations.

Patient Education

Group size: Three to four members.

Setting: Simulate the following scenarios. Have one member simulate the patient, another the clinician, and the remainder serve as coaches.

Scenario 1: You are doing physicals for the local high school's women's cross country track team. You know many healthy adolescents rarely see health care professionals. How might you use the opportunity to discuss substance use? What other health maintenance issues are important to broach, too?

Scenario 2: The patient is a 24-year-old man who is married with two children. He works second shift (3 to 11 PM) and likes to go out after work with the boys. He sees you the morning after an automobile accident, which resulted in a DWI; he has a concussion. Routine screening about 6 months ago was negative for abuse or increased tolerance.

Questions: What are your concerns? What additional information is needed to assess changes in this patient's drinking pattern? What questions will you ask? What are your goals? What would you deem a satisfactory outcome?

Processing: What are effective ways to broach the topic of substance use problems in each of these situations? For each of the previous situations, what information would you try to elicit? What information would you provide?

SETTING UP PERSONAL FILES

No discussion of professional development would be complete without mention of professional reading. As was noted at the beginning of this manual, the alcohol and drug literature provides special challenges. It is dispersed throughout the journals of many disciplines. It is not restricted to medical journals but is found also in the journals of the behavioral and social sciences. Most of the journals that health care professionals regularly read will not keep them informed about the current work. Thus, some additional effort will be required.

A PERSONAL INFORMATION SYSTEM

There is nothing so frustrating as wanting information or material you are certain is available but not knowing where to look for it. Whether for reference purposes, lecture preparation, or other teaching, the time devoted to organizing personal files is well spent.

Whatever system is devised, note the following:

- Locating an article should not be dependent on remembering where it is filed.
- Because many articles cover more than one subject, some means of cross-referencing is needed.

- Refiling should be easy.
- Each article should have a complete citation written on it.

Number system. In using this method, each article, reprint, or manuscript included in the files is given a number. Write it on the top of the article. Then simply file all your reprints in numerical order. To help you find things, create a system of index cards, with one card per topic. Simply write down the number of the reprint. Later, to pull together all material on a given topic, take the subject card and pull the items numbered on each.

There is a drawback to this system. With only numbers on the subject card, you would not be able to quickly locate a single article, even when you know the title or author. The solution to this is to put a small note on the card.

Subject files method. In this system material is placed in files according to the subject; the different subject files are arranged alphabetically. The major difficulty with this system is cross-referencing. Often articles discuss more than one topic. One inventive solution is to make multiple copies of the first page. Before copying, note the subject under which the full article is filed. Clearly indicate where each article belongs. This ensures that the papers can be easily refiled and that the full article can be located without difficulty. Place a copy of the first page in each of the other appropriate topic files.

General considerations. For either system, the potential problem is selecting subjects. The idea is to select terms that are distinct, discrete, and appropriately broad or narrow for your purposes (e.g., medical complications would probably be too broad a category for a physician or health professional but adequate for a counselor). It is also important to avoid overlapping and synonymous categories.

To keep track of the file topics, create a master list in a notebook or on 3 × 5 index cards. Do not try to depend on your memory. If you do, you will inevitably find that you have four or five files for the same materials. For example, you might have "drugs" and "abused substances," as well as subjects organized by multiple drug type and drug classes. Then you will never be quite sure where certain subjects are. Keep track of terms that you are not using by making a note ("See _____") for the subject used to incorporate that type of material.

Whether the material is within personal files or a staff library, it tends to disappear. If materials are shared with others, a few safeguards are worth the trouble. Stamp your name on the articles. If it's something treasured, make a note of who borrowed it.

Index